Constantine Stephanidis (Ed.)

Universal Access in Human-Computer Interaction

Ambient Interaction

4th International Conference on Universal Access in Human-Computer Interaction, UAHCI 2007
Held as Part of HCI International 2007
Beijing, China, July 22-27, 2007
Proceedings, Part II

Springer

Volume Editor

Constantine Stephanidis
Foundation for Research and Technology - Hellas (FORTH)
Institute of Computer Science (ICS)
70013 Heraklion, Crete, Greece
E-mail: cs@ics.forth.gr

Library of Congress Control Number: 2007930226

CR Subject Classification (1998): H.5.2, H.5.3, H.3-5, C.2, K.4.2, I.3, D.2, F.3

LNCS Sublibrary: SL 2 – Programming and Software Engineering

ISSN 0302-9743
ISBN-10 3-540-73280-2 Springer Berlin Heidelberg New York
ISBN-13 978-3-540-73280-8 Springer Berlin Heidelberg New York

Springer is a part of Springer Science+Business Media

springer.com

Printed in Germany

Typesetting: Camera-ready by author, data conversion by Scientific Publishing Services, Chennai, India
Printed on acid-free paper SPIN: 12082537 06/3180 5 4 3 2 1 0

Foreword

The 12th International Conference on Human-Computer Interaction, HCI International 2007, was held in Beijing, P.R. China, 22-27 July 2007, jointly with the Symposium on Human Interface (Japan) 2007, the 7th International Conference on Engineering Psychology and Cognitive Ergonomics, the 4th International Conference on Universal Access in Human-Computer Interaction, the 2nd International Conference on Virtual Reality, the 2nd International Conference on Usability and Internationalization, the 2nd International Conference on Online Communities and Social Computing, the 3rd International Conference on Augmented Cognition, and the 1st International Conference on Digital Human Modeling.

A total of 3403 individuals from academia, research institutes, industry and governmental agencies from 76 countries submitted contributions, and 1681 papers, judged to be of high scientific quality, were included in the program. These papers address the latest research and development efforts and highlight the human aspects of design and use of computing systems. The papers accepted for presentation thoroughly cover the entire field of Human-Computer Interaction, addressing major advances in knowledge and effective use of computers in a variety of application areas.

This volume, edited by Constantine Stephanidis, contains papers in the thematic area of Universal Access in Human-Computer Interaction, addressing the following major topics:

- Intelligent Ambients
- Access to the Physical Environment, Mobility and Transportation
- Virtual and Augmented Environments
- Interaction Techniques and Devices

The remaining volumes of the HCI International 2007 proceedings are:

- Volume 1, LNCS 4550, Interaction Design and Usability, edited by Julie A. Jacko
- Volume 2, LNCS 4551, Interaction Platforms and Techniques, edited by Julie A. Jacko
- Volume 3, LNCS 4552, HCI Intelligent Multimodal Interaction Environments, edited by Julie A. Jacko
- Volume 4, LNCS 4553, HCI Applications and Services, edited by Julie A. Jacko
- Volume 5, LNCS 4554, Coping with Diversity in Universal Access, edited by Constantine Stephanidis
- Volume 7, LNCS 4556, Universal Access to Applications and Services, edited by Constantine Stephanidis
- Volume 8, LNCS 4557, Methods, Techniques and Tools in Information Design, edited by Michael J. Smith and Gavriel Salvendy
- Volume 9, LNCS 4558, Interacting in Information Environments, edited by Michael J. Smith and Gavriel Salvendy
- Volume 10, LNCS 4559, HCI and Culture, edited by Nuray Aykin

- Volume 11, LNCS 4560, Global and Local User Interfaces, edited by Nuray Aykin
- Volume 12, LNCS 4561, Digital Human Modeling, edited by Vincent G. Duffy
- Volume 13, LNAI 4562, Engineering Psychology and Cognitive Ergonomics, edited by Don Harris
- Volume 14, LNCS 4563, Virtual Reality, edited by Randall Shumaker
- Volume 15, LNCS 4564, Online Communities and Social Computing, edited by Douglas Schuler
- Volume 16, LNAI 4565, Foundations of Augmented Cognition 3rd Edition, edited by Dylan D. Schmorrow and Leah M. Reeves
- Volume 17, LNCS 4566, Ergonomics and Health Aspects of Work with Computers, edited by Marvin J. Dainoff

I would like to thank the Program Chairs and the members of the Program Boards of all Thematic Areas, listed below, for their contribution to the highest scientific quality and the overall success of the HCI International 2007 Conference.

Ergonomics and Health Aspects of Work with Computers

Program Chair: Marvin J. Dainoff

Arne Aaras, Norway
Pascale Carayon, USA
Barbara G.F. Cohen, USA
Wolfgang Friesdorf, Germany
Martin Helander, Singapore
Ben-Tzion Karsh, USA
Waldemar Karwowski, USA
Peter Kern, Germany
Danuta Koradecka, Poland
Kari Lindstrom, Finland
Holger Luczak, Germany
Aura C. Matias, Philippines
Kyung (Ken) Park, Korea
Michelle Robertson, USA
Steven L. Sauter, USA
Dominique L. Scapin, France
Michael J. Smith, USA
Naomi Swanson, USA
Peter Vink, The Netherlands
John Wilson, UK

Human Interface and the Management of Information

Program Chair: Michael J. Smith

Lajos Balint, Hungary
Gunilla Bradley, Sweden
Hans-Jörg Bullinger, Germany
Alan H.S. Chan, Hong Kong
Klaus-Peter Fähnrich, Germany
Michitaka Hirose, Japan
Yoshinori Horie, Japan
Richard Koubek, USA
Yasufumi Kume, Japan
Mark Lehto, USA
Robert Proctor, USA
Youngho Rhee, Korea
Anxo Cereijo Roibás, UK
Francois Sainfort, USA
Katsunori Shimohara, Japan
Tsutomu Tabe, Japan
Alvaro Taveira, USA
Kim-Phuong L. Vu, USA
Tomio Watanabe, Japan
Sakae Yamamoto, Japan

Jiye Mao, P.R. China
Fiona Nah, USA
Shogo Nishida, Japan
Leszek Pacholski, Poland
Hidekazu Yoshikawa, Japan
Li Zheng, P.R. China
Bernhard Zimolong, Germany

Human-Computer Interaction

Program Chair: Julie A. Jacko

Sebastiano Bagnara, Italy
Jianming Dong, USA
John Eklund, Australia
Xiaowen Fang, USA
Sheue-Ling Hwang, Taiwan
Yong Gu Ji, Korea
Steven J. Landry, USA
Jonathan Lazar, USA
V. Kathlene Leonard, USA
Chang S. Nam, USA
Anthony F. Norcio, USA
Celestine A. Ntuen, USA
P.L. Patrick Rau, P.R. China
Andrew Sears, USA
Holly Vitense, USA
Wenli Zhu, P.R. China

Engineering Psychology and Cognitive Ergonomics

Program Chair: Don Harris

Kenneth R. Boff, USA
Guy Boy, France
Pietro Carlo Cacciabue, Italy
Judy Edworthy, UK
Erik Hollnagel, Sweden
Kenji Itoh, Japan
Peter G.A.M. Jorna, The Netherlands
Kenneth R. Laughery, USA
Nicolas Marmaras, Greece
David Morrison, Australia
Sundaram Narayanan, USA
Eduardo Salas, USA
Dirk Schaefer, France
Axel Schulte, Germany
Neville A. Stanton, UK
Andrew Thatcher, South Africa

Universal Access in Human-Computer Interaction

Program Chair: Constantine Stephanidis

Julio Abascal, Spain
Ray Adams, UK
Elizabeth Andre, Germany
Margherita Antona, Greece
Chieko Asakawa, Japan
Christian Bühler, Germany
Noelle Carbonell, France
Jerzy Charytonowicz, Poland
Pier Luigi Emiliani, Italy
Michael Fairhurst, UK
Zhengjie Liu, P.R. China
Klaus Miesenberger, Austria
John Mylopoulos, Canada
Michael Pieper, Germany
Angel Puerta, USA
Anthony Savidis, Greece
Andrew Sears, USA
Ben Shneiderman, USA
Christian Stary, Austria
Hirotada Ueda, Japan

Gerhard Fischer, USA
Jon Gunderson, USA
Andreas Holzinger, Austria
Arthur Karshmer, USA
Simeon Keates, USA
George Kouroupetroglou, Greece
Jonathan Lazar, USA
Seongil Lee, Korea
Jean Vanderdonckt, Belgium
Gregg Vanderheiden, USA
Gerhard Weber, Germany
Harald Weber, Germany
Toshiki Yamaoka, Japan
Mary Zajicek, UK
Panayiotis Zaphiris, UK

Virtual Reality

Program Chair: Randall Shumaker

Terry Allard, USA
Pat Banerjee, USA
Robert S. Kennedy, USA
Heidi Kroemker, Germany
Ben Lawson, USA
Ming Lin, USA
Bowen Loftin, USA
Holger Luczak, Germany
Annie Luciani, France
Gordon Mair, UK
Ulrich Neumann, USA
Albert "Skip" Rizzo, USA
Lawrence Rosenblum, USA
Dylan Schmorrow, USA
Kay Stanney, USA
Susumu Tachi, Japan
John Wilson, UK
Wei Zhang, P.R. China
Michael Zyda, USA

Usability and Internationalization

Program Chair: Nuray Aykin

Genevieve Bell, USA
Alan Chan, Hong Kong
Apala Lahiri Chavan, India
Jori Clarke, USA
Pierre-Henri Dejean, France
Susan Dray, USA
Paul Fu, USA
Emilie Gould, Canada
Sung H. Han, South Korea
Veikko Ikonen, Finland
Richard Ishida, UK
Esin Kiris, USA
Tobias Komischke, Germany
Masaaki Kurosu, Japan
James R. Lewis, USA
Rungtai Lin, Taiwan
Aaron Marcus, USA
Allen E. Milewski, USA
Patrick O'Sullivan, Ireland
Girish V. Prabhu, India
Kerstin Röse, Germany
Eunice Ratna Sari, Indonesia
Supriya Singh, Australia
Serengul Smith, UK
Denise Spacinsky, USA
Christian Sturm, Mexico
Adi B. Tedjasaputra, Singapore
Myung Hwan Yun, South Korea
Chen Zhao, P.R. China

Online Communities and Social Computing

Program Chair: Douglas Schuler

Chadia Abras, USA
Lecia Barker, USA
Amy Bruckman, USA
Peter van den Besselaar, The Netherlands
Peter Day, UK
Fiorella De Cindio, Italy
John Fung, P.R. China
Michael Gurstein, USA
Tom Horan, USA
Piet Kommers, The Netherlands
Jonathan Lazar, USA
Stefanie Lindstaedt, Austria
Diane Maloney-Krichmar, USA
Isaac Mao, P.R. China
Hideyuki Nakanishi, Japan
A. Ant Ozok, USA
Jennifer Preece, USA
Partha Pratim Sarker, Bangladesh
Gilson Schwartz, Brazil
Sergei Stafeev, Russia
F.F. Tusubira, Uganda
Cheng-Yen Wang, Taiwan

Augmented Cognition

Program Chair: Dylan D. Schmorrow

Kenneth Boff, USA
Joseph Cohn, USA
Blair Dickson, UK
Henry Girolamo, USA
Gerald Edelman, USA
Eric Horvitz, USA
Wilhelm Kincses, Germany
Amy Kruse, USA
Lee Kollmorgen, USA
Dennis McBride, USA
Jeffrey Morrison, USA
Denise Nicholson, USA
Dennis Proffitt, USA
Harry Shum, P.R. China
Kay Stanney, USA
Roy Stripling, USA
Michael Swetnam, USA
Robert Taylor, UK
John Wagner, USA

Digital Human Modeling

Program Chair: Vincent G. Duffy

Norm Badler, USA
Heiner Bubb, Germany
Don Chaffin, USA
Kathryn Cormican, Ireland
Andris Freivalds, USA
Ravindra Goonetilleke, Hong Kong
Anand Gramopadhye, USA
Sung H. Han, South Korea
Pheng Ann Heng, Hong Kong
Dewen Jin, P.R. China
Kang Li, USA
Zhizhong Li, P.R. China
Lizhuang Ma, P.R. China
Timo Maatta, Finland
J. Mark Porter, UK
Jim Potvin, Canada
Jean-Pierre Verriest, France
Zhaoqi Wang, P.R. China
Xiugan Yuan, P.R. China
Shao-Xiang Zhang, P.R. China
Xudong Zhang, USA

In addition to the members of the Program Boards above, I also wish to thank the following volunteer external reviewers: Kelly Hale, David Kobus, Amy Kruse, Cali Fidopiastis and Karl Van Orden from the USA, Mark Neerincx and Marc Grootjen from the Netherlands, Wilhelm Kincses from Germany, Ganesh Bhutkar and Mathura Prasad from India, Frederick Li from the UK, and Dimitris Grammenos, Angeliki Kastrinaki, Iosif Klironomos, Alexandros Mourouzis, and Stavroula Ntoa from Greece.

This conference could not have been possible without the continuous support and advise of the Conference Scientific Advisor, Gavriel Salvendy, as well as the dedicated work and outstanding efforts of the Communications Chair and Editor of HCI International News, Abbas Moallem, and of the members of the Organizational Board from P.R. China, Patrick Rau (Chair), Bo Chen, Xiaolan Fu, Zhibin Jiang, Congdong Li, Zhenjie Liu, Mowei Shen, Yuanchun Shi, Hui Su, Linyang Sun, Ming Po Tham, Ben Tsiang, Jian Wang, Guangyou Xu, Winnie Wanli Yang, Shuping Yi, Kan Zhang, and Wei Zho.

I would also like to thank for their contribution towards the organization of the HCI International 2007 Conference the members of the Human Computer Interaction Laboratory of ICS-FORTH, and in particular Margherita Antona, Maria Pitsoulaki, George Paparoulis, Maria Bouhli, Stavroula Ntoa and George Margetis.

April 2007

Constantine Stephanidis
General Chair, HCI International 2007

HCI International 2009

The 13th International Conference on Human-Computer Interaction, HCI International 2009, will be held jointly with the affiliated Conferences in San Diego, California, USA, in the Town and Country Resort & Convention Center, 19-24 July 2009. It will cover a broad spectrum of themes related to Human Computer Interaction, including theoretical issues, methods, tools, processes and case studies in HCI design, as well as novel interaction techniques, interfaces and applications. The proceedings will be published by Springer. For more information, please visit the Conference website: http://www.hcii2009.org/

General Chair
Professor Constantine Stephanidis
ICS-FORTH and University of Crete
Heraklion, Crete, Greece
Email: program@hcii2009.org

Table of Contents

Part I: Intelligent Ambients

Part III: Virtual and Augmented Environments

Part IV: Interaction Techniques and Devices

Part I

Intelligent Ambients

Creating Smart and Accessible Ubiquitous Knowledge Environments

Ray Adams[1] and Andrina Granić[2]

[1] CIRCUA, School of Computing Science, Middlesex University, London, United Kingdom
r.g.adams@mdx.ac.uk

[2] Faculty of Natural Sciences, Mathematics and Education, University of Split, Split, Croatia
andrina.granic@pmfst.hr

Abstract. Digital libraries offer substantial volumes of declarative knowledge to the information society. This paper explores the extent to which current and future digital libraries, also known as ubiquitous knowledge environments, can be made sufficiently usable, accessible and smart to support an inclusive information society and the aspiration of universal access. Using a range of converging methods to evaluate a random sample of such digital library websites, it is concluded that, whilst they act as substantial and functional repositories for knowledge, there is potential to improve, particularly in accessibility and smartness. The current methods are validated through the substantial statistical significance levels and by the meaningful patterns found in the resulting data. A new measure of system smartness is introduced and found to provide a useful metric for present purposes, though it is clear that further work will be needed.

Keywords: digital library, smart, accessible, usable, ubiquitous knowledge environment.

1 Introduction

There is little doubt that digital libraries have contributed significantly to the provision of structured, declarative knowledge to online communities, students and scholars, who need to have substantial, accessible cognitive resources at their fingertips. Such libraries represent a major investment of both applied computing science and pedagogic expertise, so providing potentially very valuable support for through the building of smart learning environments. At the moment, digital libraries are often set behind monolithic interfaces that can offer an overwhelming richness of data. But that should not blind us as to their potential to provide smart, accessible, cognitive support for human learning in the context of the inclusive knowledge society [9].

What comes after the digital library? This paper explores the possibility of creating what has been called the ubiquitous knowledge environment or post-digital library. It aims to explore the accessibility, usability and smartness of digital libraries and their user interfaces. The first component has been to conduct an expert evaluation of a

C. Stephanidis (Ed.): Universal Access in HCI, Part II, HCII 2007, LNCS 4555, pp. 3–12, 2007.

quasi-random sample of digital libraries to identify their potential to support inclusive, smart ubiquitous knowledge environments. The second component has been to conduct a literature review of ubiquitous knowledge environments development and innovations, in the light of the specific issues raised by the present data.

This work has been conducted within the framework of the ERCIM Working Group SESAMI (Smart Environments and Systems for Ambient Intelligence), raising questions like the following. Can digital libraries will become smarter and more accessible, thus creating the ubiquitous knowledge environments? The latter expression captures a possible convergence of technologies towards ambient intelligence and ubiquitous computing in the sense that such knowledge environments will move beyond the desktop or laptop to form part of our physical environment. Thus we are considering the creation of smart settings, with ubiquitous knowledge environments as a vital component. Access to the knowledge encapsulated would be accessed and processed through smarter everyday artifacts that deploy sensor data based responses in order to provide the users with relevant, user-model specific, situation-aware and context-of-use-aware knowledge at the point of use.

2 Expert Evaluations

In order to investigate the potential of smart, digital libraries, the first step is to evaluate current systems against the criteria of usability, accessibility and smartness. Usability is defined here as a suitable level of ease of use. Accessibility is defined as the lack of barriers that would prevent entry (completely or partially) to systems, their functions and contents. In universal access terms, this implicates the aspiration to achieve access by anyone, anytime and anywhere. Smartness is defined as the possession of functions and attributes by a system that would be judged to be intelligent in the case of a human operator, such that the probability of passing a cognitive version of the Turing Test would be increased. The term smart, as used here, does not necessarily imply true intelligence, merely a simulation of it.

2.1 Methods

A quasi-random sample of twenty digital libraries was generated by a Google search using the search terms "digital library". From this sample of twenty, ten were randomly selected for evaluation of usability, accessibility and smartness on the basis of the following hybrid methodology that combined a number of converging techniques.

First, the method of behavioural walkthrough provided the overall context and rationale, using a subject expert (E) to generate the data. This method simulates a user's reasoned action process at each step in the interactive dialogue, evaluating the extent to which the user's beliefs, external stimuli and intentions to perform can act as prerequisites for the next interaction step [1].

Second, the following stages of cognitive walkthrough were adapted to fit in with the above method:

1. The expert (E) considers the initial appearance of the library.
2. E identifies the subject matter definition of the digital library.
3. E conducts ten searches for topics covered by the specific library (for example, "discover relevant information on topic x, where x is covered by the specific library").
4. E uses the mechanisms provided by the library to conduct searches, for example directed searches by author, title, content, key words, extended searches, etc. using available screen objects (menu items, buttons, command-line inputs and the like).
5. E chooses the action that seems most likely to make progress toward the objective.
6. E carries out the actions and evaluates the system's feedback for evidence that progress is being made toward the current objective.
7. The above steps are used to retrieve information from the library system and to explore the extent to which each digital library interface supports "exploratory learning", i.e. first-time use without formal training.

Third, from the Web Accessibility Initiative (WAI) advice about the evaluation of the accessibility of a website, the following two points were extracted:

1. Include all pages on which people are more likely to enter the site.
2. Include a variety of pages with different layouts and functionality.

Fourth, the expert used the following four questionnaires to generate estimates of the usability, accessibility and smartness (the order of completion was randomized for each library evaluation):

1. System Usability Scale (SUS),
2. Questionnaire for User-Interaction Satisfaction,
3. Simplex accessibility questionnaire and
4. Simplex smartness questionnaire.

Fifth, the first, main page was evaluated by the use of Bobby (Watchfire WebXACT) [13] for accessibility.

2.2 Results

For each of the questionnaires, an overall score was derived and expressed as a percentage of the maximum, possible score. These data were summarized in Table 1. The data were analyzed by a one-way, analysis of variance. It is clear that the digital library websites did reasonably well on usability (System Usability Scale (SUS) and User-Interaction Satisfaction), slightly less so on accessibility (Simplex accessibility) and much less so on smartness (Simplex smartness). The overall differences were indicated by analysis of variance, ANOVA, ($F = 192.02$, df. 3, 36, $p < 0.0001$). Rated smartness was substantially lower than ratings of the other attributes, i.e. usability and accessibility. The main source of the significant difference between conditions is that due to the Simplex smartness questionnaire in relation to the others ($F= 261.9$, df. 1, 9, $p<0.0001$). However, accessibility (Simplex accessibility) was rated lower than both measures of usability ($F=261.9$ and 520.83, df. 1, 18, $p< 0.0001$). A comparison of the System Usability Scale and the Questionnaire for User-Interaction Satisfaction, both measures of usability, clearly indicated that the minor differences between them were highly likely to be due to chance ($F = 0.002$, df. 1, 19, $p= 0.96$). This agreement of results between the two questionnaires provides additional validation for the present methods, as they are clearly showing substantial overlap and correlation (see below). The sizes of the obtained F ratios indicate that these results are likely to be robust to the influence of any departures from the assumptions that accompany analysis of variance.

Table 1. Average scores (%) for each library and questionnaire

Library ID	System Usability Scale (SUS)	Simplex accessibility	Simplex smartness	User Interaction Satisfaction
01	64.00	61.11	26.25	72.14
02	78.00	67.22	24.38	75.71
03	76.00	67.50	25.63	72.14
04	70.00	62.50	22.50	70.00
05	66.00	56.67	25.63	70.00
06	62.00	52.78	23.44	70.00
07	62.00	59.72	21.56	59.72
08	72.00	52.22	12.19	66.43
09	68.00	54.17	15.94	67.15
10	70.00	59.17	25.94	65.71
Column Sums	688 mean = 68.80	593.06 mean = 59.306	223.46 mean = 22.346	689 mean = 68.90

Second, the results of the Bobby (Watchfire WebXACT) [13] test are shown in Table 2. Here, the relatively low evaluations of accessibility are confirmed at a more detailed level. Surprisingly, all ten sites were found to fail the WCAG standards, though three (01, 04, 05) were passed at priority one only.

These results point to the current status of digital libraries, as a basis for identifying where further developments could be made to enable them to contribute to the emerging information society and for universal access as a goal for society. Whilst we can conceive of a website having good accessibility accompanied by low usability, the present sample of digital websites shows the opposite problem. According to the present questionnaires, these websites showed poorer accessibility than usability, a finding supported by the use of Bobby to indicate accessibility problems at the coding level and above. However, smartness or intelligence would seem to provide the main focus for progress. If we are to move towards the goal of universal access in the information society, it is likely that we will require smarter systems and interfaces to do so.

Turning to the smartness questionnaire, a consideration of the items in the questionnaire, it is clear that some items are more demanding than are others. For example, "system recognizes my ID" does not require much smartness but "recognizes humor" seems much more demanding, requiring more "smartness". To check this possibility, each item was rated for required level of smartness and this level was correlated with the smartness scored derived for the websites, resulting is a very significant correlation ($r = 0.60$, $p < 0.001$). Clearly the digital libraries did better on the lower level items but much poorer on the higher level items. This results, validates the scale and points to those aspects of smartness that need to be improved.

Table 2. Bobby based evaluations of accessibility

		Automatic checkpoints			**Manual checkpoints**		
Library ID		**Priority 1**	**Priority 2**	**Priority 3**	**Priority 1**	**Priority 2**	**Priority 3**
		status & errors	status & errors	Status & errors	status & errors	status & errors	status & errors
01	*	√ 0	⊗ 1	⊗ 11	! 9	! 19	! 9
02	*	⊗ 15	⊗ 0	⊗ 37	! 43	! 45	! 10
03	*	⊗ 2	⊗ 1	⊗ 1	! 22	! 20	! 8
04	*	√ 0	⊗ 0	⊗ 9	! 26	! 30	! 9
05	*	√ 0	⊗ 0	⊗ 9	! 26	! 30	! 9
06	*	⊗ 1	⊗ 3	⊗ 13	! 11	! 17	! 10
07	*	⊗ 95	⊗ 3	⊗ 25	! 12	! 19	! 12
08	*	⊗ 18	⊗ 4	⊗ 19	! 7	! 15	! 8
09	*	⊗ 3	⊗ 7	⊗ 12	! 11	! 19	! 11
10	*	⊗ 1	⊗ 8	⊗ 6	! 6	! 18	! 9

* does not comply with WCAG

These results underline the need for work to develop smart interfaces for digital libraries if they are to contribute to the information society in a more accessible way. The following tables show which items of the smartness were rated as good (see Table 4) and those rated as less good (see Table 3). In the table, each item is quoted along with its question number and the total score across the ten digital libraries. Ten is the lowest possible score i.e. ten ratings of 1, where 1 is the lowest rating. A score of ten means that all ten digital libraries were given the lowest rating (1) on the given questionnaire item.

An inspection of the above, low rated items suggests that they are those that tend to require smarter performance or human-like qualities, as compared with those given slightly better ratings, which tend to require only the appropriate provision of information in response to requests. However, one of the purposes of the present research is to explore the range of possible items from those that strongly require human-like qualities and thus that simply require a response to requests for information. The distinction is not as clear-cut as would be first assumed, for two reasons. This questionnaire will be developed rigorously, according to psychometric principles. First, items may be found to share factors that relate to other distinctions. Second, new factors and items may be found that blur the presently offered distinction. On a conceptual note, users like us may not be able to distinguish human-like qualities from simulations of those qualities and so they remain of interest for ambient intelligence applications.

A consideration of the correlations between questionnaire scores, shown in Table 5 below, does not show a clear-cut profile. However, questionnaire three (smartness) shows the lowest correlation, indicating that questionnaire one (usability) and questionnaire three (smartness) are probably measuring substantially different aspects of the perceptions of these systems. Questionnaire two (accessibility) seems to relate well to questionnaire three, but apparently there is some tendency for usability and accessibility to correlate positively if not perfectly, even when they take different levels.

Table 3. Items which were given low ratings

Questions	Question number	Question score min = 10 max = 100
Recognizes finer categories of people	9	10
Uses commonsense to answer questions	14	10
Takes account of my expertise when answering questions	19	10
Responds to my emotional state	20	10
Recognizes humor	21	10
Recognizes irony	22	10
Can use numbers to make calculations	24	10
Can use logic	25	10
Uses hunches	26	10
Uses good judgment	27	10
Understands the structure of knowledge areas	29	10
Can solve problems	30	10
Can recognize patterns in data	31	10
Recognizes important changes	32	10

Table 4. Items which were given better ratings

Questions	Question number	Question score min = 10 max = 100
Can identify the meaning of received data	12	11
Has good manners	23	12
Responds to subtle details	28	13
Clarifies questions before answering	5	14
Understands that I have specific expertise	7	15
Takes account of my interests when answering questions	18	15
Uses knowledge to answer questions	13	16
Understands that I have specific interests	6	17
Provides error free messages	11	18
System recognizes my profile	2	23
System recognizes my ID	1	26
Useful help system provided	17	27
Offers more information than that requested	8	55
Answers questions	4	54
Needs only limited amount of input from the user	10	55
Provides useful feedback	16	55
Can provide search results in order of relevance	15	65
Responds to simple searches well	3	77

Table 5. Correlations between questionnaires

	Questionnaire 1 (usability)	Questionnaire 2 (accessibility)	Questionnaire 3 (smartness)	Questionnaire 4 (usability)
Questionnaire 1				
Questionnaire 2	0.58			
Questionnaire 3	-0.045	0.60		
Questionnaire 4	0.52	0.47	0.40	

2.3 Discussion

The sample of digital libraries considered here could all be seen as valuable resources that contained considerable volumes of scholarly information that were being made available to the user who was willing to use the system diligently. There was no indication that they were not highly functional and priceless sources. However, that is not the present focus. Using a variety of converging methods of expert evaluation, it is clear that the random sample of ten digital library websites could be developed further in usability, accessibility and smartness (in increasing order of potential). It is worth pointing out that usability was seen as significantly better than accessibility, demonstrating that these two measures of "user friendliness" are neither synonymous nor closely linked. The direction of the difference is also interesting, since it shows that the achievement of a reasonable level of usability can be accompanied by a significantly lower level of accessibility, whether the latter is measured by questionnaire or by an automatic evaluation system. Scores of usability and accessibility tended to be positively correlated, even though the latter was rated at a lower level than the former. Scores on the smartness questionnaire and one of the usability questionnaires were not well correlated, suggesting that the usability and smartness of a system are not synonymous.

There is considerable interest in the concept of the smart system and that is why we have set out to produce a questionnaire with which to evaluate system smartness. Without confusing simulation with reality, there might be a parallel between attempts to measure system smartness and human intelligence, the latter is a field of research that is to vast to consider here (but see [3]). If so, then the aspiration to produce a useful and valid measure of system smartness is only in its infancy. The present efforts can only pave the way for something better.

3 Literature Review of Post-digital Library Development and Innovations

In summary, the first component of this work demonstrated the potential to develop the smartness of the digital library, as well as its accessibility. It also identified those aspects of system smartness that were served well and less well by current systems. It also turned out that the functionality of these digital library systems exceeded their usability, which, in turn, was superior to their accessibility as measured by questionnaire and by the Bobby system. The second component of this work looks at current and potential developments in this field that address the issues raised by the current data, by the inspection of a set of relevant, key papers.

3.1 Key Papers

Here we have selected a sample of papers that show the way forward for such developments of accessibility and smartness. Stephanidis *et al.* [11] have argued that these two system aspects should be considered as related, arguing that digital libraries can cope with user diversity through the smart use of adaptivity. Liddy *et al.* [6] are working to provide smart access to a wide range of digital resources for a diverse range of different users. They started with Internet based, question answering services using human experts to interpret questions, to search databases and supply answers. The next stage in their work is the simulation of human operators by the application of unmediated natural language processing of texts and queries. Kling and Elliott [4] took another approach arguing that digital libraries should be designed to achieve "organizational usability", namely the effective integration of systems into the aims and objectives of current organisations. Nardi *et al.* [8] have worked to create smart agents that can extract semantics from library documents so that they can be used to infer users' high level goals, based upon simple user activities, in order to meet user requirements in a smarter manner. Li *et al.* [5] discuss one important digital library, CiteSeer, in order to evaluate the future development of this system. Their conclusions match those of the present paper to a significant extent. They argue that the new architecture of CiteSeer should be redesigned on the basis of scalability, flexibility, self-adaptivity, service-based and user-orientation, a mix of usability, accessibility and smartness. Stone *et al.* [12] present an intelligent digital library for biologists, based on advanced data mining techniques, using a framework which combines conventional library structures with an object-oriented methodology. Shang *et al.* [10] present a new intelligent agent-supported system for active, student centered learning. The important point is that this system makes use of current Internet, digital library and multiagent concepts. Lin and Hauptmann [7] show that the digital libraries can be provided with novel and innovative interfaces, reporting a wearable, digital library that can be used to support personal conversations. Such a system collects records of conversations and retrieves summaries of these conversations when needed to support new interactions. Finally, Chen *et al.* [2] provide a smart meeting room system that uses an intelligent agent based system, services, sensors, a semantic web ontology, logic reasoning, security policies and privacy policies.

3.2 Summary of Findings

The findings and objectives of the above studies can be captured by consideration of surface (interface) or the deep structures of the post-digital library, shown in Table 6.

Table 6. Overview of reviewed findings

Authors	Description	Interface	Deep structure
Stephanidis *et al.* (2000)	cope with user diversity through the smart use of adaptivity	√	
Liddy *et al.* (1994)	unmediated natural language processing of texts and queries	√	
Kling and Elliott (1994)	effective integration of systems into the aims and objectives of current organizations	√	
Nardi *et al.* (1998)	smart agents to extract semantics from library documents, used to infer users' high level goals, based upon simple user activities	√	
Shang *et al.* (2001)	a new intelligent agent-supported system for active, student centered learning that makes use of current Internet, digital library and multiagent concepts	√	
Lin and Hauptmann (2002)	a wearable, digital library that can be used to support personal conversations	√	
Li *et al.* (2006)	argue that the new architecture of CiteSeer should be redesigned for scalability, flexibility, self-adaptivity, service-based and user-orientation	√	√
Stone *et al.* (2004)	an intelligent digital library for biologists, based on advanced data mining techniques, combining conventional library structures with an object-oriented methodology	√	√
Chen *et al.* (2004)	a smart meeting room system that uses an intelligent agent based system, services, sensors, a semantic web ontology, logic reasoning, security and privacy policies	√	√

3.3 Discussion

It is clear from even a brief review that the issues and concerns identified in the first component of this work (usability, accessibility and smartness) can be addressed in a varied number of ways in order to enable digital libraries to contribute to the development of an inclusive, information and knowledge society. However, it is also clear that, if this sample is at all representative, much of the concern with accessibility and smartness is focused on aimed the interface rather than the deep structure of the digital library.

Overall, digital libraries provide an invaluable source of knowledge about a wide range of subjects. There can be few working scholars who do not make use of them. They are, at the moment, set behind monolithic interfaces that are typically accessed from the desktop or laptop environments. Surprisingly, however, the sample of libraries evaluated here clearly needed improvements in both accessibility and smartness. (The smartness questionnaire items used here are provided in tables four and five above. The accessibility and usability questionnaires are available from the authors). Clearly, if digital libraries are to form the basis for the realization of ubiquitous knowledge environments, they will become smarter and more accessible. If that can be achieved, then there would be a possible convergence of technologies like digital libraries, artificial intelligence (in the weaker sense of simulating human behavior), ambient intelligence and ubiquitous computing. The substantive contents of such knowledge environments could be unleashed into the external, physical world rather than staying on the desktop or laptop. If so, the present methods of questionnaire based evaluation would focus not only on significant components of the smart environment like the smart digital library, but more so on an evaluation of the overall, smart environments themselves. These methods, or their successors, could be used to design and evaluate better ubiquitous knowledge environments. Access to the knowledge encapsulated would be accessed and processed through smarter everyday artifacts that deploy sensor data based responses in order to provide the users with relevant, user-model specific, situation-aware and context-of-use-aware knowledge at the point of use.

Acknowledgments. This work has been carried out within project 177-0361994-1998 *Usability and Adaptivity of Interfaces for Intelligent Authoring Shells* funded by the Ministry of Science and Technology of the Republic of Croatia.

References

1. Antona, M., Mourouzi, A., Stephanidis, C.: An expert-based tool for Universal Access Evaluation. In: Proceedings of Universal Access in HCI, July, Beijing (2007). Inpress (2007)
2. Chen, H., Perich, F., Chakraborty, D., Finin, T., Joshi, A.: Intelligent agents meet semantic web in a smart meeting room. In: Kudenko, D., Kazakov, D., Alonso, E. (eds.) Adaptive Agents and Multi-Agent Systems II. LNCS (LNAI), vol. 3394, pp. 854–861. Springer, Heidelberg (2005)
3. Cianciolo, A.T., Sternberg, R.J.: Intelligence: A brief History. Blackwell Publishing, Malden, MA (2004)
4. Kling, R., Elliott, M.: Digital library design for organizational usability. SIGOIS Bulletin 15(2), 59–70 (1994)
5. Li, H., Council, I., Bolelli, L., Zhou, D., Song, Y., Lee, W., Sivasubramaniam, A., Giles, C.: CiteSeer - A Scalable Autonomous Scientific Digital Library. In: Proceedings of the 1st Int. Conference on Scalable Information Systems, INFOSCALE 06, ACM Press, New York (2006)
6. Liddy, E., Eisenberg, M., McClure, C., Mills, K., Mernit, S., Luckett, J.: Research Agenda for the Intelligent Digital Library. In: Proceedings of Digital Libraries, pp. 5–12 (1994)
7. Lin, W., Hauptmann, A.G.: A Wearable Digital Library of Personal Conversations. Joint Conference on Digital Libraries (JCDL'02). Portland, Oregon, USA, pp. 277–278 (2002)
8. Nardi, B., Miller, J., Wright, D.: Collaborative programmable intelligent agents. Communications of the ACM 41, 96–104 (1998)
9. Nikolaou, C., Stephanidis, C. (eds.): ECDL 1998. LNCS, vol. 1513. Springer, Heidelberg (1998)
10. Shang, Y., Shi, H., Chen, S.: An intelligent distributed environment for active learning. In: Journal on Educational Resources in Computing (JERIC)., vol. 1 (4), pp. 1–17. ACM Press, New York (2001)
11. Stephanidis, C., Akoumianakis, D., Paramythis, A., Nikolaou, C.: User Interaction in Digital Libraries: Coping with Diversity through Adaptation. International Journal on Digital Libraries. Special issue Alexandrian Scholars II 3(2), 185–205 (2000)
12. Stone, J., Wu, X., Greenblatt, M.: An Intelligent Digital Library System for Biologists. In: Proc. of, IEEE Computational Systems Bioinformatics Conference (CSB'04) (2004) pp. 491–492 (2004)
13. Watchfire WebXACT [Available On-line], http://webxact.watchfire.com/

Coupling Interaction Resources and Technical Support

Nicolas Barralon, Joëlle Coutaz, and Christophe Lachenal

Université Joseph Fourier, Grenoble
{Nicolas.Barralon, Joelle.Coutaz}@imag.fr

Abstract. Coupling is the action of binding two entities so that they can operate together to provide new functions. In this article, we propose a formal definition for coupling and present a graph theoretic notation so that the side-effects of the creation of a coupling can be analyzed in a formal and systematic way. We then describe I-AM (Interaction Abstract Machine), a middleware that supports the dynamic coupling of interaction resources such as screens, keyboards and mice, to form a unified interactive space. Using our notation, we illustrate how couplings are supported in I-AM.

Keywords: Multi-surface interaction, multi-instrument interaction, devices assembly, ambient intelligence, ubiquitous computing, UI development tool.

1 Introduction

Technological advances in computing, sensing, and networking, are rapidly leading to the capacity for individuals to create and mould their own interactive spaces. As envisioned by Weiser [18], interactive spaces will be assembled opportunistically by coupling private devices with interaction resources from public hot spots to access services within the global computing fabric. Interactive spaces will also take the form of autonomous computing islands whose horizon will evolve, split and merge under users' control.

From the software perspective, this ultra-flexibility calls for multi-scale infrastructures that act as a bridge between heterogeneous and dynamic sets of hardware, operating systems, and interaction resources. Projects such as Aura [15], Easyliving [3], Dynamo [10], Augmented Surfaces [11], and i-LAND [16] are early attempts in this direction. The same holds for prototypes based on proximal interaction and synchronous gestures [8, 9,12], or on physical connection [7, 13, 17]. These projects address a particular aspect of the vision where distributed and migratory user interfaces (UI) replace the conventional centralized paradigm. However, all of these systems are based on software concepts that were proposed twenty years ago when user interfaces were confined to a single computer equipped with a single screen, a single keyboard and a single pointing device.

With the exception of e-Gadget [5] and Smoblet [14], no one seems to have called into question whether such software concepts and tools are appropriate for the newly emerging forms of interaction based on coupling interaction resources. For example,

C. Stephanidis (Ed.): Universal Access in HCI, Part II, HCII 2007, LNCS 4555, pp. 13–22, 2007.

one can couple two entities, such as a wallet and home keys, by shaking them together [9]. As a result, an alarm can signal when one is separated from the other. But, what should happen when the keys are coupled with a pair of shoes? Are then the shoes coupled with the wallet?

In this article, we present a theoretic framework for reasoning about coupling [1] followed by the description of I-AM (Interaction Abstract Machine), a middleware that supports the dynamic coupling of interaction resources such as display screens and keyboards to form a unified interactive space.

2 Coupling Entities: Definition

The word "coupling" may be used to denote an act, or the result of this act.

- As an act, *coupling* is the action of binding two entities so that they operate conjointly to provide a set of functions that these entities cannot provide individually.
- As the result of an act, *a coupling* is an assembly of the source entities, that is, a new compound entity that provides a new set of functions that the source entities, alone, cannot provide.

In both cases, given two entities, the nature of the act determines the resulting set of functions. For example, in Hinckley's dynamic display tiling [8], users obtain different functions depending on the way the tablets are bumped together: if one tablet rests flat on a desk surface, and a second tablet is bumped into the base tablet, then the resulting function is the creation of a larger display. Alternatively, if the two tablets are bumped symmetrically, the same content is replicated on both displays to support face-to-face collaboration.

We express the twofold acceptation of coupling (either as an act, or as an entity) in the following formal way. Let:

- $\mathbf{E}$ be a non-empty finite set of entities and $\mathbf{F}$, the set of functions that these entities provide individually,
- *func*, the function that returns the set of functions f ($f \subset \mathbf{F}$) that an entity $e \in \mathbf{E}$ provides: $f = func(e)$,
- $\mathbf{A}$, a non-empty set of sequences of actions a,
- $\mathbf{C}$, the set of couplings between entities belonging to $\mathbf{E}$, using sequences of actions $a \in \mathbf{A}$,
- $e \in \mathbf{E}$, the compound entity that results from binding e_1 and e_2 by the way of the sequence of actions $a \in \mathbf{A}$,

then, the coupling c ($c \in \mathbf{C}$) is defined as the Cartesian product $\mathbf{E} \times \mathbf{E} \times \mathbf{A}$ in $\mathbf{E}$:

$$c: \mathbf{E} \times \mathbf{E} \times \mathbf{A} \rightarrow \mathbf{E}$$

and is denoted as:

$$c = (e_1, e_2, e): \forall f_i \neq f_1 \wedge f_i \neq f_2 : (f_1 \cap f_i = \emptyset) \wedge (f_2 \cap f_i = \emptyset) \quad (1)$$

where $e_1, e_2 \in \mathbf{E}$, $f_1 = func(e_1)$, $f_2 = func(e_2)$, $f = func(e)$

or as:

$$c = (e_1, e_2, f) \tag{2}$$

or as: (e_1, c, e_2) or $e_1 \overset{c}{\text{——}} e_2$ (3)

In notation (1), the focus of attention is the new compound entity obtained by the way of coupling. Notation (2) stresses the importance of the resulting set of functions while maintaining an explicit reference to the source entities. Notations (3) make the bond between the source entities explicit.

As suggested by the wallet, keys and shoes example, coupling two interaction resources may generate new couplings. In the following section, we present a theoretic notation to reason about causal and consequent couplings.

3 Causal Couplings and Their Consequents: A Formal Analysis

As in chemistry, couplings may have *causal relationships*: coupling an entity with a compound entity may entail a chain of reactions. Some bonds may be destroyed, possibly giving rise to multiple entities. Alternatively, additional couplings may be created. A coupling is *causal* when its creation implies, as a side effect, the creation of additional couplings. These additional couplings are called consequent couplings or simply, *consequents.*

3.1 Formal Analysis with a Graph Theoretic Notation

We represent couplings using a graph notation where nodes denote entities, and where edges express the existence of couplings. Symbols "*" and "=" denote causal and consequent couplings respectively. The "?" symbol denotes the couplings that are under evaluation (i.e. keeping them as consequents or rejecting them has not been decided yet). To express their transitory state, causal couplings, as well as consequents and undecided couplings are represented as dotted edges. Let:

- *EDGE* be the set of edges of the graph under consideration.
- $r_1(c)$ (resp. $r_2(c)$) be the first (resp. the second) interaction resource involved in the coupling *(r1, c, r2)*.
- $F(r_1, r_2)$ be the function that results from (r1, c, r2).
- $Compatible(f_1, f_2, f_3)$ returns TRUE if the functions f_1 and f_2 allow the existence of the function f_3. To be TRUE, $Compatible(f_1, f_2, f_3)$ may require the suppression of existing couplings. Although important (and challenging), this possibility is not addressed in this article.

The principle of our algorithm is the following: consider every new edge that results from the transitive closure with paths of length 2 that contain both $r_1(c)$ and $r_2(c)$. If this new edge corresponds to the creation of a coupling whose function is compatible with the functions provided by its neighboring edges, then it is created. In turn, the coupling that this edge denotes becomes a causal coupling and the algorithm is applied again.

More formally:

```
For every causal coupling c
   Build the set of nodes Nc such that :
      n∈Nc ⇔    n∈path ∧ length(path)= 2
                ∧ r1(c)∈path ∧ r2(c) ∈path

   For all n ∈ Nc and n≠r1(c) and n≠r2(c)
      if edge(n,r1(c)) ∈ EDGE
         if compatible(F(c, F(n,r1(c), F(n,r2(c))) then
                EDGE = EDGE ∪ new edge(r2(c), n)
         else
            if compatible(F(c), F(n, r2(c)), F(n, r1(c))) then
                EDGE = EDGE ∪ new edge(r1(c), s)
```

3.2 Illustration

To illustrate the algorithm, let's consider the initial configuration of couplings represented in Fig. 1. On the left, *Screen1* is coupled with *Mouse1* and *Keyboard1*, and *Mouse1* is coupled with *Keyboard1* to provide *Keyboard1* with the input focus function. This configuration corresponds to a private workstation. On the right, a public *Screen2* is coupled with a public pointing device *Mouse2*. Because *Screen1* and *Screen2* are compatible by design (resulting in the enlarge display function), *c5* is performed (for example, by a proximity detection service).

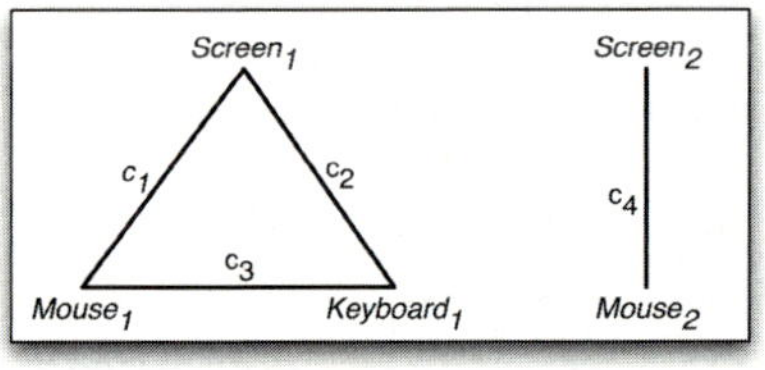

Fig. 1. Initial configuration. On the left, a private workstation; on the right, a public configuration

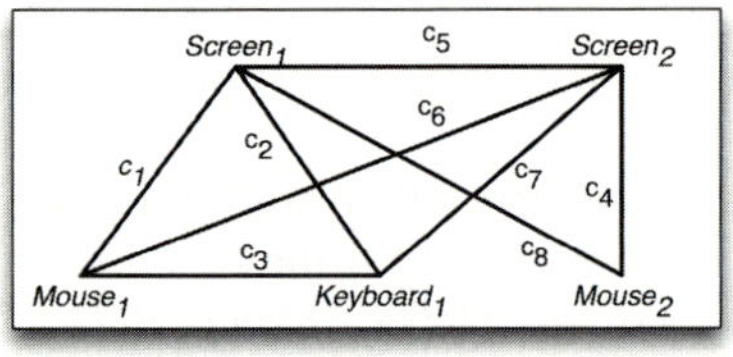

Fig. 2. Final configuration where the couplings *c6*, *c7* and *c8* are the consequents of the causal coupling *c5*

The final configuration that results from the causal coupling *c5* is shown in Fig. 2: The owner of the private workstation can manipulate digital information displayed on *Screen2* and *Screen1* using the private interaction resources *Mouse1* and *Keyboard1*. In addition, information can be designated on both screens with *Mouse2*, but for privacy reason, *Mouse2* cannot be coupled to *Keyboard1*. In a different situation where the workstations were owned by two distinct users who wanted to collaborate via a unified space, the compatibility functions would be different resulting in a distinct final configuration.

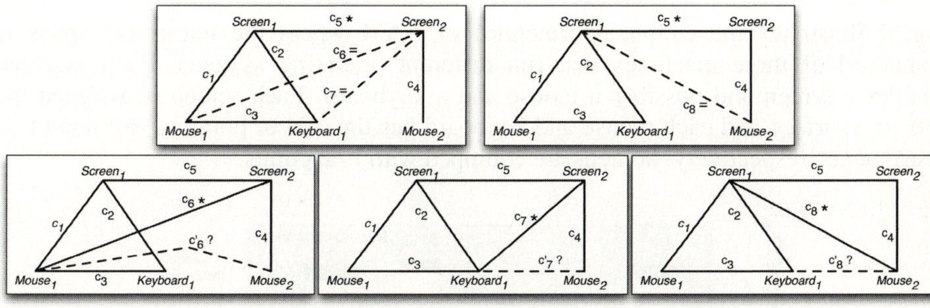

Fig. 3. Evaluation steps resulting from the causal coupling c5

Fig. 3 shows the successive steps that lead to the final configuration of Fig. 2. Fig. 3 (top left) corresponds to the generation of c_6 and c_7 that result from the transitive closure with paths c_5–c_1 and c_5–c_2 respectively. Fig. 3 (top right) shows the generation of c_8 that results from the transitive closure with path c_5–c_4. Because the function that results from c_6 is compatible with that of c_1 and c_5, c_6 is created. The same holds for c_7 and c_8 whose resulting functions are compatible with that of c_5 and c_2, and c_5 and c_4 respectively. c_6, c_7 and c_8 are now causal couplings. Fig. 3 (bottom left) corresponds to the application of the algorithm to c_6 with the evaluation of c'_6 that results from the transitive closure with paths c_6–c_4. The function that results from c'_6 is not compatible with that of c_6 and c_4 (coupling a private mouse with a public mouse to access any display area is considered as inappropriate for this particular situation). The same holds for c'_7 and c'_8 that result from the transitive closure with paths c_4–c_7 and c_8–c_2 respectively. For this particular situation, *Mouse2* cannot serve as input focus for *Keyboard1* (Fig. 3, bottom center and bottom right). In short, the causal coupling c_5 has three consequents: c_6, c_7, and c_8.

I-AM, presented next, offers a technical support for dynamically coupling interaction resources including causal and consequent couplings.

4 I-AM: Overview

I-AM is a technical instantiation of the ontology described in [4] where a computer platform is modeled as an actor characterized by a dynamic set of interaction resources. An interaction resource is a real-world physical object (with its own attributes such as shape, size and location in space) that plays a role such as that of a surface or of an instrument. Typically, a display screen is an interaction resource that plays the role of a surface whereas the keyboard plays the role of an instrument.

In I-AM, the interaction resources may be distributed across multiple machines running distinct operating systems. In this space, users can distribute and migrate user interfaces as if they were handled by a single computer. This illusion of a unified space is provided at no extra cost for the developer who can re-use the conventional GUI programming paradigm.

4.1 Technical Principles of I-AM

Fig. 4 illustrates the technical principles of I-AM where the interactive space is composed of three machines that run different operating systems. Each machine handles a screen and possibly a mouse and a keyboard. Each screen is assigned the role of a surface and each mouse and keyboard has the role of pointing and input text instruments, respectively. Screens are equipped with link points.

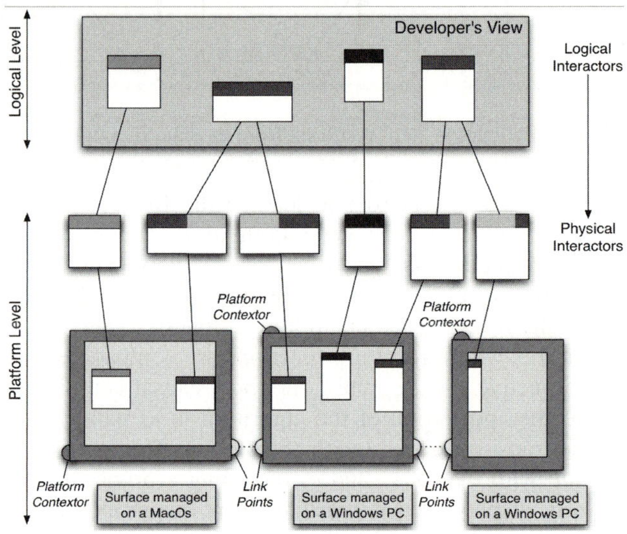

Fig. 4. Technical principles of I-AM

A link point is a reference point located at the edge of a screen. It can take the form of a physical sensor (e.g., infrared sensors, accelerometers as in Hinckley's example of synchronous gestures [8]). It can be a painted dot tracked by a computer vision system, or any conventional identifiable spot on the edge of a screen, or IR sensors or software interaction techniques [2]. Bringing two link points together, from two different screens, results in coupling the two screens. Because link points are geometric points, the screens are automatically related by geometric relations.

The bottom of the figure shows the distribution of the user interface across three screens. Some interactors such as the top left window of the developer's view, are fully rendered within a single screen whereas other interactors, such as the right most window of the developer's view, are split across two screens. In the latter case, the logical interactor of the developer's view is mapped into two effective interactors whose rendering is tightly coupled to entertain the illusion of a single surface: as the user moves one of the effective interactors using any pointing instrument of the interactive space, the other "twin" effective interactor is moved and transformed as if the twins were one single piece.

4.2 The Programmer's View

I-AM preserves the conventional GUI programming paradigm. As shown below, the programmer creates a window interactor, specifies its size and location, fills it with a picture, and asks I-AM to manage the window. The window is then mapped by I-AM on the physical configuration of the screens. With I-AM, the programmer gets UI distribution and migration between multiple surfaces for free, as well as the management of multiple instruments and cursors.

```
// My program is an IAMApp
IAMApp myiamapp = new IAMApp ();

// Create mywindow, and assign
IAMWindow mywindow = new IAMWindow();
mywindow.setCenterLocation (300, 300);
mywindow.setSize (300, 200);
…
// Ask I-AM to manage mywindow
myiamapp.addInteractor (mywindow);
```

4.3 The End-User's View

Fig. 5 and Fig. 6 show early examples of interaction techniques that allow users to mould their interactive space. Fig. 5-a corresponds to the situation where two applications are running on two independent workstations. A closed blue border outlines the screens to denote the absence of coupling. In Fig. 5-b, the screens are now coupled to provide the "single display area" function. An halo outlines the display area and a gateway shows where interactors can transit between the coupled screens.

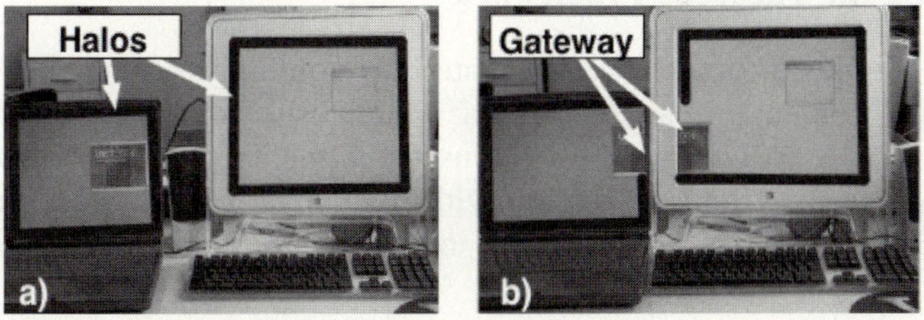

Fig. 5. (a) The PC and the Macintosh are decoupled and run two applications. (b) The two screens are coupled to form a single information space. Halos have been artificially enhanced on the pictures to increase readability.

Within an interactive space, any instrument can be used to modify any interactor. For example, in the configuration of Fig. 5-b, a PC mouse can be used to move a window created on the Macintosh and migrate it to the PC. In addition, the two mice can be used simultaneously. In Fig. 6, the user has selected the text field interactor displayed on the Macintosh screen with the PC mouse. Text can now be entered with the PC keyboard. If the text field is also selected with the Macintosh mouse, text can be entered with the Macintosh keyboard as well.

We have designed (but not evaluated) several interaction techniques for coupling screens. If the screens are equipped with infrared or if they are tracked by a computer vision system, coupling can be performed by bringing the screens in close contact. This sequence of actions *a*, is similar in spirit to Hinckley's synchronous gestures where devices are bumped against each other [8]. An alternative sequence of actions, inspired from SyncTap [12] called "Click'n Couple" [1], consists in bringing the cursors of the mice face to face, and then click the mouse buttons simultaneously (i.e. within the same temporal window).

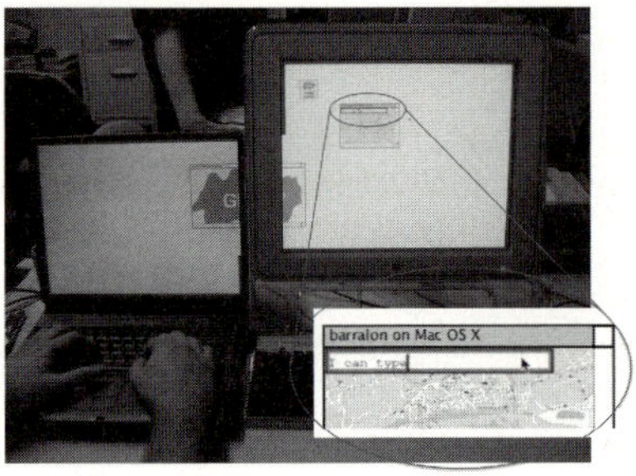

Fig. 6. Entering characters in a text field located on a Macintosh screen using a PC keyboard. Meanwhile a window is transiting through the gateway.

Having presented the technical principles of I-AM as well as the views it offers to the programmer and to the end-user, we now analyze I-AM more formally using our theoretic framework.

4.4 I-AM and the Theoretic Framework

We will use Figures 5, 6 and 7 to illustrate how couplings are handled in I-AM. In Fig. 5-a, two computers, a PC and a Macintosh, run independently. As for conventional window managers, the mouse and the keyboard of a computer are automatically coupled by I-AM to provide the "text input focus" function. The situation of Fig. 5-a is represented as two independent graphs: c1-c2-c3 and c4-c5-c6 (see Fig. 7).

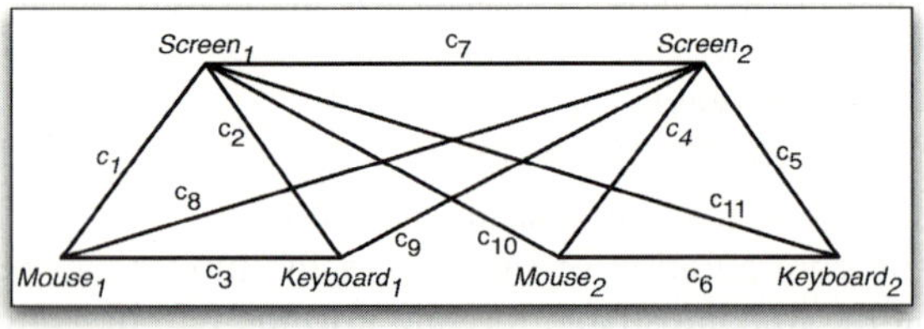

Fig. 7. The configuration that results from the causal coupling c_7 between the two screens

When the user performs any of the appropriate sequence of actions mentioned previously, *c7* is created between *Screen1* and *Screen2* (cf. Fig. 7), and a new function *f* is now available: *f* is an affine transform that supports different screen resolution and orientation, as well as bezels thickness so that windows and figures can overlap multiple screens without any deformation. Has *c7* consequent couplings?

By applying the algorithm presented in 3.1, the consequents *c8*, *c9*, *c10*, and *c11* are created because coupling *Mouse1* with *Screen2* produces a pointing function that is compatible with *f*. Similarly, coupling *Keyboard1* with *Screen2* produces a text entry function that is compatible with *f*. The same holds for *Mouse2* and *Keyboard2* with regard to *Screen1*. The configuration shown in Fig. 7 expresses the capacity for any interactor displayed on the unified surface to be coupled to the mouse-keyboard of the Macintosh as well as to the mouse-keyboard of the PC. Then, as shown in Fig. 6, characters can be entered simultaneously from any keyboard.

5 Conclusion

In summary, we have developed I-AM, a middleware that supports the dynamic coupling of interaction resources, possibly distributed across an heterogeneous set of platforms. I-AM advances the state of the art by addressing the following problems: 1) Platforms heterogeneity (running a mix of MacOs X, Windows NT and Windows XP); 2) Interaction resources heterogeneity (e.g., screens with different sizes, resolutions); 3) Platforms and interaction resources discovery; 4) Multi-surface interaction grounded on the dynamic coupling of hinged display surfaces whose spatial relations are automatically modeled and maintained; 5) Multi-keyboard, multi-pointer capabilities (so that a user can use the mouse of a PC to manipulate a window displayed on a MacOS screen and drag the window across screens boundaries as if there were a single screen).

Coupling interaction resources is not a new phenomenon. But in the GUI computer world, most couplings are pre-packaged and immutable. As we move to ubiquitous computing and ambient interactive spaces, the story is not as simple. In particular, couplings may engender new couplings. We propose a formalism using a graph theoretic notation to reason about the consequents of causal couplings in a systematic way. We use the notion of compatibility between the function returned by a consequent and the functions provided by its two neighbors. Other criteria could be used as well such as that of observability, predictability, traceability, and controllability. These issues are discussed in detail in [6] with the concept of meta-UI. Meta-UI's will allow users to build and control their own interactive spaces by coupling entities of many forms.

Acknowledgments. This work has been partly supported by Project EMODE (ITEA-if4046) and the NoE SIMILAR- FP6-507609.

References

1. Barralon, N.: Couplage de resources d'interaction en informatique ambiante. Thèse de l'Université Joseph Fourier (2006)
2. Barralon, N., Nguyen, V., Rey, G.: Techniques de couplage de bureaux: Ambient-Desktop comme illustration. In: Proceedings UbiMob'05, Grenoble, 31 mai-3 juin, pp. 193–200 (2005)

3. Brumitt, B., Shafer, S.: Better Living Through Geometry. In: Personal and Ubiquitous Computing, vol. 5(1), Springer, Heidelberg (2001)
4. Coutaz, J., Lachenal, C., Dupuy-Chessa, S.: Ontology for Multi-surface Interaction. In: Rauterberg, M., et al. (ed.) Proc. Interact 2003. IFIP, pp. 447–454. IOS Press, Amsterdam (2003)
5. Christopoulou, E., Kameas, A.: Using Ontologies to Address Key Issues in Ubiquitous Computing Systems. In: Markopoulos, P., Eggen, B., Aarts, E., Crowley, J.L. (eds) EUSAI 2004. LNCS, vol. 3295, pp. 13–24. Springer, Heidelberg (2004)
6. Coutaz, J.: Meta-User Interface for Ambient Spaces, In TAMODIA'06. In: Coninx, K., Luyten, K., Schneider, K.A. (eds.) TAMODIA 2006. LNCS, vol. 4385, pp. 1–15. Springer, Heidelberg (2007)
7. Gorbet, G.M, Orth, M., Ishii, H.: Triangles: Tangible Interface for Manipulation and Exploration of Digital Information Topography. In: Proc. of CHI'98, Los Angeles, pp. 49–56 (1998)
8. Hinckley, K.: Synchronous gestures for multiple persons and computers. In: Proc. UIST03, pp. 149–158. ACM, New York (2003)
9. Holmquist, L.E., Mattern, F., Schiele, B., Alahuhta, P., Beigl, M., Gellersen, H.W., Smart-Its Friends, A.: Technique for Users to Easily Establish Connections between Smart Artefacts. In: Proc. of Ubicomp, Atlanta, Georgia, 2001, pp. 116–221 (2001)
10. Izadi, S., Brignull, H., Rodden, T., Rogers, Y., Underwood, M., Dynamo, A.: A public interactive surface supporting the cooperative sharing and exchange of media. In: Proc. UIST 2003, pp. 159–168. ACM, New York (2003)
11. Rekimoto, J., Masanori, S., Augmented Surfaces, A.: Augmented Surfaces: A Spatially Continuous Workspace for Hybrid Computing Environments. In: Proc. CHI'99, pp. 378–385. ACM, New York (1999)
12. Rekimoto, J., Ayatsuka, Y., Kohno, M.: SyncTap: an Interaction Technique for Mobile Networking. In: Chittaro, L. (ed.) Mobile HCI 2003. LNCS, vol. 2795, pp. 104–115. Springer, Heidelberg (2003)
13. Resnick, M., Martin, F., Berg, R., Borovoy, R., Colella, V., Kramer, K., Silverman, B.: Digital Manipulatives: New Toys to Think With. In: Proc. of CHI'98, Los Angeles, pp. 281–287 (1998)
14. Siegemund, F., Krauer, T.: Integrating Handhelds into Environments of Cooperating Smart Everyday Objects. In: Markopoulos, P., Eggen, B., Aarts, E., Crowley, J.L. (eds.) EUSAI 2004. LNCS, vol. 3295, pp. 160–171. Springer, Heidelberg (2004)
15. Sousa, J., Garlan, D.: Aura: an Architectural Framework for User Mobility in Ubiquitous Computing Environments. In: Proc. IEEE-IFIP Conf. on Software Architecture, Montreal (2002)
16. Streitz, N., et al.: i-LAND: An interactive Landscape for Creativity and Innovation. In: Proc. CHI'99, ACM/SIGCHI, pp.120-127 (1999)
17. Tandler, P., Prante, T., Müller-Tomfelde, C., Streitz, N., Steinmetz, R.: ConnecTables: Dynamic Coupling of Displays for the Flexible Creation of Shared Workspaces. In: Proc. of UIST'01, Orlando, Florida, pp. 11–20 (2001)
18. Weiser, M.: The computer for the 21st century. Scientific American, pp. 94–104 (September 1991)

Learning Situation Models for Providing Context-Aware Services

O. Brdiczka, J.L. Crowley, and P. Reignier

Project PRIMA, INRIA Rhône-Alpes, Montbonnot, France
{brdiczka, crowley, reignier}@inrialpes.fr

Abstract. In order to provide information and communication services without disrupting human activity, information services must implicitly conform to the current context of human activity. However, the variability of human environments and human preferences make it impossible to preprogram the appropriate behaviors for a context aware service. One approach to overcoming this obstacle is to have services adapt behavior to individual preferences though feedback from users. This article describes a method for learning situation models to drive context-aware services. With this approach an initial simplified situation model is adapted to accommodate user preferences by a supervised learning algorithm using feedback from users. To bootstrap this process, the initial situation model is acquired by applying an automatic segmentation process to sample observation of human activities. This model is subsequently adapted to different operating environments and human preferences through interaction with users, using a supervised learning algorithm.

1 Introduction

Research in intelligent environments seeks to provide an enabling technology for a variety of new services. The key to acceptability for such services is unobtrusive behavior. Services that create distractions and unwanted interruptions are unlikely to find acceptance. Services must conform to human social conventions, and comply with rules for polite interaction. Such services must be able to perceive and make sense of human activities, and respond and learn from implicit and explicit feedback obtained through interaction with humans.

Unfortunately, human behavior is complex and unpredictable. Even within a given context, actions and reactions vary from one individual to another. Unobtrusive services must be able to adapt to individual variations and to the evolutions of preferences for a given individual. Adaptation is fundamental to unobtrusiveness in the sense that adaptation makes a system evolve with human behavior and needs. However, in order to create socially acceptable services, the user should be kept in the loop and in control whenever possible [9].

Human activity is situation dependent and does not necessarily follow plans. Services within intelligent environments need information about the current situation to respond correctly without disrupting human activity. A strong contextual model is

C. Stephanidis (Ed.): Universal Access in HCI, Part II, HCII 2007, LNCS 4555, pp. 23–32, 2007.

necessary for representing humans within the environment and their activities. The situations of this model can be decorated with system services to provide to the users in the environment. The construction process for such a model and the associated services accommodate and assimilate human preferences. We have investigated the use of machine learning methods in order to provide a technology in which naturally expressed human reactions is used as feedback to adapt the behavior of context aware services.

This article motivates and introduces a general approach for learning situation models from user feedback. In the first part of this article, we describe a method to automatically acquire an initial model with minimal human intervention. We then propose a method to adapt an existing situation model with user feedback given on appropriate system services. The proposed approach has been implemented and evaluated with experiments in our augmented meeting environment.

2 A Scenario

Bob is dreaming of a new intelligent home. The new home provides services to make Bob's life easier and more convenient. Bob hopes to reduce all that technical stuff that he needs to switch on/off, regulate, configure, etc. His ideal environment should provide entertainment and communication services with little or no configuration, adapting according to his preferences with a minimum of disruption and feedback. Bob should only need to indicate which service he wants and the system should adapt accordingly.

For instance, Bob enjoys jazz music when he is eating on the couch, but he does not want to be disturbed when eating with his girlfriend. Bob is willing to give feedback for learning to the system by giving specific voice commands in the environment or even, if needed, by clicking on services to provide on his PDA.

To satisfy Bob, the environment needs to be equipped with visual and acoustic sensors. For example, video cameras and a video tracking system and microphone array with speech detection and recognition can provide basic information about Bob's current location and activity. Of course, hand crafting of detection routines is not sufficient for Bob's dream as he wants the system to evolve, constantly adapting to his preferences. Thus a general model of the environment needs to be designed and then adapted according to Bob's remarks. The situation model has proved to be very useful for this task, being applied to various problems and domains [2].

A situation is a temporal state describing activities and relations of detected entities (persons) in the environment. Perceptual information from different sensors in the environment are associated with situations. In general, individual basic activities are first detected and then combined to situations [4]. For example, posture detection results from the video tracking system may help characterizing the situation "sitting at table". The different situations of the situation model are connected within a network. A path in this network describes behavior in the scene. System services to be provided are associated with the different situations in the network.

3 Initial Situation Model

In order to build a situation model for Bob's home, we start with an initial model describing Bob's very basic behavior. This model can be seen as default configuration of the system for the environment, being general and providing little detail. The picture below shows an example of such a default situation model for Bob's home.

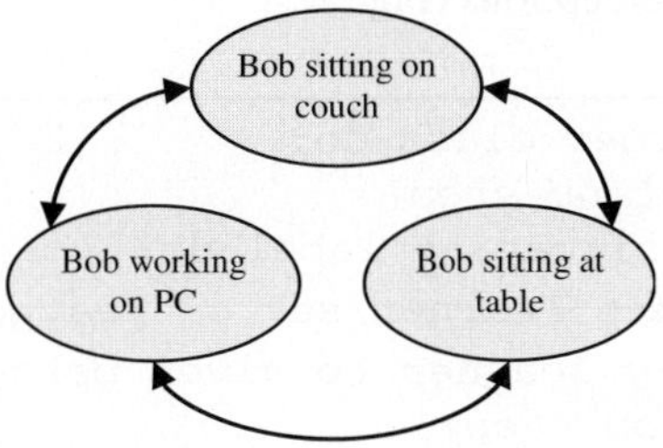

Fig. 1. Initial situation model for Bob's home

An open question, however, is from where to obtain a suitable initial model in order to minimize adaptation costs and user disruption. Normally, an expert constructs these models when setting up the system within environment. However, expert hours are expensive. An expert should at least be aided by automatic processes. In the following, we propose a schema for creating the initial situation network with a minimum of expert knowledge input. We exploit the addition of human expertise only for providing the situation labels. The derivations of the situations are, however, automatic, based on the recorded sensor signals.

The schema of the process of creating an initial situation model is depicted in Fig. 2. Given sensor recordings of Bob's activity in the environment, the automatic extraction of situations provides a first segmentation of sensor signals. This first segmentation is then labeled by an expert, integrating his expert knowledge. We assume here that expert knowledge and obtained automatic segmentation have a minimum of compatibility allowing the integration of expert situation labels. A supervised learning scheme is used to associate the situation labels with the recorded perceptions.

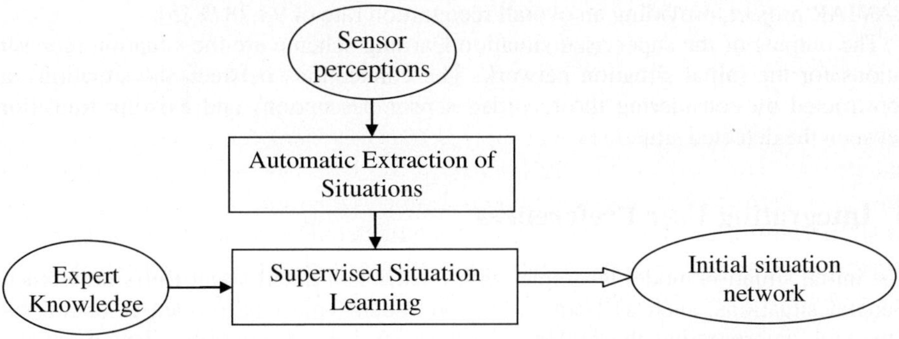

Fig. 2. Overview of the process of creating an initial situation model

The method for initializing the situation model is based on the stream of perceptual events coming from different sensors in the environment. The method detects changes in the overall event distribution and provides a first segmentation based on the detected changes. The method has been tested on audio and audio-visual recordings of small group and individual activities, producing an overall segmentation correctness of over 0.9 (Q value [10]) [3].

A supervised learning scheme [5] can be adopted to associate the situation labels with the recorded sensor perceptions (Fig. 3).

```
A. For each learner class do:
    a. {optimization step}
       For each situation label do:
         •  Select learner/set of learners
         •  Apply learner to given perceptions
    b. {validation step}
       Calculate ratio of between-situation and within-
       situation distance
    c. Repeat a.-b. until optimal ratio is obtained

B. Choose learner class with best ratio of between-
   situation and within-situation distance
```

Fig. 3. Scheme for supervised learning of situations

The idea is to use discriminant pattern recognition to recognize situations. Therefore, we first iterate over the possible learner classes (SVMs, Bayesian classifier, decision tree etc.) applicable for the task (part A). For each learner class, we select parameters and apply the learner to perceptual signals for each situation label (provided by an expert). The set of parameters that gives the best discrimination of the situations is retained (part A, step c.). Situations representations produced by the learner class with the best discrimination are retained (part B). As this is a general scheme, different forms of discriminant learning may be used interchangeably. The proposed supervised learning scheme has been evaluated on video surveillance data from the CAVIAR project, providing an overall recognition rate of 93.78 % [5].

The outputs of the supervised situation learning scheme are the situation representations for the initial situation network. The connections between the situations are constructed by considering the recorded sensor perceptions and existing transitions between the detected situations.

4 Integrating User Preferences

The initial situation model is simple, with insufficient detail about Bob's preferences. General situations, such as "Bob sitting on couch", must be refined to obtain sub-situations incorporating the preferred system services. A possible adapted situation model could look like in Fig. 4.

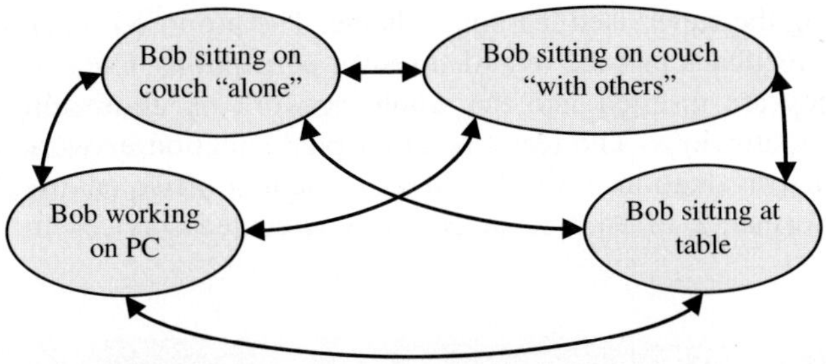

Fig. 4. Adapted situation model for Bob's home

"Sitting on couch" has been split into "Sitting on couch -alone-" and "Sitting on couch -with others-". Sensor perceptions need to be associated to the new sub-situations. Bob is, however, not interested in recruiting a system engineer implementing the new sub-situations. This refining process, and in particular the association of sensor perceptions to the new sub-situations, should hence be as automatic as possible. The new sub-situations need thus to be learned from recorded sensor perceptions as well as Bob's given feedback (via his voice or PDA) using machine learning methods. The supervised learning scheme (Fig. 3) can again be adopted to associate sensor perceptions to the new sub-situations.

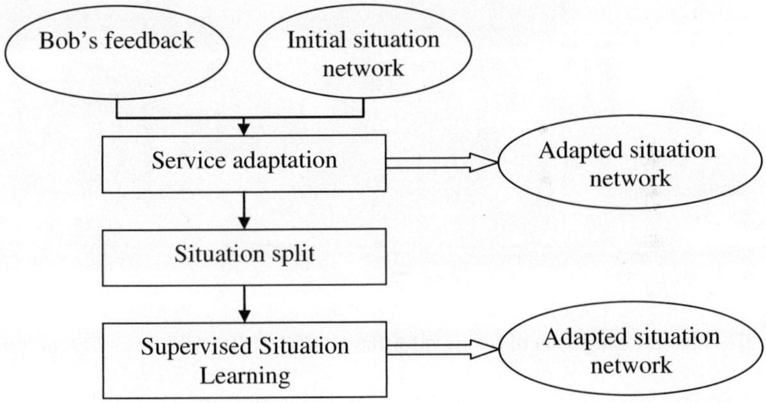

Fig. 5. Overview of the process of integrating user feedback into the initial situation model

The overall process of the automatic integration of Bob's feedback can be seen in Fig. 5. Bob's feedback and the initial situation network are the input. First, the algorithm tries to adapt simply the services associated to the given situations ("if service A is associated to S, and Bob indicates a preference for service B, then associate service B with S and dissociate service A"). If successful, the result is an adapted situation network integrating Bob's wishes. No situation split is necessary. However, if Bob's feedback indicates further that the concerned situation is too general, i.e. several distinct services are to be associated with one situation, the algorithm splits the situation into sub-situations. The sensor perceptions describing the new sub-situations are learned using the supervised learning scheme. The proposed supervised scheme is run with Bob's feedback and the recorded sensor perceptions. Once the sub-situations are learned, they are inserted into the whole network by eliminating conflicts and erasing obsolete situations. The result is an adapted situation network with new sub-situations. A first evaluation in the PRIMA augmented office environment provided an overall performance of 94.3 % of correctly executed services for the evaluated scenarios [6].

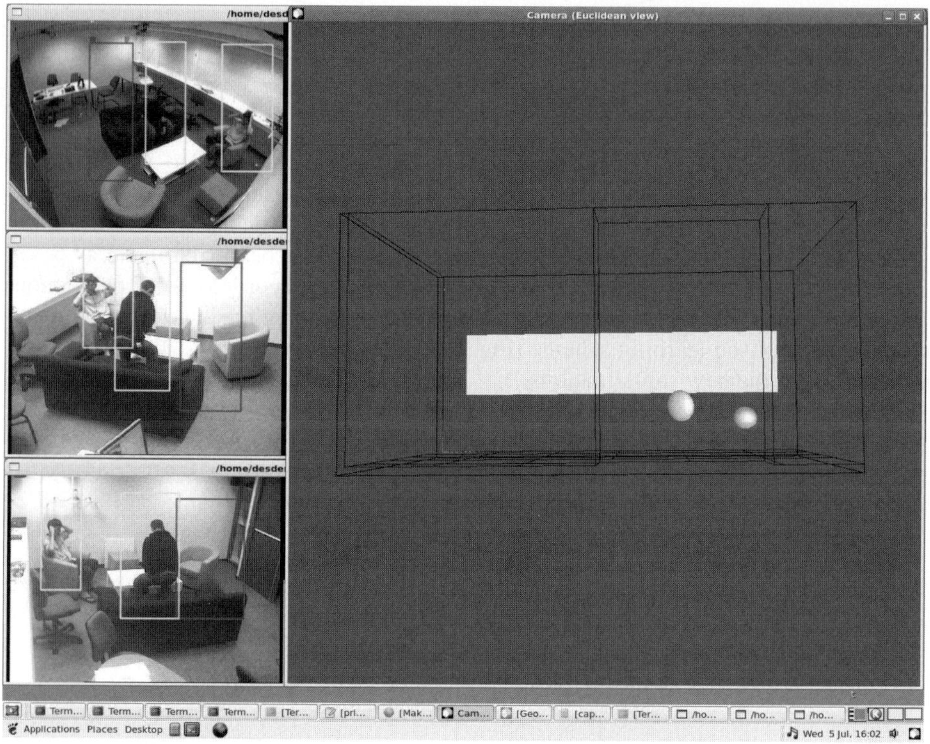

Fig. 6. 3D video tracking system fusing information of 3 2D trackers to a 3D representation

5 Experimental Evaluation

We evaluated the integral approach on 3 scenarios recorded in the PRIMA augmented home environment. The scenarios involved up to 2 persons doing different activities (introduction/address of welcome, presentation, aperitif, playing a game, siesta {1 person}) in the environment. A 3D video tracking systems [1] detected and tracked the people in the scene (Fig. 6.).

An individual activity detector [4] [8] has been applied to the extracted properties of the detected targets (persons). Additionally, the participants wore head microphones detecting whether the participant is speaking or not. A room microphone detected ambient noise in the scene. The association between video targets and head microphones has been manually done by a supervisor at the beginning of each scenario recording. The observation generated by the system for each target is a code between 0 and 52, combining posture (sitting, standing, lying), movement (gesturing, changing position, walking), speech and ambient sound. The whole system runs in real-time, i.e. 25 frames per second.

The first step of our proposed approach is to create the initial situation model. We extract the situations from the sensor perceptions, i.e. the observations generated for the targets in the scene using our automatic segmentor [3]. The automatically extracted segments and the *ground truth* for the scenarios are depicted in Fig. 7. The overall segmentation exactitude Q [10] is best for scenario 2. This can be explained by the fact that the algorithm has difficulties to distinguish ground truth segments "game" and "aperitif". In scenario 1 and scenario 3, "game" and "aperitif" are detected as one segment. As in scenario 2 "playing game" and "aperitif" are separated by "presentation", these segments can be correctly detected.

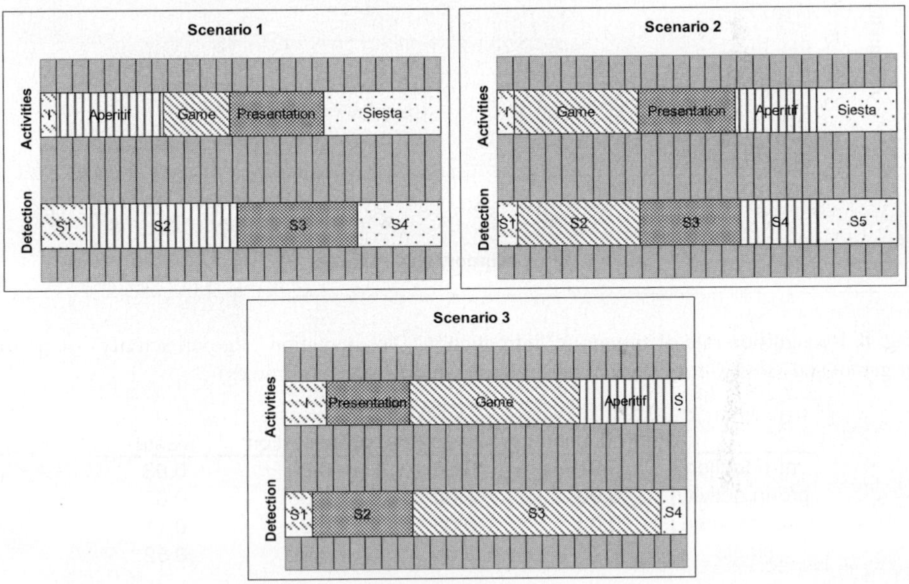

Fig. 7. Extracted situation segments and the corresponding *ground truth* for scenario 1 (Q = 0.68), scenario 2 (Q = 0.95), scenario 3 (Q = 0.74)

The supervised learning scheme is applied on the detected segments. As expert knowledge, we inject the situation labels: "introduction", "presentation", "group activity" (=aperitif or game), "siesta". We will adopt hidden Markov models [7] as unique learner class, iterating over left-right hidden Markov models of state numbers between 8 and 16 (=parameters of the class). To evaluate, we did 3-fold cross-validation, taking the detected segments + expert labels of 2 scenarios as input for learning and the third scenario as basis for recognition. As our system should be as responsive as possible, we evaluated different window sizes used for recognition. The results can be seen in Fig. 8. If we limit the observation time provided for recognition to 10 seconds (i.e. 250 frames with a frame rate of 25 frames/sec), we get a recognition rate of 88.58 % (Fig. 9). The recognition rate of "siesta" is poor due to the fact that in two of the three scenario recordings wrong targets have been created and detected when a person lay down on the couch, resulting in a disturbance of the existing target properties.

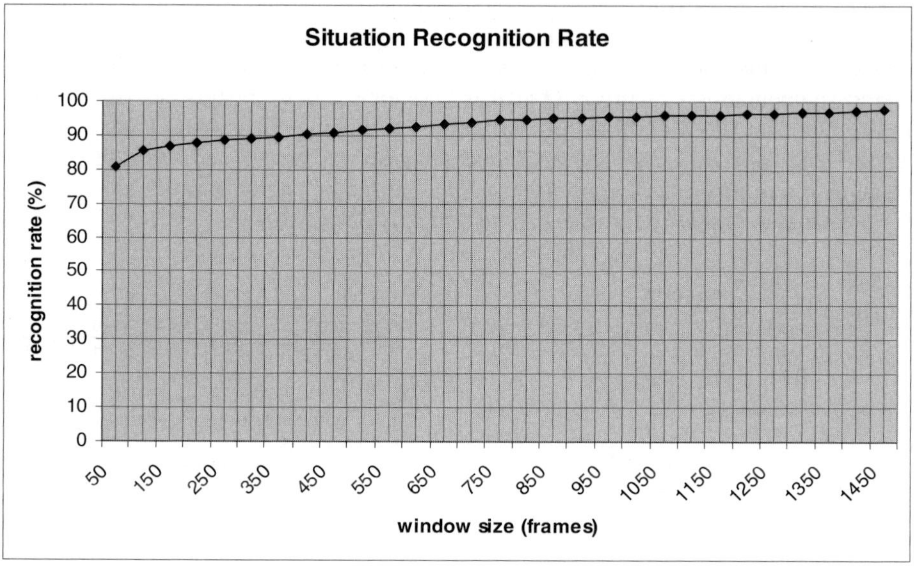

Fig. 8. Recognition rate of situations "introduction", "presentation", "group activity" (=aperitif or game) and "siesta" for different observation window sizes (in frames)

	introduction	group activity	presentation	siesta
introduction	0,97	0,00	0,00	0,03
group activity	0,00	1,00	0,00	0,00
presentation	0,03	0,03	0,83	0,11
siesta	0,40	0,00	0,08	0,52

	TP rate	FP rate	Precision	Recall	F-measure
introduction	0,97	0,07	0,41	0,97	0,58
group activity	1,00	0,02	0,98	1,00	0,99
presentation	0,83	0,02	0,95	0,83	0,89
siesta	0,52	0,03	0,72	0,52	0,61

Fig. 9. Confusion matrix and information retrieval statistics for each situation (observation window size=250 frames). The overall situation recognition rate is 88.58 %.

We have now learned an initial situation model with the situations "introduction", "group activity", "presentation" and "siesta". In order to integrate user preferences into this model, a user can give feedback to our system. The feedback is recorded and associated to the particular frame when it has been given. The initially learned model is then adapted according to this feedback (Fig. 5). For our scenarios, the user wants to integrate the following services:

- S1: Introduction → normal light and no music
- S2: Aperitif → dimmed light and jazz music
- S3: Game → normal light and pop music
- S4: Presentation → dimmed light and no music
- S5: Siesta → dimmed light and yoga music

The user gives one feedback indicating the corresponding service during each situation. As the initial situation model does not contain any situation-service associations, S1, S4 and S5 can then be simply associated to the corresponding situations. For S2 and S3, there is only one situation "group activity" which is too general in order to associate both distinct services. This situation needs thus to be split into sub-situations. The learned situation representation for "group activity" (here: a HMM) is erased and two distinct situation representations (here: HMMs) for "aperitif" and "game" are learned. The observations necessary to learn these situations are taken around the time points when the user gave the corresponding feedback. The size of the observation window used for learning the new sub-situations can be varied. We will adopt the double of the detection window size, i.e. 500 observation frames around the feedback time points to learn "aperitif" and "game". The obtained results of the 3-fold cross validation for recognition window size of 250 frames are depicted in Fig. 10.

	introduction	aperitif	game	presentation	siesta
introduction	0,97	0,00	0,00	0,00	0,03
aperitif	0,00	0,72	0,27	0,00	0,01
game	0,00	0,19	0,81	0,00	0,00
presentation	0,03	0,00	0,03	0,83	0,10
siesta	0,40	0,00	0,00	0,08	0,52

	TP rate	FP rate	Precision	Recall	F-measure
introduction	0,97	0,07	0,41	0,97	0,57
aperitif	0,72	0,08	0,70	0,72	0,71
game	0,81	0,09	0,81	0,81	0,81
presentation	0,83	0,02	0,95	0,83	0,89
siesta	0,52	0,04	0,72	0,52	0,60

Fig. 10. Confusion matrix and information retrieval statistics for each situation (observation window size=250 frames) after the split of "group activity". The window size for learning the new sub-situations is 500 frames. The overall situation recognition rate is 76.48 %.

6 Conclusion

In this paper we have described and evaluated a first approach for learning situation models in order to provide context-aware services. The obtained results are encouraging, but much remains to be done. First, the sensors necessary for a reliable sensing of Bob's activities are not sufficiently reliable and require expensive installation.

Multiple cameras, microphones or other sensors must be installed and calibrated in Bob's home. Clearly we will need automatic procedures for configuration and calibration of whatever sensors are used for such a system to be economically viable. Second, even though our results are encouraging, the error rates are still too high. Further improvements in detection and learning algorithms are necessary in order to provide a reliable system that could be accepted by Bob in his daily life. One way to alleviate this is to provide explanations to Bob. When errors occur (and corresponding system explanations are good), Bob could understand and correct wrong system perceptions and reasoning himself.

References

1. Biosca-Ferrer, A., Lux, A.: A visual service for distributed environments: a Bayesian 3D person tracker, submitted to International Conference on Computer Vision Systems (2007)
2. Brdiczka, O., Reignier, P., Crowley, J.L., Vaufreydaz, D., Maisonnasse, J.: Deterministic and probabilistic implementation of context. In: Proceedings of 4th IEEE International Conference on Pervasive Computing and Communications (PerCom) Workshops, pp. 46–50 (2006)
3. Brdiczka, O., Maisonnasse, J., Reignier, P., Crowley, J.L: Extracting activities from multimodal observation. In: Proceedings of 10th International Conference on Knowledge-Based & Intelligent Information & Engineering Systems (KES), vol. 2, pp. 162–170 (2006)
4. Brdiczka, O., Maisonnasse, J., Reignier, P., Crowley, J.L.: Learning individual roles from video in a smart home. In: 2nd IET International Conference on Intelligent Environments, Athens, Greece, vol. 1, pp. 61–69, (July 2006)
5. Brdiczka, O., Yuen, P.C., Zaidenberg, S., Reignier, P., Crowley, J.L.: Automatic acquisition of context models and its application to video surveillance. In: Proceedings of 18th International Conference on Pattern Recognition (ICPR), vol. 1, pp. 1175–1178 (2006)
6. Crowley, J.L., Brdiczka, O., Reignier, P.: Learning situation models for understanding activity. In: Proceedings of 5th International Conference on Development and Learning (ICDL) (2006)
7. Rabiner, L.A.: A tutorial on Hidden Markov Models and selected applications in speech recognition. In: Proceedings of IEEE, vol. 77(2), pp. 257–286 (1987)
8. Ribeiro, P., Santos-Victor, J.: Human activity recognition from Video: modeling, feature selection and classification architecture. In: Proceedings of International Workshop on Human Activity Recognition and Modeling, pp. 61–70 (2005)
9. Streitz, N., Röcker, C.: Prante, Th., van Alphen, D., Stenzel, R., and Magerkurth, C. Designing Smart Artifacts for Smart Environments. In: IEEE Computer vol. 38(3) pp. 41–49 (March 2005)
10. Zhang, D., Gatica-Perez, D., Bengio, S., McCowan, I., Lathoud, G.: Multimodal Group Action Clustering in Meetings. In: Proceedings of International Workshop on Video Surveillance and Sensor Networks (VSSN), pp. 54–62 (2004)

Ambient Intelligence and Multimodality

Laura Burzagli, Pier Luigi Emiliani, and Francesco Gabbanini

IFAC-CNR, Via Madonna del Piano, 10, Sesto Fiorentino, Firenze, Italy
{l.burzagli, p.l.emiliani, f.gabbanini}@ifac.cnr.it

Abstract. Ambient Intelligence (AmI) scenarios place strong emphasis on the fact that interaction takes place through natural interfaces, in such a way that people can perceive the presence of smart objects only when needed. As a possible solution to achieving relaxed and enjoyable interaction with the intelligent environments depicted by AmI, the ambient could be equipped with suitably designed multimodal interfaces bringing up the opportunity to communicate using multiple natural interaction modes. This paper discusses challenges to be faced when trying to design multimodal interfaces that allow for natural interaction with systems, with special attention to speech-based interfaces. It describes an application that was built to serve as a test bed and to conduct evaluation sessions in order to ascertain the impact of multimodal natural interfaces on users and to assess their usability and accessibility.

1 Introduction

According to the Ambient Intelligence (AmI) paradigm, present-day computers and telecommunication terminals will be replaced by an environment in which people will be surrounded by intelligent and intuitive interfaces. The environment will be aware of human needs and will be capable of proactively helping people to organize, structure, and manage their everyday activities in an invisible and unobtrusive way (see [5]).

AmI is supposed to support humans to reach their goals by engaging them in "natural" dialogues, possibly through the introduction into the intelligent environment of suitably-designed multimodal interfaces that offer the opportunity for communicating using multiple natural interaction modes such as speech, eye gaze, gestures and haptics, thus simulating the way in which human beings communicate with each other. While it will take some time to see full-featured AmI scenarios in place, the time seems mature for exploiting the capabilities of multimodal interfaces with a view to their future integration in AmI environments. In addition, interest in multimodality has recently been renewed due to the diffusion of mobile devices and to the awareness that multimodal interfaces can make, right from the present day, a valuable contribution to achieving universal access in the information society. Thus, the importance of multimodality is twofold: in the short term, it will make its contribution to providing universal access in the information society as it is structured at present; in the long term, it will serve as an essential foundation for AmI environments. However, benefits will not come automatically with the introduction of multimodal interfaces: they

C. Stephanidis (Ed.): Universal Access in HCI, Part II, HCII 2007, LNCS 4555, pp. 33–42, 2007.

will show up only if users and modalities are central during the design process. This paper attempts to outline in section 2 what challenges are to be faced when trying to design multimodal interfaces that allow for natural interaction with systems, with a closer look to speech based interfaces.

Section 3 describes an application that is based on an architecture which was introduced in [1]: it was built to serve as a test bed and to conduct evaluation sessions in order to ascertain the impact of multimodal natural interfaces on users and to assess their usability and accessibility.

2 Multimodal Interfaces

Multimodal interfaces are considered useful for interaction with AmI, especially when e-inclusion problems are taken into account. In particular, when interacting with services traditionally based on a direct human interrelation, a "human-like" dialogue could be a suitable solution to cooperate and get support from AmI, avoiding the need of learning and adapting to machine oriented user interfaces. This could be the case, for example, of the prototype service described in the paper (see section 3), which is meant to test features of multimodal interaction.

2.1 General Perspectives and Challenges

Interest in multimodality has recently been renewed[1] thanks also to the diffusion of mobile devices (which, in an evolutionary perspective, could evolve to become examples of future smart objects in AmI). Due to the fact that, at present, graphical interfaces and limited screen size oblige users to follow complex approaches in order to accomplish simple tasks, users are under-using mobile applications (as reported in [6], for example). Providing applications with multimodal interfaces might become a way to achieve more efficient, pleasant and natural interaction (see [10]). Moreover, there is general awareness that the flexibility and interaction capabilities offered by multimodal interfaces can make a valuable contribution to achieving universal access in the information society (see [9, 2, 11, 8]). All systems are supposed to achieve better usability and accessibility if users are able to interact with them through multimodal interfaces; therefore, multimodality may be of key importance for e-inclusion, by improving the usability and accessibility of information systems for a vast diversity of users, including elderly people. While there is general agreement on the fact that multimodal interfaces can make a significant contribution to rendering interaction easier, that they are easier to learn, and are preferred by users for many applications, it is worth considering that these statements are not automatically and inherently tied to injecting multimodality into interfaces. They will show up if the user and the modalities are kept central during the design process. So far, the development of user interfaces has been a technology-driven, rather than a user-driven, process: software design expects users to go through a learning and training process, to finally adapt to the product capabilities. This is especially true as computing capabilities are now

[1] In Europe the Similar network of excellence (http://www.similar.cc) comprises groups with interest in multimodality.

migrating away from the ordinary desktop computer towards mobile objects such as cell phones or PDAs. Due to limited screen size, interfaces tend to be rather complicated and it is almost inevitable that much time is spent by users in applying their attention to gaining a certain understanding of how mobile applications work. Instead, according to the modern approaches to interaction design, users should not have to adapt to machines, and machines should support users to achieve their goals. As for multimodal interfaces, this assumption has a number of implications. First of all, interfaces have to be designed from a user-centered perspective, so as to maximize user performances (along with system performance) and to satisfy user preferences. In this respect, Oviatt observes in [10] that multimodal interfaces are built using recognition-based technologies which have to interpret human behaviors that often are not even under full conscious control of users. Thus, it is virtually impossible for users (even for the most cooperative of them) to adapt to this kind of interfaces. Secondly, to achieve better matching of modalities to user needs, the context must be well defined and properly modeled. New approaches towards context modeling (see [3, 4]), could allow better shaping human activities, more efficiently anticipating their needs, more appropriately capturing attitudes to interact using different modalities and more accurate semantic interpretation of multimodal utterances. A third important point is that, in multimodal applications, the interface must be designed by respecting each modality's peculiarities, expressiveness, and interaction capabilities. Thus, it is necessary to understand how to reorganize and transform information in order for it to be appropriately conveyed by the desired modality, paying attention that the information contents are preserved across different modalities, at the maximum extent possible. This is a very difficult task, and it requires a profound understanding of the capabilities of each modality, which still need to be analyzed in depth. Actually, different modes have their own peculiarities, and these are best suited to conveying different types of information. No complete analogy exists between the different modes. For example, a speech interface is not the best one for describing the contents of a geographical map in a GIS application; it is, however, probably the most efficient if it is used in a conversational application such as a virtual travel agency or a booking centre for making appointments for medical examinations. This third aspect, along with the first one mentioned, implies that, when designing multimodal interaction, human computer interaction researchers should work as a team together with experts in different research fields, including the cognitive sciences. Moreover, it is important to keep in mind that no particular modality should be treated as a reference modality. This is what happens now in many voice-enabled applications, in which the graphical user interface has the role of "main interface" and the speech interface is treated as secondary, and it translates and describes information conveyed by windows and forms, thus loosing expressive power and giving rise to applications with poor usability. If these issues are not considered, few benefits can be expected from the introduction of multimodal interaction in applications, even if, from the implementation point of view, for some modalities, the technology seems mature enough to provide designers with tools that have the potential to bring a satisfactory and efficient multimodal interaction. In section 2.2, the principles that were discussed here at general level, in a modality independent fashion, are detailed in relation to a particular modality. The speech modality is chosen, because it is one of the most familiar to humans and because knowledge about speech interaction, both from the technological and the human factors points of view, appears to be sufficient to implement system that aim at achieving natural and human-like interaction.

2.2 Speech Based Interfaces

Among all the communication modalities, speech is probably the one to which humans are best adapted: people use their voices to exchange ideas and to communicate in their everyday life. Thus, human-computer speech interfaces have a great interaction potential, right from the present day, considering the fact that (apart from GUIs) they are the ones for which technology is more mature and readily available.

Though, enjoyable speech interfaces can be obtained if designers do not incur in the error to create them based on GUI metaphors and treat the GUI as the reference modality: there is general agreement, coming from past studies (see [7, 15] for example) that translating GUI results in speech interfaces with poor flexibility and usability. Speech interfaces can be roughly divided into two groups: menu driven and conversational ([7]).

Menu driven systems currently represent the most common type of applications with speech interaction capabilities. They enable users to accomplish their tasks by navigating through a hierarchy of successive steps. At each step, interaction possibilities are defined by a series of choices coded in menus, and users express their choice by issuing a vocal command. This theoretically represents an advance over keypad interfaces, where choices are expressed by pressing a number key, because menu driven voice systems allow a richer vocabulary and are more semantically consistent in that they eliminate the arbitrary association between a key and its corresponding function. However, the drawbacks are that their structure is so inflexible that they become tedious to use, and, moreover, their usability is poor when there are too many menu choices, because users' short-term memory gets overloaded. Even if menu driven voice systems are currently used with success in many services offered to the general public (for example they are used in many call centres), they do not appear to put users at the centre of the interaction process; moreover, going through a long series of menu options is indeed a kind of interaction that poorly respects the peculiarities of the speech modality. Given that humans interact with devices to achieve a goal (see [4]), which is certainly not represented by interacting with the computer system itself, the menu driven approach implies modelling tasks necessary to reach the goal state as a precise sequence of user actions, which is common and appropriate in GUI design. Now, it is to be observed that this is not the way humans act in the real world and that actions to be performed when trying to achieve some goal could be better modelled as an unordered set. Spoken dialogues between humans reflect the fact that humans do not usually follow a linear approach to reach their goals and tend to accomplish this by a continuous cooperation with the person who takes part in the conversation. For these reasons, conversational systems appear to offer a better model of users' behaviour and of the modality's characteristics.

During interaction with these systems, rather than asking a series of questions, the computer is supposed to cooperate with users (and not the inverse) in achieving some result. Interaction is more natural, because users can condense a sequence of menu choices into a single language utterance, which obtains its meaning both from the context and from the spoken words. This puts the user at the centre of the interaction process and highlights the importance of an appropriate modelling of context. In fact, certain expressions might have different meanings, depending on different situations. These reasons make conversational interfaces suitable for use in AmI environments, to enable access to dialogue based services. Though, designing conversational interfaces is a hard task, because it requires a knowledge in fields related to technology and computer science, as well as in fields that regard human-factors, such as linguistics, philosophy, psychology, sociology, in order to properly understand the mechanisms underlying human-human dialogues and to catch their essence. From a technological perspective, the main problem arises from the fact that dialogue inputs are uncertain, since speech recognizers have their error rates, so that one of the biggest challenges is to design interfaces that maximize the probabilities of correct understanding. To achieve this, great help comes from understanding the vocabulary, and this is attained from careful study and knowledge of the language domain in which a speech-based system will operate. Clearly, ordering a pizza is different from buying opera tickets: each domain has its own terminology, utterance structures, and interactive patterns. Also, it is important to build a model of the discourses that users employ in communicating and in performing their tasks. These can be key factors in obtaining usable, enjoyable and robust conversational interfaces.

3 System Overview

A speech based component in a multimodal interface is considered important for interaction with AmI, especially, but not only, when accessibility problems are taken into account. This is particularly true when services traditionally based on dialogues with humans need to be accessed, and this is the main reason why a prototype of a service based on speech interaction was regarded as an interesting building block of multimodal interfaces, to test some of the general considerations about the proper use of the features of the different modes.

3.1 Architectural Requirements

Designing and implementing "natural" multimodal systems is a difficult task, from both the technological and the human-factors perspective. It requires the use of suitable architectures. Their key factors should be modularity and, as pointed out in [12], the capability of easily integrating new technologies, in order to grow smoothly and facilitate evolutionary progress.

It is indeed necessary that developer teams include human computer interaction experts, as well as experts from all the fields pertaining to the modalities that the interface has to comprise (such as lexicographers and psychologists with discourse analytic training in the case of speech interfaces). If the architecture is well specified at an abstract level, the development effort can be distributed among different teams, each one focusing attention on designing the interaction for different modalities; contributions can then be integrated to form the final multimodal interface for the system.

As for architectures, a generic design approach for the development of multimodal applications that appears convincing is the one introduced by Carbonell and described in detail in [1]. It is based on a six-layer software architecture that aims to facilitate multimodal input and output processing, by matching multimodal utterances of users to appropriate methods supported by the application in question. One of the strengths of this approach lies in the fact that it neatly separates the user interface layer from the rest of the system, thus providing the possibility of designing unimodal interfaces separately from the others, possibly using, at the time of implementation, software for the generation of monomodal output and interpretation of monomodal input available on the market, and of developing the system in a cooperative fashion.

3.2 Application Description and Implementation Issues

The test application regards a public utility scenario which is potentially useful for the vast majority of citizens. It allows interaction with a booking and management service for medical examinations through a multimodal interface that combines a classical GUI with a vocal interface capable of speech recognition and synthesis. It is possible to check for available dates for medical examinations, to make, review and delete appointments, and to inspect results for examinations that were already taken. The application is based on an architecture that is essentially the one specified in [1] and described in section 3.1. It was built mainly to evaluate multimodal natural interfaces, to assess their usability and accessibility, and to evaluate their potential uses in AmI environments. While the focus of this paper is not on technology, technological aspects have naturally been considered to be important and have been exploited during the development process: in this respect, attempts have been made to design a modular application that allows for the reuse of important architectural components, such as monomodal output generators and monomodal input interpreters, with a view to future work.

During implementation, it was considered important to have the possibility for easily plugging modalities in and out, in order to better investigate how people make use of different combinations of modes, and, as previously mentioned, to facilitate collaborative work so that modalities can be implemented by different teams.

Some relevant implementation details about the application, whose overall structure is represented in Fig. 1, are reported in the following of this section.

As for the platform used, it is to be considered that the first interfaces to be integrated in the application were a GUI and a voice interface. Software development kits that provide programmers with a rich set of tools for building speech dialogue interfaces are available on the market: some examples are the Java speech API[2], the Microsoft .NET Speech Technology[3], the Philips Speech SDK[4], the IBM Via Voice SDK[5]. These toolkits all include accurate and robust speech recognizers that are reliable enough to meet general usability requirements for a speech-based interface. To achieve quicker integration, it was decided to use the Microsoft .NET 2.0 platform and Microsoft .NET Speech Technology. The platform provides assemblies that, besides

[2] http://java.sun.com/products/java-media/speech/

[3] http://msdn2.microsoft.com/en-us/netframework/default.aspx

[4] http://www.speechrecognition.philips.com

[5] http://www-306.ibm.com/software/voice/viavoice/dev/

integrating APIs that facilitate the development process of graphical user interfaces, offer the opportunity for easily integrating speech synthesis and recognition in an application. This makes it possible to focus attention on the interaction design, rather than on other implementation details, while providing an opportunity for later coding or integration of other monomodal interpreters/generators (either packed in assemblies compatible with the .NET platform or in DLLs compiled from C/C++ code). To address the general requirement expressed in [1] that a generic multimodal interface should offer the possibility for easily plugging in/out additional/existing modalities, different modalities were implemented in distinct assemblies.

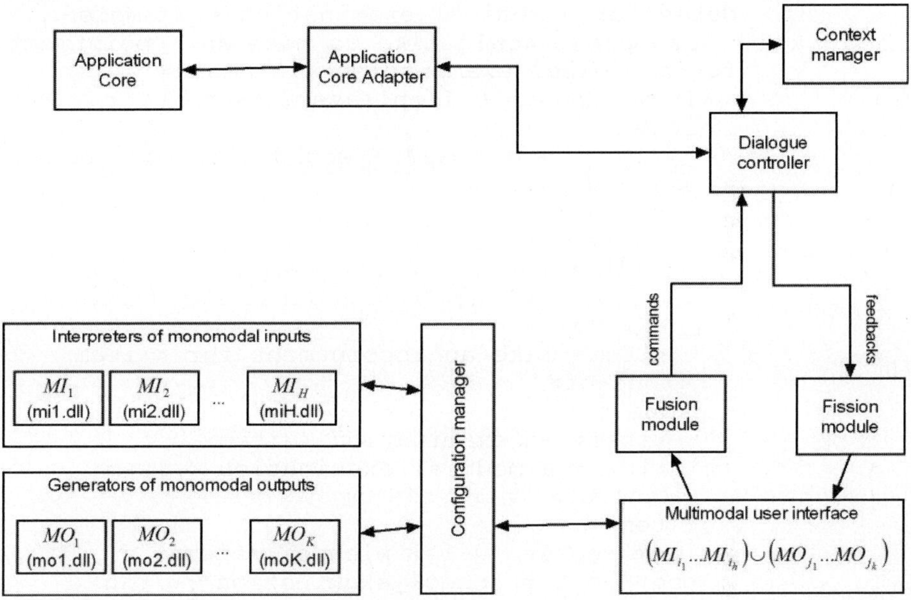

Fig. 1. Application structure

The decision as to which modalities should be included in the user interface is at the moment taken at start up time, during a configuration process based on an XML file that specifies which modalities to use, where the corresponding assemblies are to be found and how to configure the modalities. Anyway, nothing prevents loading and unloading interfaces while interaction occurs, for example as a result of adaptation processes. The configuration manager then employs dynamic loading and late binding, using reflection services (which, in the .NET universe, denote the process of runtime type discovery) to start up modalities of which it has no compile time knowledge of. While the GUI development did not require major efforts, when designing the speech interface the main point on which attention was focused was that of enabling conversational style interaction. To achieve reliable natural interaction with a speech system, it is first of all important to limit the speech recognizer's input uncertainty.

```
<?xml version="1.0" encoding="iso-8859-1"?>
<grammar root="check_dates"
        xmlns="http://www.w3.org/2001/06/grammar"
        xmlns:xsi="http://www.w3.org/2001/XMLSchema-
        instance"
        xsi:schemaLocation="http://www.w3.org/2001/06/
        grammar http://www.w3.org/TR/speech-     gram
        mar/grammar.xsd" xml:lang="en-US" ver
        sion="1.0">
        <rule id="check_dates">
          <example>I would like to check for available
        dates for a medical examination </example>
          <example>I would like to make an appointment
        for a medical examination </example>
          <item repeat="0-1">please</item>
          <item>
            <item repeat="0-1">I would like to</item>
            <one-of>
              <item>
                <item> check for </item>
                <item repeat="0-1"> available </item>
                <item repeat="0-1"> dates for </item>
              </item>
              <item> make an appointment for </item>
            </one-of>
            <one-of>
              <item> an examination </item>
              <item> a medical examination </item>
            </one-of>
          </item>
          <item repeat="0-1"> please </item>
          <tag>$.out = "check_examination";</tag>
        </rule>
</grammar>
```

Fig. 2. Example of grammar that allows phrases such as: "I would like to check for available dates for a medical examination" or "I would like to make an appointment for a medical examination". The semantic content is specified through the tag declaration.

It is then to be recalled that people are accustomed to speaking to other people, and the design must account for this preconditioned input method and take it as an "inspiration" to enable users to engage in natural and intuitive conversations with the system. As the platform supports W3C Speech Recognition Grammar Specification[6] (SRGS), it was decided to rely on grammar in order to achieve a balance between reliability and the possibility for users to pronounce articulated word sequences (see Fig. 2 for an example). Grammars basically define what the system is able to hear and interpret from the user at each segment of a dialogue, and is intended for use by speech recognizers and other grammar processors so that developers can specify the

[6] http://www.w3.org/TR/speech-grammar/

words and patterns of words to be heard by a speech recognizer, thus mitigating the effect of input uncertainty. In order to define grammars, it is necessary to properly understand the vocabulary (as described in section 2.2) by obtaining knowledge of the language domain. Even if it is typically outside the scope of the speech recognizer (and not supported by SRGS), but within the scope of a dialog manager (with the help of information coming from the context), to perform a more thorough semantic analysis, the SRGS provides syntactical support for a form of semantic interpretation through the use of the `tag-format` and `tag` declarations.

The use of grammars can help making interaction as natural and conversational as possible while reducing error rates during the recognition process. They are important to support specific groups of users with different speaking styles, such as accented people, children or elderly people, in which recognition error rates are higher (see [14]). This assumption is supported by the fact that, during our preliminary test sessions, the speech recognizer did not have any problems with users speaking English with a strong Italian accent.

4 Conclusions and Future Directions

The paper describes challenges to be faced and outlines possible directions to be followed when designing applications with multimodal interfaces that allow for natural interaction with computers, in view of future integration in AmI. In section 3, it discusses an example application designed according to the outlined directions. Of course, the application does not address all the themes involved in AmI: it deals with aspects related with natural multimodal interaction that were considered important for the development of AmI. As the application is now in place and ready to be tested, interest is in programming evaluation sessions to ascertain the impact of multimodal interaction on users, with special interest on visually impaired users, in order to check usability and accessibility. Also, it will be interesting to analyze and introduce more modalities into the application.

With a view to AmI, future directions of research will investigate the introduction of multimodal capabilities into portable devices, to allow for interaction with forms of intelligence distributed in the environment, for example by establishing wireless connections of PDAs to desktop computers playing the role of AmI. In this direction, it could be interesting to study possible benefits coming from the addition into the framework of a module handling abstract descriptions of the user interface like the ones described in [13].

References

1. Carbonell, N.: Multimodal interfaces -A generic design approach. In: Stephanidis, C. (ed) Universal Access in Health Telematics. LNCS, vol. 3041, pp. 209–223. Springer, Heidelberg (2005)
2. Carbonell, N.: Ambient multimodality: towards advancing computer accessibility and assisted living. Universal Access in the Information Society 5(1), 96–104 (2006)
3. Coutaz, J., Crowley, J.L., Dobson, S., Garlan, D.: Context is key. Commun. ACM 48(3), 49–53 (2005)

4. Crowley, J.L., Coutaz, J., Rey, G., Reignier, P.: Perceptual components for context aware computing. In: UbiComp '02: Proceedings of the 4th international conference on Ubiquitous Computing, London, UK, pp. 117–134. Springer, Heidelberg (2002)
5. Ducatel, K., Bogdanowicz, M., Scapolo, F., Leijten, J., Burgelman, J.C.: Scenarios for ambient intelligence in 2010. Technical report, Information Society Technologies Programme of the European Union Commission (IST) ((February 2001)
6. Fan, Y., Saliba, A., Kendall, E.A., Newmarch, J.: Speech interface: An enhancer to the acceptance of m-commerce applications. In: ICMB '05: Proceedings of the International Conference on Mobile Business (ICMB'05, pp. 445–451. IEEE Computer Society Press, Los Alamitos (2005)
7. Harris, R.A.: Voice Interaction Design: Crafting the New Conversational Speech Systems. Morgan Kaufmann, San Francisco (2005)
8. Maybury, M.T.: Universal multimedia information access. Universal Access in the Information Society 2(2), 96–104 (2003)
9. Oviatt, S.: Multimodal interfaces. In: Jacko, J., Sears, A., (eds.) Handbook of Human-Computer Interaction. Lawrence Erlbaum, New Jersey, pp. 286–304 (2003)
10. Oviatt, S.: User-centered modeling and evaluation of multimodal interfaces. In: Proceedings of the IEEE vol. 91(9) pp. 1457– 1468 (2003)
11. Richter, K., Hellenschmidt, M.: Position paper: Interacting with the ambience: Multimodal interaction and ambient intelligence. In: W3C Workshop on Multi-modal Interaction, 19./20.07.2004, Sophia Antipolis, France (2004)
12. Russell, D.M., Streitz, N.A., Winograd, T.: Building disappearing computers. Communications of the ACM 48(3), 42–48 (2005)
13. Trewin, S., Zimmermann, G., Vanderheiden, G.: Abstract representations as a basis for usable user interfaces. Interacting with Computers 16, 477–506 (2004)
14. Wilpon, J.G., Jacobsen, C.N.: A study of speech recognition for children and the elderly. In: Acoustics, Speech, and Signal Processing, ICASSP-96. Conference Proceedings. vol. 1 (7-10 May 1996) pp. 349–352 (1996)
15. Yankelovich, N., Levow, G.A., Marx, M.: Designing SpeechActs: issues in speech user interfaces. In: CHI '95: Proceedings of the SIGCHI conference on Human factors in computing systems, New York, NY, USA, ACM Press/Addison-Wesley Publishing Co, pp. 369–376 (1995)

Is the Intelligent Environment Smart Enough?

Laura Burzagli, Pier Luigi Emiliani, and Francesco Gabbanini

IFAC-CNR, Via Madonna del Piano, 10, Sesto Fiorentino, Firenze, Italy
{l.burzagli,p.l.emiliani,f.gabbanini}@ifac.cnr.it

Abstract. Ambient Intelligence (AmI) is considered a likely future embodiment of the information society, according to development scenarios proposed worldwide. With reference to the scenarios developed in Europe by the Information Society Technology Advisory Group (ISTAG), this position paper maintains that, up to now, the attention has been more on the smart objects that are supposed to populate the environment and their interfaces than on the "intelligence" of the entire system. The latter is of paramount importance if users are to be served according to the specifications of the AmI environments. Correspondingly, the current notion of Design for All needs to be revised in order to take into account the additional complexity of the emerging information society. Examples of the main points to be considered are offered in order to elicit discussion.

1 Introduction

According to converging worldwide agreement, the Information Society is developing towards an ambient intelligence environment in which people are surrounded by fixed and mobile intelligent objects that are interconnected through fixed and mobile networks which will allow access to information, interpersonal communication and environmental control. It is acknowledged that interaction with the intelligent environment will have to be redefined in order to guarantee certain characteristics that are considered necessary for the environment, not only to be acceptable but also usable and useful: i.e. to be unobtrusive, customizable, adaptive to different user needs, and anticipatory [1].

While most problems for integration within the present Information Society are connected with a suitable structuring of information and an accessible interface of users with the system (including an appropriate use of different modalities), integration within the ambient intelligence environment is much more complex because of the multiplicity and heterogeneity of intelligent objects in the environment, the variety of contexts of use, and the diversity of user goals.

The main purpose of this position paper is to discuss the meaning and role of "intelligence" in the emerging environment, by arguing that up to now the main emphasis of the development activity has been more in the "ambient" aspects of the emerging environment that is in the intelligent objects, their interconnection, and their interfacing [2-5], than in the intelligence of the environment as such, needed for identifying the goals of the users, how the goals become modified in different contexts and how AmI can contribute to their fulfilment in a way that is acceptable and

C. Stephanidis (Ed.): Universal Access in HCI, Part II, HCII 2007, LNCS 4555, pp. 43–52, 2007.

accessible by the users. Correspondingly, Design for All approaches that have been developed to make Information and Communication Technologies (ICT) systems and services and their interfaces accessible to all potential users need a revision and generalization at the technical approach level, in order to cope with emerging accessibility problems.

2 Design for All

2.1 The Classical Approach

Recently, due to changes in the political and social attitude towards problems of socio-economic integration and the increasing importance of information technology and telecommunication in our society, an interest in the Design for All (universal design) approach that has been developed in architecture and industrial design, has grown in connection with the problems of accessibility to ICT systems, services, and applications.

However, while in architecture and industrial design, Design for All can be conceived as an approach that leads to the design of an artefact that is accessible to all potential users (architectural barriers are a clear example), when dealing with information technology, it immediately became clear that a single artefact (for example the interface with a computer) could not be valid for all users. Therefore, even if at the conceptual level the definition of Design for All as "the design of products and environments to be usable by all people, to the greatest extent possible, without the need for adaptation or specialized design"[1] is the same in the various application environments, the implementation approach had to be carefully reconsidered.

The proposed approach, which was first applied in the design of human computer interfaces [6] and then generalized to the implementation of complete applications, is based on the concepts of adaptability and adaptivity [7;8]. The central idea is that the variety of possible users and contexts of use can be served only if the systems and services are able to adapt themselves automatically to the needs, requirements and preferences of every single user. The adaptation must be guaranteed at run time (adaptability) and, dynamically, during interaction (adaptivity). Adaptation to users is now considered an important feature of all systems and services in ICT, even if in most cases this general claim is considered to be satisfied by introducing some form of personalization under the control of the user.

2.2 Design for All in Future AmI Scenarios

The situation is much more complex if an instantiation of the information society as the one sketched in the introduction is taken into account. In fact, the information society is no longer seen as a support to the execution of activities such as accessing and manipulating information or communicating with other people, but is supposed to have an impact on all aspects of our social activities. This is clear if the socio-political factors at the basis of the deployment of the new technology and application environments as discussed in the ISTAG documents are considered[2]. According to ISTAG,

[1] See the Trace Center website at http://trace.wisc.edu/world/gen_ud.html

[2] See ISTAG web page at http://cordis.europa.eu/ist/istag.htm

AmI should: (i) facilitate human contacts; (ii) be oriented towards community and cultural enhancement; (iii) help to build knowledge and skills for work, better quality of work, citizenship and consumer choice; (iv) inspire trust and confidence; (v) be consistent with long-term sustainability – personal, societal and environmental - and with life-long learning; (vi) be controllable by ordinary people. In essence, the challenge is to create an AmI landscape made up of 'convivial technologies' that are easy to live with.

Accordingly, the main high-level design requirements of an ambient intelligence environment are that it must be unobtrusive (i.e. many distributed devices are embedded in the environment, and do not intrude into our consciousness unless we need them), personalized (i.e. it can recognize the user, and its behaviour can be tailored to the user's needs), adaptive (i.e. its behaviour can change in response to a person's actions and environment), and anticipatory (i.e. it anticipates a person's desires and environment as much as possible without the need for mediation).

It is clear from the above design requirements that Design for All in the information society must be much more than personalisation (adaptability) and adaptivity, which however are among the required features of AmI. Smart devices and (complex) services are supposed to be embedded in the environment, and must be able to provide support to users only when they need them, anticipating their desires. Moreover, this must occur in any place and context of use and in any moment. This requires the deployment of an infrastructure for supporting ubiquitous connection and computational power, but also of intelligence for identifying the goals of the users and helping users in fulfilling them. Therefore, the environment must not only be filled with intelligent objects (that is, computer-based systems), but must also be able to reason with regard to the goals of the users and to optimise the support in accordance with the resources available.

From this perspective, it is interesting to report some of the comments that ISTAG experts offer concerning the intelligence present in the environment [1]. For the Maria scenario, they report that the intelligence is in the seamless and intuitive support that Maria has as she goes around in her high-pressure world. She does not have to negotiate each step of her trip, because intelligent agents take care of most practical arrangements, even if she is always in control. This allows her to concentrate on the real purpose of her trip, in this case making her presentation. In the Dimitrios scenario, the system has to have a lot of intelligence. It must capture, process and share data about humans' lives by constructing and managing knowledge databases, while most of decision are made by agents. The seamless intercommunication of devices will generate a permanent and invisible data flow. The real role of AmI here is to expand human relationships. Mass consumption of D-Me's will create the possibility of people-based, ad-hoc networks that protect people from unwarranted interference in their lives and provide possibilities of making new contacts and interactions. It is supposed to develop a continuously changing virtual space in which amounts of virtual relations develop. Here, it is important to observe the complexity of the privacy and security problems in this environment as regards the criticality of the information to be used (database of a human's life) and the complexity of the virtual environment foreseen. Reasoning about decisions connected with the exchange or withdrawal of critical information will be of paramount importance as far as acceptance is concerned. For Carmen, the AmI approach leads to a much more efficient and user-friendly urban environment. It tries to optimise among the competing goals (e.g. individual preferences versus the good of the population) for the use of the urban space. This involves the operation of very large-scale systems, and requires societal acceptance of the legitimacy of the results (i.e. automated speed controls). Lastly, for Annette and Solomon the role of the AmI environment is to permit greater empowerment of users - starting with mentors and students - over their own tasks and processes in a learning environment. The system provides instant feedback on many different issues, which does not result from rule-based systems, but from the ability to record and review (if possible, quite literally) experiences of past and present participants. Moreover, technologies capable of supporting social (learning) processes must be deployed. The system starts with the simple provision of a network for communication and a collective corporate memory, on which gradually many different kinds of new applications can be built and to which new technological possibilities can be added. Therefore, it can be concluded that a lot of intelligence is necessary in the system in addition to what is needed to make systems and services adaptable and adaptive to the needs of the users.

3 Levels of Necessary Intelligence

While many problems connected with interaction with the present Information Society are actually linked to a suitable structuring of information and an accessible human system interface, integration within the ambient intelligence environment is much more complex, due to the interplay of different levels, e.g. the physical level with a multiplicity and heterogeneity of intelligent objects in the environment and their need for a continuous and high-speed connection, the level of identification and consideration of the variety of contexts of use, and the level of elicitation of the diversity of user goals and help in their fulfilment.

The system (intelligent ambient environment) must be able to seamlessly integrate the three levels considered above. At the lower level, all objects in the environment must incorporate intelligence and must be interconnected and able to cooperate in order to support the goals of the user. Moreover, the environment must be reconfigurable in real time, to cater for the introduction or removal of components (for example, objects that users entering the environment may have with them), by remodelling its support as a function of the available resources. This aspect of the intelligent environment is a prerequisite for its development, and the reconfiguration must take into account the variability of the contexts of use and the goals of the users.

At this level, artificial intelligence is crucial in supporting the development of basic technologies considered important in the implementation of AmI. For example, the ISTAG experts write that pattern recognition (including speech and gesture) is a key area of artificial intelligence which is already evolving rapidly. Speech recognition will have a big impact on the miniaturisation of devices and the augmentation of objects allowing hands-free operation of personal ambient devices. In the scenarios, the use of voice, gesture and automatic identification and localisation are implicitly used to synchronise systems, so that services are available when people want them. The synchronization of systems is indeed a very important aspect. In the intelligent environment, there may be different users with goals that have different importance and criticality. AmI must be able to decide how to take care of potentially conflicting needs (from the perspective of resources).

At a higher level, the AmI environment must take care of the contexts of use considered as processes, which are defined by specific sets of situations, roles, relations, and entities [9]. Recently, interest on the right definition and role of the contexts of use has grown, when dealing with both the development of user machine interfaces and with the organization and representation of information. For example, in connection with multimodality, it has been argued that the availability of different representations of the same information could be very interesting in order to avoid problems of context-related accessibility. Typical examples are car drivers who are functionally blind and motor disabled, meaning that they cannot interact with information and communication by using a screen and a pointer. But in AmI, the situation is more complex, because in the ubiquitous interaction with information and telecommunication systems the context of use may change continuously or abruptly and the same systems or services may need to behave differently in different contexts. A clear example to be considered is the complexity of the situation where a user is carrying out some activity in a room (for example, in the kitchen) and a second person enters the room. The system must reconfigure itself, not only due to the possible introduction of some additional intelligent component, but also because of the change in the context of use. The system must accommodate the original goals of two persons, and also take into account their interaction, which, for example, may redefine in real time some of their goals or change the time scale of different activities. This requires not only a complete configurability of the system and service at the level of interfaces and functionalities, but also the capacity of realizing changes in the environment and reasoning as to their impact on the context in which they are used.

When discussing the technology necessary for transforming the scenarios into reality, ISTAG experts [10] make a list of its intelligent components. They are:

(i) Media management and handling, including presentation languages that support "produce once" and "present anywhere", methods and tools to analyse content and enrich it with metadata, and tools for exploiting the Semantic Web;
(ii) Natural interaction that combines speech, vision, gesture, and facial expression into a truly integrated multimodal interaction concept, that allows human beings to interact with virtual worlds through physical objects, and that enables people to navigate the seemingly infinite information which they will be able to access;
(iii) Computational intelligence, including conversational search and dialogue systems, behavioural systems that can adapt to human behaviour, and computational methods to support complex search and planning tasks;
(iv) Contextual awareness, for instance, systems that support navigation in public environments, e.g. in traffic, in airports and in hospitals, service discovery systems that enhance the shopping experience, and context-aware control and surveillance systems;
(v) Emotional computing that models or embodies emotions in the computer, and systems that can respond to or recognise the moods of their users, and systems that can express emotions.

The above technologies are the necessary building blocks for implementing AmI environments populated by smart artefacts that can adapt to human behaviour and to different contexts, The question now is whether the list is exhaustive and what the impact of (artificial) intelligence is in really meeting the design requirements. That is, creating an environment where people can reach their goals and which they do not feel as artificial does not create problems of information overload and confusion, and is perceived as being worthy of trust and confidence.

Indeed, in addition to objects and contexts of use, there is a higher abstraction level to be considered. Most of the interaction with currently available systems is based on the performance of tasks in a set determined by the application used. In the intelligent environment, the goals of the user are the starting point. They must be inferred by the system and decomposed into tasks that are adapted to the preferences of the individual. This is really the level where intelligence plays a crucial role. The acceptability and uptake of the new paradigm will be essentially dependent on how smart the system is in inferring the goals of the users in the continuously varying contexts of use and in organising the available resources (intelligent objects in the environment) in order to help users to fulfil them. Moreover, this aspect is also very sensitive from a psychological perspective. For example, the system must be able to deal with the task of inferring the goals of the users without giving them the impression that they are under control (big brother), and must be able to support the users without giving them the impression that they are forcing them. It must "offer" possible solutions, not "impose" them. This requires a lot of ingenuity also on the part of human beings, and appears particularly difficult for a machine. However, it can also be argued that the intelligence in the system does not necessarily have to be artificial, but could and probably will also be in the network of interconnected and cooperating persons.

4 Annette and Solomon

In order to clarify the main points made above, let us now briefly discuss one of the ISTAG scenarios (that of Annette and Solomon) [1]. In the following discussion, it is taken for granted that the environment is completely functional from a technical point of view: i.e. it includes all intelligent objects necessary for carrying out the foreseen activities (sensors to monitor people's behaviour, actuators for suitably re-structuring the space, presentation systems); all the objects are interconnected through a broadband network that guarantees the necessary exchange of information, and suitable natural interaction systems are deployed. The focus is on the "intelligence" necessary, in addition to an efficient network of intelligent objects and natural interfaces, for making the scenario suitable for attaining the results described. Here as follows, the parts in italics report the scenario as described in the ISTAG document.

It is the plenary meeting of an environmental studies group in a local 'Ambient for Social Learning'. The group ranges from 10 to 75 years old. They share a common desire to understand the environment and environmental management. It is led by a mentor whose role it is to guide and facilitate the group's operation, but who is not necessarily very knowledgeable about environmental management. The plenary takes place in a room looking much like a hotel foyer with comfortable furniture pleasantly arranged. The meeting is open from 7.00-23.00 hours. Most participants are there for

4-6 hours. A large group arrives around 9.30 a.m. Some are scheduled to work together in real time and space and thus were requested to be present together (the ambient accesses their agendas to do the scheduling).

One of the complexities of this scenario has to do with the fact that it addresses a group, and not an individual. Therefore, the mentor and the ambient must be able to control both the group dynamics and the learning activity. This is why a mentor is considered necessary. He/she is not an expert in the topic to be learned. Therefore, his/her main role is apparently to work at the level of the group dynamics, while the organisation of the learning itself is mainly delegated to the AmI environment, to the group of learners, and to external experts. Additional difficulties lie in the fact that the group is not homogeneous (it includes people aged from 10 to 75 years). Obviously, the members have a different general culture, knowledge of the topic, interests, speed of learning, etc. Also, the group composition changes randomly with time, even if there are some scheduled meetings. Lastly, the space is not structured, and people can seemingly move around while the space is restructured in order to meet the needs of groups and individuals.

Therefore, the ambient must: (i) be acquainted with the topic to be taught and be able to organise it at the level of complexity suitable for the individual users, if and when they are studying individually, as a function of the user's present knowledge and culture and the goal(s) of the learning activity; (ii) know the individual users, and be able to follow them during their movements in the learning space; (iii) organise the common work on the basis of the goal(s) to be attained and the people who are in the group; (iv) reorganise the work when new persons are added to the group or leave it; (v) restructure the space as a function of the different groups that dynamically form it by making the necessary resources available; (vi) not interfere with the group dynamics. It must monitor the behaviour of individuals and the group, and support the mentor in her activity. This means that the ambient must understand what the mentor is doing, be able to reason with regard to the situation of the group, and behave accordingly.

A member is arriving: as she enters the room and finds herself a place to work, she hears a familiar voice asking "Hello Annette, I got the assignment you did last night from home: are you satisfied with the results?" Annette answers that she was happy with her strategy for managing forests provided that she had got the climatic model right: she was less sure of this. Annette is an active and advanced student so the ambient says it might be useful if Annette spends some time today trying to pin down the problem with the model using enhanced interactive simulation and projection facilities. It then asks if Annette would give a brief presentation to the group. The ambient goes briefly through its understanding of Annette's availability and preferences for the day's work. Finally, Annette agrees on her work programme for the day.

This introduces a new level of difficulty, because the ambient must not only be able to organise the learning material according to preset schemes, but must "understand" it as well, because it discusses the correctness of the work done by Annette and suggests how to clarify the controversial points.

One particularly long conversation takes place with Solomon who has just moved to the area and joined the group. The ambient establishes Solomon's identity; asks Solomon for the name of an ambient that 'knows' Solomon; gets permission from Solomon to acquire information about Solomon's background and experience in

Environmental Studies. The ambient then suggests Solomon to join the meeting and to introduce himself to the group. In these private conversations the mental states of the group are synchronised with the ambient, individual and collective work plans are agreed and in most cases checked with the mentor through the ambient. In some cases the assistance of the mentor is requested.

Even if it is not clear what "the mental state of the group are synchronised with the ambient" means and what the roles of the ambient and the mentor are, this probably implies a level of abstraction that is not compatible with suitable organisations of intelligent objects.

A scheduled plenary meeting begins with those who are present. Solomon introduces himself. Annette gives a 3-D presentation of her assignment. A group member asks questions about one of Annette's decisions and alternative visualisations are projected. During the presentation the mentor is feeding observations and questions to the ambient, together with William, an expert who was asked to join the meeting. William, although several thousand miles away, joins to make a comment and answer some questions. The session ends with a discussion of how Annette's work contributes to that of the others and the proposal of schedules for the remainder of the day. The ambient suggests a schedule involving both shared and individual sessions.

Again, the ambient is able to understand the problem under discussion and plan the work accordingly, as it is also able to segment it in individual and shared sessions. This implies an estimation of the individual's pace of learning and a careful planning for synchronising the individual sessions with the shared ones.

During the day individuals and sub-groups locate in appropriate spaces in the ambient to pursue appropriate learning experiences at a pace that suits them. The ambient negotiates its degree of participation in these experiences with the aid of the mentor. During the day the mentor and ambient converse frequently, establishing where the mentor might most usefully spend his time, and in some cases altering the schedule. The ambient and the mentor will spend some time negotiating shared experiences with other ambients – for example mounting a single musical concert with players from two or more distant sites. They will also deal with requests for references / profiles of individuals. Time spent in the ambient ends by negotiating a homework assignment with each individual, but only after they have been informed about what the ambient expects to happen for the rest of the day and making appointments for next day or next time.

This implies a high level of abstraction. The ambient is not a "big brother" that controls the activity of the member of the group and participates in the activities according to the perceived needs of the learning person. It is able to infer their possible difficulties and negotiate its level of participation with the learning person. The learning environment is not a school, but a place where people pursue a learning experience. Therefore, they have the right to learn what, how and when they want. The ambient must understand this, and negotiate with people only if it thinks that it could help in attaining their perceived goal. Moreover, as the mentor's activity is mainly related to the group dynamics, the fact that the mentor and the ambient discuss the matter of where the mentor should spend his/her time implies that the ambient has an understanding of the dynamics within the different groups.

5 Conclusions

The scenario commented above clearly shows that the usability and usefulness of AmI environments is not exclusively related to the availability of intelligent objects with natural interfaces that are efficiently interconnected through a broadband network and able to adapt themselves to the different contexts of use.

To be acceptable and useful, the AmI environment must be continuously able to obtain information not only about the users, but also about their goals, the space in which people are located, their interpersonal interactions, and the activities to be carried out in order to match the available facilities and support for fulfilling people's goals within the variable contexts of use. This is particularly true when it has to deal with groups of interacting people. Moreover, it must be able to "reason" with regard to people's goals and to their variability as a function of the context and the interaction with other people, in order to structure the activities necessary for attaining the goals in a way that is matched to the capabilities of the people and to the available resources. However, it must not give users the impression that they are controlled; instead, they should believe that they are always in control of the situation, and must have a sense of trust and confidence.

Therefore, the Design for All approach continues to be valid at the conceptual level, or, rather, it is the only reasonable possibility. This is because environments as complex as the emerging ones cannot be designed without taking into account the needs, requirements and preferences of all users. However, the underlying technical approach must be revised because, even if they are important, the concepts of adaptability and adaptivity, are not sufficient to satisfy the requirements of complex situations such as the ones described in the Annette and Solomon scenario.

The "quality" and "quantity" of the necessary intelligence and the balance between "natural" and "artificial" intelligence cooperating in the AmI environments is an open challenge at both the conceptual and technical levels.

References

1. Ducatel, K., Bogdanowicz, M., Scapolo, F., Leijten, J., Burgelman, J.C.: Scenarios for ambient intelligence in 2010. Technical report, Information Society Technologies Programme of the European Union Commission (IST) ((February 2001)
2. Coroama, V.: Experiences from the design of a ubiquitous computing system for the blind. In: CHI '06: CHI '06 extended abstracts on Human factors in computing systems, pp. 664–669. ACM Press, New York (2006)
3. Richter, K., Hellenschmidt, M.: Position paper: Interacting with the ambience: Multimodal interaction and ambient intelligence. In: W3CWorkshop on Multimodal Interaction, 19./20.07.2004, Sophia Antipolis, France (2004)
4. Johanson, B., Winograd, T., Fox, A.: Interactive workspaces. Computer 36(4), 99–101 (2003)
5. Garlan, D., Siewiorek, D., Smailagic, A., Steenkiste, P.: Project aura: Towards distraction-free pervasive computing. IEEE Pervasive computing 1(2), 22–31 (2002)
6. Stephanidis, C.: User Interfaces for All. Lawrence Erlbaum Associates, Inc. Mahwah, NJ, USA (2001)

7. Emiliani, P.L., Stephanidis, C.: Universal access to ambient intelligence environments: opportunities and challenges for people with disabilities. IBM Systems Journal 44(3), 605–619 (2005)
8. Emiliani, P.L.: Assistive technology (at) versus mainstream technology (mst): The research perspective. Technology and Disabilty 18(1), 19–29 (2006)
9. Coutaz, J., Crowley, J.L., Dobson, S., Garlan, D.: Context is key. Commun. ACM 48(3), 49–53 (2005)
10. ISTAG, Ambient Intelligence: from vision to reality. For participation in society and business, Information Society Technologies Programme of the European Union Commission (IST) (2003)

An Agent-Based Framework for Context-Aware Services

Axel Bürkle[1], Wilmuth Müller[1], Uwe Pfirrmann[1], Nikolaos Dimakis[2], John Soldatos[2], and Lazaros Polymenakos[2]

[1] Fraunhofer Institute for Information and Data Processing, Karlsruhe, Germany
{Axel.Buerkle,Wilmuth.Mueller,Uwe.Pfirrmann}@iitb.fraunhofer.de
[2] Athens Information Technology, 19.5 Km Markopoulou Ave., Peania, GR 19002
{ndim,jsol,lcp}@ait.edu.gr

Abstract. A major challenge of Ambient Intelligence lies in building middleware that can ease service implementation through allowing the application developer to emphasize only the service logic. In this paper we describe the architecture of an Ambient Intelligence system established in the scope of the European research project CHIL (Computers in the Human Interaction Loop). CHIL aims at developing and realizing computer services that are delivered to humans in an implicit and unobtrusive way. The framework presented here supports the implementation of human-centric context-aware applications. This includes the presentation of the sensors used in CHIL spaces, the mechanisms employed for controlling sensors and actuating devices, as well as the perceptual components and the middleware approach for combining them in the scope of applications. Special focus lies on the design and implementation of an agent based framework that supports "pluggable" service logic in the sense that the service developer can concentrate on coding the service logic independently of the underlying middleware. Following the description of the framework, we elaborate on how it has been used to support two prototype context-aware human centric and non-obtrusive services.

1 Introduction

The emerging Ambient Intelligence (AmI) paradigm aims at the convergence of pervasive and intelligent systems, exploiting the full range of sensors, devices and networks available to transparently provide services, regardless of time and the location of the end user [1]. AmI services are essentially context-aware services that acquire and process information about their surrounding environment. Context-aware applications execute service logic not only based on input explicitly provided by end users, but also based on information that is implicitly derived [2]. Implicit information is usually derived based on a rich collection of casually accessible, often invisible sensors that are connected to a network structure. Sensors provide information streams, which are accordingly processed by middleware components towards deriving context cues. As a characteristic example, complex perceptive interfaces and recognition algorithms process audiovisual streams and extract context relating to the identity and location of people and objects. Having an initial set of context cues, information fusion algorithms are applied to derive more sophisticated context, leading to situation recognition. Context-acquisition can then trigger the service logic of an AmI service. The latter is likely to be composed

C. Stephanidis (Ed.): Universal Access in HCI, Part II, HCII 2007, LNCS 4555, pp. 53–62, 2007.

of a rich set of invocations to soft-computing services, including commands to actuating devices, sensor control and regulation of the environment. Therefore, an infrastructure for Ambient Intelligence should at least include:

- A transparent sensing infrastructure, which is as non-intrusive as possible.
- An infrastructure for controlling sensors and actuating devices.
- A collection of perceptual components gaining elementary context cues from the various sensor streams.
- Information fusion components combining elementary context cues towards deriving more sophisticated context.
- An infrastructure for service provision.

These infrastructure and families of components can be seen as the common denominator of any non-trivial application. Building this common denominator infrastructure is a particularly challenging task. Indeed several major projects have allocated significant effort in building such hardware and middleware infrastructures [2][3][4][5][6]. As soon as these infrastructures are established, another challenge is to reuse these components to realize a variety of services. The challenge lies in building middleware that can ease service implementation through allowing the application developer to emphasize only the service logic rather than wondering about the integration with the underlying context-aware components. Such middleware is a key prerequisite for the wide adoption of Ambient Intelligence, given that it can significantly minimize the effort required to develop AmI applications.

In this paper we describe the sensing and middleware infrastructure established in the scope of the Computers in the Human Interaction Loop (CHIL) project [7] to support the implementation of human-centric context-aware applications for in-door environments. The paper is structured as follows: Section 2 gives an overview of the CHIL system architecture. Section 3 discusses the sensing infrastructure and context-aware middleware components established within CHIL. Section 4 presents the design of the agent-based framework that facilitates service access control and personalization, while also enabling service developers to plug service logic in a seamless fashion. Section 5 emphasizes two applications of the framework in the scope of two distinct services. Section 6 concludes the paper.

2 Architecture of the CHIL System

Due to the scale of the CHIL project with its large number of partners contributing to the CHIL system with a diversity of technical components such as services and perceptual components, as well as their complexity, a flexible architecture that facilitates integration of components at different levels is essential. A layered architecture model was found to best meet these requirements and allow a structured method for interfacing with sensors, integrating technology components, processing sensorial input and composing services as collections of basic services. Furthermore, the architecture described here supports flexible exchange of components and the replacement of unavailable components with simulators through well-defined interfaces.

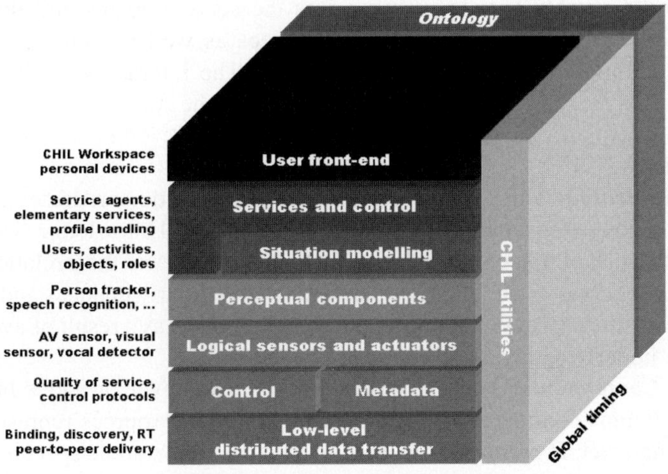

Fig. 1. CHIL architecture layer model

2.1 CHIL Layer Model

In order to realize proactive and intelligent services, both context-delivering and collaborating components have to be integrated. In our project, context is delivered both by perceptual components and learning modules. Perceptual components continuously track human activities, using all perception modalities available, and build static and dynamic models of the scene. Learning modules within the agents model the concepts and relations within the ontology. Collaboration is enabled by a set of intelligent software agents communicating on a semantic level with each other. The layered system architecture that facilitates the integration of different components is presented in Figure 1. The lower layers deal with the management and the interpretation of continuous streams of video and audio signals in terms of event detection and situation adaptation and contain the perceptual components. The upper layers of the infrastructure enable reasoning and management of a variety of services and user interfacing devices, based on agent communication. All layers use a common ontology as a backbone. A detailed description of the layers is given in the following section. The agent infrastructure of the CHIL system is described in more detail in section 4.

2.2 Description of the Layers

User Front-End: The *User Front-End* contains all user-related components such as the Personal Agents, Device Agents and the User Profile of a CHIL user. The Personal Agent acts as the user's personal assistant taking care of his demands. It interacts with its master through personal devices (e.g. notebook, PDA, smartphone) which are represented by corresponding Device Agents. The User Profile stores personal data and service-related preferences of a user.

Services and Control: This layer comprises the service agents and their management. Services include reusable basic services as well as complex higher-level services composed of suitable basic services. The interaction with other agents within this layer and the *User Front-End* layer uses the communication mechanisms of the agent platform, while communication with the other layers uses internal mechanisms.

Situation Modelling: This layer is a collection of abstractions representing the environmental context in which the user acts. An ontological knowledge-base maintains up-to-date state of objects (people, artifacts, situations) and their relationships. Additionally it serves as an "inference engine" that regularly deduces and generalizes facts during the process of updating the context models as a result of events coming from the underlying layer of *Perceptual Components*.

Perceptual Components: The *Perceptual Components* layer provides interpretation of data streams coming from various audio and video sources represented by the underlying layer. *Perceptual Components*, such as for example speech recognition, process the raw data input and generate higher-level semantics events used by the *Situation Modelling* layer and/or by the *Services and Control* layer.

Logical Sensors and Actuators, Control and Metadata, Low-level Distributed Data Transfer: These layers contain components which provide abstractions of the physical sensors and actuators, allow data annotation, storage, search and transfer of sensor data and control information.

CHIL Utilities: This layer provides functionality that is needed by several or all components in the framework, e.g. global timing.

Ontology: In order to enable the intended cognitive capabilities of the CHIL software environment, it is necessary to conceptualize entities and to formally describe relations among them. Through the ontology, CHIL software components both know the meaning of the data they are operating on and expose their functionality according to a common classification scheme.

3 Sensors Infrastructure and Context-Awareness

Sensing infrastructures are a key prerequisite for realizing context-aware AmI applications such as those developed, studied and evaluated within CHIL. Therefore, several sites within this project have constructed in-door environments comprising multi-sensor infrastructures with multiple microphones and cameras. These infrastructures are called 'smart rooms' and include at least:

- One 64 channel linear microphone array [8].
- Microphones for localization, grouped in inverse T-shaped clusters.
- Four fixed cameras, used for overall monitoring of the room.
- One active camera with pan, tilt and zoom (PTZ camera).
- A panoramic (or fish-eye) surveillance camera.

Based on these sensor infrastructures, a variety of perceptual components have been built and evaluated such as 2D (and 3D)-visual perceptual components, acoustic components, audio-visual components, as well as output perceptual components such as multimodal speech synthesis and targeted audio. Examples of such perceptual components which are operational in the AIT 'smart room' are:

- Acoustic identification and localization of the speaker [9].
- Person identification based on visual sensors [10].
- Detection and tracking of peoples' movements [11].
- Detection of speech activity [12].

3.1 Situation Recognition

Perceptual components derive elementary contextual information, and in general lack information about the overall current status of the people's interactions and environmental conditions. To be able to "fuse" many of these perceptual components together in order to determine more sophisticated and meaningful states, additional middleware interfaces have been developed to facilitate the intercommunication of these components, as well as higher layer agents which act as receptors of the whole range of the elementary context cues and process them in order to map the resulting contextual information into a complicated situation. This process is called situation recognition and is a major part of every human-centric Ambient Intelligence application.

Situation recognition, as developed in our implementation, follows the network of situation approach. This scheme allows the interconnection of distinct cases (situations), which are connected with arcs, forming a directed graph. A transition from one situation to another occurs if given constraints are satisfied. As soon as this transition is feasible, the service logic is applied, and the active state is reflected by the newly reached one. Context-awareness is hence modeled by this network. Figure 2 illustrates such a network of situations which can be used to track situations during meetings in a 'smart room'.

4 Agent Infrastructure

Ambient Intelligence services are usually based on complex heterogeneous distributed systems comprising sensors, actuators, perceptual components, as well as information fusion middleware. In projects like CHIL, where a number of service developers concentrate on radically different services, it is of high value that a framework ensures reusability in the scope of a range of services. To this end, we have devised a multi-agent framework that meets the following target objectives:

- Facilitates integration of diverse context-aware services developed by different service providers. Facilitates services in leveraging basic services (e.g. sensor and actuator control) available within the smart rooms.
- Allows augmentation and evolution of the underlying infrastructure independently of the services installed in the room.
- Controls user access to services.
- Supports service personalization through maintaining appropriate profiles.
- Enables discovery, involvement and collaboration of services.

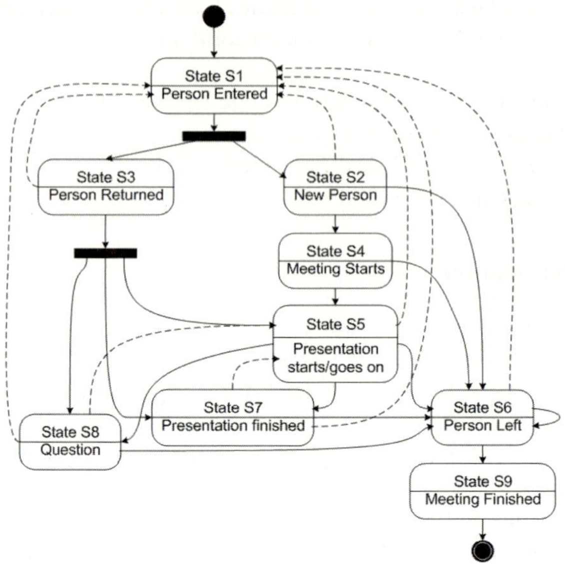

Fig. 2. An network of situations model for tracking meetings in a smart room

The CHIL software agent infrastructure, shown in Figure 3, is composed of three levels of agents. It covers the upper two layers of the CHIL architecture (cf. Figure 1). Agents and components close to the user form the level of User-Related Agents and are situated in the *User Front-End* layer, whereas the *Services and Control* layer contains the Basic Agents level providing elementary tasks and including a communication ontology as well as the level of specific Service Agents.

User-related Agents: Every person in the CHIL environment has his own Personal Agent acting as a personal secretary. Users interact with the system only via their self-adapting Personal Agents assigned during the login procedure. The Personal Agent manages interactions with its master through its associated Device Agents, whereby each device known to the system is represented by one Device Agent. It selects the input and output devices based on their availability and its master's context and preferences. Personal Agents and Device Agents act as the user interface of the different services provided by the Service Agents. Furthermore, the Personal Agent provides and controls access to its master's profile and preferences, thus ensuring user data privacy.

Basic Agents and Ontology: The main basic agents are the CHIL Agent and the CHIL Agent Manager. CHIL Agent is the basic abstract class for all agents used in the CHIL environment. It provides methods for agent administrative functionality, for registration and deregistration of the services provided by the agent instantiations, and additional supporting utility functions like creating and sending ontology-based messages, extracting message contents and logging. The CHIL Agent Manager is a central instance encapsulating and adding functionality to the JADE [13] Directory Facilitator (DF). Other CHIL agents register their services with the Agent Manager

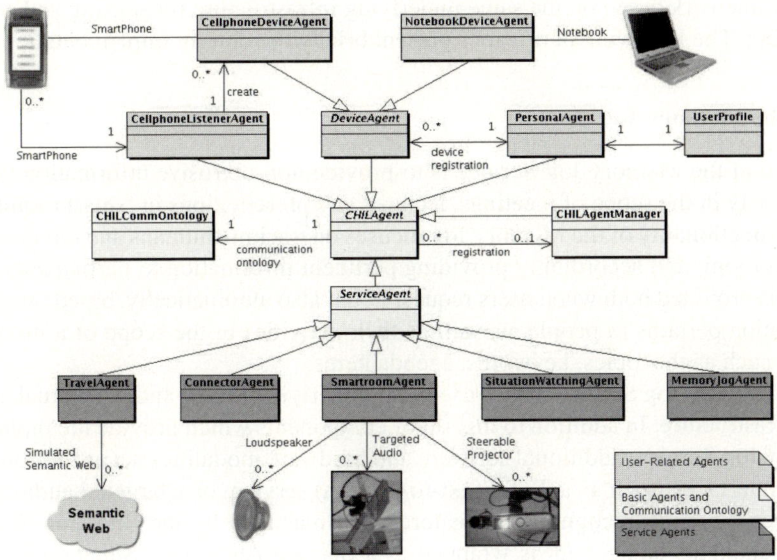

Fig. 3. Agent infrastructure

including required resources for carrying out these services. Service Agent is the abstract base class for all specific service agents.

Service Agents: Service Agents provide access to the service functionality. Based on a common ontology they map the syntactical level of the services to the semantical level of the agent community enabling the use of other Service Agents to supply their own service. The Memory Jog and the Connector Agent implement the functionality of the corresponding services. Both are described in detail in the next section. The Travel Agent can arrange and rearrange itineraries according to the user's profile and current situation. To gain information about flight and train schedules, it uses a simulated semantic web interface that gathers the required data from several online resources on the internet. The Smart Room Agent controls the service-to-user notification inside the smartroom using appropriate devices such as loudspeakers, steerable video projectors and targeted audio. The Situation Watching Agent provides access to the situation model.

5 Prototype Applications

We have exploited this architectural framework in implementing two different non-intrusive Ambient Intelligence applications, namely the 'Memory Jog' and the 'Connector'. These two applications demonstrate how this agent framework is indeed appropriate for developing context-aware applications. Specifically, implementations have shown that it is possible to use this framework to interface with situation modeling logic, as well as to invoke basic services. Nevertheless, demonstrating the full value of the framework, demands that two or more services are plugged into the same instance of the framework based on the same underlying infrastructure for sensing and context-awareness. The following paragraphs present briefly the current implementations.

5.1 The Memory Jog

The goal of the Memory Jog Service is to provide non-obtrusive information to boost productivity in the scope of meetings, lectures and presentations in 'smart rooms'. The current functionality of the Memory Jog focuses on tracking humans and their activities within a room, and accordingly providing pertinent information to participants. Information is provided both when users request it, but also automatically, based on context. Information pertains to people, as well as their activities in the scope of a meeting or lecture, such as the topics, keywords, agenda items.

The Memory Jog Service makes use of all underlying sensor and perceptual component infrastructure. In addition to this set of components which provide the input to the Memory Jog Service, additional software and hardware modalities act as the computer-human interfaces, such as a TTS (Text-to-Speech) service, or a targeted audio device. Moreover, situation recognition is featured and managed by the Situation Watching component. This component is wrapped as a Service Agent (i.e. Situation Watching Agent) and is accordingly integrated into the agent framework.

An agent implementing the service logic for the Memory Jog Service was developed by making use of all these infrastructure components. The agent was registered at the Agent Manager as a provider for the Memory Jog Service and the Agent Manager was extended by pluggable behaviors to integrate the agent into the system. The service logic includes:

- Display of peoples' identities and locations on an appropriate user interface.
- Tracking and displaying the meeting agenda.
- Automatic display of presentations on the participants' screens.
- Automatic e-mailing of presentations at the end of the meeting.
- Services invoked upon users' requests to play audio prompts, display messages to other participants, search a database based on the current contextual state.

The information provided by the Memory Jog is delivered to the user via his Personal Agent which invokes the appropriate Device Agent based on the user's preferences and context. The Device Agent filters the gathered information according to device limitations such as screen size and processing power, factors which should be taken under consideration in the case of e.g. a PDA.

5.2 The Connector

The goal of the Connector Service is to facilitate human communication during events that occur in in-door environments. It manages intelligent communication links (connections and notifications) and handles connection and notification requests, either simple requests (e.g. a meeting participant wants to talk to another) or more complex requests (e.g. a meeting participant wants to notify all other participants). The corresponding Connector Agent mediates between various Personal Agents and handles communications affecting two or more Personal Agents (Personal Agents may communicate with each other directly if there is only a direct communication between two Personal Agents). The Connector Service stores all pending connections and finds a suitable point of time for these connections to take place.

In order to describe the complex behavior of the Connector Service, we consider a sample scenario described in detail in [14]. In this scenario a meeting is scheduled in a CHIL smart room, where most of the meeting participants are already present in the meeting room. Another participant (Jeff) realizes that he will be late for the meeting and wants to inform the other participants about his delay.

Jeff uses his smartphone to trigger his Personal Agent (via the smartphone's Device Agent) which informs the Agent Manager of the delay. The Agent Manager asks the Meeting Agent for the meeting room number and a list of all meeting participants to inform them in the most efficient way. With this information the Agent Manager requests the responsible Connector Agent to deliver Jeff's message in an appropriate manner. After contacting the situation model via the Situation Watching Agent, the Connector Agent (being aware of a list of participants already in the meeting room), decides to notify them via the Smart Room Agent which is aware of the output devices available in the meeting room. The Smart Room Agent chooses to display the delay message with the central video projector. For those participants who are not yet in the meeting room, the Connector Agent informs their Personal Agents which in turn may choose an appropriate output medium for their masters (e.g. notebook, PDA, mobile phone, etc.) according to their current situation and user profile. Finally Jeff is informed again by his Personal Agent that his message has been delivered to all meeting participants.

Please note that the scenario described in [14] covers further functionality of the Connector Service and involves additional devices and agents. A detailed illustration of the complete scenario would be beyond the scope of this paper.

6 Conclusion

Common constituents of sophisticated Ambient Intelligence services are: a non-intrusive sensing infrastructure, infrastructures for controlling sensors and actuating devices, collections of perceptual components gaining elementary context cues from the various sensor streams, as well as a rich set of information fusion components combining elementary context cues towards more sophisticated context. Having these components at hand, a major research challenge is to reuse these components to realize a variety of Ambient Intelligence services. The challenge lies in building middleware that can ease service implementation through allowing the application developer to emphasize only the service logic, rather than wondering about integration with underlying components. In this paper we have presented an architecture of an Ambient Intelligence system with special focus on a distributed agent framework allowing developers of different services to concentrate on their service logic, while exploiting existing infrastructures for perceptual processing, information fusion, sensors and actuators control. The core concept of this framework is to decouple service logic from context-aware and sensor/actuator control middleware. Hence, service logic can be plugged in a specific placeholder based on well defined interfaces. The agent framework has been implemented based on the JADE environment, and accordingly instantiated within two real life smart rooms comprising a wide range of sensors and context-aware middleware components. The benefits of this framework have been manifested in the development of two radically different applications, one providing memory support during meetings and conferences, and another facilitating human communication.

Acknowledgements

This work is part of the project CHIL, an Integrated Project (IP 506909), partially funded by the European Commission under the Information Society Technology (IST) program. The authors acknowledge valuable help and contributions from all partners of the project.

References

1. Aarts, E., Marzano, S., (eds.): The New Everyday: Views on Ambient Intelligence. 010 Publishers, Rotterdam, The Netherlands (2003)
2. Dey, A.K., Salber, D., Abowd, G.D.: A conceptual framework and a toolkit for supporting the rapid prototyping of context-aware applications. Human-Computer Interaction 16 (2001)
3. Coen, M., Phillips, B., Warshawsky, N., Weisman, L., Peters, S., Finin, P.: Meeting the Computational Needs of Intelligent Environments: The Metaglue System. In: 1st Int. Workshop on Managing Interactions in Smart Environments, Dublin, Ireland (1999)
4. Johanson, B., Fox, A.: The Event Heap: An Coordination Infrastructure for Interactive-Workspaces. In: 4th IEEE Workshop Mobile Computer Systems and Applications (WMCSA 2002), Piscataway, N.J, IEEE Press, New York (2002)
5. Judd, G., Steenkiste, P.: Providing Contextual Information to Pervasive Computing Applications. In: IEEE Int. Conference on Pervasive Computing (Percom 2003), Dallas, USA (2003)
6. Saif, U., Pham, H., Paluska, J.M., Waterman, J., Terman, C., Ward, S.: A Case for Goal-oriented Programming Semantics. In: Dey, A.K., Schmidt, A., McCarthy, J.F. (eds.) UbiComp 2003. LNCS, vol. 2864, Springer, Heidelberg (2003)
7. CHIL - Computers in the Human Interaction Loop (2007), `http://chil.server.de`
8. Brandstein, M., Ward, D.: Microphone Arrays: Techniques and Applications. Springer, Heidelberg (2001)
9. Constantinides, A., Polymenakos, L., Talantzis, F.: Estimation of Direction of Arrival Using Information Theory. IEEE Computer Society Press, Los Alamitos (2005)
10. Pnevmatikakis, A., Polymenakos, L.: An automatic face detection and recognition system for video streams. In: 2nd Joint Workshop on Multi-Modal Interaction and Related Machine Learning Algorithms, Edinburgh (2005)
11. Pnevmatikakis, A., Polymenakos, L.: Kalman tracking with target feedback on adaptive background learning. In: Joint Workshop on Multimodal Interaction and Related Machine Learning Algorithms (2005)
12. Rentzeperis, E., Stergiou, A., Boukis, C., Souretis, G., Pnevmatikakis, A., Polymenakos, L.: An adaptive speech activity detector based on signal energy and lda. In: 2nd Joint Workshop on Multi-Modal Interaction and Related Machine Learning Algorithms (2005)
13. Java Agent DEvelopent Framework (2007), `http://jade.tilab.com`
14. Danninger, M., Flaherty, G., Bernardin, K., Ekenel, H., Köhler, T., Malkin, R., Stiefelhagen, R., Waibel, A.: The connector: facilitating context-aware communication. In: 7th Int. Conference on Multimodal Interfaces (ICMI'05), ACM Press, New York (2005)

An MDE-SOA Approach to Support Plastic User Interfaces in Ambient Spaces

J. Coutaz, L. Balme, X. Alvaro, G. Calvary, A. Demeure, and J.-S. Sottet

Université Joseph Fourier, Grenoble
{Joelle.Coutaz,Lionel.Balme, Xavier.Alvaro, Gaelle.Calvary, Alexandre.Demeure, Jean-Sebastien.Sottet}@imag.fr

Abstract. User interface (UI) plasticity denotes UI adaptation to the context of use (user, platform, physical and social environment) while preserving usability. Our approach to this problem is to bring together MDE (Model Driven Engineering) and SOA (Service Oriented Approach) within a unified framework that covers both the development stage and the runtime phase of plastic UI's. In particular, an interactive system is modelled as a graph of models that can be dynamically manipulated by, and/or encapsulated as services.

Keywords: User Interface plasticity, UI adaptation, Model-driven Engineering (MDE), Service Oriented Architecture (SOA), context of use, meta-UI.

1 Introduction

With the move to ubiquitous computing, user interfaces (UI) are no longer confined to a unique desktop. Instead, UI's may be distributed and migrate across a dynamic set of interaction resources that are opportunistically composed, borrowed and lent. As a result, user interfaces must adequately be plastic.

UI plasticity denotes the capacity for user interfaces to adapt to the context of use while preserving usability [7]. The *context of use* is a structured information space whose finality is to inform the adaptation process. It includes a model of the user who is intended to use (or is actually using) the system, the social and physical environments where the interaction is supposed to take place (or is actually taking place), and the platform to be used (or is being used). The latter covers the set of computing, sensing, communication, and interaction resources that bind together the physical environment with the digital world. *Usability* expresses the *useworthiness* of the system: the value that this system has in the real world [8].

From the software perspective, UI plasticity goes far beyond UI portability and UI translation. As discussed in Section 2, the problem space is complex. Software adaptation has been addressed using many approaches over the years, including Machine Learning [14], Model-Driven Engineering (MDE) [18], and Component-oriented services [17]. Our approach to the problem of UI plasticity is based on the following observations: first, every paradigm has its own merits targeted at specific requirements. Thus, in an ever-changing world, one single approach is doomed to

C. Stephanidis (Ed.): Universal Access in HCI, Part II, HCII 2007, LNCS 4555, pp. 63–72, 2007.

failure. Second, software tools and mechanisms tend to make a dichotomy between the development stage and the runtime phase making it difficult to articulate run-time adaptation based on semantically rich design-time descriptions.

Our approach to UI plasticity is to bring together MDE (Model Driven Engineering) and SOA (Service Oriented Approach) within a unified framework that covers both the development stage and the runtime phase of interactive systems. The principles of our solution space are presented in Section 3.

2 The Problem Space of UI Plasticity

As shown in Fig. 1, the problem space of UI plasticity is characterized (but is not limited to) the following dimensions: the means used for adaptation (i.e. re-molding and re-distribution); the smallest UI units that can be adapted by the way of these means (from the whole UI considered as a single piece of code to the finest grain: the interactor); the granularity of state recovery after adaptation has occurred (from the session level to the user's last action); the UI deployment (static or dynamic) as a way

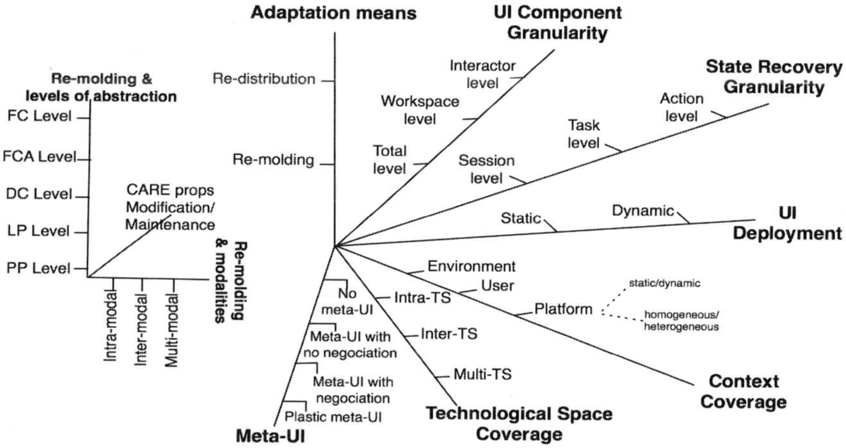

Fig. 1. The problem space of UI plasticity

to characterize how much adaptation has been pre-defined at design-time VS computed at runtime; the context coverage to denote the causes for adaptation with which the system is able to cope; the coverage of the technological spaces as a way to characterize the degree of technical heterogeneity supported by the system; and the existence of a meta-UI to allow users to control and evaluate the adaptation process. A subset of these dimensions is now developed in detail.

2.1 Two Adaptation Means: UI Re-molding and UI Re-distribution

UI re-molding denotes the reconfiguration of the user interface that is perceivable to the user and that results from the application of transformations on the user interface.

These transformations may result in suppressing the UI components that become irrelevant in the new context of use; inserting new UI components to provide access to new services, or reorganizing the UI components by revisiting their spatial layout and/or their temporal dependency. Re-molding may result in using different modalities, or in exploiting multimodality differently. For example, because of the lack of computing power, the synergistic-complementarity [9] of the source multimodal UI (as in "put that there") may be transformed into an alternate-complementarity (the user has to behave seuquentially), or complementarity itself may disappear.

UI re-molding is *intra-modal* when the source UI components that need to be changed are retargeted within the same modality. It is *inter-modal* when the source UI components that need to be changed are retargeted into a different modality. Inter-modal retargeting may engender a modality loss or a modality gain. Thus, a source multimodal UI may be retargeted into a mono-modal UI and conversely, a mono-modal UI may be transformed into a multimodal UI. As in Teresa [2], re-molding is *multi-modal* when it uses a combination of intra- and inter-modal transformations.

UI adaptation is often assimilated to UI re-molding. This is true as long as we live in a closed world where the interaction resources are limited to that of a single computer at a time. In ubiquitous computing, the platform may be a dynamic cluster composed of multiple interconnected computing devices whose interaction resources, all together, form a *habitat* for UI components. In this kind of situation, instead of being *centralized*, the user interface may be *distributed* across the interaction resources of the cluster. *UI re-distribution* denotes the re-allocation of the UI components of the system to different interaction resources. For example in CamNote, on the arrival of a PDA, the control panel of the slides-show dynamically migrates from the PC to the PDA (See Annex 1). Note that, as a consequence of re-distribution, all or parts of the UI may require re-molding.

2.2 Coverage of the Technological Spaces

"A technological space is a working context with a set of associated concepts, body of knowledge, tools, required skills, and possibilities." [12]. Examples of technological spaces include documentware concerned with digital documents expressed in XML, dataware related to data base systems, ontologyware, and so on.

Most user interfaces are implemented within a single Technological Space (TS), such as Tcl/Tk, Swing, html. This homogeneity does not hold anymore for plastic UI's since re-distribution to different computing devices may require crossing technological spaces. For example, a Java-based UI must be transformed into WML when migrating from a PDA to a WAP-enabled mobile phone.

TS coverage denotes the capacity of the underlying infrastructure to support UI plasticity across technological spaces: *Intra-TS* corresponds to UIs that are implemented and adapted within a single TS. *Inter-TS* corresponds to the situation where the source UI, which is expressed in a single TS, is transformed into a single distinct target TS. *Multi-TS* is the flexible situation where the source and/or the target user interfaces are expressed in distinct technological spaces. In CamNote, the control panel, when residing on the PC, is implemented with BIGre, a C++ homemade post-WIMP toolkit. It is a Windows-CE toolkit component when it resides on the PDA, whereas the slides display area is kept unchanged as a BIGre widget.

2.3 Existence of a Meta-UI

A *Meta-UI* is the set of functions (along with their user interfaces) that are necessary and sufficient to control and evaluate the state of interactive ambient spaces [11]. This set is *meta-*, since it serves as an umbrella beyond the domain-dependent services that support human activities in an ambient interactive space. They are *User Interface*-oriented since their role is to help users to control and evaluate the state of this space.

A *meta-UI without negotiation* makes observable the state of the adaptation process, but does not allow the user to intervene. This is the case for CamNote: as soon as a PDA enters or leaves the interactive space, UI re-distribution and UI re-molding are automatically applied. The weaving effect of the control panel that expresses its migration between the PC and the PDA is the meta-UI that allows the user to evaluate the evolution of the adaptation process. A *meta-UI incorporates negotiation* when, for example, it cannot make sound decisions between multiple forms of adaptation, or when the user must fully control the outcome of the process.

The balance between system autonomy and too many negotiation steps is an open question. Another issue is the *plasticity of the meta-UI* itself since it lives within an evolving habitat. Thus, the recursive dimension of the meta-UI calls for the definition of a *native bootstrap meta-UI* capable of instantiating the appropriate meta-UI as the system is launched. This is yet another research issue.

2.4 Summary

To summarize, the most demanding case corresponds to the following situation: all aspects of the CARE properties (Complementarity, Assignment, Redundancy, Equivalenece) are supported, from synergistic-complementary multimodality to mono-modal user interfaces. Re-molding and re-distribution are both supported and they both operate at the interactor level while guaranteeing state recovery at the user's action level. They cover all three aspects of the context of use (user, environment, platform). They are able to cross over technological spaces, and they include a plastic meta-UI. Re-molding is able to draw upon multiple modalities that may impact all of the levels of abstraction of an interactive system. And all this can be deployed dynamically.

To address the challenges raised by the development of plastic UI's, we propose a set of principles and approach that are still under development and validation.

3 Principles of Our Approach to Plastic UI's

Our principles and approach to the problem of UI plasticity in Ambient Spaces is to bring together MDE and SOA within a unified framework that covers both the development stage and the runtime phase of interactive systems. MDE aims at integrating different technological spaces using models, models transformations and mappings as key mechanisms. SOA defines the appropriate meta-model for a particular class of models: the runtime components. Services are contractually defined behaviors that can be implemented and provided by any software entity for use by any software entity, based on contracts [5]. Contracts range from a non-negotiable level (basic contracts) to a highly dynamically negotiable level (quantitative contracts) [3]. A fundamental characteristic of SOA is that the assembly of service-based software is performed from service descriptors. Discovery and linking between service providers and service customers are made belatedly, just before or at runtime. The flexibility offered by SOA fits our requirements for dynamic UI deployment. In addition, our requirements for fine grained UI components and for re-molding at multiple levels of abstraction are consistent with the modularity and re-usability principles of SOA. The following two principles demonstrate the complementary use of MDE and SOA.

3.1 Principle #1: An Interactive System Is a Graph of Models

An interactive system is a graph of models that expresses and maintains multiple perspectives on the system. As opposed to previous work, an interactive system is not limited to a set of linked pieces of code. As shown in Fig. 2, the models developed at design-time, which convey high-level design decision, are still available at runtime.

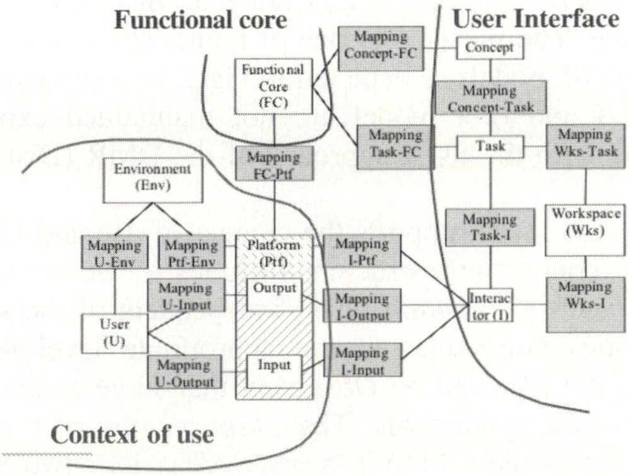

Fig. 2. A UI is a graph of models related by mappings

AUI may include a task model, a concept model, an Abstract UI model (expressed in terms of workspaces), and a Concrete UI model (expressed in terms of interactors) all of them linked by mappings. Tasks and Concepts are mapped to entities of the Functional Core of the interactive system, whereas the Concrete UI interactors are mapped to input and output (I/O) devices of the platform. Mappings between interactors and I/O devices support the explicit expression of centralized versus distributed UIs.

Transformations and Mappings are models as well. In the conventional model-driven approach to UI generation, transformation rules are diluted within the tool. Consequently, "the connection between specification and final result can be quite difficult to control and to understand" [13, p.13]. In our approach, transformations are promoted as models expressed in ATL [4, 18].

3.2 Principle #2: Close-Adaptiveness and Open-Adaptiveness Cooperate

A system is close-adaptive when adaptation is self-contained. The system is open-adaptive "if new adaptation plans can be introduced during runtime" [15]. By design, an interactive system has an innate domain of plasticity: it is close-adaptive for the set of contexts of use for which this system can adapt on its own. If it is able to learn adjustments for additional contexts of use, then the domain of plasticity extends dynamically, but this extension relies only on the internal computing capabilities of the system.

In ubiquitous computing, unplanned contexts of use are unavoidable, forcing the system to go beyond its domain of plasticity. If continuity must be guaranteed, then the interactive system must call upon a tier infrastructure that takes over the adaptation process. The role of this infrastructure is to compute the best possible solution by applying new transformations and mappings on the system models and/or by looking for the appropriate services sitting somewhere in the global computing fabric. Fig. 3 shows the functional decomposition of our run-time infrastructure [1].

The platform layer includes the hardware and the legacy operating system(s), which, together, form the habitat of the interactive system. The interactive system layer includes the interactive systems (e.g., CamNote) that users are currently running in the interactive space. The meta-UI is one of them. The structure of an interactive system may be a graph of models as depicted in Fig.2, or a subset of this graph where, for example, the AUI and task model are not maintained explicitly. This MDE approach is combined with the SOA approach of the DMR (Distribution-Migration-Remolding) layer.

The DMR middleware layer supports the context of use and UI adaptation by the way of *services*. The context infrastructure includes a *sensing layer* that generates numeric observables and a *perception layer*, independent of the sensing technology, that provides symbolic observables at the appropriate level of abstraction. The symbolic observables are received by *Observers* that serve as gateways between the "world" and the situation synthesizer. The *platform observer* gathers information about the platform (e.g., a new PDA has arrived/has left, two surfaces have been coupled) by subscribing to the services of the context infrastructure that probe the evolution of the platform. It maintains the platform model shown in Fig. 2. The *physical environment observer* maintains a model of the physical place (e.g., we are in room R, or in street S), and the *users observer* probes users (for instance their profile, or their position relative to a wall surface such that information is not projected in their back). The *interactive systems observer* subscribes to information relevant to interactive systems plastification. For instance, an interactive system may produce the event "current situation S is out of my domain of plasticity" so that open-adaptation can take over the retargeting process.

The *situation synthesizer* computes the current situation from the information provided by the observers. A situation is defined by a set of obervables that satisfies a set of predicates [10]. When the cardinality of the set of observables changes and/or when the predicates do not hold anymore, a new situation is entered. For example, in CamNote, the arrival or departure of a PDA results in a new situation. Situations form a graph. Ideally, the graph of situations results from a mix of specifications provided by developers, by users (using the meta-UI), or learnt automatically by the situation

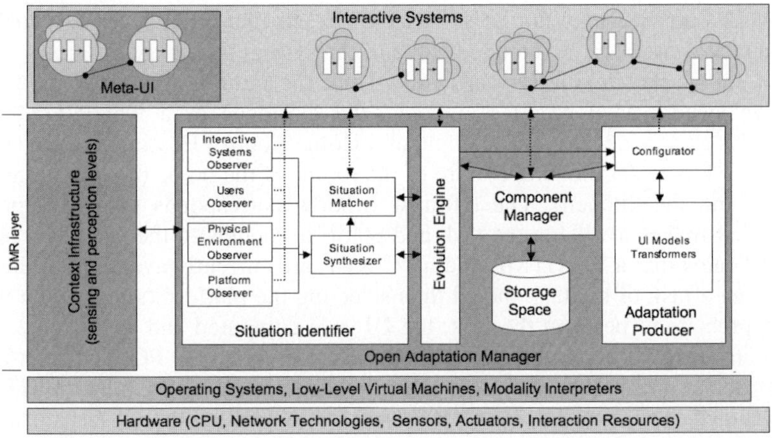

Fig. 3. The overall functional decomposition of a middleware for plastic UI's

synthesizer. In CamNote, the graph of situations has been provided by the programmer. Entering a new situation is notified to the evolution engine.

The *evolution engine* elaborates a reaction in response to the new situation. As for the graph of situations, the reaction may be a mix of specifications provided by developers and/or users (using the meta-UI), or learnt by the evolution engine. In CamNote, reactions are expressed by developers in terms of rules. For example, "if a new PDA arrives, move the control panel to the PDA". The reaction may result in retargeting all or part of the UI. If so, the evolution engine identifies the components of the UI that must be replaced and/or suppressed and provides the configurator with a plan of actions. In the case of CamNote, the plan is to "replace the PC control panel with a PDA control panel without loosing any previous work".

The *Configurator* executes the plan. If new components are needed, these are retrieved from the *storage space* by the *component manager.* Components of the storage space are described with conceptual graphs and retrieved with requests expressed with conceptual graphs. By exploiting component reflexivity, the configurator stops the execution of the "defectuous" components specified in the plan, gets their state, then suppresses or replaces them with the retrieved components and launches these components based on the saved state of the previous components. In CamNote, the PC control panel is replaced with a PDA control panel and its state is restored properly so that users can continue the slides-show at the exact slide number before migration occurred (state recovery is at the user's action level).

The components referred to in the action plan do not necessarily exist as executable code. They may instead be high-level descriptions such as task models or AUI's. If so, the configurator relies on *reificators* to produce executable code as in Digymes and iCrafter. A retrieved component may be executable, but may not fit the requirements. It may thus be reversed-engineered through *abstractors*, and then transformed by *translators* and reified again into executable code [6, 16]. Alternatively, the components storage is unable to provide an acceptable solution. In this case, if the graph that depicts the interactive system at run time includes a high-level description such as the task model, then a new CUI can be produced on the fly.

The new CUI service may not be as "usable" as expected, but at least, it makes the expected tasks possible: the intended value of the system is preserved.

Fig. 4 shows the flexibility that results from the interplay between modeling an interactive system as a graph of models, the existence of a meta-UI and of UI transformers as services. In this example of a Home Control Heating System (HHCS), the user's task is to set the temperature of the rooms of the home (i.e. the living-room, the cellar and the kitchen). The leftmost window corresponds to a very primitive meta-UI that makes available the task and platform models to the user. The platform model indicates that a PC HTML and a PC XUL are currently available in the home. By selecting a task of the task model then selecting the platform(s) on which the user would appreciate to perform the task, the UI is re-computed and redistributed on the fly, thus ensuring UI consistency. When the user deselects the PC XUL platform for the task "Select room" then the XUL UI is updated accordingly whilst the HTML UI is not changed. The meta-UI is an OSGI service as well as the UI transformers (an embedded ATL transformation engine).

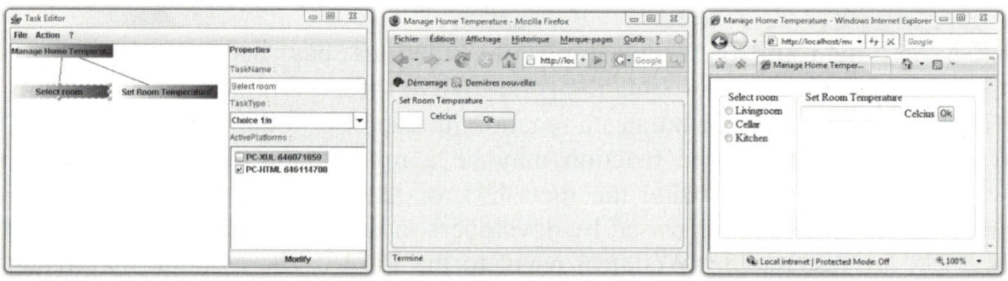

Fig. 4. A basic meta-UI making it possible for the user to redistribute the UI

4 Conclusion

In summary, the problem space of plastic UI covers many dimensions. As a solution space to this complexity, we propose the combined use of MDE with SOA where an interactive system is not simply pure code, but a graph of models related by mappings and transformations, and where general purpose functions such as UI transformers are encapsulated as services. We shown the promise of our approach with the development of early examples of applications and infrastructure. This work is still under progress.

Acknowledgments. This work has been partly supported by Project EMODE (ITEA-if4046) and the NoE SIMILAR- FP6-507609.

References

1. Balme, L., Demeure, A., Barralon, N., Coutaz, J., Calvary, G.: CAMELEON-RT: A Software Architecture Reference Model for Distributed, Migratable, and Plastic User Interfaces. In: Markopoulos, P., Eggen, B., Aarts, E., Crowley, J.L. (eds.) EUSAI 2004. LNCS, vol. 3295, pp. 291–302. Springer, Heidelberg (2004)

2. Berti, S., Paternò, F.: Migratory multimodal interfaces in multidevice environments. In: Proc. International Conference on Multimodal Interfaces, ACM Publ, pp. 92–99. ACM Press, New York (2005)
3. Beugnard, A., Jézéquel, J.-M., Plouzeau, N., Watkins, D.: Making components contract aware. IEEE Computer 13(7), 38–45 (1999)
4. Bézivin, J., Dupé, G., Jouault, F., Pitette, G., Rougui, J.: First Experiments with the ATL Transformation Language: Transforming XSLT into Xquery. OOPSLA Workshop (2003)
5. Bieber, G., Carpenter, J.: Introduction to Service-Oriented Programming (Rev2.1) (2002), http://www.openwings.org/download.html
6. Bouillon, L., Vanderdonckt, J.: Retargeting of Web Pages to Other Computing Platforms with VAQUITA. In:Proceedings of the Ninth Working Conference on Reverse Engineering (WCRE'02), p. 339 (2002)
7. Calvary, G., Coutaz, J., Thevenin, D., Limbourg, Q., Souchon, N., Bouillon, L., Vanderdonckt, J.: Plasticity of User Interfaces: A Revised Reference Framework. (TAMODIA' 2002) pp. 127–134 (2002)
8. Cockton, G.A: development Framework for Value-Centred Design. In: ACM Proc. CHI 2005, Late Breaking Results, pp. 1292–1295 (2005)
9. Coutaz, J., Nigay, L., Salber, D., Blandford, A., May, J., Young, R.: Four Easy Pieces for Assessing the Usability of Multimodal Interaction: The CARE properties. In: Proceedings of the INTERACT'95, pp. 115–120. Chapman&Hall Publ, Sydney, Australia (1995)
10. Coutaz, J., Crowley, J., Dobson, S., Garlan, D.: Context is Key. Communications of the ACM 48(3), 49–53 (2005)
11. Coutaz, J.: Meta-User Interface for Ambient Spaces. In: Coninx, K., Luyten, K., Schneider, K.A. (eds.) TAMODIA 2006. LNCS, vol. 4385, pp. 1–15. Springer, Heidelberg (2007)
12. Kurtev, I., Bézivin, J., Aksit, M.: Technological Spaces: an Initial Appraisal. CoopIS, DOA'2002 Federated Conferences, Industrial track, Irvine (2002)
13. Myers, B., Hudson, S.E., Pausch, R.: Past, Present, and Future of User Interface Software Tools. Transactions on Computer-Human Interaction (TOCHI), ACM Publ. vol. 7(1), pp. 3–28 (2000)
14. Njike, H., Artières, T., Gallinari, P., Blanchard, J., Letellier, G.: Automatic learning of domain model for personalized hypermedia applications, International Joint Conference on Artificial Intelligence, IJCA, Edinburg, Scotland, pp. 1624 (2005)
15. Oreizy, P., Gorlick, M., Taylor, R., Heimbigner, D., Johnson, G., Medvidovic, N., Quilici, A., Rosenblum, D., Wolf, A.: An Architecture-Based Approach to Self-Adaptive Software, IEEE Intelligent Systems, May/June, pp. 54–62 (1999)
16. Paganelli, L., Paternò, F.: Automatic Reconstruction of the Underlying Interaction Design of Web Applications. In: Proceedings Fourteenth International Conference on Software Engineering and Knowledge Engineering, Ischia, pp. 439–445. ACM Press, New York (July 2002)
17. Sheshagiri, M., Sadeh, N., Gandon, F.: Using Semantic Web Services for Context-Aware Mobile Applications. In: Proceedings of ACM MobiSys2004 Workshop on Context Awareness, Boston, Massachusetts, USA, (June 2004)
18. Sottet, J.-S., Calvary, G., Favre, J.-M.: Towards Model Driven Engineering of Plastic User Interfaces. In: Briand, L.C., Williams, C. (eds.) MoDELS 2005. LNCS, vol. 3713, Springer, Heidelberg (2005)

Annex 1

CamNote (for CAMELEON Note) is a slides viewer whose UI is composed of four workspaces: a slides viewer, a note editor for associating comments to slides, a video viewer also known as pixels mirror that shows a live video of the speaker, and a control panel to browse the slides and to setup the level of transparency of the pixels mirror. As shown in the picture, the pixels mirror is combined with the slides viewer using alpha-blending. Speakers can point at items on the slide using their finger.

(a)

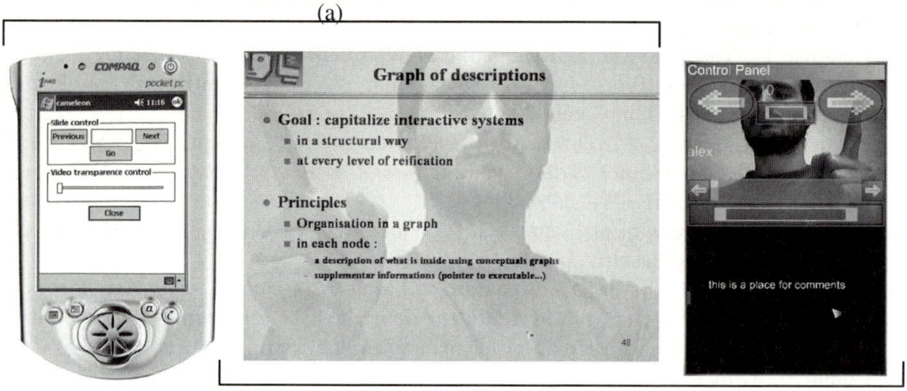

(b)

Figure a) shows a Pebbles-like configuration where the graphical UI is distributed across the surfaces of a PC and of a PDA. If the PDA disappears, the control panel automatically migrates to the PC screen. Because different resources are now available, the control panel includes different widgets, but also a miniature representation of the speaker's video is now available (cf. Figure b). During the adaptation process, users can see the control panel emerging progressively from the slides viewer so that they can evaluate the progress of the adaptation. The UI, which was distributed on a PC and a PDA is now centralized on an elementary platform. Conversely, if the PDA re-enters the interactive space, the UI automatically switches to the configuration of Figure a) and the control panel disappears from the PC screen by weaving itself into the slides viewer before reappearing on the PDA.

Whole-System Programming of Adaptive Ambient Intelligence

Simon Dobson and Paddy Nixon

Systems Research Group, School of Computer Science and Informatics
UCD Dublin IE
{simon.dobson, paddy.nixon}@ucd.ie

Abstract. Ambient intelligence involves synthesising data from a range of sources in order to exhibit meaningful adaptive behaviour without explicit user direction, driven by inputs from largely independent devices and data sources. This immediately raises questions of how such behaviours are to be specified and programmed, in the face of uncertainty both in the data being sensed and the tasks being supported. We explore the issues that impact the stability and flexibility of systems, and use these issues to derive constraints and targets for the next generation of programming frameworks.

1 Introduction

Ambient intelligence faces an uncomfortable duality. On the one hand, systems must be constructed from networks of independently-constructed and -programmed devices, often having very restricted local functionality; on the other, these systems must produce user-centric behaviour which reacts to complex scenarios in a way that retains a clear focus on the users' activities on an ongoing basis. While it is attractive to think that user-centric behaviour will simply "emerge" from the interactions of individual devices, there are strong reasons to suspect that a more directed approach will be needed in most cases. This suggests that ambient intelligence requires a "script" of some kind for each service or application being hosted, provided at the level of the network rather than the level of the individual devices.

While numerous pervasive *applications* have been demonstrated, large-scale *systems* remain elusive. It is hard to recognise what is happening in the real world; hard to translate this into meaningful adaptive behaviour; hard to ensure that the adaptive behaviours remain within an acceptable envelope; hard to ensure that individual services compose without interference; and hard to deal with the inevitable mistakes that occur when performing complex actions without explicit user instruction.

We have previously conjectured [1] that whole-system descriptions of adaptive systems provide both a more principled approach to design and a more verifiable platform upon which to perform development. Experience has borne-out this conjecture, but has also raised the significance that the uncertainty of sensor

C. Stephanidis (Ed.): Universal Access in HCI, Part II, HCII 2007, LNCS 4555, pp. 73–81, 2007.

data and task inference have for ambient intelligence applications. Our goal in this paper is to explore two questions which we believe are of critical importance for any platform for adaptive systems:

1. What impact do the low quality, diffuse and semantically heterogeneous nature of sensor data and task inference have on programming? and
2. What do these imply for the creation of middleware and other programming support frameworks for ambient intelligence?

We conclude that ambient intelligence is *not* primarily about sensing, but rather relies on leveraging information from a diverse range of sources with rich interconnections. This in turn changes the fundamental problem from being one of sensing and reasoning to one of information management and truth maintenance: a holistic view of the system's responses to its changing environment.

Section 2 explores the nature of sensing and inference in ambient systems, from which section 3 derives some criteria that must be met by any suitable programming platform. Section 4 concludes with some possible directions for future research.

2 Uncertainty in Sensing and Inference

The literature on pervasive computing and ambient intelligence contains a large number of example applications. Typically these follow a similar storyline (figure 1): a collection of sensors is fitted to an environment and used to collect data about the activities of users within that space, who may be using various electronic and networked devices. Events from these devices are used to select behaviour for the system to exhibit, which in turn is visible to and affects the environment. This closing of the feedback loop is characteristic of adaptive and autonomic systems [2].

Unfortunately this abstract description elides all the issues which make ambient intelligence problematic – and also those which make it most useful.

2.1 The Uncertainty of Sensors

Traditional applications provide a bounded context within which interaction may occur. For most systems there is very little uncertainty in these interactions: a user presses a key or selects a menu item, or doesn't. In some systems there may be errors due to lost, garbled or repeated messages which are typically handled using middleware; in almost all systems there will be operator errors which must be correctable in some way, typically with minimal impact[1]. The point is that interaction, while it may be *wrong*, is at least *definite*.

[1] Although not always: accountancy software, for example, will typically not allow an erroneous transaction to be deleted, forcing the user to explicitly record a cancelling transaction. This of course if the "correct" behaviour for this particular application domain.

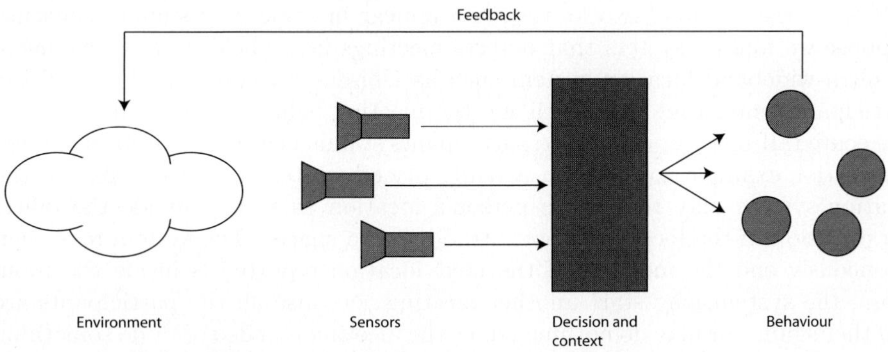

Fig. 1. Archetypal ambient intelligence applications match sensor data to a task description

Ambient interaction exhibits completely different characteristics. Interaction occurs (at least in part) by way of sensors observing "everyday" actions. Even within a single category such as location, each family of sensor has often radically different characteristics (figure 2).

System	Range	Precision
GPS	Global	1m
GSM triangulation	Global	50m
RFID	Building	room/door
Wifi triangulation	Local-area	20-50m
Ultra-wideband	Room	10-30cm
Cameras	Room	10cm

Fig. 2. The precision of location sensing can vary dramatically

First we must recognise the distinction between *precision* and *accuracy* – two terms that are sometimes used almost synonymously. A location sensor's precision describes the smallest detail it can resolve – or, to put it another way, the minimum distance that an object must move before the sensor registers a change. A sensor's accuracy describes the extent to which the location it reports for an object corresponds to that object's "real" position. For example, a Wifi location system such as PlaceLab might generally report a device's position to within 10m (precision), but might also (because of reflections or beacon misplacement) exhibit sporadic or systematic errors [3] which place a device in a totally different position unrelated to the way it is actually sensing at the physical level (accuracy). The terms apply analogously to most sensors.

This raises an interesting mis-match. The design of an application in the style of figure 1 will typically be phrased in terms such as "when A and B are in room X, perform action *1*". No single sensor is likely to provide information of sufficient precision to make this decision with any confidence.

If these issues sound exotic, they can appear in some very simple scenarios. Suppose we build a system that detects meetings being held in an office, using an ultra-wideband location system such as Ubisense[2] (figure 3). When all the participants enter the office (area A), the meeting behaviour – whatever it is – is executed. If however one of the participants stands near the door for whatever reason (for example to draw on a badly-placed whiteboard near area C), the location system may report the person's location as being outside the office: the precision of the location report straddles two spaces. The system may then erroneously end the meeting. If the next location reported is inside the room again, the system may start another meeting (because all the participants are together again), or may do nothing (since the meeting is ended) – or do something else entirely.

There are a number of issues to be teased out here. Firstly, there is an interesting interaction between the sensors' imprecisions, the layout of the real world, and the behaviour a user will observe. For the system to potentially exhibit undesirable behaviour, a user must stand in an area in which, at the location sensor's resolution, straddles two spaces, *and* those spaces must exhibit different behaviours, *and* the user must stand in the area without meaning proceed into the other space. If any of these conditions does not pertain, the system will be more likely to behave correctly: if, for example the whiteboard is moved away from the door to the other side of area A, a user standing in the zone of uncertainty is less likely to be an unwanted transient.

The underlying problem is that *we cannot assign meaning to a single action*, only to a *constellation of actions* taken in context. Some actions "just happen", and so we need to be careful that we do not designate innocuous actions as triggers for behavioural change.

2.2 From Sensing to Task

Event-driven pervasive systems address this issue by providing a model of the tasks which the application is supporting. The events received are used to "move the task along" in the manner of a workflow system. Unfortunately processes in pervasive systems tend not to be well-specified – and if they are, users will anyway tend not to follow them with the precision required of workflow. In scenarios in which the process *can* be followed precisely (such as for the computer theatre of Pinhanez and Bobick [4]) then temporally-enriched forms of workflow such as [5] can usefully be used: in less structured cases, however, experience has shown that such systems do not provide significant benefits and have problems with their expressive power.

Things become even more complicated when we consider ambient *systems* containing several applications or services. A given action may then be interpreted by several applications simultaneously, each of which may then exhibit a behaviour. These behaviours are "independent", in the sense of not affecting one another; however, they may also be "dependent" in that one application's

[2] http://www.ubisense.net

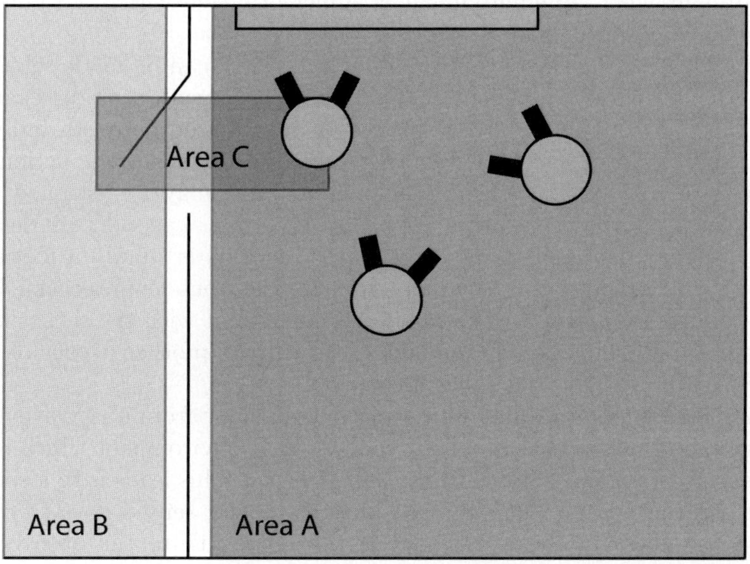

Fig. 3. There are some subtle interactions at play between sensor imprecision, behaviour and task

behaviour may detrimentally affect another's. The classic example is having two applications controlling the lighting level in a room: if they disagree on the "right" level, which is selected?

3 Designing and Programming with Uncertainty

To summarise, any data used to drive a pervasive computing system is inherently uncertain in ways that improved sensor technology will not completely address. The relationship of this data to the scenarios being supported by the pervasive systems is tentative, since an action often cannot be unambiguously assigned a particular meaning in a process that is subject to the uncertainties of users' everyday actions. This implies that *any decision taken within a task may be wrong*, in that it may be driven by data that has been mis-interpreted.

What does this imply for systems? One might take the pessimistic view that ambient intelligence is a flawed dream which cannot be achieved because of the limitations of sensing the real world. A more balanced view is that *any decision may be taken incorrectly*. This has a significant impact on programming. We can split the problem into two parts: how can we determine that a decision has been taken in error?, and what can be done if and when the mistake is detected?

Although sensors are individually imprecise, a sufficiently sensor-rich environment may be able to compensate for these individual deficiencies and develop a more accurate consensus estimate of the values being sensed. This raises a question about when an environment is sufficiently sensor-rich – a question to which we have no principled answer.

We may observe, however, that an ambient system can be made significantly richer without heavy investment in sensors. Using location as an example, a system may have many potential sources of information as to an individual's location: sensors form one part, but there are also diary entries, actions taken that correlate to locations, default behaviours that may be assumed, and so forth [6]. Such alternative sources are of low precision – people's diaries do not generally reflect their movements precisely – but this is simply a feature they share with any other sensor. We may therefore extract low-precision location information from a diary (for example) and combine it with the sensor readings we are obtaining from the environment. It is simply another aspect of context that can be "mined" for location information.

The important point is that we decouple behaviour from observations taken in isolation, and instead use a holistic model of the environment which is driven by *all* aspects of the environment that we can sense. This leads is to a somewhat different abstract model than we used in figure 1: use sensed data to maintain and refine a model of the world that is the "best fit" to the observed data. Applications and services, in this model, test scenario hypotheses against the world and activate those that are supported by the current consensus (figure 4). Scenarios are deactivated when they cease to be supported.

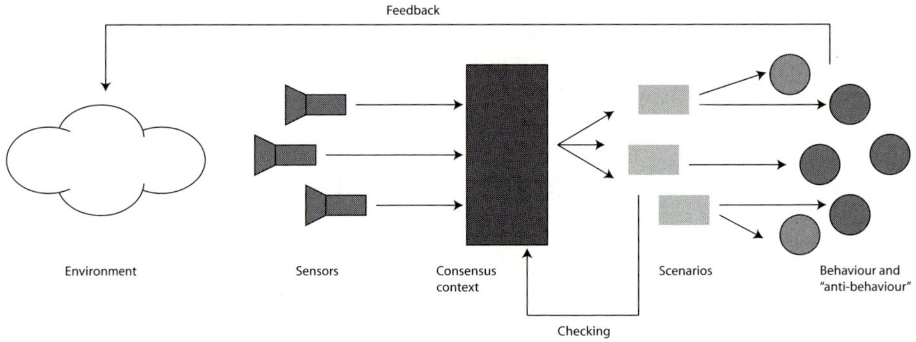

Fig. 4. We need to constantly check the validity of hypotheses, including past ones, against the evolving context

This leads to a number of general statements about programming platforms for this class of systems:

Events are too noisy to serve directly as a basis for programming. An event derived from a sensor, such as an observation of an individual in a particular space, may be issued in error. If the application reacts to this event it will react to noise, so applications must attempt to identify noise locally before performing actions. In many cases the signal-to-noise ratio will be low, and applications can become cluttered with noise-handling code at the expense of application logic. This is hard to do purely at the event level, without reference to a wider context, and suggests that "composite" event systems such as those of Hayton *et alia* [7] may not be suitable for pervasive applications.

It is important to stress that this is not a criticism of events as a *communications* construct, where they can provide a very flexible and scalable communications framework. Rather, it is a criticism of using events directly as a *programming* construct, since they seem to devolve too much of the system's complexity onto applications programmers under an abstraction model that makes it difficult to deal with locally.

Don't take anyone's word for anything. One solution to noise is to construct systems which "damp" erroneous observations by fusing observations across a range of sources. By maintaining a context model, distributed across the pervasive system, which maintains a running "consensus estimate" of values of interest, a single observation has less scope for skewing the consensus.

A corollary of this approach is that it provides a way of dealing with semantically heterogeneous data sources. Each sensor can deliver data in its lower ontology, which can then be mapped to an upper used by applications [8]. The advantage is that applications are insulated from the details of the individual sensors available, reducing the impact of changes in the sensor population. The upper ontology can present the on-going consensus estimate of values such as location, allowing context fusion to occur within the platform and away from individual applications. This is the approach we are taking with the Construct platform [9,10].

Interconnection is more important than data. Although it is a commonplace to think of ambient intelligence as pertaining to sensors, it might be more useful to think of it in terms of leveraging information from a richly-interconnected model. It is possible to build ambient intelligence with little or no traditional sensor data for example: a location-aware system could be driven by asking the user to spot landmarks, or by using default assumptions about behaviour.

By contrast, we cannot deem a system "ambiently intelligent" if it is simply driven by sensor events, taking no account of other factors. The model, its relationships and the ability to extract information through fusion is far more characteristic of the domain than the availability of sensors.

Any decision needs a mitigation strategy. No matter how successfully we perform consensus, however, it is inevitable that errors will remain, and these errors can cause major problems for applications. At a suitably abstract level, the issue is simple: a decision is made at time t, and at some subsequent time $t + \delta$ information becomes available to show that the decision was made incorrectly. The problem is then to incorporate this new information into the on-going computation. This may happen as a result of sensor error, of mis-interpreting an action intended for another service, or simply because new information arrives over time.

The classical approach to such problems is rollback as found in databases. This will no work for pervasive computing: one might literally be shutting the stable door after the horse has bolted! We must therefore investigate non-classical solutions such as, for every action a resulting from a decision, providing an action a^{-1} that can be performed if action a is determined to have been in error. Actually the situation is a bit more subtle, since the appropriate action a^{-1} is actually a function of δ, and will vary depending on when the error is recognised.

The general point, however, is that applications must be written with failure in mind. In programming language terms, mistakes are often dealt with using exceptions; in ambient intelligence, *failure is not exceptional* and so requires a different programming idiom. It is by no means clear how to provide such an idiom without cluttering a system with mitigating code.

Everything interesting comes from composition. The final criterion involves the nature of systems. While it is possible to address many of the issues we have highlighted within a single application, such *ad hoc* approaches will inevitably break down when confronted with more complex systems, and especially with systems composed of applications which are not known *a priori*. It is therefore essential that ambient intelligence is constructed on a well-founded basis which is compositional in nature.

At the present state of the art, placing two ambient services in the same space is a somewhat fraught activity. We have no way of deciding whether two systems will interact positively or interfere. Similarly, independent behaviours may be suitable to run together or may not, or one may take precedence over another. The details of a particular system are not important for the current argument: what *is* important is the idea that composing applications and services has a system-wide impact, and the results of composition should be well-definable ahead of time. This is the only way in which we can reliably deploy large-scale ambient intelligence with the degree of confidence needed by a large organisation.

4 Conclusion

Ambient intelligence involves synthesising data from a range of sources in order to exhibit meaningful adaptive behaviour without explicit user direction. The imprecisions, inaccuracies, incompleteness and contradictions implicit in sensor- and inference-driven decision-making place strong requirements on the stability and flexibility of systems, which in turn impact on the programming solutions deployed.

In this paper we have attempted to highlight some of these issues in a way that lends itself to the development of programming platforms suitable for ambient intelligence. The challenges centre around dealing with through-going uncertainty in a principled fashion, whilst providing an environment in which services may be safely composed with known impact. This involves developing tools and techniques – at design, programming and analytic levels – which can improve the confidence with which we make decisions based on often flimsy data. Exactly what sort of programming environments will emerge to address these challenges is an open – and exciting – area of current and future research across the community.

In some ways the current activity mirrors that of parallel and distributed programming. Initial approaches based on semaphores, suitable for simple applications but with rapidly intractable complexity as systems grow, were replaced by more structured approaches such as transactions and skeletons together with middleware abstractions reflecting the realities of the underlying domain. We hope that ambient intelligence will evolve similar mechanisms for manging the complexity of systems.

Acknowledgements

This work is partially supported by Science Foundation Ireland under grant numbers 05/RFP/CMS0062 ("Towards a Semantics of Pervasive Computing"), 04/RPI/1544 ("Secure and Predictable Pervasive Computing"), and 03/CE2/I303-1 ("LERO: the Irish Software Engineering Research Centre").

References

1. Dobson, S., Nixon, P.: More principled design of pervasive computing systems. In: Bastide, R., Palanque, P., Roth, J. (eds.) Human computer interaction and interactive systems. LNCS, vol. 3425, Springer, Heidelberg (2005)
2. Kephart, J., Chess, D.: The vision of autonomic computing. IEEE Computer 36, 41–52 (2003)
3. Hightower, J., LaMarca, A., Smith, I.: Practical lessons from PlaceLab. IEEE Pervasive Computing 5, 12–19 (2006)
4. Pinhanez, C., Bobick, A.: Human action detection using PNF propagation of temporal constraints. In: Proceedings of CVPR'98, pp. 898–904 (1998)
5. Allen, J., Ferguson, G.: Actions and events in interval temporal logic. Journal of Logic and Computation 4, 531–579 (1994)
6. Dobson, S.: Leveraging the subtleties of location. In: Bailly, G., Crowley, J., Privat, G., eds.: Proceedings of Smart Objects and Ambient Intelligence, pp. 175–179 (2005)
7. Hayton, R., Bacon, J., Bates, J., Moody, K.: Using events to build large-scale distributed applications. In: Proceedings of the 7th ACM SIGOPS European workshop on systems support for worldwide applications, ACM Press, pp. 9–16. ACM Press, New York (1996)
8. Clear, A.K., Knox, S., Ye, J., Coyle, L., Dobson, S., Nixon, P.: Integrating multiple contexts and ontologies in a pervasive computing framework. In: Contexts and ontologies: theory, practice and applications (2006)
9. Coyle, L., Neely, S., Rey, G., Stevenson, G., Sullivan, M., Dobson, S., Nixon, P.: Sensor fusion-based middleware for assisted living. In: Nugent, C., Augusto, J.C. (eds.) Smart homes and beyond, pp. 281–288. IOS Press, Amsterdam (2006)
10. Dobson, S., Coyle, L., Nixon, P.: Hybridising events and knowledge as a basis for building autonomic systems. Journal of Autonomic and Trusted Computing, To appear (2007)

Informative Art Display Metaphors

Alois Ferscha

Institut für Pervasive Computing
Johannes Kepler Universität Linz
Altenberger Strasse 69, 4040 Linz, Austria
ferscha@soft.uni-linz.ac.at

Abstract. Informative Art display systems have been proposed to provide users with information considered relevant at arbitrary points of work or living engagement, originating from many different –mostly geographically dislocated– sources and presented at the periphery of human (visual) perception. Having the displays operate at the periphery of a user's attention allows other user tasks to sustain primary. Much like the information presented by wallclocks, posters, paintings or windows, peripheral displays move to the center of attention only when appropriate and desirable. Abstract art has been proposed to serve as the visualization paradigm, encoding information into graphical or pictorial artwork by subtly modifying its shape, color and appearance details or its overall impression. This paper approaches a systematic elaboration of visual metaphors able to deliver information via peripheral displays in an aesthetic, artful way. In our approach, the choice of metaphors is driven by the aesthetic appeal of the visual appearance of the display as a whole, out of which certain dynamic emblems or symbols are used to conotate information in a visual style. From experiments we find, that such metaphors are considered by users as a means of personal emotional expression, and that controllable aesthetic attractiveness turns out to be the dominant factor of display appreciation. The choice of aesthetic themes, as well as the control of emblem and symbol dynamics are supported and implemented in our *peripheral display framework*, a general purpose software framework for informative art display systems.

Keywords: pervasive display systems, informative art, peripheral displays, ambient intelligence, intelligent user interfaces.

1 Hidden in Artwork

"*The rate at which computers disappear will be matched by the rate at which information technology will increasingly permeate our environment and determine our lives*" [23]. As an example from the current Pervasive and Ubiquitous Computing literature, the above to the point statement reflects an observation, that computing devices are continuing to pervade into everyday objects in such a way, that users do not notice them anymore as separate entities. Appliances, tools, clothing, accessories, furniture, rooms, machinery, cars, buildings, roads, cities, even whole agricultural landscapes increasingly embody miniaturized and wireless, thus invisible information and communication systems. Information technology rich systems and spaces are

C. Stephanidis (Ed.): Universal Access in HCI, Part II, HCII 2007, LNCS 4555, pp. 82–92, 2007.

being created radically changing the style of how we perceive, create, think, interact, behave and socialize as human beings, but also how we learn, work, cultivate, live, cure, age as individuals or in societal settings. A major issue in such technology rich settings is how we perceive information, how we interact with digital media, how we manage to sustain attentive to information of interest, how we stay aware of the dynamics and changes of information, or how we manage perceptual complexity and information overload.

Peripheral displays were proposed to provide users with information considered relevant at arbitrary points of work or living engagement, originating from many different –mostly geographically dislocated– sources, and presented at the periphery of human (visual) perception [12]. Having the displays operate in the periphery of a user's awareness allows other user tasks to sustain primary [8] [13]. Much like the information presented by clocks, posters, paintings or windows, peripheral displays move to the center of attention only when appropriate and desirable. Computational counterparts of such displays have been designed to support for group awareness in work groups in virtual [5] [6] [7] or in physical [20] [22] [23] [24] space settings, for knowledge dissemination in enterprises [17], for users of instant messaging systems [2][3], for deaf users [9], to keep in touch with family members [19], or to display a cities health information in public places [1] – to name a few. Metaphorically, abstract art has been proposed to serve as the visualization paradigm for contextual information [21], design principles and guidelines have been developed [11] [14], upon which software frameworks and development toolkits [15] [16] have been built. Evaluation guidelines have been developed [11][14] and assessment studies have been conducted, e.g. relating comprehension of peripheral displays (i.e. how well a user understands and uses such artifacts) to the time span of their use [10].

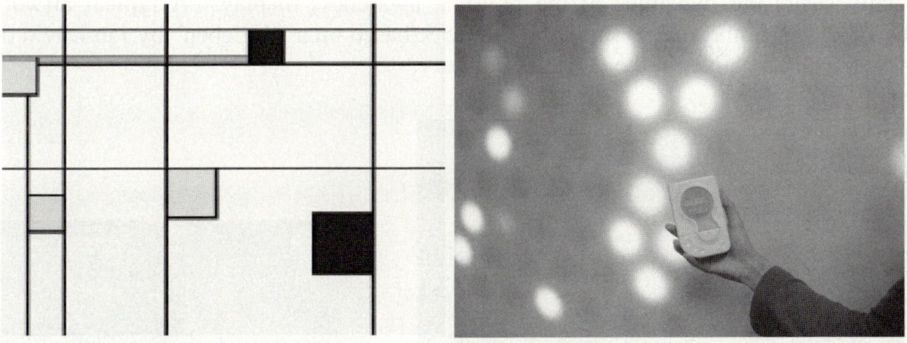

Fig. 1. Abstract Informative Art [21] (*left*), inspired by Mondrian, in real time shows the expected weather situation or urban bus traffic situation; The Hello.Wall [24] (*right*) displays abstract aesthetic patterns of mood or presence in work teams, and provides interaction patterns for personalized or group related communication among remote team members.

Informative Art [25] displays particularly addressing (i) the *cultural context* within which information is being displayed, (ii) the *aesthetic appeal* exploited to address personal emotional expression, and (iii) the *continuity of comprehension*, so as to

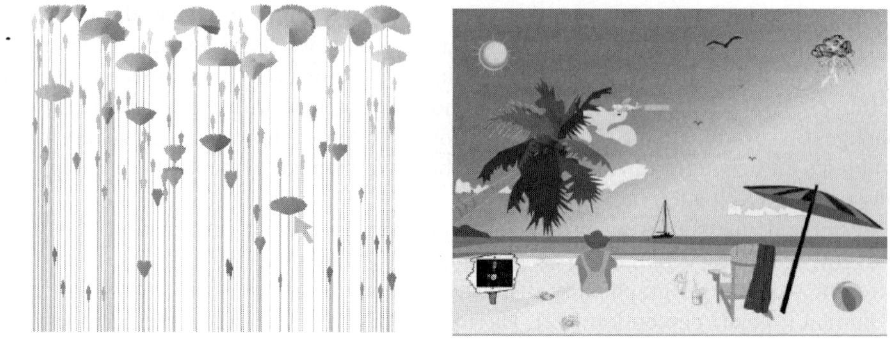

Fig. 2. Figural Informative Art like in People Garden [27], shows user activities in terms of message densities from posting onto a message board (*left*); InfoCanvas [18] (*right*) displays multiple sources of information ranging from NASDAQ Composite Index to the number of employees present at work in real time in a beach scene

deliver information free of disruption caused by abrupt changes in the visual appearance of color, light, smoothness, shininess, brightness, etc. have been studied in [5]. A software framework, the *peripheral displays framework* has been developed, that covers the path from collecting potential awareness data from sensors, to the discovery of meaning in that data, the distribution of awareness information according to publish subscribe principles and restraining it with respect to the preservation of personal interests. The so obtained awareness genotypes in the categories environment, artefact and person are then mapped to artwork phenotypes respecting cultural background, preference wrt. aesthetic appearance, and personal settings. A control engine finally steers the dynamics of the physical awareness display. A typical artwork theme of this framework is shown in Figure 3, based on a "Stilleben" by Jan David de Heem, a dutch painter in the early 17th century.

Fig. 3. Aesthetic awareness display based on "Stilleven" by Jan David de Heem with mappings of e.g. weather conditions, plant watering, garage monitoring, etc. [5]

2 Informative Art Displays

Computer displays delivering information of interest to the periphery of attention of a user, or making users aware of the remote presence of other users or their circumstances have been studied extensively in the context of Informative Art [26] [27]. The issues of designing such display systems have been outlined as of critical importance [25] in order to improve on awareness, i.e. the understanding of the activities and contextual situation of other users or entitites, as well as on connectedness, i.e. the "positive emotional appraisal which is characterized by a feeling of staying in touch within ongoing social relationships". Particularly to support the issue of distraction free perceivability of awareness displays we have developed design criteria and the corresponding framework architecture components, which we summarize as follows:

(i) *Cultural Background*: Cultural background and understanding to a high degree determines individual appreciation of visual designs and the aesthetic appeal of artwork. Our framework for awareness displays offers a choice of artwork metaphors relating to the cultural context of its use, which we call "*themes*", i.e. predefined, visually coherent images with the potential of informative connotation of the contained emblems and symbols. Our framework particularly supports original fine arts paintings (as an example see Fig. 3).

(ii) *Aesthetic Appeal*: To provide means for a personal emotional expression our framework allows to modify the appearance of color, light, smoothness, shininess, etc. in themes by means of "emotional skins". Controllable aesthetic attractiveness has turned out to be the dominant factor of display appreciation.

(iii) *Environmental Context*: The aesthetic appreciation of a piece of artwork is always based on its context of exposure. Different settings of exhibit (like e.g. living room, office, public cafeteria, etc.) conceivably raise different levels of comfort with one and the same display theme. Our framework supports adaptation of themes at run-time, so as to satisfy the respective environmental requirements

(iv) *Comprehension* and *Continuity*: From prototypical installations we have learned that spontaneous changes of the modes of display or the displayed emblems or symbols, severely disrupts the continuity of comprehension. To minimize distraction generated by the occurrence of status changes, very soft blending and smoothing techniques have to be deployed to the visuals and graphics. Updates in information must be encoded in subtle changes of the respective visuals.

(v) *Periphery* of *Perception*: A critical affordance of Informative Art displays happens to be unobtrusiveness with respect to the primary task of the user, i.e. the display must not draw the focus of the users attention (by e.g. alerting), but stay calm in the background. The flow from the periphery to the focus of the users attention (and back) should be user controlled.

The way how a certain theme metaphor is chosen to serve a particular purpose (like awareness, connectedness, etc.) with a particular contextual relevance, and appropriate level of perceivability of the display elements (theme, symbol) follows a user-centered design approach: While the theme is allowed to be chosen by the user, the symbols are derived as the result of a metaphor driven structured design process.

2.1 Themes, Symbols and Connotations

There are no general rules steering the process of finding display elements in an Informative Art display, because they are highly dependent to the individual aesthetical appreciation of a user. In our framework we hence build on a characterization of the users preferences based on the individual ranking of personal aesthetic appeal coming from color, space, shape, level of abstraction, dimension and orientation. This is being deduced from Fine Art paintings, which are at the same time potential candidates for *themes* in the Informative Art display. A *theme* in our software framework is a visually coherent pictorial presentation like an artistic drawing or painting, a photograph, a technical illustration, a computer generated 3D scene, etc., with a certain aesthetic appeal and with the potential of an informative connotation of the contained emblems and symbols. Fig. 3 shows a theme borrowed from Still Life art, where typically inanimate ("dead") subject matter of commonplace objects like natural fruits, or flowers, or objects of everyday use like drinking glasses, bottles, books, musical instruments etc. are depicted with colorful, highly detailed optical realism. We call the latter *symbols* or *emblems*, since –much like the intented (!) disguised symbolism in the artwork of the Netherlands in the 17th century– their props and setting represent carriers of connotated information delivering the overall "message". *Symbols* are the active components of an iconographic program executing in a pictorial *theme*. Further *themes* with comparably more or less detailed realism, and hidden symbols can be found in Fig. 5 – 7.

As for the design of Informative Art displays, both the themes and *emblems/symbols* should be chosen metaphorically, so as to meet the intuition of the user with respect to the connotation. Much like a metaphor in language ("*a metaphor casts a first subject as* being *or* equal *to a second subject in some way*", wikipedia.org) the *metaphor* of the *symbols* in a theme should ease to perceive the connotated information. On the other hand, when developing symbolic connotations, metaphoric symbols can be intuitively perceived (and economically described), because implicit and explicit attributes of the symbol can be used to enhance the description of the "message" to be delivered with the Informative Art display. Furthermore, aesthetic appreciation is another design constraint.

2.2 Metaphors

The main concern in our *theme* based Informative Art design approach is the choice of a *theme* which (i) meets the aesthetic appreciation of the user, and (ii) at the same time provides sufficient degree of metaphoric freedom within the contained *symbols*, to be able to encode the information to be delivered with the display. Previous work [21][23][26] has rather followed a creative artistic approach to design *themes* and *symbols*, and present the result, "as is", to the user (see Table 1). We propose to involve the user already at the time of *theme* choice, and then in a structured way encode information into *symbols* contained in that chosen *theme*. As a consequence, our Informative Art software framework allows the user to even change or reconfigure *themes* at runtime (see Fig. 4).

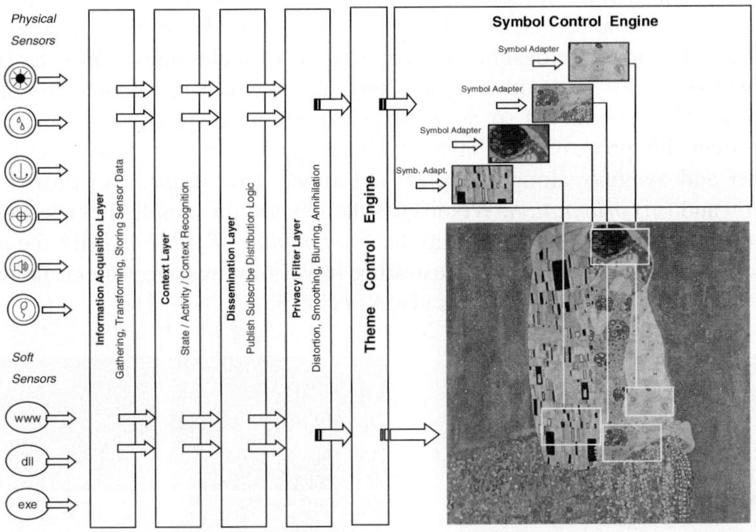

Fig. 4. Our Informative Art display framework collects information of interest via hardware or software sensors (Acquisition Layer), identifies the context (Context Layer), distributes context information according to a publish subscribe principle (Dissemination Layer) and restrains it with respect to privacy policies (Privacy Filtering Layer). The *theme* control engines generates the visual appearance from the chosen *theme*, the *symbol* control engine encodes information into symbol visuals (not necessarily rectangular), which are overlayed into the *theme*.

Table 1. Previous work in Informative Art analysed wrt *Themes*, *Symbols* and *Connotations*

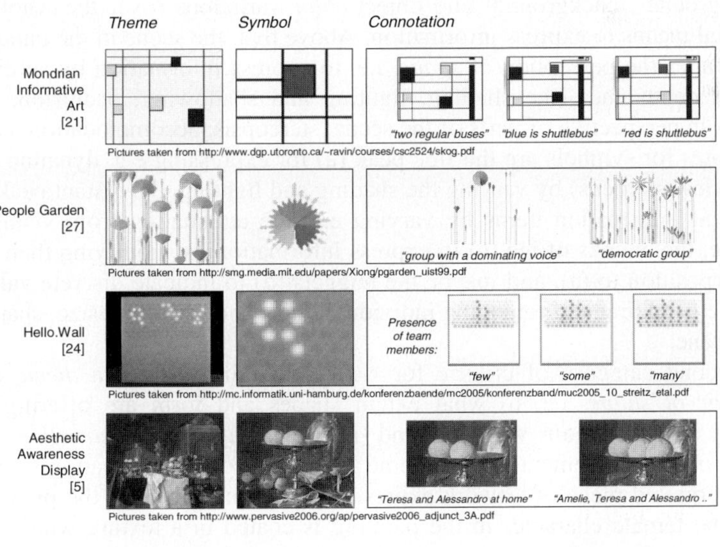

The first step towards a pictorial Informative Art display is to select a *theme* according to the users appreciation. This choice should not be influenced or affected by any constraints rooted in design, implementation or technology. Once a choice has been made (Fig. 5 – 7 could be considered as potential candidates for *themes*), a *theme* analysis is conducted so as to reveal appropriate symbols and metaphors. In order to steer this processs, we have developed guidelines for identifying metaphors in *themes* and *symbols* along (i) *color*, (ii) *space*, (iii) *shape*, (iv) *abstraction*, (v) *dimension* and (vi) *orientation*. We discuss them based on sample themes (Fig. 5 – 7).

Intuitive categories of metaphor are the (i) *metaphor of color* and (ii), the *metaphor of space*. An example of a *theme* illustrating in very impressive way combinations of ranges of color and scales of space is given in Fig. 5.

Fig. 5. Caspar David Friedrich (1774-1840), Das Eismeer (The Arctic Sea) – "Die gescheiterte Hoffnung", (1823/24), oil on canvas, 96,7x126,9 cm, Hamburger Kunsthalle, http://www.hamburger-kunsthalle.de (*left*), and a set of symbol candidates (*right*) – referred to by (a) upper left, (b) upper right, (c) lower left, and (d) lower rigth

Foreground-, background- and object-*color* variations (over the whole spectrum) are trivial means to express information. Above that, the scene in the painting encourages to alter the perception of *space*, i.e. to express information by subtle modifications of depth cues like shading, lighting and shadowing, occlusion, attenuation, changes in perspective of parts of the scene, stereopsis, accommodation and texturing. Candidates for symbols are the floe peak (a) for expressing e.g. dynamic information (at the viewers focus) by varying the shading and lighting, the distant peak (b) for less prominent information items by varying e.g. the attenuation from visible to totally invisible, the chunks of ice (c) to express information by modifying their texture and relative position to (a), and maybe the nuggets (d) to indicate discrete value information by e.g. adding and removing individual nuggets of different size, shape and color to the scene.

A second category of criteria for *symbol* identification in a *theme* are (iii) the *metaphor of shape*, i.e. to what extent shapes and form are offering degrees of freedom for harmonious variation, and (iv) the *metaphor of abstraction*, i.e. whether abstract or figural elements of the theme are exploited for information visualisation. A well interpreted piece of artwork expressing these metaphors is the picture in Fig. 6. While the female character in the painting is coated in a texture with strictly curly, circle like and roundly ornament *shapes*, the male character is coated in a strictly rectangular, geometric and squarish ornament shaped texture. Aside from what the art community has developed as interpretation of these abstract ornatment shapes in Klimts work, here it offers a broad range of possible shape variation (color, size, proximity, inclusion, alignment, direction, horizontal, vertical, inside, outside, cyclic, spin, connection, hole, crack, fissure, boundary, presence, absence, count). (b) is a good candidate for a symbol if the intent is to strictly stick to an abstract curly shape metaphor, just like (c) is for an abstract rectangular shape metaphor – (d) encourages (and supports) a mix of both. As for the degree of *abstraction*, (a) as a suggested symbol allows to combine expressive means rooted in abstract ornaments as well as figural elements. Connotating information into the facial expression of characters appears as a very rich, yet intuitively perceivable symbolic instrument.

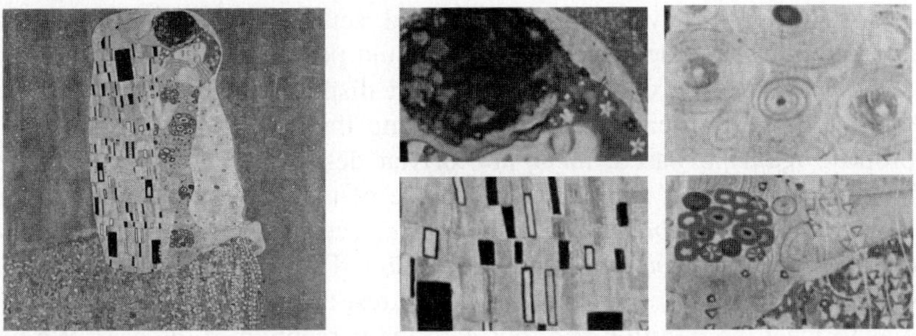

Fig. 6. Gustav Klimt (1862-1918), Der Kuß, (1907/08), oil on canvas, 180x180cm, Österreichische Galerie, Wien, http://www.belvedere.at (*left*), and a set of symbol candidates (*right*, (a), (b), (c), (d))

Symbols can also be identified with respect to the embodied (iii) *metaphor of dimension*, and (iv) the *metaphor of orientation*. A *theme*, which due to its strictly geometric composition invites to connotate any sort of information and data on a metric scale is given in Fig. 7. Straight lines, segments, string cords, rulers, tickers etc. suggest symbols like (a) and (d) to express *dimensional* values on arbitrary metric scales, while (b) or (c) (a rendered sphere) suits for connotating *orientation* data.

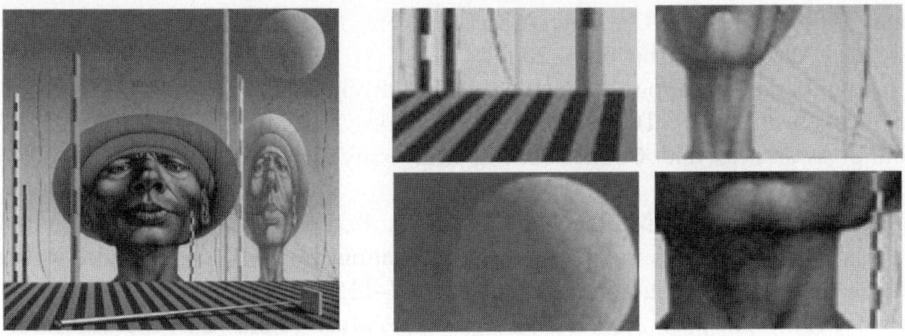

Fig. 7. Rudolf Hausner (1914-1995), Adam maßstäblich, (1972), 54,0x55,5cm, signed, http://www.artnet.com (*left*), and a set of symbol candidates (*right*, (a), (b), (c), (d))

3 Findings and Conclusion

In its earliest appearance, "Informative Art" was considered as computer augmented pieces of art or computer generated artwork, turning an aesthetical object into an information display [21]. Several contributions have appeared in the literature, addressing the issue of encoding information of interest into aesthetical art installations, using the one or the other desing driven approach. In most of these cases, the design work conducts information visualisation concepts, display strategies, as well as decorative, aesthetic and artistic composing, but not involving the user beforehand. Typically, the user is consulted once the informative art display system is ready at hand, and concerned for usability engineering studies.

The hypothesis of this work was, that users, based on their cultural background, cognitive skills, situative environment, contextual settings, but most of all their aestehtic appreciation, have dedicated, individual and personal attitudes towards the preferred overall appearance of an informative art display system. In our previous work we have found empirical evidence supporting this hypothesis [5]. Therefore, here we propose a *theme* based, *metaphor* driven design process that guarantees sovereignity of the user with respect to the choice of a display *theme*. Our process then identifies *symbols* or *emblems* out of the *theme* according to metaphors of *color*, *space*, *shape*, *abstraction*, *dimension* and *orientation*. These metaphors then help to find the right connotation of the information of interest and the respective *symbols* of a *theme* so as to meet the intuition and thus ease the perception of the user. We have used original artwork (C. D. Friedrich, G. Klimt, R. Hausner) to support our arguments for metaphor driven symbol selection. Our informative art design process is support by a fully functional informative art software framework, within which many display systems have already been built. Currently we are generalizing and formalizing the concept of *symbols* (attributes and dynamics) in a markup language, so as to achieve *theme* independence. The prospect of this generalization is to let the user (or a process in a context sensitive way) "hot-swap" from one theme to another without any symbol reconfiguration.

References

1. Ames, M., Bettadapur, C., Dey, A.K., Mankoff, J.: Healthy Cities Ambient Displays. Extended Abstracts of UbiComp (2003), http://guir.berkeley.edu/pubs/ubicomp2003/healthycities.pdf
2. De Guzman, E.S.M.S.: Thesis: Presence Displays: Tangible Peripheral Displays for Promoting Awareness and Connectedness, University of California, Berkeley (December 2004)
3. De Guzman, E.S., Yau, M., Gagliano, A., Park, A., Dey, A.K.: Exploring the design and use of peripheral displays of awareness information. In: CHI '04 Extended Abstracts on Human Factors in Computing Systems, pp. 1247–1250. ACM Press, New York (2004)
4. Ferscha, A.: Workspace Awareness in Mobile Virtual Teams. In: Proceedings of the 9th International Workshops on Enabling Technologies: Infrastructures for Collaborative Enterprises (WETICE 2000), pp. 272–277. IEEE Computer Society Press, Los Alamitos (2000)

5. Ferscha, A., Emsenhuber, B., Schmitzberger, H., Thon, P.: Aesthetic Awareness Displays. Advances in Pervasive Computing 2006. In: Adjunct Proceedings of the 4th International Conference on Pervasive Computing. books@ocg.at Vol. 207, Austrian Computer Society (OCG): Vienna (2006)
6. Ferscha, A., Johnson, J.: Distributed Interaction in Virtual Spaces. In: Proc. of the 3rd International WS on Distributed Interactive Simulation and Real Time Applications, IEEE Computer Society Press, Los Alamitos (1999)
7. Gutwin, C., Greensberg, S.: A Framework of Awareness for Small Groups in Shared-Workspace Groupware. Technical report 99-1, Department of Computer Science, University of Saskatchewan, Canada. http://www.cpsc.ucalgary.ca/grouplab/papers/
8. Heiner, J., Hudson, S., Tanaka, K.: The Information Percolator: Ambient Information Display in a Decorative Object. In: ACM Symp. on User Interface Software and Techn. pp. 141–148. ACM Press, New York (1999)
9. Ho-Ching, F.-W., Mankoff, J., Landay, J.A.: Can you see what I hear? The Design and Evaluation of a Peripheral Sound Display for the Deaf. Group for User Interface Research, Computer Science Division, University of Berkeley. http://guir.berkeley.edu/projects/ic2hear/Masters-final.pdf
10. Holmquist, L.E.: Evaluating the comprehension of ambient displays. In: CHI '04 Extended Abstracts on Human Factors in Computing Systems, ACM Press, New York (2004)
11. Hsieh, G., Mankoff, J.: Peripheral Displays Evaluation. http://www.cs.berkeley.edu/projects/io/peripheral_evaluation/
12. Ishii, H., Ullmer, B.: Tangible Bits: Towards Seamless Interfaces between People, Bits and Atoms. In: Proceedings of the Conference on Human Factors in Computing systems, pp. 234–241. ACM Press, New York (1997)
13. Mankoff, J., Dey, A.K.: From conception to design: a practical guide to designing ambient displays. In: Ohara, K., Churchill, E. (eds.) Public and Situated Displays, Kluwer, Dordrecht (2003), http://www.intel-research.net/Publications/Berkeley/072920031038_155.pdf
14. Mankoff, J., Dey, A.K., Hsieh, G., Kientz, J., Lederer, S., Ames, M.: Heuristic Evaluation of Ambient Displays. EECS Department, University of Berkeley. In: Proceedings of the SIGCHI Conference on Human Factors in Computing Systems, CA, USA, pp. 169–176. ACM Press, New York (2003), http://www.cs.berkeley.edu/projects/io/publications/660-mankoff.pdf.
15. Matthews, T., Dey, A.K., Mankoff, J., Carter, S., Rattenbury, T.: A toolkit for managing user attention in peripheral displays. In: Proceedings of the 17th Annual ACM Symposium on User interface Software and Technology UIST '04, Santa Fe, NM, USA, October 24 - 27, 2004, pp. 247–256. ACM Press, New York (2004), http://doi.acm.org/10.1145/1029632.1029676
16. Matthews, T., Rattenbury, T., Carter, S., Dey, A.K., Mankoff, J.: A Peripheral Display Toolkit. EECS Department, University of California, Berkeley Technotes, UCB//CSD-03-(2003) (1258), http://www.eecs.berkeley.edu/Pubs/TechRpts/2003/CSD-03-1258.pdf
17. McCarthy, J.F., Costa, T.J., Huang, E.M., Tullio, J.: Defragmenting the organization: Disseminating community knowledge through peripheral displays. Workshop on Community Knowledge at the 7th European Conference on Computer Supported Cooperative Work, ECSCW, pp. 117–126 (2001)
18. Miller, T., Stasko, J.: The InfoCanvas: information conveyance through personalized, expressive art. In: CHI '01 Extended Abstracts on Human Factors in Computing Systems, pp. 305–306. ACM Press, New York (2001)

19. Mynatt, E., Rowan, J., Jacobs, A., Craighill, S.: Digital Family Portraits: Supporting Peace of Mind for Extended Family Members. In: Proceedings of the SIGCHI conference on Human factors in computing systems, pp. 333–340. ACM Press, New York (2001)
20. Prante, T., Stenzel, R., Röcker, C., Streitz, N., Magerkurth, C.: Ambient agoras: InfoRiver, SIAM, Hello.Wall. In: CHI '04 Extended Abstracts on Human Factors in Computing Systems CHI '04, Vienna, Austria, April 24 - 29, 2004, pp. 763–764. ACM Press, New York (2004)
21. Redström, J., Skog, T., Hallnäs, L.: Informative art: using amplified artworks as information displays. In: Proceedings of DARE 2000 on Designing Augmented Reality Environments, pp. 103–114. ACM Press, New York (2000)
22. Streitz, N., Magerkurth, C., Prante, T., Röcker, C.: From information design to experience design: smart artefacts and the disappearing computer. interactions 12,4, 21–25 (July 2005)
23. Streitz, N.A., Nixon, P.: The Disappearing Computer. Guest Editors' Introduction to Special Issue. In: Communications of the ACM, vol. 48, pp. 33–35 (March 2005)
24. Streitz, N.A., Rocker, C., Prante, T., Alphen, D.: Designing Smart Artifacts for Smart Environments. IEEE Computer 38,3, 41–49 (March 2005)
25. Walker, K.: Interactive and Informative Art. IEEE MultiMedia 10,1, 4–10 (January 2003)
26. Wisneski, C.: Ambient Displays: Turning Architectural Space into an Interface between People and Digital Information. In: Streitz, N.A., Konomi, S., Burkhardt, H.-J. (eds.) CoBuild 1998. LNCS, vol. 1370, pp. 22–32. Springer, Heidelberg (1998)
27. Xiong, R., Donath, J.: PeopleGarden: creating data portraits for users. In: Proceedings of the 12th annual ACM symposium on User interface software and technology (UIST '99), pp. 37–44. ACM Press, New York (1999)

Usable Multi-Display Environments: Concept and Evaluation

Thomas Heider and Thomas Kirste

Mobile Multimedia Information Systems Group
Department of Computer Science
Rostock University, Germany
{th,tk}@informatik.uni-rostock.de

Abstract. The number of conference or meeting rooms with multiple displays available is on the rise. While this increased availability of displays opens up many new opportunities, the management of information across them is not trivial, especially when multiple users with diverging interests have to be considered. This particularly applies for dynamic ensembles of displays. We propose to cast the Display Mapping problem as an optimization task, where we define an explicit criterion for the global quality of a display mapping and then use computer support to calculate the optimum. We argue that in dynamic multi-user, multi-display environments, an automatic – or at least computer supported – document-display assignment improves the user experience in multi-display environments.

1 Introduction: Managing Multi-Display Environments

Multi-Display Environments[1] support collaborative problem solving and teamwork by providing multiple display surfaces for presenting information. Typical examples for such environments are meeting rooms, conference rooms, and "mission control centers", as shown in Figure 1.

One difficult task here is the *Display Mapping problem* – that is, deciding which information to present on what display in order to optimally satisfy the users' needs for information. While this task is more or less trivial in single-user, single-display situations, it becomes challenging in multi-user, multi-display settings: Users and displays are spatially dispersed so that the visibility of (semi-) public and private displays varies across users. Also, information needs may vary across users, so that finding the "best" assignment of information to displays becomes a typical optimization problem.

One solves an optimization problem by defining an objective function $q(x)$, the "quality" to maximize, and then applying a suitable optimization algorithm to compute $x_{max} = \arg\max_{x \in X} q(x)$.

In this setting the Display Mapping problem gives rise to two subproblems:

[1] See e. g. the UbiComp 2004 workshop on Ubiquitous Display Environments [1].

C. Stephanidis (Ed.): Universal Access in HCI, Part II, HCII 2007, LNCS 4555, pp. 93–102, 2007.

Fig. 1. Examples of multiple display environments. (i, left) Stanford's iRoom; (ii, right) Rostock University Smart Appliance Lab; (iii, bottom) the "Management Cockpit" at Iglo-Ola, Unilever Belgium

- What is a suitable definition for $q(x)$? I. e., what is the objective function to be maximized in order to achieve an optimal (or at least: satisfactory) solution for the Display Mapping problem?
- How should the computation of x_{max} be distributed across the members of an ensemble of displays? – This is especially interesting, when dynamic ensembles have to be considered (e.g., portable projectors carried into a meeting room, etc.).

In this paper, we outline a strategy for achieving an automated display mapping using an optimization framework, and we discuss an experimental setup for evaluating the benefit of automated multi-display environments.

The further structure of this paper is as follows: in Section 2, we motivate why an automated display mapping is necessary. In Section 3, we provide an in-depth discussion of the display mapping problem and our proposal of a global quality function q for this problem. The experimental design and first results of our evaluation of an automated display mapping in comparison to a manual assignment is described in Section 4. A discussion of the results and further work is given in Section 5.

2 The Need for Automatic Display Mapping

Why do we need automated display mapping? – Couldn't the users just do the assignment manually, using a suitable interactive interface, resolving conflicts by social protocols (negotiations)? One example for such a manual display assignment is the ModSlideShow system [7], which is designed to manage presentation slides on multiple displays. Displays can be linked and grouped into flexible configurations depending on their physical layout in the environment and on the scenarios of use. For assignment of content to displays, meeting participants drag-and-drop presentations from their note books to any of the available displays. Another example providing a similar interaction mechanism is the PointRight software developed for Stanford's Meyer Teamspace [2].

However, we do not believe that such a solution would be successful in the long run (i. e., as multiple display environments become more and more complex) because of the following issues:

1. **Interest conflicts** between users will need a computer supported negotiation mechanism: Morris et al. [8] have already observed that social protocols do not always suffice for coordinating the use of shared resources, such as display surfaces, in teams – even in relatively simple situations. They suspect that the need for coordination may increase as the number of users, the number of documents, or the number or size of the surfaces increases. Indeed, they advocate the development of specific strategies for automatizing the negotiation process.
2. The need for **dynamic realignment** of Display Mapping is caused by topic changes in the user population – in this situation, the user's focus of attention will be on the changing topic rather than on convincing the display infrastructure to change the topic.
3. In a dynamic multiple display environment, the **user will not be able to know** (and will not want to know) the **displays currently available** to him. With dozens to hundreds of possible display configurations, the user will have to rely on the infrastructure to select the best choice for him.

We call a solution process that does not require human intervention an *unsupervised* process. Although there is substantial research in multi-display environments, to our knowledge, the development of an interaction-free, automatic display assignment has not yet been addressed on a general level (i.e., independent of a specific ensemble).

In [3] we have presented a distributed optimization algorithm supporting the unsupervised display assignment. This algorithm has the further advantage that it requires only *local knowledge* at each participating device. Next, we discuss the basic properties of a quality measure – q(x) – that can be used for solving the display mapping problem.

3 Defining Optimal Display Assignment

3.1 The Basic Idea

Consider the simple Display Mapping problem outlined in Figure 2, left. There are two users u_1, u_2 sitting at a table and three display surfaces s_1, s_2, s_3 (for instance, backprojection displays or simply screens with an associated projector). User u_1 is interested in documents d_1 and d_2, user u_2 is interested in d_1 and d_3. Also, u_1 has very high interest in d_1 (maybe it is the presentation currently delivered by u_2). In this situation, considering the positions of users and display surfaces, the resulting display visibility, and the user's information needs, an optimal mapping of documents to the available display surfaces is given by the mapping outlined in Figure 2 at right: $u1$ gets optimal visibility of his most important document on $s3$ and acceptable visibility of $d2$ by looking sideways on s_1. Similarly u_2, gets acceptable visibility of $d1$ and d_3.

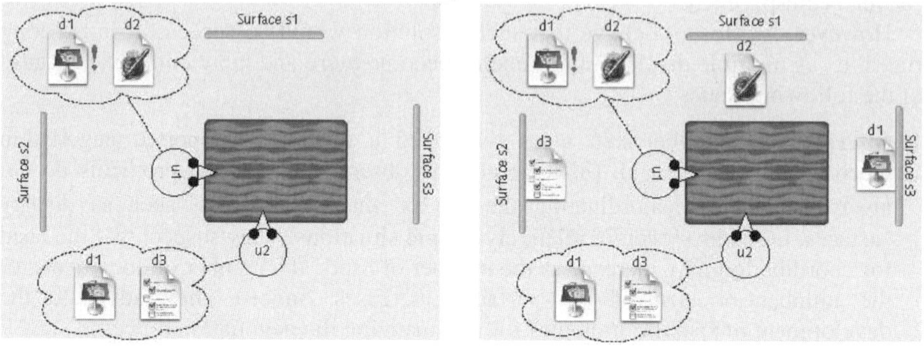

Fig. 2. Mapping documents to displays. Initial situation (left) and optimal mapping

Let D, U, S be the sets of documents, users, and surfaces, respectively. Let $impt(d, u) \in [0 .. 1]$ denote the importance of the document $d \in D$ to a user $u \in U$ and $vis(s, u) \in [0 .. 1]$ the visibility of surface $s \in S$ by user $u \in U$. Let furthermore $sm \in D \to 2^S$ be a mapping of documents to display surfaces, such that $sm(d) \in 2^S$ denotes the set of surfaces to which document $d \in D$ is assigned. Then the quality achieved by the mapping sm can be defined as

$$q(sm) = \sum_{\substack{u \in U \\ d \in D}} impt(d,u) * \max_{s \in sm(d)} vis(s,u) \tag{1}$$

This definition is based on the manifest intuition that, in a good mapping, documents with high importance (for specific users) should be assigned to display surfaces with high visibility (for this user). In addition, if a document is assigned to multiple display surfaces, only the best one for a given user is considered when computing the quality for this user (this is the "max vis" term).

Finding the optimal mapping $sm_{max} = \arg\max_{sm \in D \to 2^S} q(sm)$ requires to explore the possible document-to-surface maps in a suitable manner in order to find surface map giving the best quality.

A basic issue with the notion of multiple displays environments is whether they are modeled as a single continuous surface or as multiple loosely connected surfaces. The former model has been investigated in projects such as [9, 2], where a continuous surface is formed by mapping the edge of each display to the nearest edge of the nearest display. In our discussion, we use the latter model, where the displays can be freely distributed across a room, e.g. [10–12].

3.2 Accounting for Different Types of Displays

Since some time, steerable projectors such as the Everywhere Display [4] are being investigated for a flexible information display by several research groups (see [5] for a short overview). And our lab infrastructure too provides such a device. The introduction of steerable projectors introduces another degree of freedom in the display mapping process, as a steerable projector may be able to choose between different projection screens. We therefore need to distinguish between *Displays* (devices which can present a document) and *Surfaces* (regions in space on which a display renders a document). For some devices, the mapping from display to surface is fixed (i.e., a notebook display will always render on the notebook's screen surface; a fixed beamer will always render on the screen it is looking at), while for other devices it is variable (i.e., a steerable beamer that can pick different screens to project on).

Let Y denote the set of displays and S the set of available (display) surfaces. Furthermore, let $rend(y, s) \in [0 .. 1]$ be the rendering quality achievable by display $y \in Y$ on surface $s \in S$ (for devices with fixed display surface, *rend* will be 1 for this surface and 0 everywhere else). We now have to replace *sm* by *two* mappings: $dm \in D \rightarrow 2^Y$, mapping documents to sets of display devices, and $ym \in Y \rightarrow S$, mapping displays to surfaces. And our definition of q is changed to

$$q(dm, ym) = \sum_{\substack{u \in U \\ d \in D}} impt(d,u) * \max_{y \in dm(d)} \left(vis(ym(y),u) * rend(y, ym(y))\right) \quad (2)$$

so that we now have to look for $(dm_{max}, ym_{max}) = \arg\max_{\substack{dm \in D \rightarrow 2^Y \\ ym \in Y \rightarrow S}} q(dm, ym)$.

As a first approximation to computing *vis* and *rend*, we have chosen Lambert's law of reflection, which gives the visibility (or rendering quality) as cosine of the angle between the rendering surfaces' surface normal n_s and the vector connecting the surface and the projector (resp. the user). A similar approach has been taken by the EasyLiving Geometry model [6]. We would like to emphasize two points with respect to our definition of q:

- q has been defined completely independent from a concrete ensemble of users, displays, documents, and surfaces. It describes the globally optimal behavior for any possible ensemble. Once machinery is available for computing the optimum for q, any ensemble will be able to behave optimally – as far as q is a correct definition of an ensembles global optimum from the user's point of view.
- Our definition of q for the display mapping problem is still rather simplistic – for instance, it lacks a notion of "history", that would keep a document from confusingly hopping from display to display as the user slightly shifts position. So, q does not yet faithfully describe an ensemble's global optimum from the user's point of view. An improved definition of q is the objective of ongoing user studies (first experiments are described in Section 4 below). But even though q is not final yet, it shows that an ensemble's globally optimal behavior *can* (and should!) be defined explicitly in a way that is independent of a specific ensemble realization.

The details on the distributed algorithm we have developed for approximating q can be found in [3]. (Basically, we use a distributed version of the Greedy Randomized Adaptive Search Procedure, GRASP.)

4 Evaluation of Automatic Display Assignment

4.1 Objectives and Overall Experimental Design

Objective of our evaluations is to answer the following questions with respect to automatic display mapping in general and the definition of q specifically:

- Is it possible to predict and automatically generate a good document display mapping that would satisfy a reasonable subset of users? Are the configurations produced by the algorithm actually useful and sensible to users in multi-display environments? What benefits does automatic content distribution offer over manual distribution?
- Is it possible to do automatic content distribution in a way that users find usable, intuitive, understandable, and satisfying? How does this compare to existing techniques for assigning content to displays?
- Is it possible to develop a universal approach, or do different application domains, situations, and contexts require different assignment strategies (or even a pure manual mechanism)?

In this paper, we focus on the objective to quantify the benefit of an automatic display assignment in comparison to a manual assignment in a multi-user, multi-display environment.

The evaluations are based on two experiments:

- Calibration experiment: Objective of the calibration experiment has been to verify that a multiple display environments is able to improve performance in comparison to a single display environment. (We conducted this experiment – for which we considered the outcome as obvious – as safety measure against a seriously flawed experimental setup.)
- Evaluation experiment: Objective of this experiment is to measure the impact of manual vs. automatic display assignment on the performance of a team in solving a semi-cooperative assignment. In semi-cooperative tasks, the need of cooperation and joint use of information is not evident from the start – we think that this kind of aspect pertains to many team processes, specifically in multidisciplinary teams.

Both experiments were carried out in our Smart Appliance Lab (cf. Figure 1, right). This environment provides six projection based public displays, arranged in two pairs at three sides of the room that were used for the experiments (see Figure 3, left)[2].

---

[2] Other infrastructure available in the Smart Appliance Lab – such as steerable beamers, additional motor screens, UbiSense-based location tracking, remote-controlled lighting and HVAC, etc. – will be used in future experiments.

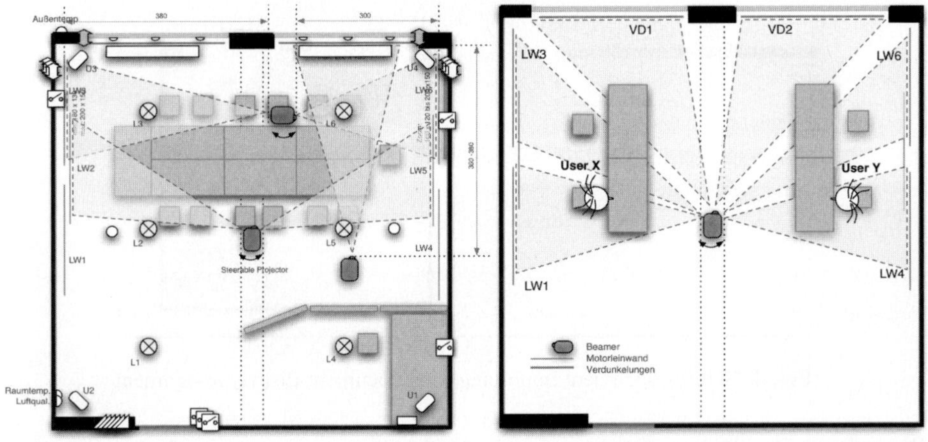

Fig. 3. Smart Appliance Lab, equipment examples (left), configuration option (right)

4.2 Calibration Experiment

Goal and Hypothesis. Objective of this experiment was to establish that multiple display environments improve the performance over single display environments. Specifically, we wanted to make sure that this performance improvement is valid for the type of tasks intended for the following evaluation experiment.

Procedure. The subjects were given the task of finding the differences between two similar pictures[3]. Subjects in group A were given a single display (which could present only one picture at a time), subjects in group B were given two displays, so they could compare both pictures side by side. We measured the time it took the participants to complete each task.

Results. Although only a few participants per group took part in the evaluation, the result was clear. The group with the option to use two displays was able to solve the task in distinctly shorter time. Also the post-experiment questionnaire showed, that all participants would prefer a multi-display environment over a single-display environment for this kind of task. This result is not very surprising and confirms our hypothesis.

4.3 Evaluation Experiment

Goal and Hypothesis. Objective of this experiment was to compare the effect of manual and automatic display assignment on task performance. Our hypotheses is that automatic assignment enables teams to solve their tasks in a shorter time, with less conflicts between team members, and with greater satisfaction.

---

[3] Source: Gregory, Richard L.: Eye and Brain – the Psychology of Seeing, Oxford University Press, 1998.

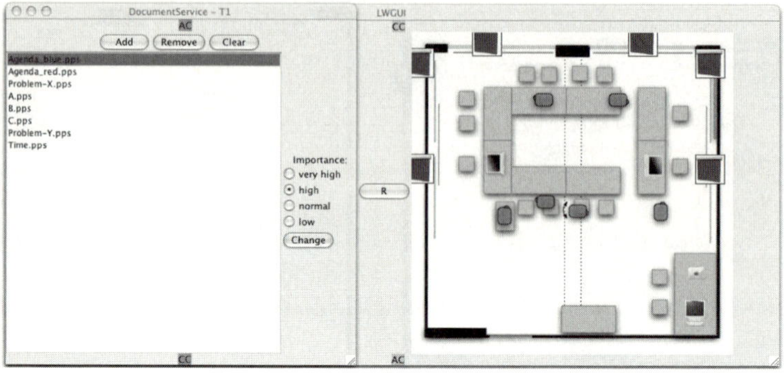

Fig. 4. GUI for document importance and document-display assignment

Procedure. For the experiments, every participant was given a simple user interface for document assignment. Manually assignment of a document to a display-surface is done through a simple "drag & drop" (Figure 4, right). For automatic assignment, the user just associates an importance value with the documents (Figure 4, left). The optimal document-display assignment is then computed using our goal function q.

In the experiment, two-person teams had to solve a semi-cooperative task as fast as possible. The seating arrangement used for a team is shown in Figure 3, right. Note that there are two pairs of displays exclusively visible to User X and Y of a team, and one display pair visible to both X and Y. The teams were assigned to two equal-sized groups, A and M, using automatic or manual assignment, respectively. The team members X and Y were given different agendas, containing different tasks for the two users. For X the task was to compare two documents A and B, for Y the task was to compare A and C. The task was a simple letter comparison, counting the number of differences in two letter sequences. In addition, X and Y had to report time information and a random key from another document Time. The seemingly unrelated tasks for X and Y were linked into a cooperative task through the shared documents A and Time – see Figure 5 for the documents.

As the agendas and task descriptions were mutually unknown, the sharing had to be discovered through a conflict in the manual assignment group. (In order to enforce resource conflicts in this simple setting, each document could only be displayed on one display at a time.)

For each team, we recorded the time required for completing the task as well as the subjective feeling of conflict and user satisfaction (using a questionnaire).

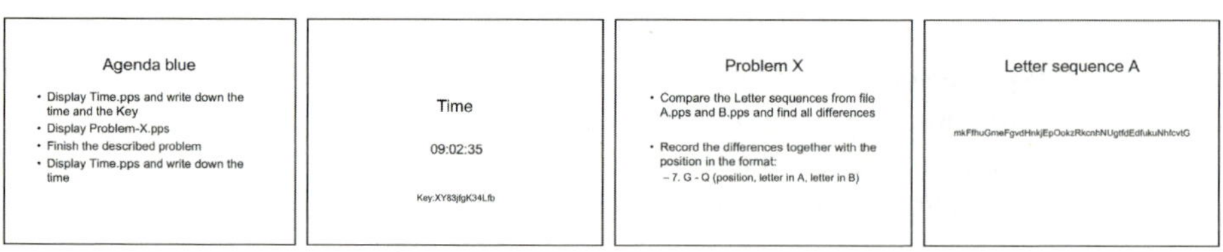

Fig. 5. Problem documents, from left: Agenda, Time, Problem-X, A

Results. Although the first tests involved only a small number of teams (experiments are ongoing), the results seem to indicate a consistent trend: in all cases, the teams from group A finished the tasks in a shorter time than the "manual" teams (group M). The satisfaction seems to be higher, and conflict is experienced less in the A teams. The M teams initially had no idea that they needed to share documents. So they unwittingly "stole" the shared documents from each others "private" displays. It required a couple of minutes, until the M participants realized that they needed to cooperate and to assign some of the documents to a display visible to both users. This process of realization and negotiation was the reason for confusion and delay. In the A group no such conflicts did arise as the system automatically displayed shared documents on a shared screen. This resulted in an overall greater satisfaction for the A group.

5 Conclusion and Future Work

In this paper, we have discussed the problem of assisting teams in effectively using multi-display environments for working together. We have claimed that the optimal behavior of such an environment can be formulated rigorously as an optimization task so that an automated solution to the display assignment problem should be possible. Providing an automated assistance in using multi-display environments is based on the hypothesis that there are situations, where an automatism streamlines and simplifies the social negotiation processes required for agreeing on the use of limited resources in a team of users.

Our – ongoing – experimental work indicates that there is indeed a noticeable effect of display assignment methods on team performance, at least for semi-cooperative tasks. An automatic display assignment here seems to (i) improve the team effectiveness (measured in time to complete a task), (ii) to reduce the level of conflict in the team (i.e., the number of arguments about resource use), and (iii) to improve the individual user experience and satisfaction.

Unfortunately, our experiments are still in a very early stage so that our results are anecdotal evidence and not yet statistically valid. Remedying this deficiency is objective of the next experimental phase. Also, other aspects such as understandability of the computed assignment and its compatibility with user expectations have to be measured. The same holds for an assessment of the usability of automatic display assignment in other team situations.

To summarize, although there are many open questions, we have shown that it seems possible that automatic display assignment provides a measurable benefit in multi-display environments, at least in some situations. Future investigations will have to show whether this benefit offers the universality and significance required to incorporate it generally into such environments.

References

1. Alois Ferscha, Gerd Kortuem, and Antonio Krüger. Workshop on ubiquitous display environments. In: Proc. Ubicomp 2004, Nottingham, England, (September 7 2004)
2. Johanson, B., Hutchins, G., Winograd, T., Stone, M.: Pointright: Experience with flexible input redirection in interactive workspaces. In: Proc. ACM Conference on User Interface and Software Technology (UIST2002), pp. 227– 234, Paris, France (2002)

3. Heider, T., Giersich, M., Kirste, T.: Resource optimization in multi-display environments with distributed grasp. In: Proceedings of the First International Conference on Ambient Intelligence Developments (AmI.d'06), Sophia Antipolis, France, September 19 -22, pp. 60–76. Springer, Heidelberg (2006)
4. Pinhanez, C.: The everywhere displays projector: A device to create ubiquitous graphical interfaces. In: Abowd, G.D., Brumitt, B., Shafer, S. (eds.) Ubicomp 2001: Ubiquitous Computing. LNCS, vol. 2201, Springer, Heidelberg (September 2001)
5. Molyneaux, D., Kortuem, G.: Ubiquitous displays in dynamic environments: Issues and opportunities. In: Ubicomp, Workshop on Ubiquitous Display Environments [1] (2004)
6. Brumitt, B., Shafer, S.: Better living through geometry. Journal for Ubiquitous Computing, (January 2001)
7. Chiu, P., Liu, Q., Boreczky, J.S., Foote, J., Kimber, D., Lertsithichai, S., Liao, C.: Manipulating and annotating slides in a multi-display environment. In: Human-Computer Interaction INTERACT '03: IFIP TC13 International Conference on Human-Computer Interaction (2003)
8. Morris, M.R., Ryall, K., Shen, C., Forlines, C., Vernier, F.: Beyond "social protocols": multi-user coordination policies for co-located groupware. In: CSCW '04: Proceedings of the 2004 ACM conference on Computer supported cooperative work, pp. 262–265. ACM Press, New York (2004)
9. Hutchings, D.R., Czerwinski, M., Meyers, B., Stasko, J.: Exploring the use and affordances of multiple display environments. In: Ubicomp, Workshop on Ubiquitous Display Environments [1] (2004)
10. Robotham, T., Hertzum, M.: Multi-board concept -a scenario based approach for supporting product quality and life cycle oriented design. In: TMCE: Third International Symposium on Tools and Methods of Competitive Engineering, pp. 763–774. Delft University Press, The Netherlands (2000)
11. Wigdor, D., Shen, C., Forlines, C., Balakrishnan, R.: Effects of display position and control space orientation on user preference and performance. In: CHI '06: Proceedings of the SIGCHI conference on Human Factors in computing systems, pp. 309–318. ACM Press, New York (2006)
12. Mark, G.: Extreme collaboration. Commun. ACM 45(6), 89–93 (2002)

Ambient Intelligence in Assisted Living: Enable Elderly People to Handle Future Interfaces

Thomas Kleinberger[1], Martin Becker[1], Eric Ras[1], Andreas Holzinger[2], and Paul Müller[3]

[1] Fraunhofer Institute for Experimental Software Engineering (IESE)
67663 Kaiserslautern, Germany
thomas.kleinberger@iese.fraunhofer.de,
martin.becker@iese.fraunhofer.de,
eric.ras@iese.fraunhofer.de

[2] Medical University Graz, 8036 Graz, Austria
Institute for Medical Informatics, Statistics & Documentation (IMI)
Research Unit HCI4MED
andreas.holzinger@meduni-graz.at

[3] Technical University Kaiserslautern, 67653 Kaiserslautern, Germany
AG Integrated Communication Systems
pmueller@informatik.uni-kl.de

Abstract. Ambient Assisted Living is currently one of the important research and development areas, where accessibility, usability and learning plays a major role and where future interfaces are an important concern for applied engineering. The general goal of ambient assisted living solutions is to apply ambient intelligence technology to enable people with specific demands, e.g. handicapped or elderly, to live in their preferred environment longer. Due to the high potential of emergencies, a sound emergency assistance is required, for instance assisting elderly people with comprehensive ambient assisted living solutions sets high demands on the overall system quality and consequently on software and system engineering – user acceptance and support by various user-interfaces is an absolute necessity. In this article, we present an Assisted Living Laboratory that is used to train elderly people to handle modern interfaces for Assisted Living and evaluate the usability and suitability of these interfaces in specific situations, e.g., emergency cases.

Keywords: Ambient Intelligence, Assisted Living, User-Interfaces, Learning, Elderly People.

1 Introduction and Motivation

In most industrialized countries, demographical, structural, and social trends tend towards more and more elderly people and single households, which have dramatic effects on public and private health care, emergency medical services, and the individuals themselves. Humans live longer, mainly because of progress in medical treatment and pharmacies. The increasing average age of the total population

C. Stephanidis (Ed.): Universal Access in HCI, Part II, HCII 2007, LNCS 4555, pp. 103–112, 2007.

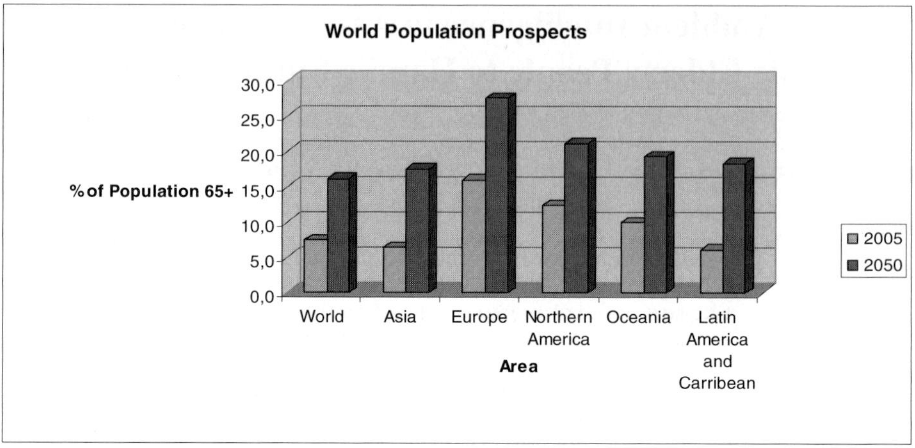

Fig. 1. Demographical Change according to the United Nations World Population Prospects: 2004 Revision, http://esa.un.org/unpp (last access: 2007-01-30)

(cf. figure 1) and the consequent rise of chronic diseases will result in a dramatic increase of emergency situations and missions within the coming years.

An exemplary study in the district of Kaiserslautern, Germany, shows that 44% of Emergency Medical Services' (EMS) system resources are dedicated to patients older than 70 years of age. This will result in even higher costs for such services or in a decrease of service quality or both. Assisted Living solutions for elderly people using ambient intelligence technology can help to cope with this trend, by providing some proactive and situation aware assistance to sustain the autonomy of the elderly, be helpful in limiting the increasing costs while concurrently providing advantages for the affected people by increasing *quality of life*. The goal is to enable elderly people to live longer in their preferred environment, to enhance the quality of their lives and to reduce costs for society and public health systems.

Today's commercially available products for emergency monitoring already use a broad range of modern technology (e.g., necklaces with emergency buttons, fall sensors in mobile phones with wireless notification of emergency services, vital data monitoring plasters, etc.). However, they are mostly closed, stand-alone systems with a limited ability to describe the actual situation, often just too difficult for the elderly people to operate and useless in emergencies.

Nevertheless, assisted living systems promise a huge potential for handicapped and elderly people suffering from all kinds of disabilities, e.g., gait changes, neurological alterations, visual acuity changes, vestibular compromise, spontaneous fractures and falls, cardiac alteration with syncope, or sudden changes in blood pressure. In our opinion this will only be the case if *three major requirements* are met:

1. They have to be ambient and unobtrusive to reach a high acceptance.
2. They have to adapt themselves to changing personal situations or capabilities of the individual and the environment to fulfill individual needs.
3. They have to provide their services in an accessible way to enhance usability.

Recent research and development in technology and software engineering produce a new generation of solutions that provide their services in a more flexible, adaptive, and anticipative manner compared to traditional products. Low energy consumption, wireless communication, non-traditional interfaces, small footprints, and the ability to sense the environment for useful information about the context of a situation allow designing and engineering solutions and applications that are ambient and unobtrusive, adaptive to the individual context, and provide easy to use interfaces for elderly and handicapped people.

2 Ambient Intelligence in Assisted Living

Systems that render their service in a sensitive and responsive way and are unobtrusively integrated into our daily environment are referred to as being *ambient intelligent* [1], [2]. Ambient Intelligence has been recognized as a promising approach to tackle the aforementioned problems in the domain of Assisted Living [3]. Living Assistance systems focusing on the support of people with special needs (elderly, disabled) in their own homes are called Home Care Systems (HCS) [4], [5].

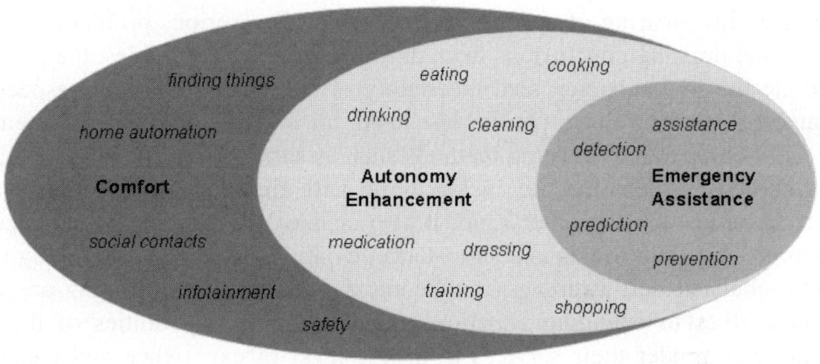

Fig. 2. Home care system domain

The aim of a HCS is to allow the assisted persons to live longer in their preferred environment at home, while retaining their independence, even when they have handicaps or medical diseases. As illustrated in Fig. 2 the HCS domain can coarsely be structured into emergency assistance services, autonomy enhancement services, and comfort services.

According to Oppermann et al. [6], AmI systems represent a new generation of systems that show the following *characteristics*:

- invisible, i.e., embedded in clothes, watches, glasses, etc.,
- mobile, i.e., being carried around,
- spontaneous (ad hoc) communication among the nodes,
- heterogeneous and hierarchical, i.e., they comprise different kinds of system nodes regarding their computational power and rendered functionality,

- context-aware, i.e., they are aware of their local environment and spontaneously exchange information with similar nodes in their neighborhood,
- anticipatory, i.e., acting on their own behalf without explicit extrinsic requests,
- natural communication with users by voice and gestures instead of keyboard, mouse, or text on screens,
- natural interaction with users by means of devices they are used to, e.g., clothing, watches, TV, telephone, household appliances. To this end the devices will be equipped with some kind of intelligence.
- adaptive, i.e., capable of reacting to all abnormal and exceptional situations in a flexible way.

With the aforementioned characteristics, AmI systems apparently bear some interesting potential for HCS. Because of its transparency, AmI technology enables novel ways of unobtrusive sensing. First, it will become possible to embed the monitoring and assistance devices invisibly in objects of our daily life, which reduces the stigmatization of these devices and thus increase their acceptance. Second, a considerable amount of sensors will be integrated in our living environment that can also be used to detect specific situations from an external perspective. With this, the availability of the sensing functionality does not depend on the actual usage of devices, e.g., the wearing of special devices, which is a serious problem these days. By fusing and drawing conclusions from different measured variables, the system can compensate the low accuracy and uncertainty of single sensor values, especially of environmental sensor values. On the one hand, an accurate automated system has a clear benefit compared to existing methods such as surveys in providing a continuous monitoring activity at home, i.e., a log along with times and durations for a wide range of activities. On the other hand, it also enables the system to recognize some mid-term or long-term trends and short-term deviations from the usual daily routine. Through enhanced self-awareness and context-awareness the systems are able to adapt themselves to changing situations (e.g., changing capabilities of the users). Thus, they can render their services at a new level of experience and enhance the quality of service.

Through early detection of upcoming or already existing problems, HCS systems can proactively assist people in preventing problems, e.g., by suggesting actions, or assisting them in critical situations, such as loss of consciousness, neurological, mental, or physical disabilities. Furthermore, the systems can provide an escalating assistance that also reduces the probability of false-positive or false-negative alarms. For instance, the system first provides early proactive assistance, e.g., by providing helpful instructions. Next, it integrates friends, family, or caregivers into the solution. In case of an emergency that cannot be prevented by the first two steps, it supports the assisted person to contact an integrated emergency medical service (EMS) and provides background information about the person's current state. The system interacts with humans in a multi-modal way using speech, gestures, and other forms of natural communication. Ideally, the users can interact with the system as they would do with other humans.

3 Challenges of Future Interfaces in Assisted Living

Besides the considerable system functionality of *Ambient Home Care Systems* (AHCS) we consider the combination of non-functional properties especially challenging. They have a major impact on the overall acceptance of the system and the chance to let elderly people learn to accustom themselves to the assistance provided. AHCS have to fulfill the following interface related requirements:

- Adaptivity: The systems need to adapt themselves to the context at runtime [6]. Adaptivity on various levels is considered an outstanding characteristic of AHCS. In order to render their service in the best possible way, the systems adapt themselves, according to the current situation, e.g. they reduce the interface complexity in case of emergencies to reduce the cognitive load. To support this, the systems must monitor their environment continuously, reason on necessary adaptations and make these adaptations, while still preserving quality.
- Natural, anticipatory human-computer interaction: AHCS have to provide human accessible interfaces for different target user groups: Especially for the people being assisted, who have limitations and handicaps, but also medical and care personnel, relatives, and maintenance operators. Multi-modal interaction paradigms that combine several modes (e.g., gesture, sound) are a good approach to enhance usability and accessibility. Anticipatory interfaces that proactively contact persons in certain situations are considered mandatory.
- Heterogeneity: Full-fledged Assisted Living systems will integrate several subsystems provided by different manufacturers. However, the user should be confronted with a homogeneous interface that integrates the services of the different subsystems in a seamlessly way.

At the same time, ethical, social, medical, and technological constraints must be considered.

- Formalization of domain knowledge: Developing AHCS requires domain knowledge to be transformed for machine processing. In many cases, this knowledge is difficult to formalize, e.g., the diagnosis of a disease pattern – decisions depend mostly on the expertise of medical staff that cannot be translated easily into information models and algorithms.
- Elderly people as the most important stakeholders: Some of the currently available solutions put a strong focus on the technological solution and neglect usability issues. Any HCS, which requires special skills from the elderly people to handle it, will fail. In addition, requirements are usually elaborated together with the end users. This is a difficult task since elderly people often have insufficient knowledge of the possible technical solutions available and are usually unaware of their increasing disabilities.
- Late learning: Still many of today's elderly people (esp. in Europe) are not used to modern IT systems and even worse, they are afraid of using them [7], [8]. Here big cultural differences become apparent. To meet this challenge, AHCS must either rely on the interaction paradigms they are used to or there must be special training programs offered to teach the users.

- Low acceptance of health assistance solutions: Assistance solutions that solely tackle health problems are hard to sell due to the negative associations raised by them and the social stigma identifying the assisted person's disabilities [9].
- Integration of available technologies: Many different electronic devices are available on the market. However, most of them do not provide standardized interfaces or integration specification. Many of these technologies have been developed for other purposes or are not intended to be integrated in larger solutions with other components. Good Usability of applications is essential [10], [11].
- Immaturity: Driven by upcoming problems due to the diverse changes, it is common sense that the assisted living domain will be a huge market. However there is only limited knowledge on how products will look, how they can be introduced to the market, who will pay for them, and how they will be accepted. To meet this challenge, the products must provide some kind of flexibility that will also affect the HCI.

4 Environment for Testing Future Interfaces for Assisted Living

Developing, testing, and training the elderly end users and measuring the impact of the assisted living solutions requires a realistic near-life environment in which training and evaluation can be performed. In order to cope with the different research and domain challenges in parallel, we have set up an Assisted Living Laboratory to analyze and develop sound assisted living solutions as well as engineering approaches.

The Assisted Living Laboratory is located at the Fraunhofer IESE in Kaiserslautern, Germany, and looks like the typical apartment of an elderly person: $60m^2$ with entrance, living room, sleeping room, bathroom, and kitchen. It plays a central role in performing research and development in the domain of assisted living. Firstly, it is used to perform accessibility and usability tests with elderly people in a realistic environment (cf. Fig. 3). Secondly, it acts as an evaluation platform for all developments. Thirdly, it provides results of the tests and evaluations in a direct feedback loop for further adjustment of research and development. Finally, it is used as a demonstration platform for representing the results of the research in demonstration scenarios.

It is equipped with different sensing, interaction, and assistance facilities to provide the basic technology and measurement environment for implementing and evaluating assisted living scenarios:

- ambient sensors and EIB[1]-based home automation with ambient sensors integrated in switches, blinds or power sockets to keep track of the elderly person's activities while using the devices.
- position tracking solutions, e.g. a smart carpet equipped with RFID[2] tags, RFID tags mounted in the ceiling, ultrasonic and radio-frequency-based movement sensors. RFID provides a lot of other possibilities [12], however, security aspects must always taken into consideration [13].
- intelligent household appliances, such as refrigerators that warn about spoiled food or cups that signal drinking activities

---

[1] European Installation Bus.

[2] Radio Frequency Identification.

- an intelligent walking aid that recognizes falls and notifies a central assistance system
- vital data monitoring devices that collect basic vital information, such as pulse, skin temperature and skin humidity in an unobtrusive manner with bracelets and transfer this information to the emergency monitoring and assistance application
- an autonomous robot transportation platform: a robotic device that can act as an assistant and which is controlled by remote users involved in emergency assistance scenarios for multimedia interaction and transportation purposes
- an interactive TV-based video-telephony system for communication with relatives, health care staff or the emergency medical service
- remote care and information applications for relatives and care personal
- audio and visual devices in several rooms for multimodal interaction with the elderly end user to provide reminders or to ask for feedback in specific situations.

Fig. 3. A view into the living room of the lab

The software application running in the Assisted Living Laboratory is called amiCA[3]. Its goal is to support elderly people so that they can live longer in a self-determined way in their preferred environment. To this end, it monitors the daily behavior of elderly people and assists them to maintain their well-known daily routine (nutrition, movement, sleeping, and other regular activities) as a fellow occupant would do. Of special interest is adequate emergency assistance integrating relatives, health care staff, and emergency medical services. AmiCA will be iteratively evolved into a full-fledged AHCS prototype within the coming years.

5 Assisting Elderly People to Handle New Technology

Learning is a lifetime process of cognitive and social change. Consequently, when referring to the support of elderly people, life long learning is not just a catch phrase, indeed it is a chance to promote learning, through their lives. Especially the new and

[3] Ambient intelligent Care and Assistance system.

ambient technology offers us both the challenge and the opportunity to support elderly people by assisting them to participate in the information society [14], [15]. However, in order to understand the issues involved in enabling the elderly to cope with the new technology, it is essential that one of the primary objectives of our research should be enabling the elderly to become aware of the benefits of new technology [16], [3], [17], [18]. To include people who are rarely involved in technological activities, such as the elderly, they must be encouraged to involve themselves in our experimental studies aimed at improving the quality of their lives. It is possible that these studies will be faced with multiple methodological challenges, some of which, together with the delicate nature of some of the issues in question, could be detrimental to the implementation of the participation of elderly people. One possibility of reaching these goals is by the application of user-centered design methods to involve elderly people in the development from the very beginning [19]. This includes usability methods [20], such as thinking aloud studies, which can provide insight into their behavior, their attitudes and their anxieties and can, most of all, provide ideas of what technology would be beneficial to them in order to enhance their daily life.

6 Evaluation Approach for Assisted Living Solutions

The impacts of the Assisted Living solutions are measured in the Assisted Living Laboratory from several perspectives: The end users' point of view (elderly person), the professional point of view (medical impact), and the technological point of view. To consider the stakeholder interests adequately, all stakeholders (medical professionals, health care staff, the end user target group, and their relatives) have already been integrated into the requirements analysis and development process. They participated in the requirements elicitation, the validation of the underlying theoretical models for the application, as well as in test and evaluation. Our *evaluation program aims* to:

1. prove the validity of our application model,
2. enable the developers to decide on optimization of the solution, and
3. enable end users/stakeholders to draw conclusions on the benefits (as well as limitations) of adopting the solution in real life.

The *Objects of evaluation* are in compliance with the aims of the evaluation program:

- the verification and validation of the assessed needs and requirements of all stakeholders,
- an empirical validation of the application model of AmiCA,
- the adequacy of specific assistance settings (technology, interfaces, interaction schemes),
- the accessibility of specific human computer interfaces in different emergency situations,

- the effectiveness of environmental sensors for activity tracking and situation recognition, and
- the effectiveness of interaction schemes to resolve upcoming or acute emergency situations.

In order to perform the evaluation process, we use a) continuous interviews of lab visitors regarding usability, acceptance, suitability, relevance, b) formative evaluations of specific objectives, c) summative evaluations of specific objectives; and d) external field tests for long-term evaluations and long term simulation data.

7 Conclusion and Future Outlook

Assisted Living Systems with Ambient Intelligence technology raise new challenges to system and software engineering. The development of Assisted Living applications requires domain-oriented interdisciplinary research. Adapted engineering approaches are required to cope with the specific characteristics of ambient intelligent systems. Our experience showed that test and evaluation of technology and prototypes should be done in controlled environment simulating real-life, such as the Assisted Living Laboratory. Further evaluation then should be done under real life conditions with different perspectives. Finally, in any Assisted Living solution including Ambient Intelligence technology, adequate information and training activities must be arranged/planned to make the elderly people aware of the ambient and unobtrusive assistance in their home environment. We found out that elderly people are the most demanding stakeholders for IT-development – even highly sophisticated systems will not be accepted when they do not address the real needs of elderly and are not very easily accessible and usable.

Acknowledgements

The work presented in this paper was carried out in the BelAmI (Bilateral German-Hungarian Research Collaboration on Ambient Intelligence Systems) project, funded by the German Federal Ministry of Education and Research (BMBF), Fraunhofer-Gesellschaft, and the Ministry for Science, Education, Research, and Culture (MWWFK) of Rhineland-Palatinate, Germany.

References

1. Aarts, E., Harwig, E., Schuurmans, M.: Ambient Intelligence. In: Denning, J. (ed.) The Invisible Future, pp. 235–250. McGraw-Hill, New York (2001)
2. Aarts, E.: Ambient intelligence: A multimedia perspective. Ieee. Multimedia 11(1), 12–19 (2004)
3. Emiliani, P.L., Stephanidis, C.: Universal access to ambient intelligence environments: Opportunities and challenges for people with disabilities. IBM Systems Journal 44(3), 605–619 (2005)
4. Burrows, M., Abadi, M.R.N.: A Logic of Authentication. ACM Transactions on Computer Systems 8(1), 18–36 (1990)

5. Bellazzi, R., Montani, S., Riva, A., Stefanelli, M.: Web-based telemedicine systems for home-care: technical issues and experiences. Computer Methods and Programs in Biomedicine 64(3), 175–187 (2001)
6. Oppermann, R., Rashev, R., Kinshuk.: Adaptability and Adaptivity in Learning Systems, In: Behrooz, A (Ed.): Knowledge Transfer vol. II pAce, pp. 173–179 (1997)
7. Phang, C.W., Sutanto, J., Kankanhalli, A., Li, Y., Tan, B.C.Y., Teo, H.H.: Senior citizens' acceptance of information systems: A study in the context of e-government services. IEEE Transactions On. Engineering Management 53(4), 555–569 (2006)
8. Monk, A., Hone, K., Lines, L., Dowdall, A., Baxter, G., Blythe, M., Wright, P.: Towards a practical framework for managing the risks of selecting technology to support independent living. Applied Ergonomics 37(5), 599–606 (2006)
9. Lester, J., Choudhury, T., Borriello, G.: A Practical Approach to Recognizing Physical Activities4th International Conference PERVASIVE (2006)
10. Holzinger, A., Sammer, P., Hofmann-Wellenhof, R.: Mobile Computing in Medicine: Designing Mobile Questionnaires for Elderly and Partially Sighted People. In: Miesenberger, K., Klaus, J., Zagler, W., Karshmer, A.I. (eds.) ICCHP 2006. LNCS, vol. 4061, pp. 732–739. Springer, Heidelberg (2006)
11. Edwards, A., Edwards, A., Mynatt, E.: Designing for Users with Special NeedsTutorial at CHI 2003. ACM Press, New York (2003)
12. Holzinger, A., Schwaberger, K., Weitlaner, M.: Ubiquitous Computing for Hospital Applications: RFID-Applications to enable research in Real-Life environments 29th International Computer Software & Applications Conference (IEEE COMPSAC), pp. 19–20 (2005)
13. Weippl, E., Holzinger, A., Tjoa, A.M.: Security aspects of ubiquitous computing in health care. Springer Elektrotechnik and Informationstechnik, e and i 123(4), 156–162 (2006)
14. Holzinger, A., Nischelwitzer, A., Meisenberger, M.: Mobile Phones as a Challenge for m-Learning: Examples for Mobile Interactive Learning Objects (MILOs). In: Tavangarian, D (Ed.): 3rd IEEE PerCom, pp. 307–311 (2005)
15. Holzinger, A., Nischelwitzer, A., Meisenberger, M.: Lifelong-Learning Support by M-learning: Example Scenarios. ACM eLearn Magazine, 5 (2005)
16. Shneiderman, B.: Human values and the future of technology: a declaration of responsibility. ACM SIGCHI Bulletin 23(1), 11–16 (1990)
17. Perry, M., Dowdall, A., Lines, L., Hone, K.: Multimodal and ubiquitous computing systems: Supporting independent-living older users. Ieee. Transactions On. Information Technology In. Biomedicine 8(3), 258–270 (2004)
18. Stephanidis, C., Savidis, A.: Universal Access in the Information Society: Methods, Tools and Interaction Technologies. Universal Access in the Information Society 1(1), 40–55 (2001)
19. Holzinger, A.: User-Centered Interface Design for disabled and elderly people: First experiences with designing a patient communication system (PACOSY). In: Miesenberger, K., Klaus, J., Zagler, W. (eds.) ICCHP 2002. LNCS, vol. 2398, pp. 34–41. Springer, Heidelberg (2002)
20. Holzinger, A.: Usability Engineering for Software Developers. Communications of the ACM 48(1), 71–74 (2005)

Multi-modal Authentication for Ubiquitous Computing Environments*

Taekyoung Kwon, Sang-ho Park, and Sooyeon Shin

Dept. of Computer Engineering
Sejong University, Seoul, 143-747, Korea
tkwon@sejong.ac.kr, {superh1,shinsy}@sju.ac.kr

Abstract. In ubiquitous computing environments, the computer technology will recede into the background of our lives for its ultimate goal, invisibility. For ensuring security and privacy in those environments, both human beings and surrounding devices should be authenticated under the interaction methods that are used for ubiquitous services. However, the invisibility of devices, the adaptiveness of interactions, and the varying performance of devices will make it difficult to achieve it. In this paper, we reconsider authentication for ubiquitous computing environments and propose a conceptual framework for resolving the difficulties.

1 Introduction

Ubiquitous computing will integrate computation into the physical environments under its ultimate goal, invisibility. In other words, the computer technology recedes into the background of our lives. The construction of ubiquitous computing environments means that human beings surrounded by real world objects are actually surrounded by various kinds of (hidden but communicating) electronic devices embedded into those objects, and they are also embodied by such tiny devices. There will be a need to change the way of interacting with computers, services, and the surrounding physical objects into more natural and casual ways. This new computing paradigm is being emphasized as an exciting revolutionary shift that makes us transfer to the next computing era called the age of calm technology [14]. Our living environments will be transformed to the spaces of intelligent and pro-active computing devices such as the so-called ambient devices, where it is unnecessary for us to continually rationalize the use of computing systems or even services. Under the goal of invisibility, we should conduct various kinds of human-computer interactions with such distinct computing devices even at the time we are not aware of using them, on the contrary to the virtual world stuffs, in the real world.

For ubiquitous service availability, we should move around and be identified by those devices very frequently. We should also be authenticated when we need to claim

* This research was supported by the MIC (Ministry of Information and Communication), Korea, under the ITRC (Information Technology Research Center) support program supervised by the IITA (Institute of Information Technology Advancement) (IITA-2006-C1090-0603-0028).

C. Stephanidis (Ed.): Universal Access in HCI, Part II, HCII 2007, LNCS 4555, pp. 113–121, 2007.

our identity or authority for security of services [3, 4]. However, there are at least three difficulties in achieving it in the ubiquitous computing environments. First, since the devices authenticating us are usually invisible, we should mind the so-called *calm adversaries*[1] around us. There exists the high risk to disclose secret information to the calm adversaries. Second, authentication should be carried out adaptively depending on the user preference as well as the available interaction methods. For example, we may not want to give a password loud when speech recognition is only possible, since we may fear that someone can hear our speech. We should mind other recognition methods and radio devices for privacy reasons likewise. Third, the communicating devices and sensing devices may vary with regard to their performance. Thus, it is feasible that the required authentication level cannot be met again.

In this paper, we reconsider authentication for ubiquitous computing environments and propose a conceptual framework for it. Multi-modality and its relation should be considered more carefully than multi-factor has been done for traditional authentication methods. This result is the main stem of our on-going work, the pro-active authentication considering human-computer interactions. The rest of this paper is organized as follows. In Section 2, we examine the current authentication technologies. In Section 3, we discuss our authentication framework for ubiquitous computing. In Section 4, we conduct a simple experiment corresponding to the pre-processing of multi-modal authentication in our framework and discuss its result. This paper is concluded in Section 5.

2 Authentication Technology

Authentication means the process of proving and verifying the claimed identity, and has been studied and applied for many years in computing environments. For authentication of human beings in those environments, three kinds of factors are usually considered, such as what we know (e.g., passwords, passphrases, or personal identification numbers), what we have (e.g., identification cards, security tokens, or software tokens), and what we are (e.g., fingerprint, retinal patterns, voice patterns, or other biometric identifier). Sometimes a combination of them is used, e.g., a bank card and a PIN, for producing better security in person authentication. This is called multi-factor authentication in the literature.

Specifically in biometric authentication, we use another term, multi-modal authentication, for describing the enhancement to increase the accuracy of authentication systems in five different ways: multiple biometrics, multiple acquisitions of the same biometry, multiple representations for the same biometry, multiple units of the same biometry, and multiple sensors for the same biometry. The multi-modality is accordingly used for describing the multiple treatments of biometric traits associated to a person in the literature [2, 13].

---

[1] Ubiquitous computing technologies could allow ill-intentioned individuals to deploy secret surveillance networks for spying on unaware victims, subsequently being used in unanticipated and illegal ways, even if they were initially deployed for legitimate purposes. Since the adversaries are invisible and utilize the calm technology, we call them the calm adversaries who can conduct data collection, coordinated analysis, and automated event correlation easily.

In this paper, we view the multi-modality as more concrete sub-categories of the multi-factor for authentication. In other words, not only biometric traits but also the other two factors are classified in more details with regard to the modality, and they could be used together.

3 Authentication for Ubiquitous Computing

3.1 A Conceptual Framework

In ubiquitous computing environments, authentication (and identification) must be conducted frequently, mostly without user's awareness, between: person-and-person, person-and-device, and device-and-device. A number of authentication events could occur for a person simultaneously whereas the human user is moving around with expecting various seamless services. Those ubiquitous services may have very different authentication requirements and security levels, while users may have their preferred authentication methods and the given devices can be lack of the required authentication methods. Privacy infringement is another major problem for authentication in such environments since physical devices as well as data packets can be captured and the related transactions can be traced easily by adversaries. Thus, it may not be trivial to apply traditional authentication methods without considering these distinct features [7, 10, 12].

We would like to propose a conceptual framework that the existing authentication methods can be used and combined consistently. In ubiquitous computing environments, there must be many surrounding (ambient) devices, e.g., wireless sensor networks (WSNs), around the person, and also many belonging devices of personal area networks (PANs). Thus in many cases, the person authentication could be the authentication of person's belongings as well. Fig. 1-(a) depicts the case that two mobile users having their respective PANs meet each other, and they are also connected to the environment networks, definitely without their awareness. The physical domain can be bound by the radio coverage of devices, but we need more to model an abstract domain that defines an authenticated boundary. We mean by the space such an authenticated domain, whereas the spaces can be layered and overlapped according to different security levels and network connectivity. For example, a user space may be constructed in the PAN layer and also linked to the user's home network layer. In case of Fig. 1-(a), there should be a number of interactions in the overlapped spaces, and their identification and authentication processes can be modeled as shown in Fig. 1-(b). Note that surrounding devices may stand by in the ubiquitous computing (UC) spaces, whereas belonging devices do in user spaces.

From now on, we handle authentication both for identification and authentication since identification is only about distinguishing an entity from the others and can be considered as a part of authentication process. In Fig. 1-(b), when a user space meet a UC space, meaning a user move into a certain environment, several authentication requests (or beacon messages) may be pushed to the user space. Such requests should contain at least available modality lists, required security levels, and random challenges. Note that the modality lists should also reflect available interfaces. These can be constructed efficiently in textual form. Depending on the communication channels that each request are sent over, awareness of corresponding devices and sometimes of the user will be necessary. The user preferences collected contextually in the PAN and sometimes the user's real time decision can then be combined with the given modality lists for constructing the reduced user space that is composed of the real time authentication factors. Fig. 1-(b), a token is rather a general term for a temporary ticket for specific services. Upon the service requests which may contain the prepared modality, specific authentication protocols could be conducted between the reduced space and the UC space. In the UC space, the user context could be fetched very in part from the PAN or through public (global) networks in an authentic manner if a need arises after identification. It is desirable to have three parts such as private, public, and anonimized parts in the user context for privacy reasons, and maintain them according to security levels. Finally, the user space can be merged with the UC space for ubiquitous services through the authenticated channels established from the reduced space. Two different user spaces can be modeled similarly for authentication, for example, simply by substituting for the UC space, respectively.

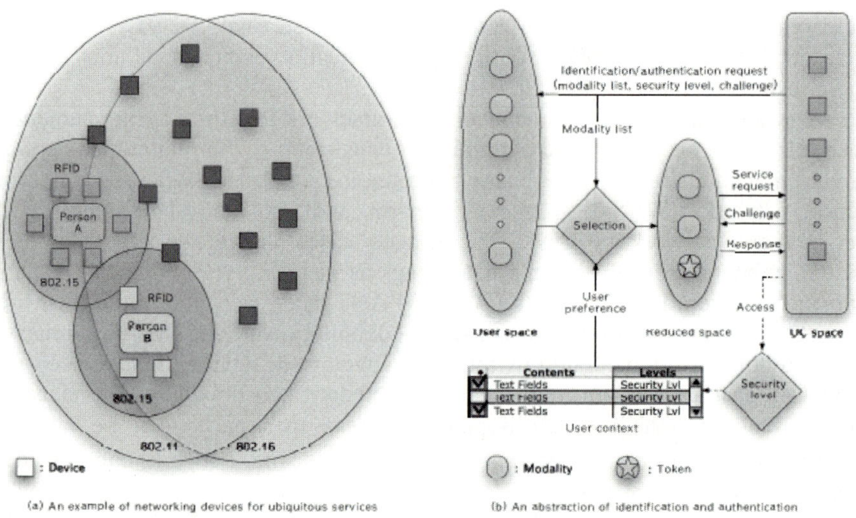

Fig. 1. Authentication for ubiquitous computing

3.2 A Scenario with Authentication Protocols

We discuss the implementation of our conceptual framework with a simple scenario by exploiting the existing authentication methods. It is assumed that a public key infrastructure (PKI) exists in a distributed manner and can be accessed by the space connected to a global network. It should also be reasonable to presume that basic PAN devices as well as biometric traits are already registered to a user's home network in an authentic manner. The home network should have several layered UC spaces. Finally we assume that a temporary ticket called a token is issued for a user by the authorities in PKIs, and stored in the user's PAN device. Let us omit the technical details in this paper; rather, we describe a single scenario with authentication building blocks only.

A simple scenario is that a human user wakes up in the morning, dresses himself up, and goes out to the office. When he wakes up, the UC spaces of his home network detect it and awake his PAN devices in a pro-active manner, according to his master context stored in the home network. A simple challenge-response protocol might be sufficient for identification requests of devices since they are already registered, but the status such as integrity and consistency of user context in the PAN and the modality of the PAN must be checked explicitly. A kind of digital signature or message authentication codes (MACs) can be used for it.

While he dresses himself up, new devices such as RFIDs of clothes are added (e.g., as a list of carried items) to the PAN. When we consider the PAN that is constructed through a specific communications mechanism such as a Bluetooth standard (IEEE 802.15.1), an RFID reader being capable of reading tags must be connected to the PAN for identifying and registering RFIDs in the PAN. A kind of blocker tags may also be necessary for privacy reasons [6]. Otherwise, the privacy-enhancing RFID authentication protocol that is based on symmetric key cryptography can be used for the purpose [9]. User's awareness is not yet required, but is soon necessary if he requests a specific broadcast service on TV that needs authorization with a password. The authentication request may be pushed by describing the required modality and security levels. Since the user must already been identified, the password can only be entered if a key pad is available around him but otherwise he can choose another input method through ambient devices. For password authentication with a broadcast center, a concrete method of IEEE P1363.2 can be applied [5]. However, if he cannot enter nor speak the password currently or his context explicitly describes that he doesn't want his awareness on this event, a different authentication method can be applied, by letting the password be encrypted by AES, an advanced encryption standard algorithm, at the previous registration phase and the encryption key be split to the PAN devices. Thus, if the user's PAN device accomplishes its authentication with the surrounding UC device as above, the split key can be transferred to the authenticated ambient device for decrypting the password.

When the user leaves for the office, he may go out trough the main gate of his house. At this time, his master context is set as roaming status for strengthening the privacy controlling security levels. It must be up to his choice to register his destination at this stage as well. While going to the office, if the user wants the same broadcast service on his PDA-like device having a fingerprint sensor, the fingerprint might be better than entering the password in a public space [8]. The fingerprint can be utilized to increase the security level: The PDA-like device captures the user's fingerprint and send its encryption along with the device authentication data to the UC device in his home network through a wider networking device such as a 3/4G cellular phone. The home device can decrypt the password of the roaming user with more authentication data in the reduced space than the above case that the user was home. For reducing the computation and network channel requirements, we can utilize a slight different method for the same goal. When encrypting the password in the home network, the super encryption of it with a key embedded into a biometric template is also prepared and stored in the home network. There are several methods to embed a cryptographic key into biometric templates and restore it using biometric samples. The key instead of the biometric sample itself then can be encrypted and transferred after capturing the user's fingerprint above. The scenario described in this subsection can be implemented with the existing authentication methods in our conceptual framework.

4 Authentication Experiment

We conduct a simple authentication experiment corresponding to the pre-processing of multi-modal authentication in our framework by considering the authentication scenario discussed in Section 3.2. More specifically, we consider the case that a human user is mobile and actually moves around both secure and insecure UC spaces, while the same security level of authentication is necessary in both spaces. For the purpose, we need a privacy-preserving location decision method. The secure UC space means that all ambient devices are authenticated and bound mutually, and the corresponding user space (concentrated on the user PAN) is secure from eavesdropping, while the insecure UC space may be insecure from those perspectives. We assume that an authorized device can only access the sensitive user context including a shared key with regard to the given security levels in the UC space.

In our experiment, we set up the UC space with ambient devices by deploying ultrasonic sensor nodes called Crickets and ZigBee sensor nodes called Berkeley Mica-Z motes. Those devices are bound by themselves through their base stations that are connected respectively in the secure UC space such as a home. We assume that a human user carries a PAN gateway that can communicate with both ZigBee devices and Crickets. Thus, we emulate the PAN gateway by connecting a Mica-Z mote with a Cricket on respective MIB-510 programming boards connected to a portable PC for the user. The list of current items, a number of pseudonyms PN_x, authentication factors, and a unique key K are stored in the Mica-Z mote, while those are made as an encrypted user profile that can be accessed by an authorized device only. We then let the user move with the emulated PAN gateway in our UC space.

As depicted in Fig. 2, four ambient ultrasonic devices named isl-1to 4 are positioned in respective coordinates such as (−60.0, 60.0), (60.0, 60.0), (−60.0, −60.0), and (60.0, −60.0). The inside of the square is assumed as the secure UC space, while the outside is not. When the user moves from the coordinate (14.3, 3.9, 47.9) to (−1.5, −88.5, 11.4), (s)he may listen to the environment where a beacon message including a random challenge R comes from. The user's Cricket estimates its location from those beacon messages but cannot decide the security level of the environment. Thus, we need a query to the environment. Note that, unless the user's Cricket transmits at all, a small degree of location privacy can be provided [11]. In other words, the environment cannot track the user yet, whereas the user's cricket estimates its location. For deciding the location, rather we can devise a privacy-preserving query protocol conducted over a distinct channel by porting our implementation to the Mica-Z mote. In that sense, the user device can query securely whether the user is in the secure UC space or not. The query can be made to an authorized device by encrypting the estimated location under K. The concrete protocol for this query is conducted over a ZigBee channel, and is depicted in Fig. 3.

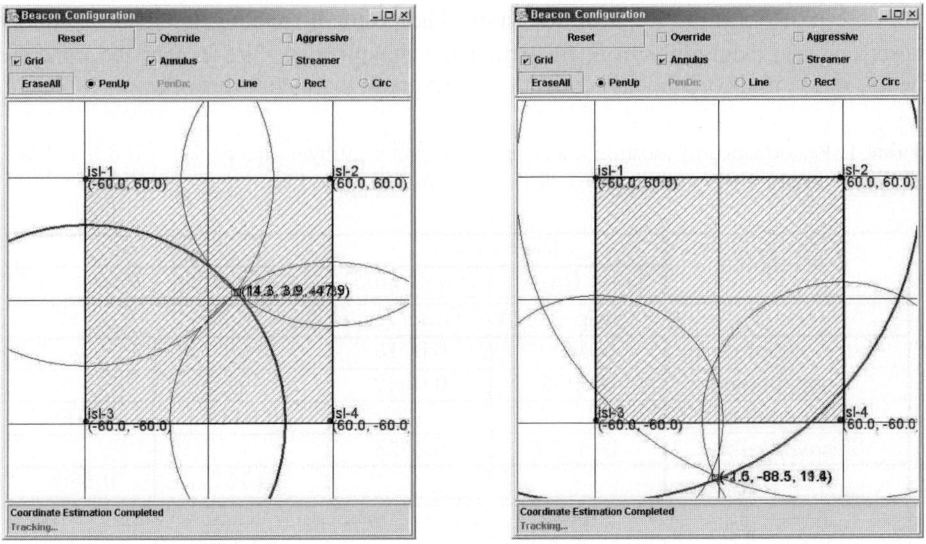

(a) A user in the secure UC space (b) A user in the insecure UC space

Fig. 2. Location detection of a mobile user

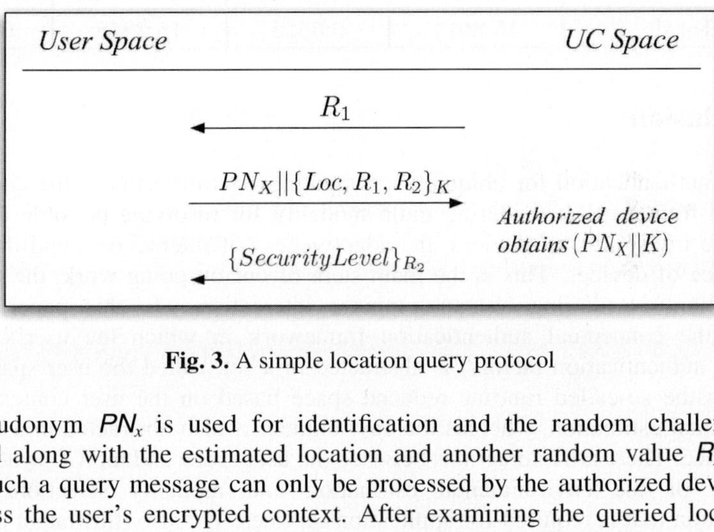

Fig. 3. A simple location query protocol

A pseudonym PN_x is used for identification and the random challenge R_1 is encrypted along with the estimated location and another random value R_2, called a nonce. Such a query message can only be processed by the authorized device which can access the user's encrypted context. After examining the queried location, the authorized device can respond with the security level of the corresponding environment by using the nonce R2 as an encryption key. For further authentication and desired application services, the user space can choose and agree on its preferred authentication modality by utilizing this critical information. Implementing and experimenting the further multi-modal authentication is our on-going work. Another on-going work is to enhance the location privacy in our authentication framework [1]. The performance of the simple location query protocol is summarized in Table 1, using the performance matrix of Atmel ATmege128L and that of CC2420 chip [15, 16]. Since the random challenge R is relayed through the Cricket in the user space, we omit the costs required for it in the Table. The protocol running time and its energy costs are very negligible from the efficiency perspectives. We expect the concrete details of the multi-modal authentication experiment in our future work.

Table 1. Performance of location query protocol (Note: 29 byte data packet and 8 byte block cipher are used for $|PN_x|=8$, $|Loc|=3$, $|R_x|=8$, $|SecurityLevel|=1$.)

Operations	User Space		UC Space	
	Time (msec)	Power (mJ)	Time (msec)	Power (mJ)
Step 2: $PN_x \| \{Loc, R_1, R_2\}_K$				
Nonce generation	0.0300	0.0010	-	-
Encryption	0.0955	0.0032	-	-
Decryption	-	-	0.0119	0.0004
Transmission	10.1574	0.3555	-	-
Receiving	-	-	10.1574	0.3860
Step 3: $\{SecurityLevel\}_{R_2}$				
Encryption	-	-	0.0477	0.0016
Decryption	0.0054	0.0002	-	-
Transmission	-	-	5.0787	0.1778
Receiving	5.0787	0.1930	-	-
Total	15.3671	0.5528	15.2958	0.5657

5 Conclusion

We study authentication for ubiquitous computing environments in the context of a conceptual framework considering multi-modality for resolving possible difficulties such as the invisibility of devices, the adaptiveness of interactions, and the varying performance of devices. This is the main stem of our on-going work, the pro-active authentication considering human-computer interactions. In this paper, first we construct the conceptual authentication framework in which the user's modality (including authentication factors) is abstracted in a set, called the user space, and is reduced to the so-called runtime reduced space based on the user context and the environmental estimation, whereas the environment is also abstracted in a set, called the UC space. There are interactions between the user space and the UC space for pre-processing of the environmental estimation and modality selection, and for authentication that is required for application services. We also illustrate a ubiquitous authentication scenario in our framework, and discuss that the presented scenario can be implemented with the current technologies in our framework. As for the environmental estimation, we present and experiment to conduct a practical protocol that queries a security level of the environment without leaking both identity and location of a user to unauthorized parties. In the simple experiment, we could observe that such a protocol can be executed in less than 50 msec under the resource-limited 8-bit processor ambient devices. It should take only several hundreds of msec even if we consider the possible transmission delay and processing delay of the encrypted user context by the authorized device, in such a resource-limited computing environment, and we could expect much more improvement from augmenting computing resources. It means that the protocol runs practically with regard to the varying performance of devices. In our future study, we will investigate more concrete details of both frameworks and mechanisms.

References

1. Beresford, A., Stajano, F.: Location privacy in pervasive computing. IEEE Pervasive Computing, pp. 46–55, (January-March 2003)
2. Bign, J., Duc, B., Smeraldi, F., Fischer, S., Makarov, A.: Multi-modal person authentication. In: Proc. of Face Recognition: From Theory to Applications (NATO-ASI Workshop) (1997)
3. Buennemeyer, T.K., Marchany, R.C., Tront, J.G.: Ubiquitous Security: Privacy versus Protection. In: Proc. of the 2006 International Conf. on Pervasive Systems and Computing, pp. 71–77, (June 2006)
4. Bussard, L., Roudier, Y.: Authentication in Ubiquitous Computing (Extended Abstract)., http://citeseer.ist.psu.edu/547343.html
5. IEEE P1363-2, Standard specifications for password-based public key cryptographic techniques (December 2002), available from http://grouper.ieee.org/groups/1363/
6. Juels, A., Rivest, R., Szyldo, M.: The Blocker Tag: Selective Blocking of RFID Tags for Consumer Privacy. In: Proc. of ACM Conference on Computer and Communications Security, pp. 103–111 (2003)
7. Kagal, L., Finin, T., Joshi, A.: Moving from Security to Distributed Trust in Ubiquitous Computing Environments. IEEE Computer (December 2001)
8. Koreman, J., Morris, A.C., Jassim, S., Sellahewa, H., Chollet, G., Aversano, G., Salicetti, S., Allano, L.: Multi-modal biometric authentication on the SecurePhone PDA. In: Proc. of MMUA workshop on Mult-Modal User Authentication, (May 2006)
9. Lim, C., Kwon, T.: Strong and robust RFID authentication enabling perfect ownership transfer, Information and Communications Security. In: Gorrieri, R., Wehrheim, H. (eds.) FMOODS 2006. LNCS, vol. 4037, pp. 1–20. Springer, Heidelberg (2006)
10. Matsumoto, M., Takagi, Y.: Mutual Authentication Method for Ubiquitous Service Environments. In: Proc. of IEEE Global Telecommunications Conf (GLOBECOM '03), vol. 3, pp. 1389–1393 (December 2003)
11. Priyantha, N., Chakraborty, A., Balakrishnan, H.: The Cricket location-support system. Mobile Computing and Networking, pp. 32–43 (2000)
12. Stajano, F., Anderson, R.: The Resurrecting Duckling: Security Issues for Ubiquitous Computing. IEEE Computer 35(4) Part Supplementary, 22–26 (2002)
13. Thian, N., Bengio, S.: Why Do Multi-Stream, Multi-Band and Multi-Modal Approaches Work on Biometric User Authentication Tasks? IDIAP research report. In: Proceeding of 2004 Internation Conf. on Acoustics, Speech, and Signal Processing (ICASSP 2004), vol. 5, pp. 893–896, (May 2004)
14. Weiser, M.: Some Computer Science Issues in Ubiquitous Computing. ACM SIGMOBILE Mobile Computing and Communications Review 3(3), 12–21 (July 1999)
15. Crossbow technology, Inc. http://www.xbow.com
16. ZigBee Specification Ver. 1.0 (2005), http://www.zigbee.org

Secure Authentication and Accounting Mechanism on WLAN with Interaction of Mobile Message Service*

Hyung-Woo Lee

Div. of Computer, Information and Software, Hanshin University,
411, Yangsan-dong, Osan, Gyunggi, 447-791, Korea
hwlee@hs.ac.kr

Abstract. In a wireless network that uses 802.1X Port Access Control, the wireless station plays the role of the Remote User and the wireless AP plays the role of the Network Access Server (NAS). However, Security problem for user authentication has been increased on existing IEEE 802.11 wireless network. However, brute force dictionary attack can be launched against the shared secret on existing IEEE802.1x (EAP-MD5, EAP-TLS, EAP-TTLS) protocols or security systems. Therefore, we overview main problem on existing EAP-MD5 authentication mechanism on Wireless LAN and propose a SMS(Short Message Service) based secure authentication and accounting mechanism for providing security enhanced wireless network transactions against those attacks.

1 Introduction

802.11's WEP(Wired Equivalency Privacy) encryption has well-known weaknesses that make it relatively easy for a determined user with the right equipment to crack the encryption and access the wireless network. A better way to protect your WLAN is with WPA(Wi-Fi Protected Access). WPA provides much better protection and is also easier to use, since your password characters aren't limited to 0-9 and A-F as they are with WEP. WPA support is built into Windows XP (with the latest Service Pack) and virtually all modern wireless hardware and operating systems. A more recent version, WPA2, is found in newer hardware and provides even stronger encryption.

WLAN security can be significantly strengthened by using 802.1X to control access point (AP) port access and deliver dynamic keys to authenticated users. Authentication Servers based on the RADIUS protocol play a key role in 802.1X. Therefore we take a closer look at how RADIUS works to better understand what's required from your RADIUS Server to support WLAN authentication.

Spread of Wireless network environment is supplied with the fast speed for the latest year. But, wireless network had tried quantitative swelling of wireless network service environment when wireless network business proprietor does not care greatly about security being used commercially first time. As a result, form and technology of

*This work is supported by 2007 Hanshin University Research Foundation.

C. Stephanidis (Ed.): Universal Access in HCI, Part II, HCII 2007, LNCS 4555, pp. 122–131, 2007.

wireless network invasion are increasing number of times. Therefore, the variety succeeds attack attempt and invasion is also increased gradually as a proportional with time.

Current wireless network is supplying Message encryption and user certification mechanism for wireless MAC frame through WEP and WPA etc. to solidify security. Through RADIUS and DIAMETER protocol, wireless network is offering user authentication and improved services. However, send-receive through existent protocol is not secure because packet sniffing for overall frame is possible. One solution is to supplement domain and limitation of certification process through service that associate except existent radio frame.

The Remote Authentication Dial In User Service (RADIUS) protocol was originally defined to enable centralized authentication, authorization, and access control (AAA) for SLIP and PPP dial-up sessions. Instead of requiring every Network Access Server (NAS) to maintain a list of authorized usernames and passwords, RADIUS Access-Requests were forwarded to an Authentication Server, commonly referred to as an AAA Server (AAA stands for authentication, authorization, and accounting). Therefore the wireless LAN based authentication architecture made it possible to create a central user database, consolidating decision-making at a single point, while allowing calls to be supported by a large, physically distributed set of NASs. However, a simplified authentication mechanism combined with mobile phone is required to enhance its performance.

In this study, we propose new protocol by associating SMS(Short Message Service) with existing RADIUS based authentication system for providing security enhanced and convenient one. The characteristics of protocol are personal information (privacy) protection and reinforcement by using the key given from SMS system. Also, we can implement easily the accounting system that is used in hand phone.

Certification way of existent wireless public network system delivers EAP-Request message to terminal including user information for transmit in AP on EAPoL packet. User terminal records EAP message including his own username on EAPoL packet and sends it to AP. And AP sends the message to RADIUS server. And RADIUS server notifies the result to AP that EAP Success message is received after examine whether RADIUS server had valid list in presented user account table. AP that receives this result is taking processes that permit internet access to relevant user.

At this procedure, the main issue is that username is exposed to malicious attacker. Username part that is stored in EAP message is transmitted to AP and RADIUS server when it is not encoded. We transmit sharable key to terminal through SMS between RADIUS server and terminal to supplement these limitation. And we propose protocol that encrypt and transmit EAP message by encrypt username using previously shared key by SMS.

In this study, we propose SMS based certification system based on ID/Password that is used in existent wireless public network. Presented system distributes secret key using AES-128 algorithm to user. And this secret key is used EAP certification procedure and EAP Message's encryption process. RADIUS server connects and achieves decryption process by using secret key that is created at user certification request process with user authentication server.

This paper explained about protocol that describe background knowledge to understand proposed protocol in Chapter 2, and proposes advanced one in Chapter 3.

And in Chapter 4, we propose a safe certification system through combination with proposed protocol. And certified method is reviewed for providing high performance through comparative analysis with existing certification system. Finally, we described about conclusion with future research topics in Chapter 5.

2 Background

2.1 NAS Mechanism with RADIUS for WLAN Authentication

When a user connects, the NAS sends a RADIUS Access-Request message to the AAA Server, relaying information like the user's name and password, type of connection (port), NAS identity, and a message Authenticator. Upon receipt, the AAA Server uses the packet source, NAS identity, and Authenticator to determine whether the NAS is permitted to send requests. If so, the AAA Server tries to find the user's name in its database. It then applies the password and perhaps other attributes carried in the Access-Request to decide whether access should be granted to this user. Depending upon the authentication method being used, the AAA Server may return a RADIUS Access-Challenge message that carries a random number. The NAS relays the challenge to the remote user (for example, using CHAP). The user must respond with the correct value to prove its asserted identity, which the NAS relays to the AAA Server inside another RADIUS Access-Request message (Figure 1).

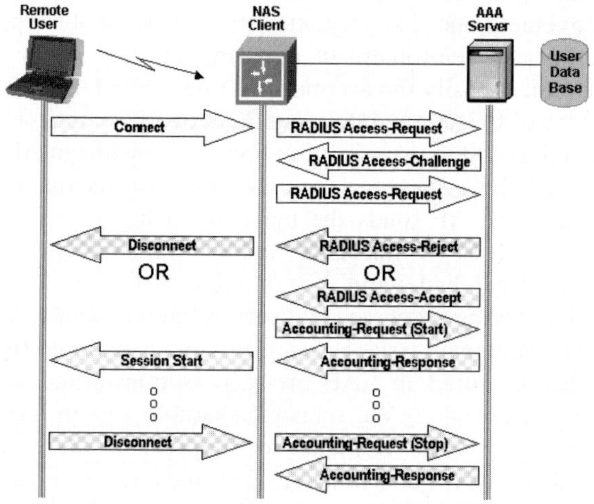

Fig. 1. NAS Mechanism with RADIUS for WLAN Authentication

2.2 IEEE 802.1X EAP-MD5 Authentication

The MD5 authentication method[1] is the simplest one available to wireless LAN users, and support is required in the EAP standard. However, the security of MD5 in a wireless environment is so blatant, that some wireless vendors have chosen not to allow MD5 as an authentication method. With MD5 authentication, the authenticator sends a challenge to the supplicant: some string, along with a serial number. The supplicant proves it knows the password by hashing the challenge, the string, and the password together and then sending the information back.

Below Figure 2 shows the simplified IEEE802.1x EAP-MD5 mechanism. In first step, station connects with AP running certification procedure of system level by Open System or Shared Key Authentication. This connection is not more that Ethernet Station connects by cable in Switch. Since, run certification procedure of user level by EAP formality.

And then AP receives EAP-Request [Identity] message transmit user name if receive EAPoL Start message from terminal, or sense truth that terminal is connected to EAPoL Packet and require to terminal. Identity item of this case user name be instead of, name etc., of SSID and AP that is AP's information are received.

AP creates RADIUS Access-Request message which is received EAP-Response [Identity] message from terminal. Then RADIUS Serve composes EAP Request message(MD5-Challenge Value (CV) : RADIUS Access-Challenge message) and send it to AP. After much more interaction between RADIUS server and Station, if Station receives EAP Success message, it can approach to outside (Internet) via AP[2].

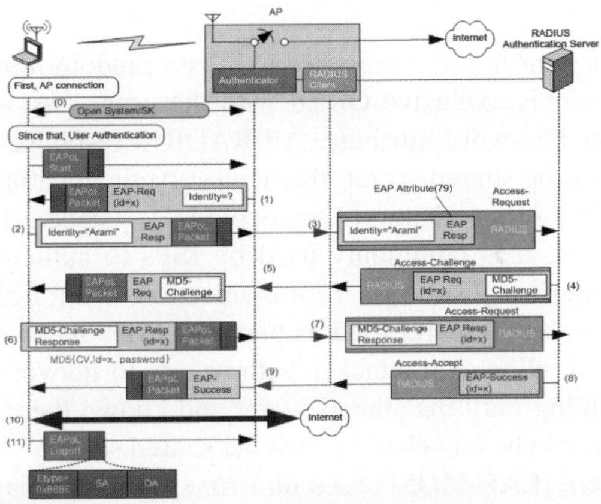

Fig. 2. IEEE802.1x EAP-MD5 Mechanism (EAP-MD5 Challenge)

Challenge-based authentication schemes, like MD5, were designed to counter the insecurity of schemes like PAP (Password Authentication Protocol), which actually send the username and password in the clear across the wire. With MD5 (or CHAP in traditional PPP), the password doesn't pass across the wire. Instead, the supplicant "proves" that it knows the password. MD5 is fine for dialup, but there are three issues that render MD5 less than optimal for wireless authentication.

First, MD5 requires that user passwords be stored in a way that lets the authenticator get at the original plain-text password. You'll sometimes hear this referred to as "reversibly encrypted." This opens up the possibility of someone other than the authentication server getting access to the file of passwords.

Secondly, MD5 only authenticates the supplicant. It does nothing to authenticate the authenticator, the wireless access point. Since wireless is especially vulnerable to impersonation, this is the major problem. Whereas impersonating a dial-up access server on the other end of a phone line is fairly difficult, impersonating wireless just means getting within a couple hundred feet of the supplicant. This lack of mutual authentication is the reason some wireless vendors have chosen not to allow MD5.

Thirdly, MD5 does not create a WEP session key. Ideally, immediately after authentication, the wireless client and access point would jump into WEP-encrypted communications, which reduces the risks of eavesdropping, impersonation, or data corruption by a hostile attacker. Other authentication methods, such as TLS and TTLS, support this but MD5 does not and therefore this limits its usefulness in the wireless world.

2.3 Vulnerability of IEEE 802.1X EAP-MD5 Mechanism

The purpose of the Authenticator is to provide a modest bit of security. The NAS and AAA Server use the Authenticator to demonstrate that both know the same secret password. The Authenticator also helps the NAS detect forgery of RADIUS responses. Finally, the Authenticator is used to obscure the user's password, inhibiting disclosure to the NAS or anyone else who might eavesdrop on the RADIUS messages.

The Authenticator sent in the Access-Request is a random number. An MD5 hash of this random number is exclusive OR'ed with the user's password and sent in the Access-Request User-Password attribute. All RADIUS response messages thereafter carry an MD5 hash of the shared secret, the request Authenticator, and other response values.The RADIUS Authentication protocol is a standard used for remote authentication of users. It is commonly used by ISPs to authenticate dial up users, although it has wider applications. Communication with a RADIUS server is mediated in part by a shared secret used as part of a MD5 hash. A design flaw in the RADIUS specification allows an attacker with access to network traffic to intercept an MD5 hash containing only the shared secret and known data. This allows a *brute force dictionary attack* to be launched against the shared secret.

Certification system (EAP-MD5) based on PAP system has many limitations. First, EAP-MD5, the original implementation of EAP, is vulnerability to man-in-the-middle attack–referred to as *MITM or monkey-in-the-middle-attacks*(taken from a popular MITM tool called monkey_jack[5]) against the AP because there is no AP/server-to-host authentication. A rogue AP placed between the EAP-MD5 supplicant and the RADIUS server can easily snatch the users employing sent to the authentication server and even authenticate users employing false credentials[6].

Second, Because Message encryption does not consist in EAP-MD5 Wireless torso that increase, is weak in hackers' Sniffing attack. And EAP-MD5 certification way uses MD5 Hash function to this Hash function too much limitations find [7]. Therefore, we propose PAP base certification system that uses SMS to prevent these limitations. Proposed system combines existing mobile phone service with wireless public network account service.

3 SMS Based Secure Authentication and Accounting System

3.1 SMS Based Secure Authentication

New SMS based certification system can provide stable wireless public network service. It can solve the vulnerability problems on EAP-MD5 certification system and also can provide message encryption on wireless transaction.

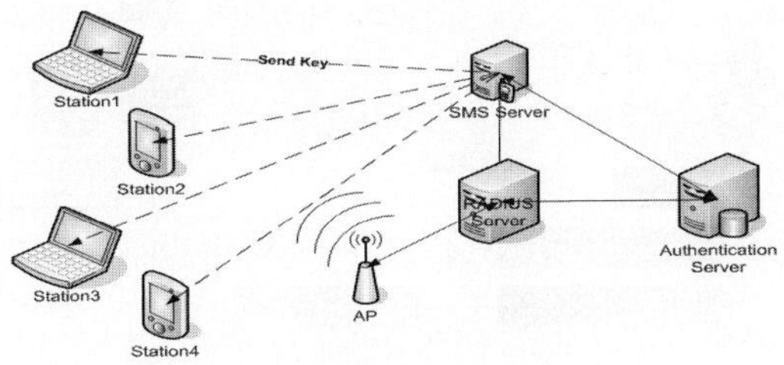

Fig. 3. SMS based Authentication Architecture

EAPoL Frame on Station. On SMS based PAP certification system, each Stations encrypts their own EAP packet using AES algorithm with Secret Key that is received by SMS message from SMS server. In this time, each entity receives EAP packet on EAPoL frame which is prescribed in 802.1x for data transmission on wireless transaction. EAP packet on EAPoL frame is used for security enhancement on wireless transaction and it contains the most important user information (User ID and Password), which is used in certification process between the Station and RADIUS Server. Encryption process executes encryption on EAP Message using AES algorithm using 128 bit key.

SMS based Authentication through AP. AP delivers frame between Station and RADIUS Server. A specific implication of man-in-the-middle attack is performed by a Rogue AP. It attacks one-way IEEE802.1x authentication mechanism which is based on EAP-MD5. To perform such an attack, Rouge AP will impersonate as a Rogue RADIUS Server by providing fake credentials in the form of always positive authentication reply to the station.

Therefore we propose an efficient defense mechanism against this vulnerability. User encrypts and sends an EAP packet using secret key that is received from AP. And then authenticated RADIUS server can decrypt message included in EAP packet.

Station that receive EAP-Request [Identity] message from AP transmits EAP-Response message as a response message. Station receives his own information from the RADIUS Server through AP.

RADIUS Server that receive EAP-Response message (UserID) creates 128 bit secret key that do Random. At this time, SMS Server transmits Secret Key to the user's Hand Phone by SMS message after comparing the user's information with that is stored in user authentication table on Authentication Server.

RADIUS Server is system that act important role that take charge decision of certification success availability and Secret Key relationship creation function in this system. RADIUS Server that accept user's ID information reads Hand-Phone information of use in User Authentication Table and give Secret Key transmission command by SMS Server. By this mechanism, we can get some effectiveness. We can keep away user's partial secret from the wired network. As the secret key is received from the SMS message, we can construct the secret sharing mechanism on the ID/PASSWORD based authentication mechanism.

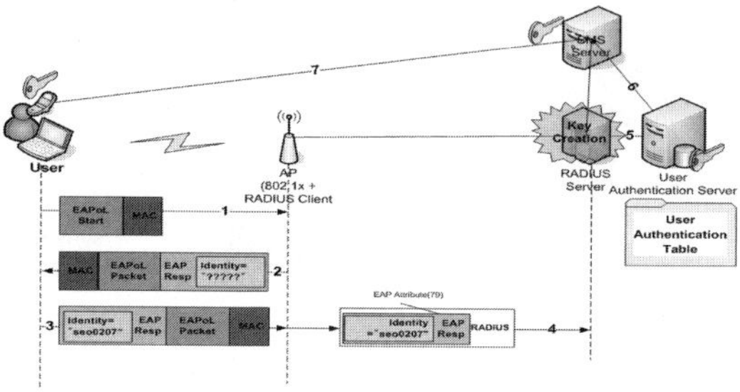

Fig. 4. Secret Key Distribution on SMS Message

Station creates hash value with user's own password, CV and seq_ID. Station transmits EAP packet including created hash value to RADIUS Server. And then RADIUS server also creates HV' using password that is stored already on his own account table and CV and seq_ID. Finally, RADIUS Server compares received HV ' value with computed HV value. Of course, encryption on EAP packet is achieved independently with commonly used MD5 hash function in this process.

User authentication table is situated to Authentication Server. It is place that necessary user information is stored in certification process of RADIUS Server and each Station on this table. Secret Key that is created in RADIUS Server is stored to Authentication Server's Secret Key field.

3.2 SMS Based Accounting Mechanism

Current wireless public network users can be connected to public network after preliminary registration are given based on ID and Password authorization process. Also, users pay money according to connection time. But, present wireless network environment cannot use network in all time and places that users want. By various kinds factor, there is a case that smooth service is not achieved. This time, existing subscribers can feel many discomforts. And network administrator also has present complaint in fare system of wireless network that make fixed amount of money and then use unlimitedness.

We can solve these users' discomfort. User who do not join in Wireless public network service transmits his own Hand-Phone number and Secret Key request message to Radius Server, and RADIUS Server transmits Secret Key to user Hand-Phone using SMS. Secret Key of user is given and encrypts individual's unique number (resident registration number Korean case) by Secret Key and transmits to RADIUS Server with joined beforehand user.

RADIUS Server that accepts user information foretells availability whether Hand-Phone subscriber's unique number and unique number that request person inputs conform. If these input two values equal, user can use wireless network service.

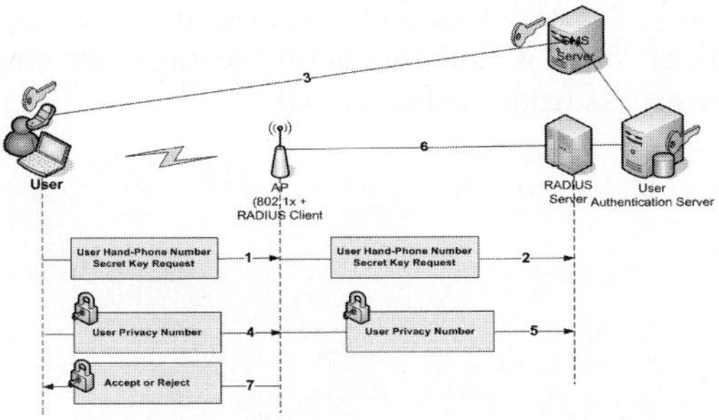

Fig. 5. SMS based Accounting Process

4 Experimentation and Analysis

4.1 Experimentation Environment

Experiment of this treatise is Fig 6. In an experiment actuality packet of EAP-MD5 certification formality after Capture actuality costs of each frame see and analyzed about techniques that is encoded by Key value that values are drawn by SMS Server and part that improve than existent system when encoded. Station's environment is Windows XP, AP used LinkSys WRT54GS.RADIUS Server used Windows 2003 servers.AES-128 Key's encryption process embodied by Matlab.

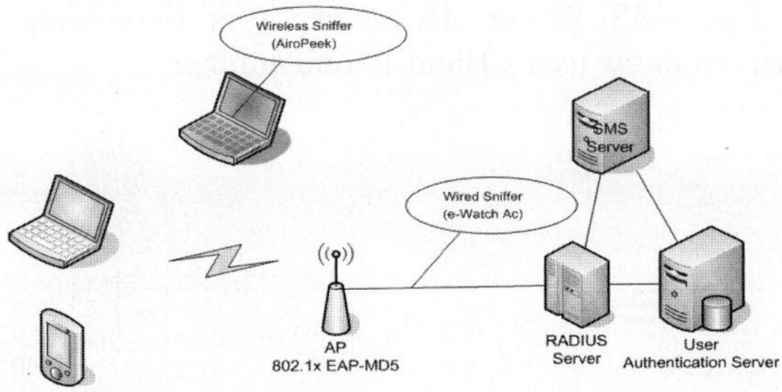

Fig. 6. Experimentation Environment

4.2 Preventing Dictionary Attack and Rogue AP Protection

WLAN access at hotspots is still a relatively new phenomenon. Most hotspots today operate on the *open access model*, in which users can sign up via their Web browsers, and pay on-demand or be billed against an existing provider account. However it doesn't protect user credentials and data transfer over the wireless connection, open access is not secure enough for most corporate users, or for individuals concerned about identity theft and other personal security issues. If we also offer wireless phone service, we can implement *SMS-based authentication* that lets us offer wireless hotspot Internet access to existing wireless phone customers, based on the information in your subscriber database (and conveniently bill customers for both on a single statement). Additionally, the AES function based on secret key from SMS can be used to encrypt/decrypt IEEE 802.1X authentication message, we can prevent dictionary attack and protect the access from the Rogue AP.

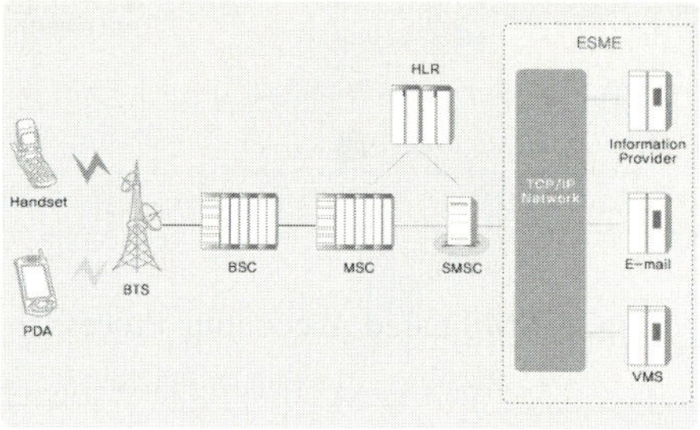

Fig. 7. Field Test Model

EAP message is recorded on EAPoL frame and is transmited to the receiver. EAPoL frame is consisted of Protocol Version (1 byte), Packet Type (1 byte), Body Length (1 byte) and EAP message.

EAPoL frame is consisted of fixed Packet length. And we can detect rogue AP by using encrypted EAP message on EAPoL frame. Attack by rogue AP is possible because there is no mutual authentication process. Rogue AP sends a message EAP-Success message to Station, Rogue AP that do not know Secret Key of Station and RADIUS Server can not encryption EAP-Success message. Rogue AP gives Secret Key to Station using SMS Server. However, it is impossible to see user's ID information and can not know user's Hand-Phone number.

Fig. 8. EAP Encryption & Decryption Result

4.3 Secure Message with SMS/EAP-Message Encryption/Decryption

Fig. 8 shows a frame sniffing result. EAP Message's frame structure can know in Fig.7. EAP Header part has 4byte's data frame all, and data of Body Type's 1byte and real EAP of Type data of EAP Body part is received. This paper encrypts EAP message entirety (header inclusive).

5 Conclusion

By using these new protocol, we can construct secure system compared with existing EAP over LAN(EAPoL). It is because user ID is encrypted by the shared key from the SMS message. User who is not joined in wireless public network can connect easily and authenticated securely to it with accounting system through hand phone. We developed EAP-Message encryption module with AES-128 encryption algorithm using these shared secret key. As a result, we can prove that secure authentication process is possible on wireless environment with proposed SMS based mechanism. For future works, we can combine wireless authentication mechanism with fingerprint certification procedure. Using it, we can propose certification system that use fingerprint to solve authentication problem happen in existing wireless certification system. Therefore, we will supplement security vulnerability in existing wireless certification system.

References

[1] Wireless LAN Security Interoperabillity Lab, What are EAP Authentication, pp. 1–2

[2] Yoon, J.-H.: Wireless LAN Security Protocols, pp. 282–283, (2005.08)

[3] Phillips Craiger J.: 802.11, 802.1x, and Wireless Security (2002.06)

[4] Trappe, W., Washington, L.C. (eds.): Introduction to CRYPTOGRAPHY with CODING THEORY, pp. 128–136. Prentice Hall, Englewood Cliffs (2001.03)

[5] Beaver, K., Davis, P.T.: Hacking Wireless Networks for DUMMIES, p. 208. Wiley, Chichester (2005)

[6] Andrew, A., Vladimirov, K.V., Gavrilenko, A.A.: “Wi-Foo“, Fifth printing p. 182. Addison-Wesley, London (October 2005)

[7] Wang, X., Yu, H.: Shandong University, How to Break MD5 and Other Hash Function

[8] Buchholz, J.J.: Matlab Implementation of the Advanced Encryption Standard (2001.11), http://buchholz.hs-bremen.de

Dynamic Conflict Detection and Resolution in a Human-Centered Ubiquitous Environment

Haining Lee[1], Jaeil Park[1], Peom Park[1], Myungchul Jung[1], and Dongmin Shin[2]

[1] Industrial & Information System Engineering, University of Ajou, Suwon, Korea
[2] Hanyang University, Ansan. 1217, Kyunggi-do, Korea
{leehaining, jipark, ppark, mcjung}@ajou.ac.kr,
dmshin@hanyang.ac.kr

Abstract. In this paper, a Conflict Control Manager (CCM) for a ubiquitous services system is presented to prevent the mode confusion of humans. CCM consists of a lock-based conflict detection module and a D-PRI (dynamic priority)-based conflict resolution. By means of CCM, the mode confusion can drastically be reduced, and, as a result, CCM can assist in designing and implementing a human-centered ubiquitous environment. Through a case study, it is observed that CCM can successfully detect and resolve the runtime conflicts caused by multiple devices interconnected in a ubiquitous environment. It can also be used to detect the potential conflict risk during the service registering phase so that computerized devices are deployed to improve the human interactions with them.

Keywords: Conflicts detection, resolution, human-centered ubiquitous environment, human interaction.

1 Introduction

As a high degree of automation is achieved with rapid development of computer technologies, the way a human works in a system has drastically changed. Two separate approaches to research related to human-involved complex system have been pursued – automatic coordination and human-computer interactions. In spite of the significant work conducted in both areas, very limited crosscutting research has been conducted in the important integration area. Furthermore, as the interaction between human and computerized systems becomes complicated, the importance of the coordination of a system and conflict management has been emphasized. As the degree of computerization increases, a large number of topics have become critical in terms of human-computer interaction. Especially, the clumsy automation without considering the human factors view cannot achieve the desired benefits of the system automation that most of information technology nowadays is associated with [1].

In the ubiquitous service system, one of the most crucial research areas from the human-computer interaction perspectives, conflicts are frequently incurred at runtime when several services are requested for a device and/or the environment variables of

C. Stephanidis (Ed.): Universal Access in HCI, Part II, HCII 2007, LNCS 4555, pp. 132–140, 2007.

different types of devices are set by different users at the same time. These conflicts may result in the deadlock of the service system. Far more importantly, they may cause the degradation of situation awareness of humans involved in a ubiquitous environment where a variety of devices are interconnected. Since a ubiquitous environment needs to be designed in a human-centered manner, it is crucial to ensure that humans can be aware of the system when an unanticipated situation occurs due to conflicts among devices.

For this reason, this paper presents a conflict detection and resolution mechanism for improving the human interaction with devices that provide services to humans in a ubiquitous environment. The main purpose of this paper is to develop a reliable and robust ubiquitous service system by detecting and resolving runtime conflicts incurred when two or more services are requested for ubiquitous access in the ubiquitous service system. A test bed ubiquitous environment is implemented with WS-ECA framework that exploits Web service technologies, and the effectiveness of the proposed conflict management system is assessed. Through a case study, it is observed that CCM can successfully detect and resolve the runtime conflicts caused by multiple devices interconnected in a ubiquitous environment.

The remainder of paper is organized as follows. Section 2 presents the related works. Section 3 analyzes the conflicts in ubiquitous services system and proposes a conflict detection and resolution mechanism. The practical implementation is presented in Section 4. Section 5 concludes the paper and discusses future work.

2 Related Work

Recently, the importance of human-computer interaction has been emphasized and several researches have been conducted. Especially, human-robot interaction has been one of active research and has received much attention from various perspectives. Several approaches toward the development of intelligent robot for man-machine interaction have been pursued [2] [3].

Situation awareness is also critical in a dynamic environment since it plays an important role in dynamic human decision making [4]. It is desirable to ensure that a ubiquitous environment can be of use to humans such that humans can enjoy benefits of services provided by devices in the system.

Recently, the coordination of multiple devices has received a large amount of attention to realize a ubiquitous environment. Especially, conflicts among devices are known to have the significant influence on the system running in consideration with humans. While a significant attempt at static conflict detection has been made by Imperial College [5], the very crucial and complex issue of dynamic conflict detection in ubiquitous service management has yet to be resolved in an effective way.

Current advances in conflict detection and resolution have been primarily focused on static, compile-time environments [5]. There exists, however, a compelling requirement to examine the very complex and unresolved issues surrounding dynamic (or run-time) conflict detection and resolution.

3 Conflict Detection and Resolution Mechanism

3.1 Conflict Classification

In the human-centered ubiquitous environment, dynamic conflicts are frequently incurred at runtime when several services are requested for a device and/or the environment variables of different types of devices are set by different services or users at the same time. We consider the conflicts that may impose negative impact on the human-centered ubiquitous environment and identify two types of conflicts: (1) resource conflicts and (2) environment variable conflicts. The resource conflicts happen when one device which is performing a service is interrupted by other services. This device should be used exclusively and not be interrupted by other services while performing its service. For example, a TV recorder is scheduled to record Channel 1 from 1:00 to 2:00pm. If another service attempts to use the same recorder to record Channel 2 from 1:10 to 1:30, a resource conflict happens.

Some variables of devices can be used to describe the environment surrounding a ubiquitous service system, such as temperature, noise level, illumination, etc. These environment variable conflicts happen when users request to change the environment variables of devices, which are common for them. For example, while a sleeping service requested by one user sets the "noise level" of his/her house to be "silent", the other user, who likes to use a cleaner at the same time, raises the "noise level" of the house to be "noisy". This is a typical example of the environment variable conflicts.

Resource conflicts can cause the mode confusion when a human uses a device that is subject to the resource conflict. On the other hand, environment variable conflicts can degrade the quality of services that a human expects to enjoy, resulting in the poor human interactions with devices.

3.2 Conflicts Detection and Resolution Mechanism

As mentioned in the previous section, all the conflicts incurred in the human-centered ubiquitous environment can be decomposed into a collection of resource conflicts and environment variable conflicts. The detection and resolution of these conflicts can be a key to ensuring that humans can be aware of the system when an unanticipated situation occurs due to conflicts among devices. In an attempt to detect and resolve conflicts, we suggest (1) lock-based conflicted detection and (2) D-PRI (Dynamic Priority) conflicts solution.

Lock-based Conflict Detection Method. The lock-based conflict detection method is devised to manage universal access to devices and their environment variables in the human-centered ubiquitous environment. Each time a service requests an access to a device or manipulates its environment variable, the service sends a lock request to the conflict control manager, which registers the lock and checks the system for runtime conflict detection. The conflict control manager can accept the lock request for an item (a service or an environment variable) if the item is currently free or there is no lock held on the item. The conflict control manager uses the lock compatibility database in which the compatibility of services is registered in terms of items when an item can acquire multiple services at the same time. For instance, services A and B can run on device 1 at the same time, or Services A and C can not run on device 1 simultaneously, to name a few. If an item is already locked by a service, a new lock to the item by other services can be granted only if the lock request is compatible. If the lock request is not compatible, the services wait for the lock timeout interval of the previous service to expire.

In summary, the lock compatibility database is used to check the compatibilities between different lock requests. Conflicts are incurred when the new requested lock on the item is incompatible with the previous one. Figure 1 shows the lock-based conflict detection mechanism. The lock-based conflict detection method enables the detection of resource and environment variable conflicts by checking the Lock Compatibilities.

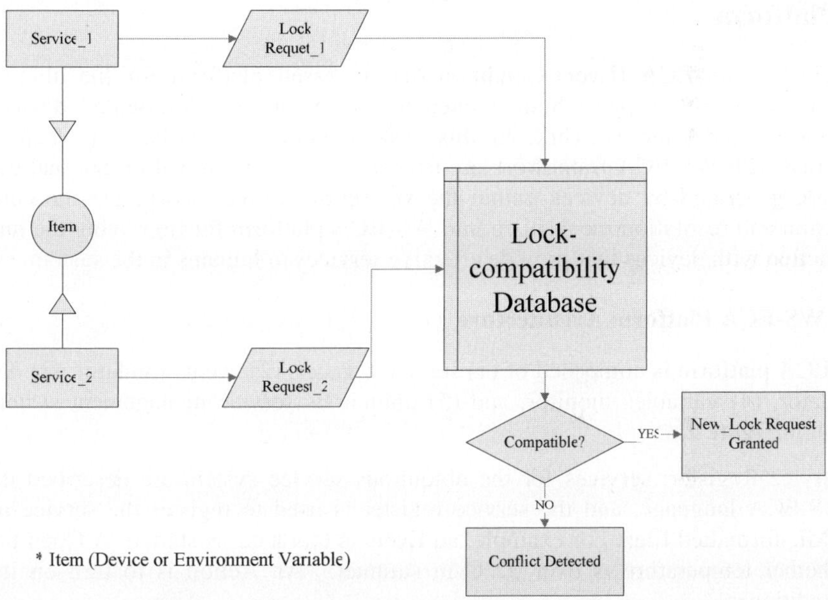

Fig. 1. Lock-based Conflict Detection Mechanism

D-PRI (Dynamic Priority) Conflicts Method. When conflicts happen, the conflict control manager decides which lock request can be granted (which service can access the devices and/or change environment variables). We suggest a D-PRI (Dynamic Priority) conflicts solution where each service is assigned a D-PRI. When conflicts happen between two services, the conflict control manager checks each service's D-PRI and allows the one of them which has the higher D-PRI to use the device and/or change environment variables. The D-PRI is decided in three ways as follows:

- Comparative way: the conflict control manager assigns each service a D-PRI by comparing its importance to the user. For example, security services have higher D-PRI than entertainment services.

- Interactive way: when conflicts between services A and B are detected, the conflict control manager sends conflict information to a user who is interested in using the services. If the user prefers service A rather than B, service A has a higher D-PRI than service B.
- User-specific way: the user-specific way uses the statistical result of the interactive way to determine user specific D-PRI. The conflict control manager examines the past records of how conflicts are resolved by individual user, and, then, statistically determines the D-PRI of each service in terms of user' preference.

It should be noted that human is considered a critical component in establishing the dynamic priorities of services. This can contribute to reflect human's preferences and behavioral history in designing a ubiquitous environment.

4 Conflict Detection and Resolution Mechanism on the WS-ECA Platform

WS-ECA is an ECA (Event-Condition-Action)-based platform for the ubiquitous services system to support human interactions among service-oriented devices in ubiquitous computing network. In this system, conflicts can happen when rules specified with WS-ECA framework are triggered by some internal or external events that are generated by devices within the environment. We incorporate the conflict detection and resolution mechanism into WS-ECA platform for improving the human interaction with devices that provide effective services to humans in the system.

4.1 WS-ECA Platform Architecture

WS-ECA platform is composed of (1) service register, (2) event simulator, (3) device simulator, (4) variables monitor, and (5) ubiquitous service management system as shown in Figure 2.

1. Service Register: services for the ubiquitous service system are described in the WS-ECA language, and the service register is used to register the service using XML-formatted files. For example, an Event is that a car is started. A Condition is whether temperature is over 32°C in summer. An Action is to turn on its air conditioner.
2. Event Simulator: the event simulator simulates the event in the ubiquitous service system by generating event messages. The event messages are sent to ubiquitous service management system to activate services.
3. Device Simulator: the device simulator activates and/or deactivates devices in the ubiquitous service system. Device's states change according to the use of the corresponding services.
4. Variable Monitor: in the ubiquitous service system, the information of environment variables such as temperature, humidity, noise level, etc. are obtained though various types of sensors. We use the variable monitor instead of sensors to collect the information of environment variables.
5. Ubiquitous Service Management System: the ubiquitous service management system is the core of the platform. It allocates and controls all the services running in the system and detects and solves conflicts.

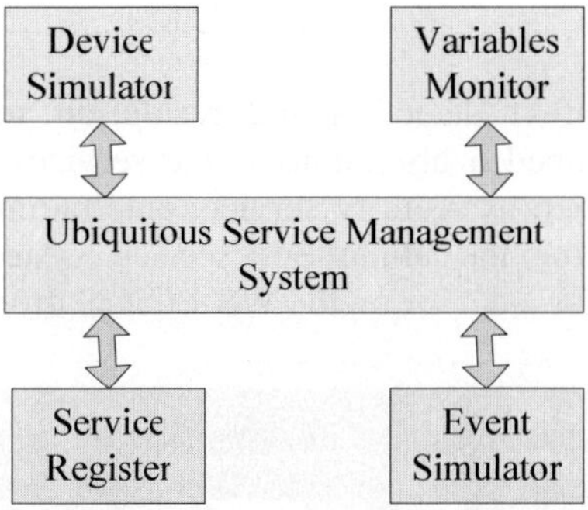

Fig. 2. WS-ECA Platform Architecture

4.2 Conflict Control Manager Architecture

The conflict control manager architecture on the WS-ECA platform is divided into four parts: (1) resource and environment variable status database, (2) lock compatibility database, (3) D-PRI database, and (4) service controller.

1. Resource and Environment Variable Status Database: the resource and environment variable status database stores the lock status of resource and environment variables.
2. Lock Compatibility Database: the lock compatibility database stores the compatibilities between lock requests.
3. D-PRI Database: the D-PRI database assigns and stores dynamic priorities which are the base of conflict resolution to different services.
4. Service Controller: the service controller grants the lock request from different services and schedules the services based on the information from the resource and environment variable status database, the lock compatibility database, and the D-PRI database.

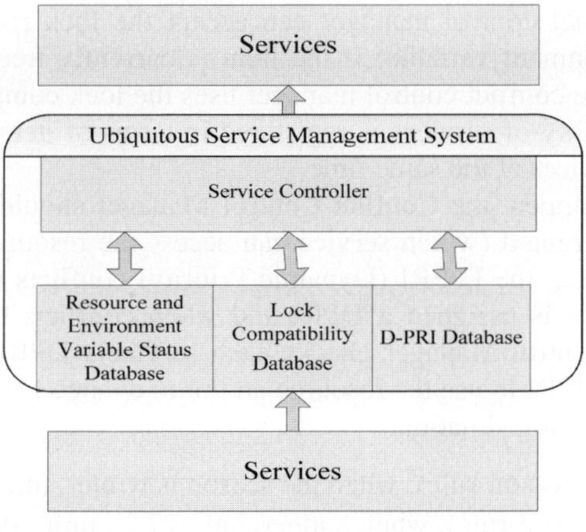

Fig. 3. Conflict-Control Manager Architecture

4.3 Implementation

Using the proposed conflict detection and resolution solution on the WS-ECA platform, we have developed a ubiquitous home services system. In this test bed, three types of services such as security service, entertainment service, and sleeping service are considered for the ubiquitous service system. Figure 4 shows the registration of ECA rule for a device on the WS-ECA platform.

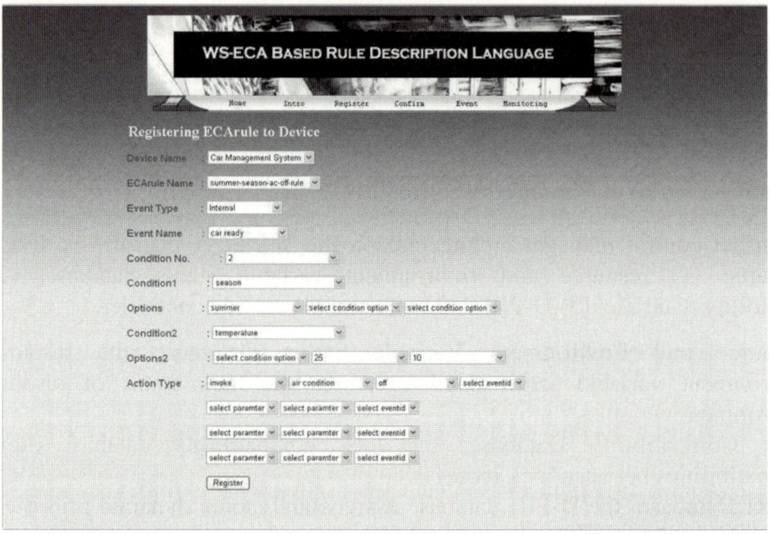

Fig. 4. ECA rule registration step

Each time a service requests an access to a device or changes its environment variable, the service sends a lock request to the conflict control manager, which is responsible for the lock registration and checking system for the runtime conflict detection. The conflict control manager can accept the lock request for an item (a service or an environment variable) if the item is currently free or there is no lock held on the item. The conflict control manager uses the lock compatibility database in which the compatibility of services is registered in terms of items, when an item can acquire multiple services at the same time.

When conflicts happen, the Conflict Control Manager should decide which Lock Request should be granted (which service can access the resources and environment variables). In this case, the D-PRI (Dynamic Priority) conflicts resolution method is applied. Each service is assigned a DPRI and when conflicts happen between two services, Conflict-Control Manager checks each service's DPRI, and allow the one who has the higher DPRI to use the resource and/or to change environment variables.

Consider the following situation.

- Service A (winter-season-rule): when the season is winter, turn on the heater
- Service B (new-season-rule): when temperature>27℃, turn off the heater

In winter season, service A is activated. Service A sends “heater-on lock request” to CCM. The heater is free at this time, CCM, thus, grants the “heater-on lock request” from Service A. When temperature becomes higher than 27℃,Service B is activated. Service B sends “heater-off lock request” to CCM. CCM checks the Lock

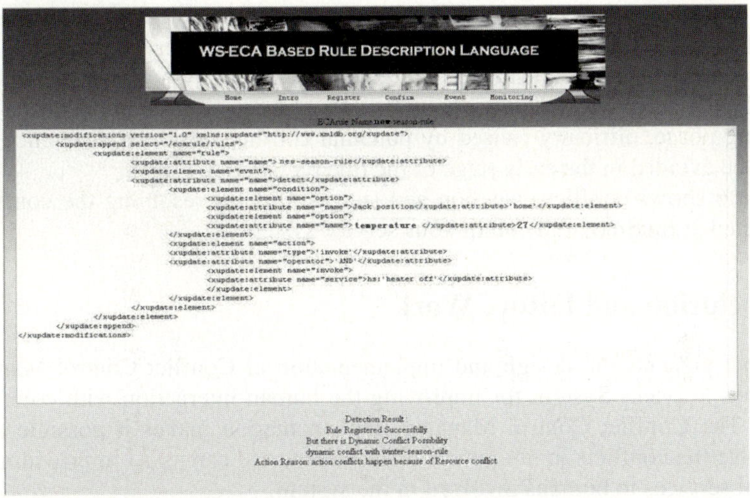

Fig. 5. Conflict detection at the registration stage

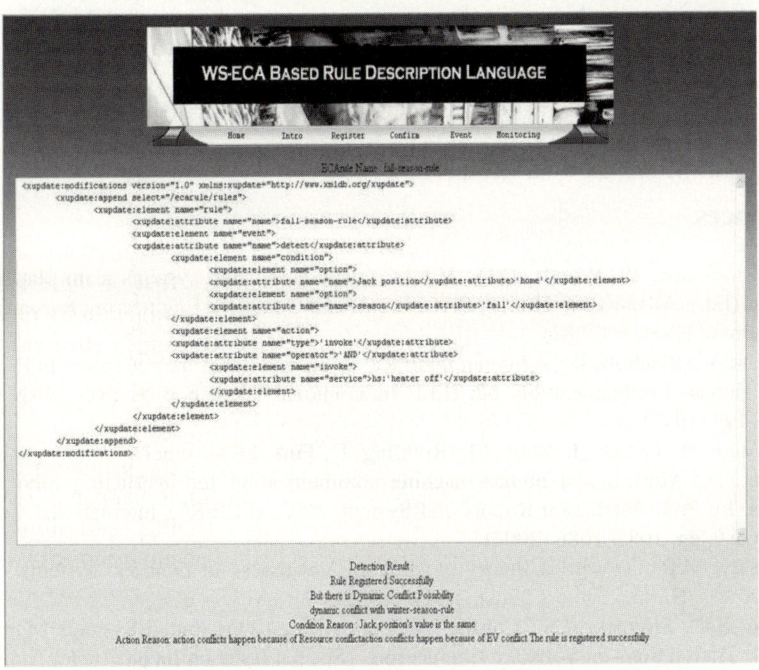

Fig. 6. Conflict detection at runtime

Compatibility Database and finds that "heater-on lock request" is incompatible with "heater-off lock request" (because "heater on" and "heater off" can not be executed at the same time). Conflict is detected. At this time, if Service B's DPRI is lower than Service A, then Service B is aborted. Otherwise, Service A is suspended and Service B is executed.

Figure 5 show both device conflict and environment variable conflict detected in the phase of Service Registration. With Conflict Control Manager implemented, runtime conflicts which occur frequently in Ubiquitous Services System can be successfully detected and solved. By employing the lock-based detection method in the services registering phase, difficulty caused by potential conflicts between difference services can also be avoided in the early stage of the rule registration phase.

Figure 6 shows conflict detection and suggestions for resolving the conflicts that are detected at runtime of the ubiquitous service system.

5 Conclusion and Future Work

This paper presents the design and implementation of Conflict Control Manager for Ubiquitous Services System for improving the human interaction with computerized devices. The Conflict Control Manager implementation makes it possible to detect and resolve the conflicts in ubiquitous environment and can assist in providing higher quality of services to humans involved in the system.

Our future work includes the establishment of a more realistic environment for evaluation of the effectiveness of human-computer interaction. By conducting a variety of experiments, human preference on services and its impact on designing and building the human-centered ubiquitous environment can be evaluated.

Acknowledgments. This work was supported by the research fund of Hanyang University (HY-2006-N).

References

1. Christofferson, K., Woods, D.D.: How to make automated systems team players. In: E. Salas (Ed.), Advances in Human Performance and Cognitive Engineering Research, vol. 2. JAI Press, Elsevier (2002)
2. Graefe, V., Bischoff, R.: A human interface for an intelligent mobile robot. In Proc. Robot and Human Communication, 6th IEEE International Workshop on (RO_MAN '97), pp. 194–199 (1997)
3. McGuire, P., Fritsch, J., Steil, J.J., Rothling, F., Fink, G.A., Wachsmuth, S., Sagerer, G., Ritter, H.: Multi-modal human-machine communication for instructing robot grasping tasks. In: Proc. Intelligent Robots and System, 2002. IEEE/RSJ International Conference on, vol.2, pp. 1082–1088 (2002)
4. Endsley, M.R.: Toward a theory of situation awareness in dynamic systems: Situation awareness. Human Factors 37(1), 32–64 (1995)
5. Lupu, E.C., Sloman, M.S.: Conflicts in Policy-Based Distributed Systems Management. IEEE Transactions on Software Engineering - Special Issue on Inconsistency Management (1999)

From Ambient Devices to Smart Care for Blind People: A Metaphor of Independent Living with Responsive Service Scenarios

Ying Liu[1] and Roger Wilson-Hinds[2]

[1] Computer Laboratory, University of Cambridge, JJ Thomson Avenue, Cambridge CB3 0FD, UK
firstname.lastname@cl.cam.ac.uk
[2] Choice Technology (UK) Limited, 7 The Rookery, Orton Wistow, Peterborough, PE2 E6YT UK

Abstract. We present a metaphor showing that blind people (users) often are living in a perplexing contexture – a chain of barriers affecting their ability to live independently. In such a context to support users' tasks in real time, current technologies may not be intuitive enough to be used for this kind of real world application. The increasingly specialised devices and rapidly advanced assistive technologies require a composite architecture of scalable non-textual reading services. We illustrate this requirement by three user scenarios at a scale of a device, an object-awareness and a real-time situated meaningful response.

1 Introduction

Universal access in a digital society is about enabling individuals, with varying degrees of less than perfect ability, to access information or facilities they require in order to function, as they choose, in their environments. It also identifies any barriers to this access, which can arise from the technologies themselves or from exclusive social contexts [9][15]. There are proactive approaches based on various metaphors [1], as well as useful techniques and methods, e.g. using ontology based semantic annotation to semi-automatically identify objects and discover their roles in support of mobility [21].

Smart care technology is sensor based technology used to aid and support human independent living [23]. Such technologies offer new potential and can give rise to new problems for universal access. Rapid deployment of wireless sensor technologies, together with hand-held and ubiquitous computing[16], sensor networks[20], data communication networks [18], mobile and wearable smart devices [7], make it possible to provide services for smart homes or remote healthcare monitoring [19]. These technologies will have a profound impact on the type, content, location, operation and functionality of care products and services [7], and all this must be integrated with the earlier information services. It is therefore crucial to adopt the concept of universal access at this initial stage of smart care research.

C. Stephanidis (Ed.): Universal Access in HCI, Part II, HCII 2007, LNCS 4555, pp. 141–150, 2007.

In this paper we are concerned with blind people (users). Collaborating with Guide Dogs for the Blind Association UK Ltd. (GDBA), we are investigating how to fully explore smart technologies to assist users' independent living.

GDBA conducted focus groups and interviews across the UK between May and September 2005, investigating users' perspectives on the provision of audiovisual information about buses [10]. The participants of the focus groups included people with visual, hearing and dual sensory impairments, and those over 65. There was unanimous agreement that the ability to identify the right bus at the outset of one's journey, including sufficient information to enable adequate pre-journey preparation, is fundamental to a stress-free and successful journey. Several participants spoke of having 'great difficulty identifying what bus to get on' or of 'not being able to see the buses in the distance' or of 'terrible problems consistently missing buses, most especially when buses are lined up one behind the other and it becomes quite impossible to identify which is which. Being able to locate the wanted bus easily and independently, even among a row of several buses, clearly emerged as a priority for these users.

We report our findings on the studies of the above case in section 2, as well as report the current available technologies and their limitations towards the solution.

In section 3, we argue that it is necessary to extend the metaphor of universal access or mobility onto the quality of independent living. The users' needs (e.g. finding a bus stop, identifying and getting on a bus) should not be considered in isolation. As an example (and several others we illustrate later), accessing to a right bus is a need. But from a wider and more useful way of thinking, a blind person may need to use a bus in order to see a doctor, or to visit their bank manager. Accordingly, users with poor health may not go to see a doctor regularly, because of the difficulty of using a bus or of finding their way around a hospital. Thus, users often are living in a perplexing contexture – a chain of barriers affecting their ability to complete a task. Assistance should be offered appropriate to users' behaviour and context. Then alternatives might be suggested. A service gateway might suggest home based healthcare or online banking services, as well as providing an information service on bus travel.

In section 4, we expand the metaphor by giving three self-manageable and integrative user service scenarios, namely talking@gadget, talking@object and talking@care.

In section 5 we highlight our future work and give conclusions.

2 Research Findings

There are many relevant technologies are developed essentially for sight needs in the hope that the technologies potentially can be used as mobility aids, e.g.:

- Sonar Canes, Sonic Guide and Sonic Pathfinder are products for detecting obstacle and hazards [24];
- vOICe developed a range of devices that translate arbitrary video images from a regular PC camera into sounds in the hope that users can "see with their ears". Such a device scans each camera snapshot from left to right, while associating height with pitch and brightness with loudness [25];

- Talking Sign is an electronic aid used to assist in orientation and navigation. The system uses infrared signals from permanently installed transmitters, to a hand-held receiver, that decodes the signal and delivers a voice message through its speaker or headset. Transmitters can be placed on signs, buildings, doors etc [26];
- GPS-talks, BrailleNote GPS MoBIC [27], and Visuaide Treker [28] are navigation systems that utilise GPS and wireless communication networks for outdoor way-finding;
- Cricket is an indoor location system for pervasive and sensor-based computing environments providing fine-grained location information - space identifiers, position coordinates, and orientation, to applications running on handhelds, laptops, and sensor nodes. Cricket is intended for use indoors or in urban areas where outdoor systems like GPS don't work well. Reportedly, it can provide distance ranging and positioning precision of between 1 and 3 cm [29].

The Ministry of Economy, Trade and Industry (METI) of Japan started a project for developing user friendly wayfinding/guidance systems for various disabilities [30]. The main objective is to develop a single device which can be used for different types of wayfinding/guidance systems. The common platform architecture, to be designed integrates functions that operate with different types of sensors and media such as GPS, infrared communication, radio communication and RFID. The platform can also incorporate new sensors' functionalities. The project is to propose the standardized system to ISO.

However, these devices and systems tend to be designed to help users to become familiar with an outdoor environment. They are not intuitive enough for new or unknown places or for access to an unfamiliar social infrastructure such as a hospital or shopping mall. They may be based on users hearing sounds bouncing off nearby objects (ultrasonic echolocation), creating a familiar pattern as the person moves, but offering little or no information regarding the objects themselves.

Users encounter objects in order to travel. That is, they must not only avoid obstacles, but also be able to find objects, such as buses, buildings and entrances. It is unclear whether such object awareness is the focus of other research programs. For example, the ASK-IT integrated project aims at establishing Ambient Intelligence in semantic web enabled services, "to support and promote the mobility of mobility-impaired people, enabling the provision of personalised, self-configurable, intuitive and context-related applications and services and facilitating knowledge and content organisation and processing" [31].

Researchers have demonstrated that information about an object and its location can be described and encoded in a RFID tag associated with the object. Users can receive information about the object through wearable devices that embed RFID readers [21]. Reportedly, a ubiquitous computing network has been developed to assist users in finding their way around indoor spaces [22]. It is based on the "Cyber Crumb" concept: the idea that tiny, inexpensive solar-powered digital chips can be used to store relevant pieces of information that can be placed along building walkways, like a trail of crumbs to follow. A wireless network of "crumbs" provides access from any point in a building to a central server that provides orientation and wayfinding information.

A location-aware sensing approach can also be used in developing applications for tracking objects, This has already been exploited in industry for resource discovery, human or robot navigation, computer games, medical applications (e.g., equipment and patient tracking or monitoring), or migration of a stream of objects.

In summary, these enabling, object-aware technologies are limited to helping users to interact with events in the environment, and are thus unable to provide specific navigation assistance in real time. It is important to remember that users' mobility is often goal driven. Dynamically correlating much of the interactive information between users, objects and the environment is a critical prerequisite for assisting individuals' travels.

Therefore a more innovative approach is urgently required to integrate existing technology as "vision aids and vision substitution" towards a multi-dimensional service oriented approach. The aim is to develop real time, personalised, non-textual reading, integrated sensory information and communication services, to augment sensory perceptions about objects, indoors and outside. There are other important reasons for this device and service integration.

Firstly, although it is necessary to know the various devices' special properties, there are too many alternative use cases to make bespoke solutions feasible. A service platform is needed to allow devices to "plug-and-play" to meet the specific needs of the various users, e.g., a device which suits a partially vision-impaired person can be completely useless for a totally blind person. Many contexts may be more difficult to understand, and can be inadequately represented in a phase of device specialisation. Consider the following combinations of many users and many disadvantageous situations (reported in [10]),

> "About 24,000 people in the UK are registered as deafblind [35]. When devices add new features, the relevant services may have to adopt the changes, e.g. incorporating vibration-tones and downloadable information in Braille formats. Approximately 10 million people in the UK have a disability [36]. Of this population, up to 70% have difficulty walking or climbing steps, an estimated 41% have a hearing loss, and 24% a vision loss [37]. A combined total of approximately three million people in the UK have sight loss, dyslexia or other reading-related disability [38]. The strong correlation between disability and age (up to one-third of the population aged between 50 and 60 have a disability) also means that the prevalence of disability in society is set to grow with predicted demographic changes in the population."

Secondly, with respect to the above combinations of users, there are many inter-related environmental contexts; the need should not be considered in isolation. For example, a blind person may need to use a bus in order to see a doctor, or to visit their bank manager; access to a bus is a need. From a wider perspective, a service gateway might suggest home based healthcare or online banking services, as well as providing an information service on bus travel.

Thirdly, the management of emerging technologies must be sustainable and coordinated, and this cannot depend only on applied research dedicated to the preservation of the technologies or, more significantly, on an organisation dedicated to changing services as technologies improve. A service architecture must be able to incorporate a new technology, upgrade a service, or create a new one. Many lessons can be learned from the past. For example, reportedly [40], as computer technology was becoming cheaply available and effectively deployable, the Nottingham Navigation Centre, a world-leading institution that focused on blind navigational technologies, was closed for lack of funding. If a service architecture had been in place, components of many ground breaking technologies that came out of the research might have been re-used, such as the sonic Pathfinder.

3 "Ideal" User Scenarios of Voice Commanded, Self-managed, Real Time Responsive Services

As we have discussed, mobility-needs may exist in a perplexing living contexture. What is needed is an integrated service, scalable to applications of technologies. We propose the following four user scenarios, showing that desired interactions between users and a smart environment require an architecture of dynamic, self-manageable and scalable service components.

3.1 A Talking Gadget

Helen is 63 and lives alone. She is totally blind and has diabetic retinopathy (a side effect of diabetes that is a leading cause of blindness among the working-age population). Because of her poor health, she needs to see her doctor regularly. Helen has heard about CareGrid services. She is cautious and sceptical about the services and having the computer and wireless kit in her home. Her other worry is how to find them if she drops them somewhere or she forgets where she has put them. However the program manager arrives at her home and explains not only how easy it is to manage and use the equipment, but also that she can subscribe to other services to make her life easier. In particular, the device Talking Gadget with tone-and-shaped touch buttons recognises Helen's face and finger print, so nobody else can unlock and use it. The gadget does many other things. She can either rent or buy the hardware, and subscribe to or cancel the services at any time. So she joins the programme and subscribes to three services.

3.2 Talking@Travel

If she presses the round button, the gadget is in the travelFinder mode. Before travelling, she tells the gadget the destination name. If she is a first time traveller to this destination, the gadget makes a plan. If she is returning to a place she has already visited, the gadget updates the plan with real time information, and tells Helen how to get there and when she will arrive. Assuming a sensor-rich external environment, when she is waiting for a bus, the gadget identifies the right bus and announces the stops when Helen is on it. As she walks around the city it tells her about the buildings she is passing.

3.3 Talking@Object

If she presses the square button, the gadget is in the objectFinder mode. The gadget comes with an ample supply of thin electronic tags that it can read. Let us assume that the technology is able to detect a tag within house-wide range and that a database of room-names to 3D locations has been created. Helen can attach a tag to any object. She only needs to use the gadget to scan the tagged object once, then tells the gadget her preferred name for the object. When she wants to know where an object is, she can ask the gadget, using this name. An alternative approach, perhaps more realistic for current technology, is that she walks around the house holding the gadget and is alerted when she comes close to the lost object. Helen can use the gadget as a "mirror" too. The gadget reads her tagged clothes and tells her their colours. She can match her new coat with a nice pair of trousers.

3.4 Talking@Care

If she presses the triangular button, the gadget is in the mode of careFinder. She can attach a set of medical devices supplied to get her health conditions checked: blood pressure, weight, pulse and blood glucose levels. The gadget wirelessly collects and transports the data to her home computer to be analysed; it also reminds her regularly to check a number of times a week at specific times. If she is not at home, the gadget stores the data temporarily and remotely transmits these to her surgery. She has asked the gadget to remember the devices in case she cannot find them.

When she goes out she uses the gadget to augment her guide dog. The gadget helps keep her informed of her changing environment, giving her greater control than ever before. The dog can help her avoid obstacles safely and can guide her home when commanded. Before subscribing to CareGrid, she always asked somebody to accompany her to hospital. Now she can make this trip more quickly and independently.

3.5 Summary

There is an incentive to invent a voice-commanded, object-aware mobile gadget with services, sufficiently and effectively connecting users via remote servers to mobility related objects in both physical and virtual space.

The gadget has an embedded voice recognizer and sensory memory, infrared and RFID sensing, a data acquisition hub, and local data storage. It is capable of peer to peer networking, hosting third party sensors, sensing around personal surroundings indoors and outside, processing real time data and distributed data streaming. It can act like a wireless data gateway programmed via a remote server to control and manage sensory data and objects. It has biometric security: face and fingerprint recognition. Users give commands to the gadget by voice, and can train the gadget to remember a tagged object by telling the name to the gadget. The remote server can manage users' contextual information, correlate personal health monitoring data, public travel information and public infrastructural information, and offer Talking@Gadget services to users as aids to improve the quality of users' independent living.

It is interesting to note that the technology relevant to each individual gadget function such as voice commanded mobile handset, voice commanded home appliance control, RFID smartphone and biometric smartphone exist. The focus of our research is on the design of such a service system.

4 Towards Developing Pervasive Assistive Entities

As noted, it is greatly challenging and also extremely hard to develop truly applicable smartcare services and associated systems. Our metaphor intends to enable service design to provision a synergy of networked communication, living environmental control and telecare components working to foster people's desire to live with utmost independence.

End-user smart service design and service oriented computing are currently unconnected developments with many their own design metaphors. That is why the establishment of smart application provision is still very difficult.

First, service oriented computing has its root in Web based services and e-commerce application domains. For example a service is provisioned in order to give value to a client, for example, to book a train ticket for a given date. This service is the provision of a *train ticket* (entity) that is to be used according to the specified constraints. A web-based service [6][8][11] is a computational entity, in this case for accessing a timetable, selecting and receiving a train ticket and making a payment over the Internet. The Service Oriented Computing paradigm [2] has been widely adopted but it does not yet fully address large-scale system design [3], even less about end-user services. Moreover, end-user services must be easy to use, and personalised or context-aware while in use [1] and, most importantly, must be secure and trustworthy [4][5].

Second, unlike current web based services which are mainly developed for reading textual information (e.g. train timetables, ticket costs), smart care services require an increasing number of sensory devices. They are driven by context - where the devices are used and how the data are acquired, processed and distributed. Thus, the specialisation of a device must be able to address the wider question of the provision of the service required to support its function. For example, Portable Braille PDAs are already available as plug-ins for PCs and GPS, but are not yet widely used. This is, most likely, due to the lack of sufficient services to support these devices.

Towards design of the services based on the scenarios, we propose the following pervasive assistive entities mapping to the scenarios in section 3.

4.1 End User Mobile Entity

This type of entity connects the end-users to merge into a unified mode of function gives the person a ubiquitous presence. This entity 1) embeds computing technology in such a way that it has an unique identifier, a built-in memory with data read/write capabilities, and support for close-range wireless ad-hoc communication, 2) extends the user' identity and presence beyond his or her immediate physical surroundings, 3) extends the users controllability around his or her physical surroundings, and 4) extends the user's informational and knowing capacity. This is used as an end-user enabled service application that can be delivered only when and where needed, can be executed and discarded as soon as the goal is accomplished.

4.2 Smart Ambient Entity

This type of entity has sensor based interfaces and posses rudimentary "intelligence" sufficient to be aware and affect the environment around it. It can be very sophisticated body area sensor networks, equipments such as smart TVs, cameras, or usual things that embed sensors or are electronically tagged/labelled such as keys, watches, pens, bags, clothes, books, furniture, windows, doors, almost all objects ranging from man-mad artefacts to natural ones, such as plants, insects, animals, and human bodies, in the real world. Although the smart/intelligent object, may be a common.

4.3 Role Based Entity

This type of entity connects an end-user service participant to merge into a unified mode of function which delegates a service session. This entity 1) embeds computing technology in such a way that it has an unique identifier, a built-in memory with data read/write capabilities, and support for close-range wireless ad-hoc communication, 2) is responsible for dynamically updating and logging the identifier's profiles or credentials files, 3) extends the informational and knowing capacity during the service session. This is used as a service actor assistive service application that can be delivered only when and where needed, can be executed and discarded as soon as the goal is accomplished.

5 Conclusions

Blind people currently still depend on very primitive aids such as canes, guide dogs or spoken directions for access to only known routes and social infrastructures. They have great difficulty in managing their daily lives and participating in social and health-critical activities. Current technologies may not be intuitive enough to be used for real world applications. Wireless sensor technologies and wearable mobile devices are rapidly integrating with ICT in providing real time information about the environment where people live. However, these advances are still largely unexplored for integrated smartcare for blind people. A more innovative approach is required to create accessible environments and new living spaces. The design scenarios show the potential of smartcare technologies to improve blind and sight-impaired people's mobility, seamlessly, indoors and outside. A smartcare service design may usefully begin with the most essential end-user service enabling entities in respect to what devices users will use, who will participate in service sessions and what physical smart-artefacts will be networked.

Acknowledgement. We gratefully acknowledge the support of EPSRC through the CareGrid grant EP/C53718.

References

1. Emiliani, P.L., Stephanidis, C.: Universal Access to Ambient Intelligence Environments: Opportunities and Challenges for People with Disabilities. IBM Systems Journal 44(3), 605–619 (2003)
2. Huhns, M.N., Singh, M.P.: Service Oriented Computing: Key Concepts and Principles. IEEE Internet Computing 9(1), 75–81 (2005)
3. Bacon, J.: Expectations and Reality in Distributed Systems. Proceedings of IASTED International Conference on Parallel and Distributed Computing and Networks, Insbruck, Austria, February vii – xiv (2005)
4. Bacon, J., Moody, K.: Adaptive Middleware: Toward Open, Secure, Widely Distributed Services. Communications of the ACM 45(6), 59–63 (June 2002)
5. Bacon, J., Moody, K., Yao, W.: A Model of OASIS Role-based Access Control and Its Support for Active Security. ACM Transactions on Information and System Security (TISSEC) 5(4), 492–540 (2002)
6. Cerami, E.: Web Services Essentials. O'Reilly (2002)
7. ESTO: Science and Technology Roadmapping: ambient intelligence in everyday life (AmI@Life)," JRC/IPT – European Science and Technology Observatory Study. (June 2003)
8. Fensel, D., Keller, U., Lausen, H., Polleres, A., Toma, I.: WWW Or What's Wrong with Web Service Discovery. Proceedings of Workshop on Frameworks in Web Service, Innsbruck, Austria, (June 2005)
9. Maxwell, C.: Global Trends That Will Impact Universal Access to Information Resources, UNESCO, (July 15 2000)
10. Nzegwu, P.: Audio and Visual Information on Buses: Moving Toward Inclusion. Guide Dogs for the Blind Association, Reading, UK (2005)
11. Preist, C.: A Conceptual Architecture for Semantic Web Services. In: McIlraith, S.A., Plexousakis, D., van Harmelen, F. (eds.) ISWC 2004. LNCS, vol. 3298, Springer, Heidelberg (2004)
12. Queue: Building Web Services. ACM Queue, (March 2003)
13. Schatz, B.R., Hardin, J.B.: NCSA Mosaic and the World Wide Web: global hypermedia protocols for the Internet. Science Magazine 265, 895–901 (1994)
14. Star, L.S.: Got Infrastructure? how standards, categories and other aspects of infrastructure influence communication. Proceedings of The 2nd Social Study of IT Workshop at the LSE ICT and Globalization, London, (April 22-23 2002)
15. Stephanidis, C.: User Interfaces for All: new perspectives into HCI. In: Stephanidis, C.C. (ed.) User Interfaces for All – Concepts, Methods and Tools. Lawerence Associates, Mahwah, NJ (2001)
16. Abowd, G.D., Hayes, G.R., Iachello, G., Kientz, J.A., Patel, S.N., Stevens, M.N., Truong, K.N.: Prototypes and Paratypes: designing mobile and ubiquitous computing applications. IEEE Pervasive Computing, (Oct-Dec 67-73 2005)
17. Zhao, F., Guibas, L.: Wireless Sensor Networks. Elsevier Morgan Kaufmann Publishers (2004)
18. Bodic, G.L.: Mobile Messaging, Technologies and Services, 2nd edn. John Wiley & Sons, Chichester (2005)
19. Dewsbury, G., Sommerville, I., Rouncefield, M., Clarke, K.: Bringing IT into the Home – a Landscape Documentary of Assistive Technology, Smart Home, Telecare, Telemedicine in the Home in Relation to Dependability and Ubiquitous Computing. Computing Department, Lancaster University, UK (2002)

20. Rhodes, B., Mase, K.: Wearable in 2005. IEEE Pervasive Computing 5(1), 92–95 (January-March 2006)
21. Ross, D.A.: Cyber Crumbs for Successful Aging with Vision Loss. IEEE Pervasive Computing 3(2), 30–35 (2004)
22. Yesilada, Y., Harper, S., Goble, C., Stevens, R.: DANTE: Annotation and Transformation of Web Pages for Visually Impaired Users. In: WWW2004, pp. 490–491. ACM Press, New York (May 2004)
23. Giroux, S., Pigot, H.: From Smart Homes to Smart Care: ICOST 2005 (Assistive Technology & Research). IOS Press, USA (2005)
24. http://www.vard.org/jour/99/36/4/lagrow.htm
25. http://www.seeingwithsound.com/voice.htm
26. http://talkingsign.co.uk/
27. http://www.SenderoGroup.com/
28. http://www.visuaide.com/
29. http://cricket.csail.mit.edu/
30. http://www.csun.edu/cod/conf/2005/proceedings/2210.htm
31. http://www.ask-it.org
32. http://www.deafblind.org.uk/deafblindness/index.html
33. http://www.drcgb.org/thelaw/casedetails.asp?category=legal&id=521
34. http://www.drcgb.org/thelaw/casedetails.asp?category=legal&id=521
35. http://www.rnib.org.uk/xpedio/groups/public/documents/publicwebsite/public_r2rreport.hcsp
36. http://www.deafblind.org.uk/deafblindness/index.html
37. http://www.drcgb.org/thelaw/ casedetails.asp?category=legal&id=521
38. http://www.drcgb.org/thelaw/ casedetails.asp?category=legal&id=521
39. http://www.rnib.org.uk/xpedio/groups/public/documents/publicwebsite/public_r2rreport.hcsp
40. http://www.wayfinding.net/navigation.htm

Crisis Rooms Are Ambient Intelligence Digital Territories

Irene Mavrommati[1] and Achilles Kameas[1,2]

[1] Computer Technology Institute, Kazantzaki str, University Campus, 26500 Patras, Hellas
[2] Hellenic Open University, 23 Sahtouri str, 26222 Patras, Hellas
{mavrommati, kameas}@cti.gr

Abstract. The study of Digital Territories provides a way to conceptualize the interactions happening in Pervasive Computing Environments. This paper will address Crisis Rooms as Digital Territories. Based on the concepts stemming from Digital Territories we will attempt to give a high level overview of issues that can be applicable in the context of the future Crisis rooms and of the interactions that happen within them.

Keywords: Crisis Rooms, Digital Territories, Human Computer Interaction, Ambient Intelligence Environments.

1 Introduction

Crisis management involves identifying a crisis, planning a response to the crisis and confronting and resolving the crisis. Crisis management can be applied in almost any field of endeavor, but it is most commonly used in international relations, political science and management. Due to the large number of considerations involved in many decisions, computer-based Intelligent Decision Support Systems (that try to realize some human/cognitive decision making functions) have been developed to assist decision makers in considering the implications of various courses of thinking.

According to ISTAG [5], Ambient Intelligence is a vision that places human beings at the centre of future development of the knowledge-based society and ICTs. AmI space consists of a set of technologies, infrastructures, applications and services operating seamlessly across physical environments (e.g. neighbourhood, home, car); thus spanning all the different spheres of everyday life. Physical space becomes augmented with digital content, thus transcending the limits of nature and of direct human perception. A new term is needed for this new kind of space, which captures its dual nature. The term “digital territory” (DT) has been coined in an attempt to port a real world metaphor into the forthcoming synthetic world.

The Ubiquitous presence of information is becoming increasingly prominent; Crisis Rooms evolve into digital environments that have a hybrid nature (digital and physical).

Visualization technologies, multimodal interfaces, collaborative tools for remote, distributed decision-making are key to a rich landscape of information. Physical space that is augmented with digital capabilities, is providing appropriate information for situated decision making. Crisis rooms are Digital Territories that act as the physical

C. Stephanidis (Ed.): Universal Access in HCI, Part II, HCII 2007, LNCS 4555, pp. 151–157, 2007.

point of convergence where decision makers converge to learn, consider and decide. A *Digital Territory* is an ephemeral AmI space [3]: it is created for a specific purpose and integrates the will of the owner (an individual or group operator) with the means to achieve it (including infrastructure, properties, services and objects) within an AmI space. A Digital Territory can be composed of sub-spaces, which are determined with respect to their services, usage, etc. A territory is usually a continuum in space; the real and digital elements of Digital Territory however, may co-exist in disparate locations (in the end, any digital element is recorded on a hard-disk or other medium which has a specific physical substance and location – although the latter may change with time, i.e. if the device is mobile). The substitute for continuity in Digital Territory is proximity; in the case of crisis management, proximity is defined as being analogous to the degree of relationship to the crisis. The elements of a Digital Territory are active, as opposed to the usually passive objects found in real world territories. Transient elements, like activities or procedures, can now become elements of Digital Territory.

2 Crisis Management Requirements

The 'total design' of Crisis management rooms (i.e. the design of physical and digital space and interactions) determines how the involved actors act (as individuals or groups), navigate and react to information [4]. It includes all aspects of Digital Territories, such as ownership, visibility of information, communication with the environment, etc. For example, the design of borders and markers (digital and physical) of a Crisis room affects how secure the exchange of information is.

Crisis management is primarily concerned with the following issues:

- Preparation and management all operations from response to recovery
- Event and incident tracking
- Personnel, material and resource management
- Emergency operation plans and procedures
- Manage personnel resources
- Document and track Incidents and Commands

Efficient and effective features for crisis management are considered the following:

- Tracking events
- Log task status to completion
- Deploy resources, then monitor, track and demobilize them
- Create standard operating procedures, checklists and notification lists
- Track resources and inventory, including strike team members
- Geographical mapping interfaces allows for geo-spatial representation of data

Usability of the crisis room environment and crisis management software is therefore very important. Robustness of the software and equipment, and design so that both of them leave no room for error, is crucial. The controls and information visualization embedded in the environment –the crisis room- has to be quick to learn and master, to use and navigate in. The same applies for the software used of course, and the way it locates and interacts with the physical environment of the room.

The security of the crisis management information is of utmost importance, while at the same time the system should allow certain information disclosure to trusted parties and actors resolving the crisis.

Crisis management is facilitated by an array of crisis management software. Rooms that are specially designed, engineered and equipped, the so called crisis rooms, bring the decision actors and teams together and facilitate them in terms of information, communication, action planning and deployment, tracking completion and receiving feedback from each action, in order to resolve the crisis.

3 The Crisis Bubble

Modern Crisis Rooms are physical spaces augmented with information and communication technology infrastructure. In the case of crisis management, one could define the crisis room as being a Digital Territory. A territory has a measurable quantity of elements which are contained within its borders. Borders are no more defined as "lines" to traverse or not. *Borders* are conceived as spaces "in-between", spaces of negotiation. *Markers* are a way of defining / denoting the boundaries, the borders and the points of negotiation and crossing.

In fact, one could apply the concept of Virtual Residence in the case of Crisis Rooms [2]. The basic elements of a Virtual Residence, that is, a "connected" room or space, the online lives of people and mobility and interoperability between different AmI environments, can be applied to Crisis Rooms as well. A Crisis Room occupies one or more physical rooms – in that way, we can model access to activities that take place in distant locations, where, for example, some member of the crisis management committee are located, or the premises of the organization under crisis. The people or organisations that own or are part of bubbles have their data online and use computers to implement several procedures. Finally, support for mobility between physical spaces or information servers and interoperability between activities (modeled as bubbles) is a prerequisite for any crisis management process.

A (digital) *bubble* is a temporarily defined AmI space within a Digital Territory that can be used to limit the information coming in or leaving with respect to a specific activity. As a direct consequence to its relationship with Digital Territory, the bubble concept clusters together all the interfaces, formats, rights and agreements etc. needed for the management of personal, group and public data and informational interactions that relate to this activity. Such contextual activity can be based on privacy, personalization, priority, location, membership, ambience, social circumstances, and time.. *Ownership* depends entirely on the purpose the bubble serves. The owner claims bubble territoriality in order to regulate the Digital Territory environment. The owner of a Digital Territory bubble can be a single person, a group, or an agent.

Within this Digital Territory, several bubbles co-exist more or less closely related to the crisis. The most important among them is the crisis bubble, which contains all data and procedures related to the particular crisis. This bubble is transient; it lasts as long as the crisis lasts and then is dissolved. Other participating bubbles are those of the actors (people, organizations, agents etc) involved in the crisis. These contain the personal or other data of their respective owner and usually will persist even after the crisis is over.

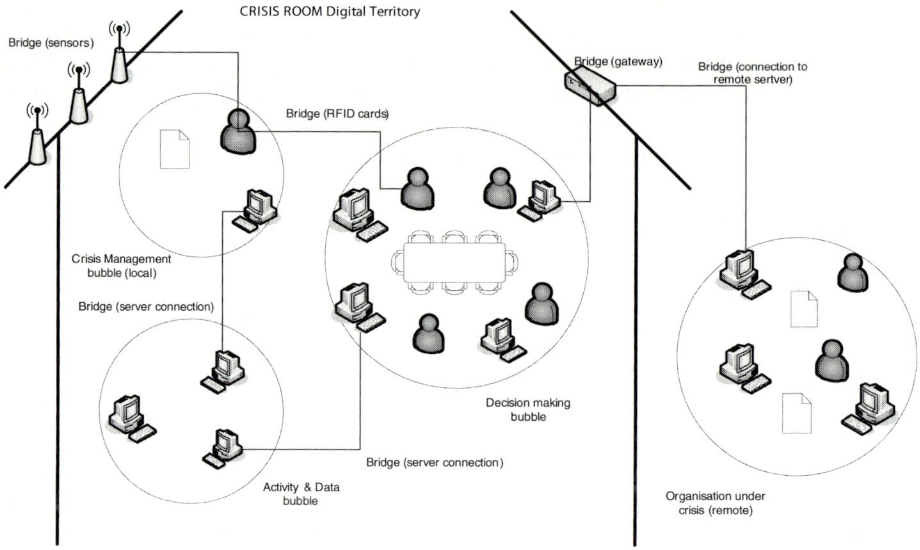

Fig. 1. Interactions within Digital Territories

Specific Interactions in Digital Territories that thus apply to Crisis rooms are (figure 1):

- interaction between bubbles and environment (through bridges)
- interaction between bubbles and markers
- evolution of bubbles as a result of these interactions
- interaction as part of the negotiation process for the specification of markers and borders
- interaction related to identity, privacy and trust negotiation

Each of the actors can be perceived as defining a 'bubble' space that contains the personal or other data of their respective owner and will usually remain even after the crisis is over. Crisis actors can isolate by closing the digital links, i.e. by manipulating the transparency of their individual bubble, so that they are made non accessible and not visible. Decisions, taken as a result of negotiation between the bubble entities, can have a direct digital and communication effect. Tracking and registration of events (physical as well as digital) is facilitated, as every action –upon the elements of the physical tangible environment- has a digital counterpart within the context of a Digital Territory.

4 Crisis Room Bridges

Bridges between physical and digital are actually elements/components of AmI spaces linking the physical and the digital and facilitating exchange of information in Crisis Room bubbles or between the Crisis Room and other environments. They may be combinations of physical and digital media, often so interwoven with everyday life that they are no longer noticed as special, novel or distinct. Bridges are discrete elements disposing of certain autonomy in their conception and internal structure. Sensors, actuators and RFIDs are examples of bridges between the physical and the digital. When one builds a bridge between the physical and the digital space, it is in fact a bridge between activities that take place in remote physical spaces in the same time. Examples of current technology and artifacts that can be used as bridges are: location based services, RFIDs, bio-implants, biometrics, user interfaces, and CCTV's, etc. When one builds a bridge between the physical and the digital space, it is in fact a bridge between activities that take place in remote physical spaces in the same time.

Bridges are of interest when they enhance Digital Territories -and therefore Crisis Rooms as such- by supporting modification of contained relationships, newly-emerging requests of DT members and enable the creation of (new) complex DTs. The need to create bridges arises from the generation of new, additional or transformed data, the need to transfer information, as well as the need to pass to a different level of hierarchy, either within a DT or between different DTs in AmI spaces. When created for generating complex DTs (i.e. by DT inter-connection), they allow consideration of new links that where not possible before.

Bridges within the context of Crisis rooms can be considered as the linking elements between the sub-elements of a crisis situation. These can be in a digital form or a physical form –for example an RFID tagged card. Via them a tangible interface to the crisis software can be facilitated for example, for reasons of speed, efficiency, geographical mapping of data visualization, etc. Resources can be inventorised and tracked easier by using augmented interfaces to the digital data representations.

5 Human Computer Interaction Issues in DT Crisis Rooms

New elements that are introduced by the nature of living and interacting within an Ambient intelligent environment lead to new HCI paradigms. Some of the issues that have an impact in AmI HCI research practice [**Error! Reference source not found.**] -and therefore the augmented space of Crisis Rooms- are:

1. A shift in the nature of interaction

Interaction in Ambient Intelligence Spaces can range from explicit to implicit interaction. Unintended user actions on the environment may result in unintended control and manipulation of the ambient applications. Ambient Intelligence Environment vision implies less direct and less conscious user input than in the current systems. This in turn raises issues of the appropriate level of transparency and visibility to the workings of the system. In concepts borrowed from Digital territories that would imply a focus to the realization of a moderated transparency level in the visualization of the Bubble metaphors, as well as possibility for the information visualization of the available and the active bridges.

2. Different interaction channels (shift in the nature of input and output devices)

The context of DT in Crisis Rooms implies the introduction of tangible manipulation controls within the environment that interface with the information and its manipulation, alongside to the Crisis management software. A value to this approach could be the replacement of complex command languages with actions from manipulating directly the objects, and making use of multimodal interface combinations to interact with the system. Crisis room and the crisis management software can be perceived in this context as one DT entity, where the elements of the physical and the digital are interacting.

3. The role of intelligence

Actors coming into play within the crisis management are agents (that can be human, software, or their combination), who are collecting and comparing data, benchmark against similar past situations and can present informed decision choices. These can also be intelligent software agents within the Digital Territory environment, facilitating actions and communication, and specific applications. In such case unexpected behavior –resulting agent intervention- that may surprise the user *must* be avoided; visibility on the workings of the intelligent system and its rationale, should be available upon request, as well as an overwrite function for the agent (the overall off switch).

4. Visibility, Reversibility of action, Error tolerance

Feedback should be provided for actions upon the physical environment which affect/manipulate digital aspects of the crisis. Syntactic correctness of sequences of actions has to be checked at all times, in order to appropriately inform users, so as to avoid errors before they are made. To be able to undo actions (reversibility of actions) is also very important in the case of error, and in order to avoid extensive delays in the handling of the crisis.

6 Conclusions

Crisis rooms involve a merge of the physical and the digital world, which come together in the context of a crisis management situation. Therefore Crisis rooms of the future will increasingly resemble Ambient Intelligence Spaces –targeted to handling specific situations. The Digital Territories study has developed concepts for this merge of the physical and digital worlds. The concepts of Digital Territories can be useful to the conceptualization and design of future Crisis rooms. In particular concepts such as borders and markers and metaphors such as bridges and bubbles can provide useful insight into the design of future crisis rooms.

References

1. Altman, I.: The environment and social behaviour: privacy, personal space, territory, crowding. Brooks/Cole Publishing Company (1975)
2. Beslay, L., Punie, Y.: The virtual residence: Identity, privacy and security. The IPTS Report, Special Issue on Identity and Privacy, No. 67, September 2002, pp. 17–23 (2004)
3. Daskala, B., Maghiros, I.: Digital Territories. Proceedings of the 2nd IET International Conference on Intelligent Environments (IE06), 5-6 July 2006, Athens, Greece. Published by IET, pp. 221 – 226, vol. 2 (2006)
4. Halkia, M.: Panel description UAHCI2006, Beijing, China (July 2007)
5. Advisory, I.S.T.: Group Working Group Report, Ambient Intelligence: from vision to reality [For participation – in society & business]. Available at (2003), ftp://ftp.cordis.europa.eu/pub/ist/docs/istag-ist2003_consolidated_report.pdf
6. Mavrommati, I., Darzentas, J.: An overview of AmI from a User Centered Design Perspective. Proceedings of the 2nd IET International Conference on Intelligent Environments (IE06), 5-6 July, Athens, Greece. Published by IET, pp.81–88 vol. 2 (2006)

Learning Topologies of Situated Public Displays by Observing Implicit User Interactions

Hans Jörg Müller and Antonio Krüger

University of Münster, Germany
{joerg.mueller, antonio.krueger}@uni-muenster.de

Abstract. In this paper we present a procedure to learn a topological model of Situated Public Displays from data of people traveling between these displays. This model encompasses the distance between different displays in seconds for different ways and/or different travel modes. It also shows how many people travel between displays in each direction. Thus, the model can be used to predict where and when people will appear next after showing up in front of one display. This can be used for example to create continuous 'shows' spanning multiple displays while people pass them. To create the model, we use Bluetooth connection data of mobile phones people carry, and employ the EM algorithm to estimate mean travel times for different paths people take.

1 Introduction

Imagine yourself strolling down a main road in your city center a hot summer afternoon. The streets are filled with digital advertising screens that show advertisements for a few tens of seconds each. You heard about personalized advertising, where people are identified and delivered individual advertisements, but you don't like that. You prefer to make use of your right to privacy and stay anonymous. As you look towards one display, you see an advertisement showing an attractive girl that states "Hot, isn't it?". You wonder what this is about, but continue walking. A few meters further, you see the same girl again that tells you "If there only was some cooling..." and now you realize how hot it really is and get curious. Some meters further, you see the same girl again telling you: "You're really lucky! Buy 'di Cultelli's' ice cream right here!". You turn your head and see that you stand right in front of an ice cream parlor. As you enjoy your ice cream you realize that you were not really identified by the advertisements but did only ride a 'green wave' of continuous advertisements. It is easy to provide such continuous 'shows' for the user if he can be identified. But because of users right to privacy, at least some users will always stay anonymous to advertising displays. Nevertheless, if a topological model of the displays is available that allows to estimate the probability that a user passes one display a certain time after he passed another, the following advertisements could be presented for certain confidence intervals of arrival probability. Thus, 'green waves' of continuous advertisement shows, related by a common design, could be created. If these are designed accordingly, like in the example, it would not matter

C. Stephanidis (Ed.): Universal Access in HCI, Part II, HCII 2007, LNCS 4555, pp. 158–167, 2007.

much if the user misses one of the advertisements. In this paper, we focus on the problem of how such a topological model can be created. We implemented and evaluated our approach in our test environment presented in figure 1. Of course, such a topological model representing the relative locations of displays could be used for many more applications, for example deciding which advertisement to show depending on the environment in general.

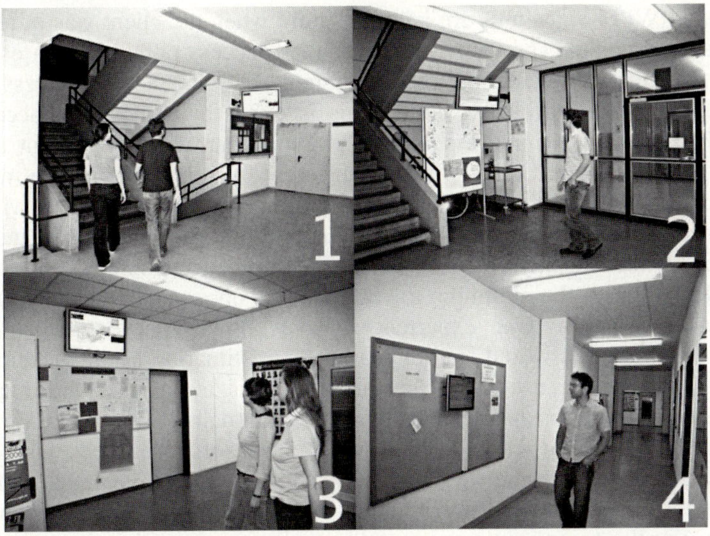

Fig. 1. The Situated Public Displays installed in our test environment at the University of Münster. Displays 1 and 2 are installed at the entrances of the building, while displays 3 and 4 are installed in hallways. The displays are used as an information system for the department and mainly show advertisements for talks, lectures, excursions etc. We have more than 10 sources of information from faculty and secretaries. More than 500 students use the system on a daily basis. The system is running for more than 15 months now, and over 340 advertisements have been posted. Each advertisement is shown on all displays for several weeks, thus there are always more advertisements available than fit on the displays. We select the advertisements that are shown in dependence on the location, time, and audience in front of the display. Most information is published as paper-based posters as well as on the displays, but the displays seem to be gradually replacing paper for urgent news.

The remainder of this paper is structured like follows. After summarizing some related work, we show how the problem fits into a more general context of self-configuring Situated Public Displays. Then we present how data obtained from people who can be identified can be used to create a topological model of the displays. This model contains the mean travel times between displays for different paths, the standard deviation and number of people that took that path. We identified people using Bluetooth sensors to identify their mobile phones. We present the algorithms we use together with the example data for our setting. Finally, we conclude and present some future work.

2 Related Work

This work builds on ideas that were introduced in the NearMe proximity estimation system [1]. NearMe estimates the proximity of different 802.11 wireless networking (Wi-Fi) enabled devices. When two devices share no common access point (long-range proximity), NearMe uses an estimation of the distance of access points the devices can connect to for estimating the distance of the devices. To achieve this, time-stamped Wi-Fi signatures are kept that store when the client was in reach of the different access points. The distance between two access points is then estimated as the minimum time difference between one signature with the first access point and another with the second access point. This is done for any pair of access points, resulting in a list of MAC address pairs and the minimum time any client was able to transition between them. Our approach is different from NearMe in two major ways. First, NearMe creates a full table of all pairs of access points together with a travel time estimate. Instead, we create a topological graph model that includes the information, which displays have to be passed to get from one display to another. Second, NearMe uses the minimum travel time ever observed to estimate the distance between access points. Our experiences have shown that because of frequent erroneous readings, this would lead to heavy underestimation of the distance between displays. We therefore use the Expectation-Maximization (EM) [2] algorithm to estimate the travel times between displays. Additionally, while NearMe uses Wi-Fi,we use Bluetooth, and while for NearMe a client software is necessary to collect the signatures, in our case the whole software runs on the displays. Predestination [3] is a system to predict the destination of car drivers from GPS data as the trip progresses. Similar to our system, it can be used to predict where a user will appear next. Location prediction is also a common problem in wireless networks, an overview can be found in [4]. In wireless networks, location prediction is used to make smooth handoffs between communication cells. Relate [5] is a system to sense the relative location of different devices with custom hardware. The spatial relations of a number of laptops on a table are sensed with ultrasonic transducers. A general overview of location systems for ubiquitous computing is provided by [6]. A more general approach to user modeling in ubiquitous computing is given by [7]. Here, Bluetooth sensors are used to detect users mobile phones and estimate users location and actions. In [8] Bluetooth sensors are employed to select advertisements not yet seen by the present audience in front of a public display. An overview of issues for self-configuration of Situated Public Displays, and a further description of Situated Public Displays as installed in Münster is provided in [9]. A collection of various works regarding Situated Public Displays is available in [10].

3 The Need for Self-configuring Situated Public Displays

Regarding the adaptation of Situated Public Displays to their environment, we distinguish between the adaptation to the immediate situation (short-term adaptation) and adaptation to the general context (long-term adaptation). Long-term adaptation is especially important when there is not enough information available for short-term adaptation. For example, it could be impossible to identify each individual user in short-term. This could be due to technical limitations, but also due to legal issues or simply because users do not like to be identified. But long-term adaptation can nevertheless generate models that allow adapting to the general population of users, although the individual users can't be identified. In theory, these models could also be created manually, but in most cases this would not be realistic. There is enormous effort involved in creating such models and no central authority available to coordinate the creation across multiple display owners. Furthermore, the necessary knowledge that should be represented in the model might simply be unavailable. A continuously changing environment would require continuous updating of such models. Therefore, we follow the autonomic computing paradigm from IBM [11] and suggest that Situated Public Displays should be self-configuring.

One question that needs to be solved to enable such self-configuration is to determine the location of the display. The location could be represented either in absolute or relative coordinates. Location could also include models of paths people usually take, to predict where people would probably appear next. Absolute location models could be achieved from classical location systems, like GPS, together with maps of the environment. Relative location models could be created by observing the people passing the displays, like presented in the next section. The location of nearby Points of Interest (POI) would be needed to provide related information to the POIs. Such a model could be created by observing the position of people known to visit a POI before and during the event. Another question is how a model of the user population passing the display at certain days and times can be created and used to adapt information presentation to this population. Such a model could be created by observing the spatio-temporal behavior of people for whom profiles are available, for example via Bluetooth sensors. A model of which kinds of information certain people and groups are interested in is also necessary to enable such adaptation. This model could be created from interaction data, for example people copying events to their calendar. Alternatively, the display could observe which items people look at, for example via face detection with a camera installed at the display.

4 Learning the Topology of Situated Public Displays

To create a topological model of the displays, we follow a similar approach to that used in NearMe for long-range proximity. In NearMe, to estimate the distance between two access points, the minimum travel time ever observed was used. This can be problematic in case of frequent erroneous readings, for example trough ceilings and walls and due to numerous other error sources. In this case that approach is quite vulnerable to heavily underestimate the real distance. In our case, due to errors we sometimes have transit times of zero or one second between displays, so taking the minimum would clearly produce wrong results. Instead, we use the Expectation-Maximization (EM) algorithm [2]. This algorithm assumes that the different travel times are created by people taking different ways between the displays. It furthermore assumes that the travel times for each way are distributed according to the normal distribution. This is a strong simplification, because for example the normal distribution has non-zero probability for negative travel times while in reality negative travel times are impossible. Nevertheless, we show that this approach still produces quite good results.

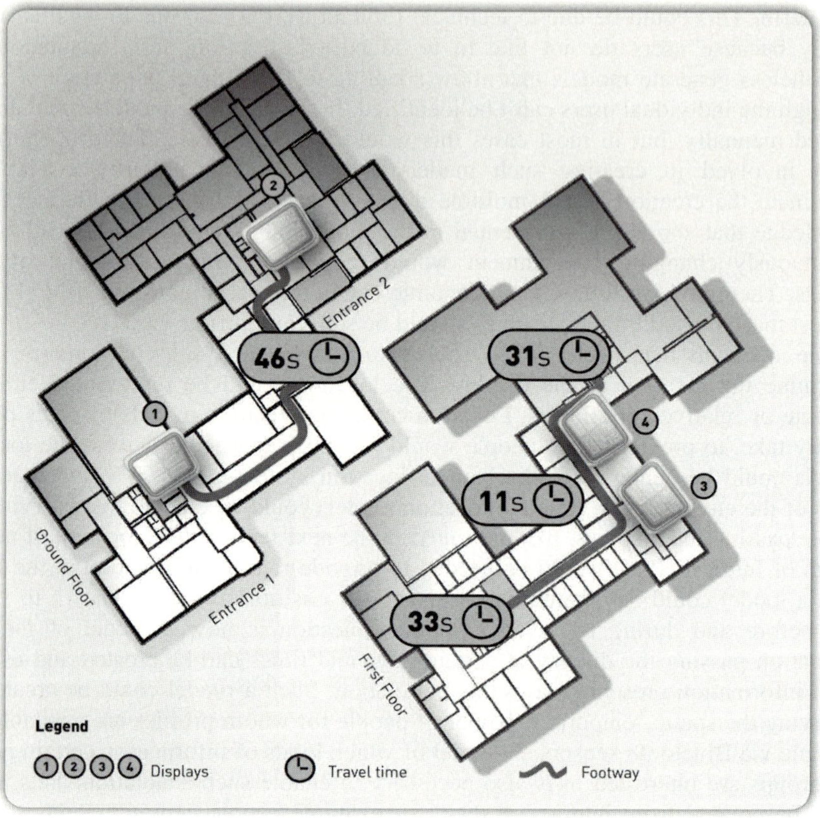

Fig. 2. A map of the test environment showing the locations of the different displays. The paths between the displays are shown together with the time needed to travel between the displays, as measured with a clock. These times are then estimated with the Expectation-Maximization algorithm.

The EM algorithm takes as input the set of travel times and the number of normal distributions (Gaussians) that should be assumed to have generated the data. It then adjusts the means and standard deviations of the Gaussians until it reaches a local maximum likelihood hypothesis for the parameters of the Gaussians. This approach has the benefit that it is quite insensitive to noise, because there is always one Gaussian with a big standard deviation to accommodate all the noise. In addition, multiple paths and transportation modes, like walking, bicycle, car, bus etc. can be identified. The main drawback is that the number of Gaussians and thus the number of paths must be known in advance. In our case the data is generated with Bluetooth sensors. A Bluetooth sensor is a device that scans for nearby Bluetooth devices and reports the Bluetooth addresses of the devices found. Users can subscribe to a service that enables interaction with the displays via their mobile phone and thus agree that their data is logged by the system. Currently, most members of our work group and a number of students use this offer. Each display is equipped with a Bluetooth USB stick and runs software that continuously scans for nearby Bluetooth devices.

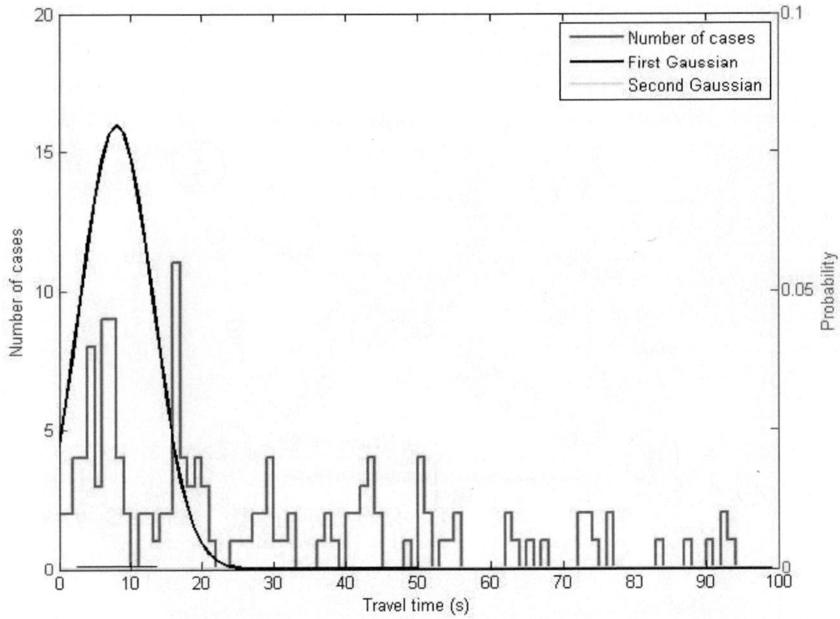

Fig. 3. Part of the travel times from display 1 to display 3, together with the EM estimations for two Gaussians. The first Gaussian (μ=8s, σ=5s) represents people who are assumed to have taken the direct way. The second Gaussian (μ=11284s, σ=63451s) represents the indirect ways and noise and is so flat that it is hardly visible. Thus, the algorithm assumes the path to take about 8 seconds to walk. Only travel times of up to 100 seconds are shown.

For all subscribed devices found it is checked whether they were present during the previous scan. If a device is found that was not present during the previous scan, a database entry is created that contains the Bluetooth MAC address, a timestamp, an "entered" flag and the name of the display. If a device that was present during the last scan is not found again, a database entry with a "left" flag is created. On our platform a scan takes 11 sec., so this is the temporal resolution with which timestamps are created. To calculate the individual travel times between displays, we cycle through all database entries with a "left" flag. From this entry, we look for the next entry with an "entered" flag, and store the time difference into the corresponding list for the pair of displays from which the entries were created. Thus, for each ordered pair of displays we obtain a set of travel times. For each ordered pair of displays we then execute the EM algorithm to estimate the mean travel times for the different paths between the displays.

First we set the number of different paths we want to identify, in our case one per pair of displays. Then we add another Gaussian to accommodate the noise that occurs for example when someone passes a display, goes to vacation, and then passes another display when he comes back. The algorithm is then initialized with random hypotheses about the means and standard deviations of the Gaussians. In the Expectation step, for each of the instances the probability that it was generated by

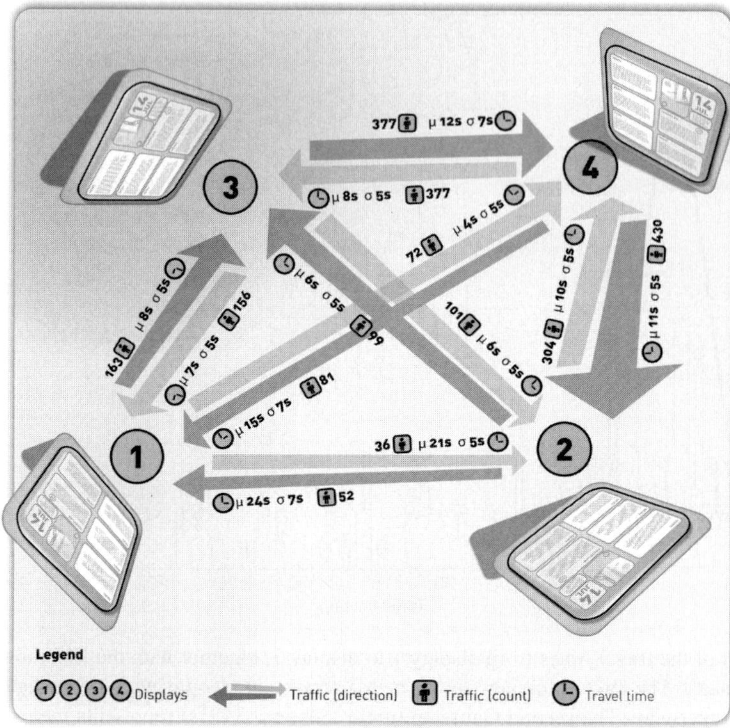

Fig. 4. The model of the displays in the test environment, as generated by the procedure presented. The model is a directed graph that contains as labels for each edge a) The mean time to walk from one display to the other b) The corresponding standard deviation and c) The people observed to have walked from the first to the second display. The model enables to predict where and when a person will probably show up next after having passed a certain display.

each of the Gaussians is calculated. In the Maximization step, new hypotheses about the means and standard deviations are built. This happens under the assumption that the instances belong to the Gaussians as calculated in the Expectation step. These two steps are repeated until the algorithm converges to a local maximum likelihood hypothesis. A graph showing the actual travel times from display 1 to display 3 together with the Gaussians that were calculated by the EM algorithm is depicted in figure 3. The data structure created by the procedure is a directed multigraph with labeled edges (see figure 4). Each display is represented as a node, and each Gaussian for a way between the displays is represented as an edge. Edges between two displays are labeled with a) How many people directly traversed from the first display to the second without passing another display in between and b) The expected mean and standard deviation of the travel time. Within four months of running the system we collected 92.827 timestamps. However, the majority of these timestamps were not actual traversals between different displays, but people sitting for example at their workplace and being repeatedly found and lost by the scanner.

Table 1. Travel times between all combinations of displays in our building. The "Measured" column gives the times we measured with a clock, "EM" gives the estimation of our procedure for the distance, and "Error" is the difference between the two. "Cases" gives the total number of traversals our system observed, and the last four columns give the time difference between leaving the first Bluetooth cell and entering the next Bluetooth cell for different mobiles we carried while measuring with the clock. In case of negative times, the second cell was entered before the first one was left, impossible trajectories are marked with "-". In case of "x" the device was not found by the display, and in cases of "*" the device was found by a third display that was not directly passed before being found by the second (target) display.

From	To	Measured	EM	Error	Cases	PEBL	K700i	6230i	6310i
1	2	46	21	25	36	23*	23*	23	37*
2	1	48	24	24	52	x	38	30*	63*
1	3	37	8	29	166	x	-53	-7	-7
3	1	33	7	26	156	15	3	15	3
1	4	48	4	44	72	-	-	-	-
4	1	43	15	28	82	-	-	-	-
2	3	41	6	35	99	-	-	-	-
3	2	38	6	32	101	-	-	-	-
2	4	31	10	21	304	-12	-11	-11	-11
4	2	27	11	16	430	36	-21	-9	-30*
3	4	11	12	-1	380	16	-2	-4	-4
4	3	10	8	2	379	-7	-18	-18	-19

In total 2257 traversals between different displays were detected. Because within our building, between each pair of displays only one path is possible (see figure 2), we used for each ordered pair of displays two Gaussians. One of these was supposed to accommodate the data from people taking the direct way, and one to accommodate the noise. To create a ground truth, we measured the time needed to traverse between the displays by walking normally (see table 1). While we did this, we carried four mobile phones with us to generate comparison data for Bluetooth cell entry and leaving with different models. The data we generated for the travel times are shown in table 1. As can be seen in the table, there is a quite constant error of about 28 seconds except for the way from display 3 to display 4 and back. The mean error is 23.4 seconds. The error stems from four main sources. First of all, of course the Bluetooth cells are much bigger than only the immediate vicinity of the display. The Bluetooth signal is lost by the system only a number of seconds after the user started to walk away, and the second display receives a Bluetooth signal a number of seconds before the user actually arrives in front of the display. This sometimes even causes the cells to overlap, as with displays 3 and 4. Second, a scan can take place only every 11 seconds, so we have an error of up to ±11 sec. due to temporal resolution. Third, quite often a mobile phone is not found by a Bluetooth scan although it is in vicinity of the display. This causes an additional error of 11 sec. per scan where the phone is not found. Fourth, Bluetooth works through ceilings and walls. So, when a user passes next to a display on a different level or on the other side of a wall, he is often detected by the display. In our case, users traversing from display 1 to display 2 on the ground floor are regularly detected by displays 3 and 4 on the first floor (see figure 2). In table 1, these cases are depicted with a "*". To deal with the first error source, it would be sensible to add a constant offset of 23 seconds to the estimation of distances. The remaining error would then be within a few seconds, but that would have to be tested against a different set of displays in another setting. Because the error from the first three sources doesn't grow with the distance between displays, the bigger the actual distance, the smaller the impact of the error.

5 Conclusion and Future Work

In this paper we presented a procedure to learn a topological model of Situated Public Displays from data of people traversing between these displays. The model contains the mean travel time between Situated Public Displays for different ways and/or transportation modes. In addition, it shows how many people traverse between Situated Public Displays in each direction. This model enables to predict where and when people would probably appear next after showing up in front of a display. This enables us to present continuous 'shows' that span multiple displays while people pass them, regardless whether people can be identified, detected, or are invisible to the system. We implemented the procedure and tested it using four different displays. We showed that the procedure works for our case and presented four main sources of errors. We plan to add additional sensors to augment the model with further information. One idea is to use display-mounted cameras with blob detection to estimate in which direction a user walked after passing the display. This information could be used to generate arrows that guide the user to a particular location. Camera information could also be used to estimate whether a user actually passed a display and when exactly he did so. We also plan to work on the generated shows that span multiple displays, and want to further investigate how to generate such shows for people invisible to the system.

Acknowledgements. We would like to thank all the people that contributed to this research: Patrick Olivier had the idea for continuous shows, Oliver Paczkowski and Oliver Meyer designed the Situated Public Display prototype. Dennis Wilmsmann implemented the Bluetooth Scanner, and Christophe Littfass created the illustrations.

References

1. Krumm, J., Hinckley, K.: The NearMe Wireless Proximity Server. In: Davies, N., Mynatt, E.D., Siio, I. (eds.) UbiComp 2004. LNCS, vol. 3205, pp. 283–300. Springer, Heidelberg (2004)
2. Mitchell, T.M.: Machine Learning Science/Engineering/Math. McGraw-Hill, New York (1997)
3. Krumm, J., Horvitz, E.: Predestination: Inferring destinations from partial trajectories. In: Dourish, P., Friday, A. (eds.) UbiComp 2006. LNCS, vol. 4206, pp. 243–260. Springer, Heidelberg (2006)

4. Cheng, C., Jain, R., van den Berg, E.: Location prediction algorithms for mobile wireless systems. In: Handbook of Wireless Internet CRC Press, pp. 245–263. CRC Press, Boca Raton (2003)
5. Kortuem, G., Kray, C., Gellersen, H.: Sensing and visualizing spatial relations of mobile devices. In: UIST '05: Proceedings of the 18th annual ACM symposium on User interface software and technology, pp. 93–102. ACM Press, New York (2005)
6. Hightower, J., Borriello, G.: Location systems for ubiquitous computing. IEEE Computer 34(8), 57–66 (2001)
7. Carmichael, D., Kay, J., Kummerfeld, B.: Consistent modelling of users, devices and sensors in a ubiquitous computing environment. In: User Modeling and User-Adapted Interaction vol. 15(3-4) pp. 197–234 (2005)
8. Payne, T., David, E., Jennings, N.R., Sharifi, M.: Auction mechanisms for efficient advertisement selection on public displays. In: Proceedings of European Conference on Artificial Intelligence. pp. 285–289 (2006)
9. Müller, H.J., Krüger, A.: Towards situated public displays as multicast systems. In: UbiqUM 2006 Workshop on Ubiquitous User Modeling, The 17th European Conference on Artificial Intelligence (2006)
10. O'Hara, K., Perry, M., Churchill, E., Russell, D. (eds.): Public and Situated Displays: Social and Interactional Aspects of Shared Display Technologies. Kluwer Publishers, Dordrecht (2003)
11. Kephart, J.O., Chess, D.M.: The vision of autonomic computing. In: IEEE Computer vol. 36(1) pp. 41–50 (2003)

A Context-Aware Service Platform to Support Continuous Care Networks for Home-Based Assistance

Federica Paganelli and Dino Giuli

Dept. of Electronics and Telecommunications, University of Firenze
via S. Marta 3,
50139 Firenze, Italy
{federica.paganelli, dino.giuli}@unifi.it

Abstract. Efficient and effective treatment of chronic disease conditions requires the implementation of emerging continuous care models. These models pose several technology-oriented challenges for home-based continuous care, requiring assistance services based on collaboration among different stakeholders: health operators, patient relatives, as well as social community members. This work describes a context-aware service platform designed for improving patient quality of life by supporting care team activity, intervention and cooperation. Leveraging on an ontology-based context management middleware, the proposed architecture exploits information coming from biomedical and environmental sensing devices and from patient social context in order to automate context-aware patient case management, especially for alarm detection and management purposes.

Keywords: care networks, home care, context model, ontology.

1 Introduction

At present, the growing percentage of elderly population in industrialized nations is progressively increasing the percentage of people affected by disabilities and chronic disease conditions. According to recent results of a survey funded by the European Commission [1], Europe and Japan will experience the most pronounced ageing trends up to 2050. The share of the above 60 age group will be around 37% in Europe and even more in Japan, and slightly lower in North America (27%). As a consequence, the increase in the share of persons surviving to very old ages (80+) may lead to an increase in the prevalence of chronic and degenerative diseases. The "Survey of Health, Ageing and Retirement in Europe" [1] provides a clear picture of the problem.

Advances in technologies and AmI context-aware system design are thus required in order to address two main objectives:

– improving quality of life of both patients and their closest relatives. In fact, chronic conditions cause limitations to everyday life activities, but they may dramatically decrease the quality of life of patient family members too [2];

C. Stephanidis (Ed.): Universal Access in HCI, Part II, HCII 2007, LNCS 4555, pp. 168–177, 2007.

– providing cost savings in long-term care services provision. Ageing and chronic conditions treatment require continuous and long-term assistance services. Such services cannot be afforded with traditional approaches, which are instead conceived for the treatment of acute health problems.

In this application scenario, services which can be provided by an AmI system have been classified into the following categories [3]:

– Emergency treatment: services for emergency detection and management
– Autonomy enhancement: services for user assistance for primary needs and/or everyday activities (nutrition, medicine taking, vital signs monitoring, etc.).
– Comfort: services allowing better life quality (e.g. education, socialization, etc.)

These services should be adaptive, easy to use, and strongly personalized according to user requirements, needs and disabilities. In most existing AmI context-aware systems, the focus is on the requirements of the person needing assistance ("patient"), whereas requirements coming from the heterogeneous community of persons which are involved in patient care and assistance are often not taken into account into system design.

On the contrary, nowadays it has been widely recognized that the care of people affected by chronic conditions requires the development of novel models, called *continuous care models*. These models need an organized system of care, based on the active role and cooperation of heterogeneous actors, including patient and his/her family, health care teams (e.g., general practitioners, physicians, nurses), and social community actors (for instance: volunteers and self-aid groups).

Moving from these issues, this work is being done as part of the KAMER project, which has the objective to design and realize an AmI service platform for home-based assistance of elderly and persons affected by chronic conditions. The main objective of the project is to design and develop a service platform aiming at improving patient quality of life by offering instruments and services supporting cooperating care network members. Care network members are, for instance, general practitioners, medical specialists, nurses, social operators, volunteers, and, above all, patient relatives. Even if they play different roles in the care network, they have some common requirements: for instance, they need to access patient records, they can be asked for intervention in critical situations (e.g. emergency) and they should be aware of responsibilities and actions of other care team members.

The paper is structured as follows: Section 2 introduces main aspects of novel continuous care models for treatment of chronic conditions. Section 3 discusses related work. Section 4 describes our reference application scenario and Section 5 illustrates the overall service platform architecture for Continuous Care Networks. Section 6 provides an overview of the Context Management Middleware. Section 7 summarizes the results and provides some insights into future work.

2 Continuous Care Models

At present, continuous care models for chronic disease conditions are being discussed, promoted and experimented at national and international level. One of the first examples is the Chronic Care Model (CCM), which is a conceptual, evidence-based framework developed in the USA. This model proposes innovative organizational aspects aiming at improving effectiveness and efficacy of assistance to patients affected by chronic conditions. Recently, the WHO has proposed the Innovative Care for chronic conditions (ICCC) framework, which extends CCM for an international community [4].

These models promote an holistic approach for continuous care of chronic conditions, including guidelines for policy planning, as well as principles for social community and health care systems organization and effort coordination.

Focusing on those aspects which are more directly related to the topic of this paper, we highlight that the above-mentioned continuous care models place point-of-care in the community and at patient home. These models emphasize the fact that effectiveness and efficiency of long-term condition care depend strongly on the capability of both patients and their relatives to manage their case (self-management) and on the collaboration of all involved care providers. Patients, family members, health care teams (e.g. clinicians, general practitioner, nurses, etc.) and social community members (e.g., social workers, volunteers) should be properly informed, motivated and prepared in order to effectively collaborate together.

From the point of view of AmI and context-aware system designers, home-based care models pose several technology-oriented challenges. Technology efforts strictly focused on patient assistance requirements provide a relevant but partial contribution in facing the problem. As a matter of fact, collaboration among different stakeholders (health operators, patient relatives, as well as social community members) and efforts coordination requirements should be taken into account in AmI and context-aware system design for continuous care.

3 Related Work

There are a number of research projects related to home-care and e-health assistance. Here we will focus on works proposing context-aware systems to support home-based assistance to chronic patients.

Most attempts have focused on specific aspects, such as health status monitoring, alert and reminders based on scheduled activities (e.g., medicine taking, training activities, etc.), patient behavior and daily activities modelling. For instance, Vivago® is an alarm system, providing long-term monitoring of user's activity profile and automatic alarm notification [5]. It consists of three main components: a wrist unit, a base station and an alarm receiving and routing software. Further systems are: Georgia Tech Aware Home, providing assistance services for the elderly [6]; CareMedia [7], which uses multimedia information to track person activities; MIT's PlaceLab [8], which includes a proactive health care application based on wearable and environmental sensing.

The Freeband Awareness project aims at the development of a context-aware infrastructure architecture [9]. The project focuses on requirements coming from the health care domain. Its reference scenarios include tele-monitoring, tele-assistance and assistance to disabled persons.

In above works, guidelines and reference models for continuous care are not yet extensively taken into account in the design of pervasive care solutions. Recently, some high-level analysis and conceptual design have been performed. Chronic care model principles have been taken into account in the conception of Pervasive Self Care, a ubiquitous computing service infrastructure conceptual framework [10]. In [2] social network analysis is applied to the study of continuous care networks. First experimentation results have been reported in [11], where a telemedicine system is used for the home care of patients suffering from Chronic Obtrusive Pulmonary Disease; its functionalities include communication facilities between patients and their care team and data sharing among the care team.

While these latter works have focused on conceptual design or on implementation of applications targeted to specific chronic diseases, the aim of this work is to design and implement a service platform supporting care teams which should be dynamically and flexibly activated to provide care services accordingly to patient situation (e.g. health status and home environment).

4 Application Scenario for Continuous Care at Home

Novel continuous care models suggest that information and communication systems should provide technological instruments in order to effectively support the activity of continuous care networks and coordinate efforts of different members: patients and families, health care teams and social community partners [4].

In this section we first provide an overview of main stakeholders usually involved in a continuous care network and their requirements, in order to motivate the service platform architecture and the Context Management Middleware for continuous care networks described in the following sections.

With the term *continuous care network* we refer to the broad range of people which is involved to different extent in the care of the elder. Care networks can be characterized, as specified in [2], in terms of: roles within networks; communication structures within networks; types of information shared; importance of shared information; individuals' comfort in sharing information. Complexity of care network management is also due to the fact that members typically have more than one place of work, belong to different organizations and do not have frequent physical contacts. Availability of shared and updated information is thus a critical aspect for these loosely-coupled teams.

Some relevant stakeholders requirements are described below:

Patient: general patient requirements include the capability of easily communicating with relatives or health operators, notifying an emergency situation and requesting an intervention. He/she might also require support for implementing his/her health assistance plan (for instance, reminding for regular medicine taking and vital sign measurements). Requirements depending on specific patient conditions (e.g. physical impairments, cognitive disabilities, etc.) have not been taken into account in this work.

Family members: providing care can have different impact on patient relatives' life. In [2] three main categories have been identified: those who make *drastic life changes* to support the elder (e.g. quitting job or neglecting hobbies and social activities); those who make *significant contributions* to care for the elder (without making important changes on their lives), those who have *peripheral involvement* in the elder's care (e.g. sporadic interaction with the elder). Relatives belonging to the first category are critical network members, as their contribution is relevant for the elder quality of life. As these family members are often involved in implementing the assistance plan, they should be aware of patient conditions, be informed about the health plan implementation (e.g. if the patient has taken his/her medicines) and be made capable of expressing the availability for an intervention (for instance when outside home).

Doctors: Doctors (especially general practitioners) are responsible to define the patient health assistance plan. Accordingly to emerging continuous care models, they should cooperate with nurses and social assistance operators in order to define an integrated assistance plan. Main requirements include the capability of accessing complete and accurate patient records and timely updating patient data (for instance during home visits). Doctors also need not to be overwhelmed by intervention requests, especially when the situation is not extremely critical and could be handled by other operators (nurses, social assistance operators), or when they are involved in critical interventions.

Nurses: They are relevant care providers and, analogously to doctors, they need efficient scheduling management. They also require access to patient records as well as information support for timely interventions.

Social assistance operators: They provide support for daily activities and social communication. Their activity can be relevant also for detecting patient attitudes and emotive state and other information which are useful for evaluating health plan implementation results but could not be automatically measured.

Call center: with this term we refer to the center which has the responsibility of managing incoming calls and alerts and planning interventions. The need is to automate, as possible, the workflow of critical situation management. This roughly consists in detecting critical or emergency situations, deciding which kind of intervention and competences are required, finding available people with needed competences, and contact them via suitable available channels (e.g. email, sms, phone, etc.).

Other community members: community members can be involved to different extent to provide their contribution. They may include volunteers, special transport service associations, shops, chemistries, etc. Their capabilities of service offering can improve the quality of life of both patients and their relatives.

In addition to patient-oriented services (i.e. emergency treatment, autonomy enhancement, and comfort), the design of a context-aware system should also offer services supporting shared care teams. We identified the following services for caregivers: communication facilities; shared access to patient related data; decision-support services and automated workflow for critical situation handling and alarm management; mutual "social awareness" about role and action of network members.

Context-awareness is a general concept, referring to the capability of a system to be aware of its physical and logical environment and to intelligently react according to this awareness. Definition of context is thus dependent on application domain and purposes. In our application scenario, context includes information on patient biomedical parameters (e.g. vital signs) and home living environment (for instance air physical parameters such as temperature and relative humidity at patient home). Even the social context (i.e. information regarding persons populating the patient care dynamic team) is considered a relevant contextual information to be exploited for context-aware assistance service delivery.

As detailed in the following sections, context management and reasoning services have been conceived and implemented to ease the development of context-aware emergency and autonomy enhancement services. Emergency detection is based on the analysis of vital signs and home environment monitoring. Emergency management is addressed in terms of alert notification planning. These tools can be easily customized for a wide range of patient disease and home living typologies. Support for automatic therapeutic intervention at home is not included since it is a capability implying deep knowledge of the specific patient case and personalized system design.

5 Context-Aware Service Platform Architecture Design and Deployment

The overall system architecture is made of the following logical components:

- Context data providers: several physiological sensors are now available which can help patient or relatives for self-measurement (e.g., oxymeter, tensiometer, glycometer, etc.). Activity sensors (accelerometer) and environmental conditions sensors can also be used to enrich system awareness of patient status.
- Context management middleware: this is a distributed architecture of computing nodes (named Context Manager Nodes) devoted to context data acquisition from sensors and analysis for emergency situation detection and handling.
- Context-aware applications: they provide care and assistance services which adapt to the contextual situation (as explained below).

The deployment configuration is hereafter described.

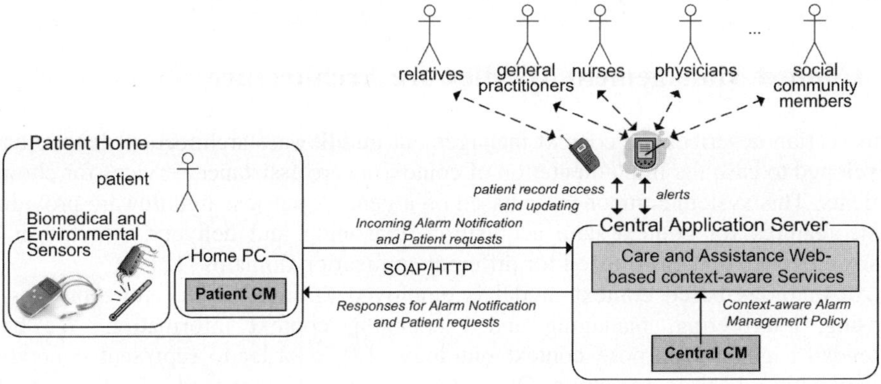

Fig. 1. Service Platform Architecture for Continuous Care

A HomePC (a Tablet PC) is deployed at Patient site. It acquires data coming from biomedical and environmental sensor networks and hosts a node of the Context Management Middleware, named Patient Context Manager (PatientCM). The PatientCM performs context data analysis in order to detect incoming emergency situations. It communicates with a Central Application Server via ADSL to send periodical status messages and up-to-date measurement values, as well as to notify alarms triggered by emergency and critical situations.

The Central Application Server is deployed in the domain of the central organization which is responsible for the integration and delivery of care and call center services (for instance, hospitals, nursing homes or municipalities). It hosts the central node of the Context Management Middleware (named Central Context Manager, CentralCM) which works to define an alert notification policy for informing care team members and require their intervention. The Central Application Server is also in charge of delivering assistance and information services.

Main services currently under development include:

- For health care team operators (doctors and nurses): a web-based application which allows team members to access and update patient records, receive alert notifications, manage alarm situations, and set their own availability status for intervention. Through this interface, care providers can notify the system about their interventions, be informed about interventions of other operators and communicate with them. These services can be accessed via desktop PC or PDA.
- For patient relatives: services include access to patient report and capability of notifying the system with their own distance from patient home and receiving alerts via phone call or sms. These services can be accessed via mobile devices with minimal technical requirements (an XHTML browser).

Even if the autonomous access of patients to services and the development of assistive technologies are not the main target of this work, some basic emergency services based on direct patient interaction can be made available by the service platform. For basic testing purposes we are planning the development of a web-based ergonomic Graphical User Interface for medicine assumption reminding and manual alarm and communication requests.

6 Context Management Middleware Architecture

This section describes the context management middleware architecture that we have developed to ease the implementation of context-aware assistance services for chronic patients. This system component is based on a general-purpose middleware providing basic features for context data acquisition, reasoning and delivery, which can be easily extended and customized for different application domains [12].

An ontology-based context model is employed throughout the entire process of sensing, interpreting, managing and exchanging context information. We have extended a general purpose context ontology [12] in order to represent contextual situations in a home care setting. Our ontology-based context model for home health monitoring and alerting in patient care networks is described in [13]. Main context modeling and reasoning capabilities are introduced here below.

The context model is composed of the following ontologies:

- the Patient Personal Ontology: includes context items about patient physical data (i.e. biomedical parameters), location and activity. These data are used by the system to automatically infer patient health status and detect alarm situations.

- the Home Environment ontology: includes context data describing the patient home environment. For instance, monitoring of environment parameters is needed in order to maintain a healthy environment and detect alarm situations.
- The Alarm Management Ontology: represents those resources that could be put in place in order to manage an incoming alarms. This ontology is used in order to instantiate the suitable alarm management policy according to the incoming alarm level, the patient identifier and the availability of care team members.
- The Social Context Ontology: represents care network resources (health teams, social community members, etc.) and their relations.

Context reasoning is used mainly for alarm triggering and management. We have defined a set of first-order rules in order to determine if an alarm has to be triggered and which alarm level should be activated, according to measured context data and corresponding thresholds. The following example shows a rule activating an alarm when both following conditions occur: hearth rate frequency is less than 40 beat/minute and systolic blood pressure is higher than 160mm/Hg:

(?parameter1 rdf:type pre:HeartRateFrequency) (?parameter1 pre:hasMeasurementResult ?value1) le(?value1, 40) (?parameter2 rdf:type pre:SystolicBloodPressure) (?parameter2 pre:hasMeasurementResult ?value2) ge(?value2,160) -> (?healthstatus pre:hasTempAlarmLevel 'HIGH')

Analogously, when the alarm has been activated, rule-based reasoning is used to determine which notification policy should be actuated for alarm handling. An alarm notification policy is a set of instructions specifying whom should be alerted and how (via sms, mail, phone call) and if acknowledge is required.

The Kamer Context management middleware is composed of context management nodes, named Context Managers (CM) and its operation is based on the above mentioned context modeling and reasoning principles. The logical architecture is similar for both the Patient Context Manager and the Central Context Manager (see Fig. 2). The Context Data Acquisition module receives context data from context providers via SOAP messages (e.g. web service-enabled sensor networks [14]), or via sensor adapters. The Ontology Manager manages the knowledge base, composed of context models and instances stored in a database, a rule-based reasoner and rule files. A Context Broker component makes context information available to external applications, by managing queries from applications and/or notifying interested applications when the context has changed. Communication among distributed components is provided via SOAP Web Services.

Specifically, the Patient Context Manager receives context data from body sensor networks and home sensors. These data are used to update the Patient Personal and the Home Environment Ontologies instances. Rule-based reasoning is applied to the knowledge base in order to detect possible alarms. If an alarm occurs, the PatientCM notifies the Central CM. Then, the CentralCM applies rule-based reasoning to the knowledge base composed by the Social Context Ontology (containing updated information about patient relatives and care providers availability) and the Alarm Management Ontology (instantiated with the information about the alarm situation to be handled). The resulting alarm notification policy is then instantiated by the Alarm Notification Application.

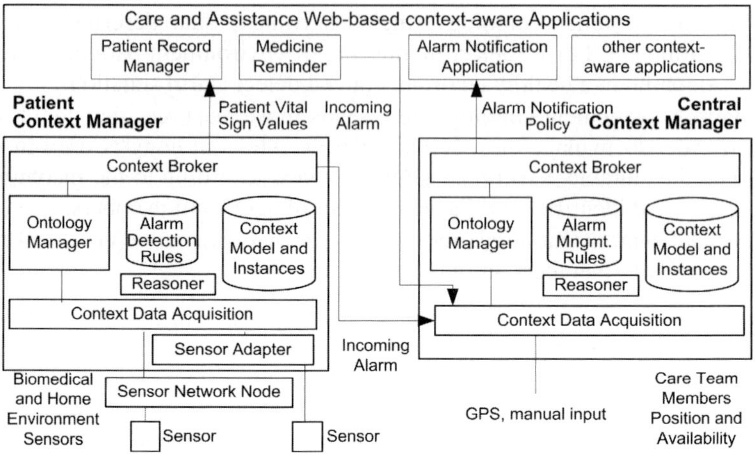

Fig. 2. Context Management Middleware Architecture

The Context Manager has been implemented as a J2EE application. Context Model and instances are encoded in OWL (Web Ontology Language) [15] and stored in a relational database (MySQL). The Ontology Manager and the reasoner are based on Jena [16], a Java framework for building Semantic Web applications.

7 Conclusions

In this paper, we have presented a context-aware service platform designed for home-based assistance of chronic patients. Main distinguishing features of this work are: the attempt to systematically take into account requirements coming from novel continuous care models into system design; the design of a service platform for continuous care networks leveraging on a Context Management Middleware and an ontology-based context model for health monitoring and alert management.

The Context Management Middleware has been described with some design details. Services for patient assistance and care network support are currently under development. Use-case testing is planned with a trial in a nursing home in the near future. This testing stage will be focused on evaluating health operators acceptance of implemented features. For this test stage, biomedical and environmental sensing will be simulated by a web application providing services for manual input or pre-defined scenario simulation for context data acquisition. A testing stage with chronic condition patients will be planned in the near future. For these tests, a sensing system for vital signs and environmental monitoring will be deployed. Test results will be reported in the conference presentation.

Acknowledgements. The Kamer Project is funded by the Regione Emilia Romagna, Italy. The partners are Hewlett Packard Italy, Cattolica University of Piacenza and the Italian National Inter-University Consortium for Telecommunications (CNIT).

References

1. Börsch-Supan, A., Jürges, H.: The Survey of Health, Ageing and Retirement in Europe – Methodology. Mannheim Research Institute for the Economics of Aging, MEA, Mannheim (2005)
2. Consolvo, S., Roessler, P., Shelton, B.E., LaMarca, A., Schilit, B., Bly, S.: Technology for Care Networks of Elders. IEEE Pervasive Computing 3(2), 22–29 (2004)
3. Nehmer, J., Karshmer, A., Becker, M., Lamm, R.: Living Assistance Systems – An Ambient Intelligence Approach. Proceedings of the 28th International Conference on Software Engineering (ICSE 2006), Shanghai, China (2006)
4. World Health Organization (WHO): Innovative Care for Chronic Conditions: Building Blocks for Action (2002), http://www.who.int
5. Korhonen, I., Paavilainen, P., Särela, A.: Application of ubiquitous computing technologies for support of independent living of the elderly in real life settings. Proc. UbiHealth 2003, The 2nd International Workshop on Ubiquituos Computing for Pervasive Healthcare Applications (2003)
6. Abowd, G.D., Bobick, I., Essa, I., Mynatt, E., Rogers, W.: The Aware Home: Developing Technologies for Successful Aging. Proc. of American Association of Artificial Intelligence (AAAI) Conference (2002)
7. Bharucha, A.J.: CareMedia: Automated Video and Sensor Analysis for Geriatric Care. Presented at the Geriatric Care Annual Meeting of the American Association for Geriatric Psychiatry, San Juan, Puerto Rico (2006)
8. Intille, S.S., Larson, K., Tapia, E.M.: Designing and evaluating technology for independent aging in the home. Proc. of the International Conference on Aging, Disability and Independence (2003)
9. van Kranenburg, H., Bargh, M.S., Iacob, S., Peddemors, A.: A context management framework for supporting context-aware distributed applications. IEEE Communications Magazine 44(8), 67–74 (2006)
10. Roussos, G., Marsh, A.: A Blueprint for Pervasive Self-Care Infrastructures. Proc. of Fourth International Conference on Pervasive Computing and Communications, Workshop on Ubiquitous and Pervasive HealthCare (2006)
11. De Toledo, P., Jimenez, S., Del Pozo, F., Roca, J., Alonso, A., Hernandez, C.: A telemedicine experience for chronic care in COPD. IEEE Transactions on Information Technology in Biomedicine 10(3), 567–573 (2006)
12. Paganelli, F., Bianchi, G., Giuli, D.: A Context Model for Context-aware System Design towards the Ambient Intelligence Vision: Experiences in the eTourism Domain. Proc. of 9th ERCIM Workshop User Interfaces For All, Special Theme: Universal Access in Ambient Intelligence Environments, Königswinter (Bonn), Germany (2006)
13. Paganelli, F., Giuli, D.: An Ontology-based Context Model for Home Health Monitoring and Alerting in Chronic Patient Care Networks. Accepted at First International Workshop on Smart Homes for Tele-Health, AINA (2007)
14. Woo, A.: A New Embedded Web Services Approach to Wireless Sensor Networks. Proc. of the 4th International Conference on Embedded Networked Sensor Systems (2006)
15. Web Ontology Language, W3C recommendation. http://www.w3.org/TR/owl-guide/
16. JENA: A Semantic Web Framework for Java [Online]. http://jena.sourceforge.net/

Architectural Backpropagation Support for Managing Ambiguous Context in Smart Environments

Davy Preuveneers and Yolande Berbers

Department of Computer Science, K.U. Leuven
Celestijnenlaan 200A, B-3001 Leuven, Belgium,
{davy.preuveneers, yolande.berbers}@cs.kuleuven.be
http://www.cs.kuleuven.be

Abstract. The evolution to ubiquitous information and communication networks is evident. Technology is emerging that connects everyday objects and embeds intelligence in our environment. In the Internet of Things, smart objects collect context information from various sources to turn a static environment into a smart and proactive one. Managing the ambiguous nature of context information will be crucial to select relevant information for the tasks at hand. In this paper we present a vector space model that uses context quality parameters to manage context ambiguity and to identity irrelevant context providers. We also discuss backpropagation applied in the network architecture to filter unused context information in the network as close to the source as possible. Experiments show that our contribution not only reduces the amount of useless information a smart object deals with, but also the distribution of unused context information throughout the network architecture.

1 Introduction

The next wave in the era of computing will be outside the realm of the traditional desktop. In the Internet of Things paradigm [1], everything of value will be on the network in one form or another. Everyday objects, such as shoes, cars, coffee cups, refrigerators, bath tubs, will be in the communication range of interconnected devices, and provide relevant context information to create a smart and proactive environment. This context information [2] is considered to be a key ingredient to create a whole range of smart entertainment and business applications that are more supportive to the user.

In a less than ideal world, however, smart objects must be aware of the usability of the imperfect context information that they are provided with [3]. If not, a smart context-aware object may mistakenly assume that the information it retrieves from other smart objects in the network (i.e. the context providers), is accurate and relevant for the purpose of its actions. Therefore, the smart object needs a way to distinguish context providers based on the relevance of the information they provide.

C. Stephanidis (Ed.): Universal Access in HCI, Part II, HCII 2007, LNCS 4555, pp. 178–187, 2007.

In this paper we first discuss how ambiguous and imperfect context is modeled and verified before usage. This model is based on several information specific context quality parameters that contribute to the diminution of information ambiguity, such as precision and up-to-dateness [4]. Other non-information specific parameters model the reliability of a context provider delivering its information to a particular smart object in the network. Secondly, given these two sets of context quality parameters, we designed an algorithm to identify and ignore invaluable context providers. To further improve the quality of the context information propagated through the network, we developed a backpropagation mechanism to inform the context providers about the usage of their information. This mechanism allows smart objects in the network to selectively redirect information to where it is considered useful. Our technique is compared to context dissemination using network hops as a boundary for propagation. After a brief period of learning, our solution reduces ambiguity by ignoring irrelevant context providers early on, and improves the bandwidth usage ratio of the valuable context information passing through a smart object in the network.

In section 2 we discuss several context quality parameters and show how they are represented in an information model that helps the smart object to decide whether information is relevant for its purposes or not, and to identify (ir)relevant context providers. In section 3 we describe the algorithm to backpropagate the information relevance to the context providers. In section 4 we conduct experiments that illustrate the improvement of the quality of the context information that passes through and is being used by a smart object. Section 5 provides an overview of related work on the distribution of ambiguous context information. We end with conclusions and future work in section 6.

2 Modeling the Ambiguity of Context Information

A smart object may rely on external context providers to take well-informed decisions. Ambiguity arises when multiple parties deliver different information due to the diverse circumstances in which they operate. In this section, we clarify the boundaries that are needed in terms of spatial and temporal relevance, accuracy and precision, and semantic interpretability to understand these situations.

2.1 Disambiguation with Context Quality Parameters

Many aspects of information quality have already been investigated in the last decade [5,6]. In this section, we will only discuss a selection of these information properties that are used as context quality parameters in our model:

1. **Accuracy:** Accuracy refers to the degree of veracity. It describes the closeness of the measured value to the actual true value, or the extent to which the provided information is correct (e.g. $36.8°C$ vs. $37.1°C$, or 99%).
2. **Precision:** This parameter is closely related to the accuracy parameter. It describes how detailed a measurement is stated (e.g. $36.9 \pm 0.1°C$). Measurements that are precise are not necessarily accurate, and vice versa.

```xml
<ContextItem>
  <ProviderUID>32afc954-a85e-c7b1-f636-123564831237</ProviderUID>
  <Class>http://localhost/context#Temperature</Class>
  <Value type='http://localhost/units#Celsius'>20.6</Value>
  <Precision type='absolute'>0.2</Precision>
  <Accuracy type='relative'>0.95</Accuracy>
  <TimeStamp>2006-09-37 09:37:41+01:00</TimeStamp>
  <Coverage>http://localhost/context#Room</Coverage>
  <Location type='http://localhost/context#Office'>02.45</Location>
</ContextItem>
```

Fig. 1. A *Temperature* information instance of a sensor on the network

3. **Spatial coverage:** This parameter defines the geographic scope of the information. For example, the temperature provided by an outside weather station is unusable for controlling the central heating in a building.
4. **Timeliness:** Timeliness refers to how current the provided information is at the time of delivery. If not sufficiently up-to-date, the temperature information may not be useful either for the task at hand.
5. **Semantic interpretability:** Some context providers may use semantically related terms, e.g. 'Corridor' and 'Hallway'. If these relationships are not understood, any relevant information specified in these terms will be neglected.

The previous parameters help to disambiguate the information itself. The following parameters describe the ability of a context provider to reliably provide useful information to a particular smart object:

1. **Objectivity:** The objectivity property describes the reliability and trustworthiness of the information source. The context provider may have specific intentions to deliver biased information.
2. **Availability:** A smart object is never sure if a context provider will be able to deliver the required information. The context provider may leave the network or its information may be dropped under way.
3. **Completeness:** This parameter reflects the amount of missing or uninterpretable context quality parameters that make the context less reliable without comparison to other available information sources.

These three subjective parameters are not set by the context provider itself, but by the receiving end. They have values between 0 and 1 and are quite likely to be different for each receiving smart object. Fig. 1 illustrates a sample of information delivered by a context provider with a specific *ProviderID.* It provides *Temperature* information using the *Celsius* scale. The *Precision* and *Accuracy* are specified in terms of relative or absolute values. The information is timestamped and the location and coverage are specified as well. Ontologies are used for semantic annotation of the *Class, Value, Coverage* and *Location* properties. Multiple values can be provided in different scales (e.g. *Celsius* and *Fahrenheit*) or specified semantically (e.g. *Office* and *Room*). For example, the context information in Fig. 1 is not relevant when requesting the *Body* temperature, because an *Office* is not semantically part of a *Body.* These relationships are modeled in an ontology as shown in Fig. 2. Subsumption (*is*-relationship) and semantic distance (*has*-relationship) in the shortest path between two concepts is used

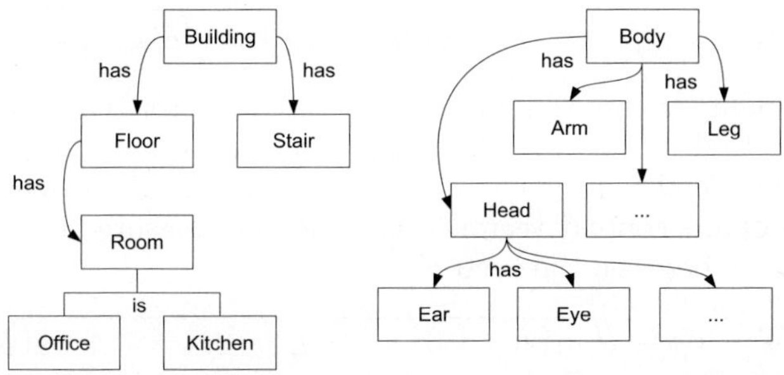

Fig. 2. Ontology specifying semantic containment

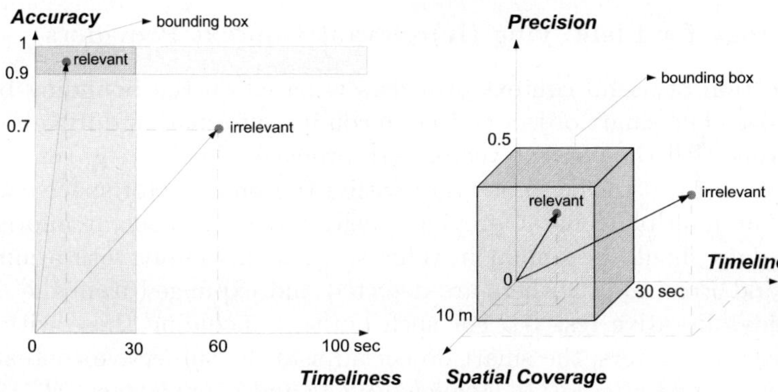

Fig. 3. A relevant and irrelevant context vector in a 2D and 3D vector space model

as a semantic metric for selecting relevant information. For unrelated concepts, the distance is defined infinite (∞). In Fig. 2, the distance between Building and Room is 2. Between Room and Office, the distance is 0 due to the *is*-relationship between the two concepts.

2.2 Modeling Context Quality in a Vector Space Model

In this section, we present a model that represents the context quality parameters in a vector space model to efficiently filter irrelevant context information.

This vector space model allows to explicate the required criteria to which delivered context information should conform. Each dimension of this model represents a context quality parameter, and for each of these dimensions a boundary for acceptable values is defined by the smart object for the task at hand. Together they form a bounding box. Two examples are illustrated in Fig. 3. Numeric parameters are represented as such. Semantic parameters use the semantic metric to represent their value in the model if conversion is not possible. Each context information instance is represented as a vector in the model. In a d-dimensional quality parameter space Q, a context vector $\overrightarrow{c}$ is defined as follows:

$$\overrightarrow{c} = (c_1, c_2, ..., c_d) \in Q \qquad with \qquad |\overrightarrow{c}| = \sqrt{c_1^2 + c_2^2 + ... + c_d^2}$$

The optimal quality vector $\overrightarrow{q}$ represents a context vector that is 100% accurate and precise, up-to-date, and completely relevant for the smart object's purposes. The value of d depends on the number of requirements of the smart object. The relevance $R_{\overrightarrow{c}}$ of any context vector $\overrightarrow{c}$ can then be measured by computing the weighted distance between the vectors:

$$R_{\overrightarrow{c}} = |\overrightarrow{q} - \overrightarrow{c}| = \sqrt{w_1(q_1 - c_1)^2 + w_2(q_2 - c_2)^2 + ... + w_d(q_d - c_d)^2}$$

The weights w determine the priority of the quality parameters. The smaller the value of $R_{\overrightarrow{c}}$ is, the more relevant the context information is.

2.3 Strategy for Identifying (Ir)relevant Context Providers

A first selection of useful context providers is based on the bounding box described above. The smart object collects incoming information during a certain period of time. All the context vectors are properly aligned (e.g. semantically converted or rescaled to the same type) within the same vector space model.

Given that multiple context providers deliver relevant context information, the actual data should be similar in value as they all comply with a minimum *Accuracy* and *Precision*. Outliers are detected and expunged from the dataset using Grubb's iterative test [7]. For such outliers, including those with undefined quality parameters, the smart object adjusts the subjective context quality parameters (*Objectivity (O)*, *Availability (A)* and *Completeness (C)*) for the corresponding context provider. When outliers in the values are detected, the *Objectivity* quality parameter of the context provider P is reduced:

$$O_P \leftarrow O_P \times \textit{Requested Relative Accuracy} \qquad with \qquad 0 \leq O_P \leq 1$$

If the requested accuracy is low and the context provider claims it complies although its value is an outlier compared to the others, then it is penalized more than if the requested accuracy would have been set higher. If some quality parameters are not provided (e.g. timestamp or location), then its information is more ambiguous and therefore its *Completeness* parameter is reduced. The *Availability* parameter describes how frequent a context provider was able to respond in time. This parameter is crucial when a smart object relies on only 1 provider. Together with the relevance value R_c of the context vector $\overrightarrow{c}$, the three subjective context quality parameters are used to determine an overall score $S_{P,\overrightarrow{c}}$ that defines a rank among the context providers:

$$S_{P,\overrightarrow{c}} = \frac{R_{\overrightarrow{c}}}{O_P \times A_P \times C_P} \geq 0$$

The smart object can then choose to use the value of the context provider with the lowest score $S_{P,\overrightarrow{c}}$ or to compute a weighted average value using these scores. The high-level overview of the algorithm is shown below:

Algorithm 1. SortContext(in: info[], **out:** context[], score[], irrelevant[])

```
(BoundingBox box, Vector optimalvector) = ComputeContextQualityBoundaries()
for each ContextItem ci in info do
    ci.vector.AlignContextVector(box)
    if (!box.Contains(ci.vector)) then
        ci.Move(info, irrelevant)
ContextItem[] outliers = info.ValueOutlierDetection()
outliers.UpdateSubjectiveParameters(box)
outliers.Move(info, irrelevant)
(context, score) = SortRescaledDistance(info, optimalvector)
```

3 Relevance Backpropagation in the Network

Our last contribution in this paper is a backpropagation mechanism to inform context providers in a large-scale and dynamic network architecture about the usage of their information. Proven technologies, such as Bloom filters [8], are used for efficient filtering of the information as close to the source as possible. Intermediate nodes will decide where to forward the information to based on feedback backpropagated by its peers. Whereas the algorithm in a neural network changes the weights of a neuron to converge the error in the output to a local minimum, does our backpropagation algorithm limit the information propagation in the network, possibly impeding the context provider completely from disseminating unused information.

A smart object forwards context information to adjacent smart objects, unless a maximum number of hops is reached. Each forwarding smart object reduces the hop counter, appends its UID to the message delivery chain, and marks the message if the information is relevant for its purposes. Backpropagation to the delivering peer is initiated whenever any of the following conditions arises:

- **Irrelevant context:** The smart object cannot use the context information for its own purposes (see Algorithm 1) and the maximum number of hops is reached or it has no other adjacent peers to forward to.
- **Unused context:** The context information is relevant along the delivery chain, but is not used that frequently. Inform the forwarding peer or the context provider to increase the transmission interval.
- **Duplicate detection:** The smart object has already received the information from another peer through a quicker trajectory. Stop sending the information along this path.

Bloom filters [8] – compact data structures for testing whether an element is part of a set – are used to check if the context information is invaluable for its own purposes and for propagation to adjacent smart objects. Algorithm 2 describes the backpropagation for context information delivery. When a *Duplicate* or *Irrelevant* backpropagation message is received, the smart object adjusts its forwarding filters. For an *Unused* message, the frequency of forwarding is reduced. The receiving peer backpropagates the message further down to the source using the labels in the message delivery chain.

Algorithm 2. BackpropagateRelevance(in: fromPeer, contextMessage)

```
(messageRelevant, messageUnused, messageForwarded) = (false, false, false)
if (InFilterReceived(contextMessage.ID)) then
   BackpropagateMessage(fromPeer, DUPLICATE, contextMessage.ID)
else
   AddFilterReceived(fromPeer, contextMessage.ID)
if (InFilterRelevant(contextMessage)) then
   messageRelevant = true
   if (InFilterUnused(contextMessage)) then
      messageUnused = true
      LabelMessage(contextMessage, UNUSED)
else
   LabelMessage(contextMessage, IRRELEVANT)
if (contextMessage.hopsLeft > 0) then
   contextMessage.hopsLeft = contextMessage.hopsLeft - 1
   for each Peer p in ForwardFilter(adjacentPeers, contextMessage.ID) do
      messageForwarded = true
      ForwardMessage(p, contextMessage)
if (not messageForwarded) then
   if (not messageRelevant) then
      BackpropagateMessage(fromPeer, IRRELEVANT, contextMessage.ID)
   else if (messageUnused) then
      BackpropagateMessage(fromPeer, UNUSED, contextMessage.ID)
```

4 Experimental Evaluation

Finding a realistic test scenario of a reasonable size without the detrimental side effects of a real-life network setup is not straightforward, especially for determining the significance of our algorithms on the outcome of the experiments. We therefore chose to simulate and compare the algorithms and mechanisms on an artificial network. The network is generated by means of a weighted location dependent wiring. For k nodes, the first one n_1 is situated in the center of a unit square. The other nodes n_j, $j = 2...k$, are randomly placed in the unit square and connected to at most m existing nodes n_i that each minimize a different function F_m:

$$F_m(n_i, n_j) = H(n_1, n_j) + w_m.D(n_i, n_j)$$

with H = number of hops to node n_1, D = Euclidean distance, and m different weights w_m = parameter that influences the geographical dependency.

4.1 Experiments

A network is generated with the following parameters: $k = 1000$ nodes, at most $m = 3$ connections with weights $w_1 = 10$, $w_2 = 5$, $w_3 = 1$, and about 100 nodes provide context information of which the characteristics are shown in Table 1. In this smart environment scenario, the *Movement* and *Wireless Body Sensors*, and the *Inhouse Thermometer* make use of the *Clocks* and *Position Beacons*

Table 1. Parametrization of the network architecture

Type	Quantity	Coverage	Update	Hops
Weather Forecast Website	5	1.0	30 min	100
Outside Weather Station	5	0.5	10 min	100
Clock	10	2.0	1 min	50
Movement Sensor	10	0.1	1 min	20
Inhouse Thermometer	10	0.1	5 min	10
Wireless Body Sensor	20	0.05	1 min	5
Position Beacon	40	0.05	2 min	3

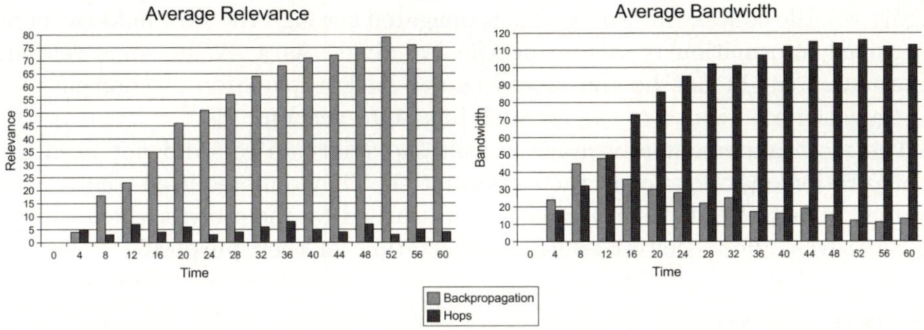

Fig. 4. Evolution of context information usage and throughput

to set their own timestamp and coverage. The *Wireless Body Sensor* is used to announce the presence of a particular person. The *Inhouse Thermometers* are used to control the central heating within a specific room related to the person that was detected. The *Clock* is also used to turn on the lights before 8:00 and after 18:00 if movement is detected in the current or nearby room.

The simulation environment assumes that all connections have similar characteristics. In the first experiment, the information is flooded in the network and only limited by the number of hops for forwarding. Filtering and backpropagation as proposed in this paper is applied in a second experiment using the same parameters and network. In Fig. 4 we compare the evolution of the average amount of valuable information for a smart object in the network (with and without backpropagation), and the average network load at a smart object.

4.2 Discussion of the Results

Clearly, the results of this experiment and the graphs in Fig. 4 are only relevant for this particular network parametrization. Nonetheless, for other experiments with different results in terms of absolute values, we could draw similar qualitative conclusions. The left figure shows that the average amount of relevant information (for a peer to which it forwards or for itself) increases up to 75%. This can be improved with larger Bloom filters. They have the characteristic of allowing false positives but no false negatives when testing membership. Bloom filters cannot handle the deletion of item either when forwarding requirements change. In that case, they are reinitialized which means that less valuable information is again being propagated.

During the initial learning phase, the backpropagation enabled scenario performs slightly worse due to backpropagation messages being sent to the delivering peers, as shown in the right figure. After the learning period, some context providers became inactive as their information was not being used, and others were limited to sending out information into certain directions. The experiment resulted into a significant drop in the overall bandwidth usage in the network.

However, we are aware that the current context propagation is not optimal. In the presence of high speed and low speed connections, it is possible that highly volatile context information is propagated through the slow links, whereas long-lived information is saturating the fast links. As a result, some relevant information might not be considered as our backpropagation mechanism does not take the bandwidth of the network links into account.

The most important advantage is that the smart objects did not need any configuration on where to get their information. They only required connectivity to other smart objects in the network and learned by themselves which context provider was able to deliver relevant information for their purposes.

5 Related Work

Buchholz *et al.* [9] identified parameters that quantify the quality of context and the uncertainty of sensed values. Henricksen *et al.* [10] identified similar imperfection aspects and proposed a graphical model and a software infrastructure for the management and use of imperfect context. In our research, we included extra parameters to explicitly deal with context distribution.

Chalmers *et al.* show in [11] how contextual information can be formulated in the presence of uncertainty using interval arithmetic for uncertain numerical context values. The authors define the *within* and *overlap* relationships to test whether a sensed value range is within a test range and to what degree two values overlap. Our work reuses the same idea in multiple dimensions, but their tree based approach differs from our semantic metric for abstract values.

Dey *et al.* [3] suggest to leverage off techniques such as Bayesian networks and neural networks, as these approaches cannot remove all the ambiguity of sensed information. The authors propose to involve mobile users in aware-environments for the refinement of imperfect context and for reducing ambiguity in context information through a process called mediation to deal with context conflicts. We envision that for large-scale networks this approach will be impractical.

6 Conclusions

In this paper, we have discussed several context quality parameters that affect the ambiguity and uncertainty of context information. We have shown how they can be represented in a multi-dimensional vector space model to allow a smart object to quickly decide whether any delivered context information is relevant for its purposes or not. We also discussed backpropagation support to provide feedback about the usefulness of the information for any of the smart objects in the network to the respective context providers. We have conducted experiments that illustrate that the amount of information that is propagated through the network but not needed by any of the smart objects on its path is significantly lower than for hop limited context propagation.

Part of our future work, is to take the timeliness of the context information into account to improve the usage of the network capacity. The goal is to achieve just in time context information delivery to the requesting smart objects. Further research will investigate how the bounding box model with its sharp boundaries can be improved by using a normal distribution of the requested context quality parameters, and how the efficiency of the relevance testing is affected.

References

1. International Telecommunication Union: ITU Internet Reports 2005: The Internet of Things 2005, 7th edition (2005)
2. Dey, A.K.: Understanding and Using Context. Personal Ubiquitous Comput. 5, 4–7 (2001)
3. Dey, A., Mankoff, J., Abowd, G., Carter, S.: Distributed mediation of ambiguous context in aware environments. In: UIST '02: Proceedings of the 15th annual ACM symposium on User interface software and technology, pp. 121–130. ACM Press, New York (2002)
4. Preuveneers, D., Berbers, Y.: Quality Extensions and Uncertainty Handling for Context Ontologies. In: Shvaiko, P., Euzenat, J., Léger, A., McGuinness, D.L., Wache, H., eds.: In: Proceedings of Context and Ontologies: Theory Practice and Applications (C&O, Riva del Garda, Italy (2006) pp. 62–64 (2006)
5. Wand, Y., Wang, R.Y.: Anchoring data quality dimensions in ontological foundations. Commun. ACM 39, 86–95 (1996)
6. Lee, Y.W., Strong, D.M., Kahn, B.K., Wang, R.Y.: AIMQ: a methodology for information quality assessment. Inf. Manage. 40, 133–146 (2002)
7. Hodge, V., Austin, J.: A Survey of Outlier Detection Methodologies. Artif. Intell. Rev. 22, 85–126 (2004)
8. Bloom, B.H.: Space/time trade-offs in hash coding with allowable errors. Commun. ACM 13, 422–426 (1970)
9. Buchholz, T., Kupper, A., Schiffers, M.: Quality of Context: What it is and why we need it. In: Proceedings of the 10th Workshop of the OpenView University Association: OVUA'03, Geneva, Switzerland (2003)
10. Henricksen, K., Indulska, J.: Modelling and Using Imperfect Context Information. In: PERCOMW '04: Proceedings of the Second IEEE Annual Conference on Pervasive Computing and Communications Workshops, Washington, DC, USA, p. 33. IEEE Computer Society, Los Alamitos (2004)
11. Chalmers, D., Dulay, N., Sloman, M.: Towards Reasoning About Context in the Presence of Uncertainty. In: Davies, N., Mynatt, E.D., Siio, I. (eds.) UbiComp 2004. LNCS, vol. 3205, Springer, Heidelberg (2004)

Managing Disclosure of Personal Health Information in Smart Home Healthcare

Umar Rashid, Hedda Schmidtke, and Woontack Woo

U-VR Lab, GIST
{urashid, schmidtk, wwoo}@gist.ac.kr

Abstract. Recent advances in ubiquitous computing have evoked the prospect of real-time monitoring of people's health in context-aware homes. Home is the most private place for people and health information is of highly intimate nature. Therefore, *users-at-home* must have means to benefit from home healthcare and preserve privacy as well. However, most smart home healthcare systems currently lack support for privacy management for home inhabitants. In this paper, we analyze the privacy needs of smart home inhabitants utilizing a healthcare system and present a conceptual framework to manage disclosure of their personal health information. The proposed framework supports sharing the most meaningful detail of personal health information at different time granularities with different recipients in different contexts. To relieve the burden of configuration, default disclosure settings are provided, and to ensure end-user's control over disclosure, the option to override default settings is included.

Keywords: Information disclosure, privacy, context awareness, home healthcare.

1 Introduction

The emerging advances in pervasive computing technologies hold great potential for improving people's quality of life. One of the most promising area of applications of these technologies is home healthcare [6, 15, 22]. In recent years, remote monitoring of patients in real-time via wearable health monitoring devices has become a special focus of interest [25]. Its promises notwithstanding, many researchers have expressed concerns about the potential privacy breaches associated with real-time health monitoring in home environment. Home remains the safest and the most private place for people [21] and health information is of highly sensitive nature as it can reveal intimate aspects about a person's life [11, 32]. Therefore, it is crucial to guarantee the respect of personal privacy in smart home healthcare [4, 22].

To date, most smart home health projects [6,15,22] have overlooked the privacy management for *users-at-home* in their design. We also found the current literature deficient in detail about guidelines how to incorporate privacy support in the design of smart home healthcare systems. To avail the promised benefits of home healthcare, smart home inhabitants should be able not only to prevent unwanted disclosure of

C. Stephanidis (Ed.): Universal Access in HCI, Part II, HCII 2007, LNCS 4555, pp. 188–197, 2007.

personal health information but moreover, to share the *most meaningful* details of information with different recipients in different contexts. In healthcare domain, trust refers to the competence as well as beneficence of the trustee [5]. We found most privacy models for ubiquitous computing systems [1, 9, 13, 17] insufficient for our purpose because they do not explicitly incorporate the competence of information recipients as a determinant for information disclosure.

In this paper, we first analyze the privacy requirements for end-users of smart home healthcare. Our analysis draws on studies in the domains of ubiquitous computing, and health information management, and on sociological readings on interpersonal relationships. Based on the requirement analysis, we construct a theoretical framework that helps the end-users manage the disclosure of personal health information in different contexts. The proposed framework is founded upon 5W1H (Who, Where, When, What, How and Why) context model proposed by Jang et al. [14]. In our application scenario, personal health information consists of raw physiological data that is collected via wearable sensors and processed stress level that is result of analysis of collected physiological data based on Oriental Medical Science [10]. To extract the most meaningful details about personal health information in emergency as well as normal situations, we classify the information at different time granularities using a variant of a clustering algorithm specified in [30]. To relieve the end-user of the burden of configuration, we provide default disclosure settings in changing contexts. However, to ensure that the end-user remains in control over the disclosure of his/her personal health information, we also include the option to override default settings.

The paper is organized as follows. In the section 2, we provide a requirement analysis for end-user's privacy in smart home healthcare. The conceptual framework to tackle privacy management in smart home healthcare is explained in section 3. Section 4 deals with an experimental demo illustrating our framework. We wrap up with a summary of current work and directions for future works in the section 5.

2 Privacy Requirements for Users of Smart Home Healthcare

Due to recent advances in ubicomp technologies, home healthcare is expected to become a usable means of health provision in the not so distant future. The concept of "smart home healthcare" deals with the use of sensors and actuators in home environment for real-time monitoring of occupants' health status. Many laboratories and companies are currently working on research projects in this field. Among these, some of the most prominent include the "Aware Home" at Georgia Institute of Technology [15], the "Center for Future Healthcare" at University of Rochester [6], and the "Intelligent Habitat for Health" at Faculty of Medicine of Grenoble [22]. However, to date, research in this domain has paid little attention to information systems and decision support for patients [16]. In particular, patients' perspective on privacy management in real-time health monitoring [4] remains under-explored in literature.

One of the prime challenges in personal health information management (PHIM) is "sharing information with individuals from social, professional, and health-care networks while maintaining personal privacy" [28]. Studies have emphasized the need for individuals' control over personal health information [31]. Surveys highlight the fact that many people consider their health information to be highly confidential [32], second only to financial information [11]. The 1993 Harris Equifax Health Information Privacy Survey found that 25% of the public scored high in general privacy concern, however, when measured specifically for medical privacy concern, 48% fell into the high concern position [12].

Use of wearable computing devices for real-time monitoring of health poses serious privacy issues for patients [20]. Real-time surveillance of personal health in home environment makes an individual's ability to preserve privacy more tenuous [4]. The classified nature of both the health information and the home signify the pressing importance of privacy management for users of smart home healthcare [21, 22]. An ethnographic study of a community living with ubiquitous computing [3] points out that:

- Users do not understand the possibilities and implications of privacy breaches in residential care.
- Users often forget that they are being monitored.
- Users trust the designers of a system to have protected them from unanticipated consequences.

The aforementioned findings indicate the gravity of the task before the system designers to offset potential privacy violations associated with home healthcare in ubiquitous computing environments. As stated by Adams and Sasse [1], "Most invasions of privacy are not intentional but due to designers' inability to anticipate how this data could be used, by whom, and how this may affect users". It is desirable to provide default privacy settings in the system to relieve the user of the burden of configuration [27]. It has also been noticed that most users are unlikely to change the default settings [27]. On the other hand, it is also important to empower people "to stipulate what information they project and who can get hold of it" [7]. Hence, the option to override default settings must be provided as well.

People's willingness to share information is likely to differ depending upon the kind of information and who is likely to view it [23]. Instead of a coarse-grained approach of denying/allowing access to personal information, ubiquitous computing systems must allow for granular control to fine-tune the details of disclosed information [13]. Patel et al. [26] discovered that most users rate family more trustworthy than the friends and colleagues. Chatfield et al [7] conducted a study to examine user's opinions on personal information exchange with an Intelligent Environment. They discovered that the biggest influence on a user's information sharing preferences was the existence of a prior relationship with the information recipient. In other words, the parameter of *social intimacy* is a determining factor in information sharing.

In the context of healthcare, trust refers to the "confidence in competence (skill and knowledge), as well as whether the trustee is working in the best interests of the trustor" [5]. People show high degree of trust in physicians to access their medical records while an overwhelming majority opposes their records to be shown to employers [11]. Confidentiality in patient-doctor relationship even outranks that in patient-family relationship [2]. Patients have high level of trust for their family physicians that gives them comfort to reveal personal and sensitive information [19, 31]. Patients reveal even those details about personal health to their doctors which they feel hesitant to share with their families. Moreover, many family members, because of low health literacy, may be unable to understand arcane technical details of health information. This suggests that in the matters of healthcare, people's willingness to share information is not only motivated by *social intimacy* to the recipient but also by the *competence* of the recipient.

Palen and Dourish [24] describe privacy management as a "dynamic response to circumstance rather than a static enforcement of rules". Lederer et al. found out that in ubiquitous computing, the recipient's identity is a stronger determinant of privacy preferences than the user's situation [18]. However, in ubicomp healthcare, users are likely to prefer privacy settings for normal situations to be set aside under emergency situations [13]. In an emergency, safety takes precedence over privacy, and most patients will probably choose a "confidentiality override policy" that would allow an authenticated healthcare provider to gain access to records that he/she would normally not be entitled to view [19]. Hence, disclosure settings of health information in smart home healthcare must make room for adapting to the changes in the user's situation.

Based upon the abovementioned observations, we specify the criteria to assess what constitutes *the most useful* information to be disclosed to a particular recipient under a particular situation in smart home healthcare. Our conclusion is that such decision is determined by the following factors:

- Social intimacy between the end-user and the recipient
- Competence of the recipient
- Situation of the end-user

3 Personal Health Information Disclosure Management

Based on the analysis of privacy needs of end-users of smart home healthcare, we present a conceptual framework that helps them manage disclosure of personal information. We use the user-centric context model of Jang et al [14] to represent the constituents of our proposed framework. According to this context model, context information is organized using the categories of involved users ('Who'), spatial circumstance ('Where'), time ('When'), involved objects, pieces of information, and services ('What'), current state ('How'), and further information on causes for user interaction ('Why'). The following components of 5W1H (Who, Where, When, What, How and Why) context model [14] are utilized for Personal Health Information Disclosure Management (PHIDM) framework:

- Personal Health Information ('What')
- Situation of the end-user represented by his/her stress level in one-minute-interval ('How')
- Competence of the information recipient ('Who')
- Intimacy between the information recipient and the end-user ('Who')

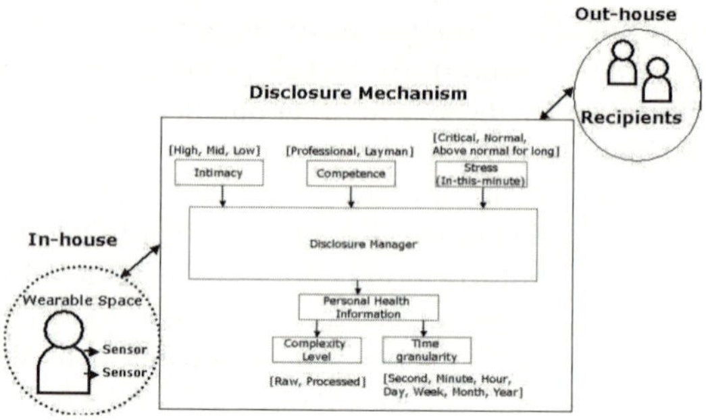

Fig. 1. Framework for Personal Health Information Disclosure Management (PHIDM)

The inputs and outputs of the disclosure mechanism are illustrated in Fig. 1. Personal health information is classified into two categories with respect to its complexity level i.e.

- Raw - physiological data ('Expert' information)
- Processed - stress level data ('Layperson' information)

Raw data consists of galvanic skin response, pulse rate, and temperature of the patient collected via wearable sensors. Processed information (stress level) is obtained by interpreting this raw data on the basis of Oriental Medical Science analysis [10].

Taking cue from Rogers et al [29], the granularity of disclosed information is set to day (24 hours) level, under normal situations. To provide a more in-depth view of the end-user's situation at different temporal granularities (second, minute, hour, day, week, month, year), we apply a variant of clustering mechanism derived from the specification provided in [30]. This corresponds to '*details-on-demand*' functionality proposed by Chittaro [8] that allows for visualization of patient's medical record at different temporal granularities on mobile devices.

Situation of the end-user is represented by the level of his/her stress during one-minute-level intervals as follows:

- Normal
- Above-normal over long duration
- Critical

Competence refers to the recipient's skills and knowledge to comprehend health information, and is categorized as:

- Professional (healthcare professionals)
- Layperson (non-healthcare people)

Based on the studies about interpersonal relations [2, 18, 23, 26] and health information privacy [11, 19, 31], we specify three levels of intimacy between the recipient and the end-user as given below:

- High (family physician, significant others, close family members)
- Medium (emergency healthcare staff, close friends)
- Low (colleagues, employers, acquaintances that need to be informed in critical situations)

Under normal situation, access to personal health information is provided *on demand* only, however, in other situations, the recipients are *notified* and provided information according to the default settings. If not overridden by the end-user, the default disclosure settings operate as follows:

If the user's stress level is critical

- Notify the High, Medium and Low intimacy contacts
- Set time granularity of disclosed information to one-minute-interval
- Set complexity of information with respect to competence of the recipient

Else if the user's stress level is above-normal for long duration

- Notify High and Medium intimacy contacts
- Set time granularity of disclosed information to the largest interval of above-normal stress (hour, day, week, month, year)
- Set complexity of information with respect to competence of the recipient

Else if the user's stress level is normal

- Allow access for information only to High intimacy contacts
- Set time granularity of disclosed information to day
- Set complexity of information with respect to competence of the recipient

The illustration of disclosure management algorithm under the modes of '*access on demand*' and '*notification*' are shown in Figs. 2.a and 2.b respectively.

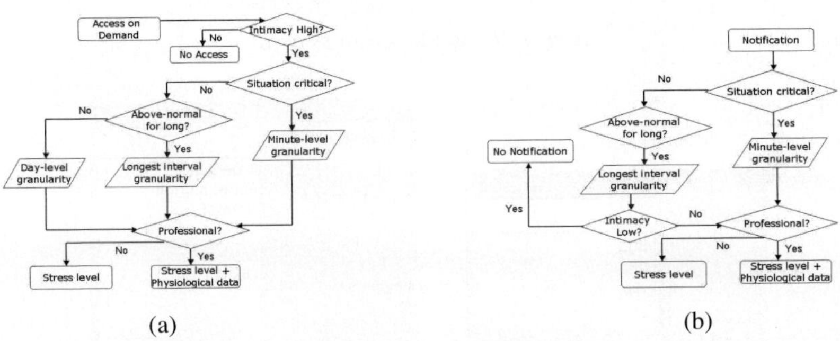

Fig. 2. Illustration of disclosure management algorithm (a). Access on Demand (b). Notification.

The physiological data of a patient (e.g. pulse rate, galvanic skin response) can be *meaningful information* to be shared with doctors. However, this information remains arcane to family members and coworkers (because of their low health literacy). Hence, it is *meaningful* to let them know about interpreted stress condition only. Similarly, it is reasonable to share stress information with employers and coworkers in an emergency. But otherwise, it is not desirable to let them access personal health information. Moreover, in an emergency situation, it is *most meaningful* for the user to disclose up-to-date, fine-grained information about stress condition, therefore, setting granularity to "minute" level. In normal situation, coarse-grained information about long-term trends of user's stress condition becomes *most meaningful*, hence, setting the granularity to "Day" level.

4 Experimental Demo

In our experimental demo, physiological data of end-users is collected from a wearable wrist type sensor system including a PPG sensor, a GSR sensor and an SKT sensor, as shown in Fig. 3. Collected data is sent to an Ultra-Mobile Personal Computer (UMPC) via blue tooth connection and interpreted into stress level on the basis of Oriental Medical Science analysis [10]. Interface to specify intimacy levels and user-specified settings (i.e. overrule the default settings) are provided on the end-user's UMPC as shown in Fig. 4. Competence of the recipients is determined by their profiles stored on their respective UMPCs.

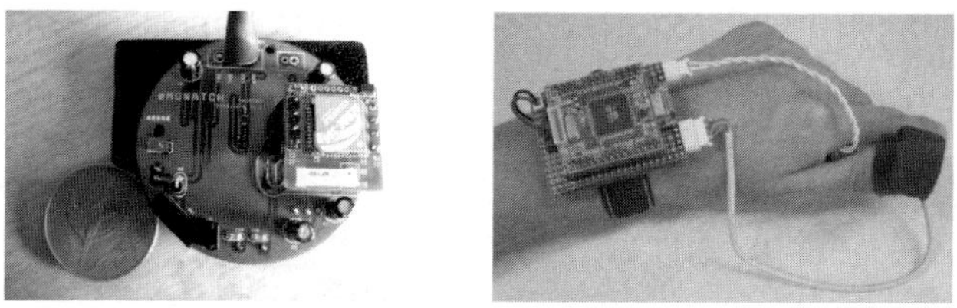

Fig. 3. Wearable sensor system

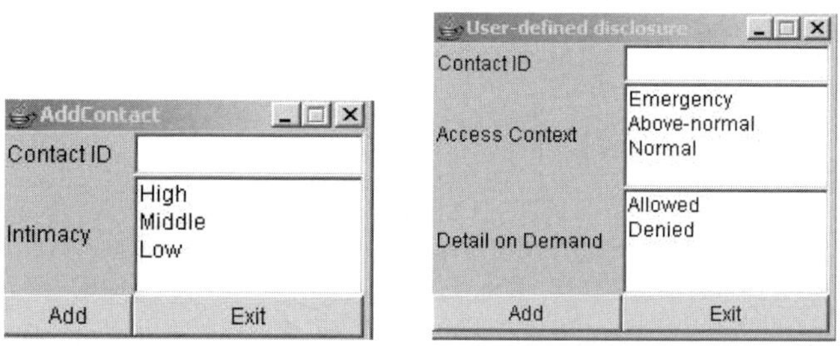

(a) (b)

Fig. 4. End-user's interface to (a) specify intimacy level of recipients (b) user-specified disclosure settings (i.e. overrule default settings)

Figure 4 shows the stress information being shown on the device of personal physician and Fig. 5 illustrates the stress information to be displayed on the device of family members (competence: 'layman' level). Figure 6 shows the data to be displayed on the devices of emergency healthcare staff under emergency situation.

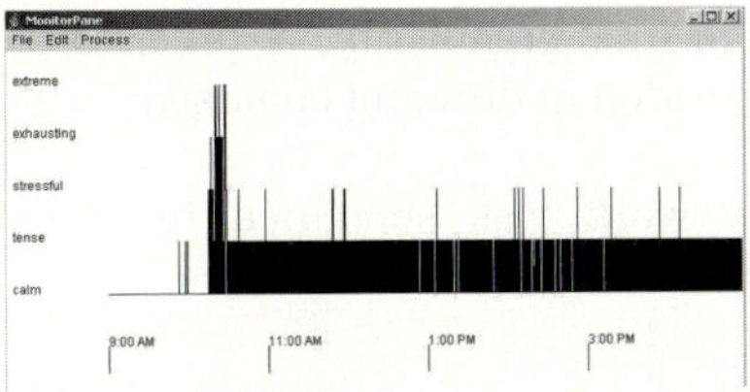

Fig. 5. Data accessible to personal physician

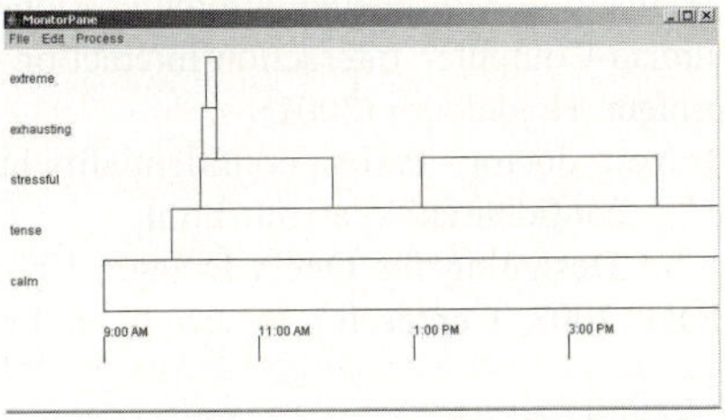

Fig. 6. Data accessible to family members (Competence level: layman)

Fig. 7. Data accessible to emergency healthcare staff and employers etc. (Intimacy level: Middle or Low)

5 Conclusions and Future Works

In this paper, we analyzed the privacy requirements for end-users of smart home healthcare and presented a conceptual framework for managing disclosure of personal health information. The primary aim of the proposed framework is not to prevent disclosure of user's health information but to share the most meaningful detail with different recipients in different contexts. It allows for fine-grained control over disclosure of health information, adapts disclosure rules with respect to end-user's context, and provides default disclosure settings to relieve end-users of the burden of configuration. The framework also includes the option to override the default disclosure rules for specific recipients and specific situations.

In future works, we intend to broaden the mechanism of personal information disclosure management from smart home to a ubiquitous smart space. In that scenario, the scope of personal information is not limited to health information but also encompass e.g. location information. This will call for taking spatial granularity into account, in addition to time granularity, in order to determine what is the *most meaningful* personal information in different contexts.

Acknowledgments. This work was supported by Seondo project, Ministry of Information and Communication, Republic of Korea.

References

1. Adams, A., Sasse, A.: Privacy in Multimedia communications: Protecting users, not just data. In: Joint Proc. Human-Computer Interaction/Interaction d'Homme-Machine (IMH-HCI 01), pp. 49–64. Springer, Heidelberg (2001)
2. BBC Health - Talking to your doctor - Patient confidentiality http://www.bbc.co.uk/health/talking_to_your_doctor/gp_confidentialitypatient.shtml
3. Beckwith, R., Lederer, S.: Designing for One's Dotage: Ubicomp and Residential Care Facilities. In: Proc. HOIT 2003, Center for Research on Information Technology and Organizations (2003)
4. Blanchard, J.: Ethical considerations of Home Monitoring Technology. Home. Health Care. Technology Report 53(4), 63–64 (2004)
5. Calnan, M., Row, R.: Trust Relations in the new NHS: theoretical and methodological challenges. Taking Stock of Trust E.S.R.C Conference, LSE (2005)
6. Center for Future Healtth http://www.futurehealth.rochester.edu/
7. Chatfield, C., Häkkilä, J.: Designing Intelligent Environments - User Perceptions on Information Sharing. In: Proceedings of the Asia-Pacific Conference on Computer and Human Interactions, pp. 570–574 (2004)
8. Chittaro, L.: Visualization of Patient Data at. Different Temporal Granularities on Mobile Devices. In: Proc. of AVI, pp. 484–487 (2006)
9. Mather, B.V., Sellen, A.: Design for privacy in ubiquitous computing environments. In: Proc. ECSCW (1993)
10. Choi, A., Rashid, U., Woontack, W.: Context-based user adaptive physiological signal analysis. In: Proc. KHCI, pp. 960–965 (2006)
11. Gallup Organization. Public attitudes towards privacy (2000)
12. Harris-Equifax.: Consumer privacy survey, conducted for Equifax by Louis Harris and Associates in association with Dr Alan Westin of Columbia University.Atlanta, GA: Equifax (1996)
13. Hong, J.I., Landay, J.A.: An architecture for privacy-sensitive ubiquitous computing. In: Proc. MobiSys 2004, pp. 177–189. ACM Press, New York (2004)
14. Jang, S., Woo, W.: Unified Context Representing User-Centric Context: Who, Where, When, What, How and Why. ubiComp workshop (ubiPCMM), pp. 26–34 (2005)
15. Kidd, C.D., Orr, R.J, Abowd, G.D., Atkesson, C.G., Essa, I.A., MacIntyre, B., Mynatt, E., Starner, T.E., Newsletter, W.: The aware Home: A living Laboratory for ubiquitous computing research. In: Proc. CoBuild'99 (October 1999)
16. Koch, S.: Home Telehealth - current state and future trends. Elsevier International Journal of Medical Informatics (2005)
17. Lederer, S., Mankoff, J., Dey, A., Beckman, C.: Managing Personal Information Disclosure in Ubiquitous Computing Environments. Technical Report IRB-TR-03-015, Intel Research Berkley (2003)
18. Lederer, S., Mankoff, J., Dey, A.: Who Wants to Know What When? Privacy Preference Determinants in Ubiquitous Computing. Extended Abstracts of CHI, pp. 724–725 (2003)

19. Mandl, K.D., Szolovits, P., Kohane, I.S., Markwell, D., MacDonald, R.: Public standards and patients' control: how to keep electronic medical records accessible but private. BMJ 322 7281, 283–287 (2001)
20. Martin, T., Jovanov, E., Raskovic, D.: Issues in Wearable Computing for Medical Monitoring Applications: A Case Study of a Wearable ECG Monitoring Device. In: Proc. 4th Int. Symposium on Wearable Computers, pp. 43–49 (2000)
21. Meyer, S., Rakotonirainy, A.: A Survey of Research On Context-aware Homes. In: Proc. Australasian Information Security Workshop Conference on ACWS Frontiers, pp. 159–168 (2003)
22. Noury, N., Virone, G., Barralon, P., Rialle, V., Demongeot J.: New trends in health smart homes: technological possibilities, societal concerns, economical constraints. In: IEEE Transactions on Information Technology in Biomedicine (TITB-119-2003)
23. Olson, J.S., Grudin, J., Horvitz, E.: A study of preferences for sharing and privacy. In: Extended Abstracts CHI2005, pp. 1985–1988. ACM Press, New York (2005)
24. Palen, L., Dourish, P.: Unpacking Privacy for a Networked World. In: Proc. CHI 2003, pp. 129–136. ACM Press, New York (2003)
25. Park, S., Jayaraman, S.: Enhancing the quality of life through wearable technology. IEEE Engineering in Medicine and Biology Magazine 22(3), 41–48 (2003)
26. Patel, S., Lai, J.: Who gets to know what when: configuring privacy permissions in an awareness application. In: Proc. CHI 2005, pp. 101–110. ACM Press, New York (2005)
27. Patil, S., Kobsa, A.: Designing with Privacy in Mind. Position paper for Workshop on Awareness Systems: Known Results, Theory, Concepts and Future Challenges. In: Proc. CHI (2005)
28. Pratt, W., Unruh, K., Civan, A., Skeels, M.: Personal Health Information Management. Communications of the ACM, Special Issue on Personal Information Management 49(1), 51–55 (2006)
29. Rogers, M.A.M., Buchan, D.A., Small, D., Stewart, C.M., Krenzer, B.E.: Telemedicine improves diagnosis of essential hypertension compared with usual care. Journal of Telemedicine and Telecare, pp. 344–349 (2002)
30. Schmidtke, H.R.: Aggregations and constituents: geometric specification of multi-granular objects. Journal of Visual Languages & Computing 16(4), 289–309 (2005)
31. Smit, M., McAllister, M., Slonim, J.: Privacy of electronic health records: Public opinion and practicalities. NAEC (2005)
32. Westin A.: How the public views health privacy: survey findings from 1978 to 2005. Privacy & American Business (2005) www.pandab.org/HealthSrvyRpt.pdf

Intelligent Privacy Support for Large Public Displays

Carsten Röcker[1], Steve Hinske[2], and Carsten Magerkurth[1]

[1] Fraunhofer IPSI, AMBIENTE – Smart Environments of the Future
Dolivostraße 15, D-64293 Darmstadt, Germany
{roecker,magerkurth}@ipsi.fraunhofer.de
[2] Institute for Pervasive Computing, ETH Zürich
Clausiusstr. 59, 8092 Zürich, Switzerland
steve.hinske@inf.ethz.ch

Abstract. This paper presents a novel concept for personalized privacy support on large public displays. In a first step, a formative evaluation was conducted in order to analyze the requirements of potential users regarding the protection of private information on large public displays. The insights gained in this evaluation were used to design a system, which automatically adapts the information visible on public displays according to the current social situation and the individual privacy preferences of the user working on the display. The developed system was evaluated regarding its appropriateness for daily usage and its usefulness to protect privacy.

Keywords: Large Public Displays, Intelligent Privacy Support, Smart Environments, Privacy-Enhancing Technologies, Context-Adapted Information Representation, Evaluation.

1 Introduction

The concept of Ambient Intelligence propagates a vision of future environments where people are supported and assisted in their everyday activities by information technologies that are very different from the computer as we know it today (Röcker at al., 2005). The envisioned technologies "will weave themselves into the fabric of everyday life until they are indistinguishable from it" (Weiser, 1991). By making numerous computers available throughout the physical environment, people are enabled and enticed to move around and interact with computers more naturally than they currently do. Instead of using traditional computers or personal mobile devices, users can access information using computational devices embedded into the environment.

As ubiquitously available displays are about to become an integral part of smart home environments, several projects aim at providing users with personalized services and information on large public displays. Many of these services are intended to provide walk-up-and-use functionality, like quickly accessing e-mails or the internet. When using such applications on large displays in public areas, the possibility of other people being able to see confidential information inevitably causes privacy concerns. Empirical evidence shows that these concerns are justified:

C. Stephanidis (Ed.): Universal Access in HCI, Part II, HCII 2007, LNCS 4555, pp. 198–207, 2007.

exploring the influence of the display size on privacy infringements, Tan and Czerwinski (2003) found that, even given constant visual angles and similar legibility, individuals are more likely to read text on a large display than on a small one. In addition to that, several other studies reported similar results and emphasized the importance of informational privacy, both in the office and in the home domain. Nevertheless, most developers still rely on social protocols or do not address privacy questions at all, when designing applications for large public displays. Until today, there are very few approaches that support users in preserving their privacy while working on large displays in public places.

2 Formative Evaluation of User Requirements

In order to provide trusted mechanisms for privacy protection, it is most crucial to involve potential users right away from the beginning of the design process. Therefore, a formative evaluation was conducted to analyse the requirements of users regarding the protection of private information when using large public displays. The goal of this evaluation was to investigate how automated protection mechanisms influence the usage of large displays in public environments.

2.1 Materials and Methods

To elicit feedback from the target user population, a scenario-driven approach was chosen. During a questionnaire-based evaluation, different scenarios were presented to the participants in a three-step process. First, and prior to the presentation of the main scenarios, the participants were asked to assess the suitability of large displays in public areas. Therefore, examples of different applications and information types were presented to the participants, which had to be rated on a five-point scale.

In the second part of the evaluation, the participants were asked to visualize a scenario, where they are working on a large public display located in a hallway of an office building. Since the display (or, more explicitly, the computer it is connected to) is integrated in the company network, the display can be used as a desktop replacement (i.e., all standard application are running on it). The scenario describes a situation, where several application windows (for example, an internet browser, a document viewer, and an e-mail program) are displayed on the public display. At the end of the scenario, the participants were explicitly reminded that passers-by are likely to see what they are doing, but also that these passers-by are mostly colleagues (i.e., people they are familiar with). In the following questions, they were asked to assess their perceived privacy while working on the display, to specify applications they would use in such a situation, and to rate the suitability of large public displays for accessing public as well as private information.

Besides this general information, we aimed at gaining specific feedback on how automated privacy protection would influence the usage of large displays in public environments. Therefore, the initial scenario was extended with a fictitious system, which automatically protects the privacy of users working on the display. The described system protects individual user privacy by automatically hiding sensitive information when other people approach the display. The participants, however, were asked not to care *how* this is achieved, but focus on the fact that they can work on the display without being afraid of potential privacy infringements.

The questions presented in the previous part were adapted to the extended scenario and had to be answered under the light of a generic privacy protection system that unobtrusively works in the background. In addition to that, the participants were asked to assess the usefulness of the presented approach and to answer several questions concerning the interface requirements of automated privacy protection systems.

2.2 Participants

Altogether, N=55 people participated in the evaluation. The gender and age distribution are shown in Tab. 1.

Table 1. Gender and age distribution of the participants

Gender Distribution			Age Distribution					
Male	Female	Total	<25	25-34	35-44	45-54	>54	Total
36	19	55	16	22	4	9	4	55
65,45%	34,55%	100, 00%	29,09%	40,00%	7,27%	16,36%	7,27%	100,00%

In addition to the standard demographical information, the participants were asked to assess their technical experience (see Tab. 2).

Table 2. Technical experience of the participants

Very Experienced	Experienced	Average	Not Very Experienced	No Experience	Total
13	16	17	7	2	55
23,64%	29,09%	30,91%	12,73%	3,64%	100,00%

It is worth noticing that in most cases there were no or only slight differences between the demographical groups.

2.3 Results

Above all, we wanted the participants to provide us with information about how suitable they consider large displays in public areas in general (see Fig. 1). We listed six applications for large public displays that had to be rated on a scale ranging from 1 (very suitable) to 5 (totally unsuitable).

Over 80% of the participants considered large displays to be suitable or very suitable for displaying rather public or general content such as advertisements or traffic information. In the case of entertainment-related content or presentations, the majority (over 60%) still classified large public displays as suitable or very suitable.

The remaining two applications, namely desktop replacement and internet browsing, however, turned out to be rather unsuitable for being displayed on large public displays: more than half the interviewees considered them to be unsuitable or even absolutely unsuitable.

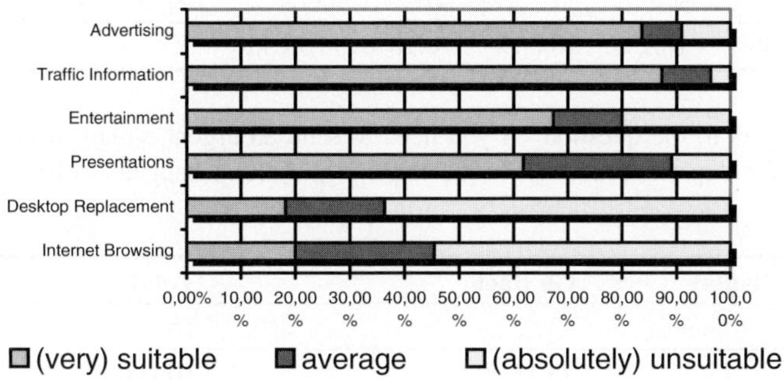

Fig. 1. Results to the answers "How suitable do you consider large displays for the following application: *app*" with *app* ∈ {advertising, traffic information, entertainment, presentations, desktop replacement, internet browsing}. The applications had to be rated on a scale from 1 (very suitable) to 5 (absolutely unsuitable).

Based on the aforementioned scenario, where the participants were asked to imagine the situation of being within a office hallway working on a large public display, we asked the participants how comfortable they would feel, using such a large display in the described situation. Less than 10% stated that they would feel comfortable or even very comfortable (see Tab. 3).

Table 3. Answers to the question "Would you feel comfortable using a large public display in an office hallway in general?", rated on a scale from 1 (very comfortable) to 5 (absolutely uncomfortable)

1	2	3	4	5	Total	Mean	Variance	Std. Error
2	3	21	14	15	55	3,67	1,0929	1,0454
3,64%	5,45%	38,18%	25,45%	27,27%	100,00%			

We further asked them whether they would use the large display for viewing e-mails or documents of private content (e.g., an e-mail from a family member). The question had to be rated from 1 (yes, always) to 5 (no, never). The result was very distinct, but not yet surprising: almost all participants would rather not use a large public display for viewing private content.

Finally, we asked the participants to consider the case in which they have to immediately send an urgent e-mail of private nature. In the described scenario, the large display is right next to them, compared to their own office, which is a few minutes away. The question was, whether they would prefer to use the large public display or rather go back to their private desktop computer instead.

Table 4. Answers to the question "Would you use the large display for viewing private content?", rated on a scale from 1 (yes, always) to 5 (no, never)

1	2	3	4	5	Total	Mean	Variance	Std. Error
0	0	1	11	43	55	4,76	0,2169	0,4657
0,00%	0,00%	1,82%	20,00%	78,18%	100,00%			

Table 5. Answers to the question "If you need to send an urgent e-mail, would you rather go back to your desktop computer or use the large display (that happens to be spatially close to you)?"

Use Large Display	Go Back	Total
12	43	55
21,82%	78,18%	100,00%

Almost 80% would rather go all the way back to their desktop computer instead of using the public computer system directly next to them. The fact that a *private* e-Mail needs to be sent certainly is the main reason for this result. Furthermore, it is worth mentioning that the answer depended on the *technical experience*: while only less than 8% of the *very experienced* users would use the large display, more than 23% of the users that are *not very experienced* and 28% of the users that have *no experience* would use the large display.

Table 6. Answers to the question "How important is privacy to you in general?", rated on a scale from 1 (very important to 5 (not important at all)

1	2	3	4	5	Total	Mean	Variance	Std.
29	24	1	0	1	55	1,55	0,5025	0,7089
52,73%	43,64%	1,82%	0,00%	1,82%	100,00%			

In this context, we asked the participants how important privacy was to them in general. Similar to the scales before, the participants could express their preferences on a scale from 1 (very important) to 5 (not at all important). Again, the results were not really surprising as almost all participants considered privacy to be important or very important (see Tab. 6).

Summing up the results, the evaluation showed that users are largely concerned with their privacy and that they are rather reluctant to use large public displays, at least without proper protection against possible privacy infringements.

In the last part of the evaluation, we extended the initial scenario and asked the participants to imagine that there would be "some kind" of privacy protection system available that is able to protect their privacy by hiding private or sensitive content whenever other people approach the large public display. In the first part of this second questionnaire we explicitly requested them to disregard *how* the system works, but to rather be not afraid of privacy infringements. We then repeated the questions of whether they would feel generally comfortable with using the large public display (Fig. 2), and whether they would use the display for displaying public and private content (Fig. 3). The light bars stand for the answers if no privacy protection system is available while the dark bars represent the existence of such a system.

In case of public content, a system designed to prevent privacy infringement resulted in the frequency of participants willing to use a large public display to almost sextuple from 5,45% to 30,91% regarding answer 1 (yes, always).

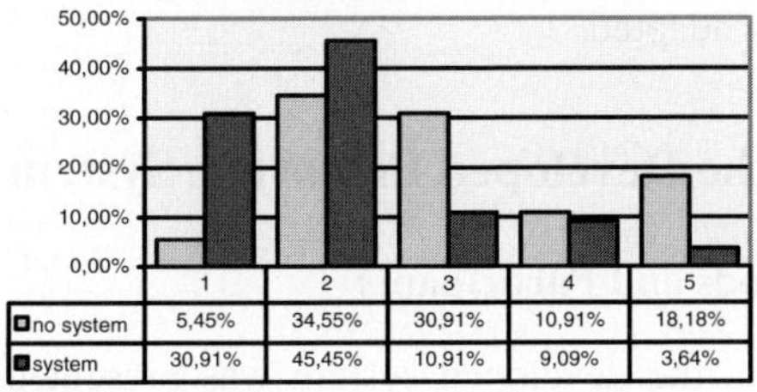

Fig. 2. Answers to the question "Would you use a large *public* display depending on whether a privacy protection system is available?", both rated on a scale from 1 (yes, always) to 5 (no, never)

In the case of private content, the result is even more obvious and distinct: while almost 80% of the participants answered that they would never (answer 5) use a large display for viewing private documents without a privacy protection system, this number shrunk to 20% given such a system. Summarizing all the listed and discussed results, it is evident that the provision of a privacy protection system can significantly increase the users' trust when using a large display in public environments.

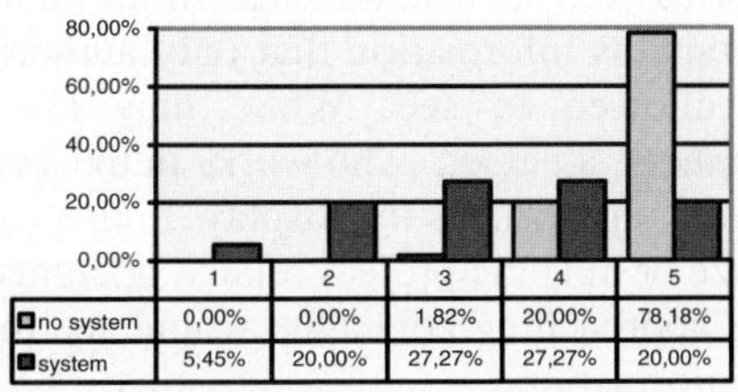

Fig. 3. Answers to the question "Would you use a large *private* display depending on whether a privacy protection system is available?", both rated on a scale from 1 (yes, always) to 5 (no, never)

3 Active Privacy Support for Large Public Displays

The insights gained in the evaluation were used to design a system for automated privacy support on large public displays. The developed application called SPIROS (see Röcker at al., 2006) gives users the freedom to spontaneously work on large public displays, without the fear of privacy infringements through passers-by. The system automatically controls the information that is visible to others, without requiring users to employ any additional equipment. This is achieved by providing users with a 'private space' in front of large displays in a shared environment. Within that personal space, the information that is visible to others is automatically controlled according to the user's individual preferences. In order to adapt the information representation to the current context, people entering the private space around a public display are automatically detected and identified using infrared and RFID technology. Based on the identity of the person(s) entering the private space and the privacy preferences of the user working on the public display, the information currently visible is automatically adapted.

4 Evaluation of the Developed Prototype System

4.1 Materials, Methods and Participants

In a second evaluation, the developed system was presented to the same group of persons who already participated in the first study. This time, the participants were asked to rate the conceptual approach as well as the implemented protection mechanisms regarding their appropriateness for daily usage and their usefulness to protect privacy.

The first part of the questionnaire briefly described the developed system. It was explained that the system scans the environment and is able to detect people passing-by the display. It is further illustrated how users can classify documents and applications and assign special actions that will be executed by the system if other persons approach the display.

For a better understanding, a concrete situation was described in form of a scenario. The participants were asked to imagine a situation, were they are viewing a project-related document as well as a news page in an additional browser window. The project document contains information that only authorized people (in this case project members) are allowed to see. While they are browsing through the confidential project document, a person, who works in the same company, but is not a member of the project team, approaches the display. In this case, the presented system would be able to minimize or hide the project-related document, but leave the browser window open. Thus, the approaching colleague would see the news website, but not the confidential project information.

4.2 Results

We first wanted to know, how comfortable the participants would feel using SPIROS compared to other approaches. Therefore, the participants were asked to rate the different approaches on a scale from 1 (very comfortable) to 5 (absolutely uncomfortable).

Figure 4 basically discloses two things:

- There is a tremendous difference between having a privacy protection system or not, and
- Users are more comfortable with the idea of using SPIROS than using *any* system.

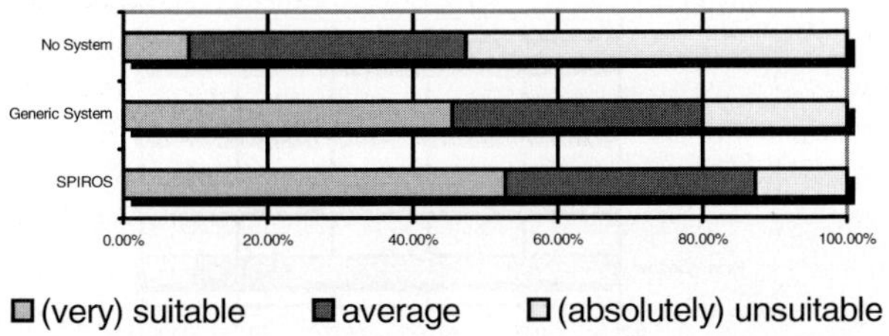

Fig. 4. Answers to the question "How comfortable would you feel working on a large display in a public environment?", rated on a scale from 1 (very comfortable) to 5 (absolutely uncomfortable)

The first premise is rather obvious: while the majority of the users would feel rather uncomfortable if no system was installed (answers *4* and *5*), only 20% felt the same way if there is a system available. The second point is less obvious but still visible: comparing the statistic means and variances of each distribution, the observable differences demonstrate the supremacy of our approach (see Tab. 7).

Table 7. Mean and Variance of the question "How comfortable would you feel working on a large display in a public environment?", rated on a scale from 1 (very comfortable) to 5 (absolutely uncomfortable)

Type of Privacy Protection	Mean	Variance
No System	3,67	1,0929
Generic System	2,67	0,8747
SPIROS	2,42	0,8615

Thus, it is not surprising that the majority would use our system: more than two third (67%) are willing to protect their privacy with SPIROS when asked whether they would use our system (the participants could answer with "yes" and "no").

Very important was also the assessment of the possible measures that can be taken by our system. We proposed four possible actions (in the order of increasing privacy protection potential) that had to be rated from 1 (very good) to 5 (very poor):

- "Show Message" (a pop-up message saying "someone is approaching" is displayed),
- "Cover Window" (a cover window with harmless content pops us and covers private or sensitive information),
- "Minimize Window" (all windows that currently display private or sensitive content are minimized), and
- "Hide Window" (completely hides all windows displaying sensitive content, i.e., they are not even visible in the task bar).

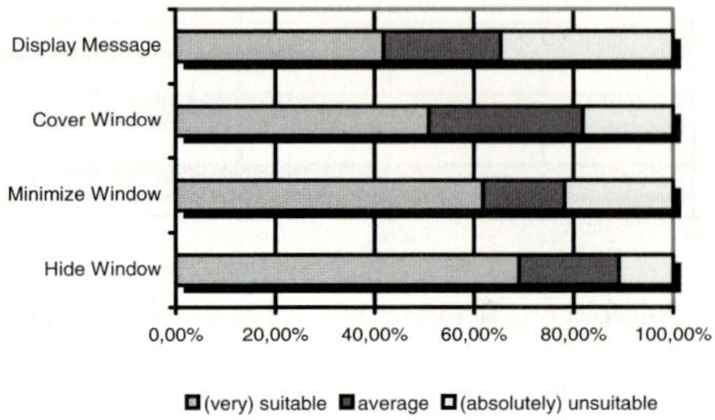

Fig. 5. Answers to the question "What do you think of each possible action?", rated on a scale from 1 (very good) to 5 (very poor)

We were rather curious to find out which action would be liked best. The feedback on displaying a message was relatively balanced: obviously, people see this action very differently. The other three actions received a better feedback: more than 50% considered the cover window to be very good or good, more than 60% thought the same of minimizing, and even approx. 70% found hiding to be very good or good. Apparently, the complete hiding of private or confidential information pleases the participants the most.

Finally, we wanted to know whether the participants would generally use SPIROS (see Tab. 8). Giving the previous findings, it is not surprising that the majority would use our system: more than two third (67%) are willing to protect their privacy with the system presented above.

Table 8. Answers to the question "Would you use such a system?"

Yes	No	Total
37	18	55
67,27%	32,73%	100,00%

The evaluation disclosed that people are much more willing to use large displays in office hallways if a privacy protection system is available and even much more so if it is SPIROS. The high user acceptance is based on the good protection of their privacy: a well and unobtrusively installed solution (i.e., if the scanners and sensors well installed and adjusted) is able to provide privacy on a very high level. This fact builds the basis for gaining the users' trust and mostly takes away their fear of using large displays in public environments.

5 Conclusion

In this paper we presented a novel concept for personalized privacy support on large public displays. In a first step, a formative evaluation was conducted in order to analyze the requirements of potential users regarding the protection of private information on large public displays. The insights gained in this evaluation were used to design a system, which automatically adapts the information visible on public displays according to the current social situation and the individual privacy preferences of the user working at the display. In a second evaluation, the developed system was evaluated regarding its appropriateness for daily usage and its usefulness to protect privacy. The results of the evaluation showed, that users are in general willing to trust system-based protection mechanisms, provided that they are well implemented. The proposed combination of pre-defined privacy profiles and context-adapted information visualization proofed to be a good trade-off between usability and adequate privacy protection.

References

Röcker, C., Hinske, S., Magerkurth, C.: SPIROS - A System for Privacy-Enhanced Information Representation in Smart Home Environments. In: Proceedings of the Second International Conference on Intelligent Environments (IE'06), Athens, Greece, pp. 267–274 (July 5 – 6, 2006)

Röcker, C., Janse, M., Portolan, N., Streitz, N.A.: User Requirements for Intelligent Home Environments: A Scenario-Driven Approach and Empirical Cross-Cultural Study. In: Proceedings of Smart Objects & Ambient Intelligence (sOcEUSAI'05), Grenoble, France, pp. 111–116 (October 12th-14th, 2005)

Tan, D.S., Czerwinski, M.: Information Voyeurism: Social Impact of Physically Large Displays on Information Privacy. In: Extended Abstracts of the ACM Conference on Human Factors in Computing Systems (CHI'03), pp. 748 – 749 (2003)

Weiser, M.: The Computer for the 21st Century. Scientific American 265(3), 66–75 (1991)

Universal Access Issues in an Ambient Intelligence Research Facility

Constantine Stephanidis[1,2], Margherita Antona[1], and Dimitrios Grammenos[1]

[1] Foundation for Research and Technology – Hellas (FORTH), Institute of Computer Science, Heraklion, GR-70013, Greece
cs@ics.forth.gr
[2] University of Crete, Department of Computer Science

Abstract. An Ambient Intelligence Research Facility is being set up at ICS-FORTH, with the goal of providing an experimentation platform for Ambient Intelligence (AmI) technologies and for studying their potential impact on users as individuals and as society. This paper discusses the opportunities that such a facility will offer towards the investigation of AmI from a Universal Access perspective, focusing in particular on issues related to Design for All.

Keywords: Ambient Intelligence, Research Infrastructure, Universal Access, Design for All.

1 Introduction

AmI presents a vision of a not too distant future where "intelligent" environments react in an attentive, adaptive and (pro)active way to the presence and activities of humans and objects in order to provide appropriate services to the inhabitants of these environments. It is an emerging field of research and development that is rapidly gaining wide attention by an increasing number of researchers and practitioners worldwide, and in Europe in particular [1]. Additionally, the notion of AmI is becoming a de facto key dimension of the emerging Information Society, since many of the new generation industrial digital products and services are clearly shifted towards an overall intelligent computing environment.

From a technological point of view, AmI targets to distribute, embed, coordinate and interactively deliver computing intelligence within the surrounding environment. AmI technologies integrate sensing capabilities, processing power, reasoning mechanisms, networking facilities, applications and services, digital content, and actuating capabilities distributed in the surrounding environment. AmI will have profound consequences on the type, content and functionality of the emerging products and services, as well as on the way people will interact with them, bringing about multiple new requirements for the development of the Information Society (e.g., [2, 3, 4]). While a wide variety of different technologies is involved, the goal of AmI is to either entirely hide their presence from users, or to smoothly integrate them within the surrounding context as enhanced environment artifacts. This way, the computing-oriented connotation of technology essentially fades-out or disappears in

C. Stephanidis (Ed.): Universal Access in HCI, Part II, HCII 2007, LNCS 4555, pp. 208–217, 2007.

the environment, providing seamless and unobtrusive interaction paradigms. Therefore, people and their social situation, ranging from individuals to groups, be them work groups, families or friends and their corresponding environments (office buildings, homes, public spaces, etc) are at the centre of the design considerations. The notions of Universal Access and Design for All (DfA) are central to this vision, since AmI aims at providing implicit, unobtrusive interaction by putting people, their social situations, and the corresponding environments at the centre of design considerations [2].

AmI is a particularly complex, multifaceted and demanding scientific domain, requiring the presence and seamless integration of most of the key technologies existing today, thus posing numerous challenges in several research areas, and requiring large scale experimentation, as well as continued collaboration of researchers and practitioners. The Institute of Computer Science (ICS) of FORTH is creating a large-scale, state-of-the-art AmI Facility, targeted to support research, experimentation and multidisciplinary scientific collaboration at an international level. Such a facility is intended, amongst other things, to support the establishment and conduct of a line of research targeted towards the provision of Universal Access to AmI technologies and environments. This paper, after briefly presenting the main characteristics of the AmI Facility currently under development, offers a preliminary discussion of some of the identified research issues and of how their investigation can be facilitated through the Facility's physical and technological infrastructure.

2 Towards a Fully Accessible AmI Research Facility

Worldwide, with the exception of few efforts in the US (e.g., Georgia Tech's Aware Home[1], MIT's House_n[2]) and in northern Europe (e.g., Philips' HomeLab[3], Fraunhofer-Gesellschaft's inHaus[4]), addressing mainly the Smart Home environment, there are no large-scale multidisciplinary facilities or laboratories where different AmI technologies are being developed, integrated and tested in a real-life context.

The AmI Facility of ICS-FORTH will act as a research nexus for studying and developing, under a human-centred perspective, related technologies, providing general-purpose and integrated solutions, and for assessing their impact on the individual, as well as on the society as a whole. The AmI Facility is also going to provide a showcase for demonstrating the potential added-value and benefits of AmI technologies in different aspects of everyday life and activities. In this direction, the AmI Facility aims at fostering the vision of AmI, facilitating multidisciplinary international collaborations, contributing towards strategic policy for an inclusive Information Society, and providing a focal point for technology transfer and dissemination of know-how to European industry.

This Research Facility will occupy a two-floor building of approximately 2500 square meters, comprising simulated AmI-augmented environments and their support

---

[1] www.cc.gatech.edu/fce/ahri

[2] http://architecture.mit.edu/house_n

[3] http://www.research.philips.com/technologies/misc/homelab/index.html

[4] http://www.inhaus-duisburg.de

spaces (e.g., computer and observation rooms), laboratory spaces for developing and testing related technologies, staff offices and public spaces. It is intended to primarily address the application domains of housing, education, work, health, entertainment, commerce, culture and agriculture (e.g., gardening, farming), through dedicated spaces simulating typical everyday environments, such as a house, a class-room, a collaborative workplace, a multifunctional doctor's office, an outdoor garden with a greenhouse and a multipurpose public "exhibition" space that can simulate diverse settings, ranging from a museum gallery to a shop section or a conference hall. The simulated house will expand on two floors which will be linked through both a staircase and an elevator and will include an open-space living room, a kitchen, a house office, two bedrooms (one for adults and one for children) and a bathroom. The house will integrate numerous application scenarios including local, remote and automated home control, safety and security, health monitoring, independent living, (tele)working and entertainment.

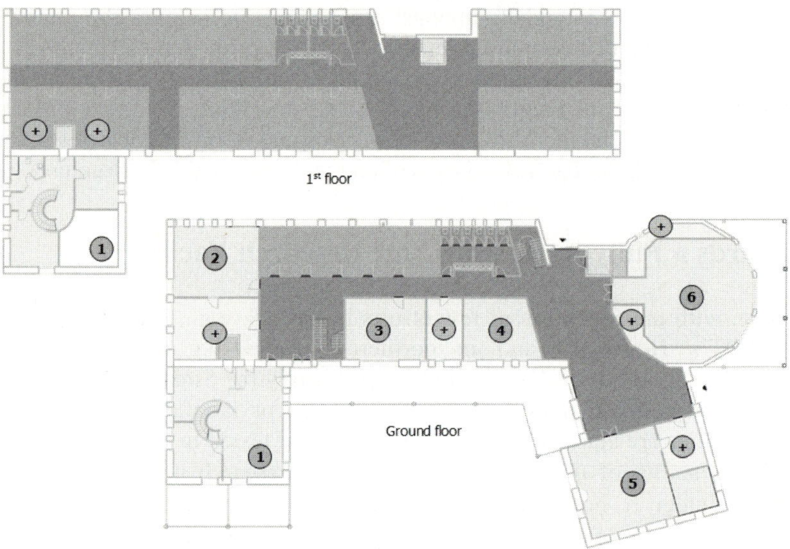

Fig. 1. Plans of the ground and first floor of the AmI Research Facility

The Facility's architectural plans of the ground and first floor are illustrated in Fig. 1. The numbered areas correspond to simulated AmI spaces as follows: (1) Home (two floors), (2) Education, (3) Workplace, (4) Health, (5) Entertainment, and (6) Exhibition. The areas adjacent to the simulated spaces (annotated with a plus symbol "+") are support rooms, where the required technical infrastructure for administering the technology and "running" the software applications resides. These rooms have a two-fold role, since they can also serve as observatories for unobtrusively monitoring the usability and accessibility of the simulated environments while being used by potential end-users ("residents").

The entire building has been designed to be accessible by people with disabilities, and follows DfA guidelines concerning stairs, elevators, ramps, corridors width, accessible bath-room facilities, multimodal signs and labels, etc. In particular, the house simulator will constitute a prototype accessible house for disabled and elderly people. Additionally, the building design takes into account issues of easy orientation and navigation in the physical environment.

The AmI simulators will be fully furnished, computationally empowered and networked, and will be equipped with a variety of interactive technologies and devices, including various types of robots, home automation equipment, cameras, presence and movement detection systems, wired and wireless sensors and sensors' network, LCD displays of various dimensions (from very small to wall-displays), video and video synchronization equipment, image projectors, intelligent telephone devices, various medical devices (e.g., electronic cardiographer, blood-pressure monitor, vital signs monitor, body temperature monitor, etc), and personal mobility vehicles.

3 Universal Access to Ambient Intelligence

AmI is perceived as a technological development which should integrate universal access characteristics in a mainstream fashion, since, in such an in fieri technological environment, accessibility and usability of interactive technologies by users with different characteristics and requirements cannot be addressed through ad-hoc assistive technology solutions introduced once the main building components of the new environment are in place [2]. AmI is also considered as offering a range of new opportunities towards Universal Access, and in particular towards the integration of disabled and elderly people in the Information Society.

One of main intrinsic benefits of AmI in this respect is identified in the emergence of new forms of interactive applications supporting every day activities by integrating (or, in some cases, substituting) limited human abilities with the intelligence spread in the environment, in such a way as to support independent living, higher quality of healthcare, easier interpersonal communication, etc (e.g., [6]). Rehabilitation applications of AmI technologies are also investigated (e.g., [7]). The concept of Ambient Assisted Living also relies on the exploitation of AmI technologies towards enhancing the independent living of the elderly and solving problems caused by the ageing of the European population [8].

AmI environments will integrate a wide variety of interactive devices, in many cases equipped with built-in facilities for multimodal interaction and alternative input/output (e.g., voice recognition and synthesis, pen-based pointing devices, vibration alerting, touch screens, etc), or with accessories that facilitate alternative ways of use (e.g., hands-free kits), thus addressing a wider range of user and context requirements than the traditional desktop computer. It is likely, therefore, that some of the built-in possibilities offered will also satisfy the requirements of disabled users (e.g., blind users will benefit from the wider availability of voice input and output), thus facilitating the design of more accessible solutions and reducing the need of Assistive Technologies.

On the other hand, AmI environments will be very interaction intensive and humans will be constantly "surrounded" by a practically infinite number of small computers of different shapes and sizes. Thus, even minor or subconscious user actions such as breathing, stretching or making a noise, might unintentionally trigger different types of sensors, be misinterpreted and result in unpredictable reactions of the "intelligent" environment. These potential problems can become much worse in the case of the disabled and the elderly, since their physical actions may considerably vary from what may be considered as "typical" or "expected".

Considering the interaction problems that most people face today when interacting with just a single "typical" computer (e.g., desktop, laptop or PDA) which has very discrete and perceptible form and input/output communication channels, it is easy to imagine the consequences of having to interact with an undefined number of "invisible" computers distributed all over the surrounding environment, each one having its own input and output styles and interaction capabilities. In order to overcome such problems, there are two main strategies that can be employed: (a) equip individual computing devices with a certain level of intelligence that will allow them to function independently, communicate and co-operate with each other aiming to best serve the user's goals and needs; and (b) provide the user with a higher and more intuitive level of control, beyond the current direct manipulation paradigm. In this context, there is a very fine balance between the level of user control and the independence of each "intelligent" machine. Providing too fine-grained user control may lead to overwhelming complexity and mental overload, while unlimited machine independence may lead to technological nightmares. In this context, there are two key prerequisites for achieving universal access: (a) to manage, orchestrate and support seamless, high-quality, unobtrusive, and fault-tolerant interaction between humans and the ambient technological environment in an efficient, effective and intuitive way, which also guarantees well-being, privacy and safety, and (b) to creatively combine the available, dispersed computing devices in order to provide useful, added-value, services, or, in other words to "put technology in good use".

Although the cost and availability of AmI technologies will be important factors for their wider spread and market success, the ultimate criterion for their public acceptance and use will be the extent to which people feel safe and comfortable using them, as well as whether it is people controlling the technology, or vice versa. Thus, Universal Access has a key role in the development of AmI environments and has the potential to make the difference between their ultimate success and adoption or their rejection by users. To this end, towards the vision of a universally accessible AmI environment, and in particular of the integration of disabled and elderly people, a number of research challenges arise [2], involving the entire development lifecycle of AmI technologies and environments, and requiring a considerable rethinking of how users are involved throughout the various design phases, as well as of how a multidisciplinary 'common vocabulary' can be achieved by the scientific community. The next section discusses some of the main challenges of Universal Access in the AmI context, outlining at a preliminary stage how a research facility such as the one mentioned in Section 2 can contribute to address them.

4 Research Challenges Towards Universal Access in AmI Environments

4.1 Understanding Human Needs in the Ami Environments

A prerequisite for the successful development of the AmI environment is that user requirements are appropriately captured and analysed. In particular, it is necessary to anticipate future computing needs in everyday life [9], and acquire an in-depth understanding of the factors which will determine the usefulness of diverse interactive artefacts in context. These requirements are likely to be more subjective, complex, and interrelated than in previous generations of technology. Under a Universal Access perspective, this implies incorporating the needs, requirements and preferences of all users, including disabled people. As a starting point towards an analysis of user's requirements in AmI, studies have been conducted through the use of scenario techniques. For example, in [10], an extension of the ISTAG scenarios [1] is presented to cater for the case in which characters in the scenarios have disabilities. On the other hand, in [11], a 'worst case scenario' exercise has been conducted in order to identify risks which could be brought about by several types of problems in AmI environments. Scenarios provide a useful starting point, but can not be considered as sufficient to fully capture future human needs and expectations in a context still difficult to grasp. In fact, currently, it appears that the analysis of the new environment presents difficulties to both to the scientific and user communities [12]. Among scientists, due to the fast technological development, there is a tendency to limit interest to the identification of research issues from an individual discipline perspective. On the other hand, for the user community, and in particular for groups such as the disabled and the elderly, it is not easy to express needs and preferences. In order to contribute to the development, users should be made aware of the technological possibilities and potential approaches to build up the new environment.

In this respect, it is planned to use the AmI facility as a vehicle to bring together multidisciplinary research teams and diverse user groups so as to start a constructive dialogue and establish a common vocabulary. This can be facilitated by the availability of a real AmI context in which to embed research and discussion [13, 14]. The main advantage is offered by the possibility of combining contextual and laboratory – based methods, with users fully immersed in a quasi-natural environment, while at the same time supporting continuous monitoring and recording of user activities in context for analysis purposes.

4.2 Understanding the AmI Context of Use

In AmI environments, the study of the context of use is of critical importance. With respect to more traditional interactive environments, the context of use in AmI is extended to include both the physical and social environment [5]. The number and potential impact of relevant factors increase dramatically with respect to conventional computing devices, particularly with respect to the (co-)presence of people, computing devices and other elements in the surrounding environment. This implies the necessity of monitoring every relevant element in context, and raises the issue of identifying the elements that should be monitored by each device, and the conditions and parameters according to which monitoring should take place. Various proposals have been put forward in the literature in order to systematically analyse and address the notion of context in AmI environments (e.g., [15]). Roughly, available models distinguish among user-oriented context (i.e., the characteristics, roles and actions of users, as individuals and as groups, within the environments), environment-oriented context (i.e., physical characteristics of the environment, such as temperature, light, noise, etc), and platform-oriented context (i.e., the characteristics of the many available interactive devices). While sensor, monitoring and recognition technologies offer the possibility to acquire massive context data, one of the bigger challenges for AmI remains how to model, reason about and exploit such data [5]. Overall, it appears that the issues related to the context of use in AmI are in need of extensive experimentation in order to test and compare different context models, improve approaches to context inference, experiment with the usefulness and usability of context-based automated action of the AmI environment, and investigate the users' awareness and acceptance of such system's initiatives. The availability of an AmI research facility will offer the opportunity to study the context of use in several ways, for example, by easily experimenting with and comparing, in the various simulated environments, different context-based approaches to automating system's action and responses, as well as with domain-oriented issues for each of the addressed domains (health, education, housing, etc).

4.3 Bridging Perspectives on 'Design for All'

In the context of AmI, Universal Access will face new challenges posed by the pursue of proactive accessibility and usability of embedded interactivity "hidden" in a variety of interconnected, multifunctional artefacts [2]. This is due to the multifunctional nature of artefacts, and to the necessity to integrate interactive behaviours in everyday objects. It will therefore be necessary to investigate how interactive functions combine with other functions of artefacts, and how the design processes of the various functions interrelate. Universal Access will need to broaden its scope, as accessibility and usability of each device in isolation will be a necessary but not sufficient condition for the accessibility and usability of the overall distributed environment. It will therefore be necessary to investigate, under a Universal Access perspective, the factors that are dynamically involved in the integration and cooperation of all elements in the technological environment. This also implies a more close study of the similarities and differences of DfA in the architectural world and in the digital world, as these worlds will no longer be clearly separated, but, on the contrary, strictly interrelated. So far, while DfA in the domain of interactive applications and services was inspired by previous approaches to DfA in the built environment, it departed from the latter in that it recognised the need of adapted and personalised interactive solutions. In the context of AmI environments, it will be necessary to establish how these two approaches coexist and combine. One of the aspects which may be more affected by this convergence is, for example, navigation in the environment and navigation support. This is likely to require new design principles and new forms of adaptation, which will need to be carefully experimented with in real settings. The ICS-FORTH AmI Facility, due to its intrinsic architectural accessibility and flexibility (moving walls, possibility of rearranging each space according to the users' needs, etc) will offer a unique opportunity to investigate these interrelationships in a multidisciplinary perspective and with the involvement and active participation of target users' representatives.

4.4 Assessing Technological Solutions

Evaluation of AmI technologies and environments will need to go beyond traditional usability evaluation in a number of dimensions, concerning assessment methods and tools as well as metrics [2]. Ubiquitous AmI technologies and systems such as personal digital assistants, wearable sensors, mobile phones, etc., challenge traditional usability evaluation methods, because the context of use can be difficult to recreate in a laboratory setting. This suggests that the evaluation of user's experience with AmI technologies should take place in real world contexts. However, evaluation in real settings also presents difficulties, as there are limited possibilities of continuously monitoring users and their activities [14]. In this respect, the AmI facility will offer an ideal experimental environment, combining user experience in context with the availability of the necessary technical infrastructure for studying the users' behavior over extended periods of time. Another relevant issue concerns the content of the evaluation. Performance-based approaches are not suitable for AmI systems, as they were developed for single user, desktop applications, and are usually applied in laboratory evaluations. Additionally, it is difficult to specify tasks that capture the complexity of everyday activities, and a more subjective view of the user experience is necessary. Qualities which may need to be taken into account in evaluating AmI technologies and environments include highly subjective factors such as attention, values, emotion, fun, privacy, and trust [2, 16]. Under a Universal Access perspective, accessibility of AmI environments is also an orthogonal concern, as AmI needs to be developed from start as fully accessible and inclusive, and the accessibility of interactive technologies will be deeply interrelated with the accessibility of the environment (see section 4.3). In the context of the above, the availability of the ICS-FORTH AmI Facility will support the involvement of users with diverse characteristics and abilities in establishing, fine-tuning and validating appropriate assessment metrics, as well as in applying such metrics in user-based experiments at various stages of the usage lifecycle of AmI technologies.

4.5 Preventing Risks

In a situation in which technology may act on the physical environment without the direct intervention of humans, it is likely that new hazards will emerge for people's health and safety [2, 11]. Possible malfunctions or even wrong interpretations of monitored data can lead to unforeseeable consequences, while the invisibility and distribution of technology could make it difficult to identify the source of the problem. This aspect is particularly important for disabled and elderly people, who will rely more heavily on the available facilities. Therefore, appropriate backup strategies must be elaborated. An important issue in this respect is the notion of redundancy (of information, communication channels, monitoring mechanisms, etc), which, through cross-checking mechanisms, can contribute towards increasing the correct functioning of the technological environment and minimising risks. It is particularly important that these backup strategies and any other mechanism developed to increase safety is tested under quasi-real conditions, such as those offered by the ICS-FORTH AmI Facility, where potential malfunctioning and misunderstandings can be safely simulated, and the effectiveness of such measures can be assessed with the direct participation of the users with different abilities.

5 Summary and Conclusions

This paper has outlined some research issues which emerge from the evolution of the Information Society towards AmI environments, and has offered a preliminary sketch of how the ICS-FORTH AmI Facility can contribute towards addressing such challenges in a multidisciplinary fashion and with the direct involvement and active participation of the addressed user communities. Table 1 below summarises the main identified contributions.

Table 1. Role of the AmI research facility towards Universal Access

Current UA Challenges	Catalytic role of the AmI Research Facility
Analysis of diverse user needs and expectations	Direct experience of AmI for diverse users, stakeholders Simulated scenarios Combination of contextual and laboratory – based methods Continuous monitoring of user activities in various environments
Study of diversity in the context of use	Experimentation and comparison of different context models and inference mechanisms in various environments Capturing the users' perception of the context of use Contexts for various environments/application domains Integration of various contexts in a single site
Design for All approaches	Elaborating and testing combined approaches to Design for All in the hybrid physical-digital environment
Evaluation and testing	Testing in quasi-real setting Availability of continuous monitoring Investigation and practice of evaluation methods and metrics for AmI Following the user experience lifecycle of AmI Technologies
Safety issues	Safe simulation of problems Assessment of backup strategies with the involvement of users

The list of relevant issues presented in this paper is by no means exhaustive. For example, social implications of AmI environment and privacy issues would also need a detailed discussion as for their investigation in quasi-real settings. However, it is believed that the discussion in this paper contributes to an understanding of the potential role of the ICS-FORTH AmI Facility towards ensuring that AmI emerges and develops in a way that is acceptable and can be adoptee in the long run by all citizens in the Information Society, as well as towards facilitating and driving a smooth transition of AmI technologies from research into real-life situations.

References

1. IST Advisory Group. Ambient Intelligence: from vision to reality. Electronically available at: (2003) ftp://ftp.cordis.lu/pub/ist/docs/istag-ist2003_consolidated_report.pdf
2. Emiliani, P.L., Stephanidis, C.: Universal Access to Ambient Intelligence Environments: Opportunities and Challenges for People with Disabilities. IBM Systems Journal, Special Issue on Accessibility 44(3), 605–619 (2005)

3. Coroama, V., Bohn, J., Mattern, F.: Living in a Smart Environment – Implications for the Coming Ubiquitous Information Society. In: Proceedings of the International Conference on Systems, Man and Cybernetics 2004 (IEEE SMC 2004), October 10-13, vol. 6, pp. 5633–5638. The Hague, The Netherlands (2004)
4. Edwards, W.K., Grinter, R.E.: At Home with Ubiquitous Computing: Seven Challenges. In: Abowd, G.D., Brumitt, B., Shafer, S. (eds.) Ubicomp 2001: Ubiquitous Computing. LNCS, vol. 2201, pp. 256–272. Springer, Heidelberg (2001)
5. Schmidt, A.: Interactive Context-Aware Systems Interacting with Ambient Intelligence. In: Riva, G., Vatalaro, F., Davide, F., Alcañiz, M. (eds.) Ambient Intelligence, pp. 159–178. IOS Press, Amsterdam (2005) http://www.ambientintelligence.org
6. Sevillano, J.L., Falcó, J., Abascal, J., Civit-Balcells, A., Jiménez, G., Vicente, S., Casas, R.: On the Design of Ambient Intelligent Systems in the Context of Assistive Technologies. In: Miesenberger, K., Klaus, J., Zagler, W., Burger, D. (eds.) ICCHP 2004. LNCS, vol. 3118, pp. 914–921. Springer, Heidelberg (2004)
7. Morganti, F., Riva, G.: Ambient Intelligence for Rehabilitation. In: Riva, G., et al. (ed.) Ambient Intelligence, pp. 283–295. IOS Press, Amsterdam (2005) http://www.ambientintelligence.org
8. Steg, H., Strese, H., Hull, J., Schmidt, S.: Europe is facing a demographic challenge. Ambient Assisted Living offers solutions. Report of the AAL Project (2005) http://www.aal169.org/Published/Final%20Version.pdf
9. Abowd, G.D., Mynatt, E.D: Charting Past, Present and Future Research in Ubiquitous Computing. ACM Transactions on Computer-Human Interaction, Special issue on HCI in the new Millenium 7(1), 29–58 (2000)
10. Antona, M., Burzagli, L., Emiliani, P.L., Stephanidis, C.: The ISTAG scenarios: a case study. In: Roe, P.R.W. (ed.) Impact and wider potential of information and communication technologies, pp. 159–187. COST, Brussels (2007)
11. Punie, Y., Delaitre, S., Maghiros, I.: Dark scenarios in ambient intelligence: Highlighting risks and vulnerabilities. Deliverable D2. Safeguards in a World of Ambient Intelligence (SWAMI) (2006) http://swami.jrc.es.pages/deliverables.htm
12. Emiliani, P.L.: Report on the Virtual Workshop of the EDeAN Proactive Assessment Special Interest Group on (November 29, 2005) http://www.edean.org/da.asp?gid=193&did=Sig5&tid=37&mid=42&levelid=1&pid=0
13. De Ruyter, B. (ed.): 365 days' Ambient Intelligence research in HomeLab. Philips (2005) http://www.research.philips.com/technologies/misc/homelab/downloads/homelab_365.pdf
14. Intille, S.S., Larson, K., Munguia, E.: Using a live-in laboratory for ubiquitous computing research. In: Fishkin, K.P., Schiele, B., Nixon, P., Quigley, A. (eds.) PERVASIVE 2006. LNCS, vol. 3968, pp. 349–365. Springer, Heidelberg (2006)
15. Preuveneers, D., Van den Bergh, J., Wagelaar, D., Georges, A., Rigole, P., Clerckx, T., Berbers, Y., Coninx, K., Jonckers, V., De Bosschere, K.: Towards an extensible context ontology for Ambient Intelligence. In: Markopoulos, P., Eggen, B., Aarts, E., Crowley, J.L. (eds.) EUSAI 2004. LNCS, vol. 3295, Springer, Heidelberg (2004) http://research.edm.uhasselt.be/ tclerckx/eusai2004.pdf
16. Theofanos, M., Scholtz, J.: Towards a Framework for Evaluation of Ubicomp Applications. IEEE Pervasive Computing 3(2), 82–88 (2004)

Designing Ubiquitous Shopping Support Systems Based on Human-Centered Approach

Hiroshi Tamura[1], Tamami Sugasaka[2], Satoko Horikawa[3], and Kazuhiro Ueda[4]

[1] Hakuhodo Inc., R&D Division, 4-1 Shibaura 3-Chome, Minato-Ku,
108-8088 Tokyo, Japan
hiroshi.tamura@hakuhodo.co.jp
[2] Fujitsu Laboratories Ltd., 1-1 Kami-Odanaka 4-Chome, Nakahara-Ku,
211-8588 Kawasaki-Shi, Japan
sugasaka.tamami@jp.fujitsu.com
[3] Univ. of Tokyo, Graduate School of Interdisciplinary Information Studies,
3-1 Hongo 7-Chome, Bunkyo-Ku,
113-0033 Tokyo, Japan
621@ze.ciao.jp
[4] Univ. of Tokyo, Graduate School of Arts and Sciences,
8-1 Komaba 3-Chome, Meguro-Ku,
153-8902 Tokyo, Japan
ueda@gregorio.c.u-tokyo.ac.jp

Abstract. We introduce our human-centered approach for the purpose of developing a ubiquitous computing system aiming at providing better experiences for shoppers at a supermarket. We focus on shopping processes by using ethnographic research techniques, understand the process with details, and construct TPM which classifies a shopper's behaviors and states of mind change into three phases. We also describe our concept design of service types for a prototype system and deal with allocation and configuration of the service types corresponding to TPM.

Keywords: ubiquitous computing, human-centered design, ethnographic research, shopping experience, shopping process.

1 Introduction

Retail outlet is a promising application area of ubiquitous computing systems. There have already been a variety of systems developed not only as research purposes but also as business purposes [1]. One of the most famous cases is the Extra Future Store by Metro AG (http://www.future-store.org/). The store has been employed a variety of embedded and mobile computing systems to improve a shopper's experience during his/her shopping trip within the store as well as to track and manage grocery store inventory from the distribution center to and within the store [2]. From the view of a shopper's experience, he/she has come to exploit the services as everyday activities, for instance, some 24 percent of shoppers utilize PSA (personal shopping assistant), which is a mobile kiosk terminal embedded with a shopping cart, and some

C. Stephanidis (Ed.): Universal Access in HCI, Part II, HCII 2007, LNCS 4555, pp. 218–227, 2007.

48 percent use the interactive kiosks furnished at a constellation of places throughout the store including greengrocery, meat, and wine floor [2].

On the other hand, not a few shoppers have rejective feeling to the service automation at a storefront due to anticipating that it will further decrease human touch services [1]. One of the reasons yielding such the affection is that the services provided by the systems are not fully suffusive for what the shoppers have expected. For instance, several systems proposed in this area adopted shopping list management as a principal service to enhance a shopper's experience [3], [4], although every shopper does not necessarily buy items according to his/her list. Rather, as [5] revealed, 93 percent of shoppers do not shop to their specified lists. It was also noted that, "on average, purchases by list shoppers exceeded the categories on their lists by about 2.5 times". Then what are the promising alternatives? We, consequently, came to believe that we had to investigate into shoppers' behaviors and states of mind change during their shopping trips for the purpose to lead design implications which would get to the point to make worthy experiences for shoppers.

Since 2003, we have promoted an empirical design project of ubiquitous computing systems at a supermarket, named SSA, or smart shopping-aid. We have secured an operating store, Bonrepas Momochi-branch (http://www.bonrepas.co.jp/) in Fukuoka City located at south-west region in Japan, as the project site. We had aimed at SSA to be truly a human-centered design project, so that we conducted a general survey regarding grocery shopping both in quantitative and in qualitative manner, thorough ethnographic researches, moment-to-moment analyses, and systems development and deployment according to the research results. In this paper, we introduce our design process and implications which will contribute to afford intrinsically useful ubiquitous computing systems at supermarkets.

2 Investigation in Shopping Process

Shopping process is a long-lasting research topic in retail marketing. According to Takahashi [6], about 70 percent of items at a supermarket and about 80 percent at a supercenter were bought without preexisting plans. Meanwhile, according to our survey conducted in the Tokyo metropolitan area in 2005, respondents who were homemakers ranged from their 30s to 40s answered that about 62 percent of them mostly planned their dinner menus at home and about 27 percent at storefronts [7]. These two facts implied a question: "Why grocery shoppers buy such many items without plans regardless majorities of them already have had their plans?" We speculated that grocery shoppers tended to gradually articulate their plans along with their shopping trips which were neither necessarily limited to at-home nor in-store but extended to the consolidation of both. One of the reasons came from another result of our survey which showed that there were almost the equal effects of major factors from both sides to their dinner menu planning (Fig. 1.). Past works had already pointed out that there existed a same kind of phenomenon, although the mechanisms

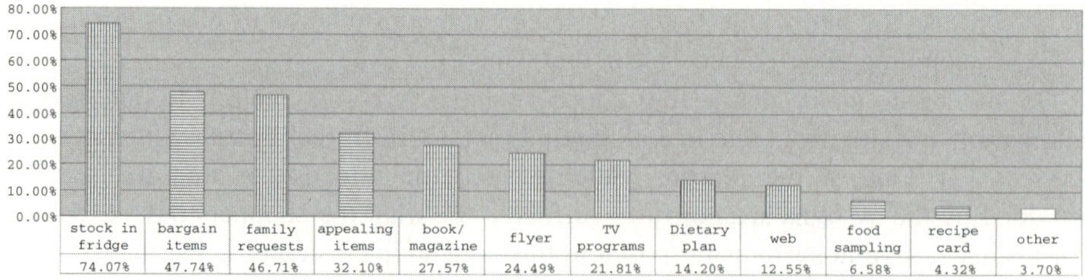

Fig. 1. Influential factors for dinner menu planning; Bars with vertical stripes are relevant to "planning at home" and ones with horizontal stripes are relevant to "planning at storefront". The survey was conducted in the Tokyo metropolitan area in January 2005. (Sample size 486, multiple answers allowed of this question)

were still at all unapparent [6]. We, therefore, decided to investigate in shopping processes which occurred widely from at-home to in-store and vice versa, and conducted thorough ethnographic researches on them.

2.1 Research Design

In-depth researches were conducted one by one with eight observees from August to September 2005. The observees were all female, were ranged from their 30s to 50s, and were chosen from trusted customers of Bonrepas Momochi-branch. We informed them that we would observe their holistic shopping processes for dinner arrangements, and requested that they should shop as same as usual. The research procedure was consisted of four steps described as follows:

- *Pre-interview at home (30-60min.)*: to interview with an observee regarding their behaviors and states of mind to everyday grocery shopping, to check whether she had her shopping plan or not, and to observe her preparation for the expedition (i.e. searching in the refrigerator),
- *Participatory observation at the storefront (20-50min)*: to take a participatory observation with her shopping trip by using contextual inquiry techniques [8],
- *Participatory observation at home (30-120min.)*: to take a participatory observation again regarding her storing, using, processing, and cooking purchased items with contextual inquiry techniques, and
- *Post-interview at home (30-60min.)*: to debrief what had not been clarified in the previous steps.

We also asked each observee to take a wearable video recording system on during the participatory observation at the storefront for posterior analysis. The camera, named Encolpia (Fig. 2.), had originally been developed for the purpose with the feature of 150-degree wide vision and real time MPEG-4 encoding functions.

2.2 Findings from the Observations

A series of observations uncovered that a shopping process at the storefront was never uniform but the process dynamically changed corresponding to each shopper's

Fig. 2. Encolpia: our original wearable video recording system equipped with 150-degree wide vision CCD. The system was designed for minimally-invasive to an observee's behavior. The bottom right is a snapshot of recorded images.

context; her behavior and state of mind abruptly transformed along with her shopping trip. Even if she had her shopping list, she never just did a rundown of it. Rather, it was used as one of the artifacts including articles, price tags, and in-store signs, with which she iteratively interacted to articulate her plan till the end of the shopping.

We discovered that there were generally three phases across two major context shifts. Observed cases which implied existence of the first phase are shown below.

- Right after starting her shopping, the observee directly went to the deli floor, closely looking at some items, saying "they're very helpful to plan my dinner menu as well as to know how to cook it!" (a homemaker in her 30s)
- As the observee already had planned her dinner menu by reference to a magazine article at home, she just looked around the meat floor right after initiating her shopping, then went to the greengrocery floor and started choosing items referring to the assortment of the meat floor in her memory. (a homemaker in her 40s)
- (An utterance from an observee) "I basically start shopping from what I don't have to forget to buy". (a homemaker in her 40s)

There seemed to exist the warm-up phase right after initiating her shopping regardless whether she had her plan or not at the moment. In this phase, she mainly replenished what she had already recognized as well as worked her plan for a main dish of the day. She was so enthusiastic to buy what she had to buy without omission that, we could speculate, she felt pretty tensed during this phase.

Observed cases which implied existence of the second phase are shown below.

- (An utterance from an observee) "Because I had decided to cook hashed rice as today's main dish, I wanted to choose an appropriate packaged beef for it. I compared several packages with each other, and decided to choose one because it seemed the most fresh." (a homemaker in her 30s)

- (An utterance from an observee; after picking up a package of aroids) "As I had decided today's main dish which packed a hard punch, I think up boiled aroids with soy and sugar as a side dish will go nicely with the main dish." (a homemaker in her 40s)

This phase was the closest to what we had conceived as the typical grocery shopping: Each observee implemented her plan by choosing and picking up specified items. In this phase, she fulfilled the plan which had been made in the previous phase as well as developed and carried out her plan for a side dish which was going to nicely with the main dish. We could see that she concentrated her mind on how she could fully suffuse her plan during this phase: i.e. to buy higher quality items with cheaper prices. We could also confirm that her state of mind in this phase got less tensed than that in the previous phase.

Observed cases which implied existence of the third phase are shown below.

- After declaring that they finished their shopping on the day, some observees still continued to look around their pathway and found what they would like to buy.
- (An utterance from an observee) "I'm always feeling that I might forget to buy what I have to buy today, so I usually scour for something tell me so in the closing stage of my shopping" (a homemaker in her 30s)

There seemed to exist the wrapping-up phase before terminating her shopping. In this phase, she tended to buy items which were not necessarily to have on the day. She was also willing to take new articles and reduced items to try them out. In other words, this phase acutely triggered her impulse buying. We could see she was relaxed and feeling fun during this phase since, we speculated, she was freed from the mission of the shopping on the day.

2.3 Findings from the Video Ethnography

We did moment-to-moment analyses of the video data of the seven observees (One is omitted due to lack of her video data). We normalized their shopping durations because they differed from each other, split them into five divisions, and plotted the items chose according to the applications in each division (Fig. 3.). As the result, "replenishment" got the highest rate in the first and the second division, "foodstuff for main dish" was the highest in the third division, "foodstuff for side dish" was the highest in the fourth division, and "replenishment" again and "others" including pure impulse buy (without any assumptions of use) were the highest in the final division. To compare this result with the result in the previous section, we could understand that the first and the second division roughly corresponded to the first phase, the third and the fourth division to the second phase, and the final division to the third phase, due to the similarities of the observed behaviors.

Consequently, we defined the three-phase model, or TPM (Fig. 4.): From the first to the second phase, it was divided in the wake of starting to buy a foodstuff for a shopper's main dish, and, from the second to the third phase, it was divided in the wake of finishing to buy what a shopper have to buy on the day.

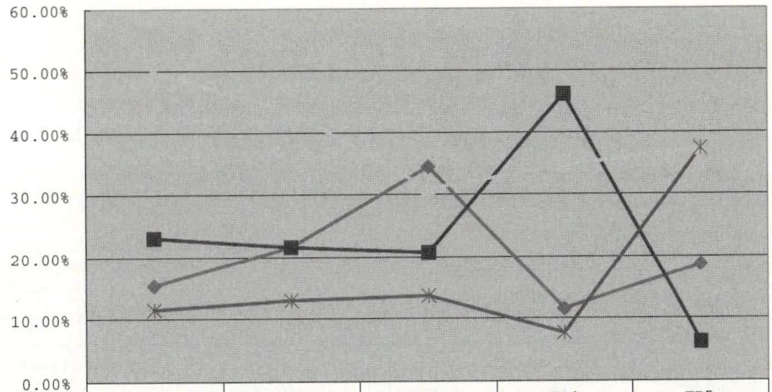

	TD1	TD2	TD3	TD4	TD5
foodstuff for main dish	15.38%	21.74%	34.48%	11.54%	18.75%
foodstuff for side dish	23.08%	21.74%	20.69%	46.15%	6.25%
replenishment	50.00%	43.48%	31.03%	34.62%	37.50%
other (e.g. impulse buy)	11.54%	13.04%	13.79%	7.69%	37.50%

Fig. 3. The rate change according to the applications of items which were added to the observees' shopping carts in five time-divisions respectively

3 Design Implications

As premises for TPM, what services are the best for each phase? Given that we would develop a mobile kiosk terminal embedded with a shopping cart which would be feasible to operate in a supermarket at that time, we described an experience scenario corresponding to each phase referring to the findings in the previous section.

3.1 Experience Scenarios

Experiences in the First Phase. I come to the supermarket with the thought that a meat dish is better for today's dinner menu because I cooked fish yesterday. I rent out a mobile kiosk terminal embedded with a shopping cart, turn on the system, and check today's fresh recommendations on the screen. I discover that every pack of pork is twenty percent reduced, so that I move to recipe recommendations on the screen and retrieve recipes of pork dishes. There are plenty of appealing pork dishes varying by parts and seasonings. Since I would like to have a hefty dish today, I choose "pork spareribs grilled with barbecue sauce" from them. I bookmark the recipe and head down to the meat floor to see pork spareribs. I pick up a carton of milk and a pack of sausages, which I have already planned to buy, on the way. While I'm passing over the egg section, I happen to remember that there are just three eggs left in the refrigerator at home, and I, therefore, take a pack of eggs which is also recommended on the screen.

Experiences in the Second Phase. I arrive at the meat floor and notice that there are two types of pork spareribs. I scan a bar-code attached to one of pricier type by using bar-code reader which is embedded to the system. There emerges a description

	Phase1	Phase2	Phase3
Behavior	•Replenishment •Planning one's main dish	•Fulfilling the plan •Developing and carrying on one's side dish plan	•To buy not necessarily to have •To buy on impulse
State of mind	•Tensed •Mission critical	•Getting calm •Concentrating on items	•Relaxed •Feeling fun

Fig. 4. The three-phase model: consecutive changes of a shopper's behaviors and his/her states of mind

regarding the article on the screen. I come to know that the type of pork has been fed on organic foods, so that it seems healthier than the other one. I decide to buy the pricier one and take a pack with adequate amounts.

Because I remember barbecue source is now out of stock at home which is necessary to cook the menu, I head down to the grocery floor. I notice that recommendations on the screen have changed from fresh foods to packaged foods. I see through them all and notice a brand of barbecue source is included. It is not the one I usually use, therefore I switch to the description of the article and know that it is totally made with organic ingredients. Although it is at a cut-rate price for this week but still a little pricier than the usual one, I decide to buy it in a sense of a tryout. While taking a bottle, I notice that three new recommendations are flashed in rotation at the corner of the screen. One of them is a jar of mustard. I think up mixing mustard with barbecue source sounds good. I remember that there remains enough amount of mustard at home, so that I don't have to buy it on this occasion.

Then I head for the greengrocery floor. I feel anything plain will be better for a side dish because the pork spareribs are somewhat greasy. I look into the screen and find that there are many recipes using in-season vegetables ready, which suit for my thought. I prefer "tomato salad with boiled spinach", so that I display the ingredients by touching the particular icon. I confirm that all the ingredients, except spinach, are stocked at home. I directly access the spinach shelf, and select a lively-leafed bunch. I also bookmark this recipe for remembrance' sake.

Experiences in the Third Phase. I have gathered most for today's dinner menu, so that I settle on the idea that I will stroll down the aisles to see what I had better buy. I again notice that instances on the screen transformed. There are new articles of the week now. I check them one by one, find a brand of low-calorie ice cream, and get happy to know my favorite mango taste is lined up. I go straight down to the ice cream freezer and two cups of mango and chocolate taste respectively for everybody in my family for after-dinner dessert.

On the way for checkout, I stop by at the tofu section and notice that there are sales rankings of the section for the last week displayed on the screen. I realize that I have not tried out the most popular one. I hesitate but bring it forward, although it seems attractive really. Then I go straight to the checkout counter.

At the checkout counter, the two recipes bookmarked are automatically printed out and I can obtain them for later use.

Looking back on the entire journey, I should say what an attractive supermarket it is!

3.1 Allocation and Configuration of Services

We identified five service types included in the scenarios. Corresponding to a shopper's dynamic process, the situation when a particular service exerts never uniform, but dynamically shifts as well. We speculated the best allocation and configuration of the service types by examining when and how the each service type would become activated.

Recipe Recommendations. As recipes are effective information to a shopper's comprehensive planning, they will tend to be used in early part of the process. Since we could know a shopper usually plans his/her main dish in the first phase and side dish in the second phase, an appropriate series of contents should be provided at each phase respectively.

Product Recommendations. Although product information seems valuable throughout the process, each phase will favor different kind of information. In the first phase, information regarding a sale on fresh food may help a shopper to develop his/her plan for a main dish. In the second phase, information which will enable a shopper to compare prices, qualities, and features of an array of choices may help a shopper to fulfill his/her plan for a main dish as well as for a side dish. In the third phase, information regarding new and luxury articles may help a shopper to suffice his/her curiosity about grocery items.

Location and Preference Based Recommendations. While the previous two service types aim at communicating from the retailer, information taking account of a shopper's unique context, including where he/she is and what he/she prefers, may contribute to provide more appropriate information to a shopper him/herself. This service type will be expected to exhibit the multiplier effect by linking up with the previous two service types.

Bookmark Functions. This service type will complement the previous three service types. Since it aims at helping a shopper return to the information which he/she saw earlier in the process whenever he/she likes, it have to be accessible at any time.

Scan-to-deliver Information. This service type will make an article itself as a trigger to retrieve its detailed description. It may be especially useful from the second phase onward because it will provide a shopper information which enables him/her to choose and to evaluate articles.

4 Subsequent Study

We developed a mobile kiosk terminal embedded with a shopping cart, named SmartCart, as the core of the prototype system. We also conducted an operation test at the project site for about two weeks in September 2006. About fifty customers used the system during their shopping trips, and about twenty among them cooperated with our participatory observations. We will introduce the details of the system as well as the evaluation of it based on the operation test in the near future.

5 Conclusion

In this paper, we reported our human-centered approach for the purpose of developing a ubiquitous computing system aiming at providing better experiences for shoppers at a supermarket.

We focused on shopping processes by using ethnographic research techniques, understood the process with details, and constructed TPM which classifies a shopper's behaviors and states of mind change into three phases. We also described our concept design of service types for a prototype system and dealt with allocation and configuration of the service types corresponding to TPM.

Although we didn't give details, we had already developed the prototype system based on the design implications stated in the previous sections and conducted an operation test at the project site. We are now investigating in the data which were acquired from the test. In the near future, we will introduce the details of the system as well as the evaluation of the system from the view of how the system had an effect on shoppers' behaviors and their states of mind.

We believe that understanding people's cognitive process, like TPM, will hugely contribute to practical applications of ubiquitous computing technologies. As Abowd and Mynatt stated, one of the most major motivations for ubiquitous computing is to support the informal and unstructured activities typical of much of our everyday lives [9]. Through the researches in applications at real retail outlets, we hope we will be able to contribute to solve such the difficult problems.

References

1. Roussos, G.: Building Consumer Trust in Pervasive Retail. In: Proc. of Int'l Workshop Series on RFID (2004) Available at http://www.slrc.kyushu-u.ac.jp/rfid-workshop/roussos-paper.pdf
2. Kalyanam, K., Lal, R., Wolfram, G.: Future Store Technologies and Their Impact on Grocery Retailing. In: Krafft, M., Mantrala, M.K. (eds.) Retailing in the 21st Century, pp. 95–112. Springer, Heidelberg (2006)
3. Newcomb, E., Pashley, T., Stasko, J.: Mobile Computing in the Retail Arena. In: Proc. of Conference on Human Factors in Computing Systems, pp. 337–344. ACM Press, New York (2003)

4. Kourouthanasis, P., Roussos, G.: Developing Consumer-Friendly Pervasive Retail Systems. In: IEEE Pervasive Computing, vol. 2(2), pp. 32–39. IEEE Press, New York (2003)
5. Thomas, A., Garland, R.: Susceptibility to Goods on Promotion in Supermarkets. In: Journal of Retailing and Consumer Services, vol. 3(4), pp. 233–239. Elsevier, Amsterdam (1996)
6. Takahashi, I.: Zouho Shouhi-sha Koubai Koudou: Kouri-Marketing he no Shazou (In Japanese). Chikura Shobou, Tokyo (1999)
7. Tamura, H., Sugasaka, T., Naito, H., Sekiguchi, M., Horikawa, S., Ueda, K.: Exploring Everyday Activities for Pervasive Decision-Aid. In: Proc. of PICMET'06. Portland International Center for Management of Engineering and Technology, Portland (2006)
8. Beyer, H., Holtzblatt, K.: Contextual Design: Defining Customer-Centered Systems. Academic Press, San Diego (1998)
9. Abowd, G.D., Mynatt, E.D.: Charting Past, Present, and Future Research in Ubiquitous Computing. In: ACM Transactions on Computer-Human Interaction, vol. 7(1), pp. 29–58. ACM Press, New York (2000)

CSCL at Home: Affordances and Challenges of Ubiquitous Computing

Lucia Terrenghi and Armin Prosch

LMU University of Munich, Media Informatics, Amalienstr. 17,
80333 Munich, Germany
lucia.terrenghi@ifi.lmu.de, aprosch@gmx.net

Abstract. Starting from an analysis of how ubiquitous computing technologies have afforded the design of novel learning experiences in different domains, we consider how such technologies can support domestic learning, thus conceiving the family as a community of practice. We exemplify such a vision with the Living Cookbook appliance: This relies on the video capture and retrieval of family members' cooking sessions, so as to enable the creation and sharing of personalized, multimedia cooking instructions. By augmenting the cooking activity with novel social and entertaining aspects, our goal is to motivate cooking and the learning thereof. We report on the implementation and evaluation of the appliance and in conclusion we discuss our results in light of their possible implications for the design of domestic technology.

Keywords: CSCL, ubiquitous computing, home, kitchen, cooking.

1 Introduction

Ubiquitous computing technologies have had an important impact on how we learn and think about the learning activity: Thanks for example to their affordances for remote communication, on site capturing of different data types, distributed display of multimodal information, the concept of the learning activity has extended in terms of space, domains, as well as in social terms, as novel scenarios of Computer Supported Collaborative Learning (CSCL) have become possible.

The research presented in this paper explores the introduction of ubiquitous computing technologies (and of digital display technologies in particular) into the home to support the domestic learning experience. In this sense we look at *learning* not as an isolated activity, but rather as a contextualized experience which happens within the domestic walls and in the mundane routines of a family. In our approach we look at the home as a learning environment: In this sense we refer to the notion of family as a community of practice [14]. From this point we consider the affordances of ubiquitous computing for supporting and augmenting such a domestic, collaborative learning process.

We focus in particular on the kitchen environment and consider how the domestic teaching and learning of the cooking activity can be enhanced and motivated by technology. We describe the Living Cookbook appliance: this aims at cultivating

C. Stephanidis (Ed.): Universal Access in HCI, Part II, HCII 2007, LNCS 4555, pp. 228–237, 2007.

communication and collaboration in the kitchen by making people's cooking experiences recordable and shareable in an interactive digital cookbook. We illustrate and motivate our design choices and report on the results of the user studies conducted to evaluate the usability of the interface and the user experience, as well as its potential for raising motivation and enhancement of learning.

2 Related Work

Ubiquitous computing technologies have motivated the research and development of several learning scenarios which have freed the learning activity and the concept thereof from the crystallized space of a traditional classroom, thus bringing it to a diversity of contexts: these encounter a variety of spatial domains (e.g., classrooms, field trips, offices, homes), social contexts (e.g., face-to-face or distance learning), as well as temporal ones (i.e., synchronous/a-synchronous communication).

The possibility of delivering and accessing information and communication on the spot, thanks to mobile devices for example, has been exploited in the design of scenarios for mobile learning (for a review in this field see [8]). This affordance in turn promises to support exploration, hands on experiences and situated learning [6], as it allows bringing knowledge *to* and *from* the field of interaction, which is not necessarily the classroom any longer. In a similar way mobile maintenance scenarios rely on the possibility of consulting experts and multimedia handbooks online, while on the field, thus allowing the mobility and connection of workers [2]. Furthermore, the opportunity of capturing and transmitting multimedia data from the field (e.g., photos, videos, sounds, as well as sensed and automatically tagged data such as temperature or time [5]) allows the creation of Reusable Learning Objects which contribute to the body of knowledge of a community of practice or organization. At the same time the advances and distribution of interactive display technologies (e.g., interactive whiteboards, large shared displays) have generated new classroom set-ups, exploiting the possibility of co-located as well as remote collaboration. These technologies allow novel formats of lecture, such as back-channel for example [15].

But while computing, communication and display technologies migrate from the office environment to other learning contexts, what are the affordances of these technologies to support collaborative learning *at* and *about* home? From our point of view some of these affordances have been neglected to a certain extent by the Ubicomp agenda when it comes to the design of CSCL scenarios for the home.

The introduction of ubiquitous computing technologies in the home has largely focused on optimization of efficiency, automation and time-saving [3]: in contrast, not much work has been done in order to integrate such technologies in a way that affords engagement and time-spending. We can also argue that the only ways in which multimedia technologies have supported time-spending in the home, e.g., home-entertainment such as TV or video games consoles, has confined users to a rather passive and not very creative role: all in all the potential of such technologies for teaching and learning support has been largely confined to content management systems for distance learning, residing on single users' PCs and dealing with curricula which are not related to the domestic context.

Taking a closer look at the kitchen, this space has traditionally been populated by a diverse range of appliances which are meant for lessening users' mechanical effort, or for maximizing the efficiency of certain tasks, or even their complete automation (for a good review see [1]). Digital display technologies, on the other hand, have had a very limited application so far. Mostly they have been used for the interface to control and coordinate electric appliances, as alternatives to or in combination with physical dials and buttons [9]. Lately some companies producing domestic appliances have been addressing the potential of digital displays and internet technology for augmenting the kitchen environment, bringing information and entertainment in the kitchen. The GR-D267DTU Internet Refrigerator by LG [7] contains a server which controls the communication to other connected appliances. On the display different functionalities are embedded: it is possible to watch TV, listen to music, or surf the internet. A microphone and a camera are built-in, thus enabling multimedia communication. In academic research some ways to augment the kitchen environment have been investigated as well. At the MIT a smart kitchen space, named La Cantina, was set up [1]: here displays are embedded in the space for different augmentation purposes. One of the proposed scenarios is instantiated in the CounterActive project [4]. This is an interactive cookbook, projected down onto the kitchen counter; the cook touches the countertop to navigate through the recipe or to glean greater details. Recipes incorporate pictures, audio and video.

It is our belief though that ubiquitous computing technologies also offer a good potential for supporting and motivating creativity and domestic learning, which has not been thoroughly exploited by the Ubicomp agenda so far: in other words, we think that these technologies afford the design of novel learning experiences which are situated in the very space and social context of the home.

3 Affording Domestic Learning and Home Communication

We refer to *domestic learning* as the leaning of familiar practices, in a familiar place such as the home. This implies, for example, the learning of how certain artifacts are to be used, their location and how they bridge social interactions. The approach we propose draws on an analysis of the mundane practices of the home and of the artifacts that support these practices, and considers how they can be augmented by digital technology so as to provide novel experiences.

A first affordance of ubiquitous computing to consider is the capture and display of multimedia content with devices that are distributed and embedded in a variety of spaces and artifacts. The instruction and apprentice of home practices within the family walls happens in a large part through storytelling, performance, observation and practical routines. Families grow and evolve as communities of practice [14], which as such rely on their members, their roles, rituals, artifacts, rules and specific locations. In co-located situations adult family members "play" the model for younger generations in the way they manage domestic activities such as cleaning, tiding up, cooking. When family members are remote from each-other, e.g., a parent is away for work, instructions are mediated via different channels: e.g., text for exchanging recipes, instruction notes next to home appliances to illustrate how to operate them, telephone calls for synchronous communication of instructions. Some work exploring how display technology can support home communication has been done in [10].

With the Leaving Cookbook appliance, we focus on how the possibility of capturing and displaying multimedia instructions "on demand" can support the collaborative learning of the cooking activity. The idea is to make people's cooking experiences recordable and shareable, so as to preserve cultural and social roots on the one hand, and stimulate cultural and generational fertilization on the other.

People often call their parents and friends to ask "What was the recipe of that dish?"; "What does the sauce have to look like?"; "How thick should it be?". Much of the communication around cooking, such as the exchange of recipes, and especially within families or close social networks, is one-to-one and supported by different media (e.g., paper, telephone, e-mail), and is a way of tightening social bindings. The emotional quality of content created by family members or intimate friends is indeed very different in comparison to the cooking sessions published in books or broadcast on TV shows, which are produced for a larger audience. TV shows afford a multimodal presentation of food preparation and take advantage of the popularity of acknowledged chefs. Still, they cannot be consulted "on-demand" as a paper cookbook, nor they can be personalized. Furthermore, TV cooking shows are often watched in spaces and time slots which are "distant" from the actual cooking activity: they are rather watched in contexts which depend on the location of the TV display and on the TV schedule.

With our appliance we aim at providing an alternative way for people to personalize their experience and, as a consequence, their communication. Similarly to the CounterActive project [4], we augment the traditional cookbook by delivering and displaying multimedia content in the kitchen. Our focus, though, is on augmentation by social and family relationships and real life experiences. Indeed, one aspect that we think it is worth considering in the design of kitchen appliances is that cooking is often social (e.g., people often cook for others or together with others) and involves several rituals and symbolic aspects. Our assumption is that the communication and display technologies available today offer the possibility to support communication and sociability of cooking, and to bring new aspects to its social and entertaining character. Below we describe the Living Cookbook appliance in further detail to exemplify how we implemented such ideas.

4 The Living Cookbook

The Living Cookbook is an application running on a tablet PC. On the tablet PC a digital cookbook is displayed, with which users can interact (see Fig. 1). On the same interface people can either author a new recipe and add it to their personal virtual book, or consult the book and learn someone else's recipe. In the authoring/teaching mode the video of the cooking session is captured by the camera. In the learning mode this video is played back and the learner can cook along.

In order to support both the teaching (recording) and the learning (playing) mode of the application with the same interface, the general conceptual model of a video recorder is adopted. In this way the interface remains consistent and users can alternatively teach or learn a recipe, without changing the operating environment.

When recording, the cook can indicate phases of activity and inactivity in the UI: When playing back, the device projects the recorded video of activities, pauses during times of inactivity, and the cook can speed up or slow down the playback of the recorded session by advancing to the next section or pausing in order to catch up.

Along the development of the project we adopted different set-ups for the implementation and evaluation of our concept: First, we instrumented the kitchen of our lab and in a following iteration we developed a portable version of the appliance, which allowed us to test it in real domestic kitchens. Below we describe our design and technical solutions and illustrate such different set-ups.

4.1 The Lab Technical Set-Up

In the first iteration we implemented and tested the appliance in the kitchen of our lab. We adopted one PC playing the role of the server and a tablet PC which was mounted on the cupboard above the stove (see Fig. 1, a). The tablet PC has a touch sensitive surface enabling the user to interact with it either with a pen or directly with her/his fingers. A beamer, connected to the server, was used for displaying the video on a wall beside the cupboard, as illustrated in the schema of Fig. 1, c.

The software of the Living Cookbook consists of two main components. In the background a custom .NET based server handles the video authoring and playback as well as the cookbook authoring. The cookbook is stored as an XML file on the server and submitted to the Flash-based user interface on request, where its content is used to build up the cookbook. The server running in our lab renders the captured video stream onto a surface in a 3D scene constructed in Direct3D, to rectify the video output. In such a 3D environment we could move a virtual camera so as to compensate the distortion introduced by the fact that the projector's image plane is not coplanar with the real-world surface onto which we project the video. We used DirectShow for both video capturing (thus allowing us to use two cameras for recording the cooking session from different viewpoints) as well as for video rendering (thus allowing us to render the video onto the virtual surface defined in Direct3D). During the recording process we compress the videos in real time and save it on the local hard disk while showing the actual recorded video to the teaching cook on the wall.

Additionally, the software incorporates a component which is responsible for handling the communication protocol and the actual communication with the client, i.e., the tablet PC. The server is accessed via TCP/IP and the communication runs over a wireless LAN connection. Initially, the client loads the cookbook when the connection is established. Later on, via the client interface a user can insert new recipes, choose already inserted recipes and handle the video. The look and feel of the interface metaphorically relates to the kitchen domain and its artifacts (e.g., users can drag plates icons on a table to set the number of portions), so as to appear familiar and intuitive for a variety of users.

The first experience trials conducted in the lab suggested that two cameras were desirable for capturing both the person and the details of food preparation [12]. Thus, the server was connected to two cameras for capturing audio and video. Furthermore, these tests elicited the need to reduce as much as possible pen-based interaction, as users are busy with handling kitchen tools and ingredients. This motivated our decision to introduce a speech recognition component (i.e., the Sphynx system, from the Carnegie Mellon University [11]). The speech input was conceived as alternative input modality to control the video recording and playback: therefore we customized the system to process certain commands only (i.e., "record", "play", "pause", "stop"). Due to the mediocre sound hardware of the tablet PC, we neither were able to use the speech recognition through the in-built microphone, nor through an external microphone connected to the tablet PC. Instead, we put the speech recognition module on the server PC and connected the external microphone to it.

Despite the results of these first trials in the lab shed some light on desirable features and potential further developments of the appliance, we realized that some of the goals of our project, i.e., the increment of motivation and support of familiar learning and communication, were hard to assess in such a setting. During the cognitive walkthroughs participants were focused on completing the task and commenting the usability of the interface, but could hardly imagine whether and how they could use it in their own kitchens and with their families (see section 5 for more details). Considering that the very space and material culture affect the perception of a household as a "familiar place", we implemented a portable version of the appliance, so that we could test the working prototype in the kitchens of families.

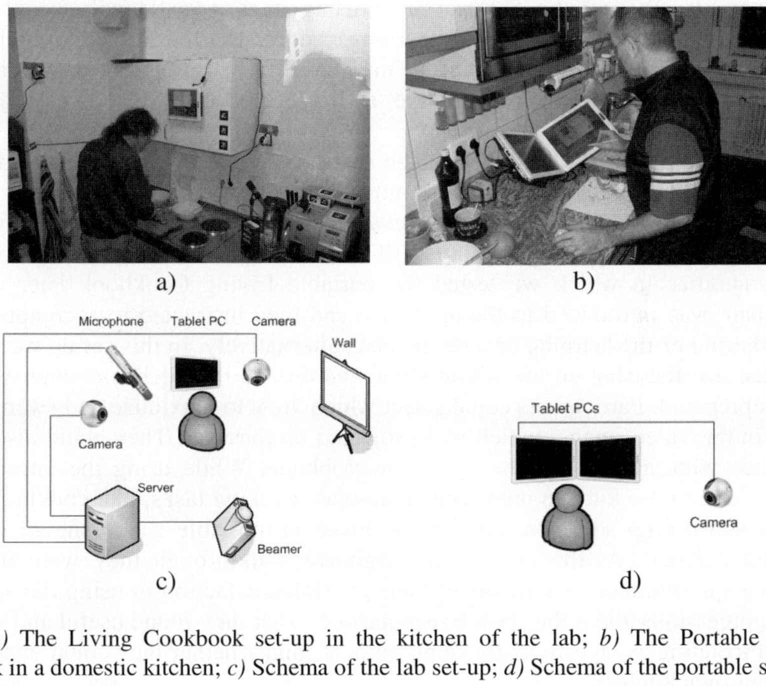

Fig. 1. *a)* The Living Cookbook set-up in the kitchen of the lab; *b)* The Portable Living cookbook in a domestic kitchen; *c)* Schema of the lab set-up; *d)* Schema of the portable set-up

4.2 The Portable Living Cookbook

The set-up for the portable Living Cookbook consists of two identical tablet PCs residing in a custom crafted metal frame, so that the physical appearance of the whole appliance suggests the shape of an open book (see Fig.1, b). This can be put somewhere on a table or on a counter, so as to more easily fit in an ordinary kitchen, the only constraints being the power cords and the camera connection. The right tablet PC displays the user interface, while the left one displays the video during recording and playback. They can either communicate through an ad-hoc or an existing wireless network. The hardware we used in this set-up afforded us compactness, but it also implied some constraints. Due to the limitations of the hardware implementation of the USB technology on these tablet PCs, we could not plug-in more than one camera (see Fig.1, d). Additionally, during some cognitive walkthroughs conducted in the lab, we also realized that the speech recognition is likely to perform poorly when there is more than one person in the environment, which often happens in a domestic kitchen. Thus, considering the above mentioned shortcomings of the sound hardware, we decided not to use the speech recognition in the portable set-up. We also did not use the video rectification here because we show the video on the second tablet PC rather than using a beamer.

5 Evaluation

Our main goals in evaluating the appliance were: i) assessing the usability of the interface; ii) assessing the experience of using it as a real family cookbook; iii) assessing its potential for domestic learning. Addressing these topics required us to think about different techniques and to involve different groups of participants. The methods we used are clearly qualitative, as it is expectable when assessing such an appliance.

In order to assess the usability of the interface we started up with conducting 6 cognitive walkthroughs in the lab set-up. Four of the participants were usability experts, thus providing a heuristic evaluation. The other 2 participants (both psychologists professionally dealing with Information Technologies) were members of the families in which we tested the portable Living Cookbook later on. Each participant was introduced to the appliance and then instructed to accomplish either the authoring or the learning of a recipe task, alternatively. In this set-up we used two cameras: one focusing on the whole scene and one on the kitchen counter where the food is prepared. Participants could select which view to maximize and swap between views in the video image, which was projected on the wall. They could also operate the video with speech input using the microphone. While using the interface they were invited to use kitchen utensils and simulate cooking tasks, like cooking water or cutting something, so as to simulate as much as possible a cooking session in a domestic kitchen. At the end of the cognitive walkthrough they were invited to answer a questionnaire asking about their general satisfaction in using the appliance; Their impressions about the speech recognition; What they found useful and what was instead irritating; Suggestions for improvements and whether they could expect using it in their own kitchen.

The results of the cognitive walkthroughs were positive regarding the graphical user interface of the appliance: testers were able to accomplish all tasks and reported a positive feedback. The speech command instead was a problem: the system recognized repetitively the instructions spoken by the researcher, thus revealing that including such a feature in a real domestic kitchen, where more people are present, would not work. Regarding their expectations of use in their personal kitchens, we had mixed answers: most of them see a possible use in the playback/learning mode, and see the utility of cooking along video instructions. A main concern, though, remain the hardware, both in terms of the space and the cables it requires, as well as the audio performance in playback mode, which is rather poor.

To better understand how such an appliance can be embedded in the familiar environment of a domestic kitchen, we installed the portable Living Cookbook in the kitchens of two of the participants of the cognitive walkthroughs. Their families were introduced to the appliance as well: we left the appliance in each kitchen for a week and asked the families to report on their use of the appliance in a diary we designed for them. One household consisted of a couple with a young baby (husband 30 years old, wife 31, child 15 months), and the other one of a couple with three children (husband 54 years old, wife 39, daughter 15, son 8, and another daughter 5). Five people in total (the two couples and the 15 years old daughter) experienced using the appliance and were involved in a subjective evaluation with in-depth interviews.

Every participant liked the idea of a family archive. The first family used the appliance in the teaching mode only, but actually the feature they liked most was the possibility to watch family members while cooking in the playback mode. They reported that in comparison to watching professional cooks on TV the videos with the Living Cookbook raise fun and intimacy for the fact that they show well-known people in ordinary activities. In the second family the parents did not enjoy using the appliance as it was perceived as an additional domestic effort, while the daughter did enjoy it. She had fun in cooking along her parents' instruction and said she would be more motivated to cook because of the entertainment added value. Both families had some criticisms in terms of usability: some buttons are too small to hit while working in the kitchen with other utensils and error corrections or editing of the instructions is not possible because the authoring/cooking activity is very sequential.

In order to better understand how "home video" can motivate the learning of cooking, we then conducted a focus group with 8 pupils, between 14 and 16 years old, who attend the course of "Household and Nutrition" in a German secondary school. In such a course they learn cooking techniques and recipes: thus, they could share their insights about learning to cook in both an institutional, as well as in a familiar educational context. We discussed topics such as the cooking as process, TV cooking shows, cookbooks, learning to cook at home with family, and how different media can support the learning activity. We then introduced them to our appliance and asked them to cook along a simple recipe we had authored, thus providing them with a hands-on experience. Their feedback was in general very positive. They stated they would be motivated to cook along the video instructions of family members because of the fun factor they recognize, while they could not imagine to use the Living Cookbook at school. They also mentioned that in comparison to TV cooking shows they would trust more the recipes of the Living Cookbook because they are likely to be dishes they have already tasted at home, and because they seem to be more doable than the ones shown by professional chefs on TV. Furthermore, some of the pupils mentioned that they would feel more comfortable and free to cook along a video than physically cooking next to their parents, as this would avoid "being bothered" by their corrections and direct feedback. Some of them also stated that by authoring their own recipe they see an advantage in learning-by-doing, which is not possible when just writing down a recipe for others. Despite they see and appreciate the value of video support for every cooking phase, they also found critical the audio performance of the hardware and mentioned this could be a problem, as you might miss some important steps when following someone's instructions (which can't be just "re-read" like in a paper based cookbook).

In summary, our different evaluation efforts have shown that assessing different aspects of a domestic appliance, which is designed for being used in family life, requires to carefully select different methods and to carefully consider the results of the tests conducted in simulating environments. The first experience trial had suggested speech command for reducing pen input [13], which turned out to be acoustically inappropriate. The cognitive walkthroughs conducted in the lab did not highlight the shortcomings of the usability of the appliance that emerged, instead, in the home set-up (e.g., size of the buttons, editing of the recipe and ingredients). These requirements became clear only when people really had to cook in their kitchens. The noise factor, provided for example by a steak frying in a pan or by other people chatting in the room, together with the poor audio performance of the hardware, revealed that the acoustics is a critical aspect of the appliance. On the other hand the fun and entertainment motivating factors we aimed at could be assessed, and were actually confirmed, only when testing the appliance in a real familiar social context, or involving specific target users (e.g., the pupils of our focus group).

6 Conclusion

In this paper we have presented our design vision about how we expect ubiquitous computing technologies to be able to afford domestic learning by leveraging social relationships, conceiving the family as a community of practice. We have instantiated our vision in the Living Cookbook appliance, and we have shown how the challenge to assess our design goals on different levels has motivated different design solutions, test environments and methods. The design of a working prototype which could be installed in real domestic environments has proved to be useful for eliciting aspects which were not considered in other settings.

In particular, the different feedback we received from different target users suggest that the affordances of ubiquitous computing for the design of domestic technologies are different in respect to the roles of its users within the family. The younger users reported a fun factor deriving from watching their parents, which as a consequence would motivate them to use the appliance and ultimately to cook more. Similarly, we can imagine that elderly people, or people living alone, would enjoy watching their relatives in their domestic environments, thus providing a sense of presence and of memory as a family photo album. Additionally, they might feel responsible to teach their recipes to the younger generation, thus getting more motivated to engage with technology and cooking. To this end we plan to extend the communication possibilities of the appliance so as to remotely and synchronously connect remote kitchens, and in turn remote family members.

While the usability of technology remains a main issue for its acceptance, we think it is important to recognize that technology can also afford time-spending and engagement when the motivation relies on users' values, such as family relationships for example. Our results are encouraging to investigate further the potential of ubiquitous computing technologies to strengthen the social bindings and the passing-on of knowledge in the home by providing novel forms of entertainment as well as capture, archival and retrieval of domestic experiences.

Acknowledgments. This research has been funded by Deutsche Forschungsgemeinschaft within the FLUIDUM project. We thank all the participants of our tests and focus group.

References

1. Bell, G., Kaye, J.: Designing Technology for Domestic Spaces: A Kitchen Manifesto. Gastronomica, pp. 46–62 (Spring 2002)
2. Dix, A., Beale, R. (eds.): Remote Cooperation: CSCW Issues for Mobile and Tele-Workers. Springer/BCS series in Computer-Supported Cooperative Work (September 1996)
3. Harper, R.: Inside the Smart Home. Springer, London (2003)
4. Ju, W., Hurwitz, R., Judd, T., Lee, B.: CounterActive: an Interactive Cookbook for the Kitchen Counter. In: The Extended Abstracts CHI 2001 (2001)
5. Kravcik, M., Kaibel, A., Specht, M., Terrenghi, L.: Mobile Collector for Field Trips in the journal Educational Technology & Society, vol. 7 (2), pp. 25–33. IEEE, Los Alamitos (April 2004)
6. Lave, J., Wenger, E.: Situated Learning Legitimate Peripheral Participation. Cambridge University Press, Cambridge, UK (1991)
7. LG GR-D267DTU freezer: http://www.lginternetfamily.co.uk/fridge.asp
8. Naismith, L., Lonsdale, P., Vavoula, G., Sharples, M.: Literature Review in Mobile Technologies and Learning, Technical Report for FUTURELAB, http://www.futurelab.org.uk/download/pdfs/research/lit_reviews/futurelab_review_11.pdf
9. Philips Home Lab: http://www.philips.com/research/ami
10. Sellen, A., Harper, R., Eardley, R., Izadi, S., Regan, T., Taylor, A.S., Wood, K.R.: Situated messaging in the home. In: Proc. of CSCW '06, pp. 383–392. Banff, Canada (2006)
11. Sphinx, Speech Recognition System, Carnegie Mellon University http://www.speech.cs.cmu.edu/
12. Terrenghi, L., Hilliges, O., Butz, A.: Kitchen Stories: Sharing Recipes with the Living Cookbook. In: Personal and Ubiquitous Computing, Springer, Heidelberg (2007)
13. Terrenghi, L.: Sticky, Smelly, Smoky Context: Experience Design in the Kitchen. In: Proc. of the Workshop on Context in Advanced Interfaces, AVI 2006, ACM Digital Library (2006)
14. Wenger, E.: Communities of Practice: Learning, Meaning, and Identity. Cambridge University Press, Cambridge (1998)
15. Yardi, S.: The role of the backchannel in collaborative learning environments. In: Proc. of the International Conference on Learning Sciences, pp. 852–858 (2006)

Non-homogenous Network, Control Hub and Smart Controller (NCS) Approach to Incremental Smart Homes

Gregg Vanderheiden[1] and Gottfried Zimmermann[2]

[1] Trace R&D Center, University of Wisconsin-Madison, USA
gv@trace.wisc.edu
[2] Access Technologies Group, Wilhelm-Blos-Str. 8, 72793 Pfullingen, Germany
gzimmermann@acm.org

Abstract. The rapid increase in memory and processing power of even simple devices is opening up new opportunities for intelligent devices and environments. However, major barriers exist to practical limitations. Many "smart environments" are currently more complex to either set up or operate than their predecessors. Environments which are simpler to use are often very complex to set up. They also often require wholesale re engineering of the environment. Proposed is a model for using a mixture of non homogeneous network technologies, a control hub and a smart controller to provide a way for users to slowly transition both themselves and their houses from current technologies to smart technologies and environments.

Keywords: Remote user interfaces, task-based user interfaces, digital home, usability, accessibility, Universal Control Hub, Universal Remote Console.

1 Introduction

The rapid advances in technology are allowing us to create products which have increasingly complex control systems. This can either be used to make products more intelligent and simpler or to add features and functionality. Although progress is being made on both fronts, the later is winning out over the former. For those looking for increased functionality and able to handle the complexity this is a positive development. For those who have difficulty dealing with technology and complexity to begin with, it is creating a crisis. Simple versions of products are disappearing and being replaced by complex, multifunction products, or even simple products with numerous additional options, setting and features.

This problem is not restricted to a small portion of the population. Increasingly the problem is being faced by consumers in general. This is also being reflected in the usability and return rates of consumer electronic products. It is widely acknowledged that complex user interfaces are an impediment for the proliferation of the digital home. "Ease of use" is the third most important aspect for home theater owners, only narrowly topped by "video quality" and "sound quality" according to a recent CEA study [1]. In the same study "ease of using remotes" was the second most important

C. Stephanidis (Ed.): Universal Access in HCI, Part II, HCII 2007, LNCS 4555, pp. 238–244, 2007.

aspect for these owners (ratio of the percentage of satisfied consumers and the percentage of those rating the attribute as important).

This lack of 'ease of use' is now directly impacting purchasing (and return) behavior. Two out of three Americans have lost interest in a technology product because it seemed too complex to set up or operate [2]. And the net profit on actual sales is now being cut down by the high percentage of products that are being returned. Den Ouden [3] found out that half of all 'malfunctioning products' returned to stores by consumers are in full working order, but customers cannot figure out how to operate the product. "No Defect Found" return rate runs as high as 90%+ (depending on product category) with consumer electronic returns costs estimated at $10B annually [1].

Philips Electronics North America's CEO Zeven reports that only 13 percent of Americans believe technology products in general are easy to use [2]. Experts have suggested having new products tested by older persons as a litmus test for ease-of-use [5]. The answer to the question "Can grandma figure out how to use it?" is a good hint for a product's usability in general.

1.1 Intelligent Homes and Intelligence in the Home

Smart homes, or just increasing the intelligence of products in the home, can help address these problems. Rather than trying to figure out how to use intelligence to add new functionality the goal should first be to make those things that people are already doing simpler. It is common for humans to first embrace new methods to achieve known tasks or to learn new tasks using old methods or tools. It is much more difficult to master new tasks and new tools simultaneously. Similarly, people are much more prone to embrace increased intelligence in their homes if it helps them to do things they currently find difficult, than if we attempt to introduce new technologies (which are more complex simply because they are un-familiar even when they are not more complex in an absolute sense.) Given the current usability crisis, the opportunity to introduce intelligence into the home has never been greater, if it can in fact make things simpler.

There are a number of barriers however in introducing intelligence into people's homes. These include:

1. Non-homogenous product technologies
2. Non-homogeneous network and connection technologies
3. Lack of interoperability even within products and technology bases
4. Investment to get started
5. Lack of transition path from existing products to smart products
6. Compelling reason to make change.

The challenges here are substantial. Developments in 4 areas however are now giving us the tools to begin addressing these issues. This paper explores the issues and then proposes a model that builds on these four developments to create a program that allows for the incremental incorporation of intelligence into the home in a fashion which can reduce complexity.

2 Six Disincentives to Adoption of Smart Environments

Although there are many barriers or disincentives to adoption of smart home/smart space technologies 6 key ones are:

2.1 Non-homogenous Product Technologies

The first problem is that homes usually have a wide variety of products from a variety of companies. Replacing them all with products from a single manufacturer is not economically practical in most cases. Also, unless you are only focusing on one general product type (e.g. home entertainment) a single manufacturer generally doesn't produce all of the products. Few companies for example sell washers, dryers, stove, lighting, heating, home entertainment and communication and computing products. And even fewer consumers purchase all of these from the same company.

2.2 Non- homogeneous Network and Connection Technologies

Within a home it is also common to find a wide range of technologies used for interconnection, communication and control including WiFi, Ethernet, Bluetooth, Firewire, USB, Powerline and IR. Trying to coordinate the functionality of products in the home with this wide a range of interconnection technologies presents a challenge.

2.3 Interoperability

In addition, different products may use different home control protocols. Such home networking protocols include, among others: Universal Plug and Play (UPnP) [6], CECED Home Appliances Interoperating Network (CHAIN) [7], HDMI Consumer Electronics Control channel (CEC) [8], HANA [9], and LonWorks [10]. Thus even products that may share a common network technology (directly or via gateway) may not work together. Users are reluctant to 'buy into' a particular technology or 'system' when they don't interoperate and it isn't clear what will win out in the end. Also, the investment to purchase a whole set of new products that are all compatible with one of the systems is a disincentive. Some of these systems do interoperate, but most consumers are unable to evaluate or configure such systems.

2.4 Investment

Replacing products with new 'smart' products is expensive. If networking is required additional expense is incurred. Often a network may exist but only in offices or select other rooms. If 'compatible' products are required in order to make a system work it can mean a sizeable investment that can be a barrier for many families.

2.5 Lack of Transition Path

Since users rarely can afford to purchase all new technologies at one time, there generally is a need to have some path for migrating from current technologies to 'smart' products. This process can take years. Yet the benefit of purchasing the first smart technology needs to come with its purchase. Thus a model where new technologies can be intermixed with older technologies is important. At the same time the technologies must work across family members who may have widely differing technical skills and interests. Thus the technologies must also support users with high feature and technology skills and preferences down through users who eschew technology and use it only as necessary.

2.6 Compelling Reason

Because of barriers or disincentives such as those above, smart technologies are generally not adopted unless there is a compelling reason to introduce them. To date, it has been technophiles that have driven adoption. However that market is limited. To really take hold, there has to be a motivation that is compelling to a much larger portion of the mainstream market.

3 The NCS Approach to Incremental Smart Homes

To address these issues it is proposed to combine several new developments to create a naturally evolving intelligence in the home. The goal is not to create a smart home but rather to introduce intelligence into the home in a gradual and natural way that matches both economic reality and the sensibilities of the average household. This model is based on new developments in networking, task modeling, and interface, some of which are available today and some of which are just emerging.

Four new developments are key to this approach.

3.1 Pluggable User Interface Sockets

The first is a new set of 5 ANSI standards that have just been released called "*Protocol to Facilitate Operation of Information and Electronic Products through Remote and Alternative Interfaces and Intelligent Agents*" (also at the FDIS stage within ISO as ISO 24752). These standards provide a technology neutral mechanism for allowing products to be read, understood and controlled by other products. They also allow the introduction and use of intelligent artificial agents to control products or groups of products (such as an audio-video (AV) system).

The standards specify communications between a Target that a user wishes to access and operate, and a Universal Remote Console (URC) that presents the user with a remote user interface through which they can discover, select, access and operate the Target. The URC is software that is typically hosted on the user's physical device, but a distributed approach is also possible. URCs can include PDAs, cell phones, special watches and assistive technologies. Target devices can include home entertainment devices, clocks, thermostats, copiers, ATMs, and elevators as well as invisible targets like Web services.

The user interface socket is a low level description of a particular target product or service and specifies its operational input and output requirements. The socket describes the functionality and state of the target as a set of typed data and command elements. The data elements on the socket provide all of the data that are manipulated by or presented to a user (including all functions, data input, indicators, and displays).

Together with the commands, they provide access to the full functionality of the Target device or service in a non-modality specific form (e.g. it does not assume a particular type of user interface or display).

3.2 Universal Remote Consoles

The introduction of user interface sockets allows individuals to purchase home electronic devices individually over time (and from different manufacturers) and have them work with an intelligent controller they purchase (or have). Because the full functionality of the products is exposed via the user interface socket, it is easy for intelligent controllers to be able to directly access the full functionality of the products, rather than having to navigate all of the menus. The user interface socket also makes the devices “more machine understandable” as well.Work on universal remote controllers is currently being carried out at the University of Wisconsin, Georgia Tech, Marquette University, Carnegie Mellon University and University of Washington. These related efforts all focus on the development of a wide range of different user interfaces that could be applied to the same target devices to better match with the needs of their users.

3.3 Intelligent and Task Based Control

The existence of interface sockets also permits the introduction of controllers that span devices and that allow direct access to functionality of the devices without having to go through the standard menus to reach that function. The ability to control the functionality of multiple products simultaneously can for example allow an individual to issue a single command such as “play Masterpiece Theater” and have the controller change multiple settings on multiple products to cause the proper channel to appear be sent to the televisions which is turned on and changed from the DVD input to the cable box and the stereo to be changed from CD to television input. This type of multi-device task oriented control requires task modeling. An evolving standard on task model representation, CEA-2018, is currently being developed by the CEA working group R7 WG12 [11], and may help to provide this capability for future generations of devices in the digital home.

3.4 Universal Control Hub

To address the problem of non-homogeneous technologies and network technologies a “Universal Control Hub concept is being developed. The Universal Control Hub (UCH) is a gateway based architecture for implementing the Universal Remote Console (URC) framework [12] [13] in the digital home. It capitalizes on the features and functionality of the URC framework without requiring URC-compliant targets and controllers. The UCH architecture was originally proposed for UPnP based home networks [14], but is also applicable to any other networking platform and any combination of them.

In the UCH architecture, the control hub is the gateway between controllers and targets that would otherwise not be able to talk to each other. Since it handles most of the URC-related technologies internally, it can be used as a transition between legacy products and products using other technologies. It can also house task based, cross product control technologies, and, by acting as a front end to products, add interface intelligence to existing products. Because the Hub can download interface sockets and other resources from the Internet, it can also adapt both to particular controller and to hardware configurations in the home.

4 NCS as a Platform for Evolving Intelligence in the Home

The combination of these technologies allow for the gradual and natural introduction of intelligence into the home, capitalizing on existing products and incorporating new target (controlled) products as well as new controllers as they evolve and/or can be afforded. The Hub would allow them to control their legacy products as well as products using different control architectures. The ability to control the household products via URC technology means that users can select and change their controller over time to meet their changing abilities. For example, if a person acquires a disability they could buy a new controller that accommodates their new limitations and provides them with the ability to continue to operate their household devices. And as people age, they can secure controllers that match their abilities and that will work with the appliances they already have. More importantly, elders can keep the same controllers that they know and are accustomed to – and use them with new products. No longer would they have to be confused and learn a new interface each time an old product (television, washer, thermostat, alarm) needed to be replaced.

As task based modeling and natural language advance, they could pick a natural language controller and have it operate the products in their environment for them. For example, a person could simply ask for television programs by name when they wanted to watch them. Or they could describe which programs they would like to have recorded and automatically have them programmed to record (all this without having to mess with finding the programs, figuring out how to ask the product to record the programs, locate the recorded programs later, etc.). Later, when they replace their clock radio, they could pick one up that was also URC or otherwise network compatible and they would find that they could now set their alarm clock by simply telling their controller (which could be, for example, just a function in their phone) what time they would like to have the alarm set to. At Christmas, they might be given a socket-enabled coffeepot, with the result being that anyone in the family can easily set it, because they can simply ask their controller to do it for them. None of the appliances would need to be intelligent beyond exposing their function and taking commands via their user interface socket.

Additional layers of intelligence and sensors can then be installed in the home in this incremental way. Using the same architecture, each of these sensors or agents could provide any central controlling unit (or each other) the ability to sense or know things. In addition, Internet services may provide supplemental descriptions of Targets that new intelligent controllers can harness to interact with Targets in a way that was not possible when the Target was purchased.

5 Conclusion

Much needs to happen before the more advanced, intelligent interfaces can come to fruition. However, the combination of these technologies can provide function today and also provide the framework for additional intelligent and easier to use interfaces to be incorporated into houses as they mature. Already simple task based controls and a variety of universal remote consoles are under development to address the needs of different users.

Acknowledgments. This work was partially funded by the US Dept of Education, NIDRR, under Grant H133E030012 (RERC on IT Access); and by the EU 6th Framework Program under grant FP6-033502 (i2home). The opinions herein are those of the authors and not necessarily those of the funding agencies.

References

[1] Consumer Electronics Association: Home Theater Opportunities – CEA Market Research Report, (September 2006) (2006) http://www.ebrain.org/crs/crs_arch.asp?crscode=CRS290

[2] Zeven, P.: Do people need the gizmos we're selling? CNET News, (December 18, 2006) (2006) http://news.com.com/Do+people+need+the+gizmos+were+selling/2010-1041_3-6144335.html

[3] Den Ouden, E.: Developments of a Design Analysis Model for Consumer Complaints: revealing a new class of quality failures. Ph.D. thesis, Technische Universiteit Eindhoven (2006)

[4] Sullivan, K., Sorenson, P.: Ease Of Use/PC Quality Roundtable: Industry Challenge To Address Costly Problems, WINHEC (2004)

[5] Ogg, E.: Can Grandma figure out how to use it? CNET News, (October 13, 2006) (2006) http://news.com.com/The+key+to+gadget+buyers+hearts+Simplicity/2100-1041_3-6125477.html

[6] Universal Plug and Play (UPnP) Forum. http://www.upnp.org/

[7] CECED Home Appliances Interoperating Network (CHAIN). European Committee of Domestic Equipment Manufacturers (CECED). http://www.ceced.org/FEDE/easnet.dll/ExecReq/WPItem?eas:dat_im=010113&eas:display=CHAIN

[8] High-Definition Multimedia Interface (HDMI). http://www.hdmi.org

[9] High-Definition Audio-Video Network Alliance. http://www.hanaalliance.org/

[10] The LonWorks Platform: Technology Overview. Echelon. http://www.echelon.com/developers/lonworks/

[11] CEA R7 WG12, Task-Based User Interface. http://www.ce.org/Standards/CommitteeDetails.aspx?Id=000011032608

[12] ANSI/INCITS 289-2005, 290-2005, 291-2005, 292-2005 and 293-2005. Information Technology - Protocol to Facilitate Operation of Information and Electronic Products through Remote and Alternative Interfaces and Intelligent Agents. ANSI, (2005) http://myurc.org/obtain-copies.php

[13] ISO/IEC FCD 24752. Information technology – User interfaces – Universal remote console – 5 parts. International Organization for Standardization (ISO), (2006) http://www.iso.org/iso/en/CombinedQueryResult.CombinedQueryResult?queryString=24752

[14] Zimmermann, G., Vanderheiden, G., Rich, C.: Universal Control Hub & Task-Based User Interfaces. URC Consortium, (2006) http://myurc.org/publications/2006-Univ-Ctrl-Hub.php

Accessibility of Internet Portals in Ambient Intelligent Scenarios: Re-thinking Their Design and Implementation

Evangelos Vlachogiannis[1], Carlos A. Velasco[2], Henrike Gappa[2], Gabriele Nordbrock[2], and Jenny S. Darzentas[1]

[1] University of the Aegean, Department of Product and Systems Design
Ermoupolis, Syros, GR83200 (Greece)
{evlach,jennyd}@aegean.gr
[2] Fraunhofer-Institut für Angewandte Informationstechnik (FIT)
Schloss Birlinghoven, D53757 Sankt Augustin (Germany)
{carlos.velasco,henrike.gappa,gaby.nordbrock}@fit.fraunhofer.de

Abstract. Internet portals are gateways to the World Wide Web, which offer an amalgamation of services, like search engines, online shopping information, email, news, weather reports, stock quotes, community forums, maps, travel information, etc. Furthermore, with the arrival of the Mobile Web, they are also frequently used in Ambient Intelligence scenarios. This paper will discuss basic design considerations inspired by systems theory fundamental principles, where the portal as a whole and its components (known as *portlets*) are analyzed. This analysis also includes a set of user requirements for people with special needs gathered in previous user studies from the authors.

1 Introduction

Internet portals have become a de-facto standard for acquiring information from the World Wide Web. Initial portal implementations were actually generic taxonomies of Web sites (e.g., Yahoo!, Excite), which through the incorporation of the search functionality became more manageable and user friendly. However, the growth of the Web demanded more personalization of these services, and nowadays is unthinkable an Internet Portal without customized entry points like Google. Despite the maturity of some user modeling systems (see, e.g., [13]; or [19]), these personalized entry points rely only on sophisticated search engines combined with a tightened selection of domains.

There are many definitions for "portal" and many web pages contain in their headings the term portal. Smith ([24]) researched the topic from an academic and industrial standpoint, and established a definition that characterizes portals as "an infrastructure providing secure, customizable, personalizable, integrated access to dynamic content from a variety of sources, in a variety of source formats, wherever it is needed." While portal has been consecrated as a paradigm for more and more applications such as e-commerce, collaborative environments and entertainment hubs, many implementation infrastructures[1] and protocols have been developed. Recently,

[1] See, e.g., Apache Portals: http://portals.apache.org/ as an Open Source set of tools.

C. Stephanidis (Ed.): Universal Access in HCI, Part II, HCII 2007, LNCS 4555, pp. 245–253, 2007.

standardizations efforts have taken place aiming at interoperability. The Web Services for Remote Portlets (WSRP) ([20]) and JSR-168 ([1]) specifications are two well-known standards in this are. JSR-168 is a standard Java interface for portlets that builds on the J2EE programming model of servlets. This is an interface between a particular Java type of UI component and its hosting container. On the other hand, WSRP is a platform independent standard messaging interface for interacting with remote compliant UI components. In both specification these UI component are named "portlets". In the context of WSRP, a portlet "is a user-facing, interactive application component that renders markup fragments that can be aggregated and displayed by a portal."

WSRP shows off the emergent Web applications paradigm: developing a Web application as a portlet, makes it pluggable to any portal that conforms to the aforementioned specifications. The blending power of Web Services, combined with the standardization of portlets makes them everywhere available. This implies that portlets UI need to be designed without being aware of the rest of the portal.

Furthermore, scenarios of m-commerce and location-based services make such systems more distributed, introducing new requirements ([22]). Ideally, a Web portal would serve at the same time both desktop and mobile clients. But this also implies that the portal infrastructure would need to be capable of serving portlets from a Universal Design point of view. Having in mind such requirements, this paper proposes a design and implementation path for portal applications from a Universal Sesign standpoint, aiming at enabling seamless access to content and services any-time, any-where and in any fashion.

The following chapters discuss the importance of accessible design of portals, especially in such heterogeneous environments (Ambient Intelligence –AmI– environments) by discussing current portals accessibility status. Then, a "whole/parts" approach for confronting such issues is presented. Finally, conclusions in form of complements and extensions to current specifications context attributes and indicative guidelines are presented.

2 Portals' Accessibility and Ambient Intelligence

The World Wide Web has surpassed its original design goals and, as the ways to access the Internet diversify (along with the range of services offered). In an aging society, it becomes increasingly important to ensure accessibility of these services to everyone, including people with disabilities.

Under the umbrella of W3C's Web Accessibility Initiative (WAI[2]) guidelines and techniques are being continuously developed to cope with accessibility problems merged from the evolution of technologies and user's requirements. In 1999, WAI released the first version of the Web Content Accessibility Guidelines ([10]). The main drawbacks from this version were:

- **Technology focus:** the guidelines were focused on the key (W3C) Web technologies at the time of publication: HTML and CSS. This affects its application to new Web technologies that have appeared since then, and even to non-W3C technologies;

[2] http://www.w3.org/WAI/

- **Usability of the document:** the language of the document might not be appropriate for some of the intended target audiences. There were also ambiguity issues related to clarification on the meaning of specific checkpoints and their priority level;
- **Organization:** there are guidelines focusing on similar issues (e.g. graceful transformation). Grouping them under more generic topics will make the document easier to handle, and the underlying concepts easier to grasp;
- **Conformance and testing:** there are a number of checkpoints that began with the words "until user agents..." which make very difficult to determine when conformance could be claimed; and
- some **errata**.

To face that, WAI is currently working on a new version of this recommendation (WCAG 2.0, [7]), technology independent and organized around four design principles: 1) Content must be perceivable, 2) Interface elements in the content must be operable, 3) Content and controls must be understandable, and 4) Content must be robust enough to work with current and future technologies. In parallel, WAI develops guidelines both for authoring tools and for user agents.

In general, it can be argued that Web accessibility shares methods and techniques with the adaptive hypermedia and the adaptive web (see, e.g., [25]; [3]; [4]; [5]; [11]). Currently, other approaches that propose adaptation of existing non-accessible Web pages have appeared ([14]; [21]; WebAdapt[3]). Some of these are also incorporating semantics in their mechanisms for offering accessibility-related annotations.

2.1 m-Portal Accessibility in Intelligent Environments

On 26th June 2006, the Yankee Group announced the results of its 2006 Transatlantic Wireless Business Survey. According to that, "the percentage of mobile workers in European small businesses continues to rise as mobile investments become a business priority. More than 50% of small business employees are classified as mobile workers, spending more than 20% of their time away from their primary workspace. This figure grew from 48% in 2005." Current generations of mobile phones and infrastructures named 2,5G and 3G are connected to digital communications infrastructures constituting a global network. Such a media can host a wide number of services including electronic commerce, known as m-commerce, pushing the ambient intelligence field.

The "ambient intelligence" term comparing with the preceding "ubiquitous computing," currently mainly implemented by mobile technology, emphasizes that "it does not solely rely on ubiquitous computing (i.e., useful, pleasant and unobtrusive presence of computing devices everywhere) but also on ubiquitous networking (i.e., access to network and computing facilities everywhere) and on intelligent aware interfaces (i.e., perception of the system as intelligent by people who naturally interact with the system that automatically adapts to their preference)." ([15])

In addition, the term mobility is quite broad and may be subdivided into three categories ([23]): "(i) personal mobility that deals with the mobility of people who

[3] http://www.webadapt.org/

may not necessarily carry a device, (ii) computer mobility that deals with the mobility of devices, and (iii) computational mobility that deals with the migration of code over physical nodes."

In case of mobile portals, the following issues arise:

- Personal mobility: a mobile portal need to communicate information to the user in a seamless way, having in mind that the mobile user has limited attention to the application, as in this case the environment might have a strong influence. This case could be somehow compared with a user with cognitive disabilities trying to acquire the same information.
- Computer mobility: the application needs to sense the location of the user and "localize" the information. Here, portals' personalization mechanism could contribute. For instance, a common user profile could be used to serve a number of portlets.
- Computational mobility: the distributed nature of a portal could be expressed in terms of Web Services and WSRP.

Venkatesh et al. [28] strongly suggest that "relevance, structure, and personalization are essential to creating a positive wireless interface experience." Therefore, personalization needs to accompany m-commerce services, to drive them to success. Dholakia & Rask [12] suggests that m-portals need to "focus on personalization, permission and specification of content in order to offer extended mobility and locability for the user." From the implementation point of view, Chen et al. [9] use the term "m-service" that extends the concept of Web Service to the wireless domain. They propose a service oriented architecture of an "m-service portal" giving emphasis to "intelligent m-services", context-aware/semantic-enabled agent-like architectures to improve adaptability and flexibility of the m-service portal.

2.2 Portals Accessibility: Evaluation Results

The accessibility of portals as a distinct type of Web application has not been subject of such wider attention as the accessibility of normal Web sites. Gappa & Nordbrock [16] realized a user study on portal accessibility with 28 users, including older persons and people with disabilities, to analyze particular requirements of portals. The results showed issues similar to those of users of mobile devices, as presented earlier. Further usability investigations will need to be carried out at the prototype level, when applying the proposed design guidelines to Web portals.

3 The Whole/Parts Approach for Portals' Design and Implementation

The whole/parts approach has been inspired from systems thinking basic principles. Systems thinking ([8]) go beyond classical analytical methods and face problems in a non reductive way. The sum of the properties of subsystems/components does not define the properties of the whole system, but is something more. The whole system also has emerging properties that determine its behavior.

Thus, in case of a Web page, the whole page can be inaccessible even though its individual components are fully accessible. Furthermore, this is typically the case with portals that aggregate portlets from different sources. Therefore, an accessible portal implies both portlets accessibility and complete portal accessibility.

Under this prism, this paper proposes a whole/parts perspective that considers portal systems as a whole and the portlets as parts that need to have some attributes, behaviors and organization for accomplishing their purpose. This perspective needs to integrate user needs with device profiles ([27]), which includes information about hardware and user agent capabilities. Of course, the equation for an intelligent environment needs to be closed with context-aware components. Then the problem space might be expressed as:

Accessible Portal Interaction = accessible communication of [accessible aggregation of (accessible portlets + accessible navigation)]

In other words, accessible portlets and navigation are necessary but not enough for composing an accessible portal as the emerging properties would probably result to an inaccessible complete portal. Thus, portlets and navigation should have such properties capable of sensing their aggregated effect on the portal as a whole. Accessible communication of the aggregated content refers to personalization/ adaptation features involving issues such as user/device modeling ([27]) and location/ context of use awareness. The following subsections will briefly discuss portals accessibility issues under such a prism.

3.1 Portal Navigation

For working on the navigation aspect of accessible portal systems, a good test case is made by investigating the case of mobile portal systems ([17]). Mobile devices can be a very good simulation platform for designers of Web portals, because they emulate different access problems due to their limited screen size and input capabilities.

For such portals, navigation is the key to success. The users need to access the information they are looking for without cognitive navigation overhead. Artificial Intelligence techniques have been used ([26]) for reducing click-distances and providing successful navigation. Similarly, in accessible Web portals, users need to interact with portlets in a transparent way and also have at their disposal powerful and useful search engines.

Authors classify portal navigation in: 1) main portal navigation, 2) inter-portlet navigation and 3) intra-portlet navigation. Further we could distinguish two kinds of hyperlinks: (i) user interface links and (ii) semantic links. Semantic links are links that provide additional information on a given topic and may lead to another Web page. User interface links are considered as the repeatable links that are provided in a toolbar paradigm and adds overhead to the actual content.

In general, for a portal page instance to be accessible, it is important to make sure that when the page is serialized by an actor it will produce an acceptable result. I.e., the windowed (portlets windows) version needs to be effectively transformed to a good structured user interface. This implies that portal systems need a mechanism to semantically communicate the portal page structure to the user agents. Consider for instance PSML[4] or an automatically generated portlet navigation, or even a separation of navigation concerns using Semantic Web technologies.

In other words, navigation should be metadata and not data. Thus a separation of the control of a Web resource from the resource itself is needed. This will allow the actors to semantically extract the navigation information and use it to guide themselves within the Web resource. The metadata can also contain more information about the structure and the content of the Web resource (i.e., pages' descriptions and relations). Furthermore, this approach could offer much towards the Semantic Web. The navigation would then be much more easily being adapted both to the actor, and to the purpose of the content (e.g., learning). Consider for instance the scenarios that aim to be personalized navigation guides.

The proposed abstract navigation language would allow fill such a gap and provide more opportunities. For example, one might consider a portal that can be accessed via speech input-output while driving. Present-day adaptive navigation techniques ([6]) could be used such as link hiding or link generation. This might allow "virtual portals" (aggregation of Web resources in a form of navigation from a set of Web resources sites) and much more.

3.2 Portal Aggregation and Interaction Layers

Portal systems consist of portlet applications that can provide completely different functionalities and serve completely different aims. Portlet applications consist of a number of portlets that have a common aim, but at the same time they are reusable and autonomous components.

In simple terms, aggregation is actually markup that creates the frames for the portlets and puts them in a given resource. Although visually presented in tabular form, the markup should use CSS techniques for layout ([2]), as recommended in accessibility guidelines ([7]).

The aggregation of the content on an interactive environment such as a portal involves an aggregated interaction as well. We can distinguish page interaction and portlet interaction because the first one refers to the interaction that happens on the portal as a whole, and the last one that happens on a specific portlet without affecting the rest of the portal. This can be seen both on a client side and on a server side manner. For instance, a client script might cause change of behavior of another portlet and consequently to the resultant portal page instance. Finally, the AJAX[5] upcoming technology is an interesting case that its accessibility is under investigation.

3.3 Portlets

Portlet interfaces may consist of hypertext and/or media content. To be accessible, these need to follow Web accessibility recommendations. Here, a distinction between portlets and Web pages needs to be made because of the former's fragmented nature.

Already, above mentioned portal specifications define portlets' attributes that affect portal as a whole. An example is the CSS classes including portlets' title. In the

---

[4] Portal Structure Markup Language: http://portals.apache.org/jetspeed-2/guides/guide-psml.html

[5] http://developer.mozilla.org/en/docs/AJAX:Getting_Started

context of intelligent and distributed environments, context-aware attributes should be introduced for extending portlets capabilities and as a result portals' services and information accessibility.

3.4 Indicative Guidelines

Following the proposed approach, related literature conclusions, best practices (see, e.g., [18]) and authors experience ([27]) some exemplary principles and guidelines for designing and developing accessible portals are suggested. This attempt is by no means an exhaustive investigation of the requirements, but aims to show the need for such a work. The proposed portlet design guidelines, mapped to WCAG 2.0 guidelines ([7]) are:

- Guideline 1.3 (*Ensure that information and structure can be separated from presentation*)
  - Follow a serializable multi-layered layout design approach.
- Guideline 2.1 (*Make all functionality operable via a keyboard interface*)
  - Make portlet controls operable through a keyboard interface. Do it in a non obstructive way.
  - Personalization and customization actions should be operable via keyboard interface.
- Guideline 2.2 (*Allow users to control time limits on their reading or interaction*)
  - Portlets must not refresh the portal page without the confirmation of the user.
- Guideline 2.4 (*Provide mechanisms to help users find content, orient themselves within it, and navigate through it*)
  - Provide a site map.
  - Do not use more than 6 main navigation buttons on a screen.
  - Provide inter-portlet navigation on the top of each page.
  - Provide way to go to inter-portlet-navigation from every portlet.
- Guideline 2.5 (*Help users avoid mistakes and make it easy to correct mistakes that do occur*)
  - Provide to your search engine with the capacity to suggest alternative keywords.
- Guideline 3.1 (*Make text content readable and understandable*)
  - When possible, use alternative modes in terms of modalities (i.e. multimedia) to offer further understandability
  - Provide internationalization
  - Provide metadata for important information to allow content adaptation
- Guideline 3.2 (*Make the placement and functionality of content predictable*)
  - Remain in portal environment and on working portlet. Provide anchors at the beginning of a portlet, so that it can be directly accessed.
  - For all external links provide visual cues and adequate title attributes.
- Guideline 4.1 (*Support compatibility with current and future user agents (including assistive technologies)*)
  - Global page information is not permitted
  - Keep every portlet entity (instance) unique on a page.

4 Conclusions and Further Work

We have proposed an initial set of accessibility guidelines that will support the design of portlets and portals in any type of environment, including AmI scenarios. Further work needs to be carried out in terms of prototyping, usability testing and incorporation of semantic information proceeding from context and device. In this regard, we distinguish between:

- **Context-aware static attributes:** user modeling attributes like those used in the Adaptive Hypermedia field ([4]; i.e., user preferences, knowledge, background, etc.)
- **Context-aware session attributes:** attributes that characterize short term interaction in ubiquitous environments, like device capabilities and context issues ([27]).

Additionally, work in the area of standardization would need to be proposed to ensure industry take-up of any proposed recommendation.

References

1. Abdelnur, A., Hepper, S. (eds.): JavaTM Portlet Specification, Version 1.0. (2003) Available online at: http://jcp.org/en/jsr/detail?id=168
2. Bos, B., Çelik, T., Hickson, I., Lie, H.W. (eds): Cascading Style Sheets, level 2 revision 1. CSS 2.1 Specification. W3C Working Draft (June 13, 2005) Available online at: http://www.w3.org/TR/CSS21/
3. Brusilovsky, P.: Methods and Techniques of Adaptive Hypermedia. User Modeling and User-Adapted Interaction 6, 87–129 (1996)
4. Brusilovsky, P.: Adaptive Hypermedia. User Modeling and User-Adapted Interaction 11, 87–110 (2001)
5. Brusilovsky, P., Maybury, M.T.: From adaptive hypermedia to the adaptive web Commun. ACM 45, 30–33 (2002)
6. Brusilovsky, P.: Adaptive Navigation Support: From Adaptive Hypermedia to the Adaptive Web and Beyond. PsychNology Journal 2, 7–23 (2004)
7. Caldwell, B., Chisholm, W., Slatin, J., Vanderheiden, G. (eds.): Web Content Accessibility Guidelines 2.0, W3C Working Draft (April 27, 2006) Available online at: http:// www.w3.org/ TR/WCAG20/
8. Checkland, P.B.: Systems Thinking, Systems Practice. John Wiley & Sons, New York (1999)
9. Chen, M., Zhang, D., Zhou, L.: Providing web services to mobile users: the architecture design of an m-service portal. Int. J. Mobile Communications 3(1), 1–18 (2005)
10. Chisholm, W., Vanderheiden, G., Jacobs, I. (eds.): Web Content Accessibility Guidelines 1.0, W3C Recommendation (May 5, 1999) Available online at: http:// www.w3.org/ TR/ WCAG10/
11. De Bra, P.: Adaptive educational hypermedia on the web. Commun. ACM 45, 60–61 (2002)
12. Dholakia, N., Rask, M.: Dynamic Elements of Emerging Mobile Portal Strategies Research Institute for Telecommunications and Information Marketing (RITIM) (2002)

13. Fischer, G.: User Modeling in Human–Computer Interaction. User Modeling and User-Adapted Interaction 11, 65–86 (2001)
14. Huang, A.W., Sundaresan, N.: Aurora: a conceptual model for Web-content adaptation to support the universal usability of Web-based services. In: Proceedings on the 2000 conference on Universal Usability CUU '00, pp. 124–131. ACM Press, New York (2000)
15. Issarny, V., Sacchetti, D., Tartanoglu, F., Sailhan, F., Chibout, R., Levy, N., Talamona, A.: Developing Ambient Intelligence Systems: A Solution based on Web Services. Automated Software Engg. 12, 101–137 (2005)
16. Gappa, H., Nordbrock, G.: Applying Web accessibility to Internet portals. Universal Access in the Information Society 3, 80–87 (2004)
17. Godwin, R., Haenel, W.: Portal Aggregation for Pervasive Devices. IBM WebSphere Developer Technical Journal (2002) Available online at: http:// www.ibm.com/ developerworks/websphere/techjournal/0210_godwin/godwin.html
18. Hepper, S., Lamb, M.: Best practices: Developing portlets using JSR 168 and WebSphere Portal V5.02. International Business Machines Corporation (2005) Available online at: http://download.boulder.ibm.com/ibmdl/pub/software/dw/wes/pdf/0403_hepper-JSR168_BestPractices.pdf
19. Kobsa, A.: Generic user modeling systems. User Modeling and User-Adapted Interaction 11, 49–63 (2001)
20. Kropp, A., Leue, C., Thompson, R. (eds.): Web Services for Remote Portlets Specification. OASIS Standard (August 2003) Available online at: http://www.oasis-open.org/committees/download.php/3343/oasis-200304-wsrp-specification-1.0.pdf
21. Parmanto, B., Ferrydiansyah, R., Saptono, A., Song, L., Sugiantara, I.W., Hackett, S.: AcceSS: accessibility through simplification & summarization. In: Proceedings of the 2005 International Cross-Disciplinary Workshop on Web Accessibility (W4A '05), pp. 18–25. ACM Press, New York (2005)
22. Rabin, J., McCathieNevile, C. (eds.): Mobile Web Best Practices 1.0, Basic Guidelines. W3C Proposed Recommendation (November 2, 2006) Available online at: http:// www.w3.org/ TR/mobile-bp/
23. Roman, G., Picco, G.P., Murphy, A.L.: Software engineering for mobility: a roadmap. In: Proceedings of the Conference on The Future of Software Engineering (ICSE '00), pp. 241–258. ACM Press, New York (2000)
24. Smith, M.A.: Portals: toward an application framework for interoperability Commun. ACM 47, 93–97 (2004)
25. Stephanidis, C.: Adaptive Techniques for Universal Access. User Modeling and User-Adapted Interaction 11, 159–179 (2001)
26. Smyth, B., Cotter, P.: Intelligent Navigation for Mobile Internet Portals Proceedings of the 18th International Joint Conference on Artificial Intelligence, AI Moves to IA: Workshop on Artificial Intelligence, Information Access, and Mobile Computing, Acapulco, Mexico, (August 11, 2003) Available online at: http:// www.dimi.uniud.it/ workshop/ ai2ia/ cameraready/smyth.pdf
27. Velasco, C.A., Mohamad, Y., Gilman, A.S., Viorres, N., Vlachogiannis, E., Arnellos, A., Darzentas, J.S.: Universal access to information services—the need for user information and its relationship to device profiles. Universal Access in the Information Society 3, 88–95 (2004)
28. Venkatesh, V., Ramesh, V., Massey, A.P.: Understanding usability in mobile commerce Commun. ACM 46, 53–56 (2003)

Engineering Social Awareness in Work Environments

Dhaval Vyas[1], Marek R. van de Watering[2], Anton Eliëns[2], and Gerrit C. van der Veer[3]

[1] Human Media Interaction Group, Twente University
The Netherlands
dvyas@few.vu.nl
[2] Intelligent Multimedia Group, Vrije Universiteit Amsterdam
The Netherlands
{rvdwate,eliens}@few.vu.nl
[3] School of Computer Science, Open Universiteit Nederland
The Netherlands
gerrit@acm.org

Abstract. A growing interest is seen for designing intelligent environments that support personally meaningful, sociable and rich everyday experiences. In this paper we describe an intelligent, large screen display called *Panorama* that is aimed at supporting and enhancing social awareness within an academic work environment. Panorama is not intended to provide instrumental or other productivity related information. Rather, the goal of Panorama is to enhance social awareness by providing interpersonal and rich information related to co-workers and their everyday interactions in the department. A two-phase assessment of Panorama showed to promote curiosity and interest in exploring different activities in the environment.

1 Introduction

Ambient intelligence, ubiquitous and pervasive computing technologies have primarily focused on the productivity and efficiency side of work environments. We believe that these technologies could be used for designing smart environments that enhance social and interpersonal relationships amongst co-workers. The issue of supporting social connections between co-workers is especially important in big organizations, where, sometimes, social awareness is neglected in the tension of heavy workloads, time clashes, a lack of social encounters between employees, and a lack of suitable platforms for establishing connections [1]. There is a deficit in the current understandings of social awareness of non-work activities and how technologies can be designed to support these. In this paper we introduce a large, artistically inspired display called Panorama, for the staff room of our computer science department. Panorama supports asynchronous, mixed initiative interaction between co-workers focusing mainly on non-critical and non-work related information and activities. Panorama attempts to mediate information about co-workers in an engaging manner to enhance social awareness within the department.

Approaches for designing smart and intelligent environments within office and work settings keep users out of the 'awareness loop', i.e. technology generates

C. Stephanidis (Ed.): Universal Access in HCI, Part II, HCII 2007, LNCS 4555, pp. 254–263, 2007.

(using sensing techniques) information about users and their environment and represents it in meaningful ways. In our approach, Panorama views co-workers as the integral and active part of the environment and utilizes different intentional and unintentional social acts for generating awareness.

Panorama utilizes two main design concepts: Self-Reflections and Casual Encounters. Self-Reflections are explicit, user-initiated interactions that allow co-workers to contribute their personal and non-critical information to the ongoing activities of the overall environment. Casual Encounters are implicit, system initiated interactions, in which Panorama collects information about the ongoing activities within the department and offers resources of potential interest from the environment.

In the rest of the paper, we will first describe some background work on technologically supported social awareness and our own conceptualization of social awareness. Next, we introduce the Panorama system and the mechanisms it uses to support social awareness. In the end we discuss the validity of our approach through a two-phase assessment of Panorama.

2 Social Awareness and Intelligent Environments

The notion of 'awareness' can be seen as an important aspect of intelligent environments. In past research, awareness is applied in two ways: system-oriented and people-oriented [13].

In *system-oriented* awareness, smart artifact or environment takes technology-initiated decisions based on the historical information and data. The focus here is on objectively observable cues and information from the environment e.g. availability, presence or geographical positions. Secondly, the importance is given to the productivity side of work. In some recent examples, awareness is supported through indications of the presence of colleagues, physical positioning, information about their daily schedules and office calendars [e.g. 3, 10, 14].

In *people-oriented* awareness, the focus is user-centric, in the sense that the system intelligence is used in a way that empowers users to make mature and responsible decisions. In some recent examples of people-oriented awareness, technology is used to provide information about workloads by representing email transactions within an office building [11], to give indications about the mood of an office setting [13] and to give indications of different activities in an office [12].

To our observation, in the system-oriented awareness the user is kept out of the 'awareness loop'. By awareness loop we mean a cycle of capturing, processing and representing the awareness information about a physical and *lived* environment. Placing our research in the line of people-oriented awareness, we believe that for enhancing social awareness, users should be seen as active contributors of awareness information. Within the social contexts social awareness is generated by different social acts of users and not solely by the technology. Technology should be used as an infrastructure to support social awareness between users.

2.1 Conceptualizing Social Awareness in Intelligent Systems

Social awareness is a very subtle aspect of our overall awareness, which can be accessed only 'indirectly' through a granular understanding of space, mediators, human conduct and culture [1]. Social awareness can only be felt; it cannot be seen or measured in a precise manner. To be aware of somebody we need to feel his or her presence in a somewhat temporary and subtle way. Because, if their presence is too apparent then we tend to take them for granted. Social awareness can be seen as a conscious feeling of belonging, relatedness, and care prompted by the environment. This sort of conceptualization leads to a reflective approach, which suggests that an intelligent awareness technology should allow users to reflect on a three–way relationship of: "how I see myself", "how I see others" and "how others see me" [7].

To design intelligent systems, we conceptualize social awareness as reflections that are supported by 'cues' and 'traces' of users' actions in a specific environment. *A trace of human activity is recognized as 'social' when it allows someone to acquaint themselves with others without receiving explicitly expressed information about them* [1, p.6]. These cues and traces users leave over the environment make it compelling and emotionally valuable for a new person. When the next person chooses the same environment, he intentionally or unintentionally adds his own cues and traces over to the same environment that eventually would turn the physical settings into a social world. Sometimes, these vague and low-fidelity cues and traces might be valued more than bold and high fidelity cues for community building. [5]

3 Panorama: A Social Awareness System

We have designed an intelligent, asynchronous, large screen display called *Panorama* (Fig. 1). Panorama transforms explicit and implicit inputs from co-workers into an artistic representation to provide information about and an impression of the social environment in the department.

Fig. 1. Panorama representing an 'Idle' environment

Panorama is not intended to provide work-schedules, project details, or any other kind of work-related information. Its goal is to allow the co-workers to leave personal, 'digitalized' cues and traces onto the environment and help them construct social awareness within the department. Our intention is to allow asynchronous communication of personal and environmental information in a meaningful way between co-workers by focusing on both: information and impression. The staff room in our department is a common place for many social activities. Most of these are closely related to the routine activities of staff members such as collecting posts, using fax machine, using coffee machine and microwave and having informal chats with co-workers. In addition, the staff room is also used for celebrating different social events like employees' birthday, approval for funding of a new project and so on. By placing Panorama in the staff room, we want the system to provide a starting point for social interaction among co-workers and to (re)kindle interest in exploring different activities in the environment.

Co-workers can electronically submit personal information to Panorama, such as personal announcements or news. Panorama uses motion and sound sensors (placed in the common area of the department) to gather implicit information from the department. It can, for example, adjust its representations based on different real-time activities detected by the sensors and captured still images or real-time video when a specific sensor is triggered. Panorama is an "intelligent" system in the sense that it transforms different types of information into an accordingly artistic and engaging representation, allowing co-workers to playfully manipulate this information (e.g. by waving in front of the camera or by submitting personalized images and messages).

In terms of presentation, Panorama shows a number of different 3D planes on which submitted or recorded images, videos and text are placed. It presents this information in a way that resembles a virtual gallery, i.e. images and videos moving along the wall and floor of the gallery in a continuous cycle. The movement indicates passing of time and it can be dynamically adjusted in speed and direction based on the sensor input. At the bottom of the screen, a number of square images provides streaming previews of the information that is in the system, providing an overview of the information. Panorama also supports scrolling text messages (e.g. news items, personal quotes) on the screen in the similar direction. Next to presenting explicit information, Panorama uses different visual effects such as particles, overlays, shaders and changing background color to implicitly mediate activity and mood in the department.

3.1 Design Methods

For designing Panorama, we wanted to understand the social dynamics of our department and co-workers' current and aspired practices of being aware of others. We used three complementary methods: Open-ended Observations, Contextual Inquiries and Cultural Probes [6]. The aim of using these ethnographic methods and tools was to get a thorough vision of co-workers' interaction dynamics, including spatial, temporal and socio-political issues within the department. As described in the previous section that social awareness can only be ephemerally observed through rich and personal experiences as conveyed by the users, we adapted our Cultural Probes methodology to focus on the social aspects of an academic department. This helped us going beyond the inspirational fascination of Cultural Probes and developing tangible design concepts.

3.2 "Shared" Initiative Interaction

Panorama supports an interaction model that allows shared control of interaction. By sharing the control between the environment and the co-workers, Panorama exploits explicit interaction (Fig. 2) – allowing co-workers to support their 'self-reflections' amongst each other; as well as, implicit interaction (Fig. 3) – utilizing the power of sensor-based proactive environment for expressing 'casual encounters'.

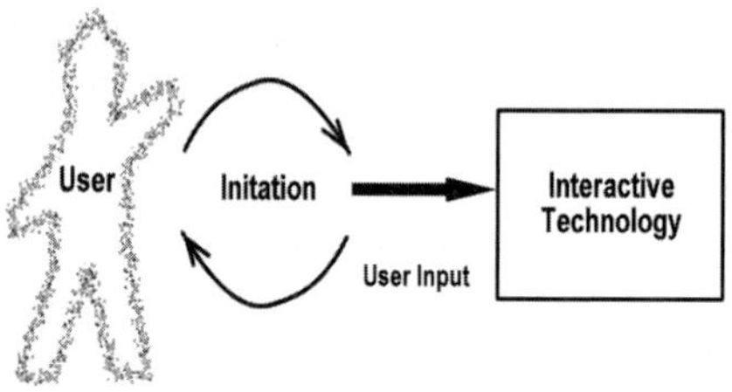

Fig. 2. Explicit Interaction: Conveying Self-Reflections to the co-workers through user inputs

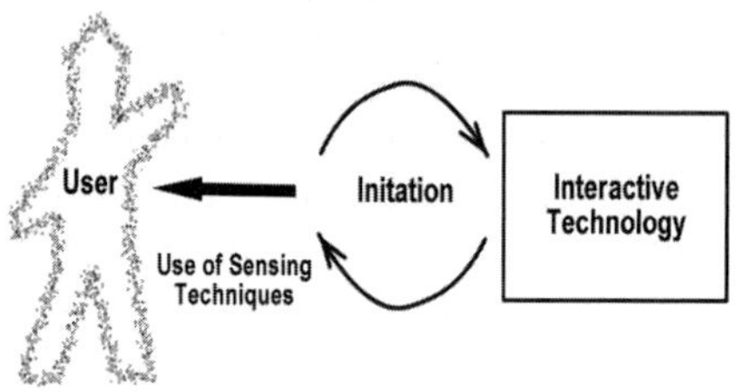

Fig. 3. Implicit Interaction: Use of sensing techniques to convey Casual Encounters amongst the co-workers

Self Reflections. For addressing the issue of self reflection, explicit user initiated interaction is used. For co-workers this means that they can contribute towards the ongoing activities of the overall environment with their personal and non-critical information or data. The technology serves as a tool that allows co-workers to support their social needs, such as sharing non-work related news (announcing the birth of a new born child), personal achievements (e.g. best paper award), personal interests (e.g. favorite books, favorite conferences), etc. In this case, the technology does not necessarily be passively receiving feeds from users. It in fact filters and alters contents and represents content in a compelling manner.

Casual Encounters. The concept of casual encounters is realized when the technology proactively pushes information about the ongoing activities within the department. Casual encounters provide an added value to the departmental social environment, especially, when during heavy workloads and frequent time-clashes physical interaction between co-workers is not possible. The technology can serve as a mechanism by which co-workers can be socially aware of each other by knowing their presence, social events and relevant non-critical activities within the department. In this case, even though users receive information from the technology, they can actively comprehend the implications of their action (either alone or in groups) upon the technology.

3.3 Representation

By conceptualizing social awareness as reflections of cues and traces of different social acts, it was important for us to consider the *meaning* that we were embedding in Panorama. Our decision of creating a representation for Panorama was based on available resources and on a number of assumptions that we regarded as facilitating social awareness.

The self-reflections (such as objects of personal interests) are represented as a flow of images using particle systems. Since these are used to form a sense of belonging and recognition, these are presented without any form of modification of the actual content. To add an artistic flavor, different particle flows are used to focus viewers' attention. The objects of self-reflections are seen as clues and traces, when interpreted within the departmental context can aid to support social awareness.

The casual encounters are represented as still images or videos generated through sensor-triggered cameras in the staff and printer rooms. To emphasize the fact that casual encounters are important and not necessarily the people involved in them, Panorama uses different level of abstractions to emphasize the peripheral nature of social awareness. This also takes into account the privacy issues that may arise when monitoring people in real-time. The videos captured by Panorama are represented in abstract forms using shaders and particle overlay effects.

The overall mood and activity level in the department is captured using different movement and sound sensors. Inspired by [11], the overall activity level is represented using different visual effects and by adjusting the speed of the information flow. Panorama uses sensor-triggered, transparent particle effects that can be shown at any layer of the Panorama interface. Increased activity level, for example, could generate more particle effects, abstraction and a higher speed of representation. We chose particle effects for their aesthetic richness to stimulate curiosity and to decrease predictability that might evolve into boredom.

3.4 Two Levels of Communication

Panorama establishes two levels of communication amongst the co-workers. This results from our two-fold aim of combining specific *information* with overall *impression* to support social awareness within the department.

Panorama provides concrete building blocks of *information* by providing the precise information such as individual announcements, achievements and so on in the form of unaltered images, texts and video streams. This way, self-reflections are mediated as a direct representation of reality, establishing detailed communication of information through the system. The movement and placement of the representation in turn are used to focus co-workers' attention. Although abstracted in part using shader techniques and other visual effects due to privacy concerns and to stimulate curiosity, casual encounters are also examples of this type of explicit communication of information. Both mechanisms aid co-workers for extracting the information about social awareness directly from what they see on-screen.

On the other hand, Panorama provides an *impression* about the overall environment by representing different set of information in certain ways to indicate the activity level within the department. Panorama uses real-time sensor input to gather information regarding overall activity in the department and based on this Panorama changes its representation. As the activity level increases, the speed, overlays and abstractions of different moving objects also increase. This sort of indications of increased activity level is generated through different social acts of the co-workers. Interestingly, for co-workers Panorama provides an indirect way of controlling its representations. This way Panorama may influence co-workers' working practices. For example, workers can adjust their ways of working after receiving indications about the overall activity level of the department.

4 Assessing Panorama

We mentioned earlier that social awareness is inherently subjective and subtle in nature and it cannot be measured in a precise manner. Methods for evaluating technological aspects of a system may be impractical or unsatisfactory when evaluating systems meant to support subjective and interpersonal aspects [15], such as understanding their social awareness. Previous research [8, 9] has shown that mixed-reality artistic interfaces can better be evaluated using a combination of argumentation ('art criticism') and informal conversation with users.

The challenge for us as designers was to understand to what extent the Panorama system helps co-workers of our department to make sense of the current environment and how this could lead to their desired experiences. We were interested knowing what kind of interpretations and meanings the co-workers construct about Panorama, their subjective understandings of Panorama, their theories of what it is and their metaphors for describing it.

To validate our understanding of social awareness, in the assessment we developed three configurations of Panorama representing three types of environments: idle, live and chaotic. These representations were created mainly to help us get a controlled view of co-workers' interpretations about Panorama.

In the three configurations we supported an increasing amount of information with an increasing number of presentation mechanisms (speed, color, visual effects). The *idle* configuration (Fig.1) provides a constant flow of information, without any extra layers or visual effects. This configuration is the basis for the next two configurations. The *live* configuration provides flashes of attention to self-reflections by moving these on a top layer, and adds particle effects and transparency to images depicting casual encounters. We regarded this configuration as the most useful combination for representing dynamics impressions and detailed information. Finally, the *chaotic* configuration provides increasing speed of movement, added multiple layers of moving objects on top of the *live* configuration, and increased amount and spread of abstract visual effects. We hypothesized that this configuration could be confusing for most users due to the relatively high visual density.

We organized our assessment in two sessions.

1. We installed a working prototype of Panorama in a laboratory setting and invited 8 participants – ranging from senior lectures, to support staff and from PhD researchers to students (see Fig. 4). Without providing any precise information about our assessment we confronted them with 3 different configurations of Panorama for an equal amount of time. During each configuration we asked participants to individually write down answers for questions related to their perceptions and understanding about Panorama, the difference between the 3 configurations and their perceived effects of having Panorama in the staff room. In the later part we asked them to discuss the suitability of Panorama in an academic department. Through this we sought to understand the social construction of meanings amongst different participants.

2. Next, we installed Panorama in our staff room (Fig. 5). As Panorama is meant to be an active part of the environment in the department, we were interested knowing how Panorama would be welcomed in the staff room. We set up Panorama next to the coffee machine in the staff room and observed what happened. We actively switched between the three configurations so that people would notice and comment on these. In some cases, we questioned people on their thoughts and interpretations, mostly about the way in which the system would affect their life at the department.

Fig. 4. Session 1 of Panorama assessment (in laboratory settings)

Fig. 5. Session 2 of Panorama assessment (in the staff room)

Results: In session 1, participants provided some interesting perspectives on Panorama. It was clear to all participants what Panorama was about. Some described it as, *"it reflects the dynamics at our department"*, *"it demonstrates what's the department in a virtual way"*, *"a lazy way to get information about the department"*, and so on. The participants showed a preference for the "live" environment – the second configuration of Panorama. The "idle" configuration was perceived as too slow when thinking of the dynamics of the department. The "chaotic" configuration, being too dense in presentation left a very little traces and indications of the detailed information about the department but provided a nice impression of a hectic environment in the department. The images of self-reflections as floating overlay objects were appreciated for focusing participants' attentions. The participants expressed their interest in recognizing people and objects. When an object or person was not recognized, the participants indicated that this would be a starting point for exploration and conversation.

In session 2 the staff members described Panorama as "nice" and "fun". In this session, we did not explicitly invite anyone. Staff members came to the room to do their routine activities like checking the post, sending fax or having coffee. Panorama initiated curiosity amongst the onlookers. Some comments were made that sparked conversations based on the artifacts and people that were depicted in the system. Both in the still images and the real time videos, most staff members liked that fact that they could see themselves. This resulted in people waiting for their images to come up in the system and manipulating the video recording by for example waving their hands. Panorama performing in its proposed environment, workers who queued for the coffee machine (Fig. 5) glanced at the system and commented aloud on what they saw. In many cases this resulted in them becoming part of 'the group' of onlookers. Curiosity was observed to be a starting point for interacting with the system, opening up ways to form a bond with the system that enabled the recognition of the information presented on Panorama. Importantly, regular activities in the staff room such as informal meetings with students were not interrupted by Panorama being present. Panorama also provided additional topics for informal talk without imposing or enforcing anything onto the people who were present.

In both sessions participants expressed the need for a higher level of direct interaction with the system, mostly thinking of the interface to be touch-screen. This could allow users to activate their channels of interest, thus filtering the available information. Interestingly, some participants asked if the system would be able to run on their desktops, supporting our proposals for a lightweight version of the system.

5 Discussion: Users in the 'Awareness Loop'

The notion of disappearance, seamlessness and intelligence coined by the ubiquitous computing [17] and ambient intelligence [4] paradigms has been fundamentally based on the technological assumptions of users' activity and intentions. This notion has been criticized for many reasons. First, it assumes the use of specific media and tools for users' seamless interaction with the environment. However, in reality our everyday encounters may involve interaction with many heterogeneous media and tools and we may use, adapt or interweave to support our activities [2]. Their technology-oriented conceptualization of context is very limited and sometime unachievable. Secondly, some of the scenarios of ambient intelligence [4] conceptualize users as 'passive receivers' of information. From the user experience perspective, users contribute as much to the interaction as the technology and the environment does [15]. And, thirdly, when technology becomes a part of our everyday used things like pillows, sofas, tables, etc., affordances of these things also change. Scenarios of ambient intelligence and ubiquitous computing assume that users will use these artifacts in their natural and traditional ways. However, as recently argued [16], affordances of an artifact emerge during the actual practice and use and they cannot be defined in a pre-deterministic ways.

Panorama uses the 'awareness' aspect to support meaningful and valuable experiences by enhancing non-work related social awareness. It extends the current application of intelligence and awareness from people's presence and activities to aspects of care, belonging and community building. Panorama acts as a tool for self-reflection and casual encounters between co-workers. In the two-phase assessment of our installation, we did not pretend to measure social awareness, as such. However, it was clear from the study that Panorama provided ways to encourage co-workers to explore different activities in the department and emphasize their presence by the active contribution of self-reflections. This confirmed our assumptions that community-level awareness can benefit more from the information related to people's values, culture and attitudes [5] then from functional and instrumental information.

6 Future Research

Taking into account the feedback gathered during the two assessment sessions, our future research for Panorama will focus on establishing better interaction mechanisms, dealing with the privacy issues and incorporating the three configurations. In order to provide direct and possibly playful interactions with Panorama we plan to incorporate touch-screen functionality. We are currently investigating the use of advanced shaders techniques to generate abstract and artful effects on real time images and video. This should further promote curiosity and at the same time deal with the privacy issues. The three experimental configurations of Panorama proved to be very useful, hinting on the future use of variable information density and indicating how lively it is at work.

References

1. Bødker, S., Christiansen, E.: Computer support for social awareness in flexible work. In: CSCW, Netherlands, vol. 15, pp. 1–28. Springer, Heidelberg (2006)
2. Chalmers, M., Galani, A.: Seamful Interweaving: Heterogeneity in the Theory and Design of Interactive Systems. In: Proc. of DIS'04, pp. 243–252. ACM Press, NY (2004)
3. Cheverst, K., et al.: Developing a context-aware electronic tourist guide: some issues and experiences. In: Proc. of CHI'00, pp. 17–24. ACM Press, NY (2000)
4. Ducatel, K. et al.: Scenarios for Ambient Intelligence in 2010. ISTAG Final Report, IPTS, Seville (February 2001)
5. Gaver, W.: Provocative Awareness. In: CSCW, pp. 475–493. Springer, Heidelberg (2002)
6. Gaver, W., Dunne, T., Pacenti, E.: Design: Cultural Probes. In: Interactions, vol. 6(1), pp. 21–29. ACM Press, NY (1999)
7. Glaser, B.G., Strauss, A.L.: Awareness Contexts and Social Interaction. American Sociological Review 29(5), 669–679 (1964)
8. Höök, K., Sengers, P., Andersson, G.: Sense and Sensibility: Evaluation and Interactive Art. In: Proc. of CHI'03, pp. 241–248. ACM Press, NY (2003)
9. Mateas, M.: Expressive AI: A hybrid art and science practice. Leonardo 34(2), 147–153 (2001)
10. McCarthy, J., Costa, T., Liongosari, E.: UniCast, OutCast & GroupCast: Three Steps Toward Ubiquitous, Peripheral Displays. In: Abowd, G.D., Brumitt, B., Shafer, S. (eds.) Ubicomp 2001: Ubiquitous Computing. LNCS, vol. 2201, pp. 332–345. Springer, Heidelberg (2001)
11. Redström, J., Skog, T., Hallnäs, L.: Informative Art: Using Amplified Artworks as Information Displays. In: Proc. of DARE'00, pp. 103–114. ACM Press, NY (2000)
12. Redström, J., Ljungstrand, P., Jaksetic, P.: The ChatterBox: Using Text Manipulation in an Entertaining Information Display. In: Proc. of Graphics Interface, pp. 111–118. Montréal, Canada (2000)
13. Streitz, N., et al.: Designing Smart Artefacts for Smart Environments, pp. 41–49. IEEE Computer Society Press, Los Alamitos (2005)
14. Tollmar, K., et al.: Supporting social awareness @ work: design and experience. In: Proc. of CSCW'96, pp. 298–307. ACM Press, NY (1996)
15. Vyas, D., van der Veer, G.C.: Rich Evaluations of Entertainment Experience: Bridging the Interpretational Gap. In: Proc. of ECCE-13, pp. 137–144. Zurich, Switzerland (2006)
16. Vyas, D., Chisalita, C.M., van der Veer, G.C.: Affordance in Interaction. In: Proc. of ECCE-13, pp. 92–99. Zurich, Switzerland (2006)
17. Weiser, M.: The computer for the 21st century. Scientific American 9, 66–75 (1991)

Case Study of Human Computer Interaction Based on RFID and Context-Awareness in Ubiquitous Computing Environments

Ting Zhang, Yuanxin Ouyang, Yang He, Zhang Xiong, and Zhenyong Chen

School of Computer Science and Engineering, Beihang Universty,
Beijing, 100083, China
zhangting@cse.buaa.edu.cn, oyyx@buaa.edu.cn,
heyang@cse.buaa.edu.cn,
{xiongz,chzhyong}@buaa.edu.cn

Abstract. Context-awareness becomes the key technology in the human computer interaction of ubiquitous computing. The paper discusses the characteristic, significance as well as function of the context, and the properties of the human computer interaction in the ubiquitous environments where the physical space fuses with the information space. These characteristics bring new requirements, that is, mobility, tractability, predictably and personality. To satisfy the demands, we present a method to realize context-awareness and the wireless interaction by using the pervasive RFID tags to track the context and using Bluetooth as the contact-less communication measure. We also construct a prototype system composed of RFID tags, BTEnableReaders and Bluetooth-enable mobile terminals. One case of application scenario is given and the experimental results show that the performance and robustness of the device are suitable for ubiquitous applications and the interaction is experienced more positively by users than the conventional method. The devices we design also can be extended to other application areas such as wearable computing, health care, disable help, and road navigation.

Keywords: Human Computer Interaction, RFID, Context, Ubiquitous Computing.

1 Introduction

Ubiquitous Computing, which makes the user utilize the communication and computing ability more easily and merges the information space with physical space, has become one of the most active research areas. This mergence is an important foundation integrating the human and the computer naturally and makes the computing environments and the software resources available for user adapt to the related history situation and context. The context is an implicit intuition in human reasoning. It normally refers to the surrounding environments of interest center [1], such as providing the original information about Where, When, What, How and the direct comprehension about this information. Radio Frequency Identification (RFID) has

C. Stephanidis (Ed.): Universal Access in HCI, Part II, HCII 2007, LNCS 4555, pp. 264–271, 2007.

become one of the most promising automatic identification technologies recently. Compared with other traditional identification technology, RFID has the advantages such as contact-less, multi-object recognition, non-line-of-sight, long distance, large store memory, programmability and penetrability. Especially, the most significant meaning embedded in the RFID technology is the fact that all the existing physical objects can enter the virtual world built by RFID networks by sticking a tag to the physical object as a unique entry. RFID is seen as a bridge between physical space and virtual reality [2] and can offer one of the foundations in the ubiquitous computing environments.

In these new ubiquitous computing environments where information access and service become pervasive, the human-computer interface differs from the WIMP (Windows, Icon, Menu and Pointer) graphic user interface. Owing to the heterogeneity of ubiquitous terminal communication devices in these environments, the interface must accommodate to variant devices of different users and provide different services based on the users' different locations, time, role and task. The context-awareness and the mobile computing interaction have become the key technology in the human-computer interaction. Since the RFID has the advantage of recording context information and Bluetooth has been embedded into many mobile terminals, such as mobile phone, PDA, notebook, digital camera, and MP3, this paper presents a case study of an implicit human computer interaction in ubiquitous computing based on RFID tags and Bluetooth enabled mobile devices.

The remainder of the paper is organized as follows. Section 2 introduces the focus point of HCI in ubiquitous computing environments and outlines our object. Section 3 presents our design concept. Section 4 details the approach and implementation of prototype system. The performance results of the original system in one application scenario are given in Section 5. The conclusions are drawn in the final section.

2 HCI in Ubiquitous Computing

Recent progress in mobile computing, signal processing and automatic recognition technologies has created a promising direction for human computer interaction research in the ubiquitous computing environments. Compared with the traditional research of the human computer interaction modalities which mainly focus on the multimode perception (e.g., speech, vision, pen, mouse, gesture, haptic), in the new environments the device is expected to possess sensation so that it can interact with the human in harmonious manner. This implicit interaction brings forward two demands; one is that humans prefer to communicate with computers socially rather than communicate by the passive and explicit input instruments; the other is that computers should communicate with humans nonverbally but intelligently which means they must be aware of the current scene situation and the context of interaction task to be capable of adapting to the current user with minimum instructions. These two demands are complementary for each other. If we make good use of the context, such as the location, temperature, time, light, noise, and people nearby, the interface will attract much less human's attention so that it will be more human-like, effective, recessive and adaptive.

The object of the human-computer interaction brought forward in this study is expected as follows: (1) Mobility, the ubiquitous environments contain heterogeneous mobile communication network infrastructures but the user can achieve accordant and transparent service no matter where he is among the ubiquitous environment. (2) Tractability, the user can inquire about internal situation and organized structure of background context process, the system should let user feel that the context is processed himself [3] and the interaction is in a natural and expressive modality. (3) Predictably, the computer should be able to understand the users' requests and future possible demands, the beforehand dispose of information does not need users' special attention and the user can even interact with the computer without training. (4) Personality, the services must be pushed according to the user's personal characters, because RFID tag has its unique ID, it has the innate advantage to identify users or computing objects.

3 Design Concept

The perceptions of the intelligent human-computer interface in ubiquitous computing environments emphasize the natural interaction between users and services embedded in the environment or available through mobile devices. In these environments the physical and virtual worlds seamlessly gear into each other. The bottleneck in reaching these scenarios appears in the natural mapping between the physical objects and their virtual counterparts [4]. The emergence of RFID opens possibilities for implementing novel user interface and enhances this mapping. The low-cost and obscure tags can be used to identify all the objects in the really world include computing device and daily commodities. It can be used as the carrier of context information needed for the human computer interaction. This context is the characteristic description of entity [3]. The entity may be the person, space or any other object related to the human computer interface, even the user or application itself. The context can be classified according to

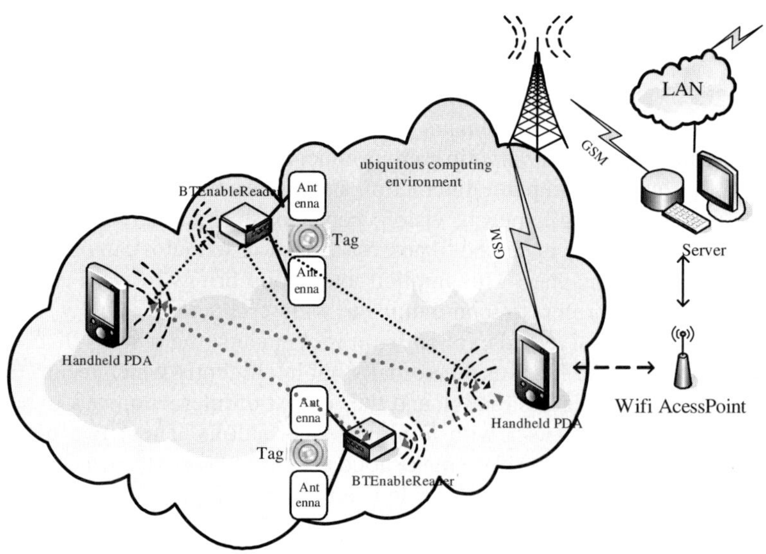

Fig. 1. Application scenario in ubiquitous computing environments

function or conception. From the functional point of view, the context's categorization is related to how the context is obtained, modeled and processed. For instance, it can be classify as low-level context with high-level context or active context with passive context. From the conceptual point of view, the context's categorization is related to how the context is cognized. For instance, it can be classify as user context, physical context and computing context. In this study we acquired the data in RFID tags through wireless mobile terminal shown in Figure 1. These pervasive tags are viewed as aggregation of context and resources or container of the URI that link to the needed context or resources, By using the information stored on RFID tags, the context of users and the state of computation objects and environments can be determined collaboratively. This context information can be used to associate interaction partners [5]. Based on the analysis of the data acquired from the tags, the system will push to users the services which agree with the current situation of interaction and the interaction will become more efficient.

The ubiquitous computing environment consists of different mobile computing devices that supply the interface for users. Because the users' situation is changing continuously, mobile computing is one of the important and broad application areas of context-awareness. When a nomadic user comes into a new environment and wants to understand his current status, the best way is to analyze the history and current context. Since the physical devices that provide available resource for user are normally in the space nearby, the PAN (Personal Area Network) is adaptive to these application scenarios very much. As one of the standards of WPAN (Wireless Personal Area Network) operating in the 2.4G ISM band [6], Bluetooth has the advantages like low-cost, opening, small-size and security. Because Bluetooth has been embedded into numerous kinds of mobile device and has become easily available, it can play an important role in the deployment of ubiquitous computing environments [7], [8]. For the communication between mobile device and computing space, we adopt Bluetooth in the environment connection layer.

4 Approach and Implementation of Prototype

Since more and more computers designed for mobile usages and the human-computer interface is expected to support the user's intentions and be aware of context, we elaborate on the implementation of an early prototype system which supports WPAN

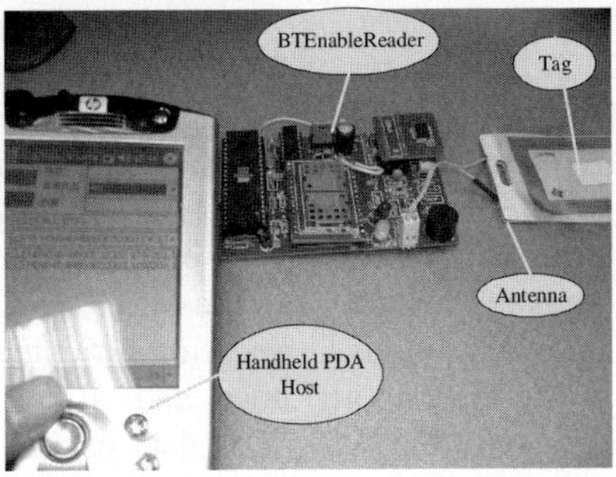

Fig. 2. Illustration of handheld host and RFID tag with reader

and is capable of associating RFID with context to trace the users' intentions in this section. Figure 2 presents the main devices for experimentation including handheld host, RFID reader, antenna and tag. The RFID reader named BTEnableReader is not only responsible for read and write of tags but also furnishes host control interface for upper layer mobile terminal's application and can be controlled by mobile host (as shown in Figure 2). Its design details are shown in Figure 3: (1) RF read/write module contains the transceiver IC S6700 [9] which handle protocol ISO/IEC 15693 communicates with responders that operate in the 13.56MHz band. (2) Real-time Clock Module is controlled by I2C bus to get time data for synchronization. (3) Memory Module is 24LC256 256K bit CMOS serial EEPROM controlled by I2C bus and used for store context history data for later query. (4) Communication Module here is equipped with an Ericsson ROK 101 007 Bluetooth chip [10] together with an onboard antenna. (5) Microprocessor Control Unit here is the 8-bit microcontroller with 8K Bytes Flash AT89C52, it also controls two LEDs for debugging purposes. In addition, the experimental responder we use is the smart-tag named "Tag-it" and supplied by TI.

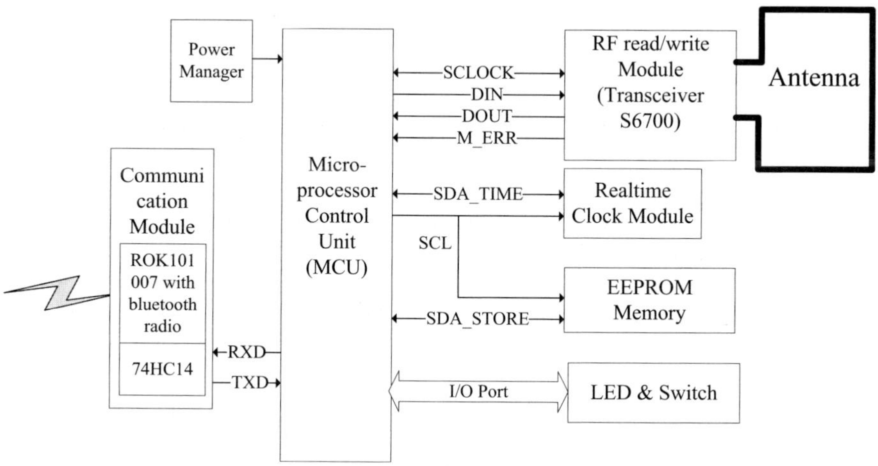

Fig. 3. Schematic diagram of BTEnableReader

As shown in Figure 4, in the physical bus drive layer we use the UART to connect the MCU with the Bluetooth hardware and set the baud rate to 57600bps. The host controller interface (HCI) defines a suit of functions to access underlying layers and Bluetooth hardware, such as baseboard, link manager, status register and event register. It hides the realization of link manager layer and supplies a uniform interface for upper application layer. The Bluetooth host can send the HCI command packet to the Bluetooth hardware and the Bluetooth hardware returns HCI event packet as the response, HCI data packet, which is classified as ACL (Asynchronous Connection-Less) or SCO (Synchronous Connection-Oriented) packet, is used for the data exchange between the Bluetooth host and Bluetooth hardware. In the BTEnableReader we design, only the ACL HCI data packet is used for context data communication in respect that SCO is more suitable for voice transmission.

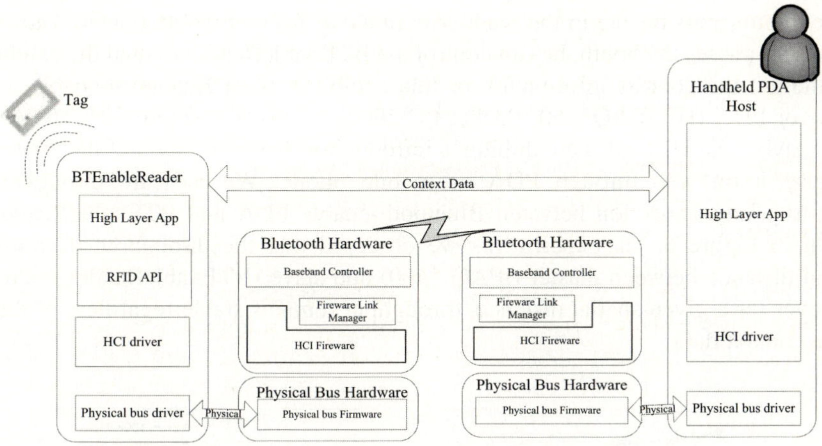

Fig. 4. Implement of software stack

5 Analysis of Interaction in Application Scenario

We present an exhibition hall as one ubiquitous computing space and use the RFID tags instead of passport barcode. The exhibition information management system consists of server center, booth reader sub-system, and mobile terminal sub-system; the whole exhibition hall is considered as one ubiquitous computing space (Figure 5 outlines the basic interaction between different partners in the space). The contexts we pay attention to include the visitor's identity, age, job, location and the nearby exhibitors. Each of visitors and the exhibitors gets one and only one RFID tag for passport identification before exhibition opening and each of gates and booths installs one BTEnableReader.

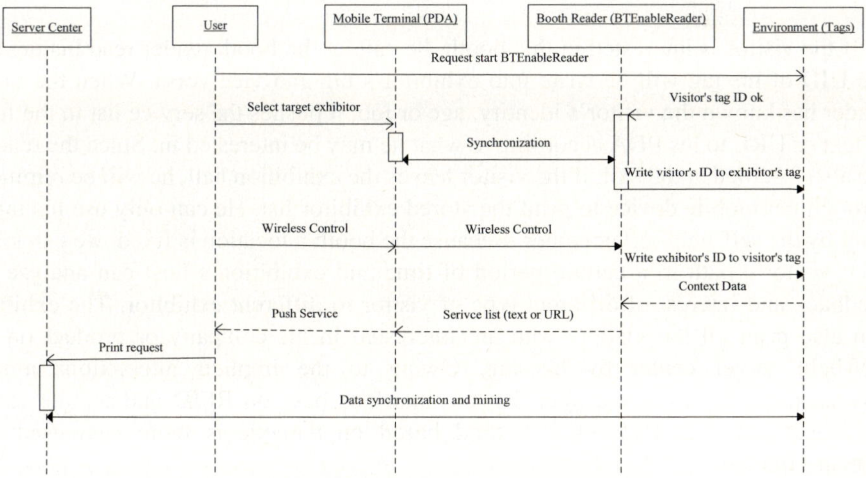

Fig. 5. Basic interaction in the scenario

The exhibitor puts his tag in the read/write range of his own booth reader. Thus when one visitor passes the booth, he can control the BTEnableReader to read the exhibitor's tag and get the context information of this exhibitor using Bluetooth-enable mobile phone or PDA (HP iPAQ5460, Pocket PC 2002, as shown in Figure 2). The context here maybe one URL of the exhibitor's introduction stored in tag and the visitor can navigate it on web through PDA or mobile phone. We measure throughput on point-to-point connection between Bluetooth-enable PDA and BTEnableReader. As shown in Figure 6, via experiments we observed that the throughput decreases as spatial distance between master (iPAQ 5460) and slave (BTEnableReader) increases. However for a given spatial distance, throughput remains stable regardless of the size of the context data.

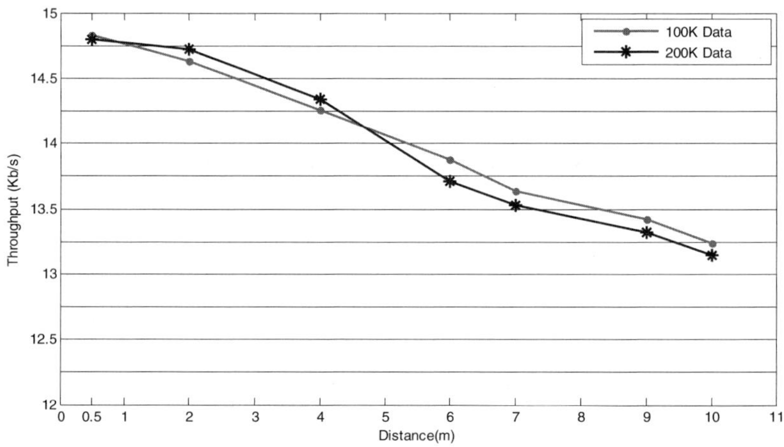

Fig. 6. Throughput of master to slave

If the visitor is interested in this booth, he can let the booth reader read his tag and the UID of his tag will be write into exhibitor's tag and vice versa. When the booth reader has known the visitor's identity, age or job, it pushes the service list in the form of text or URL to his PDA according to what he may be interested in. Since the readers are also installed at the exit, if the visitor leaves the exhibition hall, he will be reminded through the mobile device to print the stored exhibitor list. He can only use his tag to print by the self-help server center. Because the booth's location is fixed, we can know each visitor's path in a certain period of time and exhibition's host can analyze the feedback and interest of different type of visitor to different exhibitor. The exhibitor can also print all the visitors who are interested in his company or product on the self-help server center by his tag. Owing to the implicit interactions among this scenario, the users can feel that the interface base on RFID and mobile terminal compared with traditional method based on barcode is more easy-used and human-oriented.

6 Conclusion

One of the characteristics of this paper is that RFID is used to extend the way of acquirement and representation of context. The other is that we invent an embedded mobile device for test platform and this Bluetooth-enabled test bed can be applied to many real scenes and even the wearable computing. We advocated that the context sensed by RFID is an effective modality to enable a pervasive and consistent user interaction with computers across a full range of devices, and has the potential to provide a natural user interaction model.

Acknowledgments. This research is supported by the major discipline construction program of Beijing Municipal Commission of Education grant XK100060527 in China.

References

1. Mostefaoui, G.K., Pasquier-Rocha, J., Brezillon, P.: Context-Aware Computing: A Guide for the Pervasive Computing Community. In: ICPS 2004 Conference Proceedings, Beirut, pp. 38–48. IEEE Computer Society, Los Alamitos (2004)
2. Stanford, V.: Pervasive Computing Goes the Last Hundred Feet with RFID Systems. Pervasive Computing 2(2), 9–14 (2003)
3. Van Bunningen, A.H., Feng, L., Apers, P.M.G.: Context for Ubiquitous Data Management. In: Proceedings of the 2005 International Workshop on Ubiquitous Data Management (UDM'05),Tokyo, IEEE Computer Society (2005)
4. Ailisto, H., Pohjanheimo, L., Välkkynen, P., Strömmer, E., Tuomisto, T., Korhonen, I.: Bridging the physical and virtual worlds by local connectivity-based physical selection. Personal and Ubiquitous Computing 10, 333–344 (2006)
5. Siegemund, F., Floerkemeier, C.: Interaction in Pervasive Computing Settings using Bluetooth-Enabled Active Tags and Passive RFID Technology together with Mobile Phones. In: Proceedings of the First IEEE International Conference on Pervasive Computing and Communications (PerCom'03), Dallas, pp. 378–387. IEEE, Los Alamitos (2003)
6. Salminen, T., Hosio, S., Riekki, J.: Enhancing Bluetooth Connectivity with RFID. In: Proceedings of 4th Annual IEEE International Conference on Pervasive Computing and Communications, Pisa, IEEE Computer Society, Los Alamitos (2006)
7. Leopold, M., Dydensborg, M.B., Bonnet, P.: Bluetooth and Sensor Networks: A Reality Check. In: SenSys'03 Conference Proceedings, Los Angeles, ACM (2003)
8. Cano, J.C., Cano, J., Manzoni, P., et al.: On the Design of Pervasive Computing Applications Based on Bluetooth and P2P Concept. In: ISWPC 06 Conference Proceedings,Thailand, IEEE (2006)
9. Texas Instruments.: HF Reader System Series 6000 S6700 Multi Protocol Transceiver IC (RI-R6C-001A) Reference Guide. http://www.ti.com/rfid/docs/manuals/refmanuals/RI-R6C-001ArefGuide.pdf
10. Ericsson.: ROK101 007 Bluetooth Module Datasheet. www.tik.ee.ethz.ch/ beutel/projects/bluetooth/rok101007. pdf

Part II

Access to the Physical Environment, Mobility and Transportation

Accessibility and Usability Evaluation of MAIS Designer: A New Design Tool for Mobile Services

Laura Burzagli[1], Marco Billi[1], Enrico Palchetti[1], Tiziana Catarci[2], Giuseppe Santucci[2], and Enrico Bertini[2]

[1] Consiglio Nazionale delle Ricerche Istituto di Fisica Applicata "Nello Carrara", Via Madonna del Piano, 10, I-50019 Sesto Fiorentino (FI), Italy
{l.burzagli,m.billi,e.palchetti}@ifac.cnr.it

[2] Università di Roma "La Sapienza" Dipartimento di Informatica e Sistemistica, Via Salaria, 113, I- 00198 Roma, Italy
{catarci,santucci,bertini}@dis.uniroma1.it

Abstract. This paper reports the results of a study to evaluate accessibility and usability of services developed by the MAIS Designer, a new design tool that provides services suited to different mobile devices. The discussion is aimed at highlighting the methodology adopted, which is tailored to characteristics of mobile computing and the relative results obtained.

1 Introduction

One of the challenges in the application of new or innovative technologies is that its users may try to employ it in situations or ways that the designers and developers had never thought of. This is no less true in mobile computing.

The user's physical, visual and cognitive involvement/resources are likely to become constrained while s/he may perform tasks on the device in unpredictable and opportunistic ways. Furthermore, the variability of the environment/natural setting may affect the course of a task. In fact, mobile systems pose limits and offer new opportunities as compared to desktop appliances.

The present paper illustrates the method used to test the accessibility and usability of services developed by a new design tool (MAIS Designer), which is capable of implementing services adapted to various mobile devices from an abstract description of the service itself.

2 Challenges and Considerations of Design and Evaluation in Mobile Computing

The Model Human Processor model [1] has been a benchmark for a large amount of work in HCI. However, since the role and domain of devices have widened, the relationship between internal cognition and the outside world have been considered [2].

C. Stephanidis (Ed.): Universal Access in HCI, Part II, HCII 2007, LNCS 4555, pp. 275–284, 2007.

Three main models of cognition have been explored for their possible application in mobile computing: an activity theory model, a situated action model, and a distributed cognition model [3]. It is also worthwhile acknowledging the appropriateness of participatory design methods and observations of user activities in authentic everyday settings, in innovative areas such as ubiquitous computing [4, 5].

Conventional user-centered methods could be appropriately exploited in the development process of mobile applications. On the same note, some of the traditional usability evaluation techniques might become useful if they were adapted for mobile computing. For instance, several efforts are being made towards the realization of usability principles and heuristics for the design and evaluation of ubiquitous environments/systems: e.g., ambient heuristics [6] and groupware heuristics [7]. Nevertheless it would be interesting to investigate methods that go beyond the traditional task-centric approaches [8].

In this era of ubiquitous computing, the pressing need to take into account the real-world context is crucial, and evaluation methods have found it challenging, to adequately, if not completely, integrate the entire context during the evaluation process.

There are various possibilities for addressing the challenge. One option is the employment of techniques from other fields that can gain a richer understanding like ethnography, cultural probes, and contextual inquiry [2, 3]. Another possibility is to use the 'Wizard-of-Oz' technique, or other simulation techniques such as virtual reality. Methods of this type are appropriate where the mobile application is not complete.

3 The MAIS Designer

The MAIS Designer is a system for both generating and designing abstract services whose user interface is tailored so as to be appropriate for the destination device and/or channel (e.g., cell-phone, PDA, laptop, etc.) [9]. The architecture of the system consists of two main components: the Service Editor and the Interface Generator. The former permits to define user interaction graphically by exploiting an adapted version of the UML Activity Diagram; the latter generates the final interface in accordance with the device and user characteristics. Adaptation of the UML Activity Diagram mainly consists of foreseeing a predefined set of activities implemented through a set of Atomic Interaction Units (AIUs). An AIU represents a basic step in user interaction, and is modelled in terms of the data exchanged between the user and the system.

Once the service has been modelled, the Interface Generator produces a set of html pages optimized for the specific device. In this phase, several heuristics are adopted to produce a new diagram suitable for the device. A series of user interface complexity metrics are used to estimate the feasibility of the service implementation on the chosen device. Last, the system generates a real interface for the connected device.

4 Global Evaluation Methodology

The overall methodology used in evaluating the MAIS Designer has been split into two phases: the first one concerns the accessibility of the services produced by the new developing tools. The accessibility evaluation was conducted at an early stage in the implementation, so as to direct any further development in the right way.

The second phase concerns the usability of the services produced by an advanced prototype, in order to determine a final investigation into the possibility of producing accessible and usable services for mobile delivery. The accessibility and usability evaluations were performed using different methodologies: the first one was based on an elaboration of WAI guidelines to fit mobile systems specificity, while the second one was based on a set of newly proposed usability heuristics for mobile computing.

4.1 Accessibility Guidelines

In ensuring and assessing accessibility in the presented work, WAI guidelines were taken into account as the main reference. As described in [9] WAI guidelines for content [10], authoring tools [11] and user agents [12] were taken into account within the perspective of mobile characteristics.

4.2 Proposed Usability Heuristics for Mobile Computing

From the activities carried out during the MAIS project, eight usability heuristics for mobile computing, adopted for the usability evaluation reported later on, were realized:

1. Visibility of system status and losability/findability of the mobile device
2. Match between system and the real world
3. Consistency and mapping
4. Good Ergonomics and minimalist design
5. Ease of input, screen readability and glanceability
6. Flexibility, efficiency of use and personalization
7. Aesthetic, privacy and social conventions
8. Realistic error management

5 Accessibility Evaluation

The accessibility evaluation was aimed at assessing the accessibility features of simple services developed by means of the MAIS Designer. It is worth pointing out that the version of the MAIS Designer that we used in order to develop the services had been refined and/or improved on the basis of a previous evaluation, in order to realize a subsequent development step.

5.1 Methodology

Two main types of studies comprised the accessibility evaluation reported: an expert-based evaluation and a user-based evaluation, which was limited to a specific user group composed of blind and visually-impaired persons. Both studies employed the WAI guidelines mentioned in § 4.1 as heuristics cues to direct the investigation.

User Study. Four users with the following characteristics performed the test: they had a rather high level of education and were expert computer users with some knowledge of mobile devices. They were visually impaired ranging from mild to severe reduction of their sight, so that they were able to perform test by means of either screen magnifier or screen reader or directly operating on the mobile device.

The sample service was a simplified implementation of a booking service. The actual implementation was rather simple, due to the inherent limitations of the MAIS Designer in its updated but not final version.

The users were encouraged to use the service to plan a vacation using three different versions, corresponding to Notebook Generic (screen size 800 x 600), iPaq 3660 (screen size 240 x 320) and a basic cell-phone, (screen size 128 x 160).

The exploration took into account the type of devices (desktop PC, palm-top Compaq iPAQ 3760, cell-phones) and the typologies of disabilities (visual impairment and blindness). Since a screen reader was not available both for PDAs and for mobile phones, the evaluation was conducted using emulators hosted by a desktop PC. Only one user was able to conduct the test using a real PDA (Compaq iPAQ Pocket PC).

The user-based evaluation was conducted by means of a semi-structured, individual interview with disabled users (from the target user group) in front of the sample service produced by the MAIS Designer. The interviews were carried out by two experts in accessibility, who acted as moderators asking her/him to identify possible accessibility issues involved in their use in mobile contexts, and by discussing potential solutions.

After the interview was completed, the study moderator added comments on the services provided by the prototype and on the improvements suggested, assessing their compliance with the accessibility guidelines, in the view of mobile applications.

Expert-based Study. The two experts who performed the study are both e-accessibility experts and have a good knowledge of mobile devices. One of the experts is blind, and accesses to the PC by means of the JAWS 5.0 screen reader with synthetic speech output; the other is sighted.

The experts followed the same scenarios as the users, and performed the same task using the same technical set-up, so that the corresponding descriptions of the previous section are to be considered still valid. Both users have extensive experience in assessing the accessibility of systems and services, and their thorough knowledge of accessibility guidelines directed the evaluation of the sample service.

5.2 Results

Eight problems concerning device or assistive technology misbehaviour have been found, but were considered to be of no interest in this context.

Table 1. The relevant problems found by the user study

1. On the very first page, where the user chose the service and the device, the combo boxes are not tied to the corresponding label
2. The labels in the form were not read when the cursor was moved inside a text box, causing difficulties in orientation
3. The radio buttons were not enlarged with text, so that they were difficult to use, especially using the table to perform the choice between the proposed vacations
4. On the first page of the service, the selection box should be more distant from surrounding objects in order to be more visible when using the screen magnifier
5. Text contained in the table was too narrow to be easily understood. The possibility of increasing the space between cells needs to be taken into account
6. The colour combination of links and background should be more contrasted, in order to facilitate their identification
7. The fragmentation made the text difficult to enjoy and was boring, even if necessary when a device did not support the scrolling
8. Showing the table a couple of cells a time is redundant. It's simpler to linearize the table instead of having the table broken down into so many small pieces
9. The textual description, in place of the photo considered not displayable, seemed to be useless and rather confusing, as it lacked any hints about what it stands for. On the other hand, the description in a page by itself did not cause any problems
10. In one case, when a page was divided in more screenshot to fit to small screen, the form was displayed in the wrong order i.e. before of the explanatory text

Table 2. The relevant problems found by the expert user study

11. Radio buttons, used in the table for selecting the vacation, were not well rendered by the screen reader, so that it was difficult to know which row was selected
12. The table did not contain the tag needed to guarantee accessibility. Even if the table was rather simple, the lack of the appropriate tags could easily generate accessibility problems
13. In exploring the registration form, the text displayed at the side of the text box was vocalised together with the labels, and the labels were not read when the cursor was inside a text box, causing difficulties in orientation and loss of effectiveness in the use of the form
14. The text presented in the fragmented form was cut in a rough way, making it difficult to understand the meaning of the text.
15. The widely-used symbols to go from one fragment to the other ("<<" ">>") did not seem intuitive for visually-impaired people. Moreover, to navigate through the fragments of the table the words "up" and "down" were used: a better homogeny would be preferable
16. In the screenshot concerning the choice of a credit card, it is not explained what is required. Even if the task may seem intuitive, a short explanation would avoid disorientation
17. The "Cancel" button did not seem to have any evident effect in the choice of the credit card, while it was lacking in the registration form where it could be useful
18. Since the registration form was presented one field at a time, it would have been better to show the button "OK" only after the last field. The "OK" button shown after every fragment of the form caused misunderstanding, leading to sending the form before its completion.
19. Sometimes the order in which the pieces of a page were presented was wrong, as when presenting the registration form prior to a description of the chosen vacation.
20. The choice to cut the photo seems too severe, and the choice of putting the alternative text in a separate screenshot was not understood well. Furthermore, the afore-mentioned choice made the navigation more complex.

5.3 Analysis

The test produced interesting results, even if the service was simple. The main result to be emphasized is the substantial accessibility level, even if several negative comments have been reported by users and experts. Notwithstanding the aforementioned glitches, the service was found to be fully accessible in all the configurations tested.

The comments reported can be divided into four categories, in accordance with their origin: inaccurate tagging and lack of style, unsuitable choice, inaccurate implementation, wrong implementation, shown in the following table:

Table 3. Problems sorted according to the relative category

Inaccurate tagging and lack of style	1, 2, 4, 5, 6, 12, 13
Unsuitable choice	3, 9, 11, 15, 16, 20
Inaccurate implementation	7, 8, 14, 18
Wrong implementation	10, 17, 19

As can be seen from the table 3, inadequate attention has evidently been given to the correct use of accessibility tags and XHTML tags, in addition to a lack of style, which lead to important accessibility flaws such as the impossibility of correctly understanding the meaning of the fields in the forms.

Another important group of accessibility problems seems to arise from unsuitable choices made, such as the use of radio buttons to indicate a selected item, which leads to many problems related both to the users and to the assistive technology.

Inaccurate implementation seems responsible for only four problems, mainly connected to the text fragmentation, which is approached in a rather crude way.

Lastly, three errors emerged in which the order of the screenshot was wrong or the buttons did not function at all.

A final consideration concerns the distribution of reported problems between user study and expert base study: the users were chiefly able to highlight tagging and style bugs, while a minority of the other problems arose from other categories. This derived from their unusual role as evaluators: even if instructed in their role, they preferred to adapt their behaviour to functions of the service, as they are used to doing, rather than highlighting inappropriate behaviour.

6 Usability Evaluation

The usability evaluation was aimed at assessing features of sample services developed by means of a more refined version of the MAIS Designer, in order to discover the final directions for developing it.

6.1 Methodology

The usability evaluation was conducted by following the heuristic-based evaluation methodology for mobile computing that is summarized in the sequel in terms of the various parameters that constitute the methodology.

Participants and materials. The experiment involved three usability experts, as participants/evaluators, who carried out a heuristic evaluation on a mobile application for booking a journey to Florence. The application has been developed using MAIS Designer [9].

It has been used a Nokia Communicator 9500 with the following specifications: 18 MB memory, resolution of colour display 640x480, vertical and horizontal scroll, full keyboard. The application was installed on a wireless connected laptop which acted as the server.

We also prepared and provided the following materials for the participants: informed consent form, demographics questionnaire, post-evaluation form for participant's comments, a set of mobile usability heuristics, Nielsen's five-point Severity Ranking Scale (SRS) [13].

Procedure. *Pre-evaluation:* after greeting each evaluator, the goals of the study, the testing procedures, and the confidentiality issues were explained in detail by means of an Informed Consent form. Scripts, which were prepared in advance, were used for each usability evaluator so as to ensure consistency in both experts and conditions. In a demographics questionnaire, experts were asked about their level of education/academic status, relevant experience with both HCI and mobile computing, experience using mobile devices, and experience in using Nielsen's heuristic evaluation method.

A training session was conducted with each evaluator, to ensure that s/he fully understood the mobile heuristics with which the evaluators were not familiar. This involved the facilitator's stepping through each of the usability heuristics and inviting the evaluators to ask questions in order to clarify the meaning and their understanding of each heuristic.

Evaluation: the three usability experts performed the usability evaluation on the mobile application by identifying usability problems and prioritizing these according to Nielsen's five-point Severity Ranking Scale (SRS). [13]

Post-evaluation: a short debriefing, , focused on the evaluators' experiences when they were interacting with the application, was held after each evaluation session.

6.2 Results

All three participants had a high level of education and were well experienced in using mobile devices. The participants had average experience in the fields of HCI and mobile computing. Their experience in using heuristic evaluation was well distributed across three levels.

Problems identified. Most of the problems observed were of medium severity, although a significant number of catastrophic problems were found.

Table 4. Catastrophic problems (SRS 4)

1. Loss of data: For instance: the user loses data/details about him-/herself when he/she chooses to go back using “Esc”: the application should retain at least the previous settings as default
2. Some operations can be performed incorrectly without receiving error messages: e.g. entering personal details, completing the order without entering details (including the visa screen). Rather than receiving error messages, success messages sometimes appear
3. The user interface does not provide a place to enter all crucial details for users who would like to place an order
4. The interface for adding an audio file seems not to function correctly. Maybe it is not fully implemented

Table 5. Major problems (SRS 3)

5. Navigation problems, especially when the user wants to go back one page/screen back or to change the search. Usually, the user is forced to go back to the page of the initial settings
6. There are places which are supposed to provide image or video description, but there is nothing behind them
7. The user interface is rather inconsistent. For instance, by selecting “Esc” from (my) personal details, one may get the screen of “Firenze dell’arte” with the image-description which was not there at first. Moreover, while setting the device, there is a menu that pops up on the right-hand side; however, it is not available across other choices or all screens
8. It is not clear what the unique/distinct effects are of “Esc” or “Abort” or “Cancel”: for instance, cancelling the current page/screen or the current service, etc. (e.g. in selecting a credit card type). The user would have to click and then see what happens
9. The supported service(s) offers very limited/constrained options. For instance, users might want the freedom to be able to select several options and to receive information about them together (without the need to select > ok > view > esc > select > ok > view >), etc.
10. The user cannot set the type of font
11. It is not easy to understand which modality to use to interact with the interface for adding an audio file (i.e. it seems that only the device buttons can be used)
12. The pages are too long (when vertical scrolling is not restricted) or there are too many screens (when vertical scrolling is restricted). Both of these problems could be reduced, e.g. by summarizing the contents

6.3 Analysis

From Table 7, it can be observed that problems 5, 1.6, 7 and 8 have both a high severity ranking and numerous mentions from the experts. In similar manner, problems 14 to 20 have both a low severity ranking and a small number of mentions from the experts. In considering the usability problems identified by the experts, we have the impression that problem 5, 1, 6, 7, 8 should have higher priority.

Table 6. Minor problems (SRS 2)

13.The font is tiny, e.g. in the opening screen.
14.In the "home" screen where the device has to be selected, there is no way of knowing that there is an "Ok" button, which is accessible by scrolling down. Perhaps buttons should be provided on the right of every screen.
15.The words "path-image" in the title of the table can be misinterpreted/misleading. For instance, users might assume that they can click on the picture to see more.
16.Some of the screens potentially offer multiple ways of accomplishing the same operation. E.g. users might assume that they can press on the text of the radio buttons (rather than just having to select a radio button and clicking "Ok") to cause the operation to be performed.
17.The "Home" command takes the user to the page for setting the de-vice/interaction parameters, which does not really look like a homepage.
18.Some of the texts/sentences are very long: e.g. the screen after the settings screen, i.e. the second screen (above the image of Florence).
19.In the process of setting (the device, user & display), the meaning of "user" type is not clear.
20.The user is not shielded from making mistakes (e.g. inexact entries are allowed when indicating the number of persons. Using listbox/combobox might help).

Table 7. Problems sorted in accordance with their severity and in relation to the number of mentions from the experts

Problem	1	2	3	4	5	6	7	8	9	10	11	12	13	14	15	16	17	18	19	20
Mean severity of the problem	4	4	4	4	3	3	3	3	3	3	3	3	2	2	2	2	2	2	2	2
Number of experts who mentioned the problem	2	1	1	1	3	2	2	2	1	1	1	1	2	1	1	1	1	1	1	1

The other heuristics that follow in terms of violation are heuristic 5 (7 violations): "Ease of input, screen readability and glanceability" and then heuristic 6 (5 violations): "Flexibility, efficiency of use and personalization". According to [14], heuristic 5 is described as follows: "Mobile systems should provide easy ways to input data, possibly reducing or avoiding the need for the user to use both hands. Screen content should be easy to read and navigate through notwithstanding different light conditions. Ideally, the mobile user should be able to quickly get the crucial information from the system by glancing at it", whereas heuristic 6 is described as follows: "Al-low mobile users to tailor/personalize frequent actions, as well as to dynamically configure the system according to contextual needs. Whenever possible, the system should support and suggest system-based customization if such would be crucial or beneficial."

7 Conclusions

In the study reported here, the method used to test accessibility and usability of a sample service adapted to various mobile devices together with the corresponding results has been presented in the light of the afore-mentioned challenges in designing and evaluating for mobile computing.

The results showed the effectiveness of the different methods utilized for the accessibility and usability evaluation. More specifically, the WAI guidelines, which were used as heuristics cues to direct accessibility tests, were found to be appropriate in the mobile context. In turn, the usability evaluation, which was conducted by means of heuristics specialized for mobile systems, appeared to be very efficient in highlighting the usability flaws of the tested service. At the same time, the outcome of the reported work motivates us to carry out further investigations on the parameters that constitute the methodology, for the purpose of gaining a more specific understanding of the same in the light of mobile computing. Moreover, we will continue to study the applications of existing and future accessibility guidelines to new devices, software applications and assistive technologies, in both mobile computing and ambient intelligence.

References

1. Card, S.K., Moran, T.P., Newell, A.: The Psychology of Human-Computer Interaction. Lawrence Erlbaum, Mahwah (1983)
2. Alan, D., Janet, F., Gregory, A., Russell, B.: Human-Computer Interaction, 3rd edn. Prentice Hall, Englewood Cliffs (2004)
3. Abowd, G.D., Mynatt, E.D., Rodden, T.: The Human Experience. IEEE Pervasive Computing, pp. 48–57 (March 2002)
4. Rogers, Y., Scaife, M., Muller, H., Randell, C., Moss, A., Taylor, I., Harris, E., Smith, H., Price, S., Phelps, T., Corke, G., Gabrielli, S., Stanton, D., O'Malley, C.: Things aren't what they seem to be: innovation through technology inspiration. In: Proc. of ACM-SIGCHI DIS02, London, pp. 373–378 (June 25-28, 2002)
5. Strömberg, H., Pirttilä, V., Ikonen, V.: Interactive scenarios—building ubiquitous computing concepts in the spirit of participatory design. Personal and Ubiquitous Computing 8, 200–207 (2004)
6. Jennifer, M., Dey Anind, K., Gary, H., Julie, K., Scott, L., Morgan, A.: Heuristic Evaluation of Ambient Displays, ACM SIGCHI, pp. 169– 176 (2003)
7. Baker, K., Greenberg, S., Gutwin, C.: Heuristic Evaluation of Groupware Based on the Mechanics of Collaboration. In: Proceedings of the 8th IFIP Working Conference on Engineering for Human-Computer Interaction (EHCI'01). Toronto, Canada (May 11-13, 2001)
8. Abowd, G.D., Mynatt, E.D.: Charting Past, Present, and Future Research in Ubiquitous Computing. ACM Transactions on Computer-Human Interaction (2000)
9. Pernici, B. (ed.): Mobile information systems. Springer, Heidelberg (2006)
10. Caldwell, B., Chisholm, W., Vanderheiden, G., White, J.: Web Content Accessibility Guidelines 2.0 W3C Working Draft, (November 23, 2005) (http://www.w3.org/TR/2005/WD-WCAG20-20051123/)
11. Treviranus, J., McCathieNevile, C., Jacobs, I., Richards, J.: Authoring Tool Accessibility Guidelines 1.0. W3C Recommendation, (February 3, 2000) (http://www.w3.org/TR/ATAG10/)
12. Jacobs, I., Gunderson, J., Hansen, E.: User Agent Accessibility Guidelines 1.0. W3C Recommendation, (December 17, 2002) (http://www.w3.org/TR/UAAG10/)
13. Nielsen, J.: Usability Engineering. Morgan Kaufmann Publishers, San Francisco, USA (1994)
14. Bertini, E., Gabrielli, S., Kimani, S., Catarci, T., Santucci, G.: Appropriating and Assessing Heuristics for Mobile Computing. In: Proceedings of the International Conference in Advanced Visual Interfaces (AVI) (2006)

Enhancing the Safety Feeling of Mobility Impaired Travellers Through Infomobility Services

Maria Fernanda Cabrera-Umpierrez[1], Juan Luis Villalar[1], Maria Teresa Arredondo[1], Eugenio Gaeta[1], and Juan Pablo Lazaro[2]

[1] Life Supporting Technologies, Universidad Politecnica de Madrid
Ciudad Universitaria s/n
28040 Madrid, Spain
{mf.cabrera, jlvillalar@lst.tfo, mta@lst.tfo, eugenio.gaeta@lst.tfo}upm.es

[2] Instituto ITACA - UPV
Edificio 8G, Camino de Vera s/n
46022 Valencia, Spain
jplazaro@itaca.upv.es

Abstract. This paper describes the health emergency module (HEM) of ASK-IT, a European project, co-funded by the EC 6th Framework Program, within the e-Inclusion area. It identifies the functionalities and specifications of the HEM, as well as its scenarios of application, its requirements derived from the technical and legal analysis and how it interacts with other ASK-IT modules and the whole platform. Special emphasis is given to the User Interface designed, according to the specific user groups' functional characteristics.

Keywords: Safety, Emergency Management, Mobility Impaired People.

1 Introduction

There are many citizens that often require some kind of monitoring of several biological signals, which are essential for the healthcare professionals, in order to diagnose their conditions. Disruption of such bio-signals, for instance an unexpected increase of the patient's heart rate, can be interpreted as a sign of emergency. It is obvious that in these cases an emergency system, with the capability to monitor and evaluate these signals and to trigger a medical intervention, is needed. Moreover, it would be convenient to these patients to have the possibility to communicate at any time with their doctor or physician via phone, videoconference or any other mean, so they can report their symptoms, and the doctors can complete the diagnosis through the images and videos of the patient.

Emergency applications can provide a service, that enables the patient to inform an emergency medical staff in case of an emergency situation, such as a cardiac incident or an accident, in a convenient way [1]. For example, the patient is provided with a portable, wearable device, that can be used, to notify the medical staff that there is an emergency, even in case the patient is unable to use a regular or mobile phone. The

C. Stephanidis (Ed.): Universal Access in HCI, Part II, HCII 2007, LNCS 4555, pp. 285–292, 2007.

patients' medical data are stored in a database and the emergency response is decided according to the patients' personalized needs.

Another service provided by emergency applications is the remote consultation for the patient or a nurse, that lacks expertise in advanced medical treatment, in case of an emergency, in which the patient is unable to go to a clinic because of his/her remote location or the severity of his/her condition. ICT could enable the doctor to evaluate the situation and advise the patient or the nurse on his/her treatment.

Systems that monitor patients' vital signs often have the capacity to trigger an emergency event, in case some of the signals are out of the normality [2]. Nevertheless, these applications usually lack either communication resources (to forward measured data or detected alarms) or interoperability capabilities (to take advantage of the existing infrastructure, wherever the user is), which would allow better assistance to the user at any place and in any moment.

The aim of this paper is to present the health emergency module (HEM) of the ASK-IT project [3], which aims to support and promote the mobility of Mobility Impaired (MI) people, by developing an Ambient Intelligence space for the integration of functions and services across various environments. The HEM will enhance the safety feeling of the MI user, both at home and when travelling.

2 Methods

In order to have a uniform and consistent visual language, in which to express the functional specifications, the modelling approach selected for the HEM has been the use of the functional specification language Unified Modelling Language (UML) [4].

According to the user requirements, the main functionalities defined for this module are the following:

- Capture of user-triggered emergencies, coming from panic buttons, and delivery of the user alert to the third-party social or medical emergency support centre, through the ASK-IT infrastructure.
- Capture and storage of medical data, coming from wearable sensors, in order to analyse them and produce automatic alerts to be forwarded to a third-party emergency support centre, using the ASK-IT infrastructure.
- Provision of an interface for the user to request external help (human or information) for a specific task (i.e. the user is trapped in an inaccessible place, cannot open a door, is lost in a city…). The user analyses the specific problem and establishes communication with ASK-IT support centre or a relevant contact point.
- Integration with local domotics services, to exchange alarms and analyse them, combined with the user health situation and location data, to improve his/her security coverage. It is also foreseen that some personal alarms would make possible the activation of any domotic device, as an answer to the generated alert.

All these functionalities take into account an important feature regarding emergencies: the physical location of the user. Occasionally, it will be useful to know where to send the required assistance and, sometimes, to know the context of the user and analyze whether it has sense or not throwing an alert to the user.

Besides, and in order to provide these emergency services, several requirements should be taken into account, related to the manipulation of private personal and medical data, in agreement to the ASK-IT architecture [5]. This sensitive information has some limitations when it is sent and spread, as it is treated as confidential data, needing privacy guarantee. Therefore, security must be ensured, so that nobody may gain access to it, except the authorised healthcare personnel.

Finally, accessibility requirements come from the whole ASK-IT architecture, so as to provide usable tools for MI people. Also, interoperability requirements have to be taken into account, to interface with other ASK-IT modules (localisation, domotics, etc.) or external services (emergency management centres).

3 Results

According to the previous described requirements and functions, the functionality of the module was represented by a set of use cases. High-level use cases (HLUC) define the overall functionality of the HEM, whereas low-level use cases (LLUC) are described in more detail, containing all calls between modules, as they appear in the software coding, and all parameters types that are described in the ASK-IT developed ontology [6] to guarantee global interoperability. The two main scenarios identified that have been implemented are: "the user asks for help" and "system automatically triggered medical emergency". Fig. 1 shows an example of the representation diagram for the "User asks for help" use case.

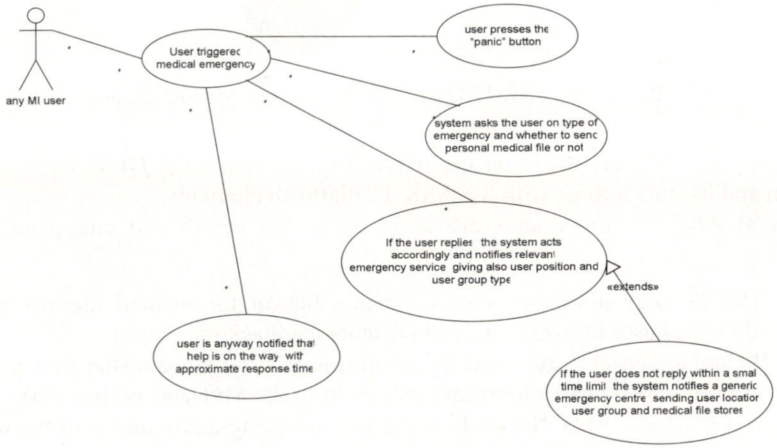

Fig. 1. "User asks for help" use case representation diagram

The HEMM architecture emanates directly from the functional specification analysis and aims at creating an information environment, that will enhance the safety

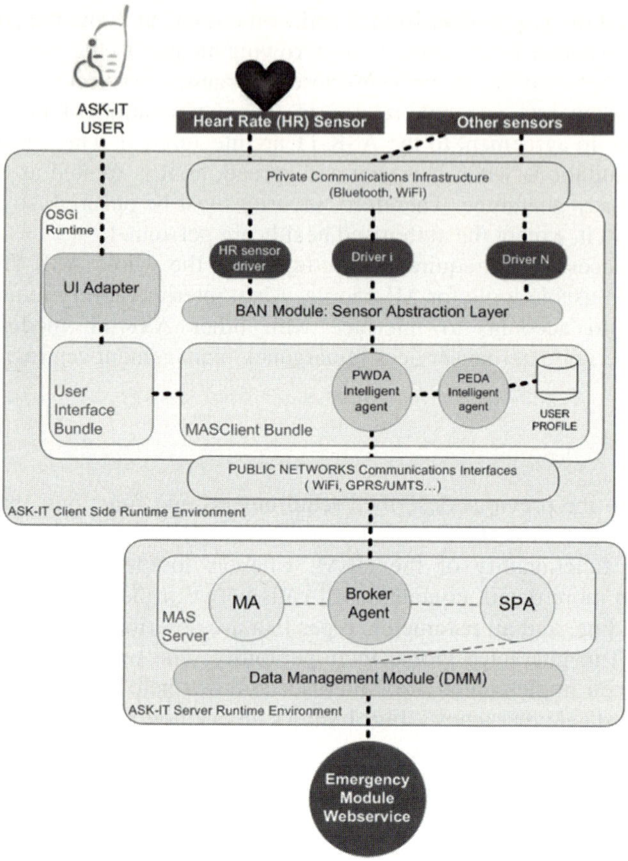

Fig. 2. The ASK-IT Health and Emergency Module chain

feeling of the MI user, while on the move. Fig. 2 depicts the HEM architecture in relation and its interactions with the ASK-IT platform elements.

Several ASK-IT components are involved in the health and emergency chain, mainly:

- ASK-IT user interface: shows a panic button for manual alarms; asks for additional user information; and presents feedback messages.
- Wearable sensors: dynamically acquire user's bio-signals (the first prototype will run with a heart-rate strap monitor from the MyHeart project [7]).
- Drivers/Body Area Network: integrates all peripherals and sensors with the user nomad device.
- PWDA intelligent agent: monitors user status and detects possible alarms.
- PEDA intelligent agent: retrieves the User Profile, to be sent to the emergency centre, if required.
- Broker intelligent agent: collects emergency calls and seeks the most appropriate service provider through the corresponding agent.

- Data Management Module (DMM): forwards the emergency request to the selected web service.
- Interface with Emergency Module (EM): receives emergency requests and assigns assistance resources to attend the user.

3.1 EM Interface

The EM module is an automatic call service, complementary to the ASK-IT architecture. It interacts with the ASK-IT framework, in order to obtain relevant information for the supporting staff in case of emergency (user positioning, medical data acquired by wearable sensors, etc.).

At present, there is a European initiative to integrate emergency service providers within the same intervention framework. This initiative is called eCall [8] and has defined an enhanced emergency call service (E112), which includes additional information (such as user location) for emergency providers.

The EM module interface has been defined, based on the eCall project; however it relies over TCP/IP data exchange (ontology, XML, web services), instead of voice/data phone calls. This way, it allows sending safely, over the communication infrastructure available (even domotic services), more significant information, like:

- Type of emergency: either manual or automatic, test or real call, etc.
- Alarm details: based on parameters as user location, confident position, alarm timestamp, etc.
- User profile: including user healthcare ID, reference healthcare centre, relevant personal data, etc.
- Medical profile: minimum/full clinical history, current bio-signals, etc.

The EM interface consists of a Web Service, which implements one main function *helpRequest* with several input parameters, in correspondence to the information listed above. The output of this function will detail the list of resources activated for attending the user, including information about the estimated arrival time.

3.2 Data Model

In case of an emergency, the ASK-IT framework collects and transmits to the emergency centre a minimum data set (MDS), containing the following information:

- when (timestamp),
- where (precise location and direction),
- who (user identification information),
- where to get more information (emergency centre data).

Additionally, if they are available, a full data set (FDS) can be sent, containing additional information related to the user's health condition and the medical bio-signals values, monitored by the sensors. The medical data is formatted according to the health-related standard HL7 [9] and contains helpful records, like:

- The medical record, detailing the different important illness suffered by the patient and which could condition the treatment.
- The surgical record, which specifies the most relevant interventions suffered for the patient, that could be of interest at the time of attending an emergency event.
- The patient's allergies. This field presents special interest by the time of administering any drug to the patient.
- The current treatments undergone by the patient, which could reveal compatibility problems with some drug administered by the emergency services staff.

In order to grant privacy for the users, a set of security requirements, that ensure confidentiality of these information have been defined and implemented:

- to store medical records in a secure way, we have to encrypt the information with a key that only the owner knows;
- to exchange medical data, we have to identify the other side of communication with an authentication service;
- to send the medical data, we have to encrypt them with a shared secret, known only by the user and the medical authorized staff or with a pair of public/private keys;
- to respect normative, all these requirements have to be implemented with standard and reliable algorithms.

Nowadays, there are many standard algorithms, in order to encrypt data and authenticate the user. The most accepted is by using X509 certificate, that contains:

- a private key, in order to store with symmetric encryption the users medical data;
- a pair of private/public key, in order to be authenticated as a user and in order to exchange sensible data over SSL connection, JADE-S platform or proprietary protocol with asymmetric encryption.
- for symmetric encryption AES with 128 bit key length and for asymmetric encryption RSA.

With AES, RSA and X509 the respect to all laws about privacy and confidentiality is guaranteed.

3.3 User Interface

This section shows the prototypes of the graphic user interfaces, developed for the HEM of the ASK-IT project. The graphical user interface for the end-users has taken into account existing guidelines, which are explained thoroughly in [10]. The approach followed usability and acceptability for mobile devices, with the purpose of providing the most efficient user interface for all future users.

Fig. 3 illustrates the "system automatically triggered medical emergency" use case, in which the ASK-IT system understands that the user is in an emergency (by wearable sensors or user not responding or other situation). It automatically triggers an alarm (the user receives warning for this and has a small time so as to abort it) to an emergency centre, sending user location, user group and medical file, stored in the

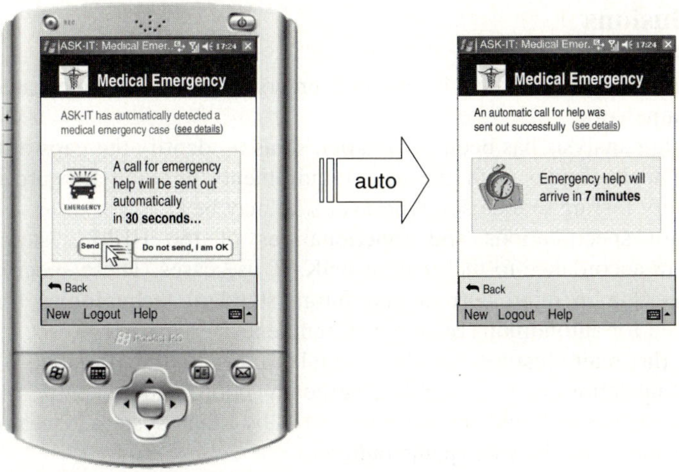

Fig. 3. The system automatically triggers an emergency

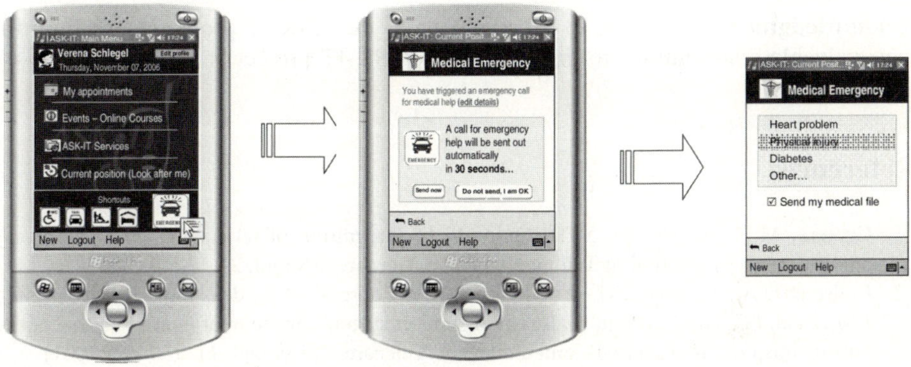

Fig. 4. The user requests help using his/her nomad device

device. The user is notified that help is on the way, with approximate response time. Optionally, it opens a voice communication line between user and centre.

The use case "User asks for help" is shown in Fig. 4.

The user is not feeling well or needs help and pushes a panic button. This should be easy to trigger but difficult to accidentally trigger. The system requests more data on type of emergency. If the user provides more data, the system contacts the most relevant emergency service and opens a communication line with it. If not, it sends notification to a generic emergency centre, sending also, if required, the user's stored medical file. The user is notified about actions and estimated time until help arrives.

4 Conclusions

This paper has described the health and emergency module integrated within the ASK-IT framework.

A thorough analysis has been carried out, so as to identify the gaps of the matching of existing technologies with the user requirements, looking forward to provide a reliable safety feeling to the user, wherever s/he may be.

The main specifications and functionalities of the HEM system have been presented, in accordance to the generic ASK-IT use cases. These specifications were defined, keeping in mind current and future standard technologies for emergency support, even for autonomous resource assignments.

One of the main features of this module relies in the provided TCP/IP-based seamless connection with a health emergency coordination centre in case of an emergency, generated either automatically by the system (wearable sensors monitorisation) or by the user (panic button).

The system, in a prototype stage, will be validated through a series of pilots in different European cities. The pilot results will verify the viability of the system and will be the basis for future improvements and fine tunings.

Acknowledgments. We wish to acknowledge to the ASK-IT project consortium for their valuable contributions to this work. The ASK-IT project is partially funded by the EC.

References

1. Cabrera, M.F., Arredondo, M.T., Quiroga, J.: Integration of telemedicine in emergency medical services. Journal of Telemedicine and Telecare 8(Suppl. 2), 12–14 (2002)
2. Rodriguez, A., Villalar, J.L., Arredondo, M.T., Cabrera, M.F., del Nogal, F., Rodriguez, J.M., Leal, G.: Transmission trials with a support system for the treatment of cardiac arrest outside hospital. Journal of Telemedicine and Telecare. 7(5, Suppl. 1), S60–62 (2001)
3. ASK IT, Ambient Intelligence System of Agents for Knowledge-based and Integrated Services for Mobility Impaired users. project. IST-511298. Annex 1- Description of work (2006)
4. Jacobson, I., Booch, G., Rumbaugh, J.: The Unified Software Development Process. Addison-Wesley, London (1999)
5. Vlachos, F., Konstantinopoulou, L., Bimpas, M., Spanoudakis, N., Kauber, M., et al.: System Architecture Concept methodologies and tools. ASK-IT Deliverable D5.7.3 (2004)
6. CERTH. ASK-IT Ontological Framework. ASK-IT Deliverable D1.7.1 (2007)
7. MyHeart project. IST-2003 507816. Annex 1- Description of work (2004)
8. eCall/E112 initiative, Communication from the Commission to the Council, the European Parliament, the European Economic and Social Committee and the Committee of the Regions - The 2nd eSafety Communication - Bringing eCall to Citizens last access: (September 2006) (http://.europa.eu.int)
9. Dolin, R.H., Alschuler, L., Beebe, C., et al.: The HL7 Clinical Document Architecture. J Am. Med. Inform. Assoc. 8, 552–569 (2001)
10. Brigitte Ringbauer, B.: Internal Deliverable ASKIT ID2.10.2_v01.doc, Simulation and mock/up of all devices for MI (2006)

Handling Uni- and Multimodal Threat Cueing with Simultaneous Radio Calls in a Combat Vehicle Setting

Otto Carlander[2], Lars Eriksson[1], and Per-Anders Oskarsson[1]

[1] FOI, Swedish Defence Research Agency
Olaus Magnus väg 42, 581 11 Linköping, Sweden
[2] Now at Motorola, Inc. IPVS, Sweden
otto.carlander@motorola.se

Abstract. We investigated uni- and multimodal cueing of horizontally distributed threat directions in an experiment requiring each of twelve participants to turn a simulated combat vehicle towards the cued threat as quickly and accurate as possible, while identifying simultaneously presented radio call information. Four display conditions of cued threat directions were investigated; 2D visual, 3D audio, tactile, and combined cueing of 2D visual, 3D audio, and tactile. During the unimodal visual and tactile indications of threat directions an alerting mono sound also was presented. This alerting sound function was naturally present for the unimodal 3D audio and multimodal conditions, with the 3D audio simultaneously alerting for and cueing direction to the threat. The results show no differences between conditions in identification of radio call information. In contrast, the 3D audio generated greater errors in localization of threat direction compared to both 2D visual and multimodal cueing. Reaction times to threats were also slower with both the 3D audio and 2D visual compared to the tactile and the multimodal, respectively. In conclusion, the results might reflect some of the benefits in employing multimodal displays for certain operator environments and tasks.

Keywords: Display technologies, Multimodal, Combat Vehicle, Simulation.

1 Background

The warning and countermeasure system (WCS) is, together with radio communication and command and control systems, of vital importance in a combat vehicle. The WCS automatically performs various countermeasures, thus saving critical time in taking action towards threats or attacks. Though the WCS is automatic the operator crew still needs to have an awareness of evolving threat situations. Carlander and Eriksson [1] showed that the driver of a Combat Vehicle 90 (CV 90) could efficiently utilize threat cueing made by 3D audio and tactile displays combining temporal and spatial positioning. The 3D audio made "threat sounds" possible to localize and a tactile belt around the torso made it possible to feel directions to "threat vibrations." Responses to the cued horizontal directions to threats were made by turning the CV 90 as to having the vehicle heading pointing towards indicated threats, and the responses were also required to be made as quickly as

C. Stephanidis (Ed.): Universal Access in HCI, Part II, HCII 2007, LNCS 4555, pp. 293–302, 2007.

possible. The overall driver performance was of high-quality in that the displays facilitated swift and accurate performance with good threat awareness. However, the 3D audio display generated greater errors and reaction times in localizing threats straight behind the vehicle compared to the tactile display and the two displays combined, respectively. That is, some front-back confusions with the 3D audio cueing were neutralized with the addition of the tactile cueing and not present with the tactile only cueing condition.

The "multiple resource theory" [2] suggests that we have independent resources for information processing and that some of these can be accessed simultaneously (parallel processes). However, parallel processeing can be interfered by handling the information by the same modality, while on the other hand multisensory processes often support and complement each other:

"… if a mosquito lands on our arm, our eyes will be drawn immediately to the source of the unexpected tactile event. In these and many other such situations, objects that are initially processed in one sensory modality "grab" our attention in such a way as to enhance the sensory processing of stimuli presented in other sensory modalities at the same spatial location … there is now convincing empirical evidence that the covert orienting of exogenous attention that is triggered by the presentation of auditory, visual, or tactile cue stimuli can facilitate the perception of target stimuli presented subsequently at the cued location, no matter what their modality. In fact, cross-modal cueing effects have now been demonstrated behaviourally between all possible combinations of auditory, visual, and tactile cue and target stimuli …"

([3], p. 3-4)

It is therefore important to consider the different sensory capabilities when designing complex information systems. Combining sensory signals reduces the variance of perceptual estimates, thus enhancing stimuli detection by cue redundancy. For instance, it has been shown that multisensory neurons are maximally activated by temporally and spatially synchronized visual, auditory, and tactile events [4]. Based on this it is easy to hypothesize that multisensory interfaces most probably improve the presentation of cues and information transfer.

Various presentation technologies now offer solutions for effectively presenting information to all our senses, also including smell and taste, e.g. [5]. However, apart from the obvious visual displays, tactile, and auditory displays are for more straightforward applications the most developed [6]. Some very useful applications of tactile displays utilize vibrations on the torso to cue directions to "the outside world." These directions are mapped to body coordinates by localized stimulations of the skin through small vibrating motors called tactors [1]. The perception of the stimulation on the skin can thus be considered analogous to the perception of auditory or visual stimulation. The tactile technology is well developed and has been studied in various operational settings, e.g. [7], [8], [9], [10], [11].

3D audio sound systems have been able to deliver high-quality, localizable sounds for quite some time [12]. Furthermore, some commercials off the shelf (COTS) alternatives are now available that even have the potential of delivering high quality 3D audio comparable to more expensive and bulky research engines [13]. Carlander and Eriksson [1] utilized a COTS system in a combat vehicle environment, and proposed that the occurred front-back ambiguities might decrease by tracking both the operator's head and the chassis of the vehicle, instead of just the vehicle, and that an improved acoustic signal would probably facilitate sound localization ability. It was also suggested that in the combined displays condition, the tactile cueing might have generated a "compelling and unambiguously perceived threat direction, leaving no room for improvement with 3D audio."

In the present study, we investigated how uni- and multimodal cueing of threat directions compare in a simulated CV 90 setting, with the vehicle driver handling the threats and incoming radio calls. A CV 90 is equipped with a 2D visual head-down display for cueing of directions to threats, mono sound for threat alerts, and a mono system for radio communication. Thus, the 2D visual display and mono sound used here were based on that presently used in a CV 90, and the tactile and 3D audio threat cueing were based on technology that easily can be implemented.

2 Methods

2.1 Participants

Twelve male students participated with a mean age of 23.0 years, ranging from 21 to 29 years. All had normal sight and hearing and no prior experience of the presentation techniques.

2.2 Apparatus

A PC equipped with an external USB soundcard, Hercules Gamesurround MUSE Pocket, was used for the threat cueing and radio communication that were presented through a pair of Sehnheiser HD 200 headphones with circumaural design. The tactile cueing was delivered by a FOI tactile torso belt and controlled from a small signal box connected to the PC parallel port. Twelve vibrating elements in the belt are based on 'clock-positions' evenly distributed on the torso, and each vibrating element thus covers 30° of the horizontal dimension. A head-down visual display was used for the 2D visual threat warnings, and a 42" plasma screen was used for the simulated terrain environment and for feedback on threat defeat status. A touch screen presented response options and was used for identification of radio call information. To compensate for head movements in the 3D audio presentation, an Ascension LaserBIRD II headtracker was used . The base for the vehicle simulation was a 6 DOF Moog motion platform, as shown in Figure 1.

The vehicle simulation was delivered from an FOI developed simulation engine - "the HiFi engine." Data from the HiFi engine was sent to a server handling threat information and presentation, with another data stream sent to the motion platform giving the exact coordinates for the simulation.

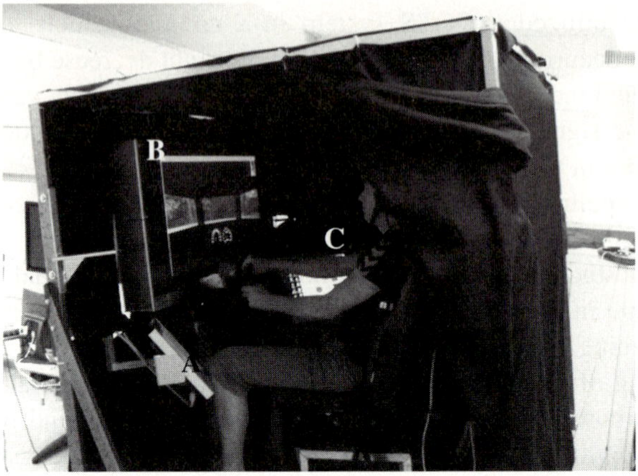

Fig. 1. The motion platform with a seated driver. At (A) is the screen presenting 2D visual information; at (B) is the out-the-window view display; and at (C) is the display presenting response options for identification of radio call information.

2.3 Design, Stimuli, and Procedure

The experiment had a 4 × 3 factorial within subjects design. It included four display conditions of threat directions cueing; 2D visual, 3D audio, tactile, and the combination of 2D visual, 3D audio, and tactile (multimodal cueing). During the unimodal visual and tactile indications of threat directions an alerting mono sound was also presented. This alerting sound function was naturally present for the unimodal 3D audio and the multimodal conditions, with the 3D audio simultaneously alerting for and cueing direction to the threat. Thus, while cueing of threat directions involved unimodal visual, auditory, and tactile displays, and the multimodal combination of these three displays, the inclusion of a mono sound with the unimodal visual and tactile displays kept the alerting function of sound presentation. That is, it is not likely that an operational cueing in a combat vehicle of threat presence would exclude sound presentation so its alerting property was kept for all display conditions. Cueing of threat directions was nevertheless unimodal in three of the display conditions. See Table 1. Threat pop-ups occurred in three sectors presented at the front (315°-45°), the side (45°-135° and 225°-315°), and the back (135°-225°), relative initial vehicle heading.

The task was to react to each threat and respond to it as quickly as possible by aligning the vehicle heading with the threat position and pushing a trigger button. Threat warnings presented with audio consisted of a beep normally used for laser warnings in a CV 90.

During the visual and tactile display conditions the radio calls were given in mono. During the 3D audio and multimodal display conditions the radio calls were given in 3D audio. The 2D visual presentation was shown on a head-down display showing a top-view of the vehicle indicated by a red cone (15 degrees wide) extending from the center of the own vehicle. The response was considered correct if the vehicle was aligned ±10° within the threat position. The threats were not visible, but after each

Table 1. Cueing of threat directions and sound alert

Cueing of Threat Direction	Sound Alert
2D Visual	Mono Sound
Tactile	Mono Sound
3D Audio	3D Audio (same as cueing of threat direction)
Multimodal (Visual, Tactile, 3D Audio)	3D Audio (same as cueing of threat direction)

threat response a text message "hit" or "miss" was overlaid on the simulated out-the-window view (Figure 1). Each threat presentation was limited to duration of 20 s or was terminated with the operator response. The time between threat response and the presentation of a new threat was randomized in the interval of 15 to 20 s. The horizontal vehicle deviation from the correct threat position at operator response was defined as localization error (LE). The elapsed time from target pop-up to having the vehicle turned ±10º from initial heading, was defined as reaction time (RT).

The participants performed a secondary task by identifying two simultaneous radio calls, given at each threat pop up. The participants were told to respond to radio calls on a touch-screen with six response buttons. That is, for each of the two simultaneous calls there were three possible responses to make on the touch-screen.

The participants were told to prioritize the main task, aligning the vehicle, but to answer the radio calls correctly and as fast as possible. The elapsed time from radio call presentation to touch screen-indication was defined as performance time (PT). Proportion of correct answered radio calls was also collected.

A block of trials consisted of using one of the display conditions, and included eight threat presentation trials in each of the three threat sectors, resulting in a total of 24 trials per participant and block. The presentation order of threats was randomized within each block of trials, and block order was balanced over participants.

Before the experiment a questionnaire was completed that included a check on the physical requirements such as normal sight, hearing, and present health condition. In between blocks of trials, questionnaires concerning the display techniques were answered, comprising perceived interpretability, mental workload, and perception of threat direction. A summarizing questionnaire was completed at the very end of the experiment. Participants responded to the questions on a seven points scale.

3 Results

Each analysis comprised twelve means (4 display conditions × 3 sectors = 12 conditions) calculated from the eight trials of each condition. Repeated measures ANOVAs were applied to the means of LEs and RTs of the threat indications, and to the PTs and proportion of correctly answered radio calls. All ANOVA *p*-values are given with the Greenhouse-Geisser corrected values.

3.1 Localization Error (LE)

The ANOVA showed a significant main effect of display condition, $F(3, 33) = 11.53$, $p < .01$, Figure 2, with no other significant effects. A Tukey HSD post hoc test showed a larger mean LE for the 3D audio condition with mean (M) = 10.1 (SE = 2.2), as compared with both the 2D visual ($p < .001$), M = 2.8 (SE = 0.4), and the multimodal presentation ($p < .001$), M = 3.0 (SE = 0.4).

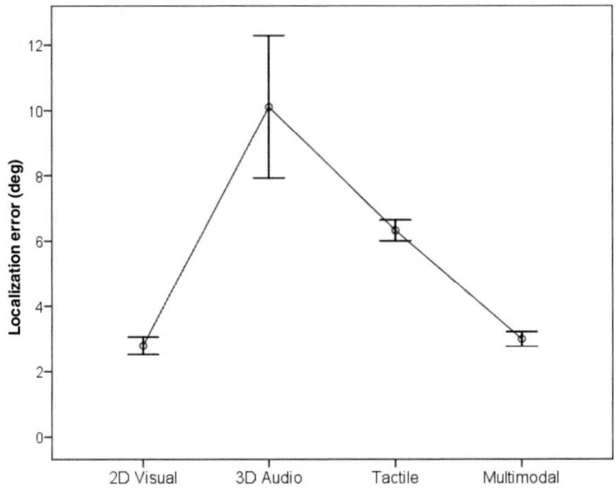

Fig. 2. Mean localization error (LE) with each display condition (±SE)

3.2 RT to Threats

The ANOVA showed a significant main effect of display condition, $F(3, 33) = 7.89$, $p < .001$, with no other significant effects (Figure 3). A Tukey HSD post hoc test

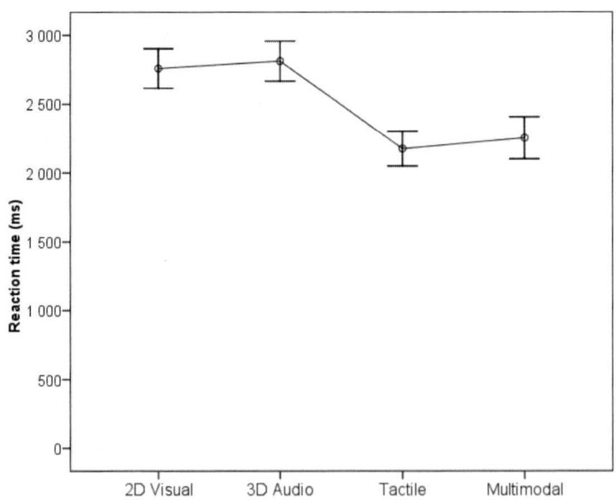

Fig. 3. Mean threat reaction time (RT) with each display condition (±SE)

showed a greater mean RT for both the 2D visual, M = 2759 (SE = 227), and the 3D audio display, M = 2812 (SE = 242), as compared with the tactile ($p< .01$), M = 2175 (SE = 204), and the multimodal presentation ($p< .05$), M = 2253 (SE = 229), respectively.

3.3 Performance Time (PT) to Identification of Radio Calls

The ANOVA showed a significant main effect of display condition for responses of radio calls $F(3, 33) = 4.00$, $p< .05$, with no other significant effects (Figure 4). A Tukey HSD post hoc test showed a greater mean PT for the 3D audio, M = 8965 (SE = 1104) compared to the tactile, with M = 7355 (SE = 1075) display condition ($p< .025$).

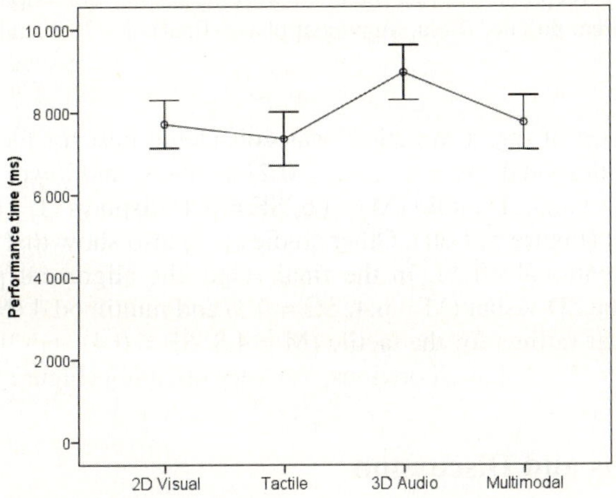

Fig. 4. Mean performance time of responses to radio calls for each display condition (±SE)

3.4 Proportion Correct Identification of Radio Calls

The ANOVA showed no significant effects. The mean values for proportion correct responses to radio calls varied between .82 and .85 (SE: .035 – .04).

3.5 Subjective Ratings

The 2D visual (M = 6.2, SE = 0.4) and multimodal (M = 6.1, SE = 0.3) displays were considered easiest to interpret. The tactile display (M = 5.5, SE = 0.4) was considered somewhat less interpretable, and the 3D audio display was considered most difficult to interpret (M = 4.1, SE = 0.4) (1 = not at all, 7 = very much). Only small differences where found for the level of mental workload, 2D visual (M = 3.8, SE = 0.4), tactile (M = 4.0, SE = 0.5), multimodal (M = 3.8, SE = 0.3), and somewhat higher for 3D audio (M = 4.4, SE = 0.4) (1 = very low, 7 = very high).

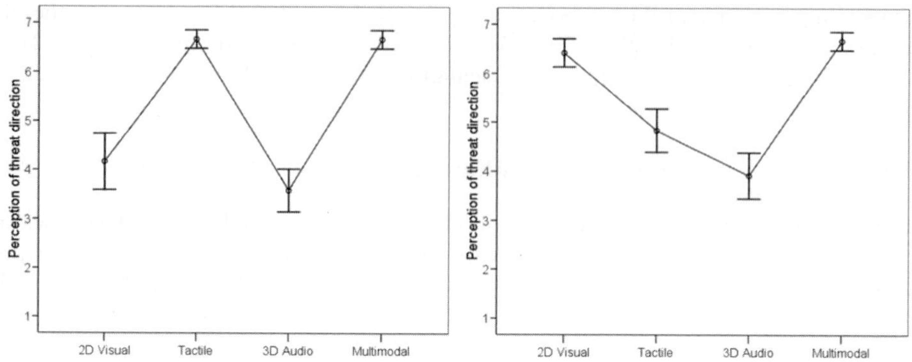

Fig. 5. Ratings of perception of threat direction with the display conditions. Left, localization phase (initial) at threat pop up. Right, alignment phase (final) (1 = Not at all obvious, 7 = Very obvious).

Initial perception of threat direction, was considered best for the tactile (M = 6.7, SE = 0.2) and multimodal (M = 6.7, SE = 0.2) displays, and lower for the 2D visual (M = 4.2, SE = 0.6) and 3D audio (M = 3.6, SE = 0.4) displays (1 = not at all obvious, 7 = very obvious) (Figure 5, Left). Other studies [11] also show that tactile cueing has a very strong attentional effect. In the final stage, the alignment phase, there were high ratings for the 2D visual (M = 6.4, SE = 0.3) and multimodal (M = 6.7, SE = 0.2) displays, and lower ratings for the tactile (M = 4.8, SE = 0.4) and 3D audio (M = 3.9, SE = 0.5) displays (1 = not at all obvious, 7 = very obvious) (Figure 5, Right).

4 Conclusions and Discussion

The results show that the 3D audio generated greater LE compared to the 2D visual and multimodal displays. Also, the RT with the 3D audio was slower compared to the tactile and the multimodal presentation, respectively. The RT with the 2D visual display was also slower compared to the tactile and the multimodal displays, respectively. The PTs for radio calls were slower for 3D audio compared to the tactile condition.

The participants performed well with the different presentation techniques, even though very little training was administered. The greater LE and slower RT for the 3D audio display cannot solely be explained by a few front – back confusion occurrences. That is, an analysis with the back sector removed showed the same pattern of results; greater LE and slower RT for the 3D audio (with less difference). Tracking both the head of the participant and the vehicle do not seem to dramatically decrease the front-back confusion occurrences. Also, altering the frequency spectra of the 3D signal do not seem to increase 3D audio performance in the combat vehicle.

The high accuracy of the 2D visual display confirms how well vision works for an in-vehicle 2D display. However, the slower RTs might indicate that the visual display is relatively poor in getting the operators attention. This is also reflected in the subjective ratings (Figure 5). Furthermore, analysis of the head-tracker data (not presented here) shows the participants used the 2D visual display more frequently when not supported by the added displays in the multimodal display condition. Thus, important time for inspection of the surrounding terrain (out-the-window-time) can be lost when using the 2D visual display. Of course, utilizing a head-down display for threat cueing is not the first choice for capturing attention. Having the visual threat cue superimposed on the out-the-window view would instead be preferable, thus making it more comparable to the tactile and 3D audio cueing.

The results are in line with the general results from Carlander and Eriksson [1] regarding the threat response performance with the 3D audio and tactile displays. The combination of sensory modalities seems to reduce localization deviations from threats or targets and decrease RTs. Also, subjective ratings from both studies show that participants perceived combination of modalities as intuitive and efficient. Combining sensory modalities in a combat vehicle setting could improve the threat awareness, or situational awareness, and overall performance. In essence, the multimodal condition of the present study has the advantage of combining the precision in the visual display when localizing threats and the attentional capture effect of the tactile display thus speeding up RT. In conclusion, the results might reflect some of the benefits in employing multimodal displays for certain operator environments and tasks.

Acknowledgements

We acknowledge the considerate cooperation of the Swedish Army Combat School in Skövde, and above all the WCS group and Jan Fredriksson for making important contributions. We also acknowledge the assistance from the technical group at FOI MSI lab, Björn Lindahl, Johan Hedström and Mattias Kindström. Fang Chen, Chalmers University of Technology, is thanked for providing valuable comments.

References

1. Carlander, O., Eriksson, L.: Uni- and bimodal threat cueing with vibrotactile and 3D audio technologies in a combat vehicle. In: Human Factors and Ergonomics Society. Proceedings of the Human Factors and Ergonomics Society 50th Annual Meeting, pp. 16–20. Santa Monica, CA (2006)
2. Wickens, C.D., Hollands, J.G.: Engineering psychology and human performance. Prentice Hall, Upper Saddle River, NJ (2000)
3. Spence, C., McDonald, J.: The cross-modal consequences of the exogenous spatial orienting of attention. In: Calvert, G.A., Spence, C., Stein, B.E. (eds.) The handbook of multisensory processes, pp. 3–25. The MIT Press, Cambridge, MA (2004)
4. Eimer, M.: Multisensory integration: How visual experience shapes spatial perception. Current biology 14(R), 115–117 (2004)
5. Yanagida, Y., Kawato, S., Noma, H., Tetsutani, N., Tomono, A.: A Nose-Tracked, Personal Olfactory Display. In: Proccedings of the Computer Graphics and Interactive Techniques 30th Conference, San Diego, CA: SIGGRAPH (July 27-31, 2003)
6. Eriksson, L., Carlander, O., Borgvall, J., Dahlman, J., Lif, P.: Operator site 2004-2005. Linköping: FOI (2005)

7. van Erp, J.B.F., van Veen, H.A.H.C., Jansen, C., Dobbins, T.: Waypoint navigation with a vibrotactile waist belt. ACM Transactions on Applied Perception 2(2), 106–117 (2005)
8. McGrath, B.J., Estrada, A., Braithwaite, M.G., Raj, A.K., Rupert, A.H.: Tactile situation awareness system flight demonstration final report. Report No. 2004-10, the US Army Aeromedical Research Laboratory (2004)
9. Rupert, A.H., Guedry, F.E., Reshke, M.F.: The use of a tactile interface to convey position and motion perceptions. In: Virtual Interfaces: Research and Applications (AGARD CP-478: pp. 21.1–21.5). Neuilly-sur-Seine, France: Advisory Group for Aerospace Research and Development (1994)
10. van Erp, J.B.F., Veltman, J.A., Van Veen, H.A.H.C., Oving, A.B.: Tactile torso display as countermeasure to reduce night vision goggles induced drift. In: Proceedings of NATO RTO Human Factors & Medicine Pan el Symposium on Spatial Disorientation in Military Vehicles: Causes, Consequences and Cures (AC/323[HFM-085]TP/42, pp. 49.1–49.8). Neuilly-sur-Seine, France: North Atlantic Treaty Organisation, Research and Technology Organisation (2002)
11. Eriksson, L., van Erp, J., Carlander, O., Levin, B., van Veen, H., Veltman, H.: Vibrotactile and visual threat cueing with high G threat intercept in dynamic flight simulation. In: Human Factors and Ergonomics Society. Proceedings of the Human Factors and Ergonomics Society 50th Annual Meeting, pp. 1547–1551. Santa Monica, CA (2006)
12. Wenzel, E., Arruda, M., Kistler, D.J., Wightman, F.L.: Localization using non-individualized head-related transfer functions. Journal of the Acoustical Society of America 94(1), 111–123 (1993)
13. Carlander, O., Eriksson, L., Kindström, M.: Horizontal localisation accuracy with COTS and professional 3D audio display technologies. In: Proceedings of the IEA 2006 conference, The Netherlands: International Ergonomics Society (2006)

Necropolis as a Material Remembrance Space

J. Charytonowicz[1] and T. Lewandowski[2]

[1] Department of Architecture, Wroclaw University of Technology
ul.B.Prusa 53/55, Wroclaw 50-317, Poland
jerzy.charytonowicz@pwr.wroc.pl

[2] Institute of Architecture and Town Planning, Technical University of Lodz,
Al. Politechniki 6, Lodz 90-924, Poland
levando@tlen.pl, archtomlew@wp.pl

Abstract. The contemporary town planning and architecture abundantly create various public, private, production, recreation, and remembrance spaces, in order to comply with the material and spiritual needs of individuals and large communities alike. Remembrance places – necropolises - are important structural elements of cities that strongly affect the human psyche. Modern forms of spatial arrangement of necropolises search for solutions which will not only provide a rational (ergonomic, economic, ecological) material shape of the burial place, but also satisfy man's mental needs connected with the burial, funeral, veneration of the dead, visits to the cemetery, irrespective of man's age and physical fitness level.

Built over the centuries and still existing necropolises are a material and spiritual cultural heritage left to us by the past generations. Mostly built of symbolic stones - "remembrance stones", they make specific "libraries" with "stone books" for the present and future generations.

Keywords: general, design for all, necropolis, burial form, new burial forms, necropolis design.

1 Introduction

Remembrance places - necropolises are important structural elements of cities that strongly affect the human psyche. The spaces of remembrance places make the last tangible traces of every man's material existence – here, each man lives in his "last home" after death.

Necropolises are necessary for the living community to satisfy man's mental and spiritual needs related to the funeral and present in the final stage of life, i.e. the old age. Traditionally, necropolises have always been consecrated places, places of veneration of the dead, family education, and intergenerational bonding, places for meditation and relaxation for the living.

Due to the fact that our beloved relatives and friends are buried there, they become specific remembrance places - places for storing information about the ancestors, the roots of the community and individuals [1].

[1] [8] J.Charytonowicz, T.Lewandowski, P.Witczak, Postulate for accessibility of remembrance places to senior and disabled persons in the information age – MKEN'2004 in Lodz, Poland.

C. Stephanidis (Ed.): Universal Access in HCI, Part II, HCII 2007, LNCS 4555, pp. 303–312, 2007.

Within the city structure, necropolises primarily play an important practical role as places where to bury human remains, and a symbolic one – as remembrance places. The multifaceted aspect of the material shape of remembrance places – necropolises, applies to every man in the world, whatever their culture and religion, irrespective of any age limits or physical fitness levels.

2 A City Within a City, or a Necropolis Within a Metropolis

The origin of any selected urbanised centre is different in each case under analysis and varies in relation to the natural conditions, historical, political, economic, social, and other contexts. However, one common characteristics – and an invariable element of each of them, regardless of the time when they were established, is the existence of a necropolis. It is an integral, historical association of two spaces: the city (metropolis) and the cemetery (necropolis), in each urban community, regardless of the time or place on Earth.

2.1 Necropolis Within the City Structure

The city and the cemetery are two historical spatial structures, each characterised by certain autonomy and discrete spatial organisation, as confirmed by numerous examples of urbanised spaces (Figure.1).

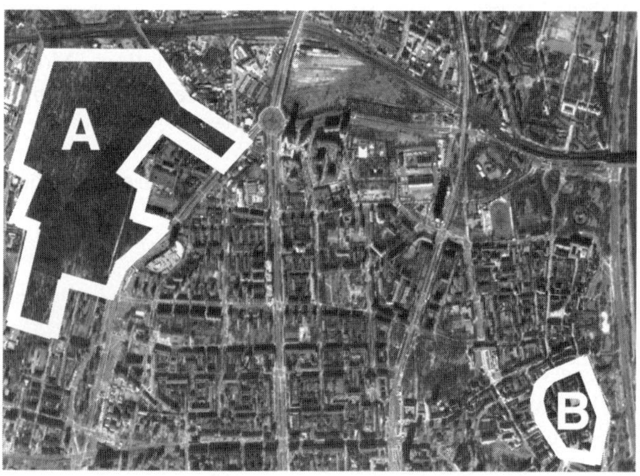

Fig. 1. Poland, Warsaw. Area A – the Powązki Cemetery is approximately 8 times greater than Area B – the Old Town [2]. The scale of land use problems is clearly visible.

Necropolis is a structural element of the city that significantly affects the external spatial organisation, in particular the adjacent city areas. Despite its certain autonomy, necropolis is fully dependent on the space availability provided by the functional and spatial arrangement of the metropolis.

---

[2] Picture of Warsaw in 1m definition, obtained from IKONOS satellite on 6.03.2002; http://www.bcgis.com.pl/

2.2 Spatial Analogies

The "city of the living" – metropolis and the "city of the dead" – necropolis are characterised by many common and analogous elements of infrastructure and spatial organisation. Some examples of such common and analogous elements of infrastructure and spatial organisation in the city space (metropolis) and the cemetery (necropolis) are shown in Table 1.

Table 1. Comparison of spatial structures: examples of common and analogous elements of spatial organisation. Space availability problem.

METROPOLIS „CITY OF THE LIVING"		**NECROPOLIS** „CITY OF THE DEAD"
man		**man**
demography		**demography**
limited area		**limited area**
urban composition	⟺	**urban composition**
communication arrangement **functional arrangement** **supplies**		**communication arrangement** **functional arrangement** **supplies**
quarter		**plot**
Home **(in Polish: DOM)**		**the last home,** **D.O.M.**[3]
man		**man**
SPACE AVAILABILITY		

Analysing the design aspects of the elements constituting the city structure, one can observe a wide range of analogies with the elements constituting the cemetery structure. Necropolis, being part of an organised urban structure, in microscale faces the same problems that are encountered in the city's macrostructure.

The scale of the problem, the complexity of each structure is relative to the size of the area it occupies and the elements of which it is comprised.

2.3 Burial of the Dead as a Demographic, Spatial, and Cultural Aspect

Many urban conurbations and cities in the world are experiencing a crisis with regard to the quality of urban structure spaces – including necropolis spaces, as reflected by their land use pathologies.

---

[3] D.O.M. - <Latin abbrev. for Deo Optimo Maximo> To God, Most Good, Most Great; an inscription on Roman temples, later also on Christian churches and tombs, Słownik Wyrazów Obcych (Foreign Words Dictionary), PWN (1977).

Globally, population growth due to longer life expectancy results in urban sprawl, and that in turn translates into a greater demand for new cemeteries within urbanised centres. Increased numbers of city dwellers directly translate into more intensive city growth, which requires more rational land use strategies and utmost spatial economies. With the passage of time, as urban populations grow, the space available for burial of the dead will be further limited. Aware of this fact, urban communities will seek alternatives to the commonly applied traditional burial forms, either by modifying them or by adopting novel solutions yet unknown. Such measures aim at developing a future spatial arrangement model for necropolises, with a view to meeting long-term increased demand for burial sites caused by demographic factors.

The search for new spatial arrangements of necropolises is still ongoing. Such burial forms are sought that in the long run would solve the problem of the scarcity of new burial places due to the shrinking availability of land within cities and urban agglomerations that might be assigned for necropolises. This phenomenon is observed in all countries in the world.

Burial is a cultural issue, too. The various cultures have developed diversified burial forms derived from their religions and the relevant religious doctrines. Religion sets out the imperatives, preferences, recommendations, permissions, or prohibitions with regard to the given burial forms, thus determining the spatial solutions of necropolises.

Great contemporary monotheistic religions and funerary rites:

- **Christianity:**
  - Catholicism: prefers traditional burial rite, permits cremation
  - Protestantism: prefers cremation, permits traditional burial rite
  - Orthodox Faith: prescribes traditional burial rite, prohibits other burial forms
- **Islam:** prescribes traditional burial rite, prohibits other burial forms
- **Judaism:**
  - reformed: prefers traditional burial rite, permits cremation
  - orthodox: prescribes traditional burial rite, prohibits other burial forms
- **Buddhism:** prefers cremation as the highest-rank burial rite, permits body dismembering and sacrificing it on altars for animals (Tibet)

Great contemporary polytheistic religions and funerary rites:

- **Hinduism:** prescribes cremation as the only burial form conducive to reincarnation

Atheists – representing approximately 29% of the global population [4], exercise many of the existing traditional and novel funerary forms: traditional horizontal or novel vertical burial, urn burial – cremation, carbonization, lyophylisation, hibernation, thanatopraxis, plastination, or burial in the outer space.

Of all the contemporarily applied funerary forms, cremation and urn burial are commonly acceptable to most religions and show the highest statistical growth dynamics.

---

[4] [9] Malherbe M., Les religions de l' Humanie, 2-eme partie: Les religions, Criterion, Paris (1990,1992) – Religie Ludzkości. Leksykon, Polish edition by Znak (1999), p. 8.

2.4 Problems of the Contemporary Necropolis Spatial Organisation

Contemporary necropolises (existing and projected) are subject to a number of assessment criteria. They are the starting point for comparative studies aimed at finding the most effective solutions for the future, paying special attention to the number of burial places available for particular forms of burial, combined with such methods of spatial organization of cemeteries that would be best both for the buried dead, and for the living people visiting the cemeteries.

Assessment criteria for spatial organization of necropolises:

- **urban development** – means logical incorporation of a necropolis into the urban structure, while maintaining the **spatial order** and highlighting the exceptional character of the necropolis within the urban structure, being always a special place, „sacred" for many communities in the world
- **economy –** translates in fact into high prices of land within cities, the logical consequence of which is searching for such burial forms that could ensure the maximum number of burial places within the smallest possible area
- **ecology** – means searching for a burial form that is neutral to the environment, and could ensure safe co-existence of a necropolis in immediate proximity to other urban facilities, and minimise materials and energy consumption necessary for the given burial form per one funeral
- **ergonomics** – means the need to adjust the entire material environment to man's psychophysical abilities, with a special focus on the needs of senior and disabled citizens, traditionally most frequent visitors to necropolises
- **availability for senior and disabled persons** – who are usually the most frequent visitors to necropolises, by considering **ergonomic** aspects of the design in order to remove architectural, urban planning, and functional barriers, as well as psychological barriers accompanying the old age and disability, thus respecting one of the fundamental human rights, that is the "right to participate in a burial, and to visit a grave" in the cemetery
- **pathology prevention** which means compliance with the binding standards and legal regulations concerning grave dimensions, minimum spaces between graves, minimum width of alleys and passages; prevention of the practices of „enhancing" the existing cemeteries through shortening of the waiting period between successive burials, or through increasing the number of graves at the expense of protective green areas; prevention of thefts and vandalism of burial sites
- **user safety and comfort** are strictly connected with the size of the cemetery (from several to several hundred hectares) as well as its legible functional and spatial organization, and the system of visual information signs which make it easier to move around the necropolis (sense of direction)
- **equipment of the cemetery with technical infrastructure, sanitary facilities, communication facilities –** access roads and parking lots adapted to the needs of all users, bus service within mega-necropolises with the fleet adapted to the needs of seniors and the disabled

- **comprehensive service** – in terms of the market economy, a necropolis is a modern enterprise offering a wide range of services to families of the dead, which manages the cemetery ensuring full transparency of data under ISO systems
- **quality of law** – legislation that takes account of modern forms of burial, spatial organization of necropolises, and land ownership
- **necropolis management model** – religious or municipal, defines the management and customer service standards, as well as spatial solutions

All the assessment criteria must take into account the **primary factor**, that is the burial form being a consequence of the religion practised and its related religious doctrine and/or outlook on life.

3 Necropolis as a Remembrance Place – "Stone Library"

For thousands of years, man has revered the dead and paid them tribute through funerary rites, burial forms, and spatial arrangement of necropolises. Traditionally, necropolises have always been consecrated places - sacrum, places of veneration of the dead, family education, and intergenerational bonding, places for reflection and memories and reveries over the passage of time and its „contemporary heroes". Primarily, necropolises are the places of remembrance of the dead.

Urban sociologists claim that "*... The cemetery is always (...) a keystone for three social groups: those who have already passed away; the living, and lastly, those to be born*"[5]. It is a unique link between generations, based on tradition, and what is vital – on the relationship between the world of the living and the world of the dead, which reflects the cultural standards of the society.

The material spatial shape of remembrance places – necropolises, has undergone and still undergoes many transformations. People continue to build tomb structures to commemorate the dead, thus referring to the long-established and powerful local traditions. Encrypted in such tomb structures is the centuries-old remembrance of the dead. The tombs represent characteristic pieces of the broad sepulchral art.
The material shape of remembrance places – necropolises – is determined by:

- **religious status** – i.e. declared non-believers (atheism), or followers of the given religion, whose faith doctrines precisely specify the preferred burial form (as described in subsection 2.3)
- **burial form** – determines the tomb's architecture, size, shape, and plots distribution, and, consequently, the form and spatial composition plan of the whole cemetery design, i.e. the spatial organisation of the necropolis
- **construction materials** and the skills of taking advantage of their properties

3.1 Contemporary Forms of Burial

The commonly practised forms of burial are historical, most ancient, timeless forms, accepted by most communities and religions. These include:

[5] [3] Jałowiecki B., Szczepański M.S., Miasto i przestrzeń w perspektywie socjologicznej, (The City and Space in Sociological Perspective) Scholar Publishing House, Warsaw (2002) p. 317.

- **inhumation** – traditional burial
- **urn burial** – cremation

Novel funerary rites are the modern burial forms that have appeared very recently. In the future, as these burial forms gain popularity, we will deal with some revolutionary changes, e.g.:

- **inhumation in the upright position**
- **carbonization** – artificial precious stone
- **lyophylisation** – garden cemetery
- **hibernation** – cold-store cemetery
- **thanatopraxis** – formolisation, embalming
- **plastination** – plastinates
- **burial in the outer space** – cemeteries in orbits, planets
- **cybernecropolis** – www.cemetery.com – virtual cemeteries

Of all commonly practised funerary rites, **cremation and urn burial deserve special interest.** There has been developed a series of novel kinds of funerals (ashes kept in urns, or strewn over the sea, from a plane, or over mountains) and burial (urns buried in pit graves, columbaria, cineraria, or remembrance gardens) which offer the widest possibilities of spatial arrangement of necropolises. Some advantages of urn burial include: reduced dimensions, low land consumption, environmental harmlessness, low cost (about 25% cost of inhumation), single urn standard. Urn cemeteries do not cause ground water pollution. Small dimensions of graves cause that the urn cemetery is perceived as very spacious. When equipped with the "piling" feature, burial places under or above the ground (columbaria), it seems one of the least land-consuming forms of burial that allows, on the saved area, to properly design such spatial development components as greeneries, traffic systems, and other facilities. Due to its space-wise functionality, ergonomic, economical, ecological, social and cultural advantages, urn burial will become the burial of the future. As indicated by statistics, this form of burial tends to be the most rapidly developing, and has already become predominant in many countries.

3.2 New Forms of Spatial Organisation of Necropolises

The modern spatial arrangement solutions for necropolises include several new types of cemeteries:

- **type 1 – "forest cemetery", "cemetery park", "cemetery garden"** – characterised by percentage dominance of greenery area over the tomb surface area, and pedestrian and motorist communications.
- **type 2 – "cemetery - town"** – a trend in cemetery design of "cities of the dead" modelled after cities of "the living", with analogous spatial development arrangements and space infrastructure components.
- **type 3 – "cemetery – sculpture"** – type of cemeteries being great artistic creations, forming original and unique spatial solutions, e.g. columbaria in the form of monumental sculptures.
- **type 4 – "multi-rite cemetery"** – type of municipal necropolises with various spatial arrangements, from traditional forms of development to the latest

tendencies of the above types 1 – 3. They are ecumenical cemeteries, managed by elective secular bodies.

- **type 5 – "virtual cemetery" –** is a burial place in the new format of virtual space. It contributes to the new phenomenon of the **duality of the cult of the dead.** A grave in the cyberspace is a multimedia form of worship of the dead within a wide social circle, while a grave in the real life space – within the narrow family circle.

3.3 "Stone Libraries"

Stone is the oldest material used by man to make tools, and the oldest natural and easily available construction material. It symbolises power, strength, durability. The world's oldest buildings which have survived until the present day are built of stone.

Fig. 2-9. Historical and contemporary spatial sepulchral buildings in the world [6]: 1 – Stonehenge/Great Britain; 2 – Jerusalem/Israel; 3 – Giza-Cairo/Egypt; 4 – Vienna/Austria; 5,7 – Modena/Italy; 6 – Barcelona/Spain; 8 – Hong Kong/China

[6] From the archive of authors.

As regards the spatial organisation of necropolises, stone has always played a leading role. Before man had learned to bury bodies of the dead, they were first covered with a stone. Next, burying ground tombs were symbolically marked with a stone. Once the Sumerians, approx. 3500 years BC, had invented cuneiform script, stone steles and tombs began to feature simple inscriptions, then extensive epitaphs – written information of the deceased. They marked the beginning of "memorial stones", or "stone libraries".

As construction skills and techniques developed, great civilisations built stone tombs and mausoleums of the rulers and their families that have never ceased to raise admiration. New masonry tools and techniques helped create unique forms of the art of sepulchral sculpture (reliefs, bas-relieves, figural sculptures, sculptural decorations), which flourished in the 19th century. Artificial stone – from the mid-20th century, concrete and ferroconcrete helped create on a grand scale novel tomb solutions.

Natural stone and artificial stone are the most popular construction materials used to build single tombs, erect great sepulchral structures, and implement whole spatial necropolis designs.

Remembrance places – real, symbolic, or virtual necropolises created over the centuries, represent the material and spiritual cultural heritage left to us by the past generations, and exert a very strong influence on the human psyche. Each necropolis is a database of the dead buried there, a picture left for posterity of the passing communities and their outstanding individuals. Most of them are comprised of written symbolic stones – "memorial stones" – and create a kind of "libraries" with "stone books" for the contemporary and future generations. These books are slowly changing their traditional sizes and formats, adjusting to the requirements and expectations of the contemporary world.

4 Conclusions

Necropolis is a material remembrance space which many people in the world immediately identify with a flat burial surface. In fact, among the contemporary spatial development and architectural solutions designed for necropolises, a strong emphasis is on spatial forms. Necropolis, just like the metropolis, prefers cubage solutions. Contemporary cemetery designs (remembrance places) are departing from horizontal surface solutions and replacing them with vertical and spatial solutions. Once again the analogy between the spatial development of the "city of the living" – metropolis, and the "city of the dead" – necropolis, becomes highly evident.

Initially, low and land-consuming sepulchral structures were built (e.g. single-level tombs), then followed by high tomb-piling sepulchral structures (e.g. multilevel tombs, vaults, tower cemeteries) that utilise all contemporarily available technical and material solutions. The floor space ratio is growing.

Some important phenomena observed in all contemporary necropolises include **minimised size of the burial casket and burial place, and vertical spatial arrangements** (compacting) aimed at increasing the number of new burial places and lessening (through concentration) possible environmental threats. These highly powerful tendencies are gaining momentum in all newly-developed and generally accessible necropolises in large urban conurbations in the world.

References

1. Heathcote, E.: Monument Builders. Modern Architecture and Death. London: Academy Editions (1999)
2. Jałowiecki B., Szczepański M.S., Miasto i przestrzeń w perspektywie socjologicznej, Wydawnictwo naukowe Scholar, Warszawa (2002)
3. Lewandowski, T.: New forms of spatial development of necropolises in Europe - Nowe formy organizacji przestrzenej nekropolii w Europie, Zastosowania ergonomii, Zielona Gora, Nr 1-2, pp. 141–158 (2004)
4. Lewandowski, T., Charytonowicz, J.: Forms of necropolises in the computer era, HCI 2005. In: 11th International Conference on Human Computer Interaction, Las Vegas, USA, (July 22-27, 2005) CD, ISBN 0-8058-5897-5 paper 53
5. Lewandowski, T., Charytonowicz, J.: Necropolis and its structural elements - Nekropolia i jej elementy strukturalne, Zastosowania ergonomii, Kwartalnik, Zielona Gora, Nr 1-3, pp. 131–145 (2005)
6. Lewandowski, T., Charytonowicz, J.: Search for new form of burial: horizontal or vertical?, Poszukiwania nowych form pochówku: poziomo czy pionowo?, Zastosowania ergonomii, Kwartalnik, Zielona Gora, Nr 1-3, pp. 261–272 (2006)
7. Charytonowicz, J., Lewandowski, T., Witczak, P.: Postulate for accessibility of remembrance places to senior and disabled persons in the information age - MKEN' 2004, Ergonomia niepełnosprawnym w wieku informacji, Lodz, Poland, pp. 77–88 (2004)
8. Malherbe, M.: Les religions de l' Humanite, 2-eme partie: Les religions, Criterion, Paris 1990,1992 - Religie Ludzkości.Leksykon, polish edition by Znak (1999)

Reconsumption and Recycling in the Ergonomic Design of Architecture

Jerzy Charytonowicz

Wroclaw University of Technology, Department of Architecture
Prusa 53/55, 50-317 Wroclaw, Poland
{Jerzy Charytonowicz,jerzy.charytonowicz}@pwr.wroc.pl

Abstract. One of the characteristics of human activity is the ability to transform the environment and create new structures. Such actions include various forms of building activities. The adjustments of the whole of material surroundings to the needs and possibilities of man is dealt with by ergonomics. The practical and specific application of the general principles of ergonomics, on the other hand, is dealt with by architecture, i.e. architects designing the *material framework for human life*. The quality of this "framework" determines the quality of human life. A widely understood design more and more often goes away from creation of the defined, finished work – object, to initiate and sustain the development process and different activities connected with the space creation. This way is related to sustainable design that is generally defined as design that meets the needs of the present without compromising the ability of future generations to meet their own needs.

Much of waste comprises valuable raw materials for further utilization and the best way to do it is to reuse the waste at the same level of this original usage. The measures to reduce material consumption in the construction industry are to be sought in the implementation of novel renewable materials of natural origin as well as the non-renewable materials, yet possible to regenerate and reuse, that is in reconsumption and recycling applied, among others, in ergonomic design of architecture.

Keywords: building activities, architectural ergonomics, sustainable design, reconsumption, recycling.

1 Introduction

One of the characteristics of human activity is the ability to transform the surrounding environment and the ability to create new structures. The manifestation of such activity comprises various forms of building activity.

The domain which deals with adapting the whole of the material surroundings of man to their needs and capabilities is *ergonomics*. Architecture, however, and architects designing material frames for man's life, whose quality determines the quality of that life, deal with practical and specific application of principles of ergonomics.

C. Stephanidis (Ed.): Universal Access in HCI, Part II, HCII 2007, LNCS 4555, pp. 313–322, 2007.

A widely understood design more and more frequently is departing from the creation of ultimately defined objects towards initiating and sustainable development processes and varied activities oriented towards the creation of architectural space. That way is related to the so called *sustainable design*. An effective implementation of sustainable design strategies requires an integrated approach to the building design, the environment surroundings and people's activity inside and outside of a structure, and this is a feature of *architectural ergonomics*.

Much of building waste becomes a valuable raw material for further use and the best thing is when it is reused at the same level as its previous use. Avoidance of disadvantageous and heterogenic storage of the waste can lead to changes in the manner building structures have been demolished so far. This will encourage a careful deconstruction and segregation of components.

Ways to diminish material absorptiveness in the building industry should be sought in implementing both new renewable materials of natural origin and the non-renewable ones but regenerative and reusable, that is in reconsumption and recycling applied in the *ergonomic architectural design*.

2 Ergonomics and Ecology in Architecture

Architecture has always reflected changes taking place in the process of evolution of societies and socioeconomic needs of human environment at a particular stage of its development, and functions and norms of architecture were moulded through centuries. Also, the underlying principle of architecture has always been creating new spatial solutions. The history of architecture, in turn, comprises a constructional order and the history of forms being a logical consequence of technical development that is a technical progress. As through the ages, when architecture was treated as a synthesis of arts, these days it is also considered one of the forms of humanization of technology and man's industrial and urbanized environment. As opposed to the past practices, when architectural objects were usually a work of one author, today's architecture is the result of works of interdisciplinary teams. [2]

Architecture, as it has been mentioned above, is a reflection of socioeconomic needs of man's environment at a particular stage of its development and also a reflection of forms of the contemporary life. It is one of the creative and conscious elements of influence on the processes of shaping a building, its surroundings, and on shaping settling arrangements, and finally whole regions. This art and its accompanying skills serve the purpose of protecting and creating optimal conditions for man's life in the direct contact with the surrounding environment. Architecture understood in that way, as art and a craft whose task is to solve specific problems, reaches into resources of various disciplines, particularly humanistic, technical, scientific, sociological, and economic – depending on a scale and complexity of analysed problems. Therefore, it has to adapt itself to a complex forms of man's life, to the fast pace of technical progress, which results from achievements of civilization, to the socioeconomic development of population and psychological tendencies specific to particular social communities. [3]

One of future trends in architecture – apart from exposing aesthetic qualities – is more effective implementation of utilitarian contents consisting in general inclusion of principles of ergonomics (e.g. "friendliness" of architecture to the handicapped) and ecology (friendliness towards the natural environment).

It is ergonomics that deals with adapting the shape of the material surroundings to man's needs and abilities in both types of environment. This domain determines the principles of proper adjustment of elements of the system: *man – technology – natural environment.* Architecture, however, that is architects who design man's material framework, deals with practical and specific application of the general principles of ergonomics. The quality of those framework determines the quality of man's life.

Transmitting the ergonomic knowledge to architects in particular is of special importance, since it is they who shape man's environment beginning from an industrial scale to a scale of a single interior detail (an industrial form), and whose design errors are for decades severely suffered by a large group of structure users.

The fundamental purpose of the contemporary and future architecture should be shaping the material environment in a manner ensuring the man appropriate standards and a comfort of life with simultaneous respect to nature – its needs and possibilities, thus with the application of the principles of ergonomics and ecology.

Interrelations between ergonomics, ecology and architecture are the easiest to notice when analysing objectives of activity and domains of interests of the above mentioned disciplines.

A widely understood ergonomics deals with adaptation of the whole of components of the material environment (abiotic environment) to man's needs (biotic factor), which is one of the elements of the global ecosystem. In other words, ergonomics aims at ensuring man safety, health environment of proper quality, and life comfort in the ecosystem of nature.

Ecology, in turn, deals with the whole of phenomena concerning interrelations between biotic elements of nature and both their animate and inanimate environment. In short, ecology concerns functioning of the animate nature in relation to the abiotic environment with particular concern for protection of ecosystems against man's destructive activities.

Concern for man and the natural environment and developing ergonomic consciousness in society is the primary task of designers in all specialities. For the sake of specificity and range of professional activity, a particular role, however, falls to architects in this respect. [1]

A shared goal of ergonomics and ecology comprises activity related to the protection of man's health and the improvement of health quality and safety of the human environment. Thus, an analysis of problems should be carried out concerning both the aspect of ecological and ergonomic design, structure building and their use. Taking the whole nature's and man's good as a direction of the ecologic and ergonomic activity it becomes clear that the overriding objective of all participants in an investment process should be a harmonious cooperation leading to building a structure fully adapted to its users' needs and abilities and to the natural environment. Therefore, ergonomics issues in the building industry should be considered in the context of such a wide cooperation, because they are not only a matter of comfort and safety of an individual man, e.g. a contractor or a user, but mainly a matter of public responsibility for the quality of performance of each participant in an investment activity.

Architectural design has always included, though with mixed effects, the context of nature. The traditional ergonomics, however, initially was concerned only with the relation *machine – man,* certainly in the anthropocentric approach.

Ergonomics of the future, in my opinion, is *eco-ergonomics* which allows for not only man's needs, but also the needs and abilities of the natural environment, whose only component he is. Hence, the historical model of the holistic ergonomics system needs to be modified into a widely understood system *man – technology – natural environment*, which will enable a more holistic view of multiaspect effects of man's technical activity.

A particularly responsible role in this respect falls to architects shaping man's material surroundings from the microscale to the macroscale, that is from the scale of an individual interior to urban and regional scales.

3 Architecture as a Generator of Building Waste

At present times, a question is raised whether architecture is still art in the traditional understanding or – as it is comprehended contemporarily – "engineering". All premises speak for the second option. Future trends point at a growing role of the economic and engineering factor, and the essence of the contemporary engineering is also – apart from an ability to create allowing for the principles of aesthetics (art) – the ability to predict effects of exploitation of technical creations and their recycling. The contemporary engineering encompasses constructing, production technology (realization), exploitation (system organization and management), and utilization of exploited technical products.

The problem of waste comes up in every dwelling and concerns all of us. As unaware consumers, we choose products affecting environment in some way or another. Analogies should be sought in the world of designers - architects responsible for taking decisions in the design process every day, in the act of building a house, a housing estate or a city. An image of a *consumption society* provides an appropriate background for considerations over the contemporary architecture whose purpose is to mould man's and nature's friendly urbanized society, ensuring a high quality of life. Designers, as part of a squandering society, are subject to similar market mechanisms and manipulations. Therefore, finding mechanisms for moulding a rational level of consumption in harmony with the surrounding natural environment comprises a challenge for architects implementing the principles of ecodevelopment. [4]

In the natural environment, there is no concept of waste. A continuous flow of matter takes place in the organic ecological cycle. The contemporary waste management in a settlement environment lacks the logic the natural flow. Waste material is still considered inconvenient in the elimination of litter which a municipal sewage facilities cannot handle. Until now, waste has not been considered as "material located in an inappropriate place" and the natural principle of transforming the waste material from one biological process into a recyclable material for another process is not accepted as well.

In the building sector, the phase of investment realization acts as the principal focus of architectural design, while the stage of use and utilization of a planned structure is given much less attention. The willingness of winning existing components of a building, recycling of building materials or whole structures is not common practice while getting rid of a building waste in "wild" dumps appears to be a standard in a building reality.

In highly developed countries, as a result of the development of social ecological consciousness, the implementation of the principles of sustainable development on the scale of the whole economy requires change in thinking, expanding the area of design decisions into a study of their environmental implications. The law on responsibility of perpetrators of environmental damage, if plainly specified and effectively enforced, changes the outlook on design and forces to seek optimal solutions harmless to the natural environment.

Ecologically conscious decisions will be connected with the sustainable resources management. This management should include both non – renewable original materials and extisting waste that would be treated as equally valuable material suitable for further processing and reusing in an investment process. Designers aware of the decisions should at the same time minimize production of non-renewable waste, adopting wasteless technologies based on existing, even already owned materials and products.

Lack of a holistic view of an investment process is the primary reason for disregard of ecological aspects in design and leads to "the surface architecture" and speculative forms of space development depending on fashion, economic situation, and ways of financing. Possibility of architect's influence on limiting investment's effect on the environment depends on how early he has become involved in the programming and designing phase of an undertaking. The earlier the environmental criteria are allowed for in the design (for example the criteria of minimizing the use of building materials or generated waste), the easier is to achieve the effect of zero influence.

Therefore, an environment-friendly design, called *holistic*, includes the whole of an investment process and the full life cycle of a structure (with the demolition phase, waste utilization and waste and material acquisition). It is design integrated with major circulations of nature management, including water, energy, air and materials, and based upon a decentralized circulation economy.

In the history of architecture, the industrial era has recorded engineering objects, factory buildings, mass housing buildings, and public utility structures all reflecting the culture of both the nineteenth and twentieth century societies. A characteristic of the architecture of that time was exploitation of the natural environment (struggle against nature), squandering natural resources in the name of civilization progress. Invariability of the planned function of buildings and its immobility characteristic to that architecture and town-planning, now – in the age of information technology civilization – has become an outdated assumption.

Buildings which enable function mobility and are easy to adapt have a prolonged technical life cycle and should not be qualified as structures for demolition. For this reason, they should be deemed environment friendly, for fundamental building constructions, used through decades, do not cause a flow of resources and generation of building waste in the course of transformations of their elements.

A form of a building imposed by an architect frequently determines potential possibilities of a structure and its capability of adaptation. A well planned building should be sensitive to social changes, sociological determinants, and changing configurations on the labour market. This is the challenge for a flexible architectural design.

Still, majority of buildings is designed with the thought of their prospective users, of their individual financial capacity, and the necessity of adaptation and adjustment of space to the users' individual needs. Majority of buildings, however, or maybe except for spectacular monuments of architecture, undergoes the process of adaptation resulting from changing habits and ways of their use. Dwellings occupants adapt and arrange space according to their own cultural models or either their own or imposed ideas concerning home or office interior. It is physical engagement of occupants that makes home live.

Perception of the user's role in an investment process changes from passive to active, particularly in the design process. The adaptation process appears to be a crucial element in the life cycle of a structure. The adaptive architecture enables the user transforming the surrounding space, meeting their expectations and current needs, diminishing considerably a useless waste stream. Prior to planning architecture of this type, first we have to plan and programme a prospective user's "design", create a proactive environment, open to a large extent. [5]

The adaptation need evidently appears in the use phase. Adaptation is a continuation of both the design phase and the construction phase. The more friendly and open a system is, the easier is to carry out transformations and make changes. When the system is closed and little flexible, it discourages from adaptation actions or even makes them impossible. It leads to the moral death of the system – we do not want to use it, despite its good technical condition. It is connected with squandering the resources, generating waste, and as a result – with a high cost of the life cycle of a structure. Therefore, the predesign, the programme phase is so important.

4 Reconsumption and Recycling in the Ergonomic Design of Architecture

An essential characteristic of design in compliance with the sustainable development is economy of natural resources and their responsible management. New technologies, capable of creating new materials and combining conventional materials in a new way, give a designer much more choices than ever before.

Such an approach is reflected by "design for minimizing waste", where a designer has to exhibit knowledge concerning the life cycle of products and materials used for production and possess information not only on a type of the materials at different levels of the product transformation chain, but also on possibilities of the usage of components obtained from recycling or elements acquired in the secondary circulation.

A crucial consequence for environment is an increase in the complexity of the applied materials. Advanced material engineering, chemistry, developing connection technologies cause that at the production stage a complex material is created, frequently with a complex structure, difficult to decompose into single elementary components.

Use of materials of that type on a wide scale will curtail the possibilities of their recycling or further processing without bearing high costs. The complexity of materials and complex technologies applied in a construction may make the structure exploitation difficult cause problems connected with repair or replacement of individual elements. The complexity concerns not only the material and technological matters, but also space design. The suggested architectural forms may be characterized by either simplicity or complexity of solutions, and frequently by unnecessary complication of form and function. This, in turn, is reflected in the amount of the used building material and waste produced.

When erecting a house from confectioned, modular building materials, an irregular plan compared to the compact plan will generate more material waste. Whereas a sensible design of a building shape will favour cutting down on squandering the building material, eliminating generation of unnecessary construction waste.

The opposition of complexity is simplification of applied solutions and elements in a manner which makes them generally comprehended, easier to replace, repair and potentially use further. Both complexity and simplification are related to the issue of material absorptiveness of products and structures. If a designer determined a possibility of using less material to achieve a desired result, the advantages of reduction of a waste stream would be noticeable both at the production and the postconsumption stage. Waste storage, energy emission and consumption at every stage of a product life cycle will drop in proportion to the amount of the product reduced material. New processing technologies, materials of better quality and an enhanced product design may have an effect on more economical use of materials and resources. [6]

In the phase of an architectural project, a choice of technology and building materials affects a construction's structure, form, and aesthetics, and determines a manner and cost of its development, and finally affects the environment.

When making a choice from among a rich assortment of building materials, we can adopt different criteria. The traditional criteria are the price, availability, mechanical durability, and safety. The ecological criteria include the degree of impact on the environment in all life phases of a material, material and energy absorptiveness, emission potential, and health and microclimate considerations. If we narrow down the issue to the waste problem, then the easiness of utilization, the possibility of biodegradation or recycling, durability and easiness of adaptation to new needs become factors of crucial importance. The influence the building materials have on the environment is connected with winning raw materials and exploitation of natural resources, pollution generated during the production process and the raw materials or ready products transportation, energy absorptiveness and emission power in the course of use, and the manner of utilization. These factors determine a list of environment friendly building materials and technologies. The list includes both the original materials, generally biodegradable and succumbing to utilization with ease, and recyclable materials – just from recycling.

It should be emphasized that biodegradable building materials will not replace completely the traditional ones. However, developing awareness of the existence of alternative materials among the investment process participants, which reduce the amount of construction waste, should be an important step towards the economy that effectively makes use of natural resources.

The promotion of "biotechnology" and "biomaterials" in architectural design is accompanied by the question to what extent in the contemporary technological world we should rely on newly obtained materials and natural resources (even if they are renewable and biodegradable resources) and to what degree we should make use of materials already produced, being in economic circulation and possible to reuse.

Promoting and applying building technologies and materials – biodegradable but possible to recycle – is in accordance with strategies of implementation of sustainable development. It is easier to obtain and maintain equilibrium on a local scale, both in the natural and urbanized environment, since obtaining natural materials, based on the local production, affects the environment less than the mass industrial production. As a result, it generates less waste and facilitates their reuse.

Nonetheless, comparing the abundance of natural resources to the potential of existing and possible to recycle building materials, priority of use should be ascribed to the already existing products, components, and objects incorporated in the structures of various buildings. Naturally, taking into consideration mixed building technologies, the use of the two material groups described above (natural resources and recycled materials) should be deemed rational.

One of the answers to the posed problems is provided by *appropriate technology.* The concept of appropriate technology puts emphasis on the implementation of more sensible approach to technology and establishes the culture of technology taking into consideration social and economic conditions in its choice and distribution. The application of appropriate technologies is connected with a right choice of technology in the production process as well as in the course of the investment realization in a specific time and place. The adequate technologies include *intermediate technologies, soft technologies,* and *low-tech technologies* being a certain counterpoint to *high-tech technologies.* [6]

Many of those new technologies are already in existence. They usually do not require a big scale and decentralization, they are capable of rapid adaptation to local conditions and increasing their self – sufficiency, which finally means their maximum flexibility. They are frequently called "soft", since their impact on the environment is seriously curtailed by using renewable resources and continuous material recirculation. These technologies embody principles governing natural ecological systems reflecting at the same time the systems wisdom. The intermediate or soft technology can be described as safe since it does not carry any risk. It relies on the use of natural, renewable materials and the consumption of tiny amounts of energy.

As far as the extent of the influence is concerned, we can distinguish two types of technologies: one of them is the independent *small – scale technology* and the other has a wider range of influence, frequently on a global scale. The first can be applied in small communities without external support, whereas the other one is based upon a social organization on a large scale. The *appropriate technology*, which includes soft techniques, is rather a technology of a small scale. It is based upon the application of processes and materials suitable for a specific climate, socioeconomic conditions and natural resources of a region and a local community.

What is peculiar about the appropriate technology is that it is characterized by creating favourable conditions supporting efficiency and pursuing social self-sufficiency, which particularly wait for scientific support and the influx of the know-how information. The idea of appropriate technologies is based upon local people struggling with every day problems. The locals understand better than experts from the outside the problems most important to them. Therefore, they may aptly suggest or create technological solutions addressing their problems. The locals may also determine priorities of solutions in order to economically and rationally manage the funds they are in possession of. Designers and experts organizing help to local communities should involve inhabitants of a specific area in the project, in its early phase. As a result, the project has a chance to be realized with consistency by the locals, be better used, and, moreover, its success would be of concern to all during the course of the whole investment.

Decisions made at each stage of the design and the investment realization have a long-term consequences. They determine functioning of a building, both in the physical, three – dimensional space-time continuum and the social space of a local community. Searching for methods of reducing harmful influence of buildings on the surroundings, we can head towards two contradictory directions: the development of highly sophisticated technologies which facilitate controlling the functioning of a building inside and outside, or the application of a simple and entirely natural solution.

The architecture of sustainable development uses every kind of technology that will rationally take up the ecological challenge of the present time. *Low – tech* means designing buildings in a simple manner, using natural resources of the local environment and at the same time respecting the laws of nature. *Light – tech*, in turn, comprises the application of original materials in an economic - or even temperate – manner, and preference for materials one hundred per cent recyclable. The solutions *high – tech* can be applied as integrating elements with the view of creating optimal life and work conditions, with the minimum use of energy and resources. Drawing conclusions from the above considerations, the right solutions should be sought within the appropriate technologies based upon the local communities. Relying on the locally obtained construction materials as well as traditional, but improved, building methods rationalizes resources management, reducing the need of transportation of mass building materials at a long distance and generating waste. The appropriate technology, frequently resulting from the process of *participatory design*, is easy to exploit, because it is understandable and accepted by local communities. Taking advantage of an informal structure of information circulation within a network of local connections, accepted technological solutions should easily develop on a regional scale, shaping the art of building of human settlements in accordance with the natural and cultural environment.

In order to create effectively operating system of resources management, it is essential to rely on mechanisms motivating people to active participation in efforts towards minimizing the generation of waste. Human factor, users' mentality and attitude are also of crucial importance. One of the programmes releasing spontaneous cooperation between people is creating more or less formal connections at the local level.

5 Final Remarks

Much of the waste comprises valuable material for further use and the best is when it is reused at the same level as it has been used. The avoidance of unfavourable, heterogenic composition of waste may lead, for instance, to changing the demolition of building structures in favour of deconstruction and segregation. Ways of hermetization of technological processes should be sought, including processes generating little or no waste. Along with emergence of economic processes, encouraging effective use of the existing resources, and introduced legislative acts, an interest in environment friendly technologies, including technologies cutting down on generating waste in the investment process, will increase among building firms and investors.

The reduction of material absorptiveness in the building industry should be sought in the decentralized production as well as the implementation of novel renewable materials (of natural origin) and non – renewable (however possible to regenerate and reuse).

What is extremely important is to study a product final life cycle, since the manner of its processing and effectiveness of use of its components influence the material absorptiveness coefficient. In each phase of a product's life the amount of energy used should be minimized and its usefulness and functionality maximized. Just carrying out the design phase properly may contribute to a considerable decrease in the material absorptiveness (both at the stage of production of building materials and erecting buildings). Also, it may significantly reduce the material absorptiveness during the structure exploitation and enable a proper maintenance of buildings, an increase in the amount of the material obtained from products recycling (evolution of home's function), and easiness of its further processing or adaptation and modernization.

References

1. Charytonowicz, J.: Architecture, Aesthetics, Ergonomics. Scientific Symposium Fine Art-Architecture. In: Conference Proceedings, Cracow, pp. 49–54 (1997)
2. Eco, U.: La struttura assenta. Introduzione alla ricerca semiologica. Casa Editrice, Valentiono Bompiani end C., Milano (1968)
3. Leśniakowska, M.: What is the architecture? Canon Agency, Warsaw (1996)
4. Świątek, L., Charytonowicz, J.: Wasteful architecture - causes of generating waste. Recycling 9, 26–27 (2004)
5. Świątek, L., Charytonowicz, J.: Methods of reducing the amount of waste at the source - appropriate architecture. Recycling 11, 12–13 (2004)
6. Świątek, L., Charytonowicz, J.: Technology versus waste. Recycling 4, 24–25 (2005)

Listen! There Are Other Road Users Close to You – Improve the Traffic Awareness of Truck Drivers

Fang Chen, Georg Qvint[1], and Johan Jarlengrip[2]

[1] Interaction Design Group, Department of Computer Science and Engineering, Chalmers University of Technology, SE-412 96 Göteborg, Sweden
[2] Human System Integration, Volvo Technology Cooperation, Sweden
fanch@cs.chalmers.se, johan.jarlengrip@volvo.com

Abstract. As the amount of good transportation on road is increasing the accidents involving heavy trucks and other road users are also increasing. To make the truck driver aware of other road users close to the truck is very important to avoid accidents. Present study tested different auditory icons that were representing different road users and presented in 3 dimensions in the truck cockpit to see if such design could improve the driver traffic awareness in trucks. A prototype system including four different type-of sound themes has been developed to present the road users such as pedestrian, cyclists, motorcycles and other vehicles. The setting was tested on subjects and integrated in a truck-simulation at Volvo Technology Corporation. An experiment was conducted to test whether these 3D sounds can improve the driver's traffic situation awareness. The results suggest that natural or realistic sounds (auditory icon) are most suitable to this application due to their intuitiveness, distinguish ability and relatively low degree of disturbance.

Keywords: 3D audio, auditory icon, traffic, driver safety, truck cabin.

1 Introduction

As the amount of good transportation on the road is increasing, accidents involving heavy trucks are often happened. Collisions between heavy trucks and invisible other road users, such as small cars, pedestrians, cyclists, motorcyclists, etc are often happened and can cause fatal accident, not to the truck driver, but other road users [1]. For most of the road users, there are misconceptions about trucks and truck drivers [2]. Vehicle industry is introducing different technologies to avoid different kind of possible fatal accident [3]. The examples of the technologies that can help driver to avoid accidents are collision avoidance/warning system, adaptive cruise control, lane tracking departure warning, side sensing (proximity) devices, etc. For all of these systems, a warning signal normally should provide to the driver. The warning signal can be provided in different kinds of modalities, such as audible or visual alarm. The timing and frequency of such warning signal presentation is a big problem and different to find the consistent opinion among drivers [2]. Besides, warnings were considered as negative feedback by the driver and should be in the minority using [2].

C. Stephanidis (Ed.): Universal Access in HCI, Part II, HCII 2007, LNCS 4555, pp. 323–329, 2007.

There are different ways to present the road information to improving the drivers' traffic awareness. One is to improve the driver's visual capacity by introducing many camera displays inside the truck cabin so the driver can have a better view of the traffic situation outside his truck, especially to those dead visual angles. Already nowadays, the driver's visual demands are considerable high [4, 5]. The amount of visual information from various devices such as navigation systems, audio systems, headway warnings and even the in-vehicle information systems tends to clutter the visual perception as well. At the same time, the audio perception has been almost blocked. The truck cabin is silent enough not to hear the traffic sounds. The "lack of sound" along with the limited view from inside the cabin significantly reduces the driver's traffic situation awareness.

A prototype that using synthesized 3D sound to simulate the traffic situation for the truck driver was designed and tested in the lab. The purpose of the study is to see whether a 3D sound system can increase the driver's traffic situation awareness by hearing different road user's location, distance, moving speed and moving direction related to the vehicle, so it can reduce the visual loading. This study is the first phase of series studies to evaluate different possibilities of providing positive information to the truck driver to avoid the potential accidents.

2 Method

Six traffic situations that have high probability of accident occurrence between truck and fellow road-users are identified, based on the limitation of truck driver's view, as user scenarios in the test. The scenarios are by Volvo Technology Corporation's internal study results, as showed in Figure 1.

In scenario 1, the shadowed area in the picture depicts the non-visible area of driver due to the masking from the right A-pillar and side rear mirror. A potential and impending collision may occur with the car from the right side. In scenario 2, the driver puts all his attention to the roundabout and has little chance to spot the car

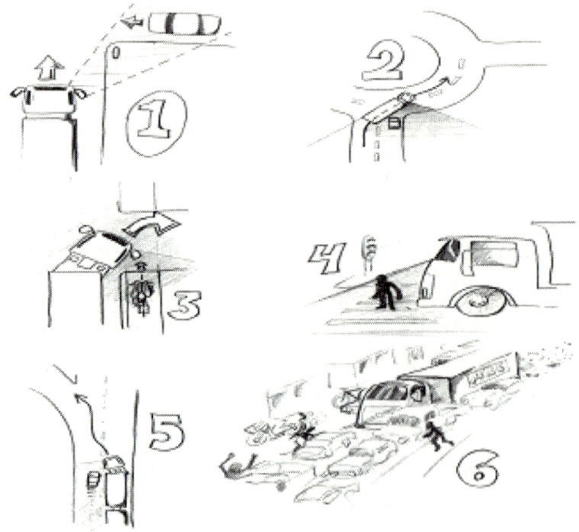

Fig. 1. The traffic scenarios that potential accident may happen

running tightly along the truck. In scenario 3, the bicycle to the right of the truck is simply too low, too close and too quiet to be recognized by the driver who intends to take right turn. In scenario 4, the driver is watching the traffic lights, and doesn't notice the old man, slowly crossing the street. He is below the driver's field of view. In scenario 5, the experienced driver properly checked his/her left rear mirror there was no sign of a car in the left lane, but as he starts to turn over, a car swiftly turns up from seemingly nowhere. In scenario 6, the traffic is moving very slowly, there is not really a risk for serious accidents, but some potential risks are exists.

Equipment

A sound engine was developed that could add 3D sound to the existing simulator. It can support sound playback for a predefined types of road users. Five types of road users were selected; car, truck, motorbike, pedestrian and bicyclist. All sounds used by the sound engine are 16 bit wav sound samples with sample rate 44100 kHz. The natural sounds that representing different objects were selected by subjective judgment. Seamlessly looping audio clips were created. The vehicle simulator at Volvo Technology Corporation is shown in Figure 2. The test driver is placed in the driver seat of a Volvo FH12 truck cab which has been detached from the chassis and placed on the floor. Three projectors, placed above the cab, together project a 140° field of view image on the curved wall in front of the cab. The wall radius from the driver's eye-point is 3.5 m to the screen.

The simulator executes traffic scenario, vehicle dynamics, data logging and graphics rendering on a Silicon Graphics Onyx2 with multiple CPUs and multiple graphic cards. The steering wheel torque is controlled from a separate PC and the I/O to and from the cab is communicated on a PC with CAN and analogue IO-interface. A single speaker, placed behind the passenger seat, is used to produce the engine sound. The quality of the engine sound is calculated from the vehicle dynamics models engine load and speed. This sound rendering is produced on a Silicon Graphics Impact2 workstation.

Fig. 2. The truck simulator at Volvo Technology Corporation

Speakers that generate the simulated 3D sound are located as to a 185 cm tall persons head as he/she is seated in the driver seat. The calibration was achieved by using white noise as speaker signal and the sound intensity was monitored and adjusted to 70dB(A) by a sound level meter set up for calibration of Loudness.

Procedure

Seven subjects participated in the experiment. Five of them were professional truck drivers and the other two were staffs from Volvo Trucks Company. All of them were males with the age between 26 to 55 years. The truck drive experience was from 2year to 30 years. None of them have problem with vision and hearing. The purpose and the design of the testing system was explained to the subjects orally and with written text, to make sure that the subjects understand it properly.

In the drive scenario, every test started with a "silent" run in the simulator i.e. the test person was obliged to make a ten minutes drive through the full scenario without aid from the 3D-sound system. After the silent drive, the 6 scenario sections were repeated in random order with the 3D-sound system on.

The experimenter took place in passenger seat to observe the drivers behavior. The subject was invited to freely comment on what he/she heard and how he/she experienced of the traffic situation and the influenced from the 3D sound system. The performance of each subject was recorded by a video camera for later observations and data analysis.

After the drive the subjects was asked to answer a questionnaire. The system acceptance in terms of usefulness and satisfaction were primarily desired to be estimated. This acceptance scale was developed by Van Der Laan's [6]. Nine basic bipolar questions with a neutral or zero reference point, implying both direction and intensity, are used to pinpoint system acceptance (See table 1). Individual item scores run from -2 to +2 as +2 are most positive and -2 are most negative. This technique provides a reliable tool for the assessment of acceptance of new technologies [6]. Finally the test ended with a conversation/interview concerning the subjects driving reactions, etc.

Table 1. The modified Van Der Laan's acceptance scale

Item 1.	useful	□	□	□	□	□	useless
Item 2	pleasant	□	□	□	□	□	unpleasant
Item 3	bad	□	□	□	□	□	good
Item 4	nice	□	□	□	□	□	annoying
Item 5	effective	□	□	□	□	□	superfluous
Item 6	irritating	□	□	□	□	□	likeable
Item 7	assisting	□	□	□	□	□	worthless
Item 8	undesirable	□	□	□	□	□	desirable
Item 9	raising alertness	□	□	□	□	□	sleep-inducing.

Among these 9 items, question1, 3, 5, 7 and 9 evaluate the usability aspects of the system, while question 2, 4, 6 and 8 evaluated the driver's satisfaction. The usefulness scale is the sum of item 1, 3, 5, 7, 9 divided by 5, and satisfaction scale is the sum of items 2, 4, 6, and 8 divided by 4.

3 Results

The result of system acceptance in terms of usefulness and satisfaction was shown in Figure 3 by using Van Der Laan's acceptance scale [6]. A bi-dimensional diagram with subjects' assessed acceptances is plotted. High experienced usefulness corresponds to above midpoint values and a high level of satisfaction is to the right of the vertical center line. According to this scale all subjects except one find the system useful and only two out of total eight subjects find it not satisfactory. The black circle top right of the chart center is the average acceptance. The absolute value should be regarded as the level of acceptance. Using the SPSS computer statistic program to analysis the date, the results showed that it is consistent and reliable within subjects (Cronbach's $\alpha = 0.688$ for usefulness, 0.827 for satisfaction).

Regarding the interpretation and audibility of the system sounds the subjective evaluation results from questionnaires are very good.

- Very easy to interpret and understand the fellow road users type, position, move direction and distance by sound
- Very audible of the sound generated from the system.

Regarding the interpretation and audibility of the system sounds the subjective evaluation results from questionnaires are very good.

- Very easy to interpret and understand the fellow road users type, position, move direction and distance by sound
- Very audible of the sound generated from the system.

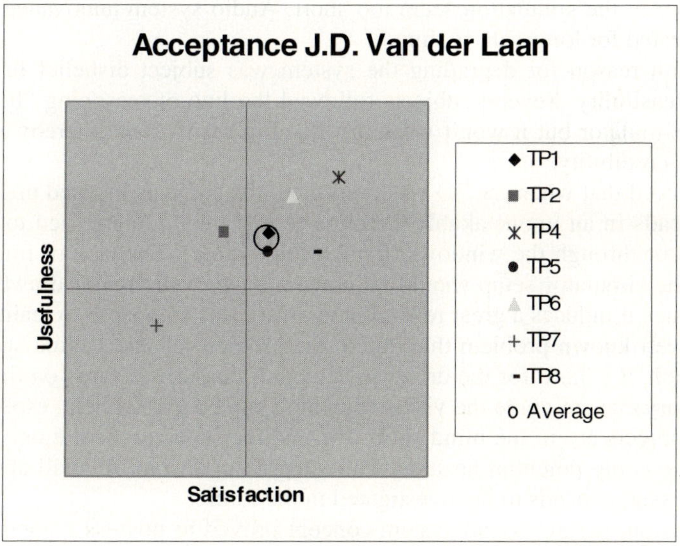

Fig. 3. Estimation of acceptance

The overall reaction to the design is very positive. It provides the users with "wow" effect. All subjects reported that they would probably use a system like this if it was available in their vehicle, but none of the subjects reported that they would use it all the time. All subjects reported that such a system is most usable in urban- or similar, dense traffic situations or in situations with reduced visibility, ex. fog, darkness or heavy snowfall. A majority of the subjects questioned the usability of the system in presence of music or radio, which was generally regarded as an almost sacred element in the daily round of a truck driver. Regarding specific sounds, the motorbike overtaking the test driver at the freeway section was auditory perceived as much faster than it was in reality. Everyone, though, recognized it as a motorbike even before it was seen.

4 Discussion

The prototype has been a valuable tool for the investigation of the 3D sound concept. It is encouraging and promising that most of the system criticism in fact has concerned in prototype implementation designs. Still, the study reported here is just a preliminary study to test the design concept. A lot more work is needed to be done.

There was an augment on what kinds of sounds should be used, earcons or auditory icons as we used in present study. To be able to answer the question, this pilot study which reported here was carried out. Most subjects select the auditory icons because it provided the intuitive information of approached objects from the sounds. A variety of factors may play an important role for the achievement of using 3D audio for enhancing traffic awareness. Usability and satisfaction estimations based on the ten minutes drive in the simulation seem too short. Audio system annoyance may be far more manifested for longer drive time.

A common reason for degrading the system was subject disbelief in the system realization feasibility. Several subjects followed the line of reasoning "It works very well in the simulator but it won't work this good in reality" and thereby assigned the concept less credibility.

It is observed that when the 3D was presented, the subjects listened up or started to turn their heads in an unmistakable direction telling way. Others tried to look in the rear mirrors or through the windows (though impossible). The lack of functional rear mirrors in the simulator setup should be noted as one of the major drawbacks of the simulator since it induces a great reduction in awareness compared to reality.

As it is well-known problem that due to the problem of many blind spot surround the huge truck, it is hard for the driver to detect all possible hazards on time visually. Using auditory cues to guide the visual searching can be a good help, especially when the hazard objects are in the blind spots, the auditory cue can be the only channel to present the existing potential hazards. The integration design in detail and the safety value of the system needs to be investigated in the future.

In conclusion, the 3D sound system concept proved to possess a good acceptance rate in terms of usefulness, satisfaction and desirability.

5 Future Work

Sound realism should primarily be improved by elaborating more advanced models for road user object dynamics and minimize the possible distraction from the sound. Some extensive user studies must be performed to statistically assure those results.

References

[1] Avedal, C., Boman, S., Lindh, C., Adolfsson, L., och Mathisson, J.: Trafikolyckor med tunga lastbilar i Göteborg – fokus på oskyddade trafikanter, Volvo Lastvagnar, Vägverket Region Väst and Trafikkontoret Göteborgs Stad, Gothenburg (2005)

[2] Roetting, M., Huang, Y.H., McDevitt, J.R., Melton, D.: When technology tells you how you drive-truck drivers attitudes towards feedback by technology. Transportation Research Part F 6, 275–287 (2003)

[3] Bishop, R.: Intelligent vehicle technology and trends. Artech House, Boston (2005)

[4] Engström, J., Johansson, E., Östlund, J.: Effects of visual and cognitive load in real and simulated motorway driving. Transportation Research Part F 8, 97–120 (2005)

[5] Victor, T., Harbluk, J.L., Engström, J.: Sensitivity of eye movement measures to in-vehicle task difficulty: Findings from HASTE. Transportation Research Part. F 8, 167–190 (2005)

[6] Van Der Laan, J., Heino, A., De Waard, D.: A simple procedure for the assessment of acceptance of advanced transport telematics. Transportation Research Part C 5, 1–10 (1996)

HMI Principles for Lateral Safe Applications

Lars Danielsson[1], Henrik Lind[1], Evangelos Bekiaris[2], Maria Gemou[2], Angelos Amditis[3], Maurizio Miglietta[4], and Per Stålberg[5]

[1] Volvo Car Corporation
Dept 94354, PV4A, S-405 08 Gothenburg, Sweden
Tel: +46 31 59 2809, Fax: +46 31 59 66 70
{ldanie25, hlind1}@volvocars.com
[2] Centre for Research and Technology Hellas - Hellenic Institute of Transport (CERTH/HIT)
L. Posidonos 17, 17455 Athens, Greece
Tel: +30210 9853194, Fax: +30210 9853193
{abek, mgemou}@certh.gr
[3] Institute of Communications and Computer Systems (ICCS) - National Technical University of Athens (NTUA), Microwaves and Optics Lab, I-SENSE group
Iroon Politechniou str. 9, Polytechnic Campus, 15773 Athens, Greece
Tel: +302107722398, Fax: +302107723557 -2291
a.amditis@iccs.gr
[4] Centro Ricerche Fiat (CRF) - Preventive Safety department
Strada Torino 50, 10043 Orbassano (TO), Italy
Tel: +390119083060, Fax: +390119083083
maurizio.miglietta@crf.it
[5] Volvo Technology (VTEC)
Dept 6400, M1.6, 405 08 Göteborg, Sweden
Tel: +46 31 666109
per.stalberg@volvo.com

Abstract. LATERAL SAFE is a subproject of the PREVENT Integrated Project, co-funded by the European Commission under the 6th Framework Programme. LATERAL SAFE introduces a cluster of safety applications of the future vehicles, in order to prevent lateral/rear related accidents and assist the driver in adverse or low visibility conditions and blind spot areas. LATERAL SAFE applications include a lateral and rear monitoring system (LRM), a lane change assistant (LCA) and a lateral collision warning (LCW). An effective Human Machine Interface (HMI) is being developed, addressing each application, on the basis of the results emerged from mock-up tests realised in three sites (one in Greece and two in Sweden), aiming to determine which is the best HMI solution to be provided in each case. In the current paper, the final HMI principles, adopted and demonstrated for each application, are presented.

Keywords: HMI, lateral safety, rear monitoring, evaluation.

1 Introduction

The target applications of LATERAL SAFE project are namely the following:

C. Stephanidis (Ed.): Universal Access in HCI, Part II, HCII 2007, LNCS 4555, pp. 330–338, 2007.

- The **Lateral Collision Warning (LCW)** application, which reduces the risk of accidents between the ego-vehicle and other obstacles in the lateral side of the vehicle. In this case, the driver is informed about dangerous relative displacement of obstacles in left and right side area of the ego-vehicle.

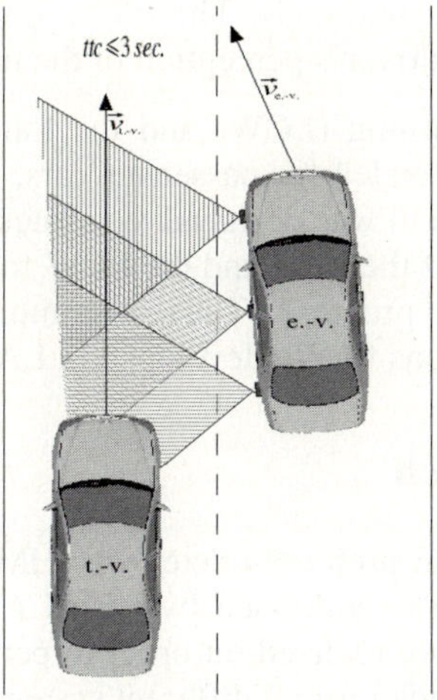

Fig. 1. "Lateral Collision Warning" application indicative scenario

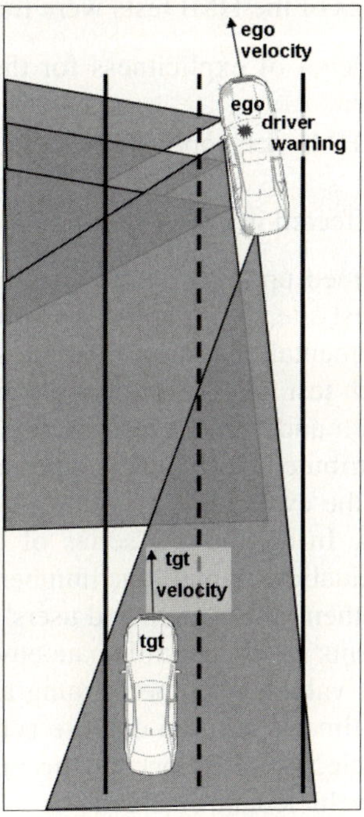

Fig. 2. "Lane Change Assistance" application indicative scenario

- The **Lane Change Assistance (LCA)** application, which provides information about vehicles approaching in adjacent lanes and vehicles present in the blind spot to assist the driver with lane change manoeuvres.
- The **Lateral and Rear Area Monitoring (LRM)** application, which reduces the risk of accidents between the ego-vehicle and other obstacles both in the lateral and rear neighborhoods. The traffic information from the sensors is used to enhance the driver's perception of the traffic situation (see figure 6).

The Lateral Collision Warning (LCW) and the Lane Change Assistance (LCA) applications were initially intended for passenger cars, whereas the Lateral and Rear Area Monitoring (LRM) system was designed as a truck application at the beginning. However, adjusted versions of the LCA and the LCW for the trucks and LRM for cars came up during the project progress. Thus, a common HMI approach has been implemented for all applications finally developed in LATERAL SAFE.

2 Background Research

In order for LATERAL SAFE project to determine HMI solutions for the support of the driver in the different tasks addressed by each LATERAL SAFE application, a series of preliminary tests were realized, in order to perform a cross-comparison of a series of HMI mock-ups intended for all different systems.

HMI mock-up tests were carried out in VTEC (desktop tests with 5 subjects), with VCC research car (10 subjects) and with CERTH/HIT car simulator (18 subjects). The main evaluation objectives of the HMI tests were the following:

- Which is the appropriate level of explicitness for the displayed visual cautionary warnings to the side mirror;
- Which is the appropriate HMI per application, based on subjective and objective evaluation measures;
- How driver behaviour is affected in case of an imminent or a cautionary warning.

The evaluation was performed upon a common evaluation plan and supplementary experimental plans for each test site, defining the type, the number and the sequence of the scenarios used, the experimental conditions and the size and profile of the sample. The scenarios selected in each test site for the assessment of the respective mock-ups were tried by the subjects with and without the system. A series of pre-test and post-test questionnaires were distributed, to evaluate user acceptance and user interface assessment, before and after the evaluation, as well as drivers' workload while testing the different HMI mock-ups. In addition, a series of objective measurements were collected during the HMI evaluation, namely the number of received warnings and the level of users' compliance to them, the system and users' failure percentage in recorded errors, the number of accidents or successful manoeuvrings, the minimum time-to-collision (TTC) and headway values when performing a manoeuvre (i.e. lane change, etc.) and the required driver time to take an evasive action in case another vehicle is drifting against the ego vehicle, which is one of the main Use Cases of LATERAL SAFE, together with the ego vehicle lane change.

The evaluation results, coming from all three types of trials, led to the determination of appropriate HMI solution for each application, presented in the following section of the current paper. These solutions however, need to be further developed and refined when going from a research system to a production system, where possibly other factors need to be considered then the ones taken into account here. The solutions presented herein give an input to this work.

3 HMI Solutions for Lateral (and Rear Monitoring) Applications

3.1 Lane Change Assistant (LCA) and Lateral and Rear Monitoring (LRM) Applications for Cars

The LCA application has two operative modes, which are adopted also by the HMI approach implemented for this application, and are the following:

- In case no actual lane change wish is detected, the presence of vehicles in the blind spot or vehicles approaching fast from behind on the neighbouring lanes is visualised by a yellow symbol (led) in the respective side mirror. This operation mode is called "**information mode**" and is beneficial for drivers who plan to make a lane change decision. The driver can acquire the information whether the LCA system judges the situation to be potentially dangerous for lane changes, by looking in the side mirror. By providing the information in the side mirrors, the risk of abuse for this function, by "blindly" relying on it, is minimised. The information provided in the side mirror covers also the lateral monitoring functionality of the "Lateral and Rear Area Monitoring" application, as this is adjusted for passenger vehicles.
- In case the driver's lane change wish coincides with potentially dangerous vehicles on the neighbouring lanes, the driver is warned by a flashing red symbol in the side mirror and with a warning sound in case the adjacent lane is occupied. This mode of operation is called "**warning mode**". The warning sound is produced by a directional sound system in the car, so that the drivers' attention is drawn to the source of danger. For detecting the driver's lane change wish, the condition of each direction indicator (on/off) is used.

The main descriptive info of the leds implemented in the side mirrors are the following:

- Symbol designed according to the working document ISO 2575.
- ISO symbol K17A.
- Symbol size > 10 x 15 mm.
- Orange/Red colour (~620/660 nm) – 2 warning levels.
- Directed towards the driver.
- Light intensity > 2000 mcd (controllable intensity: Night/Day).
- Minimum contrast: 2:1.

The side mirror led described above is implemented in the CRF demonstrator (Fiat Stilo), as shown in the following figure.

In addition, a dedicated rear view mirror is designed and realized, to integrate the selected HMI solution for the monitoring of the rear area of the vehicle (for the adjusted version of the Lateral and Rear Area Monitoring application for passenger vehicles). In the rear view mirror, there are leds that report two information levels

Fig. 3. HMI solution (side-mirror led) for the lateral area of the vehicle addressing LCA and the lateral functionality of the LRM for cars applications

(yellow or red), related to the presence of vehicles to the rear following at a close time gap (see following figure). The main characteristics of the rear view mirror leds are provided below:

- Two warning levels:
  - Level 1: One amber diode.
  - Level 2: Three red diode.
- Amber (~620 nm) and red (~660 nm) colours.
- Directed towards the driver.
- Light intensity >= 1000 mcd (controllable, Night/Day).
- Symbol size Ø >= 5 mm.
- Minimum contrast 2:1.

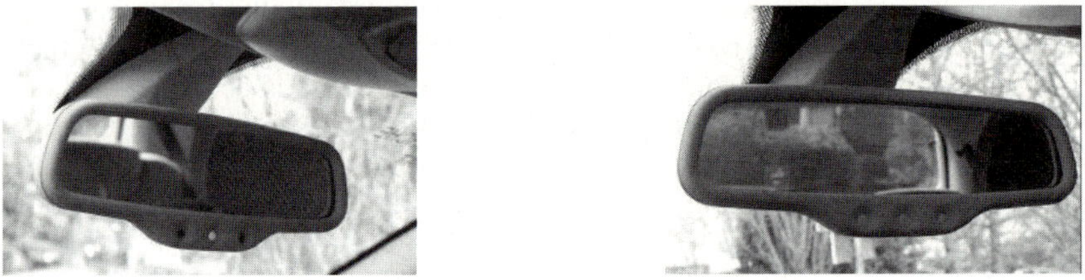

Fig. 4. HMI solution addressing the LRM application for car (rear view mirror leds)

3.2 Lateral Collision Warning (LCW) for Cars

The HMI for the Lateral Collision Warning application has been realised in the a-pillar. The used symbol has been designed following the guidelines provided by the working document ISO 2575 and using the ISO symbol K17B. A lighted warning triangle is associated to another symbol (see following figure), with the following main characteristics:

- Visual symbol size > 10 x 10 mm.
- Red colour (~660 nm).
- Light intensity >= 1000 mcd (controllable, Night/Day).
- Light directed towards driver.
- Minimum contrast: 2:1.
- Flashing.

In addition to the visual symbol, an acoustic warning is generated. The acoustic warning is generated by the application with directional features, in order warn the driver about the direction of the risk (mainly left or right and rear or front).

The HMI components integrated for the LCW functionality are shown in the following figure.

Fig. 5. HMI solution addressing the LCW application for car (a-pillar, red)

3.3 Lateral and Rear Area Monitoring (LRM), Lane Change Assistance (LCA) and Lateral Collision Warning (LCW) for Trucks

A display-based solution of LRM application is mounted on the truck dashboard, showing the objects in the surrounding area from a bird´s eye view and is implemented only in trucks (see following figures).

Fig. 6. LRM information presented to the driver in a truck

The HMI solution for the LRM application for trucks is summarised below:

- The objects behind the ego-truck, moving in the same lane, are coloured yellow under normal conditions and red if the object is very close behind the truck (headway value < 0.3s).

The objects in the adjacent lanes are normally coloured yellow. However, the colouring changes to red if the system detects that the object is closing the truck rapidly (lateral TTC < 1.5s) and combined with an acoustical LCW warning. Additionally the following strategies are followed for the colour coding change:

- Objects two or more lanes away are represented in the display, if they are closing the truck rapidly (TTC< 3s). It is coloured yellow if lateral TTC is between 1.5 and 3s and red if TTC is < 1.5s.
- If the driver intends to change lane (use of turn indicator) with an object, that is or within 1.5 s will be to the side of the truck, an acoustic LCA warning is issued and the object turns red.
- If an object is extremely close laterally (< 0.25 m) to the subject vehicle, then it is coloured red in the display.

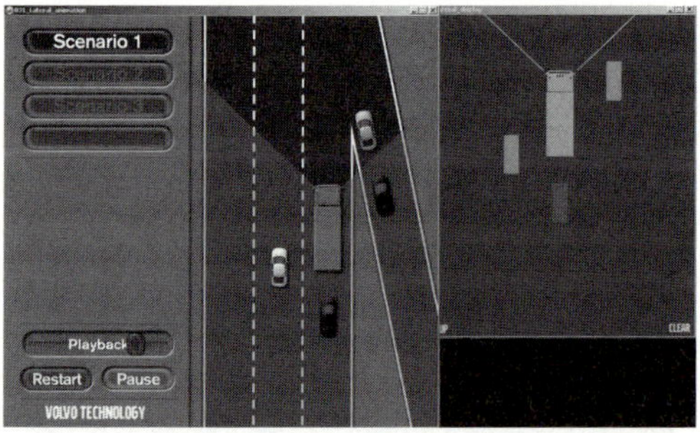

Fig. 7. LRM scenario description and information presented to the driver in a truck

Fig. 8. LRM display mounted in the truck dashboard

An algorithm for the hysteresis of warnings and highlighted objects is also implemented (minimum time is 4sec between acoustic warnings of the same type and minimum time for highlighting of objects is 2sec). Objects are not presented at all if they are moving away with relative speed > 1 s (object driving slower than truck). All objects moving are shown in the screen, using the correct speed vector information.

4 Further Steps

The HMI warning strategies and elements addressing all LATERAL SAFE project applications have been re-evaluated in the final evaluation of the project. The HMI's have been evaluated by 21 users in the VTEC demonstrator and 12 users in the CRF passenger vehicle, on specifically designed scenarios. The users have performed a series of trials with and without the system and quantitative and qualitative measurements have been collected, through subjective forms (pre- and post-questionnaires) and log files data, providing input for the final ratification and improvement of the HMI's: among others, from the warning strategies point of view, but also regarding integration and "look and feel" aspects.

Acknowledgements. We wish to acknowledge to the LATERAL SAFE Subproject Consortium of the PReVENT IP project, for their valuable contributions to this work. The PReVENT IP project is partially funded by the EC.

References

1. Bank, D., Domenico, I., Miglietta, M., Oeschle, F.: Lateral Safe Applications, Deliverable 32.8, PReVENT project, LATERAL SAFE Subproject, C.N. 050131(2007)
2. Bekiaris, E., Gemou, M.: LS HMI(s) evaluation methodology. Technical Report: PReVENT project, LATERAL SAFE Subproject, C.N. 050131 (2004)
3. Blomqvist, P., Amditis, A., Floudas, N., Polychronopoulos, A., Bekiaris, E., Gaitanidou, E., Gemou, M., van den Broek, B., Benoist, K., Appenrodt, N., Bank, D., Herzog, H.-J., Lind, H., Denielsson, L., Miglietta, M.: Requirements and specifications. Deliverable 32.3: PReVENT project, LATERAL SAFE Subproject, C.N. 050131 (2005)
4. Fahey, S.E., Wierwille, W.W.: Advisory and alarm stimuli optimisation for a drowsy driver detection system. Technical Report: NHTSA, DOT HS 808 299 Semi-Annual Report, Research on Vehicle-Based Driver Status /Performance Monitoring: Seventh Semi-Annual Research Report, National Technical Information Service, Springfield (1995)
5. Janssen, W., Nilsoon, L.: Behavioral effects of driver support systems. In: Parkes, A.W., Franzen, S. (eds.) Driving future vehicles, pp. 147–155. Taylor & Francis, London (1993)
6. Jordan, A.D.: An introduction to usability. Taylor & Francis, London (1999)
7. Levin, D.T., Simon, D.J.: Failure to detect changes to attended objects in motion pictures. Psychonomic Bullentin and Review 4, 501–506 (1997)
8. Rumar, K.: The basic driver error: late detection. Ergonomics 33, 1281–1290 (1990)
9. Sanders, M.S., McCormick, E.J.: Human factors in engineering and design, 7th edn. McGraw-Hill, New York (1992)

10. Van der Laan, J., Heino, A., de Waard, D.: A simple procedure for the assessment of acceptance of advanced transport telematics. Transportation Research, Part C 5, 1–10 (1997)
11. Wickens, C.D., Sandry, D.L., Vidulich, M.: Compatibility and resource competition between modalities of input, central processing, and output. Human Factors 25, 227–248 (1983)

INSAFES HCI Principles for Integrated ADAS Applications

Lars Danielsson, Henrik Lind, and Stig Jonasson

Volvo Car Corporation, Active Safety Electronics, Dept 94354, 405 31 Göteborg, Sweden
{ldanie25, hlind1, sjonass4}@volvocars.com

Abstract. In order to integrate several time critical warning systems, e.g. Collision Warning and Lane Departure Warning, in the same vehicle one has to deal with the problem of warning management to not overload the driver in critical situations and to make sure that driver's focus is directed to the right place. This paper presents INSAFES integration schemes to ensure these issues, and gives general as well as specific use cases based on warning systems integrated in one of INSAFES demonstrator vehicles. From these use cases are then requirements on warning management derived regarding prioritization schemes. The requirements concludes in a proposed extension of the warning management concepts derived in the AIDE project.

Keywords: Warning Management, Integrated Safety, ADAS, HMI, Automotive.

1 Introduction

The vehicles of today are being equipped with an increasing number of Advanced Driver Assistance Systems (ADAS) designed to warn/inform the driver of a potentially dangerous situation or even intervene to mitigate an impending accident. Alongside these critical active safety applications are In-Vehicle Information Systems (IVIS), e.g. telematics and communication services, infotainment (CD, Radio) and vehicle diagnostic messages, all requesting the attention of the driver. Studies have shown that allowing all these systems acting independently of each other would severely degrade the effectiveness of each individual application and increase the workload of the driver in safety critical situations [1], [2].

INSAFES is a subproject within IP PReVENT (www.ip-prevent.org) partly funded by the European Commission. The goal of INSAFES is to improve the functionality and reliability of applications developed within IP PReVENT, and to advance from stand-alone safety applications targeting one specific function to an integrated system covering a vast range of applications. To exploit synergies between different ADAS systems integrated in a vehicle INSAFES propose, in [3], integration schemes on different architectural layers, i.e. Perception, Decision and Action as defined in the ProFusion general architecture [4]. The perception layer is responsible for perceiving the surrounding traffic situation. In the decision layer, applications detect hazardous

C. Stephanidis (Ed.): Universal Access in HCI, Part II, HCII 2007, LNCS 4555, pp. 339–348, 2007.

situations and form the decisions on whether to warn, inform or intervene. The action layer is responsible for choosing the appropriate channel to convey the decision of the application to the driver or vehicle. A schematic figure of how these layers are used in INSAFES is shown in fig 1.

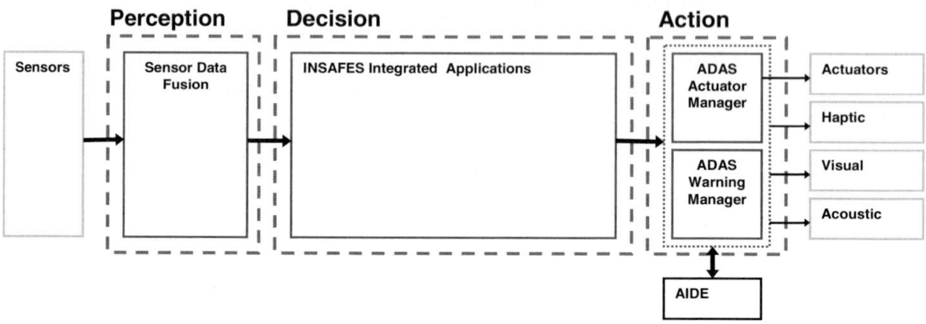

Fig. 1. INSAFES functional architecture

In order for an integrated system to be truly successful one has to deal with the problem of warning management to not overload the driver in critical situations and to make sure that driver's focus is directed to the right place.

2 Problem Formulation

The problem at hand is to find schemes to arbitrate and manage several different safety and time critical warnings integrated in the same vehicle. The applications should be integrated in such way that multiple ADAS functions and systems are allowed to interact with multiple warning devices. The aim is to minimize the reaction time and workload for the driver in a complex multi warning and information situation. The integration shall allow for a unified HMI towards the driver and to limit the number of different HMI channels needed.

INSAFES propose to form ADAS Human-Machine-Interface (HMI) strategies, in order to overcome the problems mentioned above. These strategies are incorporated in an ADAS Warning Manager (ADAS-WM), which is responsible for managing the information and warnings going to the driver from all integrated safety and time critical ADAS applications.

Other current projects such as the AIDE (Adaptive Integrated Driver-vehicle InterfacE) project are also investigating HMI integration. The focus of the AIDE project is to develop general principles and strategies for management and integration of IVIS applications. In some aspects, also ADAS applications are considered, though we argue that the AIDE ICA base architecture [5] is proposed to be extended to be able to handle time and safety critical warnings within an automotive electrical architecture. Within INSAFES, development is exclusively directed towards HMI management strategies for time and safety critical warnings with high priority and which are also crucial for the primary driving task. The management and integration of IVIS and non time critical ADAS is handled through the base AIDE ICA architecture.

3 Applications, HMI and Integration

Within INSAFES three different demonstrators are developed, a Volvo truck, FIAT car and a Volvo car, each demonstrating different applications and HMI solutions. Prioritizations of applications and use cases in terms of safety impact for the INSAFES project are defined in [6]. In this paper we use the demonstrators, developed at Volvo Cars (VCC), to show a possible solution to the problem of an integrated HMI and to give examples of use cases for an ADAS Warning Manager.

3.1 HMI Integration

In the vehicle there exists several different HMI modalities, visual, audible and haptic available to convey information and warnings from ADAS applications. Fig 2 shows placement of all visual HMI modules and a description of each is followed below. Additionally is a 4 way directional sound system integrated in the vehicle.

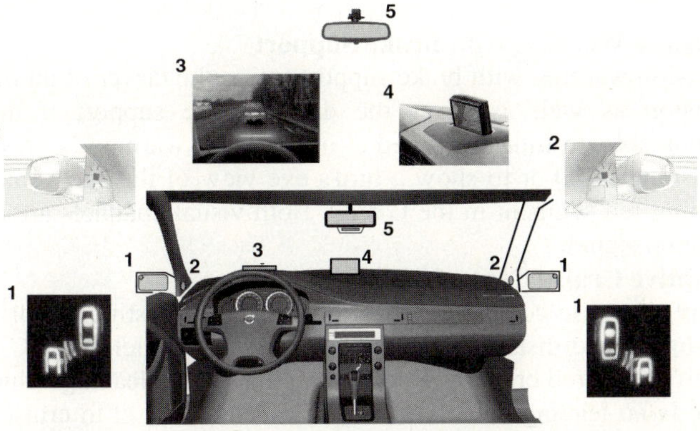

Fig. 2. Visual HMI channels distribution in the vehicle as seen from the driver. 1. Side Mirror Visual Module (SMVM), 2. A-pillar Console Visual Module (ACVM), 3. Head Up Display (HUD), 4. General Warning and Information Display (GWID), 5. Rear-end Monitoring Visual Module (RMVM).

The distributed visual HMI channels, shown in fig 2, follows a user centered approach by directing the driver's attention to the target area. Each of the HMI devices are explained in more detail below:

1. Side Mirror Visual Module (SMVM), shows a amber lit ISO 17a symbol beneath the mirror glass in the upper outer part of the side mirror. Used to inform the driver of events in the lateral area. As the side mirrors constitute the boundaries of the driver's perception area, these warning devices are only used for low priority warnings.

2. A-pillar Console Visual Module (ACVM), shows a amber light in the a-pillar console and is used to warn the driver of events in the lateral area.
3. Head Up Display (HUD), projects a row of horizontal red light onto the windscreen in front of the driver. This is suggestive to the brake lights of a preceding vehicle and directs the attention of the driver to events in front of the car.
4. General Warning and Information Display (GWID), is a general warning and information device. The GWID will in default mode be used for infotainment issues, e.g. radio and navigation, but as a warning is issued, a pop-up window will show the warning.
5. Rear-end Monitoring Visual Module (RMVM) has the same strategy as the HUD but focuses on events behind the car.

The effectiveness of the HUD (for forward collision warning applications (is investigated in [7]. The SMVM, ACVM and RMVM are developed within the LATERAL SAFE project and evaluation results are presented in [8].

3.2 Applications

The integrated ADAS applications utilizing these HMI channels defined in Section 3.1 are the following:

- **Collision Warning with Brake Support**
  Collision warning with brake support warns the driver of an impending front collision as well as gives the driver brake support if the collision is unavoidable, to limit the speed at impact. The warning is presented either as a flashing HUD or to show a bird's eye view of the ego-vehicle including a flashing red segment in the GWID. Both visual channels are combined with an audio signal.
- **Adaptive Cruise Control (ACC)**
  Adaptive cruise control is a comfort function assisting the driver in keeping an appropriate distance and speed to leading vehicles. ACC lets the driver specify a desired cruising speed and a time gap to leading vehicle. As long as there is no leading vehicle in front the vehicle is set to cruise at the desired cruising speed. The ACC application automatically reduces the speed to keep the desired time distance to slower vehicles in front. However, if the system determines that the needed brake power to slow down to the desired speed is too large a Brake Capacity Warning (BCW) is issued by flashing the HUD and an audible warning to encourage the driver to take over.
- **Lane Departure Warning (LDW)**
  Lane Departure Warning detects and warns the driver with an audio signal, if the driver unintentionally drifts over to adjacent lanes.
- **Lateral Collision Warning (LCW)**
  Warn the driver if there is an imminent danger of collision from the side. The driver will be alerted by an audio signal and a flashing light in the ACVM. Alternatively, the GWID will show the warning in similar manner as for CWBS.

- **Curve Over Speed Warning (CSW)**
  Curve over speed warning helps the driver to keep an appropriate speed while entering a curve. If the system decides that the current speed of the vehicle is too high for a safe and comfortable curve taking maneuver a warning is issued. This is made by an audio signal and a popup warning in GWID.
- **Lane Change Assist (LCA)**
  LCA system informs the driver of vehicles approaching in the left and right adjacent lanes to assist the driver while making a lane change maneuver. The information is given via the SMVM or alternatively a popup in the GWID.
- **Blind Spot Detection (BSD)**
  Detects and informs the driver of vehicles in the left and right blind spot. BSD uses the same HMI channels as the LCA application.
- **Lateral and Rear-end Monitoring (LRM)**
  Lateral and Rear end Monitoring supplies the driver with a holistic perspective of the traffic scenario in the left and right adjacent lanes as well as behind the own vehicle. LRM helps the driver to be aware of where other vehicles are in the lateral and rear end area. Information about the surrounding traffic is either given in the GWID or using the SMVM in combination with RMVM.

4 INSAFES Warning Manager Strategies

In this section we derive and motivate the concepts and requirements of the INSAFES ADAS Warning Manager. One key requirement is to be able to prioritize between warnings of both different and same level of criticality. In aide in this discussion we define different warning criticality levels as, Informatory (Low Priority), Alert or Cautionary Alert (Medium Priority) and Imminent Warning (Highest Priority). Other aspect are the interaction with IVIS applications and synchronization issues between different warning devices. All this aspects are motivated by means of identified use cases highlighting the need for warning management in integrated vehicles.

Here we also propose an extension to the basic AIDE/ICA architecture to handle the identified requirements.

4.1 Use Cases and Requirements

To derive the requirements of the ADAS Warning Manager this section gives some illustrative use cases. These use cases are identified situations that drivers may experience while driving such cars as the one described in Section 3. Linked to each use case is a set of requirements. The notation system will here refer to the INSAFES integrated functions.

Table 1. ADAS Warning Manager use cases and requirements

Nr.	Use Case	Requirements
1	The ego-vehicle starts to drift out of its lane, an event that triggers an Alert Warning from the system. Simultaneously, the system also detects a high risk of collision with a braking vehicle in front, which results in an Imminent Warning. The ADAS-WM therefore suppresses the Alert warning an gives the Imminent warning. 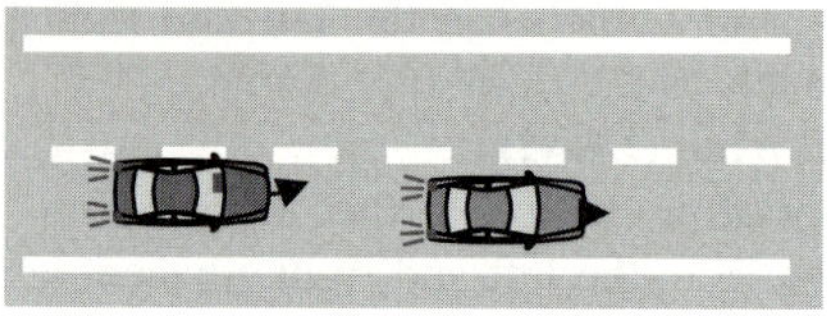	Req 1) When two functions want to use the same modality at the same time the highest priority warning shall be prioritized Req 2) Warnings shall not be stored or delayed.
2	The ego-vehicle is using Adaptive Cruise Control (ACC) on a highway. As the vehicle in front makes an emergency braking, the system first issues an Imminent warning due to the increased risk of collision. Immediately afterwards, the ACC function requests the driver to take over in order to obtain maximum break power. This results in an Alert Warning. Both warnings are in default mode using the same warning devices. However, in this use case, the driver has disabled the audible warning for collision warning. Consequently, the ADAS-WM is enabling a visual warning, followed by an audible warning. The ADAS-WM will suppress consecutive warnings for the same modality within a defined time period.	Req 3) Warnings of several modalities shall be prioritized per modality. Req 4) If a warning has been issued, all lower or same priority warnings shall be suppressed for that device during a defined time period (seconds).
3	The driver is negotiating a lane change operation but fails to recognize the issued Alert Warning, stating a car in the adjacent lane. When the system detects that the ego-vehicle is drifting out of its lane, the ADAS-WM will trigger an Imminent Warning due to the increased risk of a lateral collision collision.	Req 5) It shall be possible to combine two low priority warnings to provide a higher or same priority warning.

	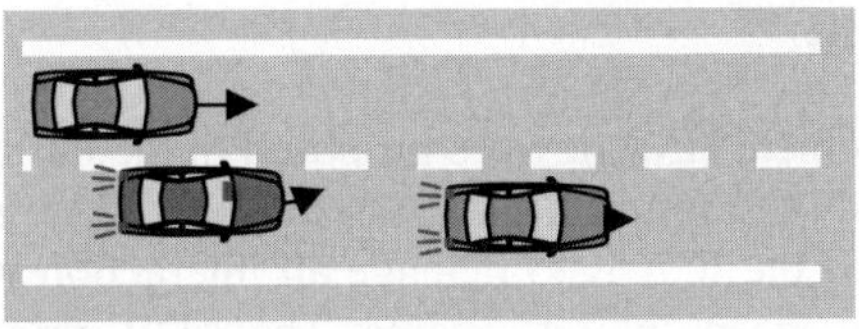	
4	The system issues an Imminent Warning due to a braking car in front while the driver is listening to music and is looking away. If the music is not muted the driver could fail to react on the warning.	Req 6) A warning device that is possible to trigger from both the ADAS-WM and other units (such as IVIS applications), shall incorporate an internal prioritization on output, allowing direct activation of warnings. Req 7) Other sound sources shall be muted while an audible warning is issued.
5	The system detects an fast overtaking car in an adjacent lane, resulting in an Informative Warning. As the car enters the blind spot area of the ego-vehicle, another Informative Warning is issued. The ADAS-WM enables the same warning device for both warnings.	Req 8) The ADAS-WM shall have a consistent approach to warning presentation.
6	The driver gets a navigation message just after a warning is provided and thereby starts to make an avoidance maneuver.	Req 9) The vehicle general HMI manager shall be informed about the warning provided to the driver and stop and delay IVIS messages during a specified time (few seconds). After the delay IVIS messages shall be repeated with updated information.
7	The system issues a Imminent Warning due to a hard braking car in front, while the driver is inattentive. The driver brakes hard and manages to stop the ego-vehicle with only a few meters remaining to the vehicle in front.	Req 10) The latency from activation of a warning state to activation of the HMI device shall be less than 100 ms. Req 11) Warnings of different modality triggered by the same warning state shall be started within a 100 ms period with 85% confidence.

4.2 ADAS WM Architecture Concepts

Current concept for management of in vehicle HMI devices proposed in the basic AIDE concept relies on the Interaction and Communication Assistance (ICA) module discussed in [5]. The general objective of the ICA is to manage all interaction with the driver with the in-vehicle systems by an accept/inhibit scheme. The ADIE principle is that all in-vehicle system (applications) asks the ICA for the use of a certain HMI channel. The ICA determines whether to accept the request or inhibit the system from using the HMI channel (based on certain criterions) and communicates this decision back to the application. If the application receives an affirmative response the application proceeds to take control of the HMI channel. This scheme is shown in Fig 3.

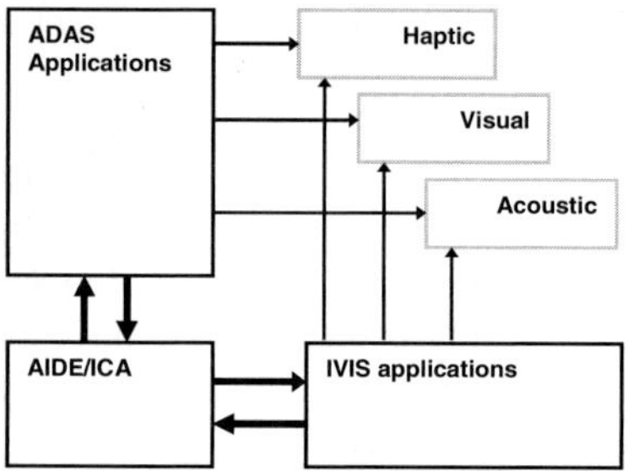

Fig. 3. Schematic view of AIDE HMI management concept

This is a very suitable scheme for IVIS and non time critical ADAS application but introduces an longer latency in the system for time and safety critical ADAS applications as it has to wait for a reply from the ICA in order to give its warning to the driver. Instead INSAFES propose to use the following scheme shown in Fig. 4. Here time and safety critical ADAS applications are managed separately by the ADAS Warning Manager (ADAS-WM). The link is still present to AIDE and the ICA module which, in this scheme, is responsible for coordination of IVIS and non time critical ADAS applications in much the same way as before. The main differences in the INSAFES proposal are shown in that the ADAS-WM only informs the ICA that it will use a certain HMI channel and will not wait for a reply. Further on the INSAFES proposal adds the possibility to add a local prioritization module in each HMI channel indicated with a red box in the HMI modules in Fig 4.

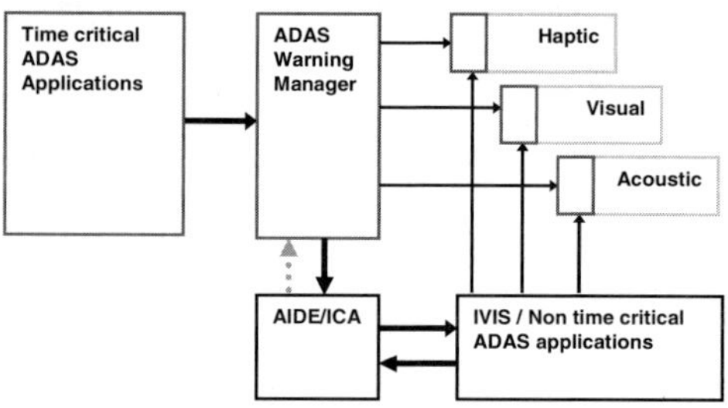

Fig. 4. Schematic view of INSAFES ADAS Warning Manager scheme

Fig. 5 shows a comparison between the described schemes in terms of latency in a likely automotive implementation where different applications can be situated at different networks and the communication has to go through a gateway. Here we clearly see drawbacks with the basic AIDE architecture compared to the extensions proposed by INSAFES.

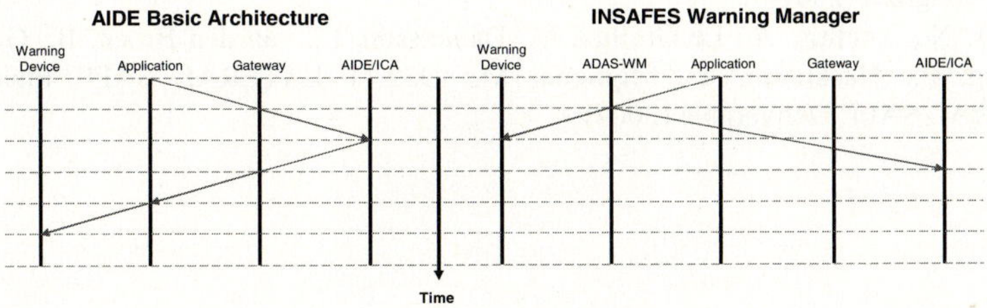

Fig. 5. Latency comparison between the basic AIDE architecture and the INSAFES proposal

5 Conclusions

The HMI integration scheme proposed in this papers allows for incorporation of general ADAS HMI arbitration and prioritization strategies for time and safety critical warnings. By tight integration in between ADAS applications and Warning Manager and direct access to warning devices latency can be reduced to an acceptable level. Using the possibility of local prioritization in the HMI devices in combination with the AIDE ICA module ensures an effective, unified HMI towards the driver with limited distractions.

Acknowledgements

We wish to acknowledge to the INSAFES Subproject Consortium of the PReVENT IP project, for their valuable contributions to this work. The PReVENT IP project is partially funded by the EC.

References

1. Lansdown, T.C., Brook-Carter, N., Kersloot, T.: Distraction from multiple in-vehicle secondary tasks: vehicle performance and mental workload implications. Ergonomics 47(1), 91–104 (2004)
2. Wierwille, W.W.: Demands on driver resources associated with introducing advanced technology into the vehicle. Transpn Res. C 1(2), 133–142 (1993)
3. Sjögren, A., Amditis, A., Polychronopoulos, A.: FUNCTIONAL INTEGRATION: POSSIBILITIES AND CHALLENGES - INSAFES PROJECT. In: 13th World Congress & Exhibition on Intelligent Transport Systems and Services (2006)
4. Strobel, T., Coue, C.: D13.4 Compendium on Sensor Data Fusion, ProFusion project deliverable (2004)

5. Amditis, A., Andreone, L., Polychronopoulos, A., Engström, J.: Design and Development of an Adaptive Integrated Driver-Vehicle Interface: Overview of The AIDE Project. In: Proc. IFAC 16th World Congress Prague Czech Republic (2005)
6. Bekiaris, E., et al.: D60.2 User needs, application scenarios and functional requirements, INSAFES project deliverable (2006)
7. Lind, H.: An efficient Visual Forward Collision Warning Display for Vehicles, SAE 2007 World Congress (2007)
8. Floudas, N., Amditis, A., Le Guillux, Y., Danielsson, L., van den Broek, B., Gemou, M., Stalberg, P., Hackbarth, T., Miglietta, M.: D32.11 LATERAL SAFE Final Report, LATERAL SAFE Deliverable (2007)

Sonification System of Maps for Blind

Gintautas Daunys and Vidas Lauruska

Siauliai university, Vilniaus str. 141, 76353 Siauliai, Lithuania
vidas.lauruska@tf.su.lt

Abstract. Presentation of graphical information is very important for blind. This information will help blind better understand surrounding world. The developed system is devoted for investigation of graphical information by blind user using a digitiser. SVG language with additional elements is used for describing of maps. Non-speech sounds are used to transfer information about colour. Alerting sound signal is issued near two regions boundary.

Keywords: blind, sonification, digitiser, maps.

1 Introduction

With the increasing usage of multimedia systems, there is a real need for developing tools able to offer aids for visually impaired or blind people in accessing graphical information. This technological development opened new prospects in the realization of man-machine interfaces for blind users. Many efforts have been devoted to the development of sensory substitution systems that may help visually impaired and blind users in accessing visual information such as text, graphics, or images.

Some of them are based on transformation of visual information to auditive signal. These approaches assume a sufficient knowledge of both visual and auditory systems. At present time, we can consider that the various solutions suggested for text access are acceptable. However, the information presented in the form of graphics or images presents a major obstacle in the daily life of blind users.

1.1 Transformation of Visual Information

One of approaches is based on the sound screen concept [1]. Its principle rests primarily on the auditive localization of virtual sound sources (VSS). The sense of hearing presents many analogies with the parameters intervening in the vision. The human being exploits this resource very much, in particular with the speech which transports important semantic components, just like the text with the vision. If all the parameters intervening in hearing are not used by the speech, on the other hand, the music exploits all the related resources at artistic ends. However, an important advantage with visual space is that one can represent a particular semantic in a graphical form. Whereas, there is no equivalent graphical representation of auditive semantic in the sound space. Here, as an alternative solution, we propose an audiodisplay system based on sound localization which allows to represent some

C. Stephanidis (Ed.): Universal Access in HCI, Part II, HCII 2007, LNCS 4555, pp. 349–352, 2007.

graphic information in the sound space. The basic idea is to project graphics on a virtual sound screen.

Other approach is coding scheme based on a pixel-frequency association [2]. The sensory substitution model can now be summarized as follows. According to our model of vision, the acquired image matrix is first convolved by an edge detector filter and, second, converted into a multiresolution image. Then, coupling between the model of vision and the inverse model of audition is achieved by assigning a specific sinusoidal tone to each pixel of this multiresolution image; the amplitude of each sine wave is modulated by the grey level of the corresponding pixel. Finally, according to the inverse model of audition, the left and right complex sounds consist of weighted summations of these sinusoidal tones.

In the TeDUB project (Technical Drawings Understanding for the Blind) [3] the system was developed, which aim is providing blind computer users with an accessible representation of technical diagrams. The TeDUB system consists of two separate parts: one for the semi-automatic analysis of images containing diagrams from a number of formally defined domains and one for the representation of previously analysed material to blind people. The joystick was used for navigation through drawings. Very interesting approach and ideas are combining haptic and auditory [4].

1.2 SVG Format

Mapping represents a perfect application of SVG (abbreviation for Scalable Vector Graphics), because maps are, by nature, vector layered representations of the earth. The SVG grammar allows the same layering concepts that are so crucial to Geographic Information Systems (GIS). Since maps are graphics that depict our environment, there is a great need for maps to be informative and interactive. SVG provides this interaction with very high quality output capability, directly on the web. Because of the complexity of geographic data (projection, coordinate systems, complex objects, etc.), the current SVG specification [5] does not contain all the particularities of a GIS particularities. However, the current specification is sufficient to help the mapping community produce open source interactive maps in SVG format.

Nowadays vector graphics format is widely used to store digitized maps. Often rich interactive maps are published in web using SVG file format. SVG is an XML markup language for describing two-dimensional vector graphics. It is an open standard created by the World Wide Web Consortium. The available fill and stroke options, symbols and markers enable higher quality map graphics. Most suitable software for browsing interactive SVG maps is plug in Adobe SVG Viewer, available for all major platforms and browsers (Linux, MacOSX, Solaris, Windows) which can be downloaded free from the Adobe SVG homepage [6]. Exist and commercial products as MapViewSVG from ESRI [7].

The analysis of SVG technology application in education is presented in A. Neumann paper [8]. Already were attempts to apply SVG formats of maps for blind users [9].

2 Method

Our aim was to develop widely available graphical information presentation system for blind user. We tried to use most common and cheapest hardware and open source or free software components.

First we consider the system hardware. Computer mouse is optional graphic-input device. The device use relative motion, so when the user hits the edge he or she need merely pick up the mouse and drop it back. It is convenient during usual work with computer applications, but maps exploration system is one of exceptions. In our application we need devices which give absolute coordinates. For graphical input we selected digitiser (tablet). Other hardware is a standard PC computer with sound card and speakers.

For graphical information description we selected SVG language because of reasons as was described earlier. Because we aimed achieved high interactivity, we don't use standard products with SVG implementation as Adobe SVG Reader. We developed software using Visual C++ environment from Microsoft Visual Studio.NET.

As a XML based language, SVG supports foreign namespaces. It is possible to define new elements or add new attributes. Elements and attributes in a foreign namespace have a prefix and a colon before the element or attribute name. Elements and attributes in foreign namespaces that the SVG viewer does not know, are ignored. However, they can be read and written by script. Foreign namespaces are used to introduce new elements (e.g. GUI elements, scale bars) and for the attachment of non-graphical attributes to SVG graphic elements [8]. The SVG file prepared for our system could be seen on other SVG viewers.

3 Maps Sonification System

Important and coherent points during design process were to choose intermediate structures for parsed SVG code storing and define additional elements to SVG specification. Selected graphical features are projected into indexed bitmap. The index of pixel colour also is a key to text and nonverbal sounds, which are bounded to selected region of map. For each region text about it features for speech synthesis is prescribed. The musical melodies can be attached during SVG editing or selected automatically in run-time. They help for user navigation over the map and also bring features of jocosity. The melodies are played when digitiser's pen is over selected region.

For easier navigation through the map, the alerting system about region boundaries was implemented. System permanently tracks, how far user input coordinates are from region contours. The intermediate bitmap helps for this purpose. If user's pen is near boundaries an alert signal is issued. The volume of alert signal depends on distance from boundary. Volume is increased, when pen of digitiser is closer to boundary.

The parsing of SVG document was implemented using XML parser Expat [10]. Graphical rendering to intermediate bitmap was implemented with Windows GDI functions. We used DirectX for output of non-speech sounds, which are musical melodies and alerting tonal signals. Speech synthesis currently is implemented using free product - Microsoft SAPI 5.

4 Conclusions

Our investigation has demonstrated that SVG format is flexible and it is suitable for combining graphical and other kinds of information about maps. The conversion of graphical information to auditory signals can be implemented via generation of intermediate bitmap layer. The software prototype which uses SVG format files as input was implemented using Microsoft Visual Studio.NET. Usability test is our nearest future task. To improve speech synthesis quality and include language choice menu is other our task. It seems that MBROLA tool [11] is suitable for the purpose.

Acknowledgement. This research is supported by FP6/IST STREP project Multimodal Collaboration Environment for Inclusion of Visually Impaired Children (MICOLE).

References

1. Liard, C., Beghdadi, A.: An Audiodisplay Tool For Visually Impaired People: The Sound Screen System, International Symposium on Signal Processing and its Applications (ISSPA), vol. 1, pp. 108–121. Kuala Lumpur, Malaysia (2001)
2. Capelle, C., Trullemans, C., Amo, P., Veraart, C.: A Real-Time Experimental Prototype for Enhancement of Vision Rehabilitation Using Auditory Substitution. IEEE Trans. Biom. Eng. BME-45, 1279–1293 (1998)
3. Horstmann, M., Hagen, C., King, A., Dijkstra, S., Crombie, D., Evans, D.G., Ioannidis, G., Blenkhorn, P., Herzog, O., Schlieder, Ch.: TeDUB: Automatic Interpretation and Presentation of Technical Diagrams for Blind People. In: Hersh, M. (eds.): CVHI'2004, Granada, Spain (2004)
4. Jansson, G., Larsson, K.: Identification of Haptic Virtual Objects with Different Degrees of Complexity. In: Wall, S.A., Riedel, B., Crossan, A., McGee, M.R. (eds.): Eurohaptics 2002. In: Conference Proceedings, Edinburgh, pp. 57–60 (2002)
5. Scalable Vector Graphics (SVG) 1.1 specification.http://www.w3.org
6. Adobe downloads page.http://www.adobe.com/support/downloads/main.html
7. ESRI homepage.http://www.esri.com
8. Neumann, A.: Use of SVG and EcmaScript technology for E-learning purposes. In: ISPRS Workshop Tools and Techniques for E-Learning, pp. 37–48. Potsdam, Germany (2005)
9. Campin, B., McCurdy, W., Brunet, L., Siekierska, E.: SVG Maps for People with Visual Impairment. In: SVG OPEN Conference (July 2003)
10. The Expat XML parser.http://expat.sourceforge.net
11. The MBROLA project homepage.http://tcts.fpms.ac.be/synthesis/mbrola.html

An Accesible and Collaborative Tourist Guide Based on Augmented Reality and Mobile Devices

Fidel Díez-Díaz, Martín González-Rodríguez, and Agueda Vidau

The Human Communication and Interaction Research Group (HCI-RG)
Department of Computer Science, University of Oviedo, Calvo Sotelo, s/n, 33007 OVIEDO – Spain
fideldd@yahoo.es, martin@uniovi.es, avidau@gmail.com
www.hci.uniovi.es

Abstract. The goal of this project is to provide support for a system of geolocation powered by augmented reality, offering also advanced services such as, context awareness mobile applications and natural interaction related to the concept of ambient intelligent which favour the creation of intelligent environments whose services fit dynamically the demand, not always made explicit, of the user. A design and a development of a location system is obtained that provides extra services based on the positional information of the different system's users. In this way, the user receives specific information of the place where he or she is located. This service is based on the Global Positioning System, from now on GPS. The aim with this platform is to locate, guide and give information to blind people, although it is open to any kind of people. It will allow the users to see information related to a place, to write comments about it and leave objects for the rest of the users to read and see. The information will be shown as a written text and as an oral one and in every moment the location of the user will be traced thanks to the virtual positioning of him or her on a map.

Keywords: context-awareness; location-awareness; natural-interaction; mobile devices; ambient intelligent; GPS.

1 Introduction

The proliferation of devices with communication and process capacity (mobile phones, PDAs, Set-top boxes of digital TV, household-electric…) it has given rise to the birth of a series of new technologies, evolution which it was known later like distributed computing and like mobile computing, and that today is included under the name ubiquitous computing.

These technologies look for to create transparent environments to the user in whom these devices with limited capacity of process and intermittent communication cooperate of intelligent form. In this way, the movable devices are aligned like a perfect technological ally to accede to the mentioned information.

C. Stephanidis (Ed.): Universal Access in HCI, Part II, HCII 2007, LNCS 4555, pp. 353–362, 2007.

To the question: Do you have computer in your house? The answer would be affirmative in the great majority of the cases. In just a short time they will comprise of our vital surroundings in a high amount. They will be interlocked and they will increase the capacities of daily or new objects, others will control our habitat and many will make the human scope of interaction with a great part of the rest of the world: email, e-commerce, e-services... so that its absence will be lived like vital handicap (like blindness, deafness...) It causes that the services that supports a computer are a problem of crucial importance. On its ergonomics, versatility... will depend that that new "sense", in much superior at sight, hearing... is useful for the accomplishment of the human like being social in the Society of the information.

By all of it, it is necessary to develop projects able to interact with the human and with the own surroundings in which it lives and it moves. Reason why the best way to obtain it is through the mobile devices, that can be moved with the own human. In addition to this, if we added to a system of location and context awareness surroundings to him to the context, at any moment it will be known where he is the human and what or who is surrounding to him.

With this project it is tried to create a support platform to increased reality cradle in GPS and wireless networks to increase the interactivity of the users among them and with the own surroundings.

So thanks to this platform, will be able to be made different applications, simply with a change of information (SD card), the base will be the same for all.

The augmented reality[3], is centered in integration between the computer and the physical surroundings that surround him and tries that the computer harnesses its activities providing to him in every moment nonintrusive information about the real objects with whom interacts and by means of a pursuit of the same ones.

In this project a "Visit Guided" by the city of Oviedo is developed, but of equal way it could have been on any other city or town of Spain, as well as a "Stroll attended for blind", "Asturian mountain Routes", "Jurassic Visit".... The number of possible applications that can be made with this platform is very high, thanks to the ubiquitous computing, the GPS location system, the context awareness surroundings....

Not only the tourists and visitors are the adressees of the new services based on the information technologies and the communications that can be conceived. Seeing data of establishments and tourist resources, it is possible to raise three types of users[2] like tourist/visitors,final adressees for products and services, propietary of the tourist sector, hotel, restorers, wholesale, propietary of sport facilities, etc. And national, autonomic and local administrations public. In them public resides the management of the cultural goods, the protected natural spaces, etc.

In the great majority of the tourist destinies, the tourist information bureaus provide great part of the information of the tourist destiny, as well as the way to accede to her. Even though strategically they are located in the destiny, all the tourists do not find them accessible, in addition the schedules to attention to the client not always satisfy the necessities with the tourist. All it leads to the necessity to make available of the client so valuable information so that it is consumed without barriers of time or space. [1]

2 State of the Art

In the market some tourist guides for mobile devices exist. Varied as far as the mobile device for that they are prepared, as far as the systems of location, the offered services, etc. All of them with its strongpoints and their errors to correct.

There are more or less basic objectives that all the systems try to obtain, nevertheless all the guides do not obtain it, and although they obtain it, are guides in whom by one either another reason is more easy to ask to someone that to look for the information in the own mobile device. The tourist guides who fulfill the basic objectives have certain similarity as far as the interfaces and in the external vision of the system, but as far as the internal structure of the same one, had in the great majority of the cases to the used system of location, there are remarkable differences.

Also another fundamental point of disjunction exists, is the mobile device with which the visit can be made: mobile telephones (with or connectionless to Internet), pocketpc, pda (both with or without GPS, with or without GPRS, with or without WIFI...) etc. Are obvious that it is not possible in the same way to treat all these different devices in his essence, although all of them are mobile devices after all.

2.1 State of the Art

2.1.1 State of the Art

SMIT [4] is a "Mobile System of Tourist Information" for mobile terminals, as much mobile telephones as PDA' s with WIFI, but these PDA' s if they were pocket PC must have installed the java virtual machine because it is J2ME application, by the other side they were palm, we would not have to install this virtual machine.

As main functions of this system emphasize the following ones:

- To look for information.
- To draw up the best route to its destiny or to draw up routes of interest specifically designed to optimize its time in mobility.
- To locate itself by corner (although also bluetooth can use a GPS).
- To reproduce videos, images, sounds....
- To also look for generic, customized, radial information from the point where we were and by resources.

2.1.2 Advantages

Basically SMIT is a tourist guide who takes advantage of some the characteristics of a mobile phone. For example, all the information downloading from servers, by that it can be continuously updated. Because it is an J2ME application, does not demand a special mobile phone.

Operative in more of 80% of the mobile terminals and wireless in general, it allows to take to the information to any site with universal vocation, offering to the tourist and the citizen the best way to know all the resources in its surroundings (sanitary centers, monuments, hotels, restaurants, museums, parks, pharmacies, parkings, beaches…).

2.1.3 Disadvantages

As all the data download directly from Internet, it is necessary to use a connection of data from the mobile phone. This limits to much the use of any program that demands more or less permanent connection. Still more, if we are going to download images, videos and audio files.

At a graphical interface level, it is very little intuitive and it is looked excessively like an interface of an PC aplication(interminable menus, for example). It is not a serious problem in himself, since it would be possible to be solved with facility leaving free users by some city and registering how they try to use the application (usuary that, to power to be, did not know anything of computer science nor of mobile phones). But meanwhile, it does not seem the sufficiently comfortable thing to use.

That the guide is done in J2ME would work on the mobile phones, but according to http://geomovil.info also it would work in PDA' s, but it says nowhere that only work in PDA' s with Palm O.S., because in PDA' s with Pocket PC operating system(PPC) it would not work because there would be to install the java virtual machine.

2.2 WALLIP

2.2.1 Introduction

WALLIP [5] project is an initiative of several companies of the CAV (Community Autonomous Basque).

It allows to the development of mobile applications with contex awareness of location and the preferences of the user, that will allow to provide suitable suggestions to him frequently and to facilitate their interaction to him with the surroundings, extending its own perception. In this project the platform has been developed, three services (one of mobility, another one for location and another one for management of profiles, all of them integrated in the platform) and two applications of test, a Tourist Assistant and an application of Operation and Maintenance, using a SOA architecture based on Services Web.

2.2.2 Advantages

Wallip allows to know the device positioning independently connection system that it uses at every moment. This location will make the own platform combining the data of the network with geographical information.

The aplication allows to offer the information that is considered necessary for the development of its activity, like people just arrivals to a city and which they do not know the surroundings that surround to them.

The objective of the Tourist Assistant is to provide information on the Points of Tourist Interest near a user based on the position in which they are updated of automatic way at the moment that the user changes of position.

The user can develop his activity of tourist and interact with the application to see with more detail the information of context of his surroundings that interest to him, as a photography of the interest point or to enter in the web page of the interest point.

2.2.3 Disadvantages

At the moment of start the project, the implementation of a Web Service on mobile devices very was not developed, reason why it was necessary to limit the roll of PDA's clients of Web Services.

The Tourist Assistant works with networks Wi-Fi and GPRS, so in a city or town that did not have the cover of these networks would not work in. Nowadays it is normal to find networks Wi-Fi and GPRS in the city, like many mobile phones and PDA' s that already come adapted to be able to use these networks, but we extended the field of vision with respect to a guided visit, and not only we were centered in a visit to a big city, but also to a visit through field, like they can be, mountain routes, routes by the towns of Asturias… we can see that it fails the guide in that way.

One of the main disadvantages, is that, different rolls are recognized and from different visitors in a same zone, but they cannot interact with others, nor to share opinions through Tourist Assistant.

2.3 AMIGUIDE

2.3.1 Introduction

Project EUREKA (http://www.eureka.be), called AMIGUIDE [1], and coordinated by Foundation IBIT, offers an interactive tourist guidance system for PDA' s equipped with wireless communications, with the possibility of downloading information multimedia through points of cover Bluetooth and Wi-Fi from the interior of hotels, and through GPRS from the outside. The guide allows to accede to services of location based on the position of the user, who obtains by the GPS system. Therefore and within the present context, project AMIGUIDE has two primary targets:

- Indoor surroundings: Wireless technologies such as Wi-Fi and Bluetooth.
- Outdoor Surroundings: GPRS from cellular telephones or from PDAs.

2.3.2 Advantages

- A new vision which the physical surroundings that surround to us turn the interface to access to the information and to the services that can demand the users.
- The user can plan his trip from an only access point. Thinking in the immense time that implies to prepare a trip, he is desirable that the user has an intelligent agent that he makes in his place this task.

2.3.3 Disadvantages

- When downloading information, the velocity of the downloading will depend on the occupation of the bandwidth. All the application is based on the downloading information through the network, either by WiFi or GPRS, this implies that the application depends on the free bandwidth, whatever with more connections, the less rapidity of data transmission.
- In order to obtain data you depend to have cover in the networks, as much WiFi as GPRS so in a city or town that did not have the cover of these networks would not work in.

2.4 PATRIMONIO MÓVIL

2.4.1 Introduction

The project (accessible in http://www.patrimoniomovil.com and in the tourism web of Salamanca http://www.salamanca.es) [6] has consisted of starting up a service for visitors, that is based on the access to the interactive multimedia information from several platforms (Internet, mobile telephone or PDA).

The user can receive and consult information on the cultural and historical-artistic patrimony of Salamanca, as well as of events and activities in the city.

The application combines the information consultation before the trip and during it: by means of his web page, the visitor can select the contents that interest to take to him with himself during their visit.

It is possible to find applications stops:

- PDA. Once loaded the information, has access to the services of:
  - Mobile Itinerary
  - Monument guide
  - Notebook of the tourist
  - Web page offers connection to Internet from the points destined for it.
- WAP. In this web page it is possible to be acceded to Events Agenda, Mobile Itinerary, Itinerary Alternative, Monument Guide, Information to the Visitor, Help and Supplies and Promotions.
- SMS. With the short messages can be received informtation of the Events Agenda, of Mobile Itinerary, Alternative Itinerary, Monument Guide and Information to the Visitor.
- MMS. If it is had a terminal multimedia, in addition to the services already mentioned, they are possible to be sent postal and to be participated in games.

2.4.2 Advantages

- The starting of service with easy system of consultation information through devices as the mobile phone or the PDA can make the visit to the city simpler and interesting.
- The system of short messages and multimedia has to its favor the ease of use and the great acceptance that first have had between the users.
- The application combines the information consultation before the trip and during it.

2.4.3 Disadvantages

- It is necessary to consider that the profile of the user of this service, is the one of a person with a certain technological culture: the service implies navigation by Internet, handling of a PDA with a concrete operating system, procedure of contents selection and downloading directly of the computer or from the downloading points in the city, etc. This process is easy for one that is familiarized with a PDA or a similar device, but to other users can not be so obvious.
- The navigation web system by mobile phone account with the barrier of the little use of the new services of data. A good help system, that it provides precise and truthful information on the service, the procedure to use it and the cost of himself can stimulate navigation by Internet with the mobile phone.

- The reception of information through short messages presents an obvious disadvantage: the capacity and the limitation of the user interface.
- If in the course of a route always is desired to consult something had to send sms to a number ready to it in order that the wished information is facilitated, the mechanism can be something tedious and uncomfortable.

3 Application

Our Project Vadinia makes use of such kind popular devices to make the interaction with physical environment around us more accessible for everybody. Geographic information is modeled for a multimodal interaction approach using small handheld devices powered by geographic location devices which informs the application about the exact geographic location of the users through the interactive experience.

Fig. 1. Application capture that shows the main form of it

Knowledge about the environment is easily edited in a Context Markup Language (CML) which renders its contents in real time using visual and auditory interfaces, providing an accessible interface for users with different kinds of disabilities. Although the standard interaction with the system is performed though the graphic pointing device of the hand held device (the Stylus in the Pocket PC) it can also be fully operated using the device buttons, providing a full interaction experience for visually disabled users.

This information displayed is powered by the use of Augmented Reality techniques also offering context awareness services and natural interaction; which are related to the concept of ambient intelligent, encouraging the creation of intelligent environments whose services fit dynamically the demand, not always made explicit, from the user.

Designers or Vadinia applications can model the semantic of the geographic information in one or several CML documents with references to the different kind of multimedia objects supported by the system. They can be textual information, images and sounds, which are displayed whenever the user enters inside the range of coverage of a POI (Point of interest) included in the CML. Semantic meta data about this information is also broadcast through the auditory channel. This meta data provides extra semantic meaning for objects (such as images) that certain kind of users (such as blind people) can not perceive.

Once designed, the whole geographic model can be zipped into a single file that can be stored in the memory of the hand held device and loaded into the Vadinia application. Depending on the amount of information modeled, this file can be included in an external memory card.

Nevertheless, dynamic information is distributed and managed through a small network of handheld devices. Small pocket computers powered by wireless networks (Wifi) provide areas of coverage for specific zones of the geographic environment. Inside those zones, users might receive live information from the environment (for instance, are the traffic lights in the green status?) but also information from other users, enabling basic social exchange capabilities and encouraging the future development of collaborative geographic context aware systems.

Fig. 2. Application capture that shows an interest point with his description and the possibility of write comments and view comments of others turist

Users of Vadinia-based technologies can use their own view of the the information provided by the system, editing it and submitting it to the system so other users can get information updated by users who have visited the areas before. This approach enables a collaborative editing system for geographic objects, where several users can collaborate to provide life and accurate information for each piece of modeled environment.

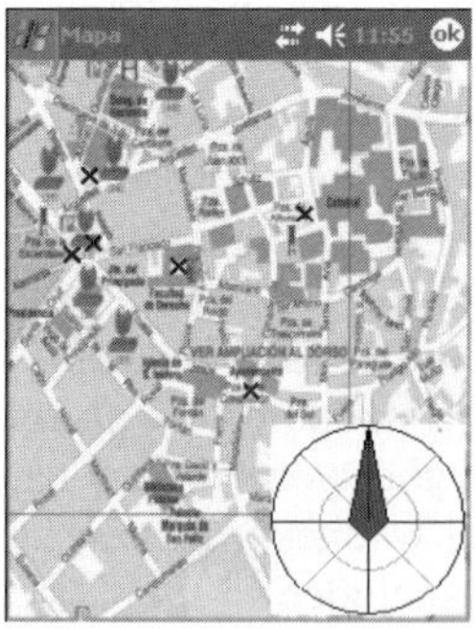

Fig. 3. Application capture thar shows the map. the interest points (the blue crosses) and a compass to view the direction

Vadinida works in any pocketpc device running Compact Framework 2.0 and powered by a Wifi and Bluetooth connection. Current user location is obtained using GPS antennas (Global Positioning System) in open sky environments (such as cities, archaeological sites, etc.) and Bluetooth antennas inside buildings.

In order to test Vadinia, we have developed an interactive tourist guide of the city of Oviedo, capital city of the province of Asturias (Spain). The guide includes context aware information about the main monuments and buildings of the town describing their history using text, images and sounds. Users can also attach their own images and texts to the objects discovered during their visit.

In the worl of this application, exists a type of user, with a good defined function in which to the system interaction it talks about. The normal user can make the following operations:

- To begin a visit with or without GPS.
- To see map, satellites, height and position. Thanks to a map, knoledge at any moment where are the interest points and where is the own user.
- To select zone with or without WiFi.
- To configure port COM, the baudrate and the language.
- To see and to select the interest points and the user objects.
- To raise an object and to write a description of itself.
- To extend the image of a interest point and an image of user object.
- To write and to see commentaries on a interest point and an user object
- To see the description of an user object and an interest point.
- To write and to modify a user name on a commentary of a user object and on an interest point.
- To enter a zone with or without WiFi.
- To see and to listen the information of the zone and the interest point where on is.

4 Conclusions

The mobile devices that are used mainly at the moment are mobile telephones and PDA' s. These two devices tend to integrate themselves, and the market already offers some models that connect both concepts.

Vadinia works by an operating system that at the moment already brings many mobile telephones and many PDA' s, not depending on same telephony company so the cover at any moment of the visit is not lost, and not centered nly in great cities with cover in all of it.

Don't forget that the accessibility and usability of the user interface represent a key factor of success. Vadinia has surpassed numerous tests of usability and accessibility with different types of users with different ages and different knowledge from mobile devices, its interface is not looked like the typical applications of PC, avoiding endless scrolls in reduced screens. Thanks to Vadinia a new concept of museum routes can be installed and be maintained. But not only in museums, also in urban nuclei, archaeological exhibitions and enclosures, commercial amusement parks, hotels and zones services can be conceived that suppose an increase of data traffic for the operator, a new form of attraction and promotion for the final user service and a customized information for the client.

The use of the information and communications technologies represent a different way to satisfy necessities of day by day, can collaborate to improve the security in the displacements and also to find new services that suppose an incentive at the time of showing preference for a tourist destiny or another one. By all these reasons, public administrations beings have to deliver a special attack in promoting and creating necessary the enterprise weave so that this type of innovating and differentiating services is a reality.

References

1. Amiguide (ambient intelligent guide). http://www.ibit.org/home/proyectos/proyecto.php?idioma=es&id=548
2. Ana M[a] Bernardos Barbolla. Servicios móviles de localización : Aplicaciones en el sector turístico. CEDITEC, (2003)
3. Barfield, W., Caudell, T.: Fundamentals of Wearable Computers and Augmented Reality (2000)
4. Smit (sistema móvil de información turística). http://geomovil.info/index.html
5. Larizgoitia, I., Lago, A.B., Wallip, I.V.: Desarrollo de una plataforma de servicios de valor añadido. CISTI, II (2006)
6. Patrimonio móvil. http://www.patrimoniomovil.com

The Use of Kaizen Continuous Improvement Approach for Betterment of Ergonomic Standards of Workstations

Ewa Gorska and Anna Kosieradzka

Warsaw University of Technology
Narbutta 85, 02-524 Warsaw, Poland
{e.gorska, a.kosieradzka}@wip.pw.edu.pl

Abstract. The paper describes: elements of a continuous improvement system in an enterprise, teamwork as an approach towards solving problems at workstations (especially problems concerning ergonomic issues) and methods and techniques used in ergonomic standards improvement at the stages of problem identification as well as search and implementation of the solutions. Requirements and conditions for efficient implementation are substantiated for improvements such as: training system, motivational system, system of applying and evaluation of applications, financial support of the implementation process and 5S program as a starting point for ergonomic improvements. Theoretical considerations will be illustrated with examples of improvements implemented in Polish enterprises.

Keywords: ergonomic standards, continuous improvement, kaizen, 5S, workstation organization, process improvement.

1 Introduction

Currently the essence of long-term business strategy in USA and highly developed European countries is reaching an increase in efficiency with simultaneous increase of the quality of professional life. It is one of the reasons why reaching strategic and operational goals of the organization together with subjective treatment of employees, with their needs, abilities, aspirations and expectations taken into consideration, becomes the fundamental and crucial objective.

The paper presents results of theoretical and empirical research indicating relationships that occur between continuous improvement of processes with workstation organization compliant with kaizen philosophy against the increase of ergonomic and occupational safety standards levels.

2 Kaizen the Continuous Improvement Philosophy

Kaizen is a philosophy that revolutionized the Japanese economy over the last 30 years. After publishing of the famous book by Masaaki Imai „*Kaizen – The Key to Japanese Competitive Success*" [1], translated to 14 languages and sold in over

C. Stephanidis (Ed.): Universal Access in HCI, Part II, HCII 2007, LNCS 4555, pp. 363–372, 2007.

180000 copies, Kaizen philosophy gained popularity in many countries, and the word "kaizen" became a part of many languages. The book appeared to be a crucial factor to understand the basis of Japanese economical success.

Kaizen is a way of thinking and managing. Its essence is the continuous improvement of processes in an enterprise through small steps performed by all employees. It is considered to be the basis of competitive success of an enterprise by the enthusiasts of this management philosophy.

Rapid pace of change in the field of technology enforces implementation of innovation, sudden changes of considerable reach that are meant to radically improve the results of work upon the enterprises. Innovations require large amounts of financial resources and a considerable effort for its implementation and maintenance, otherwise the reached improvement in productivity is not permanent. Proccess of implementing new ideas is more efficient when it is supported with kaizen activities (Fig.1).

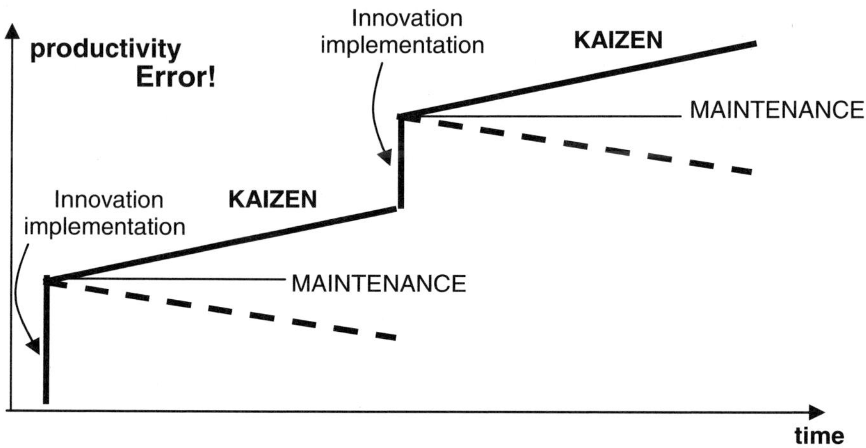

Fig. 1. Increasing productivity as a result of implementation of innovation and continuous improvement (kaizen)

Kaizen is a slower but permanent improvement of things, starting from simple improvements of tools and working methods, finishing with improvement of whole processes performed by all employees achieved with small steps in a way that does not require considerable investments. Active participation of every employee is a foundation of this theory.

3 Small Group Activity

The practical aspect of kaizen philosophy is a, so called, small group activity, these groups bear different names (e.g. quality circles, efficiency improvement groups, faultless work groups, professional training groups, problem-solving groups, occupational safety groups, efficiency committees, discussion groups etc.). Such groups should be created autonomously that means they are created from the employees initiative who set the working area and improvement goals for themselves. In case of more complex problems, which require interdisciplinary analysis, a task force is created that consist of employees from different organizational cells who perform related activities. Such teams are usually created by the management and dissolved when they fulfill their task. Small Group Activity is based on the following premises (Tab. 1):

Table 1. Characterization of Small Group Activity

Manner of operation	- voluntary participation - small numbers and uniformed membership - the rank-and-file initiative inspired by employees - continuous actions - teamwork
Manager's role	advisor, promoter, coordinator, instructor, sometimes leader.
Aims	- productivity, quality and punctuality improvement - working methods improvement - improvement of safety and working conditions - decreasing the production nuisance for natural environment human potential development - increase of employee engagement
Tasks	- losses reduction - cost reduction - quality improvement - shipment punctuality improvement - maintenance improvement - economizing material and energy usage - improvement of working methods, facilitating work - promoting „good work" mentality - communication improvement
Tools	Simple and effective teamwork and problem-solving techniques: brainstorming, Ishikawa chart, Pareto chart, correlation chart, 5 times „why", 5W1H, FMEA, flow charts and sheets, random observation, checklists etc.

Usually the subjects of small group activities are successive steps of the 5S method. 5S is an organized program, that involves all employees to keep clean, orderly, well organized and safe workplaces.

Owing to the use of 5S practices enterprise gains the following benefits: decreasing delays and the number of faults, reducing the number of errors and mistakes, improving quality, improving occupational safety, decreasing the number of equipment breakdowns, better control over production flow, increase of working safety, increase of working discipline, increase in teamwork share.

5S activities are the basis for implementing any improvements in an enterprise, especially complex systems such as JIT, TPM, TQM and complex system of Total Quality, Environment and Safety Management.

Table 2. Steps of 5S method

SEIRI - SORT	Remove unnecessary items form workplace.
SEITON – SET IN ORDER	Sort necessary items, locate everything at the point of use.
SEISO - SHINE	Carefully clean your workplace and keep your tools clean.
SEIKETSU - STANDARDIZE	Create procedures (standards), which will help for the rules to became a routine.
SHITSUKE - SUSTAIN	Sustain the high level of working discipline. When training people, try to make them take the rules of sustaining as their own. Sustain by making 5S the second nature.

4 Implementation of the Kaizen Philosophy

Implementing the kaizen philosophy requires the following elements:

1. Creating organizational structure (appointing a steering committee and secretariat, selecting promoters of productivity and appointing small groups).
2. Elaborating training program (training leaders and trainers, training in methods of productivity improvement, training in technical reference improvement, training in ergonomics and occupational safety).
3. Introducing a formal system of placing improvement proposals
4. Elaborating proposal evaluation and motivational system (financial gratification, non-financial gratification methods).
5. Elaborating procedures supporting the process of improvements implementation in the organizational and financial aspect
6. Documenting and presenting solved problems (photographical records, history of problem solving, competitions).

Problem solving done by small groups is usually performed by the following action plan:

1. Formulating the problem that is to be solved.
2. Organizing the group.
3. Determining the action plan for team members.
4. Solving the problem (collecting data, analyzing data, collecting ideas concerning the improvements, selecting the most suitable idea, assigning tasks to separate group members),
5. Implementing the solution.
6. Collecting and evaluating the results.
7. Standardization and elaborating of the documentation.

Standardization is necessary to elaborate an improved algorithm for performing particular work. This documentation is used as a basis of communication, employee training and further process improvement. The aim of standardization is to create a base for continuous improvement. If the improvements are introduced without creating a new working standard, then there usually a comeback to the old system occurs.

Documentation of standardized work should include:

- Organizational standards (sequential tasks of operators, tact time and lead time, level of work-in-process that grants continuous production);
- Quality standards (requirements concerning qualitative and technical features of the product)
- Ergonomic and occupational safety standards.

5 Ergonomic Requirements Set for Processes and Workstations

Practice shows that usually implemented organizational solutions are not verified according to ergonomic standards, which does not grant safe and hygienic working conditions as well as the comfort of work. It means that new solutions leading to the increase in productivity do not always fulfill legal requirements and are performed at the expense of employee's stress and physical effort. While designing new organizational solutions it is forgotten that human beings will be part of them, human beings that have limited biomechanical and psycho-physical abilities. These abilities have a significant influence on the success of proposed improvements as well as employees attitude towards work, psycho-physical efficiency and biomechanical conditionings have influence on the effects of introduced changes.

In conformity with Ergonomics field of interest, every organizational solution should be verified according to:

- Nuisance of physical work, in which workload, static load and monotypic actions are of great importance,
- Psychical nuisance, load on central nervous system connected with information acquiring, decision making and performing taken decisions as well as the monotony of tasks,
- Spatial planning of machines, devices and equipment at workstations, consistent with employee's limb reach and sight range,
- Construction and placement of the indicating and steering devices that includes quality, strength, size, shape, location, movement and time of using the devices as well as methods of locating them according to frequency, sequence, functionality, importance and adequacy of location,
- Environment of working processes, which can either favor or disrupt the solutions consisting of: lighting, noise, vibrations, microclimate, air pollution, radiation.

Fundamental requirements that should be fulfilled by the working space are:

- Devices and equipment should be chosen and placed in a way that does not enforce unnatural body positions, they should be in the reach of limbs and in sight range and should not limit the freedom of movements,

- Manual tasks should be performed at the height of an elbow bend in right angle,
- Use hands only within the area determined by the height of an arm and elbow,
- Reach no higher than that the height determined by a palm of a hand stretched up and no lower than the height of a lowered hand hanging loosely,
- Check whether the adjustment of a chair allows putting elbows in the working area,
- Ensure that feet are placed flatly, with their whole surface on the floor or a footrest,
- Observation area is located beneath the horizontal sight line,
- Monitors are placed in front of you and never in the lateral sight area.

It is crucial to remember that in accordance with current regulations a disabled person with proper qualifications should be able to use any workstation.

Thus the list of requirements for workstations should be extended, in order to assure accessibility and safety for a user with different types of disabilities, which means:

- adjusting communicational paths to the needs of a disabled person
- adjusting object to the needs of particular disabled person and assuring a proper sanitary background
- adjusting equipment and devices to the type of person's disability
- using objects, which can decrease or eliminate the lack of particular abilities of the disabled person,
- using equipment that will help the disabled person to perform certain tasks (sensory disability).

Above all the workstation cannot:

- enforce the worker to non-physiological, long-lasting and forced positions
- overload the static-dynamic system,
- require nervous tensions,
- cause excessive energy expenditure,
- force to long-lasting and monotonous psychical concentration.

It is crucial to remember that, according to modern ergonomic postulates, equipment and devices at workstations should be adjusted to individual needs of the user as well as to his or hers expectations and cause the feeling of comfort and esthetical delight.

Action directions:

- Ergonomic take of esthetical aspects connected with esthetical shock and delight
- Need to adjust products and working spaces to individual needs and expectations of users,
- Need to express and emphasize identity and dissimilarity,
- Ecology and environmental and living standards.

It indicates that:

– Every worker has an individualized workstation, adjusted to his or hers abilities, psycho-physiological needs and anthropometrical features,
– Tasks to be performed are planned in a way to activate both cerebral hemispheres.

The further part of the paper presents solutions that connect both kaizen improvements and ergonomic postulates. The solutions have been implemented in Polish industry with the help of the paper's authors.

6 Examples of Kaizen Improvements with the Compliance of Ergonomic Requirements

Example 1. Improvement of the Electronic Ballasts Assembly Process [3]

Before the improvement the process was divided into two areas. The first area included milling of electronic systems, the second area included assembly of ballasts. Assembly process included placing the electronic system in a steel housing and closing the housing, it was operated by two people. The whole process was operated by 8 people (Fig.2), without the actual capacity taken into consideration (resulting from the current needs).

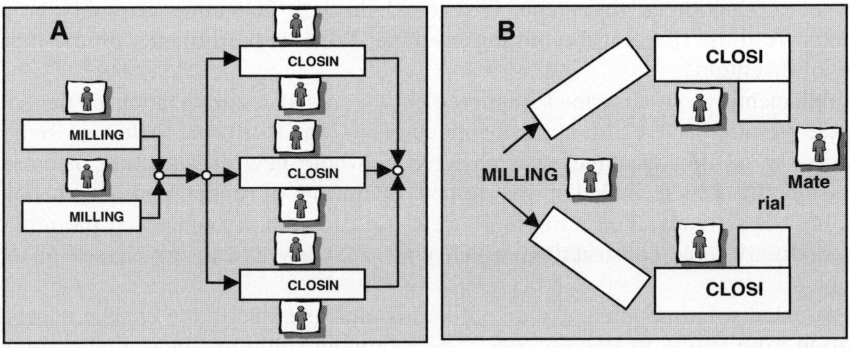

Fig. 2. Final assembly socket before (A) and after (B) the improvement

The aim of the project was to increase productivity at the final assembly socket by 50%.

On the basis of *Lean Manufacturing* principles the assumptions for the project were formulated:

– Reducing the time of production cycle and increasing productivity of the resources by waste reduction, non-value adding task elimination and rationalization of value adding operations,
– Adjusting the production pace to product demand.

Proposed solution assumes joining the operations of milling and closing in one socket. With the maximum demand for ballasts the socket will be operated by three workers and a material supplier. Two milling machines will be operated by one operator, what will help to reduce the time of operators inactivity during automatic work of the machine.

Assembly of lower and upper part of housing, up till now, performed at two different workstations, will now be done sequentially at one workstation. It will allow to eliminate unnecessary manipulative tasks. In the old solution the number of taking and giving back the object was equal 6, due to occurrence of three upper housing assembly workstations and three lower housing assembly workstations. In new solution the number was reduced to two identical workstations (each performs the assembly of lower and upper housing). Assuming a standardized time of manipulation equal 1 second, it helps to save up to 4 seconds in a typical working cycle. Furthermore joining assembly operations at one workstation does not require the synchronization of operators work, because they work simultaneously, do not wait for each other and possible differences in efficiency do not cause the rise of work in process or interruptions. Additional effect of joining the operations is reducing the monotony of operators work, what can influence the quality of production and the number of failures. Materials are supplied by a material router, who can operate many sockets – in presented case it is the fourth worker from the socket.

It is important to emphasize the flexibility of presented solution. Every time when the demand drops it is possible to reduce the worker number to three (two operators and a material supplier). Each operator prepares elements for assembly. Continuous flow of production in the socket is realized through collecting assembly products directly from the space at the milling machine. Work is performed with the minimal level of inventory.

Implementing the described improvements included reorganization of the socket, worker training and elaborating the documentation. Conveyor belt was removed, location of milling machines was changed, a whole new organization of assembly workstations, which included the joined operation of upper and lower housing assembly, was made. The same tools were used for the assembly and the remaking included only table construction, which was necessary due to the change of tables' height.

Presented solution demanded an ergonomic analysis due to the change of working position from sitting to standing one. The following solutions improving ergonomics of work were used: anti-tiredness matting and special footwear improving working comfort.

As a part of kaizen activities housing feeders were designed and manufactured. Performing additional activities as a part 5S program resulted in defining fields for work-in-process and necessary tools. Work standardization included preparing sheets with description of the new method and working sequence. During the reconstruction of sockets, trainings for employees from different workstations were performed.

Example 2. Improvement of the Fuses Welding Process

In this process traditional fuses are being manufactured, in such product after the fuse-wire is blown it is necessary to change the fuse. One of the operations in the fuse assembly process is welding the fuse-wire (which conducts electricity) to a ceramic body (filled with quartz sand). The process is operated by one worker, who walks through one workstation to another.

Welding operation is a bottleneck of the process – it is the longest operation and it causes work-in-process to occur. Welding machine used in the process was earlier adjusted to allow the worker to freely walk from one workstation to another. Worker needs to put the ceramic body and fuse wire under the snout of welding machine and than press a pedal to start it. Object needs to be held in the air and pressed to the snout.

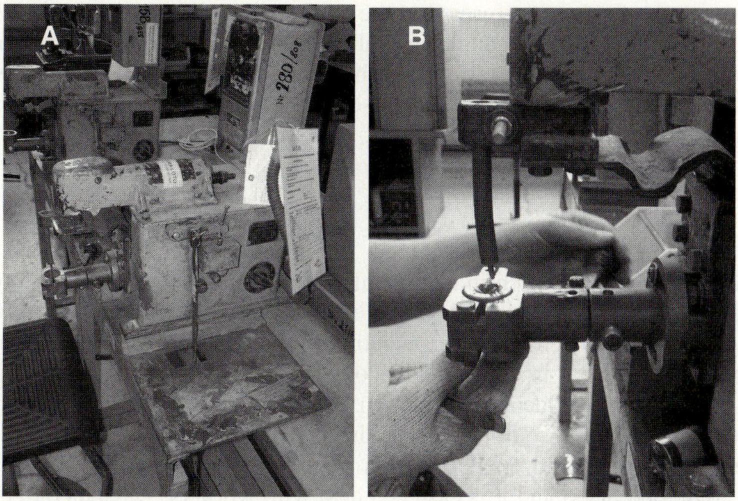

Fig. 3. Welding machine (a) and welding operation with pressing the element to the snout (b)

Even though the operation lasts only 95 seconds it is very exhausting for the worker. Pressing the object and keeping hands above shoulder line causes a major static load for the worker, in addition the pedal is located 15cm above the floor, so the worker needs to press it in the midair. Worker's exhaustion causes extension of the operation time near the end of the shift and a lower productivity of the line. The worker sometimes needs to stop the work to rest.

The assumptions of the small improvement project are:

- Decreasing the welding operation time and reducing work-in-process,
- Decreasing the static load of the worker.

Proposed solution includes redesigning the workstation according to anthropometrical body measures and ergonomic improvements. Workstation will be still operated by one employee.

Working space will be lowered in a manner to enable the worker to keep arms below the shoulder line. The assembly line is operated solely by women thus the working space will be placed at the height suitable for the elbow height of a 95 centile woman and a chair with height adjustment together with a footrest will be introduced.

Elbow-rests will be installed at the workstation, which will decrease static load of arms during the welding operation. Height of the elbow-rests is adjustable so that every person can adjust it to self body measures. Employees have to adjust the height of the chair and elbow-rests before the shift starts.

In present situation pressing the foot-pedal, that starts welding, takes 3 seconds. In production of one element the fuse-wire is welded about 25 times. Pressing the pedal located above the floor causes major static load, employee changes the leg with which the pedal is pressed what causes another extension of the operation time.

Proposed solution includes installing a footrest with adjustable height to which the foot-pedal will be fixed. Thus the employee has the possibility to put the hill on the footrest without the necessity to hold the leg in the air in an enforced position.

Tests with the footrest performed at the workstation allowed to shorten the time of pressing the pedal up to 1 second and elbow-rests caused the decrease of welding time. Finally the average operation time has been reduced form 95s to 40s. Planned production during one shift was 260 fuses but after implementing the solutions it raised up to 300 products during one shift.

7 Conclusion

There are many proofs which indicate that ergonomic solutions bring many benefits: increase safety, convenience and comfort of use, allow to keep health and well-being, help to fulfill the needs and expectations of employees. When implementing solutions, which result in improving economical results (increase in productivity, quality, punctuality, reducing production cycle time, reduce inventory etc.), it is crucial to assure that the equipment, machines and processes have ergonomic features, because working standard created in this manner is permanent (there is no coming back to “old” practices) and it is easier to deal with workers’ resistance to change due to assuring working comfort.

References

1. Górska, E.: Ergonomics– designing, diagnosis, experiments, OW PW, Warsaw (2002)
2. Imai, M.: Kaizen–The Key to Japanese Competetive Success. The Kaizen Institute Ltd., London (1986)
3. Kosieradzka, A., Maciągowski, D.: Improvement of production organization at Philips Lighting Poland S.A. based on lean manufacturing approach, Enterprise Management no 1/2005, Wyd. Polskie Towarzystwo Zarządzania Produkcją, Opole, pp. 47–58 (2005)

Development and Application of a Universal, Multimodal Hypovigilance-Management-System

Lorenz Hagenmeyer[1], Pernel van den Hurk[1], Stella Nikolaou[2], and Evangelos Bekiaris[2]

[1] Institute for Human Factors and Technology Management, University of Stuttgart, Nobelstr. 12, 70569 Stuttgart, Germany
[2] Helenic Institute of Transportation, 6th km. Charilaou - Thermi Road, 57001 Thermi, Thessaloniki, Greece
Lorenz.Hagenmeyer@iat.uni-stuttgart.de

Abstract. States of hypovigilance cause severe accidents. Technical compensation can be provided by hypovigilance management systems (HVMS). In this paper, existing HVMS are discussed and the need for the development of a novel universal, multimodal HVMS is deducted. The development of such a system is presented and its application is illustrated with two application scenarios.

Keywords: HMI, Safety, Sleepiness, Vigilance.

1 Introduction

Human beings need to sleep. Sleep is not a matter of choice, it is essential and inevitable. The longer someone remains awake, the greater the need to sleep and the more difficult it is to resist falling asleep. Sleep will eventually overpower the strongest intentions and efforts to stay awake (NCSDR/NHTSA, 1998).

Today's "24 hour society" seems to pressure many individuals to sacrifice sleep in favor of other activities, without realizing the negative effects this has on their health and ability to perform a wide range of tasks. Sleepiness reduces alertness and with this, vigilance, and attention, so that the ability to perform is impaired. The speed at which information is processed and the quality of decision-making is also affected (Reissman, 1996).

In addition, as much as 10% of the general population suffers to some degree from sleep disorders, such as: hypersomnia, narcolepsy, daytime functioning in insomniacs and sleep apnea (Backhaus & Riemann, 1999). Sleep disorders may cause extreme tiredness, loss of concentration and a pronounced inability to function normally in one's daily routines.

Both involuntary and voluntary sleep deprivation cause the related phenomena of hypovigilance and, therefore, are among the key causes of serious accidents: According to NASA Aviation Safety Reporting System, approximately 21% of the aviation incidents are fatigue-related. In a similar way, most nuclear accidents (among them Chernobyl and Three-mile Island) have clear fatigue-related causes (Mitler et al,

C. Stephanidis (Ed.): Universal Access in HCI, Part II, HCII 2007, LNCS 4555, pp. 373–382, 2007.

1988). Moreover, more than 40% of automotive accidents on US-highways can be related to hypovigilance (Garder, 1998).

Obviously, the support of technical systems in states of hypovigilance is desirable. In fact, such systems basically are present and are known under the name of *Hypovigilance Management Systems* or *HVMS*.

In principles, HVMS measure the state of vigilance of the respective user and take according measures if a critical state of vigilance with respect to the work task of the user is reached. On the one hand, the user is warned and informed about his/her state of vigilance, on the other hand the system might try to keep the user awake for a certain time (if at all possible) in order to enable the user to finish dangerous actions (e.g. to get off the road when driving tiredly).

However, it has to be mentioned that the systems known so far are mostly in a research state of development. They mainly base on single-sensor approaches and lack reliability. Moreover, most of these systems are not comprehensive, i.e. they focus on one part of the system, e.g. the sensors and neglect the other elements of a HVMS or include only rough approaches to these. Finally, the systems present are restricted to single use contexts such as the car. However, as was outlined above, hypovigilance is a problem in many different use contexts. Therefore, a universal system is needed (Hagenmeyer, 2007).

Clearly, there is a need for the development of a more reliable system that is universal in terms of its utilizability in different use contexts both with respect to the sensors used and the human machine interface (HMI).

2 Development of a Universal HVMS

Such a system was developed within the Sub-Project 4 of the SENSATION Integrated Project, a 6th Framework-Programme research project, co-funded by the DG Information Society of the European Commission, which aims at promoting the health, safety and quality of life of people and protecting the environment by reducing hypovigilance-related accidents and thus the impact on environment through the application of novel micro and nano sensors and related technologies, of low-cost and high-efficiency, for human physiological state monitoring.

Sub-Project 4 “Industrial Applications” of the SENSATION Integrated Project aims to integrate the developed project sensors in multisensorial platforms and use them to detect and predict human operator hypovigilance to promote safety, comfort and quality of life.SP4 involves three major areas of work:

- Development of hypovigilance detection, prediction correlation and operator warning algorithms.
- Development of multi-sensorial systems for hypovigilance detection, prediction, sleep management and operator warning.
- Verification of the developed applications in a series of industrial Pilots and specification of future research needs.

The innovation of Sub-Project 4 is the target to overcome the limitations and restrictions of the existing prototypes and systems, by fulfilling four major requirements:

- To be autonomous: to provide automatically a diagnosis about the user's state.
- To be non-supervised: interpretation of the diagnosis must be performed by an intelligent decision making module and this information should be displayed to the user without any on-line intervention of an expert.
- To be non-intrusive: this excludes all wired sensors.
- To be able to operate in non-constrained environment: as a consequence, such sensors will have to cope with environmental non-controlled conditions.

2.1 Basic Structure of the SENSATION HVMS

The basic structure of the SENSATION HVMS is depicted in figure 1.

Relevant data for the measurement of the vigilance state of the user is gathered by different sensors. In order to reduce traffic on the system communication network, these sensors include a basic pre-processing of data. The sensors communicate with the central system via defined networks: Sensors used close to the body are connected to a body area network (BAN); other sensors such as cameras on the dashboard of a car are directly connected to the local area network (LAN).

The pre-processed data coming from the sensors to the expert system, in a first step, will be combined by means of according algorithms to a vigilance vector, i.e. a vigilance value on a simple scale augmented by the certainty of this value. The warning strategy is implemented in a decision-of-action-to-take-manager; with respect to the use context, it takes the actual vigilance state of the user into account in combination with surrounding variables such as risk level of the actual situation. The action decided in this way is communicated to the user through the respective HMI-elements, which are connected to the expert system though the same BAN/LAN-structure that serves the sensors.

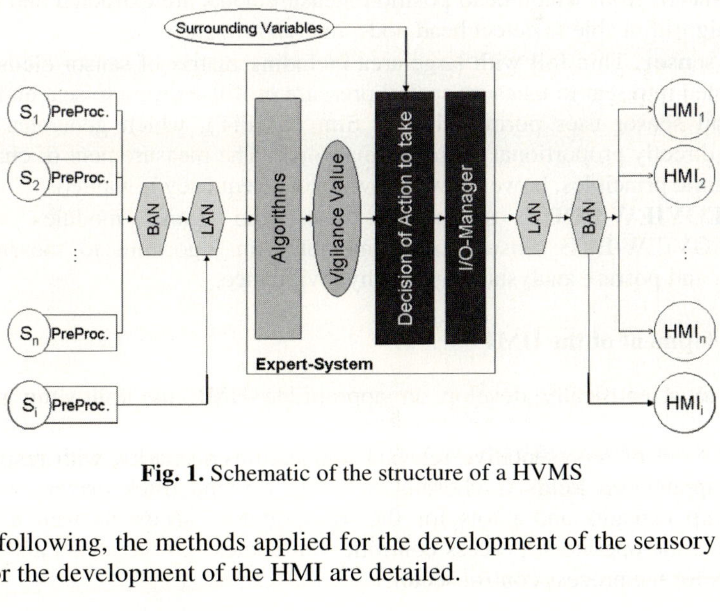

Fig. 1. Schematic of the structure of a HVMS

In the following, the methods applied for the development of the sensory system as well as for the development of the HMI are detailed.

2.2 Development of a Novel Set of Sensors

The HVMS is the central decision system which receives hypovigilance-related measurements from the integrated processing algorithms, which sequentially process signals from a series of novel high-end technology sensors developed within the Sub-Project 2 of the SENSATION Integrated Project and have been selected upon their ability to provide real-time signal processing of physiological parameters related to hypovigilance. Those sensors are listed and briefly described below:

- **STEREOVIEW-EYE sensor.** Video camera platform including 3 cameras for stereovision purpose for different human being supervision application. It includes high performance generation of CMOS camera, targeting driver's eyelid and eye gaze measurement.
- **CAPSENSE sensor.** A capacitive sensor setup targeted at measuring the posture of a seat occupant. The seat can be in a passenger car or the seat of a controller in a plant control room for example. The sensor has the ability to measure whether the seat is occupied at all, if the person is moving on the seat, the head position of the person and some other characteristics.
- **ENOBIO sensor.** Dry electrode for electrophysiology which can be used to measure EEG or other biopotential signals. The novel aspect of this electrode is the electrode skin interface which is provided by a large number of Carbon Nanotubes (CNT) forming a brush-like structure. The aim of this design is to eliminate both the need for gel and the skin preparation needed in traditional electrode applications, hence simplifying the recording of EEG.
- **EARSEN sensor.** It measures the heart beat rhythm, using the difference in absorption taking place when a blood pulse (containing arterial blood) passes between the emitter and receiver of the sensor. Moreover, it includes an inclinometer, from which head position measurements are extracted and processed by an algorithm able to detect head nods, inattention, etc.
- **SEFO sensor.** Thin foil with large area including matrix of sensor elements to be assembled into seat to measure spatial pressure profile exerted to seat and backrest. Seat foil sensor uses porous electret film (EMFiT), which generates electrical charge directly proportional to the normal force. The measurement of charge leads to dynamic principles, however with low corner frequency if wanted.
- **STEREOVIEW-BODY sensor.** It uses the same modules with the STEREOVIEW-EYE sensor but it integrates an algorithm to measure driver activity and posture analysis related to hypovigilance.

2.3 Development of the HMI

In order to scientifically develop an appropriate HMI, the following method is followed:

Firstly, a set of representative relevant applications scenarios with respect to the potential application fields is chosen, including car and truck drivers, locomotive drivers, ship captains and pilots for the transportation sector as well as machine operators, crane operators, process controllers in nuclear power plants and air traffic controllers for the process control sector.

Then, basic requirements categories for the HMI-design with respect to HVMSs are defined. These address requirements and restrictions of the warning strategy, the technical framework, the risk level of the tasks as well as additional aspects, such as the warning not only of the user but of third parties as well. On the basis of this catalogue of basic requirements, all of the chosen scenarios are analysed and, in an additional step, they are clustered to basic requirement groups for warning strategies and HMI-elements. The result of this step of the development process is the deduction of the smallest set possible of basal requirement groups both with respect to warning strategies and HMI-elements.

On the basis of these basal requirement groups, according warning strategies are developed with respect to warning modes necessary and surrounding conditions in order to warn the user as effectively as possible.

Finally, the technical implementation of these warning strategies, i.e. the physical HMI-elements, is developed. Again, the smallest set possible of different HMI-elements is to be designed with respect to the basal requirements and, hence, to the application scenarios.

With the method described above, a multimodal, universal HVMS has been developed which is applicable in all of the application scenarios mentioned:

Upon activation, the system starts in *normal mode* in which a status indicator informs the user about the hypovigilance state monitored and indicates that the system is working properly. Such continuous information should be presented in a way that it is not disturbing the user but should be recallable at any time; a traffic light like status indicator was chosen for this purpose.

The *warning mode* is activated when the user reaches a critical level of hypovigilance. Within this mode, depending on the current hypovigilance state of the user, either a cautionary or an imminent warning is displayed with the aim to stop the user conducting the work task and, by doing so, avoid accidents.

According to Wickens et al. (1998), an effective warning must first draw attention and then inform about the hazard, the potential consequences and give recommendations on how to react. Optionally, a feedback might be required from the addressee in order to confirm the reception of the information. Therefore, for cautionary warnings, the attention of the user is drawn by a complex sound according to DIN ISO 7731 (2002) in combination with a haptic vibration pulse and a bright flash.. Then, more complex information about the hazard, its potential consequences and according countermeasures are presented by means of speech messages. These were preferred vs. text displays because of their higher compatibility with most work tasks in respect of the mobility of the user and interference with the work task itself. Finally, feedback from the user is demanded which is to be given via a push-button. In case no feedback is given, the warning is repeated. If still no feedback is received or if the user reaches a more critical hypovigilance level, an imminent alarm is given which follows the same structure. However, the stimuli to draw attention are intensified by an increased volume, higher pitch and vibration frequency. Moreover, the speech messages are adapted, emphasizing the urgency to quickly react to the warning.

After an imminent warning was given and confirmed, the system switches into the *vigilance maintaining mode* aiming to support the user safely stopping his/her work task, e.g., safely driving to the next exit. The user is informed about the activation of the vigilance maintaining system (VMS) as well as its restricted, short term usefulness by a speech message. The VMS then stimulates the user by means of so called "Landström Sounds": Landström et al. (1998) showed that specific disharmonious sequences of sounds, each lasting around 4 seconds, that are presented in irregular intervals of up to 5 minutes significantly enhance wakefulness. Moreover, a high level of acceptance by the participants could be observed.

The above warning strategy was implemented as a finite state machine in SWITCHBOARD, a software package developed at Fraunhofer IAO with various I/O-capabilities. It runs on a central computing unit which integrates the sensor signals and, computes a vigilance value and decides about the actions to take (compare to the "expert system" in fig. 1). The sensors and HMI-elements were developed in a close-to-body configuration and are connected to the central computing unit via a body area/local area network. A screenshot of the implementation of the warning strategy is depicted in fig. 2.

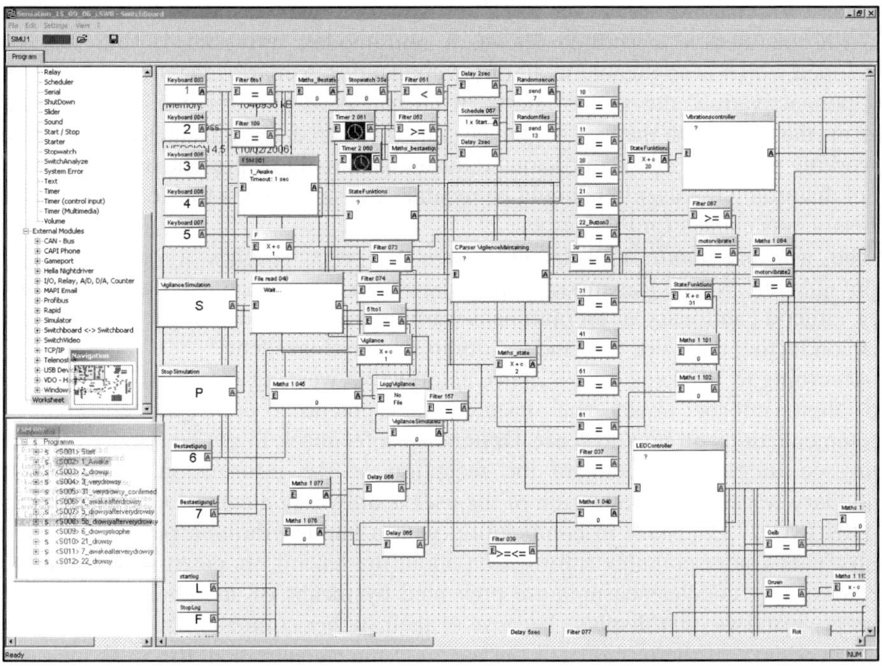

Fig. 2. Screenshot of the SWITCHBOARD-implementation of the warning strategy

The status indicator, visual master alarm and feedback button were integrated in a wrist worn device. (compare to fig. 3; for presentation purposes, all LEDs are activated). Green, yellow and red LEDs were activated according to the respective vigilance state of the user (i.e. awake, sleepy, very sleepy). A flashing white LED in the center of the device was activated in case of imminent alarms. It was integrated in a button which serves for user feedback. Finally, additional buttons for the repetition of speech messages and for volume control were built in.

Fig. 3. Wrist worn HMI-device

Haptic stimuli were presented by a belt mounted vibration device and acoustic stimuli were presented by a standard ear phone.

In this way, a mobile universal system was created. It can effectively be employed in all application scenarios indicated. However, for non mobile workers, the HMI-setup easily can be "translated" into stationary devices in order to achieve a better usability. For example, in a car, the status indicator might be integrated in the rear view mirror or dashboard, the feedback button might be integrated in the steering wheel, the vibration unit could be mounted on the belt and acoustic stimuli might be given by means of the loud speakers.

In the following, two application examples are given, the car driver and the industrial worker.

3 Car Application of the SENSATION HVMS

The Sub-Project 4 deals with a very challenging target; to develop a driver hypovigilance monitoring system that will incorporate the following features:

- Real-time driver hypovigilance monitoring and warning.
- Vehicle-independent, based on driver physiological and behavioural measurements.
- Unobtrusive and user friendly.
- Effective hypovigilance warning and interaction.
- Integrated system using 'smart' high-technology sensors.
- Innovation: driver hypovigilance-related movements monitoring.

To achieve this challenge, an innovative hypovigilance detection algorithm has been developed, which processes hypovigilance-related measurements from a combination of high-end technology sensors developed within the SENSATION Sub-Project 2, presented in Section 2.2 of this paper.

Moreover, the HVMS system of the car application follows the same strategy described within Section 2.3, but incorporates vehicle integrated modules, such as:

- personalized smart-card for driver identification and driving style recording, integrated at the rear-view mirror of the vehicle.

- visual output of the three warning strategy levels, above the smart card reader, also integrated at the rear-view mirror.
- visual output for critical stage warning, visualized at the rear view mirror as a flashing triangle.
- seat-belt vibrator for haptic warning output.
- sound warnings through tones and speech messages through the car speakers.

The figure below, demonstrates the SENSATION driver hypovigilance monitoring car demonstrator setup.

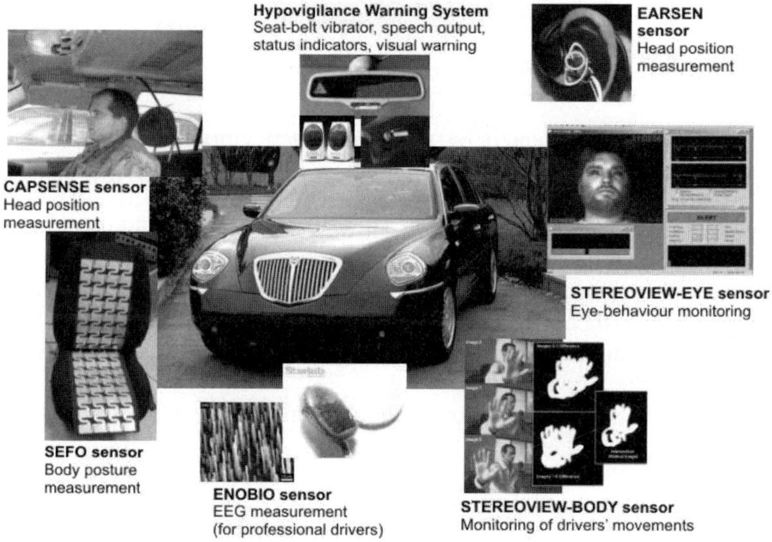

Fig. 4. SENSATION car application HVMS

4 Industrial Worker Application of the SENSATION HVMS

For an experimental evaluation of the HVMS with high practical relevance, a typical work task of an industrial worker such as rim band welding was selected: It is monotonous, has a long duration, has a high complexity, involves working memory, imposes external control on the industrial worker and is often lowly automated. Moreover, these tasks are often conducted in night shifts.

A rim band is a metal component of a television screen. Its function is to counter the vacuum induced tensions in the glass tube, thus increasing strength and safety of the tube. Furthermore, the rimband holding the tube is mounted into the television or monitor housing by means of stackable lugs welded to the rim band.

Welding rim bands and stackable lugs to rim bands are repetitive positioning tasks which are carried out in a three-shift schedule. It requires mobility and is known to produce different kinds of mistakes (Bonnet, 2000).

This work task was reproduced in a controlled laboratory environment (see fig. 4).

Fig. 5. Setup of the reproduced rim band welding station

Usability experiments were conducted with 24 students. These were divided into three parallel groups which were controlled for sex and chronotype: control group (no warnings), treatment group (warnings of the SENSATION HVMS) and positive control group (random warnings).

A baseline measurement was conducted in the late afternoon. After a night of sleep deprivation, the actual measurements were conducted.

Most participants found the HVMS easy to use (12/13). The functions were easy to learn (12/14) and were easy to remember (12/13). All participants found it easy to understand the speech messages (13/13). The content was clear (12/13) and easy to remember (12/13). Two out of six participants in the random warning group declared that they followed the warning message(s). In the Sensation warning group, five out of seven participants declared that they have followed the instructions. A high compliance to the warnings of the HVMS can be deducted.

The experiment indicates that the use of HVMSs could support hypovigilant workers. However, it should be mentioned that such technical assistance should only be provided when no other countermeasures against sleepiness such as proper shift design and sleep hygiene are effective.

References

Backhaus, J., Riemann, D.: Schlafstörungen. Fortschritte in der Psychotherapie. Göttingen: Hogrefe (1999)

Bonnet, M.: Sleep Deprivation, pp. 53–71. W.B. Saunders Co, New York (2000)

DIN ISO 7731. Gefahrensignale für öffentliche Bereiche und Arbeitsstätten. Akustische Gefahrensignale (2002)

Garder, P.: Continuous Shoulder Rumble-Strips - A safety evaluation. In. CSRS Seminar, Linkoeping (August 1998)

Landström, U., Englund, B., Nordström, B., Aström, A.: Laboratory Studies of a Sound System that Maintains Wakefulness. Perceptual and Motor Skills 86(1), 147–161 (1998)

Löher, L., Hagenmeyer, L.: Gestaltungsrichtlinien für die Nutzerschnittstelle von Hypovigilanz-Management-Systemen. In: Innovationen für Arbeit und Organisation, pp. 39–42. GfA-Press, Dortmund (2006)

Reissman, C.J.: The Alert Driver. A Trucker's Guide to Sleep, Fatigue, and Rest in our 24-Hour Society. American Trucking Associations, Alexandria (1996)

Wickens, C.D., Gordon, S.E., Liu, Y.: An introduction to human factors engineering. Addison Wesley Longman, New York (1998)

Towards Cultural Adaptability to Broaden Universal Access in Future Interfaces of Driver Information Systems

Rüdiger Heimgärtner[1], Lutz-Wolfgang Tiede[1], Jürgen Leimbach[2], Steffen Zehner[2], Nhu Nguyen-Thien[1], and Helmut Windl[1]

[1] Siemens AG, Im Gewerbepark C25, 93055 Regensburg, Germany
[2] Siemens AG, VDO-Str. 1, 64832 Babenhausen, Germany
{Ruediger.Heimgaertner, Lutz-Wolfgang.Tiede, Juergen.Leimbach, Steffen.Zehner,Nhu.Nguyen-Thien, Helmut.Windl}@siemens.com

Abstract. This paper elucidates and discusses some aspects of cultural adaptability which aid usability and universal access. We describe the concept, influence and Use Cases of cultural adaptability in driver information and assistance systems exemplified by a portable navigation system. Thereby, the reasons, advantages and problems of using adaptability regarding the driving safety and the driver preferences will be addressed. Differences in the amount of information for map display and in interaction behavior which depend on the *cultural* background of the users (e.g. attitude, preference, skill etc.). We explain how cultural adaptability can improve usability and how it has a share in universal access. Finally, a short outlook into the future of adaptive driver information and assistance systems closes our reflections.

Keywords: cultural adaptability, cultural user interface design, adaptive HMI (Human Machine Interaction/Interface), driver navigation systems, driver information systems, driver assistance systems.

1 Necessity and Benefit of Cultural Adaptability

Today driver information and assistance systems are very complex both in functionality and in usage. Generally, the design and development of user interfaces for vehicles includes manifold aspects e.g. information visualization, haptic technology etc. which are challenges to HMI designers and software developers. Driver information and assistance systems have to integrate a lot of data from several models and sources such as driving situation model, driver preference model, driver intention model and driving history as well as vehicle data [4]. Within the infotainment systems of a car, alongside other components – including radio, telephone, CD or DVD player and telematics unit – especially the car navigation system demands many highly interactive activities from the driver. Furthermore, it also provides many important and calculated pieces of information together with vehicle data to other devices (e.g. data about the driving situation). In this sense, the driver navigation system plays a prominent role of intersection within the round dance

C. Stephanidis (Ed.): Universal Access in HCI, Part II, HCII 2007, LNCS 4555, pp. 383–392, 2007.

of driver information and assistance systems. Therefore, it will be used as an exemplary system in this paper to elucidate cultural adaptability.

In order to calculate for example the optimal route, it is necessary to take into account all factors relating to the driver: preferences, mental and physical state as well as outside aspects such as weather, road conditions etc. Interaction between the driver and the system takes place not only before travel, e.g. when the destination is entered, but also whilst driving. This interaction includes the observation and reaction to the maneuver guidance and making decisions about a desired alternative route in the case of traffic jams. However, in addition to the traditional human factors, the cultural diversity and the corresponding emotional appeal include one inescapable factor: the configuration of the interface between the driver and the navigation system must prevent the driver experiencing an excessive mental workload [11]. The information presented to the driver needs to be suitable for the specific driving situation, the driver workload as well as the cultural driver preferences (e.g. to reduce information complexity).

In this case, adaptability is an appropriate solution because the driver does not have the opportunity to manually adapt the setup of the information presentation according to the special requirements depending on the situation. Especially for stressful situations, the HMI of the driver information system has to be adaptive to reduce the mental workload of the driver [12], depending on the driver's cultural background [14]. According to the principle of cross-cultural adaptation of HMI, the culturally dependent behavior of the driver has to be measured and recorded over time in order to obtain information about the parameters necessary to be able to culturally adapt the HMI [2]. Either the system suggests the adequate form of information presentation to the driver (Computer Supported Adaptation) or it adapts it automatically (Automatic Adaptation) whilst the driver is actually concentrating on driving [8]. E.g. difficult routes with high rate of accidents can be avoided most notably for beginners by analyzing the routes as well as the driving behavior and by adapting the route calculation and the information presentation according to the recognized facts.

The concept of adaptability is found in the HMI roadmaps of most automobile manufacturers nowadays: the basic concepts of adaptability for future projects have to be developed anyway. Moreover, the engineering process necessary to obtain adaptability, promotes the usability of the devices. To achieve cultural adaptability at all, i.e. to be able to perform adaptation by the initiative of the system according to the cultural differences in HMI dependent on the user needs, the cultural differences must be determined by intercultural usability engineering [6]. Including such methods from the beginning of HMI design and development also reduces costs in future developing and planning for product (regional) variants as well as increases usability [5].

Furthermore, adaptability will go along with good usability [7] by adapted user and system models, shorter training times by fast adaptation to the driver as well as in less distraction from traffic and mental workload by automatically optimizing and adapting the HMI according to the current driving situation to increase driving safety [12]. The acceptance of intercultural adaptive intelligent user interfaces is guaranteed, when the user is aware of the changes in the user interface driven by the system or when the changes are very small and happen over a long period of time so that the driver does not recognize them because he is familiarized slowly (except in dangerous situations where the system must adapt immediately and automatically according to driving situation). The resulting effect of improved usability by cultural adaptability is that many more drivers are able to use the same systems in the car more easily and with contentment which contributes to universal access.

To make driver information and assistance systems culturally adaptive, at least the following steps are necessary:

Step 1: The cultural differences in using the systems have to be determined during the analyzing phase of the product development process. This gives first insight into the different user preferences and system requirements for markets with different cultures (cultural preferences).

Step 2: The results have to be taken into account in the design phase for new products and the system architecture has to be modified and extended according to the adaptations necessary to support the cultural needs of the user for existing products. This allows the end-user to manually adapt the system according to individual cultural preferences (personalization).

Step 3: At runtime, the system has to detect the user preferences during operating and controlling the system in different driving situations in order to determine the tendency of the cultural attitudes of the driver and to adapt the HMI accordingly and automatically (adaptability).

Integrating all the three steps emerges as the most potent effect to help broadening universal access because the system is able to adapt itself to the special needs of *many more users* than those who would be covered by driver information and assistance systems that only dispose default parameters (without cultural adaptability).

1.1 Cultural HMI Patterns (Step 1)

To be able to adapt a system manually by personalization or automatically by adaptability to the cultural needs of the user, the first step is to investigate what must be adapted, i.e. to find out the differences in the cultural needs of the users as well as the cultural differences in HMI on all levels of HMI localization (user interface, functionality, and interaction) concerning Look & Feel. In this context, topics such as presentation of information (e.g. colors, time and date format, icons, font size) and language (e.g. font, writing direction, naming) or dialog design (e.g. menu structure and complexity, dialog form, layout, widget positions) as well as interaction design (e.g. navigation concept, system structure, interaction path, interaction speed) are affected [13].

One promising method to accomplish this task is to observe and analyze the interaction of users, from different cultures, with the system by an appropriate automated analysis tool [2]. From this, cross-cultural usability metrics can be derived, which can be used for cultural adaptability. The "Intercultural Interaction Analysis" tool (IIA tool) was developed to automatically obtain quantitative data regarding cultural differences in HMI by simulating use cases of navigation systems [3]. The main objective was to observe and analyze the interaction behavior of users from different cultures with a computer system to determine different interaction patterns according to the cultural background of the users (if any).[1] A quantitative study using

[1] For detailed information about the IIA tool, please refer to [2].

this online tool has shown that there are different *cultural interaction patterns* that can be measured quantitatively by a computer system using *cultural interaction indicators* that depend on the interaction behavior imprinted by the culture of the user. The cultural differences, which were found, are *statistically discriminating enough* to enable computer systems to detect different cultural interaction patterns automatically and to relate users to a certain culture behavior, which in turn makes *cultural adaptability possible* in the first place. The most classifying interaction indicators regarding the cultural preferences of the users can be summarized in the following categories: number of tasks, time period between display of information, display time of the presented information, number of mouse clicks and key presses, number of acknowledged system messages, number of refused system messages, number of list entries, time to finish task cases, number of mouse moves, number of interaction breaks, number of initiated functions, number of interactions, interaction times.[2]

This preparatory work contributes to the first step to broaden universal access in future driver information and assistance systems: now we have first knowledge about the cultural differences in the interaction behavior of the user with the system.

1.2 Scope of Cultural Adaptability (Step 2)

The interaction strategies within in-car devices/systems are connected to their main functions and divided into primary functions such as driving, navigating and secondary functions e.g. listening, talking, phoning, entertaining etc. All these are interacting.

Use Cases, which need massive interaction, are e.g. destination input, map interpretation and maneuver guidance [2]. According to the Use Cases, there are several areas in driver information and assistance systems where adaptability is reasonable, e.g. maneuver generation, voice guidance (instructions and timing), guidance pictograms, map display, dynamic routing / traffic message data handling (e.g. by TMC), multimedia / multimodal HMI in general, destination input, speech recognition, help concept controlled by speech, interaction management and dialog management. Therefore, cultural adaptability does not only concern the look and feel of the user interface, but also the interaction devices (e.g. *EasyCo*, a HMI concept based on touch pad and handwriting recognition [10]) as well as the number and the kind of system functions that can dynamically change according to the driver preferences, the driver state and the driving situation. To be able to take into account these complex information structures simultaneously and to let the driver's mental workload be as low as possible at the same time, it is necessary to employ cultural adaptability additionally to cultural pre-settings or profiles. Automatic adaptation affects country-specific aspects including format, modality, menu structure, content of menu, alternative routes (scenic, sporty, short, fast…), guidance, map display, language, advice for beginners or experts, number of messages, length of texts, number of hints, degree of entertainment or ratio of information to entertainment, etc.

---

[2] For a description of the results and the test setting in more detail, please refer to [3].

Special Use Cases, which can be solved by cultural adaptability, are the following:

- Adapting the scrolling speed of list boxes according to the speed of the touch drive usage
- Showing the right information (relevance) and the right amount of information (quantity) according to driving conditions
- Knowing the characteristics of the road in advance (virtual horizon) supports driving with foresight: the driver is warned by getting information in good time (anticipative driving)
- Changing the lower-beam headlamp such that the light automatically falls into the direction of the curve
- Using intelligent automatic gearing (especially on mountain roads)
- Calculating routes according to the driver preferences e.g. differences in gender
- Computing destination time and optimizing computation of routes according to fast or slow drivers
- Automatically showing of lanes and/or guidance information in the head-up-display.

Knowing those Use Cases for cultural adaptability enables to extend the architecture of such systems by the parameters and values as well as the adaptability algorithms to enable adaptability according to the needs of the driver to fulfill the step 2 on the way to universal access.

1.3 Demonstration of Cultural Adaptability (Step 3)

To demonstrate worldwide cultural adaptability, the first prerequisite is to manage that the adaptive HMI supports international fonts (e.g. Unicode). Furthermore, it is necessary for the design of a cultural adaptive system to take into account the differences of the desired cultures where the product will be sold. Tables consisting of the differences between the desired *cultures* (countries, ethnic groups, dialects, gender, age, preferences etc.) must be created. The results need to be integrated into the mental driver model and implemented in prototypes. The represented cognitive models of the user (driver) have to be adjusted according to the desired country.

The results of the online study using the IIA tool have been implemented in this way in a mobile navigation system based on Windows CE building a cultural adaptive HMI demonstrator to proof the concept of cultural adaptability of the HMI. In Figure 1 you can see the map display of this demonstrator exemplifying information density and information coding for Chinese (left picture) and for German (right picture) users. It is possible to adjust the number of POI according to the needs of the users: reducing disturbing or increasing information as needed. Moreover, colors can be adapted to the recognized culture of the user to provide familiarity and to avoid confusion: according to the interaction of the user with the demonstrator, the number of POI (many vs. few) as well as the color design is changed, e.g. main roads (yellow vs. white), highways (green vs. blue), calculated route (red vs. yellow). Further research should deliver more specific information to enable the development of these models in greater detail and to generate a sophisticated future adaptive HMI concept. Now, tests are done to verify the adaptive algorithm and to get the level of user acceptance and the usability of adaptive HMI to fulfill step 3 on the way to universal access.

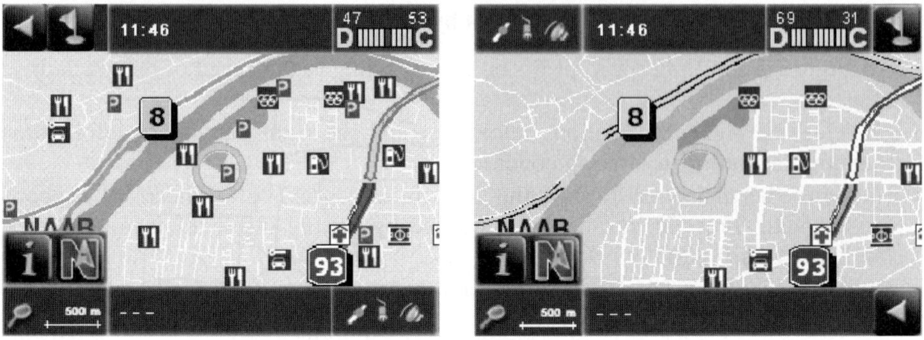

Fig. 1. Different number of POI and colors according to different needs of information density and information coding between Chinese and German users

2 Broadening Universal Access (Integration of Steps 1-3)

The objective of cultural adaptive HMI in driver information and assistance systems is the situation-referential adaptation of cultural aspects of the Graphical User Interface (GUI) and Speech User Interface (SUI). For cultural adaptive HMI user models are employed, which are averaged over all users of a cultural group (e.g. information dimming or multi-modal dialogs according to the different requirements in China and Germany respectively, according to the current situation and context). Additionally, there are some target user groups of drivers that have their own characteristics or "culture" of using such systems in the vehicle e.g. driving beginners vs. experienced drivers, old vs. young people, female vs. male users, HMI developer vs. HMI user drivers, vehicle of brand A vs. vehicle of brand B drivers (regarding HMI paradigm and motto), professional vs. hobby drivers, vehicle type A (e.g. truck) vs. vehicle type B (e.g. car) drivers, vehicles with or without cargo loading / trailers, drivers with handicaps, cheap vs. expensive car drivers, pragmatic vs. hedonic drivers and drivers of different countries and nationality.

These items are connected to the culture of the driver. However, in this sense, the meaning of the usual conception of *culture* as ethnical determined is extended to the *individual culture* of the driver (e.g. individualistic but culturally influenced style of eating, driving, interacting, using a device etc.). The individual driving behavior including aspects such as fast, stressed, hectic, sporty, or unsteady driving depends on the kind of cultural imprinting of the driver related to the group he belongs to (beginners, intermediates, professionals, experts), or gender and on the cultural background (using bumpers for parking, buzzer frequency, interaction times, interaction frequencies, etc. cf. e.g. [14]). The data collected about driving contains important information about the preferences of the driver such as the preferred type of routes, average speed, default tours, short or long tours, along rivers or hills, etc. Moreover, the interaction styles can vary strongly (e.g. reasonable, rational, arbitrary, sequentially fast, well-considered, haptic, visual, auditory, linguistic, etc.). By associating these aspects with the cultural models, implications can be made to culturally adapt the HMI and the functionality of such systems. For example, accidents are caused statistically by very young as well as very old drivers because they are not so experienced or need more time to interact with the system and to react in the right way according to dangerous events during driving (partly because of lacking technological knowledge and partly because of physical handicaps and lower mental flexibility) respectively. Here the interaction differences of old vs. young drivers have to be regarded depending on their cultural imprinting. Another aspect concerns the differences in the amount of information to display as well as the differences in interaction behavior which depend on the culture of the users (e.g. at country level like Chinese vs. German drivers).

Therefore, the "culture" of special driver groups has to be considered in the design of driver information and assistance systems. If such a system "knows" those cultural preferences of the driver, it can adapt itself to the cultural expectations of the driver regarding the driver behavior. In this sense, cultural adaptability broadens universal access, because many more users (even physically handicapped or mentally less flexible people) can use the same device (than without using cultural adaptability).

3 Discussion

It is problematic that an automatic adaptation (adaptability) depends on maximum data when observing new users: the system needs more data in order to be able to release information about the user as well as to be able to infer the characteristics of the user regarding information presentation, interaction and dialogs. Furthermore, the knowledge gathered about the user can be *misleading* or simply false. Hence, the reliability of assumptions can be a problem [9]. The behavior of the system has to be in accordance with the beliefs of the user to prevent unexpected situations. Another problem is that legal restrictions also have to be taken into account. Only the effects of driver actions are allowed to be permanently stored, but not the log file of the personalized driving sessions themselves [1]. As long as no solution is available, which can achieve meaningful adoptions from minimum data automatically; it remains necessary to investigate standard parameters and their values very early in the development process, long before runtime, in order to integrate them into the system. Therefore, it is necessary that the system already has corresponding user-knowledge (standard parameters) before the user's first contact with the system occurs. Before using the system for the first time, it must be adjusted e.g. to the nationality of the user (which indicates the main affiliation of the user to a cultural group) and the corresponding cultural parameters can be placed simultaneously as standard parameters for the desired country. Furthermore, the adaptive system also obtains adequate characteristics of the user more quickly at runtime, because there is "more time" to collect the culture-specific data for the user, since a basic adaptation to the most important user preferences has already been performed before runtime (by putting the standard parameters into the system). Thus, designing an appropriate system according to the user in the design phase helps to avoid the problems rising from adaptability. Additionally, there are many open questions that have to be addressed very carefully: How many dynamic changes are optimal for and will be accepted by the user? When does a hidden adaptation occur? How can this be prevented? How much does the user trust the adaptive system? E.g., adaptability should not surprise the user but it must be in accordance with his mental model.

Therefore, sudden changing must be prevented or space limits for the automatic enlargement of buttons for handicapped users have to be taken into account during the design process. Nevertheless, even if answering those questions demand higher development costs or increased effort, this is no argument against adaptive automotive systems since adaptability is necessary and beneficial (cf. chapter 1).

4 Conclusion

It is necessary to apply adaptability in driver information and assistance systems because:

- It is hard for the driver to handle the functional and informational complexity of such systems in extreme driving situations: the mental workload, which is caused by all possible senses (i.e. resulting from visible, audible, haptical, etc. information), simply exceeds the mental capacity of the driver.
- The mental workload should be held in acceptable limits in dangerous driving situations if the system adapts the information flow with the user automatically. Due to this fact, adaptability has also to take into account external input sources (e.g. from pre-crash sensors).
- The output modality has to be adapted automatically to achieve the lowest workload (e.g. using of different displays).

It is also necessary to *adapt culturally* in driver information and assistance systems because

- The driver preferences have to be considered and covered, which depend on the cultural background of the driver.
- The cultural background of the driver also determines the behavior in certain (especially dangerous) driving situations.
- There are many different groups of drivers, which exhibit their own "culture" (e.g. interaction behavior cf. [2]) whether regarding groups at international level (e.g. countries) or within the national level (e.g. social, ethnic, or driver groups).
- The local market for cars has changed more and more to a worldwide market, future infotainment systems have to handle the demands of various drivers and various cultures. This aspect can only be covered within a single system, if this system is adaptable and configurable.

The cultural differences in HMI found using *special combinations of cultural interaction indicators* are *statistically discriminating enough* to enable computer systems to detect different cultural interaction patterns automatically and to relate users to a certain culture behavior, which in turn makes *cultural adaptability possible* in the first place.

To design cultural adaptive systems some formation principles in the vehicle context have to be taken into account:

- The distraction potential (the mental, visual and audio workload) of the driver must be held as low as possible.
- The HMI must be simple and safe in order not to reduce the driving security.

- The reason for the adaptation (e.g. the current driving situation) and the kind of adaptation (e.g. structuring menus or renaming soft keys etc.) must be comprehensible for the driver at all times. Therefore, the frame of reference is not allowed to be altered too strongly.
- The frequency of the adaptation has to be kept as low as possible.
- Multi-modal dialog design requires that the driver can choose the modality freely anytime.
- The possibility that all haptically usable interaction elements can be accompanied by verbal output has to be guaranteed in following the motto "speak what you see".
- The interruption and resumption of dialogs and interactions has to be possible.

Using methods of artificial intelligence help to fulfill the steps to get cultural adaptability to broaden universal access applying the cross-cultural adaptive HMI principles [2] such as learning the differences in the interaction of the users of different culture, classifying interaction patterns according to culture, determining the user preferences according to culture, adapting HMI according to the user preferences, learning user preferences by observation of HMI over time and integrating knowledge from observation into the system's user model.

5 Future Outlook

The examples of cultural differences in the map display according to information density and color-coding (as shown in 1.3) are first realizations on the way to cultural adaptability in HMI. However, stronger interactive invasive changes require more complex systems. A layer approach for intelligent services, comprising the architecture and the priorities of at least two models must be employed. The data-oriented driving situation model describes the current driving situation which is defined by the values of the variables of the vehicle such as speed, lateral and longitudinal acceleration as well as the position of the vehicle (traffic jam, highway, parking place etc.) or the reason for driving (business, spare time, race etc.) and so on. The driver workload model contains information about the mental or physical stress of the driver indicated by variables such as heart rate, galvanic skin response values or error clicks and task failures. Thus, infotainment solutions for cars will change dramatically in the near future. Constantly increasing functions (e.g. Advanced Driver Assistant Systems, Autonomous Driving) combined with a large number of nomadic devices (e.g. MP3 player, personal navigation systems, mobile phones) are requiring flexible, safe and adaptable HMI solutions for the world market. Therefore, the design of future driver information and assistance systems will take into account more strongly the culturally influenced personal preferences and needs of the drivers using methods of cultural adaptability to broaden universal access.

Acknowledgments

We thank Wolfgang Gall, Thomas Gallner, Hans-Peter Reiters, and Dr. Hans-Wilhelm Rühl for the fruitful discussions whose ideas influenced this paper significantly. Furthermore we like to thank everyone who was and is supporting the cultural adaptability project.

References

1. De Bra, P., Aroyo, L., Chepegin, V.: The Next Big Thing: Adaptive Web-Based Systems. Journal of Digital Information, vol. 5(1)
2. Heimgärtner, R.: Research in Progress: Towards Cross-Cultural Adaptive Human-Machine-Interaction in Automotive Navigation Systems. In: Day, D., del Galdo, E.M. (eds.) IWIPS 2005. Proceedings of the Seventh International Workshop on Internationalization of Products and Systems, The Netherlands, pp. 7–111. Grafisch Centrum, Amsterdam (2005)
3. Heimgärtner, R.: Measuring Cultural Differences in Human Computer Interaction as Preparatory Work for Cross-Cultural Adaptability in Navigation Systems. In: Useware 2006, VDI-Bericht Nr. 1946, VDI-Verlag, Düsseldorf, pp. 301–314(2006)
4. Heimgärtner, R., Holzinger, A.: Towards Cross-Cultural Adaptive Driver Navigation Systems. In: Workshops-Proc. HCI UE Usability Symposium Vienna 2005, pp. 53–68 (2005)
5. Holzinger, A.: Usability Engineering for Software Developers. Communications of the ACM (ISSN: 0001-0782) 48(1), 71–74 (2005)
6. Honold, P.: Interkulturelles Usability Engineering. Eine Untersuchung zu kulturellen Einflüssen auf die Gestaltung und Nutzung technischer Produkte. VDI-Verlag, Düsseldorf (2000)
7. Jameson, A.: Adaptive Interfaces and Agents. In: Jacko, J., Sears, A. (eds.) Human Computer Interaction Handbook, pp. 305–330. Erlbaum, New Jersey (2003)
8. Kobsa, A.: Adaptivität und Benutzermodellierung in interaktiven Softwaresystemen. In: 17. Fachtagung KI, Springer, Berlin (1993)
9. Kobsa, A.: User modeling in dialog systems: potentials and hazards. AI & Society, vol. 4 (3), pp. 214–240
10. Nguyen-Thien, N., Basche, B., Hostmann, D., Pichl, O.: EasyCo – Ein innovatives Bedienkonzept für Car-Multimedia- und Navigationssysteme. In: Useware 2004: Nutzergerechte Gestaltung Technischer Systeme, VDI-Bericht Nr. 1837, pp. 47–55. VDI-Verlag, Düsseldorf (2004)
11. Piechulla, W., Mayser, C., Gehrke, H., Konig, W.: Reducing driver's mental workload by means of an adaptive man-machine interface. Transportation Research Part F: Traffic Psychology and Behaviour, vol. 6(4), pp. 233–248
12. Recarte, M.A., Nunes, L.M.: Mental Workload While Driving: Effects on Visual Search, Discrimination, and Decision Making. Journal of Experimental Psychology: Applied, 9 (2), pp. 119–137
13. Röse, K., Liu, L., Zühlke, D.: Design Issues in Mainland China: Demands for a Localized Human-Machine-Interaction Design. In: Johannsen, G. (ed.) 8th IFAC/IFIPS/IFORS/IEA Symposium on Analysis, Design, and Evaluation of Human-Machine Systems, pp. 17–22. Preprints, Kassel (2001)
14. Xie, C.-q., Parker, D.: A social psychological approach to driving violations in two Chinese cities. Transportation Research Part F: Traffic Psychology and Behaviour, vol. 5(4), pp. 293–308

A Multi-modal Architecture for Intelligent Decision Making in Cars

Qamir Hussain[1] and Ing-Marie Jonsson[2]

[1] QHC Consulting Ltd. Dublin, Ireland,
[2] Ansima Inc., Los Gatos, CA, USA
qhussain@qhcconsulting.com, ingmarie@ansima.com

Abstract. This paper describes a software architecture named "Gatos" engineered for intelligent decision making. The architecture is built on a distributed multi-agent system cougaar. Gatos provides a solution for sensor fusion. We propose using multiple sensors to monitor driver status, driving performance, and the driving environment in order to address bad driving behavior. Our approach for a Driving Monitor is based on both monitoring and regulating driver behavior. The system is designed to intervene and to interact with the driver in real time (if possible) to regulate their behavior and promote safe driving. A prototype is implemented using a driving simulator, but infrastructure buildup and new in-vehicle technologies make this a feasible solution for vehicles on the road.

Keywords: software agents distributed computing, multi-agent, parallel computing, driving simulator, driving behavior, driver status, driver monitoring.

1 Introduction

We are investigating how different aspects of driver state, traffic and driving environment affect driving behaviors. To address this, we are running numerous studies using driving simulators [1-5], paying particular attention to how drivers interact with and react to different types of speech based in-vehicle systems. One of the goals of these studies is to identify how to interact with a driver in real time without having a negative impact on driving performance. If a driver is found to be in a state not consistent with safe driving, it then might be necessary to intervene and influence the driver to move into a state that is consistent with safe driving performance. A driver's state can be measured in various ways. Sensors such as EEG are useful for identifying novelty, complexity, and unexpectedness, as well as emotional excitement and anxiety[6]. Unfortunately EEG is awkward to use in a vehicle because the sensors have to be attached to the scalp. Autonomic activity, including heart rate, blood pressure, blood pulse volume, respiration, temperature, pupil dilation, skin conductivity, and more recently, muscle tension (electromyography (EMG)) is relatively easy to measure. Certain measures of autonomic activity have proven reliable at distinguishing basic emotions. Heart rate increases most during fear, followed by anger, sadness, happiness, surprise, and

C. Stephanidis (Ed.): Universal Access in HCI, Part II, HCII 2007, LNCS 4555, pp. 393–400, 2007.

finally disgust, which shows almost no change in heart rate[7-9]. Heart rate also increases during excitement, and mental concentration. Decreases in heart rate indicate relaxation and can be induced by attentive visual and audio observation, as well as the processing of pleasant stimuli [6]. Blood pressure increases during stress and decreases during relaxation.

Combined measures of multiple autonomic signals show promise as components of an emotion recognition system. Many autonomic signals can also be measured in reasonably non-obstructive ways (e.g., through user contact with mice and keyboards; [10]). In the same manner our approach to monitor driver state is based on non-intrusive sensors that can be placed in a car, in the steering wheel, in the seat, in the seatbelt, in the rearview mirror and on the dashboard. The Driving Monitor does not base assessment of driving behavior on the driver state alone, the system also uses sensory input from two other sources 1) the system also gathers driver behavior information such as speed, lane position and distance to other road users and objects and 2) information from the driving environment such as road layout, traffic and weather.

The Driving Monitor can be implemented in a driving simulator. This is our first choice since it gives the possibility to work within a closed and ideal world assumption. All information ranging from driving behavior to traffic and weather is available to the system. The system can also be implemented in a vehicle. This, however, reduces the number of input sources radically. Instead of having full access, we have to rely on information available via CAN bus, other attached sensors such as cameras, GPS and maps for road layout, and third party sources for traffic and weather information. The 'real world' version of the Driving Monitor is hence limited when compared to the simulator version.

The Driving Monitor relies on creating an aura around the car and the drivers. This aura indicates the active safety area of the car., see Figure 1.

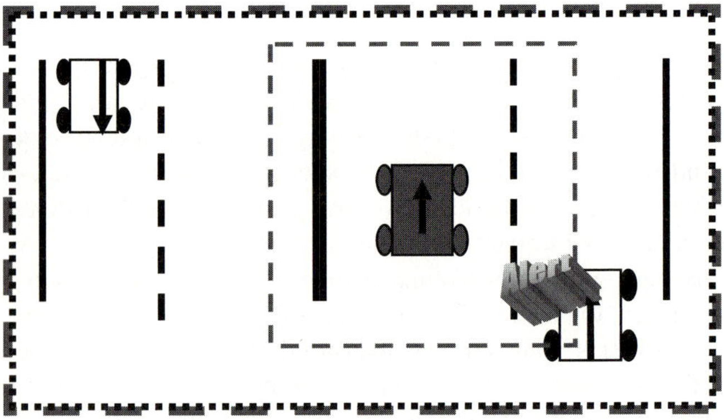

Fig. 1. Overview of Driving Monitor

The subject vehicle is surrounded by a dotted rectangle red in the illustration above (Figure 1) (this could be a sphere instead). This rectangle denotes the active area, and all activity is monitored within this area. The driver state and driving behavior are monitored by sensors within the car, and the driving environment is tracked and monitored using a combination of sensors in the car and the instrumented infrastructure. The active area observed by the Driving Monitor can change dynamically based on driver actions or driving performance to give flexibility in the amount of data used. For instance:

1. When the driver is reversing the active area is shifted to be behind the car and driver.
2. When the driver is making right or left turns (or changing lanes) the active area shifts to the left or to the right accordingly.
3. When the driver is driving slowly the active area shrinks.
4. When the driver is speeding the active area grows as a greater distance needs to be considered for safe driving.

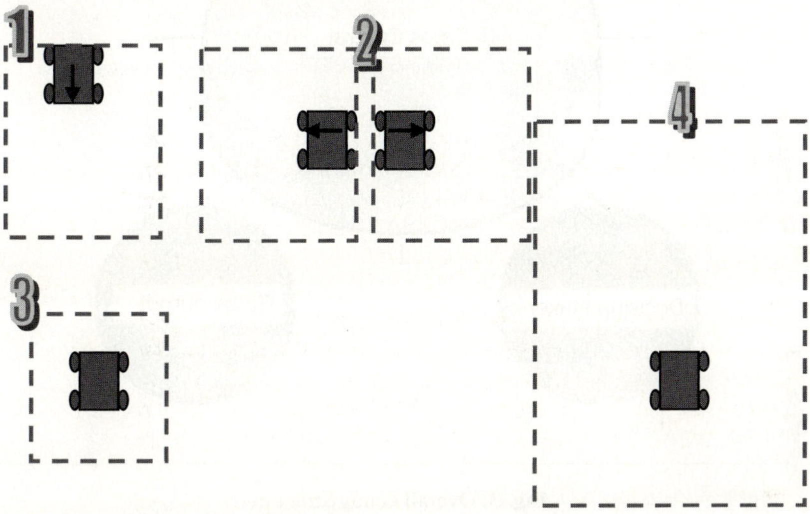

Fig. 2. Some configurations of the active are for the Driving Monitor

The interactions initiated by the Driving Monitor should, among other things, be affected by the location of the alerts. Identified threats located in the drivers blind spots should most likely be presented to the driver differently than threats in the driver's field of vision, be it in front or behind the driver.

2 Gatos

The task that Gatos is presented with is to build software that can combine input from many different sensors, working at different speeds, and making intelligent decisions to help maintain safe driving. Agent oriented solutions, and especially fine grained distributed agent systems are well suited for tasks like this. With a hierarchy of agents, there is one agent per sensor, and that agent is responsible for monitoring its inputs sending its data to the agent that is at the next level of hierarchy. The receiving agent takes this and input from many other sensors. It combines the inputs, makes calculations and finally delivers a regular stream of decisions regarding driver state, driver behavior, driving environment or a combination thereof. This agent's decision making capabilities are scriptable making it possible to update the agent's decision base and reasoning base at run time.

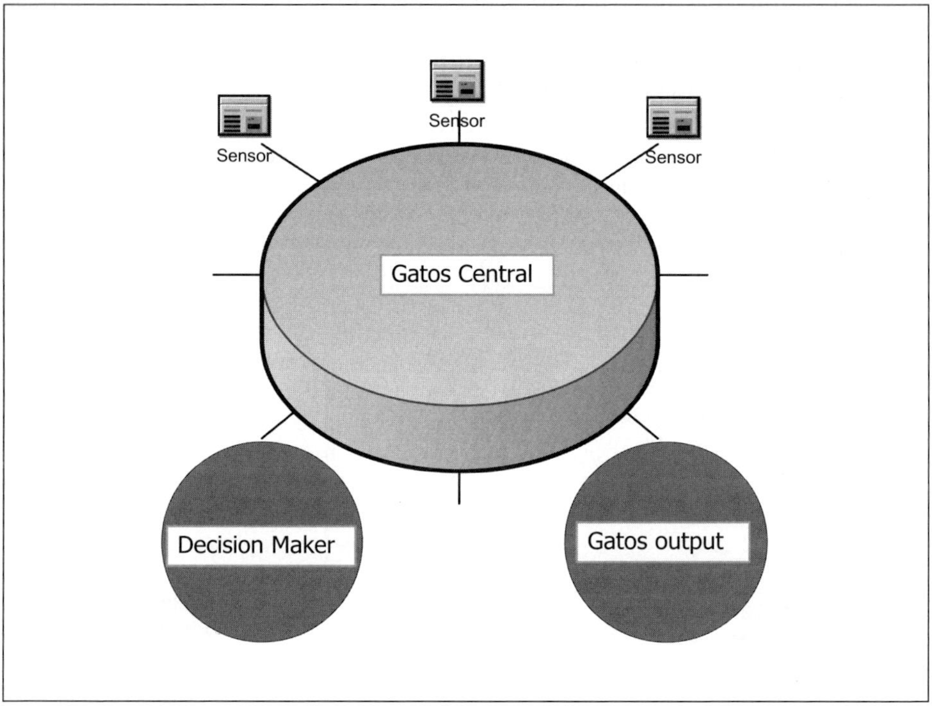

Fig. 3. Overall Gatos Structure

2.1 Distributed Architecture

From the outset it was decided to use a distributed architecture so that devices could be added dynamically and if devices left the system during runtime through failure the system would continue to function albeit with reduced capability.

2.2 Cougaar

Cougaar was chosen as the backbone over other agent systems due to its flexibility and ability to function as a true distributed system.

Cougaar also had many other properties that made it an excellent choice for the backbone of Gatos. Chief among these is that it's a true agent platform where the granularity of agents is defined by the application built on Cougaar and not by Cougaar itself [11, 12]. It is also general purpose giving us flexibility in how to use it in Gatos. The range of communication protocols supported by Cougaar made integration with the driving simulator easy.

2.3 Properties of Gatos

Gatos is an agent based prototype application; it serves as an architecture that integrates sensors and learning subsystem which makes a final decision about driver status based on presentation of complex information to the driver.

Gatos is designed to be a distributed system providing:

- Fault tolerance
- Dynamic discovery of new devices, applications and resources
- Reliability
- Graceful degradation
- Redundancy

Gatos is built on top of cougaar which forms the backbone of the system.

2.4 Inner Working of Gatos

All components within Gatos are Cougaar agents that can be removed at runtime without adversely affecting the execution of the overall system. The most interesting and crucial agents within Gatos are the decision maker and the Gatos monitor

2.4.1 Gatos Decision Maker

The decision maker is the intelligence of the system. This subsystem receives inputs from all other information gathering agents. This information is gathered, logged and passed to the decision maker. At regular intervals the decision maker component tries to ascertain the level of urgency or otherwise of the state of system. At the end of each decision interval a decision is made. All decisions, along with reasons for the decision are sent to the Gatos output agent and Log agent where they are filtered and logged before being finally output to the appropriate device.

Gatos decision maker makes inferences on several streams of data and based on pre-defined heuristics decisions are made as to the standard of driving at regular intervals.

Inside the decision maker we have experimented with different learning approaches to improve the decision making process. Using reinforcement learning algorithms has the added advantage that bad driving patterns can be detected without the need to explicitly define rules beforehand.

The decision maker relies on pre-defined rules using physiological data [8] to determine the emotional state of the driver. The corresponding corrective spoken/audio output [2-4] is then selected for the driver personality in question. This spoken output has a different pitch and different choice of phrasing for different personality types to perform the same corrective action.

2.4.2 Gatos Monitor

The Gatos monitor agent is the hub of Gatos system; it receives information from CanBus/Driving simulator and outputs to the central decision maker and log agent.

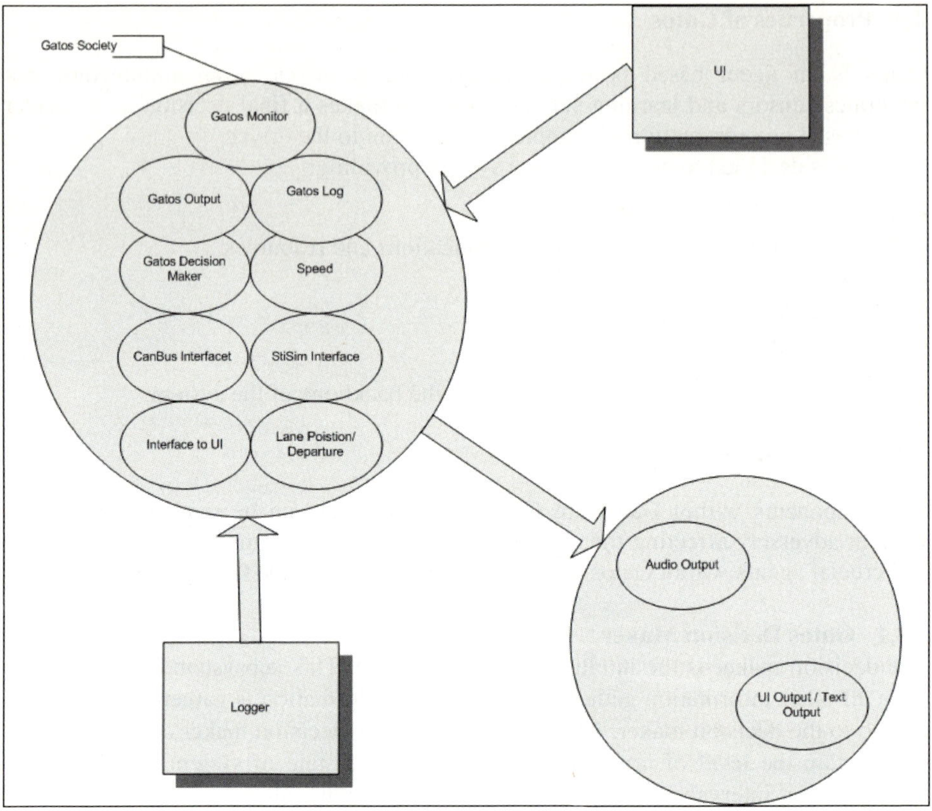

Fig. 4. Inner workings of Gatos

3 Gatos and the Driving Simulator

Gatos was interfaced with a driving simulator. Information from the simulator and a set of physiological sensors fed data to the Gatos monitor. A simulator was chosen so that the Gatos system could be prototyped quickly before interfacing into real car. In this way, ideas could be tested and prototyped before being implemented in the 'real world' scenario.

4 Conclusion and Discussion

The Gatos prototype worked well in simulation. However, there was a steep learning curve in working with Cougaar. Further refinements to the system need to be made before interfacing with a real car; in particular stress testing the parallel capability of Gatos, so that monitoring of the driver could be improved.

With regard to driver safety Gatos allows for an interdisciplinary approach to the study of driver monitoring. The system gives experimenters an approach to monitor driver behavior using multiple sensors to monitor driver status, driving performance, and the driving environment to address bad and dangerous driving behavior.

The other key aspect of Gatos is intervention on part of the decision making agent. This further opens up the field of study of driver reaction to instruction. The automotive industry has long been interested in driver workload and how to best measure and calculate driver workload [13]. Looking at drivers' reaction to interactions (different voices and different ways of presenting the same content) is a relatively new field [1, 4, 5]. There are still many aspects of how linguistic and paralinguistic properties of speech based systems in cars affect drivers.

For the other two domains of information, driver behavior and driving environment, there are both commercial and research approaches that use sensors to convey information to the shop, the driver or other drivers. Information about driving behavior is currently logged in "black boxes", and there is an ongoing debate on who owns the data and for what it should be used. Most automobile makers are investigating the area of communicating cars, where cars communicates with both instrumented infrastructure such as street signs, road markings and road signs, and with other vehicles, such as BMW's initiative of having cars convey information of road hazards to cars close by [14].

The prototype being based on data derived from a simulator means that assumptions have been made. It is at best an approximation of how a car and driver might function in the real world. However, it does allow for experimentation of scenarios that are difficult or dangerous to do in the real world. With this prototype we now have an experimental setup that allows us to continue to investigate how driver status, driving behavior and driving environment interacts to influence driver performance.

References

1. Nass, C., et al.: Improving Automotive Safety by Pairing Driver Emotion and Car Voice Emotion. In: CHI '05 extended abstracts on Human factors in computing systems, ACM Press, New York, NY (2005)
2. Jonsson, I.-M., Zajicek, M.: Selecting the voice for an In-car information system for older adults. In: Human Computer Interaction International 2005, Las Vegas, Nevada, USA (2005)
3. Jonsson, I.-M., et al.: Don't blame me I am only the Driver: Impact of Blame Attribution on Attitudes and Attention to Driving Task. In: CHI '04 extended abstracts on Human factors in computing systems, Vienna, Austria (2004)
4. Jonsson, I.-M., et al.: Thank you I did not see that: In-car Speech-Based Information Systems for Older Adults. In: Conference on Human Factors in Computing Systems, ACM Press, Portland, Oregon, USA (2005)
5. Jonsson, I.M., et al.: Got Info? Examining the Consequences of Inaccurate Information Systems. In: International Driving Symposium on Human Factors in Driver Assessment, Training, and Vehicle Design, Rockport, Maine (2005)
6. Frijda, N.: The Emotions. Cambridge University Press, Cambridge (1986)
7. Cacioppo, J.T., et al.: Psychophysiology of emotion across the life span. Annual Review of Gerontology and Geriatrics 17, 27–74 (1997)

8. Ekman, P., Levenson, R.W., Friesen, W.V.: Autonomic nervous system activity distinguishes among emotions. Science 221, 1208–1210 (1983)
9. Levenson, R.W., Ekman, P., Friesen, W.V.: Voluntary facial action generates emotion-specific autonomic nervous system activity. Psychophysiology 27, 363–384 (1990)
10. Picard, R.W.: Affective computing, vol. xii, p. 292. MIT Press, Cambridge, Mass (1997)
11. BBN-Technologies, Cougaar Architecture Document. vol. 1-74 (2004)
12. Helsinger, A., Thome, M., Wright, T.: Cougaar: A scalable, Distributed Multi-Agent Architecture. In: International Conference on Systems, Man and Cybernetics, The Hague, Netherlands (2004)
13. Angell, L., et al.: The Driver Workload Metrics Project, National Highway Traffic Safety Administration (2006)
14. BMW. BMW Talking Cars of the Future (2003) [cited; Available from: http://www.worldcarfans.com/news.cfm/newsID/2030808.001/country/gcf/bmw/bmw-pushes-lightweight-technology-with-magnesium

Usability in Location-Based Services: Context and Mobile Map Navigation

Kristiina Jokinen

University of Tampere and University of Helsinki, Finland
kristiina.jokinen@helsinki.fi

Abstract. The paper discusses usability and communicative capability of mobile multimodal systems. It reports on the evaluation of one particular interactive multimodal route navigation system and discusses the challenges encountered in this task. The main questions concerned the user's preference of one input mode over the other (speech vs. tactile/graphics input), usefulness of the system in completing the task (route navigation), and user satisfaction (willingness to use the system in the future). The user's expectations and real experience of the system were analysed by comparing the users' assessments before and after the system use. Conclusions concerning system design are drawn and discussed from the perspective of the system's communicative capability, based on the view of the computer as an interactive agent.

Keywords: usability, human-computer interaction, mobile context.

1 Introduction

Evaluation of speech-based interactive systems is needed for forming and refining system design as well as for assessing the impact, usability and effectiveness of the overall system performance. It is important for potential purchasers of commercially available systems, funding agencies who want to develop core technology, and researchers to guide and focus their research. However, the more complex systems we need to evaluate, the more complicated it is to determine appropriate features that determine the user's assessments. Especially for systems that exploit such highly human-related skills like talking, providing information, and presenting visual pictures and maps, evaluation is not a straightforward matter of getting a task done but also involves the user's experience of the system and interaction itself.

The usual way of evaluating interactive systems is to interview users after they have used the system for particular tasks, collect the evaluation forms, and use a weighted function of task-based success and dialogue-based cost measures to assess the system's functioning and suitability. The standard criteria are usefulness (what the system is for), efficiency (how well the system performs), and usability (user satisfaction). The system's performance and the user's subjective view of the usage of the system are taken into account, with the goal to maximize the objective function of usability. For instance, following the Paradise framework [1], the overall objective is to maximize user satisfaction by maximizing task success on the one hand and

C. Stephanidis (Ed.): Universal Access in HCI, Part II, HCII 2007, LNCS 4555, pp. 401–410, 2007.

minimizing the costs on the other hand (efficiency and qualitative analysis). On the other hand, [2] points out that interaction design is moving from standard usability concerns towards aspects of interaction that deal with fun, enjoyment, aesthetics and user experiences: "attractive things work better". Also various evaluation studies (see below) show that the users seem to tolerate difficulties such as long waiting times and even mere errors, if the system is interesting and the users motivated to use it

Considering practical systems, [3] points out the need to measure the quality of the service. The users also evaluate what is the value of the system for the users in helping them to complete the task, and to the evaluations need to find ways to quantify the value. One way to do this is to find out what is expected of the system by the users, i.e. evaluation does not only concern what is the quality of the system's performance perceived by the users, but what quality features are desired from the system. The main question focuses on selecting appropriate parameters: what are the quality features that provide reliable information of the system design and the user perception of the system. It is not unproblematic to determine the features, and their direct impact on the system may be difficult to operationalise. Once the features are determined, however, their impact can be quantified by calculating the difference between the user's expectations and experience before and after the use of the system, and checking how the different features have contributed to the overall change.

In multimodal and ubiquitous computing scene, location-based services are a growing service area. The ubiquitous computing paradigm [4] envisages that pervasive and mobile communication technologies will be deployed through a digital environment which is aware of the presence of mobile and wireless appliances, is sensitive, adaptive and responsive to the users' needs, habits and emotions, and is also ubiquitously accessible via natural interaction. In this context, multimodality provides realistic interaction means for practical applications: the use of text, speech, pictures, touch, and gaze allow natural input/output modalities for the user to interact with the back-end application. Multimodal systems are considered more natural than unimodal systems for several reasons. Besides bringing flexibility to interaction as the users can choose the modality that best suits to their particular situation, the interaction is also easier and enjoyable, since the users can exploit the interaction strategies they have learnt in human-human communication. Different modalities also bring in different benefits: it is easier to point to an object than refer to it by speaking, and in noisy environments it is useful to combine speech and graphics (see an overview in [5]).

However, their evaluation of such systems is often difficult due to many system components, and also due to problems in assessing system quality, performance and usability in objective terms, and providing clear metrics for system comparison. The system architecture can be distributed in the network, and the users need not sit in front of one computer terminal but operate with the system in a mobile context. Furthermore, the usage situation is challenging because of the novelty of the devices and because of the systems can be used both as traditional information searching tools and as applications enabling communicating with other, human and computer agents. The system should be useful and work well, but also questions concerning the user's expectations of the application as an enjoyable and understanding partner are brought in, together with the user's experience of the quality of service. In all these cases, an important requirement for usable and enjoyable interaction seems to be the system's communicative competence [6]: success of interaction measured in terms of dialogue and cooperation principles. As a promising approach to designing interactive systems, it is also critical when assessing trust and reliability of the system in general. It measures the system's capability to provide services and appropriate information that the user finds useful and reliable, in a manner that that takes into account the user's focus of attention: it does not interrupt the user's task goals nor intrude their privacy.

The paper will be structured as follows. Section 2 provides arguments for the "system as a communicating agent" view, and also gives a short overview of the Constructive Dialogue Model as a design framework. Section 3 discusses special aspects of location-based services in relation to the system's understanding of the context in order to provide contextually approriate information for supporting users in their tasks. In Section 4, the route navigation system MUMS and its evaluation results are briefly reported as an example case of a system usability. Finally, Section 5 draws conclusions concerning system design and the system's communicative capability.

2 Complex Systems as Communicating Agents

Due to technological and social development, our interaction with the environment has become more complex, and automatic systems require more sophisticated knowledge management and adaptation to various user needs. The challenge that speech and language technology faces in this context is not so much in producing tools and systems that enable interaction in the first place, but to design and build systems that allow interaction in a natural way: to provide models and concepts that enable experimentation with complex natural language interactive systems, and to test hypothesis for flexible human-computer interaction. Since interaction can take place via speech, text, and signing, special attention is also to be paid to multimodality.

Context-aware communication promises to build environments that understand social context and learn the preferences of individual users, adapting its decisions accordingly. Research projects are concerned e.g. about how to make communication with the house reality, while chatbots and conversational avatars are introduced as the future web surfing method. There are also many initiatives which focus especially on mobile, ubiquitous, and location-aware services, enabling "invisible intelligence" in systems and applications of our everyday life (such as cars, home appliances, factory automation, mobile phones), as well as reinforcing research and development in these areas, and trying to establish successful global standards.

Ubiquitous computing paradigm changes communication, too. Novel aspects for human-human as well as human-computer interaction are brought forward: systems exploit such highly human-related skills like talking, providing information, and presenting visual pictures and maps, and the computer is not only a tool but an agent which the users interact with. For instance, [6] argues in favour of the change of design paradigm for interactive systems, while the studies by [7] show how the users anthropomorphisize, i.e. assign human characteristics to the computer.

Also social interaction changes. The users may want to share their own (digital) data among friends and colleagues, and learn from the other members of the community by navigation, intelligent browsing, and direct interaction. Virtual communities are created where interaction is rapid but not necessarily face to face, and one's identity may be hidden behind different roles. This kind of on-line communication presupposes off-line processing of vast data which consists of various types of digital data such as texts, music, photos, videos, and emails. The organisation of data should be automatic and fast, and allow human intervention in directing and guiding the process according to individual preferences and needs. Interaction management with the application should thus support off-line organisation of the data and its retrieval according to some topical principles which relate to the conversational topic that the speakers are talking about. Recognition of the dynamically changing topic is thus of vital importance, in order for the system to provide rapid information retrieval and appropriate monitoring of and assistance in the conversation.

3 Context Understanding

Rational cooperation can be seen as emerging from the partners' communicative capabilities that maintain interaction on the basis of relevant and truthful information. Communicative behaviour is based on the speakers' observations about the world and on their reasoning, within the dialogue context, about the new information being exchanged in the dialogue contributions. In human-human interaction, this is related to the partners' shared goal, consideration on each other, and mutual trust that they both follow the same communicative principles. In human-computer interaction, cooperation manifests itself in the system properties that enable the user to interact with the system: robustness of data processing and appropriate presentation of the information user [8].

Human-human communication involves smooth coordination of a number of knowledge sources: characteristics of the speakers, topic and focus of the conversation, meaning and frequency of lexical items, facial expressions, prosody, communicative context, physical environment, world knowledge, etc. The following human-human dialogue between a service agent and a customer (Interact corpus, [9]) exemplifies these aspects: the overall dialogue structure is non-deterministic, and the agent's guidance shows flexible and considerate interaction strategy.

A: I'd like to ask about bus connection to Malmi hospital from Herttoniemi metro station – so is there any possibility there to get a bus?
L: Well, there's no direct connection – there's the number 79 that goes to Malmi but it doesn't go to the hospital, it goes to Malmi station
A: Malmi station? oh yes – we've tried that last time and it was awfully difficult
L: well, how about taking the metro and changing at Sörnäinen, or Hakaniemi if that's a more familiar place
A: Well Hakaniemi is more familiar yes
L: Ok, from there you can take the bus 73
A: 73?
L: Yes it leaves Hakaniemi just there where you exit from the metro to the bus stops, next to the market place
A: So it's by the market place that 73 leaves from?
L: Yes
A: And it's not there where the other buses leave from in front of Metallitalo?
L: No, it's there right when you come out from the metro

A: And it goes to the hospital?
L: yes, it has a stop just by the hospital
A: Ok, it must be a better alternative than the bus we took to the station, we didn't know which way to continue and nobody knew anything and we had to take the taxi…
L: what a pity – there would have been the number 69 though. It leaves close to the terminal stop of number 79 and goes to the Malmi hospital.
A: I see, so 79 to the station and then 69?
L: yes
A: Are they on the same stop?
L: well not on the same stop but very close to each other anyway
A: close to each other? Ok, well thank you for your help.
L: thank you, goodbye
A: goodbye

Since the customer had found the route via Malmi station "awful", the agent senses her frustration and introduces a simpler route via Hakaniemi using metro and bus. When the customer returns to the earlier frustrating experience, the agent provides information of this option, too, following the customer's requests. It is this kind of sensitiveness to the partner's needs and attention to their emotional state that characterizes cooperation in human communication.

The dialogue also shows another type of cooperation, related to the context in which the dialogue takes place. The speakers make frequent references to the physical environment (*change in X*, *close to each other*, *Hakaniemi*, *Malmi station*), and the spatial and visual environment directs their interpretation and generation of the language. In other words, language is *grounded* in the communicative context. Grounding is a part of natural communication, exemplified by frequent situational and contextual references, and the whole range of different modalities used in processing and manipulating information (gestures, pointing, nodding, gazing, etc.). Grounding is regarded as one of the most important problems in AI, see [10] for a discussion.

In ubiquitous, location-based services, such as map navigation, way-finding, information search, spatial information is frequently referred to. From the technical point of view, location-aware systems can be seen as responding to the grounding problem in that they enable the environment and the user's location be taken into account in the interaction design. However, the necessary context is usually included by the designers in the general usage scenario, or the system explicitly asks the user for relevant contextual information. These techniques can lead to user frustration, since the assumed context may not be the one the user is in, and the system's repeated requests for the same information sound unnatural and irritating. The systems thus need to interact by making dynamic references to the physical environment and by presenting information in accordance with the information flow of the dialogue and the knowledge of the speakers. Moreover, multimodal pointing, gestures and gazing are used in efficient and accurate reference expressions since purely verbal expressions may become rather clumsy.

Moreover, in mobile situations, the user's full attention is not necessarily directed towards the device and the service that the device provides; rather, it is often divided between the service and some primary task such as meeting people. The applications thus need to be tailored so that they are easily available when the users want them and when they can use them. This requires awareness of the context and the user's emotional state, so as to support their needs but intrude them as little as possible.

4 Evaluation of an Interactive Navigation System

Let us briefly study one location-based service, the multimodal map navigation system MUMS and its evaluation as an example of the usability issues dealing with cooperation in context. The MUMS system [11] is a multimodal route navigation system which aims at providing the user with real-time travel information and mobile navigation in Helsinki. It has been developed in a technological cooperation project among Finnish universities, supported by the Finnish Technology Agency TEKES and several IT-companies. The main goal was to build a robust practical application that would allow the users to use both spoken language commands and pen-pointing gestures as input modalities, and also output information in both speech and graphical modes. The system is based on the Interact-system [9] which aimed at studying methods and techniques for modeling rich natural language based interaction in situations where the interaction had not been functional or robust enough.

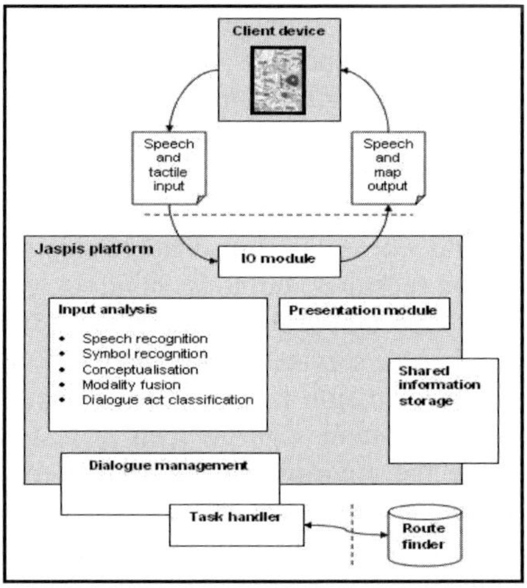

Fig. 1. General architecture of MUMS [11]

Figure 1 presents the general architecture of the system. The PDA-client only has a light-weight speech synthesizer, while the server handles all processing of the information. The touch-screen map can be scrolled and zoomed, and the inputs are recorded simultaneously and time stamped for later processing. The map interprets all pen input as locations: a tap denotes a coordinate location and a circled area a number of possible locations. The architecture is described in more detail in [11].

A screenshot of the system output is given in Figure 2. It corresponds to a situation after the user asked for information (*I want from the Opera to …<here>*), and the system provides spoken and graphical answer "*The tram 7 leaves from the Opera stop at 13:46. There are no changes. The arrival time at the Railway Station is at 13:56*".

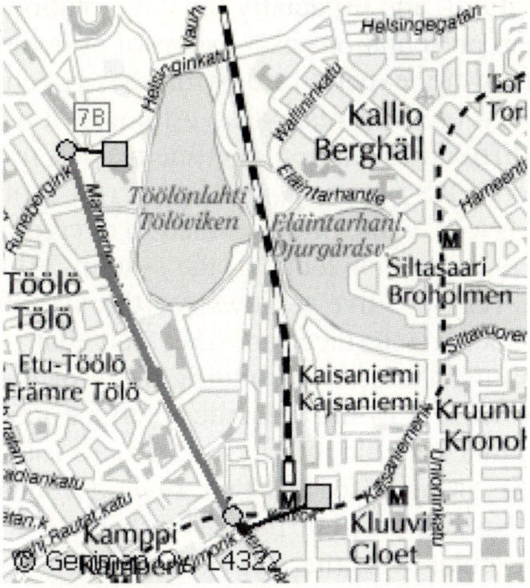

Fig. 2. MUMS example screen shot

The evaluation consisted of 17 users who had varying levels of experience with speech and tactile interfaces but none had used the MUMS or a similar system before. Before the actual evaluation sessions, they all were given a 15 minute crash-course in using the system. The users were given various scenario-based tasks ([12]) that dealt with using the system to find means of public transportation to get to certain places. They were also divided into two groups depending on the background information given to the users about the system they were to use: one group was instructed to interact with a speech interface that also had a tactile input option, while the other group was instructed to interact with a tactile system with spoken dialogue capabilities. The tasks given to both groups were exactly the same, but a priming effect on the users' behavior and expectations was expected: advanced knowledge would have impact on the users' evaluation. The expected and observed performance of the system was measured by asking the users to fill in the evaluation form twice. First they were asked to fill in their expectations of the system performance after the crash course before the actual tasks, and then again after the finishing the tasks. The same evaluation form was used to evaluate the system performance.

The evaluation questions were organized into six groups: the user's perception of the system's speech and graphical interface, the user's perception of the system's functionality and consistence, the user's perception of the system's responses and their appropriateness, the user's perception of system taking the user into account and the easiness of completing the task, the user's eagerness in future use of the system, and general questions of the overall assessment of the system. The results concern the differences in the perceived performance measures and the overall change between expectations and actual use. The latter corresponds to the actual differences in the measurement of how big the users' surprise or disappointment was as compared to what they had expected. The evaluation is reported elsewhere in detail (see e.g. [13]).

The general tendency in the evaluation is clear: user expectations were fulfilled and the system seems to have offered a genuinely positive experience. Speech and tactile input were considered natural, and especially the combination of synthetic speech and graphical map and route representations as a means of system output was praised. The biggest disappointments were experienced with the system's speed and accurate indication of how quickly it presents responses. Although it is possible to speed up the system somewhat, it is difficult to shorten the time needed for input analysis and data transfer over the mobile GPRS network: more powerful mobile devices are needed. However, the system's novelty value often seemed to overcome technical problems.

As expected, the users' prior knowledge of the system influenced their evaluations. The speech group gave very positive reviews for the system's multimodal aspects: they enjoyed using the tactile interface, and they felt that the system's speech and graphical representation contribute to the intelligibility of the system's output. They also seemed to be more willing to use a tactile interface unimodally than the tactile group, i.e. they believed that a tactile interface was more usable even if not combined with speech. The tactile group also felt that several modalities make interaction flexible and the system easy to use, but they were happier with the system's overall performance, and in particular with the rate of how often the system interprets user input correctly. The tactile group seem to believe that both tactile and speech are important, and a unimodal tactile interface would not be as usable as the multimodal one. There was also some evidence that the tactile group was more willing to use a unimodal speech system than the speech group, but these results were not significant.

It is interesting how the priming effect comes to play a role in the evaluation. For instance, the speech group seemed to feel, more than the tactile group, that the system was slow, even though the response time of the system is not affected by the form of user input. This points to the fact that speech presupposes rapid and understandable communication, and especially, if the users' prior expectations lead them to believe that the system is meant for spoken interaction, the speed of the system is important. The speech group also perceived the use of the map more positively than the tactile group (it was pleasant to look at, intuitive to use). The tactile group was more critical towards the map qualities, and in fact, the difference between the user's expectations and perceived system qualities was in absolute terms negative. Analogously, the tactile group was slightly more positive at the use of speech input and output than what they had expected, whereas the speech group was disappointed with the use of speech only system. Both groups, however, expected the system to take the user into consideration in a more individual way: this shows that the users expected a more personalized and "intelligent" system. As a whole, however, users felt the system was very easy to learn to use, and were very enthusiastic about using it again in the future.

5 Conclusions

The paper has discussed natural language communication as an important aspect of an interactive system's functionality and usability, and has also presented some evaluation results of a multimodal route navigation system to support these claims.

Evaluation focused especially on the user experience, and compared the users' expectations with real experience concerning the system properties and functionality. It is shown that the users' predisposition towards the system and prior information about the system capabilities affect the evaluation. The study also found interesting group differences that are useful to keep in mind when designing applications. For instance, younger users (under 35 years of age) were more disappointed at the interest value of the system, whereas the older ones did not consider this so important but assessed the system more on the basis of its technical features. Prior experience also seemed to make the users more critical: less experienced users regarded the novelty value of the system high and did not pay so much attention to the practical usability issues, as did the more experienced users. Although the evaluation differences may not always be pinpointed down to prior knowledge, age, or gender differences, it is important to notice that the goal of building one single practical system that would suit to most users is not reasonable. Rather, there is a need for adaptive systems that allow the users to use different modalities when interacting with the system, and can also tailor their responses according to user preferences.

User's perception of the system also depends on the system's communicative capabilities related to the task: natural intuitive interaction vs. quick and simple prompts. In general, system properties like understandability and pleasantness of the speech output are especially highly evaluated after the task. The users were unanimous that the system with both speech and tactile information is preferable whereas unimodal input and output would not be as good. However, compared with the speech group, the tactile group was surprised at the system capabilities and also had a positive experience concerning the system's functionality: the system is seen as helpful and considerate, it is cooperative and functions in a consistent way, it understands what is spoken and interaction succeeds with the first try. These aspects are commonly related to speech interfaces where inadequate performance of the speech recognizer causes problems. In our evaluations, however, speech recognition worked in a similar fashion for both groups, so the differences cannot be associated solely to speech recognition problems. Rather, the answer seems to lie in the predisposition of the users and their expectations concerning whether they interact with a speech interface that uses tactile input, or with a tactile interface that can speak as well. As mentioned above, the users automatically adjust their assessment of the system communicative capabilities with respect to what can be expected from a speech system as opposed to what can be expected from a tactile system that just happens to have speech capability. The use of (spoken) language seems to bring in tacit assumptions of fluent human communication and expectations of the system possessing similar communication capabilities. The results thus corroborate with the findings of [7] that the users project human-like properties to the computers, and more so if the system speaks and can be spoken to, supporting the observations in [8] that spoken interactive systems are regarded as agents.

When dealing with the present-day interactive services, the users are often forced to adapt their human communication methods to the needs of the technology. Simultaneously, with the development of ubiquitous environment, a growing number of interactive applications will appear, and expectations for fluent and intuitive communication get higher. For intelligent interaction, it is thus necessary to support intelligent information processing and the system's communicative capability: to understand and provide natural language expressions, recognise what is new and old information, reason about the topic of interaction, and adapt to the user's different dialogue strategies.

Acknowledgments

The author would like to thank the PUMS project partners for their collaboration in the system development and Topi Hurtig for the implementation of the system. Thanks go also to the test users, especially the group from the Helsinki City Transportation Authority for their helpful comments and participation in the evaluation.

References

1. Walker, M., Litman, D., Kamm, C., Abella, A.: PARADISE: A framework for evaluating spoken dialogue agents. In: Procs of the 35th Annual Meeting of the Association of Computational Linguistics, pp. 271–280. Madrid, Spain (1997)
2. Norman, D.A: Emotional Design: Why We Love (Or Hate) Everyday Things. In: Basic Books, Cambridge, Mass (2004)
3. Möller, S.: A New Taxonomy for the Quality of Telephone Services Based on Spoken Dialogue Systems. In: Jokinen, K., McRoy, S. (eds.) Procs of the 3rd SIGDial Workshop on Discourse and Dialogue, pp. 142–153. Philadelphia, U.S (2002)
4. Weiser, M.: The Computer for the Twenty-First Century. Sci Amweican, pp. 94–10 (1991)
5. Jokinen, K.: Interaction and Mobile Route Navigation Application. In: Meng, L.A., Zipf, S. (eds.) Map-based mobile services - usage context, interaction and application, Springer series on Geoinformatics, Springer, Heidelberg (2006)
6. Jokinen, K.: Communicative Competence and Adaptation in a Spoken Dialogue System. In: Procs of the 8th Int Conf on Spoken Language Processing (ICSLP), Jeju, Korea (2004)
7. Reeves, B., Nass, C.: The Media Equation. Cambridge University Press, Cambridge (1996)
8. Jokinen, K.: Constructive Dialogue Management - Speech Interaction and Rational Agents. John Wiley & Sons (forthcoming)
9. Jokinen, K., Kerminen, A., Kaipainen, M., Jauhiainen, T., Wilcock, G., Turunen, M., Hakulinen, J., Kuusisto, J., Lagus, K.: Adaptive Dialogue Systems: Interaction with Interact. In: Jokinen, K., McRoy, S. (eds.) Procs of the 3rd SIGDial Workshop on Discourse and Dialogue, pp. 64–73. Philadelphia, U.S (2002)
10. Harnard, S.: The Symbol Grounding Problem. Physical D42, 335–346 (1990)
11. Hurtig, T., Jokinen, K.: On Multimodal Route Navigation in PDAs. In: Procs. of the 2nd Baltic Conference on Human Language Technologies Tallinn, pp. 261--266 (2005)
12. Kanto, K., Cheadle, M., Gambäck, B., Hansen, P., Jokinen, K., Keränen, H., Rissanen, J.: Multi-Session Group Scenarios for Speech Interface Design. In: Stephanidis, C., Jacko, J. (eds.) Human-Computer Interaction: Theory and Practice (Part II), Mahwah, New Jersey, June. Lawrence Erlbaum Associates, vol. 2, pp. 676–680 (2003)
13. Jokinen, K., Hurtig, T.: User Expectations and Real Experience on a Multimodal Interactive System. In: Procs of the Interspeech Conference, Pittsburgh, U.S (2006)

Performance Analysis of Acoustic Emotion Recognition for In-Car Conversational Interfaces

Christian Martyn Jones[1] and Ing-Marie Jonsson[2]

[1] University of the Sunshine Coast, Queensland, 4558, Australia
[2] Department of Communication, Stanford University, California 94305, USA
cmjones@usc.edu.au, ingmarie@csli.stanford.edu

Abstract. The automotive industry are integrating more technologies into the standard new car kit. New cars often provide speech enabled communications such as voice-dial, as well as control over the car cockpit including entertainment systems, climate and satellite navigation. In addition there is the potential for a richer interaction between driver and car by automatically recognising the emotional state of the driver and responding intelligently and appropriately. Driver emotion and driving performance are often intrinsically linked and knowledge of the driver emotion can enable to the car to support the driving experience and encourage better driving. Automatically recognising driver emotion is a challenge and this paper presents a performance analysis of our in-car acoustic emotion recognition system.

Keywords: In-car systems, emotion recognition, emotional responses, driving simulator, affective computing, speech recognition.

1 Introduction

Cars are becoming feature rich with numerous interactive technologies embedded such as audio/video players, satellite navigation, hands-free mobile communications, climate controls and performance settings (suspension, semi-automatic gearbox etc). Attention theory suggests that speech-based interactions are less distracting to the driver than interactions with a visual display [1]. The introduction of speech-based interaction and conversational systems into the car highlights the potential influence of linguistic cues (such as word choice and sentence structure) and paralinguistic cues (such as pitch, frequency, accent, and speech rate which provide acoustic indicators of emotion). Driving presents a context in which a user's emotional state plays a significant role. The road-rage phenomenon [2] provides one undeniable example of the impact that emotion can have on the safety of the roadways. Considering the effects of emotion, and in particular that positive affect leads to better performance and less risk-taking, it is not surprising that research and experience demonstrate that happy drivers are better drivers [3]. The emotion of the car-voice has also been found to impact driving performance. Results from a study pairing the emotion of the car-voice with the emotion of the driver showed that matched emotions positively

C. Stephanidis (Ed.): Universal Access in HCI, Part II, HCII 2007, LNCS 4555, pp. 411–420, 2007.

impacted driving performance [4]. With a focus on driving safety and driving performance, these results motivate our research to investigate the design of an emotionally responsive car.

2 Affective Computing and Acoustic Emotion Recognition

The field of affective computing is growing with considerable research interest in automatically detecting and recognising human emotions [5], [6], [7]. Emotional information can be obtained by tracking facial motion, gestures and body language using image capture and processing [8]; tracking facial expressions using thermal imaging [9]; monitoring physiological changes using biometric measurements taken from the steering wheel and seat/seat-belt [10]; and also analysing the acoustic cues contained in speech [7]. Our research considers in-car affective computing where the car can recognise driver emotion and respond intelligently to support the driving experience such as offering empathy or providing useful information and conversation. In-car speech controlled systems are already commonplace with voice-controlled satellite navigation, voice-dial mobile phones and voice-controlled multimedia systems. Therefore we have adopted a speech based emotion recognition system for the in-car device.

Most emotions in speech are associated with acoustic properties such as fundamental frequency, pitch, loudness, speech-rate and frequency range [11]. The emotion recognition (ER) system presented in this paper uses 10 acoustic features including pitch, volume, rate of speech and other spectral coefficients. The system then maps these features to emotions such as boredom, sadness, grief, frustration, extreme anger, happiness and surprise, using statistical and neutral network classifiers. The emotion recognition system uses changes in acoustic features representative of emotional state whilst suppressing what is said and by whom. It is therefore speaker independent and utterance independent and can be readily adapted to other languages. Using a test set of previously unseen emotive speech, the overall performance of the emotion recognition system is greater than 70% for five emotional groups of boredom, sadness/grief, frustration/extreme anger, happiness and surprise. The emotion recogniser can track changes in emotional state over time and present its emotion decisions as a numerical indicator of the degree of emotional cues present in the speech.

3 The Emotional In-Car Conversation Interface

The emotive driver project builds on previous research which assessed the feasibility of automatically detecting driver emotions using speech [12] and developed a conversational interaction between the driver and car using driver emotion recognition and intelligent car response [13]. With knowledge of driver emotion the car can modify its response both in the words it uses but also the presentation of the message by stressing particular words in the message and speaking in an appropriate emotional state. As the car alters its 'standard' voice response it will be able to empathise with the driver and ultimately improve the wellbeing and driving performance. A previous study on pairing the emotional state of the driver with the emotional colouring of the car voice shows that pairing the emotions has an enormous positive influence on driving performance [4]. The same study reported that the engagement and amount of conversations was significantly higher when the emotions were paired. To pair emotions between the driver and car voice requires accurate automated emotion recognition. In this paper we extend the emotive driver project to provide quantitative analysis of the performance of our acoustic emotion recognition engine within a simulated car setting.

4 Experimental Method

The experimental study involved recording conversations between the driver and the car which we analysed to test the performance accuracy of the automatic acoustic emotion recognition. The experiment consisted of an 8 day study at Oxford Brookes University, UK using 41 participants, 20 male and 21 female. Participants were all in the age group 18 – 25, all driving with a mixed informational and conversational in-car system.

The experimental study used the STISIM driving simulator [14] for the driving session with the in-car information system. The driving simulator displays the road and controls such as speedometer and rev counter, and provides a rear-view mirror and control buttons for side-views left and right. Participants are seated in a real car seat and control the driving simulator using an accelerator pedal, a brake pedal, and a force-feedback steering wheel. All participants experienced the same pre-defined route and properties for both driving conditions and the car. The drive lasted approximately 20 minutes for each participant.

Engine noise, brake screech, indicators, sirens etc together with the output from the in-car information system was played through stereo speakers. The in-car information system was described as a system that would present two types of information to the drivers, informational and conversational. The informational part of the system related to road conditions, traffic and driving conditions such as 'the police often use radar here so make sure to keep to the speed limit'. The second part focuses on engaging the driver into conversation and was based on self-disclosures. Self-disclosure is elicited by reciprocity; the system will disclose something about itself and then ask the driver a question about the same (or similar) situation such as 'I like driving on mountain roads, what's your favorite road to drive on?'. Engaging drivers in conversation can be useful for reasons such as, detecting the driver's emotional state, gathering information on driver preferences to personalize the in-car information system, and as a potential aid for drowsy drivers.

Speech from the participants was recorded using an Andrea directional bean with 4 microphones placed in front and about 1.5 meters away from the driver. This microphone is typical of those used in the cars of today and provided a clean acoustic recording without overly sampling the car noise. The driving sessions were also videotaped from the front left of the driver to show driver hands, arms, upper body, head and eye motion, and facial expressions. Drivers self-reported emotions via questionnaires collected in the experiment. The questionnaires were based on DES (Differential Emotional Scale) [15], a scale based on the theory and existence of ten basic emotions.

The participants exhibit a range of emotions including boredom, sadness, anger, happiness and surprise; however for most of the drive the participants have a neutral/natural. In the absence of a distinct neutral/natural emotional state in the emotion recognition system we record average driver emotion as somewhere in between bored and sad. When challenged in the drive by obstacles in the road, other drivers, difficult road conditions and pedestrians, we observe strong emotions (aroused emotional states) from the drivers.

The performance of the automatic emotion recognition system was assessed by comparing the human emotion transcript against the output from the automatic acoustic emotion recognition system using a 2 second window analysis. The human transcripts were created by trained experts in recognising affective cues in speech. These experts did not take part in the driver study and are familiar with the emotion classifications of boredom, sadness/grief, frustration/extreme anger, happiness and surprise used by the automatic emotion recognition system. The experts were asked to listen to the speech soundtrack for each drive and report on the perceived emotional state of the driver.

The human evaluators used to transcribe the soundtracks for the rolling visual analysis and to report on the 2 second window analysis are employees of Affective Media Limited, UK. They are researchers in the product development team and have at least 2 years experience working in acoustic affective computing. They complete listening studies blind and are given unlabeled speech soundtracks. They have no knowledge of the driving experiment or the emotion recognition output. Although listener studies are subjective and the potentially the emotional transcripts could vary from one listener to another, we report that there is commonality in the classifications across human subjects for the five emotional groups of boredom, happiness, surprise, anger/frustration and sadness/grief.

5 Experimental Results

The 2 second window analysis is a detailed comparison between the automatically generated output of the emotion recognition system and the emotional transcript created by the human listener. The human listener considers in sequence each two second window of recording from the drive. For each two second window they report on the emotional state of the driver speech in terms of boredom, happiness, surprise, anger/frustration, sadness/grief (when the driver speaks); presence of the in-car voice, background car noise including engine noise, brake screech, doors and crashes; windows of no sound and other information such as other voices, non-speech sounds, Table 1.

In parallel to the human study, the emotion recognition system is presented with the driver soundtrack. The emotion recognition system is configurable and can classify any size of sound window. For this comparison the ER system will output an emotional classification for every 2 second window to allow for direct correlation

Table 1. Example human listener transcription (for participant 19) showing start and end time in seconds for the 2 second analysis speech segment; listener decision (1) on the emotional content of the 2 second window using acoustic emotion cues (not emotional cues from words spoken); whether the speech is that of the driver (blank) or the in-car conversational system (1); in-car noise such as tyre screech, indicator ticks, wheel knocks and engine noise; no sound present (1); and additional information such as what the driver says

start	end	bored	happy	surprise	anger	sadness	car voice	car noise	no sound	comments
…	…									
476	478							knocks		
478	480						1			what types
480	482						1			
482	484								1	
484	486	1				1				
486	488	1				1				neutral
488	490								1	uh
490	492	1								erm
492	494	1			1					old people
494	496	1				1				
496	498	1				1				
498	500	1				1				
500	502	1				1		screech		
502	504								1	
504	506	1				1				
506	508								1	
508	510	1				1				
510	512	1				1				

with the human transcript. The ER system outputs a continuous measure between 0 and 1 for each emotion including boredom, happiness, surprise, anger/frustration and sadness/grief, Table 2. Note multiple emotions can be present within a 2 second window and therefore it is possible to have high emotion levels for happiness and surprise, surprise and anger, boredom and sadness etc.

The ER system classifies all acoustic sounds as emotions. This can be useful for non-speech sounds such as sighs, non-words and hums/whistles [13]. However the ER system will also classify brake screech, crashes and the in-car voice. In the 2 second window study we assume that the ER system processes speech only and we use only those windows which are not corrupt by high levels of non-speech.

Each two second window from the human listener transcript is compared directly with the ER output by an additional human subject. This subject then rates the correlation between the ER output and the listener using the following criteria: 'exact' = both ER and human report same emotion; 'equivalent' = ER and human report equivalent emotions such as happy and surprise, boredom and sadness; 'mismatch' =

Table 2. Example acoustic emotion recognition output (for participant 19) showing start and end time in seconds for the 2 second analysis speech segment; automatic decision on the emotional content of the 2 second window (note '---' indicates insufficient speech for classification or no speech present) and additional information such as what the driver says (not recognised by the system but presented here to assist correlation with the human listener transcription)

start	end	bored	happy	surprise	anger	sadness	comments
...	...						
476	478	---	---	---	---	---	0
478	480	---	---	---	---	---	what types
480	482	---	---	---	---	---	0
482	484	---	---	---	---	---	0
484	486	0	0	0	0	1	0
486	488	1	0	0	0	0	neutral
488	490	---	---	---	---	---	uh
490	492	1	0	0	0	0.349	erm
492	494	0	0	0	0	1	old people
494	496	1	0	0	0	0.217	0
496	498	0	0	0	0	1	0
498	500	1	0	0	0	0	0
500	502	---	---	---	---	---	0
502	504	---	---	---	---	---	0
504	506	1	1	0	0	0	0
506	508	---	---	---	---	---	0
508	510	1	0	0	0	0	0
510	512	1	0	0	0	0	0

the ER and human differ in their judgement of emotion; 'no emotion correct' = ER returns a no-emotion present output ('0' for all emotions) which is confirmed by human transcript; 'no emotion mismatch' = ER returns a no-emotion present output ('0' for all emotions) which is in disagreement with human transcript; 'no classification' = ER does not detect speech in the window ('---' for all emotions) whereas human listener has report speech (this can be the case when there is little speech or speech is very quiet), Table 3.

The totals for each criteria for every 2 second window of the driver soundtrack are calculated and form the performance accuracy of the ER system. This provides a quantitative analysis of the correlation between the classified emotions of the emotion recognition system and that of the human listener. However it should be noted that any mismatches between the ER system and human may not indicate an error with the ER output but rather a misclassification by the human listener.

Table 3. Example comparison between the human listener transcription and the automatic emotion recognition output (for participant 19) for each 2 second window. 'Exact' = both ER and human report same emotion; 'Equivalent' = ER and human report similar emotions; 'mismatch' = the ER and human disagree; 'no emotion correct' = both ER and human report no emotion; 'no emotion mismatch' = ER and human disagree on whether emotion is present; 'no classification' = ER and human disagree on whether speech is present

		Emotion Recognised			No Emotion Recognised			
start	End	Exact	Equiv	Mismatch	Correct	Mismatch	No Class	comments
…	…							
476	478							0
478	480							what types
480	482							0
482	484							0
484	486	1						0
486	488	1						neutral
488	490							uh
490	492	1						erm
492	494			1				old people
494	496	1						0
496	498	1						0
498	500	1						0
500	502							0
502	504							0
504	506		1					0
506	508							0
508	510	1						0
510	512	1						0

6 Discussion

The project is ongoing and we continue to process all 41 participants of the in-car emotional conversation experiment to provide an overall performance score for the emotion recognition system. We are able at this stage to present an example performance measure for one male driver and one female driver. Early indications suggest that the emotion recognition performance with these two drivers is representative of the overall performance for all 41 participants. The results are obtained from the 2 second window analysis.

Performance Evaluation (for female participant 19). The human listener report 81 frames of driver speech from the 696 two second windows in the soundtrack. Of these 44 are 'exact' = both ER and human report same emotion; 13 are 'equivalent' = ER and human report equivalent emotions such as happy and surprise, or boredom and sadness; 12 are 'mismatch' = the ER and human differ in their judgement of emotion; 0 are 'no emotion correct' = ER returns a no-emotion present output which is confirmed by human transcript; 0 are 'no emotion mismatch' = ER returns a no-emotion present output which is in disagreement with human transcript; 12 are 'no classification' = ER does not detect speech in window whereas human listener has report speech (this can be the case when there is little speech or speech is very quiet).

83% two second windows were recognised by the ER system as the appropriately matching emotion to the human listener. 64% are exact matches with the transcript from the human listener and another 19% are equivalent recognitions eg happy for surprise, boredom for sadness etc. The error rate is 17%, however note that this is a comparison between the ER system output and the opinion of the human listener. The human listener may on occasion be wrong with the emotional classification.

Out of a total of 81 two second windows in which human listener has reported driver speech, the ER system detects 85% as speech windows, missing 15% of speech windows. Of the 69 windows detected by the ER system, 64% correspond exactly with the human listener emotion recognition. A further 19% are equivalent recognitions between human listener and ER system eg happy for surprise and boredom for sadness. The error rate is 17%, however note again that this is a comparison between the ER system output and the opinion of the human listener.

Performance Evaluation (for male participant 19). The human listener report 97 frames of driver speech from the 698 two second windows in the soundtrack. Of these 56 are 'exact' = both ER and human report same emotion; 10 are 'equivalent' = ER and human report equivalent emotions such as happy and surprise, boredom and sadness; 14 are 'mismatch' = the ER and human differ in their judgement of emotion; 0 are 'no emotion correct' = ER returns a no-emotion present output which is confirmed by human transcript; 4 is 'no emotion mismatch' = ER returns a no-emotion present output which is in disagreement with human transcript; 13 are 'no classification' = ER does not detect speech in window whereas human listener has report speech (this can be the case when there is little speech or speech is very quiet).

83% two second windows recognised by the ER system as the appropriately matching emotion to the human listener. 70% are exact matches with the transcript from the human listener and another 13% are equivalent recognitions eg happy for surprise, boredom for sadness etc. The error rate is 17%, however note that this is a comparison between the ER system output and the opinion of the human listener.

Out of a total of 97 two second windows in which the human listener has reported driver speech, the ER system detects 87% as speech windows, missing 13% of speech windows. Of the 84 windows detected by the ER system, 67% correspond exactly with the human listener emotion recognition. A further 12% are equivalent recognitions between human listener and ER system eg happy for surprise and boredom for sadness. The error rate is 21%, however note that this is a comparison between the ER system output and the opinion of the human listener.

There is a strong correlation between the emotional transcript created by the human listener and the emotion output returned automatically by the acoustic emotion recognition system. However there are occasions where the speech is masked by car noise (such as engine noise, sirens and brakes). Other times, the automatic system could not disambiguate between emotional states so that the driver was assessed to be in one of two emotional states - bored or sad (negative emotions with low arousal), or - happy or surprised (positive emotions with moderate arousal).

7 Conclusions

In-car speech recognition systems are becoming commonplace, enabling drivers to navigate using GPS, speed-dial on mobile communications and control audio and video. There is the opportunity for richer driver-car interaction if the car can recognise and respond to driver emotion. Our earlier studies have shown that driver emotion and driving performance can be correlated and matching the emotional tones of the car voice with the emotion of the driver can increase driver safety. Here we report a quantitative performance analysis of our acoustic emotion recognition system. The emotion recognition system can classify into 5 emotional groups of boredom, happiness, surprise, frustration/anger, sadness/grief with an average accuracy of 65% when comparing the automated classification with that of human listeners. An average of 15% of additional recognitions are equivalent, for example happiness is confused with surprise, or boredom with sadness, and the emotional response by the car remains appropriate. Less than 20% of driver speech is incorrectly recognised for emotion state. The performance is sufficient to allow the in-car system to respond to driver emotion with empathy in order to support and improve driving.

8 Future Work

The quantitative performance analysis is ongoing however a number of other research challenges remain. Some drivers did not converse with the car. We need to consider why drivers do not talk to the car. Are they too engaged in the task of driving? Are the questions posed by the car inappropriate? Are they uncomfortable talking to the car? Do they not like the car voice? Using automatic emotion recognition we hope that the car can detect driver emotion and adapt voice, conversation and vehicle parameters to support the driving experience. However there are additional questions to answer. Previous studies consider varying the paralinguistic cues only [16], however should the content of the response also change, and how? Should the car become less or more talkative depending on driver emotion? Should the car alter the telemetry, climate, music in the car in response the mood of the driver? How fast should the system change? Further research will consider automatically adapting the emotion of the car-voice to match the user. Empathy communicates support, caring, and concern for the welfare of another [17]. A voice which expresses happiness in situations where the user is happy and sounds subdued or sad in situations where the user is upset would strongly increase the connection between the user and the voice [4]. Mood must be taken into account to make the car-voice an effective interaction partner. Drivers in a good mood when entering a car are more likely to experience positive emotion during an interaction with a car-voice than drivers in a bad mood. Therefore it seems that emotion in technology-based voices must balance responsiveness and inertia by orienting to both emotion and mood. The research continues towards developing an intelligent conversational in-car system which can recognise and respond to driver emotion to support the driving experience.

Acknowledgments. We wish to thank Affective Media, UK for assistance in developing the ER technologies and help with the analysis of the driver speech data.

References

1. Lunenfeld, H.: Human factor considerations of motorist navigation and information systems. In: Vehicle Navigation and Information Systems Conference Proceedings, pp. 35–42 (1989)
2. Galovski, T., Blanchard, E.: Road rage: a domain for psychological intervention? Aggressive Violent Behavior 9(2), 105–127 (2004)
3. Groeger, J.A.: Understanding driving: Applying cognitive psychology to a complex everyday task. U.K. Psychology Press, Hove (2000)
4. Nass, C., Jonsson, I.-M., Harris, H., Reaves, B., Endo, J., Brave, S., Takayama, L.: Increasing safety in cars by matching driver emotion and car voice emotion. In: Proceedings of CHI 2005, Portland, Oregon, USA (2005)
5. Cowie, R., Douglas-Cowie, E., Tsapatsoulis, N., Votsis, G., Kollias, S., Fellenz, W., Taylor, J.G.: Emotion recognition in human-computer interaction. IEEE Signal Proc, pp. 32–80 (2001)
6. Humaine Portal.: Research on affective computing http://www.emotion-research.net/
7. Jones, C.: Project to develop voice-driven emotive technologies, Scottish Executive, Enterprise transport and lifelong learning department, UK (2004)
8. Kapoor, A., Qi, Y., Picard, R.: Fully automatic upper facial action recognition, IEEE International Workshop on Analysis and Modeling of Faces and Gestures (AMFG 2003) held in conjunction with ICCV 2003. Nice, France (2003)
9. Khan, M., Ward, R., Ingleby, M.: Distinguishing facial expressions by thermal imaging using facial thermal feature points. In: Proceedings of HCI 2005, pp. 5–9. Edinburgh, UK (2005)
10. Healey, J., Picard, R.: SmartCar: Detecting driver stress. In: Proceedings of ICPR 2000, Barcelona, Spain (2000)
11. Nass, C., Brave, S.: Wired for speech: How voice activates and advances the human-computer relationship. MIT Press, Cambridge, MA (2005)
12. Jones, C., Jonsson, I.-M.: Speech patterns for older adults while driving. In: Proceedings of HCI International 2005, Las Vegas, Nevada, USA (2005)
13. Jones, C., Jonsson, I.-M.: Automatic recognition of affective cues in the speech of car drivers to allow appropriate responses. In: Proceedings of OZCHI, Canberra, Australia (2005)
14. STISIM drive system: Systems technology, Inc. California http://www.systemstech.com/
15. Izard, C.: Human Emotions. Plenum Press, New York (1977)
16. Isen, A.M.: Positive affect and decision making. In: Lewis, M., Haviland-Jones, J.M. (eds.) Handbook of emotions, pp. 417–435. The Guilford Press, New York (2000)
17. Brave, S.: Agents that care: Investigating the effects of orientation of emotion exhibited by an embodied computer agent, Doctoral dissertation. Stanford University, CA (2003)

In-Vehicle Information System Used in Complex and Low Traffic Situations: Impact on Driving Performance and Attitude

Ing-Marie Jonsson[1] and Fang Chen[2]

[1] Ansima Inc., Los Gatos, CA 95033, USA
[2] Interaction Design Group, Department of Computer Science and Engineering, Chalmers University of Technology, SE-412 96 Göteborg, Sweden
ingmarie@ansima.com, fanch@cs.chalmers.se

Abstract. This paper describes a study where drivers' responses to an in-vehicle information system were tested in high and low density traffic. There were 17 participants in a study that was run using a driving simulator. Data was gathered for a comparison of how drivers react to an in-vehicle information system in low density traffic, complex traffic, and without system. Participants were also asked for their subjective evaluation of trust of the system and how they perceived it influenced their driving performance. Results show gender differences for both driving performance and attitude.

Keywords: Driving simulator, traffic density, in-vehicle system, cognitive load, trust, driving performance.

1 Introduction

Drivers use cognitive resources for attention, memory and decision making while driving. Complex traffic situations and unfamiliar road designs require additional resources. The measurement of cognitive resources in use while driving (cognitive workload) involves assessing how much mental effort an individual expends. This can be obtained by assessment techniques based on behavioral measures, performance measures, and self reported perception of mental effort load [1]. The concept of cognitive abilities and cognitive workload are important for the driving task, since even the smallest distraction or diversion of cognitive resources can have disastrous effects [2]. Interactions with in-car information systems (a secondary task) require cognitive resources and can distract from the primary task of driving task regardless of the intent of the system[2, 3].

Cognition is the processing of information from around us and includes perception, attention, pattern matching, memory, language processing, decision making, and problem solving. The conventional definition of cognitive load is the amount of mental resources needed to perform a given task [4-6]. User interfaces are no exception and all types, speech based, displayed based or tactile, make cognitive demands on their users. Confronted by a user interface, people must learn new

C. Stephanidis (Ed.): Universal Access in HCI, Part II, HCII 2007, LNCS 4555, pp. 421–430, 2007.

concepts, retain information in short-term memory and learn the rules of the system. They must create and refine a mental model of the system and how to use it. In particular systems that use purely speech based interfaces places even more challenges on memory and attention. Information presented in speech is serial and non-persistent[7].

Successful speech based interface designs for vehicles must consider the limitations of human cognitive processing. An interface should not require users to hold too many items in short-term memory and they should not require users to learn a complex set of commands too quickly. In particular, there are three design challenges to consider for a speech based interface:

1. *Complexity*: How complex are the rules and commands and mental model that the user is required to learn? Is it familiar or a totally new concept?
2. *Memory load*: Are users required to hold information in their short-term memory? How much new commands and procedures do they have to learn?
3. *Attention*: The user's attention will be divided since the primary task is driving. If they are distracted, can they continue their interaction with the system when they are ready to do so? Is it easy for the user to attend to the most important information?

For the study described in this paper we consider attention, since this is the process of selecting what to focus on (if there are multiple possibilities available). The way that information is presented to users can have a significant effect on how they attend to the information[8, 9]. It is important to keep in mind the user's goals, priorities, and decision criteria. This makes it possible to optimize the presentation of information and not challenge the user's ability to attend to more important tasks.

All in-vehicle information systems require divided attention, and situations might arise that demand the driver's focused attention. In-vehicle systems must accommodate this need by providing the driver with control over the pacing of the interaction. Drivers might exert such control by using a pause/resume feature, or by a longer silence, after with the system clarifies the conversational context so that the driver can continue with the dialog. Rinalducci, Mouloua, and Smither [10] investigated the interaction between perceptual and cognitive abilities and driving. They studied three age groups, 19-34, 35-59, and 60 years and older. Their results show that young drivers have a reserve of cognitive resources to be tapped into when needed, and that this reserve diminishes over time. Older drivers have fewer resources to spare for other activities. Young drivers can deal with multiple pieces of information, whereas older drivers tend to focus on one source of information [11]. Rabbit [12] found that older drivers are more distracted by irrelevant information than young drivers.

To learn more about when, in what situations, and for which age-groups, an in-vehicle information system is most useful; we decided to design a study. In particular, we wanted to investigate the usefulness of in-vehicle information system during different traffic densities. This paper presents a study that compares how driving performance and attitude is affected by information from an in-vehicle information system in complex traffic and low traffic situations. It is interesting to see how information from an in-vehicle system is perceived during situations of complex traffic where one would hope the system would be most helpful. This is compared to how the system is perceived during low traffic situations. The experiment was conducted using a driving simulator to avoid potential dangerous situations while driving in real traffic.

2 Experimental Method

The study was designed to investigate how drivers react to spoken information and suggestions presented from in-car information systems during high traffic and during low traffic. In particular to track changes in behaviors and changes in driver state in relation to simple or complex traffic events. Would the system seem more helpful and useful in complex traffic situation or while driving in areas with little to no traffic?

The study also enabled us to investigate the effect of context, and constancy and how drivers react to information from the speech system during driving induced load (complex traffic situations), no load (simple to no traffic), and when the system simply omitted to provide any information.

2.1 Traffic Events and Driving Environment

To enable replication of the study in different locations, the study design took into consideration regional and cultural differences with respect to complex traffic events such as traffic circles and "right-of-way" regulations. This study would benefit from being run with different age groups, results from previous studies show that older adults react favorably to information from in-vehicle systems [13, 14]. It is important, especially when testing older age groups, to make sure to include a test battery of cognitive abilities and mobility in the pre-screening. For younger age groups this would be helpful, however, we did not consider it necessary since the participants were all University students.

We selected the following five traffic events to be used for the study since they are relatively unbounded:

1. Left Turns for right hand side driving and Right Turns for left hand side driving
2. Overtaking
3. Merging
4. Crossing busy intersection

These traffic events were repeated and used in the driving course for the study.

2.2 Experimental Design

Within-subjects experiment design was used, where all participants experienced all conditions. All participants were randomly assigned from the age group 18-25 (10 male and 7 female). They were all university students, pre-screened to have a valid driver license.

A 60,000 ft driving course was especially designed for the study containing randomized placement of multiple instances of the four selected traffic events. The four traffic events were combined with complex traffic or low density traffic and form the study conditions. Please see table 1 for a description of the 8 conditions based on a 4x2 (traffic events x traffic density) table.

Table 1. Conditions for the study (Traffic event X traffic density)

Condition	Light Traffic	Heavy Traffic
A	Left Turn/Right Turn	
B		Left Turn/Right Turn
C	Overtaking	
D		Overtaking
E	Merging	
F		Merging
G	Crossing/Stop&Go	
H		Crossing/Stop&Go

With four repetitions of each condition, the driving course contained in total 32 traffic events. These were placed at randomized intervals throughout the driving course.

Table 2. Order of Repeated Traffic Events (Conditions)

F	D	G	E	B	A	H	C
C	A	D	B	G	F	E	H
B	H	C	A	F	E	D	G
A	G	B	H	E	D	C	F

The in-vehicle information system was designed to give information about the upcoming traffic situation for half of the traffic events, balanced across conditions. The locations for the omitted prompts were randomly selected. The result was an in-vehicle system that contained 16 information prompts, 2 for each condition.

The driving simulator used in the experiment was STiSIM from Systems Technology Inc. Participants were driving for approximately 25 minutes, and they sat in a real car seat and 'drove' using a Microsoft Sidewinder steering wheel and pedals consisting of accelerator and brake. The simulated journey was projected on a wall in front of participants and was set to daylight and sunshine. The simulator was instrumented to automatically record driving performance parameters. While driving, the in-vehicle information system offered advice and suggestions at selected traffic situations as described above. The informational prompts of the system were recorded by a female voice talent in a calm and non-emotional voice. Typical prompts used by the system were "There is road work head, merge left", "Right lane is closed ahead, merge left", and "There is a busy intersection ahead".

The design of the study enabled us to collect data for comparisons of driver reactions in three different situations:

1. Responses in Light and Heavy Traffic
2. Responses when assisted by the in-vehicle system
3. Responses in Light and Heavy Traffic when assisted by the in-vehicle system.

2.3 Measures

There were three sets of measures derived from the collected data; prior driving experience, driving performance and attitudinals. All attitudinal measures are indices derived from questionnaire data by using factor analysis. The reliability of the derived indices are then verified by Cronbachs alpha.

Prior driving experience: Information about participants' real life driving experience was collected as part of the first questionnaire. Participants were asked to self report how many years they had been driving, the number of miles they typically drive per week, the number of accidents they had had, and the number of citations they had received.

Driving Performance: The simulator, STISIM Drive, automatically generated and gathered a large variety of data on driving behavior. In this study, we focus on five measures for the most dangerous behaviors: number of collisions, number of off-road accidents, swerving, and obedience to the most important traffic laws (adherence to traffic lights, stop signs and speed limits). The three measures were uncorrelated.

All of these negative behaviors are much more common in a driving simulator than in actual driving; indeed, we would be startled to find even two occurrences of these behaviors if the experiment involved real drivers. One key reason for dramatically higher rates in simulator studies is that we create extremely difficult courses so that we can find variance in driving performance: A simple course would fail to generate any variance in poor driving behavior.

State when driving with the In-vehicle Information System: The self-report of state when driving with the in-vehicle information system was an index based on terms that were rated using 10-point Likert scale [15] (1 = Describes Very Poorly to 10 = Describes Very Well). Participants were asked "How well do the following words describe how you felt when driving with the in-car information system?" We created an index based on factor analysis that included the following terms: I felt calm driving, I was at ease driving, I felt content driving, I felt comfortable driving, I felt confident driving, I was relaxed driving, I felt secure driving and I felt indecisive driving reverse coded. The index was very reliable (alpha = .95)

Trust of the in-car information system: In general, one can distinguish trust and credibility even though these two concepts are linked. When a source is considered trustworthy, or better when an individual trusts a particular source, it is more probable that this individual will accept pieces of knowledge (beliefs) coming from that source. Trustworthiness is a property of a source while credibility should be considered a property of a piece of information.

The questionnaire focused on trust and contained items from the Individualized Trust Scale [16]. All of these scales are based on pairs of adjectives which anchor seven-point Likert scales. The pairs of adjectives are antonyms. We created an index based on factor analysis with the following items: dangerous-safe, distrustful-trustful, trustworthy-untrustworthy, not deceitful-deceitful, reliable-unreliable, honest-dishonest. The index was very reliable (alpha = .73).

Perceived influence of the In-vehicle Information System: The perceived influence of the in-vehicle information system was an index of terms rated using 10-point Likert scales (1 = Describes Very Poorly to 10 = Describes Very Well). Participants were asked "How well do the following statements describe the in-car information systems influence on your driving?" We created an index based on factor analysis with the following terms: I was a more alert driver, I drove more carefully, I was a safer driver, I was a more confident driver. The index was very reliable (alpha = .79)

Perceived Usefulness of In-Vehicle System: Participants were asked two post – experiment questions before debriefing 1) did they think that the system was most useful in complex traffic situations, in low traffic situations, or in both, 2) did they want the system turned on or off.

3 Results

The effects of the in-vehicle information system, when used in a driving simulator, on attitude and driving performance were evaluated by a one-way ANOVA with gender as the between-participant factor. Significant results are indicated in ***bold and italics***.

3.1 Prior Driving Experience

Data shows that there were no major differences between the participants' prior driving experience, except that female drivers often drove with passengers in the car as opposed to male drivers that more often drove alone (see table 3). When asked where they normally drive, most participants listed Motorway and Urban, as their normal drive scene.

Table 3. Prior Driving Performance

	Gender	Mean	Std Dev	F	Sig.
Age	Male	24.90	2.64	1.59	.23
	Female	28.29	7.97		
Years of Driving	Male	5.5	1.72	1.38	.26
	Female	4.29	2.56		
Accidents	Male	1.3	1.57	1.27	.28
	Female	.57	.79		
Tickets	Male	.60	.97	1.39	.26
	Female	.14	.39		
Passenger	***Male***	***2***	***.47***	***5.4***	***.03***
	Female	***2.6***	***.54***		

3.2 Driving Performance

For overall driving: that is the average for the entire driving course, a factor analysis of all driving performance parameters found one reliable index, **bad driving**. This index consisted of "collisions", "stop sign tickets", "centerline crossings", "road edge excursion", and "speed exceedances" reverse coded. It is interesting to note that female drivers showed worse overall driving performance for the "bad driving" index than male drivers, see table 4.

Table 4. Driving Performance

		Mean	SD	F	Sig.
Bad Driving	***Male***	***32.1***	***8.57***	***4.63***	***.05***
	Female	***43.0***	***12.31***		
Bad Driving High Traffic	Male	15.20	6.42	2.59	.13
	Female	19.86	4.91		
Bad Driving Low Traffic	Male	7.9	2.93	3.58	.08
	Female	12.6	7.1		
Bad Driving With System	Male	10.2	2.25	.140	.71
	Female	10.6	2.05		
Bad Driving Without System	***Male***	***11.5***	***5.33***	***7.22***	***.02***
	Female	***18.14***	***4.48***		

For driving performance in both complex and low traffic situations, the data shows no significant differences between male and female drivers on the 'bad driving" index, see table 4.

Looking at the data on driving with the in-vehicle system and driving without the system, there are significant differences. Female drivers once again show significantly worse driving performance driving without the system. There are no differences between female and male drivers in the "bad driving" index when driving with the system. It is however interesting to note that the difference in "bad driving" disappears when driving with the system, see table 4.

There are no significant differences between female and male drivers listening to the system in complex traffic situations. Once again the data show almost no difference in "bad driving", see table 5. Similarly, there are no significant differences between male and female drivers when driving in low traffic and non-complex situations with the system. There is however a trend in the data that shows female drivers as worse drivers.

It is interesting to note that while there is virtually no difference in complex traffic situations, female drivers perform much worse than male drivers in low traffic situations with the system, see table 5.

The data show that there are no significant differences between male and female drivers on the "bad driving" index when driving without the system in complex traffic situations, see table 5. On the other hand, when driving in low density traffic, there is a significant difference in driving performance between male and female drivers. Female drivers once again show much worse driving performance in low density traffic, this time driving without the system see table 5.

Table 5. Driving Performance Traffic Density X Speech System

		Mean	SD	F	Sig.
Bad Driving High Traffic With System	Male	7.1	3.38	1.01	.330
	Female	8.86	3.76		
Bad Driving Low Traffic With System	Male	7.3	2.36	3.95	.07
	Female	9.5	1.98		
Bad Driving High Traffic Without System	Male	6.9	3.3	2.78	.12
	Female	9.3	2.1		
Bad Driving Low Traffic Without System	***Male***	***6.8***	***2.25***	***6.01***	***.03***
	Female	***10.4***	***3.15***		

Interesting trends to note in the data are: female drivers definitely drive worse overall, and especially when driving without the system. These differences seem to be exaggerated when driving in low density traffic, see tables 4 and 5.

3.3 Drivers Perception of the In-Vehicle System

Participants self-reported on how they felt while driving with the in-vehicle system. The index for "Calm and Relaxed while Driving" and the data show that female drivers felt significantly calmer and more relaxed driving with the system, see table 6.

Table 6. Influence of In-Vehicle System

		Mean	SD	F	Sig.
Calm and Relaxed	***Male***	***42.89***	***13.48***	***5.35***	***.04***
	Female	***57.97***	***12.86***		
Trust of System	***Male***	***28.86***	***8.87***	***7.31***	***.02***
	Female	***40.81***	***9.11***		
Positive Influence of System	***Male***	***13.37***	***6.68***	***5.89***	***.03***
	Female	***21.76***	***7.49***		

The index for "trust of the in-car information system" clearly shows that female drivers trusted the system more than male drivers, see table 6. This is a finding that confirms previous simulator studies with in-vehicle systems [14, 17-19], female drivers tend to appreciate speech systems in cars more then male drivers.

Participants were also asked to rate the influence of the in-vehicle system on their driving performance and driving experience. The data shows that female drivers perceived the system to have a more positive influence on their driving performance, than male drivers, see table 6.

Finally, we asked participants if they thought the system more helpful in low or high density traffic and if they would have the system turned on in their cars. Male drivers wanted the system to be mainly turned off, but could see potential of having the system turned on in low traffic situations to alert them of upcoming traffic events. They did not like the system in high traffic situations, and thought that it distracted them from focusing on the driving task. Female drivers, on the other hand, wanted the system turned on and found the system useful in both high and low traffic situations.

4 Conclusion

Data shows clearly that the in-vehicle information system, tested in this experiment, was perceived to be more helpful in low traffic situations than in high traffic. This is confirmed by both driving performance data and questionnaire data. It is also clear that female drivers would benefit the most from this type system. The data shows a significant improvement in driving performance when the system is in use, and female drivers felt more calm and relaxed when driving with the system than did male drivers. This confirms previous studies that show the same; female drivers tend to like in-vehicle information systems more than male drivers [14, 17-19]. Female drivers also perceived that this system had a positive influence on their driving performance.

There are still many open questions related to this research; How would other age groups react to this type of in-vehicle system? Would there be a different reaction using a male voice? What other linguistic and para-linguistic cues might influence perception and performance? What would be the reaction to a dialogue system, interactive system? What is the long term reaction to this type of system? What is needed for the system to build trust instead of becoming annoying? These and many more questions need to be investigated for a better understanding of how in-vehicle systems impacts driving performance.

References

1. Angell, L., et al.: The Driver Workload Metrics Project. National Highway Traffic Safety Administration (2006)
2. Hanowski, R.J., et al.: Driver responses to unexpected situations when using an in-vehicle information system, in Development of human factors guidelines for advanced traveler information systems and commercial vehicle operations, Cener for Transportation Research, Virginia Polytechnic Institute and State University: Blacksburg, VA (1997)
3. Lee, J.D., et al.: Design alternatives for in-vehicle information displays: Message style, modality, location, in Development of human factors guidelines for advanced traveler information systems and commercial vehicle operations. Federal Highway Administration, Washington DC (1996)
4. Paas, F., van Merrienboer, J.: Instructional control of cognitive load in the training of complex cognitive tasks. Educational Psychology Review 6, 51–71 (1994)
5. Paas, F., van Merrienboer, J.: Measurment of cognitive load in instructional research. Perceptual and Motor Skills 79, 419–430 (1994)
6. Sweller, J., van Merrienboer, J., Paas, F.: Cognitive architecture and instructional design. Educational Psychology Review 10, 251–296 (1998)

7. Mayer, R., et al.: When less is more: Meaningful learning from visual and verbal summaries of science textbook lessons. Journal of Educational Pshychology 88, 64–73 (1996)
8. Mayer, R., Chandler, P.: When learning is just a click away: Does simple user interaction foster deeper understanding of multimedia messages? Journal of Educational Psychology 93, 390–397 (2001)
9. Mayer, R., Moreno, R.: Nine ways to reduce cognitive load in multimedia learning. Educational Psychologist 38, 43–52 (2003)
10. Rinalducci, E.J., Mouloua, M., Smither, J.: Cognitive and perceptual factors in aging and driving performance, F.D.o. Transportation, Editor. Department of Psychology, University of Florida, Orlando, pp. 1–26 (2003)
11. Brouwer, W.H.: Older Drivers and Attentional Demands: Consequences for Human Factors Research. In: Human Factors and Ergonomics Society-Europe, Chapter on Aging and Human Factors, Soesterberg, Netherlands (1993)
12. Rabbitt, P.: An age-decrement in the ability to ignore irrelevant information. Journal of Gerontology 20, 233–238 (1965)
13. Jonsson, I.-M., Zajicek, M.: Selecting the voice for an In-car information system for older adults. In: Human Computer Interaction International 2005, Las Vegas, Nevada, USA (2005)
14. Jonsson, I.-M., et al.: Thank you I did not see that: In-car Speech-Based Information Systems for Older Adults. In: Conference on Human Factors in Computing Systems, ACM Press, Portland, Oregon, USA (2005)
15. Likert, R.: A Technique for the Measurement of Attitudes. Archives of Psychology, vol. 40 (1932)
16. Rubin, R.B., Palmgreen, P., Sypher, H.E.: Communication Research Measures: A Sourcebook, p. 400. Guilford Press, New York (1994)
17. Nass, C., et al.: Improving Automotive Safety by Pairing Driver Emotion and Car Voice Emotion. In: CHI '05 extended abstracts on Human factors in computing systems, ACM Press, New York, NY (2005)
18. Jonsson, I.-M., et al.: Don't blame me I am only the Driver: Impact of Blame Attribution on Attitudes and Attention to Driving Task. In: CHI '04 extended abstracts on Human factors in computing systems, Vienna, Austria (2004)
19. Jonsson, I.M., et al.: Got Info? Examining the Consequences of Inaccurate Information Systems. In: International Driving Symposium on Human Factors in Driver Assessment, Training, and Vehicle Design, Rockport, Maine (2005)

Changing Interfaces Using Natural Arm Posture – A New Interaction Paradigm for Pedestrian Navigation Systems on Mobile Devices

Ceren Kayalar and Selim Balcisoy

Sabanci University
Computer Graphics Laboratory
Istanbul, 34956 Turkey
ckayalar@su.sabanciuniv.edu, balcisoy@sabanciuniv.edu

Abstract. This paper presents a new interaction technique, which is based on arm posture recognition, for mobile computing devices to switch between different visualization modes seamlessly. We implemented a pedestrian navigation system on Pocket PC, which is connected to a GPS receiver and an inertial orientation tracker. In the global coordinate system, user's position is tracked with GPS data, and in the local coordinate system user's arm posture is mapped into two application dependent states with inertial orientation tracker data. Hence, natural interaction and different levels of information is provided by processing orientation tracker data. As unnecessary computation and rendering increase power consumption in small devices, we introduced another state to our system, which saves battery according to the user's idle arm posture.

Keywords: Context-aware retrieval, mobile computing, interaction techniques, posture recognition.

1 Introduction

Location based services are becoming more available for different use cases, most notably navigation and information services. Vehicle based navigation systems became commercially successful systems as they can provide accurate data consistently. Most car navigation systems combine GPS and car telemetry data with Geographical Information Systems (GIS) data. One important advantage of vehicle systems is the available infrastructure to access the telemetry and other electronic systems (radio, lights, phone) and estimate the user context and adjust the system accordingly by adjusting the visual and audio characteristics, such as loudness of the radio, of the system if necessary.

Pedestrian navigation systems also require precise estimation of a user's context, which consists of environmental entities affecting the interaction between a user and an application. Context-aware systems use context to provide relevant services to the user, where relevancy depends on the user's task such as walking around, gazing in a particular direction [1].

C. Stephanidis (Ed.): Universal Access in HCI, Part II, HCII 2007, LNCS 4555, pp. 431–440, 2007.

With the advent of more capable mobile terminals such as mobile phones and PDAs it has become possible to perform visually appealing 2D and 3D renderings in real-time [15]. These can be maps, task specific applications (rescue, cultural heritage), and interactive guides; and have variable visual complexity. The size constraints of mobile devices make them cumbersome with minimal space for user interfaces. Moreover users expect to retrieve information using mobile computing devices with less effort. Therefore creating natural interaction techniques for mobile devices is an important challenge. One such interaction technique is to utilize users hand posture or gestures to trigger tasks, switch between applications or play games. With the advent of camera phones, first examples of such interfaces begin to be developed [13]. Even the computer vision algorithms are adequate for simple gesture recognition tasks on limited performance terminals; those techniques have not become mainstream, because of their high power consumption.

In this paper we are investigating context estimation methods for PDAs. In case of tour-guide applications we can simplify the context of a mobile user into three: investigation, navigation and idle. In the investigation state user is analyzing the façade of a building or an artifact in detail, where the application should present detailed visual information, if possible, using an Augmented Reality framework [6, 14, 17]. However at the navigation state the application should present 2D or 3D maps of the area with task specific data: street layout, names etc. The application is expected to detect also the idle state conditions when the user is not looking to the screen and trigger power save actions such as CPU clock adjustment. We propose to use a single orientation sensor to estimate the context of the user. This estimation is based on a novel posture recognition technique. The location will be computed using data from GPS sensor.

We first give a review on related work. In section three we describe our recognition method in detail. Afterwards we present a prototype system and case study to illustrate our ideas. The final chapter concludes the paper and presents our ideas on future research.

2 Related Work

Location based services require estimation of mobile users location with adequate accuracy. Depending on application's needs this accuracy can be between kilometers or centimeters. Moreover most of the services require orientation data, at least the heading. GPS is the most prominent technology around for delivering up to centimeter accuracy (Differential-GPS). However, the fact that it only works outdoors is a major drawback. An example GPS based guide application is developed by Burigat and Chittaro [4]. Several alternative positioning technologies such as GSM-Triangulation, Wireless LAN Triangulation can estimate one's position indoors, using access points with well known positions [5, 9]. A recent work of Peternier et al. [12] presents an integrated mobile mixed reality system using Wireless LAN technologies. Another possibility is to track walking data for positioning purposes. There are several research groups working on walking behavior and pedestrian tracking [11, 7].

Until now all location based services we have investigated rely heavily on precise position and orientation of the user in global coordinate frame. However to create natural interfaces for handheld devices we need to recognize upper body postures, most importantly the position and orientation of the terminal relative to user's head.

Recognition of upper body postures and gestures is studied by several research groups: Amft et al reporting a Hidden Markov Models based gesture recognition algorithm up to 94% success rate for eating and drinking arm gestures [2].

Bao and Intille developed a system to detect everyday physical activities using five body-worn wire-free biaxial accelerometers with high accuracy (84%) [3]. They report that even with two sensors – thigh and wrist their recognition performance does not deteriorate. Similarly Lee and Mase report up to 91% success rate with their wearable sensors for activity recognition [10].

Widgor and Balakrishnan implemented a novel text input technique for mobile phones using one 2 DOF tilt sensor (acceleration sensor) to recognize user hand actions [18]. They report that 20 to 50 Hz sampling rates should be required for robust tilt implementation.

3 Posture Recognition

As presented in the previous section, all of the orientation sensor work is based on either to assist precise tracking and positioning of the user in space or gesture recognition using several sensors.

Our goal is to create a stable differentiation mechanism between several hand postures and map them to several application dependent contexts.

The developed recognition algorithm is based on state transitions triggered by time-line analysis of orientation and angular velocity of the sensor. The orientation and angular velocity are the natural arm posture data of a pedestrian, which can be used as context widgets for a context-aware application.

The angle between user's forearm and upper arm is obtained from the orientation sensor as pitch angle, α, and analyzed to recognize different postures. We have gathered sample data from mobile users with various walking speeds, while moving their hands between three postures:

- *vertical*, where pitch angle is around 0°,
- *horizontal*, where pitch angle is around 90°,
- *idle*, where the hand may move freely (Fig. 1).

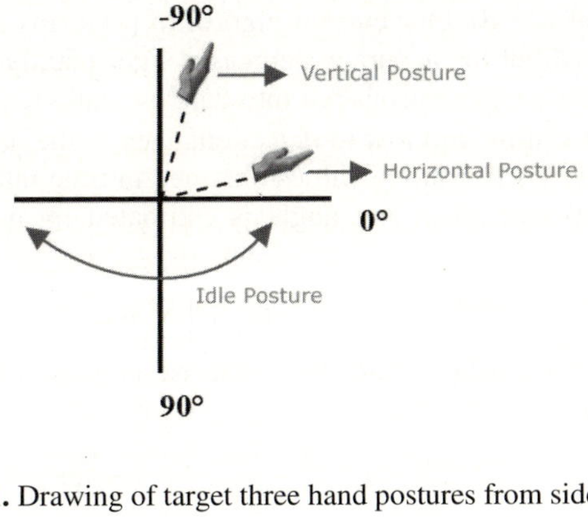

Fig. 1. Drawing of target three hand postures from side view

Fig. 2 shows pitch angle measurements of the user's arm movement in three different conditions: standing, walking, and running. Transitions between diverse arm postures can be inferred from the top left plot of Fig. 2: For $0s \leq t < 5s$, the posture is on idle state. After this interval the user moves her hand up and stabilizes on horizontal posture until $t \approx 10s$. For $10s < t < 20s$, the user moves her hand down, stabilizes on idle state and moves her hand up. For $20s \leq t < 27s$, vertical posture is observed, and so on.

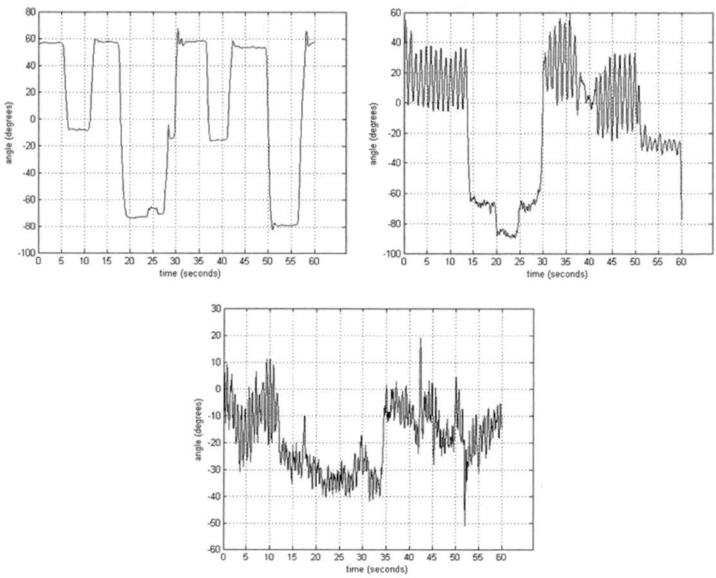

Fig. 2. Pitch Angle Measurements while user is standing (top left), walking (top, right) and running (bottom)

The measurements indicate that with the increase of velocity the noise on the measured signal increases significantly. The noise can be observed on the top right plot of Fig. 2, where the transition from idle posture to horizontal posture is not clearly recognizable at $t \approx 40$. Our current algorithm performs acceptably with users walking with low speed but the accuracy decreases significantly with increased speed due to the high frequency noise introduced into data by walking and running motion.

We implemented a sliding window to detect changes of the hand on pitch angle, α. A window, which contains five angle values obtained in time interval [t-1, t-5], is created at each time step and upcoming angle is estimated by multiplying them with increasing weights.

$$0.1*\alpha_i + 0.1*\alpha_{i+1} + 0.1*\alpha_{i+2} + 0.2*\alpha_{i+3} + 0.5*\alpha_{i+4} = \alpha_{estimated} . \quad (1)$$

The $\alpha_{estimated}$ angle is compared with the measured angle α_{i+5} to identify if the hand is moving up or down.

$$\alpha_{i+5} > \alpha_{estimated} \rightarrow \textit{downside change} . \tag{2}$$

$$\alpha_{i+5} < \alpha_{estimated} \rightarrow \textit{upside change} . \tag{3}$$

$$\alpha_{i+5} \approx \alpha_{estimated} \rightarrow \textit{no change}, \begin{cases} \alpha_{i+5} \rightarrow \text{-}90°, \textit{vertical} \\ \alpha_{i+5} \rightarrow \quad 0°, \textit{horizontal} . \end{cases} \tag{4}$$

However using the pitch angle in one single direction is not sufficient enough to have robust posture recognition. We have also evaluated the case, where the user performs short tilts (rotations around the longitudinal axis) causing an inference on the state transition. For such cases, a filter is implemented on the system which increased the state transition accuracy.

Fig. 3 shows plots of sample pitch and tilt angle measurements of the same motion and corresponding state estimations. For 7s< t <9s, tilt angle is increasing and decreasing instantly (top right plot, Fig. 3) which affects the pitch angle. In spite of the fact that the user holds her hand stable around -20° during angular data measurement, the top left plot of Fig. 3 shows that the pitch angle is changing up to 20°. Same erroneous measurement can be observed for 11s < t < 15s. These unexpected changes cause inaccurate state estimation (bottom left plot, Fig. 3). Therefore, estimation accuracy is increased (bottom right plot, Fig. 3) by introducing the system with a tilt angle filter, which locks the state to the previous one if major changes occur on tilt angles.

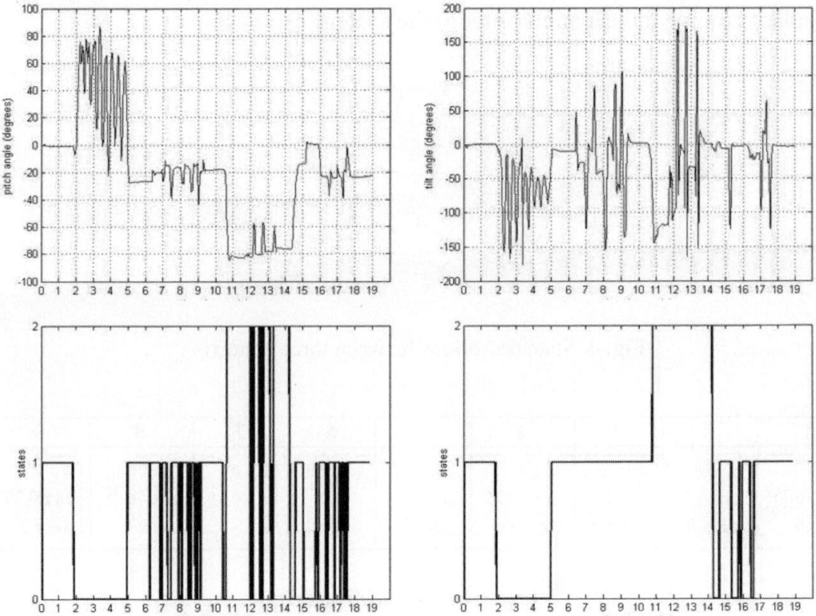

Fig. 3. Sample pitch angle measurement (top left), Tilt measurement of the same posture (top right) causing erroneous estimation – 0: idle state, 1: navigation state, 2: investigation state (bottom left) and increased estimation accuracy with tilt filter (bottom, right)

The system becomes unstable and produces erroneous results when users perform other occasional movement patterns. Therefore we have introduced an additional data, angular velocity, to the recognition system. The change of angular velocity together with the angle allows us more stable recognition results.

Finally we developed a finite state machine to map all possible postures into one of the three states: investigation, navigation and idle (Fig. 4). The investigation state is when a user holds a mobile terminal in vertical position to use it in an Augmented Reality context. In this condition the user needs to investigate point of interest buildings and receives environmental information according to her gaze direction in the local coordinate frame. The navigation state is when a user holds a mobile terminal in horizontal position to use it to render maps or GIS information. Thus, the user receives environmental information in the global coordinate frame. There is a third idle state, where the user is not in either posture and moves her hand freely. In this state, rendering is minimized to save battery power.

The conditions satisfying the state transitions in Fig. 4 are defined in the table in Fig. 5. In this algorithm, the estimated pitch angle value is compared with the angular value perceived from the orientation sensor at that time step. If they are approximately equal, user's arm posture is estimated to be stable and either in investigation or navigation state (3rd and 6th columns of the table in Fig. 5). Other enumerated transitions include conditions which define possible changes between states, i.e. while arm posture is on idle state and the user moves her hand upwards, then it is possible to switch state to navigation or upside change on arm posture continues and state is switched to investigation. The state estimation algorithm is empowered by introducing angular velocity and tilt angle filter to the system.

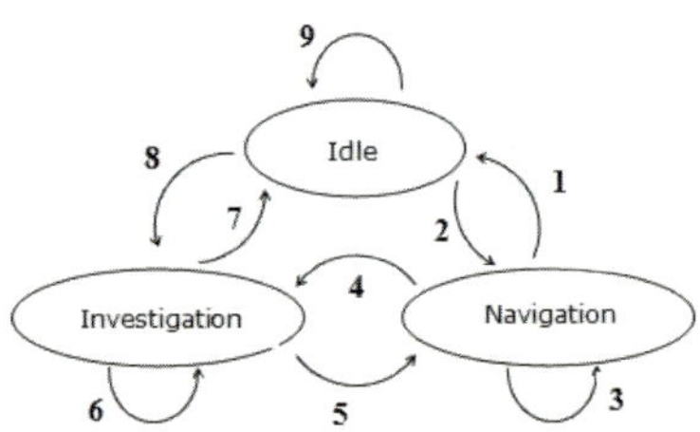

Fig. 4. State transitions between three contexts

1	2	3	4	5	6	7	8	9
$\alpha > 0°$	$\alpha > 0°$	$\alpha \approx 0°$	$\alpha < 0°$	$\alpha < 0°$	$\alpha \approx 90°$	$\alpha > 0°$	$\alpha < 0°$	$\alpha > 0°$
$\omega < -0.75$	$\omega > 0.75$	$\omega \approx 0$	$\omega < -0.75$	$\omega > 0.75$	$\omega \approx 0$	$\omega > 0.75$	$\omega < -0.75$	$\lvert\omega\rvert > 0.75$
$\Delta\alpha < 0$	$\Delta\alpha > 0$	$\Delta\alpha \approx 0$	$\Delta\alpha < 0$	$\Delta\alpha > 0$	$\Delta\alpha \approx 0$	$\Delta\alpha > 0$	$\Delta\alpha < 0$	$\Delta\alpha \neq 0$

$$\omega = angular\ velocity\ (rad/s)$$

$$\Delta\alpha = \alpha_{true} - \alpha_{estimated}$$

Fig. 5. Description of state transitions

Unexpected arm movements of the user can affect the accuracy of the system. While the user holds the PDA in horizontal or vertical position (navigation or investigation state) and suddenly performs fast upward or downward movements with her hand, i.e. waving to somebody, the system is stabilized in the former state with a tolerably accuracy rate.

4 System Setup and Case Study

We have developed an integrated hardware and software system to demonstrate our ideas. We have connected two inertia sensors over RS232 port to a Pocket PC separately. This enabled us to verify our algorithm with more than one sensor technologies. For outdoor case study we also connected a GPS sensor over Bluetooth wireless link (Fig. 6).

The recognition and estimation software is developed in C++. For the case study we have developed an OpenGL|ES based application, also reading the GPS data and orientation data from communication ports. Our OpenGL|ES implementation is based on Vincent Platform [16] and GLUT|ES Windowing libraries [8] (Fig. 7).

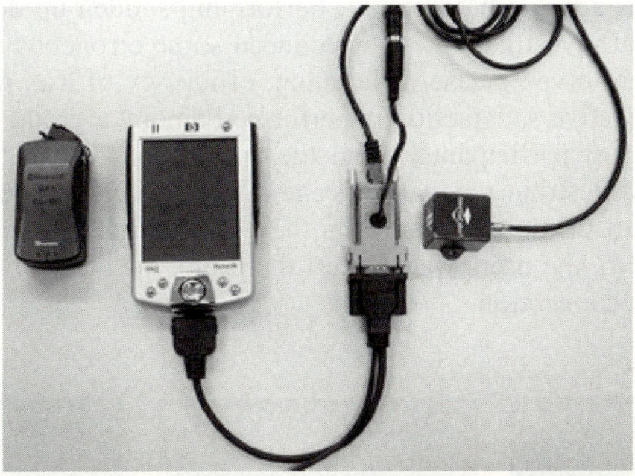

Fig. 6. Hardware prototype: Bluetooth GPS receiver, HP iPAQ Pocket PC h2200 with a RS232 connection to InertiaCube2 (left to right)

We have implemented a prototype navigation system, which guides visitors in downtown Istanbul between Istanbul Biennale venues. However we have experienced serious problems with using both of the orientation sensors we experimented (MTx orientation tracker from Xsens and InterSense's InertiaCube^2) as mobile devices. Both require either large battery packs to operate without a power supply over a long time or a 6V DC power adapter connection. Therefore we have limited the posture recognition experiments in indoors use cases in form of a campus guide (Fig. 8). Note that the investigation mode is not a live video image annotated with data, but a snapshot displayed when the user directs her Pocket PC to the computer science building. For MTX the pitch angle and velocity is acquired from the sensor, for InterSense's InertiaCube^2 we have to compute the angular velocity. For both sensors we experienced stable posture recognition and state switch.

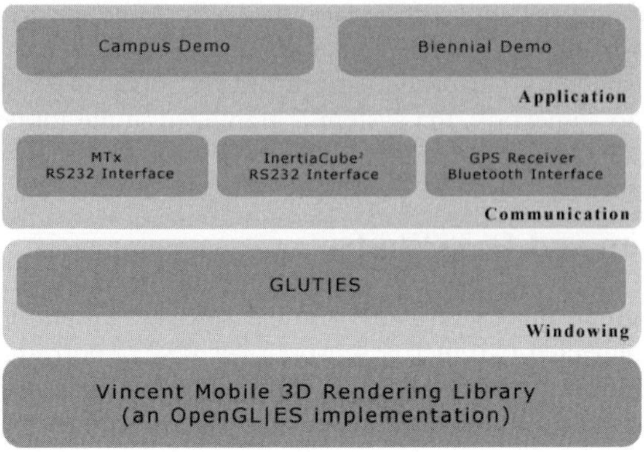

Fig. 7. Software Architecture

We performed a user study to examine the accuracy of our system. In this test, all possible state transitions emphasized in Fig. 4 are performed. The overall accuracy rate is calculated as approximately %87. Performing sudden up-down movements in navigation state and investigation state produced some erroneous results. A usability test covering the prototype's ease of learning, efficiency of use, memorability, error frequency and subjective satisfaction is performed among a group of people aged between 20 to 25. Most participants found the application dependent state transitions appropriate for a pedestrian navigation system, and concluded that once orientation trackers became part of mobile computers they can be used to create natural interaction techniques. Also, the users want to test the prototype outdoors completely with a robust battery pack connection.

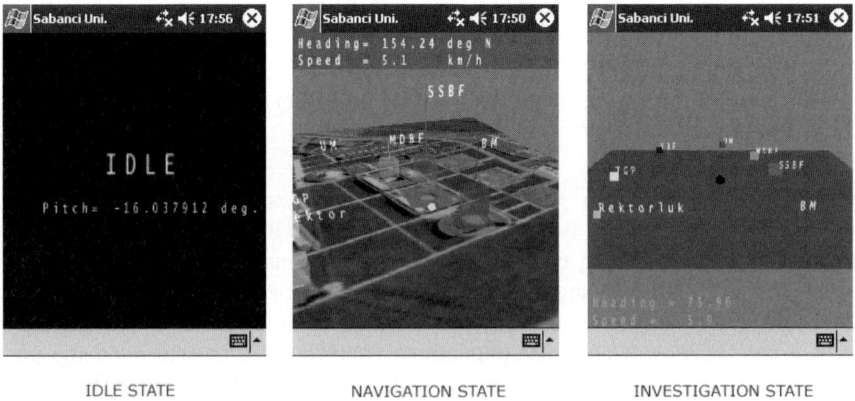

Fig. 8. Seamlessly changing interfaces (Demo video can be downloaded from http://graphics.sabanciuniv.edu/Movies/Mobile.avi)

5 Conclusions and Future Work

We have implemented a recognition algorithm with one orientation sensor attached to a Pocket PC to distinguish between two different postures of the hand and an idle state. This data can be used to differentiate between three states to switch between different applications seamlessly. We tested our approach on two different orientation sensors.

In the global coordinate frame, we used GPS sensor data to locate the user, acquire her gaze direction, embed GIS data and provide information about point of interest buildings. In the local coordinate frame, we used orientation sensor data to allow the user interact with the mobile device while performing natural arm postures and perceive information on different user interfaces. By combining these interaction techniques of global and local coordinate frame, we provide a context-aware interaction framework for pedestrian navigation systems on mobile devices by seamlessly changing graphical user interfaces.

Our work shows that once orientation sensors became part of mobile terminals, they can be used to create natural interaction techniques with mobile terminals.

In future we plan to improve our technique to recognize postures while the user is walking and running. Therefore, a robust battery pack connection must be supplied to the system to test the prototype outdoors completely. Also, we want to improve Augmented Reality context of our system by implementing an investigation state with real-time camera input of the environment, where the buildings are annotated with virtual text labels.

References

1. Abowd, G.D., Dey, A.K., Brown, P.J., Davies, N., Smith, M., Steggles, P.: Towards a Better Understanding of Context and Context-Awareness. In: Gellersen, H.-W. (ed.) HUC 1999. LNCS, vol. 1707, Springer, Heidelberg (1999)
2. Amft, O., Junker, H., Troster, G.: Detection of eating and drinking arm gestures using intertial body-worn sensors. IEEE Symposium on Wearable Computers (2005)
3. Bao, L., Intille, S.S.: Activity Recognition from User-Annotated Acceleration Data. In: Ferscha, A., Mattern, F. (eds.) PERVASIVE 2004. LNCS, vol. 3001, pp. 1–17. Springer, Heidelberg (2004)
4. Burigat, S., Chittaro, L.: Location-aware visualization of VRML models in GPS-based mobile guides. In: Web3D '05: Proceedings of the tenth international conference on 3D Web technology, pp. 57–64. ACM Press, New York (2005)
5. Cheng, Y., Chawathe, Y., Lamarca, A., Krumm, J.: Accuracy characterization for metropolitanscale wi-fi localization. Third International Conference on Mobile Systems, Applications and Services (2005)
6. Feiner, S., MacIntyre, B., Höllerer, T., Webster, A.: A touring machine: Prototyping 3D mobile augmented reality systems for exploring the urban environment. In: Proc. ISWC'97. Cambridge, MA, USA, pp. 74–81 (1997)
7. Foxlin, E.: Pedestrian Tracking with Shoe-Mounted Intertial Sensors. IEEE Computer Graphics and Applications, Nov/Dec (2005)
8. GLUT|ES - The OpenGL|ES Utility Toolkit, (as of April 2006) http://glutes.sourceforge.net/

9. Howard, A., Siddiqi, S., Sukhatme, G.S.: An experimental study of localization using wireless ethernet. In: Proceedings of the 4th International Conference on Field and Service Robotics, Lake Yamanaka, Japan (2003)
10. Lee, S., Mase, K.: Activity and Location Recognition Using Wearable Sensors. IEEE Pervasive Computing 1(3), 24–32 (2002)
11. Lee, S., Mase, K.: Recognition of Walking Behaviors for Pedestrian Navigation. In: Proc. of IEEE International Conference on Control Applications, Mexico City, Mexico (2001)
12. Peternier, A., Vexo, F., Thalmann, D.: Wearable Mixed Reality System In Less Than 1 Pound. Eurographics Symposium on Virtual Environments (2006)
13. Rohs, M.: Real-world interaction with camera-phones. In: International Symposium on Ubiquitous Computing Systems (2004)
14. Schmalstieg, D., Reitmayr, G.: Augmented Reality as a Medium for Cartography. In: Cartwright, W., Peterson, M., Gartner, G. (eds.) Multimedia Cartography, 2nd edn. Springer, Heidelberg (2006)
15. Shimada, S., Tanizaki, M., Maruyama, K.: Ubiquitous Spatial-Information Services Using Cell Phones. IEEE Micro (2002)
16. Vincent Mobile 3D Rendering Library (as of April 2006), http://sourceforge.net/projects/ogl-es
17. Wagner, D., Schmalstieg, D.: First Steps Towards Handheld Augmented Reality. In: Proc. Seventh IEEE International Symposium on Wearable Computers (2003)
18. Widgor, D., Balakrishnan, R.: TiltText: Using Tilt for Text Input to Mobile Phones, UIST 2003, CHI Letters, vol. 5(2) (2003)

Ergonomics of Contemporary Urban Necropolises

T. Lewandowski[1] and J. Charytonowicz[2]

[1] Institute of Architecture and Town Planning, Technical University of Lodz,
Al. Politechniki 6, Lodz 90-924, Poland
levando@tlen.pl, archtomlew@wp.pl

[2] Department of Architecture, Wroclaw University of Technology
ul.B.Prusa 53/55, Wroclaw 50-317, Poland
jerzy.charytonowicz@pwr.wroc.pl

Abstract. The contemporary ergonomics can accuraely describe psychophysical capabilities of the human body, thus greatly contributing to the process of improving the living quality and parameters. Many everyday activities, relating to the man's work, leisure, communication, or social relations, are subject to ergonomic rules and principles, and the same is true of urban and architectural space of urbanized centres as a material space of such activities. It is here that man actively satisfies his needs to engineer his space and facilities necessary for him as an individual – e.g. dwelling houses, and as community – e.g. necropolises. Modern forms of spatial arrangement of necropolises search for solutions which will not only provide a rational - ergonomic material shape of the burial place, but also satisfy mental needs of the man connected with the burial, funeral, cult of the dead, visits to the cemetery, irrespective of the man's age and ability. Among important problems to be solved we should pay special attention to the question of accessibility of the cemetery space to the elderly and the disabled. Therefore all elements constituting the structure of necropolis must allow for ergonomic designing factors.

Keywords: ergonomics of space of contemporary memory places, design for all, the disabled, design of necropolises, new burial form.

1 Introduction

From the ancient times until today, science has perceived man as a combination of the spirit (psyche) and body (soma-physis). Specialist sciences separately and specifically study each aspect of man's **mental** (psychology, sociology, anthropology, culture science, and other) and **somatic** activities (medicine, anatomy, engineering, and other) and create a picture of such activities characteristic of the given specialisation field.

Urban planning (on macro scale), architecture, and ergonomics (on human scale) define the frames and shape the processes of man's spatial and material existence, with a special focus on man's psychophysical needs and capabilities.

C. Stephanidis (Ed.): Universal Access in HCI, Part II, HCII 2007, LNCS 4555, pp. 441–450, 2007.

2 Urban Planning, Architecture, and Ergonomics in the Context of Spatial Organisation of Urban Necropolises

Urban planning, as a science of programming and planning cities (urban structures) creates formal and legal frames for architecture in the form of urban planning concepts. It satisfies the diversified functional needs of all urbanised space - city users. Specifically, it focuses on the public space and the architectural objects that form it. It creates, implements, and oversees public spaces and facilities, including remembrance places – necropolises.

Urban planning pursues to build a logical, finite, and functional city structure, taking into account the following criteria: economics, sustainability, ergonomics, security, and accessibility to all users. With regard to city space, the overarching objective is to create „spatial order", i.e. a consistent and logical, adequately scaled neighbourhood of the diverse functionalities of city structures and each of their components.

Architecture, the art of forming (creating) space to satisfy man's material and spiritual needs relating to designing and erecting buildings, consistently follows the urban planning regulations it is subject to. Architectural design combines into a cohesive whole a facility's function (intended use), form (aesthetics), structure (materials and structural solutions), and economic assumptions of the investment project. It needs to apply the achievements of many sciences: construction, construction statistics and physics, urban planning, economics, and sociology, psychology, culture, and other. The area of design activities relates to both public and private spaces. **A well designed architecture and urban plan evokes the assumed psychophysical feelings, which distinguishes it from the other objects in that space.**

If architecture is the art of shaping (creating) space in order to satisfy man's material and spiritual needs, then **ergonomics** is a science that adjusts the whole material environment to man's psychophysical capabilities. Many domains of man's everyday activities related to work, relaxation, dwelling, communication, and relationships with other people are subject to ergonomic laws and principles. Ergonomics significantly affects the processes of improving and human life quality and parameters.

Ergonomics is further categorised into the following domains of specialisation[1]:

- **conceptual ergonomics** – introduces ergonomic principles at the development stage of concept proposals or designs
- **corrective ergonomics** – corrects work conditions by modernising the existing work stations
- **physical ergonomics** – relates to human physical capabilities
- **cognitive ergonomics** – related to man's mental capabilities
- **organisational ergonomics** – optimises sociotechnical processes
- ...?

[1] http://www.iea.cc/

The contemporary ergonomics deals with the following aspects:

- Newborn man
- Living and working man
- Elderly man with limited psychophysical fitness – disableds
- Dead man – in relation to living man, a phenomenon strongly affecting the human psyche – this is a new research area

Demise ergonomics – is a genuine proposal for the name of a new ergonomic domain of specialisation to deal with the dead man in relation to the living man. It will help to show a full picture of man's activities in ergonomic studies and complement them with to date undescribed research areas as part of the comprehensive approach to human life from birth to death.

Remembrance places - necropolises are important structural elements of cities that strongly affect the human psyche. Within the city structure, necropolises primarily play an important practical role as places where to bury human remains, and a symbolic one – as remembrance places. The multifaceted aspect of the material shape of remembrance places – necropolises, applies to every man in the world, whatever their culture and religion, irrespective of any age limits or physical fitness levels.

Modern forms of spatial arrangement of necropolises search for solutions which will not only provide a rational (ergonomic, economic, ecological) material shape of the burial place, but also satisfy man's mental needs connected with the burial, funeral, veneration of the dead, visits to the cemetery, irrespective of man's age and physical fitness level. Among the important problems to be solved we should pay special attention to the question of accessibility of the cemetery space to the elderly and the disabled. Therefore all elements constituting the structure of necropolis must allow for ergonomic design factors.

3 Selected Ergonomic Aspects of Spatial Organisation of Urban Necropolises

The space of "cities of the dead" – necropolises - is shaped analogously to that of "cities of the living" - metropolises, and is subject to the same criteria, standards, rules and space engineering processes as city structures. It boasts the same infrastructural components and spatial organisation, and poses similar engineering problems.

3.1 Seniors and Disableds – Necropolis Accessibility Issue

"Each man is a physical, psychic, and mental entity.(...) We are all deficient in certain periods of life,(...) we get old and become increasingly weaker and mentally less effective. If (...) we want to realistically consider the shape of the environment we

engineer to satisfy human needs, it is imperative that we consider the needs and capabilities of the disabled." [2]. (Figure 1)

Fig. 1. Life pyramid. *" W e are all deficient in certain periods of life,"* [3].

Increased numbers of elderly people (seniors), who, as they get older and less healthy are included in the group of disableds, and increased numbers of the disabled in the whole society require that the urban space be adjusted to the needs of these groups of users.

To this end, all necropolis components must take into account the **ergonomic design factors** which help remove **architectural, urban planning, and functional barriers** and **psychological barriers** that arise in relation to disability and the old age. The activities intended to remove tangible constraints (architectural, urban planning, and functional barriers) and intangible constraints (mentality) can be defined as one of the forms of active social rehabilitation and an effort to help the disabled fully return to the society to the extent possible. In practice, this means the need to apply the knowledge comprosed in the science known as **„ergonomics",** one that is frequently forgotten by architects, urban planners, cemetery managements, and many other specialists. We often speak of ergonomically designed objects of everyday use, which, set aside the marketing slogan, have nothing to do with ergonomics. At the same time we forget about ergonomics, whose rules, if applied at the design stage of urban configurations, and their later redevelopments, would and could facilitate everyday life by making urbanised spaces accessible to disableds, seniors, and people that are naturally less fit.

Special attention should be paid to the issue of satisfying the psychic and spiritual needs related to the burial:

- the right to participate in funerals
- the right to visit tombs

as well as the tangible needs in the meaning of accessibility to all spaces in the city – including necropolises – by disableds. In effect of the existing barriers these rights are frequently denied or their exercise is largely hindered.

---

[2] Syrkus H., Społeczne cele Urbanizacji (Social objectives of urbanisation), PWN, Warsaw (1984) p. 639-640.

[3] Syrkus H., Społeczne cele Urbanizacji(Social objectives of urbanisation), PWN, Warsaw (1984) p. 639.

Therefore, we more and more frequently notice the needs of the elderly people and the disabled. Architects and urban planners design urban spaces so that this group can actively and independently play an active role in the life of the society by adjusting the urban spaces and cemeteries with their adjacent areas to the needs of these social groups.

Fig. 2. Old age and partial disability – accessibility issue[4]

Traditionally, seniors are the most frequent visitors to necropolises, they care of the tombs, greenery, meet and farewell the people close to them – relatives and friends. In this way they get ready to "get on the other side" – the symbolic "better side of life".

3.2 Effect of the Burial Form on the Spatial Arrangement of a Necropolis

An increasingly important problem for most urban centers, both in Europe and worldwide, is **shrinkage of grounds** designed for necropolises, and the related **problem of the burial form.**

The burial form and its ergonomics determine the architectural form of the grave, its size, shape, and division of cemetery sections, which together make up the layout of the cemetery that is the spatial organization of the necropolis.

The interrelation is presented in Table 1, e.g. comparison between the traditional pit and the urn burials (See Table 1).

Various burial forms have produced diversified size standards relating to funerary caskets (urn, coffin, funerary bag, etc.), or burial places (single level, multilevel) thus determining the diversity of plots and whole necropolises.

Some important phenomena observed in all contemporary necropolises include **minimised size of the burial casket and burial place, and vertical spatial arrangements** (compacting) aimed at increasing the number of new burial places and lessening (through concentration) possible environmental threats. These highly powerful tendencies are gaining momentum in all newly-developed and generally accessible necropolises in large urban conurbations in the world.

[4] http://www.plfoto.pl/autor kaiser_souza

Table 1. The interrelation between traditional pit and urn burials – pictures at a scale of the actual sizes and proportions [2,3] [5]

EFFECT OF THE BURIAL FORM ON THE SPATIAL ARRANGEMENT OF A NECROPOLIS			
	inhumation	urn burial	comments
„packing of the body" coffin / urn	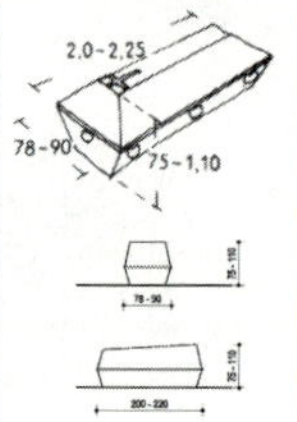		a coffin is 39 times – for its volume 21 times – for the area greater than an urn
grave	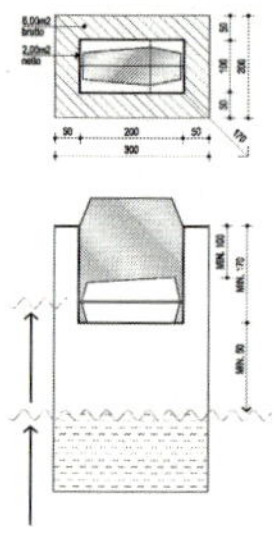	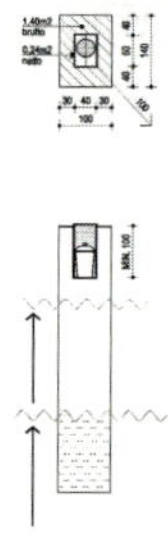	the area of a single inhumation is 8 times – net 4 times – gross greater than the area of a single urn grave and more shallow by 41%
section	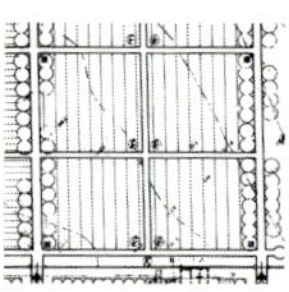	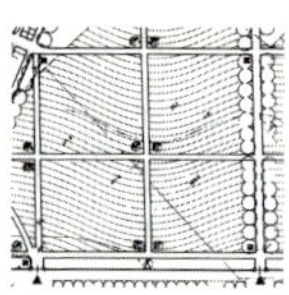	traditional cemetery sections are characterized by a rigid rectangular design of the rows urn cemetery sections offer the possibility of soft, curvilinear arrangement of the rows
urban design	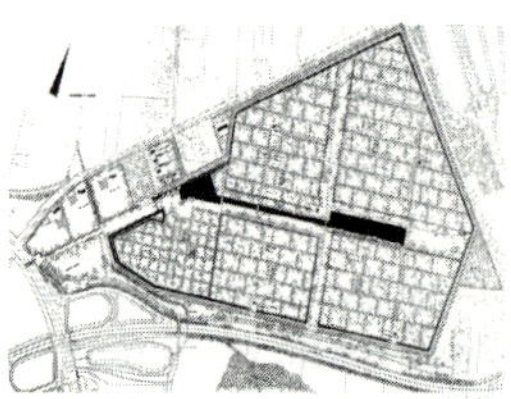 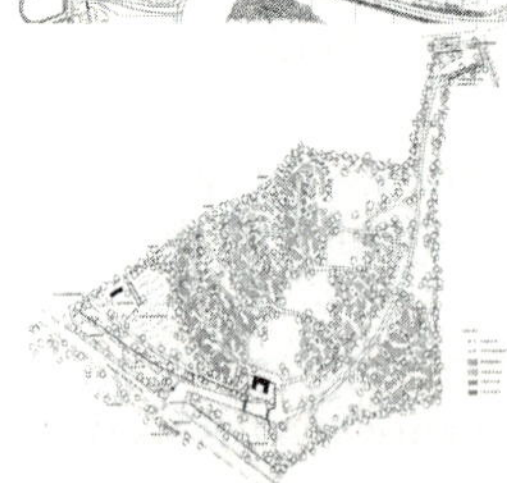		big-dimensional inhumation occupy the whole area of the cemetery („stone cemeteries") small-dimensional urn graves allow to diversify the structure of the cemetery by introducing large green areas („green, woodland cemeteries")

[5] Drawings by Tomasz Lewandowski, [1], [10].

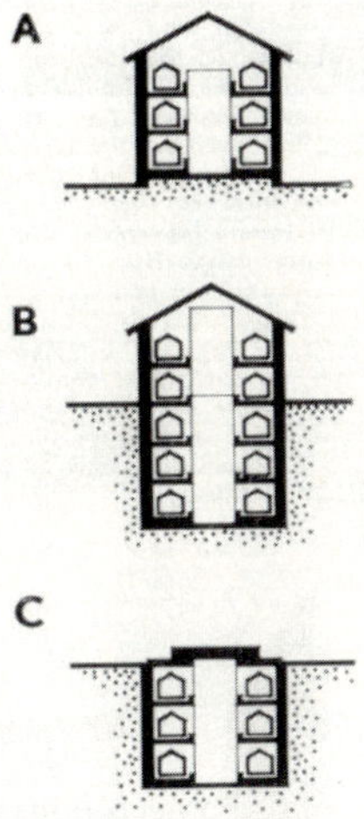

Fig. 3. Verticality of spatial arrangements (compacting) aimed at increasing the number of new burial places - type A,B,C [6]

3.3 Urn and Cybernetic Burial

Cybernecropolis – www.cemetery.com – In the time of development of the information society, and easy access to the Internet, there have appeared cybernecropolises, that is necropolises organized in the fashion of real-world cemeteries. Cyberspace cemeteries are necropolises in a new format. Though virtual, they may be the only place where we can find biographies of the deceased, photographies, memories, or listen to their voice, or watch films about them – everything recorded in an adequate format. Cybernecropolises make use of all advanced multimedia facilities of the commonly known web pages. They are built similarly to real-world cemeteries. Each commemorated deceased person has a virtual grave on which a visitor may put virtual flowers or a stone (Judaism), light a virtual grave lamp, and sign in the guestbook for visitors to the tombstone. Graves are grouped in virtual cemetery sections arranged alphabetically or by selected categories, e.g. by religions, casualties of accidents and disasters, soldiers killed in action, people who died of specific diseases, practising a definite profession, being a celebrity in their lives.

Cybernecropolises allow us – whenever and wherever – to visit persons who have already passed away. The solution's versatility has been highly appreciated by all Internet users, especially by handicapped persons or those who are temporarily not able to visit their relatives' graves. It is evidenced by the numbers of Internet users visiting virtual cemeteries. According to an administrator of one of the web pages, there are about half a billion of them in the world.

[6] Robert Auzelle, Dernieres Demeures. Conception Composition Realization Du Cimetiere Contemporain, Paris (1965), p.256.

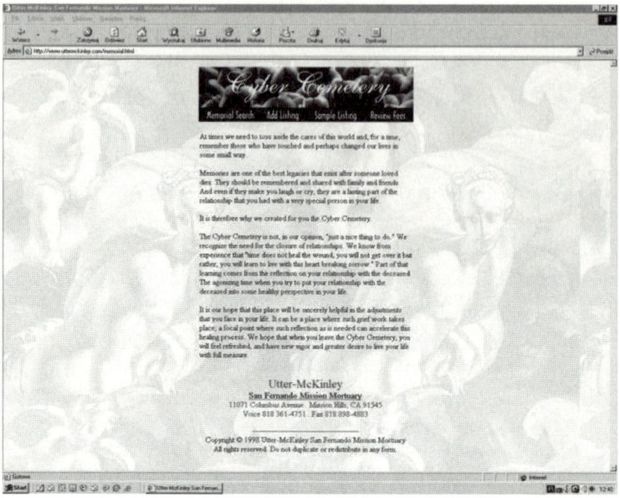

Fig. 4. Website of Cybernecropolis in the USA

In the macro-scale, a cybernecropolis is an enormous multimedia encyclopaedia – a database of the buried people, and representation of our contemporary society left for future generations.

Cybernecropolis and burial in the cyberspace – due to its multimedia nature, versatility of solution, high speed of construction and transformation, and unlimited accessibility – seems to be the burial of the future in the virtual space, that would operate in parallel with other forms of the real space.

In authors' opinion, the fullest and generally most accepted form of burial, as well as a compromise solution, will be an urn and cyberspace (UC) burial. A tomb on an urn cemetery will be the best form of commemorating a deceased person within a limited family circle. It will be complemented with a cyberspace grave as a multimedia, unlimited and common form of worshipping the person in a wider social circle.

3.4 Formal and Legal Conditions and Urban Necropolises Management Models

An important role in engineering quality necropolis space is played by formal and legal requirements that sanction the operational and organisational rules of the urban plan.

The legal regulation in force in many countries in the world (e.g. in Poland) are outdated and do not meet the contemporary needs by not applying the ergonomic design and usage rules, common standards of accessibility to the disabled, infrastructure, new forms of burials or tombs, new burial technologies, new forms of ownership, or new necropolis management systems. Outdated legal regulations enhance the pathologies in the necropolis space use and the monopoly of secular and clerical circles on the funerary market.

A contemporary necropolis in the context of free market economy is a modern enterprise that offers a full range of services to the late man's family and manage the cemetery in a transparent way to the **ISO standards**. An important role is played by the preferred necropolis management model. Two models are predominant: denominational and council model.

In the **denominational model,** cemetery management is entrusted to a denominational commune that each time creates diversified rules and regulations for the necropolis operations. This model gives rise to a series of pathologies which slow down the processes of adjusting such spaces to the existing standards, including the needs of the disabled, as exemplified by denominational cemeteries in Poland.

In the **council model,** cemetery management is entrusted to a specialised public utility that usually manages all municipal cemeteries, and a council-owned funeral company. This model guarantees unified rules and regulations for all necropolises, full data transparency, personal and decision control over the management. It expedites the management procedures, changes to and unification of the accessibility standards for all users. Examples of this model and its effects on the high quality of necropolises in European cities include Prague/Czech Republic, Budapest/Hungary, Vienna/Austria, Warsaw, Częstochowa/Poland.

4 Conclusions

We shape the tangible urban space, but the tangible urban space shapes us, too. [7]. As the demand for high quality of the surrounding space increases, the awareness of these relationships will exert a strong influence on new projects and their implementation.

On the material (somatic) plane, research projects in town planning, architecture and ergonomics should take special regard of satisfaction of mental needs of the man, in order to provide a complete image of the man in the studies.

Demise ergonomics – is a genuine proposal for the name of a new ergonomic domain of specialisation to deal with the dead man in relation to the living man. It will help to show a full picture of man's activities in ergonomic studies and complement them with to date undescribed research areas as part of the comprehensive approach to human life from birth to death.

References

1. Ehlgőtz, R.: Competitions of Horticultural Architecture.Cemeteries-Memorial places-Chapels. Berlin/Hamburg, Paul Parey Verlag, pp. 9–37 (1965)
2. Lewandowski, T.: New forms of spatial development of necropolises in Europe – Nowe formy organizacji przestrzenej nekropolii w Europie, Zastosowania ergonomii, Zielona Gora, Nr 1-2, pp. 141–158 (2004)

[7] Theodor Heuss – first President of the Federal German Republic between 1949-59 literally said: "first people shape houses, then houses shape people", Herbert Kuldschun, Erich Rossmann „Budownictwo dla upośledzonych fizycznie", Arkady (1980) p.110.

3. Lewandowski, T., Charytonowicz, J.: Forms of necropolises in the computer era, HCI, 11th International Conference on Human Computer Interaction, Las Vegas, USA, (22-27 July) 2005, CD, ISBN 0-8058-5897-5 (2005) paper 53 (2005)
4. Lewandowski, T., Charytonowicz, J.: Necropolis and its structural elements – Nekropolia i jej elementy strukturalne, Zastosowania ergonomii, Kwartalnik, Zielona Gora, Nr 1-3, pp. 131–145 (2005)
5. Lewandowski, T., Charytonowicz, J.: Search for new form of burial: horizontal or vertical?, Poszukiwania nowych form pochówku: poziomo czy pionowo?, Zastosowania ergonomii, Kwartalnik, Zielona Gora, Nr 1-3, pp. 261–272 (2006)
6. Charytonowicz, J., Lewandowski, T., Witczak, P.: Postulate for accessibility of remembrance places to senior and disabled persons in the information age – MKEN', Ergonomia niepelnosprawnym w wieku informacji, Lodz, Poland (2004) pp. 77–88 (2004)
7. Robert Auzelle, Dernieres Demeures. Conception Composition Realization Du Cimetiere Contemporain, Paris (1965)
8. Syrkus, H.: Społeczne cele Urbanizacji, PWN, Warszawa (1984)
9. Wejchert, K.: Przestrzeń wokół nas, Fibak Noma Press, Katowice (1993)
10. Neufert, E.: Podrecznik projektowania architektoniczno-budowlanego (2nd Polish ed.) Warszawa, Arkady, p. 531 (1995)

The Use of Virtual Reality to Train Older Adults in Processing of Spatial Information

Dyi-Yih Michael Lin and Po-Yuan Darren Yang

Cogvitive Aging and Digital Interaction Design Lab
Dpet. of Industrial Engineering and Management
Shou University
Kaohsiung 840, Taiwan
dlin@isu.edu.tw

Abstract. The present study examined the effect of virtual reality/VR on training older adults in spatial-based performance. Navigating emergency escape routes in a local hospital was exemplified as the taks domain. 15 older adults and 15 college students participated in an experiment where VR, VR plus a bird-view map, and two-diemtional/2D map presentations were manipulated as within-subject treatment levels of training media. The results indicated that the older subject was less advantaged in identifying the correct turns leading to the emergency exits. While the older subject was also found to have more difficulty in recalling route landmarks, the 2D and VR-plus-map presentations produced significantly stronger spatial memory than the pure VR media for both age groups. When mental rotation was evaluated, the older subject was able to achieve comparable performance if emergency routes were trained by the VR, and the VR-plus-map presentations. Detailed implications were discussed for the design of training media with age considerations.

Keywords: virtual reality, training, cognitive aging, spatial performance.

1 Introduction

An increasing number of older populations have been a major trend in many societies. Research in aging has shown that normally age is negatively correlated with cognitive functioning, which usually impedes the older adults from quality independent living. In principal, the age-related decline in cognitive function can be accounted for by four basic mechanisms, including processing speed, working memory, sensory function and inhibition [1]. The processing speed theory suggests that nearly all age-related variance on almost any kind of cognitive tasks can be explained by a generalized, decreased speed of performing mental operations [2]. With respect to working memory, [3] indicated that older adults were deficient in terms of the on-line cognitive resources available at any given moment required for information processing activities involving storage, retrieval, and transformation. Another piece of evidence demonstrating cognitive decline with age is that nearly all of the age-related variance was mediated by human sensory functioning, including visual and auditory

C. Stephanidis (Ed.): Universal Access in HCI, Part II, HCII 2007, LNCS 4555, pp. 451–459, 2007.

acuity [4]. [5] pointed out that with age, people have more difficulties in focusing on target information and inhibiting attention to irrelevant material.

Among the various cognitive deficits, spatial cognition has been identified as one of the most significant factors that mediate the older adults' cognitive function and computer-based work [6]. It has also been found that increased age is associated with declined human spatial ability, such as spatial perception, spatial organization, spatial memory, and mental rotation [7]. However, there exists potential for older adults to change this disadvantage as literature has shown that spatial ability can be improved if appropriate learning strategies are adopted [8].

In light of the increasingly widespread application of the virtual reality/VR technology as a training media [9] [10], enhancing older adults' spatial cognition appears more promising. VR is a class of computer technology that enables a simulated three-dimensional model where participants can get the sense of presence and interact intuitively with the environment and/or objects within the model in a real-time manner [11]. There is empirical evidence indicating that those who experienced a VR interface outperformed those who experienced traditional web pages in terms of how oriented they do E-mall shopping [12].

Despite the existing literature supportive of the use of VR as training media in relation to spatial ability, issues concerning how this computer technology that enables Euclidean-based presentation would assist older adults in spatial processing still remain unresolved. For example, to what extent could a VR media improve the declined spatial cognition for the elderly to the level comparable to that for the young counterpart? As compared with other traditional means of spatial presentations such as the two-dimensional map, does the VR play a more effective role in enhancing processing of spatial information, particularly for the elderly people? If yes, is the VR-based training associated with facilitation of spatial processing with respect to a specific aspect of spatial abilities? By addressing these issues, the present study was aimed at examining the effect of using VR as training media on processing of spatial information for the older adults.

2 Methodology

2.1 Experimental Design

The present study employed a 2x3 factorial design where age and training media were the two independent variables. Age was a quasi between-subject factor, which consisted of two treatment levels, namely, older and young groups. Training media was designed as a repeated-measure factor with each subject him/herself as a blocking factor to reduce as much individual-difference confounding as possible. The training media was defined to consist of three levels of display treatment, including a pure VR presentation, a VR plus bird-view map presentation, and a traditional two-dimension map presentation.

2.2 Subjects

30 subjects, 15 older adults and 15 college students participated in the experiment. The older subjects, aged from 65 to 74 years old with a mean of 68.6 and a standard

deviation of 2.85, were recruited from participants of a computer-learning program administered by a local social welfare institute. All the older subjects were proficient in basic computer operations and all were Mandarin literate with a senior high school diploma or above. The young subjects were graduate students in engineering and management of a local university, who were frequent computer users. The young subjects were aged from 23 to 26 years old with a mean of 24.3 and a standard deviation of 0.9.

2.3 The Training Systems and the Performance Measures

Three training systems associated with the aforementioned media of the VR, the VR plus bird-view map, and the two-dimension map were developed. Navigating through escape routes in fire alarm emergency was exemplified as the application domain as it requires successful processing of spatial information. For each training media, fabricated were four escape routes, which comprised such landmarks as fire extinguishers and signs to safety exits, by using the spatial layout of a local hospital as a blueprint. The number of the landmarks was designed to fall within the range of 7 ± 2 items, which have long been identified as the limit of human working memory (Miller, 1956). Figure 1 shows one example of the four escape routes presented in a two-dimension map, in which the route was exhibited by a solid orange line with an arrow indicating the subject's current location, and the fire extinguishers and the signs to the exit were displayed by a red square and a green circle respectively.

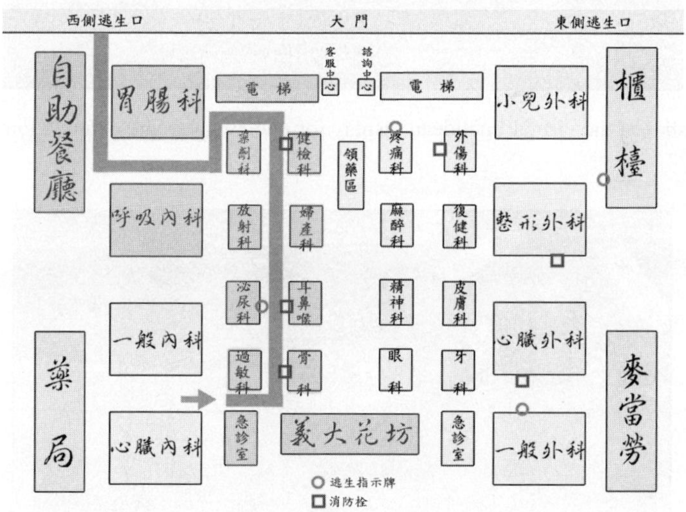

Fig. 1. One example of the escape route exhibited in the two-dimension map media

Instead of the map-like presentation, the VR system enabled a simulated, three dimensional view of the Euclidean scenery of the escape routes. The VR system was developed by 3D Studio Max (Version 7.0) and EON (Version 3.0). By pressing the designated arrow function keys on the computer keyboard, the subject was able to move forward and backward, to make right/left turns along the mimic Euclidean space of the escape routes. Figure 2 illustrates a snap display of the VR system. The VR plus bird-view map media was identical to the VR media except that a bird-view map associated with the concurrent navigation location in the escape route was provided in the upper-left corner in the VR display, as exhibited in Figure 3.

Three aspects of spatial processing performance resulting form the three different training media were evaluated. Spatial memory assessed how accurately the subject could recall the landmark information along each escape route and was operationally defined by the hit rate of test questions. Spatial orientation assessed how successfully

Fig. 2. Snapshot of the virtual Euclidean display for one escape route exhibited in the pure VR training media

Fig. 3. Snapshot of the VR plus bird-view map display for one escape route

the subject could navigate through the trained routes and was operationally defined the hit rate of questions concerning the correct turns that should be made for a particular route. Mental rotation assessed how well the subject could orientate him/herself when the test direction was opposite to that experienced during the training session. Because the pilot test of the present study revealed that mental rotation was negatively correlated with response time ($r = -0.31$, $p < 0.003$), this performance measure was operationally defined as $R_i = N_i(T_m/T_i)$, where R_i denotes the adjusted hit rate of mental rotation for subject i; N_i denotes the raw hit rate for subject i; T_m denotes the mean response time for the age group subject i belonged to; T_i denotes the response time spent by subject i.

2.4 Procedures

First, each subject of both age groups was briefed with experimental instructions and received two warm-up exercises. Then the subject proceeded to the training session in which he/she was required to undergo the 12 escape sessions (3 training media x 4 escape routes for each media) that were presented in a random order. During each session, the subject was asked to memorize the displayed escaping information, including the current location, and the shortest escape route associated with the location and the landmarks along this particular route. The pilot test of the present study revealed that for the young age group, a 5-minute, 5-minute, and 1-minute training duration for the VR, the VR plus bird-view map, and the two-dimension map conditions respectively represent averaged exposure time with which the subject felt sufficient to complete the task for each route presentation. For the older group, the averaged exposure durations were 10 minutes, 10 minutes, and 3 minutes for the VR, the VR plus bird-view map, and the two-dimension map media respectively. A rest period between alternations of the 12 training sessions was provided to each subject, who determined how long the break he/she would need. After the training session, the subject was then instructed to complete a paper-and-pencil test in which questions concerning the aforementioned three aspects of spatial performance had to be answered. The experimenter recorded the time spent by the subject in answering the mental rotation questions to derive the time adjusting factor for the performance measure of R_i.

3 Results and Analysis

Table 1 lists the descriptive statistics for the three performance measures. Before conducting the ANOVA, the assumptions of data normality and equal variances were examined. The Shapiro-Wilk test indicated that the data for the three performance measures under the 6 age and training media combinations follows a normal distribution with all p values larger than 0.05. The Barlett's test indicated that the p values for the three performance measures were all larger than the 5% criterion, suggesting that the data normality shares with an equal variance. Both preliminary confirmations justify the use of ANOVA for the subsequent analysis.

Table 1. Means and (standard deviations) for the three performance measures as a function of age groups and training media

	Older group			Young group		
	VR	VR + Map	Map	VR	VR + Map	Map
Spatial memory	0.36 (0.15)	0.56 (0.14)	0. 57 (0.15)	0.65 (0.22)	0.67 (0.20)	0.75 (0.23)
Spatial orientation	0.45 (0.18)	0.63 (0.20)	0.55 (0.21)	0.77 (0.20)	0.72 (0.23)	0.73 (0.26)
Mental rotation	0.43 (0.18)	0.45 (0.18)	0.43 (0.18)	0.63 (0.31)	0.62 (0.35)	0.62 (0.34)

The ANOVA analysis considered subject as a random-effect variable nested within the factor of age group, denoted as subject(age). Therefore, the main effect of age used subject(age) as the error term, and the main effect of training media and the interaction of age x training media used media x subject(age) as the error term.

Spatial memory. The ANOVA results indicated that the interaction of age x training media was not present ($F_{[2,56]}$ = 3.50, p < 0.143); therefore, the two main effects of age and training media need to be further examined. The age impact was observed, with the older subject reaching a significantly lower retention level than the young counterpart concerning how accurately the landmarks information could be recalled (0.49 vs. 0.69, $F_{[1,28]}$ = 22.99, p <0.0001). The effect of training media was also significant ($F_{[2,56]}$ = 5.55, p < 0.006), with the two-dimension map resulting in the highest retention hit rate, followed by the VR plus bird-view map, and the VR in a descending order. A post-hoc Tukey's analysis pointed out that the significance was mainly derived from the difference of mean hit rates between the two-dimension map and the pure VR media (0.66 vs. 0.51, p < 0.005). Nevertheless, the difference between the two-dimension map and the VR plus bird-view map (0.66 vs. 0.62), and the difference between the VR plus bird-view map and the pure VR (0.62 vs. 0.51) were neither significant.

Spatial orientation. The ANOVA results indicated that the interaction of age x training media was not significant ($F_{[2,56]}$ = 1.67, p < 0.20). Although the VR plus bird-view map resulted in the best orientation score, followed by the two-dimension map and the pure VR media (0.68 vs. 0.64 vs. 0.61), the differences were only due to a chance result ($F_{[2,56]}$ = 1.20, p < 0.31). However, the age effect was found significant, evidenced by the fact that the older subject was apparently disadvantaged as compared with the young counterpart in terms of how successful the orientation score was achieved (0.54 vs. 0.74, $F_{[1,28]}$ = 19.36, p < 0.0001).

Mental rotation. The ANOVA results indicated that the main effect of age was significant ($F_{[1,28]}$ = 5.71, p < 0.024) and so was the main effect of training media ($F_{[2,56]}$ = 15.00, p < 0.001). Nevertheless, the age x training media interaction was also significant ($F_{[2,56]}$ = 3.60, p < 0.034), and the presence of the interaction called for further justification of the two main effects. The Tukey's test revealed when the age effect was examined at each media level, the young subject significantly outperformed the older counterpart in successfully rotating mental images for the two-dimension map training treatment (0.62 vs. 0.43, $p < 0.03$). For the pure VR, and the VR plus bird-view map conditions, the older subject reached a comparable level of performance in mental rotation and the age differences were merely due to a chance result. On the other hand, when the results were examined in terms of media effect at each age level, the Tukey's rest found that for the young subject, the three paired-comparisons among the three training media were not significant. For the older subject, the significant difference occurred only when the VR plus bird-view training media was contrasted with the two-dimension map, with the VR plus bird-view map supporting a higher mental rotation score (0.45 vs. 0.43, $p < 0.005$).

4 Discussion

In general, the results of the present study were consistent with the existing literature in cognitive aging, pointing out a performance pattern where the older adults are indeed confronting an unfavorable condition in processing spatial-based information. As indicated by the results, outperformed performance in spatial memory and spatial orientation for the older subject were both evident, regardless of the type of training media that were employed.

Nevertheless, the disadvantage in spatial processing for older adults seems to be non-universal, and dependent on which aspect of spatial cognition being taken into account. This viewpoint of differentiated spatial faculty has its root considering the finding where the older subject was capable of achieving comparable level of performance in mental rotation when the VR-based training technique was adopted. It appears that training provides the older adults with an optimistic venue where their spatial abilities can be confidently exercised, but only when appropriate training media and spatial components are carefully selected.

The contingent training effect may be related to the processing essences underlying the different cognitive ability components. Specifically, the processing of spatial memory and spatial orientation requires development of an accurate world-centered cognitive map that comprises an evolving hierarchy of landmark objects, routes, and topology. Although the VR training media enables a three-dimension presentation, the display exhibits only an ego-centered view of the scenes of the navigation routes, which provides little information with respect to the topological knowledge essential to form the cognitive map. This display characteristic explains why the VR treatment resulted in the least desirable hit rates in spatial memory and spatial orientation. For those older adults who are disadvantaged at spatial cognition, the particular difficulty in recalling the landmarks information and navigating the escape route observed in the experiment is reasonably expected.

Instead of demanding world-centered knowledge, successful processing of mental rotation requires strengthened display of the front views for each intersection so that correct navigation turns can be made when the moving orientation is opposite. It is likely that equipped with the Euclidean-based presentation, the older adults will receive sufficient information needed to make accurate navigation decisions so that their rotation scores can fare as successful as those for the young counterpart. This explains why in the experiment, the difference in rotation performance between the older and young subject was only due to a chance result. Considering the rationale, it is not surprising that the training media of VR plus bird-view map that combines both topological and front-perspective information would result in the most desirable spatial-based performance, and at least for the rotation performance for the older adults.

5 Conclusions

In summary, the present study examined the effect of training older adults on processing spatial information by different spatial-related display techniques. The findings indicated that the older adults are in general more disadvantaged than their young counterpart. Although a traditional two-dimension map help retain the spatial memory and help navigate the escape route to the best effects, the older adults still have more difficulty in these two spatial tasks than the young adults. However, optimistic potential exists as the results suggest that the disadvantage is contingent upon the specific components of spatial cognition trained associated with appropriate training media. The older adults can benefit from the training in mental rotation so that they are capable of navigating as oriented as the young adults if the Euclidean display-based VR media is adopted.

Despite of the promising results, a number of caveats need to be noted. First, the training tasks designed in the present study represent only a very short period of exposure. A more valid interpretation requires a much longer duration of training session. Secondly, the fidelity of the VR interface may also influence the subject's perception towards the simulated Euclidean space and therefore in turn confound the performance data. More sophisticated VR interfaces have to be developed for future research.

Acknowledgments. The present study received funding supports from the National Science Council, Taiwan under grant NSC95-2221-E-214-041.

References

1. Park, D.C.: The Basic Mechanisms Accounting for Age-related Decline in Cognitive Function. In: Park, D.C., Schwarz, N. (eds.), Cognitive Aging: A Primer. Psychology Press, Philadelphia, pp. 3–21 (2000)
2. Salthouse, T.A.: The Processing-Speed Theory of Adult Age Differences in Cognition. Psychological Review 103, 403–428 (1996)
3. Craik, F.I.M., Byrd, M.: Aging and Cognitive Deficits: The Role of Attentional Resources. In: Craik, F.I.M., Trehub, S. (eds.) Aging and Cognitive Processing, pp. 191–211. Plenum Press, New York (1982)
4. Lindenberger, U., Baltes, P.B.: Sensory Functioning and Intelligence in Old Age: A Strong Connection. Psychology and Aging 9, 339–355 (1994)
5. Hasher, L., Stoltzfus, E.R., Zacks, R.T., Rypma, B.: Age and Inhibition. Journal of Experimental Psychology: Learning, Memory and Cognition 17, 63–169 (1991)
6. Kelly, C.L., Charness, N.: Issues in Training Older Adults to Use Computers. Behaviour and Information Technology 14, 107–120 (1995)

7. Spencer, W.D., Raz, N.: Differential Effects of Aging on Memory for Content and Context: A Meta-Analysis. Psychology and Aging 10, 527–539 (1995)
8. Holley, C.D., Dnsereau, D.F.: Spatial Learning Strategies. Academic press, New York (1984)
9. Li, J.R., Khoo, L.P., Tor, S.B.: Desktop Virtual Reality for Maintenance Training: an Object Oriented Prototype System (V-REALISM). Computers in Industry 52, 109–125 (2003)
10. Wilson, J.R.: Virtual Environments Applications and Applied Ergonomics. Applied Ergonomics 30, 3–9 (1999)
11. Pimentel, K., Teixeira, K.: Virtual Reality: Through the New Looking Glass, 2nd edn. McGraw-Hill, New York (1995)
12. Lin, D-Y.M., Lu, P-H., Guo, C-J.: E-malls Interface Design: A Comparison of Navigation Performance between Hypertext and Virtual Reality. Ergonomics Study 7, 39–46 (2005)

Using Personas and Scenarios as an Interface Design Tool for Advanced Driver Assistance Systems

Anders Lindgren[1,*], Fang Chen[1], Per Amdahl[2], and Per Chaikiat[2]

[1] Department of Computer Science and Engineering, Chalmers University of Technology, SE-412 96 Gothenburg, Sweden
anders.lindgren@chalmers.se
[2] Department of Computer and Information Science, Linköping University, SE-581 83 Linköping, Sweden

Abstract. When looking at the traditional way of conducting human factors research within the active safety area, focus often tends to be on drivers' cognitive capacities like; situation awareness, workload and behavioural adaptation. This research is of course invaluable but other important issues that tend to be forgotten are: What are the drivers' needs and how should an interface be designed to satisfy those needs? This paper describes the process of defining requirements for a dynamic graphical interface for ADAS using a rather new method, *Personas*, as a starting point in the design process. Based on the Personas different scenarios and narratives were created and used in a workshop to specify user needs and requirements in the interface design for Advanced Driver Assistance Systems.

Keywords: Advanced Driver Assistance Systems (ADAS), User Centered Design, Personas, Scenarios, Interaction Design, Traffic Safety.

1 Introduction

Advanced Driver Assistance Systems (ADAS) have the function of actively assisting the driver in avoiding accidents by providing information about current and upcoming traffic situations and helping the driver take proper actions before a potential accident occurs. In order to reach the intended safety benefits of these systems it is of vital importance that drivers understand them in order to cooperate with the vehicle and the surrounding traffic environment. This requires research on how the driver and vehicle perform in different situations. It is important to look at driver behaviour while taking physical limitations and requirements of the driver and vehicle into account. The early development and testing stages of ADAS often focus on technical aspects concerning the system implementation. This leaves questions like when, where, how and why one should present warnings to the driver to be considered later. One major issue that arises when considering how warnings best are presented to the driver in a given situation is what modality or combination of modalities to use. Also, the outlines for test scenarios are often narrowed down to measures of system performance in aspects

C. Stephanidis (Ed.): Universal Access in HCI, Part II, HCII 2007, LNCS 4555, pp. 460–469, 2007.

of the drivers' cognitive capabilities in relation to their perception of system presentation and responses. This may result in test environments lacking the naturally rich context and individual variability of the driver [12]. When looking at the traditional way of conducting human factors research within the active safety area, focus often tends to be on drivers' cognitive capacities like; situation awareness and workload [11] or behavioural adaptation [16]. This research is of course invaluable but other important issues that tend to be forgotten are; what are the drivers' needs and how should an interface be designed to satisfy these needs? An alternative approach to the traditional way of development and testing is to use a more user centered approach. A user centered approach to design basically involves finding out as much as you can about the targeted users and then use this information when designing. The idea behind this approach is that the real users and their goals should be the driving force behind the development of a product, not the technology [13]. Not knowing who you are designing for increases the risk of ending up with a product that makes nobody sufficiently satisfied [4]. According to Cooper [3] you will have far greater success if choosing to design for just one specific person, a Persona. A persona is a hypothetical archetype of real users described in great detail and defined by their goals and needs, rather than just demographics. The key is to choose the right individuals, whose needs are representative for the needs of a specific set of constituents. It is also important to know how to prioritize needs to address without significantly conflicting with the needs of the secondary users [4]. When a design team talks about users in general there is a big possibility that each team member's ideas of the user's needs and goals are quite different. The detailed description of a Persona helps to prevent this. The embodiment of the user needs and goals through personas makes it easier for the design team to know who they are designing for. It also gives them a common understanding of the users that is easier to talk about and remember than a list of features and vague descriptions of the users [2]. Grudin & Pruitt [7] has brought up issues on why scenarios are rarely used in design since they lack of empirical grounding. They suggest that grounding the scenarios in ethnographic studies, contextual inquiries, demographic data or other information directly gathered from the user would certify a sufficient level of realism. Further, Grudin and Pruitt denote that Personas is a good foundation for scenario building and data collection. Scenarios can be used in multiple ways. They may serve as starting points for group brainstorming to raise questions about which assumptions that can be made but also be used for requirement analysis for software, as partial specification of functionality, to guide design and to identify and plan evaluation tasks that can be further elaborated in a usability test etc [15]. Grudin and Pruitt [8] comments that Personas alone can aid design but that the method is more powerful when complementing other quantitative and qualitative methods rather than replacing them. This paper describes the development of a dynamic graphical interface for ADAS using Personas as a starting point in the design process. Based on the Personas, different scenarios and narratives were created and used in a workshop to gather user needs and requirements for the interface design of Advanced Driver Assistance Systems.

2 Methods: Study 1

2.1 Personas

Every other year a pool of car manufacturers make a customer survey in order to map their customers and users. Information collected by this survey is used within design, marketing and branding and includes a large database with demographic information about costumers' hobbies, age, gender, income etc. This information collected from a major Swedish automotive company was used to delimit the user group for this study (drivers between 35-65 years of age). The information was also used in a later stage of the persona development process when adding demographic information to the created characters. A series of 14 semi-structured deep interviews were conducted (5 women and 9 men), with similar educational background and living in cities of comparable size. The subjects were between 35 and 65 years of age (M 47; SD 13) and they all had drivers' licenses. The purpose with the interviews was to gather information on the drivers' attitudes, goals, needs and behaviour. The questions used were inspired by considerations and results from earlier studies made by [9]; [19] and [18], which used a variant of the Driver Behaviour Questionnaire (originally developed by [14]). The questions were organised in four main groups: in relation to the car; distractions and secondary tasks, concerning themselves as drivers; and general questions. The interviews lasted for approximately one hour and were audio recorded with the interviewees' approval. The number of interviews was not decided in advance. Instead the interview series ended when the information from the interviews was found redundant. All interviews were transcribed on a phrase level which focuses on what principally has been said rather than on the respondents' exact words [10]. This resulted in an extensive list of expressions in a chronological order. The expressions were later revised and sorted under significant categories in a first version of a so called *Affinity Diagram* (see table 1), a technique for understanding and grouping large amounts of data (more information on affinity diagrams can be found in for example [6]).

Table 1. Some categories of the affinity diagram: (translated from Swedish by the authors)

Safety	Car-dependency	Easily influenced
Environment	Hobby mechanic	Attentive
Space favouring	Technology hostile	Analytic
Practical usage	Self-conscious	Educating
Joy rider	Absent driver	Self-confident
Confident driver	Foreseeing	Preventive
Easy annoyed driver	Competitive	Considerate

The categories derived from the affinity diagram where then used as starting points for the development of the Personas. Each category served as an attribute to different members of the Persona cast and was used to express certain personality properties that became salient, such as issues concerning attitude, safety and behaviour. Several rough Personas were created and refined as overlapping attributes were found. The expressions for each category in the diagram also functioned as the foundation for the narrative descriptions of the personas described more in detail later. As soon as a unique Persona emerged, a photo was chosen from a public database and added to the document. This was done in order to make the Persona more tangible and easier to refine. The statistical information from the customer survey and interviews was used to give the personas demographic attributes in accordance to real facts.

2.2 Scenarios

As mentioned earlier, the Personas were the base for the creation of the scenarios. A template was used to extract the scenario information from the Personas and interviews. This structured the information and certified a minimal level of detail and attributes. The template was divided into three different parts; Outer Variables, Inner Variables, and Narratives.

2.2.1 Outer Variables

Outer variables are a revision of traditional road scenarios often used when setting technical specifications on automotive systems. Examples of these variables are information on road structure, road environment, road- and weather conditions and traffic situations. In order to find these variables, specific traffic situations had to be created. These situations also had to meet two criteria; normal driving situations (not accidents or critical incidents) and situations where one or several ADAS could come to be used.

2.2.2 Inner Variables

Inner variables were based on personal information from the Personas. Each Persona was exposed to each situation and the different characteristics of the Personas were taken into consideration when refining the scenarios. This part added information about the Personas' goals, characteristics, intentions and possible secondary tasks performed while driving.

2.2.3 Narratives

Creating the first two parts of the template resulted in a structured list of facts. To add more detail and a lively description, information from the other two parts of the scenario template was used. This was done in the form of narrative stories. These narratives were then read through and commented by four people both from the earlier interview series and people not earlier involved in the study. This was made in order to ensure that the narratives were understandable and easy to relate to.

3 Results: Study 1

3.1 Personas

The persona creation process resulted in a final persona cast of four members; Claes, Kristina, Mats and Camilla. For a full description of all Personas and scenarios, see [1].

Claes is a 64 year old man who values his family. He is an experienced driver. Other people see him as a rational, practical and self confident man with authority. He can easily get annoyed with drivers of other vehicles and believes that he is foresighted and has full control of his driving. Although he is interested in new technologies he has trouble keeping up with all the new gadgets.

Kristina is a 62 year old woman with a calm laid back attitude. She thinks that most problems will solve themselves. She is often perceived as a person with a laisser-faire attitude and sometimes even a bit nonchalant. Kristina sees her car as a means of transportation and has no interest in new technologies, especially not within the automotive area. She often talks in her cell phone while driving and sometimes she has problems staying within speed limits.

Mats is a middle aged man (44 years old) and an early adopter of new technology. He is an entrepreneur, always is on the run. He is a self confident driver that often mistrusts others in traffic. Mats drive a lot as part of work and he is generally very interested in new technology. He has a habit of using his cell phone while driving and he also eats and smokes a cigarette during his sometimes long trips.

Camilla is a 38 year old woman. She got her drivers licence rather late in life, and does therefore not yet feel fully comfortable drivin. Other people describe her as a caring person; she cares for the environment and has a need of being in control. Camilla has little driving experience and tends to become unsure in complex traffic situations.

3.2 Scenarios

Personas were used as the base for creating scenarios. No ADAS was explicitly considered when creating the scenarios, but rather situations used were situations where ADAS may be active. The reason for this was to focus on already existing situations that the interviewees face in real traffic and not create new situations based on system technology. Described below are results from the Outer- and Inner variables followed by a description and the results of the creation process of the narratives.

3.2.1 Outer Variables

Two traffic situations were created, both on roads with high speed limits. The main difference was the level of traffic density where one situation was normal highway driving with low traffic density and the other normal highway driving with high traffic density.

3.2.2 Inner Variables

The result of adding the Personas to the road situations gave an enhanced picture of what the situations looked like based in the goals, characteristics, intentions and possible secondary tasks that were carried out by the Personas.

3.2.3 Narratives

All four Personas were given two narratives each (high/low traffic density highway driving). Below, one of the eight final narratives is presented. For a full description of all narratives see [1].

Highway Driving: Mats

Mats has been spending all morning in a meeting with an important client and the meeting took much longer than expected. Mats has just got back on the highway after picking up a burger and a cup of coffee at a fast food restaurant. He has to hurry to make his afternoon construction site inspection in time. He has never been to the site before and has therefore put in the address of the site location in his navigation system. Mats is now cruising the highway following the general traffic speed, zipping coffee, eating his burger, listening to the radio and glancing at the navigation system waiting for it to tell him when it is time to choose the next exit from the highway.

4 Methods: Study 2

4.1 Workshop

Based on the Personas and scenarios created in Study 1, a workshop on human factors, interaction design and vehicle safety was held with eight participants. Attending were three experienced system developers, two human-machine interaction engineers, one PhD student in technical psychology and two masters students in interaction design. The workshop lasted for approximately two hours and was documented both through notes and audio recordings. Participants were briefed of the recordings and told how the material would be treated confidentially. The workshop started with a PowerPoint presentation of the four Personas and a list of 15 ADAS that are already implemented or about to reach the market in the near future. Next the participants where encouraged to individually select and rank the ADAS that they believed would be relevant for each Persona. The four Personas were presented on wall-hanged posters together with the different ADAS. Each participant was given nine black stickers per Persona that they used to mark which ADAS they thought was most relevant to the Persona. There were no rules on how to distribute the stickers other than that nine stickers had to be used for each Persona. As an example, participants could mark one ADAS with 4 stickers if they thought this system was extremely relevant for that Persona. The results where then summarised and participants were asked to comment on what basis they chose the different systems and how they found the systems feasible from the Personas' point of view. These comments were noted on the Persona posters so that they would be visible during the rest of the workshop. Next, participants were divided into two groups with as equal expertise as possible between the groups to discuss two topics; 1) what information the Persona needed from the ADAS, and 2) how this information could be presented. Participants were encouraged to focus on normal day to day driving and not emergency situations. Each group received scenarios with narratives for two Personas and was given 10 minutes per scenario for discussions. After completing the session, both groups presented and discussed their results during a joint session. The results were then analysed and transcribed at a phrase level focusing on what principally has been said rather than on the respondents' exact words [10].

5 Results: Study 2

The results from the workshop showed that the four Personas had different needs, and this was reflected in what type of ADAS would be useful for them. However most of the selected systems were thought to be relevant for two personas or more. Of the eight systems that had the overall highest ranking, five systems were selected to be relevant for two Personas or more; Adaptive Cruise Control (ACC), Blind Spot Information System (BLiS), Driver Monitoring Systems (DM), Forward Collision Warning (FCW), Parking Assistance (PA). These ADAS are presented in table 2 together with the summarised ranking. Note that the highest ranking possible for a system is 72 per Persona (8 participants x 9 stickers).

Table 2. Summary of individual rankings for the different ADAS

Persona	ACC	BLiS	DM	FCW	PA
Claes	28	15	13		6
Kristina		12	14	22	12
Mats	19		5	18	6
Camilla		17			19
Total	47	44	32	40	43

Discussing the question about information presentation for the Personas all participants agreed on that there was a need for different levels of system transparency depending on the driver. The major ADAS requirements on information presentation for each Persona were:

Claes: Because of his interests in new technology, he should be given information of the system status. He should not be given detailed information that he may think could interfere with his way of driving. Information should be adapted to the current traffic situation.

Kristina: Kristina believes that she is always in total control of her vehicle. Therefore the ADAS should not require any interaction that is not absolutely unavoidable.

Mats: He is often stressed and distracted by secondary tasks while driving. ADAS information should therefore be presented in a way that does not interfere with these secondary tasks. Because of Mats's interest in technology, the interface should support personalisation of system settings.

Camilla: Camilla is an insecure but very careful driver. She would have most use of a transparent interface that provides her with additional information. This is totally different from Kristina who wants total control of the vehicle, and hence very little system interaction. Care should, however, be taken when presenting information to Camilla. The system should not require attention to be re-focused from the current traffic situation.

6 Discussion

One of the goals using Personas is to achieve a common understanding of the target group by getting to know the individuals in the cast of Personas. For the Personas to be useful they need to mediate the information necessary for practitioners to make reasonable assumptions about them. The target group of this study was rather voluminous (approximately three million people only in Sweden). How was it then possible to create the Persona cast from only 14 interviews? The intention was never to point out that these and only these types of drivers are represented in the target group. However, during these 14 interviews obvious patterns and dissimilarities were found within areas like; attitudes, goals, needs, and confidence. Other behavioural differences concerning normal driving, secondary tasks and distraction also emerged. More details and attributes would most certainly have been detected if the sample was larger but the interview series were considered completed when the amount of new information derived from the questions decreased. It is of course possible that the lack of new information could be caused by the preparation and conduction of the interviews. Critique may be directed towards the fact that the kind of subjective statements gathered in interviews do not show any statistical significance. This study does, however show that Personas brought up issues and considerations about ADAS that may not surface through more traditional experimental research. This is an argument for using Personas as a complementary method in system development where both human and technical aspects [8] have to be considered. The method for gathering and transcribing information during the interviews should also be discussed. The transcription of the recorded interviews was followed by the affinity diagram that were then used when naming categories and sorting information into each category. Within these categories differences emerged that could be translated into salient personal characteristics. Other methods such as observations and questionnaires could have been used to complement the interviews. It could have been an advantage to perform user observations prior to the interviews in order to note the interviewee's actual behaviour and motivations in certain situations such as highway driving or driving while performing a secondary task. Scenarios are often used in system development to show the hypothesised functionality of the system or as a tool for creating test cases. When focusing too much on the system, the description of the user tent to falter [16]. Since the scenarios have their origin in the Personas the quality of the scenarios are dependent on the quality of the Personas. It is therefore of crucial importance to develop the Personas using a sufficient amount of appropriate information [7]. We also believe that the narratives have to be accompanied by the Persona (serving as the main actor) and scenario template to be fully understood. The Personas and the scenario templates should be seen as pre-requisites for understanding the narratives. We believe that if all parts (Personas, scenarios, and narratives) are read, this would serve as a good base for discussions and workshops. When a design team talk about the users in general there is always the possibility that each team member's ideas of the user's needs and goals are different and do not overlap at all. The introduction of the Personas can potentially help prevent this by providing a common ground. According to Blomqvist and Arvola [2] this embodiment of users' goals can make it easier for a team to focus on the user and to reach a common understanding of the user. This does of course not ensure that participants in the design teams are unbiased based on previous experiences. Team members may also have influenced each other during discussions and there is always a risk that some thoughts and ideas will no surface due to people being shy or worried about how their opinions would be received. Another potential issue is that the homogenous background (automotive industry, human factors and interaction design) of the design team might bias the discussion. This could have both positive and negative effects. On the positive side, the team members are knowledgeable on the focus area, user interfaces for systems in vehicles. On the other hand, the team may also oversee information and ideas that people with different background could have identified.

In conclusion, we do not claim to have found every aspect of individual driver differences but we believe that the uses of Personas in the methodology have brought important aspects of individual differences, and driver group differences to the surface.

Acknowledgements

This study was sponsored by the OPTIVe project within the Swedish IVSS research foundation and was also collaboration between Chalmers University of Technology and Linköping University.

References

1. Amdahl, P., Chaikiat, P.: Personas as drivers: An alternative approach for creating scenarios for ADAS evaluation. Unpublished master's thesis, Linköping University, Linköping, Sweden (2007)
2. Blomquist, Å., Arvola, M.: Personas in Action: Ethnography In An Interaction Design Team. In: Proceeding of the second Nordic conference on Human-Computer Interaction, NordiCHI, Aarhus, Denmark, October 19-23, 2002, ACM Press, New York (2002)
3. Cooper, A, The Inmates Are Running The Asylum – Why High-Tech Products Drive Us Crazy And How To Restore Sanity. Sams Publishing (2004)
4. Cooper, A., Reimann, R.: About Face 2.0 – The Essentials Of Interaction Design. Wiley Publishing Inc, Chichester (2003)
5. Federal Motor Carrier Safety Administration, Concepts of Operations and voluntary Operational Requirements for Forward Collision Warning Systems (CWS) and Adaptive Cruise Control (ACC) Systems On-Board Commercial Motor Vehicles. Retrieved August 10, 2006 htm (2005), from http://www.fmcsa.dot.gov/facts-research/research-technology/report/forward-collision-warningsystems
6. Gaffney, G.: [www]. Affinity Diagramming. In: Usability Techniques series: Retrieved August 10, 2006 (1999), from http://www.infodesign.com.au/ftp/AffinityDiagramming.pdf
7. Grudin, J., Pruitt, J.: Personas, Participatory Design and Product Development: An Infrastructure for Engagement. In: Proceedings of the Participatory Design Conference 2002, pp.144–161 (2002)
8. Grudin, J., Pruitt, J.: Personas: Practice and Theory. ACM Press, New York (2003)
9. Lajunen, T., Parker, D., Summala, H.: The Manchester Driver Behaviour Questionnaire: a cross-cultural study. Accident Analysis and Prevention 36, 231–238 (2004)

10. Linell, P.: Transkription av tal och samtal: Teori och praktik, Arbetsrapporter från Tema K (1994)
11. Ma, M., Kaber, D.B.: Situation awareness in driving while using adaptive cruise control and a cell phone. International Journal of Industrial Ergonomics 35, 939–953 (2005)
12. McCall, J., Trivedi, M.M.: Driver Monitoring for a Human-Centered Driver Assistance System. In: proceedings of the 1st ACM international workshop on Human-centered multimedia, Santa Barbara, California, USA, October 27, 2006, pp. 115–121. ACM Press, New York (2006)
13. Preece, J., Rogers, Y., Sharp, H.: Interaction Design: Beyond Human-computer interaction. John Wiley & Sons, Inc, New York (2002)
14. Reason, J.T., Manstead, A.S.R., Stradling, S.G., Baxter, J.S., Campbell, K.: Errors and violations on the road: a real distinction? Ergonomics 33, 1315–1332 (1990)
15. Rosson, M.B., Carrol, J.M. (2002). Scenario-Based Design. In: J. Jacko & A. Sears (Ed.), The Human-Computer Interaction Handbook: Fundamentals, Evolving Technologies and Emerging Applications. Lawrence Erlbaum Associates, pp. 1032–1050, (2002)
16. Rudin-Brown, C.M., Parker, H.A.: Behavioural adaptation to adaptive cruise control (ACC): implications for preventive strategies, Transportation. Research Part. F 7, 59–76 (2004)
17. Shneiderman, B.: Promoting universal usability with multi-layer interface design. In: proceedings of 2003 Conference on Universal Usability, Vancouver, British Columbia, Canada, pp. 1–8. ACM Press, New York (November 2003)
18. Westerman, S.J., Haigney, D.: Individual differences in driver stress, error and violation. Personality and Individual Differences 29, 981–998 (2000)
19. Özkan, T., Lajunen, T., Summala, H.: Driver Behaviour Qusetionnaire: A follow-up study. Accident Analysis and Prevention 38, 386–395 (2006)

Pedestrian Navigation System Implications on Visualization

Thorsten Mahler, Markus Reuff, and Michael Weber

Institute of Media Informatics, University of Ulm, Ulm, Germany
{thorsten.mahler,markus.reuff,michael.weber}@uni-ulm.de

Abstract. With the technical advances in mobile computing electronic maps and guiding systems become widely available for everywhere usage. The computing power allows for guides and even decision support systems. But mobile devices are used on the move and therefore become a secondary task. To reduce cognitive load and to reduce attention intensity visualizations and interaction patterns are needed that are fast and comprehensible. We present a pedestrian navigation system that uses a zoomable interface together with the Halo visualization approach for off screen locations. A user trial with 24 participants indicate that this approach reduces the device interaction immensely leaving more attention to the primary task.

1 Introduction

1.1 Motivation

Nowadays navigation systems getting more and more common. New cars come equipped with one. PDAs and soon mobile phones are offered, in combination with needed hardware, with such systems. With the technological progress navigation systems become available for a wide range of non expert users. So the task for user interface designers is to make such systems comprehensible and easy to use for everybody.

Furthermore navigation systems are detached from their traditional vehicles and thus open the door for new navigation tasks. The classic navigation task, think of car navigation for example, is to find the best route from one starting point to a certain destination. It involves traffic monitoring and dynamic rerouting in case of traffic jams or other exceptional occurrences. It's task is to guide the passenger to a predefined location. In our opinion this task completely changes if we switch to pedestrian navigation: In a way people walking already completed the navigation task just described; they are at or near their destination already. There are two possibilities now. They are in a unknown surrounding thus their task would be to explore the surrounding and/or second they try to complete a higher task.

We think of higher task as the purpose the users went to a specific area and identified two different classes: First clearly defined goals like buying a new pair of trousers or getting a brand new book. And second vague tasks like browsing, going shopping, exploring a new location or simply sightseeing. Both lead to explorational

C. Stephanidis (Ed.): Universal Access in HCI, Part II, HCII 2007, LNCS 4555, pp. 470–478, 2007.

navigation: That is because the first class has a clearly defined goal but no direct destination and the second undetermined locations. So the task here is clearly of supportive nature. Thus the ideal interface would indicate the user worthwhile locations. But it would not directly guide him to one of these locations but would let the user decide which path to take.

1.2 Background

Considerable research is done on the field of mobile computing in general and on visualization techniques in particular. Mobile computing solutions differ from desktop solutions. The reason therefore lies in technological constrains as well as their application.

PDAs typically have only limited resources in means of memory and computing power. Their input devices are inadequate and hard to use especially while moving. The limited size results in smaller display and lower resolution as well as different aspect ratios [Chittaro, 2006].

The nature of mobile computing has to be taken into account as well: color recognition is highly dependent on the environment and surrounding and the usage of mobile solution is different especially while moving. Additionally mobile devices are used while fulfilling a special task and may therefore demand as few attention as possible [Pascoeetal., 2000]. The application has to be comprehensible and easy to use to keep the requirements on human perceptual and cognitive capacities low and therefore the application less distractive.

Therefore research and experiments are done on how the mobile input can be arranged and generalized. For example Rinner et al. show different approaches and a comparison especially taking in account the users cognitive load and discuss especially the antipodal goals of excellent results versus low specification. Which system is better depends on the use case of course but generally the introduction of preferences and personalization show promising results to reach both goals, good results and easy input [C.Rinner, 2005].

On the other hand research is done on suitable visualizations for mobile devices. General concepts have been identified in the past few years like Overview + Detail or Focus + Context which are applicable for a wide range of visualizations [Chittaro, 2006]. Other work focuses especially on pedestrian navigation and how to support the navigation itself. For example May et al. analyzed how route are generally described by users [May et al., 2003]. Especially for pedestrian navigation visualizations evaluation were done to extract general rules. So participants found an overview for general route very useful. A change of scale, zooming was highly appreciated and automatic scrolling and an egocentric view could be identified as indispensable [Gartner, 2004].

Special pedestrian navigation solutions take the general consideration for mobile output in account. An example therefore is the REAL system. It combines an indoor and outdoor navigation support system relying on GPS data for outdoor navigation. The visualizations are computed on a server and distributed to the used device. Orientation and position is taken into account as well as soft factors as cognitive load or walking speed. The presentation is adapted to these constraints. The used maps are detailed accordingly and zooming is adapted automatically. [Baus et al., 2002]

Another system developed for pedestrian navigation is the Lol@ city guide. Its purpose is to guide tourists through Vienna city center. In contrast to the REAL system it does not use continuous zoom but a overview and a detailed map. The interesting thing abut Lol@ is the fact that it is not only a guide but more of a decision support system. It incorporates interesting locations into the map by showing symbols. [S.Uhlirz, 2002]

A problem for system that does not visualize routes but points of interest is that these points often lay outside of the current map area. A solution for the off-screen problem provides the Halo system. It solution is to simply draw circles around the of screen destinations. Yet from the visible arc alone the user can estimate the position that is the center of the virtual circle. The visualization was tested through a flash prototype with five participants [Baudisch and Rosenholtz, 2003].

1.3 Objectives

From these considerations and previous work arise requirements for pedestrian navigation interfaces. As we focus on the evaluation of pedestrian navigation evaluation we took the following objectives as necessary for our implementation.

- **Support with the navigation task:** The systems purpose is to support the user with the navigation task rather than guide him to a specific location.
- **Low cognitive charge:** Drawing little attention is a crucial point for every supporting applications especially for a navigation system. The user should focus on the primary task instead of focusing on the interaction with the device.
- **Simple and comprehensible handling:** To ease the handling the system should automatically choosethebest viewfor everyposition but nonetheless leave the user in charge of the navigation system.
- **Simple and comprehensible visualization:** The mapping between visualization and reality has to be easy and fast.

Based on these considerations we developed a pedestrian navigation visualization prototype. Its interface was tested in an adjacent user trial.

2 Interface

For the visualization we chose a zoomable user interface which is easy to handle and to understand. All the visualizations are based on exact maps. We used coloring to improve the contrast and to highlight different elements. So we used white for the buildings and a light ocher coloring for streets and lanes and squares. Additionally we used a light blue for the river running through the area. The only other color we used is red for the POIs (Points of Interest) so we use only a few colors to ease distinction. The decision in favor of exact maps with only the coloring as modification was mad to provide the user with an exact and above all a distortion-free view. Otherwise the distance estimation for the user would be complicated and tampered. For the visualization of the POIs we used a simple red coloring and, in case of off screen location we used the Halo circles. For interaction we provide the user with zoom, pan and roll function. These interactions can performed whenever the users likes to. But we use an egocentric view together with automated panning and rolling whenever the user is moving. All movements are picked up by a GPS receiver. So although the user can navigate by himself we try to keep interaction as low as possible by using automation. The interaction with the map can be performed by the keys on the PDA. The user can chose which modes (pan, roll, zoom) can be controlled with the PDA keys. Per default we used zoom as we thought this to be the best preference to easily get an overview as well as a detailed map. Additionally the automatic user centric view supports this choice. So as long as the user relays on the automatic rolling and panning the user interface is manageable with only one hand.

3 Prototype

For our prototypical implementation we chose a standard PDA with display resolution of 640x480 pixels. The operation system installed is the Windows Mobile 5.0 OS. Via bluetooth we connected the device to a GPS-Receiver.

After evaluation of different developing and runtime environments we decided in favor of C# with the .Net Compact Framework and Mobile DirectX for the software. We chose these techniques as it combines powerful visualization environment with data connectivity on the one hand and a modern programming interface on the other.

The positioning of the person is done by periodic examination of the GPS signal transmitted by the extern receiver. The application uses this data to automatically roll and pan the map section so that map always is oriented according to the direction in which the user is heading. Additionally the section is scrolled when the user moves on resulting in a map that always shows the user position centered.

The Halo Circles are implemented as transparent overlays which are scaled and position according to the user position.

4 UserStudy

To study the effectiveness of the presented visualization we conducted a live test with 24 participants involved. Most of the participants have a strong background

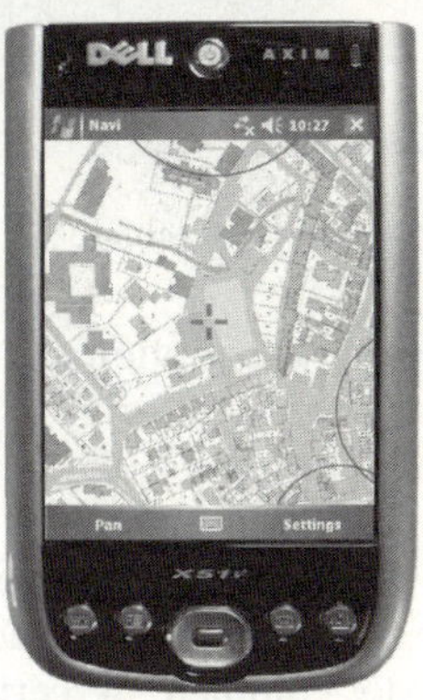

Fig. 1. Lab screenshot of the Halo Implementation

Fig. 2. Captured Interface of the Halo Implementation: First Task Completion

in computing but not necessarily in HCI and mobile computing. All participants were not familiar with the place the survey was conducted so that they were forced to use the application. Every participant was asked to complete three tasks in the way of the user test. All his movements and interactions with the device where logged for later evaluation. In the end every participant could fill in a questionnaire for feedback.

4.1 Study Setup

Every participant had to complete the following three tasks:

1. Navigation to an unknown location: Go to the residents' center of the city council. It is marked red on the map.
2. User's choice: Go to the travel agency that seems the easiest to be reached. There are two of them. They are marked red on the map.
3. Navigation to a known location: Go back to the bakery directly.

The distance between the start and the city council is a minimum of approximately 480 meters. From there to the travel agencies it is 210 respectively 350 meters. The way back from the first agency is 380 meters from the second only 135 meters.

The tasks where alternately to be completed with or without Halo support. Additionally the computer chose in turn if two or just one task was Halo supported. So in Scenario 1) the proband had Halo support for task 1 and 3. In Scenario 2) only task 2 had the Halo support enabled.

Fig. 3. Frame capture of Navigation

Fig. 4. Framecapture of Evaluation

In the beginning every person was handed out a one page description of the prototype UI and information about the accomplishment of the user trial. That included the three different interaction possibilities zoom, pan, roll and how to use them (button and pen). This was done by a short description and a picture of the prototype. In short the function of the Halo circles were reproduced and the users position explained (little purple circle in the middle). The task description included how the device would behave, that it would ask them do complete a certain navigation task and would indicate its completion. And that afterwards it would switch to the next task automatically.

4.2 Evaluation

Facts about the user group: From the questionnaire we know that only 5 persons out of 24 participants own a PDA and eleven are familiar with PDAs and only 3 claim to be experts in use of PDAs.

Only two of the participants use a navigation system regularly. Nine have used a navigation system rarely. 13 use a navigation system for the first time.

We also questioned the participants about their ability of orientation in an unknown town and the use of maps: 15 people, more than half the groups, stated their sense of orientation as good or very good. 6 think they would do ok and two think they are not good at that at all.

So we are dealing with a group that has not much experience in using a PDA and especially are not very experienced in using navigation systems. But surprisingly for us a vast majority thinks that they are good in navigation with maps.

User Interface evaluation: The vast majority (23 of the24 subjects) rated the overall usability as good. They did not have problems with the system and its principles. But what we ware especially interested in is the evaluation of the visualization especially if the Halo approach performs well in a real user test.

Halo performance: We first asked whether the Halo circles would ease navigation with the result shown in Table 1. In both groups there is a preference in favor of the Halo approach. In the first group which used the Halo circles for two of the three tasks this preference is even stronger. So we concluded that the repeated use of the Halo system increases the ease in pedestrian navigation. We tested this hypothesis with an F-Test and found it to be very significant (p=0.008).

Table 1. Result to: Does Halo ease navigation?

Grade	1	2	3	4	5	6
Group 1	7	4	0	0	0	1
Group 2	5	3	2	1	0	1

Halo influence on orientation: In a second step we asked whether Halo had an influence on the orientation especially on the soft factors. We asked the subjects whether they felt supported by the Halo approach and felt more certain (Table 2 shows the results). Again we can state a preference for the Halo approach and it is once more stronger with the first group. We tested our hypothesis whether Halo increases the certainty of the subjects with the F-Test and found it to be significantly increased(p=0.0314).

Table 2. Result to: Does Halo increase degree of certainty?

Grade	1	2	3	4	5	6
Group 1	6	4	1	0	1	0
Group 2	1	4	3	0	0	4

Navigation with maps: In the next section we asked the participants about navigation with maps. Not surprisingly a majority of 21 out of 24 persons stated that orientation would be greatly improved by the electronic map. This is a result reflects the results of the first part in which 15 persons stated to be very good in orientation and reading maps. Nonetheless a majority of 21 persons prefers Halo to the plain map visualization (Table3). This is a preference for Halo we could not expect in such clearness after the user group evaluation.

Route: As we regularly logged the positions we could evaluate the routes taken by the participants as well. For visualization we used the magnalox [Magnalox, 2006] service: This website visualizes GPS data in combination with real maps (for an example see figure 5). We compared the routes taken with and without Halo support for every task.

Table 3. User preference usual map vs. Halo

	Map	Halo
Group 1	1	11
Group 2	2	10
Total	3	21

For the first task there is no measurable significant difference between the two groups. We think the reason for that is that most of the participants needed this first task to become familiar with the device and the software.

Fig. 5. Routes taken by the participants

For the second task we could not find significant differences as well. The reason for that is simply that the different destinations were to close to the current position of the user. Therefore the Halo circles could not make a difference here.

But for the third task we could make a difference between the two groups: 9 out of the 11 participants (82%) using the Halo system for this task decided for the shortest way. In contrast to that only 6 out of the 11 (55%) participants not using the Halo approach took the shorter route. Two persons even went back on the route they used before which was considerable longer. So nearly half of the participants not using the Halo system chose a longer route. They preferred an already known route or used main streets instead of the shorter way along the side street.

Time: A hard to measure value is the time. The absolute time needed to complete all three task varied from 12 up to 24 minutes. And although the time needed depends on the route taken it is also dependent on the velocity of walking. So we compared the time needed for one task relative to the overall time.

As with the route we have no strong evidence in favor or against the Halo approach with the first task. We only could measure a weak significance in favour of Halo (p=0.0625). For the second task the differences between the two approaches are too small to be evaluated which is clearly due to the short distance.

But for the third task we could make out a significant improvement by Halo (p=0.007). We used the Mann-Whitney test this time as we are dealing with relative values. So using the Halo approach tends to result in shorter navigation time.

Attention: A most interesting thing we could find is that participants using Halo do not have to interact with the device in a degree the map users do. This is best shown with the clicks the users do: Halo users needed only a fraction of the clicks (only about one third, see table 4). Note that these users had exactly the same possibilities to interact with the system. So they did get the information from the system without further interaction. Not needing to interact results in less attention drawn from the user.

Table 4. Number of clicks

Destination	City Council	Travel Agency	Bakery
w/o Halo	418	113	239
Halo	140	96	69

5 Conclusions

We presented our implementation of a GPS based pedestrian navigation system. In our user trials we could show that the zoomable interface together with the Halo visualization makes is difference in user acceptance: The Halo visualization eases navigation and improves the certainty of a navigation decision made. Even more although a vast majority of participants judged themselves to be good navigators with maps in general a majority of 21 out of 24 preferred the Halo visualization. Remarkably the visualization with Halo reduced the user interaction significantly. And with the reduction of the device interaction we reduce the attention leaving more resources to the primary task.

Surprisingly to us more precise maps were not used despite the considerably slower moving speed compared to car navigation for example. The possibility to zoom into the map for a better understanding of the near surrounding was not often used. Instead the users preferred a larger map to get a better overview. A reason for this could be that the goals of the users trials were well defined. We think that the user's task of exploring the area would change that.

6 Future Directions

We plan to further develop the prototype as for one the study led to very promising result and the user questioning afterward showed possible directions for improvements: The integration of landmarks for example could further improve navigation. We asked the participants about this and 17 out of 24 think this would lead to a further improvement. Additionally we plan to further investigate how the direction of the destination could be integrated in the visualization. Additionally we plan to further improve the interaction by focusing on implementing alternative ways of user input.

References

[Baudisch and Rosenholtz, 2003] Baudisch, P., Rosenholtz, R.: Halo: a technique for visualizing off-screen objects. In: CHI '03: Proceedings of the SIGCHI conference on Human factors in computing systems, pp. 481–488. ACM Press, New York (2003)

[Bausetal., 2002] Baus, J., Krüger, A., Wahlster, W.: A resource-adaptive mobile navigation system. In: IUI '02: Proceedings of the 7th international conference on Intelligent user interfaces, pp. 15–22. ACM Press, New York (2002)

[C. Rinner, 2005] Rinner, C., Raubal, M.: B. S, User interface design for location-based decision services. In: 13th International Conference on Geoinformatics. [Chittaro, 2006] Chittaro, L (2006).Visualizing information on mobile devices. Computer, vol. 39(3) pp. 40–45 (2005)

[Gartner, 2004] Gartner, G.: Location-based mobile pedestrian navigation services -the role of multimedia cartography. In: International Joint Workshop on Ubiquitous, Pervasive and Internet Mapping. ICA (2004)

[Magnalox, 2006] Magnalox, magnificent gps logs and annotated tracks. [Online; accessed 08-September-2006] (2006), http://www.magnalox.net/

[May et al., 2003] May, A.J., Ross, T., Bayer, S.H., Tarkiainen, M.J.: Pedestrian navigation aids: information requirements and design implications. Personal Ubiquitous Comput. 7(6), 331–338 (2003)

[Pascoe et al., 2000] Pascoe, J., Ryan, N., Morse, D.: Using while moving: Hci issues in field work environments. ACM Trans.Comput.-Hum.Interact. 7(3), 417–437 (2000)

[S. Uhlirz, 2002] Uhlirz, S., Lechthaler, M.: LoL@ - City Guide. Prototyp einer kartenbasierten UMTS-Applikation. In: Geowissenschaftliche Mitteilungen, Schriftenreihe der Studienrichtung Vermessungswesen und Geoinformation TU Wien 58, 171–182 (2002)

A DIYD (Do It Yourself Design) e-Commerce System for Vehicle Design Based on Ontologies and 3D Visualization

L. Makris, N. Karatzoulis, and D. Tzovaras

Informatics & Telematics Institute
1st Km Thermi-Panorama Road, PO Box 361,
GR-57001 Thermi-Thessaloniki, Greece
{lmak, nkaratz, tzovaras}@iti.gr

Abstract. The state of the art in vehicle configuration is still very much characterized by a face-to-face sales situation. In addition, web browsers are becoming market places. But direct sales over the internet, without contact with a sales person constitute still a small segment of the market, of only a few percent for European manufacturers. The internet is more used as a medium to gather information. A standardised DIYD vehicle configuration is thus a must for European manufacturers today. This paper presents an Intelligent DIY e-commerce system for vehicle design, based on Ontologies and 3D Visualization, that aims at enabling a suitable representation of products with the most realistic possible visualisation outcome. The platform, designed for the automotive sector, includes all the practicable electronic commerce variants and its on-line product configuration process is controlled by an ontology, that was created using the OWL Web Ontology Language.

1 Introduction

This paper presents an intelligent and user-friendly e-commerce solution, by adopting additional technologies, such as a configuration utility, supported by an intelligent help desk system and 3D visualisation in a virtual reality environment. The focus of this paper is on the automotive sector; however the intention is that the system to be developed will be suitable for suppliers, and wholesalers, from other sectors, such as clothing, bicycles, etc. The conception of the system is as generic as possible, in order to facilitate knowledge transfer to other industrial sectors.

The technical contribution of this paper is to present how to: (i) integrate and develop a product Visualisation Tool, capable of handling different media types (2D and 3D), (ii) introduce a novel configuration module, which is capable of integrating different functionalities, input and output devices, and (iii) provide enhanced workflow mechanisms and tools for an easy integration into modern legacy systems (ERPs).

The implementation of this work has started in the context of the CATER European project (CN 035030), funded under the 6th EU framework, which aims to aims to deploy intelligent agents and knowledge management based N-business systems, that will support modular personalisation of the automotive products to the explicit as well as emotional needs and wants of the international clients, as well as mass

C. Stephanidis (Ed.): Universal Access in HCI, Part II, HCII 2007, LNCS 4555, pp. 479–487, 2007.

customisation and reverse engineering of product fulfilment and flexibility of services, to meet the needs of customers, suppliers, sales, marketing and the concurrent engineering team and, within this framework, to develop a customisation database structure and functionality with exemplary product data for vehicle configuration.

The described platform, called hereafter CATER platform, has been designed for industrial automotive design products, that can be configured on-line. The main modules of the CATER platform are the **Intelligent Configurator Module** (and its ontology structure) and the **3D Visualisation Module**. These two modules combined, comprise an advanced automotive design system, that offers different products and services to customers, based on their demand and not on a fixed product line.

The paper is structured as following: in section 2 the intelligent configurator module is presented, with special focus on its architecture and ontology structure. In section 3 the 3D visualization module is analysed and in section 4 the e-shop solution and its integration with existing ERPs, is discussed. Finally, section 5 presents some experimental results and concludes the paper.

2 Intelligent Configurator Module and Ontology

The Intelligent Configurator module is a web based application, that allows the user to assembly vehicles, based on the available vehicle parts, that are being stored in the systems repository, maintained by the vehicle manufacturer. Figure 1 displays the Units of the Configurator module.

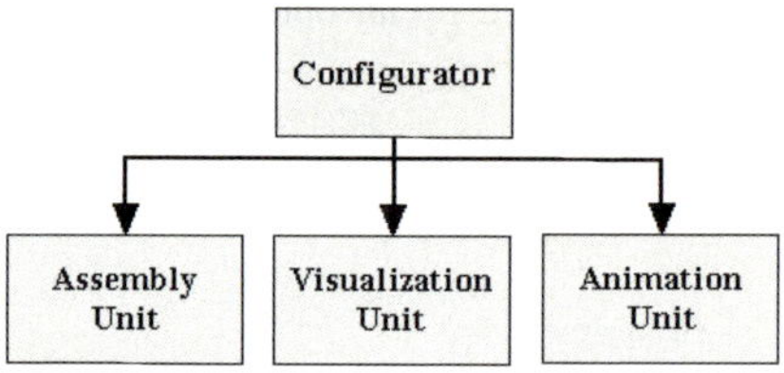

Fig. 1. The Units of the Configurator Module

The Assembly Unit allows the user to insert individual 3D objects to the scene, that can consist of a fully functional vehicle. The user can compose the desired vehicle according to his/her needs, by selecting the vehicle's parts. The vehicle part and the texture selection processes are being controlled by the restriction mechanisms, that are generated from the system Ontology [1, 2, 3]. The main functionalities of the Assembly Unit are the following: (i) Insertion of 3D object parts, (ii) Selection of texture and (iii) Assembly process based on rules (e.g. weight).

The purpose of the Visualization Unit is to record and store the 3D object assembly steps in real-time. The assembly sequence is being stored in the 3D animation repository for future reproduction.

The Animation Unit allows the reproduction of the vehicle parts assembly processes, that are stored in the animation system repository. In the Animation Unit the user can control the viewpoints and the playback of the loaded vehicle assembly process. The web interface of the Configurator Module is depicted in Figure 2.

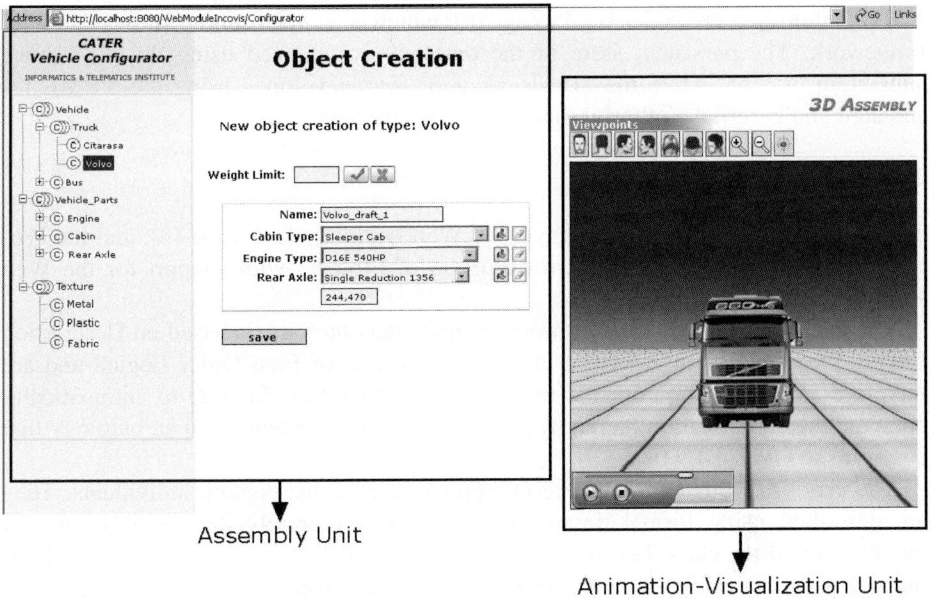

Fig. 2. The web interface of the Configurator

2.1 Configurator Architecture

The Configurator is implemented (Figure 3) using Java programming language. The system runs on Apache Jakarta Tomcat [4], as Java Servlet, and is based on the Jena framework [5], which is a Java framework for building Semantic Web applications.

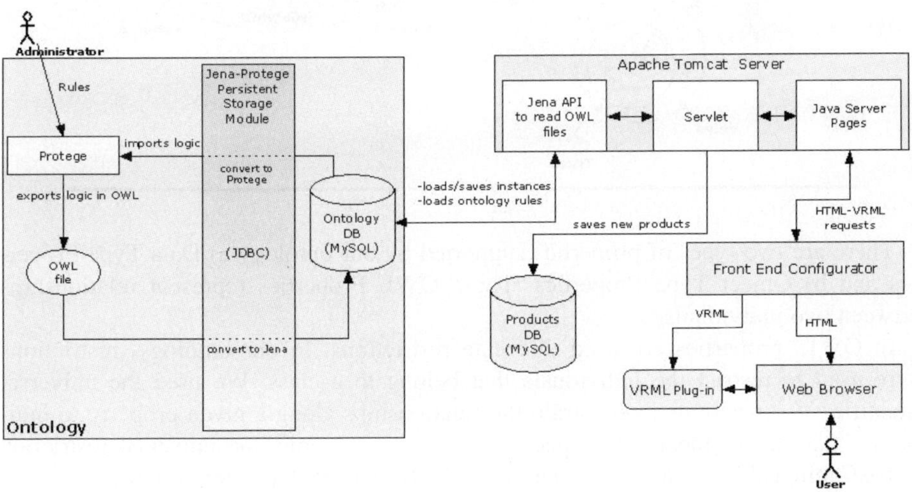

Fig. 3. Configurator Architecture

The ontology is created using Protégé [6], which is an open source knowledge-base framework. The persistent store of the ontology is achieved using the persistence subsystem of Jena, while the 3D visualization was developed using the VRML [7] standard and External Authoring Interface (EAI) mechanisms.

2.2 Ontology Development

The ontology was created using the OWL Web Ontology Language [8], and the Protégé OWL-Plugin [9], which is an extension of Protégé, with support for the Web Ontology Language (OWL).

The OWL-DL profile, used in order to create the ontology, is based on Description Logics. Description Logics are a decidable fragment of First Order Logic2 and are therefore amenable to automated reasoning. It is therefore possible to automatically compute the classification hierarchy and check for inconsistencies in an ontology that conforms to OWL-DL [10].

The classes of this Ontology are interpreted as sets that contain individuals. They are described using formal descriptions, that state precisely the requirements for membership of the class. For example, the class "Vehicle" contains all the individuals that are of type Vehicle in the CATER domain. The taxonomy of the classes is being achieved using the superclass-subclass model hierarchy.

Table 1. Example of the class hierarchy of the class "Vehicle" and an example of an Object Type Property for the individual "vehicle_1"

Class Model	Object Type Property
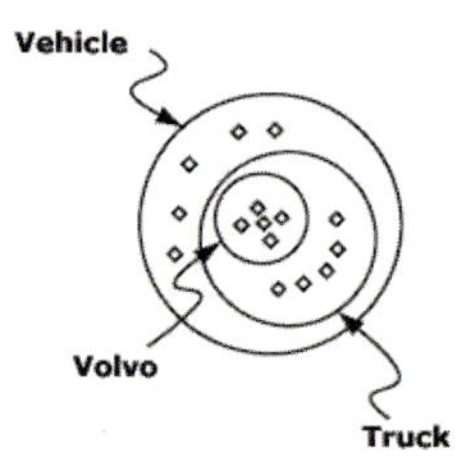	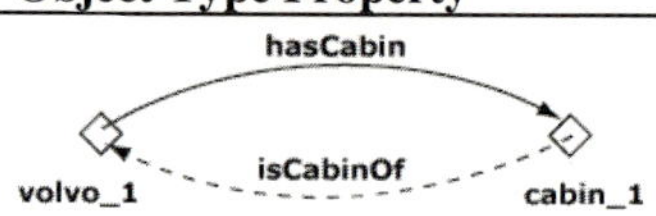

There are two types of properties supported by our ontology a) Data Type Properties and b) Object Type Properties. These OWL Properties represent relationships between two individuals.

In OWL, properties are used to create restrictions. In our ontology, restrictions were used to restrict the individuals that belong to a class. We used the universal quantifier ∀ restrictions to constrain the relationships along a given property to individuals that are members of a specific class. For example, the universal restriction ∀ hasCabin cabin_1 describes the individuals, whose hasCabin relationships are members of the class Cabin.

Cardinality restrictions were used to define the order in which the individual object parts should appear during the 3D assembly process (i.e. real-time animation). The cardinality restrictions provided the way to describe the class of individuals that have at least, at most or exactly a specified number of relationships with other individuals or datatype values.

The hasValue restrictions, denoted by the symbol ∍, were used to describe the set of individuals that have at least one relationship along a specified property to a specific individual. For example, when we wanted to predefine the dimensions of an individual object, we used a hasValue restriction (dimensions ∍ "40-50-80").

2.3 Ontology Reasoning

Ontology reasoning was achieved using the Jena OWL reasoner (Figure 4). The Jena OWL reasoner can be described as instance-based reasoner, that works by using rules to propogate the if- and only-if- implications of the OWL constructs on instance data. Reasoning about classes is done indirectly - for each declared class a prototypical instance is created and elaborated. The sub-class and sub-property lattices are cached using the embedded OWL reasoner. Each domain, range, sub-property and sub-class declaration is eagerly translated into a single query rewrite rule. The result of a query to the graph will be the union of the results from applying the query, plus all the rewritten versions of the query to the underlying graph [11].

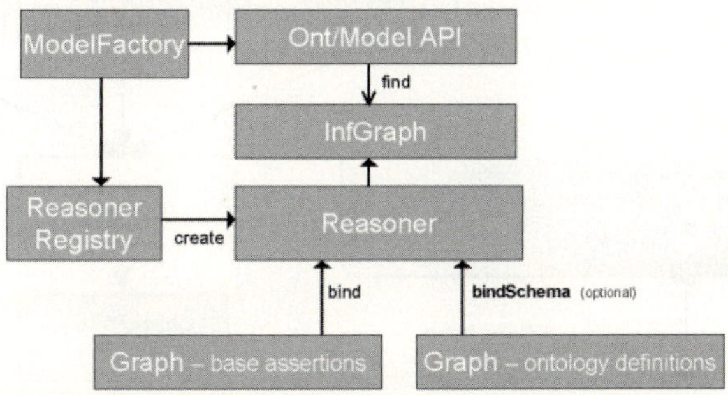

Fig. 4. The Jena Inference API layering [12]

3 3D Visualisation Module

The 3D Visualization Module is realized on the Visualization and Animation Units. The structure of the individual 3D scenes, supported by the 3D Visualization Module, can be seen in Figure 5.

The 3D scene contains the viewpoints, the lighting of the 3D world, the background, the 3D objects and the object functionalities (interactions), that are created dynamically, according to the ontology specifications. The user interaction with the 3D scene is achieved by the use of predefined VRML Protos. For every 3D object that is inserted in the 3D scene an animation, representing its assembly process, is dynamically generated.

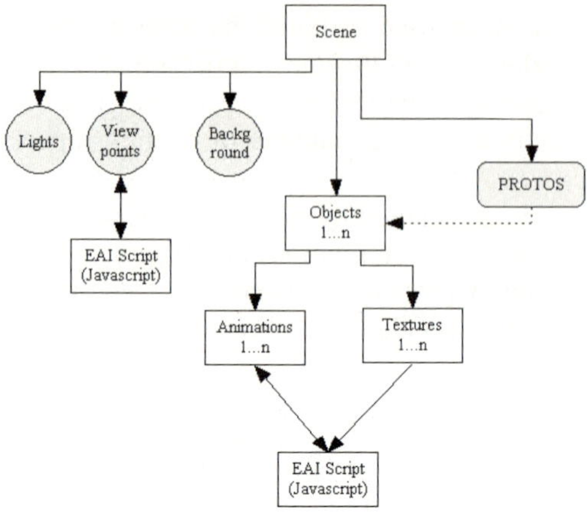

Fig. 5. The 3D scene structure of the 3D Visualization Module

The playback functionalities of the assembly process are controlled by a panel (Figure 6), that was developed using several VRML sensors (TouchSensor & PlaneSensor).

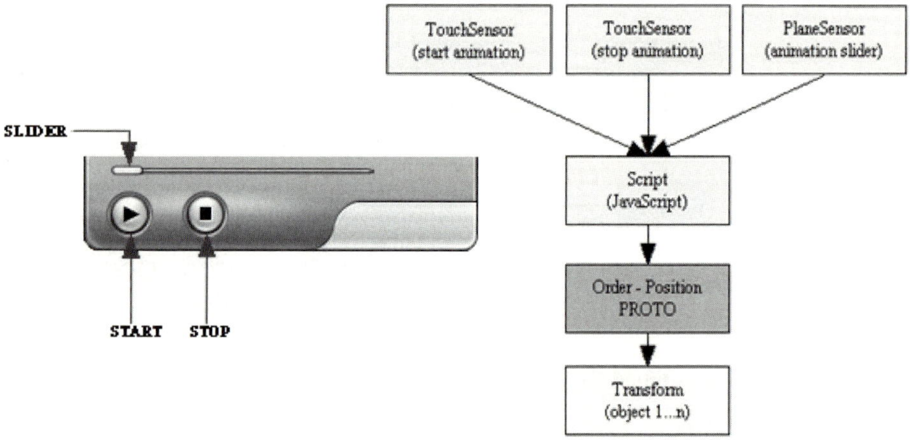

Fig. 6. The assembly process control

4 The e-Shopping Platform in Practice

The use of the CATER platform "brings" advantages to both suppliers and buyers, regarding (i) the cutback of transaction costs, (ii) the use of automated supply procedures, (iii) economies of scale, (iv) wide access on both local and international markets, (v) dynamic real-time price mechanisms/modules and (vi) the use of compatible/expandable technologies.

The requirements of the described CATER platform for automotive products, that together with the Intelligent Configurator Module and the 3D Visualisation Module comprise the advanced 3D Shop system, are:

- search and present all the available products, based on multi-criteria search engines;
- group products into multilevel categories (set by the e-shop administrator);
- make offers/ sales and promote them;
- update both the product catalogue and all items' availability (set by the e-shop administrator);
- create/use shop baskets (by the end buyers);
- provide several convenient pay/ receive methods;
- provide a secure e-payment credit card transaction (with the use of HTTPS and SSL protocols).

However, the efficiency and overall quality of an e-commerce service depends "heavily" on its automatic connection with the existing ERP (Enterprise Resource Planning) system for the catalogue, prices, stock and product update. In order to integrate all the available ERP data with the e-shop database, a powerful staging mechanism is developed and securely transfers all necessary data. This staging process uses a smart "track changes" algorithm, to enhance the update speed.

There are two staging processes, Real Time Staging and Off Line Staging (that uses an automated batch process). The characteristics of the two staging "methods" are compared in the following table.

Table 2. Staging Procedures Comparison

	Real Time Staging	**Off Line Staging**
Data Update	(+) All data are updated at all times	(-) All data are updated at specifically defined time periods
Infrastructure	(-) Reliable, high speed, technical infrastructure is necessary, available on a 24x7x365 basis	(+) Not so advanced technical infrastructure is necessary
Security	(-) The system can be secure but certain "protective" actions must be taken	(+) Security is obvious

The previous table shows that a real time staging procedure should be followed only if the nature of the commodity traded imposes the constant database update. In our case, an every day off line procedure is chosen for both security and convenience reasons.

Yet, if we try to deduct a general case example we must notice that each company's and product's needs, concerning the use of an e-market, are different; therefore the connectivity solutions (between an e-shop and an ERP) provided vary, depending on: (i) the ERP used (it can be a widely used international ERP such as SAP, Oracle Applications, etc. or it can be a custom made system, that fits to specific needs), (ii) the transaction volume and the form of the data transferred, (iii) the importance of the information transferred (regarding time, safety etc. aspects), (iv) the use of unilateral or bilateral communication and (v) whether it is an on-line or a batch transfer of data.

5 Experimental Results and Conclusions

E-commerce services offered through a B2C (business to consumer) or B2B (business to business) system, provide the necessary infrastructure for real time e-business and an added value package of services, that guarantee faster and more efficient buy and sell transactions, access to a broadened database of buyers/suppliers and business opportunities, through the development of new partnerships.

In conclusion, in this paper we presented an interactive and user-friendly e-commerce solution for the vehicle sector, but appropriate for other sectors as well. Volvo Technology Corporation (VTEC) has been the end-user responsible for using and testing the CATER platform, so a number of its vehicles were integrated in the platform for evaluation and testing purposes.

Finally, the main contribution is that our approach integrates additional technologies, such as an intelligent configurator module and a 3D visualisation environment aiming at enabling a suitable representation of products, in order to achieve the most realistic possible visualization and simulate a realistic shopping procedure.

Acknowledgements

We wish to acknowledge to the CATER project Consortium for their valuable contributions to this work. The CATER project is partially funded by the EC.

References

1. Kompatsiaris, I., Mezaris, V., Strintzis, M.G.: Multimedia content indexing and retrieval using an object ontology. In: Stamou, G., Kollias, S. (eds.) Multimedia Content and the Semantic Web: Methods, Standards and Tools, pp. 339–371. Wiley, Chichester (2005)
2. Tsampoulatidis, I., Nikolakis, G., Tzovaras, D., Strintzis, M.G.: Ontology Based Interactive Graphic Environment for Product Presentation. In: Proc. CGI 2004, pp. 644–647, Heraklion, Crete, Greece (June 2004)
3. Mezaris, V., Kompatsiaris, I., Strintzis, M.G.: An Ontology Approach to Object-Based Image Retrieval. In: Proc. IEEE International Conference on Image Processing (ICIP 2003), Barcelona, Spain, vol. II, pp. 511–514 (September 2003) http://www.iti.gr/db.php/el/publications/details/532.html
4. Apache Jakarta, http://jakarta.apache.org/
5. Jena, A Semantic Web Framework for Java, http://jena.sourceforge.net/
6. Protégé, An Ontology Editor and Knowledge-base Framework, http://protege.stanford.edu

7. Web 3D Consortium, VRML Standard, http://www.web3d.org/x3d/vrml/
8. Protégé OWL Plugin, http://protege.stanford.edu/plugins/owl/
9. The OWL Web Ontology Language, http://www.w3.org/TR/owl-features/
10. Horridge, M., Knublauch, H., Rector, A., Stevens, R., Wroe, C., Practical, A.: Guide To Building OWL Ontologies Using The Protégé-OWL Plugin and CO-ODE Tools, Edition 1.0, The University of Manchester (August 2004)
11. Carroll, J., Dickinson, I., Dollin, C., Reynolds, D., Seaborne, A., Wilkinson, K.: Jena: Implementing the Semantic Web Recommendations, Digital Media Systems Laboratory, HP Laboratories Bristol (2003)
12. Jena 2 Inference Support, http://jena.sourceforge.net/inference/

WATCH-OVER HMI for Vulnerable Road Users' Protection

Katrin Meinken[1], Roberto Montanari[2], Mark Fowkes[3], and Anny Mousadakou[4]

[1] University of Stuttgart
Institute for Human Factors and Technology Management
Nobelstr. 12, 70569 Stuttgart, Germany
katrin.meinken@iat.uni-stuttgart.de
[2] University of Modena and Reggio Emilia
Dipartimento di Scienze e Metodi dell'Ingegneria
via Fogliani 1, 42100 Reggio Emilia, Italy
montanari.roberto@unimore.it
[3] MIRA Limited
Watling Street, Nuneaton, CV10 0TU, UK
mark.fowkes@mira.co.uk
[4] Centre for Research And Technology – Hellas
Poseidonos av. 17, 17455 Alimos, Athen, Greece
amousa@certh.gr

Abstract. WATCH-OVER is a European project, aiming at the enhancement of road safety and the impairment of traffic accidents involving vulnerable road users (VRUs), such as pedestrians, bicyclists and motorcyclists, in urban and extra-urban areas. The project carries out research and development activities, in order to design an integrated cooperative system for accident prevention. In this paper, the concept of the Human Machine Interface of the WATCH-OVER system is discussed and its user-centred approach, based on a user requirement survey, is described. Regarding the HMI, the basic functionalities and elements, as well as the preliminary guidelines that endorse the WATCH-OVER system approach, are presented.

Keywords: Vulnerable road users, HMI, road safety, Powered Two-Wheeler's.

1 Introduction

Throughout the last 30 years, the overall volume of road traffic has tripled (European Commission, 2003). Even though the number of road deaths has fallen by half in these years, it is still at an unacceptable high number. New on-board information and communication technologies offer considerable potential for reducing the number of traffic accident victims. The WATCH-OVER project aims at avoiding road accidents that involve VRUs, namely pedestrians, bicyclists and motorcyclists, by developing an integrated cooperative system for accident prevention. This topic is in line with the

C. Stephanidis (Ed.): Universal Access in HCI, Part II, HCII 2007, LNCS 4555, pp. 488–496, 2007.

ambitious target of the EC, to reduce the total number of road fatalities by 50 % by 2010.

WATCH-OVER is a specific targeted project, co-funded by the European Commission Information Society Technologies (IST), that started its activities in January 2006. The core of the system, based on sensor and communication technologies, is the interaction of an on-board module and a user module, in order to cover a wide traffic scenario, including blind spots. Current sensor technologies cannot "see" behind obstacles and have a limited view of lateral and longitudinal areas. The main difficulty in detecting VRUs is therefore the limited "visibility" of car drivers and of in-vehicle sensor based systems. WATCH-OVER aims at improving these soft spots, by combining the most promising communication technologies with the most promising sensor technologies. Besides focussing on the exploitation of these advanced communication and sensing technologies, the main focus of the project is the design and development of the human machine interface (HMI) for both the driver and the vulnerable road user. Therefore, different solutions for the HMI have to be found: One would be an in-vehicle device, whereas the others would be based upon wearable devices for pedestrians, bicyclists and motorcyclists.

To set up an effective HMI, which meets the demands of the future users, it is essential to consult existing guidelines and specifications on the one hand, and to carry out a thorough examination of user requirements and identify specific traffic scenarios, in which the system is considered as valuable, on the other hand. The present paper describes the user-centred development procedure, based on general guidelines and regulations and on the results of a conducted user needs survey, concerning HMI, including the requirements of an effective warning strategy.

2 System Architecture

The WATCH-OVER project focuses its activities on the design and development of an integrated cooperative vehicle-user system, for the prevention of accidents involving VRUs, in urban and extra-urban scenarios. The system architecture is based upon the cooperation of innovative wireless short range communication technologies and vision sensor technologies. This cooperative platform shall extend the actual coverage of the state of the art technologies and will be open to integrate localisation technologies. Therefore, the following specifications are considered as important and will be integrated in the design of the WATCH-OVER system:

- The extension of the "protection concept" by an effective warning and/or intervention strategy.
- Increased vehicle speed range (up to 50 km/h), at which the system is operable.
- A high reliability of signal recognition in each scenario.
- Timely performance of the detection and localisation of VRUs.
- Low cost and low power consumption of components.

– Increased processing speed (more than 10 Hz).
– Increased sensor coverage (0–20m).

The key challenge in implementing these attitudes into the system architecture is to cover the various urban and extra-urban traffic scenarios, involving a variety of VRUs, in very different conditions. Thus, the in-vehicle module of the WATCH-OVER system is intended to enable the following functionalities:

– Real-time detection of pedestrians, bicyclists and motorcyclists, equipped with the WATCH-OVER module.
– Calculation of the relative positioning of the vehicle vs. VRU (relative motion analysis).
– Detection of dangerous situations.
– Appropriate warning of the driver, providing information only in really dangerous situations.

The vulnerable road user module on the other hand is conceived to:

– Promptly answer to vehicle's stimulus, delivering its identification parameters.
– Send back self-localisation parameters.
– Give feedback to the VRU with an appropriate HMI.

The modules for the VRUs are designated to be integrated into wearable objects, like helmets, shoes, watches, rucksacks or consumer electronics.

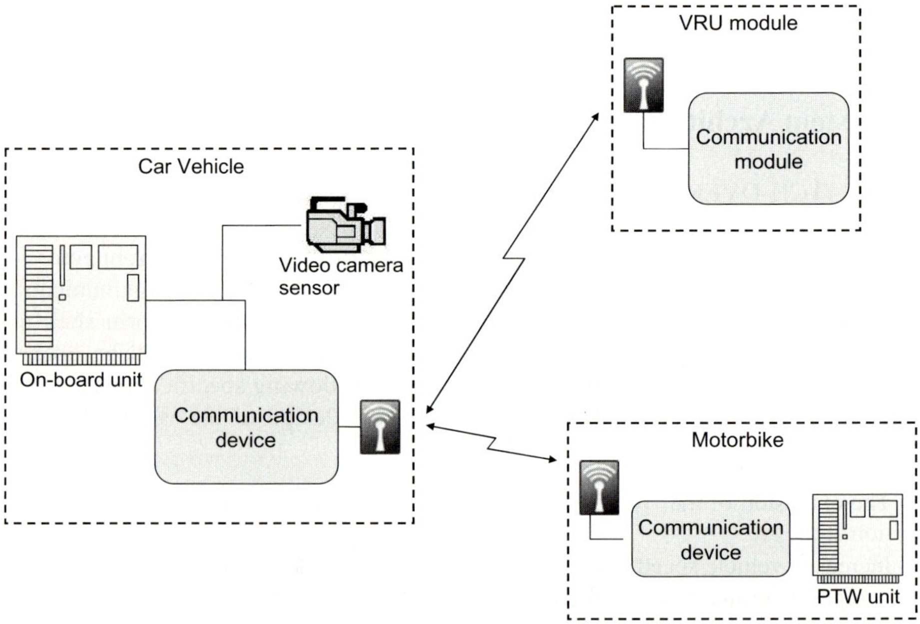

Fig. 1. WATCH-OVER system architecture and components

3 HMI Concept and Warning Strategy

To derive the concept for the HMI of the WATCH-OVER system, different sources had to be considered. Not only general guidelines for HMI design and common requirements for warning strategies were consolidated but also the specific user requirements, related to the WATCH-OVER topics, were examined.

3.1 Appliance of Preliminary Guidelines

General guidelines for in-vehicle systems were used, together with specific guidelines for the design of warning devices, to derive the basic HMI and warning concept. In 2001 the European Commission concluded a process, which started on 1999, for the development of a set of guidelines for the design of safety on-board information systems. This document is named "European Statement of Principles on Human Machine Interface (HMI) for In-Vehicle Information and Communication Systems" (ESoP) and was updated in December 2006. Considering that the driver's primary task is the safe control of the vehicle in a complex and dynamic traffic environment, the primary goal of the principles is to fulfil the requirements. All contemplated guidelines summarise essential safety aspects, to be considered for the HMI for in-vehicle information and communication systems. These guidelines apply to all components and aspects of a system that the driver will interact with while driving. The most important declarations need to be included in the WATCH-OVER system, such as that:

- The system must comply with relevant regulation and standards.
- The system supports the driver and does not increase driver distraction from driving task.
- The system shall not require uninterruptible sequences of interaction.
- The system does not distract or visually entertain the driver.
- No part of the system should obstruct the driver's view of the road scene.
- The system response (e.g. feedback, confirmation) following driver input should be timely and clearly perceptible.
- Information which has the highest safety relevance should be given priority.
- The behaviour of the system should not adversely interfere with the display or controls required for the primary driving task and for road safety.

Thus, the main goal of the WATCH-OVER HMI must be to avoid driver confusion and overload. Only information that will assist the driver more than distract him/her in complex traffic scenarios in urban and extra-urban areas should be provided by the HMI.

3.2 Warning Strategy

The WATCH-OVER warning strategy follows the approach of Wickens et al. (2004), as they state in their work that "the goal [of a warning] is to get the user to comply with the warning and, therefore, use the product in a safe way, or avoid unsafe behaviour." In order to ensure a secure handling of the future system, four elementary requirements have to be attended to:

- The warning must be noticed.
- The warning must be perceived (read/heard).
- The warning must be understood.
- The warning must be accepted.

By applying these criteria, an efficient design of a warning strategy will first of all draw the attention of the driver or the vulnerable road user. Then, it has to be assured that the warning message is not only physically perceived, but, moreover, cognitively understood and then accepted by the driver or the vulnerable road user. The system has also to give information about the identified risk and about possible and recommendable actions, in case they are not obvious.

3.3 User Requirements

The definition of user requirements is an essential step in designing a system, intended to effectively serve the needs of the future user. The user requirements have to be considered since the beginning of the project and are of immediate importance for the development and implementation of the system's hardware and software architecture. In WATCH-OVER, user requirements have been defined through 154 questionnaires, answered by non-technical experts from 9 countries (Austria, Chech Republic, France, Germany, Greece, Italy, Poland, Switzerland, the Netherlands), who were pedestrians and drivers themselves and commute regularly with cars, motorcycles and bicycles. According to the answers given to HMI related questions, the following HMI requirements arise:

In case of no accident risk

1. the system should only inform the driver of the presence of VRUs (location, distance, etc.) after explicit demand;
2. the visual information should appear on the head up display or on the instrument cluster;
3. the system should inform the driver of the presence of VRUs, regarding the distance and the heading of the vulnerable road user on demand only.

In case of an acute accident risk due to the presence of a VRU

4. the system should warn the driver;
5. the warning should be a tone/beep or an icon on the display;
6. secondary important information provided includes the relative position, the weather, the height of the pedestrian and the momentum;
7. these information (see item 5 and 6) should be presented by an icon on display or by a tone/beep.

Also, previous projects demonstrate that driver assistance systems designed to prevent accidents with VRUs are highly attractive. Users' assessments on different HMI's of dissimilar systems show that following conclusions should be considered important in HMI development and therefore for the development of the WATCH-OVER system as well:

- The allowance for false alarm should be very low.
- If a driver perceives too many false alarms, the warning will be ignored (Lee, See 2004).
- The warning should be given acoustically and therefore must be heard.
- Mere visual information may not be noticed in-time, and might possibly decrease safety due to its distraction effect. A combination with visual information might be useful, because of redundancy.
- The warning should be given with adequate timing, in order to allow the driver to react well considered.

3.4 WATCH-OVER HMI Concept

In the course of the identification of the user requirements, an expert's workshop has been held, in order to discuss the implementation of the WATCH-OVER HMI. One main objective was to find an approach that limits the number of false alarms or even completely avoids them and to evade issues of an information overload. Therefore, it is crucial to be coherent throughout the warning strategy and by this avoid redundancy. The WATCH-OVER HMI concept provides a continuous evaluation of the risk level by the system. If the risk level is approaching a prior specified threshold, the system will warn the driver or the VRU respectively. The thresholds will be identified according to the different risk levels.

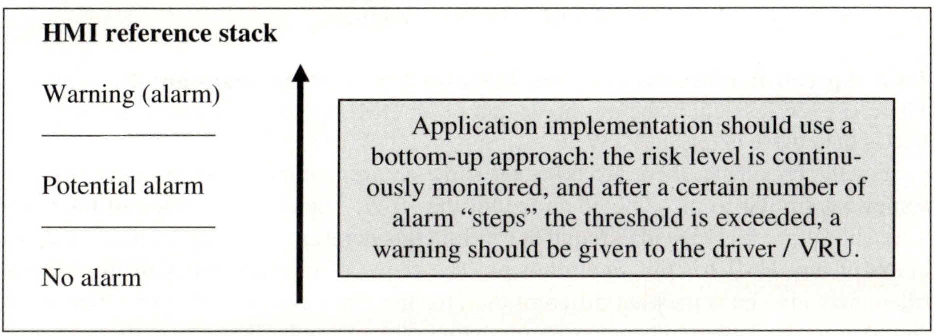

Fig. 2. HMI approach followed within the WATCH-OVER project

The above discussed concept is introduced, in order to avoid the development of a system, that could potentially distract the driver or the VRU, instead of assisting in already complex traffic situations. If the HMI interface is too pervasive, with an intensive visual or acoustical output presented to the user, it may lead to switching the system off altogether. Therefore, it is necessary to eliminate false alarms, as well as an overload of information in all cases, if possible.

Through the HMI, the communication with the user will be established. Thus, the HMI constitutes the physical representation of the warning strategy. It is important that the HMI set-up is adaptable to both the personal preferences of the user, as well as to his/her cultural background, in order to guarantee a good acceptance. That means, e.g. that the driver or the VRU should have control of the loudness of auditory information, due to the likelihood of distraction or of a noisy surrounding. Or that, concerning the exploitation of the international market, internationally and/or nationally agreed standards, related to icons or symbols, should be used and speech output has to be at least in a language that the user is able to understand.

3.4.1 Special Requirements for the HMI for VRUs: Powered Two-Wheelers

Both the ESoP and other guidelines concern mainly the automotive sector. The research in the domain of Powered Two-Wheeler's (PTWs) is rather limited and most studies concerning the safety aspect do not deal with information systems at all. However, the neighbouring area of automotive research is well explored and the guidelines for this area may be used to some extent for PTWs, although some modifications are necessary.

There are some important differences between the PTW domain and the automotive domain. The PTW-driver is, for instance, much more affected by rain, wind and noise, since a standard PTW is not sheltered. This means that the design of a PTW information system has to take into consideration such things as dirty or wet displays or helmet visor and high noise levels, due to rain, wind, high speed or city traffic. Hence, the automotive design guidelines have to be utilised in a very conservative manner in the PTW-domain. The recommended limit should always be used rather than the legal limit: for instance the font size on displays could be augmented, in comparison to the minimum accepted size and the sound level for warning signals and other information should be adjustable to the noise environment inside a helmet.

The automotive guidelines may hence represent an important help in designing for PTWs, but every decision has to be made with keeping in mind the vital differences between the PTW and the automotive driving conditions.

3.4.2 Special Requirements for the HMI for VRUs: Pedestrians and Bicyclists

There is even less guidance on the design of an HMI for the pedestrian and bicyclist VRUs than there is for the PTW.

For the bicyclists, there are however some environmental considerations, that are somewhat similar to those noted above for the PTW. The exposed nature of the environment for the bicyclist also requires careful consideration, with regard to implementation of any HMI for this environment. The range of characteristics of the bicycle riders may also be somewhat different than for the PTW riders, with no restriction on age, due to the lack of licensing requirements, for example. There are also practical considerations with regard to HMI packaging and implementation for the bicyclist without the availability of any regular power sources and other electrical equipment and displays, that would be available on the PTW on the majority of most bicycles. An HMI that is self-powered and potentially worn by the user should be considered.

In this respect, this may have similar requirements to the HMI for a pedestrian who has, additionally, even less constraints in terms of legal requirements, licensing and power availability, than the bicyclist.

In both cases, HMI that can deliver readily understood warning requirements to the user, in a clear and unambiguous manner, must be sought. This must consider all potential sensory modalities, that could be realised in such an operational setting. These, potentially, must be understandable to users across a wider range of age, than that for the automotive and PTW users.

4 Conclusions and Outlook

The WATCH-OVER European project aims at designing and developing an integrated cooperative system for the prevention of accidents, involving VRUs in urban and extra-urban areas. The project is co-funded by the European Commission and is supported by EUCAR. The project Consortium is composed of 13 project partners from six different European countries, presenting vehicle and PTW manufacturers, automotive suppliers, technology and research centres for the development and testing phase.

The system is based on the cooperation of communication and sensor technologies and will provide users with an in-vehicle module, to warn drivers of approaching VRUs on the one hand and wearable modules, that call attention of VRUs to critical traffic situations, on the other hand. One major challenge in the development process is the design of an efficient HMI, that is of assistance in dangerous scenarios and does not distract the driver's or vulnerable road user's attention from the driving task or the surrounding traffic.

The development phase of the WATCH-OVER HMI has just started and will therefore be further addressed and investigated within the ongoing project activities. Executable prototypes of the HMI are planned to be tested and validated with driving simulators. The cooperative platform of different modules – in-vehicle and VRU-sided – will significantly help to further enhance road safety and to accomplish the goal of reducing the number of road fatalities.

Acknowledgements. We wish to acknowledge to the WATCH-OVER project Consortium of the PReVENT IP project, for their valuable contributions to this work. The WATCH-OVER project is partially funded by the EC.

References

1. Andreone, L., Bekiaris, E.A., Guarise, A., Mousadakou, A. (2006), D2.1 Requirements and use cases, WATCH-OVER project, (July 2006)
2. Andreone, L., Guarise, A., Lilli, F., Gavrila, D.M., Pieve, M. (2006), Cooperative Systems for Vulnerable Road Users: The Concept of the WATCH-OVER Project, 13th ITS World Congress, London (2006)
3. Barber, C.: Psychological aspects of conventional in-car warning devices. In: Stanton N (Ed.), Human Factors in Alarm Design, pp. 193–205. London: Taylor & Francis (1994)
4. European Commission, Commission Recommendation of 21 December 2005 on safe and efficient in-vehicle information and communication systems: A European statement of principles on human machine interface (2006)
5. Hagenmeyer, L., Marberger, C., Bekiaris, E., Nikolaou, S.: Preliminary Guidelines for the Personalization of the HMI of Hypovigilance-Management-Systems. Conference Proceedings HCI (2005)
6. European Commission; Communication from the Commission - European road safety action programme - Halving the number of road accident victims in the European Union by 2010: a shared responsibility COM/2003/0311 final
7. ISO, 8: Road vehicles – Ergonomic aspects of transport information and control systems – Specifications and compliance procedures for in-vehicle visual presentation (1500)

8. Lee, J.D., See, K.A.: Trust in Automation: Designing for Appropriate Reliance, Human Factors, vol. 46(1)
9. Lerner, N.D., Kotwal, B.M., Lyons, R.D., Gardner-Bonneau, D.J.: Preliminary Human Factors Guidelines for Crash Avoidance Warning Devices. National Technical Information Service, Springfield (1996)
10. Marberger, C., Dangelmaier, M., Bekiaris, E., Nikolaou, S. (2004). User centred HMI development for the AWAKE vigilance monitoring system. In: Conference Proceedings FISITA (2004)
11. Oltersdorf, K.M., Mayer, B., Maximov, K. (2003), D02.3 User Needs Investigation Results, PROTECTOR project (February 2003)
12. WATCH-OVER web site: http://www.watchover-eu.org
13. Wickens, C.D., Lee, J.D., Gordon Becker, S.E., Liu, Y.: An introduction to human factors engineering. Pearson Education, Upper Saddle River, New Jersey (2004)

Improvement Approach of the Automation System in Aviation for Flight Safety

Takafumi Nakatani[1], Kenichiro Honda[2], and Yukihiko Nakata[2]

[1] Nagoya R&D Center, Technical Headquaters, Mitsubishi Heavy Industries, Ltd.
1, Takamichi, Iwatsuka-cho, Nakamura-ku, Nagoya 453-8515 Japan
[2] Nagoya Aerospace Systems Works, Mitsubishi Heavy Industries, Ltd.
10, Oye-cho, Minato-ku, Nagoya 455-8515 Japan
{takafumi_nakatani, kenichiro_honda, yukihiko_nakata}@mhi.co.jp

Abstract. Next generation cockpit concept aiming to reduce the risk of pilot-error-induced accident was studied. This new cockpit concept, called Human-Centered Cockpit incorporates several ideas which aim to improve the pilot's situation awareness for the terrain and the aircraft situation without increasing the pilot's cognitive workload. This concept is built on task analysis and accident analysis, and through several times of the airline pilot reviews using partial task simulation of new functions, design issues were identified and the design was brushed up. Fully functional cockpit simulator was finally developed to evaluate the effectiveness of this cockpit concept in the realistic commercial aircraft operational environment from preflight to spot-in, including the ATC. Six pilots participated in the final evaluation and the result showed that this cockpit concept enhances the pilot's situation awareness in the actual operation environment, and improves the pilot's cognitive workload in flight.

Keywords: Human Factors, Flight Deck, CFIT, and Situation Awareness.

1 Introduction

The mission of air transportation service is carrying people and loads to safety to the destination. However, as the statistics [1] shows, rate of hull-loss accident remains almost stable from middle of 1970's to today. This fact and continuous growth of the commercial traffic in the future imply that the number of the aircraft accident will continue to increase if proper action will not be taken by the manufacturer and/or the operator.

On the other hand, about 70 percents of the accidents are said to be due to the pilot error [1]. Introduction of the highly-automated glass-cockpit has been contributing to the reduction of the pilot workload, however, it does not lead to the reduction of the accident rate, and on the contrary, it induces new type of the human error unseen in the past due to improper interaction between the highly-automated system and the pilot.

This study is aimed at improving flight safety by building "Human-Centered Cockpit". This design concept is built on task analysis and accident analysis, and the

C. Stephanidis (Ed.): Universal Access in HCI, Part II, HCII 2007, LNCS 4555, pp. 497–506, 2007.

goal is achieved by repeating the evaluation and modification based on the Human-Centered Design Process. This process is applicable also to the service in which a specialist is engaged and which is involved safely.

"Human-Centered Cockpit" is a cockpit trying to eliminate any possible causes of human-factor-induced aircraft accidents, by optimizing the interaction between human and machine in a highly automated aircraft control system.

This study is trying to establish and propose the "Human-Centered Cockpit", as a next generation cockpit improving the man-machine interface in the glass cockpit. The study focused not only on working out the improvement ideas and evaluating their effectiveness, but also on how to integrate them into the cockpit and pilot procedure for practical use in the actual operational environment without imposing "special" effort to the pilot.

2 Approach

In order to extract the aspect and essential factor of human-factor-induced aircraft accidents, pilot task analysis and accident analysis were conducted. And the design subject to which priority should be given was defined.

2.1 Task Analysis

The pilot task in real operation was classified for every flight phase, in order to analyze the relation between a pilot work load and that outside environments (control command, weather, air-traffic environment, etc.) and airframe system condition.

Not only the generalized task but the task data when flying using a full flight simulator were used for the data of task analysis.

Pilot behavior, eyes movement, and dialogue were recorded in simulation flight. And the flow of the task in real time, the volume of a pilot work load, and the characteristics of those were captured.

About the situation with especially issue, a phase and its details were specified from pilot's interview. Based on them, the subject for reduction of a work load and human error prevention was extracted.

As a result, a pilot's main tasks are the command inputs to the auto pilot system. Although the work loads at the time of normal condition or cruise phase decreased by the auto pilot, at the time of Approach and Landing phase or Non-normal condition, the work load became large. Especially the volume of cognitive processing is increasing rather compared with manual control.

2.2 Accident Analysis

The accident supposed that human factors are the cause in formal accident reports, such as NTSB, was extracted. For them, correspondence with the primary factor of the accident and design items were supposed and classified. What summarized the analysis result is shown below.

Table 1. Primary factor of the accident and design items

Design items	Num.	
Airframe situation awareness	56	>Situation Awareness
- Maneuver condition / trend	23	
- A/P, A/T	19	
- Control surface	4	
- Icing	3	
- Fuel residual quantity	2	
- Engine	2	
- Pitot system	2	
- Warnings	1	
External world situation awareness	22	>Situation Awareness
- Geographical feature	11	
- Traffic, airspace	6	
- Weather	3	
- etc.	2	
Intelligibility of design logic	20	>Communication Gap (Human - machine)
- A/P A/T Mode	9	
- Warning operation	3	
- Override to A/P	2	
- Override to Safety Lock	2	
- Work load	2	
- The relation of PF/PNF steering	1	
- FMS input	1	
Appropriateness of a command	17	>Communication Gap (Human - machine)
- Intentional reconfirmation	8	
- Setting error	7	
- Prediction of a command result	2	
Appropriateness of decision-making	10	>Situation Awareness
- RTO, G/A, etc.	5	
- Management at the time of critical-system failure	1	
- Outside circumference -> judgment of the control direction	1	
- Under SIGMET	1	
- Collision avoidance	1	
- Criticality judgment at the time of A/P failure	1	
Reliability and redundancy of a design	12	
- A/P	2	
- Control system	2	
- Backup at the time of critical-system failure	2	
- Warning system	2	
- System related to the situation awareness of a critical system	1	
- Communications system	1	
- Bad weather	1	
- Meter	1	
Certification level	5	
- Bird-strike reinforcement	1	
- Performance at the time of bad weather	1	
- The phenomenon outside assumption	1	
- Backup when Manual Recovery is difficult	1	
- The performance warranty at the time of icing	1	
Support of the improvement in communication accuracy	4	>Communication Gap (Human - Human)
- ATC	2	
- Between crews	2	

The starting points of error chains are various. In many cases, according to the disagreement concerning situation awareness of pilots, the chain of errors was not stopped. Even if it sees the number of cases, there are extremely many primary factors concerning "airframe situation awareness" and "external world situation awareness."

In the breakdown of "airframe situation awareness", lack of situation awareness related to maneuver condition (energy state), that trend, and an automatic pilot system has become the primary factor of an accident in many cases. Besides, by the primary factor of "external world situation awareness", it turns out that there are many cases of loss of the situation awareness about the terrain. This is in accord with the occurrence tendency of accidents.

There are many primary factors related to the scheme of the autopilot among "design logic." The case has close relation with the above "loss of situation awareness."

2.3 Define the Design Object

As a result of being the above analysis, it became clear that a work load increase phase and the frequent occurrence phase of accidents were in accord. It is the phase of approach & landing. Besides, it is CFIT (Controlled Flight into Terrain) which has one of the strongest relevance of a human error as an accident event, and the issue is in "situation awareness" and "communication gap." Communication gap is a barrier which exists in the situation of various communications, such as an interface between a pilot and auto pilot, a pilot and a pilot, a pilot and a controller.

Then, it made into the design objective to cut off the error chain which leads to an accident by reducing various kinds of work loads in Approach and Landing phase, and giving room to a pilot's cognitive resource.

3 Function Level Concept Study

Accident cause investigation was conducted for the human-factor-induced accidents including those described in the FAA Human Factors Team report [2]. The investigation result showed that;

- Most of the accidents can be avoided if the pilot could realize the situation well before the warning.
- Warning system informs the pilot of the imminent hazard as a last resort, though, it cannot be an ultimate accident stopper.
- The improvement of the situation awareness especially for the aircraft automation system and the terrain in normal operation, ie. cutting off the error chain on the root cause is a key issue to cope with the human-factor-induced accident.

We suggested several new function ideas focusing on the improvement of the auto-pilot situation awareness and the terrain awareness well before the warning situation. Some of the main items are shown below.

3.1 3D Terrain View Overlay on PFD

CG-based 3D Terrain View using the EGPWS terrain database is overlaid behind the Attitude Indicator instead of the blue/brown artificial horizon, to enhance the terrain awareness. Normally the Attitude Indicator shows the conventional blue/ brown artificial horizon, and the 3D view automatically pops up when i) altimeter setting is in manual setting mode (which is certainly selected by the pilot when the aircraft is below the transition altitude), ii) flap is set to other than "up" position, or iii) EGPWS caution/warning alert is active, and pops down automatically when descending to Decision Height or Minimum Descent Altitude, in order to enhance the pilot to look out the actual external view. Manual on/off push button is also equipped.

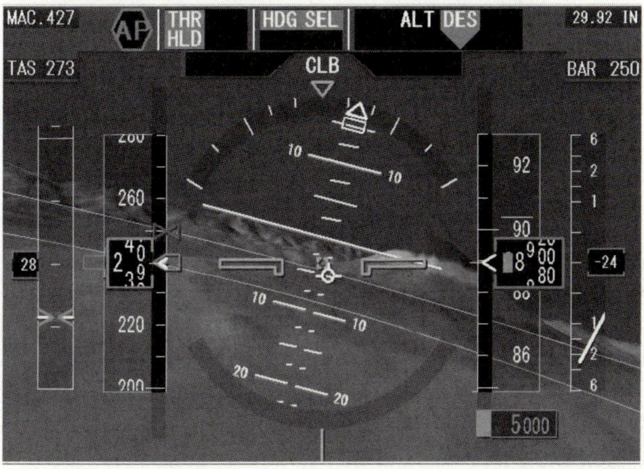

Fig. 1. 3D Terrain View Overlay on PFD

3.2 Vertical Profile Display

This display aims at improving the terrain awareness and the vertical flight plan/path awareness. Terrain cutout and vertical flight profile along the expected lateral path are displayed with the aircraft position and vertical trend vector, as an aid to visually check the deviation from the planned vertical profile or to determine the VS (Vertical Speed) or FPA (Flight Path Angle) value when VS or FPA mode is engaged.

Lateral displayed range is linked to that of the nose-up lateral flight path map, and vertical range is fixed in an optimized value for each lateral range so that the display can show the entire vertical profile within the selected lateral range.

The expected lateral path used for cutting the vertical flight profile and the terrain, depends on the engaged lateral mode. When the LNAV (Lateral Navigation) mode is engaged, the display shows the cutout along the FMS lateral flight plan course, and for other modes, along the current track. (Fig. 2)

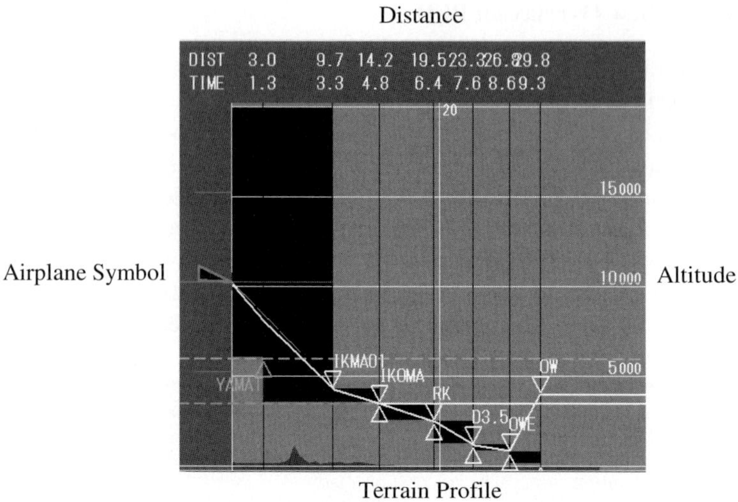

Fig. 2. Vertical Profile Display

3.3 Full-Time Speed Management (S-MNG)

S-MNG is an automatic speed command function which commands appropriate speed, according to the altitude, flight phase, and flap setting, and speed constraint at the waypoint. S-MNG is not a part of the FMS, and is available in any flight situation from takeoff to landing, unlike the conventional speed management system available only when the FMS vertical navigation is active (ie. the pilot is required to set the speed bug during the final approach which is said to be the highest workload phase.).

4 Evaluation

It is impossible to guarantee inhibition of the human-factor-induced accidents by design improvement, and it is also difficult to show a quantitative effect. It is because all of the complicated situation or Slip which result in an accident cannot be assumed and it cannot reappear, either.

Occurrence probability of human's general Error, for example, the selection error by a mistake is made in reading is set to 3x10-3 (it is based on WASH-1400 [U. S. Atomic Energy Commission]). At least in order to check the reduction efficacy of the occurrence probability of a simple error, it is necessary to perform 3000 examinations or more. To design evaluation, it is unreal.

Therefore, the developed cockpit system was evaluated by the commercial pilots to confirm if the system is designed to be an effective situation awareness improvement tool for practical use in the actual operational environment.

4.1 Method

Six pilots participated in the evaluation. Four of them are the airline pilots all belong to the flight operating engineering section in the large transport carrier, and each has following background;

- Boeing 777 Captain,
- Airbus 320 Captain,
- Boeing 777 First Officer, and
- Boeing 747-400 First Officer.

Other two are the flight test pilot usually operating the business and military jet on the aircraft manufacturer.

Subjective rating method was taken for the evaluation of the effectiveness of the developed cockpit system in the aspects of the situation awareness, workload, safety and operational acceptance. In addition, heuristic comments were provided to help understanding the reason for each given rating.

Before the evaluation flight, pilots received a handout-based tutorial for the cockpit system and operation including the control method of the Navigation Unit, and took an introductory full flight in the function simulator to be familiar with overall procedures. (Fig. 3)

Fig. 3. The function simulator

After the introductory flight, each two of them were seated on the left and right seat on the function simulator, and made an evaluation flight, simulating the normal IFR flight operation from the preflight to the post-flight, except for unusual many times of the flight plan changes aimed to increase the workload. Mission profile is shown on Fig. 4. Left and right pilots cooperatively performed all of the operational procedures of the developed systems (ie. the display system, the auto flight control system and the navigation unit system) in a real time from the preflight to the post flight. In order to provide equal opportunity to operate the Navigation Unit for both the left and right pilot, they changed their PF (Pilot Flying) and PNF (Pilot Not Flying) duties in flight.

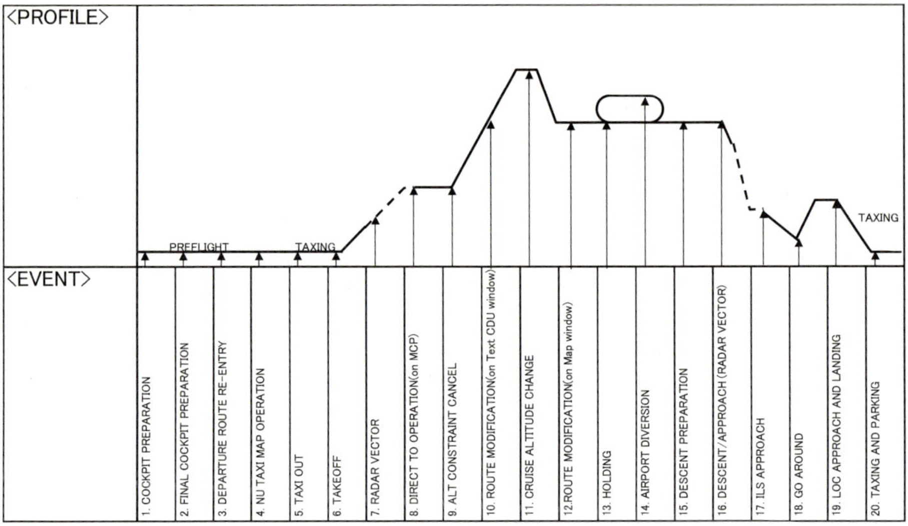

Fig. 4. Mission profile for the evaluation flight

4.2 Result

The result of the subjective rating is summarized in Fig. 5.

In view of the aircraft situation awareness, the effectiveness of various improvement functions was positively accepted. Heuristic comments also supported the rating result;

- VPD is an effective tool to recognize the aircraft situation.
- VPD is especially useful on the non-precision approach, which requires the pilot to decide appropriate descent path looking into many "step down" altitude constraints.

The cockpit was also evaluated to be effective for the terrain situation awareness improvement. Heuristic comment showed that the VPD, the 3D Terrain View Overlay, and the Navigation Unit display contributed to this rating;

- Terrain perspective view and ILS approach tunnel on the 3D Terrain Overlay function are very effective to avoid the CFIT accident.

Effectiveness rating for the task workload was split among the pilots. Heuristic comments were mainly described for the full time speed management function;

- Full time speed management function eliminates the speed bug setting task and contributes to the reduction of the task workload.

– Full time speed management does not always reduce the task workload, because call out action may be required in order to avoid unintended speed command change.

Negative impact for the task workload by the introduction of new function was not pointed out, except for a comment that new training system needs to be established suitable for this new cockpit system.

On the other hand, the effectiveness for the reduction of the cognitive workload was very positively accepted. Heuristic comments supported the rating result in the following reasons;

– VPD and NU display provide much better cognition for the flight plan and improve the cognitive workload.
– N1 indication on the PFD is effective for the reduction of the cognitive workload especially in manual flight.

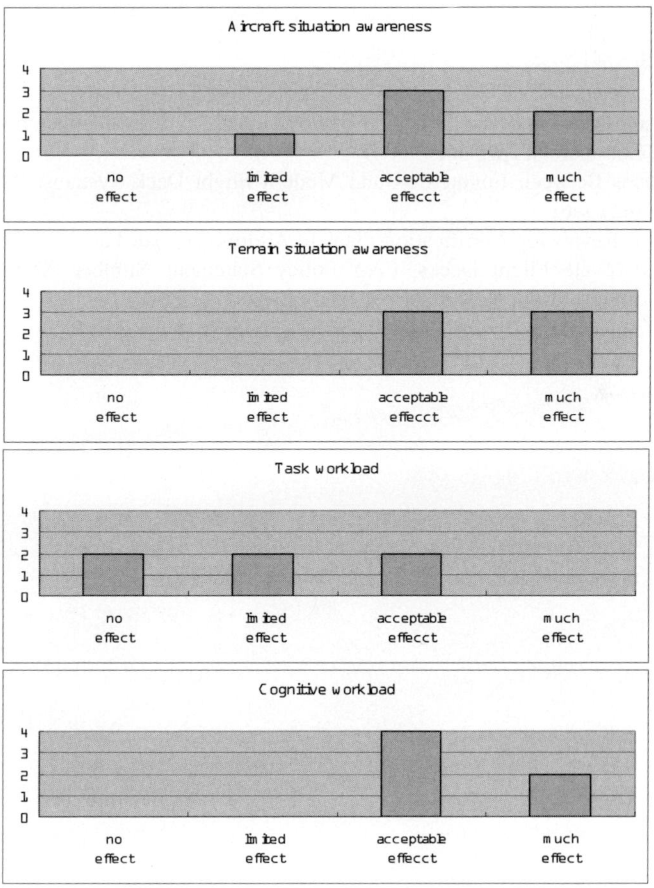

Fig. 5. The result of the subjective rating

5 Conclusion

Human-Centered Cockpit system, incorporating many ideas to improve the situation awareness aiming to reduce the risk of pilot-error-induced accident was developed. This design concept is built on task analysis and accident analysis, and the goal is achieved by repeating the evaluation with the commercial pilots and modification. The subjective rating and heuristic comments showed that the developed cockpit system improves the aircraft/terrain situation awareness. Contribution factor for the reduction of the task workload was not confirmed, however, the system was evaluated to reduce the cognitive workload without inducing negative task workload by the additional function.

Acknowledgments. This study was performed by Mitsubishi Heavy Industries, Ltd. with the help of the Japanese Ministry of Economy, Trade and Industry (METI) and Japan Aircraft Development Corporation (JADC).

References

1. Statistical summary of commercial jet airplane accidents-Worldwide operations 1959–2005. By Boeing Commercial Airplane (2006)
2. The Interfaces Between Flightcrews and Modern Flight Deck Systems. By FAA Human Factors Team (1996)
3. Guidance for Reviewing Certification Plans to Address Human Factors for Certification of Transport Airplane Flight Decks. FAA Policy Statement Number ANM-99-2, Federal Aviation Administration, Department of Transportation (1999)

Addressing Concepts for Mobile Location-Based Information Services

Wolfgang Narzt, Gustav Pomberger, Alois Ferscha, Dieter Kolb, Reiner Müller, Horst Hörtner, and Ronald Haring

Johannes Kepler University Linz, Altenbergerstr. 69, A-4040 Linz, Austria
Siemens Corporate Technology, Otto-Hahn Ring 6, D-81730 Munich, Germany
Ars Electronica Futurelab, Hauptstr. 2, A-4040 Linz, Austria
{wolfgang.narzt, gustav.pomberger, alois.ferscha}@jku.at,
{kolb.dieter, reiner.e.mueller, jan.wieghardt}@siemens.com,
{horst.hoertner, roland.haring}@aec.at

Abstract. Emerging mobile location-based information services enable people to place digital content into the physical world. Based on three technical components (1) mobile devices, (2) wireless networking and (3) location-sensing the implementation of location-based services can be considered state of the art. In contrast, we observe a lack of conceptual work in terms of user interface issues, like designing indirect (one-to-any) addressing models, handling information overflow and avoiding spam. Every user is able to arbitrarily place information anywhere without structure or restrictions, and is confronted with an information mess in return. The focus of this paper concentrates on a novel addressing concept for mobile location-based information services, which systematically structures both direct and indirect addressing methods and supports the users in finding or filtering the information they are interested in.

Keywords: Mobile Location-Based Services, Spam, Addressing Concepts.

1 Introduction

A heterogeneous manifold of mobile devices and wireless networking technology satisfy the rapidly rising need for mobility and autonomy concerning unbounded world wide information exchange. Whereas laptop computers, personal digital assistants and mobile phones can be regarded as mature mobile device technology, the next generation of transportable perception units is close to be released from the research labs (i.e., wearable computers, head-mounted see-through displays and even tangible objects). Combined with various wireless transmission technologies, like GSM, GPRS, UMTS and WLAN these mobile devices are commonly used for synchronous (e.g., voice and video telephony) and asynchronous communication (e.g., SMS and MMS).

Recently, miscellaneous location sensors (e.g., GPS, cellular triangulation, ultrasonic sensors, etc.) extend such services and enable users to annex position coordinates to messages and consequently to store information at a desired place 1611.

C. Stephanidis (Ed.): Universal Access in HCI, Part II, HCII 2007, LNCS 4555, pp. 507–516, 2007.

Neglecting uncertainty issues concerning positioning accuracy, limited field coverage, fragmentary wireless connectivity and power consumption, the three components mobile devices, wireless networking and location-sensing are regarded as the enabling core technologies for mobile location-based services 2. However, based upon these technical prerequisites it is necessary to develop concepts and user interaction paradigms for organizational issues concerning such services, in order to make the perception of information adequate for the users 11:

2 Organizational Issues

Basically, we can identify four different organizational issues which extend or structure the pure functionality of mobile location-based information services:

First, the type of *addressing* inevitably differs in location-based services: Information is not only delivered to a set of selected predefined phone numbers but to any receivers (e.g., distinguished by their group memberships) who locally pass by the information. Thus primarily, the type of addressing is indirect (one-to-any) implicating that the number and identity of the recipients is unknown to the author of information.

Second, the *context* a recipient is associated with when examining information may affect his perception, meaning that e.g., information is only relevant on certain conditions or that the content of information is presented differently to the user 5. Context can be regarded as a diversified term, representing any identifiable state due to sensory input. To rise above or fall below a threshold of any technically measurable quantity may change a potential context 19. Time is a simple example of a quantifiable value allowing recipients e.g., to perceive information only during a period.

Third, and closely related to the feature of context-sensitivity of mobile location-based information services is the term *smartness* 16: Information is not always supposed to present static content – it can also dynamically adapt content or provide executable content for active manipulation. Basically, we distinguish three different types of smartness: (1) Information contains self-changing elements, like a ticker showing the consecutive progress of time (*dynamic content*). (2) The recipient himself is able to influence the content of information, e.g., by a click on a button, like in a poll where he changes statistical content by his vote (*influenced content*). (3) Users are able to trigger actions through interactive elements or the information itself executes code when it is perceived (*executable content*).

Bringing smart elements to mobile location-based information services opens up the door for developing an unlimited variety of distinctive content. Consequently, the service needs an *extension* concept for the core functionality, which appears to be the fourth organizational issue in mobile location-based information services. An extension concept must enable third-party developers to easily design their own (smart) elements, and it has to provide a mechanism to make these self-developed elements accessible to all users without forcing them to download new software versions or to restart their system. Users should not recognize if an element has just recently been developed by a third party or if it is a basic element like plain text.

These four issues addressing, context, smartness and extensibility enrich the functionality of mobile location-based information services. They are considered to represent the organizational layer, a more focused layer above the technical layer as illustrated in Fig. 1.

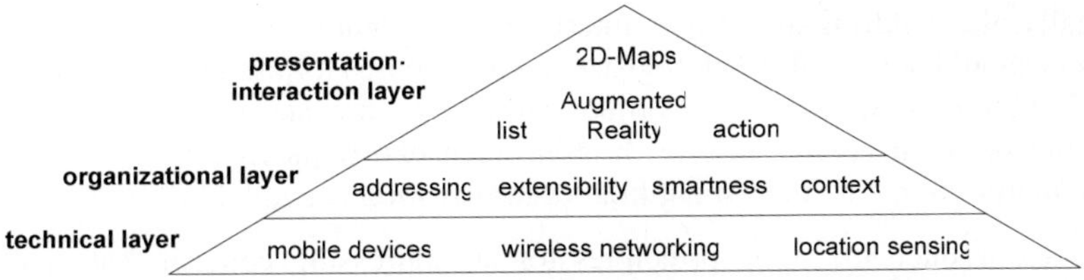

Fig. 1. Layer Model

The top layer contains presentation and interaction paradigms. It uses the technical components and concepts of the layers below to adequately present information.

Generally, location information can be shown in a bird's eye view on a 2D-map, in a simple list showing only the information the user is close to or even in an augmented reality (AR) view 15. Future scenarios even dismiss conventional display metaphors. They supersede the device screen for perception and present information in an alternative manner: Text may e.g., appear acoustically or a door may open when the user approaches information without forcing the user to peer at a display.

However, this paper focuses on *addressing* concepts in the organizational layer and gives an idea how information can be filtered by the user in the top layer.

3 Addressing Concept

The classical sender-receiver model for dispatching information does not meet the requirements in mobile location-based information services, anymore. Information is enriched by location and is predominantly designated to all passers-by within a defined radius. However, if everybody is capable of placing information to any location the service will predictably become unusable due to information overflow.

An exaggerated use of this service leaves the users stuck in an unstructured information mess where the entropy of most messages is null. Thus, mobile location-based information services urgently need a flexible and structured addressing concept for avoiding scenarios like this.

- An addressing concept must be capable of dealing with distinctive user communities or groups of interest for constricting the set of recipients and for avoiding spam. Users must be capable of joining communities or selecting terms of interest in order to find or filter the required information.
- Self-evidently, the concept must be scalable to millions of simultaneously online users. And it must be globally expandable all over the world, in contrast to locally bordered, non-interoperable isolated solutions. The possibility for building autonomous applications should be preserved, though.
- The use of smart elements enforces an extended model for access control. Information is not only characterized by read- and write-privileges, it can also define execution rights for selected users or groups.

- Finally, the handling of the user interface must comply with simplicity paradigms. Users should not run through registration procedures to join groups or communities (although registration is sometimes inevitable for access control). Interaction should be intuitive and answer the following two requests a user might make: "I am interested in …" and "What kind of information is available here?"

We first introduce the basic principles for an addressing concept that meet all the requirements stated above on the example of direct addressing, where users select one or more recipients from their private address book. Afterwards, we extend this concept to indirect one-to-any addressing based on the principles of direct addressing.

3.1 Direct Addressing

Similar to mobile telecommunication services we propose a distributed provider model where users can join the provider of their choice. This proven model guarantees scalability of the service as each provider only handles a limited number of clients.

Every user carries a world-wide exclusive identification number which consists of the unique identification of the provider plus an internal number:

```
<User-ID> = <Provider-ID>.<number>
```

The identification number grants independence from the used mobile devices and transport technology. It is the task of the provider to map this abstract number to a specific IP-address, MAC-address or phone number. The identification number is also used to mark location-based information. Messages stored at a particular provider also obtain this tuple for unambiguous identification, whereupon the second part has to be disjoint from that of the registered users:

```
<Message-ID> = <Provider-ID>.<number>
```

A user who wants to position directly addressed information – no matter where on the earth – sends a message with an associated geo-position and the list of recipients to his provider. The provider assigns a new ID to this message and separates the message into a small header and a body. The header contains the new message ID, the location and the list of recipients. The rest (i.e., the main part of a message including text, pictures, video, sound and smart elements) is part of the body. Header and body are separately stored at the provider, and the header information is delegated to all those providers that can be identified in the tuple numbers of the recipients list. So, all involved providers of the recipients are aware of the location-based message but only the provider of the creator stores the whole content (see Fig. 2).

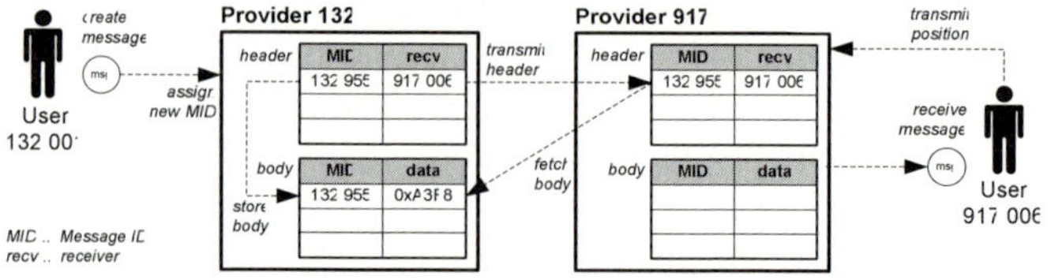

Fig. 2. Direct Addressing Concept

Once, the recipient is logged in at his provider and repetitively transmits his current geo-position he continuously (but only once per message) receives header information for messages with local proximity from his provider. Being aware of nearby information now, the recipient can request his provider to retrieve the whole content. Due to the tuple of the message ID the provider knows where the matching body is stored and indirectly transmits the content to the requesting user.

3.2 Indirect Addressing

Indirect addressing betokens the assignment of location-based information to one or more publicly accessible user groups. The creator of a message is consequently unable to anticipate the identity or even the quantity of the recipients. Indirect addressing therefore enables users to widely spread information to a large audience, which imposes mechanisms to prevent unregulated penetration (spam!).

Different from direct addressing where a provider model and a distribution mechanism of header information establishes a world-wide mobile location-based information service in an easy way, indirect addressing appears to be more complex. The propagation of header information does no longer seem to be applicable for messages that are addressed to different types of potential groups rather than to registered individuals, thus requiring a more elaborate concept for indirect addressing. Let us have a look at the groups: Basically, we distinguish global and local groups.

- *Global groups* are applicable all over the planet. They are typically kept general (e.g., tourism, traffic, etc.) and are uniquely identified. For more flexibility global groups can be structured hierarchically.
- *Local groups* are only valid within a restricted region. They are typically exclusive (e.g., students on a campus) but are also uniquely numbered. It is absolutely possible that different regions with different local groups overlap.

The concept now works as follows: Every region is represented by an appropriate server (*region server*) the virtual regional boundaries of which are registered centrally, so that a region server can quickly be found due to its geographical extent. (This look-up mechanism operates similar to the well known domain name service DNS where IP addresses can be found due to a network name.) Providers – which continuously receive geo-positions from their connected clients – can consequently identify one or more region servers that cover the area a client is currently residing in. As clients are only connected to their providers the information about the local groups is indirectly passed to the clients via their providers (see Fig. 3).

So, as the client moves around he is continuously kept informed about regional services and available local groups. Generally, it is not necessary to join a local group via a registration mechanism – everybody (neglecting special privileges for the time being) may automatically perceive the messages addressed to local groups. In this spirit, local groups are primarily used to logically structure information. Users are just required to filter the provided information they are interested in, which in a first simple attempt refers to the previously inflicted requirement where users may ask: "What kind of information is available here?"

Global groups cannot be stored using the same mechanism as local groups do. A world-wide region server for global groups would have no boundaries and would have to serve every single connected client in the world. Instead, the local region servers provide information for global groups. They simply integrate selected global groups into their group hierarchy and declare thereby that information for global groups can be found at their covered area. This concept now satisfies the user request: "I am interested in ..." meaning that a user just once declares his global interest (by selecting a global group) and automatically receives appropriate location-based messages from every region server which supports the selected global group. Users do not have to permanently check for a suitable group when crossing region borders.

Having this concept of global and local groups, let us now examine the creation-, storage- and propagation mechanism for messages addressed to these groups: The appealing fact is that the mechanism for indirect addressing works very similar to the one for direct addressing, presuming that region servers can store information separated into a header and a body in the same way as providers do. Even the used data structures and storage models remain unchanged for indirect addressing.

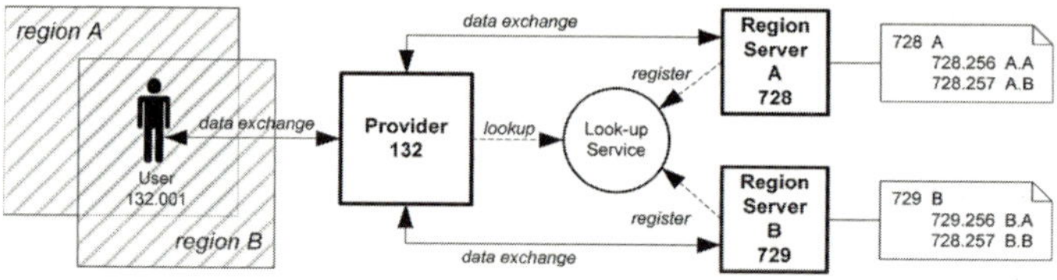

Fig. 3. Region Server Concept

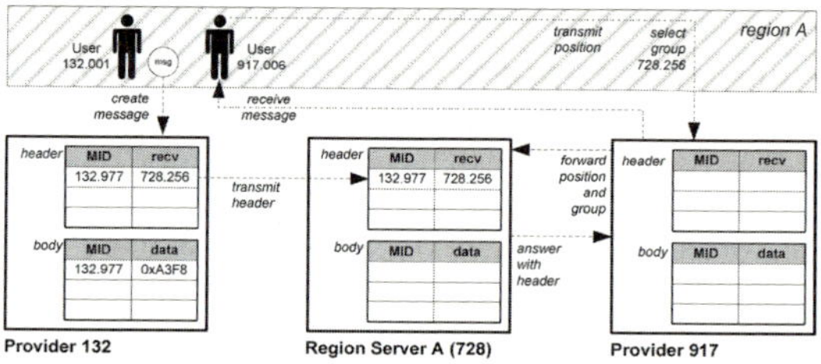

Fig. 4. Indirect Addressing Concept

Like in direct addressing, messages to local or global groups are stored at the provider of the creator. The message is separated into a header and a body with the difference that the recipient is no longer a single user but one or more local or global groups. Nevertheless, the recipient is a sequence of dot-separated numbers with a prefix denoting the destination server to which the header has to be transmitted no matter if this is a provider or a region server, thus letting the original mechanism for storing directly addressed messages also work for indirectly addressed ones (see Fig. 4).

An approaching user of a different provider is indirectly informed via his provider about an active region server and the local and global groups available. A selection of one or more of these groups is forwarded to the region server which resends all appropriate message headers. Hereby, the provider itself does not store any data as Fig. 4 shows. Again, the prefix of the message id reveals the server holding the body.

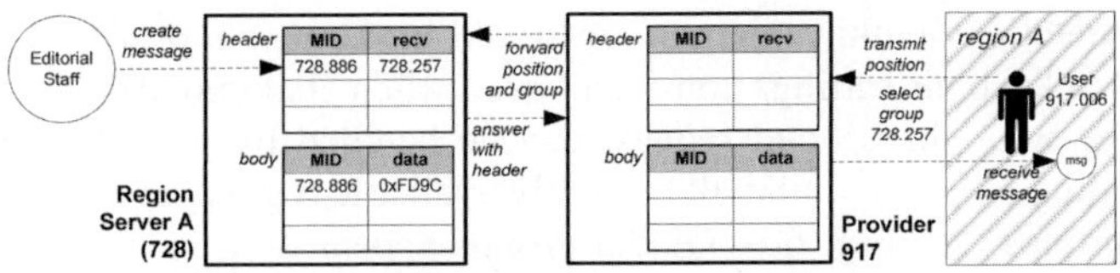

Fig. 5. Editorial Content on Region Server

The main purpose of a region server, however, is not to handle messages created by users of the system. As the succeeding section will show users should usually be hindered from creating indirectly addressed messages in order to prevent spam. Moreover, region servers should provide editorial content for its local and global groups for reading and execution. Therefore, messages are directly stored at the region server, without the need for propagating their headers. Message retrieval as shown in Fig. 2 remains unchanged (see Fig. 5).

4 User Interaction

Regardless, what kind of visualization method is used for perceiving location-based messages (be it a two-dimensional geographical map, a simple list view or an augmented reality scene) the search and filtering interfaces are detached from these methods and can be applied equally.

We suggest an interaction paradigm that reflects the two user requests initially stated: “I am interested in …” and “What kind of information is available here?”

The first request can be handled by providing a selectable folding tree containing all global groups (see Fig. 6a). By default, nothing is selected in order not to confront the user with the load of globally addressed information.

A selection within this tree enables users to automatically perceive the requested information type all over the world. Even when crossing region borders these settings guarantee the reception of equally grouped messages without requiring any further user interaction. Users are not supposed to pay attention when crossing region boundaries and to repetitively search for suitable topics of interest (groups) when entering a new region. With this mechanism users may e.g., express their interest in traffic messages, travel around and automatically receive all regional traffic messages no matter which local traffic management (region server) provides them.

a) b)

Fig. 6. a) “I am interested in …”, b) “What kind of information is available here?”

The user selections within this tree are stored in the user's profile at his provider, enabling him to keep his settings consistent even when changing devices.

In the same way, the second request can be handled by providing an analogous selectable folding tree containing all currently available region servers and their (local and global) groups (see Fig. 6b). Global groups appear both in the first folding tree and in the second, with the difference that the second tree denotes all those groups that are actually available at the current location. The first tree always lists all global groups regardless if information for those groups is currently available or not. However, the selection mechanism is the same for both trees.

These simple folding trees represent the interaction interface for users hiding the complex addressing concept presented in the previous sections and supporting them in finding or filtering the desired information.

5 Related Work

Location-based services are emerging as the focal point of investigation for an increasing number of research labs and industry 3789101314172021:

TagandScan 22 is a service for mobile phones that enables users to mark real physical locations with electronic tags. The tags contain a title, a description, the time and location when and where the tag was created. The position of the mobile phones is determined by triangulation of signal strengths within the GPRS network. The advantage of TagAndScan is based on the fact that the service works with conventional mobile phones without any additional hardware equipment. However, tracking is inaccurate. In cities tags can be positioned with an accuracy of about 100 meters whereas in rural areas a user has to consider several kilometers offset – too much for a detailed graphical representation.

HotTown Geobots 12 is an approach of attaching context-aware services to objects or persons moving in a physical space. The software architecture provides location-based information in a heterogeneous wireless network. The backbone of the architecture is a Geobot, a virtual representative of a physical object, which is aware of its current location and is additionally capable of serving information to other objects floating in a physical space. The Geobots do not exist as objects in the real world, instead they are modeled as software entities in a virtual world controlled by a location server. Users who physically enter this world (e.g. detected by GPS) must register at the location server and are consequently aware of where Geobots are located. The architecture enables parallel interaction in the physical and the virtual world. A new Geobot positioned in the virtual world immediately affects the real world because it becomes known to the users connected to the location server.

Google Earth 7 provides location-based information and offers a rudimentary filtering mechanism for finding the desired information. However, this concept only considers global filtering attributes and does not refer to local peculiarities.

All approaches have substantial similarity to the mobile location-based information service presented in this paper. However, our system offers a wide spectrum of features like extensibility, smartness, an elaborate plug-in mechanism enabling third party developers to dynamically throw in customer-dependent smart elements, and – most important – a scalable and world-wide applicable addressing concept, an attribute which cannot be found in any comparable communication service.

6 Future Work

Due to the emerging field of location-based information services and the associated rising information mess and spam problem, addressing and filtering concepts inevitably gain in importance. Our future work primarily concentrates on a widespread user evaluation test in the first half of 2007 where numerous students will be granted access to this service on the university campus using notebooks, handhelds and cell phones in order to give us feedback concerning the usability of this service, especially the addressing concept.

Furthermore, we plan to extend the addressing concept by contextual features. Groups (and the messages attached to these groups) may be conditionally restricted or extended, in order to prevent or grant access to messages. As an example, a group may be associated with the condition: "only for adults over 18 years". Since the group is usually visible to every user, the providers (who are able to evaluate the attribute age) automatically prevent the contents to be transferred to the corresponding users.

7 Conclusion

Now, that the technical basis for mobile location-based information services is established, concepts for higher level organizational issues have to be developed in order to successfully design accredited commercial applications.

This paper has introduced one major higher level concept concerning addressing issues, meeting requirements such as scalability, global practicability, diminishing intrusiveness, handling distinctive user groups and employing access privileges. We have presented a flexible group system with local and global groups where users are able to automatically be member of or be incorporated via registration. We have shown the scalability of the addressing concept by outlining a provider and region server model with a header propagation mechanism as the key idea for distributing messages globally. And finally, we have given an idea of an interaction mechanism complying simplicity in finding or filtering information the users are interested in.

This concept enriches mobile location-based services with great demand and high potential for the future indispensable in private and business fields.

References

1. Beigl, M., Gellersen, H.-W.: Smart-Its: An embedded platform for Smart Objects, Smart Objects Conference, Grenoble, France (2003)
2. Benford, S.: Future Location-Based Experiences. JISC: Technology and Standards Watch (2005)
3. CityNeo verified (August 2006), http://www.cityneo.com

4. Espinoza, F., Persson, P., Sandin, A., Nyström, H., Cacciatore, E., Bylund, M.: GeoNotes: Social and Navigational Aspects of Location-Based Information Systems. In: Ubiquitous Computing, pp. 2–17. Springer, Heidelberg (2001)
5. Ferscha, A., Hechinger, M., Mayrhofer, R., Rocha, M., Franz, M., Oberhauser, R.: "Digital Aura", Advances in Pervasive Computing, 2nd Int. Conference on Pervasive Computing (Pervasive 2004), Austrian Computer Society (OCG), Vol. 176, pp. 405–410, (April 2004)
6. Gellersen, H.-W., Schmidt, A., Beigl, M.: Adding Some Smartness to Devices and Everyday Things. In: Proceedings of IEEE Workshop on Mobile Computing Systems and Applications 2000 (WMCSA '00), Monterey, CA, IEEE Press, New York (December 2000)
7. Google Earth verified (August 2006), http://earth.google.com
8. Google Maps verified (August 2006), http://www.google.com/gmm/index.html
9. Gutwin, C., Penner, R., Schneider, K.: "Group awareness in distributed software development", ACM conference on Computer Supported Cooperative Work, (November 2004)
10. Holmquist, L.E., Falk, J., Wigström, J.: Supporting Group Collaboration with Inter-Personal Awareness Devices, Personal Technologies, vol. 3(1 and 2) (1999)
11. Jones, Q., Grandhi, S.A., Whittaker, S., Chivakula, K., Terveen, L.: Social awareness and availability: Putting systems into place: a qualitative study of design requirements for location-aware community systems, ACM conference on CSCW (2004)
12. Kanter, T.G.: HotTown Geobots. Attaching Context-Aware Services to Moving Locations. IEEE Internet Computing 2003 7(2), 43–51 (2003)
13. LocatioNet verified (2006), http://www.locationet.com
14. Mobiloco verified (August 2006), http://www.mobiloco.de/html/index.jsp
15. Narzt, W., Pomberger, G., Ferscha, A., Kolb, D., Müller, R., Wieghardt, J., Hörtner, H., Lindinger, C.: A New Visualization Concept for Navigation Systems. In: Stary, C., Stephanidis, C. (eds.) User-Centered Interaction Paradigms for Universal Access in the Information Society. LNCS, vol. 3196, pp. 440–451. Springer, Heidelberg (2004)
16. Narzt, W., Pomberger, G., Ferscha, A., Kolb, D., Müller, R., Wieghardt, J., Hörtner, H., Lindinger, C.: Pervasive Information Acquisition for Mobile AR-Navigation Systems. In: Proceedings of the 5th IEEE Workshop on Mobile Computing Systems and Applications, Monterey, California, USA, pp. 13–20, (October 2003)
17. Plazes.com (verified August 2006), http://beta.plazes.com
18. Ravi, N., Borcea, C., Kang, P., Iftode, L.: Portable Smart Messages for Ubiquitous Java-enabled Devices, 1st Annual International Conference on Mobile and Ubiquitous Systems: Networking and Services, MobiQuitous (2004)
19. Rossi, G., Gordillo, S., Lyardet, F.: Design Patterns for Context-Aware Adaptation. In: Proceedings of the 2005 Symposium on Applications and the Internet Workshops (SAINT-W'05) (January 2005)
20. SociaLight (verified 2006), http://www.socialight.com
21. Sohn, T., Li, K., Lee, G., Smith, I., Scott, J., Griswold, W.G.: Place-Its: A Study of Location-Based Reminders on Mobile Phones, UbiComp'05: Seventh International Conference on Ubiquitous Computing, pp. 232–250 (September 2005)
22. TagAndScan 2005 (verified August 2006), http://www.tagandscan.com/

Ergonomic Design of Children's Play Spaces in the Urban Environment

Przemysław Nowakowski and Jerzy Charytonowicz

Wroclaw University of Technology, Department of Architecture
Prusa 53/55, 50-317 Wroclaw, Poland
{Przemyslaw Nowakowski, przemyslaw.nowakowski}@pwr.wroc.pl,
{Jerzy Charytonowicz, jerzy.charytonowicz}@pwr.wroc.pl

Abstract. Any space available to children can be used as a playground. Such places are getting more and more diminished and isolated from the nearby surroundings. Creating spatial enclaves, apart from undeniable measurable advantages (e.g. safety), causes various negative social and organizational consequences (age discrimination, monotony, uniformization, loosened and deteriorated interpersonal relationships). However, the arranged playgrounds may become a means of an effective psychophysical and social development and rehabilitation of the handicapped children. The paper discusses the following issues: evolution of housing needs of children of all ages, with special concern for spatial requirements connected with children's increased mobility; role of a dwelling, the importance of a child's room and the importance of conditions of acquiring independence and autonomy; the importance of the play environment in the open urban space and the role it plays in the family life and in the life of individual children, and problems of its evolution in the circumstances of the progressing urbanization.

Keywords: designing for children, playgrounds, home and urban environment.

1 Introduction

The human rest environment is comprised by flats and their surrounding areas used mutually by their occupants. The environment is supposed to enable realization of changing needs of groups of people varied by age and psychophysical abilities.

The model of flat with rooms allocated individual people and generations became established in the nineteenth century. At that time, it was becoming more and more common to allocate separate rooms to children. Through the whole 19th century, attempts were being made to disseminate that division between children's and adults' activities. Children's intensive motor activity or noisiness they produce are elements of family life usually unwelcome by adults, especially in a more representative part of a flat. In such circumstances, children's living needs can be satisfied only in "children's rooms", which most often belong to the smallest rooms of a flat. It generally leads to a rigid division between the adult and children's world, intergenerational isolation and narrowing down the living space within a flat [2].

C. Stephanidis (Ed.): Universal Access in HCI, Part II, HCII 2007, LNCS 4555, pp. 517–526, 2007.

Also, the contemporary building regulations legitimize the established model of a flat divided into rooms for children and for adults.

Urbanization processes, particularly the development of motorization cause the external areas intended for rest and play continually get diminished. Children's and adults' kinetic activities are more and more uncontrollably superimposing on areas performing functions which basically preclude the possibility of relaxation.

In Europe, the first public municipal "gardens of entertainment and kinetic plays for children" emerged at the end of the 19th century in Poland, thanks to the initiative of the Polish socially engaged doctor Henryk Jordan. They were patterned then on American solutions. Playgrounds adjacent to homes became more widespread in the interwar period. However, it was not until World War II that every housing estate was to be completed by that kind of facility [3]. More complex play units began to emerge in the western countries, especially from the beginning of the 70. The normative records valid at that time, conditioning the number, size and manner of equipping the play sites on the number of flats within a housing estate, assured children a sufficient access to free space.

The "quality" evolution of flats and urbanized spaces unfortunately progresses in parallel with deterioration of the "quantity" features. In flats, children are still being allocated small rooms, and on housing estates the free spaces are more and more being adopted for other purposes, mainly parking lots.

Still, the functional programmes of majority of playgrounds do not include the equipment that kinetically stimulate physically handicapped children. Those playgrounds and their attractions are thus accessible to them to a limited degree.

The contemporary challenge is making much more space accessible to children at different ages and in different psychophysical form, and some dispersion of the play equipment. First of all, it pertains to hitherto allotted grounds in bigger green areas (in parks) or big yards. Furthermore, play areas should be attractive not only to small children, but also to school children and adults. Mobility and convertibility of selected elements in a play ground, serving its users' imagination and skills, may, however, help avoid weariness.

At present, it can be noticed that children are more often treated as equal partners of adults, and a better identification of children's needs and recognition of the influence upbringing has on their subsequent, adult lives are conducive to the evolution of contact between successive generations. Thus, a change in the relation of adults and children should be reflected in both the living and urbanized spaces.

2 Spaces Intended for Play and Their Significance for the Structure of a Dwelling, a City, Family Life, Rehabilitation and Integration

A child gets to know her/his environment as s/he becomes independent kinetically. The urbanized space can be divided into the following areas: a flat (including child's own room, annexes for playing in other rooms), semi – open spaces (e.g. staircase), and areas encircling a house (the entrance area, the yard), the interior of a housing estate, quarters of a building (with playgrounds, parks, and nearby shops), a district with a school and recreational buildings). Children look closely at the material and social surroundings and search in it some ways of understanding their environment, satisfying their needs, and thus shaping an appropriate behaviour. All those things, in turn, contribute to identification with place and people.

In child's imagination almost every surrounding space may serve playing. It can be a flat as well as free green areas, but also farm buildings, streets, squares, parking lots, or even wastelands, building gaps and ruins. Adults, for various reasons, perceive playing sites for children in a limited way. The function of such places more and more frequently is performed by enclosed and marked spaces, supplied with special equipment. Two types of playing space can by distinguished – not only from the architectural, but also educational point of view – „playground" as an artificially allotted one – functional acreage and "playing space" as a multifunctional space, enabling children a considerable motor freedom and invention when playing.

Territorial divisions made by adults and limitations of motor freedom connected with them are generally not respected by children, and every near patch of land can be a stimulus to varied kinetic activities.

It should be mentioned that a specific lifestyle of parents and prestigious character of a flat may negatively influence a child's proper, unfettered psychophysical development. Also, it should be remembered that – considering a progressing limitation of freedom in the area of further use of an urbanized environment - as the child is growing older, a role of the living environment with the surrounding area is becoming more and more significant. There are other factors shaping that influence such as: the development of motorization, prevention of criminogenic situations, and raising standards of general public safety. Unfortunately, the world of children's motor activity with yards, squares, streets, gardens, and parks is becoming more and more confined to allotted and enclosed play grounds designed rather according to adults' than childrens' view of environment (e.g. aspects of safety).

Adapting a dwelling to children's needs should be a well – thought – out action, which all members of family – as well as children – judge and take part in. Surprisingly, even relatively young children are capable of expressing their preferences and participating in the decision – making process concerning interior design [5]. A quality of living together can be affected by the following factors: psychological attitude towards a child's presence and activity, accepting the fact that the whole flat is a place of gaining experience, a learning and playing field, expression of clear rules of coexistence, explanation of bans, avoiding a division between adults and children, and a selection of equipment meeting raised durability and safety requirements.

Designing space for children should be based upon recognizing their needs and identifying activities they may perform. Typical functions will include: satisfying basic existential needs (e.g. changing a baby, toilet, sleep, feeding and maintenance) and spiritual needs (e.g. learning, static and motor plays).

Childrens' proper psychophysical development and their motor activity related to it requires support from an urbanized environment and therefore it should be included into the "playing space". Adopting such a solution should find acceptance not only among urban designers, but also estate owners, co – tenants , teachers as well as parents. They can focus on such activities as: removing limitations and sometimes bans on playing in yards and nearby green areas, removing fences around neighbouring multifamily houses and green areas, adapting undeveloped areas (building gaps, wastelands, ruins, etc.), converting the existing open spaces into areas attractive to both children and adult users, and finally traffic calming and regulation.

In the industrialized countries, there is a well developed infrastructure for children's play. The infrastructure expresses a concern of city and a housing estate management for satisfying motor needs of children and their parents. Those tendencies, however, can be usually deemed as a peculiar "alibi" for adults who – wishing to maintain peace and quiet – brush aside lively and noisy children and close them in enclaves. Additionally, such actions reinforce loosened interpersonal relationships between members of different generations (children – adults) and between neighbours (families and their neighbours). Atomisation of families and an atrophy of social relationships between co-tenants can become soothed in a universal "playing space" facilitating the establishment and development of interpersonal contacts in relations children – children, children – adults, and adults – adults. The nearness of playing site to home (as a meeting place) can favour making spontaneous and lasting acquaintances or even friends. Such meetings do not require special preparations from adults and children. Children's contacts may turn into lasting friendships between whole neighbouring families. A nearby playground, often popularly called a yard, may then become a multifunctional space, conducive to the development of widely – understood interpersonal relations, later shifted to homes.

Additional equipment enabling the use of space for play by handicapped children may have practical implications not only for the parties concerned with it, but also for the whole society. Yet, it stimulates the psychomotor activity (being a supplement to motor rehabilitation exercise) and mixing with other children helps develop and strengthen interpersonal contacts and bonds. The proximity of a playing space may have a considerable therapeutic, educational, and integrating significance to children in an impaired psychophysical condition. In a sociological sense, both healthy and handicapped children playing jointly permit to accustom the phenomenon of disability from the youngest age, and at the same time give their carers a chance to participate in a social life.

3 Children in the House Environment

In the industrialized countries, dwellings with a number of rooms equal to a number of household members are commonly accepted. That means that children usually have their own rooms. Also, the rooms usually belong to the smallest parts of a dwelling. Additionally, every child does not always have a separate room. In families of limited means and with many children each room is occupied by more than one person. In those circumstances, satisfying such needs as a natural seclusion from the environment, intimacy, freedom of play (especially the loud one) and the need for concentration during studying are difficult, and sometimes even impossible.

Granting a child a separate room is a significant parental decision. A child's room performs various functions, which in the case of adults are carried out within the whole space of a dwelling – in different rooms (a living room, a study, a dining room, a bedroom, etc.). A child, however, is supposed to fulfil most of his/her living needs in his/her own room. That room is one of the rooms exploited most in a house. Once a child reaches a schooling age, the time of using of such a room extends during the day. Then, to traditional children's plays its new forms should be added, such as plays with a computer, and new obligations: studying and doing homework. The size of child's room should also provide an opportunity for an unfettered kinetic activity and a mutual play of a child with his/her peers or adults. If it is not possible, and additional area for play should be determined and separated in other part of a dwelling. Making other parts of a flat accessible to children (in particular those smallest ones) is recommended especially in respect of a necessary visual and audial contact and supervision by an adult – a parent or a carer.

To children furniture has not only a utilitarian role, but also symbolic; it can serve as a landing field for planes, a fortress, an observational tower, etc. Thus, it can be a means (a pretext) of individual creation of ideas and images and an inspiration to arrangement of one's own room interior. Arrangements and forms of furniture should be free and flexible – easy to adjust to changing children's needs, so that the furnishings would "grow" with their users (Fig. 1). Important elements supplementing elementary furniture (a bed, a table, a chair, a wardrobe, a bookcase, etc.) can be special furnishings for plays, particularly kinetic: exercise equipment, a ladder at a wall, a slide, and a swing, etc. That equipment enables children's kinetic activity at home, especially during the rainy weather.

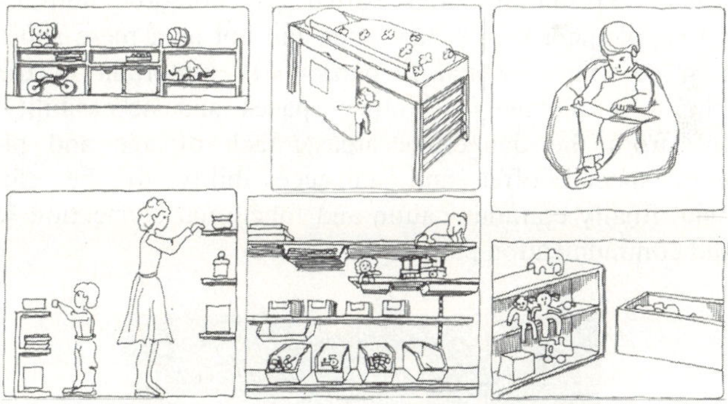

Fig. 1. Examples of furniture in children's rooms [3]

Furnishing of a child's room with furniture for adults is undoubtedly not a recommended solution, in particular with the heavy one and with a more prestigious design. They are difficult to adapt to children's kinetic needs and the size of their bodies. Such furnishings do not favour creating a specific and individual atmosphere in the room.

4 Creating Playing Spaces in the External Environment

Already in the 70. of the 20th century in the industrialized countries playing spaces were much more considerably varied. A great significance in that process had also family initiatives. They focused not only on creating new playgrounds or modernizing the existing ones, but also on creating alternative programme solutions. From this current, thematic infrastructures are derived, e.g. adventure, architectural, educational and prointegrating. However, additional infrastructure that will help children in an impaired psychophysical condition use the playing space is still lacking.

Although many ideas are relatively old and repeatedly imitated, they still seem to be interesting to a majority of users so far devoid of similar facilities at all. Generally, standard solutions are applied, with equipment mostly prefabricated, sold on the market in large quantities. They are universal and independent of the environment. A mass duplication of the same conceptions often make playgrounds monotonous, and thereby less appealing to children.

At present, a selection of playing equipment varied as regards their programmes and aesthetics matching an individually shaped surrounding is one of the most interesting tendencies. Moreover, such equipment inspires its users' creativity and imagination when playing. The "prointegrating equipment" does not have to be more costly than the standard one, but at the same time it can be an interesting alternative to typical solutions.

Designing an interesting playground for children requires fulfilling many conditions, e.g. "participatory design" (with children's participation and taking into consideration their expectations and varied psychomotor abilities), treating a playground as a supplement to a richer offer and not as a mere substitute, location close to a place of living (which is particularly important in the case of the handicapped children), openness to other spaces and accessibility to all users (seperating only from the dangerous areas), lack of age and physical ability discrimination (a special offer and its accessibility to the elderly and the handicapped), and finally communication and functional connection with other play spaces (hardened communication pathways).

Fig. 2. Application of natural, low processed building materials

Fig. 3. Use of water for playing

The programme of furnishing a playground with playing equipment and facilities should provide for the need for creating various options of play, not imposing the one and only solution (Fig. 2, 3). This can be assured by: the usage of natural building materials (trunks, boulders, rock, sand, etc.), the usage of flowing waters (ditches, gutters, fountains, cascades, etc.) and still waters (ponds), creating the open wings and auditoria (in the form of faults and resistance walls, platforms, arenas and viewpoints), the use of multifunctional, mobile and convertible equipment, the use of free materials (pieces of wood, chests, cases, car tyres, cardboard boxes, old pans and other safe scrap materials).

As far as the aesthetic qualities are concerned, the following features should be taken into consideration: individualized programme of equipment for every playing complex, facilities individual and unique by nature, supplementing the equipment with elements appealing to senses (smelling and colorful plants, green tunnels, etc.), diversification of land level (avoiding flat surfaces) through the use of reclaimed pits and building heaps (financial savings), the division of larger acreage into functional annexes (e.g. sandpits in quiet areas, equipment for kinetic plays in "loud" areas, large and small size equipment).

The design of greenery should provide for: varied selection of plants (trees, bushes, grass, flowers), functional issues (isloation from noise and excessive insolation, providing fruit trees and bushes, avoiding poisonous and prickly trees and bushes).

Considering issues related to the safety of usage one should remember about the elimination of a potential threat of an accident (injuries, slips, falls, stumbles), protection against poisoning by harmful plants or preparations (paints and varnish), isolation from the traffic, and a convenient connection with pedestrians' pathways, easiness of evacuation and escape (elimination of barriers, divisions, and partitions on communication pathways), keeping clean, neat and tidy (sand sifting and change, removal of broken glass and pieces of metal, etc.), regular security check, and social control thanks to houses in a near neighbourhood [1, 4, 5].

The above mentioned requirements also have a considerable significance to the handicapped children. What is important for them is not only an opportunity to spend free time on active playing, but also prophylactic, remedial, educational and social considerations. An easy access to a playing space has a special significance for prophylaxis and rehabilitation – both physical and mental. Properly designed playgrounds may therefore stimulate kinetically the disabled children, and a varied selection of materials and textures may influence the development of their sensory sensitivity. Moreover, a play, especially with other children, apart from its integrating qualities and mobilizing to an increased effort, helps get away from daily worries and inefficiencies (Fig. 4, 5).

What presents a considerable challenge to playing space designers is finding a unique *genius loci*. An individual and unique character of the place, responding also to users' functional and aesthetic needs, creates a sense of place and the place identity. A sense of place favourably influences users' behaviour, affects their imagination, and releases the feeling of identity with a particular place. Unique features of a place can be obtained through: the use of unique features of a particular space and its surrounding physical context (spatial relations, the character of the nearby buildings, a slope, directions and communication pathways, the existing greenery, orientation towards the sun and the wind.)

Fig. 4. Educational facility in open space

Fig. 5. A child sitting in a wheelchair playing with sand

5 Psychological Aspects

With time a small child learns to attach not only to the household members, but also to material objects and places, where she/he is staying. Child's growing independence can be realized and expressed through taking possession of those objects and places.

Both children and parents can make use of that ability to develop a child's individual character. The control over some elements of the surrounding helps a child better understand mutual interaction between the social world and the material environment. A bit older children develop their own associations with objects, places, and spaces. Some of the feelings are positive, negative or neutral, and some are a combination of those reactions. As a child is becoming more and more mobile, his/her activity, at the beginning in a flat, and later outside, will exhibit intentions and motives of action, reflecting the development of identity with place. Even a small child not only knows which objects are his possessions, but s/he can better and better determine where they should belong to, how they should be used and when they can be used by others. This ability is also completed by expectations related to the material surroundings, which become expressed directly, especially when they are not fulfilled [3, 4].

A slow metamorphosis of a totally dependent child into a separate individual, different from others, is supported and continually confirmed by acquiring the ability of coexistence with the nearest surroundings, especially when it includes objects, places and spaces "belonging" to the child. It can be stated that a child's room with all its objects and the ability of making it a place beyond parents' control is a place having a considerable significance to the child's development, the development of his/her place identity, and also his/her own identity. When children are able to discriminate between themselves and others and the surrounding space, home and its surroundings indeed become their world. Apart from creating their personal world, children learn also that spaces and places are shared, and that the surroundings is not static, but it is continually changing, because it is being changed by the presence of other people. Being a child carries many spatial limitations, which are slowly but steadily removed as a child displays her/his own responsibility and dexterity in the surrounding world. Already very young children can gradually discover who controls particular areas and learn to respect the spatial autonomy and privileges, especially of the older household members. For example, they may first learn that the access to the bathroom is not possible, because it is occupied, or that they cannot enter their parents' bedroom, because its door is locked. However, as children grow up, their ability to coexist and interact with the surroundings evolves, and they acquire both the ability to control their actions and autonomy in particular places at home. The spatial autonomy essentially influences the development of psychological independence. A certain degree of control over the material environment (at least within the boundaries of a child's own room) is indispensable for a healthy psychophysical development.

What bears an immense significance to child's development is the part of his/her room, performing the role of a deep hiding place. A peculiar niche or hideout, understood literally and figuratively, is supposed to enable him/her effective isolation from the surrounding space and his/her relatives, and satisfy the child's need for privacy. A place like this allows the child to struggle with his/her own problems and a bad mood, maintain secrets, and concentrate during studying. The intimacy sphere appears to be equally important to both younger and older children. Own room has a particular role in a teenager's life, whose experience of opposition and rebel against the surrounding world is inherent in their existence. On the other hand, the above mentioned places may become a means of initiating interesting (also group) games and plays of dramatic nature, involving dressing up (disguising, identity changing, impersonating other characters) and arranging little puppet theatres.

6 Conclusion

Home comprises a fundamental environment in a child's life, because it is a place, in which most of the cognitive and learning processes take place. Many of those early personal observations and perceptions will last and survive to the adult life, so will a great part of the place identity moulded in childhood. Experiences gained in childhood to a large extent may determine particular behaviours in the future life environment, e.g. in own home.

Progressing urbanization cause the free space for children to diminish. Children's movement freedom is particularly limited by the development of motorization. Such monofunctional spaces as pavements, roadways, parking lots, market places and others should be adapted to safe and free presence of other people, including children. When designing playgrounds, it is essential to provide for the needs of all age groups, and also expectations of people with an impaired motor ability (e.g. the disabled children and the elderly). It is then possible to avoid age segregation and functional ascribing selected areas to particular generation groups (children, parents, grandparents) and ability discrimination (including those kinetically handicapped).

Typical dwellings, in which the role of a living room - a prestigious place for adults – is often overestimated, should be "open" to children's needs (kinetic in particular). The main part of a dwelling (e.g. the living room) does not need to be reserved for "show off" and used on special occasions only, and children's activity space does not need to be confined to only a child's room. Moreover, a change in a stereotypical lifestyle of the adult household members is recommended. It should happen through acceptance of children's visible presence, e.g. presentation of children's artefacts, changes in arrangement giving children an easy access to objects and materials for playing in different areas of home. Freedom of movement can also be assured by the arrangement of lights and other controls at the level easily accessible to children. In such a situation, the household members themselves and their home send visiting guests a symbolic message that children and their actions are valuable and significant to the family life.

External playing spaces located in the neighbourhood of houses can thus be a good supplement to space intended for children's motor activity inside buildings and in individual dwellings.

References

1. Burkhardt, Ch., Kuerner, P.: Kind und wohnen. Leske + Budrich, Opladen (1994)
2. Internet Encyklopedia. Panstwowe Wydawnictwo Naukowe, Warsaw (2006)
3. Oesterle-Schwerin, J.: Mit Kindern wohnen. Bauverlag GmbH, Wiesbaden (1976)
4. Rui Olds, A.: Child Care Design Guide. McGraw-Hill, New York (2001)
5. Weinstein, C.S., David, T.: Spaces for Children. Plenum Press, New York (1987)

Towards an Accessible Europe

Maria Panou[1], Evangelos Bekiaris[1], and María García Robledo[2]

[1] Centre for Research and Technology Hellas – Hellenic Institute of Transport (CERTH/HIT)
L. Posidonos 17, 17455 Athens, Greece
Tel: +30210 9853194, Fax: +30210 9853193
{mpanou, abek}@certh.gr
[2] SIEMENS, S.A.
Ronda de Europa, 5 - B 3,
28760 Tres Cantos, Madrid, Spain,
Tel: +34 91 514 45 02
maria.garcia-robledo@siemens.com

Abstract. Mobility is a right that we all have. However, being able to travel by yourself, without the need of another person's assistance, is not always the case with mobility-impaired (MI) users. The reason for this is the non-accessible environment, which prevents an MI person from moving around, using and changing transportation means, having access to the proper information (on timetables, routes, etc.). Nevertheless, there exist certain accessible points and transportation means available in most European countries, but the people mostly in need of them do not have the proper information about it. ASK-IT IP aims to eliminate these barriers, by offering information about accessible content (transportation means, points of interest, etc.), following a 'design for all' concept and taking advantage of both location-based and infomobility services.

Keywords: accessibility, infomobility, disability, pilot sites, mobility-impaired.

1 Introduction

The population in Europe with problems using information and communication technology is estimated to be 22.25% (with different types of problems) [1]. Today, although ICT services are exponentially expanding in the area of transportation, there are many barriers for elderly and disabled people. For example, inter-modal and personalised accessibility information (content) along each route, for the above functionality to operate (referring to accessibility of pavement, transportation means, bus stops or parking lots, point of origin and destination), does not exist. Also, route guidance systems, which are useful for all, but are mostly needed by travellers with disabilities, lack an 'accessible route' functionality.

During the last years, significant attention has been given to the rights and opportunities of disabled people in most European cities. Most of the latest developments follow the accessibility instructions (e.g. accessible building entrances,

C. Stephanidis (Ed.): Universal Access in HCI, Part II, HCII 2007, LNCS 4555, pp. 527–535, 2007.

pavement, special transportation vehicles, etc.) and the services for the disabled persons are increasing continuously. To be in line with the technological trend of our days, and to really support the free mobility of those users, all these content and services have to be interconnected and offered as a global accessible service, that the user will be able to access at any time and from any place. The population needs and deserves a 'design for all' solution to access easily both the internet and mobile services, in order to be informed about accessible transport and accommodation, events and sites of interest, receive advice on getting there and, generally, about important issues of their travel. The travellers need reliable services that are available on call throughout a journey or service request. The most affected user groups are those people that suffer from limitations in moving freely, varying between functional limitations and activity limitations.

1.1 What ASK-IT Does

ASK-IT Integrated project, which is co-funded by the European Commission, has promised to support and promote the mobility of MI people, enabling the provision of applications and services and facilitating knowledge and content organisation and processing. MI people related infomobility content is collected, interfaced and managed, encompassing many areas, such as personal services, e-work and e-learning, social services, transport, tourism and leisure. The main benefit of ASK-IT services for the MI users is their accessibility in terms of content and HCI. In summary, ASK-IT offers its citizens (MI or not) rich, reliable, localised, personalised and dynamic (without having to maintain local web site, info is always fresh and just in time) services on localisation (where am I), guidance (how to go there), leisure (nearest preferred restaurant), work (ability to have business data access from any public or allied PC), social relations (networking with groups I belong to), etc.

The target groups of ASK-IT are people with a wide variety of functional impairments, such as people unable to walk (i.e. wheelchair users), with hearing problems, learning difficulties, visually-impaired persons, elderly and illiterate, as under circumstances literacy is required to find your way in the transportation network.

The integrated ASK-IT system and services are to be tested in 8 interconnected sites Europewide, to prove that the MI travelers can have full travel accessibility information, which will affect their daily transportation. The selected core ASK-IT sites are: Athens/Thessaloniki, Bucharest, Genova, Helsinki, Madrid, Newcastle and Nuremberg, while there is one more satellite site (i.e. covering only a few services and 1 user group category), The Hague.

2 Site-Specific Services and Their HCI

The above-mentioned pilot sites where selected with an open procedure, allowing all interested cities to take part. The final selection was performed, based on a commonly applied scoring scheme, according to the feedback provided by the sites themselves, in terms of already available content, infrastructure, local support, etc.

ASK-IT does not start from scratch to develop services and gather accessibility content in its eight pilot sites. The pilot sites have already certain transport-related web services available for people with various types of disabilities, as well as relevant content for various points in the city and transportation means, that has been gathered in the framework of other, mostly national, initiatives. Unfortunately, in most cases, this info remains unused or underused, due to the low users' awareness about them, the missing sustainability strategies, or the lack of appropriate platforms to support these services. These services are being connected to the ASK-IT platform, following the ASK-IT ontology, while the available content is extended (by gathering new data) and transformed in web applications. Indicative examples of existing PC-based applications for disabled users, in the ASK-IT pilot sites, follow below.

One of the services that is being adapted and connected to ASK-IT is the route guidance functionality within the airports of Frankfurt and Athens. With this service, the traveler is able to view in his/her mobile phone or PDA, his/her position and destination within the airport in order to reach the assigned gate. A clear indication of the route to follow is also shown.

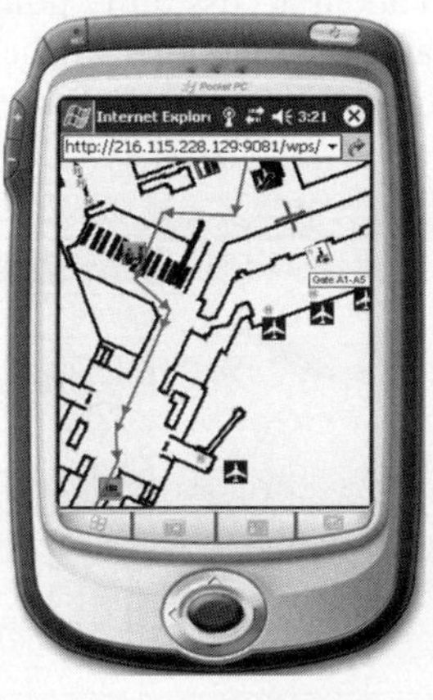

Fig. 1. Route guidance application in the airport of Frankfurt, given on a PDA

An available web service in Nuremberg is that with info about public transportation, timetables, maps. There is a specific section 'Mobility for All', through which the users can find accurate info about accessible elevators and toilet facilities in subway stations, accessible vehicles, low-floor-trams and low-floor-busses. Finally, touristic information is available about sightseeing and appropriate transportation.

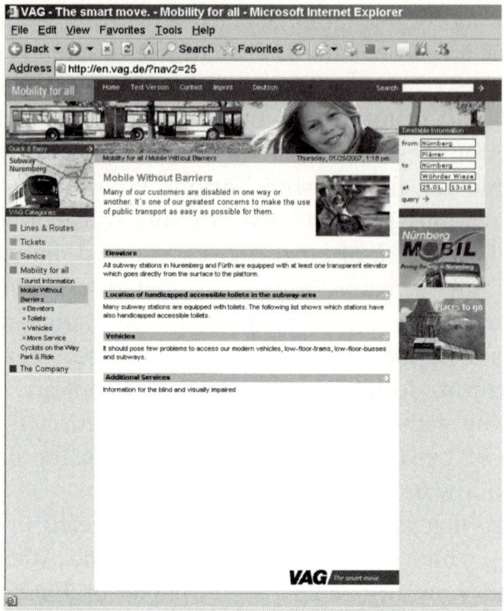

Fig. 2. On-line public transportation service for the city of Nuremberg

A database with information about accessibility points in the city of Genova (60km of pedestrian routes of the main tourist points in the city) presents to the user the detailed accessibility level of the route that has to follow to reach a specific place.

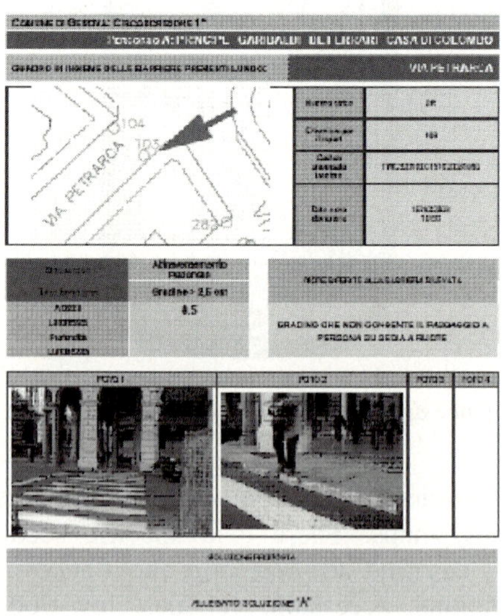

Fig. 3. PC application with accessibility info of points in the city of Genova

A similar PC application for the city of Athens is presented below, which is available in the form of a database with built-in, easy-to-use user interface. It presents the accessibility level of certain points of interest (POIs) and, more specifically, of public buildings and buildings of residents affairs and of the connected transportation means to reach them, from 10 municipalities (priority to those near disability organisations) in Athens. In total, 124 buildings (banks, schools, medical clinics, ministries, post offices, city halls, etc.) were examined for their accessibility level, which are to be connected and enhanced within ASK-IT [2]. After the assessment, the buildings were assigned different colours, according to their level of accessibility (green: fully accessible; yellow: semi-accessible, i.e. in most cases there was possible to get in with a wheelchair but the interior might have some problems, such as small steps or narrow corridors and there is no accessible toilet in; red: non-accessible, i.e. the wheelchair could not pass from the entrance). Screenshots of the application follow below.

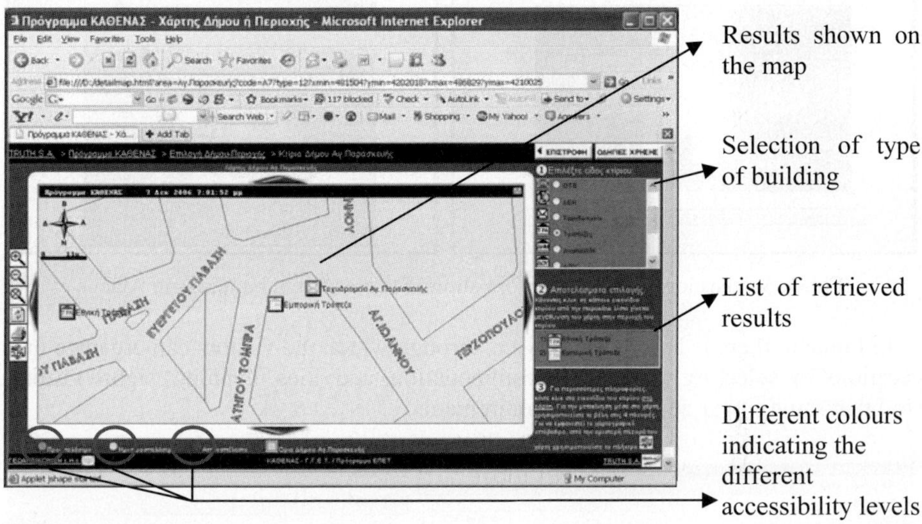

Fig. 4. PC-application, presenting the accessibility status of buildings in Athens and the connected transportation means to reach them

As shown in the picture above, different symbols are used to represent types of building. By clicking on a POI on the map, more detailed information is available. A short description of the accessibility barriers is included (in case of semi- or non-accessible buildings). The detailed transportation means that pass near this POI are indicated, as well as the distance of their stations from it. Finally, pictures of the exterior and interior space are provided. In this way, the disabled user is fully informed about each building, before visiting it, and can avoid unpleasant and unexpected situations, when he/she is already there. It has to be noted that all the examined buildings were visited by a wheelchair user during the assessment, for more profound results. Examples of UIs presenting the detailed information follow in Fig. 4 below.

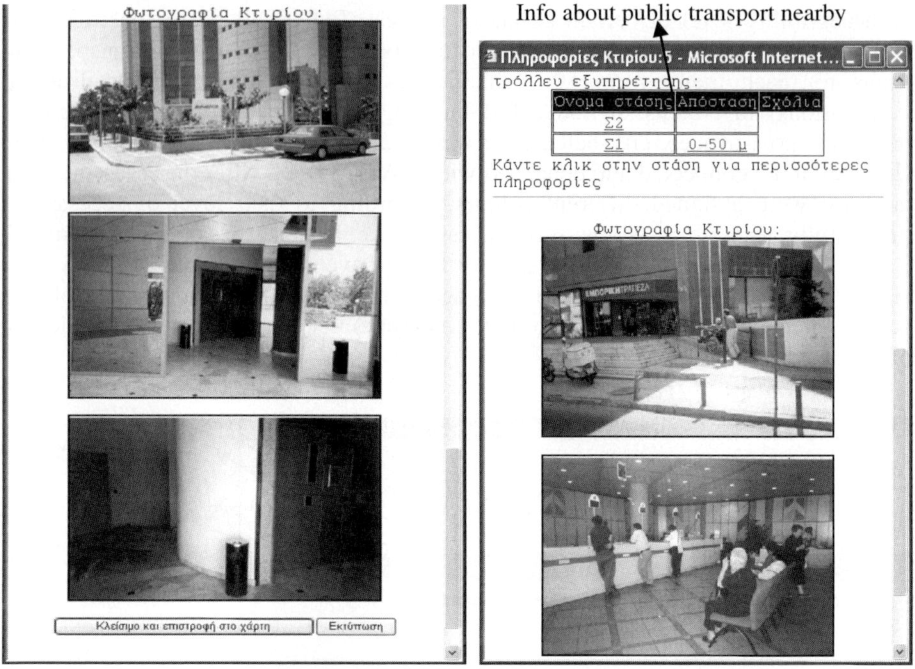

Fig. 5. Screenshots of detailed information of two different buildings in Athens

In Finland, there is an on-line service, through which the visitors can organize their vacations by selecting facilities (accommodation, activities planning, sights visiting, etc.) that satisfy their accessibility requirements.

Fig. 6. Screenshots of the Finnish on-line service for accessible travel planning

Each user can build his/her profile by selecting the preferred type of activities; among the profile parameters, there are several accessibility parameters that the user can select. The visitors have also the possibility to see the location of the travel service on the map and make an on-line booking and e-payment of the selected facility.

In Newcastle, technical know-how for indoors navigation is available, using trilateration techniques, allowing the system to know the user's location relative to the reference points. This is especially interesting for the blind and visually-impaired users.

Fig. 7. Navigation system application on the PDA

At the Netherlands, there is an existing on-line service with content about the reachability, accessibility and usability of buildings in Rotterdam. Search is possible by the name and address of the building or by the building category. A small map is also available for each building.

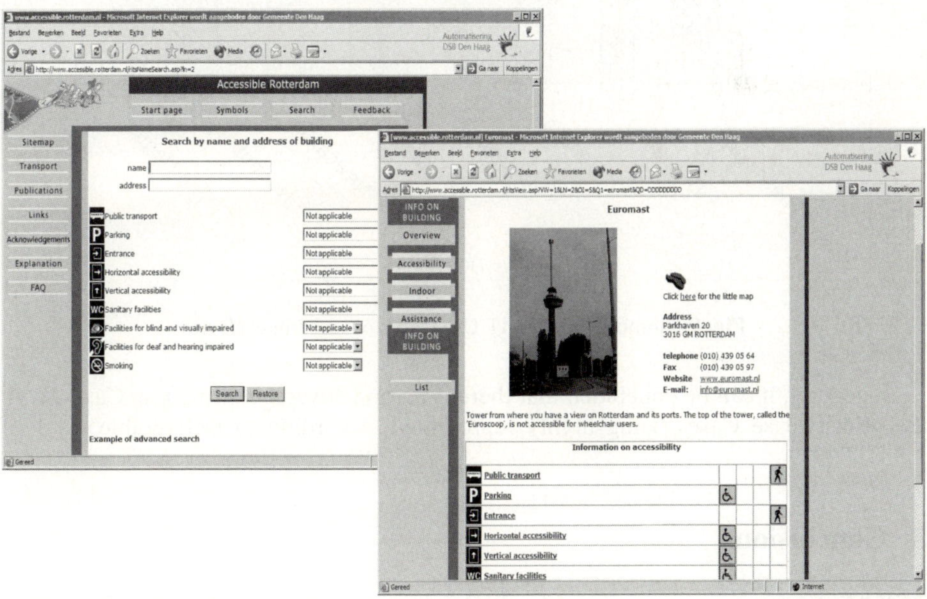

Fig. 8. On-line service with accessibility info of PoIs and transportation in the Netherlands

The examples of the PC-based services that were presented above, show that there is available infrastructure to start with, thus there is indeed a strong potential in strengthening the concept of independent mobility for the MI travelers through ASK-IT. Furthermore, ASK-IT sites plan to offer their citizens the same level of services when traveling to another ASK-IT site, through automatic roaming of service and transfer of the user personalisation profile with him/her, in his/her mobile or PDA. However, the diversity of content details, structure and furthermore, HCI concepts of all these services, makes their integration into the ASK-IT platform, with a unified HCI, a major challenge.

2.1 Use Cases Satisfied by the Pilot Sites

In ASK-IT, 42 detailed Use Cases have been determined. Each pilot site has generated the application scenarios that are to be performed at the tests, with clear correlation to the use case(s). Thus, the number of Use Cases satisfied in each site are determined and presented below, allowing a comparison among the sites. As it is expected, The Hague, as a satellite site, fulfills the lowest number of use cases.

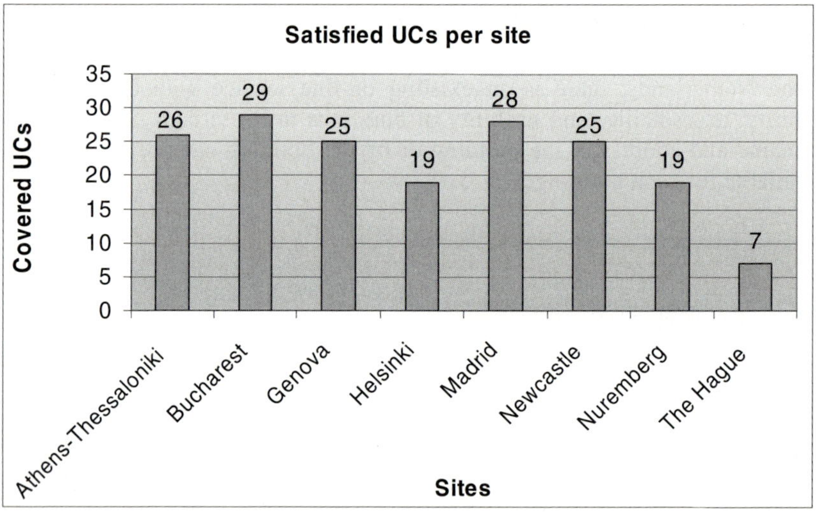

Fig. 9. Number of ASK-IT Use Cases covered in each site

In general, it can be concluded that there is a good coverage of the Use Cases, with the priority Use Cases being highly represented, according to Deliverable 4.1.1 of ASK-IT [3].

3 Conclusion

ASK-IT creates a new society of advanced sites throughout Europe. Through a common ontological framework, it interconnects the services of hundreds of service providers from across Europe. This is the only way to prove that full travel accessibility for MI users can be achieved in a reliable, seamless and viable way, using a range of available technologies and communications networks.

Currently, the existing web services and content are being interconnected to ASK-IT ontological framework and new content is being gathered. The ASK-IT pilots are expected to start in September 2007 and last for about 9 months, with 50 mobility-impaired users testing ASK-IT system and services in each site, of which 5 will have travel to other pilot sites (international trip) and 15 will use the system for longer (maximum 2 weeks), in order to test the long-term effects (user learning and personalisation issues). In the Satelite site, 10 users will participate in the short-term tests and 20 in the long term ones.

The aim is to demonstrate ASK-IT feasibility, interoperability and viability and provide adequate feedback to the development team for system optimization.

ASK-IT services will be offered through a unique and self-adaptive (according to user needs and wants, but also the context of use) interface through PC, PDA, intelligent phones, as well as, in-vehicle. The transition of proprietary, single services and even devices HCI to an integrated, self-adaptive and multi-platform HCI concept, applied and tested Europewide, constitutes one of ASK-IT key innovations.

Acknowledgments. We wish to acknowledge to the ASK-IT project pilot sites for the provision of the material related to their site. Also, EC (DG IST, eInclusion unit) is thanked for its financial support.

References

1. Gill, J.M.: Smart Cards: Accessibility and Social Inclusion. National Smart Card Project, March, 37 pp. Also (2004), at http://www.tiresias.org/reports/national_smart_card_project.htm
2. Panou M., et al.: KATHENAS Deliverable ‘Accessibility assessment of public buildings, public buildings and rest infrastructure of the city of Athens, for disabled persons’, 2000.
3. Bekiaris, et al.: ASK-IT Deliverable 4.1.1 ASK-IT pilot sites selection and profile (November 2006)

Nomad Devices Adaptation for Offering Computer Accessible Infomobility Services

Laura Pastor[1,2], María García[2], Luis Reigosa[2],
Maria Fernanda Cabrera-Umpierrez[1], Alexandros Mourouzis[3],
and Brigitte Ringbauer[4]

[1] Life Supporting Technologies – Technical University of Madrid (UPM)
Ciudad Universitaria
28040 Madrid, Spain
{lpastor,chiqui}@lst.tfo.upm.es
[2] SIEMENS, S.A.
Ronda de Europa, 5 - B 3,
28760 Tres Cantos, Madrid, Spain
{maria.garcia-robledo, luis.reigosa}@siemens.com
[3] Foundation for Research and Technology –Hellas (FORTH)
Vassilika Vouton, P.O. Box 1385,
71110 Iraklio, Crete, Greece
mourouzi@ics.forth.gr
[4] Universitaet Stuttgart (IAT)
Nobelstr. 12,
70569 Stuttgart, Germany.
Brigitte.Ringbauer@iat.uni-stuttgart.de

Abstract. This paper describes the adaptation approach for users with disability of nomad devices within the ASK-IT European project funded by the EC 6th Framework Program within the e-Inclusion area. The devices, software and hardware modules involved are described. The User Interface (UI) configuration, defined according to the functional characteristics of specific user groups, is analysed along with the technical specifications of the devices and the provided services. Finally, the current mock-ups of the system for different nomad devices are illustrated.

Keywords: nomad devices, disability, infomobility, user interface.

1 Introduction

User Interface research and development is a rapidly evolving field. New interaction approaches, methods and techniques are continually being produced and modified, with important consequences on users' view of, navigation in, and interaction with computers. In parallel, a transition from desktop computers to nomad devices with mobile phones and palmtops is obtaining a significantly greater market penetration than conventional PCs. Taking also under consideration the recent efforts to provide computer-based interactive applications and services accessible by the broadest

C. Stephanidis (Ed.): Universal Access in HCI, Part II, HCII 2007, LNCS 4555, pp. 536–545, 2007.

possible end user population, including people with disabilities, one can conclude that the design and development of the User Interface requires the revision of currently prevailing HCI assumptions, such as that of designing for the “average” user in a desktop environment. This assumption needs to incrementally be replaced by the more demanding and challenging objective of designing to cope with diversity in the end user population, the access media and devices, the contexts of use, etc. [1]. The technological development of nomad devices generates the possibility, but also the need, to explore these systems and optimize them for the benefit of people with disability. By enhancing the technical performance of this area, pursuing high levels of "infomobility", significant opportunities for disabled users can be envisioned.

ASK-IT[1] (Ambient Intelligence Systems of Agents for Knowledge Based and Integrated Services for Mobility Impaired People) is a European Integrated Project (IST-2003-511298) within the IST 6th Framework Program in the e-Inclusion area. The driving vision behind the project is to develop services based on Ambient Intelligence (AmI) and Information and Communication Technologies (ICT) that allow mobility impaired people to move independently, lead a quality life, and as a result, establish and secure economic and social inclusion. These services include the provision of relevant and real time information, primarily for travelling, but also for use at home and at work. Nomad devices allow content access at any time, at any place, and across multiple networks. These devices combined with the ASK-IT platform aim to cover a wide range of the mobility impaired users personal needs [2]. ASK-IT provides applications and services in five main areas: (i) transportation, tourism and leisure; (ii) personal support; (iii) work; (iv) business and education support; and (v) social relations and community building [3].

The key challenge here is to ensure the delivery of high-quality user interfaces, by effectively addressing diversity in the following three dimensions: (a) target user population; (b) categories of delivered services and applications; and (c) deployment computing-platforms (e.g., mobile phones, PDAs and laptops). In this context, alternative interfaces are designed and constructed, demonstrating multimodal intuitive interaction, according to the appropriately identified configuration parameters. Finally, specific configuration tools are developed, to further enable end-user customise and individualise the delivered interfaces.

2 Contents

2.1 Hardware and Software User Interface Solutions Relevant to the Platform

In this section we consider four different aspects related to the UI Configuration: device form factors, operating system, runtime software and networking technology selected for the system.

Three *device form-factors* have been specified for the initial application development; these are expected to be useful for supporting the targeted scenarios. These devices are the following [4]:

---

[1] http:// www.ask-it.org

- Smart Phone: This form factor, representing today's most common nomad device, are full-featured mobile phones with personal computer like functionality, rich displays, and miniature keypads for text entry. Voice input and output capabilities are also inherent to this form factor.
- PDA (Personal Digital Assistant): This form factor represents a richer user input/output modality than Smart Phones, with larger touch screens and more powerful processors; the trade-off is their larger total size. Both the size and feature-sets of PDAs are typically supersets of Smart Phones.
- Tablet PC: This form factor represents the largest display areas among nomad devices and the most flexible user input mechanisms, at the cost of larger size than Smart Phone and PDA form factors.

Choice of selected *operating systems* is based on the features needed or preferred by end-users as well as on the potential commercial exploitation. The following operating system choices have been made for the initial developments [4]:

- Operating systems allowing Java development: Based on the Mobile Information Device Profile (MIDP), combined with the Connected Limited Device Configuration (CLDC), is the Java runtime environment for today's nomad information devices such as phones.
- Symbian OS: Widely used Smart Phone operating systems available on many devices.
- Windows Mobile OS: A widely used operating system for mobile devices including Smart Phones and PDAs.
- Windows Tablet PC: A version of Windows OS with specific "Tablet" functionality enhancements facilitating interaction with and without keyboard.

A "*run-time*" is a programming system that lies on top of an operating system and aids in the development of rich software on the system. The following three device developments are the most popular [4]:

- Native code development (C/C++): This represents the native communication with the underlying operating system. Some native code development might be necessary for the target device HW & operating systems. This is particularly important in the area of interfacing higher level code (Java and C#/CLR) with lower level functionality, such as custom networking interfaces.
- Java development (Java language, Java run-time): Java is the name for both the programming language and run-time environment. Java is a popular development language for servers, desktops and mobile device applications.
- CLR/C# development: The CLR (Common Language Runtime, also commonly known as ".NET") is an ISO and ECMA standards complaint run-time for servers, desktops and mobile devices. It supports a wide variety of programming languages, but the two most popular are C# and Visual Basic.

Target HW and Operating Systems support some sub-set of the following *networking technologies* [4]:

- GPRS/UMTS: It represents data communications over wide-area mobile networks.
- Wi-Fi support: It represents the Wireless LAN communications models.

- Bluetooth/Zigbee support: It represents optimized communications for body area network and personal area network technologies.

Some additional support technologies, such as RFID and A-GPS might be used.

The following table depicts the correspondence between the selected operating systems and both the aforementioned run-time (development) environments and the target platforms.

Table 1. Correspondence between the selected operative systems and (a) popular run time environments (*top*), and (b) the target platforms considered in ASK-IT [4] (*bottom*)

OS / Runtime	OS with MIDP	Symbian	Windows Mobile	Tablet PC (Windows)
Native Code (C/C++)		X	X	X
JVM (Java)	X	X	X	X
CLR (C#)			X	X

OS / Target device	OS with MIDP	Symbian	Windows Mobile	Tablet PC (Windows)
Smart Phone	X	X	X	
PDA			X	
Tablet PC				X

Regarding the specific devices that will be used in the Project by mobility impaired users, the following models have been considered:

- Smart Phones: Nokia N92, Nokia 9300i[2].
- PDAs: Fujitsu-Siemens Pocket LOOX N550 (04/06)[3], Fujitsu-Siemens Pocket LOOX T830 (07/06)[4], Qtek9090[5].
- Tablet PCs: Fujitsu-Siemens Stylistic ST5022 (see[4]), Fujitsu-Siemens LIFEBOOK P1510 (see[4]).

The UI configuration of the final system will take into consideration the functional limitations of the user, the type of service that needs to be supported in each case, and finally, the benefits offered by each one of the pilot devices.

2.2 User Interface Approach

The approach that will be followed for the development of the ASK-IT UI across the whole project is depicted in Figure 2. Within the ASK-IT project, a series of mock-ups are built: Route guidance, e-commerce & e-payment, domotics, ADAS/IVICS, medical, e-working & e-learning and assistive devices. After this, the final integration of the User Interface in the ASK-IT devices should be managed [5].

[2] http://www.forum.nokia.com/devices
[3] http://www.nseries.com/nseries/
[4] http://www.fujitsu-siemens.com/
[5] http://www.qtek.es/

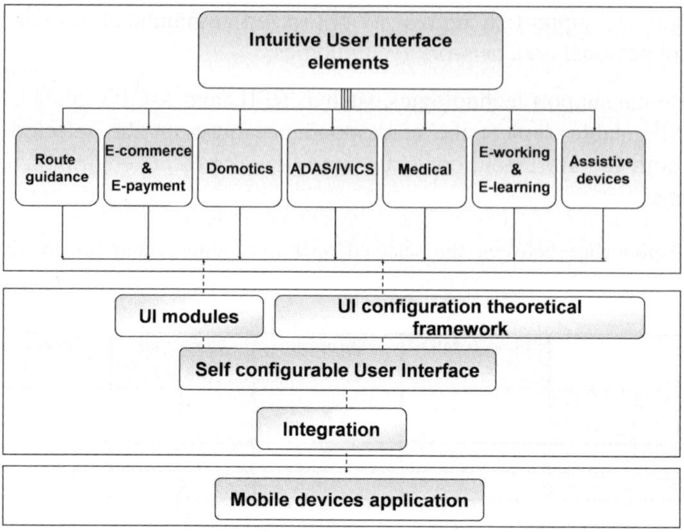

Fig. 1. Block diagram, showing the build-up of the ASK-IT UI modules [5]

2.3 Configuration of the ASK-IT User Interface

Most of the systems reported in the literature in the area of content adaptation for small devices consist of tailoring several presentations of the same content to different kind of devices. The difficulty of such an approach is that it requires a lot of human efforts in authoring and storing the different content variants [6]. Some studies tried to resolve this problem by providing mechanisms that allow a more dynamic adaptation. Unfortunately most of the proposed models are device dependent and include already presentation based information, which is not suitable for all types of devices [7].

ASK-IT is adopting a more abstract approach. This is done by providing a device independent model which excludes presentation information from the content. Some key user characteristics to be analyzed and co-related with the UI configuration parameters consist of the level of computer expertise, the relevant task expertise and the particular known user-preferences. The notion of *automatic software adaptation* reflects the capability of the software to adapt, during runtime, to the individual end-user, as well as to the particular context of use, by delivering the most appropriate interface solution [6]. For the implementation of the UI adaptation in ASK-IT, the *Decision Making Specification Language* (DMSL), which includes a method for automatic adaptation-design verification, was found to be a useful solution [6].

2.4 Interface Design Guidelines Applied to ASK-IT Nomad Devices

This section will list some of the main design guidelines that will be applied to ASK- IT nomad devices interfaces.

Half of Shneideman's eight interface design guidelines [8] apply to nomad devices without explicit changes [9]:

- *Enable frequent users to use shortcuts*: As the frequency of use increases, so does a user's desire to reduce the number of interactions [10].
- *Offer Informative feedback:* For every operator action, there should be some system feedback, substantial and understandable by the user [9].
- *Design Dialogs to yield closure:* Users should be given the satisfaction of accomplishment and completion [9].
- *Support Internal Locus of Control:* Systems should be designed such that users initiate actions rather respond to them [9].

Fig. 2. ASK-IT PDA mock-ups: the system is offering informative feedback to the user *(left)*, ASK-IT Use of shortcuts *(right)* [10]

Figure 2 shows an example of two of these guidelines. The screen on the left is a domotic mock-up offering informative feedback to the user with information about the status of the light in the house. The screen on the right is illustrating the use of shortcuts.

The remaining four guidelines require modifications and/or an increased emphasis on use with nomad devices [11]:

- *Consistency:* Across multiple platforms and devices for the same application. On the other hand the specific characteristics of the platforms and devices have to be taken into account [11].
- *Reversal of actions*: Allowing easy reversal of actions may be more difficult for mobile devices because of a lack of available resources and computing power [12].
- *Error prevention and Simple error handling*: This need becomes more critical due to the more rapid pace of events in the mobile environment [9].
- *Reduce short term memory load*: interfaces should be designed such that very little memorization from the user side is required during the performance of tasks. Using alternative interaction modes such as sound can be beneficial [13].

Additional guidelines for mobile device design [9]:

- *Design for multiply and dynamic contexts*: The usability or appropriateness of an application (e.g., brightness, noise levels, weather) can change depending on location, time of day and season [14].

- *Design for small devices*: As technology continues to advance, mobile platforms will continue to shrink in size and include items such as bracelets, rings, earrings, buttons, and key chains [9].
- *Design for limited and split attention*: Interfaces for mobile devices need to be designed to require as little attention as possible [15].
- *Design for speed and recovery:* For mobile devices and applications, time constraints need to be taken into account in initial application availability and recovery speed [9].
- *Design for top-down interaction:* To reduce distraction, interactions, and potential information overload, a better way of presenting information might be through multilevel or hierarchical mechanisms [16].
- *Allow for personalization:* Since nomad devices are more personal, it is more likely that a user of mobile applications will personalize the device and its applications to his or her preferences [9].
- *Design for enjoyment:* Aesthetics is also part of designing an overall enjoyable user experience with mobile devices [9].

3 Results

This section shows some design prototypes for several nomad devices interfaces currently available for the ASK-IT project.

Figure 3 shows an ASK-IT prototype using a PDA as a nomad device. The system requests both a user name and a password in order to identify the user. Once the user has entered the system, the PDA screen shows a menu with the user name, the date and local time, the entry to the user profile and three different domain-spanning options (See Fig. 3): My appointments, Events-on-line courses and Current Position (Look after me). Additionally the entry to all available ASK-IT services is given. In this particular example, the user is selecting the option "ASK-IT Services". The ASK-IT services are grouped on application domain related categories: Route Planning, Points of interest, Domotics, Assistance and My Car. Figure 4 (left) shows the categories for the ASK-IT Services menu.

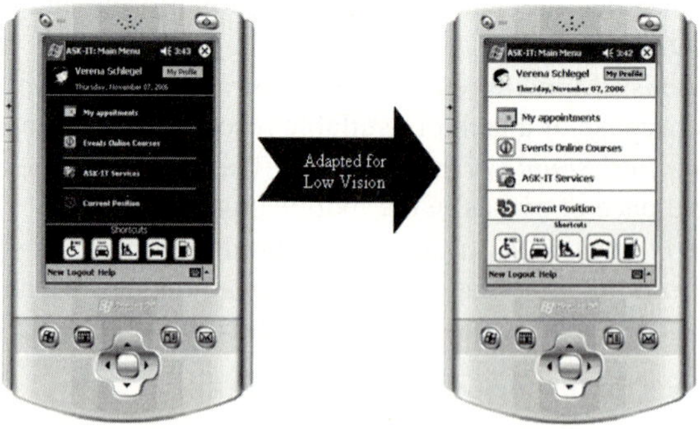

Fig. 3. Two versions of a User Interface from an ASK-IT use case. The mock-up is adapted for visually impaired users [10].

Fig. 4. ASK-IT Services menu *(left)* and ASK-IT Domotics menu *(right)* [10]

If the user is choosing the option "Domotics" from the menu (see Fig. 4, left), the device will list the rooms in the house that the users will be able to interact with (see Fig. 4, right).

Figure 5 illustrates an ASK-IT prototype for a Tablet PC. The screen is divided into six different areas: a welcome area, help and log-out buttons at the top; a navigation area to the left; shortcuts button area; system status area; an information area, which provides the data and position of the user, at the bottom; and a content area, in the centre.

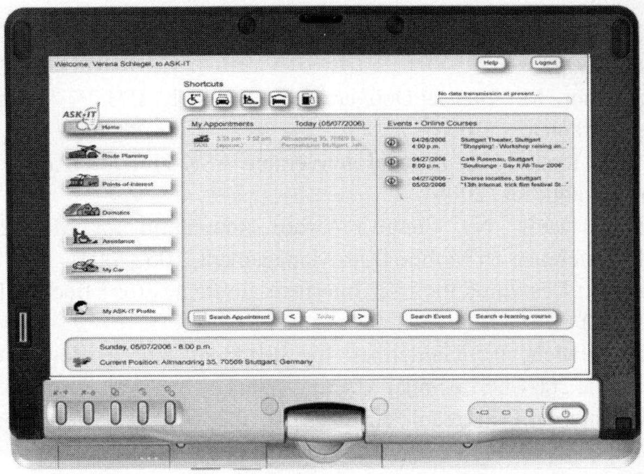

Fig. 5. ASK-IT Tablet PC screen prototype [10]

4 Conclusions

This paper builds on the importance of supporting adaptation of the user interface to different devices and diverse user needs. This is particularly relevant in the case of nomad devices - mobile phones, PDAs and Tablet PCs - as they allow the user to access information at any time and at any place. Several hardware and software User Interface design options have been described. Some of the currently available mock-ups for the nomad devices UI have been depicted. The underlying idea is to keep similarity when possible, but to adapt the UI when needed.

The *Decision Making Specification Language* (DMSL) is a useful solution to adapt the software at runtime onto the individual end-user, as well as to the particular context of use. The design of a user interface has a significant social impact. This paper has presented the guidelines for the user interfaces adaptations for nomad devices and its particular application to mobility impaired users within the ASK-IT project that will help them to improve their access to information and quality of life.

Acknowledgments. We wish to acknowledge to the ASK-IT IP project Consortium for their valuable contributions to this work. The ASK-IT IP project is partially funded by the EC.

References

1. Stephanidis, C., Savidis, A.: Unified User Interface Development. In: J.Jacko & A Sears (eds.) The Human-Computer Interaction Handbook, NJ: Lawrence Erlbaum Associates (2003)
2. Gardner, M.: Nomadic devices. Toward simpler, Standarized Integration into Vehicles Via a Nomadic Gateway (2006), http://www.motorola.com/mot/doc/6/6462_MotDoc.pdf
3. Annex, A.I.: 1- Description of work, version 13 September 2006 Approved by EC on 13 (September 2006)
4. Alcaine, P., Salmre, I.: Internal Report ASKIT-SIE-WP33-R1-V11 Target Devices Specifications (2006)
5. Bekiaris, E., Gemou, M., Internal Deliverable, A.S.K.-I.T.: ID3.2.1-final.doc, Definition of Configuration Parameters (2005)
6. Savidis, A., Lilis Ioannis, L.: Internal deliverable ASK-IT-ID3.2.2.doc, UI Configuration according to user abilities (2006)
7. Lemluma, T., Layaïda, N.: Context Aware Adaptation for Mobile Devices, IEEE International Conference on Mobile Data Management, 106 (2004)
8. Schneiderman, B.: Designing the User Interface: Strategies for Effective Human Computer Interaction (1997)
9. Gong, J., Tarasewich, P.: Guidelines for handheld mobile device interface design. Proceedings of the 2004 DSI Annual Meeting (2004)
10. Ringbauer, B.: Internal Deliverable ASKIT ID2.10.2_v01.doc, Simulation and mock/up of all devices for MI (2006)
11. Ringbauer, B.: Smart Home Control via PDA - an Example of Multi-Device User Interface Design. In: Sloane, A. (ed.) Proceedings of the Home oriented Informatics and Telematics Conference (HOIT 2005), London, Springer, Heidelberg (2005)
12. Satyanarayanan, M.: Fundamental Challenges in Mobile Computing, Proceedings of the fifteenth annual ACM symposium on Principles of distributed computing, pp. 1–7 (1996)
13. Chan, S., Fang, X., Brzezinski, J., Zhou, Y., Xu, S., Lam, J.: Usability For Mobile Commerce Across Multiple Form Factors, Journal of Electronic Commerce Research, 3(3) (2002)

14. Kim, H., Kim, J., Lee, Y., Chae, M., Choi, Y.: An Empirical Study of the Use Contexts and Usability Problems in Mobile Internet, Proceedings of the 35th Hawaii International Conference on System Sciences (2002)
15. Poupyrev, I., Maruyama, S., Rekimoto, J.: Ambient Touch: Designing Tactile Interfaces for Handheld Devices, Proceedings of the 15th annual ACM symposium on User interface software and technology, pp. 51–60 (2002)
16. Brewster, S.: Overcoming the Lack of Screen Spaces on Mobile Computers, Personal and Ubiquitous Computing, vol. 6, pp. 188–205 (2002)

GOOD ROUTE HMI for Actors Involved in Dangerous Goods Transportation

Marco Santi[1], Katrin Meinken[1], Harald Widlroither[2], and Evangelos Bekiaris[3]

[1] University of Stuttgart
Institute for Human Factors and Technology Management
Nobelstr. 12, 70569 Stuttgart, Germany
marco.santi@iao.fraunhofer.de,
katrin.meinken@iao.fraunhofer.de
[2] Fraunhofer-Institute for Industrial Engineering
Nobelstr. 12, 70569 Stuttgart, Germany
harald.widlroither@iao.fraunhofer.de
[3] Centre for Research and Technology Hellas – Hellenic Institute of Transport (CERTH/HIT)
L. Posidonos 17, 17455 Athens, Greece
Tel: +30210 9853194, Fax: +30210 9853193
abek@certh.gr

Abstract. GOOD ROUTE is a European project developing a cooperative system for routing, monitoring, re-routing, enforcement and driver support of dangerous goods vehicles, based upon dynamic, real time data, in order to minimise the Societal Risks related to their movements, whereas still generating the most cost efficient solution for all actors involved in their logistic chain. In this paper the theoretical background for the Human-Machine Interface of the GOOD ROUTE system is discussed, different actors are characterised and their user needs are described. Basic functionalities and elements as well as the preliminary guidelines that endorse the GOOD ROUTE system approach are presented.

Keywords: Dangerous Goods, communication and interaction, information and warning strategies, user centred design, user needs, requirements analyses.

1 Introduction

Several thousands of trucks are carrying dangerous goods across Europe on a daily basis. They utilise urban roads, rural roads, highways, tunnels and long bridges. Due to different national regulations and individual policies of infrastructure operating companies they are not allowed to use some of them. As a consequence secondary roads and alternative ways are used. In addition, unforeseen events like traffic jams or accidents sometimes force truck drivers to taking different routes as well. But the actual accident risk and impact when using secondary roads or other alternative ways is not calculated.

C. Stephanidis (Ed.): Universal Access in HCI, Part II, HCII 2007, LNCS 4555, pp. 546–555, 2007.

The GOOD ROUTE project aims at developing a cooperative system for Dangerous Goods vehicles. GOOD ROUTE is a specific targeted project co-funded by the European Commission Information Society Technologies (IST) and started its activities in January 2006. The GOOD ROUTE system will help to route, monitor, re-route and support the truck driver, based upon dynamic, real time data, in order to minimise risks related to their movements still generating the most cost efficient solution for all actors involved in the logistic chain. Figure 1 summarises GOOD ROUTE's aims in a greater detail by listing GOOD ROUTE's core uses cases.

- Automatic notification of the infrastructure and issue/booking of permission of passage.
- Provision of navigation and optimal route guidance to the driver by a cooperative system that fuses data from the vehicle on-board sensors, the infrastructure and the other equipped vehicles.
- Re-routing to the safest route, in case of need for re-routing due to an accident, incident, denial of passage, etc.
- Re-routing to the safest route, in case of need for re-routing due to change in business goals.
- Automatic enforcement, by providing key data (vehicle speed, profile, total weight per axle, etc.) to a local/central check-point.
- Provision of real-time information to all stakeholders in the DG logistics chain (dispatcher, transporter, client, recipient, etc.), regarding vehicle position and status, expected arrival time, cargo level and condition, as well as any unforeseen malfunction.
- Automatic and semi-automatic accident notification and key info (type of cargo, level of loading, location of different compartments' loading, etc.) provision to all support teams of the logistic chain.

Fig. 1. GOOD ROUTE use cases

The aim of this paper is to give an initial overview of the development of optimal user interfaces for both the drivers of the Dangerous Goods vehicles and the operators of different control centres involved in the transportation of dangerous goods. The user interfaces will provide appropriate information and warnings, without enhancing actors' workload or other unnecessary behavioural adaptations. The development of GOOD ROUTE's user interfaces (UI) follows a user-centred design approach (ISO, 1999) where user needs, requirements, and already available interfaces and procedures are analysed first before designing new human-machine interface (HMI) solutions. The procedure of developing GOOD ROUTE HMIs is based on general guidelines and regulations including the requirements for effective warning strategies.

2 Theoretical Concepts

2.1 Human-Machine Interface (HMI)

"All components of a work system for functional interaction between humans and a technical system are combined under the term human-machine interface." (Spath, Braun & Hagenmeyer, 2006, p. 1617). This definition states that two parties, namely humans and technical systems, interact with each other. Interaction in turn is based on communication processes, where information between two parties are exchanged and processed. Once processed, some sort of reaction takes place, which in turn is the exchange of information. Interaction in the context of development of HMIs therefore can be seen as a continuous process of information exchange between technical systems and humans.

The interface, typically also called user interface (UI), consists of all system aspects that a user comes into contact conceptually, communicatively and physically. (Moran, 1981, in Sarodnick & Brau, 2006). It is therefore the medium enabling the exchange of information.

2.2 Information

Many definitions of the term information can be found in scientific literature. Dependent on the context they differ significantly from each other. In the context of Communication Psychology and Symbolic Interactionism (Georg Herbert Mead, 1863 – 1931) all entities enclosed in a certain communication process need to share a "common ground" (Frindte, 2001, p. 27) so that information is interpreted correctly with respect to the communication context. Therefore, communication of information itself does not necessarily imply any responses. The further course of the interaction process is determined depending on how the recipient interprets the information or message in a certain context.

The latter aspect is very important for the design of user interfaces. Only if the presentation of information matches context and recipients' characteristics, successful interaction will take place. While developing information strategies, the analysis of user needs and requirements are very important in order to find the above mentioned common ground of communication.

The presented paper focuses mainly on the part of receiving information from the GOOD ROUTE HMI. The human actor is able to receive information on three independent channels, namely the visual channel, the auditory channel and the tactile channel. All of them are not equally appropriate in all situations and have to be carefully chosen depending on the context, the user needs and the information that is being received by the actor.

2.3 Warnings

Laughery and Wogalter state the purpose of warning at several levels while pointing out that warnings belong to the category of communication. "Most generally, warnings are intended to improve safety, that is, to decrease accidents or incidents that result in injury, illness or property damage. At another level, warnings are intended to influence or modify people's behaviour in ways that improve safety. At still another level warnings are intended to provide information that enables people to understand hazards, consequences and appropriate behaviours, which in turn enables them to make informed decisions."

Warning signals announce imminent hazards or hazardous situations that require appropriate actions in order to eliminate or at least control the hazard or hazardous situation (DIN EN 842, 1996). Whereas in most communication situations misunderstandings can be easily overcome by asking, repeating or rephrasing, a hazardous situation will generally require all necessary information to be communicated within the first attempt. Therefore, they have to be thoroughly designed.

The GOOD ROUTE warning strategy follows the approach of Wickens et al. (2004). They state: "the goal [of a warning] is to get the user to comply with the warning and, therefore, use the product in a safe way, or avoid unsafe behaviour." In order to ensure a secure handling of the future system, four elementary requirements have to be attended to:

- The warning must be noticed.
- The warning must be perceived (read/heard).
- The warning must be understood.
- The warning must be accepted.

By applying these criteria an efficient design of a warning strategy will first of all draw the attention of the actors involved in the transportation of dangerous goods. Then it has to be assured that the warning message is not only physically perceived, but moreover cognitively understood and then accepted by the recipient. The system also has to give information about the identified risk and about possible and recommendable actions in case they are not obvious.

2.4 Alerts

In comparison to warnings, alerts are signals showing the start or the existence of a dangerous or hazardous situation (DIN EN 842, 1996). It requires immediate actions in order to limit negative consequences. While developing information and warning strategies, alerts must be given high priority.

3 HMI Concepts for Different Actors

Different actors are involved in the handling of Dangerous Goods transports. These are namely:

- drivers of dangerous goods trucks;
- logistics enterprise control centre operators;
- infrastructure control centre operators;
- fire station control centre operators;

Since the above listed actors belong to different user groups with different user needs, different work environments and different backgrounds regarding education, expertise, training and responsibilities within the logistic chain, HMI concepts have to be designed for the addresses user group specifically.

3.1 Drivers

The transport of dangerous goods is carried out by specially trained truck drivers in order to be licensed operating a dangerous goods vehicle. The vast majority of required driving skills do not differ from regular truck drivers. Also general user needs can be considered as being similar to those of regular truck drivers. Though, one central difference in driving behaviour pertains to the freedom in choosing the route that the dangerous goods truck driver can use safely and in accordance to local regulations. As mentioned above, regulations differ between countries and infrastructure operating companies. The most important differences exist for the accepted quantity and quality of the load and the time of passage. Closely connected to these differences are regulations on how to obtain permissions and on enforcement actions. In Switzerland for instance the current practice is to get permission days before the dangerous goods truck actually passes a certain infrastructure. The Frejus Tunnel in Italy on the other hand doesn't require registration time ahead. Necessary paper work is done just before the truck in question passes the tunnel. Therefore, truck drivers and the logistics enterprise need an extensive database storing these different regulations in order to plan routes appropriately. The GOOD ROUTE system will provide the truck driver with all necessary information utilising existing on-board HMI and additional third party devices like Personal Digital Assistants (PDA).

Driving a vehicle is generally characterised as a dual task condition (Santi & Juch, 2004) where the primary task is a regulatory task mainly involving visio-motoric coordination aiming at the safe control of the vehicle in a complex and dynamic traffic environment. The secondary task instead applies to all actions acquiring and sending information from and to a driver information system which are not related to the pure driving task. The field of HMI development within GOOD ROUTE pertains mostly to the area of secondary task operations.

Generally to be considered, and therefore highly applicable for Dangerous Goods truck drivers as well, are guidelines for the design of warning devices to derive the basic HMI and warning concept. In 2006, the European Commission updated its set of guidelines for the design of safety on-board information systems (European Commission, 2006).

All guidelines summarise essential safety aspects to be taken into account for the HMI for in-vehicle information and communication systems. These guidelines apply to all components and aspects of a system that the truck driver will interact with while driving. The most important declarations need to be included in the GOOD ROUTE truck driver HMI:

- The system must comply with relevant regulations and standards.
- The system supports the driver and does not increase driver distraction from driving task.
- The system shall not require uninterruptible sequences of interaction.
- The system does not distract or visually entertain the driver.
- No part of the system should obstruct the driver's view of the road scene.
- The system response (e.g. feedback, confirmation) following driver input should be timely and clearly perceptible.
- Information which has the highest safety relevance should be given priority.
- The behaviour of the system should not adversely interfere with the display or controls required for the primary driving task and for road safety.

Thus the main goal of the GOOD ROUTE truck driver HMI must be to ensure that the driver will experience neither confusion nor overload. Only information that will assist the driver more than distract him in complex traffic scenarios should be provided by the HMI. Since truck drivers will receive both, information, e.g. "Successful booking of permission of passage." and warnings, e.g. "Accident ahead. Slow down!", information and warning strategies utilising the existing on-board HMIs will be developed.

3.2 Logistics Enterprise Control Centre Operators

One of the most important tasks of control centre operators working for logistics enterprise is the routing of dangerous goods vehicles. Surveys conducted in Germany resulted in no specific HMI solution already being in use for this particular task. Instead, logistics enterprises use commercially available standard routing software. Asking for their user needs they communicated high demands for route planning software providing specific information for the planning of routes for dangerous goods transports. Companies are especially missing the above mentioned information about restrictions applying to different countries and infrastructure operating companies. As commercial routing software is widely available it is suggested to enhance their databases with detailed information on policies and procedures.

Control centre operators of logistics enterprises in Germany rarely monitor the status and position of their dangerous goods vehicles. In case of any unforeseen incident the truck driver contacts his or her company via cell phone.

Since no safety related actions can be taken by control centre operators of logistics enterprises, GOOD ROUTE's HMI development for this user group will mainly focus on information strategies.

3.3 Infrastructure Control Centre Operators

In Europe many road infrastructure elements, such as tunnels and bridges are individually operated and monitored by specially trained personnel. Typically one control centre operates one infrastructure element. Due to the aforementioned differences in state policies and regulations defined by the infrastructure operating companies itself, the handling of dangerous goods transportation varies accordingly.

Despite this heterogeneity they all monitor a well defined area. User needs surveys and on-site observations at two infrastructures, namely Gotthard Road Tunnel (Switzerland) and Frejus Tunnel (Italy), were conducted in order to formulate the core questions needed to be answered with the help of the GOOD ROUTE HMI:

- Who is coming when?
- What is the quantity and quality of the load?
- What is the driver's nationality?
- Whom is the driver working for?
- Where is the driver headed to?
- Are there any safety related problems with the dangerous goods truck?

Control Centre operators of infrastructure elements have high demands for well designed information and warning strategies. Appropriate information is necessary in order to manage the traffic efficiently. Warnings and possibly even alerts will have to be handled in cases of malfunctions of the dangerous goods truck.

Although the core questions presented above need to be answered for a vast majority of the infrastructure operating companies, differences in policies and procedures prevent the development of a unified HMI for infrastructure control centre operators.

3.4 Fire Station Control Centre Operators

Also involved in the logistics chain are fire station control centre operators. The major difference to aforementioned actors is that they are typically not interested in every single dangerous goods truck passing a road segment they are assigned to. User needs surveys in Greece and Germany successfully resulted in a well defined set of requirements:

- Only incidents or very dangerous transports should be reported through the GOOD ROUTE system.
- An easy way is requested to pass on key information to the rescue team.
- The exact location is required. A map giving an overview of the area where the incident occurred is highly appreciated.
- Information about the quantity and quality of the load has to be available immediately. That also includes a loading status of all individual compartments.
- An automated identification of the dangerous goods substance linking to existing databases informing about how to handle the substances in question would safe time and is therefore highly requested.
- The knowledge of the driver's nationality is important for communication purposes. It is also important to know the drivers' logistic enterprise's origin and information about a company located at minor distance in order to be contacted for help processing the dangerous goods load.

Analysing these requirements, the HMI development for fire station control centre operators have to focus on warnings strategies. Figure 2 shows a paper prototype developed after analysing the above mentioned user needs and requirements.

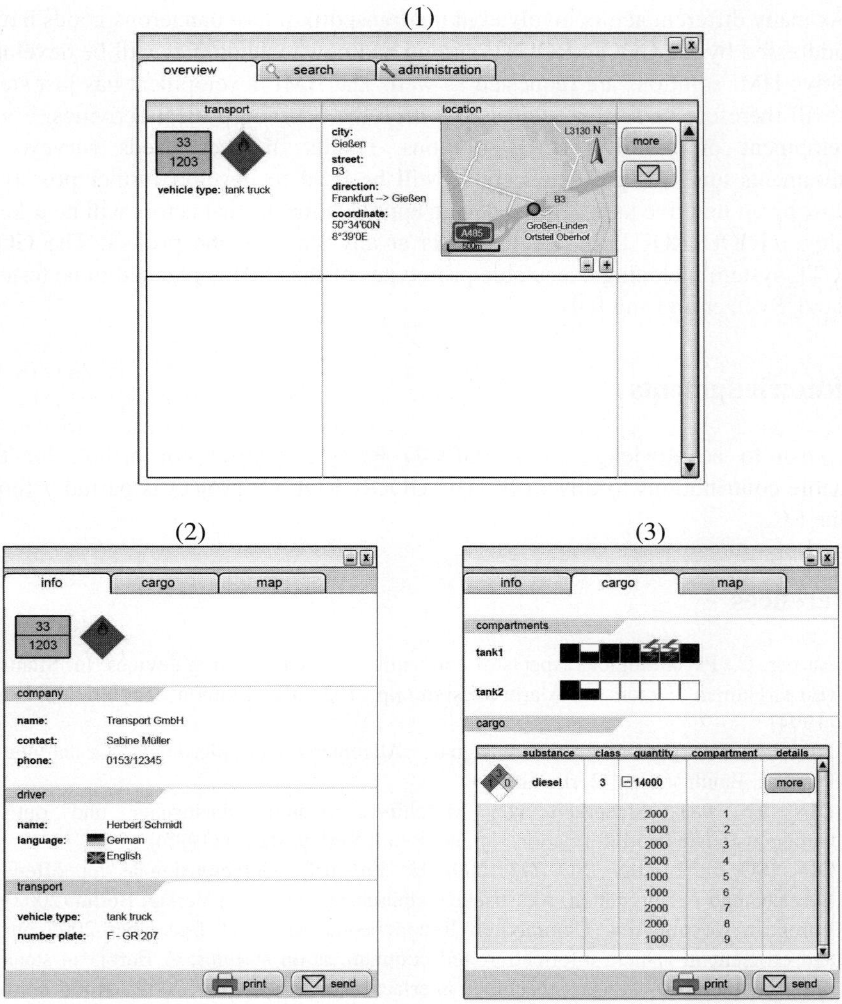

Fig. 2. Paper prototype of the fire station control centre HMI. The overview tab (1) presents basic information about the substance and the location of the dangerous goods truck. Clicking on "more" links to the details tab (2) showing information about substance's hazardousness, company contacts, information about the driver and details about the vehicle. The cargo tab (3) is showing details about the compartment filling.

4 Conclusions and Outlook

The GOOD ROUTE project aims at developing a cooperative system for the routing, monitoring and re-routing (in case of need) of dangerous goods vehicles, that will minimise the Societal Risks related to their movements, while still generating the most cost efficient solution for all actors involved.

As many different actors involved in the transportation of dangerous goods have to be addressed by the GOOD ROUTE system and new technologies will be developed, intuitive HMI solutions are requested as well. The HMI development has just started and will therefore be further addressed within the ongoing project activities. For the development of intuitive HMI solutions, results of user needs surveys and requirements analyses presented above will be used to develop further prototypes. Following an iterative user-centred design approach means that actors will be asked to evaluate GOOD ROUTE's developments at any stage of the project. The GOOD ROUTE system including executable prototypes of the HMI is planned to be tested in Finland, Switzerland and Italy.

Acknowledgments

We wish to acknowledge to the GOOD ROUTE project consortium for their valuable contributions to this work. The GOOD ROUTE project is partially funded by the EC.

References

1. Barber, C.: Psychological aspects of conventional in-car warning devices. In: Stanton N (Ed.), Human Factors in Alarm Design, pp. 193–205, London: Taylor and Francis (1994)
2. DIN EN 848, Optische Gefahrensignale. Allgemeine Anforderungen, Gestaltung und Prüfung. Beuth Verlag: Berlin (1996)
3. DIN EN 981, Sicherheit von Maschinen. System akustischer und optischer Gefahrensignale und Informationssignale. Beuth Verlag: Berlin (1997)
4. DIN ISO 7731, DIN ISO 7731:2002-03 (Entwurf). Gefahrensignale für öffentliche Bereiche und Arbeitsstätten. Akustische Gefahrensignale. Beuth Verlag: Berlin (2002)
5. European Commission, Commission Recommendation of 21 December 2005 on safe and efficient in-vehicle information and communication systems: A European statement of principles on human machine interface. Retrieved 01, 2007, from Europe's Information Society Thematic Portal Web Site: esafety/doc/esafety_forum/hmi/ agenda_and_other_papers/l1964_en.pdf (2006), http://ec.europa.eu/information_society/activities/
6. Frindte, W.: Einführung in die Kommunikationspsychologie. Beltz Verlag: Weinheim und Basel (2001)
7. ISO, ISO 13407: Benutzer-orientierte Gestaltung interaktiver Systeme. Berlin: Beuth (1999)
8. Santi, M., Juch, S.: Die Ablenkungswirkung von Fahrerinformationssystemen - Validierung und Weiterentwicklung eines Messinstruments zur Erfassung von Ablenkungswirkung durch Fahrerinformationssysteme und Risikokompensation bei der Verwendung von Fahrerinformationssystemen - Eine experimentelle Untersuchung -. Unpublished diploma theses, Friedrich-Schiller-University of Jena, Germany (2004)

9. Sarodnick, F., Brau, H.: Methoden der Usability Evaluation. Huber: Bern (2006)
10. Spath, D., Braun, M., Hagenmeyer, L.: Human Factors and Ergonomics in Manufacturing and Process Control. In: Salvendy, G. (ed.) Handbook of Human Factors and Ergonomics, 3rd edn. pp. 1597–1625. Wiley, New Jersay (2006)
11. Wickens, C.D., Lee, J.D., Gordon Becker, S.E., Liu, Y.: An introduction to human factors engineering, 2nd ed. Pearson Education, Upper Saddle River, New Jersey (2004)

An Empirical Study of Developing an Adaptive Location-Based Services Interface on Smartphone

Kuo-Wei Su, Ching-Chang Lee, and Li-Kai Chen

Department of Information Management, National Kaohsiung First University of Science and Technology, Kaohsiung City, TAIWAN, R.O.C.
kwsu@ccms.nkfust.edu.tw

Abstract. A mobile market shows that the global LBS (Location-Based Service) market is noticeable and continues to grow rapidly. With the coming of mobile applications, the requirement of the small screen interface (SSI) is even more reinforced because of the need for more functions and contents on the devices. This research explore an empirical study of user access to PoI's (Point of Interest) information of the map view display (MVD) and list view display (LVD) meeting the user's needs base on the principle of adaptive and intuitive visualization on Smartphone. Further, the prototype of LBS on smartphone was emulated by VB.Net program, which interfaces are evaluated through objective measurement and subjective investigation. Our study's results appear cognition of symbols that affects operating performance, so the suggestion is towards using LVD more effectively than MVD on LBS applications. The findings of the study will be helpful to enrich functionality and customization of the LBS appearance on smartphone.

Keywords: Location-Based Service, Point of Interest, Map View Display, List View Display, Adaptive Visualization, Small Screen Interface.

1 Introduction

About recently years, mobile networks are widely deployed in global mobile market (including Taiwan) and income from telephony services had proven to be significant to mobile operators. As well as according to figures from market researchers Canalys point out shipments of converged smart mobile devices, namely smart-phones and wireless handhelds, rise by 170% year-on-year in first part of 2005 in Europe and Middle East as, in contrast, standard mobile phone shipments rise by only 11% [1]. By the way, in some countries such as Japan and South Korea, mobile Internet use is growing rapidly. For example, NTT DoCoMo reports, that the number of i-mode subscribers now exceeds 38 million, which is nearly half of all cellular phone subscribers in Japan [12]. Reed stated "telecommunication companies are making huge investments and they know LBS technology is a key application from which they can generate revenue"[15]. While mobile users operate the add-value service, they suffer some possible problems of the lack of screen space. The display of dynamic PoI information on the map shall be tailored to the needs of users, thus the PoI information

C. Stephanidis (Ed.): Universal Access in HCI, Part II, HCII 2007, LNCS 4555, pp. 556 – 564, 2007.

must be simple and intuitive without overly complex information. The objectives of the study are listed below:

(1) To develop two kinds of displays in a prototype of LBS interface, which displaying dynamic PoI's information in the map in an adaptive and clear way base on meeting the design principles of mobile interfaces. (2) To evaluate and compare performance of the prototype through the rigid experimental evaluations.

2 Related Concepts

LBS can provide various services to a user based on the user's location. This add-value service in the broadest sense is any service or application that extends spatial information processing or geographical information services (GIS) capabilities, to end users via the internet and/or wireless network [7]. The Open Geospatial Consortium (OGC) stated LBS is defined as a wireless-IP service that uses geographic information to serve a mobile user, or any application service that takes advantage of the position of a mobile device [13]. These services help to answer questions such as "Where can I find a Chinese restaurant?" or "Where is the nearest friends?" etc. For example, in Japan, NTT DoCoMo expresses a "friends finder" service on its iMode system [10]. Therefore these are usually combined with a digital map associated to the user location. Previous studies have proved that a visual communication of geographic information in the form of maps is high on the users' wish list of LBS [8]. During this visualizations process, cartographic methods and techniques are applied. These methods and techniques can be considered as a kind of grammar that allows for the optimal design of maps, depending upon the application (Figure 1) [9].

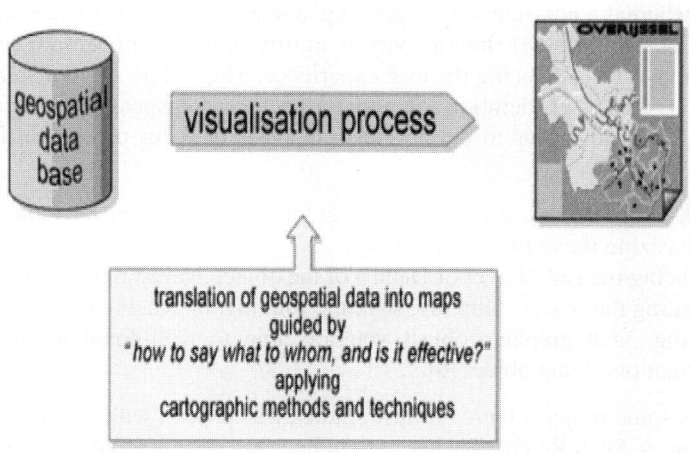

Fig. 1. The cartographic visualizations process

Representations may be presented symbolically, graphically, or iconically and are often differentiated from other forms of expression (textual, verbal or formulaic) by virtue of their synoptic format and with qualities traditionally described by the term ´Gestalt´. The adaptive geovisualization service will produce mobile maps which the user gets the possibility to specify the information he needs for his purpose, the system selects the necessary data and omit unimportant details. Dunlop, Ptasinski, Morrison, McCallum, Riseby, Stewart present two types of views providing both map and list-index information access: (1) MVD (Fig 2a) (2) LVD (Fig 2b)[4].

Fig. (2a). MVD

Fig. (2b). LVD

In the past one of the problems with using menus is that they take up a lot of space on the screen. Two solutions are the use of pull-down or pop-up menu [14]. Most windowing systems provide a system of menus consisting of implicit or explicit pop-up menus [11]. As well as Crampton describes taxonomy of interactive functions in geo-visualization and argues that a highly interactive map provides many of theses functions, whereas a non-interactive map (e.g. a scanned raster map) does not offer any interaction possibilities [3]. Interactivity is mostly used to compensate for the small displays and not for enhancing the user experience. Thus while small display interface design processes, consideration of user aspect is indispensable. Reichenbacher expressed graphical means to put a visual emphasis or focus on several features are [16]:

- highlighting the object using a signal color, e.g. pink or yellow (color)
- emphasizing the outline of the object
- enhancing the LoD(Level of Detail) of the object against that of other objects
- animating the object (blinking, shaking, rotating, increasing/decreasing size)
- clicking on a graphics object you are able to drill-down to more detailed information of that object [6].

Whereas some projects there are few studies which dealt with the map displays on mobile devices. Such Reichenbacher has studied the process of adaptive and dynamic generation of map visualization for mobile users [16]. Besides, Jern plays a major role in a dynamic user interface enabling the user to take a more active role in the process of visualizing and investigating data [6]. Graphics and icons can help support the function of the table of contents. In addition to the many new tools to highlight their functionality, they can be even more effective as guides through and around a product.

3 A Prototype of a MVD/LVD Mobile Visualization

Prior to actually touring through the unknown city, a user may plan the sightseeing tour in a restaurant and request information related to the sights PoI. Consequently, the most important feature is the list of available PoIs and related detailed dynamic information.

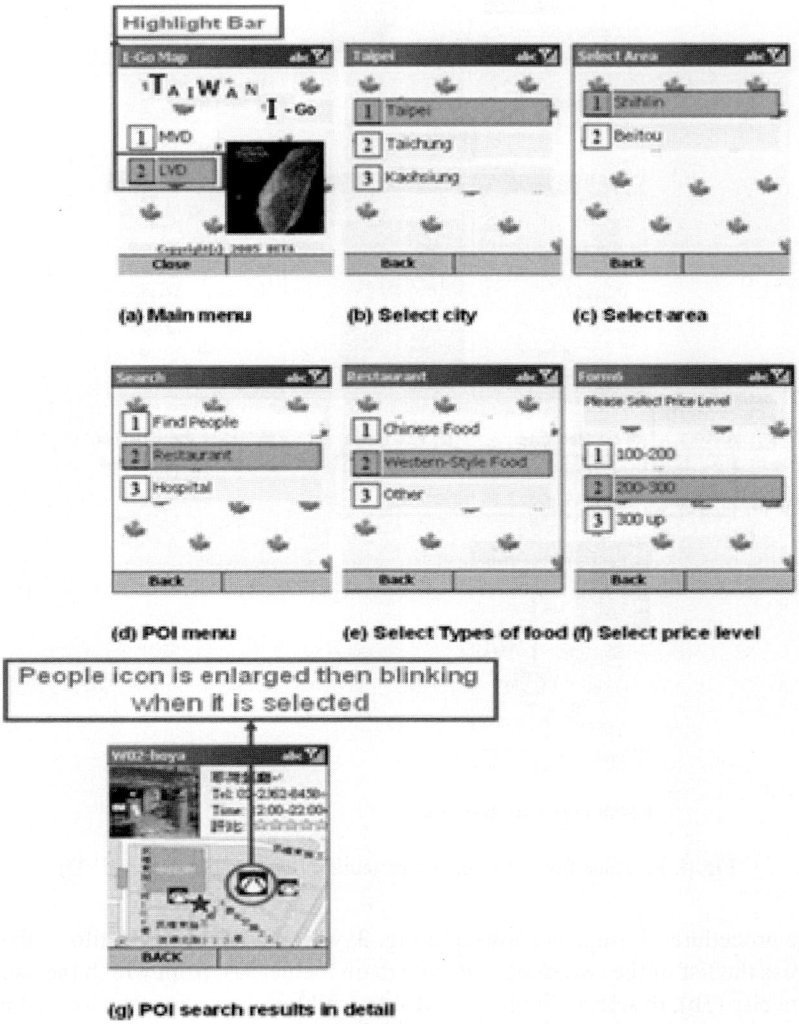

Fig. 3. Interface flow of a generic restaurant finder application (LVD)

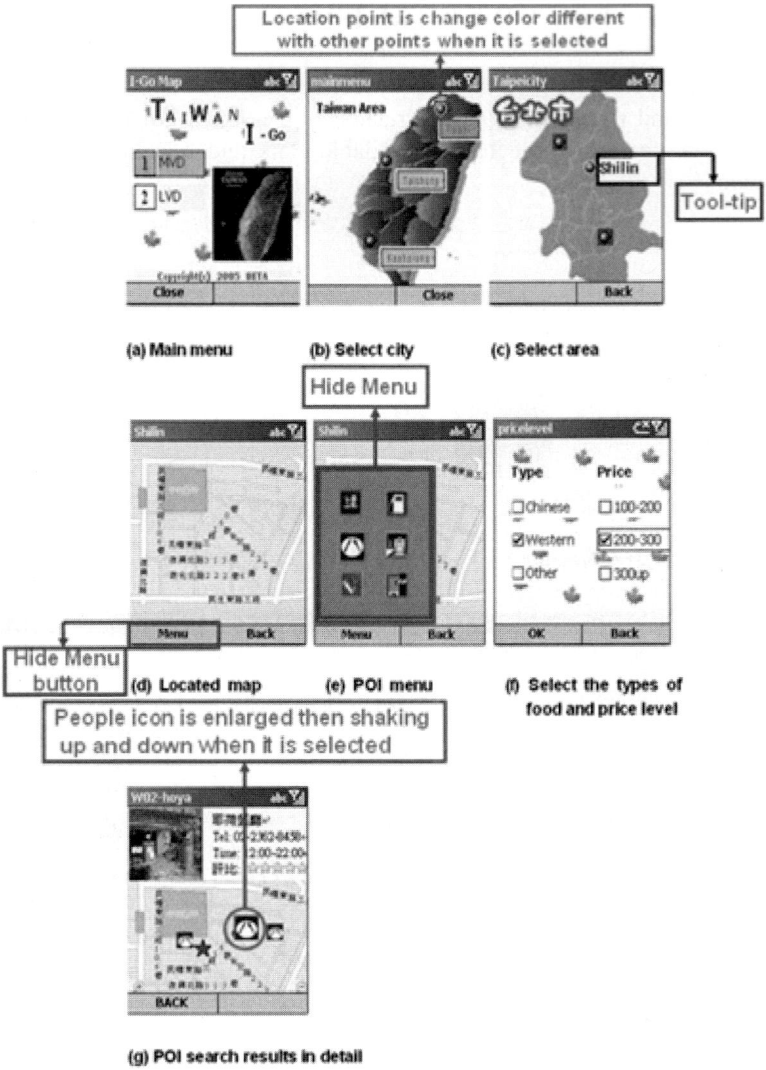

Fig. 4. Interface flow of a generic restaurant finder application (MVD)

The procedure of usage is showed in Fig. 3, which LVD in LBSI allows the users to access the list of the two selections of a main menu (3a), from which the users can select a city (3b), to select which located area (shihlin) (3c), show the located map of shihlin (3d), after clicking menu button, to select the icon of restaurant in Hide Pop-up POI menu (3e), user can choose one of three types of food which is favorite and your preference price level (3f), all the icons of restaurants will be showed in visible area on screen, on the map individually, it is enlarged then shaking up and down when the icon is selected that user will focus on it as well as the usage of a pop-up information box that gives further details about the identity of a selected restaurant(3g).

(1) The LVD provides rapid way to access information by method of query filters which are predefined for different types of attractions and designed for step by step selection as lists for choice (see figure.3).

(2) MVD can provide utilized information by icon of query filters (see figure.4).

4 Design of Experiment

4.1 Subjects

The participants were undergraduates. Hence, we assumed that the variance of different groups were all equal. Each participant was randomly assigned into one of two groups, the control group or experiment group. Table 1 gives a summary of the profile of the subjects.

Table 1. Profile of the subject

Average	22 Years old	
Gender	Male (50%)	Female (50%)
Smart-phone Experience	Yes (50%)	No (50%)
LBS Experience	Yes (0%)	No (100%)

Participants are parted two groups, there are six subjects in each group. Each group based on two guiding tasks of POI directions successfully. These sets of tasks, referred to as task 1 and 2, were randomized across the two environments (see Table 2). Each ordering of the tasks and environments were replicated 6 times, requiring 12 participants in total.

Table 2. Within-subject design of the experiment

Display / Task	LVD	MVD
Task 1	Group 1	Group 2
Task 2	Group 2	Group 1

4.2 Experimental Variables

Two independent variables are considered in the study:

(1) The type through MVD or LVD interfaces of LBS on smart-phone; and (2) Through two different tasks which include service of friend finder and restaurant finder for accessing POI information. The following dependent variables were measured to characterize user efficiency and usability:

1. Operating time: time of operation the tasks of finding their POI (friends or restaurants).
2. Clicks: times of clicks of assigned task performance in all procedure.
3. Error of clicks: error times of clicks of assigned task performance in all procedure (other clicks without correct route which include backward).

4.3 Research Hypothesis

The hypotheses were tested in the SPSS V12.0 software using the repeated measurement General Linear Model (GLM). The significance level was set to 5% and the level of multiple comparisons was independent T-test. Our hypotheses for the experiment were that below:

1. By operating time, which display provided better user performance between LVD and MVD?
2. By clicking times, which display provided better user performance between LVD and MVD?
3. By error of clicking times, which display provided better user performance between LVD and MVD?

4.4 Experimental Procedure and Data Collection

Each user was first asked to familiarize with the interface for approximately 5minutes. No manual was at hand. The experimenter stressed that it was a prototype service and that automatic location of the user's present location was not implemented. The user was asked to accomplish each task while "talking aloud". Since clarifications regarding an opinion were seen as important, only accuracy was considered and completion times were measured. If difficulties occurred, the user was first given a hint by the experimenter and if this information did not suffice, the user was guided through the task before starting with the next.

- Objective: time taken to complete the individual questions, the number of clicks needed to be followed to complete a task (refereed to here as clicks), and fill in questionnaire completed later.
- Subjective: degree of user satisfaction, user comments and suggestions.

5 Results and Discussion

In this chapter, the performance of all participates was evaluated by these three indicates: operating time, Clicks, Error of clicks and post-questionnaire.

5.1 Operating Time, Clicking Time and Error of Clicking Time Aspects

As shown in Table 3,

Table 3. The t-test for average operating time, clicking times and error of clicking time of independent populations (α=0.05)

Dependent Variable	Operating Time		Clicking Time		Error of Clicking Time	
Independent Variable	LVD	MVD	LVD	MVD	LVD	MVD
Mean	42.58	77.05	6.08	8.42	1.17	3.52
Standard Deviation	35.76	35.51	2.234	2.151	2.855	4.981
Sample Size	12	12	12	12	12	12
Degree of Freedom	22		22		22	
T-value	-2.369		-2.606		-1.659	
P-value	0.027*		0.016*		0.111*	

1. The operating time when using LVD is significantly different from that of MVD ($p<.05$). from the sample means for the two groups, one can see the using LVD group spent significantly less training time than MVD group.
2. The click time when using LVD is significantly different from that of MVD ($p<.05$). From the sample means for the two groups, one can see the using LVD group spent significantly less clicking times than MVD group.
3. There is no significant difference in error of clicking times when using LVD versus MVD visualization.

As a result of measurement clearly indicate LVD visualization was more effective than MVD visualization.

5.2 Questionnaires Aspect

Participants are given the questionnaires to response their opinions. These suggestions and comments are summarized below. Although the visualization of MVD (pictorial) was reasonably effective in providing users with overview of some aspect of their LBS functions, also giving them sufficient access to necessary details of events, the MVD was less effective than the visualization of LVD. Majority of the users commented that if there were pop-up legends it would be acknowledge more helpful. Users are asked about content of display; some users suggested that more extra information should be increase about PoI which shows information of restaurant as possible as in detail.

Acknowledgements. The authors would like to thanks the financial supporting from National Science Council (NSC 94-2622-E-327-002-CC3) and OleMap Inc. in TAIWAN.

References

1. CANALYS, 2005. Changing times in the smart mobile device market. Canalys website, company press release, 29th September 2005.
2. Colbert, M. (2002). A Diary Study of Rendezvousing: Group Size, Time Pressure and Connectivity. Mobile HCI, Springer-Verlag.

3. Crampton, J. W. (2002): Interactivity types in geographic visualization. Cartography and Geographic Information Science, 29(2): 85 - 98.
4. Dunlop, M, Ptasinski, P., Morrison, A., McCallum, S., Riseby, C. & Stewart, F. (2004). Design and development of Taeneb City Guide - From Paper Maps and Guidebooks to Electronic Guides. Proc.
5. Fithian, R., Iachello, G., Moghazy, J., Pousman, Z., and Stasko, J. The Design and Evaluation of a Mobile Location-Aware Handheld Event Planner. In Proceedings of Mobile HCI 2003 (Udine, Italy, 8-11 September, 2003). Springer-Verlag, Berlin, 2003,145-160.
6. Jern M (2000). Collaborative Visual Data Navigation on the Web. Invited Keynote Lecture to INFVIZ 2000, IEEE International Conference on Information Visualization, London, IEEE Computer Science Press
7. Koeppel, I. (2000): What are Location Services? - From a GIS Perspective, Sun Microsystems. 2001.
8. Kölmel, B. and Wirsing, M. (2002): Nutzererwartungen an Location Based Servcies - Ergebnisse einer empirischen Analyse, in A. Zipf and J. Strobl (Eds.),
9. Kraak, M. J. (2001) Settings and needs for web cartography. In Web cartography: developments and prospects, edited by Kraak, M. J. and Brown, A., (Taylor & Francis: London) Chapter 1, pp 1-7
10. Levijoki, S. (2000). Privacy vs Location Awareness, Department of Computer Science, Helsinki University of Technology. 2002.
11. Marcus,1992: A. Marcus. Graphic Design for Electronic Documents and User Interfaces. ACM Press, New York, 1992.
12. NTT Docomo (2003) Subscriber growth. NTT Docomo, accessed June 1, 2003, http://www.nttdocomo.com
13. OGC (2003): OpenGIS Location Services (OpenLS): Core Services, OGC 03-006r1, Open GIS Consortium.
14. Preece, J., 1995. Human-computer Interaction, Wokingham, England: Addison- Wesley. Co.
15. Reed .C (2001). Are mobile wireless location -based services hype or reality? Business Geographics http://www.geoplace.com/bg/ 2001/0201/0201mob.asp
16. Reichenbacher, T.: Mobile Cartography – Adaptive Visualization of Geographic Information on Mobile Devices. Dissertation submitted at the Institute of Photogrammetry und Cartography, Technical University, Munich, 2004.
17. Spiekermann, S. (2004), Location-Based Services, Morgan Kaufmann, chapter 1, pp. 9–26.
18. Tamminen, S., Oulasvirta, et.al.: Understanding mobile contexts. Proceedings of Mobile HCI 2003, Udine, Italy. Springer-Verlag, Berlin (2003) 17-31.

Augmented Ambient: An Interactive Mobility Scenario

Veronica Teichrieb, Severino Gomes Neto, Thiago Farias, João Marcelo Teixeir, João Paulo Lima, Gabriel Almeida, and Judith Kelner

Virtual Reality and Multimedia Research Group, Computer Science Center, Federal University of Pernambuco
Av. Professor Moraes Rego S/N, Prédio da Positiva, 1º Andar, Cidade Universitária, 50670-901 Recife, Pernambuco, Brazil
{vt, spgn, mouse, jmxnt, jpsml, gfa, jk}@cin.ufpe.br

Abstract. This paper presents the Augmented Ambient project that aims to construct a highly interactive mobility scenario based on augmented reality applications running on heterogeneous multimedia devices. Mobility is made available through ambient networks, which are dynamic computer networks. A case study has been performed about a virtual museum, where users join a service network that includes art pieces visualization, broadcast interview, chat, and remote live auctions. These services are implemented in Desktop, Pocket PC and Symbian OS platforms. Each one has its own limitations related to processing power and content exhibition, which are considered during media exchange. The application development process for each supported platform is detailed in the text that presents also some libraries built to simplify and speed up the development, namely OgreAR, OGRE port for Pocket PC and CIDA, beyond the ambient networks related software infrastructure.

Keywords: augmented reality, ambient networks, mobility, interaction techniques.

1 Introduction

This paper presents the Augmented Ambient (A2) project, that aims to construct a highly interactive mobility scenario based on Augmented Reality (AR) [1] applications running on heterogeneous multimedia devices and made available through dynamic computer networks, named Ambient Networks (AN) [2]. A2 approaches the emerging area of pervasive computing and communications, aimed at providing both platform and paradigm for all the time, everywhere services as a natural outcome of the advances in wireless networks, mobile computing, and interactive user interfaces (UIs). It proposes an architecture for service distribution and validation, and content adaptation which will be used in some classes of devices (cell phones, Personal Digital Assistants (PDAs), and notebooks) to access advanced communication services. It is also proposed a framework to build AR-based services running on mobile devices.

A case study has been performed, where some services are released by creation of dynamic networks as result of incoming users to the virtual museum area network.

C. Stephanidis (Ed.): Universal Access in HCI, Part II, HCII 2007, LNCS 4555, pp. 565–574, 2007.

Offered services are users VoIP intercommunication, access to virtual auctions, visualization of virtual art pieces and live conferences and interviews watching. Therefore, users can meet each other, build networks dynamically to exchange ideas and discuss opinions, participate in auctions and watch live interviews.

Using AR-based applications, visitors may realize art pieces that are not physically in the museum ambient. These pieces have been inserted on fiducial markers that are part of a complex and sophisticated system composed by a Head Mounted Display (HMD), a webcam and a device that can be a notebook, a PDA or a cell phone. In the PDA's and cell phone's case, they will work as a "Virtual Magnifier", displaying virtual content when the user points the camera to the desired marker.

Different media types can be displayed by devices depending only on processing and exhibition power. In this case, beyond images, users can watch videos, listening audio tracks or see virtual objects that "in fact" do not exist in real world.

AN have been proposed in order to allow competition in a context where exists a need for resource sharing, service releasing and cooperation between networks. They represent a new point of view in the network area that aims to enable the creation of a brand new solution to wireless and mobile networks, permitting a good quality, scalable, easy to use, and not expensive communication service provision.

The remainder of this paper is organized as follows. Section 2 presents some related work, including mobile AR systems and AN systems. Section 3 gives an overview of the A2 project. The defined and built AR frameworks are described in Section 4; there have been developed AR applications for the Desktop and Pocket PC platforms. Issues related to the interaction methods and techniques applied are presented in Section 5. Finally, Section 6 highlights the contributions of this work.

2 Related Work

A2 project involves many knowledge areas in an interdisciplinary way. To understand the research, as well as the conception and development of A2, some works were reviewed, like Höllerer and Feiner [3], which provides a detailed introduction to mobile AR technology with in-depth reviews of important topics, such as wearable display, tracking, user interaction, heterogeneous UIs, collaboration, wireless communication and AR challenges. Further subsections detail aspects related to concepts and experiences that compose A2 project.

2.1 Mobile Augmented Reality Systems

A benefit of A2 project is its development of many mobile AR services/applications on a single project. In a similar way, the work of Reitmayr and Schmalstieg [4] should be cited. Concerning A2 services, there are relevant experiences related with them.

Resembling to interview service the most relevant works are Billinghurst et al. [5] (focused in AR teleconferencing) and the Tangible Teleconferencing study [6]. The first one discusses the technology used and the expected advantages achieved. Beyond, it presents the use of ARToolKit in this kind of research, reviewing 3D Live project and exploring the concept of AR remote collaboration. The second one uses some fiducial markers to interact with the application, manipulating the position and orientation of virtual objects and allowing the user a full view of them; it is also analog to the way one interacts on the A2 virtual auction service. The concept used in the application developed by Woods et al. [7], in which the user plays a game locating patterns containing solar system planets, is very similar to the one present in A2 visualization service, as well as the Handheld Augmented Reality Displays work [8].

A2 project relies strongly on AN technology. Due to this, other AR works using this technology were researched, like the study named Face to Face Collaborative AR on Mobile Phones [9], that has developed a peer-to-peer (P2P) communications layer to allow devices to interact and collaborate each other. The mentioned study also works with a port of ARToolKit to Symbian OS [10], as well approached by A2.

2.2 Ambient Networks

AN is a novel networking concept that has its goals validated through technical solutions developed by proof of concept activities [11]. As A2 is one of them, it has some features related to areas (multi-access networks, content adaptation, network composition and policy-based management (PBM) being studied to deliver an integrated and flexible architecture to AN projects.

Internet was designed for wired links and fixed end systems, but the widespread use of mobile devices and the popularity of wireless communications have led to heterogeneous networks with different access solutions (as WLANs (Wireless Local Area Networks), Bluetooth, 2.5G or 3G cellular systems). A2 uses wireless technologies, such as Bluetooth and wireless LANs to increase its services availability.

In order to make a service capable of receiving multiple types of connections, media adaptation is essential permitting multimedia delivery and presentation on mobile devices. A2 client applications are responsible for device and network capabilities detection, informing the application server so it can adapt the media accordingly.

Network composition is a key concept of the AN project, aimed at enabling control-plane inter-working and sharing of control functions among networks. Composition can be thought of as a mechanism for automatic negotiation of roaming and/or Service Level Agreements (SLAs), which today are done manually.

PBM is used to address the problem of complex network infrastructures administration, in an automated way. Policies can be used, for example, to manage and control the access to network resources by high-level abstract levels of rules and decisions. As A2 was developed using the X-PBMAN (Policy-based Management for Ambient Networks) prototype framework [12], it adheres to the P4MI, a P2P Policy Management Infrastructure, an enhanced version of the PBM framework developed by the IETF (Internet Engineering Task Force).

3 System Overview

A2 project conception may be detailed by many aspects, like services, software modules, topology and AN infrastructure. A case study has been performed about a virtual museum, where users make use of AN concepts to join a service network that includes art pieces visualization (pictures, sculptures etc.), broadcast interview, chat between users and remote live auctions. These services are implemented in three platforms: Desktop (notebooks and compact PCs), Pocket PC (PDAs and Smart Phones) and Symbian OS Series 60. Each platform has its own limitations related to size, processing power and content exhibition that are considered during media exchange, improving the service use experience.

To get access to the services, users perform a composition with the museum network. In this process, an initial authentication takes place and then an automatic network configuration occurs. After composition, services may be accessed in a seamless way, as being local. If a required service does not belong to the current network, it will compose with the network that offers the requested service, without notification to the user that must not be concerned with the service location or provider.

In visualization service, exposed trackable markers are recognized and used to recover data that will be rendered at marker's position and orientation. The information about what content will be displayed on each marker and the media object itself may be acquired through requests by the service protocol at startup or at the right moment of markers' detection, at runtime. When a device with a lower processing and/or exhibition power asks for a virtual object, this will be transmitted with some changes, such as fewer polygons, fewer files to transmit, and lower resolution textures.

Interview service uses fiducial markers, as well, to show up the 3D model of the interviewer. The actor's image is based on video channels that are interpolated by an image server using the markers' orientation to establish the correct mix between video flows acquired by cameras surrounding the actor. Due to the huge amount of processing involved in audio and video handling, only the Desktop platform implements completely this service (remaining ones have only audio transmission implemented).

Chat service allows users from distinct museum areas to communicate through voice messages. Voice interaction was chosen in order to override the usual text based interaction, which is harder to use with smaller devices and rather impossible in the desktop version, since the user can not use a keyboard and will be wearing data gloves and a HMD. The choice of voice codecs that control media exchange differs among platforms according to their processing power. The negotiation to choose the appropriate codec is under charge of the chosen protocol, the H323, that holds an open implementation ported to the Pocket PC platform. In virtual auction service users may place a bid and offer a higher price to an object, and manipulate objects through a tangible interface build upon a cube of markers, using an AR-based interface. This cube may be used to scale and inspect the virtual object chosen by the user. The suggested interface for the auction service is easy to handle and allows more immersive interaction to users in all platforms. The application development process for each supported platform in the A2 project is detailed in Section 4.

3.1 Hardware and Software Setup

In A2's case study, some hardware items were specified in order to arrange the test environment. A HP iPAQ H5500 PDA, a Nokia 6600 cell phone and a miniaturized board (ADL855PC) running a multimedia dedicated operating system were used as client platforms, all of them having an integrated camera, due to the AR interface. As support equipment and backend infrastructure, PCs were used to process the services and act as media servers.

The topology of A2 is composed by a policy server for the museum network, one more for the auction network, an auction's application server, and a visual applications server. This network was interconnected using gigabit Ethernet (IEEE 802.3z), required for large amounts of data generated by the cameras, which will be composed in a central server in order to redistribute an optimized data flow to the clients.

The network infrastructure of A2 was built using the X-PBMAN [13]. Its general architecture is focused on the role and implementation of the Ambient Control Space (ACS). The ACS may present three types of implementations in PBMAN: PDN (Policy Decision Network) ACS, User ACS and PEP (Policy Enforcement Point) ACS.

The better way to understand the infrastructure of A2 is following data path of an offered service, as seen in Fig. 1 – the visualization service for the Pocket PC. As the sequence of explanations evolves, each concept presented will be explored.

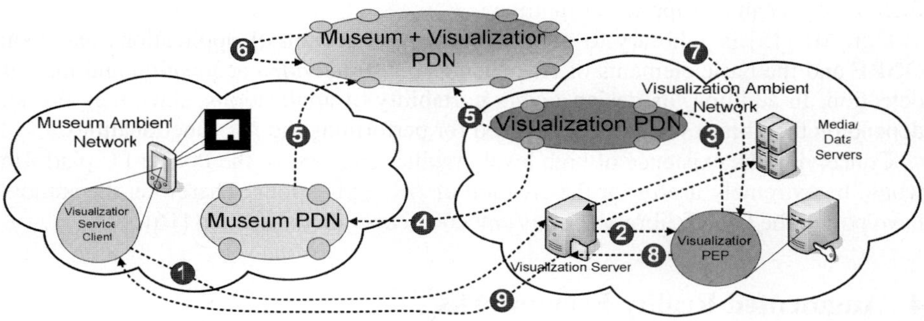

Fig. 1. Data path of the visualization service

The Visualization Service Client tries to access the Visualization Server (1); since the Visualization Server is located at a different network from the one where the user is (e.g. the server is at the Visualization AN and the user at the Museum AN), request is forwarded to the Visualization PEP (2). PEP agents are software and/or hardware services providers, which must enforce right of use, security, and accounting policies.

The Visualization PEP sends a request to the Visualization PDN (3) that detects the user is subscribed to Museum AN, and negotiates a composition with the Museum PDN (4). In case the negotiation is successful, the Visualization PDN and Museum PDN proceed to create a new PDN ring and republish all relevant information (5); the new PDN performs a policy selection process and the Auction service is granted (6).

To finish the process, the PDN sends a response to the Visualization PEP (7) that responds to the Visualization Server for it to resume its pending session with the Visualization Client (8). Finally, the Auction Server sends the adapted information located at the media server, according to the device capacity, about the item that the client wants to display (9). In order to compose all the proposed services, some software modules were developed for A2 and other existing libraries were used, as well. On the client's application side, the libraries used were OGRE, CIDA [14], OgreAR [15] and the OGRE port for Pocket PC [16]. Chat service uses OpenH323 and PWLib libraries to transmit data and develop tasks such as encode and decode voice chunks.

On Pocket PC platform, to construct graphics interfaces and the OGRE port, Klimt and OpenGL ES libraries were used. OpenGL ES was also used on Symbian OS platform. ARToolKit Plus was used to manipulate and detect markers, as well as an ARToolKit port for Symbian OS. At last, X-Peer was used to distribute application data, and also to provide media server and PDN communication. Some aspects about software modules created during this project are better described in the next subsections.

3.2 Support Libraries

Some libraries were developed around the conception and implementation of A2 services. CIDA (Chaotic Interaction Devices Abstraction) is an input devices management platform developed by the authors that provides an abstraction layer between interactive systems and interaction devices [14]. Through this platform, all devices having required features to interact with the application (buttons, axes, degrees of freedom etc.) can be supplied at runtime.

OgreAR [15] is a library to provide an interconnection of applications based on OGRE and the basic elements of AR, such as real-time video acquisition and marker detection. In addition, its design favors portability of applications, since they do not depend on the libraries that are being used for performing the AR functionalities.

Conceiving the existence of high level graphics engines for the Pocket PC platform would be extremely useful for the creation of AR applications. Therefore, the authors have ported the OGRE library for this embedded operational system [16].

4 Augmented Reality Frameworks

This section presents some libraries used to construct the A2 services. They were catalogued to make part of an AR framework, valid for all platforms enclosed by A2, with the purpose of accelerating the development process and make it easier.

4.1 Desktop Platform Development

The Desktop platform has an adequate profile for services which demand more processing and visualization capabilities. However, this platform mobility is a little compromised by the quantity of equipments the user must carry and their weight.

In this profile notebooks or miniaturized computers can be used. Fig. 2 shows the hardware and software setup for this platform. Connected to these devices, an HMD is used for 3D visualization and a camera captures the environment image for the AR interface. As input devices, a data glove is used for gesture based interaction and a tracker for capturing hand movements and passing this data to the application.

In order to manipulate the services, a management interface was created, based on objects modeled using physical simulation, that when handled, enable the corresponding services, send services to the background or finalize them. The PhysX was the physics engine used, chosen among others because it provides both hardware and software implementations. All integration with these objects is done through the data glove and tracker, which are accessed using CIDA. The software modules used on this platform architecture can be clearly seen in Fig. 2.

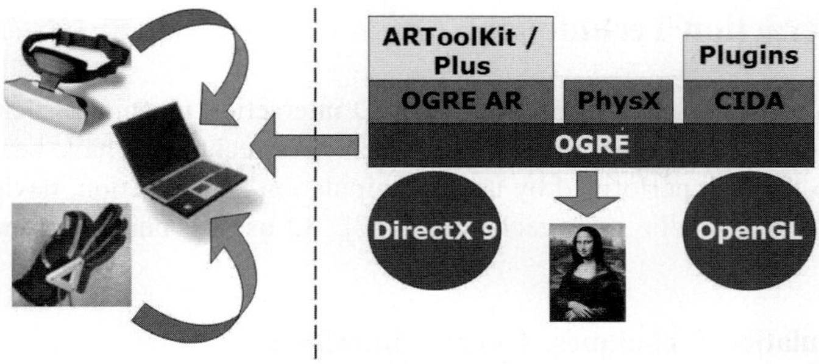

Fig. 2. Desktop platform setup

4.2 Pocket PC Platform Development

Initially, OGRE was ported and used as the underlying graphics infrastructure also on the Pocket PC. However, the low frame rates of the demos, which ranged between 6.561 and 13.390 frames per second (fps), made the use of the engine with AR applications unworkable. The absence of hardware acceleration on the device impacts on the fps reached. Marker tracking is done with ARToolKitPlus. Some screenshots of the A2 services running on Pocket PC are shown in Fig. 3.

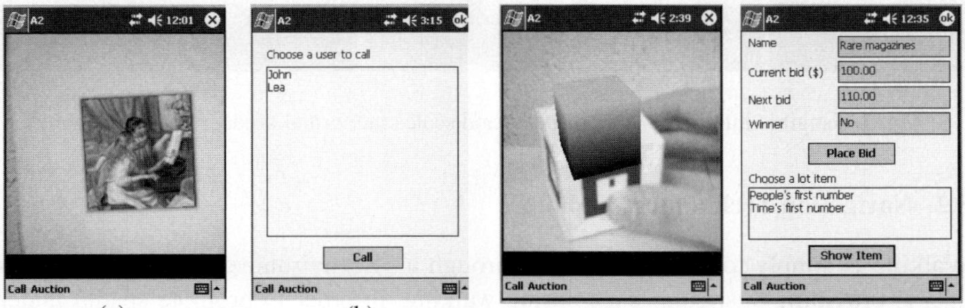

(a) (b) (C) (d)

Fig. 3. A2 services on Pocket PC: a) visualization; b) chat; c and d) auction

Some services are not offered, since the performance is insufficient, especially in the case of video exhibition. Therefore, the interview service is not available, and in the visualization service, only the pieces of art are presented, without additional video information about it (Fig. 3a). In the auction service, the objects related to each lot item are much simpler than the ones used in the Desktop platform (Fig. 3c and Fig. 3d). The chat service is the same provided to desktop users (Fig. 3b). The user interacts using the pen and the touch screen. Due to all these factors, the UI is simple. It is also different from the desktop UI. The communication is done via Wi-Fi.

5 A2 Interaction Techniques

This section presents information about the 3D interaction techniques that have been specifically developed for A2 project . VR interaction techniques have been classified according to the task performed by user: manipulation and selection, navigation, system control and symbolic input techniques [17]. A2 uses techniques from these four categories.

5.1 Manipulation Techniques: Tangible Interfaces

Tangible UIs (TUIs) are the ones where users interact with physical objects, tools, surfaces and spaces to interact with systems, which is a very intuitive and natural way. In AR systems, physical objects are mapped in a one-to-one relation with virtual objects operations. These systems are based on fundamentals of TUIs being complemented with a visualization display. A2 project uses TUIs, as illustrated in Fig. 4.

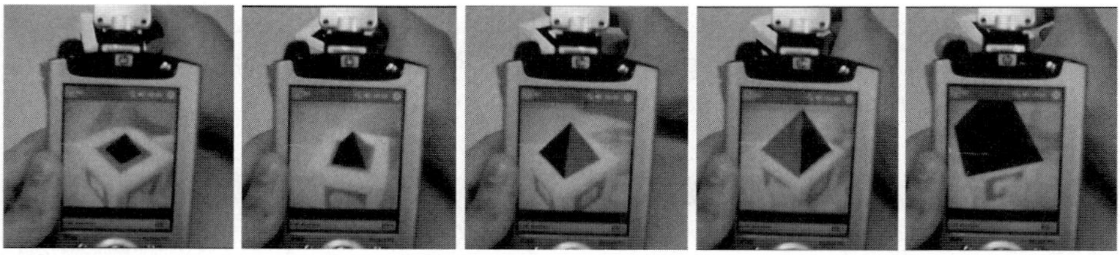

Fig. 4. Tangible interface – user inspects and scales the virtual object rotating the cube

5.2 Navigation Techniques: Walking

Walking is simply to physically walk through a 3D environment. An important aspect is providing vestibular cues during walking, in order to promote spatial understanding (especially in mobile AR systems that rely on user's interaction with the real world along the virtual one). Real walking is not always practical or feasible, since it is limited by space and technology. A2 uses the walking technique since users may utilize the system during movement, as illustrated in Fig. 5a. In A2 the 3D objects may be visualized and manipulated by the user according to its physical location in the virtual museum. A user wearing the Desktop platform is shown, interacting through walking.

5.3 System Control Techniques: Gesture Commands

Spontaneous gesticulation, mimic and symbolic gestures are used as input, implying more learning for the user. Fig. 5b shows a user wearing a data glove and making two postures, namely an open hand and a closed hand posture, respectively.

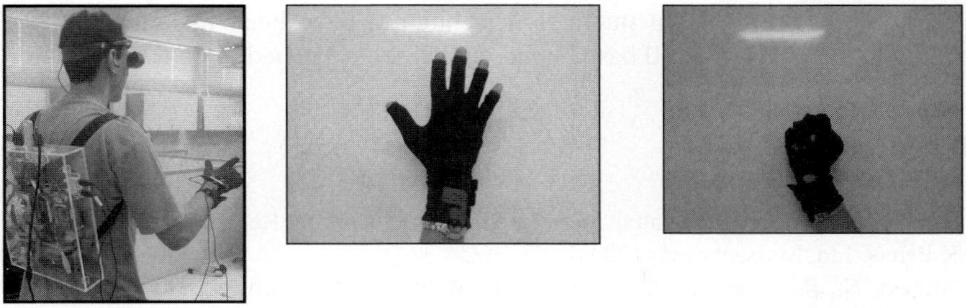

(a) (b)

Fig. 5. Navigation techniques: a) user wearing mobile Desktop platform; b) gesture commands

The gesture commands were included in A2 using a data glove, which can detect many pressure degrees for each finger, and a tracker. The combination of one or more finger sensors activations performs a gesture. User can freely combine one of these actions with a movement of the tracker to perform actions.

5.4 Symbolic Input Techniques

In many situations symbolic input would be useful, such as leaving a brief, precise annotation, entering filenames for open/save operations, adding labels to virtual objects, specifying numeric properties (e.g. thickness, position) and setting parameters in a scientific visualization. These applications could be generalized in scenarios that involve immersive virtual or augmented worlds where a common text/number-input technique would be demanded and where speech input alone would likely not suffice.

These techniques for 3D UIs are necessarily different from traditional ones (e.g. keyboards) because of the inherent differences between 3D (non-desktop) and 2D UIs. Mobile computing (Pocket PC platform onto A2) uses pen-based input in which user writes characters, symbols, or other gestures with a pen/stylus on device.

6 Conclusion

This paper has presented A2, an interdisciplinary project that gathers research areas like AR, HCI and AN to allow more interactive multimedia services using innovative interfaces onto the last mobile network generation, beyond 3G, expected to be available for popular use in five to ten years.

Using three platforms (Desktop, Pocket PC and Symbian OS) that represent the different levels of mobility and processing limitations, it prooves that content adaptation and the others AN concepts have worked fine on top of the designed architecture.

Frameworks were assembled, with several parts implemented by the authors, to make the interface, the interaction model and the services intercommunication with AN. In this case study, the described topology has been used to test and prove the concepts cited in this paper. As expected, the Symbian OS platform requires some workarounds, since the device used has lower memory capacity and the system itself is more complex to be developed and tested. Some libraries have been developed in order to make A2 work properly, beyond the AN related software infrastructure.

Finally, some well known interaction techniques have been implemented in A2 according to the platform used based upon guidelines suggested by in the literature.

References

1. Bimber, O., Raskar, R.: Spatial Augmented Reality: Merging Real and Virtual Worlds. A K Peters, Ltd. Massachusetts (2005)
2. Niebert, N., Schieder, A., Abramowicz, H., Malmgren, G., Sachs, J., Horn, U., Prehofer, C., Karl, H.: Ambient Networks: An Architecture for Communication Networks Beyond 3G. In: IEEE Wireless Communications, pp. 14–22. IEEE Press, New York (2004)
3. Höllerer, T., Feiner, S.: Mobile Augmented Reality. In: Karimi, H., Hammad, A. (eds.). Telegeoinformatics: Location-Based Computing and Services. Taylor and Francis Books Ltd. London (2004)
4. Reitmayr, G., Schmalstieg, D.: Data Management Strategies for Mobile Augmented Reality. The International Workshop on Software Technology for AR Systems (2003)
5. Billinghurst, M., Cheok, A., Prince, S., Kato, H.: Real World Teleconferencing. Computer Graphics and Applications. IEEE 22(6), 11–13 (2002)
6. Hauber, J., Billinghurst, M., Regenbrecht, H.: Tangible Teleconferencing. In: Masoodian, M., Jones, S., Rogers, B. (eds.) APCHI 2004. LNCS, vol. 3101, Springer, Heidelberg (2004)
7. Woods, E., Billinghurst, M., Looser, J., Aldridge, G., Brown, D., Garrie, B., Nelles, C.: Augmenting the Science Centre and Museum Experience. In: International conference on Computer graphics and interactive techniques in Australasia and SouthEast Asia, pp. 230–236. ACM Press, New York (2004)
8. Wagner, D., Schmalstieg, D.: Handheld Augmented Reality Displays, IEEE VR Workshop on Emerging Display Technologies, pp. 35–36 (2006)
9. Henrysson, A., Billinghurst, M., Ollila, M.: Face to Face Collaborative AR on Mobile Phones. IEEE / ACM International Symposium on Mixed and Augmented Reality (2005)
10. Henrysson, A., Ollila, M.: UMAR – Ubiquitous Mobile Augmented Reality. International Conference on Mobile and Ubiquitous Multimedia, pp. 41–45 (2004)
11. WWI Ambient Networks. Available: Ambient Network site. (visited on February, 2007) http://www.ambient-networks.org/
12. Kamienski, C., Sadok, D., Fidalgo, J.F., Lima, J., Ohlman, B.: On the Use of Peer-to-Peer Architectures for the Management of Highly Dynamic Environments. Annual IEEE International Conference on Pervasive Computing and Communications Workshops (2006)
13. Kamienski, C., Fidalgo, J.F., Sadok, D., Lima, J., Pereira, L., PBMAN,: A Policy-based Management Framework for Ambient Networks, IEEE International Workshop on Policies for Distributed Systems and Networks, pp. 76–79 (2006)
14. Farias, T., Teixeira, J.M., Rodrigues, C.E., Pessoa, S., Costa, N., Teichrieb, V., Kelner, J., CIDA,: an interaction devices management platform. Symposium on Virtual Reality. SBC, Porto Alegre, pp. 271–284 (2006)
15. Farias, T., Lima, J.P.T., Teichrieb, V., Kelner, J.: OgreAR: construction of augmented reality applications using high-level libraries. Technical Report, Avaiable: grvm/en/pdfs/RelatoriosTecnicos/2007/TR_1-200702_OgreAR.pdf (2007), http://www.gprt.ufpe.br/
16. Lima, J.P., Farias, T., Teichrieb, V., Kelner, J.: Port of the OGRE 3D Engine to the Pocket PC Platform, Symposium on Virtual Reality. SBC, Porto Alegre, pp. 65–76 (2006)
17. Bowman, D.A., Kruijff, E., LaViola, J.J., Poupyrev, I.: 3D User Interfaces: Theory and Practice. Addison Wesley Longman Publishing Co., Inc, Redwood City (2004)

A New Approach for Pedestrian Navigation for Mobility Impaired Users Based on Multimodal Annotation of Geographical Data

Thorsten Völkel[1] and Gerhard Weber[2]

[1] Mobile Communication and Service GmbH, Lise-Meitner-Str. 2,
24937 Flensburg, Germany
t.voelkel@hci-research.de

[2] Technical University of Dresden, Mommsenstr. 13, 01062 Dresden, Germany
g.weber@hci-research.de

Abstract. Although much effort is spent in developing navigation systems for pedestrians, many users with special needs are mostly excluded due to a lack of appropriate geographical data such as landmarks, waypoints, or obstacles. Such data is necessary for computing suitable routes which might differ from being the shortest or fastest one. In this paper, the concept of multimodal annotation of geographical data for personalized navigation is described. Direct input by the user is combined with data derived from the observation of the user's LOM-Modality (Location, Orientation, and Movement) to annotate geographical data. Based on this data and data derived from other users of the same user group, suitable routes even in unknown territory can be calculated.

Keywords: multimodal annotation, pedestrian navigation, mobility impairment.

1 Introduction

Carrying out an independent and autonomous life seems usual for most people around us. However, many disabled and elderly people face immense problems in overcoming difficulties imposed by our common environment. For example, for people restricted in their mobility due to impairment, a task such as covering a specific distance for buying daily life products may become a heavy burden. In this context, the navigation problem is divided into two parts, namely, micro-navigation and macro-navigation. Distances up to 10 meters are covered within micro-navigation which includes the avoidance of nearby hazards and obstacles whereas all distances above are covered within macro-navigation. The navigation to a remote destination which is not perceivable by the traveller is thus a task including both micro-navigation and macro-navigation.

Travel aids and assistive technologies have been developed to guide elderly and visually impaired people in unknown environments. For example, the MOBIC travel aid [19] is based on geographical information systems (GIS) and the Global Positioning System (GPS) for guidance for distances greater than 50 meters which has

C. Stephanidis (Ed.): Universal Access in HCI, Part II, HCII 2007, LNCS 4555, pp. 575–584, 2007.

been defined as the starting distance for macro-navigation at the time of system development. The difference to the distances used within the introduction for macro-navigation is due to a higher accuracy of state-of-the-art GPS systems.

MOBIC also provides a component for pre-journey planning, on which the later navigation relies. The MOBIC system proved successful for distances over 50 meters; however, there is a gap between the immediate environment of the traveller which can be sensed by other travel aids such as the long cane and the provided support for long distances. Approaches to close this gap, which are also used for indoor navigation, incorporate beacons which provide additional information about the environment. Although promising results have been reported [16], such systems require immense investments regarding necessary infrastructure and are therefore only available at special places.

Using current GPS systems, promising results have been reported to support navigation for instance for visually impaired people [13]. However, one of the most important problems – as was also reported for the MOBIC system – is the acquisition of specific data including obstacles, specific waypoints, and landmarks [5, 14]. The additional information is necessary to adaptively calculate the best route for people with special needs and provide accurate route descriptions. Although the direct and shortest route might seem the best choice for people without impairments, for instance blind people try to avoid crowded cross-ways. Consequently, a route avoiding such cross-ways – though it might be of longer distance – becomes more suitable. A recently developed solution [11] uses machine learning methods for route planning and takes additional information into account to fit the requirements of disabled travellers. User specific information such as the type of handicap is derived from a user model and used within a fuzzy decision system where an appropriate route is calculated using a modified version of the A*-Algorithm. Although additional data is used for the calculation of appropriate routes, the problem of the acquisition of specific geographical data remains an untreated problem.

The paper is structured as follows. An extensive overview of assistive technologies for navigational support for mobility impaired and in particular visually impaired travellers is given in section 2. The requirements of mobility impaired travellers regarding pedestrian wayfinding are presented in section 3 together with a discussion of standard route calculation algorithms and their adaptation to the specific needs of the intended user group as discussed in the following. In section 4, the concept of multimodal annotation of geographical data is introduced which is used to acquire necessary data for the calculation of optimal routes. Finally, a conclusion is given in section 5.

2 Travel Aids for Navigational Support

The navigation and wayfinding problem for mobility impaired and particularly visually impaired people has been tackled by many research projects and commercial product developments. Most systems have been developed to solve one specific part of the wayfinding problem, namely either micro-navigation or macro-navigation. Electronic travel aids can thus be classified in the following schema:

- primary vs. complementary travel aids,
- support for micro-navigation and / or macro-navigation,
- dependencies upon environmental installations.

Considering the first classification, primary travel aids can be used on their own. Consequently, primary travel aids must offer support for micro-navigation for travellers who are not able to sense their direct environment directly. For instance, blind travellers need a travel aid such as a long cane or a guide dog to avoid nearby obstacles and hazards. Long canes and guide dogs are thus primary travel aids; the Ultrasonic Cane [9] is an example for a primary electronic travel aid respectively.

Complementary electronic travel aids normally support the part of the navigational task related to reaching a remote destination beyond the immediate perceivable environment (macro-navigation). Examples for complementary travel aids include GPS-based systems such as the MoBIC travel aid [19], Trekker [10], and Drishti [15]. Other complementary electronic travel aids which rely upon environmental installations include Talking Signs [4] which is discussed in detail below, and Talking Braille [16], being mainly a solution for the problem of 'where am I?' by providing environmental information accessible within short distances from RFID beacons.

The MoBIC travel aid and Trekker are complementary travel aids which do not rely upon environmental installations. The MoBIC travel aid is based on a geographical information system (GIS) and the Global Positioning System (GPS). It is intended to increase the mobility of blind and elderly travellers. The MoBIC travel aid is mainly used for macro-navigation, thus it can be classified as complementary to primary travel aids including the long cane or guide dog which are used to avoid obstacles and hazards within micro-navigation distances. The MoBIC travel aid consists of two components, namely the MoBIC Pre-Journey System (MoPS) and the MoBIC Outdoor System (MoODS). The MoPS allows travellers to plan their routes and to access information about the environment using a standard PC. The system uses different digital maps which have to be enriched by additional information bein particularly important for blind and elderly travellers such as the type of surface underfoot, or entrances usable by wheelchairs. During route planning, user preferences such as choosing the safest route instead of simply following the shortest path where incorporated into the route calculation.

The pre-planned route is used by the MoODS to assist the traveller during the navigational task. The system provides information and feedback to the traveller whenever a change in direction is needed or when the traveller explicitly asks for it. Field trials revealed promising results for elderly and blind travellers. Main drawbacks of the system include the exclusive support for great distances above 50 meters and the lack of additional specific geographical data for optimal route calculation. Consequently, only pre-planned routes could be used without the possibility for a dynamic adoption to changing parameters.

Trekker is a commercially available complementary system developed by the New Zealand based company Humanware. Trekker offers GPS based navigation support for blind travellers based on map data and personal points of interest stored on a PDA. This data can be updated by using internet based resources, for example, points of interest of other users can be imported and used. Additionally, Trekker offers an offline mode for travellers to explore routes in advance comparable with the functionality of the MoPS. Although Trekker is one of the most sophisticated systems on the market, it does not support an adaptation of the underlying geographical data by the user. Consequently, the functionality regarding the calculation of optimal routes is restricted.

Examples for systems relying upon environmental installations include Talking Signs and Talking Braille. The Talking Signs system relies upon remote infrared signage deployed at important locations or public transportation means. The traveller uses a receiver which must be pointed towards the direction of the signage to access the specific information. The information is then presented using synthetic speech. Consequently, the traveller receives information about location itself and the direction where the place is located.

The Talking Braille system also conveys information about specific locations by using a receiver and synthetic speech. However, Talking Braille uses RF signals to transmit the information which does not permit to obtain the direction of the specific location. The main drawback of both systems, although they offer many benefits to make cities more accessible, is the need to deploy beacons within the environment which is additionally very cost intensive. A usage of the system in environments without preliminary installations is also not possible.

To sum up, regarding current electronic travel aids, the main problem is lack of appropriate geographical data to fit the requirements of disabled people. Most systems still rely upon inappropriate map data; an acquisition of additional geographical data or related annotations is not possible. Consequently, a methodology for the acquisition of such data is needed.

3 Pedestrian Navigation for Mobility Impaired People

Mobility impaired people form a very heterogeneous user group with a broad range of different requirements concerning pedestrian navigation and wayfinding. A definition of the term "mobility impairment" in a way that fits in the context of the discussion is needed to narrow the user group. In most cases, mobility impairment is defined as a motion impairment limiting the movement of parts of the body [21]. This definition must be broadened to include the intended user groups. We thus will rely upon the following practical definition for mobility impairments for the following discussion:

> *Mobility impairments include all functional limitations which affect the ability of a person to reach a remote destination independently. A physical, cognitive, or sensory impairment or a combination of them may lead to mobility impairment.*

The above definition allows a broader context regarding the term of 'mobility impairment'. Although wheelchair bound people are the most prominent group of mobility impaired users, our definition allows for inclusion of other users such as blind people who are limited in their mobility by the inability to sense their environment visually. However, part of the mobility impairment of blind people can be compensated by the use of specific travel aids such as the white cane or a guide dog. Additionally, many elderly people have problems when navigating in an unknown environment due to a slight loss of sight or cognitive disabilities such as dementia [1]. These people are hence mobility impaired and can benefit significantly when travel aids offering appropriate navigational instructions in a suitable presentation form are available [6].

Pedestrian navigation in particular concerning mobility impaired travellers imposes additional requirements upon navigation systems compared to car navigation. Car navigation mostly relies upon a network of well-known streets whereas pedestrian navigation is more complex due to an increased network size as pedestrians are able to use paths that are not accessible for cars. Assuming that the available map data is sufficient, pedestrian navigation is then reduced to the problem of finding a route in a network from one initial point *S* to a destination point *D* with minimum cost. This problem has been treated extensively within the past decades and is referred to as the shortest path problem.

The most well-known algorithm for solving the shortest path problem is Dijkstra's algorithm [2] which calculates the shortest path from one starting location to all other locations in the network. This calculation can be accelerated when only the shortest path from one starting point to one destination point is of interest. The corresponding algorithm is called the A*-Algorithm [7] and is the most commonly used shortest path algorithm in geographical networks. As the result of these algorithms is the route with minimal costs, it strongly depends on the weightings associated with the branches of the network graph. The weightings are normally correlated with the distance of the real path section or the time necessary to traverse it. Fig. 1 shows a simple example of a network graph with weights associated with the branches.

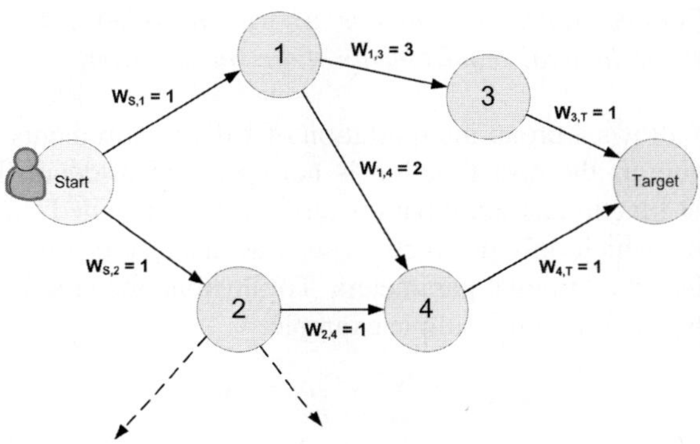

Fig. 1. Example for a simple network graph

The above presented distance metrics provide appropriate results for most pedestrians navigating in unfamiliar environment. However, they do not fit the heterogeneous requirements of mobility impaired travellers, as the assumption that the suitability of a path only depends upon distance or traversing time cannot be adhered. For example, people bound to a wheelchair are not able to surpass stairs. Therefore, a route including a section which can only be passed by traversing stairs must not be the result of the route calculation algorithm. On the other hand, regarding blind travellers, it even depends on the current situation which routes are appropriate. If a blind traveller is accompanied by a guide dog, escalators must be avoided as the guide dog is not able to use them. In this case, stairs or elevators are suitable alternatives. In contrast, if the blind traveller uses only a long cane, escalators are a suitable option.

The complexity of route calculation increases significantly when additional means of public transportation such as busses, railways, or tramways are considered. The inclusion of these transportation means leads to an increased network graph. In this context, the navigation is sometimes referred to as multimodal [3], meaning the availability of different modes of transportation. The usage of public transportation also leads to new constraints regarding the convenience rating of routes. Although a bus stop might be closest with respect to a desired destination, taking the next bus stop might be a better choice for a traveller using a wheelchair if the way backwards goes downhill instead of uphill. Furthermore, big squares and plazas impose additional problems upon navigation systems. As specific fine grained geographical data are normally not available, only poor support for micro-navigation is offered by most navigation systems.

Routes calculated by currently available navigation systems do not provide optimal routes for mobility impaired travellers regarding the above mentioned requirements. Consequently, we need an adapted definition of 'optimal route' before the aspect of missing geographical data is discussed in more detail in the next section. We thus defined the term 'optimal route' in the context of pedestrian navigation for mobility impaired travellers as follows:

> *A route from an initial location S to a destination D is optimal if the value of a specified cost function is minimal compared to the value of other possible routes. The specified cost function expresses a metric depending on the parameters distance, time, convenience as well as other related parameters derived from the individual requirements of the specific user.*

The definition allows a broad interpretation of what requirements must be fulfilled by an optimal route as the cost function is not specified in detail. However, it also constricts the cost function as these parameters must be included. In contrast to most navigation systems which only use metrics such as distance or time, the here defined cost function relies on additional parameters. To illustrate the creation of suitable cost functions, consider the following simple example:

$$W_{Path} = \sum_{i,j} f_{i,j}(w^{u}_{i,j}, w^{c}_{i,j}, d^{\sim}_{i,j})$$

The function W_{Path} calculates the value of the cost for the whole path as the sum of the cost $f_{i,j}$ of each section / branch linking intermediate locations i and j. The cost $f_{i,j}$ of a section depends on a convenience weighting $w^{u}_{i,j}$ derived from the personal profile of the user, on a collaborative convenience rating $w^{c}_{i,j}$ which is accessed remotely and associated with the user group of the traveller, and on a temporal / distance metric $d^{\sim}_{i,j}$ for the section. The last parameter is used to verify calculations which are based on the previous convenience parameters. Although a route might lead to a maximum convenience rating (which would result in a minimum cost value), it might have a very high distance rating, that is the distance of the resulting route is comparably high. Consequently, a very high value of the distance metric might lead to an exclusion of specific routes as it is not reasonable for a traveller to traverse a very long route to reach a nearby destination.

The convenience ratings indicate a measurement of appropriateness for the individual traveller and the associated user group. Consequently, the result of the cost function represents a metric which depends on the correlation of all parameters required by a specific user. The cost function thus varies dependent on the current user's profile and situation.

4 Multimodal Annotation of Geographical Data

To enable navigation systems to calculate optimal routes for mobility impaired travellers, additional geographical data are necessary. In the majority of cases, these specific data are neither part of the underlying maps nor of the geographical database. One of the biggest problems is the acquisition of the geographical data including obstacles, specific waypoints and landmarks as well as their annotation with meta-data, which is particularly important regarding the derivation of parameters for the cost function used to calculate optimal routes.

The here introduced technique of multimodal annotation builds a conceptual framework for both the acquisition and application of specific geographical data and corresponding metadata. The general concept is to annotate and enrich the basic geographical data with additional information associated with predefined user profiles. The concept is based on two integral parts. Firstly, annotation data is derived semi-automatically by analyzing the user's LOM-Modality. The LOM-Modality combines the user's location, orientation and movement into one modality which allows for drawing conclusions using arbitrary combinations of all three spatial dimensions to annotate the underlying geographical data. Secondly, direct input by the user is used to derive geographic information. This approach stands in contrast to classical approaches where spatial information is solely considered as context [17, 18] but offers many benefits as the user's location, orientation, and movement can be comprehended as an integral part of the interaction.

Annotation examples derived via direct input include information about the ground surface, the slope of a path section, specific points of interest (POI), small sound samples, or even images. Considering the last example, especially elderly people benefit substantially when guided along a route using photographs of landmarks compared to the use of standard paper based maps [6]. Automatically derived annotations using the LOM-Modality include specific convenience weights for path sections indicating the suitability for specific user groups. For instance, if a user needs significantly longer than the average for covering a specific distance, the route might therefore not be appropriate. Additionally, specific paths which are used more often than others by different users can be associated with a high convenience rating. However, annotations derived by analyzing the user's LOM-Modality might lead to improper conclusions regarding in particular the weighting of path sections. As the system is not able to determine the reason of the time difference which varies significantly from the average, direct input by the user is needed to decrease the grade of uncertainty. Combining information derived from the LOM-Modality and from direct user input thus leads to a semi-automatic annotation procedure.

Annotated data is related to the user from whom it was derived. However, this data is only suitable within the known environment of the user and does not permit the navigation in unknown terrain. Derived data is therefore transmitted to a central database where the annotations of all users are assembled and associated with specific user group profiles. A traveller navigating in unknown environment is then able to access the data remotely to broaden the data basis for the calculation of an optimal route concerning his specific requirements. The usage of collaboratively derived annotations in combination with personal annotations leads to the concept of stereotype based navigation.

The resulting system consists of a mobile device carried by the traveller and a central server where the collaborative annotation data is stored. The software of the mobile component is build on top of a standard PDA phone such as the generally available T-Mobile MDA [20]. A central server part is responsible for the management of collaboratively acquired annotation data. The overall system architecture is presented in Fig. 2.

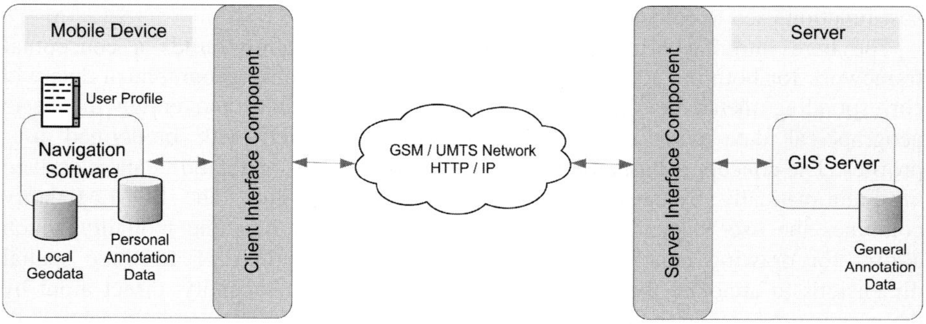

Fig. 2. Overall System Architecture

The presented approach has some important advantages compared to the assembly of proprietary hardware. For example, by using the standard PDA phone, GSM and UMTS channels are available to access the central database remotely without the need to connect to any WLAN hotspots. The central server is thus accessible in all areas where a normal mobile network is available. Additionally, a lower financial investment is necessary which makes such devices affordable for many mobility impaired people. The comparably low price and the fact that the device is not noticed as obtrusive assistive technology might decrease the inhibition threshold for many mobility impaired people regarding its usage.

5 Conclusion and Future Work

In this paper, the concept of multimodal annotation of geographical data is presented which leads to a data based allowing for the calculation of optimal routes for mobility impaired travellers. The annotation data is acquired by using direct input from the user in conjunction with an analysis of the user's LOM-Modality. Additional information is requested from the user in case results of the automatically acquired data are contradicting. The calculated routes are not necessarily optimal in terms of distance or time needed to pass them but rather in terms of a predefined convenience rating derived from a personal user profile of the traveller and a central server component.

Standard GPS receivers are used for the localization of the traveller. Although the GPS systems matured significantly, the accuracy of the localization is in particular in urban environments still unsteady. Concerning pedestrian navigation, this fact might lead to annotations related to false locations and improper navigational instructions. One possible solution is the application of step sensors in conjunction with a digital compass to build a hypothesis about the current location of the traveller as has successfully been shown in [8]. This approach is similar to techniques used in actual car navigation systems which combine the sensor data of a GPS receiver with the velocity of the car and the steering of the driver to calculate the most likely location of the car. However, user tests can also be carried out without the application of additional sensors as the standard Wizard-of-Oz technique can be applied to the evaluation of navigation systems as has been shown recently for an indoor navigation system [12].

As yet, a conceptual model has been build within our ongoing research. We are currently gathering additional user requirements while the system is being implemented. Future research includes the refinement of the system and evaluation phases with users to verify the benefits of the here presented concept of multimodal annotation of geographical data.

References

1. Blackman, T., Mitchell, L., Burton, E., Jenks, M., Parsons, M., Raman, S., Williams, K.: The accessibility of public spaces for people with dementia: a new priority for the 'open city'. Disability and Society 18(3), 357–371 (2003)
2. Dijkstra, E.W.: A note on two problems in connexion with graphs. Numerische Mathematik 1, 269–271 (1959)
3. Fragouli, M., Delis, A.: Navigation and multimodal transportation with easytransport. IEEE Intelligent Systems 20(2), 54–61 (2005)
4. Golledge, R.G., Marston, J.R., Costanzo, C.M.: Assistive devices and services for the disabled: Auditory signage and the accessible city for blind and vision impaired traveler, Technical Report UCB-ITS-PWP-98-18, Department of Geography, University of California (1989)
5. Golledge, R.G., Marston, J.R., Loomis, J.M., Klatzky, R.L.: Stated preferences for components of a personal guidance system for nonvisual navigation. Journal of Visual Impairment and Blindness 98(3), 135–147 (2004)
6. Goodman, J., Gray, P., Khammampad, K., Brewster, S.: Using landmarks to support older people in navigation. In: Brewster, S., Dunlop, M.D. (eds.) Mobile Human-Computer Interaction – MobileHCI 2004. LNCS, vol. 3160, pp. 38–48. Springer, Heidelberg (2004)

7. Hart, P.E., Nilsson, N.J., Raphael, B.: A formal basis for the heuristic determination of minimum cost paths. IEEE Transactions of Systems Science and Cybernetics 4, 100–107 (1968)
8. Hosokawa, Y., Takahashi, N., Taga, H.: A system architecture for seamless navigation. In: Proceedings of the 24th International Conference on Distributed Computing Systems Workshops - W7: EC (ICDCSW'04), Washington, DC, USA, pp. 489–504. IEEE Computer Society Press, Los Alamitos (2004)
9. Hoyle, B., Fowler, J., Waters, D., Withington, D.: Development of the electronic guide cane for enhanced primary mobility for the vision impaired. In: Online Proceedings of the Euro-Assist-CVHI 2004 Conference and Workshop on Assistive Technologies for Vision and Hearing Impairment (2004)
10. Humanware Trekker 3.0 GPS orientation system. Retrieved December 4th (2006), at http://www.humanware.ca/web/en/Trekker3.asp
11. Karimanzira, D., Otto, P., Wernstedt, J.: Application of machine learning methods to route planning and navigation for disabled people. In: MIC'06: Proceedings of the 25th IASTED international conference on Modeling, indentification, and control, pp. 366–371, Anaheim, CA, USA. ACTA Press (2006)
12. Liu, A.L., Hile, H., Kautz, H., Borriello, G., Brown, P.A., Harniss, M., Johnson, K.: Indoor wayfinding: developing a functional interface for individuals with cognitive impairments. In: Assets '06: Proceedings of the 8th international ACM SIGACCESS conference on Computers and accessibility, pp. 95–102. ACM Press, New York (2006)
13. Loomis, J.M., Marston, J.R., Golledge, R.G., Klatzky, R.L.: Personal guidance system for people with visual impairment: A comparison of spatial displays for route guidance. Journal of Visual Impairment and Blindness 99, 219–232 (2005)
14. May, A.J., Ross, T., Bayer, S.H., Tarkiainen, M.J.: Pedestrian navigation aids: information requirements and design implications. Personal Ubiquitous Computing 7(6), 331–338 (2003)
15. Ran, L., Helal, S., Moore, S.: Drishti: An integrated indoor/outdoor blind navigation system and service. In: Proceedings of the Second IEEE International Conference on Pervasive Computing and Communications (PerCom'04), pp. 23–30. IEEE Press, New York (2004)
16. Ross, D.A., Lightman, A.: Talking braille: a wireless ubiquitous computing network for orientation and wayfinding. In: Assets '05: Proceedings of the 7th international ACM SIGACCESS conference on Computers and accessibility, pp. 98–105. ACM Press, New York (2005)
17. Schilit, B., Adams, N., Want, R.: Context-aware computing applications. In: Proceedings of the IEEE Workshop on Mobile Computing Systems and Applications, Santa Cruz, CA, US, pp. 85–90. IEEE Computer Society, Los Alamitos (1994)
18. Schilit, B.N., Theimer, M.M.: Disseminating active map information to mobile hosts. IEEE Network 8(5), 22–32 (1994)
19. Strothotte, T., Fritz, S., Michel, R., Raab, A., Petrie, H., Johnson, V., Reichert, L., Schalt, A.: Development of dialogue systems for a mobility aid for blind people: initial design and usability testing. In: Assets '96: Proceedings of the second annual ACM conference on Assistive technologies, pp. 139–144. ACM Press, New York (1996)
20. T-Mobile MDA PDA phone. Retrieved December, 12, 2006 at http://www.t-mobile.de/shop/handy/0,4855,2963-_5540-0-1-0,00.html
21. University of Illinois Medical Center. Definition of "mobility impairment". Retrieved December, 6th (2006), at http://uimc.discoveryhospital.com/main.php?id=3246.

A Proposal for Distance Information Displaying Method of a Walking Assistive Device for the Blind

Chikamune Wada and Miki Asonuma

Graduate School of life Science and Systems Engineering, Kyushu Institute of Technology
Hibikino 2-4 Wakamatsu-ku, Kitakyushu, Fukuoka, 808-0196, Japan
wada@life.kyutech.ac.jp

Abstract. In this paper, we propose a device that indicates the direction of an obstacle that is encroaching into the path of a visually impaired person who is walking. Our proposed system, which would resemble a pair of eyeglasses, first detects an obstacle and then indicates its direction and distance to the wearer through puff of air to the forehead. This paper describes the preliminary testing for presenting distance information.

Keywords: Blind, Walk, Assistive device, Tactile, Distance.

1 Introduction

When a visually impaired person uses a cane to assist in navigating throughout daily life, some obstacles that protrude into a pathway or are located above the waist go undetected. These include such obstacles as truck rearview mirrors, signboards, and other types of raised barriers. These types of unexpected obstacles present a dangerous hazard to the visually impaired. Numerous devices have been developed in order to solve these problems. However, for one reason or another they are seldom used[1,2]. We believe that one possible reason is that these devices do not precisely indicate the obstacle's direction and distance from the user. We have therefore set out to develop a new system which presents the user with the obstacle's direction relative to the users facial orientation[3].

Figure 1 shows an imaginary illustration of our device. We decided upon an eyeglass appearance so that it would be more aesthetically acceptable to the general public.

In figure 2, both top down and side views can be seen of the device's basic outline and how it would be worn. Figure 2 also offers a brief overview of how to operate the system. Specifically, a puff of air would be presented to the lower left part of the forehead when an object was detected in the lower left vicinity of the wearer. The wearer would then turn his/her head until the device indicated that the obstacle had shifted to a position directly in front.

Since we found it necessary to have the vibrator in constant contact with the skin, this resulted in an unpleasant feeling of vibration, though the vibration was easy to

C. Stephanidis (Ed.): Universal Access in HCI, Part II, HCII 2007, LNCS 4555, pp. 585–594, 2007.

control. In order to overcome this problem, we decided to stimulate the skin of the forehead with air.

Obstacle information requires distance information in addition to information regarding direction. As for a method of displaying distance information in other assistive devices for the visually impaired, a change in vibratory frequency or a different stimulation pattern of the vibratory motor has often been used. However, the above methods are not intuitive, since the user must learn the relationship between the frequency change/stimulation pattern and distance.

Inversely, we hypothesized that if there were a relationship between the kind of stimulation and the sense of distance caused by the stimulation, the user would not need to learn the nature of the relationship, since it would be known intuitively.

Therefore, in this paper, we have examined the relation between air stimulation and the sense of distance resulting from air stimulation.

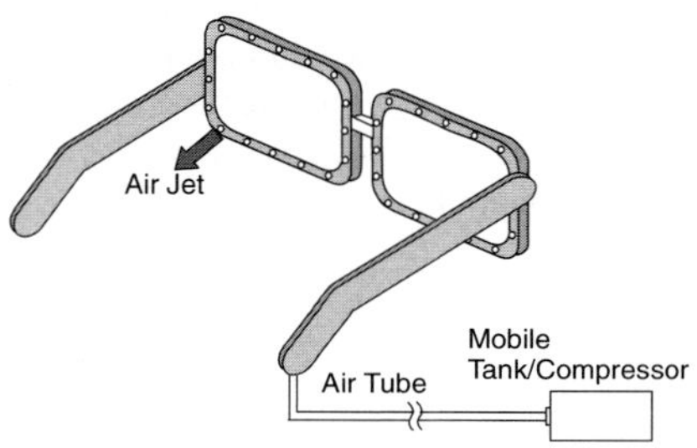

Fig. 1. Imaginary figure of our device

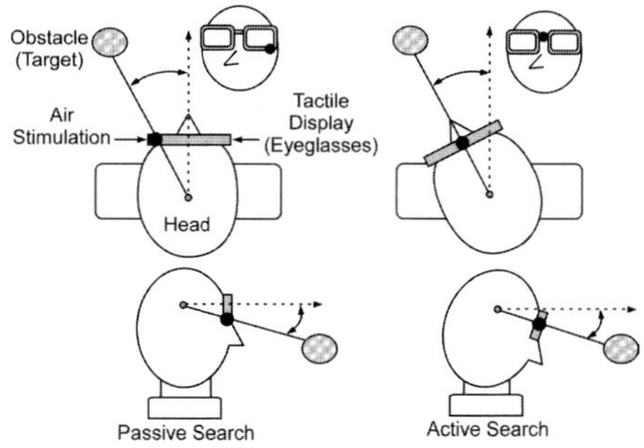

Fig. 2. Display method of our device

2 Appropriate Distance to Avoid Obstacle

If the visually impaired knew there was an obstacle which was 10 m in front of him/her, he/she would have to gather the obstacle information for a long time. Inversely, even if the visually impaired knew the close obstacle, he/she might not be able to avoid it. Then, we hypothesized there is an appropriate distance to be presented for the visual impaired.

In this experiment, two distances were measured: the distance between the obstacle and the non-visually impaired subjects when they avoided the obstacles; the distance between the obstacle and the visually impaired subjects when they avoided the obstacle with the white cane.

Figure 3 and 4 show the experimental procedures for the visually impaired subject and for the non-visually impaired subject, respectively. Two visually impaired subjects and five non-visually impaired subjects took part in this experiment. All subjects were asked to walk and avoid the obstacle. This trial was repeated ten times for all subjects. The trace of walk was recorded by a video camera, and Xf and Xg and Ys were measured from the recorded movie. Xf meant the distance between the subject and the obstacle when the subject passed by it. Xg meant the meant the distance between the subject and the guideline. Ys meant the distance between the subject and the obstacle when the subject started to avoid.

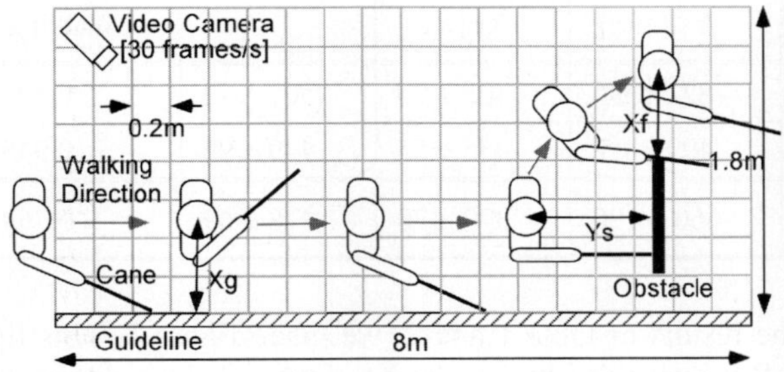

Fig. 3. Procedure of obstacle avoidance experiment for the visually impaired subject

Figure 5 shows two examples of trace in the case of visually impaired subject. Lower trace shows the result of subject A and upper shows the result of subject B. In the case of this figure, walking speeds were 0.52m/s and 1.02m/s. Table 1 shows the average results for two visually subjects. Figure 6 shows the relationship between Ys and walking speed. From this graph, it was found that there was a strong correlation between Ys and walking speed (r>0.8). Then, Ys could be estimated by walking speed (shown by 'v') and the formula for estimation was decided to be Ys(v)=-0.77v+1.25.

Table 2 shows the average results for the non-visually impaired subjects. From this table, non-visually impaired subjects started to avoid the obstacle at the point of about 3.43m far from the obstacle.

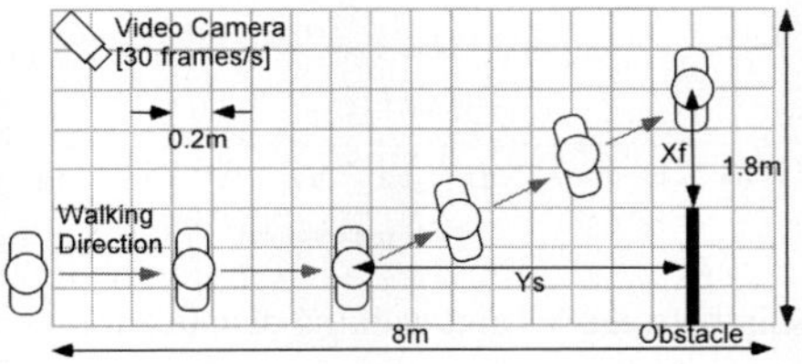

Fig. 4. Experimental procedure of obstacle avoidance for the non-visually impaired subject

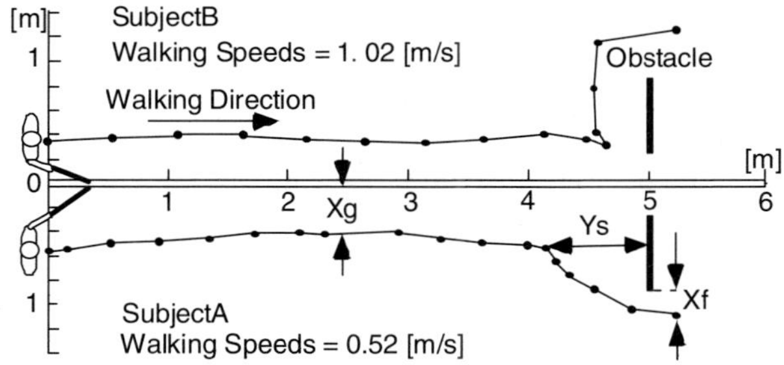

Fig. 5. Example of traces of the visually subjects

Table 1. Average results of Ys, Xf, Xg and walking speed for visually impaired subjects

Subjects	Ys [mm]	Xf [mm]	Xg [mm]	Walking speed [m/s]
A	821 ± 98	305 ± 24	507 ± 72	0.592 ± 0.061
B	499 ± 95	435 ± 55	449 ± 95	0.945 ± 0.152
Average	660 ± 190	370 ± 78	478 ± 69	0.769 ± 0.213

Combining the results of table 1 and 2, we made figure 7. This figure consists of four areas. Area B was decided by Ys and Xf of table 2. Area A was out of other three areas. Area C and D were decided by Ys(v) and area B. The visually impaired subjects did not enter the area D because their white canes hit the obstacle. Non-visually impaired subjects walked on the area B. Then, we concluded the visually impaired had to start avoiding the obstacle when they had entered area C. Therefore, we thought that the visually impaired had to know the obstacle within about 0.5m and 3.5m in front of them.

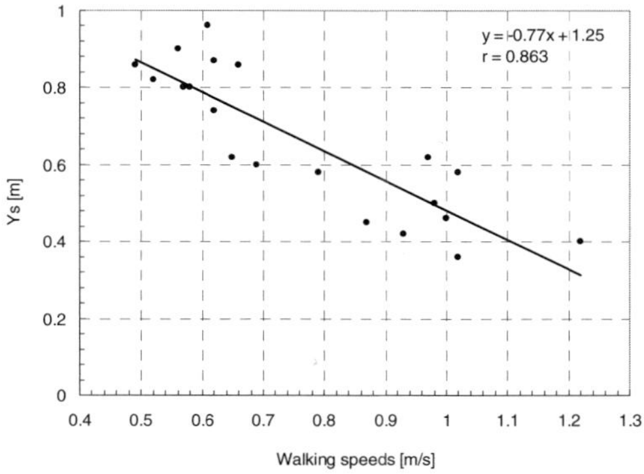

Fig. 6. Relationship between Ys and walking distance for the visually subjects

Table 2. Average results of Ys, Xf, and walking speed for the non-impaired subjects

Subjects	Ys [m]	Xf [m]	Walking Speed [m/s]
C	3.79 ± 0.85	0.298 ± 0.01	1.04 ± 0.16
D	3.31 ± 0.23	0.320 ± 0.10	1.35 ± 0.09
E	4.46 ± 0.37	0.410 ± 0.17	1.33 ± 0.04
F	2.89 ± 0.33	0.512 ± 0.07	1.18 ± 0.10
G	2.72 ± 0.16	0.512 ± 0.04	1.24 ± 0.09
Average	3.43 ± 0.77	0.410 ± 0.11	1.23 ± 0.15

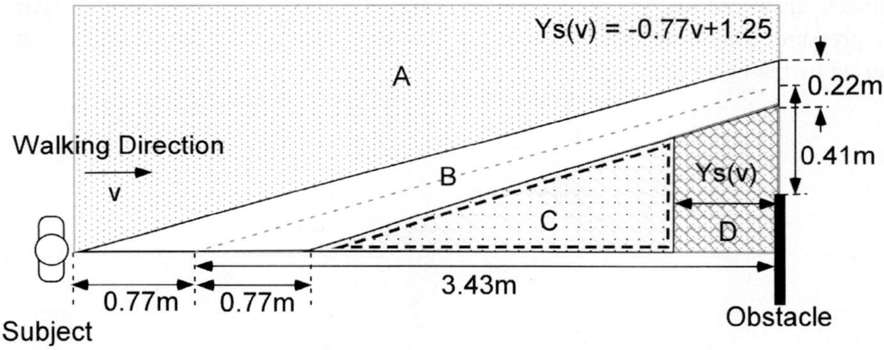

Fig. 7. Concept of obstacle avoidance

3 A Sense of Distance Caused by Air Stimulation

Testing was done to examine the relation between air stimulation pressure and the sense of distance created by the air stimulation (figure 8). First of all, we examined whether or not a subject sensed a distance of an arm's length when the air stimulation was presented. Next, the subject was asked to walk as far as he/she imagined the distance to be after air stimulation of various pressures was presented. This was done in order to investigate the relation between the distance and the strength of stimulation.

3.1 Air Pressure and the Sense of Arm Length

Figure 9 shows a block diagram of our experimental setup. Computer operated solenoid valves controlled the airflow and airflow stimulation was supplied through nylon tubing (outer diameter:1.8 mm, inner diameter:1.0 mm, length:1.5 m). An electrical regulator was used to change air pressure by means of a computer. Twenty kinds of air pressure were presented randomly (0.02 – 0.19MPa). The air duct was located 35mm above the midpoint between the two eyes and placed 10mm in front of the forehead. The duration of air stimulation was between 0.1 to 0.5 sec.

After the subject's forehead was stimulated by a puff of air, using the method of constant stimuli, he/she was asked if they imagined the distance of an arm's length. The five non-visually impaired subjects wore eye masks and headphones to shut out the noise of the air jets. Each subject repeated this experiment 15 times for one intensity of air pressure, resulting in an overall total of 300 trials per subject.

Figure 10 shows the example of result of one subject (subject A). This graph indicates the relationship between air pressure and the rate that subjects imagined the distance of an arm's length (when stimulation time = 0.5s). From this graph, subject A could imagine an arm's length at a probability of 73%, when the air pressure was 0.152MPa. Table 3 shows results for all subjects. In this table, arm length of subject was also shown. Results obtained for all subjects indicated that the rates for which subjects answered that they imagined an arm's length exceeded 70% for the mean of air pressure. Therefore, we hypothesized that the sensation of arm length could be caused by the mean of air pressure.

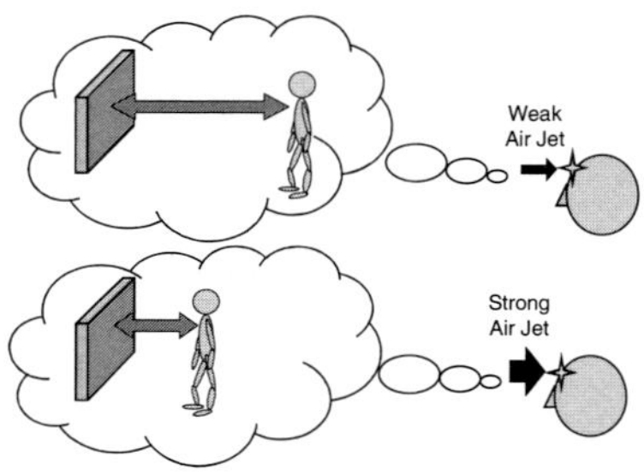

Fig. 8. Sense of distance

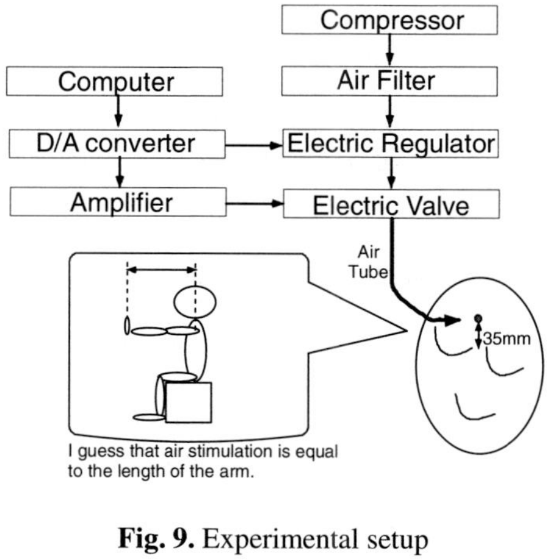

Fig. 9. Experimental setup

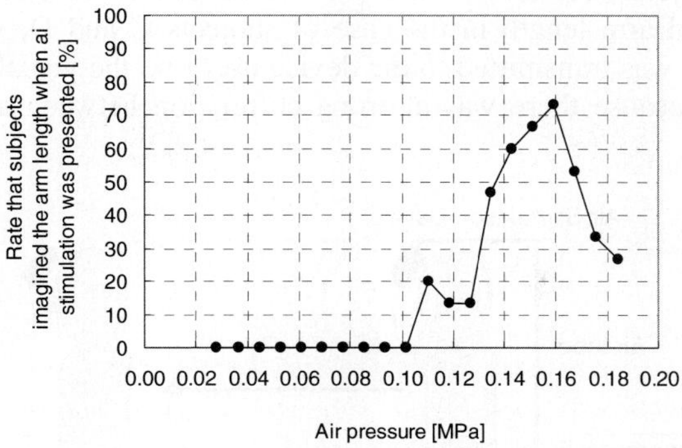

Fig. 10. Relationship between air pressure and the answer rate for subjects who guessed that the air pressure was equal to an arm length. (at stimulation time = 0.5s)

Table 3. Air pressure and probability when the subject imagined his/her arm length and arm length of subject. (stimulation time = 0.5s)

Subject	Air pressure when the subject imagined his/her arm's length [MPa]	Probability [%]	Arm length[m]
A	0.152	73	0.72
B	0.115	86	0.74
C	0.122	73	0.72
D	0.109	86	0.72
E	0.089	100	0.73

3.2 Air Pressure and the Sense of Distance

Figure 11 shows the graphic for this phase of testing. The same air stimulation system as in section 3.1 was used. After a subject's forehead was stimulated by a puff of air, he/she was asked to first imagine the distance length and then to walk as far as the imagined distance. Afterwards, the distance walked by each subject was measured.

Ten kinds of air pressure (0.02 – 0.20MPa) were randomly presented to the subjects. The five non-visually impaired subjects wore eye masks and headphones to shut out the noise of the simulation system. Each subject performed 10 trials for one kind of air pressure.

Figure 12 shows the relationship between walking distance and air pressure of one subject (subject A). Black dots indicate the average values while bars indicate standard deviations. The curve was drawn by using a method of statistical polynomial fit. As the air pressure increased, the walking distance decreased. Specifically, there was a strong correlation (r>0.9) between air pressure and walking distance. In section 3.1, in the case of subject A, the mean of air pressure was 0.152MPa and the arm length was 0.72m. From figure 13, we estimated a walking distance of 0.71m when the air pressure was 0.152MPa. Similarly estimation was done (table 4). Moreover, there was a strong correlation (r>0.9) between air pressure and walking distance for all subjects. Although there was some difference between estimated walking distance and arm length in the case of subjects C and D, we thought that distance information was transmitted to the device user (ex. the visually impaired) by using air pressure because there was a strong correlation between air pressure and walking distance.

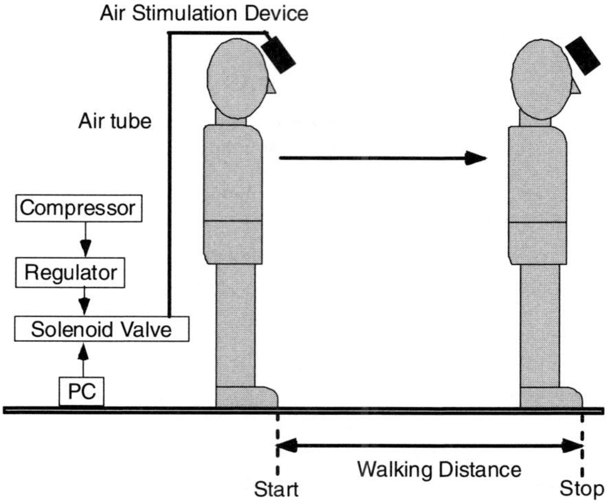

Fig. 11. Experimental setup and procedure

Figure 13 shows the relationship between walking distance and air pressure when the stimulation time was changed for all subjects. The curve was drawn by using a method of statistical polynomial fit. In order to present a feeling of a certain distance (ex. 1.5m), this graph shows that we must use strong air pressure for a short stimulation time (ex. 0.1 s) or weak air pressure for a long stimulation time (ex. 0.5 s). In this manner, the air pressure was found to depend on the stimulation time.

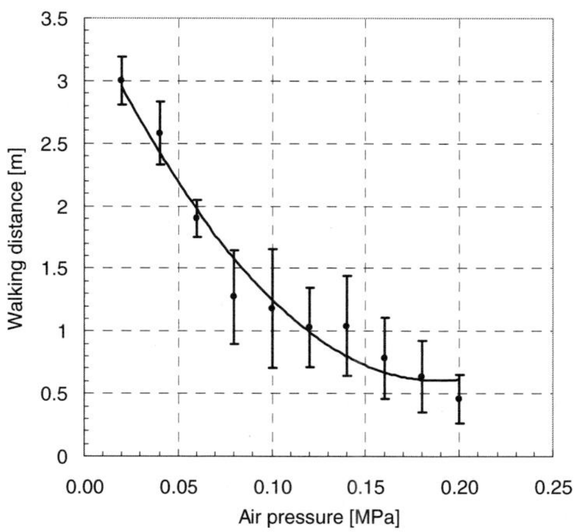

Fig. 12. Relationship between walking distance and air pressure (stimulation time = 0.5s)

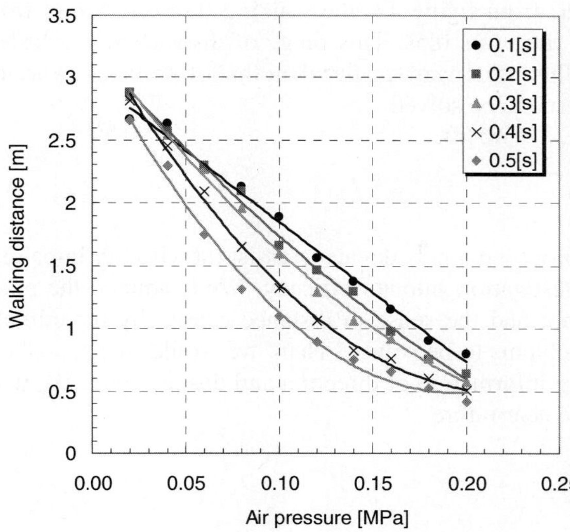

Fig. 13. Relationship between walking distance and air pressure (All subjects)

Table 4. Estimated walking distance and arm length of subject. (stimulation time = 0.5s)

Subject	Estimated walking distance [m]	Arm length[m]
A	0.71	0.72
B	0.77	0.74
C	0.113	0.72
D	0.114	0.72
E	0.90	0.73

Table 5. Statistical polynomial fit and coefficient at each stimulation time

Stimulation time [s]	Statistical polynomial fit [m]	Correlation coefficient
0.1	$Y = 0.091X^2 - 11.225X + 2.970$	0.575
0.2	$Y = 9.639X^2 - 14.493X + 3.090$	0.659
0.3	$Y = 31.688X^2 - 19.917X + 3.285$	0.707
0.4	$Y = 58.797X^2 - 26.007X + 3.363$	0.751
0.5	$Y = 71.155X^2 - 27.734X + 3.190$	0.809

Table 5 shows the approximate formulas for figure 13. The correlation coefficient was found to decrease as the stimulation time was shortened. This was because perception of air stimulation was difficult when air stimulation time was short. In view of the strong correlation ($r>0.8$), the optimal air stimulation time was thought to be 0.5s. Moreover, from figure 13, the walking distance varied from 0.5m to 2.7m when stimulation time was 0.5s. This range of distance was a little bit shorter than that of figure 7. This value was smaller than that of previous experiment. Prolonging this range is the issue to be solved.

4 Conclusion

In this paper we proposed a new device to assist the visually impaired and carried out a preliminary investigation into its efficacy. We examined the relation between air stimulation pressure and the sense of distance caused by the stimulation. However, there are some problems to be solved. Then, we would like to make an experimental setup of presenting information of direction and distance, and evaluate the efficacy of our proposal in the near future.

References

[1] Kay, L., Sonars, A.: With Acoustical Display of Spatial Information, Animal Sonar Systems, Press, New York, pp. 769–813 (1980)
[2] Shoval, S., Ulrich, I., Borenstein, J.: Navbelt and the GuideCane, IEEE Robotics and Automation Magazine, pp. 9–20 (2003)
[3] Asonuma, M., Matsumoto, M., Wada, C.: Study on the use Air Stimulation as the Indicator in an Obstacle Avoidance System for the Visually Impaired, SICE (2005)MA2-14-2(CD-ROM) (2005)

Specification of Information Needs for the Development of a Mobile Communication Platform to Support Mobility of People with Functional Limitations

Marion Wiethoff[1], Sascha M. Sommer[2], Sari Valjakka[3], Karel Van Isacker[4], Dionisis Kehagias[5], and Evangelos Bekiaris[6]

[1] Delft University of Technology, Faculty TPM, Transport Policy and Logistics organisation, Jaffalaan 5, 2628 BX Delft, Tel: +31 15 278 1716, Fax: +31 15 278 2719
m.wiethoff@tudelft.nl

[2] Johanniter-Hospital Radevormwald, Neuropsychology, Germany,
sascha.sommer@johanniter-einrichtungen.de

[3] National Research and Development Centre for Welfare and Health, Finland
Sari.Valjakka@stakes.fi

[4] Information Society Open To ImpairmentS, Athens, Greece
karel@e-isotis.org

[5] Centre for Research and Technology Hellas / Informatics and Telematics Institute, Greece
Dionisis.Kehagias@iti.gr

[6] Centre for Research and Technology Hellas / Hellenic Institute for Transport, Greece
abek@certh.gr

Abstract. Opportunities for people with functional limitations are increasing. ICT provides a number of possibilities to receive care, to travel, to work, to educate oneself, to inform oneself and to meet other people. In this paper, the methodology for defining user requirements for supporting people with functional limitations through ICT (the ASK-It Concept) is presented. The methodology covers various domains. A case example as an illustration of the process is used: a communication platform to support social relations and communities. The methodology is built upon the definition of user groups, the elaboration and implementation of relevant action and activity theory principles, and is successively developed with the content modelling procedure, in order to provide a formal description of user information needs in a computer understandable and interoperable format.

Keywords: Virtual communities, Content requirements, Action theory, Activity Theory, Functional limitations.

1 Introduction

According to the Eurostat statistics, 25.3% of the European Union (15 countries) population are "severely hampered" (9.3%) or "hampered to some extent" (16.0%). More specifically, these figures refer to "hampered in daily activities by any physical or mental health problem, illness or disability" [1]. For these people, it is particularly

C. Stephanidis (Ed.): Universal Access in HCI, Part II, HCII 2007, LNCS 4555, pp. 595–604, 2007.

difficult to participate in the society. Their quality of life would improve substantially if they could participate, and the society could benefit from their contribution. The transdisciplinary project ASK-IT is developing an ambient intelligence system that provides information to people with functional limitations.[1] This addresses one of the main aims of the European Commission: increasing the participation of all members of the society (e-Inclusion). The idea is that people with functional limitations can benefit substantially from information on accessibility of all types of services and infrastructure in our society [2]. For instance, a wheelchair user who has information on accessibility of a café can choose an accessible café to meet people. A visually impaired person who receives timely relevant information on actual arriving times of a tram can decide to take it. Important is that applications presented to the users are personalised, self-configurable, intuitive and context-related. ASK-It aims at supplying useful and timely information about mobility barriers and suitable offerings to overcome them on a mobile phone or a PDA-like device. Users will receive accessibility information tailored to their personal user profile. The information needs for every goal-directed action depend generally on the complex interaction between, on the one hand, the individual (physical abilities, psychophysiological capacities, cognitive resources etc.) and, on the other hand, relevant factors of the environment (objects in a scene, available tools, implicit and explicit context rules etc.). Riva suggested accordingly to focus on relevant user activities when analysing requirements for ambient intelligence environments [3]. The psychological frameworks Action theory and Activity theory are approaches to conceptualize goal-directed human behaviour. Action theory enables the division of complex actions into smaller behavioural units [4]. Activity theory stresses, moreover, the social context of human behaviour [5].

In order to develop these services, the user requirements need first to be established. This paper concerns this first stage: the route from an activity-centred specification of service content requirements to the translation of the identified requirements into a machine-readable format. The methodology for defining user requirements is presented briefly and applied to developing a communication platform to support social relations and communities of people with functional limitations. The methodology is built upon the definition of user groups together with the elaboration and implementation of relevant action and activity theory principles.

2 Theoretical Framework for the Specification of Requirements

The Content Areas and the User Groups

The following areas are defined for which ASK-IT will develop services for the users with functional limitations: "Transportation" to identify detailed transportation-related data content requirements, e.g. what barriers might exist across different transport modes, what effect uncertainties (such as delays), "Tourism and leisure" to identify

[1] ASK-IT: Ambient intelligence system of agents for knowledge based and integrated services for users with functional limitations. Integrated project co-funded by the Information Society Technologies programme of the European Commission. Project number IST 511298; duration 2004 – 2008).

everything related to what a tourist who visits the specific area or city would need to know (e.g. hotels, museums, interesting places, embassies etcetera), and leisure content addresses all sectors that are used in every day's life not only by tourists but by residents also. "Personal support services": finding and booking a (local) personal assistant for travelling or special care. "Work and education": Accessibility to schools and working environments and distance learning and -working. "Social contacts and community building": any content to enable making contacts with other people and with people with similar functional limitations, access to meeting places and access to virtual communities.

The user groups are classified on the basis of *functional* limitations. The ICF codes are applied that take into consideration the interaction between health conditions and contextual factors, and provide an adequate basis for the definition of user groups that has been proven to be appropriate in previous projects [6, 7]. User groups were defined accordingly in two stages: first a main group classification, and second a nested sub group classification of different levels of severity. The one exception is the wheelchair user group which is classified as a separate main user group, because their functional requirements differ considerably from other users with lower limb limitations. The resulting user group classification has the following main groups: (1) lower limb impairment, (2) wheelchair users, (3) upper limb impairment, (4) upper body impairment, (5) physiological impairment, (6) psychological impairment, (7) cognitive impairment, (8) vision impairment, (9) hearing impairment, (10) communication production/receiving impairment.

Implementation of Action Theory and Activity Theory into the Process of User Requirements Definition

Sommer et al. [8] described in detail the methodological approach for defining the user requirements, based on Action theory and Activity theory. The central issue in the methodology is the analysis of various types of goal-directed human behaviour [3] in hierachical-sequential action patterns and being organized by higher levels of action regulation.

Activity Theory [9, 10] considers, in particular, organisational issues and the social cultural environment to be very important. In the theory 'activity' is defined as the 'minimal meaningful context for understanding individual actions' [5]. The activity entails: tool, subject, object, rules, community and division of labour. The object is the entity (or goal) that actors manipulate. The actors interact on the object with the help of artefacts (tools), within a context of roles, and under a set of community rules. This definition of an 'activity' is used in the current project to define the elements that need to be incorporated in our scenarios (see further). For the sake of the present focus on mobile work, the space- time setting is added to define the context of mobile work, i.e. synchronous vs. asynchronous, same vs. different location, mediated by what type of tool, under which rules, and who participates.

Figure1 shows, as an example for a hierarchical-sequential action process, the flow of actions and operations of a person taking part in a virtual conference (an a-synchronous meeting with other members of the virtual community, aimed at exchanging mobility information for this user group). Decomposing complex goal-directed actions in this manner enables, with sufficient detail, to identify specific support needs of users with different types of functional limitations. For the social contacts context, it would involve knowledge about the specific patient communities or peer groups available for your user group, or specific communication opportunities if your communication options are limited (speech impairments, hearing or visual impairments).

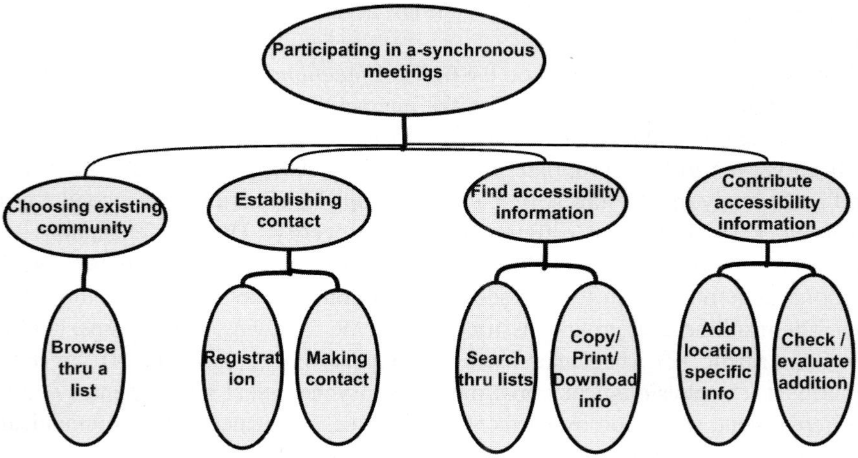

Fig. 1. Example of a hierarchical-sequential action process: A person participating in a virtual conference

Then, the hierarchical sequential action process is transformed into a set of matrices. The first matrix (Matrix 1) involves the *preparation* of activities (e.g. registering for starting up a virtual conference). The second matrix (Matrix 2) involves the *execution* of activities (e.g. actually contributing to the virtual conference). The ASK-IT service is aimed to provide assistance at both these two stages. Each row in the matrices corresponds to a specific activity, action or operation. The columns of these matrices specify for each user group separately the information requirements, specifically for that activity, action or operation. For instance, for "browsing through a list", information elements contain for the severely visually impaired people: "accessible mailing list". The attributes describe in a structured way the environmental factors, which make / do not make accessible operations possible. To each action a set of user group specific attributes can be mapped, e.g. accessible steps to a meeting place.

Then, Matrix 3 is produced. This matrix defines for each information element the characteristics of the attribute (type of variable, e.g. a value, a description), and the prioritisation (essential, important, nice, neutral) of the attribute. Table 1 shows the translation of the action process "Find accessibility information" and "add location specific information at the location through a storage unit" into required information elements for the visually impaired people: Matrix 3.

Table 1. An extract of the Social contacts and community building Matrix 3 for the visually impaired users

Information need	Information element	Conditions / Attribute	Value / type	Value limit	Priority
Find accessibility information	Accessible dedicated mailing list	Name	Text		Important
		Description	Text	See W3C guidelines	Important
	Accessible supporting document repository	Name	Text		Important
		Description	Text	See W3C guidelines	Important
	………				
Add location specific information through a storage unit	Voice driven Recording equipment	Available	Yes/No		Nice

3 Content Modeling Procedure

The goal of the content modelling procedure is to provide a formal description of user information needs in a computer understandable and interoperable format, based on the content requirements as presented in table format (see Table 1). The outcome of the modeling procedure is a set of computer-interpretable models that represent the user information needs. These models describe the pieces of information that should be exchanged between the user and different data sources or heterogeneous applications. By imposing a set of constraints on data, a common delivery format is dictated. Thus, when a user with a functional limitation requests a new service, the common data format, which acts as an information filtering facility, guarantees that the user gets access only to valid data values. XML was chosen for representing models, because it is by far the most supported content representation language today. An XML-schema is a definition of the structure of an XML document. Given an XML document and a schema, a schema processor can check for validity, i.e. that the document conforms to the schema requirements.

The procedure for moving from the content requirement matrices to the XML schemes involves the transformation of the matrices into a *tree* structure, consistent with the notation of an XML schema. Each concept related to a specific user information need is encoded as an information element composed of several attributes, related to values of information that the user desires to know in order to be able to read. In Table 2, an example of one *information element* and its *attributes* are shown: this example is for supporting reading for the visually impaired. The full description of the content modelling procedure is presented in [8].

Table 2. Division of information elements into attributes and their description

Information Element	Attributes
Reading	Screenreaders Visual aids Audio signals Sound volume control for the use of a product with voice output (in a public area) Etc.

The next step is to create the corresponding XML-Schema document. The latter is actually a representation of a collection of elements as the one described in Table 2. A graphical representation of an arbitrary information element comprised of three attributes, is illustrated in Figure 2. This tree-like graphical representation is provided by the XMLSpy authoring tool, which supports automatic generation of XML code by knowledge engineers, without requiring a deep knowledge of XML. The corresponding XML-Schema document that describes the element of Fig. 2 is given in the code segment of Figure 3. The author creates the tree, which is illustrated in Figure 2 using a set of an appropriate graphical user interface, while the authoring tool automatically generates the code shown in Figure 3.

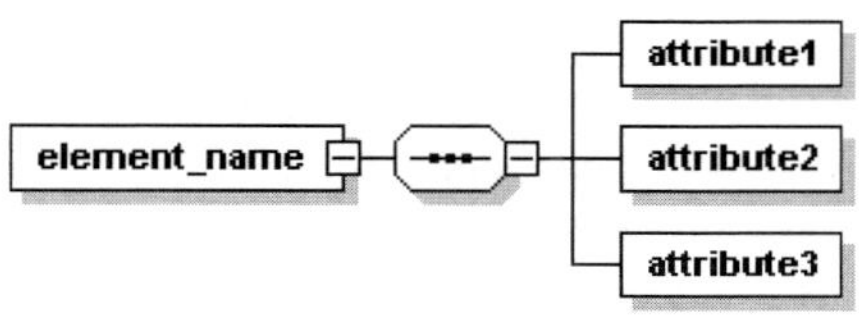

Fig. 2. A XMLSpy-generated graphical representation of an element with three nested elements as attributes

```
<xs:element name="element_name">
  <xs:complexType>
    <xs:sequence>
      <xs:element name="attribute1"/>
      <xs:element name="attribute2"/>
      <xs:element name="attribute3"/>
    </xs:sequence>
  </xs:complexType>
</xs:element>
```

Fig. 3. An element with attributes in XML-Schema

In the example shown in Table 2 each element is specified by the xs:element identifier. Since the element 'element_name' consists of three elements (i.e. more than one other element), it is a complex data type. This is specified by the identifier xs:complexType. The xs:sequence literal represents an ordered collection of elements that describe the list of three attributes that constitute the 'element_name' in Fig. 3. Primitive XML data types can also be encoded in any schema in order to describe simple data values of the various structural elements. For example, in order to represent temperature in Celsius degrees, the xs:decimal type, which is suitable for representing decimal numbers, would be used. The application of the transformation of the content requirements into the XML tree-like structures will eventually result in tree representations.

4 Application of the Methodology: Social Contacts and Community Building Content

Social contacts are very important for any person and in particular for people with functional limitations, for whom it is not always easy to make and maintain contacts. Evidence summarized by [11] suggests that ICT s have a positive impact on the tendency to join groups and increase interpersonal connectivity, and that people and institutions are no longer connected primarily by geography, but are instead living in networked societies and Internet is a complement to people's ongoing activities of life [12]. To be part of a community will enable people to support each other, and to inform themselves. Additionally is the valuable opportunity to disseminate knowledge about accessibility and other relevant issues and enrich the content of the ASK-IT device. After all, ASK-IT users know best how accessible their immediate environment is, and can help others by sharing this knowledge.

Currently, there are many different websites for numerous communities of people with functional limitations and their families.

There are already many tools available, electronic message boards, chatting facilities, web logs, internet sites on accessibility. While most of these tools are fully known and used by people with disabilities, their accessibility is sometimes cumbersome, hence it needs to be addressed and clearly specified in any community that will be established (e.g. many websites are not accessible for visually impaired people). In this respect, various assistive technologies should be able to use the content provided through these communities and propagate them in an accessible manner (through speech, Braille, etc.) to the end-user.

In the following, a usage scenario is presented that will better illustrate how ASK-IT will support the social environment of a person with functional limitations.

> Josephine (29) lives in Dortmund in a flat on the ground floor, together with her older sister. She is tetraplegic due to a heavy car accident when she was 15 years old. Being a very social person before the accident, Josephine has since then insisted on being able to take up her social life again. However, meeting people on public places has proven to be quite difficult due to the fact that Josephine cannot "afford" to arrange for a meeting in a place she doesn't know due to the fact that her electric wheelchair requires that the meeting place is on the same level as the street, or has a ramp or elevator via which she can enter the place. So, apart from meeting friends on the spot, she also meets others by using MSN and SKYPE. Furthermore, she is a member

> of a few virtual communities, e.g. the local and the national community of wheelchair users. She makes use of ASK-It which is linked to http://rollidriver.de/ to plan her trip in Germany and to chat with other wheelchair users about accessibility, the daily hassles, and also she contributes her information about accessibility of her direct environment. Of course, the information is provided by ASK-IT, but validating and other contributions from the user community improve the quality. She can submit her information when she is on the road, and ASK-IT adds the localization information automatically, or later at home. On the other hand, if she wants to know accessibility details of buildings in other cities, she makes use of ASK-IT to find out. So, with the help of the ASK-IT system Josephine finds accessible public places, where to meet people such as cafes, restaurants etc. corresponding her individual accessibility needs. After that she could utilise the virtual community in arranging the meeting with other people or e.g. discussing the menu and meals of an accessible Italian restaurant proposed by the ASK-IT service.

User requirements focus on needs during a personal- and community meeting preparation: both synchronous and a-synchronous, and both virtual or in real life (physical meeting). Following content was desired to be available to enable respectively a successful preparation of such a meeting, and the actual taking place of the meeting:

- (Preparing) personal/community meeting, synchronous contact: In case a real-life meeting is to take place, the user should be provided with information on the accessibility of the premises where the meeting will take place.In case that technology is being utilised to enable such intermediated synchronous contact (e.g. video conferencing, chat session, messaging, etc.), the degree of accessibility of such tools and their incorporation with assistive technology should be clearly indicated. In addition, the end-user should be informed on the specific devices s/he will need to establish such synchronous contact, and to what extent the offered services will be accessible for all kinds of end-users. For all content provided, the use of a clear, unambiguous and easy understandable language, including pictorial language, ought to be used.
- (Preparing) personal/community meeting, a-synchronous contact: While traditional tools such as letters, magazines, etc. should ensure that the content is readable and easily understandable, there are no real content requirements, apart from the overall required use of a clear, unambiguous and easy understandable language -including pictorial language- that ought to be used. However, where various tools that support such a-synchronous contact are envisaged to be used, the service provider will have to inform in advance the user on how accessible their services are, and what additional devices might be required to use certain tools. This information should be provided in an accessible format through the various accessible channels (devices such as mobile devices, and internet) where the end-user will look for and obtain such information. In addition, the various tools should support the application or where possible have assistive technology already incorporated.

5 Discussion and Conclusions

The above described content definition and modeling procedure has been successfully applied in the framework of the ASK-IT project. The matrix structure based on action and activity theory principles facilitated the systematic and extensive content requirements specification. Comprehensive content requirement matrices were produced. The tables include user group specific attributes for all identified actions and activities. A difficulty was the wide variety of relevant activities for some domains, and hence the huge quantity of information needs related to their performance by people with various types of functional limitations. That was not the case for the field of social contacts and community building. The extensive lists of content requirements were, furthermore, evaluated and prioritized by representatives of the different user groups. Only those attributes with "essential" and "important" priority for the user group in question were translated into XML schemes.

Morganti and Riva emphasized recently that the focus of Ambient Intelligence for rehabilitation should be the support of the users' activities and interactions with the environment [13, p. 285]. The integration of action and activity theory principles has indeed proven to be a suitable theoretical framework for the specification of content requirements for an ambient intelligence-based tourist information service for users with functional limitations. The content requirements matrices provide, for each user group, a structured representation of information elements in the form of classes with attributes and limit values. This approach facilitates the subsequent creation of XML schemes, because the input for the content modeling procedure is immediately available in a format that can be converted into a machine-readable language without difficulties.

References

1. Simoes, A., Gomez, A.: User groups classification and Potential demography of MI in Europe. ASK-It Deliverable D1.1(511298) (2005)
2. United Nations: Barrier-Free Tourism for People with Disabilities in the Asian and Pacific Region. United Nations Publications, New York (2003)
3. Riva, R.: The Psychology of Ambient Intelligence: Activity, Situation and Presence. In: Riva, G., Vatalaro, F., Davide, F., Alcaniz, M. (eds.) Ambient Intelligence, pp. 17–33. IOS Press, Amsterdam (2005)
4. Frese, M., Zapf, D.: Action as the Core of Work Psychology: A German Approach. In: Dunnetee, M.D., et al. (eds.) Handbook of Industrial and Organizational Psychology, 4th edn. pp. 271–340. Consulting Psychologists Press, Palo Alto (1994)
5. Kuutti, K.: Activity theory as a potential framework for human computer interaction research. In: Nielsen, J. (ed.) Usability Engineering, Academic Press, London (1993)
6. World Health Organization: International Classification of Functioning, Disability and Health (2001)
7. TELSCAN project: Inventory of ATT System Requirements for Elderly and Disabled Drivers and Travellers, Deliverable 3.1 (1997)

8. Sommer, S.M., Wiethoff, M., Valjakka, S., Kehagias, D., Tzovaras, D., Tzovaras, D.: Development of a Mobile Tourist Information System for People with Functional Limitations: User Behaviour Concept and Specification of Content Requirements. In: Miesenberger, K., Klaus, J., Zagler, W., Karshmer, A. (eds.) ICCHP 2006. LNCS, vol. 4061, pp. 305–313. Springer, Heidelberg (2006)
9. Engeström, Y.: Learning by expanding. Helsinki, Orienta-Konsultit (1987)
10. Kuuti, K.: Work processes: scenarios as preliminary vocabulary. In: Carroll, J.M. (ed.) Scenario-based design: Envisioning work and technology in system development, John Wiley & Sons, New York (1995)
11. Otis, Nancy, Johanson, G.: Community Building And Information And Communications Technologies: Current Knowledge, Nancy Otis & Graeme Johanson (April 2004)
12. Wellman, B.: The Global Village: Internet and Community. Idea&s - The Arts & Science Review, University of Toronto, vol. 1(1), pp. 26–30 (2004)
13. Morganti, F., Riva, R.: Ambient Intelligence for Rehabilitation. In: Riva, G., Vatalaro, F., Davide, F., Alcaniz, M. (eds.) Ambient Intelligence, pp. 283–295. IOS Press, Amsterdam (2005)

Intuitive Map Navigation on Mobile Devices

Stefan Winkler, Karthik Rangaswamy, and ZhiYing Zhou

Interactive Multimedia Lab
Department of Electrical and Computer Engineering
NationalUniversity ofSingapore (NUS)
Singapore 117576
{winkler,elerk,elezzy}@nus.edu.sg

Abstract. In this paper, we propose intuitive motion-based interfaces for map navigation on mobile devices with built-in cameras. The interfaces are based on the visual detection of the devices self-motion. This gives people the experience of navigating maps with a virtual looking glass. We conducted a user study to evaluate the accuracy, sensitivity and responsiveness of our proposed system. Results show that users appreciate our motion-based user interface and find it more intuitive than traditional key-based controls, even though there is a learning curve.

Keywords: Virtual map navigation, user interface, motion detection, pose estimation.

1 Introduction

Mobile phones and PDA's are becoming increasingly powerful and provide more and more functionality to the user. However, the user interface (UI) is still severely limited due to the small form factor of these devices. Using the small, un-ergonomic keys for control in applications other than calling is tedious and not always intuitive.

In order to overcome these problems, we have developed novel, motion-based user interfaces for mobile devices, which are based on the detection of the 3D self-motion of the device using the integrated camera. Possible movements involve translation and rotation with a total of 6 degrees of freedom. These movements can then be used to control applications on the device.

3D motion tracking using the phone's built-in camera forms the backbone of this work. The process involves motion detection, computing the pose of the phone in 3D space from the motion registered, and tracking [1]. The process has to run in real-time under the constraints of the limited memory and computing resources available on a hand-held device [2].Work on this subject is very recent, and the current studies focus mainly on gaming [3]. We have presented a car racing game using motion-based interaction elsewhere [4]. Here we extend this concept to virtual map navigation, which also benefits greatly from this new way of interaction. Arhippainen et al. [5] investigated a similar problem involving

C. Stephanidis (Ed.): Universal Access in HCI, Part II, HCII 2007, LNCS 4555, pp. 605–614, 2007.

gesture-based control for scrolling and zooming maps on mobile devices with motion feedback from sensors and accelerometers. However, these sensors are not always available on standard mobile devices. Since a camera is available with almost all phones in the market today, we propose to use visual motion detection and pose estimation to achieve our goal.

For the work described in this paper, we use fiducial markers as references to simplify the detection of the phone's motion. These markers can be carried in personal wallets, printed on maps, or fixed on traveller log books, which are often used for route planning. The pose of the phone in 3D space can be estimated with respect to the marker by analyzing the frames returned by the camera for any detected markers and determining the transformation from marker to camera coordinates. The vectors in the transformation matrix are mapped to various types of interactions that drive applications on the mobile device.

To test our interface, we developed an application for navigating virtual maps that involves standard controls for scrolling across the map as well as zooming in and out to see the map at different resolutions. We define specific device movements that translate into these basic controls. We designed three such user interfaces and conducted a user study to compare the performance of our motion-based interfaces with traditional key-based controls.

The paper is organized as follows: Section 2 introduces the system specifications and the system design. Section 3 explains the three user interfaces we designed and how the user can control the application with them. Section 4 discusses the user-study conducted and the results of the survey. Concluding remarks are given in Section 5.

2 System Overview

Our application runs on a Hewlett-Packard rw6828 PocketPC equipped with a 416 MHz Intel PXA272 processor and 64MB RAM, running Windows Mobile 5.0 OS. The phone has a built-in 2-megapixel camera, which is used to track the markers at a video resolution of 176x144 pixels.

The marker tracking is implemented with ARToolkitPlus[6],a modified version of ARToolkit[7] that is compiled for the mobile platform. ARToolkitPlus accepts the frames from a DirectShow FrameGrabber filter and returns the 3D position and pose vectors of the phone if a marker was detected. These vectors are then mapped to different controls on the user interface to drive the application. The complete flow of control in the system is summarized in Figure 1.

Maps are downloaded from Google Servers on the Internet whenever the user scrolls to unexplored regions or zooms to a different resolution of the map. The Map-Navigation application was developed in C++, making use of the Direct3D Mobile libraries for displaying maps as textures on a vertex grid. The vectors obtained from ARToolkitPlus are used to translate a virtual camera over the map textures by a pre-defined offset for every rendered frame, thus giving the notion of continuous scrolling. Zooming is implemented by a similar operation to view different resolutions of the map.

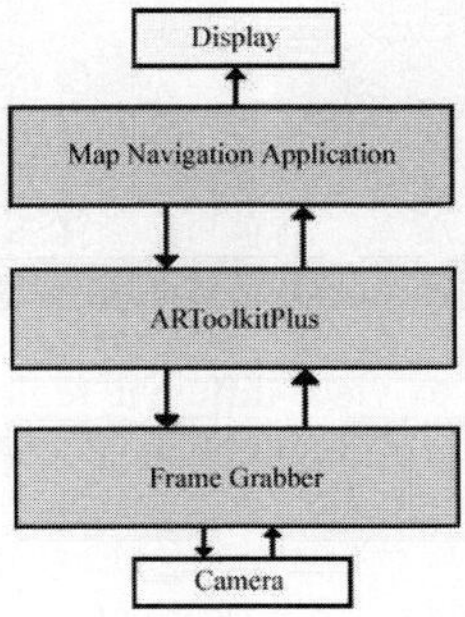

Fig. 1. Control flow in the system

Figure 2 shows the Map-Navigation application running on our PocketPC with a marker in the background that helps with pose estimation. A small video feedback window on the top-left corner of the application displays the camera view. This window is provided so that the user can keep track of the marker and maintain it within the field of view of the camera. It also helps the user to scroll the maps in arbitrary directions, which will be explained in Section 3.

Fig. 2. ID-encoded ARToolkitPlus marker used for computing the pose of the mobile device in 3D space

Furthermore, the mobile device can be rotated by any arbitrary angle to view a specific section of the map in landscape or portrait mode or any orientation in between, as shown in Figure 3; the orientation of the virtual map does not change, similar to how real maps would behave under a looking glass.

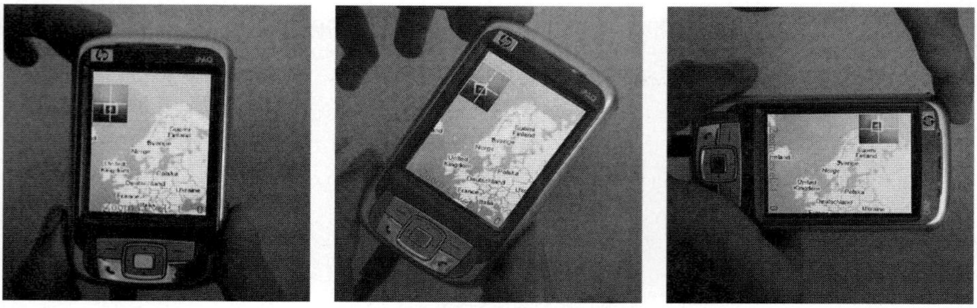

Fig. 3. The phone can be rotated to view different regions of the map, whose orientation remains fixed, as shown here for three different phone poses

3 Interaction Methods

In terms of interaction, the well-established key-based interfaces are robust enough to navigate maps, but allow only a limited set of discrete movements and generally restrict the user's freedom. In our implementation, the user instead moves his phone over a pre-defined set of markers that are constantly being tracked by the phone's camera. Moving the phone over a given marker performs a particular operation, like scrolling the map in a certain direction, or zooming to a different level of detail on the map. To zoom in or out, the user has to move the phone towards or away from the marker, for example. In order to aid the participant in controlling zooming, we provide a 'zoom-meter' whose arrow-head indicates the zoom level as a function of the distance between the phone and the marker. This helps people to know the current resolution of the map and to get a feel of how far they have to move in order to get to the next level of resolution. The definition of zoom levels is explained in more detail below.

Although many different UI designs are possible with such a setup, we restrict ourselves to three designs for the time being. Our goal was not to find the best user interface design, but to get a general idea of how people view such user interfaces when compared to using keys on the phone.

3.1 Key-Based Setup

For comparison purposes, we implemented a simple key-based interface for scrolling and zooming the virtual map. The maps can be scrolled with the four directional keys on the phone along the four cardinal directions. Two other keys are allocated for zooming in and out of map resolutions incrementally.

3.2 Five Marker Setup

This is the most basic setup involving four markers that guide continuous scrolling of the map along the four cardinal directions and one marker for zooming, as shown in Figure 4. The marker located in the center aids in zooming, where the user moves the phone towards or away from it. This requires that only one marker be visible within the camera field of view at any instant for unambiguous selection of the corresponding operation. The distance between the phone and the marker along the depth direction is used as a scale to fix the zoom levels for the application. The phone cannot be moved too close to the marker as the complete area of the marker has to be visible within the camera's field of view. On the other hand, the phone cannot be moved too far away either as the marker pattern might not be detected accurately. These two conditions impose physical limits within which we confine all the zoom levels for the application.

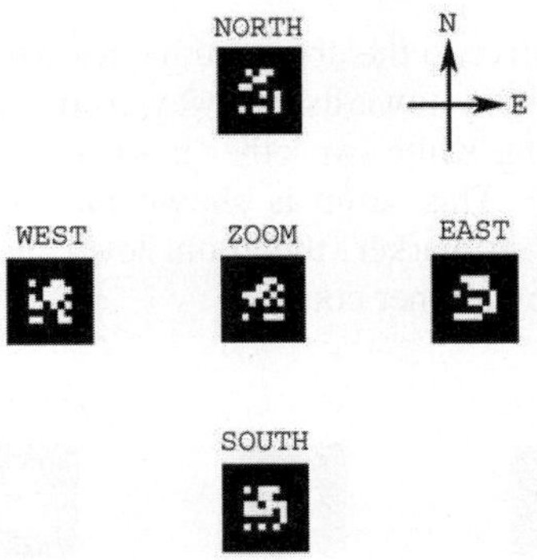

Fig. 4. Five-marker setup for map navigation

We split the detectable range (maximum distance minus minimum distance) into as many segments as we have zoom levels in the application. In the current implementation, four zoom levels are implemented, from country level to city level. In this case, a direct jump from any given resolution of the map to any other is possible just by moving the phone more than a segment's length in order to skip the resolution(s) in-between.

3.3 Single Marker Setup

Five markers may be considered an unnecessary burden and also restrict the scrolling to one of the four cardinal directions. Therefore, we designed a user interface wherein both the scrolling and zooming operations can be achieved with a single marker.

For scrolling, the user has to move the phone over the marker such that the map scrolls in a direction defined by a vector drawn on the marker plane from the optical axis to the center of the marker center. As a result, scrolling is possible in any direction. Scroll speed is based on the relative distance of the marker from the optical axis. At the optical axis the scroll speed is zero, but it increases as the marker moves away from the axis in proportion to the distance between the marker-center and the axis on the marker plane.

The zooming operation here is very similar to zooming in the five-marker setup, i.e. moving the phone towards or away from the marker. Either the user can fix the marker at a place and move the phone over it or hold the phone at a constant distance from his view and move the marker in the background.

A limitation to the zooming operation in this setup is that as the phone is moved closer to the marker, the usable scroll movement range is reduced as the marker area in the camera view increases. As a solution, the scroll speed is set to constant at these zoom levels, and the users only have to move the marker center relative to the optical axis in their preferred scroll direction. Additionally, a thresholded region around the axis is defined where the scroll speed drops to zero. The user can move the marker center to this region to stop scrolling.

3.4 Three Marker Setup

We provided another alternative to the above strategies wherein zooming need not be controlled by moving the phone towards or away from the marker. In this setup, a single marker aids in scrolling while two other markers are used for zooming in and out of the map respectively. This setup is shown in Figure 5. Whenever the user moves his phone over a zoom marker, the zoom level increments or decrements in fixed time intervals defined by a timer count.

Fig. 5. Three-marker setup for map navigation

Alternatively, the markers can also be fixed to a cube which can be moved by the user, with the phone held at a constant distance from the cube, as shown in Figure 2. A sample cube with markers attached to its faces is shown in figure Figure 6. The system is designed to tolerate more than one marker in the field of view, especially when the cube is rotated. The display freezes whenever more than one marker is seen by the camera, and the system waits until only one marker appears in the field of view.

Fig. 6. A cube with markers attached to three of its faces

4 User Study

We designed a user study in which people could evaluate each of the interfaces introduced above individually. The goal of the study was to evaluate the intuitiveness of the interface, the comfort in usage and the responsiveness of the system. These aspects were tested for both scrolling and zooming operations.

The initial group of people who tested our interfaces felt that the five-marker setup was quite similar to the key-based interface except for the automatic scrolling and zooming. Five markers were a burden to carry along with the phone, especially when the scrolling operation seemed redundant compared to scrolling with keys on the phone. This was the reason that led to the design of the single and three marker setups and the expulsion of the five marker setup from the user study.

12 male participants and 4 female participants between 16 and 28 years of age took part in the study. Almost all of them had experience with a map navigation application on the PC platform, while only one of them had used it on a mobile PDA. Owing to this lack of experience, we let the users experiment with our key-based interface for map navigation on the mobile phone for some time in order to give them a feel of the application on a mobile platform. Once they were comfortable, they were asked to navigate the map with the single-marker and the three-marker setup. The three-marker setup was fixed on a cube for easy handling. The order in which the interfaces were tested were key-based, single-marker and finally three-marker setup.

The participants were then asked to rate scrolling and zooming of the map with each interface independently a scale from 0 to 10 for intuitiveness, comfort and responsiveness. The average ratings of all participants is shown in Table 1.

Though the average ratings in Table 1 did not allow us to draw any conclusions, the individual ratings were wide-spread. Hence, we felt that rather than choosing an interface based on the above ratings, it would be wise to identify what led to the users decisions in making their ratings.

The ratings for the intuitiveness of the interfaces are quite similar for key-based and single-marker setup, while the three-marker setup suffered in zooming. This was expected, because the three-marker setup was designed with the accuracy and ease of the zooming operation in mind, which is reflected in the ratings for system's responsiveness and comfort in zooming with the single-and three-marker setups.

Table 1. Average Ratings (scale of 0-10)

	Key-based Interface		Single-Marker Setup		Three-Marker Setup	
	Scroll	Zoom	Scroll	Zoom	Scroll	Zoom
Intuitiveness	7.3	7.3	7.3	7.1	7.3	6.4
Comfort	6.8	6.7	7.3	6.0	6.4	6.3
Responsiveness	6.2	6.3	6.6	5.9	6.5	6.3

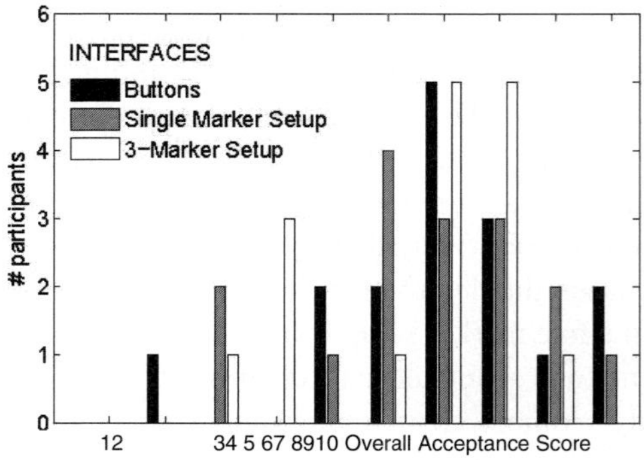

Fig. 7. Bar plot showing the distribution of overall acceptance scores given by the participants to each interface

Clearly, the single-marker interface was much more comfortable than both the key-based and the three-marker setup for scrolling. Although the scrolling methodology was the same for the single-and the three-marker interfaces, we felt that the lower rating for the three-marker setup in terms of scrolling might have been influenced by the number of markers involved in the operation and the order of testing the interfaces. In their feedback, the participants who favored the single marker setup felt that it was more intuitive than the three marker setup and carrying one marker along with their phones was easier than carrying three markers on a cube.

On the other hand, people who favored the three-marker setup argued that the single-marker interface was too sensitive to use in the first attempts, especially during zooming, which took some getting used to. The ratings for the responsiveness of the zooming operation confirms this. Participants felt that human hands are not always steady, and they found it difficult initially when they had to scroll maps by moving the phone and at the same time hold it at a steady distance from the marker in order to maintain the zoom level. In comparison, they found the three-marker interface to be rather straightforward, as scrolling and zooming were handled by distinct markers, and it took less time to get used to it.

The preference ratings for the additional features we provided in the application, namely the video feedback window, map rotation with tilting the phone and the 'zoom-meter', are shown in Figure 8 as bar plots. People found especially the rotating window feature, which is not normally found in other mobile map navigation applications, to be very useful. As for the video feedback window and 'zoom-meter', the participants felt that they were indispensable to controlling the application and thus more of a requirement than a feature.

The ratings of the participants were also heavily affected by their experience with such interfaces, especially in similar applications where user interaction is constrained by online downloading of data and network speed. People have used keys on the phone all along and when switching to markers, the more time they spent with marker-based interfaces, the more they got adapted to using them. Yet the scores for the key-based interface are not so high either, and people seemed to be ambivalent, which is also seen in Figure 7. Hence, we believe that with adaptation and experience, people would find virtual map navigation and other similar applications easier to handle with markers than with keys on the phone.

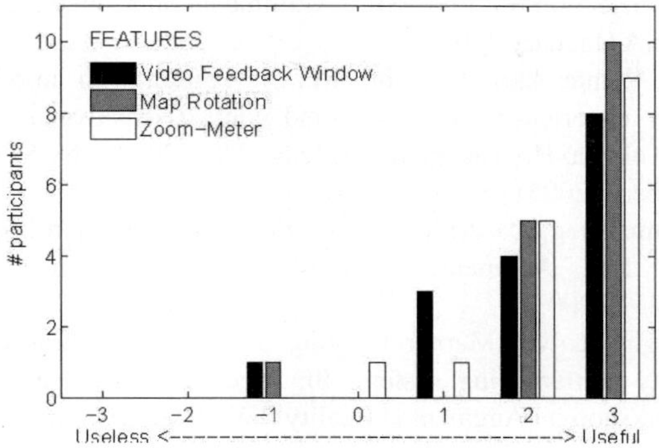

Fig. 8. Bar plot showing feature preference ratings for the video feedback window, map window rotation with tilting the phone, and the 'zoom-meter'

5 Conclusions

We proposed intuitive motion-based interfaces for an online virtual map navigation application. The application runs on mobile devices with a built-in camera, and the phone becomes a virtual looking glass over the map. The interface is based on pose estimation from fiducial markers extracted from the frames captured by the phones camera using ARToolkitPlus. We developed different user interfaces to control the application, and we conducted a user study to evaluate their accuracy, sensitivity and responsiveness. The results show that the motion-based interfaces are well appreciated for their intuitiveness and perform equally well when compared with a key-based interface even for a first trial. Adaptation and experience would certainly give our proposed interfaces a lift in performance and general acceptance in comparison to working with keys on the phone.

In spite of all the possibilities to make markers 'mobile', they still represent a considerable burden and inconvenience. Our future work focuses on enhancing the system with marker-less methods of detecting the phones pose and movement in 3D space with techniques like feature tracking and optical flow. We are also investigating applications for combining our map navigation techniques with a GPS device.

References

1. Foxlin, E.: Motion tracking requirements and technologies. In: Stanney, K.M., ed.: Handbook of Virtual Environment Technology. Lawrence Erlbaum Associates, Hillsdale, N.J., USA, pp. 163–210 (2002)
2. Moehring, M., Lessig, C., Bimber, O.: Optical tracking and video see-through AR on consumer cell phones. In: Proc. Workshop on Virtual and Augmented Reality of the GI-Fachgruppe AR/VR, pp. 193–204 (2004)

3. Drab, S.A., Artner, N.M.: Motion detection as interaction technique for games & applications on mobile devices. In: Pervasive Mobile Interaction Devices (PERMID) Workshop, Munich, Germany (May 2005)
4. Winkler, S., Rangaswamy, K., Zhou, Z.: Intuitive user interface for mobile devices based on visual motion detection. In: Proc. SPIE Multimedia on Mobile Devices. Volume 6507., San Jose, CA, USA (January 2007)
5. Arhippainen, L., Rantakokko, T., Táhti, M.: Navigation with an adaptive mobile map-application: User experiences of gesture-and context-sensitiveness. In: Murakami, H., Nakashima, H., Tokuda, H., Yasumura, M. (eds.) UCS 2004. LNCS, vol. 3598, pp. 62–73. Springer, Heidelberg (2005)
6. Wagner, D., Schmalstieg, D.: ARToolkit on the Pocket PC platform. In: Proceedings of the 2nd IEEE Intl. Augmented Reality Toolkit Workshop (ART032), Tokyo, Japan(October 14–15 2003)
7. Kato, H., Billinghurst, M.: Marker tracking and HMD calibration for a video-based augmented reality conferencing system. In: Proceedings of the 2nd IEEE and ACM International Workshop on Augmented Reality (IWAR), San Francisco, CA, 85–94 (1999)

Part III

Virtual and Augmented Environment

An Interactive Entertainment System Usable by Elderly People with Dementia

Norman Alm[1], Arlene Astell[2], Gary Gowans[3], Richard Dye[1], Maggie Ellis[2], Phillip Vaughan[3], and Alan F. Newell[1]

[1] School of Computing, University of Dundee, Dundee, Scotland, UK
{nalm, rdye, afn}@computing.dundee.ac.uk
[2] School of Psychology, University of St Andrews, St Andrews, Fife, Scotland, UK
aja3@st-andrews.ac.uk, mellis@computing.dundee.ac.uk
[3] School of Design, University of Dundee, Dundee, Scotland, UK
{g.g.gowans, p.b.vaughan}@dundee.ac.uk

Abstract. As the population profile in most part of the world is more and more weighted towards older people, the incidence of dementia will continue to increase. Dementia is marked by a general cognitive decline, and in particular the impairment of working (short-term) memory. Finding ways to engage people with dementia in stimulating but safe activities which they can do without the help of a carer would be beneficial both to them and to their caregivers. We are developing an interactive entertainment system designed to be used alone by a person with dementia without caregiver assistance. We have piloted a number of interactive virtual environments and activities both with people with dementia and professionals in the field of dementia care. We report the results of this pilot work and consider the further questions to be addressed in developing an engaging, multimedia activity for people with dementia to use independently.

Keywords: Dementia, assistive technology, cognitive prostheses, multimedia, touchscreens.

1 Introduction

Dementia is a progressive, irreversible disorder and age is the greatest risk factor for developing it. The most common cause of dementia is Alzheimer's disease, which is characterised in the early stages by memory problems and failure to learn new information. Over time, all aspects of cognitive function are affected and daily living skills erode. People with dementia gradually lose the ability to keep safe, keep busy and care for themselves.

Left to their own devices, people with mild to moderate dementia may become lost and confused if they go out of the house, and at home may start activities, such as cooking or running a bath, which they fail to complete. These situations present considerable risks and reducing these places significant demands on caregivers, who

C. Stephanidis (Ed.): Universal Access in HCI, Part II, HCII 2007, LNCS 4555, pp. 617–623, 2007.

are typically family members. As dementia progresses, people are commonly confused and disorientated. Many attempt to leave the unfamiliar nursing or residential settings full of apparently unknown people. Their agitation and distress present a challenge to caregivers and highlight the difficulties of keeping people occupied.

Finding safe, stimulating activities that engage people at all stages of dementia would therefore be beneficial not only to them but also to their caregivers [3]. Participation in activities is important for stimulating and maintaining cognitive and social skills [8]. In addition, previous studies have shown positive effects of activity on reducing agitation and engendering a sense of well-being in people with dementia [4]. Engaging activity for people with dementia also provides caregivers with well-earned breaks from constant caring.

In our previous work, we demonstrated that people with dementia are comfortable in front of a touchscreen computer and will use the system when prompted. We have shown that a carefully designed system can tap into well-rehearsed cognitive and social scripts and use them to engage people with dementia [1,2]. We developed such a system to prompt and support conversations between people with dementia and caregivers using a hypermedia structure. Hypermedia is ideal for tackling the short-term memory problem of people with dementia, as there is no penalty for 'losing the place' [5,6]. Users are encouraged to explore and get lost in the system to make the most of the material. Thus wherever the user is within the interface is the right place to be. This is excellent for people with dementia whose short-term memory is extremely impaired, and who are unable to remember where they have just been.

Using multimedia technology it is possible to include text, photographs, graphics, sound recordings and film recordings. These contents can be linked in various dynamic and flexible ways to promote the user's engagement. The user is invited to interact with the material presented in a more lively way than by just looking at text and pictures on a page. In addition hypermedia provides abundant opportunities for users to make decisions as they explore the system.

The way that hypermedia operates fits well with the multiple trace theory of how memories are stored and accessed [7]. In this theory older memories are accompanied by multiple traces within the brain, which facilitate retrieval by providing more ways to access the memories. However, people with dementia have extreme difficulty accessing memories at will. Hypermedia provides multiple prompts from across a range of stimuli to tap into these multiple access routes and facilitate retrieval of stored memories.

Hypermedia offers further possibilities for creative interventions for people with dementia to access self-generated activities, which are safe and enjoyable. The main challenges in developing such a system are impaired short-term memory and problems learning new skills and information. Our solution with the conversation support system was to take the here-and-now state of people with dementia and design the system around this. We are repeating this approach in our new project, 'Living in the Moment'.

2 Iterative Design Process for an Interactive Entertainment System

We began by developing virtual environments for users to navigate, and also a set of virtual activities. We wanted to assess the general usability of these for people with dementia. We also wanted to investigate ways to prompt people with dementia to make use of the touchscreen to carry out activities unaided. In our evaluations we first obtained the views of professionals in the field as to appropriate content for such a system. We then had people with dementia try out a variety of prototype interfaces to determine which content worked best, and to begin to gain an understanding of what sort of prompting mechanisms might begin to enable them to use such a system on their own, without a carer present. The three studies we undertook were: dementia professionals trying out virtual environments, people with dementia trying out virtual environments, and people with dementia trying out virtual activities, with and without a helper present.

2.1 Dementia Professionals – Virtual Environments

Respondents were recruited at the UK Alzheimer's Society Annual Conference. Thirteen people completed a questionnaire after trying out the virtual environments. Three navigable virtual environments were created: a museum, a pub, and a botanical garden. The environments were presented through a 20-inch touch-screen monitor. The VR environments were viewed at a resolution of 1280 x 1024 pixels. Written prompts were included to indicate places to touch the screen (see Figure 1). A brief questionnaire about the virtual environments was compiled comprising the following questions: Did you try out the virtual reality environments?; Which, if any, did you prefer and why? Do you think they add to the experience?; Why?; Any additional comments; Suggestions for other VR environments.

Participants were invited to use the computer by themselves for as long as they liked. When they had finished each user was asked to complete the brief questionnaire about the virtual environments. Most respondents gave general comments about the VR environments. One respondent commented, "I like to see things that are related to the person with dementia's life". Another commented on the nature of the VR contents, stating that it was "Good to see moving pictures". Of the thirteen respondents, eight expressed a preference for one of the three VR environments. Of these eight, five preferred the botanical gardens. The reasons for this included reference to the contents such as "beautiful to look at"; "excellent music"; and "lovely scenery". Finally, one respondent commented, "the range of possibilities is greater than the other environments".

Eleven respondents commented on the additional value of having VR environments. Responses were addressed to three areas. First was the experience itself where respondents commented that it was 'very realistic' and "the garden – more real looking and multidimensional. Provides a choice of where to go and what to look at more closely, etc.". A second group of comments referred to the engaging properties of the VR environments, such as "an escapism into a relaxing, enjoyable and engaging environment". Further comments in this vein were "holds the attention' and "stimulates memories, gives enjoyment through several senses – colour, movement and sound". The third group of comments referred to the appeal of the VR experience and the possibility for giving back some control to people with dementia. These included "greater variety and therefore more possibilities for everyone"; "it brings fun and a sense of achievement - you can make things happen; and "you can control what you are looking at".

One respondent additionally comment that the activity provided "Confidence building opportunities". Other additional comments referred to the ease of navigation, the size of the control buttons and the ion screen instruction. Some respondents made suggestions for additional VR environments, which included: shopping; dancing; roller skating; fairground rides; animals (a zoo); and seasonal scenes.

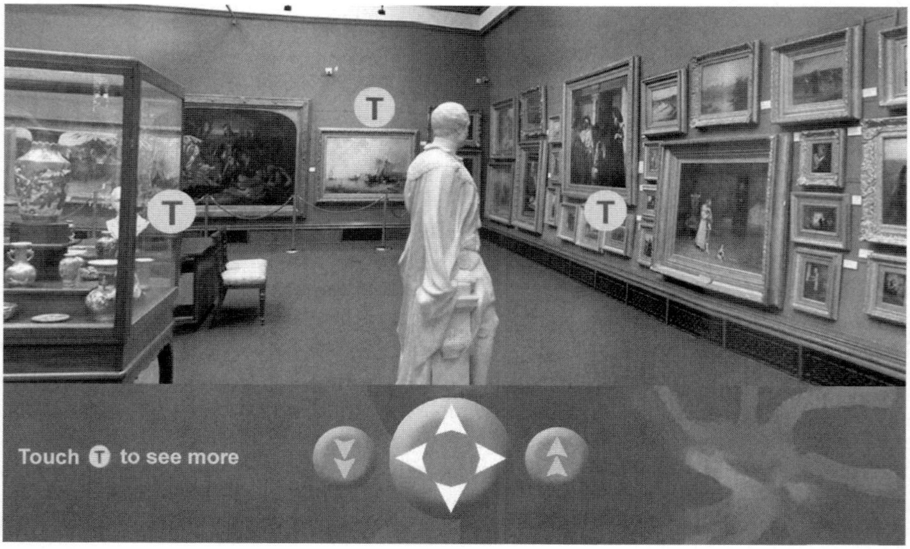

Fig. 1. The virtual museum. Other environments tried were a pub and a botanical garden.

2.2 People with Dementia – Virtual Environments

Five people with dementia (2 men) were invited to look at the virtual environments in a day care setting. The touch screen system as described above was taken to a Day Centre for people with dementia. Each participant was invited to look at the VR environments with a member of the research team. In addition, each participant was encouraged to use the touch screen individually and explore the environments. When they had finished each participant was interviewed.

All of the people with a diagnosis of dementia appeared to enjoy looking at the VR environments and 3 out of the 5 tried using it independently. All participants spontaneously commented about the experience both when using it and afterwards. It was apparent that the botanic garden was the most popular environment with this group, just as it had been with the dementia care professionals. The participants with dementia commented on the contents, for example "lovely garden", "beautiful flowers", and "looks like a good pint " (in a pub VR environment). One person went further in relating to the experience with the comment "I'll sit here (bench in garden) for a while". Another person commented on the totality of the experience, saying "the music is in time with it all" (in the VR botanic garden). A final group of comments reflected the user's reaction to the experience including "amazing", "wonderful", "clever".

2.3 People with Dementia – Virtual Activities

Six people with dementia (2 men) were invited to try out the virtual activities hosted on the touch screen in a day care setting. A number of virtual activities could be undertaken on the touch screen platform. These included games requiring moderate skill, games of chance, creative activities, and viewing short video clips. In all cases the activities were designed to be enjoyable without the use of working memory.

Most of the users engaged well with the activities. We learned a great deal about how to structure the interaction to avoid confusion or boredom. Activities with a clear and always present goal worked best. Activities which were familiar, not surprisingly, also worked well. Activities which were less successful involved occasional pauses when it was not clear what to do next, or just what was happening. Comments from users included "That's brilliant! I'd be there all day!", "Isn't that lovely? Can I take this home?", "Not bad considering I didn't know what I was doing".

We tried out a number of ways of prompting users through the activities. The spoken prompts did not work well. These relied on synthetic speech. The system used was quite understandable to most people, but our users with dementia simply ignored it. This interesting outcome relates to work being done on difficulties older people in general may have with understanding synthetic speech, and will be followed up. We tried leaving the users alone with the system, once we had got them started with it. We could see what they were doing from the next room with the video camera. Surprisingly, a number of the users managed to interact with a variety of prototype systems with minimal prompting. A combination of prominent visual prompts, such as an onscreen button flashing, and an occasional text message, seemed to work very well. This has encouraged us that a final system, may not need to include prompting which is overly intrusive. We will continue to investigate this important aspect of the project.

3 Discussion

Evaluation of our three initial VR environments by a group of dementia care professionals and a group of people with a diagnosis of dementia was positive and provided useful feedback for the development of the Living in the Moment project. Of particular interest were the comments relating to the engaging properties of the stimuli. The dementia care professionals directly commented on the way the system captured attention and provided an engaging experience. These observations were further supported by the comments of the users with a diagnosis of dementia, who were able to imagine themselves in the environments, for example sitting on a bench in the botanic garden or having a pint of beer in the pub environment.

A number of useful comments were also made about the ease with which one could navigate around the environments. These included comments about the size of the arrows and on screen prompts for where to touch. We are currently carrying out detailed investigation of how best to prompt people with dementia to initiate and maintain interaction with the touch screen when they are using it alone.

It is intended that the finished Living in the Moment system will provide a way for people with dementia to independently engage in activities that they can no longer participate in outside of the care environment, for example shopping and cooking. VR is one way to provide people with a diagnosis of dementia with opportunities to re-experience activities they previously enjoyed in a safe and risk-free situation. The evidence from this pilot work suggests that people with dementia respond positively to the environments and with adequate prompting can explore them independently. We plan to develop a network of interconnected VR environments each containing activities to occupy and stimulate people with dementia. We have begun to create a virtual garden environment, which could be explored and also which could host a number of activity areas (See Fig. 2).

Fig. 2. A virtual garden, which can be the jumping off point for a variety of activities

It is further hoped that Living in the Moment will be an enjoyable experience, which provides opportunities for people with dementia to exercise autonomy over their activities. This would assist families and others who care for people with mild to moderate dementia by providing safe and positive ways to occupy their relatives, creating a well-earned respite from the heavy demands of keeping people with dementia active and stimulated. In addition, it will help to address the problems of safety for people with dementia with as little infringement on their rights and autonomy as possible.

Acknowledgments

We are grateful to everyone at the Alzheimer's Society Annual Conference in York (UK) and at the Alzheimer Scotland Dundee Project who took part in this pilot work. The Living in the Moment project is funded by the Engineering and Physical Sciences Research Council (EPSRC).

References

1. Alm, N., Astell, A., Ellis, M., Dye, R., Gowans, G., Campbell, J.: A cognitive prosthesis and communication support for people with dementia. Neuropsychological Rehabilitation 14(1–2), 117–134 (2004)
2. Astell, A.J., Ellis, M.P., Alm, N., Dye, R., Campbell, J., Gowans, G.: Facilitating communication in dementia with multimedia technology. Brain and Language 91(1), 80–81 (2004)
3. Gori, Pientini, Vespa.: The selection of meaningful activities as a treatment for day-care in dementia. Arch Geron Ger, pp. 207–212 (2001)
4. Lou, A.: The use of music therapy to decrease agitated behaviour of the demented elderly: the state of the science. Scandinavian Journal of Caring Sciences 15(2), 165–173 (2001)
5. Maddy, D.: Brouwer-Janse User centred design, the contour of multimedia, theoretical and empirical developments, Academia Research Monograph 19. Ch12. Luton: John Libbey Media (1996)
6. McKerlie, D., Preece, J.: The hypermedia effect: more than just the sum of its parts. In: Proceedings of the St.Petersburg HCI Conference, pp. 115–127 (1992)
7. Nadel, L., Moscovitch, M.: Consolidation, retrograde amnesia and the hippocampal formation. Current Opinion in Neurobiology 7, 217–227 (1997)
8. Tzrinski and Higgins Therapeutic play activities: building cohesion and socialization among nursing home residents. Activities, Adaptation and Ageing, vol. 25(3–4), pp. 121–135 (2001)

VRfx – A User Friendly Tool for the Creation of Photorealistic Virtual Environments

Matthias Bues, Günter Wenzel, Manfred Dangelmaier, and Roland Blach

CC Virtual Environments, Fraunhofer IAO, Nobelstr. 12,
70569 Stuttgart, Germany
{Matthias.Bues, Guenter.Wenzel, Manfred.Dangelmaier,
Roland.Blach}@iao.fraunhofer.de

Abstract. By using VR, industrial designs and architectural studies can be evaluated in early stages of development. In order to judge visual appearances and surface materials, a high visual quality is crucial. Today's programmable graphics hardware allows rendering of photorealistic effects in real-time. Basically, this functionality can be ex-ploited in VR, but the amount of work for model creation must be by orders of magni-tudes lower than what's acceptable for computer games. Thus, a tool is needed which allows efficient preparation of design models from the digital process chain for high-fidelity VR models and which is easy to use for people who are familiar with model-ing or CAD software. In this article, we describe the software tool VRfx. which ad-dresses this task.

Keywords: Virtual Environments, Industrial Design, Real-Time Shading, Photorealism.

1 Introduction

Today, VR is a well established review tool and communication medium. While industrial designers and architects were very interested in VR from the beginning on, most industrial applications in product design concentrate on CAD and numerical visualization so far, where visual realism is of limited relevance. The ongoing development of real-time graphics processing units (GPUs) has brought not only impressive increasings in throughput, but also fundamental enhancements of functionality. Particularly, the two major stages of the graphics pipeline are no longer hard-wired; instead, they are replaced by programmable processing units. This makes it possible to use many rendering algorithms which could not be implemented on the classical, hard-wired graphics pipeline, leading to a variety of visual effects which now can be used in real-time rendering.
The following image shows some examples:

The main application domain which pushes GPU development is computer games. Many of the visual effects known from there are applicable in VR, too. However, a major difference between computer games, where the digital model (i.e. the game

C. Stephanidis (Ed.): Universal Access in HCI, Part II, HCII 2007, LNCS 4555, pp. 624–632, 2007.

Fig. 1. Examples of Realtime Shading Effects

content) is the product itself, and VR applications, where the digital model is only a medium in the design process, is that the acceptable amount of work to create or prepare the model is by orders of magnitude less.

The conventional workflow for VR visualization projects in the industrial design and architecture domains is characterized by the following steps:

1. Model creation using animation software (e.g. 3DStudio MAX or Maya)
2. Export to a data format readable by VR software (e.g. VRML 97)
3. Manual optimization and (rarely) application of special effects
4. Presentation / review in the immersive environment

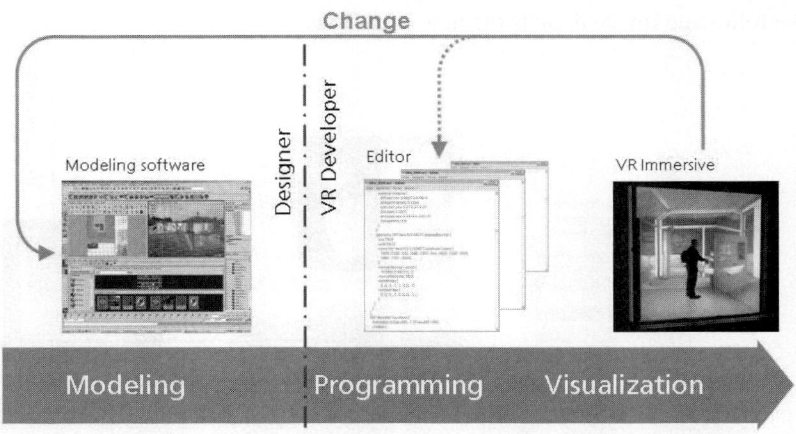

Fig. 2. Conventional workflow

The modeling tools mostly used in the industrial design and architecture domains (e.g. 3D Studio MAX, Maya, etc.) provide advanced material and shading possibilities themselves, however, most of them cannot be described in typical real-time data formats and are therefore lost in step 2. Visual effects therefore have to be added in step 3. Any change in the result requires iterating the entire process chain again, which leads to a very long iteration loop which can't be traversed very often during the project. In addition, step 3 always requires specialized VR know-how, resulting in design decisions often made by programmers rather than the designers since these do not have direct access to the VR model. This limits the achievable quality and, more important, the accordance with the designer's intentions. Also, no changes (e.g. of surface and material properties) are possible during the VR review session, which also limits the usefulness in collaborative scenarios, where direct changes applicable by and visible to all participants are particularly desirable.

2 The VRfx Approach

To overcome the above limitations, we specified and implemented an improved workflow and the associated tools. Major objectives were to give designers direct control over the final result, and to eliminate the unidirectional character of the traditional workflow. It consists of the following major steps:

1. Model creation using animation software (e.g. 3DStudio MAX or Maya)
2. Export to a data format readable by VR software (e.g. VRML 97)
3. Applying materials and special effects using the target VR tool, on the desktop or in the immersive environment.

Presentation is no longer a separate step as it can take place at any time during the creation process without a finalizing step.

The following image depicts the new workflow:

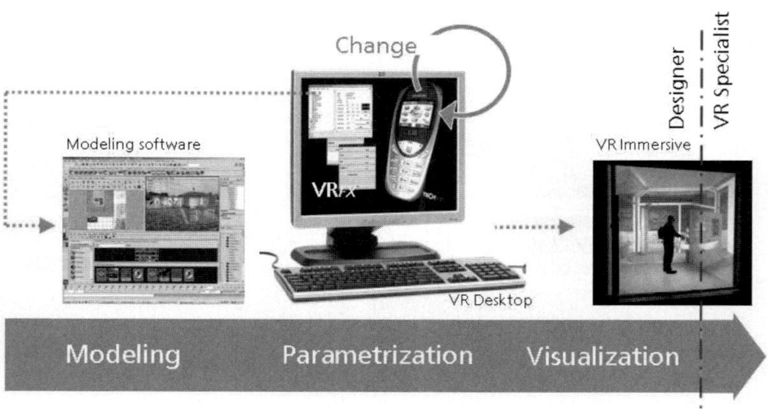

The resulting VRfx process is characterized by the following properties and features:

- Visual Fidelity: Photorealism by full support of current PC graphics hardware.
- "What you see is what you get": each change is visible immediately in real time, on the desktop as well as in the VR environment. This avoids the long iteration loop of the conventional workflow.

- No dedicated "Editor" and "Player" component. Any modification can be made in any working environment from desktop to PIcasso [13] to CAVE, single-user and collaborative. Changing between these is possible at any time.
- Comfort: intuitive graphical user interface.
- Flexible process integration: support of numerous input data formats, expandability and avoidance of a proprietary "native" data format. The VRfx session format contains only references.
- Cross-platform: Linux (preferred for, but not limited to immersive environments) and Windows (preferred for desktop mode), allowing easy integration into the designer's workflow

There are other tools, commercial as well as experimental, which address the same task. Tools like Virtual Design 2® [1] from vrcom und DeltaGen® from RealTime Technologies [2] provide scene editing functionalities analog to VRfx, but both follow the "Editor/Player" approach, which spans a long iteration loop between scene editor and immersive environment. VirtoolsTM [3] and Quest3DTM [4] are complete development environments, addressing VR developers rather than designers and modellers.

Another approach is to leave all scene editing on the modeller software side and specifying an exchange format which holds more visual effects than typical exchange formats like VRML, and provide an exporter plugin for the modelling software and a VR capable player which displays the scene in the immersive environment. This approach is actually a variant of the "Editor/Player" scheme, and it is limited to a particular modelling tool. An example is VR4MAX [5].

3 Functional Aspects of VRfx

3.1 User Interface

The most important design criteria for the graphical user interface of VRfx were intuitive access by users who are familiar with modelling tools like 3D Studio MAX, and a direct, undelayed visual feedback of all changes in the 3D view which is a prerequisite for fine tuning of material properties by the designer. The GUI main window is vertically divided into two halves, from which the left shows a tree view of the objects in the scene (geometry, materials, light sources, functional objects), the right shows the editable properties of the selected object. This holds for shader materials, too, which expose their adjustable parameters only, thereby hiding most of the technical complexity of the shader. From the designer's view, a shader is a material which can be simply applied to a surface like a texture.

The GUI is available on the desktop as well as in an immersive environment. In the latter, it can be displayed on a mobile device (e.g. a tablet PC) or on a Sensing Surface [6], i.e. a virtual desktop which is displayed on an arbitrary textured object in the VR scene, in which case the interaction takes place through the 3D input device. In collaborative sessions, each client has its own GUI window.

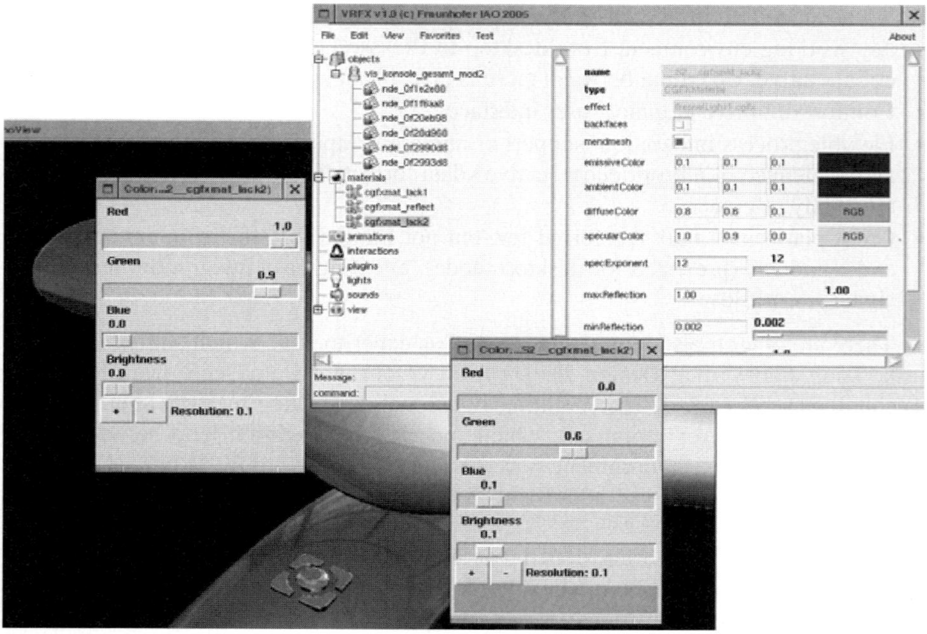

Fig. 3. VRfx GUI

3.2 Data Integration

To maintain maximum flexibility in data integration, we wanted to avoid a proprietary data format containing all scene information and resources (geometry, textures, shader effects). Instead, the VRfx scene description (called session file) contains only references to these data, and the values of modifiable object properties. This allows to change external resources without any change in the session file. In the particular case of geometries, the only limitation is that object identifiers (i.e. node names) in the model which are referenced in the session should not change.

Geometry files can be of any data format supported by the scene graph, which are currently VRML97, Inventor, OBJ, flt, and a few less important others. Many normalmap-based effects require an additional local coordinate system (the tangent space) at each vertex. As long as vertex normals and at least one set of texture coordinates is provided in the model data, the associated tangents and binormals are generated automatically. Normal map textures can either be used from external sources or computed internally from bump maps.

3.3 Interactions

Spatial interaction with virtual prototypes, such as operating switches of appliances, can play an important role in the review of a virtual prototype. Like the visual appearance, they should be specifiable without need for programming. VRfx provides a simple event mechanism which allows to change properties of arbitrary objects when entering or leaving dedicated sensitive volumes (called trigger volumes) with head or hands of the user's avatar. This functionality is completely accessible through the GUI. More complex semantics which cannot be described with the current simple event model can be implemented as TCL scripts which can be imported as plugins. Script objects have the same property interface as other objects so that they can be accessed seamlessly through the GUI.

In addition, complex animations can be imported from VRML files which allows using the functionality of modelling tools to specify animation paths. For this, VRfx integrates a complete VRML97 runtime environment which is based on the open source VRML library libVRML97 [7]. The nodes of a loaded VRML scene and their fields are accessible in VRfx which allows to connect them to the interaction event mechanism.

4 Technical Aspects of VRfx

4.1 Overview

The implementation of VRfx is based on the VR framework Lightning by Fraunhofer IAO [8]. It provides an application development environment with a two-layer API consisting of a scripting layer and a C++ API. Most basic system components (particularly the visual renderer, the script interpreter, and the device server) are encapsulated as dynamic shared objects therefore exchangeable. The current VRfx implementation uses TCL as scripting language and OpenGL Performer [9] as scene graph renderer, which was extended by shader functionality. As any scene graph node can be linked to an instance of the Lightning object pool, they are accessible through VRfx, especially to apply materials and shaders to them.

4.2 Shader Support

The programmable stages of the GPU are capable of executing short programs for each vertex or fragment (corresponding to a pixel), respectively. These programs are usually written in C-like high level languages like Cg [10], OpenGL Shading Language [11], and HLSL [12]. However, a complete shader effect consists of more than a vertex and a fragment program. References to external resources (mostly textures) must be specified. The mapping of effect parameters and other renderer state variables to program parameters must be defined, and other state variables of the graphics pipeline which are important for a particular effect must be specified; an example for this is the blending mode for transparency effects. Another issue is multipass effects which rely on rendering the geometry multiple times with different vertex/fragment programs (e.g. the fur effect in Fig. 1) and state settings; a comprehensive effect description method should support this. Figure 5 gives an overview of the elements of a shader effect.

As we wanted to expose shader effects simply as materials to the user, we needed an effect description which included all of these elements. A first prototype was a material object in Lightning which accepted vertex and fragment programs as well as texture resources through the its field interface. The renderer bindings were specified through a simple, script-based mechanism.

While this approach already allowed to implement a variety of effects, it was too inflexible and proprietary, which was the reason to move to the CgFX format from NVIDIA, which allows a self-contained specification of shader effects with all required components. In addition, CgFX allows to specify different implementations of an effect as so-called *techniques*, which makes it possible to write hardware independent effects; the renderer chooses the best technique for the hardware it is running on at execution time.

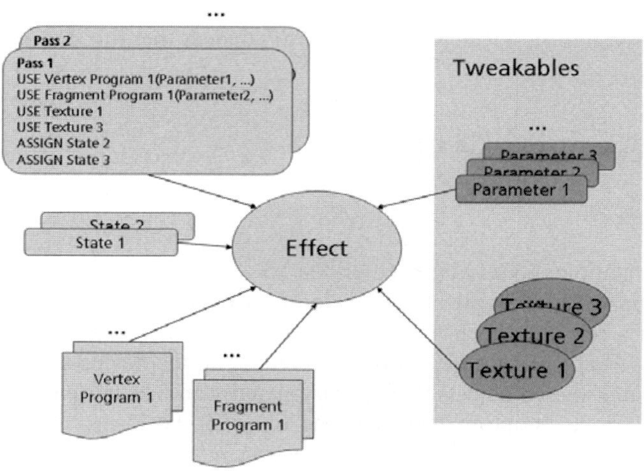

Fig. 4. Components of a shader effect

The editable properties of a CgFX effect (called tweakables) can have an additional description of their representation in the graphical user interface, which is used in VRfx. While the CgFX specification is not complete (e.g. some of the renderer binding semantics are not part of the specification), CgFX effects can often be exchanged between applications with very few adaptations. More important is the fact that the CgFX format is sufficiently comprehensive to allow external developers to create new shading effects and use them without modification of the target renderer.

To add shader and especially CgFX support to the Performer scene graph, its draw traversal was extended so that the separate Model and View matrices (which are collapsed to a single Modelview matrix in standard OpenGL) are tracked.

5 Example Scenario

Since VRfx enriches internal and external communication of design concepts and sketches with a visual fidelity which is close to a real physical model, it is an adequate tool in a wide range of applications from industrial design or architecture to marketing. Whatever it is used for in a particular project, two main parties are involved – the modeller and the customer.

An important fact is that the modeller often is an external contractor who works offsite on his desktop on the creation or adaptation of geometry data and the composition of the materials, while the customer has direct access to the final platform, the virtual environment. However, desktop and immersive displays differ considerably in display characteristics that significantly affect the appearance of a material: e.g. resolution, brightness, contrast and color density. Therefore it is essential to constantly adjust the appearance of materials between the modeller's desktop and the final platform. VRfx therefore offers the possibility to connect several application instances – e.g. one on the desktop of the modeller the other in the VR environment. External resources (geometry and textures), which make up most of the data volumes, are distributed prior to the collaborative session. The only data that has to be shared in real time are the parameters of the current session. As a result, exactly the same content is presented on all VRfx instances while all changes are visible directly. Both sides have full access to the GUI and all its interaction features and have their own, independent navigation. In a collaborative session between an external modeller and customer, the modeller can apply changes to the scene remotely, while both parties immediately see the result.

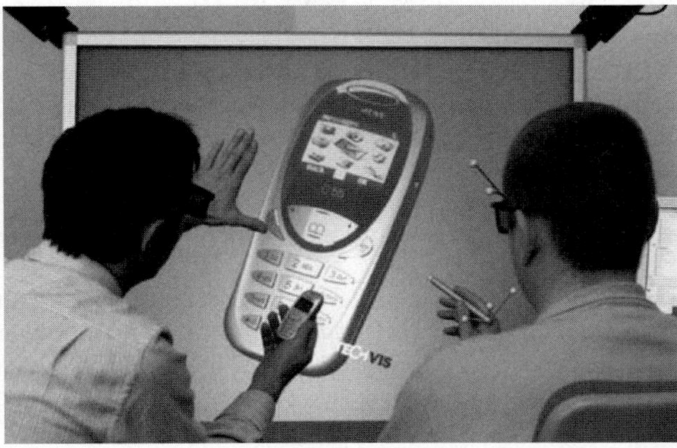

Fig. 5. Scenario for fine tuning in VRfx: Two designers consult an external modeller off-site about the materials of a mobile phone prototype

6 Conclusion and Future Work

So far, VRfx was used in a variety of visualization projects; the results and user feedback obtained so far indicate that the proposed workflow actually facilitates the creation of VR presentations and leads to an improved quality of the results. Users with different background skills levels are working with the tool; the depth of work ranges from pure assembly and preparation of models to the development of own CgFX shader effects. Next steps in development are:

- Support for more input data formats, e.g. the JT format which is well established as a visualization exchange data format in the CAD world, and Collada, a data exchange format of growing importance in the digital content creation domain.

- More comfortable handling of complex scenes by additional structuring mechanisms beyond the scene graph hierarchy.
- Extended model to describe interactions to provide more flexibility without the need for scripting.
- Support more shader description formats, e.g. RenderMonkey from ATI
- Integration of diffuse global illumination by internal computation of light maps
- Integration of raytracing, at first for single objects only, in combination with hardware based rendering of the rest of the scene [16].

References

1. Virtual Design 2. http://www.vrcom.com
2. DeltaGen. http://www.realtime-technology.de
3. Virtools. http://www.virtools.com
4. Quest3D. http://www.quest3d.com
5. VR4MAX - Real-time VR for 3ds max and Autodesk VIZ. http://www.vr4max.com
6. Bues, M., Blach, R., Haselberger, F.: Sensing Surfaces - Bringing the Desktop into Virtual Environments. In: Proceedings of IPT & EGVE Workshop, Zürich, Springer, Heidelberg (2003)
7. Morley, C., McDaniel, B. libVRML97 library. Maintained by http://www.openvrml.org
8. Blach, R., Landauer, J., Rüsch, A., Simon, A.: A flexible prototyping tool for 3D realtime user-interaction.Virtual Environments. Conference and 4th Eurographics Workshop held simultaneously with IEEE YUFORIC Germany (1998)
9. Rohlf, J., Helman, J.: IRIS Performer: A High Performance Multiprocessing Toolkit for Real-Time 3D Graphics, Computer Graphics (SIG-GRAPH '94 Proceedings), pp. 381–394 (July 1994)
10. NVIDIA Corporation: Cg Toolkit. http://developer.nvidia.com/object/cg_toolkit.html
11. Segal, M., Akeley, K.: The OpenGL Graphics System: A Specification (Version 2.0), http://www.opengl.org/documentation/specs/version2.0/glspec20.pdf
12. Gray, K.: The DirectX programmable graphics pipeline. Redmond, Microsoft Press (2003)
13. Hoffmann, H., Stefani, O., Dangelmaier, M.: Mobile and Desk integrated Virtual Reality. International Conference on Human Computer Interaction (HCI 2005), Las Vegas (2005)

Effects of Virtual Reality Display Types on the Brain Computer Interface System

Hyun Sang Cho[1], Kyoung Shin Park[2], Yongkag Kim[1], Chang S. Kim[3], and Minsoo Hahn[1]

[1] Digital Media Laboratory, Information and Communications University, 517-10 Dogok-dong, Gangnam-gu, Seoul 135-854, S. Korea
haemosu@icu.ac.kr

[2] Multimedia Engineering, Dankook University, San 29 Anseo-dong, Cheonan-si, Chungnam, 330-714, Korea

[3] Digital Ocean & Virtual Environment Center, Korea Ocean Research & Development Institute, 1270 Sa2 dong, Ansan 426-744, Korea

Abstract. This paper presents the study of evaluating VR display types on Brain Computer Interface (BCI) performance. In this study, a configurable virtual reality BCI system was used for users to control the virtual environment to execute the ubiquitous computing home facilities. The study evaluated various VR display types: 2D arrow cue, 3D virtual reality, 3D fully immersive CAVE system, and 3D CAVE cue. The task involved users to imagine left or right arm movements for rotating the direction in the virtual environment and move forward by using a direction locking device. The result shows that there was no significant improvement on BCI classification rate even by enhancing the immersion of VR displays. Instead, the level of simulator sickness was increased. This result indicates a new improved display type is needed for the ubiquitous computing environment control BCI system.

Keywords. Brain Computer Interface, Virtual Reality, Ubiquitous Computing Environment, Immersion, Display Types.

1 Introduction

Brain computer interface (BCI) is a direct communication method between the human brain and computing devices. BCI extracts the information from human brain wave using electroencephalogram (EEG). The most commonly used brain input signals are evoked potentials, such as Visual Evoked Potential (VEP), Slow Cortical Potentials (SCPs), and Event Related Desynchronization (ERD) or Event Related Synchronization (ERS) of μ (8~12Hz) and β (13~30Hz) rhythm [3][6]. ERD refers to the spectrum band comparison of left and right side sensorimotor (parietal) cortex. This phenomenon is a spectral power decrease of μ rhythm (8~12Hz) or β rhythm at opposite side motor cortex (i.e. C3 and C4 of international 10-20 system) when a person moves his/her left or right arm or simply imagines such a movement [2]. The μ-rhythm ERD starts 2.5 seconds before the movement-onset, reaches a maximal desynchronization

C. Stephanidis (Ed.): Universal Access in HCI, Part II, HCII 2007, LNCS 4555, pp. 633–639, 2007.

shortly after the movement-onset, and then recovers to the baseline level within a few seconds. Since ERD/ERS is triggered by human imagery of motion without physical movements, it is possible to be used for motion disabled people. With the advent of emerging ubiquitous computing technology, it is possible to create a smart home environment that allows motion disabled people to control their surrounding objects.

Virtual reality provides realistic spatial information of real world, and it offers rich and immersive sensory feedbacks that draw user's attention. Virtual reality can offer the recovery of life for motion disabled people by giving the feeling of presence. There have been a few attempts that BCI is used as a control interface for virtual reality or the real environment, such as a training BCI tool for disabled people to operate wheelchair or robot arm [8]. However, most of them use the one degree of freedom (DOF) BCI system because the error rate of BCI classification is much higher with 2-DOF BCI system. It is also observed that the user controllability of the system is dramatically reduced when more than 2 DOF classifications are simultaneously used in the virtual environment, which results in user's simulation sickness [4].

Over the last year, we have developed a virtual reality BCI system for disabled people to control a ubiquitous home environment. This application used the motor imagery based BCI using ERD signal detection of μ and β rhythm at external skull region of parietal lobe to catch users' intention of left or right direction turns in the virtual environment [3][6]. In this system, we provided a direction locking mechanism to enhance the user controllability and help reduce simulation sickness. That is, a user could lock the direction when he/she wanted the direction to go forward, and the user could unlock (i.e., release the direction locking) so that he/she could turn left or right directions (i.e., rotate in the virtual environment). We have developed a pedal-like direction locking device for normal people and a simple eye-blink detector for motion disabled people [4].

This paper presents a study on the effects of VR display types on ERD-based BCI performance. The goal of this study is to investigate which VR display type is the most effective for users to control the ubiquitous computing home environment. It measured the subject's BCI decision classification rates and simulation sickness questionnaires (SSQ) [5] while different VR display types were given: 2D arrow cue on the monitor, 3D virtual reality on the monitor, 3D virtual reality in the fully immersive CAVE system, and 3D virtual reality in the CAVE with the cue. This paper first describes the virtual reality BCI system designed for disabled people to control their ubiquitous computing home facilities. Next, it describes the study method and the results. Then, it concludes with the future research directions.

2 The Virtual Reality Brain-Computer Interface System

Fig. 1 shows the overview of our virtual reality BCI system for ubiquitous computing home controls. The system consists of the brain signal processing, the virtual environment, and the controller for ubiquitous computing home facilities. The brain signal processing includes QEEG-8 8-channel EEG measurement equipment by Laxtha Inc. and a brain signal collection and processing unit. We use the international 10-20 system for the EEG electrode placement attached on the human brain. A reference and a ground electrode are attached to the user's lower jar below a right ear. The data is

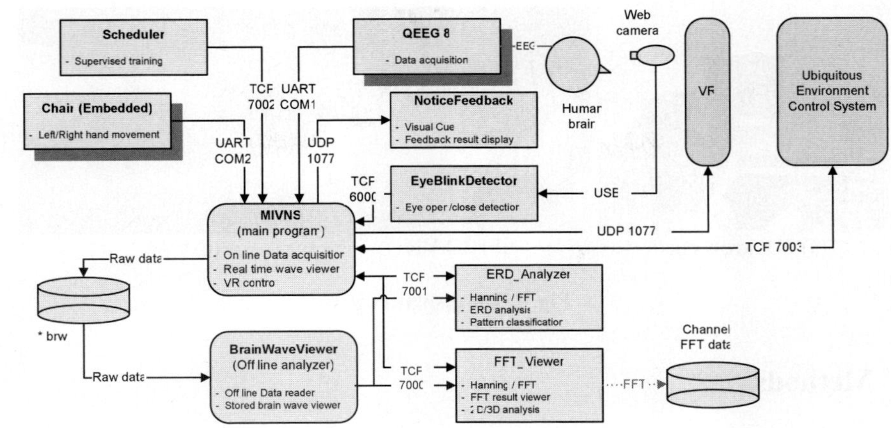

Fig. 1. The system architecture of the virtual reality BCI system for ubiquitous computing environment controls

sampled at 128 Hz and processed in every one second using a Fast Fourier Transformation (FFT). Thus, the frequency range after FFT is 0~63 Hz and the resolution is 1 Hz.

The brain signal processing consists of a functional module for frequency analysis, feature extraction, pattern classification, training session and data analysis. The modules are connected via UDP and TCP communication with UART. The additional direction locking mechanism is provided to support free VR navigation – i.e., a user can freely move around the virtual world by moving forward and turning left or right. For a direction locking mechanism, an eye blink detection or foot-pedal device is used. The embedded chair gets the additional signal from user. We also provide a rich data visualization tool to display online and offline brain wave for further analysis. We support the user training session and the brain wave analyzer to build up customized feature extractions and classifications for each subject in order to reduce the subject dependency [7]. The Scheduler randomly generates left or right arrow direction cues and supervises the user training session by predefined training schedule. The ERD Analyzer detects the user's intention from brain signals two seconds after the user imagines left or right arm movements. It then sends the classification result to the main program, and to the notification feedback display. Raw brain signals from the 8-channels EEG equipment and the classification results from the ERD Analyzer are saved in the local storage. The BrainWaveViewer restores the saved data and send the date to other modules for offline analysis.

The virtual environment was implemented using Ygdrasil (YG) [1]. YG is a framework for rapid construction of networked virtual environments. It can run on Linux, Windows, and SGI machine. This virtual environment contains two lamps and one curtain in a room. In this environment, users can turn left or right in the rotation degree of 22.5° and go forward in one-foot step. The lamp lights are on and the curtain moves upward when the user approaches these objects.

(a) 2D arrow cue (b) 3D VR (c) CAVE

Fig. 2. VR display t ypes

3 Methods

We conducted an experiment of six participants using our virtual reality BCI system to evaluate the effects of the VR display types. We evaluated subject's BCI performance on a 2D visual arrow cue for the subject's base condition, and then a 3D free VR navigation on a 17'' LCD monitor, and a 3D free VR navigation in a fully immersive CAVE system. We expect the immersion can enhance the user's concentration and consequently the BCI correct classification rate. Five male and one female graduate student volunteered as participants in this study. The ages of the participants were 23 to 37 years old. They had high level computer experience and their typical computer usage time was more than three hours a day. However, none of them had prior experience with EEG equipment, BCI, and VR system. That is, all participants were novice users to VR and BCI.

The experiment involved a simple BCI test using left or right arrow direction cues presented on a 17'' LCD monitor to measure the subject's ERD patterns. This study was required to find the reference for the subject's baseline characteristics. In this test, all subjects were given three sessions at different time. Each session consisted of five training trials with a 5-minute break in between the trials. For each trial, the subjects were randomly given left or right direction cues by the automatic cue generator (shown in Fig 2 (a)). The subject imagined left or right lobe body movement such as fingers as soon as he/she saw the arrow cue. Then, the system detected the user's intention, and then it displayed the BCI classification feedback on the monitor. This test was conduct at the ICU Digital Media Lab.

In the actual experiment, the subjects freely decided their navigating direction in the virtual environment using our BCI system within a 5-minute session while the different VR display types were presented –i.e., a 17'' LCD monitor versus a fully immersive CAVE-like system. This study was conducted at the Digital Ocean & Virtual Environment Center (DOVE) of the Korea Ocean Research and Development Institute (KORDI). KORDI's MoVE (Motorized multi-purpose Virtual Environment) system has four 3.2 x 2.4m size movable screens. The system runs on a SGI Onyx350 workstation with 6 CPUs (64bit RISC MIPS R16000A 800MHz), 4 pipes and 1 GB texture memory. The subjects were given the task three times for each condition (3D VR on the monitor and then in the CAVE) and a 5-minute break between the task session.

Table 1. The correct BCI classification rates by subject's ERD of the μ rhythm (%)

Subject	2D cue		3D VR		3D CAVE		3D CAVE cue	
	left	right	left	right	left	right	left	right
A	62.22	44.63	65.56	29.53	72.59	34.30	65.23	38.17
B	54.65	53.64	76.58	36.68	59.31	50.66	N.A.	
C	66.36	56.34	54.39	70.48	61.70	53.80	66.24	60.05
D	66.56	53.01	59.87	34.61	68.49	34.73	52.93	60.24
E	80.53	49.95	52.51	49.81	69.83	39.43	N.A	
F	73.23	51.80	67.48	37.76	69.37	37.34	57.06	63.96
Average	59.41		52.94		54.30		57.99	

In this test, a button on a tip of wooden bar tied on the chair arms was provided to the subjects to lock or unlock the direction and to indicate their intention of moving direction after the BCI uses. When a user pushed the left and right button together, the chair embedded controller sent a direction locking toggle command to the system. When the system was under the lock mode, the user could go forward if he/she pushed either left or right side buttons. Then, when the system was under the unlock mode, the user could press left or right button after the BCI decision to indicate which way they wanted to turn. Finally, the subjects were asked to answer simulation sickness questionnaire (SSQ) [5] at the end of the tasks for each condition.

In the follow-up experiment, four subjects came back and performed the same VR navigation task while the left or right direction cue was randomly given by the experimenter verbally, i.e., without the button operation. Before this test, they first experienced two other VR applications: the Ocean and the Digital Goguryeo. Then we also evaluated simulation sickness questionnaire (SSQ) before and after VR experience.

4 Results and Discussions

Table 1 shows the study results, and the average correct classification rate was 59.41% (2D cue), 52.94% (3D VR), 54.30% (3D CAVE), and 57.99% (3D CAVE with the randomly given cues). We wanted to find out if BCI classification rate would become higher by more immersive VR display types in our BCI system. However, the classification rate was still quite low regardless of the conditions. We think this low classification rate seemed to be due to a short user training time (i.e., 3 sessions in the 2D direction cue test) and the system did not adopted no machine learning method. We found that each subject had unique ERD pattern of μ and β rhythm in the 2D cue test. Some of them would show better direction classification on the μ rhythm, and others showed the β rhythm tendency. In particular, most subjects had shown lots of body movements in the CAVE that affected the β rhythm. Thus we used the μ rhythm for BCI classification to all our subjects in the rest of the experiments.

Unlike our expectation, the study results show the BCI classification rate widely varied by the subjects. Overall relatively high classification rate was found on 2D cue (for left or right side). Also, overall BCI classification rate was slightly better in the CAVE than on the 3D VR Monitor. The classification rate was quite low for the right

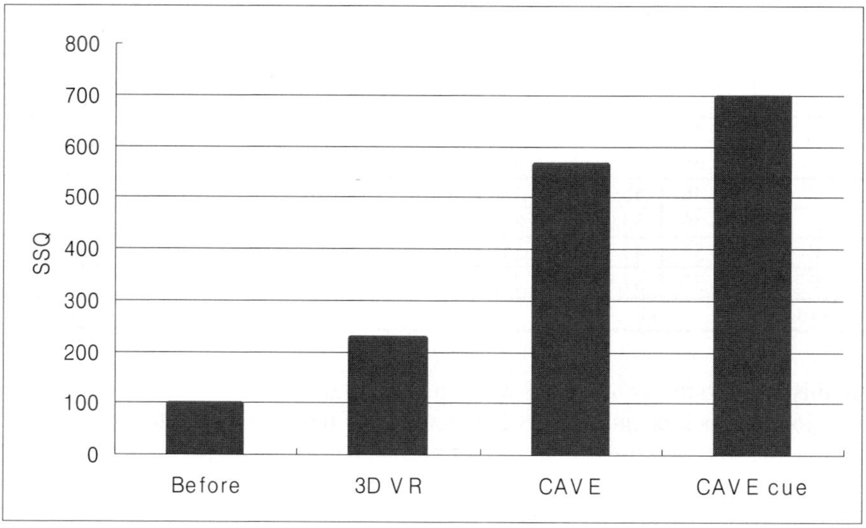

Fig. 3. Participants' average value of SSQ

side compared to the left side, and indeed the subjects said they had to concentrate on the task to make the correct rotation to the right. Furthermore, the classification rate got slightly better in the 3D CAVE cue condition where the subjects were given the left or right cues randomly by the experimenter.

Interestingly, CAVE seemed to be a source of simulation sickness when using our BCI system due to greater immersiveness. According to SSQ results, most subjects felt disorientation after the CAVE experience. This result might be because they were novice to the CAVE system as well. We also believe that user simulation sickness seemed to be intensified by low BCI classification rate. Some subjects also reported that free navigation in a narrow VR space (even in the Digital Goguryeo) made them feel severe fatigue

5 Conclusions and Future Work

This paper presents the effects of VR display types on the BCI performance. This study is intended to investigate the suitable display types for the ubiquitous computing environment control BCI system. The study evaluated subject's ERD of the μ rhythm on BCI to detect left or right direction decisions under 2D arrow cue, 3D virtual reality, 3D full immersive CAVE system, and 3D CAVE cue conditions. We expected that the large amount of visual feedback and immersiveness could help users to concentrate on the task thereby increasing BCI classification performance. However, the study results showed no significant difference among the VR display types. Instead, severe user simulation sickness was observed in the fully immersive CAVE system even if the locking mechanism was provided or the cue was given.

The SSQ results showed that most subjects felt simulation sickness in the fully immersive CAVE system. This result might be because the subjects were not familiar with the CAVE and the BCI system. However realistic temporal-spatial visual feedback is essential in the BCI system. In the near future, we will support a streaming of real video images from a ubiquitous computing home robot (Ubiquitous Robotic Companion, URC) [9]. Users simply instruct the destination to the autonomous mobile robot and receive the actual moving video from the robot. We believe this real video streaming will give users high immersiveness with less simulation sickness. We will also support the environment map with the current user position and the object information (such as, TV contents or the state of washing machine) combined with the main video stream. Furthermore, we will develop the context-aware service model for appropriate system operations in the ubiquitous computing home environment. We will also continue to improve BCI classification rates by adopting machine learning methods or artifact removals and develop a user training program to our BCI system for further evaluation studies.

Acknowledgements. I appreciate participants' heartful and active participation in this experiment. This research was supported by the MIC (Ministry of Information and Communication), Korea, under the Digital Media Lab. support program supervised by the IITA (Institute of Information Technology Assessment).

References

1. Pape, D., Anstey, J., Dolinsky, M., Dambik, E.J.: Ygdrasil-a framework for composing shared virtual worlds. Future Generation Computer Systems 19(6), 141–149 (2003)
2. Gert Pfurtscheller and Christa Neuper, Motor Imagery and Direct Brain–Computer Communication. In: Proceedings of the IEEE, vol. 89(7) (July 2001)
3. Guest Editorial, Brain–Computer Interface Technology: A Review of the Second International Meeting, IEEE Transactions on Neural Systems and Rehabilitation Engineering, vol. 11(2) (June 2003)
4. Cho, H.-s., Goo, J., Suh, D.-j., Park, K.S., Hahn, M.: The Virtual Reality Brain-Computer Interface System for Ubiquitous Home Control. In: Sattar, A., Kang, B.-H. (eds.) AI 2006. LNCS (LNAI), vol. 4304, Springer, Heidelberg (2006)
5. Prothero, J.D.: The Role of Rest Frames in Vection, Presence and Motion Sickness, Doctorate dissertation (1998), http://www.hitl.washington.edu/publications/r-98-11/thesis.html
6. Wolpaw, J.R., et al.: Brain–Computer Interface Technology: A Review of the First International Meeting. IEEE Transactions on Rehabilitation Engineering, vol. 8(2) (June 2000)
7. Polak, M., Kostov, A.: Development of Brain-Computer Interface: Preliminary. In: Proceedings - 19th International Conference - IEEE/EMBS October 30 - November 2 (1997)
8. Moore, M.M.: Real-World Applications for Brain–Computer Interface Technology. IEEE Transactions on Neural Systems and Rehabilitation Engineering, vol. 11(2) (June 2003)
9. Oh, S.R: Network-based new intelligent robot paradigm: ubiquitous robotic companion. IEEE Workshop on Advanced Robotics and its Social Impacts (2005)

A First Person Visuo-Haptic Environment

Sabine Coquillart

i3D - INRIA Rhône-Alpes - LIG
Montbonnot, 655 avenue de l'Europe, 38334 Saint-Ismier Cedex, France
Sabine.Coquillart@inria.fr

Abstract. In real life, most of the tasks we perform throughout the day are first person tasks. Shouldn't these same tasks be realized from a first person point of view in virtual reality? This paper presents a first person Projection-based Visuo-Haptic Environment, and virtual prototyping and data exploration applications taking advantage of the first person visuo-haptic features of this configuration.

Keywords: virtual reality, 6dof force feedback, projection-based virtual environments, co-location, virtual prototyping, scientific visualization.

1 Introduction

In real life, most of the tasks we achieve throughout the day are first person tasks (ie. with co-location). Shouldn't these same tasks be realized from a first person point of view in virtual reality?

In Virtual Reality, one can distinguish mainly between two classes of configurations, HMDs and Projection-based Virtual Environments. Both allow for first person visualization due to head tracking. However, when haptic feedback is added, first person manipulation is not easy to maintain with Projection-based Virtual Environments for two major reasons. First, because there are not many types of force feedback devices and most of the existing ones are either heavy, invasive and expensive, or only work within a limited space. The second difficulty comes from the configuration itself. Most of the benefits of Projection-based Virtual Environments become constraints when the integration of force feedback is concerned. The large size of the visualization space is very important to increase presence and immersion but few force feedback devices work in large enough spaces. Most force feedback devices are constructed of large rigid parts which, when located in the field of view, may occlude the scene. Moreover, these parts can create inconsistencies in visualization when they are placed behind the virtual objects of the scene.

This paper presents the Stringed Haptic Workbench, a new First Person Visuo-Haptic Environment based on a two-screen workbench. This virtual environment is enriched with a Stringed Haptic Interface. Several applications have been developed using this new environment. They take advantage of the first person visualization and haptic manipulation.

C. Stephanidis (Ed.): Universal Access in HCI, Part II, HCII 2007, LNCS 4555, pp. 640–643, 2007.

2 The Stringed Haptic Workbench

The Stringed Haptic Workbench [3] is a first person visuo-haptic environment, it integrates a SPIDAR haptic device with a two-screen workbench. The SPIDAR [1] is a stringed haptic system which has two critical advantages: it allows for large manipulation spaces and it is visually non intrusive. Several version of the SPIDAR exist including a 3dof (translations) version which makes use of 4 strings and a 6dof (translations and torques) making use of 8 strings. The strings are activated by motors controlled by a computer. See [3] for more details on the motor positioning. Figure 1 shows the Stringed Haptic Workbench with an operator touching a car wheel.

The Stringed Haptic Workbench opens a door to new applications requiring a realistic integration of first person visualization and haptic feedback. Two applications have already been developed on the Stringed Haptic Workbench: a virtual prototyping application simulating putty application on a car body [2], and a scientific visualization application for geosciences.

Fig. 1. Stringed-Haptic Workbench: touching a cube (with special fx)

3 Simulation of Putty Application on a Car Body

The automotive industry has increasing demands for new virtual reality prototyping tools in order to decrease the time and the cost of the conception stages. The application described here concerns putty application on a car body. In the conception stage, car designers need to evaluate the application of putty onto metallic junctions of the car body. In this task, the operator uses a putty gun. The putty comes out from the nose of the gun, when the trigger is pushed, and is applied to the junction. Quality, time and ergonomics are considered at the evaluation of the task. With physical mock-ups, when "critical regions" (defective junctions or parts of a junction) are detected, a new mock-up has to be built and tested again after the problem is corrected. The Stringed Haptic Workbench can be used to simulate putty application on virtual mock-ups in order to avoid costly physical mock-ups. See [2] and Figure 2 for more details.

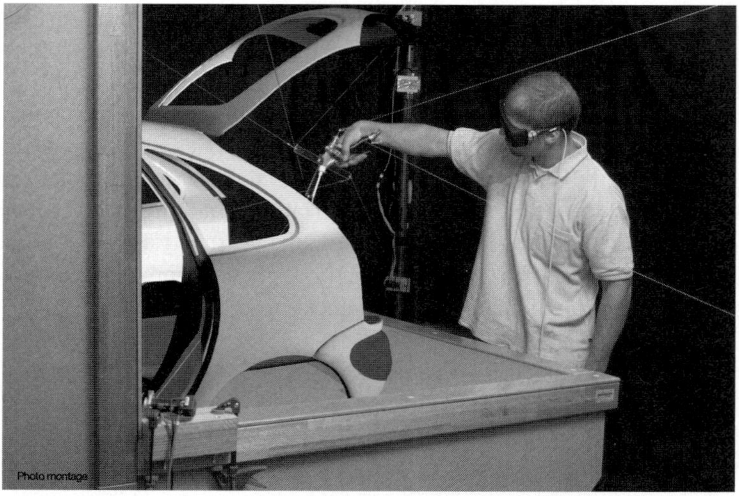

Fig. 2. Putty application on a Citroën Picasso car (data © PSA Peugeot Citroën) (with special fx)

4 Data Exploration

Data exploration is another major virtual reality application. Regardless of the data source (large scientific computation programs or experimental data), exploration application are often required to analyze large and complex data sets. In most case,

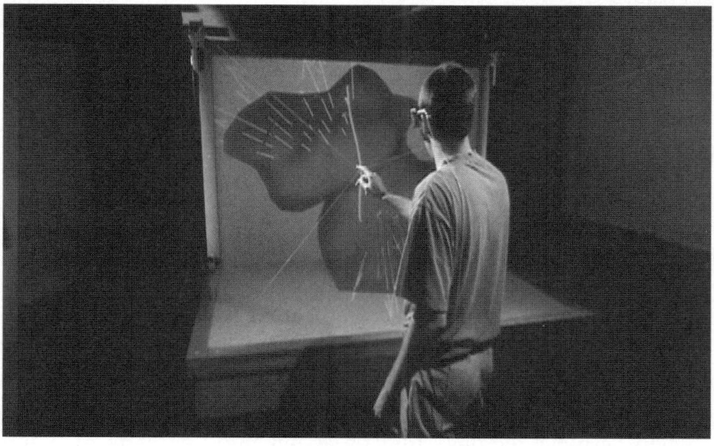

Fig. 3. Analysis of streamlines of a meteor entering water (data ©CEA)

even a large field of view is not sufficient to visualize the complexity of the potentially multi-dimensional data. This problem might be resolved by rendering different dimensions on different sensory channels. The Stringed Haptic Workbench is an ideal configuration for this purpose. Some information can be rendered on the visual channel while other can be rendered on the haptic one. Figure 3 shows such an application where an operator is exploring streamlines of a meteor entering water.

5 Conclusion

The Stringed Haptic Workbench is a flexible configuration that provides first person visualization together with first person haptic feedback. The main advantage of the Stringed Haptic Workbench is the size of its visual and haptic spaces. It allows direct haptic manipulation in a large space, while the occluded visualization space is negligible. And the occultation is minimal so that any part of the visualization space is visible.

Two applications, virtual prototyping and data exploration, have been developed. Informal evaluations have assessed and confirmed the configuration benefits. Other applications are under consideration.

Acknowledgments. The author thanks Ambroise Guabello, Mathias Lorente, Michaël Ortega, Nicolas Tarrin and Thomas Vincent, for their participation to the "Stringed Haptic Workbench" project, and Inna Tsirlin for a careful reading of the paper. The author thanks also PSA Peugeot Citroën, BRGM, and CEA for fruitful collaborations on the Stringed Haptic Workbench. This work was partly funded by the ANR projects Geobench and PERF-RV2. Certain parts of the paper were already published in [2] and [3].

References

1. Hirata, Y., Sato, M.: 3-Dimensional Interface Device for Virtual Work Space. IEEE/RSJ International Conference on IROS (1992)
2. Ortega, M., Coquillart, S.: Prop-based Haptic Interaction with Co-location and Immersion: an Automotive Application. In: HAVE'05 (2005)
3. Tarrin, N., Coquillart, S., Hasegawa, S., Bouguila, L., Sato, M.: The Stringed Haptic Workbench: a New Haptic Workbench Solution. In: EUROGRAPHICS'03 (2003)

AKROPHOBIA Treatment Using Virtual Environments: Evaluation Using Real-Time Physiology

Marcel Delahaye[1], Ralph Mager[1], Oliver Stefani[1], Evangelos Bekiaris[2], Michael Studhalter[1], Martin Traber[1], Ulrich Hemmeter[3], and Alexander H. Bullinger[1]

[1] COAT-BASEL, University of Basel,
Wilhem-KleinStr. 27,
4052 Basel, Switzerland
Marcel Delahaye, Oliver Stefani, Ralf Mager, Alexander Bullinger
key@coat-basel.com
[2] CERTH-HIT: Centre for Research and Technology Hellas (CERTH),
Hellenic Insitute of Transport (HIT)
6th Km Charilaou - Thermi Rd. PO Box 361
57001 Thermi, Thessaloniki, Greece
abek@certh.gr
[3]Philipps-Universität Marburg,
Klinik für Neurologie
Rudolf Bultmann Strasse 8
D-35032 Marburg
PD Dr. Ulrich Hemmeter
hemmeter@med.uni-marburg.de

Abstract. In the present paper a VR (Virtual Reality) exposure treatment program for Acrophobia (fear of heights) is introduced and evaluated against an in vivo exposure with the same success rate. During the VR exposure psychophysiological parameters (heart rate, respiratory rate) are collected. VR offers the good opportunity to study psychophysiological effects under almost standardized conditions. The findings reflect partly the somatic correlates during an anxiety attack. Beside the opportunity of standardized circumstances other advantages of VR techniques are discussed (cost effectiveness, enhancement of the narration process, higher user acceptance).

Keywords: VR therapy, Acrophobia, presence physiological correlates, narration process, desensitization.

1 Introduction

Psychotherapy has become a big research and application field for VR in the last decade. One newly defined field within this “Cyberpsychology” is the treatment of phobias in VR [1], [2].

Despite the fact that a lot of somatic symptoms are included in the diagnostic criteria of anxiety and panic disorders there are only little research efforts focusing on psychophysiological parameters [3]. An objective measurement would also alleviate a valid evaluation of the therapeutical effect [4].

C. Stephanidis (Ed.): Universal Access in HCI, Part II, HCII 2007, LNCS 4555, pp. 644–651, 2007.

VR offers the opportunity to focus on psychophysiological parameters such as heart and breathing rate under standardized circumstances. The virtual environment guarantees more controllable conditions compared to an in vivo exposure in the real world (other people, weather, etc.).

A clinical trial study was performed at the University of Basel comparing Acrophobia desensitization in Virtual Reality vs. desensitization in vivo. 67 participants were recruited via advertisement in the local newspaper. Special emphasis was given to the selection of the participant. Patients with phobia were only allowed to participate if they had no other psychiatric comorbidity.

2 Experimental Setup

The experimental setting can be described as following: while patients with acrophobia are confronted with their fear in VR (outside elevator), they had to rate their subjective discomfort (anxiety level) every three minutes on a the "SUD-score" scale [5]. At the same time the heart and respiratory rate are measured.

3 Aims of the Study

First goal was to demonstrate that a VR program with a simple HMD system has the same effect for the treatment than a "lege artis" in vivo confrontation.

Second goal was to show that during desensitization physiological parameters will reflect the progress of the therapy.

Third goal was to describe the benefit of VR tools for the narration during the desensitization process.

4 Description of the Measured Data (Dependent Variables)

Beside the subjective anxiety level, heart rate and respiratory rate are measured.

5 SUD Score

Participants had to rate their level of anxiety (0 – 100) every two to three minutes or at every change of the height. "0" equals total relaxation and "100" equals fear of death.

6 Heart Rate

Heart rate was measured via ECG at 250 Hz and recorded the whole duration of the exposure. After different corrections the interbeat-intervals were calculated. From these the heart frequency was calculated in the beat-to-beat-modus. After a visual evaluation and a half automatic correction of the artefacts the mean heartbeat was composed and lowered on a frequency of 0.1Hz. With respect to other studies [6], [7] we were expecting a higher heart beat frequency due to higher sympathetic nervous system activation during the exposure and an adaptation of the heart beat frequency with increasing habituation.

7 Respiratory Rate

An impedance pneumogram was the basis to calculate the respiratory rate. Breathing was measured via ECG electrodes and recorded with 250 Hz. The percentage of clippings due to movement and speech was calculated and corrected. After a filtering and detrending of the row value a correction of the aorta pulsation was performed. As maximum signals were missing (due to the clipping) the period lengths were calculated for thorax movements above threshold with respect to the resting respiratory position rate for positive und negative zero trials. After that a transaction of gasps per minute was following as well as a floating averaging and a downsampling to 0.1 Hz. The validity of the data is sufficient although the best quality is achieved during speech and motion free periods.

Due to influences from the central cortex we are expecting a inclination of the breathing rate during exposure [8], [9]. In total were three different measuring times during each VR exposure session:

1.	2.	3.
Baseline (before the exposure): reading a neutral text	First two minute interval on maximum height	Last two minute interval on maximum height (after habituation = significant decline of the SUD)

8 Results

During the study three major questions were addressed:

1. Do patients feel anxiety during the VR confrontation?
2. What are the psychophysiological correlates?
3. Is the treatment in VR as successful as an in vivo exposure?

Ad 1: Do Patients Feel Anxiety During the VR Confrontation?

Paired t- test for "SUD" (measuring the anxiety level) comparing first and second measurement during first therapy session:

Paired t test

N=31

Variable	Obs	Mean	Std. Err.	Std. Dev.	95% Conf. Interval	
1. Measurement	31	0.26	0.25	1.4	-0.25	0.78
2. Measurement	31	48.2	3.93	21.88	40.17	56.22
Diff	31	-47.93	4.00	22.32	-56.12	-39.75

Null hypothesis:	mean SUD 1 - mean SUD 2 ≥ mean(diff) ≥ 0

Alternative hypothesis:	mean(diff) < 0
	t = -11.956
	P = 0.000

Conclusion: Null hypothesis has to be rejected: VR exposure leads to an inclination of anxiety.

Ad 2 a) Are There any Correlation During the VR Exposure with Heart Rate?

Paired t test
N=25

Variable	Obs	Mean	Std. Err.	Std. Dev.	95% Conf. Interval	
1. measurement	25	87.78	1.99	9.98	83.65	91.90
2. measurement	25	88.94	1.68	8.42	85.46	92.42
Diff	25	-1.16	1.44	7.20	-4.14	1.80
Null hypothesis:		mean(Messung 1 - Messung 2) ≥ mean(diff) ≥ 0				
Alternative hypothesis:		mean(diff) < 0				
		t = -0.8106				
		P = 0.2128				

Conclusion: Null hypothesis cannot be rejected! Even though it would have been expected, the VR exposure does not affect the heart rate. The second measurement does not show a significant difference compared to the first measurement (baseline).

Ad 2 b) Are There any Correlation During the VR Exposure with Respiratory Rate?

Paired t test

N=28

Variable	Obs	Mean	Std. Err.	Std. Dev.	95% Conf. Interval	
1. measurement	28	15.40	0.49	2.61	14.38	16.41
2. measurement	28	16.00	0.33	1.77	15.31	16.69
Diff	28	-0.59	0.49	2.60	-1.60	0.40
Null hypothesis:		mean(Messung 1 - Messung 2) ≥ mean(diff) ≥ 0				
Alternative hypothesis:		mean(diff) < 0				
		t = -1.2204				
		P = 0.1164				

Conclusion: Null hypothesis cannot be rejected! The VR exposure does not affect the respiratory rate. In parallel to the heart, there is no positive correlation between the exposure and the respiratory rate.

Ad 2 c) Comparison of the Heart Rate at the Beginning and After the Exposure – the (physiological) Habituation Effect: Measurement 2 & 3

Paired t test

N=13

Comparison 2nd with 3rd measurement				
Variable	**Mean 2nd measurement**	**Mean 3rd measurement**	**T-score**	**P value**
1. session	87.15	83.76	3.217	0.0037
2. session	86.48	83.39	3.0964	0.0046
3. session	83.11	82.67	0.3051	0.3827
Null hypothesis:		**Mean (second measurement- third measurement) ≥ mean(diff) ≥ 0**		
Alternative hypothesis:		**mean(diff) < 0**		

Conclusion: The null hypothesis has to be rejected for the first and second therapy session. It can be concluded that the heart rate slowed down after the exposure. A physiological habituation effect can be interpreted!

Ad 2 d) Comparison of the Respiratory Rate at the Beginning and After the Exposure – the Physiological Habituation Effect (Measurement 2 & 3)

Paired t test

N=14

Comparison 2nd with 3rd measurement				
Variable	**Mean 2nd measurement**	**Mean 3rd measurement**	**T-score**	**P value**
1. session	15.69	15.18	1.50	**0.07**
2. session	15.72	15.40	0.89	**0.19**
3. session	16.49	16.09	0.77	**0.22**
Null hypothesis:		**mean(second measurement- third measurement) ≥ mean(diff) ≥ 0**		
Alternative hypothesis:		**mean(diff) < 0**		

Conclusion: The null hypothesis cannot be rejected for none of the therapy session. A trend for the first session can only be concluded in the way that the respiratory rate slows down after the exposure. A physiological habituation effect can be interpreted with caution!

Ad 3: Is the Treatment in VR as Successful as an in Vivo Exposure?

During the planning of the study we faced the problem that it is difficult to find clear criteria for the evaluation of the effects. We consider a VR (N= 35) as well as an in vivo treatment (N= 32, control group) successful when 6 or more points are achieved on the following scale:

Yes = 1	No = 0

1. Confirmation of the subjective benefit of the therapy after the third session
2. Confirmation of the permanent subjective benefit
3. Achievement of maximum height during therapy
4. Augmentation of 30 % of the achieved height compared to the beginning of the sessions
5. Achievement of maximum anxiety level (SUD = 100)
6. 30% reduction of the symptoms (first and last session)
7. Permanent reduction of the symptoms (first and last session)
8. Achievement of maximum height during follow up (in vivo)
9. Reduction of the avoidance behaviour

Kriterium	In vivo	VR	Signifikanztest P-Wert
Success (6 or more points)	15/25	24/32	0.262 n.s.
Drop-outs	7/32	3/35	0.175 n.s.

The results clearly demonstrate that the null hypothesis can not be rejected and therefore is no difference in the success rate between the VR and the in vivo exposure. Compared to other exposure treatments the drop-out rate is very low.

Conclusion: The advantages of VR treatment can be summarized as follows. There is a clear effect of the VR treatment. The success rate is comparable with an in vivo confrontation. Standardized circumstances present another advantage as they allow to measure psychophysiological correlates. Partly the results are in accordance with the clinical criteria for anxiety indicating that somatic effects rise occur during anxiety attacks and adapt with habituation of the anxiety.

Other advantages of VR treatment are drawn from the experience of the therapists during the exposure and can be summarized as following. A well known problem in traditional psychotherapy is the low ability of the patient to introspection. Very often it is difficult for patients to verbalize their feelings and initial thoughts when they experience a panic attack. It is highly important for a successful psychotherapy to know details about the development and progress of the phobia. In cognitive – behavioral psychotherapy it is not required to explore the "absolute last reasons" of the phobia (e.g. childhood), but is binding to embed the phobia in a macroanalytic background (first onset, family background, critical life events, etc.). This is crucial for the recovery and it helps the person to integrate the phobia in his/her biography. Therefore the big advantage of VR treatment can be seen in supporting the process of introspection.

Surveys estimate that for special phobias the prevalence lies between 10-20% of the population [2]. To treat the fear of flying, heights, tight spaces, etc. VR exposure therapy is a safe and successful procedure. Its popularity is justified by its lower costs than in vivo exposure, its ability to have total control of the environment, the repeatability of any phobic stimuli and its safety. In controlled stages patients will be exposed to virtual environments using stereoscopic displays as HMDs or projection based systems, where the virtual environment elicits progressively higher levels of anxiety. Each stage can be repeated until the patients anxiety has lessened and they feel ready to move to a higher level.

The demand for cost effective treatment as a common argument for the implementation of VR scenarios in treatment and should be mentioned. But, beside cost effectiveness. VR also offers a big variety of application scenarios which almost never occur in real live. In our simulation for the treatment of Acrophobia, the patients have to cross a barrow which lies between two skyscrapers. By fulfilling this scenario the patient can generate different mental scenarios how to overcome his/her fear. In general VR scenarios can be used very creative. As already mentioned this is especially important for the detection of unknown thoughts. For patients it is very often difficult to explain their fears. VR scenarios can be used to identify these "internal dialogues" and enhance the introspection/ narration process.

References

[1] Bullinger, A.H., Angehrn, I., Wiederhold, B., Mueller- Spahn, F., Mager, R.: Treating Agoraphobia in a Virtual Environment. Annual Review of Cyber Therapy and Telemedicine 3, 93–100 (2005)

[2] Stefani, O., Mager, R., Mueller- Spahn, F., Sulzenbacher, H., Bekiars, E., Wiederhold, B., Patel, H., Bullinger, A.H.: Cognitive ergonomics in virtual environments: development of an intuitive and appropriate input device for navigating in a virtual maze. Applied Psychophysiological Biofeedback 30(3), 205–216 (2005)

[3] Hemmeter, U., Stoermer, R., Mager, R., Kuntze, M., Mueller-Spahn, F., Hennig, J., Amditis, A., Bekiars, E., Bullinger, A.– H.: Modification of virtual reality combined with a mental task stimulates cortisol in volunteers. Neuropsychobiology 51(3), 165–172 (2005)

[4] Orr, S.P., Roth, W.T.: Psychophysiological assessment: clinical applications for PTSD. Journal of Affective Disorders 61, 225–240 (2000)

[5] Kuntze, M.F., Bullinger, A.H.: Höhenangst und andere spezifische Phobien. Verlag Hans Huber. Bern (2001)

[6] Emmelkamp, P., Felten, M.: The process of exposure in vivo: cognitive and physiological changes during treatment of acrophobia. Behavior Research and Therapy 23, 219–223 (1985)

[7] Sarlo, M., Palomba, D., et al.: Blood phobia and spider phobia: two specific phobias with different autonomic cardiac modulations. Biological Psychology 60, 91–108 (2002)

[8] Martinez, J.M., Papp, L.A., et al.: Ambulatory monitoring of respiration in anxiety. Anxiety 2, 296–302 (1996)

[9] Wilhelm, F.H., Kochar, A.S., et al.: Social Anxiety and Response to Touch: Incongruence between self-evaluative and physiological Reactions. Biological Psychology 58, 181–202 (2001)

Multimodal Augmented Reality in Medicine

Matthias Harders, Gerald Bianchi, and Benjamin Knoerlein

Virtual Reality in Medicine Group
Computer Vision Lab
ETH Zurich
Switzerland
mharders@vision.ee.ethz.ch

Abstract. The driving force of our current research is the development of medical training systems using augmented reality techniques. To provide multimodal feedback for the simulation, haptic interfaces are integrated into the framework. In this setting, high accuracy and stability are a prerequisite. Misalignment of overlaid virtual objects would greatly compromise manipulative fidelity and the sense of presence, and thus reduce the overall training effect. Therefore, our work targets the precise integration of haptic devices into the augmented environment and the stabilization of the tracking process. This includes a distributed system structure which is able to handle multiple users in a collaborative augmented world. In this paper we provide an overview of related work in medical augmented reality and give an introduction to our developed system.

Keywords: Augmented Reality, Haptics, Medicine, Training.

1 Introduction

While the potential of virtual reality for training of medical procedures is widely acknowledged and pursued [1,2], the use of augmented reality (AR) [3] for teaching purposes in healthcare is in its infancy. Most research aims at using augmented reality technology for intuitive intra-operative surgical navigation by merging the real operating scene with virtual organs segmented from pre-operative radiological data. Moreover, all these projects are limited to the merging of visual data with the real world. Key point of our activities is the adaptation of visual AR to educational needs and includes the integration of haptic feedback into such a system.

The driving force of our current research is the development of surgical training systems using AR techniques. In this setting, high accuracy and stability are a prerequisite. Misalignment of overlaid virtual objects would greatly compromise manipulative fidelity and the sense of presence, and thus reduce the overall training effect. This situation becomes even more critical, if collocated haptic feedback is integrated into the system. Calibration errors or excessive latencies in generating feedback would lead to the loss of spatial and/or temporal synchronization making the interaction disturbingly unnatural. Unfortunately, so far no systems are available

C. Stephanidis (Ed.): Universal Access in HCI, Part II, HCII 2007, LNCS 4555, pp. 652–658, 2007.

which would meet the high demands for stability, accuracy and response time. In the following we provide an overview of current state-of-the-art in augmented reality in medicine and follow with a description of our visuo-haptic collocated augmented reality framework.

2 Related Work

Most related activities focuses on intra-operative surgical navigation. These systems can be distinguished with respect to the applied image augmentation paradigm.

In the first category, the view of conventional optical instruments commonly used by physicians is enhanced with additional information. In the Microscope-Assisted Guided Intervention (MAGI) system [4], 3D information from pre-operative images is overlaid in both eyepieces of a neurosurgery microscope resulting in a stereoscopic view of the augmented scene. Similar work has been described in [5], where ultrasound, CT or MRI images are added into the view of a surgical microscope. In [6] preliminary results are reported on the enhancement of endoscopic images in laparoscopic surgery. Related work has also been proposed in [7], where the use of AR is explored to compensate for the drawbacks of minimally invasive surgery, such as restricted workspace and limited endoscopic view. To this end, pre-operative CT volume data are rendered directly onto the endoscopic images. In [8] a stereoscopic endoscope is used to display the reconstructed 3D coronary tree in order to guide the surgeon's gestures during minimally invasive cardiac surgery.

An alternative strategy of displaying AR information is to capture images of a patient's body from a fixed camera located in the operating room and to show subsequently augmented images on a monitor. For guiding neurosurgical procedures, a live video sequence of the patient is combined with a previously segmented MRI model in [9]. Likewise an image guidance system for breast surgery, where 3D ultrasound images are overlaid on the patient has been developed in [10]. Another example of a guidance system has been proposed in [11], where the position of a needle inside the body is displayed via a monitor during liver punctures.

In the third class of systems, the view of a surgeon is directly enhanced – typically with semi-transparent mirrors. In [12] a stereo pair of images is generated by a monitor and reflected on a half-silvered mirror, thus optically combining the virtual data with the view of the real scene. A related system has been proposed in [13] to provide a superimposed slice view of the brain on the patient. Based on a similar principle, in [14] a handheld device with a transparent mirror merges images from ultrasound with the user's view. In the Camera Augmented Mobile C-arm (CAMC) system, X-ray and video camera images are combined [15]. The optical axis of a camera attached to the C-arm is aligned via a double mirror system, thus merging the X-ray and the camera images. Based on this system, a needle guidance application has been developed [16]. Instead of a mirror, a semi-transparent display is placed over the patient in the MEDical Augmented Reality for PAtients (MEDARPA) system [17]. The surgeon's head, the display and the surgical instruments are tracked in order to update the augmented images.

The fourth alternative for AR visualization is the rendering of augmented images via a head-mounted display (HMD). In [18] a system has been described that displays stereoscopic ultrasound slice images properly aligned with the scanned patient via two cameras mounted on the user's head. Accurate and stable registration is obtained with a combined visual and magnetic tracking approach. The system has also been extended to ultrasound-guided biopsies of breast lesions [19]. In the Reality Augmentation for Medical Procedures (RAMP) system [20] three cameras are mounted on the user's head. One is used for tracking the head pose and the other two for generating the stereoscopic view, which is enhanced by virtual objects. The system has also been extended to display anatomical structures in the brain for image-guided neurosurgical planning and navigation [21]. Furthermore, an HMD and a head-mounted operating microscope are combined in [22] to enable surgeons to perceive augmented images for oral implantology. In contrast to the aforementioned *video see-through* approaches, an *optical see-through* HMD is used in [23] to visualize human anatomical joints in motion by overlaying the virtual anatomy of the knee joint on a leg model. Instead of tracking the user's head, the location of the leg model is optically tracked around the joint.

Nevertheless, most AR based medical applications have been designed for visual navigation purposes. Anatomical structures or medical images are the common virtual information used to be overlaid on the surgeon's view. However, only few groups have explored the potential of this technology for the development of multimodal systems, which could be used in medical education. An example of an AR based medical training system for forceps delivery has been described in [24]. The system simulates the contact between the 3D fetus model and real forceps in order to train forceps placement and to analyze the mechanical effects of the instrument on the fetus. Fetal head deformations are calculated via Finite Element Analysis to evaluate the pressure and the traction force of the forceps on the fetus. However, deformations are not computed in real-time and no haptic feedback is provided to the user. A similar system [25] combines AR visualization with a physical mock-up of the female torso (including the fetal head). The simulator provides real-time physiological values such as blood pressure, heart rates or oxygen supply. Moreover, a sensor is mounted on the fetal head measuring user interaction during forceps delivery. The AR system is used to overlay a view of the virtual uterus as well as the virtual fetal head on the real images. Unfortunately, all these projects are limited to merging of visual data with the real world.

3 Visuo-Haptic Collocated Augmented Reality System

The basic paradigm of our multimodal AR setup is to capture a view of the real scene with a head-mounted camera, superimpose virtual objects in the image, and display the augmented scene with a head mounted display. To ensure exact alignment between real and virtual world, the system needs to estimate the relative position between the virtual objects and the user's head. Therefore, accurate estimation of the head pose with respect to an arbitrary world coordinate system in which the virtual objects are placed is necessary. Our AR system comprises an optical position tracking device OPTOTRAK 3020 manufactured by Northern Digital Inc., a head-mounted

FireWire camera and a camera-mounted marker. The optical tracker consists of three fixed linear cameras which detect the infrared LEDs attached to a marker. By triangulation, the optical system measures the 3D LED position with a RMS accuracy of 0▷2*mm* at an optimal distance of 2▷25*m*. From these measurements, the orientation and position of the marker are computed. Since camera and marker are rigidly attached to each other, the camera-marker transformation is fixed and estimated by an offline process using Hand-Eye calibration [26]. Experimental results have shown a back-projection error around 2 pixels, which is a sufficient starting point for applying hybrid tracking based on image-space error minimization. Given the camera-marker transformation and the marker pose, the AR system can estimate the camera pose within the tracker coordinate frame. The IR tracking data are inherently noisy due to the inaccurate measurements of the LED positions. The precision of the measurements becomes even more limited when the head-mounted marker moves. As a consequence, the registration between the real and the virtual world is affected, causing instabilities of virtual objects in the augmented images. Therefore, we correct the estimated camera pose of the IR optical tracker with a vision-based approach [27]. A back-projection error of less than 0.7 pixels can be achieved in less than 1*ms* computation time. Moreover, using additional refinement of 3D landmark positions, the error can be further reduced to about 0.3 pixels. This estimated camera pose then finally allows the visual alignment of the virtual and the real world. Overview images exemplifying our system are shown in Figure 1.

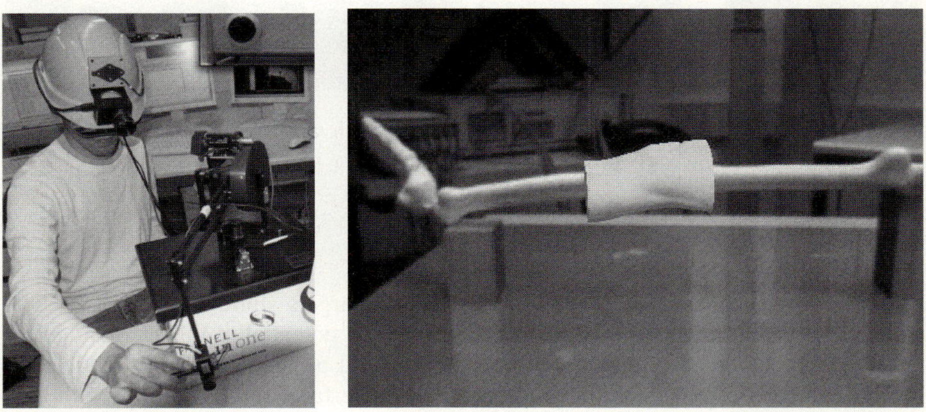

Fig. 1. View depicting head-mounted camera, markers and the haptic device (*left*). View of augmented scene example with virtual tissue overlaid on real plastic bone (*right*).

In order to allow simultaneous interaction with real and virtual objects in a multimodal augmented reality environment, visuo-haptic collocation is a prerequisite. This for instance allows interaction with virtual and real objects in the augmented scene via the same tool (see Figure 2). In order to align the virtual representation of the haptic interaction point with the correct physical location in the real world, the relationship between the haptic and the world coordinate system needs to be determined. The first step of our calibration procedure is to collect 3D point measurements in the coordinate systems of the haptic device and the optical tracker. After acquiring 3D point correspondences, the *absolute orientation problem* needs to be solved [28]. Since additional errors in the estimation of the haptic-world transformation are introduced due to inaccuracies in haptic encoder initialization, a two-staged optimization process is followed. The final calibration results yield an alignment error below 1.5*mm* within the whole workspace of the device.

Finally, to provide sufficient performance for the simulation the entire system was distributed to multiple machines. To this end, a specialized communication model was developed, which ensures high consistency in time for the exchanged data and facilitates extensions for multiple users and integration of different applications. A number of prototype simulations have been developed with the presented visuo-haptic AR setup, allowing simultaneous interaction with real and virtual deformable objects as well as collaborative interaction with multiple users.

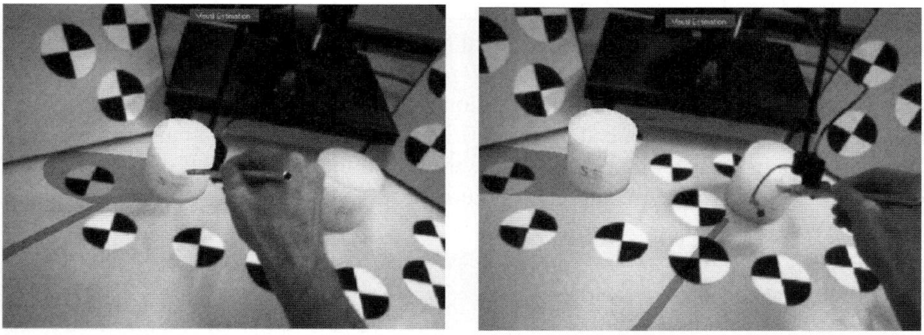

Fig. 2. Concept of visuo-haptic collocation. Interaction with virtual (*left*) and real deformable object (*right*) with the same tool.

4 Conclusion

Most research in medical augmented reality targets intra-operative surgical navigation. Within this context, we have explored the potential of this technology for the development of multimodal systems, which could be used in medical education. To this end, we examined the integration of haptic interfaces into AR setups with high accuracy and stability. In this paper we provided an overview of the current state-of-the-art in medical augmented reality and gave a description of our developed prototype system. Future work of our research will focus on the application of our visuo-haptic AR environment to education for orthopedic interventions.

Acknowledgments

This work has been performed within the frame of the Swiss National Center of Competence in Research on Computer Aided and Image Guided Medical Interventions (NCCR Co-Me) supported by the Swiss National Science Foundation.

References

1. Liu, A., Tendick, F., Cleary, K., Kaufmann, C.: A Survey of Surgical Simulation: Applications, Technology, and Education, Presence, vol. 12(6), pp. 599–614. MIT Press, Cambridge (2003)
2. Basdogan, C., Sedef, M., Harders, M., Wesarg, S.: Virtual Reality Supported Simulators for Training in Minimally Invasive Surgery, IEEE Computer Graphics and Applications (2007)
3. Azuma, R.T.: A Survey of Augmented Reality. Presence: Teleoperators and Virtual Environments 6(4), 355–385 (1997)
4. Edwards, P.J., King Jr., A.P., Maurer, C.R., de Cunha, D.A., Hawkes, D.J., Hill, D.L.G., Gaston, R.P., Fenlon, M.R., Chandra, S., Strong, A.J., Chandler, C.L., Richards, A., Gleeson, M.E.: Design and evaluation of a system for microscope assisted guided interventions (magi). In: Taylor, C., Colchester, A. (eds.) MICCAI '99: Proceedings of the Second International Conference on Medical Image Computing and Computer-Assisted Intervention. LNCS, vol. 1679, pp. 842–851. Springer, Heidelberg (1999)
5. Giraldez, G.J., Talib, H., Caversaccio, M., Gonzalez, M.A.: Ballester. Multimodal augmented reality system for surgical microscopy. In: Proceedings of SPIE Medical Imaging, vol. 6141, pp. 537–544 (2006)
6. De Buck, S., Van Cleynenbreugel, J., Geys, I., Koninckx, T., Koninck, P.R., Suetens, P.: A system to support laparoscopic surgery by augmented reality visualization. In: Niessen, W.J., Viergever, M.A. (eds.) MICCAI 2001. LNCS, vol. 2208, pp. 691–698. Springer, Heidelberg (2001)
7. Feuerstein, M., Wildhirt, S., Bauernschmitt, M.R., Navab, N.: Automatic patient registration for port placement in minimally invasive endoscopic surgery. In: Duncan, J.S., Gerig, G. (eds.) MICCAI 2005. LNCS, vol. 3749, pp. 287–294. Springer, Heidelberg (2005)
8. Mourgues, F., Vieville, T., Falk, V., Coste-Manière, E.: Interactive guidance by image overlay in robot assisted coronary artery bypass. In: Ellis, R.E., Peters, T.M. (eds.) MICCAI 2003. LNCS, vol. 2878, pp. 173–181. Springer, Heidelberg (2003)
9. Grimson, W.E.L., Lozano-Perez, T., Wells, W.M., Ettinger, I.G.J., White, S.J., Kikinis, R.: An automatic registration method for frameless stereotaxy, image guided surgery, and enhanced reality visualization. In: Transactions on Medical Imaging, pp. 430–436 (1996)
10. Sato, Y., Nakamoto, M., Tamaki, Y., Sasama, T., Sakita, I., Nakajima, Y., Monden, M., Tamura, S.: Image guidance of breast cancer surgery using 3-d ultrasound images and augmented reality visualization. IEEE Trans. on Medical Imaging 17, 681–693 (1998)
11. Nicolau, S.A., Pennec, X., Soler, L., Ayache, N.: A complete augmented reality guidance system for liver punctures: First clinical evaluation. In: Duncan, J.S., Gerig, G. (eds.) MICCAI 2005. LNCS, vol. 3749, pp. 539–547. Springer, Heidelberg (2005)
12. Peuchot, B., Tanguy, A., Eude, M.: Virtual reality as an operative tool during scoliosis surgery. In: First International Conference on Computer Vision, Virtual Reality and Robotics in Medicine (CVRMed), pp. 549–554 (1995)
13. Masamune, K., Masutani, Y., Nakajima, S., Sakuma, I., Dohi, T., Iseki, H., Takakura, K.: Three-dimensional slice image overlay system with accurate depth perception for surgery. In: Delp, S.L., DiGoia, A.M., Jaramaz, B. (eds.) MICCAI 2000. LNCS, vol. 1935, pp. 395–402. Springer, Heidelberg (2000)
14. Stetten, G., Chib, V.: Overlaying ultrasound images on direct vision. Journal of Ultrasound in Medicine 20(3), 235–240 (2001)

15. Navab, N., Bani-Kashemi, A., Mitschke, M.: Merging visible and invisible: two camera-augmented mobile c-arm (CAMC) applications. In: Augmented Reality, 1999 (IWAR '99) Proceedings. 2nd IEEE and ACM International Workshop, pp. 134– 141 (1999)
16. Mitschke, M., Bani-Hashemi, A., Navab, N.: Interventions under video-augmented X-ray guidance: Application to needle placement. In: Delp, S.L., DiGoia, A.M., Jaramaz, B. (eds.) MICCAI 2000. LNCS, vol. 1935, pp. 858–868. Springer, Heidelberg (2000)
17. Schwald, B., Seibert, H.: Registration tasks for hybrid tracking system for medical augmented reality. Journal of WSCG 12, 411–418 (2004)
18. Bajura, M., Fuchs, H., Ohbuchi, R.: Merging virtual objects with the real world: seeing ultrasound imagery within the patient. In: SIGGRAPH '92: Proceedings of the 19th annual conference on Computer graphics and interactive techniques, pp. 203–210 (1992)
19. State, A., Livingston, M.A., Garrett, W.F., Hirota, G., Whitton, M.C., Pisano, E.D., Fuchs, H.: Technologies for augmented reality systems: Realizing ultrasound-guided needle biopsies. In: SIGGRAPH, pp. 439–446 (1996)
20. Sauer, F., Khamene, A., Bascle, B., Schinunang, L., Wenzel, F., Vogt, S.: Augmented reality visualization of ultrasound images: system description, calibration, and features. In: Augmented Reality, 2001. In: Proceedings. IEEE and ACM International Symposium, pp. 30–39 (2001)
21. Maurer, C.R., Jr Sauer, F., Hu, B., Bascle, B., Geiger, B., Wenzel, F., Recchi, F., Rohlfing, T., Brown, C.M., Bakos, R.S., Maciunas, R.J., Bani-Hashemi, A.: Augmented reality visualization of brain structures with stereo and kinetic depth cues: system description and initial evaluation with head phantom; Medical Imaging 2001: Visualization, Display, and Image-Guided Procedures, pp. 445–456 (2001)
22. Birkfellner, W., Figl, M., Huber, K., Watzinger, F., Wanschitz, F., Hanel, R., Wagner, A., Rafolt, D., Ewers, R., Bergmann, H.: The Varioscope AR - a head-mounted operating microscope for augmented reality. In: MICCAI '00: Proceedings of the Third International Conference on Medical Image Computing and Computer-Assisted Intervention, pp. 869–877 (2000)
23. Baillot, Y., Rolland, J., Lin, K., Wright, D.: Automatic modeling of knee-joint motion for the virtual reality dynamic anatomy (vrda) tool. Presence: Teleoperators and Virtual Environments 9, 223–235 (2000)
24. Lapeer, R., Chen, M.S., Villagrana, J.: An augmented reality based simulation of obstetric forceps delivery. In: Third IEEE and ACM International Symposium on Mixed and Augmented Reality, 2004. ISMAR 2004., pp. 274–275 (2004)
25. Sielhorst, T., Obst, T., Burgkart, R., Riener, R., Navab, N.: An augmented reality delivery simulator for medical training. In: International Workshop on Augmented Environments for Medical Imaging - MICCAI Satellite Workshop, pp. 11–20 (2004)
26. Bianchi, G., Wengert, C., Harders, M., Cattin, P., Székely, G.: Camera-Marker Alignment Framework and Comparison with Hand-Eye Calibration for Augmented Reality Applications, ISMAR 2005, pp. 188–189 (2005)
27. Bianchi, G., Jung, C., Knörlein, B., Harders, M., Székely, G.: High-fidelity visuo-haptic interaction with virtual objects in multi-modal AR systems. In: Proc. ISMAR (2006)
28. Bianchi, G., Knörlein, B., Székely, G., Harders, M.: High Precision Augmented Reality Haptics. In: Proc. Eurohaptics (2006)

New HCI Based on a Collaborative 3D Virtual Desktop for Surgical Planning and Decision Making

Pascal Le Mer and Dominique Pavy

France Telecom Div. R&D – 2, avenue Pierre Marzin, 22307 Lannion, France
{Pascal.lemer, dominique.pavy}@orange-ftgroup.com

Abstract. Today, diagnosis of cancer and therapeutic choice imply strongly structured meeting between specialized practitioners. These complex and not standardized meetings are generally located at a same place and need a heavy preparation-time. In this context, we assume that efficient collaborative tools could help to reduce decision time and improve reliability of the chosen treatments. The European project Odysseus investigates how to design a Collaborative Decision Support Systems (CDSS) for surgical planning. We present here an activity analysis and the first outcomes of a participatory design method involving end users. Especially a new concept of Graphic User Interface (GUI) is proposed. It tries to make use of Virtual Reality technologies to overcome issues met with common collaborative tools.

Keywords: 3D Graphic User Interface, Collaborative Decision Support System, Surgical planning, Virtual Reality Technologies.

1 Introduction

Today, diagnosis of cancer and therapeutic choice imply strongly structured meeting between specialized practitioners. These complex and not standardized meetings are generally located at a same place and need a heavy preparation-time in order to take the best decision as promptly as possible with the available part of the medical history.

However, a lot of reasons such as delocalised skill centres, home constraints or busy schedules, don't allow practitioners to attend all the meeting they could be expected for. Thereof, several overview studies [1] or technical experiments [2] underline the potentiality of collaborative tools to reduce decision time and improve reliability of the chosen treatments. Indeed looking for the most experienced second opinion is crucial in decision making activity. But despite striking needs, a large deployment of distance collaborative tools didn't really yet occurred in medical communities, even though tremendous tools are easy to implement and exist since several years. From our point of view, this situation could be partly explained by unsuitability of the available tools as well as a lack of network infrastructures to share efficiently medical histories.

C. Stephanidis (Ed.): Universal Access in HCI, Part II, HCII 2007, LNCS 4555, pp. 659–665, 2007.

In the European project Odysseus (Eureka 3184) INRIA, IRCAD and France Telecom R&D investigate how to design a Collaborative Decision Support Systems (CDSS) for surgical planning. And the project priorities are focused on adequacy of the CDSS with both activity and infrastructure aspects.

We present here ergonomic requirements pointed out from several analysis. Then we explain how we assume that 3D and more generally Virtual Reality techniques could contribute to overcome unsuitability of existing collaborative tools. And finally, we describe a first prototype of Graphic User Interface (GUI) designed to contribute to an iterative participatory design method [3] involving end users.

2 Activity Analysis and Requirements

2.1 Decision Making Is Not a Lonesome Activity

Practitioners we have interviewed in several hospitals are requested each day if not several times a week for medical opinions. The majority of these opinions are asked in order to talk about a complex situation or to reach a consensus in the close practitioners' circle. And whether they are inside or outside the hospital, they are used to talking by phone. It is the only collaborative tool really used between dispersed practitioners.

In the specific context of cancer treatment, structured and co-localised meetings are usually organised in the majority of the French and European hospitals. The aim of these meetings is to provide a reliable diagnosis and follow therapeutic choices along the treatments.

Odysseus project focuses on this last specific use case activity. Indeed, we assume there is a strong need of distance collaboration before, during and after these meeting. Before the meetings, practitioners need to prepare relevant elements of the medical histories with a team physically dissipated. During the meeting skill centres could be delocalised as well. And after a meeting practitioners could need to call for details about a treatment or a surgical operation.

In order to determine delocalised activity requirements, we first investigated co-localised ones. Features we have observed are the following:

- Number of the attendees
- Length of the meeting
- Time dedicated to each patient
- Non-usual attendees number for each meeting
- Time dedicated to remind each patient history
- Content of the medical history
- Collaboration steps
- Rhythm of a meeting

2.2 Iterative Participatory Design Method

From our opinion, introduce a collaborative system for distance decision making activity, requires at least do not change the way of working. That is to say it is mandatory to keep in mind to fit with the original co-localised activity. Then in a second time latent needs will appear progressively and changes of way of working could be consider. Indeed we assume that using a CDSS might imply not easy to anticipate changes in the way of working.

However only co-localised decision meeting exist today. Thereof it is very difficult to obtain from practitioners expected functionalities for such a system. The main reason comes from the difficulty for everybody of projecting himself onto other way of working. Above all, these difficulties increase when opportunity of making use of new technologies such as 3D are mentioned.

In such a situation an iterative method seems to be appropriated. Therefore we have decided to design a prototype bound to initialize an iterative participatory design method [3] involving end users.

2.3 Expected Functionalities of a Collaborative Tool

Without real requirements from practitioners, the first step of the design method is to draw up hypothesis on activity expectations. Hereunder are the ones identified during several interviews with practitioners:

- Allow diagnosis and decision (e.g. therapeutic choices) in a short time for each patient
- Reduce memory efforts by introducing persistency of context between meeting
- Combine in the same interface face to face communication and data sharing phases
- Maintain confidentiality of medicals information
- Allow connectivity both within the Hospital Information System (HIS) and outside
- Ensure compatibility across different HIS application formats
- Bring in the patient in the loop

Seeing that these requirements depend strongly on the efficiency and the acceptability of the user activity, we decided to focus our efforts on the Graphic User Interface (GUI) design. Especially we decided to explore the potentiality of VR technologies to improve the efficiency and the acceptability of collaborative tools. And in a second time we tried to find technical solutions about the infrastructure aspects.

3 Prototype of Collaborative Virtual Desktop for Decision Making

3.1 GUI Based on VR Technologies

We have noticed through several interviews with practitioner the wish to keep richness and expressiveness found in the co-localised working environment. This striking need lead us to investigate current studies that try to explore alternative design to the pervasive desktop paradigm (i.e. WIMP [4]) by using 3D. For instance desktops such as Task Gallery [5], Looking Glass (http://www.sun.com/software/looking_glass/), or more recently BumpTop [6] try to recapture real word capabilities to work with documents.

However these previous works don't take care of group activity. Thereof our approach consist not only in following existing works but also in taking into account collaborative decision requirements in the GUI design.

The main result of this work is a prototype of shared desktop developed upon a collaborative middleware [7]. It allows sharing medical contents such as DICOM pictures, office data format or 3D models of patients. Let us see how 3D technologies could contribute to bring closer a real and a virtual shared activity.

Hereunder two snapshots of the prototype's GUI (figure 1). The left snapshot shows a shared space of the desk (i.e. a public view). And the right snapshot shows a "private" point of view in which the user can see the shared space (i.e. right bottom corner of the snapshot) and is own working space. In the both view, documents are represented either opened by an applicative windows or by icons (i.e. partial data view). In the "public view" icons could be moved between a helical menu, a desktop or an auto-distorting visual display represented as half-circle wall. The principles are the same in the "private view".

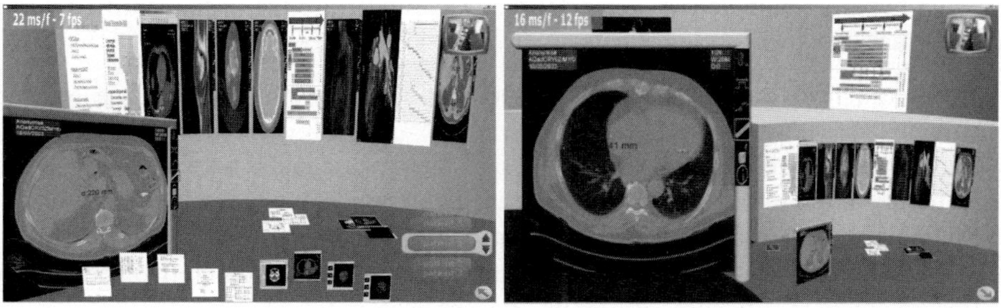

Fig. 1. CDSS user interface – Left image: public space; Right image: private space

Such a 3D dynamic space organisation gave us the opportunity of imagine new kinds of interactions. Various benefits in relation with practitioner's activity are expected from the following set of proposal:

Quick reminder. For each patient electronic record available in the public view, the spatial organization is get back as left at the previous meeting. We think that's a good mean to remind rapidly the patient context.

Optimized interactions. A new "drag and throw" technique is proposed in order manipulate document almost as quickly as in reality. It's a mean to avoid the time lost with the common windows interactions (i.e. close, minimize, etc.).

All patient electronic record at a glance. Data are represented on a dynamic helical menu. This new mean of setting data allows a direct interaction in a delimited display surface whatever the number of data and the number of hierarchical levels.

Smooth transition between a public and a private space. By the mean of a camera movement, user can extend is point of view between both public and private spaces.

Smooth transition between a face to face communication and sharing phases. A scalable display of users' videos allows focusing the activity either on the communication or on the study of the patient electronic records.

Allow exchanges between the private and the public spaces. The double view (private and public) allows a seamless functionality of uploading. This could contribute to a feeling of "non-computerized" activity, which could help to transpose real meeting habits.

3.2. Infrastructure and HIS compatibility

To preserve the benefit of a shared virtual desk approach, infrastructures issues should be "hidden" to end user, whether they are inside or outside the hospital. Thereby, Figure 2 proposes to integrate two network equipments: the HIS connector and a conference service. These equipments are designed to be integrated in common HIS architectures.

HIS connector. By the mean of a such kind of equipment, practitioners outside the HIS are able to upload or download patient electronic records in agreement with HIS security policy.

Conference service. All the data and the communication flow pass through this equipment. This kind of equipment could contribute to enhance planning decision meeting activity throughout new functionalities such as automatic staff report or dedicated data storage. Indeed data storage becomes increasingly a real brain-teaser for HIS administrator.

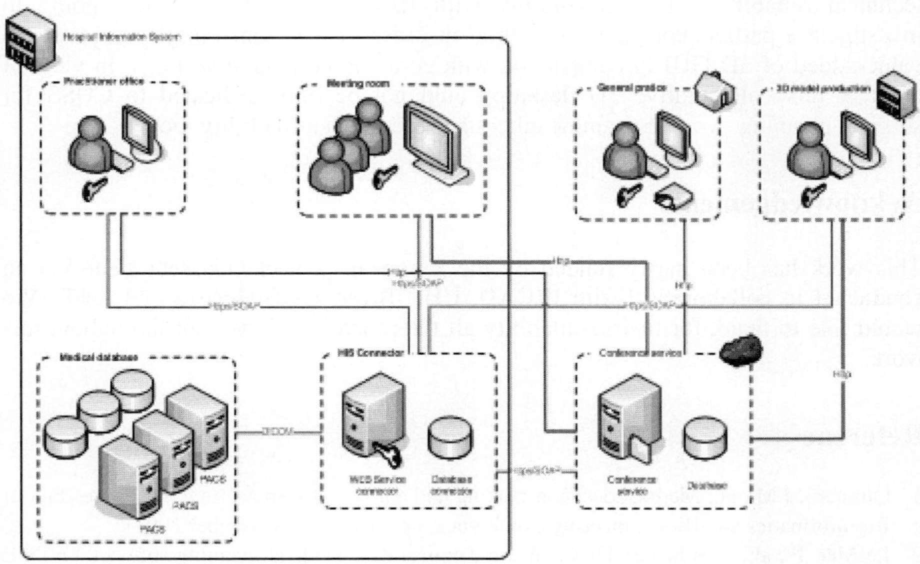

Fig. 2. Service architecture for distance activity

4 Discussion and Future Works

Throughout this study, we have catch sight of the activity's complexity. We have brought to light the profound reshaping needed by distance collaboration as well. But most of all we are now confident in the benefit of a suitable tool for surgical planning and decision making.

The main question we are now addressing is the value-added of our 3D GUI in comparison with common collaborative tools. Indeed our prototype seems to by efficient (i.e. reliability, compatibility with HIS data format, etc.) for a clinical experiment inside the hospital. However a lot of obstacles exist to evaluate and improve the concept of 3D collaborative desktop as CDSS for surgical planning.

Indeed, some practitioners are very reluctant to computerize their activity for performance or schedule reasons. What could be easy to understand. However clinical experiment requires the agreement of a whole team to give interesting results.

Given that the level of acceptability of our system is not easy to evaluate. In order to avoid an experiment breakdown, future works will focus on a participatory design method with small groups of practitioners. We intend to take things step by step. Firstly we will examine co-localised collaborations using the virtual desk as visual display support (e.g. using large tactile screen). And in a second time we will investigate distance collaborations upon patient electronic records previously studied by instance. Thanks to these methods we hope to answer the question of the suitability of a collaborative 3D desk.

5 Conclusion

We have designed a 3D collaborative virtual desktop dedicated to surgical decision activity. The system seems to by efficient regarding expected functionalities, technical reliability and compatibility with HIS aspects. We are now going to investigate a participatory design method in order to work on usability aspects and value-added of 3D GUI in comparison with common collaborative tools. In view of the fact this collaborative 3D desktop could not be only dedicated to CDSS for surgical planning, we will examine other use-cases such as mobility too.

Acknowledgements

This work has been partly funded by the European project Odysseus (Eureka) en conducted in collaboration with IRCAD, CHU-Brest, HUG-Geneva and LIFL. We would like to thank for their availability all the practitioners we met throughout this work.

References

1. Quintero, J.M., al.: Medical decision-making and collaborative reasoning. In: Proceeding of Bioinformatics and Bioengineering Conference, pp. 161–165 (November 2001)
2. Le Mer, P., al.: Argonaute 3D: a real- time cooperative medical planning software on DSL network. In: Proceeding of MMVR12, pp. 203–209, Newport Beach, California, USA (January 2004)

3. Muller, M., Kuhn, S.: Special Issue on Participatory Design, CACM 36:6 pp. 24–28 (June 1993)
4. Myers, B.: A taxonomy of window manager user interfaces. IEEE Computer Graphics and Applications 8(5), 65–84 (September/October 1988)
5. Robertson, G., al.: The Task Gallery: A 3D Window Manager. In: Proceeding of CHI. pp. 494–501 (2000)
6. Agarawala, A., Balakrishnan, R.: Interacting with Large Surfaces. CHI 2006. In: Proceedings, pp. 1283–1292, Montréal, Québec, Canada, (April 22–27 2006)
7. Louis Dit Picard S., Degrande S., Gransart C., Saugis G. and Chaillou C.: VRML data sharing in the Spin 3D CVE. In: Proceeding of Web3D 2002 symposium, pp. 165–172, Tempe, Arizona, USA (February 2002)

Measurement and Prediction of Cybersickness on Older Users Caused by a Virtual Environment

Cheng-Li Liu[1] and Shiaw-Tsyr Uang[2]

[1] Department of Industrial Management, Vanung University
No. 1 Van Nung Rd., Chung-Li, Tao-Yuan, Taiwan
johnny@vnu.edu.tw
[2] Department of Industrial Engineering and Management
Ming Hsin University of Science and Technology

Abstract. Recently the development of network technology is quickly, there are more and more VEs can be browsed on the Web, such as video games, digital museums and electronic shops. Therefore, the older web-users can easily immerse in a VE at home and become the fastest growing group of internet users. In general, these visitors browse the web-VEs on the field of TFT-LCD display. This study found that the SSQ scores of cybersickness increased significantly with increasing navigation rotating speed and exposure duration on older participants whilst the device of TFT-LCD displays are used to present the VE. Therefore, the cybersickness-predicting model was designed by fuzzy sets including speed of navigation rotation, angle of navigation rotation and exposure duration to evaluate the symptom of cybersickness for older users on TFT-LCD display in VE.

Keywords: Cybersickness; Virtual environment; Navigation; Elders; Fuzzy sets.

1 Introduction

1.1 A Fastest Growing Group of Virtual Environment Users: Elders

A virtual environment (VE) is a computer generated three dimensional models, where a participant can interact intuitively in real time with the environment or objects within it, and to some extent have a feeling of actually being there. The participant's interaction is through control of the viewpoint, using controls to move or re-orient objects in the model or through virtual controls (switches, handles, buttons, etc.) on the virtual objects [20]. In the past, because the limitation of bandwidth and deliver speed of network, it was difficult to browse VE on the Web. Recently the development of network technology is quickly, there are more and more VEs can be browsed on the Web, such as video games, digital museums and electronic shops. Therefore, the older web-users can easily immerse in a VE at home. Although the percentage of older adults using the Web currently is less than the percentage of younger individuals, surveys indicate this may not be the case for long [9]. Demographically, older users are fastest growing group of internet users. Critically, individuals just younger than the current group of retirees, dubbed the silver tsunami,

C. Stephanidis (Ed.): Universal Access in HCI, Part II, HCII 2007, LNCS 4555, pp. 666–675, 2007.

are expected to greatly increase the number of older web users in the near feature [8]. In fact, the web-VR has become the expressing tool of multiple experience of human life. It provides a comfortable environment where the older users, even act inconveniently, could browse VE through internet at home. Several researches have shown that an important and troublesome problem with current virtual environment technology is the tendency for some users to exhibit symptoms that parallel symptoms of classical motion sickness both during and after the VE experience [3, 22]. Its main symptoms are eye strain, disorientation, and nausea [14, 28]. Previous researchers have found that there are 80% to 95% of users will experience some level of disturbance during exposure to VEs, with between 5% and 30% experiencing symptoms severe enough to discontinue exposure [5, 6, 27, 29].

One of the most interesting questions about the causes of cybersickness is why some people get sickness in certain situations while other does not. Reason and Brand reported that age differences play a factor in motion sickness susceptibility [17]. They stated that motion sickness susceptibility was greatest between the ages of 2 to 12 years of age, decreased rapidly from 12 to 21 years of age, then more slowly until 50. They claimed that around 50 years of age, motion sickness is almost nonexistent. However, few studies have focused on the effects of age on VE sickness. Recently, Arns and Cerney found that older users often appeared to suffer more severe cybersickness than younger users in a driving simulator [1]. Knight and Arns also found that an increased incidence and severity of sickness among older users and lower incidence and severity of sickness in younger users in a 4-wall projection screen (CAVE) [13]. Therefore, the age plays a factor on cybersickness in VEs, but for what individual reasons elders suffer more severe cybersickness in VEs. The problem has seldom been discussed in the last decade.

1.2 Effects of Navigation Processing on Cybersickness with TFT-LCD Display

Because vection and sickness can be generated by watching moving scenes in VEs, the effects of navigation on the level of cybersickness becomes one of interesting lines of research. Although the effects of navigation methods have been studied in many researches [19, 23], we know of fewer studies that have purposely investigated the effects of navigation processing (e.g. speed, rotating speed, rotating angle etc.) especially for older users on cybersickness. Hu et al. reported that an increase in vection sensation and sickness symptoms in subjects exposed to a rotating drum rotating at 60°/s along the yaw axis [10]. Reid et al. also reported that vection generated during an exposure to an optokinetic drum rotating along the yaw axis caused symptoms of nausea in over half participants [20]. Muller et al. found that rotating speeds from 10°/s to 200°/s along the pitch axis of an optokinetic projection of random-dots [16], sickness symptoms occur after 3-8 sec. of exposure. Reinhardt-Rutland described that viewers of a stationary disc with a rotating circumference at 22.8 °/s could experienced an illusion of rotating motion of the stationary disc in the opposite direction (roll axis) [21]. We can find that most these studies concern vection-induced sickness were not in VE. Although, Lo and So found that the presence of scene oscillation in VE, both nausea ratings and SSQ scores increased at significantly higher rates than with no oscillation [15]. While individual participants exhibited different susceptibilities to nausea associated with

VR simulation containing scene oscillations along different rotational axes, the overall effects of axis among participants were not significant. However, this study was discussed on the field of Head-Mounted Display (HMD), not TFT-LCD display. As describing in previous section, some VEs browsed on the Web like digital museums have established as the tour metaphor extended this to the 'virtual tour' on-line, which can be browsed by the older user easily. The virtual tour can take the form of an entire museum complex rendered in three-dimensions, giving the visitor to the museum the impression of being taken on a guided tour of a museum and its exhibits [24, 33]. In general, the visitors browse the digital museum on the field of TFT-LCD display at offices, home or somewhere. Whilst the device of TFT-LCD display is used to present the virtual environments, this set-up does not physically enclose user, it retains the potential to simulate environments that may psychologically involve the participant. Whether the symptoms of cybersickness that are due to navigation processing on the field of TFT-LCD display will follow on older users?

1.3 Objective

In the style of VE on Web (e.g. digital museum and electronic shop), users are navigated to zoom in or zoom out along the fore-and-aft axis, and rotating scene along yaw or lateral axis, but seldom rotating scene along the fore-and-aft axis. For example, user can immerse in VRs by clicking and holding mouse button, then moving and dragging to rotate scene along yaw or pitch axis, or Zoom in by [SHIFT key] / Zoom out by [CTRL key] in the QuickTime or JAVA player. The symptoms of cybersickness are expected to occur for participants navigated in VE due to speed and angle of the rotating scene and exposure duration. In fact, when the scene rotates at angle 90 along yaw axis, it is the same as rotating along pitch axis. Therefore, the effect of navigation rotating along pitch axis could be discussed as a special case of navigation rotating along yaw axis. The purpose of this study was to discuss and analyze the effects of navigation rotating speeds, angles and exposure duration on cybersickness for older users caused by an immersing virtual environment on TFT-LCD display. Then a Cybersickness-predictive model with fuzzy sets including navigation rotating speeds, angles and exposure duration would be designed. The critical values of navigation rotating speeds, angles and exposure duration inducing cybersickness obtained by an experiment could be defined as crisp values of fuzzy sets.

2 Methods

2.1 Participants

Sixteen female elders between 55 and 65 years of age participated in the experiment, and were paid NT$500 as compensation for their time. All were consenting volunteers without color blindness. Participants of the same gender were used in this study because it has been reported that gender can have a significant effect on susceptibility to cybersickness [2, 26]. Regan and Price reported that repeated exposure to the same virtual environment with separation of less than seven days could significantly affect the levels of cybersickness [18]. Therefore, they had not been exposed to any VE within the previous 2 weeks.

2.2 Apparatus and the VE

The virtual scene was constructed using a virtual environment developing software (VIZARD) running on a personal computer. Images were presented on a 19" TFT-LCD display. The VE was a classroom which contained tables, chairs, bookcases and so on. All participants were exposed to the same VE which could freely zoom in and zoom out the scene along the fore-and-aft axis and rotating along yaw and pitch axis., but each participant was exposed to one of sixteen condition combined by 4 different navigation speeds and 4 different navigation angles. During exposure to VE, the participant must search and confirm some objects listed as check boxes stick on the right side of window, some listed objects could be find out in the scene, but some could not (see Figure 1).

2.3 Experimental Design

The experiment investigated four levels of navigation rotating speed along yaw axis: 15°/s, 30°/s, 45°/s and 60°/s, four levels of navigation rotating angle: 0°, 30°, 60° and 90° and four levels of exposure duration: 5 min., 10 min., 15 min. and 20 min. A randomized block design with 4 × 4 Latin squares was used. In other words, a Latin square design is based on experimental units that have a row-and-column block structure [25]. In this study we block on navigation speed (the row) and navigation angle (the column). Therefore, four levels of exposure duration are defined as treatments. Each treatment appears once in every low and once in every column. Sixteen participants were randomly assigned in one condition. In order to reduce the bias from participants, the scene of VE was controlled by the researcher according to the experiment step of design. The participants just kept their viewpoint on the screen. After the exposure, participants were asked to complete a post-exposure Simulator Sickness Questionnaire (SSQ) documenting the severity levels of 28 sickness symptoms [12].

Fig. 1. An example view of the virtual environment

3 Results and Model Design

3.1 Results

The analysis of variance in the scores of SSQ was shown in Table 1. Results Of the ANOVA indicate that the F of 55.48761 for SSQ scores from effect of exposure duration was statistical significantly at $p < 0.0001$ level, the F of 5.844658 for SSQ scores from effect of navigation rotation speeds was significant at $p < 0.05$ level, but SSQ scores from effect of navigation rotating angles was not significant. In order to investigate the results in advance, Figure 2 was drew to show the plots of total sickness severity mean scores of three factors in four levels by the SSQ. We can find that older participants would increase incidence and severity of sickness with increasing exposure time. The present result supports the original hypothesis and is consisted with some previous studies [15]. On the other hand, Figure 2 shows that the total sickness severity mean scores increased as the rotating speeds increased from 15 to 45°/s, but decreased at 60°/s. Why did the scores decrease at 60°/s, not increase? After investigating and inquiring, we found that older participants can't concentrate attention and will tend to move view toward elsewhere when navigation rotating speed is too quick. So, the total sickness severity scores decrease. On the other hand, although the difference of navigation rotating angles was not significant, the SSQ scores remain steady around the total mean score (21.99125), the effect of navigation rotating angles should not be ignored. Therefore, the three factors, navigation rotating speed, navigation rotating angle and exposure duration, would be defined as fuzzy sets to develop a Cybersickness-predictive model.

Table 1. ANOVA for the effects of navigation processing in SSQ scores

Source	SS	DF	MS	F-value	P^a (<0.05 significant level
Navigation rotating speed	100.238075	3	33.41269	5.844658	0.032588663
Navigation rotating angle	17.543075	3	5.847692	1.022897	0.446290961
Exposure duration	951.633275	3	317.2111	55.48761	9.25E-05
Error	34.30075	6	5.716792		
Total	1103.715175	15			

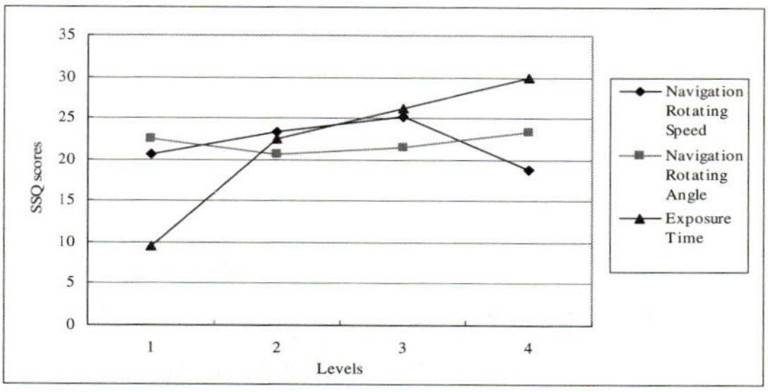

Fig. 2. Plots of total sickness severity mean scores of three factors in four levels

3.2 Cybersickness-Predictive Model

Fuzzy set theory was proposed by Professor L.A. Zadeh in 1965 [31]. A fuzzy set is the best thought of as an extension of the traditional set theory in which elements either do or do not belong to a given set. Because a clear boundary exists between set members and non-members, traditional sets are often referred to as crisp sets [4, 11]. However, it would seem more appropriate to distinguish between levels of events rather than to assign every event to either member sets or non-member sets. For example, if we abruptly define the rotating speed exceeding 30°/s is quick, the symptom of cybersickness would be induced and user should be warned. Why is it that a 30.1°/s is completely "quick," while a 29.9°/s is not "slow" at all? Therefore, the fuzzy sets used to develop a cybersickness-predictive model should be adapted. The model was designed as illustrated in Fig.3, and it was consisted of four components.

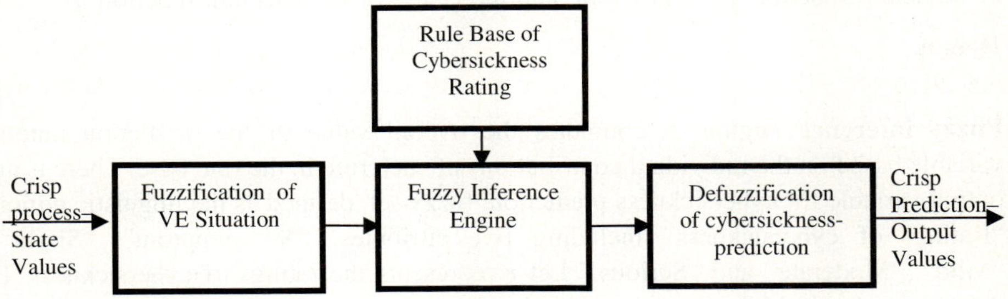

Fig. 3. The structure of a cybersickness-predictive model

Module of Fuzzification of Navigation States. It converts current values of navigation states into fuzzy sets, including three linguistic variables: speed of navigation rotation, angle of navigation rotation and exposure duration. First, we defined the fuzzy set which represents the linguistic notion "Speed of navigation rotation," along yaw axis. The fuzzy set is described by three attributes: "Slow speed" (SS), "Medium speed" (MS) and "Quick speed" (QS). The results of previous experiment indicate that the mean SSQ scores of navigation rotating speed on the level of 15°/s was 20.6, 30°/s was 23.4. According to the Kennedy and Lane's study, when the total sickness severity score is smaller than 7.5, the symptom of nausea would be seldom [12]. When the total sickness severity scores is between 7.5 to 22.5, at least one symptom of nausea would occur. When the total sickness severity score is bigger than 22.5, the symptoms of nausea would increase quickly. Therefore, the total sickness severity scores 7.5, 15 and 22.5 could be used to define the center of Fuzzy sets. For example, if the total sickness severity scores is smaller than 7.5, the membership value of $\mu_{\tilde{S}_{SS}}$ is equal to 1. Hence, using the method of linear interpolation the center of membership function $\mu_{\tilde{S}_{SS}}$ could be gotten is 5.5°/s. Similarly, the center of membership function $\mu_{\tilde{S}_{MS}}$ is 11°/s and the center of membership function $\mu_{\tilde{S}_{QS}}$ is 25°/s.

Second, fuzzy set $\tilde{A}$ was defined to represent the linguistic notion "*Angle of navigation rotation,*" includes two elements of the domain: "Small angle" (SA) and "Large angle" (LA). Using the method as described in previous section, we have that the center of membership function $\mu_{\tilde{A}_{SA}}$ is 30° and the center of membership function $\mu_{\tilde{A}_{LA}}$ is 75°. Finally, the fuzzy set $\tilde{D}$ was defined as the linguistic notion "*Exposure duration.*" The fuzzy set is described by three attributes: "Short exposure duration" (SD), "Medium exposure duration" (MD) and "Long exposure duration" (LD). We have that the center of membership function $\mu_{\tilde{D}_{SD}}$ is 4 min., the center of membership function $\mu_{\tilde{D}_{MD}}$ is 7 min. and the center of membership function $\mu_{\tilde{D}_{LD}}$ is 10 min.

Fuzzy inference engine. It computes the overall value of the prediction output variable based on the individual contributions of each rule in the rule base. There is an output variable for cybersickness prediction, fuzzy set, defined as the linguistic notion "Ratings of cybersickness" including five attributes: "No symptom", "Slight", "Mild", "Moderate" and "Serious." Let *r* represents the ratings of cybersickness. If the value of *r* is high, it means that the symptom of cybersickness is significant. Therefore, we can define these five membership functions, $\mu_{R_{NO}}, \mu_{R_{ST}}, \mu_{R_{MD}}, \mu_{R_{MO}}, \mu_{R_{SE}}$, as triangular functions in the continuous domain [-25,125]. Let us consider the i-th rule of the form as

$$\text{Ri: IF w } is \text{ S}^{(i)} \text{ AND x } is \text{ A}^{(i)} \text{ AND y } is \text{ D}^{(i)} \text{ THEN r } is \text{ R}^{(i)}, \tag{1}$$

where $S^{(i)}$, $A^{(i)}$, $D^{(i)}$ and $R^{(i)}$ are the linguistic values taken by w, x, y and r in the i-th rule. According to the fuzzy logic theory, the concept of "quantization" and "uniform" is used to discretize the domain into six segments by five judgment criterions: 0, 25, 50, 75 and 100 [32].

Rule Base of Cybersickness Rating. It is a set of fuzzy if-then production rules. An if-then production rule describes the causal relationship between navigation states and prediction output variables. The rule base was composed of ten-eight rules: three attributes of the linguistic variable "speed of navigation rotation," multiplied the two attributes of the linguistic variable "angle of navigation rotation" and multiplied the three attributes of the linguistic variable "exposure duration." The relations are shown in Table 2.

Table 2. Rule base for Ratings of cybersickness

Rule No.	IF			THEN	Rule No.	IF			THEN
	Navigation Speed	Navigation Angle	Exposure Duration	Cybersickness Ratings		Navigation Speed	Navigation Angle	Exposure Duration	Cybersickness Ratings
1	Slow	Small	Short	No	10	Medi	Large	Short	Mild
2	Slow	Small	Medium	No	11	Medi	Large	Medium	Moderate
3	Slow	Small	Long	Slight	12	Medi	Large	Long	Serious
4	Slow	Large	Short	Slight	13	Quick	Small	Short	Slight
5	Slow	Large	Medium	Mild	14	Quic	Small	Medium	Mild
6	Slow	Large	Long	Moderate	15	Quic	Small	Long	Moderate
7	Medium	Small	Short	No	16	Quic	Large	Short	Moderate
8	Medium	Small	Medium	Slight	17	Quic	Large	Medium	Serious
9	Medium	Small	Long	Mild	18	Quic	Large	Long	Serious

Module of defuzzification of cybersickness prediction. It converts the set of modified prediction output values into a single point-wise value. The degree of fulfillment of the premise of each rule is calculated by combining the membership functions $\mu_S(w)$, $\mu_A(x)$ and $\mu_D(y)$ into one membership function, $\mu_R(r)$.

$$\forall\, w, x, y: \mu_R(r) = \min(\mu_S(w), \mu_A(x), \mu_D(y)) \tag{2}$$

The final vigilance performance value r* using the Center-of-Area method (in the literature also referred to as the Center-of-Gravity method) is given by

$$r^* = \frac{\sum_{i=-25}^{125} r_i \cdot \mu_R(r_i)}{\sum_{i=-25}^{125} \mu_R(r_i)}, \tag{3}$$

it is a well-known defuzzification method [7].

4 Conclusion

The main findings of this study are: (1) the SSQ scores of incidence and severity of sickness increased significantly with increasing navigation rotating speed and exposure duration on older participants whilst the device of TFT-LCD display is used to present the virtual environments. However, the total sickness severity mean scores increased as the rotating speeds increased from 15 to 45°/s, but decreased at 60°/s. The reason is that older participants can't concentrate attention and will tend to move view toward elsewhere when navigation rotating speed is too quick. So, the total sickness severity scores decrease, (2) the difference of SSQ scores from navigation rotating angles was not significant, (3) the cybersickness-predicting model was designed by fuzzy sets including speed of navigation rotation, angle of navigation rotation and exposure duration. This model could evaluate the symptom of cybersickness for older users on TFT-LCD display in VE.

Acknowledgments. The author would like to thank the National Science Council of the Republic of China for financially supporting this work under Contract No. NSC95-2221-E-238-005.

References

1. Arns, L.L., Cerney, M.M.: The Relationship Between Age and Incidence of Cybersickness among Immersive Environment Users. IEEE Virtual Reality Conference, pp. 267–268 (2005)
2. Biocca, F.: Will simulation sickness slow down the diffusion of virtual environment technology. Presence 1(3), 334–343 (1992)
3. Bowman, D., Kruijff, E., LaViola, J.J., Poupyrev, I.: An introduction to 3-D user interface design. Teleoperators and Virtual Environments 10, 96–108 (2001)
4. Campbell, C.S., Massaro, D.W.: Perception of visible speech: influence of spatial quantization. Perception 26, 627–644 (1997)
5. Cobb, S.V., Nichols, S.C., Ramsey, A.D., Wilson, J.R.: Virtual reality induced symptoms and effects (VRISE). Teleoperators and Virtual Environments 8, 169–186 (1999)
6. DiZio, P., Lackner, J.R.: Circumbenting side effects of immersive virtual environments. In: Smith, M., Salvendy, G., Koubek, R. (eds.) Design of computing systems: Social and ergonomic considerations, pp. 893–896. Elsevier Science Publishers, Amsterdam (1997)
7. Driankov, D., Hellendoorn, H., Reinfrank, M.: An introduction to fuzzy control. Springer, New York (1996)
8. Fox, S.: Wired seniors: A fervent few inspired by family ties. Retrieved October 5, 2006 (2001) from http://www.pewinternet.org/pdfs/PIP_Wired_Seniors_Report.pdf
9. Hanson, V.L.: Adapting web pages for older adults. In: Proceedings of the 11th International Conference on Human-Computer Interaction (2005)
10. Hu, S., Davis, M.S., Klose, A.H., Zabinsky, E.M., Meux, S.P., Jacobsen, H.A., Westfall, J.M., Gruber, M.B.: Effects of spatial frequency of a vertically striped rotating drum on vection-induced motion sickness. Aviat. Space Environ. Med 68, 306–311 (1997)
11. Kasko, B.: Fuzzy engineering. Prentice-Hall, New York (1997)
12. Kennedy, R.S., Lane, N.E.: Simulator sickness questionnaire: an enhanced method for quantifying simulator sickness. The. International Journal of Aviation Psychology 3(3), 203–220 (1993)
13. Knight, M.M., Arns, L.L.: The relationship among age and other factors on incidence of cybersickness in immersive environment users. In: Proceedings of the 3rd Symposium on Applied Perception in Graphics and Visualization APGV '06, Massachusetts, pp. 162–162. ACM Press, Boston (2006)
14. Lathan, R.: Tutorial: a brief introduction to simulation sickness and motion programming. Real. Time. Graphics 9, 3–5 (2001)
15. Lo, W.T., So, R.-H.Y.: Cybersickness in the presence of scene rotational movements along different axes. Applied Ergonomics 32, 1–14 (2001)
16. Muller, C.H., Wiest, G., Deecke, L.: Vertically moving visual stimuli and vertical vection – a tool against space motion sickness. In: Proceedings of the 4th European Symposium on Life Sciences Research in Space. Trieste, Italy (1999)
17. Reason, J.T., Brand, J.J.: Motion sickness. Academic press, London (1975)
18. Regan, C.: An investigation into nausea and other side-effects of head-coupled immersive virtual reality. Virtual Reality 1, 17–32 (1995)

19. Regan, E.C., Price, K.R.: The frequence and severity of side-effects of immersion virtual reality. Aviat. Space Environ. Med. 65, 527–530 (1994)
20. Reid, K., Grundy, D., Khan, M.I., Read, N.W.: Gastric emptying and the symptoms of vection-induced nausea. Eur. J. Gastroenterol. Hepatol 7, 103–108 (1994)
21. Reinhardt-Rutland, A.H.: Peripheral movement, induced movement, and after effects from induced movement. Perception 10, 173–182 (1981)
22. Rich, C.J., Braun, C.C.: Assessing the impact of control and sensory compatibility on sickness in virtual environments. In: proceedings of Human Factors and Ergonomics Society 40th Annual Meeting. Human Factors and Ergonomics Society, Santa Monica, CA, pp. 1122–1125 (1996)
23. Riecke, B.E., Vastfjall, D., Larsson, P., Schulte-Pelkum, J.: Top-down and multi-modal influences on self-motion perception in virtual reality. In: proceedings of 11th International Conference on Human-Computer Interaction 2005. Las Vegas, Nevada (2005)
24. Sherwood, L.E.: Moving from experiment to reality: choices for cultural heritage institutions and their government. In: Jones-Garmil, K. (ed.) The Wired Museum: Emerging Technology and Changing Paradigms, pp. 129–150. American Association of Museums Press, Washington (1997)
25. Snedecor, G.W., Cochran, W.C.: Statistical Methods, 7th edn. Iowa State Univ. Press, LA (1980)
26. So, R.-H.Y., Finney, C.M., Goonetilleke, R.S.: Motion sickness susceptibility and occurrence in Hong Kong Chinese. In: Hanson, M. A., Lovesey, E. J., Robertson, S. A. (eds.): Contem porary Ergonomics 1999. London: Taylor & Francis, London (1999)
27. Stanney, K.M., Mourant, R.R., Kennedy, R.S.: Human factors issues in virtual environment: A review of the literature. Presence 7, 327–351 (1998)
28. Stanney, K.M.: Handbook of Virtual Environments. Earlbaum, New York (2002)
29. Wilson, J.R., Nichold, S.C., Ramsey, A.D.: Virtual reality health and safety: Facts, speculation and myths. VR News. 4, 20–24 (1995)
30. Wilson, J.R.: Virtual environments applications and applied ergonomics. Applied Ergonomics 30, 3–9 (1999)
31. Zadeh, L.A.: Fuzzy sets. Information and Control 8, 338–353 (1965)
32. Zadeh, L.A.: Outline of a new approach to the analysis of complex systems and decision processes. IEEE Transactions on Systems, Man, and Cybernetics 3, 28–44 (1973)
33. Zorich, D M.: Beyond bitslag: integrating museum resources on the internet. In: Jones-Garmil, K. (ed.) The Wired Museum: Emerging Technology and Changing Paradigms, pp. 171–201. American Association of Museums, Washington (1997)

VR, HF and Rule-Based Technologies Applied and Combined for Improving Industrial Safety

Konstantinos Loupos[1], Luca Vezzadini[2], Wytze Hoekstra[3], Waleed Salem[4], Paul Chung[5], and Matthaios Bimpas[1]

[1] Institute of Communication and Computer Systems (ICCS), Athens, Greece
[2] Virtual reality & Multimedia Park (VRMMP), Turin, Italy
[3] TNO Defense,Security and Safety, Netherlands
[4] Fraunhofer-Institut für Fabrikbetrieb- und automatisierung IFF, Magdeburg, Germany
[5] Loughborough University, Leicestershire, England

Abstract. Industrial safety can be regarded as a major issue of industrial environments nowadays. This is why industries are currently spending huge amounts of resources to improve safety in all levels by reducing risks of causing damages to equipment, human injuries or even fatalities. This paper describes how Virtual Reality, Human Factors and Rule-based technologies are used in the framework of the VIRTHUALIS Integrated Project towards industrial training, safety management and accident investigation. The paper focuses mainly on the VR system specification and basic modules, while at the same time it presents the main system modules that synthesize the tool as a whole.

Keywords: Virtual Reality, Virtual Environments, Human Factors, Rule based technologies, industrial safety.

1 Introduction

It is widely known that any wrong operation or mal-function in any industrial environment can lead to accident causing property damages, human injuries and even fatalities, especially when discussing over industries involving dangerous or explosive materials or substances. Therefore nowadays there are significant amounts of money spent from industrial sectors in order to reduce accidents and the reasons that may lead to possible accidents.

Some of the typical and practical safety issues currently present into industrial sites can be listed below:

- Training for control room operators;
- Emergency teams training;
- Assessment of the impact of plat modifications
- Managers' assistance in defining the impact of their decisions on operators' work

The VIRTHUALIS (Virtual Reality and Human Factors Applications for Improving Safety) Integrated Project (IP) is an EC funded project, focusing on industrial safety and currently involves 48 partners including research, industry and

C. Stephanidis (Ed.): Universal Access in HCI, Part II, HCII 2007, LNCS 4555, pp. 676–680, 2007.

other consultation partners ranging in 14 European countries. The main objectives of the VIRTHUALIS IP are to reduce hazards in production plants and storage sites by addressing end-users' practical safety issues through the development of an innovative technology. In general, VIRTHUALIS aims in providing the chemical and petrochemical industries with the necessary tools for efficient life-cycle design, production, use and recovery.

The project scientific and technological objectives can be summarized as follows:

- To sensibly reduce accidents and incidents in the process industry;
- To enhance system operability within the overall life-cycle;
- To reduce costs associated with safety production.

VR technology as a rapid and diversifying field can be regarded as one of the key technologies regarding visualization and/or user interaction through massive advances in computer science, human/computer interfaces and visualization technologies. Its increasing use in various fields has not only aided in major improvements but it has also contributed to the identification of advantages in different application areas (sych as the industrial sector). Additionally the usage of VR technologies has been proved ideal as an effective design and training tool thanks to the immersivity (the sense of "being there") and interactivity support. VR technologies are currently used in a wide area of applications such as archaeology [4], entertainment [5], architecture [6], automotive [7], etc. VR simulator users can use the technology and interact with the virtual world in a variety of ways and this is what indeed defines the technology versatility. In a typical VR system, the user can have fully immersive view with the aid of Head Mounted Displays (HMDs) while at the same time interacts with the system/virtual world via an interaction device.

One of the breakthroughs that VIRTHUALIS offers is the combination of VR with Human Factors (HF) technologies to achieve the aforementioned objectives, supported by the usage of Rule-Based systems. HF technologies in general represent studies on how humans behave physically and psychologically related to particular environments, products and services [2]. By immerging sharp-end operators, teams, safety analysts, managers into Virtual Environments (VEs) suitably modelled for the specific analysis to perform, it will be possible to experience safety-critical situations amplifying people capabilities and enabling them to suitably exploit HF concepts when performing safety analyses. At the same time the support from Rule-Based technologies comes when there is need to make the system as dynamic as possible and create rules that it must comply with and follow. This provides the ideal solution since the information (or rules) are not "hard" coded into the system but can be altered and adjusted depending on the exact application or application scenario (case study).

This paper provides a description of the overall system focusing on VR technologies and their widening when combined with HF and Rule-Based technologies.

2 System Description and Modules

2.1 Main System Modules

The system is based on distributed modules that communicate with each other via the network communication and has been design as such to maximize its extensibility.

Ideally the system has been designed to be operating in a desktop or CAVE system. Its main structure consists of two main modules: the master and the satellite applications. These are supported by some more external modules that provide additional capabilities to the system as a whole. The diagram below shows the main system architecture and main modules included in it.

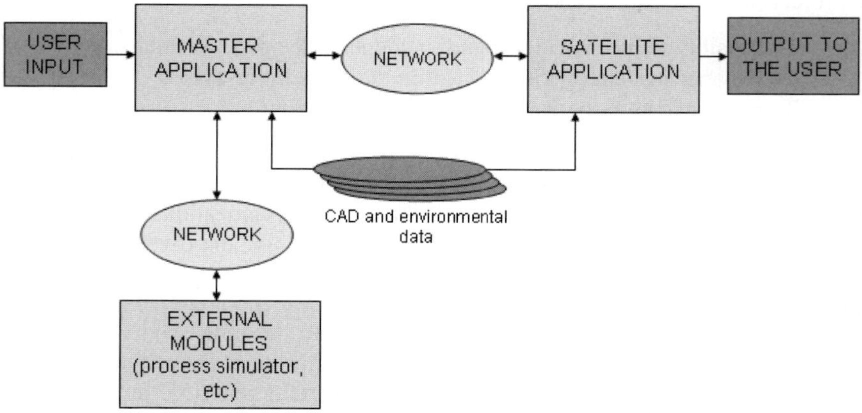

Fig. 1. Main System Architecture

The master application is the module responsible for handling the main part of data processing. It handles all models' states, user actions (including user interface) and keeps all system state attributes up to date. It is not handling any model or image rendering but rather keeps in memory of the scene graph sub-module that is kept synchronized with the related sub-module of the satellite application (mainly done in order to improve overall system performance). At the same time the master application monitors the user responses/actions and reacts to update the suitable sub-modules. This synchronization is achieved through network communication. The master application (and the satellite application as well) also include a logging sub-module responsible for logging all user actions and system states in order to keep an exact log of the simulation for replay or other functions.

The satellite application is the module in charge of handling and rendering the visualization data. This module receives the transmitted data over the network and then the synchronized scene graph sub-module (in synch with the master application's same module), updates the local data, renders the related models and outputs the result on the output device (monitor, projection, etc).

2.2 Additional System Modules

Apart from the master and satellite applications (modules), there exist some system modules that operate in parallel but are not directly linked to the system's operation as a whole. These are the recording module, the process simulator and the rule-based computing system.

The recording module is responsible for monitoring all system actions/states and receiving data from both the master and satellite applications (can be one or more). The module is "smart" enough for being able to select and filter if a message sent from the master or any satellite application has to be recorded or not. This module can be used for helping trainees and trainers to evaluate the operation of the system and monitor the user performance or reproduce/replay the whole simulation.

The particular function that the process simulator is responsible for is to simulate the chemical process performed in the plant (in the absence of the actual plant). The system (master application) communicates with the process simulator to update it (on user actions, etc) and be also updated (on system state changes). For instance whenever the user opens a valve, the master application notifies the process simulator of this (via the network) and the simulator takes this under consideration in the simulation of the whole chemical process. It then, in turn communicates the results of these actions to the master application so that the whole simulation cycle is updated (on the results of the user action – valve opening).

Finally the Rule-Based module is the module responsible for responding in predefined ways when certain (user or system) conditions occur and is the module that has been designed using rule-based technology. The general idea for its operation is that it includes an internal set of attributes representing the parameters to be monitored. In case that an event occurs (user or system internal action) the module checks if the action is related to any rules and acts accordingly. This module can be used in various ways: as a process simulator substitute, to affect the environment, to apply plant-specific behavior and to help monitor the execution (and right order) of procedures [2].

Having described the system as a whole the bullets below can summarize its capabilities and features up to its current state:

- Realistic simulation of the industrial environment (supporting fire, smoke, light conditions, etc);
- User interaction supporting VRPN devices;
- Advanced user interface (UI) for various tasks execution and scenario start/stop;
- Communication to external process simulators (for plant operation simulation);
- Interface to related CAD systems and plant creation tools;
- Rule-based computing mechanisms to implement scenario-driven dynamic simulations;
- Logging and re-play functions;

3 Conclusions and Future Works

This paper has described the general architecture including main building blocks for an interactive 3D system that is currently being developed to improve training for process industry. To ensure adaptability and maximize extendibility, the system has been based on distributed architecture and independent modules. The system is based on three main modules: the master application, the satellite application and the external modules, while the communication and synchronization between them is achieved via usage of advanced networking protocols.

The system under development is expected to be applied to industrial sites in order to reduce hazards in production plants and sites. This will be done with the construction of some applications applied mainly to the "Risk Assessment" safety action. Later this application will be enhanced such as to support other safety actions (Training, Safety management and accident investigation). The first prototype for the first aforementioned safety action ("Risk Assessment") is expected to be completed in the next four months.

References

1. http:// www.virthualis.org
2. Salem, W. (et al) - Enhancing the Trainee's Awareness in a Virtual Training Environment. IMCL, conference, April 19-21, 2006, Amman, Jordan (2006)
3. Prof. Paul Chung (et al) – The Integration of VR and Rule-Based technologies to improve process safety. ESREL, 18-22 September 2006, Estoril, Portugal (2006)
4. Sideris, A., Roussou, M., Gaitatzes, A.: Virtual Reconstruction of the Hellenistic Asklepieion of Messene using Scientific and Educational Scenario-based Approaches. In: Proc. 9th Annual Meeting of the European Association of Archaeologists, St. Petersburg, Russia, September 10-14, 2003 and Imeros Journal for Culture and Technology (4) (2004)
5. Bates, J.: Virtual reality, art, and entertainment, Presence: Teleoperators and Virtual Environments. Winter 1(1), 133–138 (1992)
6. http://www.uwm.edu/People/jstagg/
7. INTUITION NoE WG –CRF: Research Position Paper: Towards Virtual Product Creation: the role of VR in the Automotive & Transport Industry, 21/02/, INTUITION NoE WG2.3 (2006)

Adaptive Virtual Reality Games for Rehabilitation of Motor Disorders

Minhua Ma[1], Michael McNeill[1], Darryl Charles[1], Suzanne McDonough[2], Jacqui Crosbie[2], Louise Oliver[2], and Clare McGoldrick[2]

[1] School of Computing and Information Engineering,
[2] Health and Rehabilitation Sciences Research Institute,
University of Ulster, U.K.
m.ma@ulster.ac.uk

Abstract. This paper describes the development of a Virtual Reality (VR) based therapeutic training system aimed at encourage stroke patients with upper limb motor disorders to practice physical exercises. The system contains a series of physically-based VR games. Physically-based simulation provides realistic motion of virtual objects by modelling the behaviour of virtual objects and their responses to external force and torque based on physics laws. We present opportunities for applying physics simulation techniques in VR therapy and discuss their potential therapeutic benefits to motor rehabilitation. A framework for physically-based VR rehabilitation systems is described which consists of functional tasks and game scenarios designed to encourage patients' physical activity in highly motivating, physics-enriched virtual environments where factors such as gravity can be scaled to adapt to individual patient's abilities and in-game performance.

Keywords: Serious games, Virtual Reality, adaptive games, motor disorder, therapeutic exercise, bilateral training.

1 Introduction

The use of VR technology and computer games in motor rehabilitation has been shown in the literature to be an effective way of providing enjoyable and motivating tasks which can be graded to facilitate the rehabilitation process. To date the application of VR to rehabilitation has focused extensively on using the technology to encourage patients to practise active functional tasks in virtual environments. Many studies [1], [2] have identified the benefits of using VR in rehabilitation to improve balance, endurance, dexterity, speed and range of motion.

Currently, most VR applications in rehabilitation simulate real life activities such as grasping and manipulating objects or performing everyday tasks e.g. pick-and-place virtual objects [1], [3], [4], shop in a virtual mall [5], or cross a street [6]. These VR systems help patients enhance improve functional ability and realise greater participation in community life. However, object animations in most VR therapy systems are pre-rendered and hence not realistic in terms of physical simulation.

C. Stephanidis (Ed.): Universal Access in HCI, Part II, HCII 2007, LNCS 4555, pp. 681–690, 2007.

1.1 Physically-Based Simulation

Physically-based simulation creates realistic motions of virtual objects based on the laws of physics. The behaviour of virtual objects and their responses to external force and torque are simulated in a physically realistic manner. Physics simulation models objects with physical properties, such as mass, inertia, barycentre, joint limitations, restitution and surface friction — it can make objects in virtual worlds not only *look real* but *act real*. Typical dynamics simulation includes collision detection and the simulation of gravity, friction force, torque, and kinematics in motor actions. Physics can be applied to rigid bodies or deformable bodies such as human tissues. Rigid body dynamics plays an important role in VR motor rehabilitation and is especially needed when dextrous manipulation of virtual objects is concerned.

The advantage of using VR in clinical settings is that by virtue of its programmability, environments and the type and difficulty of tasks can be modified according to the user's capacities and therapeutic goals. Physics simulation provides more flexibility on experiment configuration in which not only object positions, orientations, size can be modified but also gravity, restitution, force and torque damper, and joint limitations can be reliably modified [7], thereby creating a very individualised set of rehabilitation tasks which would be impossible to achieve with the user's residual motor control in the physical world. These tasks can then be reliably recreated over a period of several weeks or months and patient outcome can be assessed. The addition of physics to the VR therapy may increase patients' experience of immersion in virtual environments, which may in turn increase engagement and activity enjoyment and thereby improve clinical outcome.

The quality of physics that is required in a simulation is application specific. In the cognitive and affective domains of learning where the focus of training is more on attitudes, high physical fidelity is not always required. However, in medical simulation such as surgery planning and training, high quality physical fidelity is so important that without it the skills acquired in the virtual world may not transfer to the real one. Recent research suggests that physics fidelity may be important for motor rehabilitation. Viau et al. [1] compared movement kinematics of identical tasks of reaching, grasping, transporting, placing and releasing a ball in a real and a virtual environment. Their results showed that there is a slight change in motor patterns when grasping and placing a ball in the two reality conditions for both healthy subjects and hemiparesis patients with motor deficits, which was mainly due to lack of collision handling in the VE. Their interpretation of the results is that both healthy subjects and individuals with motor deficits used similar movement strategies in pick-and-place tasks in the two conditions, and they concluded that training of arm movements in VR may be a valid approach to the rehabilitation of patients with motor disorders. However, the results also suggest that physics simulation in VR rehabilitation may reduce the difference of movement strategies in the virtual and real world, which may be an important factor in the transferability of virtual skills to the real world.

2 Adaptive Rehabilitation

Ideally, rehabilitation should be targeted to the individual needs of patients. Patients have a wide range of abilities and tasks which are impossible for some can be trivial for others. It is usual to tailor a stroke rehabilitation session to individual patients according to the type of injury (left/right hemiplegia) and their capabilities. Typically this is done by assessing the patient in a number of standardised tests prior to the rehabilitation session. The therapist can then create a suitably challenging set of exercises for the patient. A key principle in rehabilitation is matching therapeutic tasks to the patients' abilities in order to enable them to improve residual capabilities without causing fatigue and frustration. This is a time-consuming part of the physiotherapist's duties, as constant monitoring is required to ensure the tasks remain adequately challenging throughout the sessions, which typically last for several weeks.

2.1 Adaptivity

Adaptation is one technique that VR therapy systems can exploit to benefit a group of users with a wide range of abilities. In order to maintain patient motivation, rehabilitation tasks should be set at an appropriate level of challenge. Also, for the patient to stay engaged in the process, he or she should experience a feeling of immersion in the virtual environment. Charles et al. [8] applied flow theory to adaptive game design, and they suggested that the game should find a balance between the annoyance of an activity that is perceived as trivial and the frustration of one that is perceived as too difficult. This is even more important in the context of VR motor rehabilitation due to the repetitive nature of the exercises and the limitations of the users (patients).

A physiotherapist will typically design motor therapy exercises for a patient based on a number of factors, including the patient's age, gender, culture background, usual handedness, and his or her medical condition (e.g., time since stroke, left or right hemiplegia and cognitive, sensory, and motor abilities based on standardised tests such as the Line Cancellation Test). Not only the difficulty level of the exercises but also the body parts activated during the task may be adapted to individual patient's needs. For example, tasks may be developed to train a specific movement such as wrist extension in order to increase range of motion or endurance of the wrist joint. This data, taken together, forms an individual patient profile which can then be used to initially configure the system to present a suitably challenging, individualised rehabilitation session. Various elements of the simulation can be configured from this profile data, including the number and type of objects, their sizes, speed, mass, distance between objects and the patient, distance of object transportation etc. Additionally, data collected during the rehabilitation session can be used to further improve the patient experience. Such in-session data (e.g., the time taken to perform a task or achieve a goal in a game, the accuracy rate or stimuli-response time) can be used to evaluate the initial configuration of the system. If tasks are not being successfully completed then the objects or game elements in the simulation should be configured to make them easier. Objects can be made larger (easier to grasp), for example, or moved closer to the patient (easier to reach). Alternatively, if activities are being completed much too quickly it may be that the activity is too easy for the patient, and corresponding changes can be made to make the task more challenging.

The ability to dynamically adjust the difficulty of the simulation is a key benefit since in addition to offering a tailored solution which suits the patient's individual needs it also decreases the dependence on human therapists to monitor and provide similar solutions.

2.2 User Profiling

We have constructed a patient model using traditional symbolic classifiers based on patients' age, time since stroke, left/right hemiplegia, impairment and functional measurement, and hemispatial neglect. Table 1 below shows the profile of three patients participating in the study. For each patient, three motricity index and ARAT scores are given, representing their status before training, post training, and 6 weeks after training. Patients 1 and 3 have no hemispatial neglect, while patient 2 has a mild deficit. Table 2 shows how we use patient profile to setup parameters in VR simulations initially.

Table 1. Examples of patient profiling: Motricity Index [9] is for impairment measurement, and Action Research Arm Test (ARAT) [10] is for functional measurement

	Patient #1	*Patient #2*	*Patient #3*
Age	76	62	42
Gender	M	F	M
Years since stroke	4	4	1
Usual handedness	R	R	R
Left/Right hemiplegia	L	L	L
Motricity Index	77,77,81	62,73,77	77,79,77
ARAT	3,6,11	4,11,19	54,53,54
Hemispatial neglect	None	Left-sided	None

3 A Framework for VR Motion Therapy

Fig. 1 shows our framework for VR post-stroke motor rehabilitation. Rehabilitation tasks consist of functional tasks, such as wrist extension, reaching, grasping and catching, and game simulations. The system allows users to interact with virtual objects in real-time through multiple modalities and to practice specific motor skills. Users of the system are stroke patients with motor deficits and physiotherapists who, as operators, are responsible for initialising the system and controlling the scripting of tasks. Input devices include ordinary devices, mouse and keyboard for operators and a range of real-time motion tracking devices - two 5DT Ultra DataGloves which capture finger flex and hand postures (Fig. 2c); Four Ascension MotionStar wireless magnetic sensors (Fig. 2a) are used to track the patient's hand, arm and upper body movements.

Output involves visual, audio and haptic modalities. The dual output visual interface includes a desktop monitor for operators and a high resolution head-mounted display (HMD) equipment, Virtual Research 1280 stereo (Fig. 2b), for patients. Haptic interface is a possible extension of the system but it is not our current concern.

The device drivers interface the specialised hardware with the software components which include a 3D graphic engine based on OGRE [11], dealing with loading of mesh data, rendering, scene management and the user interface, and a rehabilitation engine which creates functional (task-based) or non-functional

Table 2. Initial setup of parameters of VR therapy based on patient profile

Impairment measures	*Parameters of VR therapy*	*Goals*
Motricity Index (Elbow flexion score, Shoulder abduction score) ARAT (gross movement score)	Size of target area on x-z plane (initial coordinates of falling oranges in the catching task), range of mice positions in the whack-a-mouse game	Range of movement Gross movement
ARAT	Size of oranges in the catching task	Gross movement, accuracy
ARAT	Size of basket in the catching task	Gross movement, accuracy
Hemispatial neglect L/R hemiplegia Usual handedness	Loci of oranges in the catching task, Loci of mice and dogs in the whack-a-mouse game	Movement of affected arm Attention of affected side
Motricity Index (pinch grip score) ARAT (grasp, grip, & pinch score)	Size of objects (cube, ball, cylinder, cup) in the pick-and-place task	Accuracy, dexterity Hand/finger movement
Motricity Index (elbow flexion score, shoulder abduction score) ARAT	Gravity in the catching task, Length of time that the mouse is stationary in the whack-a-mouse game	Speed Accuracy
Motricity Index (elbow flexion score, shoulder abduction score) ARAT (gross movement score)	Time between falling oranges in the catching task	Speed

(game-based) activities. We use Ageia PhysX [12] to handle dynamics simulation, e.g., articulated structures, robust CD, and friction/contact modelling. A wrapper called NxOgre [13] is used to integrate PhysX with OGRE. The databases consist of mesh data of 3D models and patient profiles which may be used to automatically adapt the tasks to specific therapeutic needs.

The dynamic adaptation part of the system uses patient profile data and patient progress data to select tasks and initially configure the difficulty level of the tasks and the game. This continues in-session, as all patient interaction with the system is recorded and analysed for in-game adaptation. Hence the system can provide data on progress for individuals that may be collated across the recovery period or across individuals to provide a database on patient progress. The data analysis module enables visualization of patients' movement trajectories and displays joint angles, range of movement and velocities. Currently this occurs off-line, after the rehabilitation session has finished.

3.1 Functional Training

Previous study shows that pyramidal tract (e.g. fingers, lower limb) is often impaired after stroke, whereas more proximal areas may be less profoundly affected. [14] It is therefore common for people with stroke to exhibit problems with manipulative movements, on the contra-lateral side, following unilateral stroke. The functional training part of the VR therapy focuses on manipulative movements of fingers, hands and arms such as reaching, grasping, placing, and wrist extension. The 3D position and orientation of the user's hand, elbow, and shoulder are sampled via using three magnetic sensors. Sensor 1 is placed on the volar aspect of the hand, at the base of the head of the 3rd metacarpal bone, Sensor 2 is placed on the posterior aspect of the elbow, just above the olecrannon process, and Sensor 3 is placed on the anterior aspect of the shoulder, on the greater tuberosity of the humerus.

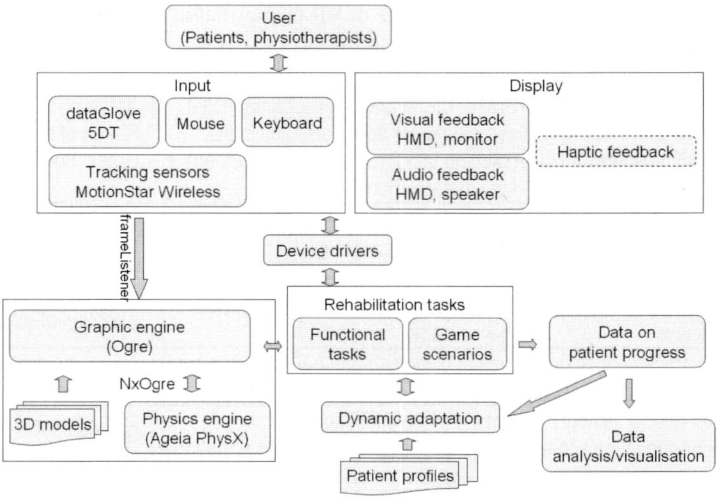

Fig. 1. A framework for physically-based VR rehabilitation

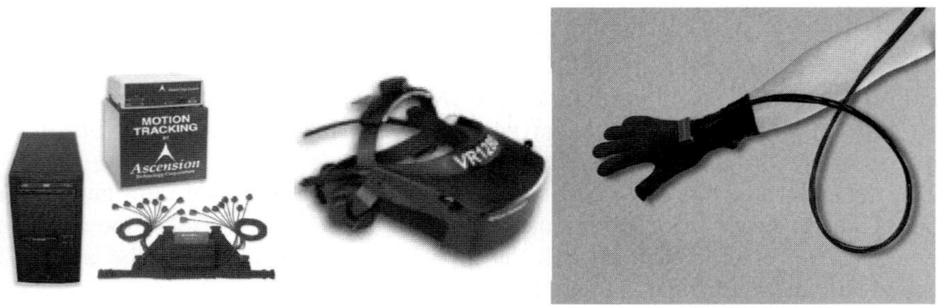

a. MotionStar wireless b. VR 1280 HMD c. 5DT data glove

Fig. 2. Hardware

In the functional training part we simulate a virtual kitchen where subjects are asked to manipulate virtual objects of various shapes and sizes at different locations, such as a typical pick-and-place task by reaching and touching a start marker, grasping a virtual cup, and placing it on a saucer some distance away. When the virtual hand, controlled by the tracking sensors and data glove, intersects with any object in the VE, an auditory signal is played and the object changes colour to indicate success (collision between hand and object detected). Patients use the hand of their hemiplegia side to perform the task.

3.2 Bilateral Training

Traditional therapies of upper limb rehabilitation following stroke primarily focus on unilateral strengthening exercises and functional training of the paretic limb. Recent studies in neuroplasticity and stroke rehabilitation have suggested that bilateral training may prove beneficial [15], by activating similar neural networks in both hemispheres when voluntary movements of the intact limb are initiated. A catching task has also been developed, where the user holds a virtual basket with either one hand or two (for bilateral upper limb training) to catching falling oranges which fall at random onto a target area (Fig. 3). The position/orientation of the virtual basket is controlled by a sensor attached either on the user's hand if one hand is used to perform the task, or on a real object, a real basket, for example, which the user holds with both hands. If the patient tilts the basket, he or she may not able to catch the oranges and the ones already in the basket may fall to the ground. The target area on the x-z plane, the falling speed of oranges (controlled by simulating gravity in the virtual environment), the time between oranges falling and the size of oranges and the basket can all be adjusted to suit individual patient's needs. All sensor data is recorded to disk, allowing post-therapy visualisation of the trajectories and analysis of joint angles, velocity, acceleration and range of movement.

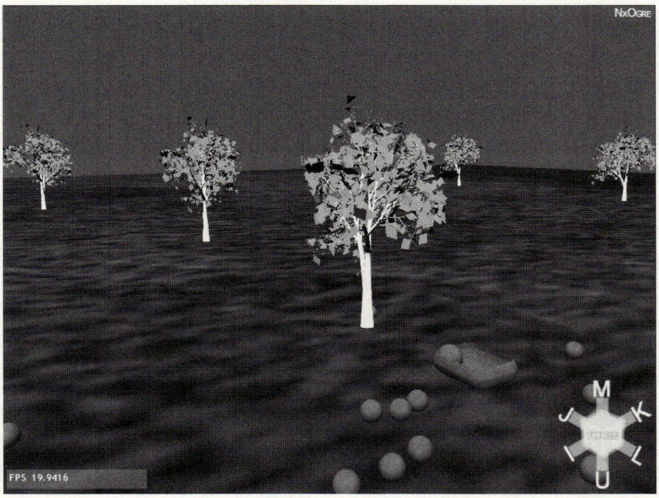

Fig. 3. A functional catching task

3.3 An Adaptive Game for Motor Rehabilitation

We have developed an adaptive VR "whack-a-mouse" game for post-stroke therapeutic exercises as shown in Fig. 4. The aim of this game is to encourage gross movement and to improve accuracy and speed of users' upper limb movement. It has also been designed to improve patient's visual discrimination and selective attention, important aspects of stroke rehabilitation where the patient exhibits hemi-spatial neglect. The mouse appears at a random location on the table top, stays there for a certain number of seconds (the actual time it stays still depends on the patient profile), and then re-appears on another part of the table. While the mouse is stationary the patient tries to hit it using a virtual hammer which is controlled by the position and orientation of sensor 1 on the patient's hand. This simulation encourages faster, grosser and less accurate movement than the functional tasks described earlier.

Fig. 4. A 'whack-a-mouse' game

Initial configuration of the game is done automatically based on the profile of the player. For example, the game will be configured to be easier for patients with serious upper extremity motor impairment, i.e., the mouse will stay still for a longer period of time for them than for patients with minor motor impairment. The locus of stimuli will also depend on if a) the patient has right or left-sided hemiplegia and b) if the patient exhibits hemi-spatial neglect. For left-sided hemiplegia patients, the random positioning of the mouse is biased towards the right; similarly for the left. If the patient also exhibits hemi-spatial neglect this bias can be increased. It is important that patients are given a chance to familarise themselves with the game and not be presented initially with something that is too difficult, which could lead to disengagement. Therefore we tend to be conservative with the initial setup.

Patients will learn as they play and their progress of learning may be different. Therefore, the configuration that we use at the beginning of the game may no longer be appropriate as the game proceeds. The length of time that the mouse is stationary and the locus of mouse and dog adapts dynamically to patient performance. The mouse appears more frequently in the quadrant where the patient has more misses and seems to have difficulty due to either motor deficit or attention deficit.

There are, therefore, a number of adaptive elements of the game which change dynamically according to how well or badly the user is performing. The game has been programmed to enable automatic progression between three levels (Beginner, Intermediate and Expert) under preset conditions. At the Beginner level the time that the mouse is stationary is set automatically according to the patient profile. At the Intermediate level, the time adapts to the patient's performance (to begin with, the speed is the same as in the beginner level). The game progresses according to a simple accuracy test based on the number of mice hit and the number missed, where

$$\text{accuracy} = \frac{\text{miceHit}}{\text{miceHit} + \text{miceMissed}}$$

When the accuracy rate drops below a certain threshold, the length of time that the mouse remains still for increases which has the effect of slowing the game, making it easier; and when the accuracy rate exceeds a certain threshold, this time decreases, making the game harder. The Expert level contains both a mouse and a dog which appear simultaneously: patients must hit as many mice as possible and try to avoid hitting the dog. Hitting a mouse increases the score by one, but hitting a dog decreases it by one. This aspect to the game forces patients to search for and hit only the mouse when both mouse and dog are present, in order to improve visual discrimination and selective attention, which can be important aspect to patient rehabilitation particularly for patients with hemispatial neglect.

The player, level of game, score, and adapted speed are shown in the upper-right corner of the screen to give the user real-time feedback. Overall performance data such as score, accuracy rate, and the length of game-play sessions are also shown to the user when the game is over or on entry to the next level, and this data is also written to a session log file for the user. The next time the patient uses the system this information will be used to configure the game. Further, the physiotherapist can analyse this data to assess how the patient is progressing over a number of sessions. Besides the performance feedback, multiple sensory feedback is given. When a mouse is hit, it squeaks and its colour changes to red, and when a dog is hit, it barks and its colour changes to red. To create an element of competition, but also to give feedback to the patient, the user can view the highest scores of all the users and also his or her personal best scores of each game level.

4 Conclusion

This paper has shown how adaptive VR games can contribute to motor therapy by providing motivating tasks that can automatically adapt to individual patient's capabilities. We discussed the potential for the integration of physics simulation techniques into VR games for upper limb motor rehabilitation. A physically based VR framework with adaptive game configuration based on data collected before-game and in-game was described which is currently being used by a number of hemiplegia patients with various levels of severity. The integration of physically-based simulation with conventional clinical therapy and game-like scenarios adds richness to the virtual environment which has the potential for improving patient outcome. Initial feedback is very positive, with patients reporting that they enjoy playing the game. Further work is necessary to determine just how much the introduction of physics into the game simulation actually influences patient outcome, but we believe that adaptive game technology has much to offer motor rehabilitation.

References

1. Viau, A., Feldman, A.G., McFadyen, J., Levin, M.F.: Reaching in reality and virtual reality: a comparison of movement kinematics in healthy subjects and in adults with hemiparesis, Journal of NeuroEngineering and Rehabilitation, 1.11 (2004)
2. Holden, M.K., Dyar, T.A., Schwamm, L., Bizzi, E.: Virtual Environment-based Telerehabilitation in Patients with Stroke, Presence - Virtual Rehabilitation, M. Alexa and J. Marks (Eds), 14.2, pp. 214–233 (2005)

3. Kuttuva, M., Boian, R., Merians, A., Burdea, G., Bouzit, M., Lewis, J., Fensterheim, D.: The Rutgers Arm: An Upper-Extremity Rehabilitation System in Virtual Reality, Proc. of the 5th International Workshop on Virtual Rehabilitation (IWVR05), Catalina Island, California, U.S.A, pp. 94–103 (2005)
4. McNeill, M.D.J., Pokluda, L., McDonough, S., Crosbie, J.: Immersive virtual reality for upper limb rehabilitation following stroke, IEEE International Conference on Systems, Man and Cybernetics, October pp. 2783–2789 (2004)
5. Rand, D., Katz, N., Shahar, M., Kizony, R., Weiss, P.L.: The virtual mall: development of a functional virtual environment for stroke rehabilitation, Abstracts of the 55th Annual Conference of the Israeli Association of Physical and Rehabilitation Medicine (2004)
6. Katz, N., Ring, H., Naveh, Y., Kizony, R., Feintuch, U., Weiss, P.L.: Interactive Virtual Environment training for safe street crossing of right hemisphere stoke patients with unilateral spatial neglect, ICDVRAT 2004: Proceedsings of the Fifth International Conference on Disability, Virtual Reality and Associated Technologies, Oxford, UK (2004)
7. Ma, M., McNeill, M., McDonough, S., Crosbie, J., Oliver, L.: Physics Fidelity of Virtual Reality in Motor Rehabilitation. Virtual: a Real Success: Proc. Of the 8th International Conference on Virtual Reality (VRIC—Laval Virtual), S. Richir and E. Klinger (Eds.), pp. 35-41, Laval, France, (April 2006)
8. Charles, D., McNeill, M., McAlister, M., Black, M., Moore, A., Stringer, K., Kücklich, J., Kerr, A.: Player-centred game design: player modelling and adaptive digital games, DIGRA2005: Proceedings of the Second International Digital Games Research Conference, pp. 285-298, Vancouver, Canada, (June 2005)
9. Demeurisse, G., Demol, O., Robaya, E.: Motor evaluation in vascular hemiplegia. European Neurology 19, 382–389 (1980)
10. Lyle, R.C.A.: Performance test for assessment of upper limb function in physical rehabilitated treatment and research. Int. J Rehabil 4, 483–492 (1981)
11. OGRE: Object-oriented Graphics Rendering Engine (2007), http://www.ogre3d.org
12. Ageia: Ageia PhysX SDK (2007), http://www.ageia.com
13. NxOgre (2007), http://www.nxogre.org
14. Smyth, M., Wann, J.: Interactive interfaces for movement rehabilitation in virtual environments, Proceedings of the third International Conference Series on Disability, Virtual Reality and Associated Technologies (ICDVRAT), Alghero, Sardinia, Italy (September 2000)
15. Lewis, G., Byblow, W.: Neurophysiological and behavioural adaptations to bilateral training intervention in individuals following stroke. Clinical rehabilitation 18, 48–59 (2004)

Controlling an Anamorphic Projected Image for Off-Axis Viewing

Jiyoung Park[1] and Myoung-Hee Kim[1,2]

[1] Dept. of Computer Science & Engineering, Ewha Womans University, Seoul, Korea
[2] Center for Computer Graphics and Virtual Reality,
Ewha Womans University, Seoul, Korea
lemie@ewhain.net, mhkim@ewha.ac.kr

Abstract. We modify a projected image so as to compensate for changes in the viewer's location. We use the concept of a virtual camera in the viewing space to achieve a transformable display with improved visibility. The 3D space and virtual camera are initialized and then the image is translated, rotated, scaled and projected. The user can modify the position and size of the image freely within the allowable projection area. They can also change its orientation as seen from their viewpoint, which can be off the axis of projection.

1 Introduction

Modern displays produce high-resolution images on the compact screens of portable devices, which many people now use on a daily basis. There has also been progress on the development of image projectors, which are now smarter and more portable, but the way in which they are used remains relatively unchanged. It is often difficult to find a place to put a projector and screen, because of the many objects that clutter our environment. Most portable projectors require the projector itself, or a mirror, to be rotated in order to adjust the position of the projected image; this is cumbersome, and projectors are still heavier than other portable devices. Furthermore, after the projector and screen have been set up, viewers must sit near the axis of projection to see a true image. It would be better if projected images could be moved and tilted easily, like televisions and monitors, to suit the viewer.

In this paper, we present a method of controlling a projection-based display so as to compensate for changes in the viewer's location. We use the concept of a virtual camera in the viewing space to achieve a transformable display with improved visibility.

2 Related Work

Many smart displays allow images to be modified in order to increase the convenience of using a projector, and to allow the viewer to move around an ordinary environment. The most ubiquitous facility is automatic keystone correction [1] [2], which is currently available on many commercial projectors. Keystone correction adjusts the projected image to fit the projection surface, but takes no account of the user.

C. Stephanidis (Ed.): Universal Access in HCI, Part II, HCII 2007, LNCS 4555, pp. 691–698, 2007.

However, recent research on the interactive use of projected images allows images to be adjusted manually or automatically under software control.

Pingali et al. [3] developed the Everywhere Display system which allows interactive images can be cast on to a floor or wall. They made a prototype that combines a projector, a pan/tilt mirror, and a camera. The mirror is used to deflect the image from the projector on to different surfaces, and they process the projected image to compensate for the perspective distortion. Similarly, in the PRIMA project [4], the Steerable Camera Projector (SCP) was developed as part of an interactive environment. The SCP is itself motorized, and does not use a mirror like the Everywhere Display [3] [5]. Tapia et al. [6] have used the Everywhere Display projector in a prototype ubiquitous video communication system, which involves the perception of eye contact. The system locates a person's face using miniature video cameras embedded within walls and cabinetry, and then projects an image of that face on to an appropriate surface where it can be seen by another person. This allows eye contact between people who are moving around while also communicating over long distances.

Instead of using a steerable mirror or moving the projector, some researchers position the projector in a location where it can be seen from anywhere in the workspace, and then allow the user to control the projected image within the range of adjustments supported by the projector. Cotting et al. [7] project images which the user can rotate and scale under the control of a laser pointer. The PaperWindows [8] system supports interaction on various sizes of paper using a projector and a vision tracking system. In this case the projector is placed above the workspace, windows are projected on to the paper, and the user's interactions are inferred using computer vision.

The increased portability of the latest projectors, which may be hand-held, has motivated a new line of research. Beardsley et al. [9] have developed an interactive projection technique for a hand-held projector. They measure and correct the projector motion, so that the projected image appears to be static. However, by allowing the projector motion to affect the cursor, they give the user a convenient way of interacting with the image that requires no extra hardware. Cao et al. [10] have developed another interaction method which uses a pen and a hand-held projector. Blaskó et al. [11] simulated a wrist-worn projection display with a fixed projector and proposed a method of interaction that exploits this wearable projector.

In most of these projection-based display techniques, the projectors are carried by the user, or the users move to a position where they can see the screen, because it is usually assumed that the user should always be in front of the display. If the projected image is warped, that is done to suit the projection surface, and not the user's position and viewing direction. This does not assist the user who wants to move about. In this paper, we present a method to control a projected image using the concept of a virtual camera. Our system allows projected images to be easily be moved and scaled and rotated, creating anamorphic images which appear correct when viewed by the user, even if he or she is in an off-axis position. The user continues to see an undistorted image even if they change their position and viewing direction.

3 Display Control Using a Virtual Camera

Our method of display control involves the translation, rotation and scaling of the image. A display initialization step sets up a 3D space and a virtual camera. Then, under the real-time control of the user, the image is transformed and projected. In this step, the user can modify the position and size of the image freely within the allowable projection area. We also provide a rotation that modifies the direction of the display to accommodate the user's viewpoint, which avoids the user having to move to the axis of projection in order to see an undistorted image. We render images using DirectX. When the transformation that control the projected image is changed, a transformation matrix is modified and applied to the rendered picture.

3.1 Display Initialization

By using a 3D virtual space and a virtual camera, we can control the position, size and orientation of the image without touching the physical projection system. In the initialization step, a 3D virtual space is created. As shown in Figure 1, we position a screen on which the original image is displayed, and a virtual camera is generated and located where it will see the correct interpretation of the projected anamorphic image. The virtual camera acquires images of the 3D space, including the virtual screen. Figure 2 shows a projector displaying an image acquired by such a virtual camera. The virtual camera is positioned at the user's viewpoint, and changes to the camera's position and viewing direction generate the spatial transformations that are used to modify the real projected image.

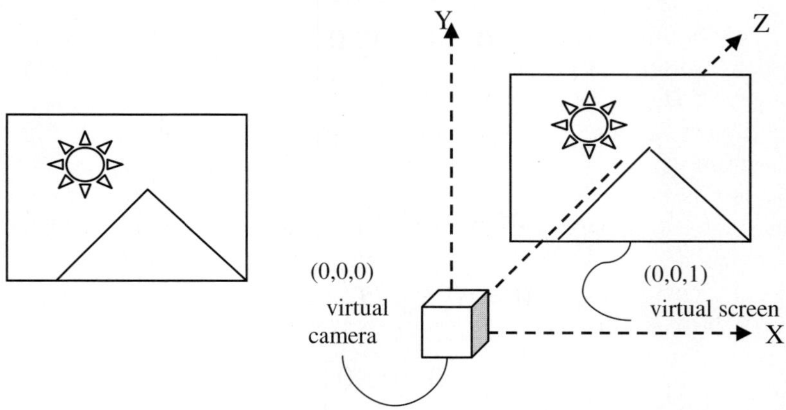

Fig. 1. Original image to be projected (left). The camera and screen in virtual space (right).

3.2 Translation and Scaling

To move the image, we create a translation matrix, as shown in Equation (1), where t_x and t_y are the translation parameters for the x and y-axis respectively. To change the scale of the projected image, a scaling matrix is created using the parameter s, as

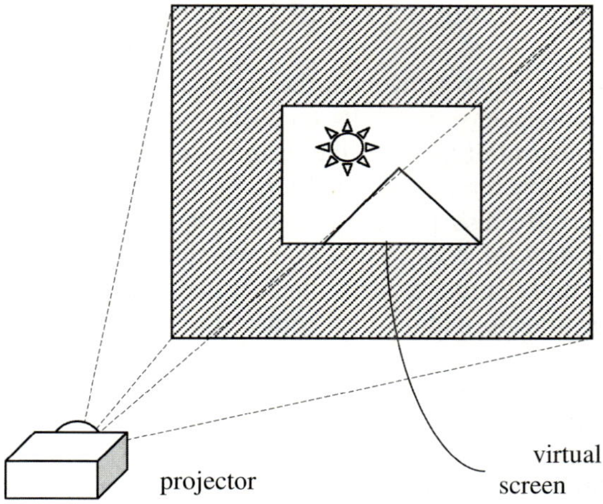

Fig. 2. Projecting a 3D scene on to a planar surface

shown in Equation (4). The translation and scaling parameters are provided by real-time input from the user, who activates a controller such as a mouse. As new parameters arrive, the transformation matrices are re-composed and applied to the existing projection matrix *M*, which is obtained from Equation (2). The new projection matrix *M'* (Equation (3)) replaces *M*. An example of a transformed display is shown in Figure 3. The dashed lines correspond to the virtual screen before transformation.

$$T' = \begin{bmatrix} 1 & 0 & 0 & 0 \\ 0 & 1 & 0 & 0 \\ 0 & 0 & 1 & 0 \\ tx & ty & 0 & 1 \end{bmatrix} \tag{1}$$

$$M = S_m R_m T_m \tag{2}$$

$$M' = S_m R_m T' T_m \tag{3}$$

$$S' = \begin{bmatrix} s & 0 & 0 & 0 \\ 0 & s & 0 & 0 \\ 0 & 0 & 1 & 0 \\ 0 & 0 & 0 & 1 \end{bmatrix} \tag{4}$$

$$M' = S' M \tag{5}$$

Fig. 3. Translation (left) and scaling (middle and right) of the image

3.3 Rotation in 3D

We use an anamorphic image to allow the user to see an undistorted image even if they are not located in front of the screen. An anamorphic image appears correct only when seen from a particular off-axis perspective, or when viewed through some transforming optical device such as a mirror [12]. A familiar example of a plane anamorphosis is the markings on roadways which are elongated on the road so that they look normal when foreshortened by a driver's point of view.

Constructing a plane anamorphic image requires a perspective transformation. We assume the user's eye corresponds to the virtual camera. We generate a viewing transformation matrix based on four vectors which describe the position and orientation of the virtual camera. These vectors are the position, the viewing direction, and a rightward-facing and an upward-facing vector, which are written as $p=(p_x, p_y, p_z)$, $d=(d_x, d_y, d_z)$, $r=(r_x, r_y, r_z)$, and $u=(u_x, u_y, u_z)$ respectively. When the user modifies the position and viewing direction of the virtual camera, the view transformation is modified. By applying the new view transformation at the rendering stage, we can generate a perspective image that appears undistorted to the user. As shown in Equation (6), a new view transformation matrix V' is created and then the transpose of V' replaces the existing viewing matrix V. The image after rotation about the three virtual camera axes is shown in Figure 4.

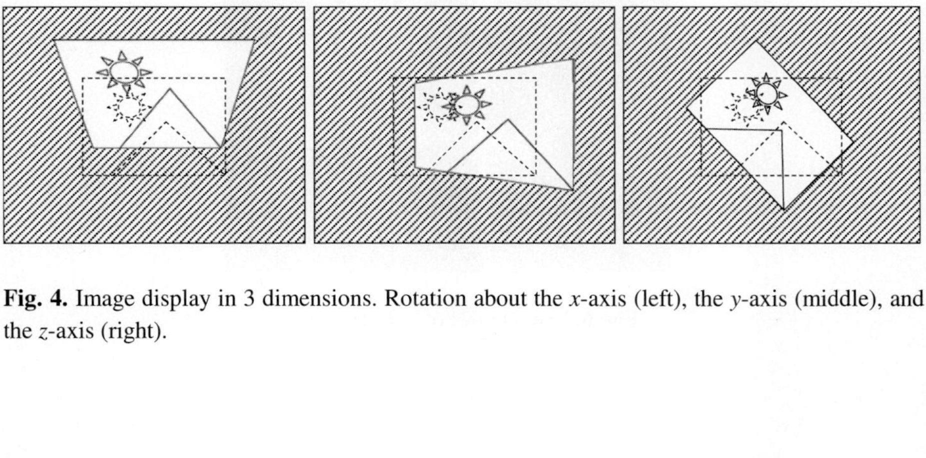

Fig. 4. Image display in 3 dimensions. Rotation about the *x*-axis (left), the *y*-axis (middle), and the *z*-axis (right).

$$V' = \begin{bmatrix} r_x & u_x & d_x & 0 \\ r_y & u_y & d_y & 0 \\ r_z & u_z & d_z & 0 \\ (-p \cdot r) & (-p \cdot u) & (-p \cdot d) & 1 \end{bmatrix} \tag{6}$$

$$V = (V')^T \tag{7}$$

4 Experimental Results

We used a wireless space mouse as the display controller. The mouse has three buttons: translation is linked to the left button, scaling to the middle button, and the right button changes the viewing direction. The coordinates of the screen center are (0,0,0)

Fig. 5. User control of a ceiling display

Fig. 6. User control of a wall display

and the center of the virtual screen is (0,0,1). At initialization, the eye position is (0,0,0) and the viewing vector is (0,0,1). When the user moves the cursor with the right button pressed, the direction vector is calculated from the position of the cursor (x,y,0) to the center of the virtual screen (0,0,1). Then the view transformation matrix is modified by the vectors and the image is projected so that it appears undistorted from the user's position.

We have used this technique to generate a ceiling and wall displays, as shown in Figures 5 and 6.

5 Conclusions

We have proposed a method for controlling a projected image using a virtual camera. A user can move and scale the image, and change its apparent axis of projection. This allows a user more flexibility of movement and posture while looking at a projected image. The proposed method does not need a special projector or controller, which allows it to be easily integrated with existing devices.

It is not easy to specify a 3D rotation with the space mouse. Therefore, we do not currently support rotation about the z-axis using the mouse, and we need a better interface and method of interaction to adjust the image intuitively. In future work, we plan to detect the user's face and then to calculate the viewing transformation automatically.

Acknowledgement. This work was supported by the Korean Ministry of Information and Communication under the Information Technology Research Center (ITRC) Program.

References

1. Sukthankar, R., Stockton, R., Mullin, M.: Automatic Keystone Correction for Camera-assisted Presentation Interfaces. In: International Conference on Multimedia Interfaces (ICMI) (2000)
2. Raskar, R., Beardsley, P.: A Self-correcting Projector. In: Proceedings of IEEE Computer Vision and Pattern Recognition (CVPR), pp. 504–508 (2001)
3. Pingali, G., Pinhanez, C., Levas, A., Kjeldsen, R., Podlaseck, M., Chen, H., Sukaviriya, N.: Steerable Interfaces for Pervasive Computing Spaces. In: Proceedings of IEEE International Conference on Pervasive Computing and Communications (PerCom'03), pp.315–322 (2003)
4. PRIMA project. http://www.inria.fr/recherche/equipes/prima.en.html
5. Pinhanez, C.: The Everywhere Displays Projector: A Device to Create Ubiquitous Graphical Interfaces. In: Proceedings of Ubiquitous Computing 2001 Conference, pp. 315–331 (2001)
6. Tapia, E., Munguia, I.S.S., Rebula, J., Stoddard, S.: Concept and Partial Prototype Video: Ubiquitous Video Communication with the Perception of Eye Contact. In: Dey, A.K., Schmidt, A., McCarthy, J.F. (eds.) UbiComp 2003. LNCS, vol. 2864, Springer, Heidelberg (2003)

7. Cotting, D., Ziegler, R., Gross, M., Fuchs, H.: Adaptive Instant Displays: Continuously Calibrated Projections Using Per-Pixel Light Control. In: Proceedings of Eurographics 2005, pp. 705–714 (2005)
8. Holman, D., Vertegaal, R.: Altosaa,r M., Troje, N., Johns, D.: PaperWindows: Interaction Techniques for Digital Paper. In: Proceedings of ACM CHI 2005 Conference on Human Factors in Computing Systems, pp. 591–599 (2005)
9. Beardsley, P., Baar, J.V., Raskar, R., Forlines, C.: Interaction Using a Handheld Projector. IEEE Computer Graphics and Applications 25(1), 39–43 (2005)
10. Cao, X., Balakrishnan, R.: Interacting with Dynamically Defined Information Spaces Using a Handheld Projector and a Pen. In: Proceedings of UIST 2006 – the ACM Symposium on User Interface Software and Technology, pp. 225–234 (2006)
11. Blaskó, G., Coriand, F., Feiner, S.: Exploring Interaction with a Simulated Wrist-Worn Projection Display. In: Gil, Y., Motta, E., Benjamins, V.R., Musen, M.A. (eds.) ISWC 2005. LNCS, vol. 3729, pp. 2–9. Springer, Heidelberg (2005)
12. Anamorphic Image. http://www.physics.uoguelph.ca/morph/morph.html

An Anthropomorphic AR-Based Personal Information Manager and Guide

Andreas Schmeil and Wolfgang Broll

Fraunhofer FIT, Collaborative Virtual and Augmented Environments Department, Schloss Birlinghoven, 53754 Sankt Augustin, Germany
Andreas.Schmeil@googlemail.com, Wolfgang.Broll@fit.fraunhofer.de

Abstract. The use of personal electronic equipment has significantly increased during recent years. Augmented Reality (AR) technology enables mobile devices to provide a very rich user experience by combining mobile computing with connectivity and location-awareness. In this paper we discuss the approach and development of an Augmented Reality-based personal assistant, combining the familiar interface of a human person with the functionality of a location-aware digital information system. The paper discusses the main components of the system, including the anthropomorphic user interface as well as the results of an initial prototype evaluation.

Keywords: Augmented Reality, Mobile Computing, Virtual Humans, Anthropomorphic User Interfaces, Digital Assistants, Environment Model, Location Based Systems.

1 Introduction

Mobile electronic devices are being used more and more in every day life. Mobile phones, PDAs and laptop computers have replaced more traditional media and tools. Thus many people use laptop computers instead of desktop PCs today, and PDAs and smartphones have replaced traditional paper-based organizers. Another development we can observe today is the increasing availability of location-based services. In recent years mobile providers have started providing navigation and other cell based services. The popularity of such services has also increased with the introduction of new connectivity technologies such as WiFi, WiMax and UMTS. However, most available devices and systems share these problems:

- Compared to having a real assistant, many tasks are very cumbersome and time-consuming, due to the limited user interface provided by the devices.
- The range of applications and services are limited, due to limits of the existing devices and displays used in them.
- Existing devices are difficult to use if you want to use your hands for another task or if you need them free.
- Users do not benefit appropriately from available location information, as it is mostly not integrated with the organizer functionality.

C. Stephanidis (Ed.): Universal Access in HCI, Part II, HCII 2007, LNCS 4555, pp. 699–708, 2007.

Fig. 1. A virtual anthropomorphic assistant in a mobile environment

The work presented in this paper aims to overcome these shortcomings without the use of complex user interfaces. Interacting with a virtual anthropomorphic character should in theory be similar to communicating with a real assistant (or person), as these types of interface present information in a very natural way. To foster this experience they have to be part of the real world, i.e. by augmenting the real environment rather than being an autonomous interface element on a display. Mobile Augmented Reality (AR) enables us to use virtual assistants as part of the user's local environment almost anywhere and anytime (see figure 1).

In this paper we describe the development of an intuitive multimodal user interface that combines AR technology with a mobile personal assistant. The second part of the paper provides a brief overview of related work, pointing where our approach goes beyond the current state-of-the-art. Section 3 presents our approach in detail, including the hardware setup, the development of the virtual assistant, the environment model and the user interface. In section 4 we describe and discuss the results of our initial field trials. Section 5 provides conclusions and future directions.

2 Related Work

In contrast with previous work which either developed an AR information and navigation system or an anthropomorphic assistant, the work presented here concentrates specifically on combining these two technologies.

Mobile augmented reality systems such as the Touring Machine [6] and the applications developed within the OCAR project [11] provide information about the mobile environment by superimposing text into the user's view. The user interfaces of these systems are mostly based on two-dimensional GUIs operated by touchpads, which according to our experience are often considered as somewhat awkward and rather difficult to use. Furthermore, reading requires the user's complete attention.

Augmented reality systems make use of virtual characters for digital storytelling throughout a city [8] and for guiding school children to outdoor locations with virtual learning content [12]. However, when the user requires additional information and further interactivity the situation becomes more complex. Virtual assistants have mainly been used in virtual reality environments so far. Virtual assistants are in most cases restricted to one specific task. The anthropomorphic assistant Hamilton [13] was designed to arrange furniture in a virtual environment. MAX [9] demonstrates how to assemble a construction kit. Both assistants understand voice commands and interpret hand gestures. Within the research project Virtual Human [16] an interactive learning application was developed: two anthropomorphic characters (a teacher and student) explain requested content in a new and interesting manner.

Welbo [1] was the first anthropomorphic assistant in AR and took the form of a little robot that floats around a living room – the robot was visible to those wearing the HMD. Welbo points at virtual objects and rearranges them upon voice commands. Other virtual characters functioned as game characters [3], test subjects for object design [2] and behavior-driven presenters [4]. However, an anthropomorphic assistant that fulfils tasks for everyday life, as our assistant does, has not yet been developed.

Most AR systems work with small manually entered data sets. Therefore, only little research has been done in the field of databases for mobile AR applications or in the use of environment models and the management of such systems. However as the trend towards location-aware services and assistants grows there is a need for research into storing location based information. The Nexus project [7] explores the creation, definition and development of environment models from heterogenic data sources.

The problem with many of the environment models created so far is that they often only contain geometric and physical data, so data about meanings etc. has to be added manually using keywords. In contrast, as our work is focused on the development of an anthropomorphic assistant the environmental model contains information about the objects and how they can be presented.

3 Our Approach

We decided to combine personal information management (PIM) functions with the functionality of a local guide to demonstrate how a mobile user can benefit from an omnipresent anthropomorphic assistant. The approach includes the following five major components, which will be introduced in detail later: the hardware setup, the virtual character, our developed environment model, the software system, and the multimodal user interface.

3.1 The Mobile AR System

Our mobile AR setup uses a notebook computer with a 2 GHz processor and an ATI Mobility FireGL V3100 graphics accelerator operating under Windows XP. In outdoor settings, the user's position is tracked by a Holux GPSlim236 GPS receiver. For the time being we abandoned the option of using differential GPS or hybrid outdoor position tracking. For orientation tracking an InterSense InertiaCube3 is used.

Indoors, the user's position and orientation is tracked by a combination of ARToolKit tracking and the InertiaCube3. For accessing the tracking devices and for combining the provided data into stable 6-DOF tracking information we use the MORGAN [10] AR/VR framework, which also provides support for the seamless transition between multiple tracking systems (e.g. outdoor and indoor tracking). By doing this the user can roam freely between indoor and outdoor environments. The notebook computer and the GPS receiver are mounted on a backpack worn by the user.

The virtual assistant is superimposed onto the user's view by using a Shimadzu DataGlass 2/A display, this is a monoscopic optical see-through head-worn display. For safety reasons (especially regarding the use in the outdoor environment), we decided for a monoscopic optical see-through display. For head tracking, the InertiaCube3 and an external active GPS antenna are mounted to the sides of the display. For indoor use – which requires the tracking of the ARToolKit markers – an additional camera is mounted to the display. For speech input and output (from the assistant) we chose a one-ear headset, to reduce magnetic interferences. The alternative input device, a common PC wheel-mouse connected with the laptop computer via BlueTooth, is either carried in one hand or in a (jacket) pocket.

Unlike most other mobile AR configurations, our setup works perfectly without a helmet. For the hardware designated to be head-worn components were chosen that are light-weight and small in size. Moreover, putting on and taking off the modified display and the one-ear headset is very easy. This layout is a prototype and we expect to make some modifications over time so that it is more suitable for daily use.

3.2 The Virtual Character

For the rendering of the anthropomorphic character, we extended the MORGAN framework by the open source character animation library Cal3D [14]. As the anthropomorphic assistant places or removes objects from her pockets it was necessary to develop a system that enables her to take out objects like a calendar (for scheduling appointments), a notebook (for writing down notes) and a pen. Further, our software component facilitates the scheduling of all the described animation functions, thus allowing the creation of whole sequences of animations.

Further, in order to equip the assistant with a natural voice, we extended our framework with a component for speech synthesis and output based on Loquendo TTS. The virtual assistant seems more alive to the user and becomes human-like, i.e. anthropomorphic. This impression is further improved by the synchronization of speech and gestures. The assistant appears more acceptable and trustworthy to the user, thus reducing any inhibitions they have when it comes to interacting with it.

The assistant is equipped with elementary movements like walking or running in any desired speed and can nod, shake the head and point into specific directions. During the presentation of objects specifically designed animations are executed, synchronized with speech output. However, to ensure flexibility, the synchronization of presentations cannot be controlled by the application. Rather, it has to be specified in a modifiable database where all information about the world is defined.

3.3 An Environment Model

For the virtual assistant to be a local guide for the user, extensive information about the real world, i.e. the user's current environment, is required. We developed a lightweight, yet powerful environment model. It is based on the widespread XML format GPX [15]. GPX defines waypoints, routes and tracks. We extended the waypoints to utilize them as local environment models.

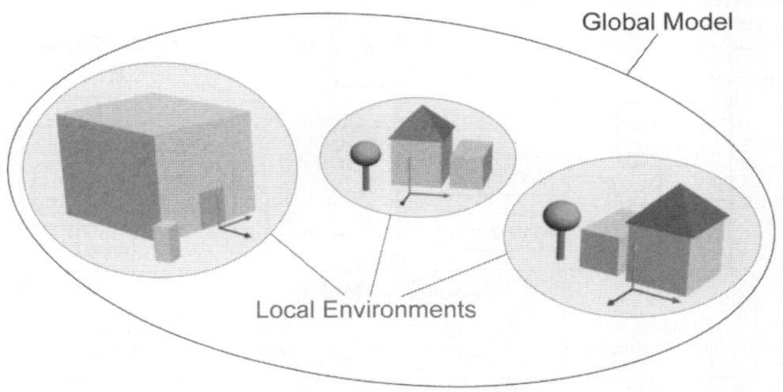

Fig. 2. The sum of all local environments builds a global environment model

An augmented waypoint, i.e. a local environment, is defined as a limited area that can contain objects. Every local environment has its own Cartesian coordinate system in which the contained objects are transformed. Figure 2 illustrates this concept. Besides this transformation, a name, an elevation, a description, a comment, and a type an augmented waypoint provides the following additional information:

- the extent of each object in the local environment: a VRML scene
- a name, a comment, and a description of each contained object
- position and orientation of ARToolKit markers used for indoor tracking
- specific information for the assistant (information about actions to execute for presenting objects or the waypoint itself, data for synchronizing speech and gestures, position to take in for presentations).

We developed an XML schema for an augmented waypoint. An object's information is linked with its 3D data through the unique VRML identifier of the object. The assistant presents an object by reading out aloud its description. Waypoint-specific animations are defined as actions. For the synchronization of gestures and speech, the appropriate action is started when the speech output reaches a corresponding label, which is embedded in the text. For navigation tasks the assistant gets information about the structure of pathways in the user's environment in form of GPX routes.

For the purpose of an anthropomorphic assistant describing and presenting objects to the user, an environment model based on a complex object hierarchy (as found in [7] or [11]) is not needed. When presenting an object by reading a pertinent text, metadata about the object is not needed. Furthermore, since the environment of a mobile user changes continuously, we considered the use of flexible multiple VRML scenes instead of one large global 3D model more appropriate.

3.4 The Software System

Figure 3 gives an overview of the components running within the MORGAN framework. The MARA application controls the assistant, manages the user's personal information and handles all aspects of interaction, while the MORGAN Viewer's purpose is to render the scene graph including the virtual character.

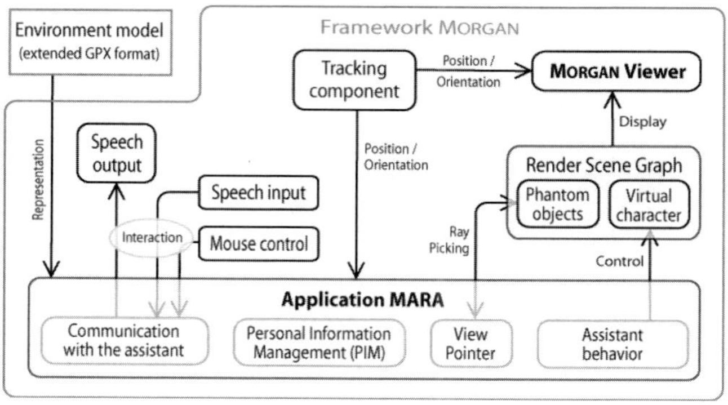

Fig. 3. The modular software system

The tracking component provides continuously updated information about the user's position and viewing direction. The viewer uses this information to set the view point for rendering, the application MARA keeps the assistant informed about the user's whereabouts. The assistant is therefore able to move towards the user while talking to him, to follow him and to turn to him while presenting an object. Using the information about the user's viewing direction we realized a view pointer, allowing the user to select objects simply by gazing at them. For the personal information management (PIM) functionality of the system, the internal database comprises a set of appointments and an ordered list of notes. Appointments can be associated with locations, i.e. with waypoints. The assistant is able to guide the user to an appointment at a desired time, simply by walking ahead. For the navigation a route is planned using paths defined in the environment model.

The MARA application also controls the assistant's behavior. We realized it as a 2-level hierarchical state machine. The higher level states represent the implemented functions:

Idling	Calendar	Notebook	Introduction	Presentation	Guidance

The lower level states correspond to the several steps of the particular functions; e.g. scheduling an appointment requires the specification of a time, a reminder, and an optional location in succession. The assistant displays the current state with distinct gestures and tells the user about ongoing actions. In general, transitions between states are expressed by single animations, e.g. pulling out or putting away a calendar. Figures 4 and 5 provide examples on how the behavior and the current state are projected by the anthropomorphic assistant. Upon receiving a help command the assistant informs the user about the current state and any inputs which may be expected from the user. State transitions are mostly caused by user actions, but also by the expiration of time intervals or the end of ongoing actions of the assistant.

Fig. 4. The virtual assistant with the calendar waiting for input

Fig. 5. The virtual assistant presenting the portal of a castle

3.5 Multimodal Interaction

To control the system, i.e. to interact with the assistant, two distinct types of interaction are needed:

- communicating with the anthropomorphic assistant
- selecting (real world) objects

As a consequence, the interaction is inherently multimodal. We decided to use speech input as the main user interface for communicating with the assistant. This approach comes closest to communicating with a real person and thus promises a high user acceptance, allowing the user to converse with the virtual assistant.

Our speech input component uses IBM's ViaVoice speech recognition software to transform spoken words, phrases and continuous text into written text and commands. To increase recognition rates we used multiple grammars, one for each function. The user can quickly cancel the current function and change to another mode by issuing short commands. Different phrases with the same meaning can be associated with the same annotation. The system switches automatically between the grammars at high-level state transitions. The listing in figure 6 shows the intuitive character of the interaction with the assistant.

Situations may occur, in which the user is not able to or does not want to use speech interaction. For these situations, we developed a secondary user interface, utilizing an ordinary PC wheel-mouse. To keep the interaction intuitive, the left mouse button is always used for confirmation or for giving an affirmative answer, while the right mouse button always stops or cancels the current action, dismisses a selection, or negates a question. The wheel is used to change the selection or alter the value that is currently of interest. To keep the user interface as natural as possible, the mouse interaction is designed to function without an on-screen menu. Mouse control and speech input are both usable at the same time, and the user does not need to switch modes. The entire functionality is available through both input methods, with one solitary exception – dictating notes.

User:	Schedule an appointment.
Assistant:	Okay. At what time?
User:	At 16:30.
Assistant:	Aha, 16:30. Shall I remind you of it 15 minutes earlier?
User:	No, 10 minutes earlier.
Assistant:	Alright, 10 minutes earlier. Where is it? At building C5?
User:	No.
Assistant:	At the canteen?
User:	Yes.
Assistant:	I schedule an appointment at 16:30 at the canteen.

Fig. 6. Dialog between user and assistant

The user selects an object by simply gazing at it for two seconds. The assistant then utters the name of this object and points at it. The help function is accessible at any time, either by saying “help” or by pressing the middle mouse button. The assistant tells about the current state or action and gives interaction hints.

4 Evaluation

We evaluated the system in an outdoor setting at our campus. The assistant had information about several waypoints and paths between them. Some of the augmented waypoints contained objects that were selectable (and presentable) separately.

Evaluation Procedure. The evaluation focused on both the functionality of the system and the interaction methods used. The test persons had to make appointments, take notes, let the assistant repeat the notes, make the assistant describe an object or a waypoint and guide the user to an appointment. In order to evaluate the speech interface against mouse input the subjects had to undertake all functions once by speech interaction and once by mouse control. The second part of the evaluation was the completion of a questionnaire. The subjects were asked to rate individual aspects of the user interface as well as the sustainability of the overall approach.

Test Group. 13 volunteers participated in the evaluation (7 male, 6 female). The age varied between 16 and 45. Nine participants were frequent computer users, also nine participants said they used the PIM functionality of their mobile phones, five were frequent PDA users, and four indicated they used in-car navigation system.

Results. In order to ensure a fair study the speech recognition system was not trained to recognize any specific voice. Nonetheless, recognition rates varied strongly from user to user. As would be expected the subjects rating of the speech interface was heavily influenced by the number of recognition errors. The mouse as an alternate input method was considered rather feasible. One important finding is that the amount of time taken to complete a task was similar for both input methods. Also, the view pointer for the selection of objects was generally considered intuitive.

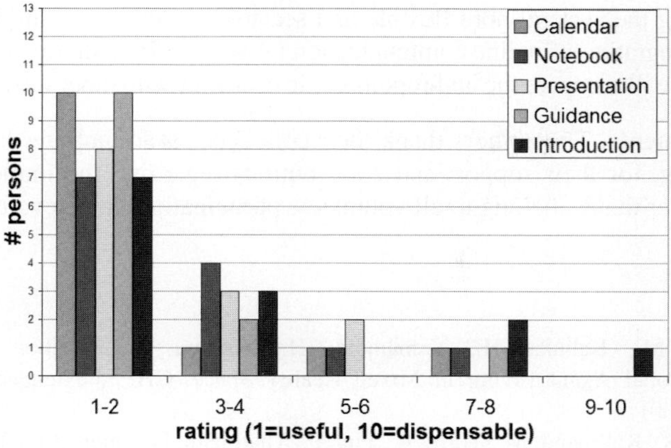

Fig. 7. Rating of the implemented functions

As figure 7 illustrates, the selection of the functions implemented in the system was found to be useful. The users also liked the idea of the assistant being both a secretary and a local guide. All test persons appreciated the help function and considered it user friendly.

About half of the users declared that the assistant's state and behavior were not always clear. That was mostly due to the limited field of view (FOV) of the display and its sensitivity to bright daylight. The assistant could only be seen in a small area and was, due to contrast issues, not always visible in bright daylight. As a result, only half of the users accepted the assistant as a proper substitute for a human assistant. The other half were pleased with the speech (and mouse) interface and considered the virtual character a side-product. Also, some subjects stated that they would appreciate more visual and acoustic feedback from the assistant and eventually visual head-up information, apart from the virtual character.

The study points to people liking the idea of an anthropomorphic assistant; however it also points to there being a need to improve speech recognition, the display and to make the system more wearable.

5 Conclusions and Future Work

In this paper we introduced MARA – our omnipresent personal virtual assistant, representing a first step towards integrating PIM functionality with services that are usually offered by personal guides and secretaries. We developed this by combining mobile AR technology, an anthropomorphic user interface representation in the local environment of the user, an intuitive multi-modal user interface, and a location-aware application. We evaluated our approach in an outdoor setting. Based on our findings we would expect that such a system would enjoy wide user acceptance. Anthropomorphic characters in mobile AR systems however require significant improvements in underlying technologies (especially with the quality of the head-worn displays) in order to form a good alternative to more traditional user interfaces.

Our intention is to modify the system to take into account the findings of the evaluation. This includes supporting additional awareness and feedback mechanisms as well as making the system more flexible and scalable (as suggested in [5]). Next steps include the integration of online communication (email, VoIP). Additionally, in a further evaluation we will compare the anthropomorphic character with other interface options.

Acknowledgments. The authors thank their colleagues at Fraunhofer FIT, especially Jan Ohlenburg, for their support and contributions regarding the implementation of MARA. Further thanks belong to all volunteers participating in the evaluation.

References

1. Anabuki, M., Kabuka, H., Yamamoto, H., Tamura, H.: Welbo: An Embodied Conversational Agent Living in Mixed Reality Space. CHI ', extended abstracts, pp. 10–11 (2000)
2. Balcisoy, S., Kallmann, M., Torre, R., Fua, P., Thalmann, D.: Interaction Techniques with Virtual Humans in Mixed Environments. Proc. of International Symposium on Mixed Reality, Yokohama, Japan (2001)
3. Barakonyi, I., Weilguny, M., Psik, T., Schmalstieg, D.: MonkeyBridge: Autonomous Agents in Augmented Reality Games. In: Proc. of ACM SIGCHI International Conference on Advances in Computer Entertainment Technology (ACE'05), Valencia, Spain (2005)
4. Barakonyi, I., Schmalstieg, D.: Ubiquitous Animated Agents for Augmented Reality. In: Proc. of ISMAR'06, Santa Barbara, CA, USA (2006)
5. Broll, W., Schäfer, L., Höllerer, T., Bowman, D.: Interface with Angels: The Future of VR and AR Interfaces. IEEE Computer Graphics and Applications 21(6), 14–17 (2001)
6. Feiner, S., MacIntyre, B., Höllerer, T., Webster, A.: A Touring Machine: Prototyping 3D Mobile Augmented Reality Systems for Exploring the Urban Environment. In: Proc. ISCW '97, pp. 74–81, Cambridge, MA, USA (1997)
7. Hohl, F., Kubach, U., Leonhardi, A., Rothermel, K., Schwehm, M.: Nexus – An Open Global Infrastructure for Spatial-Aware Applications. In: Proc. of MobiCom '99, Seattle, WA, USA (1999)
8. Holweg, D., Schneider, O.: GEIST – Mobile Outdoor AR-Informationsystem for historical education with digital storytelling. BMBF Virtual Reality Status Conference, (2004)
9. Kopp, S., Jung, B., Leßmann, N., Wachsmuth, I.: Max – A Multimodal Assistant in Virtual Reality Construction. KI – Künstliche Intelligenz 4/03, special Issue on Embodied Conversational Agents. Bremen, Germany, pp. 11–17 (2003)
10. Ohlenburg, J., Herbst, I., Lindt, I., Fröhlich, T., Broll, W.: The MORGAN Framework: Enabling Dynamic Multi–User AR and VR Projects. In: Proc. of VRST'04, pp. 166–169 (2004)
11. Reitmayr, G., Schmalstieg, D.: Collaborative Augmented Reality for Outdoor Navigation and Information Browsing. In: Proc. of Symposium Location Based Services and TeleCartography 66, 53–59 (2004)
12. Sephton, T.: Teaching agents for wearable augmented reality systems. In: Fensel, D., Sycara, K.P., Mylopoulos, J. (eds.) ISWC 2003. LNCS, vol. 2870, pp. 250–251. Springer, Heidelberg (2003)
13. Wachsmuth, I., Lenzmann, B., Jörding, T., Jung, B., Latoschik, M., Fröhlich, M.: A virtual interface agent and its agency. In: Proc. of the First International Conference on Autonomous Agents, pp. 516–517. ACM Press, New York (1997)
14. Cal3D website: http://cal3d.sourceforge.net
15. GPX website: http://www.topografix.com/gpx
16. Virtual Human website: http://www.virtual-human.org

Merging of Next Generation VR and Ambient Intelligence – From Retrospective to Prospective User Interfaces

Oliver Stefani[1], Ralph Mager[1], Evangelos Bekiaris[2], Maria Gemou[2], and Alex Bullinger[1]

[1] Center of Applied Technology in Neuroscience
Wilhelm Klein-Strasse 27, 4025 Basel, Switzerland
{ols, ram, bua}@coat-basel.com
[2] Center for Research and Technology Hellas
Hellenic Institute of Transport
6th km. Charilaou-Thermi Road
57001 Thermi, Greece
{abek, mgemou}@certh.gr

Abstract. In this paper we present current and future approaches to merge intelligent interfaces with immersive Virtual Environments (VEs). The aim of this paper is to substantiate the introductory presentation in the session "Facing Virtual Environments with innovative interaction techniques" at HCI 2007. Although VEs and multimodal interfaces tried to make Human-Computer-Interaction as natural as possible, they have shown serious usability problems. We describe concepts to aid users in supporting their personal cognitive and perceptual capabilities, where the Virtual Environment will adapt dynamically and in real-time to the users' physiological constitution, previous behaviour and desires. With our concept, human performance can be significantly enhanced by adapting interfaces and environments to the users' mental condition and their information management capacity. Health and usability problems caused by stress, workload and fatigue will be avoided. We intend to encourage discussions on this topic among the experts, which are gathered this session.

Keywords: Virtual Reality, Sensors, Ambient Intelligence, Adaptive interfaces.

1 Introduction

1.1 Adaptive Interfaces

One of the main aims of Virtual Reality is to make interaction with computers less difficult. New interaction approaches and techniques are continually being produced and modified - with important consequences on the interaction with computers. Taking also into consideration the recent efforts to provide computer-based interactive applications that are accessible by a broad end user population, including people with disabilities, one can conclude that the design of the User Interface

C. Stephanidis (Ed.): Universal Access in HCI, Part II, HCII 2007, LNCS 4555, pp. 709–714, 2007.

requires the revision of currently prevailing HCI assumptions, such as designing for the "average" user in a desktop environment. These assumptions need to be replaced incrementally by the more challenging objective of designing for the diversity in the end user population, the access media and devices, the contexts of use, etc. Depending on their characteristics, systems that adapt to users are contemplated as adaptive interfaces, user modelling systems, software agents or intelligent agents. The term "user-adaptive" system is often used for describing the entire family of the aforementioned systems.

Another approach to cater for diversity in the end user population is based on providing users with the opportunity to explicitly specify desired properties of the user interface. Systems offering such functionality are known as user-adaptable systems. The main advantage of such systems is that they allow the user to decide how the system will be displayed. One frequent objection to such an approach is that, in many cases, it is not possible for the user to know the best configuration settings for his/her requirements. Thus, the adaptability of such a system is under-utilised, since it is a time-consuming and complicated task. The main difference between the user-adaptive and the user-adaptable systems can be summarised in that user-adaptive systems adapt their behaviour to individual users on the basis of processes of user model acquisition and application, that involve some form of automated learning, inference, or decision making; while user-adaptable systems allow the individual user to explicitly tailor the user interface, by choosing options that determine, for example, the appearance of the system.

The emerging field of "Augmented Cognition" aims at revolutionizing the way humans interact with computer-based systems by coupling traditional electromechanical interaction devices (e.g., mouse, joystick) with psychophysiological methods (e.g., respiration, heart rate, EEG, functional optical imaging), where human physiological indicators can be used in real time to drive system adaptation. [1]

1.2 Multimodal Interfaces

Multimodal interfaces include more than the traditional keyboard and mouse. Natural input modes are used such as voice, gestures, haptic interaction and facial expressions. As described in [2], multimodal interfaces should follow several guiding principles, e.g. to be predictable and not unnecessarily complex and they should provide for modality switching. Multimodal interfaces should adapt to user's needs, abilities and the environment. Our approach will base its developments on the generation of new user-adaptive interfaces, fusing information from various modalities by measuring continuously both, the physiological and the behavioural status of the user.

1.3 Physiological Sensing

Using real-time neurophysiologic techniques within a virtual environment in the form of a closed-loop-system is relatively new. The general feasibility has already been demonstrated within the EU co-funded project VIEW of the Future (IST-2000-26089). A possible undesired health impact of these combined technologies was investigated thoroughly in the course of the EU co-funded project AGILE (QLK6-CT-2002-00118; target group: Elderly people). In the EU co-funded project RESPECT (QLRT-2000-00038) the question whether users might suffer health-related symptoms caused by the assessment tools themselves (the physiological measurement equipment) was addressed. It has been shown that the modular test-battery developed by COAT-Basel, which measures various physiological parameters, is a valid and valuable new test instrument of satisfactory acceptance by the targeted test population.

2 The Problem

Several existing interface technologies offer users various modes of interaction within a VE (speech, gestures, spatial motion, etc.). They are supported by traditional interaction devices like joysticks or tracking devices. Users are able to listen to spoken prompts and audio, to view information on high end graphical displays and to get tactile and haptic feedback from their interaction devices. They can talk, move and use force input to interact with the virtual world. Nevertheless, many 3-D input devices (e.g. data gloves) have shown usability problems [3]. The rapid decrease of prices for hardware, such as PCs and digital video projectors, leaded to an increasing spread of VEs to industries, SME's, hospitals, universities and soon to private homes.

There was a public demonstration of an immersive VR-System at the International Conference of Human Computer Interaction, 2003, in Crete, where visitors (delegates of the Human Factors and Ergonomics community) gave expert feedback on the design, usability and utility of the system exhibited. Many participants found the technology still difficult to use and had various problems to interact with the environment. There were many responses of how the technology should be improved, including the comment to "link technology with brain/mind/hand research." [4]

Interaction within VEs has many user specific parameters that affect the usability of the VE. The parameters are defined using calibration processes for devices and by explicit settings, using user preferences. In the last case it is hard for inexperienced users to identify and set their preferences within a VE [5]. However, it might be possible for the system to identify the user preferences by observing the psycho-physical and behavioural condition of the users, while practicing in the VE. In addition, although immersive virtual environments and multimodal interfaces try to make Human-Computer-Interaction as natural and effective as possible, it still lags far behind the much more natural and efficient human interpersonal communication and interaction. One major reason for this is that humans are able to adapt to each other, in order to maximise efficiency of communication and interaction, whereas artificial worlds and interfaces expect the "ideal" user. Another major problem when designing and developing new interaction techniques for 3-D environments is the lack of specific best practice guidelines [6]. Furthermore, accurate interaction with complex virtual environments has been shown to fail when a stressful situation is encountered. Efficient interaction can not be guaranteed if workload and fatigue is too high. Simulator sickness, information overload, dizziness and severe health problems have already been investigated in several research activities.

3 The Challenge

We aim, by measuring the mental and physical condition of the user and his/her behaviour, to adapt and personalise the multimodal virtual environment in real-time, to avoid health problems caused by anxiety, stress, workload and fatigue, as well as to enhance the user's satisfaction and comprehension of the VE. In this way, human performance while interacting with virtual multimodal environments could be tremendously enhanced, within an Ambient Intelligence Environment, where the interface and VE adapt to the users mental and physical condition, level of expertise, individual preferences, needs and wants.

New multimodal and adaptive interfaces and virtual environments could improve the usability of VEs by providing natural, intuitive and efficient interfaces for all kinds of users. They could increase the sense of realism, enrich the experience and the sense of presence, protect the users' health and manage his/her stress and fatigue levels in the VE. Interfaces and environments developed would adapt to the user, based on psycho-physiological, behavioural and personal preferences and related parameters, which would be derived from a multimodal measurement system. The multimodal measurement system would monitor the user regarding his/her physiological state (measuring autonomic body functions and EEG) and psychological state (monitoring behaviour, mimics and gestures), taking also into account explicit user profile parameters and preferences. The challenge is also to adapt multimodal interfaces (i.e. change from visual feedback to acoustic feedback or vice versa), according to the user's mental condition and his/her information management capacity; to identify mental workload and fatigue to prevent usability and health problems; to increase the sense of realism and to enrich the experience and the sense of presence of a user in a Virtual Environment and to improve the usability of VEs by providing natural, intuitive and efficient interfaces.

4 Potential Applications

4.1 Product Design and Engineering

Immersive Product Design and Engineering applications are complex human-machine interactive environments that have been shown to fail, due to stressful situations, to information overload and cyber sickness. Validation of geometry is the most common use of immersive virtual reality. Inspection of integrity, interferences between parts, accuracy and functionality are complex tasks to be performed by the operator. Depending on the user's individual workload, visual, audio or haptic feedback could be given to the user, in order to operate in the environment most efficiently. Additionally, the system could identify which senses of the user suffer from an information overload and provide alternative modalities to transfer the information more ergonomically to the user. Self adapting applications and interfaces will empower the user's ability to successfully accomplish the task. Cyber sickness can be detected before the user will get seriously sick.

4.2 Health and Medicine

Surveys estimate that fear of flying exists in 10-20% of the population. To treat the fear of flying, heights, tight spaces, etc. VR exposure therapy is a safe and successful procedure. Its popularity is justified by its lower costs than in vivo exposure, its ability to have total control of the environment, the repeatability of any phobic stimuli and its safety. In controlled stages patients can be exposed to virtual environments using stereoscopic displays as HMDs, where the virtual environment elicits progressively higher levels of anxiety. Each stage can be repeated until the patients anxiety has lessened and they feel ready to move to a higher level.

Adaptive VEs could refine and sustain medical treatments of anxieties. An individualized level of anxiety can be generated by the VR-system, based on the patients' level of fear, which can be derived from the objective physiological measurement system. A real-time evaluation kit can be used to monitor the physiology of the patient. He/she will be monitored during all phases of therapy, to ensure that the client is not becoming too anxious. At the same time, the environment should not be too boring for the patient. If the patients' anxiety becomes overwhelming, he/she will always be able to return to a less stressful level or exit the environment completely. The closed loop computational system, in which the computer adapts to the state of the patient would significantly improve the success of the treatment.

4.3 Training and Education

After unpredictable events, like earthquakes, terrorist attacks, etc, procedural knowledge is often unusable for a first aid. In these particular circumstances, strategic knowledge is the key for taking quick and effective decisions. Several organisational psychologists have shown how the human capability to deal and to utilise strategic knowledge is directly connected to the personal capability of the subject to cope with anxious situations. A pragmatic case for these considerations is represented by people operating in the civil protection organisations. Their skills are put in action mainly in unstructured situations, where procedures wouldn't help much to face such complex and multi-differentiated circumstances. A system able to perform adaptations, based on psychophysiological feedback parameters coming from the user, can be of big advantage in a variety of applications for the civil protection operators. Psychophysiological feedback parameters coming from the students during the training sessions using the VR will be utilised for adapting the VR training scenarios, strategies and system parameters accordingly. The approach of utilizing the students' emotional relevance, provided by the multimodal measurement system developed in the project, will be beneficial for the training of unpredictable and risky events, because it will be able to adapt the involvement level of the training scenario, in order not to be too scary for the trainees and monitor the trainees awareness level, in order to provide them real-time feedback during critical situations (self-consciousness during the performance of safety related tasks).

5 Future Work

We intend to develop/enhance and integrate micro- and nanosensors into Virtual Environments which are capable of sensing user-related input (i.e. physiology) and behavioural input/data from the user, as well as from the VE system. Development of knowledge-based (semi)-automated systems, capable of processing behavioural data in real time and actuating the integrated VE proactively (user pattern recognition leading to predictive behaviour estimations by the system) will therefore be needed. Furthermore a feasible user and decision model and a sensor fusion model (to extract higher level user state and behaviour) will be developed. Reasonable adaptation mechanisms to support user needs in complex VE's need to be provided.

6 Conclusion

We presented state of the art approaches to integrate multimodal interfaces, adaptive interfaces and immersive Virtual Environments. We discussed current barriers and problems with interaction in virtual environments. The challenge to be tackled and promising applications which could benefit from this approach are described in detail. We provide concepts to aid users in supporting their personal cognitive and perceptual capabilities, where the Virtual Environment will adapt dynamically and in real-time to the users' physiological constitution, previous behaviour and desires. The intention of this paper is to substantiate our introductory talk and to encourage further discussions on this topic.

References

1. Interview with Dylan Schmorrow found at: http://www.augmentedcognition.org/faq.htm
2. Raman, T.V.: Multimodal Interaction Design Principles For Multimodal Interaction, CHI, Apr. 5-10, 2003, Fort Lauderdale, USA (2003)
3. Stefani, O., Karaseitanidis, I.: Designing 3D Input Devices for Immersive Environments, IEEE SMC 2004 Conference Proceedings IEEE Conference on Systems, Man & Cybernetics Den Haag, The Netherlands 2004-10-10 - 2004-10-13). 2004, pp. 6280–6285, (2004)
4. Stefani, O., Patel, H., Hoffmann, H., Haselberger, F.: Extending the Desktop Workplace by a Portable Virtual Reality System, IPT 2004 Conference Proceedings, Ames, USA (2004)
5. Burdea, G.C.: Force and touch feedback for virtual reality. John Wiley & Sons, Inc, New York (1996)
6. Patel, H. Stefani, O., Sharples, Hoffmann, H., Karaseitanidis, I., Amditis, A, Human centred design of 3D interaction devices to control virtual environments, accepted at the International Journal of Human-Computer Studies (2005)

Steady-State VEPs in CAVE for Walking Around the Virtual World

Hideaki Touyama and Michitaka Hirose

Graduate School of Information Science and Technology, University of Tokyo
tou@cyber.rcast.u-tokyo.ac.jp

Abstract. The human brain activities of steady-state visual evoked potentials, induced by a virtual panorama and two objects, were recorded for two subjects in immersive virtual environment. The linear discriminant analysis with single trial EEG data for 1.0 seconds resulted in 74.2 % of averaged recognition rate in inferring three gaze directions. The possibility of online interaction with 3D images in CAVE will be addressed for walking application or remote control of a robotic camera.

1 Introduction

The brain computer interface (BCI) is a communication channel with which the computer or machine can be operated only via brain activities [1]. In recent, the walking from thought via motor imagery tasks was demonstrated and the feasibility of the BCI in immersive virtual environment was presented [2].

The steady-state visual evoked potential (SSVEP) [3], which is one of the event related potentials, can be used in order to infer user's gaze-direction. Trejo et al developed a realistic demonstration for control of a moving map display [4]. However, the previous works on BCI based on SSVEP have been performed only on a computer monitor [5, 6]. In immersive virtual environment with SSVEP, the authors made a demonstration on brief position control of a 3D object in real time [7].

The purpose of this paper is to present a result of a preliminary study to detect the SSVEP in CAVE [8] for walking around the virtual world or for remote control a robotic camera in real world.

2 Experimental Method

A virtual panorama and two cubes were used as visual stimuli in our experiment. These visual stimuli were presented in CABIN, which is an extended multi-screen display system from CAVE to have a five-screen configuration. Two virtual cubes illuminated with constant frequencies of 6.86 Hz and 4.80 Hz, respectively, floating in a virtual panorama generated by OpenGL Performer, SGI.

The subject was sitting on a luxury arm chair about 2.0 m in front of the front screen, wearing a LCD shutter glasses to obtain stereoscopic scenes (Fig. 1, left).

C. Stephanidis (Ed.): Universal Access in HCI, Part II, HCII 2007, LNCS 4555, pp. 715–717, 2007.

Adopting non-invasive electroencephalogram (EEG) technique, three electrodes (O_1, O_2 and O_z) were attached over visual cortex. The EEG signals were amplified and were band pass filtered between 0.5 and 30 Hz. The analogue data was sampled at 100 Hz in an A/D converter to be stored in a PC.

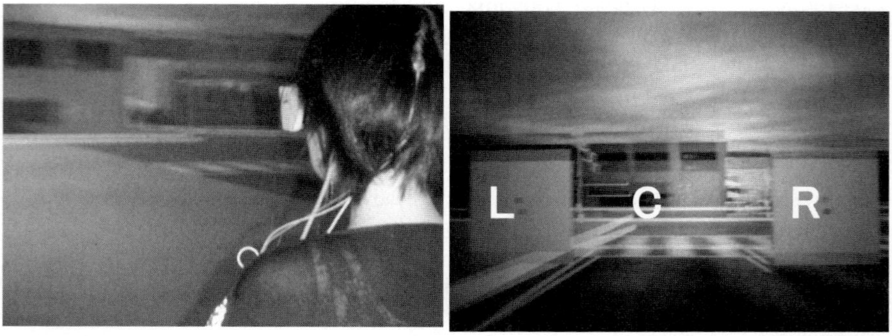

Fig. 1. (left) A subject in immersive virtual environment, and (right) a virtual panorama and two visual stimuli inducing steady-state VEP

For all two subjects, three types of experimental task were imposed. The task 1 was to gaze (and focus attention to) a left visual stimulus (virtual button) of 6.86 Hz illumination ('L' in Fig. 1, right), and task 2 was a centre fixed point ('C'), and task 3 was a right stimulus of 4.80 Hz illumination ('R'). These tasks were performed by turns. One trial lasted 30 seconds, and after that the subject took about one minute rest.

3 Multi-class Classification

The recorded EEG data was analyzed in offline in the following procedures; (1) The extraction of features of steady-state VEP, (2) The estimation of recognition rates.

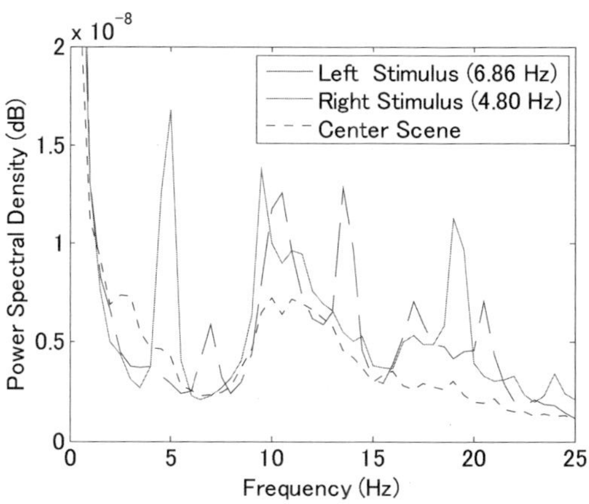

Fig. 2. Estimated power spectral density averaged for one

The features were extracted from the linear combination of voltage value of three electrodes on visual cortex, expecting the reduction of environmental noise. The features in brain activities induced by three visual stimuli (a left, a right button and centre virtual scene) were successfully extracted by frequency analyses. It was found that, for two buttons, the clear SSVEP was obtained with the data averaged, while, as expected, no significant signals were detected for centre scene (Fig. 2).

In investigating the single trial data, the power spectral densities from 3 Hz to 25 Hz were used to construct a feature vector. In the estimation of recognition rate, we adopted the linear discriminant analysis, and a leave-one-out method was applied. With 1.0 seconds of single trial EEG data, the averaged rate was 74.2 % for two subjects, while with 2.0 seconds the rate was 77.9 %.

4 Future Works

One of our future goals might be to implement and evaluate a BCI system for walking via SSVEP, detecting user's gaze-directions and attention, in order to achieve multi-dimensional movement in 3D virtual space. The method described in this pilot study would be useful to perform walking in a virtual world and remote control of a robotic camera only via human brain activities.

Acknowledgement. This research is partly supported by Special Coordination Funds for Promoting Science and Technology, "IRT Foundation to Support Man and Aging Society".

References

[1] Wolpaw, J.R., et al.: Brain-computer interfaces for communication and control. Clinical Neurophysiology 113, 767–791 (2002)

[2] Pfurtscheller, G., et al.: Walking from thought. Brain Research 1071, 145–152 (2006)

[3] Kuroiwa, Y., et al.: Visual Evoked Potentials with hemifield pattern stimulation, Their use in the diagnosis of retrochiasmatic lesions, Arch. Neurol. 38, 86–90 (1981)

[4] Trejo, L.J., et al.: Brain-computer interfaces for 1-D and 2-D cursor control: designs using volitional control of the EEG spectrum or steady-state visual evoked potentials, IEEE trans neural Syst. Rehabil. Eng. 14(2), 225–229 (June 2006)

[5] Middendorf, M., et al.: Brain-Computer Interfaces Based on the Steady-State Visual-Evoked Response. IEEE Transactions on Rehabilitation Engineering 8(2), 211–214 (2000)

[6] Cheng, M., et al.: Design and Implementation of a Brain-Computer Interface With High Transfer Rates. IEEE Transactions on Biomedical Engineering 49(10), 1181–1186 (2002)

[7] Touyama, H. et al.: Brain computer interface via stereoscopic images in CAVE, 12th International Conference on Human-Computer Interaction (HCI International, to appear (2007)

[8] Cruz-Neira, C. et al.: Surround-screen projection-based virtual reality: The design and implementation of the CAVE, ACM SIGGRAPH'93. In: Proc. pp. 135–142(1993)

Part IV

Interaction Techniques and Devices

An Eye-Gaze Input System Using Information on Eye Movement History

Kiyohiko Abe[1], Shoichi Ohi[2], and Minoru Ohyama[3]

[1] College of Engineering, Kanto Gakuin University, 1-50-1 Mutsuura-higashi, Kanazawa-ku, Yokohama, Kanagawa 236-8501, Japan
abe@kanto-gakuin.ac.jp

[2] School of Engineering, Tokyo Denki University, 2-2 Kandanishiki-cho, Chiyoda-ku, Tokyo 101-8457, Japan
ohi@d.dendai.ac.jp

[3] School of Information Environment, Tokyo Denki University, 2-1200 Muzaigakuendai, Inzai-shi, Chiba 270-1382, Japan
ohyama@sie.dendai.ac.jp

Abstract. We have developed an eye-gaze input system for people with severe physical disabilities such as amyotrophic lateral sclerosis. The system utilizes a personal computer and a home video camera to detect eye gaze under natural light. It also compensates for measurement errors caused by head movements; in other words, it can detect the eye gaze with a high degree of accuracy. We have also developed a new gaze selection method based on the eye movement history of a user. Using this method, users can rapidly input text using eye gazes.

Keywords: Eye-gaze input, Communication aid, Natural light, Gaze selection, Welfare device.

1 Introduction

Recently, the eye-gaze input system was reported as a novel human-machine interface [1,2,3,4,5,6,7]. The operation of this system only requires the user eye movements. Using this system, many communication aid systems have been developed for people with severe physical handicaps such as amyotrophic lateral sclerosis.

Eye-gaze input systems commonly employ a non-contact-type eye-gaze detection method. Infrared or natural light can be used as the light source for eye-gaze detection. The detection method that uses infrared light can detect an eye gaze with a high degree of accuracy [1,2,3]. However, it requires an expensive device. The detection method that uses natural light requires an ordinary device such as a home video camera or a personal computer; therefore, a system using this method is cost-effective [4]. However, the systems that operate under natural light often have a low accuracy. Therefore, they are capable of classifying only a few indicators. This problem can be resolved by using multi-camera systems [5].

C. Stephanidis (Ed.): Universal Access in HCI, Part II, HCII 2007, LNCS 4555, pp. 721–729, 2007.

We have developed a new eye-gaze input system with multi-indicators. This system utilizes a personal computer and a home video camera to detect eye gaze under natural light [7]. The system is not only inexpensive but also user-friendly, thereby making it fit for personal use. A new eye-gaze input system, which employs multi-indicators (12 indicators), was developed for text input. It can input English or Japanese text at a faster rate by using the information obtained from the eye movement history of a user.

This paper presents the evaluation experiments of the proposed eye-gaze text input system.

2 Eye-Gaze Detection Methods by Image Analysis

The eye-gaze input has to detect the eye gaze of users. Several eye-gaze detection methods have been studied [1.2.3.4.5.6]. The method of iris tracking is the most popular detection method under natural light by image analysis [4.5.6]. However, it is difficult to distinguish the iris from the sclera by image analysis. Therefore, the degree of accuracy of this method is not very high. We propose a new method for detecting the eye gaze in both the horizontal and vertical directions by image analysis. The proposed method can detect the eye-gaze of users from a single eye image captured using one home video camera and does not require special devices such as infrared lights. The horizontal eye-gaze is detected by the limbus tracking method that is extended by image analysis [7], and the vertical eye-gaze is detected by the change in the light intensity distributions in the eye image associated with eye movement.

We now describe our eye-gaze input detection method in detail.

2.1 Horizontal Eye-Gaze Detection

The overview of the proposed horizontal eye-gaze detection method is shown in Fig. 1 (a). This method detects a horizontal eye-gaze by image analysis based on the limbus tracking method. The difference in the reflectance between the iris and the sclera is used for detecting the horizontal eye-gaze; in other words, the eye gaze is estimated by a difference between the integral values of the light intensity on areas A and B, as shown in Fig. 1 (a).

We define this differential value as the eye-gaze value, and it indicates the value of the horizontal eye-gaze. The eye-gaze value and the angle of sight are nearly proportional to each other. Therefore, if the eye-gaze input system is calibrated using this relation, the horizontal eye-gaze of the users can be estimated. This method is simple and it is robust against the noise in an image of the eye such as the fluctuation of light. Therefore, the system using this method can rapidly detect the horizontal eye-gaze at a high sampling rate.

2.2 Vertical Eye-Gaze Detection

Vertical eye-gaze detection requires a different process as compared to that used in horizontal detection, since a major part of the sclera is hidden by the change in the eyelid shape with eye movement. We focus on the vertical movement of the iris for the detection of the vertical eye-gaze. The light intensity distribution from the eye image changes with the iris movement. The vertical eye-gaze can be detected by using this change.

Concretely speaking, the system stores eye images gazing on the indicators aligned vertical. The light intensity distributions (the results of one-dimensional projection) are calculated using these eye images as the reference data. The vertical eye-gaze of the users can be detected by pattern matching using these reference data. The overview of the proposed vertical eye-gaze detection method is shown in Fig. 1 (b). This figure describes a detection method for the three eye-gaze directions, namely, top, center, and bottom.

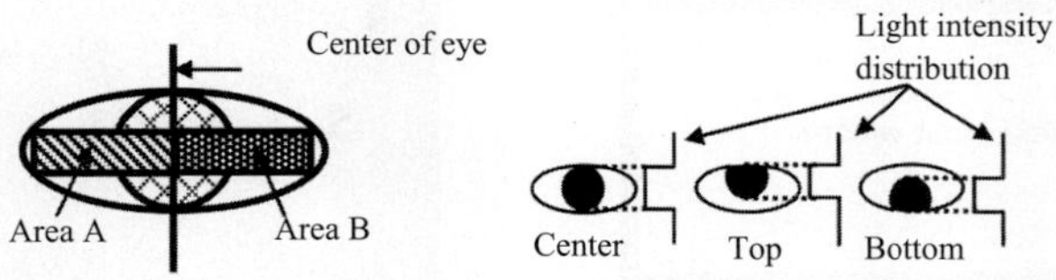

(a) Horizontal detection (b) Vertical detection

Fig. 1. The overview of eye-gaze detection

3 Proposed Eye-Gaze Input System

3.1 System Configuration

The proposed eye-gaze input system comprises a personal computer, a home video camera, and an IEEE1394 interface for image capture from the video camera. The personal computer runs an image analysis software for eye-gaze detection in the Windows XP platform. This system does not require an exclusive image processing device.

The video camera used in this system records the images of the user's eye from a distant location (distance between the user and camera is approximately 70 cm) and then this image is enlarged. The head movements of the user induce a large error in the measurements. Therefore, this system must compensate for the user head movement. Methods such as tracing a marker on glasses have been developed for the compensation of head movement [6]. We compensated for the head movement by tracing the location of an inner corner within the eye.

The proposed system executes the eye-gaze detection process every 200 ms (CPU: Pentium 4; clock frequency: 2.2 GHz). The hardware configuration of this system is shown in Fig. 2. A screenshot of the proposed system is shown in Fig. 3 (a). The center of the display is assigned to the workspace. The workspace is used for displaying an application software window. Therefore, this system can input text while the application software is running.

Users must calibrate the system before using it as described above. After adjusting the camera location, the calibration begins. While the calibration is being performed, users gaze at each of the five indicators shown in Fig. 3 (b). If the calibration terminates successfully, the users can select each indicator by an eye gaze.

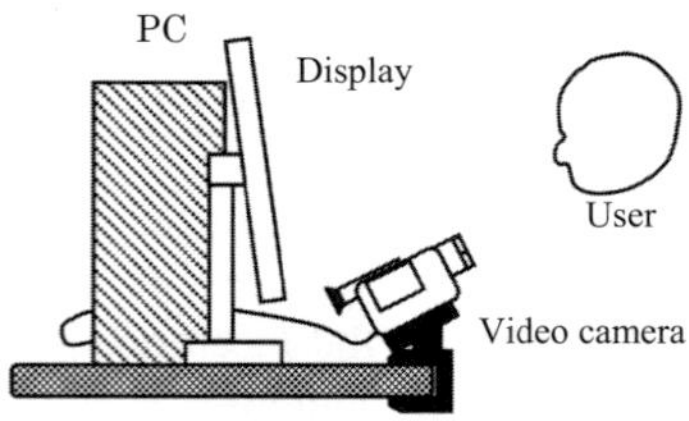

Fig. 2. Hardware configuration

(a) (b)

Fig. 3. Screenshot (a) and indicators for calibration (b)

3.2 Text Input by Eye Gaze

The text input method by using the above system is described below. Our proposed eye-gaze detector is capable of classifying 12 indicators on a display. However, around 60 indicators are required to input Japanese text (our mother tongue). Similarly, 12 indicators are insufficient for English text input. This is because the English language contains upper- and lowercase letters and symbols. Moreover, control keys are required for text input.

We designed an interface for Japanese and English text input, as shown in Fig. 4. This interface requires two selections: one for character input and another for character group selection, for example, "groups A to E." Fig. 4 shows the text input method used in this system. Alphabets and symbols ("Etc." in Fig. 4) are selected by using two selections; however, commonly used characters (for example, "Space") are selected by using one selection.

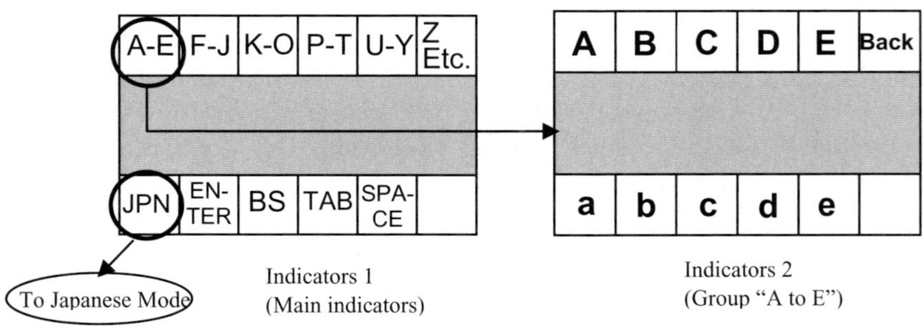

Fig. 4. Interface for English text input

4 Eye-Gaze Input Method Using Eye Movement Information

The eye-gaze input decision requires the detection of not only the location of a user's gazing point but also the user's command for an indicator (assigned character) selection. An input decision can be made either by blinking on gazing or by using eye fixations (measuring the time for which the eye fixates on a target such as the indicators). Blinking occurs as a physiological phenomenon. Therefore, it is difficult to classify the conscious blinking of a user. Hence, we consider the method involving the use of eye fixations for the eye-gaze input decision. In this method, if the user gazes at an indicator for more than a defined period of time, the state of the user's eye gaze is classified as "gazing." Then, the gazed indicator is selected for input.

However, we confirmed that many input errors occur by directly using this method. When the user gazes at an indicator, the eye gaze of the user drifts around a gazed indicator. If the speed of eye movement is very slow during this drifting, the eye-gaze input system makes an erroneous decision for estimating the gazed indicator. In order to resolve this problem, we have developed methods for eye fixation detection. This method detects eye fixations using the information on the eye movement history (or gaze state history) of users. We now describe the methods we have developed for eye fixation detection. One of these methods has already been reported, while the other is a completely new method for eye fixation detection.

4.1 Method 1 (Our Conventional Method)

We have reported the eye-gaze input method that uses the gaze state history of users. In this method, the gaze state is defined by including two states such as the initial and continuous states. Hence, if the users gaze at an indicator for more than a defined period of time, we define this state as the initial state. After the initial state is completed, the user's state changes to the continuous state. Although the users gaze at the same indicator in these states, eye-gaze measurement errors may occur due to unexpected eye movements such as those associated with blinking. Therefore, the gazed indicator is determined based on the entire continuous state; the majority number of gazed indicator is extracted as the user's decision. A schematic illustration of this input decision is shown in Fig. 5.

In this figure, the small rectangles indicate a character assigned to an indicator. The measurement ranges of the initial and continuous gaze states are five and 10 samples, respectively.

By using method 1, we confirmed that five subjects could input text at an average rate of 6.9 characters/min. However, this method should count the same indicators (e.g., five samples) for classifying the initial gaze state. Therefore, if the user's gaze drifts out of the gazed indicator, the system resets the process of classifying the initial gaze state and restarts the process from the beginning. Further, method 1 does not confirm whether the indicators of a candidate input at the initial and continuous gaze states are equal or not. Therefore, method 1 has the disadvantage of causing input errors when the indicators of the candidate input are not equal.

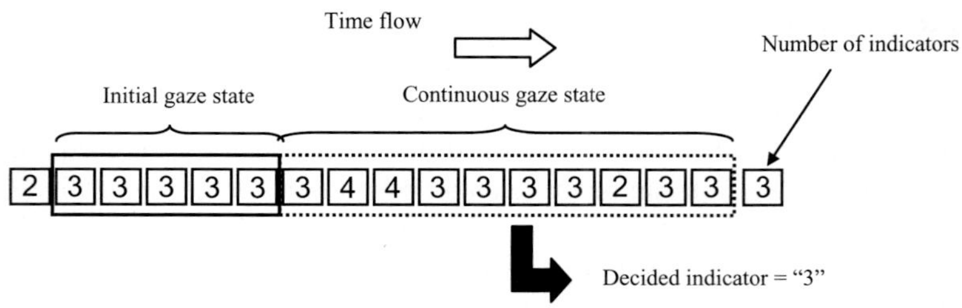

Fig. 5. Input decision based on eye movement history. (Method 1)

4.2 Method 2 (Our Proposed Method)

To eliminate the disadvantages of method 1, we have developed a completely new eye-gaze input method using the gaze state of users. By using this method (method 2), users can input text at higher speed and with greater accuracy as compared to that using method 1. Method 2 measures the gaze state history using two gaze states as effectively as method 1. The majority numbers of gazed indicator in each state are extracted as the candidate inputs. If these two indicators are equal, the candidate input is selected. By using method 2, the input decision process is not reset even if the user blinks or a drifting eye movement occurs.

In the state where the user is tracing an indicator, adjacent gaze selection data are random; in other words, the eye-gaze input is not predetermined because the two candidate input indicators are not equal. A schematic illustration of this input decision is shown in Fig. 6. In this figure, the small rectangles indicate a character assigned to an indicator. In addition, a user's gaze is fixed on a selected indicator after an eye-gaze input decision. This gaze state was investigated in an experiment. The length of this state depends on the user. This eye fixation induces input errors. Users can set the measurement ranges of the two states for the eye-gaze input decision. Therefore, users should appropriately adjust these ranges to decrease input errors.

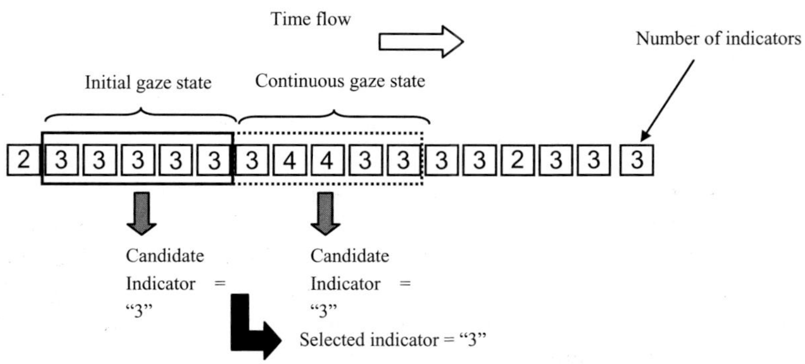

Fig. 6. Input decision based on eye movement history. (Method 2)

5 Evaluation Experiment for Proposed System

The evaluation experiments were conducted with five subjects using method 2 as described above. In these experiments, the measurement range for the eye movement history is varied. It changes to 12, 10, 8, 6, or 4 samples. The experiment includes two measurement steps (initial and continuous gaze states), as shown in Fig. 6. We confirm the following experimental parameters: rates of gaze selection, rates of text input, and errors in gaze selection. Prior to the experiments, the subjects memorized the input text, which was as follows: "I am using our eye-gaze input system." It contains 37 characters and requires 68 gaze selections for input. The experimental system is calibrated at the beginning of the experiments.

When a user commits an error during the text input, it can be corrected by the following two procedures. In case the input error occurs during group selection

Table 1. Rate of gaze selection [selections/min]

Subject	Measurement range [samples]				
	12	10	8	6	4
A	19.4	23.5	25.3	32.7	34.6
B	20.1	23.4	25.9	34.3	33.0
C	20.4	24.0	28.4	30.1	22.9
D	16.2	19.5	18.6	29.2	24.1
E	17.5	22.7	23.8	22.6	34.5
Average	18.7	22.6	24.4	29.8	29.8

Table 2. Rate of text input [characters/min]

Subject	Measurement range [samples]				
	12	10	8	6	4
A	10.6	12.8	13.8	17.8	18.8
B	11.0	12.7	14.1	18.7	18.0
C	11.1	13.0	15.5	16.4	12.4
D	8.8	10.6	10.1	15.9	13.1
E	9.5	12.4	13.0	12.3	18.7
Average	10.2	12.3	13.3	16.2	16.2

Table 3. Errors in gaze selection [counts]

Subject	Measurement range [samples]				
	12	10	8	6	4
A	0	4	8	2	2
B	0	4	2	0	3
C	2	0	0	10	37
D	0	8	12	9	35
E	0	0	5	28	9
Average	0.4	3.2	5.4	9.8	17.2

(indicators 1, as shown in Fig. 4), the subject must gaze at "Back" (on indicators 2) in order to return to indicators 1. If an input error is noticed after text input, it can be corrected by gazing at "BS" (backspace) on indicators 1, following which the subject can input the correct character.

The gaze selection and text input rates are shown in Table 1 and Table 2, respectively. These rates include the time required for error correction. We define over-selection counts as errors in the text input. The errors in gaze selection are shown in Table 3.

6 Discussion

We summarize the obtained results as follows: From Tables 1 and 2, it is evident that the rate of text input by a subject increases with the narrowing of the measurement range of the eye movement history. However, it appears that there is a decrease in the rates of gaze selection and text input by subjects B, C, and D when the measurement range is reduced to four samples. This is due to the increase in the errors when the measurement range of the eye movement history is narrowed, as shown in Table 3. In other words, there is a decrease in the required gazing (dwell) time. We surveyed the comments about these errors. Subjects B, C, and D say that many errors occur on selecting the correction indicator and therefore input correction is unsuccessful.

As shown by the above experimental results, the average input rate is the highest when the measurement range of the eye movement history is either four or six samples. In these cases, subjects can input text at an average rate of 16.2 characters/min. Hence, our system can input text at a rate that is comparable to that of a conventional infrared eye-gaze input system without requiring word prediction [3]. The proposed system analyzes the image of an eye taken under natural light, and it does not employ an exclusive device for this purpose; therefore, it has a lower sampling rate than most conventional systems that employ infrared light [3]. The sampling time of the proposed system is approximately 200 ms; under such conditions, the user can input English text at a comfortable rate.

Apart from the reported results, we also observed that subject A was able to input text at the largest rate when the measurement range of the eye movement history was four samples. This result shows that the optimum parameters are different for individual subjects. Therefore, it is desirable to vary the measurement range when this system is utilized.

7 Conclusions

We present a new eye-gaze input system based on the user's eye movement history, which is suitable for personal use. This system is also compact and easy to use since it does not require exclusive image processing units or sensors.

In the evaluation experiments, the measurement range of the eye movement history is varied. The results for five subjects show that the optimum parameter for text input is approximately six samples (1.2[sec.]), and the average rate of English text input is approximately 16.2 [characters/min]. This result shows that the text input rates are approximately 2.5 times greater than that in our previous system. The results also indicate that the rate of text input using the proposed system is comparable to that of a conventional system that employs infrared light.

We will attempt to conduct additional evaluation experiments in the future. The change in the error rate will be researched in a prolonged experiment. We will also develop a new eye-gaze input system that is more comfortable to use and inputs at a greater rate. The new system will be capable of dynamically altering the arrangements of indicators by utilizing the character occurrence rate [2].

References

1. Huchinson, T.E., White Jr., K.P., Martin, W.N., Reichert, K.C., Frey, L.A.: Human-computer Interaction using Eye-gaze Input. IEEE Trans. Systems, Man, and Cybernetics 19,7, 1527–1534 (1989)
2. Ward, D.J., MacKay, D.J.C.: Fast Hands-free Writing by Gaze Direction. Nature 418, 838 (2002)
3. Hansen, J.P., Torning, K., Johansen, A.S., Itoh, K., Aoki, H.: Gaze Typing Compared with Input by Head and Hand. In: Proc. of the Eye Tracking Research and Applications Symposium on Eye Tracking Research and Applications, pp. 131–138 (2004)
4. Corno, F., Farinetti, L., Signorile, I.: A Cost-effective Solution for Eye-gaze Assistive Technology. In: Proc. IEEE International Conf. on Multimedia and Expo, 2, 433–436 (2002)
5. Wang, J.G., Sung, E.: Study on Eye gaze Estimation. IEEE Trans. on Systems, Man and Cybernetics 32,3, 332–350 (2002)
6. Kim, K.N., Ramakrishna, R.S.: Vision-based Eye-gaze Tracking for Human Computer Interface. In: Proc. IEEE International Conf. on Systems, Man and Cybernetics, 2, pp. 324–329 (1999)
7. Abe, K., Ohi, S., Ohyama, M.: An Eye-gaze Input System based on the Limbus Tracking Method by Image Analysis for Seriously Physically Handicapped People. In: Adjunct Proc. 7th ERCIM Workshop "User Interface for All", pp. 185–186 (2002)

Handheld Haptic Display with Braille I/O

Tomohiro Amemiya

NTT Communication Science Laboratories
3-1 Morinosato Wakamiya, Atsugi, Kanagawa
2430-198 Japan
t-amemiya@avg.brl.ntt.co.jp

Abstract. This paper describes the implementation of a handheld haptic display using verbal and nonverbal communication technologies for visually impaired pedestrians. Wearable and mobile human-computer-interface technologies provide the means to use the display in daily life. Six ring-mounted vibrators for the finger-braille method, one of the commonly used communication methods among deaf-blind people in Japan, and a textual input interface designed on the basis of the braille input method, are adopted as the verbal I/O interface. As the non-verbal I/O interface, a perceptual force attraction method, which can convey "pull" or "push" sensations on handheld devices, is adopted for intuitive way-finding. The handheld haptic display with these technologies integrated has the potential to support wayfinding not only for blind people but also for sighted people.

Keywords: force display, sensory illusion, wearable computer, Finger-Braille, brailler.

1 Introduction

Nowadays, highly sophisticated mobile devices, such as mobile phones, PDAs, and portable media players, are available. However, their interfaces are designed for visual and auditory modalities. Because of the need for an accessible design (e.g., the HCI for the blind) and the limitations of screens, the haptic channel is attracting attention as a new interface for handheld devices that can be intuitively interpreted (e.g., [Poupyrev et al. 2002; Luk et al. 2006]). In addition, the braille input-output (I/O) method is suitable for mobile computing since it requires just six-key input and six-dot output. In this paper, a method for developing a handheld haptic device using braille I/O and a force feedback technique is proposed.

2 Verbal I/O: Braille Interfaces

Considering the space limitations for the "keyboard" and "screen" in handheld devices, a braille input/output method has potential to be an effective human computer interface in mobile devices. Braille input can be done with a chord keyboard, which can be used

C. Stephanidis (Ed.): Universal Access in HCI, Part II, HCII 2007, LNCS 4555, pp. 730–739, 2007.

as the "keyboard" for text-entry in wearable computers [Lyons et al, 2004]. As braille output, the finger-braille method requires just six fingers to read characters via tactile sensation (as six-bit information), which can be used as the "screen".

2.1 Interface Using Finger-Braille Method

In the finger-braille method, verbal information is transmitted by tapping a deaf-blind person's fingers, to which are assigned to the digits of braille [Fig. 1(a)]. This method enables deaf-blind people to obtain information as if they are listening in real time. People who have experience with braille input can read messages using the finger-braille method with a little training.

Glove-style interfaces cover the palm or the fingertips, which have the highest tactile sensitivity. Therefore, ring-shaped interfaces were developed, which always allow the user to obtain the original tactile sense information. The interface prototype consists of six DC motors whose frequency is 116 Hz. The vibrators are controlled by wristwatch computers (WatchPad 1.5, IBM Japan and Citizen Watch), which are connected to the main computer wirelessly [Fig. 1(b)]

(a) Finger-Braille Method. A Finger-Braille transcriber (left) taps the fingers of a deaf-blind person (right).

(b) Prototype of Wearable Finger-Braille Interface.

Fig. 1. Verbal output interface: Wearable Finger-Braille Interface

Figure 2(a) shows the vibration profile measured by an acceleration sensor when the interface was worn on the fingers. The vibration was started with 50-ms delay after pulse input. The measured frequency of vibration was approximately 80 Hz.

Experiments were conducted to determine the character recognition rate (Japanese braille code). The stimulation of one character was presented with 200-ms duration. The participants were five deaf-blind people who usually use the finger-braille method. The results showed that they can read 87.6 % of Japanese braille characters on average [Amemiya et al. 2004a]. Figure 2(b) shows the number of stimulated fingers vs. recognition rate. Sometimes the subject felt a non-vibrated finger was vibrated when the neighboring finger was stimulated. This indicated that the finger-braille method would be an effective way to transmit verbal information to the user on wearable devices, especially in phonogramic languages such as Japanese.

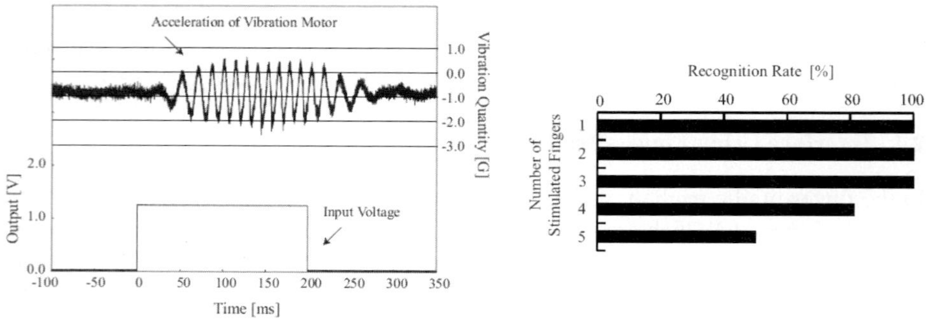

Fig. 2. Evaluation of verbal output interface

2.2 Interface Using Braille-Input Method

The author designed a mobile chord keyboard called OBOE (Oboe-like Braille interface for Outdoor Environment) on the basis of the braille-input method. Although portable braille-based note-takers, such as BrailleLite, are now used worldwide, they are designed for use on a desktop. The "oboe-type" interface is good for outdoor use and can be used while walking or navigating. A glove-style interface (e.g., [An, et al. 2004; Rosenberg & Slater, 1999]) was not used because the glove covers the fingertips, preventing users from experiencing the natural touch. In the prototype, the buttons are the same as the mechanical switches used in keyboards for desktop computers (ALPS Electric Co., Ltd.). By feeling the click, users can clearly and easily confirm their input operations, which is an important feature for handheld devices, as reported in [Silfverberg 2003], and is lacking in acceleration sensors and touch sensors. The prototype has eight keys as shown in Fig. 3. Six keys are for the six-dot braille input and the other two keys are function keys, such as Backspace, Space, and Enter. The body of the device is an acrylate resin tube with a diameter of 35 mm, length of approximately 220 mm, and weight of approximately 150 g [Amemiya et al. 2004b].

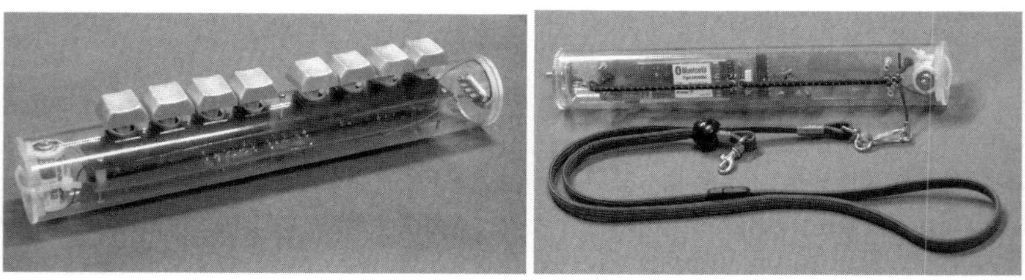

Fig. 3. Verbal input interface: OBOE

The device was evaluated by measuring input speed and error rate. In the experiment, there were five trials to examine the effect of learning. Six nonblind subjects participated in the experiment. All the subjects were male, right-handed, and had no experience using braille typewriters. The average age of the subjects was 23.6 years. The experiment consisted two sessions, a non-semantic session (practice for Japanese braille code) and a semantic session (predefined short phrases).

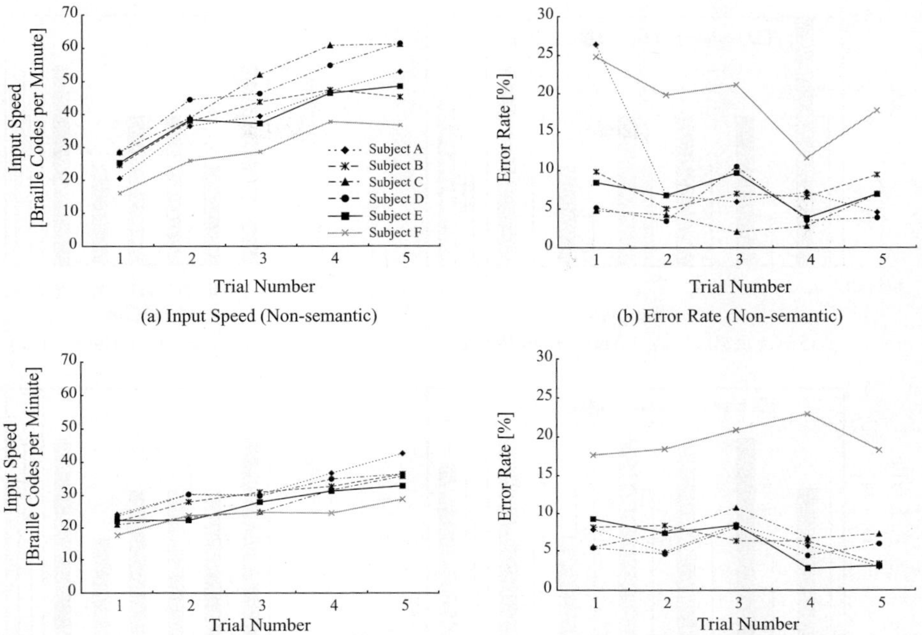

(a) Input Speed (Non-semantic)

(b) Error Rate (Non-semantic)

(c) Input Speed (Semantic)

(d) Error Rate (Semantic)

Fig. 4. Learning effect of OBOE

The experiment showed that novices to braille could input 50.9 braille codes per minute (Bpm) on average in the non-semantic session and 35.4 Bpm in the semantic session. The error rate, calculated by Soukoreff's metrics [Soukoreff et al. 2003], was 8.2 % in the non-semantic session and 6.8 % in the semantic session. The learning effect in terms of input speed and error rate is shown in Fig. 4. The input speed was 110% up in the non-semantic session and 60 % up in the semantic session. The error rate was 38 % down in the non-semantic session and 25 % down in the semantic session.

The results of a questionnaire are shown in Fig. 5. The average scores for fatigue were 1.8 at the beginning of the experiment and 3.3 at the end of the experiment. The average scores for muscle strain ranged from 2.3 at the beginning of the experiment to 3.5 at the end. These results suggest the necessity for ergonomic improvements. The average score for usability were 3.0 and that for preference was 3.2.

Another experiment with two subjects who had experience with finger-braille transcribing was carried out. The transcriber subjects showed a higher input speed of 112.4 braille codes per minute, and a lower error rate, 3.6 %, than the novices with a little learning in the semantic session (p<.01). The transcriber subjects commented that, in the non-semantic session, using characters that rarely appear in usual Japanese sentences slowed them down. (e.g., "Dya" is almost always replaced by "jya" in a Japanese sentence, but the user had to input this character in the tutorial session.) They also commented that they tended to make mistakes when using little finger since little finger is not used in transcribing finger-braille method.

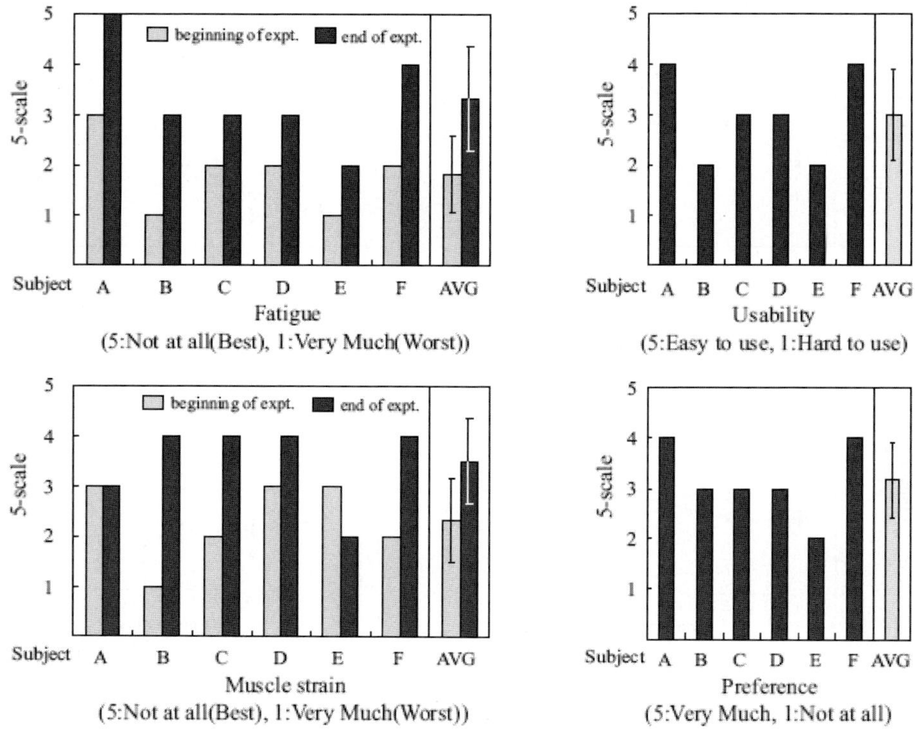

Fig. 5. Results of the rating questionnaire about OBOE

The experts (braille transcribers) could input 112.4 Bpm, and the error rate was 4.1 %. With OBOE, experts can achieve 80 % of the 135.9 Bpm input speed reported for chording gloves in [Lee et al., 2003]. This indicates that the braille input method with clear click feedback is an effective way to input commands to computers for mobile use.

A strap attached to the input device lets the device dangle from the neck when not in use so that it can be used together with a blind cane.

2.3 Navigation Aid with the Verbal I/O

As a first evaluation of the navigation aid system with verbal I/O, an experiment with a blind person was conducted using PATIO, which is an outdoor positioning system comprising 1,349 RFID transmitters in an area of 1,700 m^2 [Amemiya et al. 2004a]. The blind subject, who can read finger-braille, wore a wearable computer, two receivers for RFID signals, and a verbal I/O, as shown in Fig. 6.

The subject was instructed to walk 50 m on a sidewalk obstructed by a signboard (W 800 mm x D 130 mm x H 2,000 mm) in PATIO. The task for the subject was to avoid the signboard only using haptic verbal information. The subject could ask the questions using OBOE to an experimenter if he wanted and could read the answers through finger-braille interface from the experimenter. Two kinds of information were provided through the finger-braille interface: verbal information (braille information) and non-verbal information indicating the street curbs (e.g., vibrating all fingers of the left hand when the distance between the subject and the left curb of street was within 1,500 mm). In the experiment, the information was normally nonverbal for walking support, but no information was given until errors occurred. The verbal information was given when the subject was in side a 3,600 mm-square area in front of the signboard. The mode change was indicated by vibrating all fingers three times.

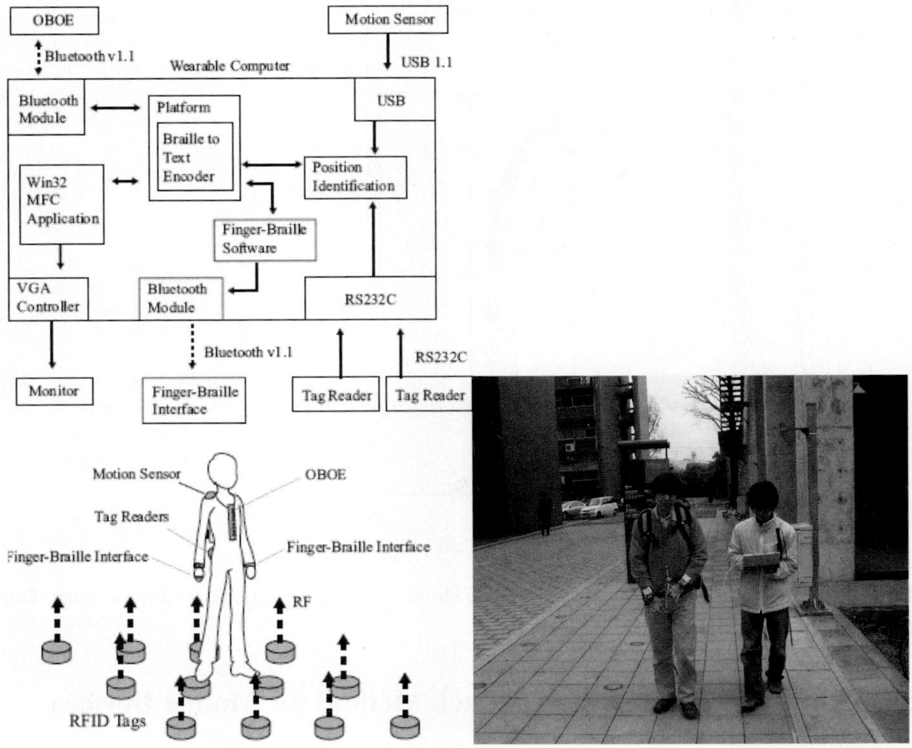

(a) System

(b) View of experiment. The blind subject (left) wore the wearable navigation system with the verbal I/O and the experimenter (right) walked beside the subject.

Fig. 6. Navigation system and view of experiment

As shown in Fig. 7, the subject successfully avoided the signboard. However, it took much time to do so because the verbal information was not suitable for the task. Verbal information requires converting the words or sentences into direction information. In a task like this one, nonverbal information is helpful and enables the user to navigate the correct route sooner. The following section presents the non-verbal I/O for intuitive navigation.

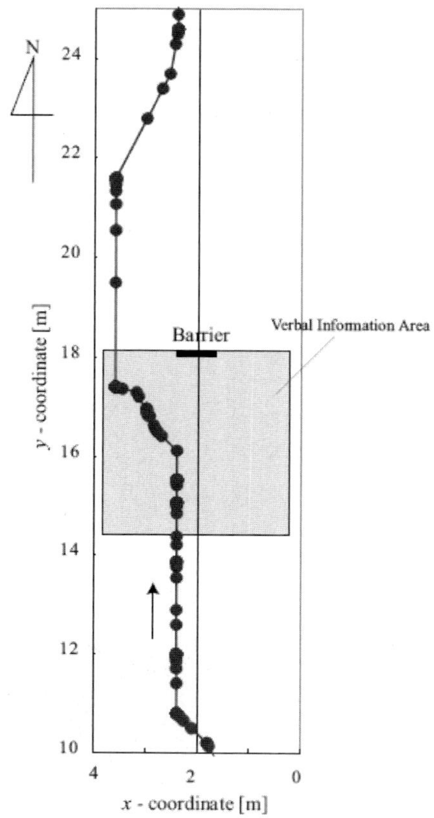

Fig. 7. Results for navigation system. Blue line shows the walking trajectory of the subject. Dots indicate the time stamp (1 sec).

3 Non-verbal I/O: Force Feedback Method for Mobile Devices

Nonverbal information enables users to navigate routes without distraction. However, no handheld force feedback devices had been proposed before our work because force devices require grounding to generate translational and continuous force sensation; Prior mobile force feedback devices are just torque sensation [Tanaka et al. 2001; Yano et al. 2003]. To convey a pulling or pushing sensation in handheld devices, the author proposed exploiting the kinesthetic illusion induced by characteristic of human perception when a small object moves periodically and prismatically with asymmetric acceleration in the handheld device [Amemiya et al. 2005]. A one-degree-of-freedom haptic device based on a crank-slider mechanism was constructed that converts the single-speed rotational cyclic movement of a motor into asymmetric translational cyclic movement with asymmetric acceleration as shown in Fig. 8. The side-to-side force generated by the arm in the mechanism is cancelled out by the mirror-symmetric pairs of the crank-slider mechanism [Amemiya et al. 2006a]. The mechanism can be miniaturized to a palm-sized one [Amemiya et al. 2006b]. The method conveys the force sensation by means of kinethestic illusions.

Experiments were conducted to determine the percent-correct scores judging a "pull" or "push" force at several motor rotational frequencies. For all subjects, the frequency of 10 Hz yielded the best percent-correct scores (exceeding 90 %) [Amemiya et al. 2005]. That indicates that the force feedback method is effective for transmitting the nonverbal information to the user for mobile and wearable use.

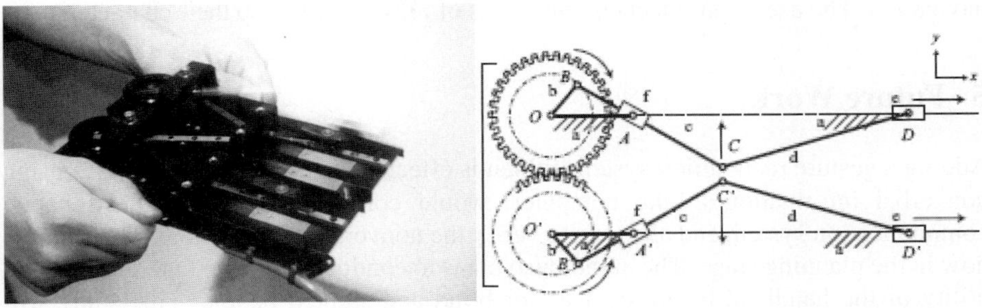

Fig. 8. Nonverbal output interface: Perceptual Attraction Force

4 Handheld Haptic Display

The above-mentioned technologies can be integrated into a handheld device to support blind pedestrians; they can be used simultaneously and make a handheld device small enough and light enough for practical use. Figure 9 shows some examples of integrated systems.

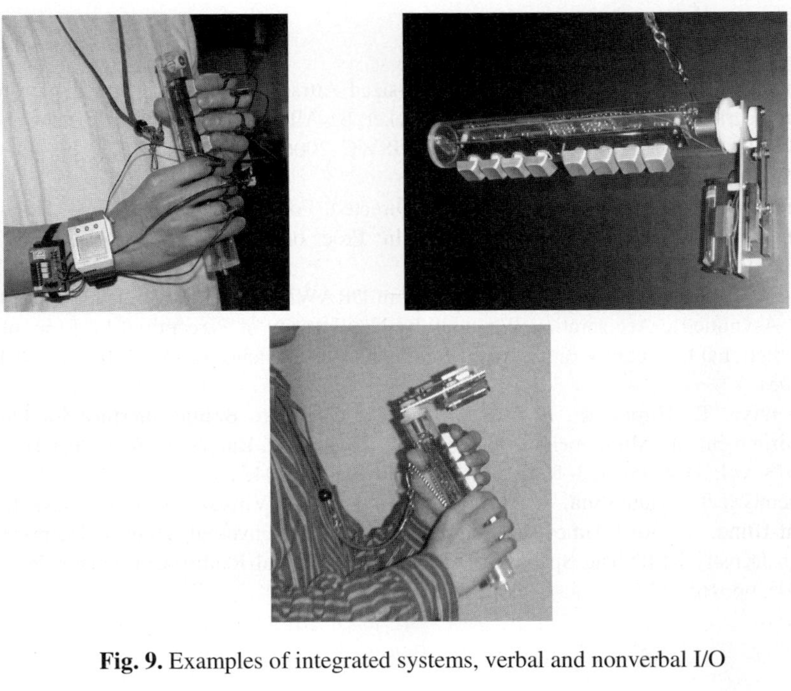

Fig. 9. Examples of integrated systems, verbal and nonverbal I/O

The haptic handheld display with braille I/O has the potential to support not only way-finding for blind people but also for sighted people. The author confirmed that just changes in a vibrational stimulus pattern of the finger-braille interface can guide users along a desired direction [Amemiya et al. 2004a]. Therefore, even users who cannot read braille (or finger-braille) code can be guided by the vibration stimulus patterns as rotational information and by the "pull" sensation as translational information for navigation. The users can select combinations of I/Os according to their characteristics.

5 Future Work

Adding a gesture recognition system, which is effective for inputting commands using nonverbal information to the computer, would complement the handheld haptic communication system and allow us to verify the nonverbal input system. This work is now in the planning stage. The author also plans to conduct a user study to evaluate the utility of the handheld haptic devices for blind and sighted people. That study will examine various aspects, such as the usefulness of feeling pulling sensations while reading finger-braille messages and of text-input while feeling a pulling sensation. One of our final goals is to embed a miniaturized version of the proposed system in blind canes.

Acknowledgments. I wish to thank Drs. Michitaka Hirose, Koichi Hirota, and Satoshi Fukushima for discussion on development the Wearable Finger-Braille Interface, and Drs. Taro Maeda, Hideyuki Ando, and Ichiro Kawabuchi for development of force feedback mechanisms.

References

1. Amemiya, T., Ando, H., Maeda, T.: Palm-sized Attraction Force Display Exploiting the Nonlinearity of Perception. In: Cruz, I., Decker, S., Allemang, D., Preist, C., Schwabe, D., Mika, P., Uschold, M., Aroyo, L. (eds.) ISWC 2006. LNCS, vol. 4273, pp. 115–116. Springer, Heidelberg (2006b)
2. Amemiya, T., Ando, H., Maeda, T.: Directed Force Perception When Holding a Nongrounding Force Display in the Air. In: Proc. of EuroHaptics 2006, pp. 317–324, (2006a)
3. Amemiya, T., Ando, H., Maeda, T.: Phantom-DRAWN: Direction Guidance using Rapid and Asymmetric Acceleration Weighted by Nonlinearity of Perception. In: Proc. of 15th International Conference on Artificial Reality and Telexistence (ICAT 2005), pp. 201–208 (2005)
4. Amemiya, T., Hirota, K., Hirose, M.: OBOE: Oboe-like Braille interface for Outdoor Environment. In: Miesenberger, K., Klaus, J., Zagler, W., Burger, D. (eds.) ICCHP 2004. LNCS, vol. 3118, pp. 498–505. Springer, Heidelberg (2004)
5. Amemiya, T., Yamashita, J., Hirota, K., Hirose, M.: Virtual Leading Blocks for the Deaf-Blind: A Real-Time Way-Finder by Verbal-Nonverbal Hybrid Interface and High-Density RFID Tag Space: In Proc. of IEEE Virtual Reality Conference 2004 (VR 2004), pp. 165–172, (2004a)

6. An, S.S., Jeon, J.W., Lee, S., Choi, H., Choi, H.-G.: A Pair of Wireless Braille-Based Chording Gloves. In: Miesenberger, K., Klaus, J., Zagler, W., Burger, D. (eds.) ICCHP 2004. LNCS, vol. 3118, pp. 490–497. Springer, Heidelberg (2004)
7. Hirose, M., Amemiya, T. (2003). Wearable Finger-Braille Interface for Navigation of Deaf-Blind in Ubiquitous Barrier-Free Space. In: Proc. of 10th International Conference on Human-Computer Interaction (HCI International 2003), vol. 4 pp. 1417–1421
8. Lee, S., Hong, S.H., Jeon, J.W.: Designing a universal keyboard using chording gloves. In: Proc. of Conference on Universal Usability 2003, pp. 142–147. ACM Press, New York (2003)
9. Luk, J., Pasquero, J., Little, S., MacLean, K., Levesque, V., Hayward, V.: A Role for Haptics in Mobile Interaction: Initial Design Using a Handheld Tactile Display Prototype. In: Proc. of Conference on Human Factors in Computing Systems (CHI 2006), pp. 171–180. ACM Press, New York (2006)
10. Lyons, K., Starner, T., Plaisted, D., Fusia, J., Lyons, A., Drew, A., Looney, E.W.: Twiddler typing: one-handed chording text entry for mobile phones. In: Proc. of Conference on Human Factors in Computing Systems (CHI 2004), Vienna, Austria, pp. 671–678. ACM Press, New York (2004)
11. Poupyrev, I., Maruyama, S., Rekimoto, J.: Ambient Touch: Designing tactile interfaces for handheld devices. In: Proc. of UIST'2002, pp. 51–60. ACM Press, New York (2002)
12. Rosenberg, R., Slater, M.: The Chording Glove: A Glove-Based Text Input Device. IEEE Transactions on Systems, Man, and Cybernetics-Part. C 29(2), 186–191 (1999)
13. Silfverberg, M.: Using mobile keypads with limited visual feedback: Implications to handheld and wearable devices. In: Chittaro, L. (ed.) Mobile HCI 2003. LNCS, vol. 2795, pp. 76–90. Springer, Heidelberg (2003)
14. Soukoreff, R.W., MacKenzie, I.S.: Metrics for text entry research: an evaluation of msd and kspc, and a new unified error metric, Conference on Human Factors in Computing Systems (CHI 2003), Lauderdale, Florida, pp. 113–120. ACM Press, New York (2003)
15. Tanaka, Y., Masataka, S., Yuka, K., Fukui, Y., Yamashita, J., Nakamura, N.: Mobile Torque Display and Haptic Characteristics of Human Palm. In: Proc. of ICAT 2001, pp. 115–120 (2001)
16. Yano, H., Yoshie, M., Iwata, H.: Development of a Non- Grounded Haptic Interface Using the Gyro Effect. In: Proc. of HAPTICS 2003, pp. 32–39 (2003)

Nonverbally Smart User Interfaces: Postural and Facial Expression Data in Human Computer Interaction

G. Susanne Bahr[1], Carey Balaban[2], Mariofanna Milanova[3], and Howard Choe[4]

[1] Florida Institute of Technology, Melbourne, Florida, U.S.A.
[2] University of Pittsburgh, Pittsburgh, Pennsylvania, U.S.A.
[3] University of Arkansas at Little Rock, Little Rock, Arkansas, U.S.A.
[4] Raytheon - Network Centric Systems (NCS), Plano, Texas, U.S.A.
gbahr@fit.edu, balabancd@upmc.edu, mgmilanova@ualr.edu, choe@raytheon.com

Abstract. We suggest that User Interfaces (UIs) can be designed to serve as cognitive tools based on a model of nonverbal human interaction. Smart User Interfaces (SUIs) have the potential to support the human user when and where appropriate and thus indirectly facilitate higher mental processes without the need for end-user programming or external actuation. Moreover, graphic nonverbally sensitive SUIs are expected to be less likely to interfere with ongoing activity and disrupt the user. We present two non-invasive methods to assess postural and facial expression components and propose a contextual analysis to guide SUI actuation and supportive action. The approach is illustrated in a possible redesign of the Microsoft helper agent "Clippit" ®.

1 Introduction

Vygotzky presented the notion that higher mental processes such as decision making, deduction and inference are mediated by various types of tools including symbol systems, materials, human behaviors (1926, 2006). 68 years later, Jonassen described the term cognitive tool as a group of generalizable computer based tools that facilitate human cognitive processing (1994). We suggest that User Interfaces (UIs) can be designed to serve as cognitive tools based on a model of nonverbal human interaction (See Figure 1). Such *Smart* User Interfaces (SUIs[1]) have the potential to support the human user when and where appropriate, and thus facilitate higher mental processes without the need for end-user programming or external actuation. In the particular case of *graphic* user interfaces (GUIs), nonverbally sensitive SUIs are expected to reduce disruptions of their users during high levels of engagement. Nonetheless, the SUI approach is intended to augment user interfaces whether tangible, ambient or graphic. The mapping of our human-centered nonverbal model to SUI systems is seen in Figure 2.

[1] The word Sui translated from Latin means "I merged". In the context of the Smart User Interface application, the user and interface merge on the level of nonverbal, behaviorally expressed communication.

C. Stephanidis (Ed.): Universal Access in HCI, Part II, HCII 2007, LNCS 4555, pp. 740–749, 2007.

In this paper we first present our model assumptions about nonverbal human signaling, then our technical approach and last but not least, a hypothetical application of our SUI approach to an existing GUI helper agent (Microsoft's "Clippit" ®). Our technical approach is comprised of two main parts: the sensing and classification of nonverbal data focused on postural assessment and facial expressions, and a conceptual model of contextual integration and analysis for interface actuation or inhibition. The final section addresses the implications of the SUI approach for the redesign of Microsoft's "Clippit" ®: We explore the problem of user frustration in three use case vignettes and the potential of "Clippit" ® as a nonverbally smart helper agent.

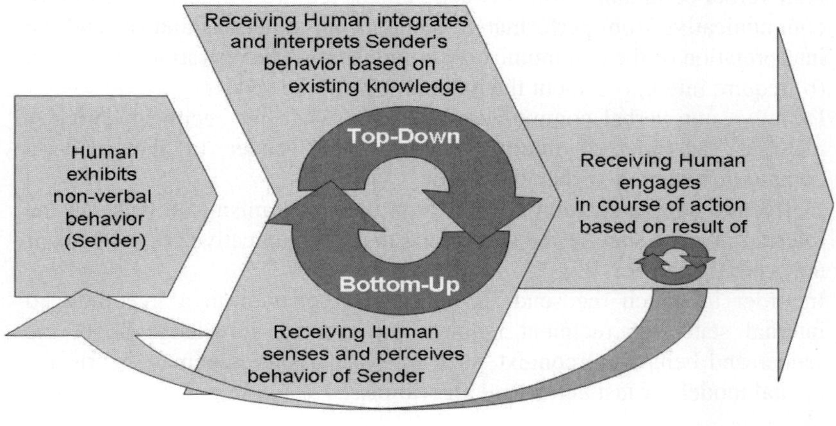

Fig. 1. Model of Human Nonverbal Communication

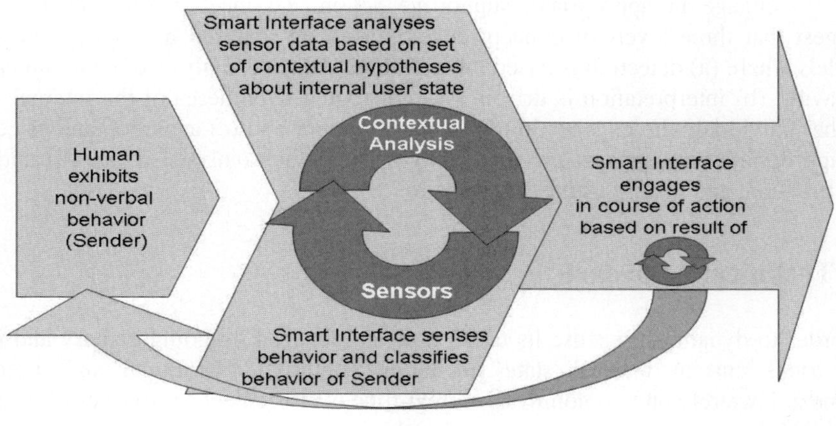

Fig. 2. Model of Human-Smart User Interface Nonverbal Communication

2 Assumptions and Concept Development

As a first step to explore the problem space of "what makes an interface really smart," we propose model and architecture based on nonverbal communication that rest on the following five principles:

1. Human actions (e.g., posture, gesture and facial expression) are purpose driven and serve communicative functions. One aspect is explicit communication, an intentional signaling component of the action (e.g., frenetic activity to show "I'm busy"). Another aspect is implicit communication, where the action unconsciously conveys the degree of engagement, concentration and desire for interaction or isolation.
2. Non-verbal communication between humans requires (a) discrimination of communicative from performative components of actions and (b) and the interpretation of the communicative components. The operations of (a) and (b) require inferences about the internal state of the sender.
3. Effective non-verbal communication occurs when the recipient correctly matches the inferred internal state of the sender to the sender's communicative non-verbal expression.
4. Ineffective communication occurs when there is a mismatch between the inferred internal state of the sender and the communicative components of non-verbal behavior.
5. In order to match the sender's non-verbal behavior to a hypothesized internal state, the recipient requires pre-existing knowledge about the sender and behavioral context, such as expectations, schemas, heuristics, mental models or fast and frugal algorithms.

Based on our five assumptions, the following challenges for designing SUIs emerge: SUIs are unobtrusive interfaces that are effective if they (a) recognize and distinguish communicative behaviors from noise, (b) interpret relevant data correctly and (c) engage in appropriate, supportive action. To meet these challenges, we suggest that three levels of concept development are required involving contextual models where (a) detection is based on contextual data and analysis of communicative behavior, (b) interpretation is driven by a contextual hypotheses of the internal state of the individual who engages in non-verbal behavior and (c) actuation and selection of appropriate user support are guided by a contextual analysis of (a), (b) and the internal state and history of the SUI system.

3 Technical Approach

In order to dynamically sense its user's type and level of on-going activity and infer the user's current internal state (including cognitive, attentional and affective elements), we rely on two noninvasive, real-time measurement approaches of postural and facial expression components. In this section we present the nonverbal components' measurement and analyses, followed by a possible use case and its conceptual mitigations based on a stepwise, dynamic, contextual analysis of user state in light of user history and system state.

3.1 Postural Data: Introduction

A comparative psychology tradition focused on classifying properties of directed somatic movements of organisms in relation to stimuli (Fraenkel & Gunn, 1961). As a first response a *taxis* was defined as a directed change in orientation relative to the location of a stimulus or the environment. Directed movements that produced orientation toward a stimulus or environment were termed a positive *taxis* (i.e., approach response or attraction). Directed movements producing an orientation away from a stimulus source were termed a negative taxis.

Orienting responses also are also expressive, serving as a form of non-verbal communication. Posture and gesture are recognized as components of nonverbal communication (e.g., Bull, 1987). For example, a person listening carefully to a phone conversation assumes a posture and affect that we associate with immersion, while a person put on hold during a phone conversation listening to music and advertisements assumes a different pattern of posture and affect. Similarly, a person intently playing a pinball machine or video game signals immersion in the task. One must not forget that cognitive engagement generates the need to orient toward and act relative to events and objects of priority and importance. The orienting movements can therefore be conceptualized as conveying information about (1) the parsing of continuous events into parts for processing and action (Zacks and Tversky, 2001) and (2) the relative magnitude of cognitive resource allocation to the event. These automatic movements or static postures are also nonverbal communicative expressions of engagement.

3.2 Postural Data: Technical Approach

The Dynamic Postural Assessment Chair (Balaban et al., 2004, 2005) has ultra-thin 16×16 pressure sensor arrays (Vista Medical, FSA pads) mounted between the padding and cloth upholstery of an office chair seat and back. Data collection and processing are performed in real time on a personal computer with interface software written in LabView (National Instruments). The raw data from the seat and back pressure sensor arrays are used to calculate eleven variables in real-time involving Seat Torsion, Base of Support, Seat and Back pressures derivatives, three-dimensional measures of the centers of pressure, and temporal assessments of path lengths. A global postural engagement response is identified by examining the linear correlation in a 9 second window between the variables and the number of relevant GUI objects in motion.

A positive *globally postural engagement response* is defined as any time when the correlation coefficient (r) for any of these calculations is greater than 0.71 (Balaban et al., 2004, 2005). During this state, the user observes the overall screen and the information displayed to assess the global situation. Global engagement responses disappear when attention and the task requirements shift towards a need to assessment and task execution at the local level. During this state, the user engages with the interface and shifts from the observer to the actor role. Depending on the task difficulty, the user returns to a state of global engagement or alternatively disengagement, at the end of local activity phase. All three path lengths variables are inversely related to task difficulty indicating that a seated user shows little postural sway during a difficult task.

Four distinct patterns of user posture in relationship to user activity have been documented: Low levels of user activity while assessing global situation, low levels of user activity while assessing global situation in a highly aroused state, high levels of activity and alertness during local assessment and low levels of activity and low attention to task.

3.3 Facial Expression: Introduction

Charles Darwin in his seminal work *Expression of the Emotions in Man and Animals* laid the foundation for the study of facial expressions as indicators of affect. His approach of relating facial expressiveness to evolution draws attention to the complexity of facial patterns made possible by the increasing mobility of facial muscles along the phylogenic ladder. For instance, Redican (1982) speaks of the mask like quality of many species compared to the wide range of expressiveness in primates. Likewise, humans are capable of displaying a wide range of facial activity, which, according to the classic tradition of Charles Darwin and later Paul Ekman and Carroll Izzard, is a reflection of their internal state. (For review, see Cornelius, 1996.) Current research questions the direct link between internal state and facial expression and provides examples involving the masking of feelings as a result of social pragmatics and social monitoring. Because the later are less likely implicated in personal computing with graphic user interfaces, we base our approach on the use of facial expression as indicators of internal states in the classic tradition.

3.4 Facial Expression: Technical Approach

MPEG4 is a standard used primarily to compress audio and video digital data. The idea behind MPEG4 based *face animation* is to transmit the commands that convey changes in facial expressions that allow the recipient to synthesize the facial image with the corresponding affect without transferring the image (Pandzic & Forchheimer, 2002). MPEG-4 specifies a face model in its neutral state, a number of feature points as reference points, and a set of Face Animation Points (FAP), each corresponding to a particular facial action. The FAP value for a particular FAP indicates the magnitude of the corresponding action, e.g., a big versus a small smile (Lever, 2003; Parke & Waters, 1996). Deforming the face model in its neutral state according to the specified FAP values for the corresponding time instant generates a particular facial action sequence (Johnson, Shaw & Ganeshan, 1999).

In order to quickly detect profile views of faces in images our approach uses a cascade of boosted classifiers and an extended set of Haar-like features. Haar-like features are intended to be a computationally efficient way to simulate early features of the human visual system, such as edge and line features. Individually each feature is a weak classifier, but combined they form a series of strong classifiers. Because later classifiers in the cascade rarely need to be evaluated, the cascade takes few computations on average.

This algorithm performs rapid object detection with a cascade of boosted classifiers on Haar-like features. It requires a large database of training images and a significant number of processor hours to construct a classifier so we used a pre-built classifier library.

Automatic tracking of human faces from image sequences is an important and challenging task in computer vision. We have implemented a real time face tracking system with Conditional density propagation algorithm, which is a robust technique for tracking objects through video sequences in the presence of clutter. The Condensation algorithm overcomes the major limitation of the Kalman filtering by allowing the probability density representation to be multi-modal, and therefore capable of simultaneously maintaining multiple hypotheses about the true state of the target. This allows recovery from brief moments in which the background features appear to be more target-like (and therefore a more probable hypothesis) than the features of the true object being tracked. The recovery takes place as subsequent time-steps in the image sequence provide reinforcement for the hypothesis of the true target state, while the hypothesis for the false target is not reinforced and therefore gradually diminishes (Ahlberg, 2002). To extract the facial feature of the person in front of the camera, we implemented a version of Motion Estimation Algorithm. A new location for the control point is found by identifying the pixel computationally closest to the original control point. The set of new control points are the facial animation parameters which are based on important facial regions like eyes, nose and mouth and produce reasonable results. Once we calculate a set of new control points (the FAPs) we create a dynamic video map of these facial animation parameters and transmit them to the receiver. See Figure 3 for an example of a video map that is comprised of only the control points. A single feature point must be mapped to many vertices along the real face model. Influenced points are a list of vertices in a vicinity of a feature point that must move along with this feature point. Individual weights may be assigned to each influenced point, usually proportional to the 1/ (distance from the reference point). This technique of mapping one feature point to multiple vertices reduces the complexity of computations without compromising the results (Condensation Algorithm, 2006). The novelty of our approach lies in the consideration of few facial regions critical for affect expression and capture. We reliably captured and animated fear, joy, sorrow (sadness), distress, surprise, interest, boredom, calm, disgust, frustration and anger.

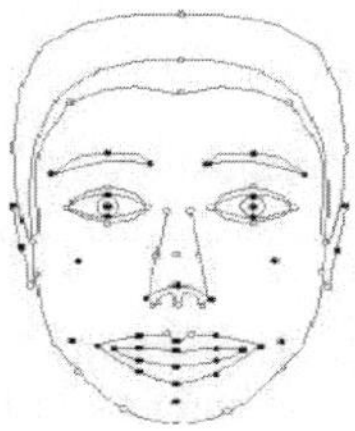

Fig. 3. Face Video Map

3.5 Proposed Integration and Contextual Guidance

As seen in the previous sections, nonverbal data are rich sources of user state. Moreover, the recognition of certain facial expression appears to be a universal phenomenon common across cultures (Ekman, 1994). Nonetheless, judging facial expressions out of context can lead to contradictory meanings (Knapp & Hall, 2006); Likewise, postural information and engagement indices without conjoint facial expressions require clarification and may prove difficult to interpret whether SUI action (or action suppression) is appropriate. As a result, the emergent nonverbal data of inferred user states must be analyzed jointly.

We suggest that the combinations of facial and postural data are sufficient to screen for supportive action activation or suppression as seen our user state hypothesis table (Table 1). Valid combinations of engagement indices derived from postural data and facial expression are indicated by the abbreviated entry for smart action recommended (SAR). Invalid combinations and no action recommended states are indicated by the entry "No action".

Table 1. Emergent Nonverbal States and Smart Action Recommendation

Postural State→ / Facial Expression ↓	Assessing global situation	Taking local action	Low activity & attention to task
Joy	No Action	No Action	SAR
Distress	SAR	SAR	SAR
Surprise	No action	No action	No action
Interest	No action	No action	Invalid
Boredom	SAR	SAR	SAR
Calm	No action	No action	SAR
Disgust	SAR	SAR	SAR
Frustration	SAR	SAR	SAR
Anger	SAR	SAR	SAR

Traditional research on facial expressions has focused on six affect universals: fear, happiness, sadness, surprise, disgust and anger (Fridlund, Ekman, & Oster, 1987). In addition, our MPEG4 model has reliable captured facial expression with cognitive and non-affective components that appear relevant to human computer interaction: Interest, Boredom, Frustration and Calm. We eliminated the Sadness and Fear dimensions from our analysis because it appears unlikely that even highly advanced systems will be capable to address these dimensions satisfactorily. In addition the global assessment indices were collapsed to eliminate redundancy with facial expression data.

Of all the possible combinations of engagement indices and facial expression, several reasonable hypotheses emerge where system support may be desirable. Clearly, each state is highly context dependent comprised at a minimum of user state, ongoing user activity and system state. A comprehensive treatment of this problem space is beyond the scope of this paper. Hence we present an exploratory use case starring a Smart Clippy Interface Support.

3.6 Implications for Clippit®

As a possible application of our nonverbal-contextual approach to *Smart* User Interfaces, we present the smartening of the semi-retired “clippit” ®. The Microsoft

14. Knapp, M.L., Hall, J.A.: Nonverbal communication in human interaction 6th ed. Thomson Wadsworth (2006)
15. Luening, E.: Microsoft tool Clippy gets pink slip. Retrieved October 15, 2005, (2001, April 11), from http://news.com.com/2100-1001-255671.html
16. Lever, N.: Real-time 3D Characteranimation. Focal press, Woburn, MA (2003)
17. Pandzic, I.S., Forchheimer, R.: MPEG4 Facial Animation. John Wiley & Sons Publishers, Hoboken, NJ (2002)
18. Parke, F.I., Waters, K.: Computer Facial animation. Wellesley, MA: A.K. Peters Ltd (1996)
19. Redican, W.K.: An Evolutionary on Human Facial Displays. In: Ekman, P. (ed.) Emotion in the Human Face, 2nd edn. Cambridge University Press, Cambridge (1982)
20. Thurrott, P.: Microsoft Office XP reviewed. Retrieved December 8, 2006, (2002, January 22), from http://www.winsupersite.com/reviews/
21. office10_whatsnew.asp
22. Vygotsky, L.S. (ed.): Educational Psychology, 1st edn.(reprint) Pentagon Press, New Delhi, India (1926–2006)
23. Zacks, J.M., Tversky, B.: Event structure in perception and conception. Psychological Bulletin 127, 3–21 (2001)

Towards a Physical Based Interaction-Model for Information Visualization

Roland Blach[1], Günter Wenzel[1], Manfred Dangelmaier[1], and Jörg Frohnmayer[2]

[1] CC Virtual Environments, Fraunhofer IAO, Nobelstr. 12,
70569 Stuttgart, Germany
[2] Merz Akademie, Pathway New Media, Teckstr. 58,
70190 Stuttgart, Germany
{Roland.Blach, Guenter.Wenzel, Manfred.Dangelmaier}@iao.fraunhofer.de,
joerg.frohnmaier@merz-akademie.de

Abstract. The ongoing process of collection and storage of knowledge with computer technology leads to highly complex information environments. The efficient access to information and the structure itself gets more and more complicated. The presented work investigates the usefulness of physical based interaction and representation behavior in immersive environments for information visualization. A framework will be presented for the mapping of physical behavior on abstract data entities and interaction. This framework is applied to an early prototype for market research.

Keywords: Information Visualization, Virtual Reality, Virtual Environments, Physical Based Modeling.

1 Introduction

The ongoing process of collection and storage of knowledge with computer technology leads to highly complex information environments. The efficient access to information and the structure itself gets more and more complicated. Techniques for handling information have been researched mainly for desktop environments [7], but the framed 2D-screen is often a restricting factor for the layout of and the navigation in data spaces.

Immersive environments might have the potential to overcome some of these shortcomings. These environments differ from conventional desktop in the sense that they embed the user in a computer generated data environment. These systems have the following key properties e.g. as described in [12]:

- 3D-Representation and perception
- Spatial interaction in real-time
- Sense of Presence

C. Stephanidis (Ed.): Universal Access in HCI, Part II, HCII 2007, LNCS 4555, pp. 750–758, 2007.

Well known examples are systems which drives head mounted displays or 3D stereoscopic multi-wall environments as e. g. CAVE-systems [8].

Information visualization in immersive environments is still in its infancy. Chen describes in [6] the challenges for information visualization in general. In immersive environments, which have to be real-time by definition, two of the ten problems, he presented are specifically prominent:

- Scalability: Large data sets to be visualized
- Usability: Interaction with complex structures without loosing the context

In this paper we will focus on the second topic; the interaction with abstract structures in spatial environments. Our approach is also related to the "paradigm shift from structures to dynamics" and the "problem of prior knowledge", which are addressed in Chen's collection of challenges.

2 Related Work

Physical based modeling has become quite common in interactive environments. The main reason to enhance these environments with physical simulations, is the general lack of behavioral realism. Games are the most prominent example where physics is used for enhancement of the realism of the scenery for better engagement but also to give users a greater variety of interactions, e. g. all objects in the scene manipulate other objects in a physical consistent way, if they collide with each other. In virtual environments physics has also been used to create more realistic behavior most prominent examples are e. g driving simulators [2] or assembly planning [1]. The interaction between user and systems is only affected so far as e. g. in training situations realistic behavior is necessary for the training purpose itself.

The first implementations of information visualization applications have been basically pure representational approaches, where the immersive technology was used to fly through these structures in search of new perspectives shown by e. g. [9] or [16]

Physical based system modeling is a general approach toward a more realistic representation of real world behavior. For our research, the usage for abstract data items with no real world equivalent is more interesting. For the 2D visualization of graphs spring and mass approaches have been used with good results [11]. An approach which is very close to ours, is the work of Osawa [15], which incorporates thermodynamics to represent content proximity. He has designed the interface also in an immersive environment. However Osawa does not use the physical behavior for the interface itself.

Physical interface behavior has also been introduced in the research area of immersive environments as pure interaction metaphors very often applied to assembly scenarios as e. g. [13] or [10].

3 Conceptual Framework

3.1 Physical Based Modeling Revisited

User and information items are seen as part of the same environment where the user is able to interact with all items consistently. Here, interaction and the behavioral representation of information items will be based on rigid body dynamics. Due to the abstract nature of the data the physical behavior is not predefined by mimicking real world behavior. Therefore it can be devoted purely to the task of information transfer, that is interaction and interface. This left many design options open which have to be filled in by the application developer. The compelling properties of rigid body dynamics are that they draw on every day's experience but expose more autonomous behavior, which can be exploited for better adapted behavior of the environment. Rigid body physics consists of the following basic principles which if applied to many bodies, are able to form complex behavioral pattern:

- Position and velocity
- Inertia (mass, inertial tensor)
- Force (gravity, springs, damping, etc.)
- Energy

Position and velocity describe the actual state of the entity. Inertia is a form of memory where the behavioral impact of the past is kept. The forces work on this state and interact with the past state consistently, defining the future state. The energy is an additional attribute which collects the overall potential of change in the future taking into account the velocity and the mass. Forces can also have different reference systems regarding their point of application:

- Forces which work on objects and are moving with the object
- Forces which work in reference to space, e. g. force fields

They can expose different time behavior:

- Permanent forces (often force fields)
- Impulses which apply a force only for an infinite small amount of time
- Forces which change over time (e. g. controlled engines)

So how can these properties be exploited as basic design principles for information items and user interaction in spatial and interactive environments?

3.2 Representation

If we consider the kinetic state position and velocity as describing factor of information entity properties, the spatial dimensions have to expose a specific semantics. The forces describe internal or external constraints, which respect the historical state of the item. In the following table a selection mappings for common physical concepts and potential semantics will be presented.

Table 1. Mapping between physical concept and interpretation

Physical concept	**Abstract interpretation**	
Inertia, Mass	Ability of attribute to resist changes (or the amplification factor of its own history)	Parameters of items. Changes the influence of forces on state (position and velocity)
Position	Proximity	The space is only used for layout purpose. A single attribute is mapped on distance. Freedom of configuration.
	Attributes are mapped on spatial axes	Useful for multidimensional representations. If time is one of the axis processes can be frozen.
Velocity	Change	Represents processes. Representation can be via animation (the speed might be controllable) or as a static item attached to the entity as e.g. flow field vector arrows where the length describes the velocity.
Forces between Items		
Attraction	Positive Relation	Can depend on mass
Repulsion	Negative Relation	Can depend on mass
Spring	Preset equilibrium state	Here a desired situation can be manifested in the parameters of the spring. The spring pulls or pushes the connected items to the desired state.
Force Fields		
Gravity	Principal ordering force (top and bottom)	Often constant, but can also vary over space
Viscosity Friction Air drag	Stabilizing force via negative feedback dependent on velocity	Linear or nonlinear

The above described interpretation schemes are understood to be principal. Detailed design can fine tune the applied rules. A good example is viscosity or air drag, which depend linearly or nonlinearly on the velocity. A useful enhancement is the ability to collide with other items. Obviously this is especially helpful if items should not share the same space with each other. The reaction on a collision can also be chosen deliberately.

3.3 Interaction

To stay in consistency with the representation, interaction has also to work on the above described principles. The user can interact with the information items scene via change of forces, velocity or position. All three different types have impact on the semantics as well as on the implementation.

- **Impose forces:** User changes constraints of the environment.
  The items adapt to new constraints. The new spatial configuration reveals the effects on the modeled system.
- **Change velocity**: User modifies the history of the item.
  The items adapt to its new history. The new spatial configuration reveals the effects of the changed history.
- **Change position**: User forces the item into new position.
  The other items adapt to this new forced configuration or expose broken constraints. The new spatial configuration reveals the effects of a forced change in item location. This could mean that this is only possible with infinite power, which is a kind of "magic" interference from outside the system.

Positional changes are the most critical type for the implementation, because if they are applied naively, it breaks with constraints of the underlying physical simulation, which can lead to numerical instabilities. This can also exploited as a feedback for the user that an important constraint is affected

The here presented framework is a starting point for the exploration of possible mappings between physical concepts and interaction and information representation. In the next section an application prototype is described where these mappings are partially used.

4 Application Prototype

Our application example is a market exploration tool. We have identified actors in the market and want to present various level of relations as e. g. "sells products to", "has

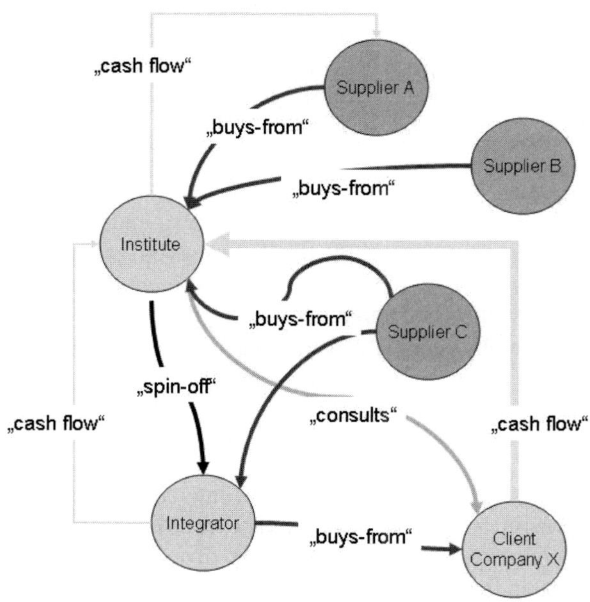

Fig. 1. A simple example of some market actors and their interrelations

common projects with" or "is spin of from" and relations which have also values as e. g. "cash flow between actors". This application case is a synthetic example which is at the moment not based on an economical validated method for market description.

The abstract model of this application case is a directed graph structure with several semantic partially weighted link types which connect the nodes.

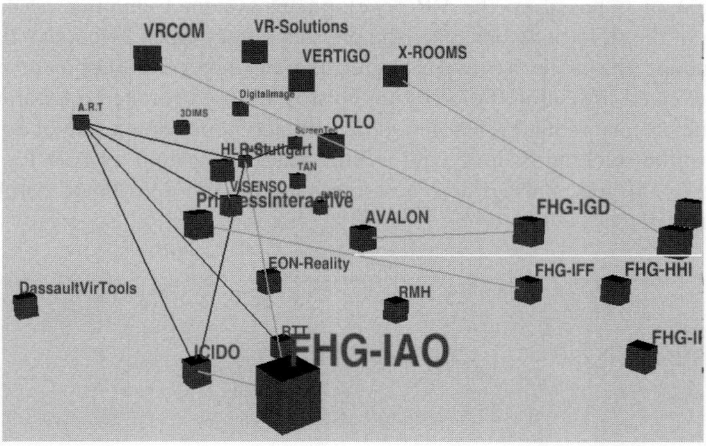

Fig. 2. Graph network. The nodes are actors in the market and the links describe a specific semantic relation.

If the mappings from the described concept are applied the following principles can be found in the application:

- Nodes represent actors in the market which have the attributes "will for cooperation", "client dedication" and "budget to spend", which are mapped to mass for different link types.
- Links act as attraction forces between the actors. The semantic of the link defines the relation of attribute to the mass property. The defined links are "is spin-off", "buys from", "has funded projects", "has bilateral projects" and "cash flow" as the only weighted link.
- Proximity is the general measure which represents a combination of the meanings of the links. The closer the nodes, the better the actual cooperation.

Possible interactions consist of the creation and parameterization of nodes and links and the superposition of links types. The user can also grab nodes, which refers to the "positional change", to see the limits of the proximity imposed by the structure of the overall system. At this stage user can explore the market actors and their relations in regard to the actual cooperation.If several layers of links are superimposed, a complex force structure acts on the items and can show an equilibrium state. This could reveal qualitatively a possible market configuration, where several dependencies are taken into account. Obviously the different force layers have to be normalized. Here an economical theory has to provide a normalization scheme, which makes the effects comparable. Also unstable configurations can immediately be recognized.

4.1 Technical System Description

The application is based on the VR-development system Lightning 2.5 [3] For the simulation of the rigid body behavior, the physics library Open Dynamics Engine [14] was integrated. The target hardware platform is an immersive 3D-powerwall system which is operated in seating. Polarization glasses are used for stereo separation of the images. The projectors have a resolution of 1400x1050 on screen size of 2.66 m x 2.0 m. The position tracking is done with a video tracking system by A.R.T., which can track up to ten targets. Furthermore a wireless mouse and a keyboard can be used as interaction devices.

Fig. 3. Powerwall integrated into media based meeting room

5 Conclusion and Future Work

The useful application of immersive environments for information visualization and its benefits are still not clear. Although some interesting properties are acknowledged there has been still no productive environment developed. The freedom of mapping more information dimensions to the interactions space comes along with more complexity of the interface. Physical based modeling promises to induce more autonomy of the environment with still comprehensive behavior. In case of abstract data representation many design questions remain still open. We have presented a framework for the mapping of dynamic principles of rigid bodies to information entities and the interaction. This has been applied to a simple graph structure for market research.

The next steps for the future have to be the development of an application prototype to perform user evaluations. This feedback will help us to refine the conceptual framework and possibly to extend it with other metaphors of real-world dynamics. Here we can imagine to exploit the dynamic laws for situations which cannot be done in the real-world, e.g. as springs which expose forces only in one direction as described [4]. The non-realistic physical based modeling might open up new options for better interfaces to information environments.

Acknowledgments. The work has been partially supported by the FhG-IAO VISUM project.

References

1. Banerjee, A., Banerjee, P., Ye, N., Dech, F.: Assembly Planning Effectiveness Using Virtual Reality. In: Presence: Teleoperators and Virtual Environments, vol. 8(2), pp. 204–217. MIT Press, Cambridge (1999)
2. Bayarri, S.M., Fernandez, M.: Perez: Virtual reality for driving simulation. In: Communications of the ACM 39(5), 72–76 (1996)
3. Blach, R., Landauer, J. M., Simon, A., Rösch, A.: A Flexible prototyping Tool for 3D Real-Time User-Interaction. In: Proceedings of the Eurographics Workshop, pp. 195–203 (1998)
4. Blach, R., Hoffmann, H., Stefani, O., Dangelmaier, M.: Interacting with hierarchical information structures in immersive environments In: 2003 HCI Jacko, J.A. et al.: HCI International 2003. Proceedings of the 10th International Conference on Human-Computer Interaction. vol.1: Theory and Practice (Part I). Mahwah/NJ.: Erlbaum, 2003, pp (1118)-1122
5. Bowman, D.A, Kruijff, E., Laviola, J.J., Poupyrev, I.: 3D User Interfaces Theory and Practice. Addison-Wesley, Boston (2005)
6. Chen, C.: Top 10 Unresolved Information Visualization problems. In: IEEE Computer Graphics and applications VoL.Juli/August 2005, pp. 12–16 (2005)
7. Card, S.K., Mackinlay, J.D., Shneiderman, B.: Readings in Information Visualization – Using Vision to Think. Morgan Kaufmann, San Francisco (1999)
8. Cruz-Neira, C., Sandin, D.J., DeFanti, T.: A. Surround-screen projection-based virtual reality: The design and implementation of the CAVE. In: Proceedings of SIGGRAPH 93, Annual Conference Series, pp. 135–142 (1993)
9. Ebert, D., Shaw, C.D., Zwa, A., Miller, E.L., Roberts, D.A.: Minimally-immersive Interactive Volumetric Information Visualization. In: Proceedings of IEEE Symposium on Information Visualization, InfoVis'96 (1996)
10. Fröhlich, B., Tramberend, H., Beers, A., Baraff, D.: Physical-Based Manipulation on the Responsive Workbench. In: Proceedings IEEE Virtual Reality 2000, pp. 5–11 (2000)
11. Fruchterman, T.M.J., Reingold, E.M.: Graph Drawing by Force-directed Placement. In: Software – Practice and Experience 21(11), 1129–1164 (1991)
12. Kalawsky, R.S.: The science of Virtual Reality and Virtual Environments. Addison-Wesley Publishing Company, New York (1993)

13. Koutek, M., van Hees, J., Post, F.H., Bakker, A.F.: Virtual Spring Manipulators for Particle Steering in Molecular Dynamics on the Responsive Workbench. In: Proc. Eurographics Virtual Environments 2002, Barcelona, pp. 53–62 (2002)
14. ODE Library, http://www.ode.org
15. Osawa, N.: A multiple-focus browser for network structures using heat models, The 59th National Convention of Information Processing Society of Japan, 5K-09 (1999)
16. Risch, J.S, et al.: The Starlight Information Visualization System. In: Card, S.K., Mackinlay, J.D., Shneiderman, B. (eds.) Readings in Information Visualization – Using Vision to Think, pp. 551–560. Morgan Kaufmann, San Francisco (1999)

A Note on Brain Actuated Spelling with the Berlin Brain-Computer Interface

Benjamin Blankertz[1,2], Matthias Krauledat[1,2], Guido Dornhege[2], John Williamson[3], Roderick Murray-Smith[3,4], and Klaus-Robert Müller[1,2,⋆]

[1] Technical University Berlin, Berlin, Germany
[2] Fraunhofer FIRST (IDA), Berlin, Germany
[3] University of Glasgow, Glasgow, Scotland
[4] Hamilton Institute, NUI Maynooth, Ireland

Abstract. Brain-Computer Interfaces (BCIs) are systems capable of decoding neural activity in real time, thereby allowing a computer application to be directly controlled by the brain. Since the characteristics of such direct brain-to-computer interaction are limited in several aspects, one major challenge in BCI research is intelligent front-end design. Here we present the mental text entry application 'Hex-o-Spell' which incorporates principles of Human-Computer Interaction research into BCI feedback design. The system utilises the high visual display bandwidth to help compensate for the extremely limited control bandwidth which operates with only two mental states, where the timing of the state changes encodes most of the information. The display is visually appealing, and control is robust. The effectiveness and robustness of the interface was demonstrated at the CeBIT 2006 (world's largest IT fair) where two subjects operated the mental text entry system at a speed of up to 7.6 char/min.

1 Introduction

Brain-computer interfaces (BCIs) translate brain signals into control commands. The measured brain signals reflect, to some extent, the intentions of a subject. The control commands may be used for a computer application or a neuroprosthesis. There is a variety of BCI systems being developed that use signals recorded from the scalp, the surface of the cortex, or from inside the brain. It has been shown that invasive BCI systems enable monkeys, and recently also humans, to operate a robotic arm ([3,4]). Furthermore it was demonstrated that noninvasive BCI systems enable healthy subjects as well as patients to control an internet browser or simple word processing software ([5,6,7]).

Since a principle motivation of the development of BCIs is to provide paralyzed patients with independent communication tools, BCI-driven spelling devices are an important topic in BCI research. The Tübingen BCI group developed a system that could

⋆ The studies were partly supported by the *Bundesministerium für Bildung und Forschung* (BMBF), FKZ 01IBE01A, by the SFI (00/PI.1/C067), and by the IST Programme of the European Community, under the PASCAL Network of Excellence, IST-2002-506778. This publication only reflects the authors' views. This paper builds upon [1,2], but also presents new material.

C. Stephanidis (Ed.): Universal Access in HCI, Part II, HCII 2007, LNCS 4555, pp. 759–768, 2007.

be operated by patients suffering from amyotrophic lateral sclerosis ([8]). Binary decisions of the BCI were used to select letters in a procedure where the alphabet was iteratively split into halves. The achieved spelling rate was about 0.5 char/min. With a similar front-end but a different BCI approach, a spelling application of the Graz group could be operated by one patient suffering from severe cerebral palsy at about 1 char/min ([9]). In [10] a spelling application is proposed that is based on a three-class BCI. While one class can be used to scroll through the alphabet which is presented on two 'assembly lines' left and right of the cursor, the other two classes are used to select the character from either the left or the right line. Since scrolling is uni-directional, missing the desired character necessitates scrolling through the whole alphabet for another chance. Two out of three BCI-trained users are able to operate the device at spelling speed 2.35 resp. 1.62 char/min (average for 5 words).

Furthermore there are BCI spelling devices that are based on the detection of potentials that are evoked by external stimuli rather than endogeneously altered mental states. Most prominent is the approach proposed by Donchin et al. ([11]) using the P300 component. Here all characters are presented in a 6×6 matrix. The symbol on which the user focuses her/his concentration can be be predicted from the brain potentials that are evoked by random flashing of rows and columns. The role of directing the gaze to the desired letter is so far not investigated. Further developments (e.g., [12,13]) suggest that high spelling rates can be achieved using this approach. In the online experiments that have been reported so far, many repetitions of the stimuli have been used in order to increase the signal-to-noise ratio for P300 detection. Accordingly the spelling speed could not exceed about 6 char/min even at 100% classification accuracy. Nevertheless offline analyses show that in principle fewer averages could be used, such that up to 15 char/min could be possible. Still, this has to be shown in practice.

Although the proof-of-concept of BCI systems was given decades ago (e.g. [14]), several major challenges are still to be faced. One of those challenges is to develop BCI applications which take the specific characteristics of BCI communication into account. Apart from being prone to error and having a rather uncontrolled variability in timing, its bandwidth is heavily unbalanced: BCI users can perceive a high rate of information transfer from the display, but have a low-bandwidth communication in their control actions, cf. Fig. 1 (a).

The Berlin Brain-Computer Interface (BBCI) is an EEG-based BCI system which operates on the spatio-spectral changes during different kinds of motor imagery. It uses machine learning techniques to adapt to the specific brain signatures of each user, thereby achieving high quality feedback already in the first session ([15]). The mental text entry system *Hex-o-Spell* which is presented here adapts modern, dynamic text entry methods into a suitable form for brain-computer control.

The idea for Hex-o-Spell was taken from the Hex system ([16,17], see Fig. 1 (b)), which was designed for use on mobile devices augmented with accelerometers, where tilt control was used to maneuver through a hexagonal tesselation. The system adapted the response dynamics in order to make control behaviour for likely actions easier than unlikely ones, without altering the ideal path for any given word trajectory. This was intended to maintain a level of stability in the patterns required to generate letter sequences, such that the user could "bootstrap" from closed-loop to open-loop control.

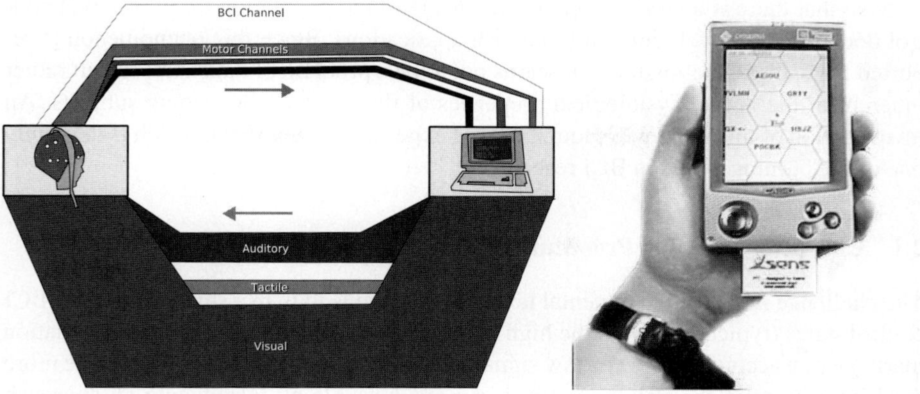

Fig. 1. (a) Left: Asymmetry of BCI communication. (b) Right: Text entry system *Hex* for mobile devices.

The adjustment was based upon a continuously-updating language model which inferred the next character given the previous text sequence. Hex-o-spell was adapted from this original system, replacing the two-dimensional tilt control with a rotation/forward switching input (see Section 2.1) and introducing layout rearrangement in place of the adaptive dynamics (see Section 2.2). In BCIs, where there is enormous asymmetry in the bandwith of the channels in the control loops (see Fig. 1 (a)), high-quality language models are essential to extract every drop of salient information from the user, using the large display bandwidth to make the user aware of the effect of their actions in combination with the language model. Although these introduce continual changes which may be difficult to predict (from the point of view of the user), the consequent reliance on continuous feedback may be tolerable given the extremely limited bit rates. Users have to move so slowly that they have plenty of time to search the space for changes.

2 Methods

The decoding of mental states from brain activity as used in the Berlin Brain-Computer Interface system is described in another contribution in this volume, see [18], and in earlier publications ([15,19]). In short, the BBCI detects the user-specific spatio-spectral changes of the EEG during motor imagination of, e.g., the left or the right hand or the feet. Applications are controlled by a continuous control signal. Typically this is the graded classifier output which discriminates two motor imagery classes. It has been demonstrated that the machine learning approach which is realized in the BBCI allows to achieve high quality feedback already in the very first session without subject training ([15,19,20]). Bit rates (measured during one dimensional cursor control) range between 6 and 40 bits per minute. The intention-to-control delay is difficult to quantify. The reaction time from stimulus presentation to significant BCI control is between 750 and 1750 ms with a large intra-subject trial-to-trial variability (compared to 300 to 450 ms in a 2 alternative forced choice task with finger movement responses to visual stimuli).

Note that there is a non-negligible percentage of the population for which BCI control does not work well enough to control applications. Since this phenomenon is reported from all BCI laboratories it seems not to be a problem of data analysis but rather inherent in the neurophysiological properties of the scalp EEG in some subjects. An investigation of this issue will require a large experimental approach which is definitely one of the burning issues in BCI research.

2.1 Character Selection Procedure in Hex-o-Spell

The challenge in designing a mental text entry system is to map a small number of BCI control states (typically two) to the high number of symbols (26 letters plus punctuation marks) while accounting for the low signal to noise ratio in the control signal. The more fluid interaction in the BBCI system was made possible by introducing an approach which combined probabilistic data and dynamic systems theory based on our earlier work ([16]) on mobile interfaces.

Here we take the example that the text entry system is controlled by the two mental states *imagined right hand movement* and *imagined right foot movement.* The initial configuration is shown in the leftmost plot of Fig. 2. Six hexagonal fields surround a circle. In each of them five letters or other symbols (including '<' for backspace) are arranged. For the selection of a symbol there is an arrow in the center of the circle. By imagining a right hand movement the arrow turns clockwise. An imagined foot movement stops the rotation and the arrow starts extending. If this foot imagination persists, the arrow touches the hexagon and thereby selects it. Then all other hexagons are cleared and the five symbols of the selected hexagon are moved to individual hexagons as shown in the rightmost screenshot of Fig. 2. The arrow is reset to its minimal length while maintaining its original direction. Now the same procedure (rotation if desired and extension of the arrow) is repeated to select one symbol. Note that there are only

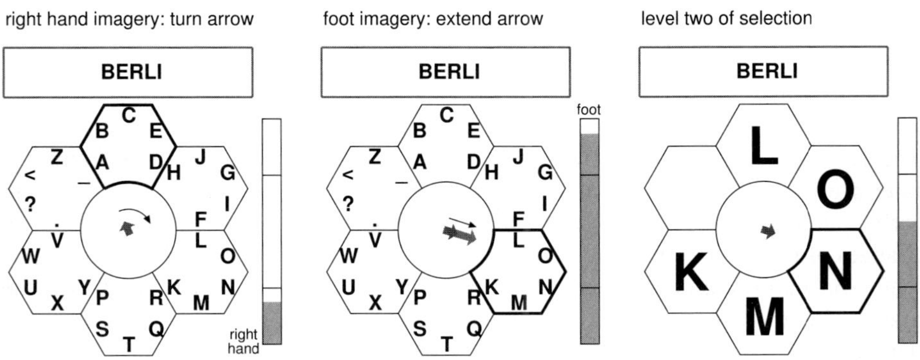

Fig. 2. The mental text entry system 'Hex-o-Spell'. The two states classified by the BBCI system (bar on the right in each screenshot) control the turning and growing of the arrow respectively (see also text). Letters can thus be chosen in a two step procedure. If the classifier output is undecided (bar on the right between the thresholds), the arrow maintains its direction and its length dimishes continuously to minimum.

5 symbols for choice in the second step, cf. rightmost screenshot of Fig. 2. Choosing the empty hexagon makes the application return to the first step without selection. This transition allows a sort of limited undo. Misspelt characters can be erased by selecting the backspace symbol '<'.

There are several parameters that can be adapted to the specific capacities of the user, like the turning and the growing speed of the arrow.

2.2 The Language Model

A language model can ease the use of text entry systems effectively if it is incorporated in an intuitive way. The language model determines a probability distribution on all symbols, given the letters that have been written so far. Such probability distribution can be used to construct (and dynamically adapt) the decision tree, such that more probable symbols and be reached faster.

The implemented language model is a modified partial predictive-match (PPM) model ([21,22]), which comes close to the maximum possible compression for English ([23]). A tree of probabilities is stored, giving $P_{\mathrm{PPM}}(X_N \mid X_{N-K}, \ldots, X_{N-1})$ as probability for the N-th letter, given the K previous letters. In the Hex-o-Spell implementation this PPM model (with K =2) was combined with a modified PPM where the prefix is variable length, and runs from the start of the word. I.e., we used the probability $P_{\mathrm{vPPM}}(X_N \mid X_1, \ldots, X_{N-1})$ of the N-th letter in a word, given all previous letters of that word. These two probability models are combined by a relative weighting that depends on the relative position of the letter in a word. The relative weights for P_{vPPM} decrease linearly from 1 for the first letter to 0.5 for the 6th and all subsequent letters. The language models have been trained on a large corpus of German newspaper articles and some novels.

From an information-theoretic point of view the whole arrangement of symbols to the positions in the six hexagons should be controlled by the language model ([17] describes how this optimisation was carried out for the original Hex system). We decided not to do so, since such policy would reduce the potential for learning and require significant search times. S/he would need to search the whole screen before each selection to find the desired symbol. Instead we keep the grouping of the symbols to the six hexagons fixed (e.g. letter 'A' to 'E' are always in the topmost hexagon, see Fig. 2). Only the arrangement of the symbols within one hexagon is controlled by the language model. In this arrangement the probability of a letter according to the language model is matched with the rank of the position which reflect how easy that position can be reached. The symbol that is in 'straight-forward' direction can be reached most easily, since in this case the user just needs to go on with the 'go straight' command. For the position clockwise next to it, switching to the turn state is required for a 60° turn, and so on, cf. Fig. 3. On the other hand the language model dictates that after one symbol has been selected the arrow will point to that hexagon which contains the most probable next letter.

The right part of Fig. 3 illustrates the language model (here trained for the German language as described above) during the writing of the word 'BERLIN'. In the very first step the language model reflects the distribution of letters beginning a word. The second row shows the situation when the second letter is selected. According to the

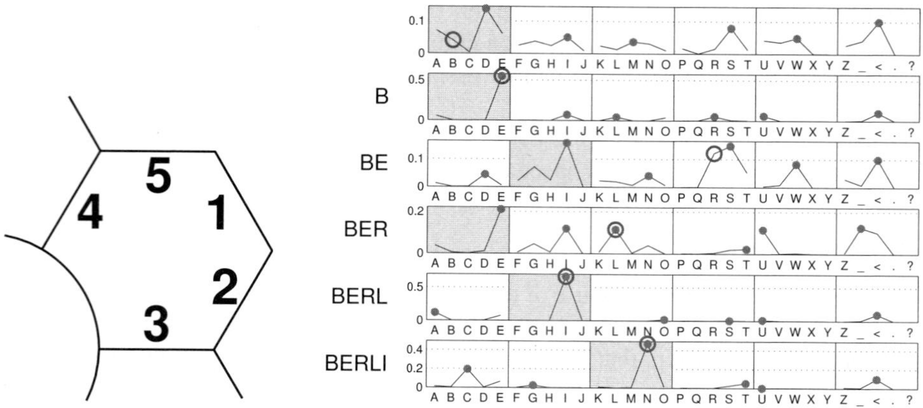

Fig. 3. Language model at work: The sketch on left shows the ranking of the positions within one hexagon. The position that can be reached in straight-forward direction from the center is the easiest to go to (no state switch needed). Then the ranking proceeds clickwise. The figure on the right illustrates how the language model influences the operation during the spelling of 'BERLIN'. Each row corresponds to the selection of one letter. Groups of five subsequent characters are placed within one hexagon, see leftmost screenshot of Fig. 2. Shading indicates the group containing the most probable letter, i.e. these characters are in the hexagon to which the arrow initially is directed to. The ranking of probabilities within each group determine the relative position of the corresponding characters within one hexagon as indicated in the left subplot. A circle marks the letter that actually needs to be written. (The probabilities were extracted for the German language.).

language model, the letter 'E' is the most probable second letter in a word starting with 'B'. This has to following two consequences. After selection of 'B' (using the 'go straight' state in the end) the arrow is reset pointing to the hexagon containg the 'E', and the 'E' is placed in 'straight forward' direction within the hexagon (topmost position). This way the mere continuation of the previous mental state (corresponding to the 'go straight' command) leads to the selection of 'E'. In the example the probability of the backspace symbol was chosen to be 0.1. In practice this value is set according to the control capability of the user.

2.3 Comments on the Design of Hex-o-Spell

Hex-O-Spell is unusual in that it uses that the user applies binary control to produce discrete output, but does so through a continuous control process. Control is effected by imagining motor movements; but these are based upon the feedback from the interface, which has a continuously changing state. This state is the result of the integration the output of the classifier identifying the imagined movements, which is integrated and then thresholded to into a decision between rotation/forward motion with fixed speeds. Fig. 4 shows the structure of this control loop.

Hex-o-Spell could also be modified to work as a T9-style system, with only a single transition for each character rather than a pair. Given that PPM models can compress

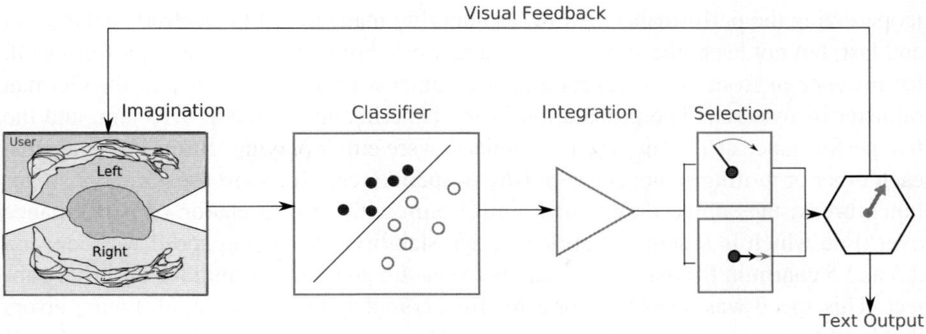

Fig. 4. The structure of the control loop in Hex-O-Spell, indicating the transformation of a discrete user intention into a continuous variable which is fed back to the user, while simultaneously generating discrete symbols

English to approximately 2 bits per character and choosing one from six transitions gives ~ 2.585 bits, this should be quite practical. [24] describes a functioning entry system using only four transitions followed by a decoding step. Despite of its increment of information transfer rate, it has to be explored whether BCI users are interested in this form of predictive text entry. There are anecdotal reports of patients who preferred a slower spelling system than using a system which suggested word completions based on a probabilistic model.

Hex-o-Spell is effectively a *timing*-based interface. The time at which the transition from the rotation state to the forward state occurs determines the letter which is selected. The rate of communication is bounded by how accurately the user can make these transitions, given the noise properties, delays and unfamiliarity of interaction present in an EEG interface. The time to traverse $60°$ should be calibrated against the reaction time of the user and the system; if the traversal time is much shorter than the reaction time, selection will become impossible. The language model, which adapts the layout, acts to minimize the time required for a selection, trading-off the minimization of the time required to rotate to the appropriate position for selection against the time required to scan the new layout and find the new locations of symbols. The "calmness" of this adaptation strategy means that the user is not always in a tightly-coupled loop with the system; rather than being a flying-like control task, the interaction is broken into smaller chunks which the user can proceed through at their own pace. This is one advantage over systems such as Dasher [25], which although extremely efficient control is possible with continuous, relatively noise-free input devices such as mice or eye trackers, but is less suited to the discrete, pulse-like control present in a BCI.

3 Results

On two days in the course of the CeBIT fair 2006 in Hannover, Germany, live demonstrations were given with two subjects simultaneously using the BBCI system. These demonstrations turned out to be BBCI robustness tests *par excellence*. All over the fair pavilion, noise sources of different kinds (electric, acoustic,...) were potentially jeopardizing the performance. A low air humidity made the EEG electrode gel dry out and last, but not least, the subjects were under psychological pressure to perform well, for instance in front of several running TV cameras or in the presence of the German minister of research. The preparation of the experiments started at 9:15 a.m. and the live performance at 11 a.m. The two subjects were either playing 'Brain-Pong' against each other or writing sentences with Hex-o-Spell. Except for short breaks and a longer lunch break, the subjects continued until 5 p.m. without degradation of performance over time which is a demonstration of great stability. The typing speed was between 2.3 and 5 char/min for one subject and between 4.6 and 7.6 char/min for the other subject. This speed was measured for error-free, completed phrases, i.e. all typing errors that have been committed had to be corrected by using backspace. The total number of characters spelled in error-free phrases was up to 560 per subject per day.

For a BCI driven text entry system not operating on evoked potentials this is a world class spelling speed, especially taking into account the environment and the fact that the subjects did not train the usage of the BBCI text entry interface: the subjects used Hex-O-Spell only twice before.

4 Discussion

Compared to spelling applications that have so far been coupled to BCIs ([10,26,8]) Hex-o-Spell is by far most sophisticated in terms of HCI principles. Conjoint with the powerful BBCI this mental text entry system allowed to achieve world class spelling performance. Hopefully this demonstration initiates the advancement of BCI applications from its rather simple state to more intelligent designed front-ends.

One of the aims of Hex-o-Spell is to make the best use of the language model to reduce the effort required to enter text, without inducing enormous cognitive load or extensive training time. There are four common approaches to introducing language models into text entry systems: post hoc interpretation (e.g. as used in T9); adaptive target resizing (as in Dasher [25]); dynamics adjustment (as in the original Hex); and layout re-ordering (used in Hex-o-Spell). Target resizing is simple to understand, but the visual display fluctuates rapidly and significant space is required to display the resized alternatives. The reinterpretation approach allows for more powerful language modeling (because subsequent letters can affect estimates of previous ones), but the lack of predictability of output can be confusing for users. Adaptive dynamics can be used to produce an efficient and visually stable display, but is less suitable for the one dimensional control inputs present in the BCI interface. The rearrangment strategy does require visual search at every new letter input, but the minimal reorganization algorithm used in Hex-o-Spell significantly reduces the impact of this. Compared to other potential entry styles, such as Dasher or grid selection mechanisms, Hex-o-Spell is also very visually compact; the hexagonal display can potentially be used as a small overlay on top of a text being edited, giving the user an overview of the context in which they are editing.

The prospective value of BCI research for rehabilitation is well known. In light of the work presented here we would advocate a further point. BCI provides stimulation to HCI researchers as an extreme example of the sort of interaction which is becoming more common: interaction with 'unconventional' computers in mobile phones, or with devices embedded in the environment. These have a number of shared attributes: high-dimensional, noisy inputs, which describe intrinsically low-dimensional content; data with content at multiple time-scales; and a significant uncontrolled variability. The mismatch in the bandwidth between the display and control channels (as explained in the introduction) and the slow, frustrating error correction motivate a more 'negotiated' style of interaction, where commitments are withheld until appropriate levels of evidence have been accumulated (i.e. the entropy of the beliefs inferred from the behavior of the joint human-computer system should change smoothly, limited by the maximum input bandwidth). The dynamics of a cursor, given such noisy inputs, should be stabilized by controllers which infer potential actions, as well as the structure of the variability in the sensed data. Hex-o-Spell demonstrates the potential of such intelligent stabilising dynamics in a noisy, but richly-sensed medium. The results suggest that the approach is a fruitful one, and one which creates the potential for incorporating sophisticated models without *ad hoc* modifications.

References

1. Müller, K.-R., Blankertz, B.: Toward noninvasive brain-computer interfaces. IEEE Signal Processing Magazine 23(5), 125–128 (September 2006)
2. Blankertz, B., Dornhege, G., Krauledat, M., Schröder, M., Williamson, J., Murray-Smith, R., Müller, K.-R.: The Berlin Brain-Computer Interface presents the novel mental typewriter Hex-o-Spell. In: Proceedings of the 3rd International Brain-Computer Interface Workshop and Training Course, 2006, pp. 108–109, Verlag der Technischen Universität Graz (2006)
3. Hochberg, L.R., Serruya, M.D., Friehs, G.M., Mukand, J.A., Saleh, M., Caplan, A.H., Branner, A., Chen, D., Penn, R.D., Donoghue, J.P.: Neuronal ensemble control of prosthetic devices by a human with tetraplegia. Nature 442(7099), 164–171 (July 2006)
4. Carmena, J.M., Lebedev, M.A., Crist, R.E., O'Doherty, J.E., Santucci, D.M., Dimitrov, D.F., Patil, P.G., Henriquez, C.S., Nicolelis, M.A.: Learning to control a brain-machine interface for reaching and grasping by primates, Public Library of Science Biology, vol. E42 (2003)
5. Kübler, A., Kotchoubey, B., Kaiser, J., Wolpaw, J., Birbaumer, N.: Brain-computer communication: Unlocking the locked in. Psychological Bulletin 127(3), 358–375 (2001)
6. Wolpaw, J.R., Birbaumer, N., McFarland, D.J., Pfurtscheller, G., Vaughan, T.M.: Brain-computer interfaces for communication and control. Clinical Neurophysiology 113(6), 767–791 (2002)
7. Dornhege, G., del Millán, J.R., Hinterberger, T., McFarland, D., Müller, K.-R. (eds.): Toward Brain-Computer Interfacing. MIT Press, Cambridge, MA in press (2007)
8. Birbaumer, N., Ghanayim, N., Hinterberger, T., Iversen, I., Kotchoubey, B., Kübler, A., Perelmouter, J., Taub, E., Flor, H.: A spelling device for the paralysed. Nature 398, 297–298 (1999)
9. Neuper, C., Müller, G., Kübler, A., Birbaumer, N., Pfurtscheller, G.: Clinical application of an eeg-based brain-computer interface: A case study in a patient with severe motor impairment. Clinical Neurophysiology 114(3), 399–409 (2003)
10. Scherer, R., Müller, G.R., Neuper, C., Graiman, B., Pfurtscheller, G.: An synchronously controlled EEG-based virtual keyboard: Improvement of the spelling rate. IEEE Transactions on Neural Systems and Rehabilitation Engineering 51(6), 979–984 (2004)
11. Farwell, L.A., Donchin, E.: Talking off the top of your head: toward a mental prosthesis utilizing event-related brain potentials. Electroencephalography and Clinical Neurophysiology 70, 510–523 (1988)

12. Kaper, M., Ritter, H.: Generalizing to new subjects in brain-computer interfacing. In: Proceedings of the 26th Annual International Conference IEEE EMBS, San Francisco, pp. 4363–4366 (2004)
13. Krusienski, D.J., Sellers, E.W., Cabestaing, F., Bayoudh, S., McFarland, D.J., Vaughan, T.M., Wolpaw, J.R.: A comparison of classification techniques for the P300 speller. Journal of Neural Engineering 3(4), 299–305 (December 2006)
14. Elbert, T., Rockstroh, B., Lutzenberger, W., Birbaumer, N.: Biofeedback of slow cortical potentials. I. Electroencephalography and Clinical Neurophysiology 48, 293–301 (1980)
15. Blankertz, B., Dornhege, G., Krauledat, M., Müller, K.-R., Kunzmann, V., Losch, F., Curio, G.: The Berlin Brain-Computer Interface: EEG-based communication without subject training. IEEE Transactions on Neural Systems and Rehabilitation Engineering 14(2), 147–152 (2006)
16. Williamson, J., Murray-Smith, R.: Dynamics and probabilistic text entry. In: Murray-Smith, R., Shorten, R. (eds.) Proceedings of the Hamilton Summer School on Switching and Learning in Feedback systems. LNCS, vol. 3355, pp. 333–342. Springer, Heidelberg (2005)
17. Williamson, J.: Continuous Uncertain Interaction, Ph.D. thesis, Department of Computing Science, University of Glasgow (2006)
18. Müller, K.-R., Krauledat, M., Dornhege, G., Curio, G., Blankertz, B.: Machine learning and applications for brain-computer interfacing. In: Proceedings of HCI International, Beijing, P.R. China, 2007, submitted (2007)
19. Blankertz, B., Dornhege, G., Lemm, S., Krauledat, M., Curio, G., Müller, K.-R.: The Berlin Brain-Computer Interface: Machine learning based detection of user specific brain states. Journal of Universal Computer Science 12(6), 581–607 (2006)
20. Blankertz, B., Dornhege, G., Krauledat, M., Kunzmann, V., Losch, F., Curio, G., Müller, K.-R.: The berlin brain-computer interface: Machine-learning based detection of user specific brain states. In: Dornhege, G., del Millán, J.R., Hinterberger, T., McFarland, D., Müller, K.-R. (eds.) Toward Brain-Computer Interfacing, MIT press, Cambridge, MA in press (2007)
21. Bell, T., Cleary, J., Witten, I.: Data compression using adaptive coding and partial string matching. IEEE Transactions on Communications 32(4), 396–402 (1984)
22. Cleary, J., Teahan, W., Witten, I.: Unbounded length contexts for PPM. In: DCC-95, pp. 52–61. IEEE Computer Society Press, Los Alamitos (1995)
23. Teahan, W.J., Cleary, J.G.: The entropy of English using PPM-based models. In: Data Compression Conference, pp. 53–62 (1996)
24. Dunlop, M.D.: Watch-top text-entry: Can phone-style predictive text-entry work with only 5 buttons? In: Brewster, S., Dunlop, M.D. (eds.) Mobile Human-Computer Interaction – MobileHCI 2004. LNCS, vol. 3160, pp. 342–346. Springer, Heidelberg (2004)
25. Ward, D.J., MacKay, D.J.C.: Fast hands-free writing by gaze direction. Nature 418(6900), 838 (2002)
26. Wolpaw, J.R., McFarland, D.J., Vaughan, T.M., Schalk, G.: The Wadsworth Center brain-computer interface (BCI) research and development program. IEEE Transactions on Neural Systems and Rehabilitation Engineering 11(2), 207–207 (2003)

EOG Pattern Recognition Trial for a Human Computer Interface

Sara Brunner[1], Sten Hanke[2], Siegfried Wassertheuer[2], and Andreas Hochgatterer[2]

[1] University of Applied Sciences Linz – FH Linz Medizintechnik
[2] Austrian Research Centers GmbH – ARC
sten.hanke@arcsmed.at

Abstract. The setup of a human computer interaction electrooculography (EOG) measurement trail for developing pattern recognition algorithms is described. With an easy to wear EOG measurement device we relized performance tests with a group of normal individuals as well as with one individual suffering from multiple sclerosis (MS). The individuals had to perform different eye movement patterns for coding information to control the environment. Different patterns of recognition in the time domain have been tried and implemented to perform online performance tests. The aim is to develop an EOG based communication device passed on pattern recognition algorithms for user with limited functionality.

Keywords: Electrooculography, EOG, pattern recognition, human computer interface.

1 Introduction

The bulk of human computer interactions occur via standard input devices like keyboard or mouse. An EOG-input device could enable handicapped people who are not able to use standard input devices, to use the computer [4,5].

We developed a new possibility to apply electrodes in an effective, but simple way to the users face. Due to the trigger generation via pattern recognition the device will be usable even from persons suffering from amyotrophic lateral sclerosis (ALS) or multiple sclerosis (MS) [4,5].

To obtain a stable human machine interface that is independent of the current eye position, we investigated if eye movement patterns can be used to encode distinct commands.

We studied if EOG-signals, measured by the EOG-head device could provide sufficient signal-to-noise ratio for subsequent signal processing, even if no conductive paste is used and the skin is not pretreated.

Three different approaches of pattern recognition in time-domain has been developed, tested and evaluated. Finally, an online pattern recognition was realized in Matlab.

C. Stephanidis (Ed.): Universal Access in HCI, Part II, HCII 2007, LNCS 4555, pp. 769–776, 2007.

Patients suffering from ALS, high cervical spinal cord injury, or advanced cases of MS are highly constricted in their motility and communication, and are therefore excluded from interacting with computers and communication systems. Our system provides a comfortable solution for communication with eye movements even if the eye movements are already influenced by any kind of disease [1].

During the study there appeared several questions concerning performance and feasibility for recapitulating the different patterns. One of these questions was the usability for ALS or MS patients and their efficiency for generating and repeating different eye movement patterns.

We also wanted to have a look at the coherence between the generated eye movement and the submitted information. The study was aimed to clarify what kind of eye movement patterns will be generated and how easily they can be distinguished using different appendages of pattern recognition algorithms.

2 Material and Methods

So far six healthy subjects and one MS-patient have been tested. The MS-patient is able to move his head and to speak slowly but cannot move his limbs. Presently he uses a head-mounted mouse for computer control. Table 1 gives information on the different subjects involved in the experiments. The head circumference was important, due to a different head circumference there will be a different positioning and pressure of the measurement electrodes because of the fixed head device (Figure 1). This could cause a different magnitude of the EOG signals which should, as a demand, have no influence on the pattern recognition. The head circumference was measured above the eyebrows and above the ears, and was used only for orientation.

Table 1. Participants of the experiment ranged by age

	Sex	**Age**	**Head Circumference [cm]**	**Diseases**	**Glasses/ Lenses**
Subject 5	male	17	56.0	No	No
Subject 1	female	18	53.0	No	Yes
Subject 3	male	20	58.0	No	No
Subject 7	female	22	56.0	No	Yes
Subject 2	male	27	58.0	No	Yes
Subject 4	female	29	53.0	No	No
Subject 6	male	41	54.5	MS	Yes

For getting a huge number of different eye movement sequences, the subjects had to code 18 different terms, divided into four groups. Each pattern was recorded three times per session, and two sessions were held within a month. The length of recorded data was limited to three seconds (600 data points).

The first group was the ‘direction’ block: the subjects had to code ‘left’, ’right’, ’up’, ’down’ and ‘enter’. The second block was a ‘number’ block, where numbers from one to five had to be converted into eye movements. The third block contained the commands 'yes', 'no', 'help' and 'switch light' and the fourth block was the 'color' block, containing 'red', 'blue', 'yellow' and 'green'. The subjects could choose freely how to code the terms, but were not allowed to use the same eye movement sequence twice in one block. The subjects recorded their eye movement sequences in order to remind them at the second session, when they had to redo the same movements for each command.

For a convenient handling of the EOG electrodes we developed a comfortable, simple head device which allows easy application of five gold cup electrodes to the subjects face without abrading the skin or using conductive paste. The electrodes were placed at the two outer canthi (horizontal EOG), above and under the right orbit (vertical EOG) and at the forehead (common electrode).

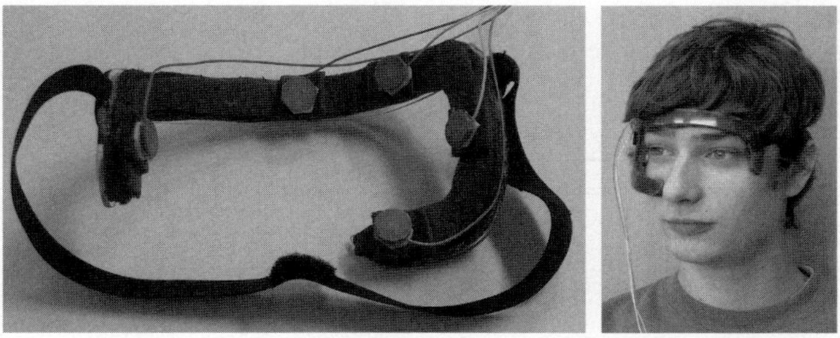

Fig. 1. Left: Five gold cup electrodes are integrated into the prototype of the EOG-Head Device, which is ergonomically designed for human heads. Right: A subject wearing the Head Device.

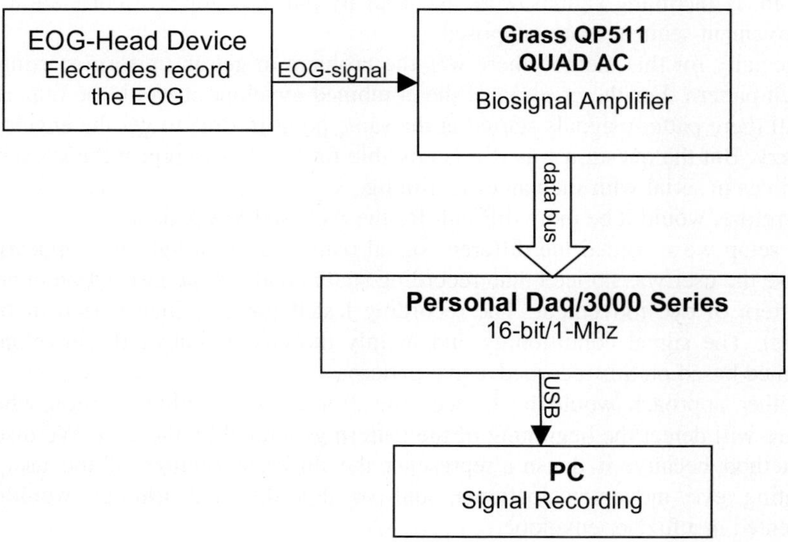

Fig. 2. Structure of the measurement chain [4,5]

For the horizontal and vertical measuring channel the two corresponding electrodes and the common electrode of the head device were connected respectively with the *Grass QP511 Quad Amplifier System* via a 3-lead input cable (*CAB-21572*). The electrode signals were amplified (factor 5000) and bandpass filtered (1 Hz – 300 Hz)[2], before they were sampled with the 16-bit/1-MHz analog-to-digital converter *iotech Personal Daq/3000 Series*. The sample rate was defined with 200 Hz. The digital data were imported with *Matlab – Data Acquisition Toolbox*.

The first step in our analysis was to investigate the repeatability of the individual eye movement patterns, which was rated by the similarity of the repeated patterns. Then we evaluated three different procedures to classify the eye movement patterns:

1) The first method was to evaluate the correlation coefficient of reference patterns (one for each term) and the actual signal. All signals for correlation were 600 data points long. Signals were counted as 'equal' when the correlation coefficient was bigger than 0.6 with a confidence level of 90 percent.

$$r = \frac{\sum_{i=1}^{n} x_i y_i - n\overline{xy}}{\sqrt{\left(\sum_{i=1}^{n} x_i^2 - n\overline{x}^2\right)\left(\sum_{i=1}^{n} y_i^2 - n\overline{y}^2\right)}}, \quad -1 \le r \le 1 \tag{1}$$

Formula for the calculation of the correlation coefficient. [3].

2) From three recorded signals of one coded term an 'envelope' was built with tolerance (20 percent in amplitude, 10 data points in time). The aim was to get out of three generated signals, a signal course where all of the three generated patterns are fitting in. If incoming signals were enclosed by the 'envelope', a correlation of the eye movement sequence was supposed.

Especially for this method there was the problem to get an uniform starting point for each pattern. For the creation of the combined envelope it would be important to have all there pattern signals started at the same point in time to get the envelope not too fuzzy. But the question was if it is possible for the user to repeat the same pattern three times in serial with such an exact timing.

Therefore, would it be more difficult for the ALS and MS patients?
In our setup we recorded the different signal patterns after a light was appearing. In that case the user was noticed that recording started and got the instruction to perform the pattern of eye movement. The recording lasted for a defined period of time (3 seconds). The signal conditioning and mainly the calculation of the envelope was performed based on this recorded signal patterns.

Another approach would be to start the 3 seconds recording session when the software will detect the beginning of the pattern generated by the user. We discarded that method because it doesn't represents the different timings of the user when generating eye movement patterns, and so this different timings wouldn't be represented in a fuzzier envelope.

3) For the third procedure, five levels were defined and each band got a corresponding value. The levels have been defined in that way that they are uniformly distributed

over the signal amplitude. For the horizontal EOG the levels were at 0, 0.2, 0.4, 0.6 and 0.8 mV; for the vertical EOG the levels were at 0, 0.1, 0.2, 0.3 and 0.4 mV with corresponding values 0, 0.25, 0.5, 0.75 and 1. An algorithm converted the signal into a sequence of values, which was then used to classify the pattern.

For the implementation of the online-pattern recognition we decided to use the correlation coefficient within the algorithm. The measurement chain was the same as described above, only the Matlab-script was changed so the signals were processed online. For pattern recognition, the subject repeated one eye movement sequence three times. The correlation coefficients of each pattern with each other pattern were computed and the sum of the two coefficients for one signal was calculated. The signal with the highest value correlated best with both other signals and it was thought that this signal would even be the best reference pattern for the following signals. The best data set got normalized and saved as reference pattern. Continually 600 values of the incoming EOG-signal were normalized and compared with the reference pattern. If the correlation coefficient was greater than 0.6, the algorithm recognized the reference pattern.

The online-algorithm was tested with two subjects. They made eye-movement-sequences built with less than three gazes changes and repeated them. For testing false-positive results the subjects were asked to look around the room or to read some text at the computer monitor.

3 Results

Our tests indicated that simple patterns can be better reproduced than complex ones: the data show an inverse relationship between the complexity of the pattern and the

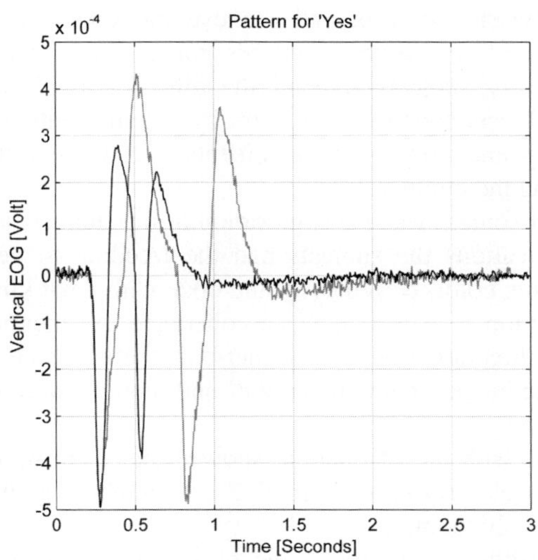

Fig. 3. For coding 'Yes' the subject made two blinks. The graph shows two out of six data sets. The correlation between these two signals is as low as 0.14, although the subject believed it repeated the movements in the same way.

probability of a correct reproduction. The best pattern reached a correlation coefficient between 0.93 and 0.99 for all six repeats, while for some complex patterns it was as low as 0.07. We were surprised to find that vertical movements can be repeated more easily than horizontal ones, even if the horizontal ones have greater amplitudes.

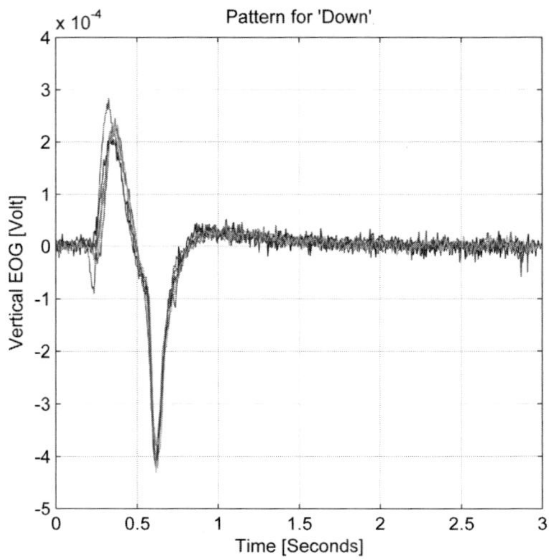

Fig. 4. The subject coded the term 'Down' by moving its eyes down and back to the middle position. The figure shows all six data sets which are highly congruent.

The relation between the term and the eye movement sequence showed that different subjects used the same sequences for coding terms. Especially in the 'direction' block every subject included the direction information in his/her eye movements. The subjects coded the numbers by counting either with blinks or with changes between up and down eye movements, e.g. three blinks or up-down-up-movement for coding the number three.

Interesting in that context was the exploration of the subjects to generated patterns. Without any specifications the subjects had the freedom to decide which kind of information (direction, color, etc.) they would code with what kind of eye movement. We had the assumption that there may be coherence. As mentioned, the coherence was apparent in the direction block but furthermore there was no appreciable relation. The terms within the blocks 'communication' and 'colors' were coded differently by every subject.

But the first trails with the MS patient showed that there maybe differences. The MS-patient built an exception: He coded every number by its own without any obvious context between them.

The best classification results were achieved with the correlation approach. Due to normalized data the influence of time delay within the eye movement sequences on the correlation coefficient was minimized. We got good results even with the envelope approach, but the algorithm could not compute an appropriate 'envelope' for every signal. As the third method, conversion between signal and assigned value, was too strict an identification of the pattern was hardly ever possible.

The online pattern recognition led to a probability of pattern recognition of 80 percent. The false-positive results were less than 5 percent. As the system was tested only with one pattern each session, false identified patterns were not obtained. The probability of correct assignment could be enhanced up to 95% by using simple, easy repeatable eye-movement-sequences.

4 Discussion

The EOG-Head Device is a useful, easy to handle tool for applying electrodes to the face. It allows EOG-recording with minimal preparatory work and required space, which is an advantage over already available gaze-tracking-systems or EOG-based control systems.

Due to the similar frequencies of different eye movements we could not achieve satisfactory results with pattern recognition in frequency domain. We analyzed the frequency spectrum of the eye movements 'left-right-middle' versus 'right-left-middle' and 'left-middle' versus 'right-middle'. The frequencies were all in the range of 0 to 15 Hz and a significant difference between them was not observable.

Our tests indicated that for a successful transfer of this technology from the laboratory to the bedside, certain minimum criteria have to be met. For example, the patients must be able to repeat the pattern often enough to train the system with sufficient ease. This is not a restriction for healthy subjects, and the technology holds the promise of a flexible, gaze independent human machine interface.

It has to be investigated if eye movements can be trained in order to improve the correlation between EOG-signals derived from subjectively equal eye movements. Therefore, it will be important to make the pattern recognition as fuzzy as essential but give the chance to distinguish between similar patterns. The similarity of the patterns depends on the possibility to repeat and replicate the single pattern. Therefore, in the following studies it should be clarified which patterns could be reproduced and are still to be distinguished in automatic detection. Furthermore it must be clarified if for MS and ALS patients some patterns are more difficult to replicate like it seems according to the pilot survey.

A possible experiment design could have five default eye movement sequences with three gaze changes each. The subjects will have to train these movements with a feedback mechanism. At first the goal could be to repeat the pattern three times, so that the computer can accept them as 'equal'. Advanced subject will have to repeat the same eye movements within a longer period of time (e.g. every 15 minutes) to see if people are able to train their eye movements.

While the data are currently evaluated in MATLAB, the final online pattern recognition algorithm will be implemented in a microcontroller MSP430 connected to a wireless transmission unit.

References

1. Jacobs, L., Bozian, D., Heffner Jr., RR., Barron, SA.: An eye movement disorder in amytrophic lateral sclerosis. Neurology 31, 1282–1287 (1981)
2. Oster, PJ., Stern, JA.: Electrooculography. In: Martin, I., Venables, PH. (eds.) Techniques in Psychophysiology, John Wiley & Sons, New York (1980)
3. Papula, L.: Mathematische Formelsammlung für Ingenieure und Naturwissenschaftler, 8. Auflage, Vieweg & Sohn Verlag Wiesbaden (2003)
4. Hanke, S., Mina, S., Morgenstern, U., Bammer, M., Poll, R.: Utilization of an EOG based controlling device with Body Area Network connectivity. In: proceedings DGBMT 2005 Nuernberg Germany (2005)
5. Hanke, S., Mina, S.: EOG controlled computer system with Body Area Network connectivity. In: proceedings OEGBMT 2004 Graz Austria (2004)

Continuous Recognition of Human Facial Expressions Using Active Appearance Model

Kyoung-Sic Cho and Yong-Guk Kim

Department of Computer Engineering, Sejong University, Seoul, Korea
nopnse@sju.ac.kr, ykim@sejong.ac.kr

Abstract. Recognizing human facial expressions continuously is useful since it has many potential applications. We have implemented a continuous facial expression recognition system using Active Appearance Model (AAM). AAM has been widely used in face tracking, face recognition, and object recognition tasks. In this study, we adopt an independent AAM using Inverse Compositional Image Alignment method. The evaluation of this system carried out with the standard Cohn-Kanade facial expression database. Result shows that it could useful for many applications.

Keywords: Active Appearance Model (AAM.), Facial Expression Recognition, Object Tracking, Inverse Compositional Alignment Method.

1 Introduction

Facial expression recognition is one of the crucial ways to infer human emotion. Facial emotions are basically categorized into six facial expressions (surprise, fear, sadness, anger, disgust, happiness). The process flow of the present system is shown in Figure 1. Facial expression images are captured from a web camera. Active appearance model includes various shape and appearance parameters. With these images, AAM instance is generated, and its emotion is classified by EFM.

We first review the AAM in section 2. Then, the process of EFM classifier is described in Section 3. The performance of the system is evaluated using Cohn-Kanade facial expression database in Section 4. Finally, we will summarize our work in Section 5.

2 Active Appearance Model

AAM is firstly proposed in [2]. Typical applications of AAM are for modeling and recognizing the faces. And yet, AAM is also effective in modeling other object. In addition, its model can be transferred to other application. AAM created once for face recognition, for example, can be useful for facial expression recognition or tracking faces [1]. The main purpose of AAM is building a new model instance by finding the best matched parameters between input images and the model with a fitting algorithm.

C. Stephanidis (Ed.): Universal Access in HCI, Part II, HCII 2007, LNCS 4555, pp. 777–783, 2007.

The fitting algorithm, which is a non-linear mode, iterates itself until the parameters of both shape and appearance satisfy some particular values. For instance, when the parameter of shape is measured, we can fit an input image on the coordinate frame of the model. After such match, the error between the instance of the model and pixels within the shape of input image could be acquired. This error would be applied for the fitting algorithm in order to update the parameters. Iterating this process would make optimized parameters through fitting algorithm. We adopted an Inverse Compositional Image Alignment, one of fitting algorithm used this system will be illustrated in section 2.2.

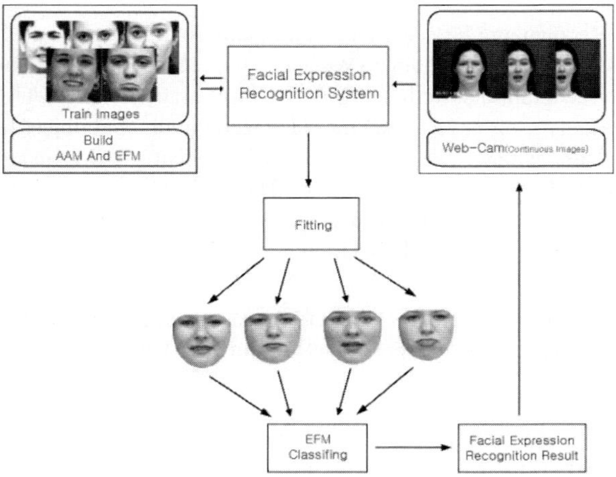

Fig. 1. Facial expression recognition system

2.1 Model Instance

Firstly, the shape of the AAM is created by combining the vectors which is made by marking on images manually.

$$\mathbf{s} = \mathbf{s}_0 + \sum_{i=1}^{n} p_i \mathbf{s}_i \tag{1}$$

In equation (1), p_i means the parameters of shape, s_0 indicates a base shape, and s_i represents shape vectors. The eigenvectors for the shape can be obtained by using Principal Component Analysis (PCA). They are the n eigenvectors corresponding to the n largest eigenvalues. Before applied PCA, AAM usually use Procrustes analysis in order to normalize Landmark points marked manually [1].

Secondly, the appearance of the AAM is defined by a pixel in a base mesh. Like the shape, appearance is also generated by the linear combination of the pixel intensity.

$$A(\mathbf{x}) = A_0(\mathbf{x}) + \sum_{i=1}^{m} \lambda_i A_i(\mathbf{x}) \tag{2}$$

λ_i indicates the appearance parameters, A_i represents the appearance vectors, and A_0 is a base appearance. After finding both the shape parameters and the appearance parameters, the AAM instance is generated by locating each pixel of appearance to the inner side of the current shape with piecewise affine warp. A model instance is indicated as equation (3).

$$M(\mathbf{W}(\mathbf{x};\mathbf{p})) = A(\mathbf{x}) \tag{3}$$

The parameters of both shape and appearance are obtained by a fitting algorithm. Figure 2 shows the process of creating the model instance.

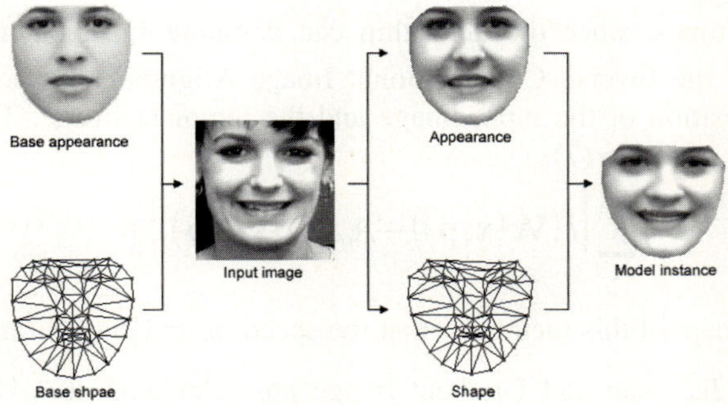

Fig. 2. Generation of an AAM instance

2.2 Inverse Compositional Image Alignment

The aim of the image alignment is to find a location of a fixed template image on an input image. Lucas and Kanade first proposed the Image Alignment Method [3]. Their algorithm is to locally align on the fixed template on an image, shown by equation (4).

$$\sum_{\mathbf{x}} \left[A_0(\mathbf{x}) - I(\mathbf{W}(\mathbf{x};\mathbf{p}))^2 \right] \tag{4}$$

The parameter $\mathbf{p}$ plays a role in minimizing errors between the fixed template $A_0(\mathbf{x})$ and the input image $I(\mathbf{x})$. In $\mathbf{x} = (x, y)^{\mathbf{T}}$ is the coordinator of pixel. The parameter $\mathbf{p}$ was linear, although $I(\mathbf{x})$ was non-linear. Thus, this formula is a non-linear optimization problem. To solve this problem linearly, Lucas-Kanade algorithm assumed that $\mathbf{p}$ was already known. Then, the algorithm increases the difference of $\mathbf{p}$ repeatedly, marked $\Delta\mathbf{p}$ in (5).

$$\sum_{\mathbf{x}} \left[A_0(\mathbf{x}) - I(\mathbf{W}(\mathbf{x};\mathbf{p}+\Delta\mathbf{p}))^2 \right] \quad \textbf{(5)}$$

The way of increasing $\mathbf{p}$ is that adding $\Delta\mathbf{p}$ to $\mathbf{p}$. When changing the value of $\mathbf{p}$, the performance of Lucas-Kanade algorithm is very slow because three parameters, Jacobian, gradient image, and Hessian Matrix have to be computed over and over. To improve this performance, Forwards Compositional Image Alignment method is introduced. In this algorithm, $\mathbf{p}$ is changed by combining the $\mathbf{W}(\mathbf{x};\mathbf{p})$ and $\mathbf{W}(\mathbf{x};\Delta\mathbf{p})$ as mentioned in equation (6).

$$\sum_{\mathbf{x}} \left[A_0(\mathbf{x}) - I(\mathbf{W}(\mathbf{W}(\mathbf{x};\Delta\mathbf{p});\mathbf{p}))^2 \right] \quad (6)$$

In Forwards Compositional Image Alignment method, we do not need to compute Jacobian every times, since the algorithm can compute Jacobian in $(\mathbf{x};0)$. In this paper, we adopt the Inverse Compositional Image Alignment method, in which we exchange the position of the input image and the template image. The ICIA can be formulated as an equation (7).

$$\sum_{\mathbf{x}} \left[I(\mathbf{W}(\mathbf{x};\mathbf{p})) - A_0(\mathbf{W}(\mathbf{x};\Delta\mathbf{p}))^2 \right] \quad (7)$$

The main advantage of this method is that the speed of updating parameters $\mathbf{p}$ can be very fast, since Jacobian and Gradient Image are calculated at $A_0(\mathbf{x})$. Once those values are acquired at the initial stage, we can use those values whenever updating a new warp parameter. Figure 3 shows three images of tracking a face using this method.

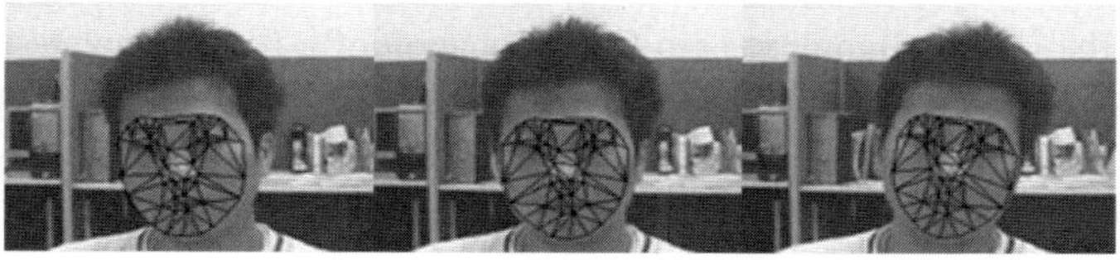

Fig. 3. Real time face tracking using ICIA

3 EFM Algorithm

Let Y be a random vector representing the lower dimensional feature. Let $w_1, w_2, \ldots, w_L$ and $N_1, N_2, \ldots, N_L$ denote the classes and the number of images within each class, respectively. Let $M_1, M_2, \ldots, M_L$ and M be the mean of the classes and the grand mean. The within-and between-class covariance matrices Σ_w and Σ_b are defined as follows:

$$\Sigma w = \sum_{i=1}^{L} P(w_i) E\{(Y - M_i)(Y - M_i)^t \mid w_i\} \tag{8}$$

$$\Sigma b = \sum_{i=1}^{L} P(w_i)(M_i - M)(M_i - M)^t \tag{9}$$

The EFM firstly diagonalizes the within-class covariance matrix Σw.

$$\Sigma w \Xi = \Xi \Gamma \text{ and } \Xi^t \Xi = I, \tag{10}$$

$$\Gamma^{-1/2} \Xi^t \Sigma w \Xi \Gamma^{-1/2} = I, \tag{11}$$

where Ξ, Γ are the eigenvector and the diagonal eigenvalue matrices of Σw, respectively. The EFM then proceeds to compute the between-class covariance matrix as follows:

$$\Gamma^{-1/2} \Xi^t \Sigma b \Xi \Gamma^{-1/2} = K_b, \tag{12}$$

The EFM diagonalizes the new between-class covariance matrix K_b.

$$K_b \Theta = \Theta \Delta \text{ and } \Theta^t \Theta = I, \tag{13}$$

where Θ, Δ are the eigenvector and the diagonal eigenvalue matrices of K_b, respectively. The overall transformation matrix of the EFM is finally defined as follows:

$$T = \Xi \Gamma^{-1/2} \Theta \tag{14}$$

4 Experiments and Performance

Facial expressions used, for the present study, were 4: neutral, sadness, happiness, and surprise. AAM model was established using 498 face images, and each image marked by 68 landmark points. For 54 neutral, 50 sadness, 50 happiness, and 50 surprise images, the EFM model was set up. Experiments were divided into two evaluations: one was an evaluation about how correctly each model classified images of facial expressions, and another was a test about how exactly the system analyzed sequential images including various facial expressions.

4.1 Performance Evaluation

For the performance evaluation, we employed 5 Cross Validation method, in which we took 1/5 facial expression images as a test set, and then used the rest as the EFM train set. Thus, the number of tests was five times, and each result is shown in Table 1 and 2. The result shows that the worst cases were for the neutral and sadness facial expressions. In the confusion matrix, note that the error was large between the neutral and sadness cases. It seems that it is rather difficult to distinguish between two subtle facial expressions.

Table 1. Recognition Result

	Test Image No.	Success No.	Rate(%)
Neutral	54	46	85.1
Sadness	50	41	82.0
Happiness	50	46	92.0
Surprise	50	45	90.0
Total	204	178	87.2

Table 2. Confusion Matrix

	Neutral	Sadness	Happiness	Surprise
Neutral	46	6	0	2
Sadness	8	41	0	1
Happiness	2	2	46	0
Surprise	5	0	0	45

4.2 Continuous Expression Image Analysis

Since the Cohn-Kanade database consists of sequential images of a facial expression, we are able to test our system for the continuous facial expression recognition cases using it. For instance, Figure 4 shows how the happiness expression evolves from the neutral one, in particular, between image sequence 4 and 7. Here, the horizontal axis represents the sequence number of the images, whereas the vertical axis indicates EFM distance between the facial expression ranks. After the sequence 7, the happiness expression becomes a dominant one with a large distance from the other expressions. The system can process 15 frames per second.

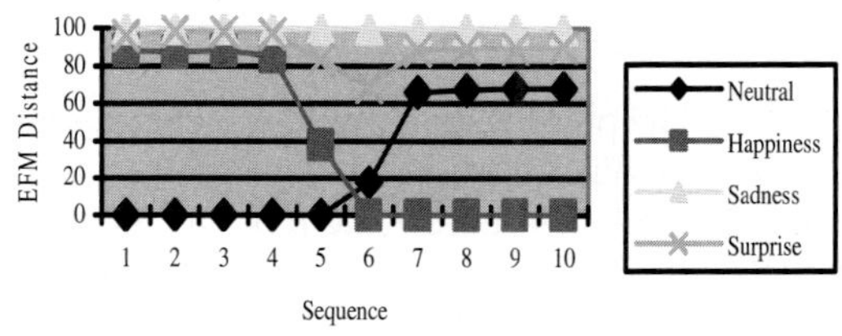

Fig. 4. Recognition of the surprise facial expression

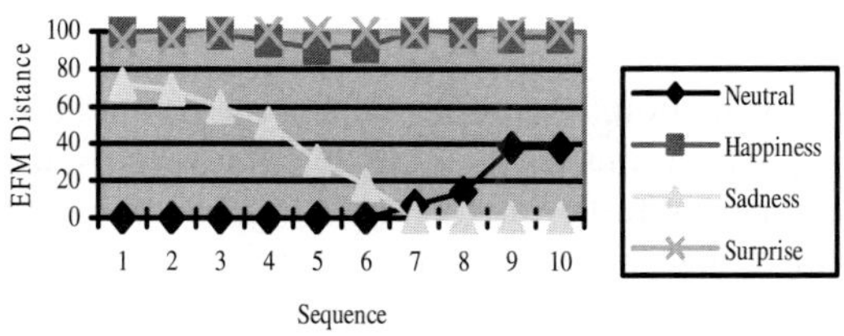

Fig. 5. Recognition of the sadness facial expression

Figure 5 shows that the sadness expression makes a distance from two expressions (happiness and surprise), as time goes by from sequence 2 to 6. And the neutral expression drifts from the bottom to upward direction. However, note that the distance between the neutral expression and the sadness one is not very far even at sequence 10, indicating that two expressions are, in a way, similar. This observation confirms the result of Table 2, in which the system appears to be confusing between two expressions.

5 Conclusions and Discussion

In this paper, we describe how real-time facial expression recognition system using AAM and EFM was implemented, and conducted two tests in order to examine the performance of the system. The result suggests that the system carried out facial expression recognition very well and it also operates in continuous facial expression recognition task. It is known that facial expression tends to accompany with head motion, we are working on a project that the head tracker is combined with the present facial expression tracker.

Acknowledgements. This work was supported by Seoul City Cluster Project.

References

1. Matthews, I., Baker, S.: Active Appearance Models revisited. International Journal of Computer vision, pp. 135–164 (2004)
2. Edwards, G.J., Taylor, C.J., Cootes, T.F.: Interpreting Face Images using Active Appearance Models. In: Proc. International Conference on Automatic Face and Gesture Recognition, pp. 300–305, (June 1998)
3. Lucas, B., Kanade, T.: An iterative image registration technique with an application to stereo vision. In: Proceedings of the International Joint Conference on Artificial Intelligence, pp. 674–679 (1981)

Robust Extraction of Moving Objects Based on Hue and Hue Gradient

Yoo-Joo Choi[1], Je-Sung Lee[1], and We-Duke Cho[2]

[1] Seoul University of Venture and Information, Department of Computer Science and Application, Seoul, Korea
yjchoi@suv.ac.kr, mpegman@paran.com
[2] Ajou University, Center of Excellence for Ubiquitous System, Suwon, Korea
chowd@ajou.ac.kr

Abstract. This paper presents a new method for robustly extracting moving objects in an environment with varying illuminations. The proposed method applies background subtraction scheme based on hue and hue gradient to minimize the effect of the illumination change. First, we train the background images in the HSI color space and build the Gaussian background model with respect to the hue and hue gradient. Next, image subtraction is performed between the trained background image and the current input image based on the Gaussian background model. Finally, the morphological operations are applied to remove the background noise. In this paper, we compare the previous subtraction schemes to our method applied to both the hand and body tracking in order to prove the robustness of the proposed method in sudden illumination changes.

1 Introduction

As the ubiquitous computing paradigms become more widely spread, intuitive human-computer interactions that do not employ cumbersome interaction devices has gained positive attention. In particular, vision-based interfaces have been an active and growing research area for the last decade due to the advantage of a vision-based approach, which promotes easy interaction for the users through natural motion and eliminating the use of any input devices. The vision-based interface offers various technical challenges for motion tracking which requires exact extraction of the human body from the video images and analyzing the variable appearance of human forms in the high dimensionality of the state space.

Robustness is an important feature of the user interface. Robustness of the vision-based interface is generally dependent on the accuracy of the human extraction from the input video images and the exact analysis of the human motion based on the segmented human body images. The segmentation of a human body in the input video images should be insensitive to the changes in the background and illumination. The background subtraction method is usually used to separate the human body region from the background. The numerous background subtraction methods based on different color models have been presented to reduce the effect of the illumination [1,3,4,5,6].

C. Stephanidis (Ed.): Universal Access in HCI, Part II, HCII 2007, LNCS 4555, pp. 784–791, 2007.

In this paper, we present a new background subtraction scheme based on hue and hue gradient to robustly extract a moving object in an environment with varying illuminations. The HSI color model is divided into hue, saturation and intensity factors. The hue factor generally represents the unique value of color itself while minimizing the effect of the illumination. The hue gradient image maintains the feature of the background image while reducing the effect of the shadow and illumination changes. Therefore, we propose the background subtraction scheme based on hue and hue gradient. In the proposed method, we train the background images in HSI color space and build the Gaussian background model with respect to hue and hue gradient. Next, background subtraction is performed between the trained background image and the current input image based on the Gaussian background model. Finally, morphological operations are applied to remove the background noise. We prove the robustness of the proposed method by comparing the results of the previous schemes with those of our scheme in the varying illumination environment.

The rest of the paper is organized as follows. We briefly summarize the features of the previous vision-based approaches in Section 2 and address background modeling based on hue and hue gradient in Section 3. Section 4 presents our background subtraction approach. Experimental results are shown in Section 5 and finally Section 6. concludes the paper.

2 Related Work

Vision-based interfaces can be categorized into two classes [2]. One is the marker-based approach and the other is the marker-free approach which generally uses the background subtraction techniques. The marker-based approach is able to extract the motion information by simply tracking the markers. However, this approach requires the user to wear a special suit with many markers and tracking these markers when multiple markers are occluded is prone to errors. In the marker-free approach, the special suit with markers is not necessary and the human body is generally extracted by applying the background subtraction techniques.

Previous background subtraction techniques have exploited the statistical color differences between an input video image and the background reference image. The background reference image is built during a certain period of the initial time [1,3,4, 6]. Hong and Woo [1] exploited the RGB and the normalized RGB color space for the background subtraction to reduce the shadow effect. Elgammal et al. [3] applied the chromaticity coordinates, that is, the normalized RG color space, for detection of the target without detecting its shadow. Thakkar[4] et al. proposed a novel technique for automatically extracting a moving object in gray-scale images captured by a moving camera. They basically exploited the intensity values for comparison of adjacent frame differences. Their approach can miss the motionless object because they use the adjacent frame differences to obtain the moving object area. Lee et al. [5] exploited the YCbCr color model to extract the skin color range among multiple moving objects. Lee [6] used the gray-scale intensity value in the moving object segmentation. He combined the pixel-based frame difference approach and the background difference approach and focused to connect the broken boundary of the moving objects. His approaches can also miss the motionless object.

3 Background Modeling Based on Hue and Hue Gradient

3.1 HSI(Hue-Saturation-Intensity) Color Space

The HSI color model was designed with graphic designers and artists in mind and how they perceive and think colors. The HSI color model consists of the saturation(the pureness of a color), hue(the color in itself) and intensity(the brightness of the color). This color model is represented by the basic triangle coordinate as shown in Fig. 1.

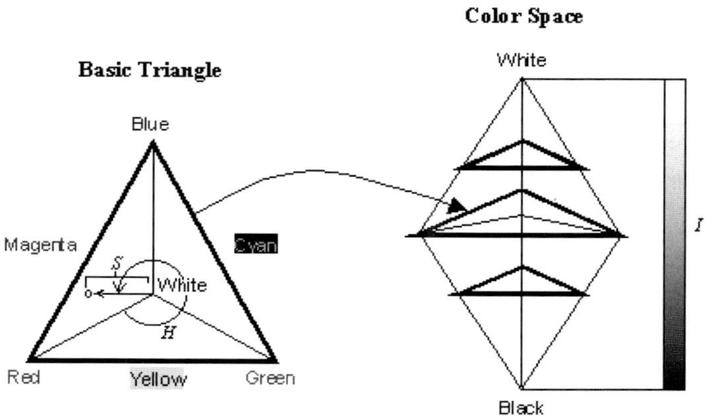

Fig. 1. HSI Color Model

Hue(H) is the angle of the vector over the basic triangle, starting from red (0 degrees). Saturation(S) is the proportional size of the module of the projection of the vector over the basic triangle. Intensity(I) is the distance from the end of the vector to the basic triangle. HSI color is converted from the RGB color space as Eq. 1.

$$H = \begin{cases} \theta & if \quad B \le G \\ 360 - \theta & if \quad B \succ G \end{cases}$$

$$\theta = \cos^{-1}\left(\frac{\frac{1}{2}[(R-G)+(R-B)]}{[(R-G)^2 + (R-B)(G-B)]^{1/2}} \right) \quad (1)$$

$$S = 1 - \frac{3}{(R+G+B)}[\min(R,G,B)]$$

$$I = \frac{1}{3}(R+G+B)$$

3.2 Background Modeling

We train the background images in HSI color space for fifty frames and all pixels of the static background scene image are modeled as a Gaussian distribution with respect to the hue and the hue gradient during background training. Each pixel of the background reference image is modeled as follows.

$$<\mu(H_i),\sigma(H_i),\mu(\Delta H_i),\sigma(\Delta H_i)> \tag{2}$$

where, $\mu(H_i)$, and $\sigma(H_i)$ are the vectors of the mean and standard deviation of pixel i's hue channel in HSI color space. $\mu(\Delta H_i)$, and $\sigma(\Delta H_i)$ are vectors of the mean and standard deviation of pixel i's hue gradient. Hue gradient is evaluated as Eq. 3.

$$\Delta H_{(x,y)} = \sqrt{(H_{(x+1,y)} - H_{(x,y)})^2 + (H_{(x,y+1)} - H_{(x,y)})^2} \tag{3}$$

where, $H_{(x,y)}$, $H_{(x+1,y)}$ and $H_{(x,y+1)}$ are the hue channel values in pixels (x, y), (x+1, y) and (x, y+1), respectively. The mean and standard deviation of the hue and hue gradient are gradually updated for the training as Eq. 4 and Eq. 5. Fig. 2 depicts the gradual progress to build the Gaussian background model.

Mean Update:

$$\begin{aligned}
&\mu(H_i(0)) = H_i(0) && t=0\\
&\mu(H_i(t)) = (1-\alpha)\mu(H_i(t-1)) + \alpha H_i(t) && t\geq 1\\
&\mu(\Delta H_i(0)) = \Delta H_i(0) && t=0\\
&\mu(\Delta H_i(t)) = (1-\alpha)\mu(\Delta H_i(t-1)) + \alpha\Delta H_i(t) && t\geq 1
\end{aligned} \tag{4}$$

Variance Update:

$$\begin{aligned}
&\sigma^2(H_i(0)) = (H_i(1) - \mu(H_i(0)))^2 && t=1\\
&\sigma^2(H_i(t)) = (1-\alpha)\sigma^2(H_i(t-1)) + \alpha(H_i(t) - \mu(H_i(t)))^2 && t\geq 2\\
&\sigma^2(\Delta H_i(0)) = (\Delta H_i(1) - \mu(\Delta H_i(0)))^2 && t=1\\
&\sigma^2(\Delta H_i(t)) = (1-\alpha)\sigma^2(\Delta H_i(t-1)) + \alpha(\Delta H_i(t) - \mu(\Delta H_i(t)))^2 && t\geq 2
\end{aligned} \tag{5}$$

where, t is the frame number and α is the constant for the weighted averaging.

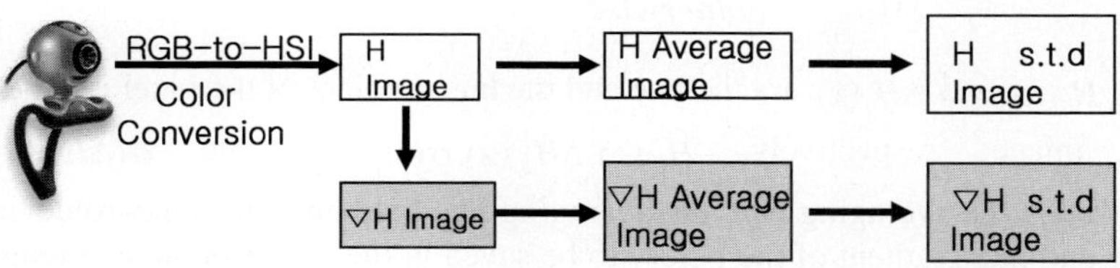

Fig. 2. Gradual Progress to build the Background Model

4 Moving Object Extraction Based on Background Subtraction

The general background subtraction technique is to subtract a current image from the reference background image. The proposed method exploits the hue and hue gradient of the pixel as the cue for the subtraction. Fig. 3 shows the overall procedure of the background modeling and background subtraction for the moving object extraction.

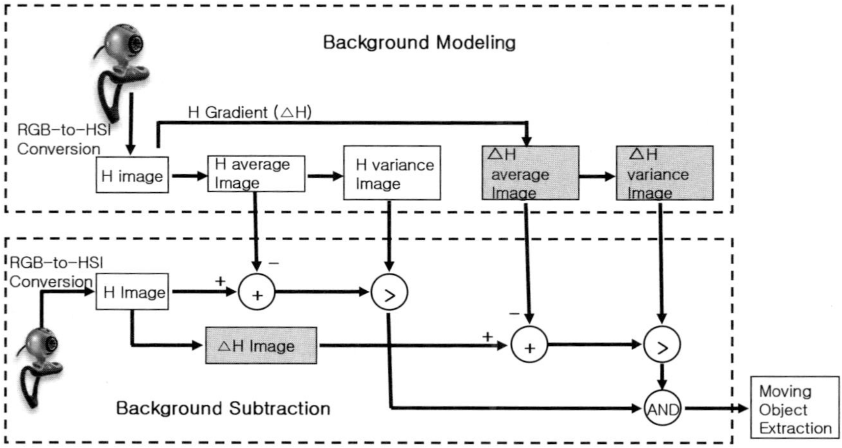

Fig. 3. Overall Procedure for the proposed subtraction

In order to extract the moving object, we compute the hue channel value and the hue gradient for each pixel of the current image frame. We then compare the computed hue and hue gradient values with those of the background model for each pixel as Eq. 6. If the subtraction values are greater than the threshold values which are determined based on the background variance images, those pixels belong to the moving object region.

$$R_i(x) = \begin{cases} 1, & \text{if} \quad |H_i(x) - H_{b_i}(x)| > \omega_1 \sigma(H_{b_i}(x)) \ \ \text{and} \\ & \quad |\Delta H_i(x) - \Delta H_{b_i}(x)| > \omega_2 \sigma(\Delta H_{b_i}(x)), \\ 0, & \text{otherwise} \end{cases} \tag{6}$$

where, $H_i(x)$ and $\Delta H_i(x)$ are the hue and the hue gradient of the pixel *i* in the current frame image, respectively. $H_{b_i}(x), \Delta H_{b_i}(x), \sigma(H_{b_i}(x))$ and $\sigma(\Delta H_{b_i}(x))$ are respectively the averaging hue, the averaging hue gradient, the standard deviation of the hue and hue gradient of the pixel *i* to be saved in the background averaging image and variance image. ω_1 and ω_2 are the constants that determine the threshold ranges. Finally, we apply the morphological opening and closing operations to remove the noise and enhance the quality of the moving object.

5 Experimental Results

5.1 Hand Tracking

We captured 320 x 240 24bit RGB images from the normal Web Cam called the Logitech QuickCam Chat for the hand tracking. We trained the background scene for fifty image frames with respect to the RGB, normalized RGB, hue and hue gradient.

In order to prove the robustness of the proposed method, we compared the results of the previous methods with those of the proposed method in the sudden illumination change made by switching the auxiliary light off. Table 1 shows the experimental results for the hand tracking. The background training was performed in the bright illumination condition and the first row of Table 1 shows the subtraction results in the same illumination condition as that for the background training. After turning the auxiliary light off, we performed the subtraction schemes without re-training the background scene. The second row of Table 1 shows the subtraction results after the sudden illumination change. The contour of the hand was robustly extracted by applying the proposed subtraction scheme.

Table 1. Comparison of background subtraction schemes for the hand tracking in the sudden illumination change

	Original Image	RGB-based Subtraction	Normalized RGB-based Subtraction	H-based Subtraction	H and H- Gradient Subtractio n
1	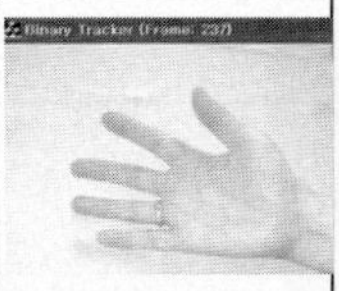	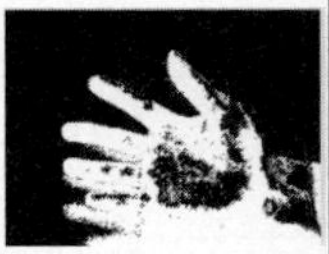	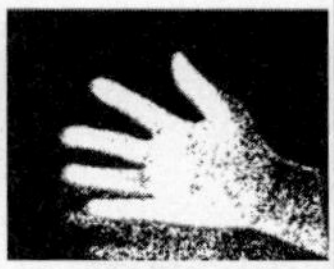		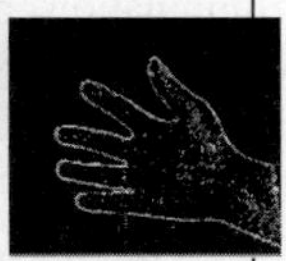
2			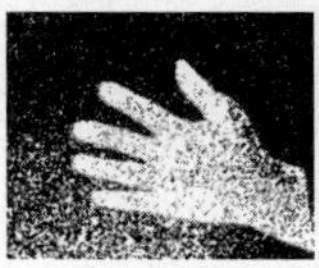		

5.2 Body Tracking

The experimental environment for the body tracking was installed as shown in Fig. 4. 640 x 480 frame images were captured in 30 FPS by two Dragonfly2 IEEE 1394 digital cameras. The projector and screen were installed in order to simulate a magic mirror. The moving human body was simultaneously extracted from the two synchronized frame images captured by two stereo cameras for 3-D tracking.

The experiment for the body tracking was performed in the same way as the hand tracking. We made a sudden illumination change by switching the auxiliary light off after the background training and the first body tracking. We then performed the body tracking without the new background modeling. The experimental results are as shown in Table 2. Among the previous subtraction schemes, the hue-based subtraction showed the most robust subtraction result. Table 2 compares the hue-based subtraction with hue and hue gradient-based subtraction. In sudden illumination change, the result of the hue-based subtraction included a lot of background noise, while the proposed subtraction scheme only produced a little amount of the background noise

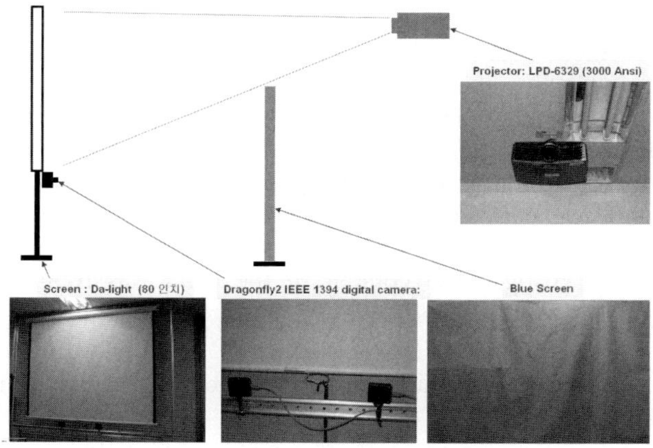

Fig. 4. Experimental environment for the body tracking

Table 2. Comparison of background subtraction schemes for the body tracking in the sudden illumination change

	H-based Subtraction		H and H-Gradient Subtraction	
1				
2				

6 Conclusions

This paper proposed a new background subtraction scheme based on hue and hue gradient. The proposed scheme was applied to the hand tracking and the body tracking to prove the robustness in the illumination change. The robustness of the proposed scheme was compared with those of the previous background subtraction schemes. The proposed scheme showed the most robust results in the hand and the body tracking during the sudden illumination change. In the proposed scheme, the background model is effectively built by gradually updating the averaging and variance images during the background scene training. The effect of the illumination change is minimized by exploiting the hue gradient as the cue of the background subtraction.

For the future work in the area of body tracking, we would like to extract the body feature points and track the body segments based on the extracted feature points in real time. The exact real-time body segment tracking has been an active challenge due to the errors from the segments occlusion and the high computation for the pose estimation. Real-time tracking of the body segments can be applied to many potential applications such as the magic mirror for the virtual dress room and gesture-based game interfaces.

Acknowledgements. This work was supported by the Ubiquitous Computing and Network(UCN) project, the Ministry of Information and Communication (MIC) 21st Century Frontier R&D Program in Korea.

References

1. Hong, D., Woo, W.: A Background Subtraction for a Vision-based User Interface. In: Proc. of PCM03-CD, 1B3.3 (2003)
2. Woo, W., Kim, N., Wong, K., Tadenuma, M.: Sketch on Dynamic Gesture Tracking and Analysis Exploiting Vision-based 3D Interface. In: Proc. of SPIE PW-EI-VCIP'01 4310, 656–666 (2001)
3. Elgammal, A., Duraiswami, R., Harwood, D., Davis, L.S.: Background and Foreground Modeling using Non-parametric Kernel Density Estimation for Visual Surveillance. In: Proc. of the IEEE 90(7), 1151–1163 (2002)
4. takoor, N. , Gao, J.: Automatic Video Object Detection and Recognition with Camera in Motion. In: Proc. of IEEE International Conference on Image Processing (2005)
5. Lee, K.-M., Lee, Y.-M.: Adpative Model-based Multi-object Tracking Robust to Illumination Changes and Overlapping. Journal of the Korea Information Science Society(Software and Applications) 32(5), 449–460 (2005)
6. Lee, H.S.: Moving Object Segmentation using Space-oriented Object Boundary Linking and Background Registration. Journal of the Korea Information Science Society(Software and Applications) 32(2), 128–139 (2005)

An Adaptive Vision System Toward Implicit Human Computer Interaction

Peng Dai, Linmi Tao, Xiang Zhang, Ligeng Dong, and Guangyou Xu

Tsinghua National Lab on Information Science & Technology, Tsinghua University, 100084 Beijing, China
{daip02,dongligeng99}@mails.tsinghua.edu.cn,
{linmi,xiang-zhang,xgy-dcs}@tsinghua.edu.cn

Abstract. In implicit human computer interaction, computers are required to understand users' actions and intentions so as to provide proactive services. Visual processing has to detect and understand human actions and then transform them as the implicit input. In this paper an adaptive vision system is presented to solve visual processing tasks in dynamic meeting context. Visual modules and dynamic context analysis tasks are organized in a bidirectional scheme. Firstly human objects are detected and tracked to generate global features. Secondly current meeting scenario is inferred based on these global features, and in some specific scenarios face and hand blob level visual processing tasks are fulfilled to extract visual information for the analysis of individual and interactive events, which can further be adopted as implicit input to the computer system. The experiments in our smart meeting room demonstrate the effectiveness of the proposed framework.

Keywords: Implicit human computer interaction, visual processing, dynamic context Analysis.

1 Introduction

Implicit human computer interaction is the fundamental HCI technology for pervasive computing. Unlike traditional human computer interfaces, computer systems are required to detect users' actions by multi-modal sensors and further understand users' intentions according to the current context of the environment, which can be considered as the implicit input to the systems and implicit output is provided for the users adapting to current situation. Implicit human computer interaction will enable the users to obtain services from computers without being distracted due to the operations involved. As the results, computers will become better tools and be possible to provide ubiquitous information services to the users. The pre-requirement to carry out implicit HCI is to generate implicit input according to users' actions. Therefore computers are required to understand users' actions and behaviors from the low level sensor data, i.e. to bridge the semantic gap. Fig. 1 illustrates the implicit HCI between human and computer systems in a smart meeting room environment.

C. Stephanidis (Ed.): Universal Access in HCI, Part II, HCII 2007, LNCS 4555, pp. 792–801, 2007.

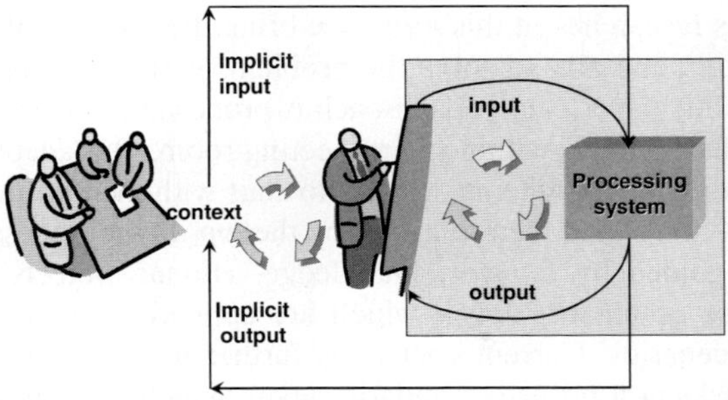

Fig. 1. Implicit human computer interaction

Visual information plays a vital role in implicit human computer interaction due to their expressiveness and unintrusiveness. In real-life applications visual processing can be performed at various granularity levels, which should be determined by current context. Therefore computer vision system has to be adaptive and complies to the requirements of dynamic context environment. Smart meeting room is adopted here to serve as a test-bed for exploring human-centered visual computing, which works in a dynamic context environment. Human individual and group actions are inferred and taken as implicit input, and multiple visual processing modules are effectively integrated to generate reasoning cues.

Although a lot of research efforts have been devoted to individual and group actions analysis in meeting room scenarios, such as Multimodal Meeting Tracker from CMU [1] and AMI System from IDIAP [2], still the problem of implicit HCI has not attracted much attention and few efforts were made to investigate visual processing problems in the light of context aware computing. In CMU's CAMEO system [3], individual states and meeting states were inferred by Finite State Machine models separately, where only users' standing-sitting states were considered and fixed visual processing mechanism was used. In [4] and [5] Layered Hidden Markov Models were used for the recognition of individual and group actions in meeting scenarios based on audio-visual information, where only fixed background subtraction and skin detection was used and no tracking modules were introduced. Hakeem and Shah [6] proposed an ontology and taxonomy framework for the offline classification of meeting videos, where head and hands were tracked with manual initialization and adjustment. Al-Hames and Rigoll [7] employed Dynamic Bayesian Network to recognize group actions in meeting video sequences based on audio-visual features, among which only global motion features were adopted as visual cues. Most of the research work mentioned above performed offline event analysis, and vision systems were designed in predetermined and fixed context. Recently Trivedi et al [8] tried to solve the issue of dynamic context analysis and presented a distributed vision system paradigm for dynamic context capture in indoor environments, where multiple sensors were set and various visual modules such as human detection, tracking and identification were integrated. In their system, variations of user's locations and face orientations were used to drive the top-down control for the best perspective selection among multiple cameras, which shares some characteristics with our concept of implicit input, but it seems lack of context aware mechanism.

Unlike previous researches in this topic, we bring the concept of implicit HCI into smart meeting room, and aim to solve the problem of visual computing in dynamic context model. In this paper, a novel approach is proposed to detect and track users at appropriate granularity levels within smart meeting room. Our adaptive vision system is operated in a bidirectional scheme, namely to start with the bottom-up processing at a coarse granularity level and then followed by the top-down processing at the refined granularity level guided by *a priori* knowledge. Human objects are detected and tracked at a coarse granularity level, which are applied as global features to infer current meeting scenarios. Current context is further used to control face and hand blob processing tasks at a refined granularity level, which provides local features for the analysis of individual and interactive actions.

The rest of the paper is organized as follows. Section 2 gives the system overview. Section 3 presents our approach of human detection and tracking. Section 4 describes the context-driven blob processing tasks. Experimental results are presented in Section 5 and conclusions are drawn in Section 6.

2 System Overview

The meeting room is equipped with multiple sensors so as to acquire the audio-visual information about the environment, as is illustrated in Fig. 2. In our current work, only three fixed cameras are considered in the vision system, which are set to acquire video frames from three distinct perspectives.

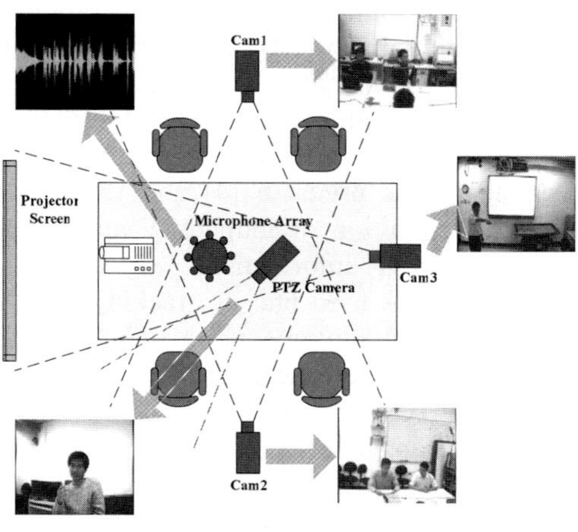

Fig. 2. Multimodal sensor setting in smart meeting room

Dynamic context model in meeting scenarios is defined in a multi-layer structure. The bottom layer includes human presence states and their individual actions such as raising hand to ask questions, looking at someone, nodding or shaking head etc. The intermediate layer includes those interactive events among participants. In the top layer, three typical types of group meeting scenarios are defined: *presentation*, in which one participant gives speech in front of the projector screen and others keep seated; *discussion*, during which four participants are all seated and talking over some topic; *meeting break*, when some participants are not seated and perform random activities.

In this paper, a novel framework is proposed for adaptive visual processing in smart meeting room. In our framework, visual processing and dynamic context analysis are tightly integrated and organized in a bidirectional loop, as is shown in Fig. 3. For the start of the scheme, human detection and tracking functions are performed to extract features about individual states such as human presence and standing-sitting states, based on which overall meeting scenarios, i.e. the meeting context, are inferred. In this regard this kind of features is of global. The meeting context possesses a selectivity mechanism to guide the follow-up visual tasks, i.e. to look into what type of visual features next. For example, only when the meetings proceed to specific scenarios such as presentation and discussion, face and hand blob processing tasks are to be fulfilled so as to analyze individual actions and interactive events. Further, during presentation and discussion, iconic actions (e.g. raising hand and pointing), focus of attention and attitudes need to be analyzed.

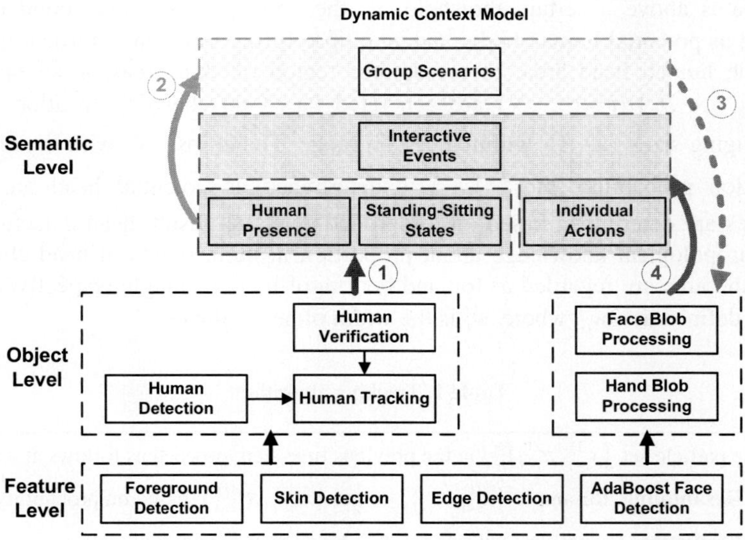

Fig. 3. Vision system structure

Context model can further be used for the guidance of proactive services in smart meeting room, such as dynamic control of camera network and microphone arrays.

3 Human Detection and Tracking

According to the requirements of implicit HCI, computer systems should be capable of detecting and understanding users' actions and intentions so as to provide proactive services, which means vision system should firstly find out user presence in the environment together with total number and their states (e.g. standing or sitting). Therefore human object detection and tracking is the starting point of our system. In our vision system, multiple visual cues such as motion, color, gradient and facial gray features are combined for human presence detection and object tracking.

In order to reduce the search space of human detection modules, foreground detection is firstly applied to extract rough areas of foreground objects. Unlike static background approaches in existing literatures about meeting processing, a behavior analysis oriented consistent foreground detection method [9] is adopted to generate moving objects in indoor environment. Different from traditional Gaussian mixture model (GMM) based methods, this algorithm maintains two background models, the original background and the run-time background, based on which foreground and background pixels are separated effectively. Connected component analysis is performed on the detected foreground pixels, which derives a set of foreground objects.

Skin detection is performed in the upper half part of the foreground objects. Skin color model is constructed in HSV color space, and skin and non-skin pixels are classified according to the distribution of hue and saturation. If the size of detected skin area is above a certain threshold λ, the corresponding foreground object is regarded as potential human body, and an ellipse fitting function is further applied to determine human head area. In a neighbor region of skin areas, a set of ellipses $X_i = [x_i, y_i, w_i, h_i]$ $(i = 1, \ldots, N)$ are generated based on changing locations (x_i, y_i) and changing sizes (w_i, h_i) within a certain range. The ellipse X_i with the maximum observation probability $p(y^{edge} \mid X_i)$ is determined as potential head area. Body rectangles are determined based on foreground detection result, head detection result and anthropological knowledge about proportion. Bottom points of head ellipse and foreground area are regarded as top and bottom of body rectangle respectively. Body width is defined as $3w_i$, where w_i is the width of head ellipse.

Table 1. Tracking algorithm

With the particle set $\{x_{t-1}^{(i)}, \pi_{t-1}^{(i)}\}_{i=1}^{N}$ at the previous time step, proceed as follows at time t:

Step 1: **Resampling**. Resample $\{x_{t-1}^{(i)}, \pi_{t-1}^{(i)}\}$ to get $\{x'^{(i)}_{t-1}, \pi'^{(i)}_{t-1}\}$ based on probability $\pi_{t-1}^{(i)}$

Step 2: **Prediction**. Propagate each sample $x_{t-1}^{(i)}$ by a linear dynamic model:

$x_t^{(i)} = Ax'^{(i)}_{t-1} + w_{t-1}^{(i)}$, where $w_{t-1}^{(i)}$ is a Gaussian random variable

Step 3: **Observation**. For each sample $x_t^{(i)}$, calculate its weight according to color and edge cues: $\pi_t^{(i)} = p(y_t^{color} \mid x_t^{(i)}) p(y_t^{edge} \mid x_t^{(i)})$

Step 4: **Estimation**. Estimate the mean state of the particle set by $E[x_t^{(i)}] = \sum_{i=1}^{N} \pi_t^{(i)} x_t^{(i)}$

Step 5: **Adjustment**. If the highest weight of the sample set $\pi_{t\ \max}^{(i)} < \eta$, adjust head or body object based on detection results and restart the sampling procedure

Detected head ellipsis and body rectangles are tracked and updated through video sequences by a multi-cue Particle Filter tracker. Head ellipsis and body rectangles are defined as state vectors and tracked respectively. Either for head or body tracking, a set of samples $\{x_t^{(i)}, \pi_t^{(i)}\}_{i=1}^{N}$ are maintained and updated, and the mean state of the sample set can be adopted as the estimated state of the current object. Detailed algorithm is given in the following Table 1.

In order to make our approach tolerant to the various noises in real environment, an AdaBoost face detector [10] is applied to verify those potential human objects during tracking procedures. An appropriate sub-window is generated within the neighbor area of tracked head ellipse and the AdaBoost face detector is applied to search face rectangles in the sub-window. Once the face detected, the target object is verified to be valid human object.

4 Dynamic Context Driven Blob Processing

Human presence detection not only detects the number of users in the environment, but also estimates their locations. From users' locations in the smart meeting room, we can infer their individual states and current group scenarios.

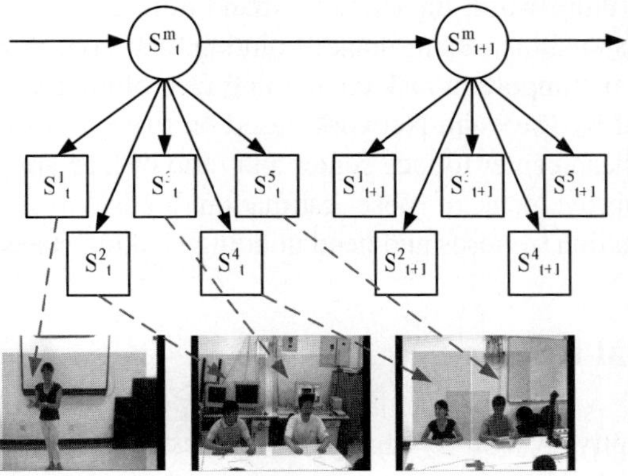

Fig. 4. Dynamic analysis of meeting scenarios

Human standing or sitting states are classified according to the detected head ellipsis and body bounding rectangles. If the ratio of body height to head height is over some certain threshold, the human state is considered as standing, otherwise is sitting. Human presence and their standing-sitting states are adopted as global features for the understanding of overall meeting scenarios.

Based on our meeting room settings, five interest areas are defined in the context model, where participants stay most of time during meetings. Dynamic Bayesian Network (DBN) is applied here to infer meeting scenarios from global features at the five interest areas. The human presence and states S_t^i $(i = 1, \cdots, 5)$ in each interest area is identified as *nobody*, *standing person* or *sitting person*. Meeting scenario state S_t^m (i.e. presentation, discussion or break) can be inferred from previous scenario and current observations. DBN model is illustrated in Fig. 4, and online filtering tasks are performed instead of offline sequence recognition, which means meeting scenario estimation S_t^m is generated at each time step synchronously.

The results from meeting scenario analysis can be further used as the top-down guidance for the blob level visual processing. Overall meeting scenario information is still insufficient for implicit HCI, thus individual actions and interactive events need to be detected and analyzed. Presentation and discussion scenarios contain all the useful information about meetings, therefore individual actions and interactive events and corresponding blob level visual processing are only required in these two scenarios.

Blob level visual processing includes hand blob and face blob processing, which can be used as visual cues for the analysis of individual actions or states, such as detection of iconic hand actions (e.g. raising hand for QA, pointing to a specific direction), head nodding or shaking and users' focus of attention.

Tracking of hand blobs appeals to color based Mean-Shift algorithm. Skin color model is applied to the human body areas to detect hand areas. To track the detected hand rectangles, probability maps are generated based on skin color model and Mean-Shift algorithm is performed, which generates hand trajectories along video sequences. In our future work, the extracted hand trajectories can be used to classify users' hand actions such as raising hand, pointing, and speech related actions. Pose estimation is the most important task concerning face blob processing. Currently face poses are estimated by Bayesian Network based on two types of rough observations, vector angle from head center to face center and ratio of face area to head area. Future work includes improvement of pose estimation algorithm and extension to the simultaneous estimation of poses and head nodding-shaking states.

5 Experimental Results

The proposed adaptive vision system has been tested in our smart meeting room environment. Visual information is captured synchronously from the three fixed cameras. Fig. 5 shows the intermediate results from various visual processing modules such as foreground detection, skin detection, ellipse fitting and face detection.

Fig. 6 shows the result of meeting scenario analysis from one of the extracted meeting samples, in which a scenario sequence 'break-discussion-speech-discussion-break-speech-discussion-break' is recognized. The first and the last breaks mean the starting and ending of the meeting respectively. The red-marked 'speech' scenario between 'break' and 'discussion' is false detected, during which one person is walking in front of the projector screen while the other three are seated. Within current scenario reasoning model, such kind of situation might be inevitably classified as a 'speech' scenario due to its deficiency of other observation cues. Recognition rate can be improved by incorporating more cues and modifying analysis model in the future.

Fig. 5. Intermediate results (1st column: raw images; 2nd column: foreground detection; 3rd column: skin detection; 4th column: ellipse fitting; 5th column: face detection)

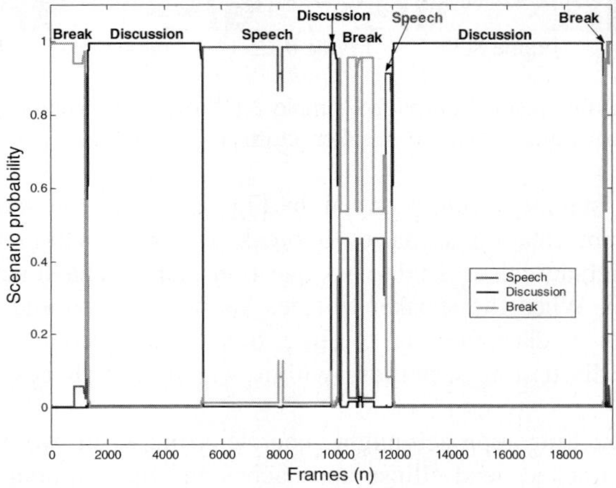

Fig. 6. Scenario analysis result from meeting 1

Visual processing result from video sample 1 is given in Fig. 7. The meeting proceeds from break to group discussion scenario. As we can see, only human head and body blobs are detected and tracked when participants enter the room before meeting starts, which is displayed in the top row. While after the discussion scenario begins, face and hand blobs are detected and tracked along the video sequence, as is shown in the bottom row.

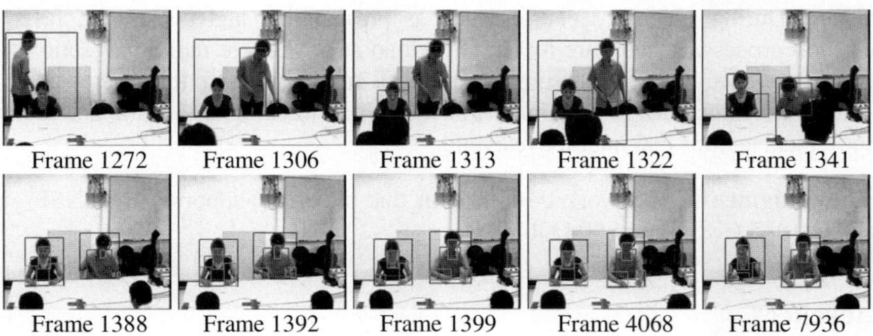

Fig. 7. Visual processing result from video sample 1 (1st row: break scenario, each participant takes the seat before meeting starts; 2nd row: discussion scenario)

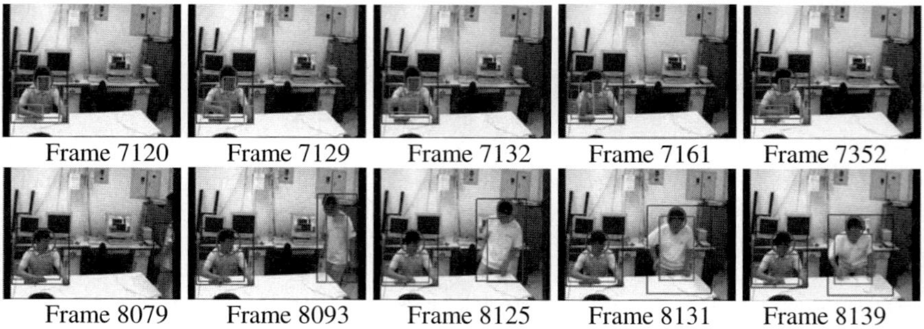

Fig. 8. Visual processing result from video sample 2 (1st row: presentation scenario, audience raises question; 2nd row: break scenario, speaker returns to his seat)

Another video sample result is given in Fig. 8, where the meeting procedure transitions from presentation scenario to break scenario. Within the presentation scenario, one participant raises hand to ask questions, and his hand actions are tracked with our approach. When the speaker finishes his presentation and gets back to his seat, the scenario is classified as meeting break and becomes a link between presentation and discussion scenarios, within which only heads and bodies are tracked.

However, our tracking approach might generate errors when two heads get close to each other or the tracked head ellipse approaches an object similar to human head. Cooperative reasoning structure is considered for future algorithm improvement.

6 Conclusion

In this paper, a novel adaptive visual processing framework is proposed toward implicit human computer interaction in smart meeting room. Visual functions and context analysis tasks are tightly integrated in a bidirectional way. Initially potential human objects are detected and tracked to generate global features such as human presence and standing-sitting states, based on which overall meeting scenarios are analyzed. During specific scenarios such as presentation and discussion, face and hand blob processing tasks are to be fulfilled so as to analyze individual actions and interactive events, which can also be regarded as implicit input to the system.

Future work includes improvements of multi-blob tracking algorithm, and analysis of individual actions and interactive events.

Acknowledgments. The work described in this paper is supported by CNSF grant 60673189 and CNSF grant 60433030.

References

1. Bett, M., Gross, R., Yu, H.: Multimodal Meeting Tracker. Proc. RIAO (2000)
2. Carletta, J., Ashby, S., Bourban, S.: The AMI meeting corpus: A pre-announcement. In: Proc. Workshop on Machine Learning for Multimodal Interaction (MLMI), (July 2005)

3. Rybski, P.E., De la Torre, F., Patil, R., Vallespi, C., Veloso, M., Browning, B., CAMEO,: Camera Assisted Meeting Event Observer. In: Proc. Int. Conf. on Robotics and Automation (ICRA'04), vol. 2, pp. 1634–1639, (May 2004)
4. McCowan, I., Gatica-Perez, D., Bengio, S., Lathoud, G., Barnard, M., Zhang, D.: Automatic Analysis of Multimodal Group Actions in Meetings. IEEE Trans. on Pattern Analysis and Machine Intelligence (PAMI'05), vol. 27(3) (March 2005)
5. Zhang, D., Gatica-Perez, D., Bengio, S., McCowan, I.: Modeling individual and group actions in meetings with layered HMMs. IEEE Trans. on Multimedia, vol. 8(3) (June 2006)
6. Hakeem, A., Shah, M.: Ontology and taxonomy collaborated framework for meeting classification. In: Proc. 17th Int. Conf. on Pattern Recognition (ICPR'04), vol. 4, pp. 219–222 (2004)
7. Al-Hames, M., Rigoll, G.: A Multi-Modal Graphical Model for Robust Recognition of Group Actions in Meetings from Disturbed Videos. In: Proc. IEEE Int. Conf. on Image Processing (ICIP'05) (2005)
8. Trivedi, M.M., Huang, K.S., Mikic, I.: Dynamic Context Capture and Distributed Video Arrays for Intelligent Spaces. IEEE Trans. on Systems, Man, and Cybernetics—PART A: Systems and Humans, vol. 35(1) (January 2005)
9. Jiang, L., Zhang, X., Tao, L., Xu, G.: Behavior Analysis Oriented Consistent Foreground Object Detection. In: Proc. 2rd Chinese Conf. on Harmonious Human Machine Environment (HHME'06) (2006)
10. Wang, Y., Liu, Y., Tao, L., Xu, G.: Real-Time Multi-View Face Detection and Pose Estimation in Video Stream. In: Proc. 18th Int. Conf. on Pattern Recognition (ICPR'06), vol. 4, pp. 354–357 (2006)

Detailed Monitoring of User's Gaze and Interaction to Improve Future E-Learning

Heiko Drewes[1], Richard Atterer[1], and Albrecht Schmidt[2]

[1] Media Informatics Group, Ludwig-Maximilians-University München, Germany
[2] Fraunhofer IAIS, Sankt Augustin and B-IT University of Bonn, Germany
{Heiko.Drewes,Richard.Atterer}@ifi.lmu.de,
Albrecht.Schmidt@acm.org

Abstract. In this paper, we investigate how to use future interaction technologies to enhance learning technologies. We examine in detail how tracking the mouse pointer and observing the user's gaze can help to monitor the use of web applications and in particular E-learning applications. To improve learning and teaching, it is of interest to understand in what order and to what extent users read texts, how much time they spend on individual parts of the teaching materials, and where they get stuck. Based on a standard web browser as an application platform, extended with a gaze tracking facility, we conducted studies to explore the feasibility of this novel approach. The concept includes an extension of current technologies to allow JavaScript code running in the browser to access the current gaze position of the user. Our work shows how pieces of web technology and eye gaze tracking can be put together to create a new platform for E-learning that provides additional benefits for learners and teachers.

Keywords: User monitoring, eye-gaze user interfaces, interaction tracking, reading detection, E-learning.

1 Introduction and Motivation

For learners and teachers, the use of electronic media has become common in education. E-learning systems are available for many different domains and are often used in addition rather than as replacement for traditional media (e.g. books and exhibits). The provision of multimedia content in an appropriate form has been a focus in research over the last decade. Systems often combine the presentation of static information (e.g. text, graphics and photos), animated information (e.g. dynamic graphics and movies) and interactive elements (e.g. simulations, navigation options). Additionally, means for assessing the progress in learning are included (e.g. tests at the end of a section or chapter). Monitoring the use of online learning materials is a basic source to understand what the learner has seen and what learning strategies she or he follows. Traditional and web-based systems achieve this at the page level by logging the URLs that have been requested and how long the user spent on certain pages. However, the information received is rather coarse as a single page may

C. Stephanidis (Ed.): Universal Access in HCI, Part II, HCII 2007, LNCS 4555, pp. 802–811, 2007.

contain text, images and photos. Similarly, it is hard to tell how long a person looked at the page, as the interval between accessing two URLs does not necessarily yield information on how long the person has been reading or interacting with the page.

Novel technologies such as gaze-tracking systems that allow the normal use of a desktop system while recording the user's gaze path are becoming widely available. Additionally, WWW technologies such as AJAX create new options for detailed tracking of interaction with digital media [1] using a standard web browser. We combined both approaches to research usability. In this paper, we show that theses technologies also offer new means for the creation of novel user interfaces for E-learning and E-teaching.

Current WWW technology provides a platform-independent format to deliver and display content, which is accessible from everywhere. For this reason, we expect that a majority of E-learning application will make use of web technologies for content provision and delivery, even if used from a DVD or on the intranet. Research to utilize the web as a platform for E-learning is manifold, for an example see [12].

Camera devices will become a standard hardware for computers in the same way that speakers are now. Many new computers and mobile phones already have build-in cameras. As processor power and memory is also steadily increasing, we expect that gaze tracking technology will be available in the future at little extra cost.

Previous research exists on how to use the gaze information to model the user's meta-cognition and use this for intelligent pedagogical agents [7]. Our approach presented in this paper follows a more pragmatic approach and looks at concrete enhancements for E-learning systems.

In the remainder of the paper, we first analyze potential scenarios of future E-learning. The scenarios are the basis for the implementation of a framework. A technological proof of concept for general tracking technologies and gaze tracking in particular shows the feasibility of the approach. We include one specific example where we developed an algorithm, which uses gaze-tracking technology for reading detection.

2 Scenarios

Detailed monitoring of interaction and gaze for the presented learning material can give benefits to both learners and teachers. The following scenarios show how they benefit from the combination of eye gaze tracking and web activity tracking.

2.1 Author and Teacher Benefits

Using the envisioned system, the author or content creator has additional options to monitor the system's use by the learner at her or his disposal. For every object (e.g. text, graphics, animations), the author can decide to record the time the user gazed on an object as well as the order in which elements have been read or watched. For text objects, there are options to make reading compulsory (e.g., continuing is only possible once the text has been read) and to record the intensity of reading (e.g. was the text skimmed, read word by word, or not read at all).

Similar to the `onmouseover` event in JavaScript, there is also an `ongazeover` event to trigger other activities. For example, if there is a diagram with explaining text, a part of the diagram can be highlighted depending on the keyword that was just read in the text. On a similar note, when looking for a while at a detail of the diagram, the corresponding explanatory text is highlighted. Jacob [11] initially investigated such approaches in 1990. He displayed a sea map with positions of ships and information on an individual ship, which corresponded to the gaze position of the user.

As soon as a lesson is online, the teacher has access to statistics how much time the learner's gaze spent on each page and on elements in the page. This information is available for individual learners and accumulated for a whole course. The value is much more reliable than the time the lesson was displayed on the screen because any time the learner spent e.g. at the coffee machine or chatting with colleagues does not contribute to the time spent for the lesson. The report also states how well the user read a text.

All this knowledge on the use of materials and the learner's behavior can help the teacher to improve the learning material, creation of tests, and the revision of teaching materials. If information is available on how long the user needed to read a certain paragraph, whether she or he re-read it multiple times or just skimmed through it, this can provide the basis for deciding on the inclusion of additional material, rewriting of paragraphs or restructuring of the course. The order in which users look at material, the general behavior (e.g. first skimming, then reading) as well as the viewing times of pictures, graphics and photos can give additional information that helps to restructure the online teaching materials or to create questions on comprehension.

2.2 Learner Benefits

To make online learning more efficient and to personalize the presentation of information tracking, the user's learning behavior in detail can provide essential clues.

When learners log onto the E-learning system, they also get statistics on how much time they spent on different lessons up to now. Texts provide feedback (e.g. through changes of the background color) on how intensively they have been studied so far. This makes it easy to go on when interrupted during learning, especially with lengthy texts. It also gives the freedom to work through the material in any self-chosen order without forgetting something.

When looking at details of the material, explanations appear automatically – there is no need to grab the mouse and position the cursor over the object of interest. Animations and videos start automatically the moment the learner looks at them, and stop the moment the gaze moves away [10]. This minimizes distraction during reading as animations and videos can pause when not looked at.

3 Future Technologies for E-Learning

3.1 WWW and AJAX

The worldwide web has been used as a way of providing services for many years. Whereas at first, the emphasis was mainly put on providing information to users of the WWW for their consumption, and to give access to this information via search facilities, in recent years web-based applications have gained more and more importance. Together with the types of tasks the web is used for, the technologies behind the WWW have been improved. Today, browsers are capable of executing complex JavaScript programs efficiently, and technologies like AJAX make web-based GUIs more similar to the GUIs of desktop programs. Thus, the web is now well suited for more types of applications, including remote E-learning.

E-learning systems of the future will be able to use an established application platform (the web browser) as their development target, and the users will benefit from the advantages of this platform, in particular its independence of operating system, screen resolution and standardized technologies.

We assume that in future things like key presses and mouse movements, which are available to web applications today (in the form of JavaScript `onkeypress`, `onmousemove` etc. events), will have been extended to include support for the capture of eye gaze data in future browsers. Previous work in this area concentrated on tracking mouse movements [13] and deducing from it the probable gaze direction of users in the absence of hardware eye tracking [1] [14].

3.2 Eye Gaze

Nowadays, eye-trackers work with a video camera in combination with an infrared LED. The light from the LED creates a reflection on the user's eyeball. As the eyeball is a nearly perfect sphere, the reflection stays stable on the same position, independent of the direction of the gaze. Image recognition detects the center of the pupil and after calibration (i.e. looking at the corners of the screen), the direction of the gaze can be calculated using the vector from the reflection point to the center of the pupil. As the detection of a black pupil inside a brown iris is difficult because of low contrast, many eye-trackers use the white-pupil-method: If infrared light illuminates the eye, the eye background (retina) reflects the light and causes a white pupil to appear for the infrared camera device.

To allow free head movement in front of the display, without use of a chin rest, the eye-tracker can be combined with a head-tracker. Head-trackers are also video-based. Commercial systems combining both technologies, such as the Tobii 1750 Eye Tracker [1] and the Eyefollower [2] are still expensive today, but work quite well.

One intrinsic problem of eye tracking is accuracy. The eye constantly performs micro-saccades which results in noisy position data. Another effect arises from the fact that the retina only has a small area of high resolution (fovea), which is about 1 degree of visual angle [8]. To see something clearly, the eye needs to move to bring the object of interest into this high-resolution area, but not necessarily into the center. On average desktop displays, the accuracy is around 30 pixels, which is about the size of standard icons and buttons, but twice the height of a line of text.

---

[1] http://www.tobii.com

[2] http://www.eyegaze.com

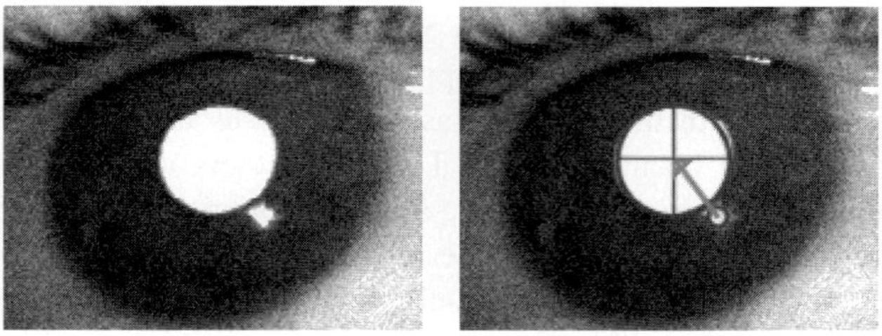

Fig. 1. How eye gaze detection works. The small white spot is the reflection of the LED.

4 Reading

Psychologists intensively researched the reading process, which is understood in detail [2]. Nowadays, many researchers in the field of human computer interaction are interested in reading [6]. Practical applications are activity recognition (e.g. is someone reading, as presented in [3] and [4]) or a reading assistant introduced by [5].

Gaze-assisted E-learning systems need basic modules, so we focused on compulsory reading and on extracting values, which tells how intensively a text was read. In contrast to related work, the suggested algorithms can not only provide information on whether or not someone is reading, but also on which part of the text was read and how long the reading of a certain part took.

4.1 Compulsory Reading

One possibility to detect whether a text was read is to use the reading detection from [3] or [4], collect the x and y coordinates and find out whether these coordinates completely cover the text area. This will result in a rather complex algorithm and as the error rate for reading detection is still above 10 percent, a reliable result cannot be guaranteed – skimming the page would likely be detected as reading.

In an initial experiment, we recorded the eye gaze of several test readers. Figure 2 shows a typical result of our commercial gaze-tracking system called ERICA[3].

We can see that the gaze moves in saccades with brief fixations and revisits. A preliminary evaluation of the data gives saccade lengths of around 30 pixels within a line and backward saccades, which are slightly smaller than the length of the line. The geometry of the system results in the 1° visual angle being 36 pixels wide. Thus, the angle of the forward saccades is about the same as the angle of the fovea, the area with high resolution on the eye's background [8]. It is interesting to note that consequently, the first fixation points in a line are about half a degree ahead of the beginning of the line, and the last fixation is the same distance away from the end of the line.

The algorithm presented here uses the fact that the gaze visits the text in sequential order. As traditional reading always works in sequential order independent of the scripture used, the algorithm can be applied to right-to-left scripts (Arab) and to vertical scripts (Chinese).

---

[3] http://www.eyeresponse.com/

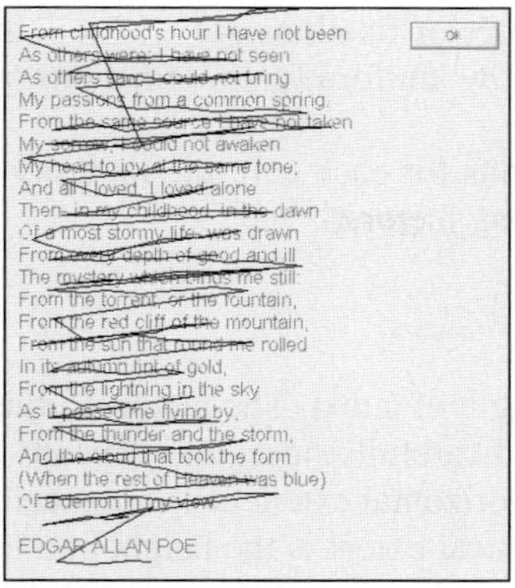

Fig. 2. Gaze trail reading a text

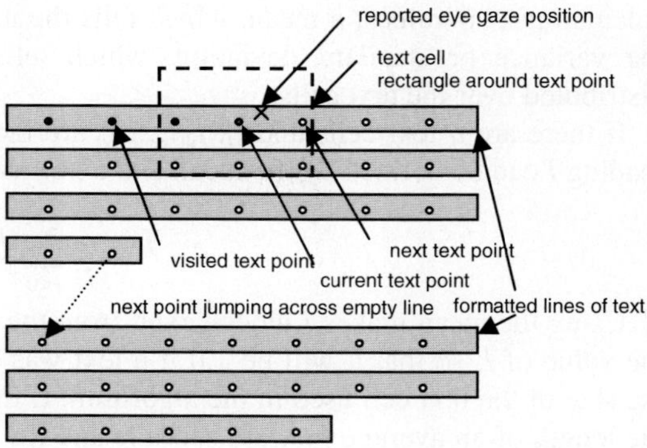

Fig. 3. Illustration of the reading detection algorithm

The basic parameters of the algorithm are the width w and the height h of the rectangle around the gaze position and the distance d of the text points. The algorithm starts with a point, which is $d/2$ from the beginning of the first line. As soon as this point is within a rectangular area around the reported gaze position, it is marked as read. Then the algorithm chooses the next point on the same line, d ahead of the previous one. In case of a line wrap, the next point is at the beginning of the next line. Once the gaze visited all points, the text was read completely.

By design, this algorithm allows the reader to take a break, perhaps to have a look at the system clock, before continuing to read. It is also robust against calibration shift because the dimensions of the rectangle can be relatively large without decreasing the reliability. A problem of this algorithm is the case that some words or lines are left out by the reader. For this reason, the system should provide feedback on the portion of text being read, for example by a change of the background color.

Another problem arises with very short texts, which can be read with one glance. To detect reading in a line of text there should be at least two, better three fixations. Together with the fact that the first and last fixation points are 0.5 degrees from the beginning and end of the line and that the fixations steps are around one degree, a line should have a minimum length of 3° visual angle. This is about 100 pixel on the system used.

4.2 Reading Intensity

For a teacher or pedagogical agent it can be of value to know how intensively a text was read and how much effort was required to read a part. There are two common ways to visualize the user's gaze. One method is drawing the gaze path (as done in Figure 2) and the other method is to use heat maps. Both methods provide too much information and it is difficult to find rules based on this data.

We introduce a method to reduce the data to a few values. The algorithm starts with formatting the text to find text points and surrounding rectangles. Every fixation inside the rectangle increases a counter for this area. It is also possible to accumulate the fixation time. This mechanism is like a low-resolution heat map. The data allows calculating two values, a mean, which tells the number of fixations per text cell, and the variance or standard deviation, which tells how uniformly the fixations are distributed over the text cells.

If there are n text cells and $f_1, f_2, \ldots, f_n$ are fixations for each cell, the intensity of reading I can be defined by the mean and a normalizing factor c:

$$I = \frac{c}{n}\sum_{i=0}^{n} f_i$$

Using the mean makes I independent from the length of a text. The factor c adjusts the value of I, so that it will be 1.0 if a text was read carefully once, and depends on the size of the text cell used in the algorithm. If the horizontal extent of the text cell is the length of an average forward saccade and the vertical extent is the height of a text line, c is 1. If the text cells are bigger and they overlap, one fixation is counted multiple times, because it is inside several text cells and the factor c will correct this.

To decide whether a text was read carefully, I is not enough, because reading half of the text twice results in the same value as reading the whole text once. Consequently, a second parameter D is necessary to know whether the gaze positions are distributed equally over the text cells. The variance provides such a parameter.

$$D = \frac{1}{n}\sum_{i=0}^{n} (cf_i - I)^2$$

If the text cells were all visited equally, D will be close to zero, otherwise D will be higher. A perfect read will result in $I = 1$ and $D = 0$.

5 Prototype and User Study

We conducted a user study on a stand-alone system to show that compulsory reading and detecting of reading intensity work reliably. To prove the technical feasibility of the concept, we then extended the functionality of our monitoring tool UsaProxy [1] to receive the eye gaze data via a separate TCP connection. Additional code evaluated the gaze data to generate the `ongazeover` events.

5.1 The Architecture of the Monitoring System

The special extensions to the JavaScript event mechanism outlined in section 3.2 do not exist yet. In order to be able to experiment with possible application areas and to evaluate whether our approach to E-learning applications works in practice, we designed an architecture that makes eye-tracking data available to the code running within a browser. Due to the technical restrictions of today's computers, a system needs to be specially prepared and the different components need to be set up independently, but this will not pose a problem with future, integrated systems, and from the point of view of the web application programmer, the environment is very similar to our envisioned future computer.

Figure 4 shows the overall design of the system: a standard web browser accesses the website, which provides the E-learning application; it can be located on any server on the Internet. In addition to the web browser, special eye tracking software is installed locally. Our UsaProxy HTTP proxy [1] is the key to make eye-tracking data

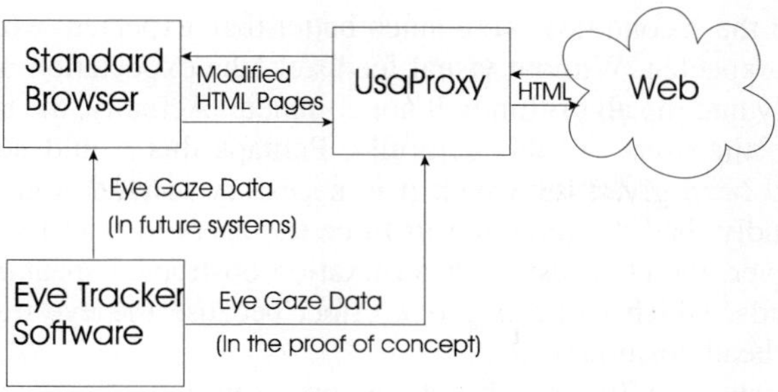

Fig. 4. Overall design of the system

available to the browser: the web browser is configured to access the WWW via UsaProxy. UsaProxy simply passes on the requests of the browser and waits for the responses of the server. However, it modifies the HTML pages before passing them to the browser. The modification causes the browser to execute the JavaScript parts inserted by UsaProxy in the context of every page, regardless of which server it came from. Once it executes, this JavaScript code contacts UsaProxy, polling it for new events. This mechanism can be implemented in a way that cross-browser compatibility is possible.

The gaze tracking software that is also running on the local machine can now be interfaced to UsaProxy as well: via a special HTTP-based API, it can repeatedly contact UsaProxy and supply the current gaze position. UsaProxy can immediately pass this information to the browser.

5.2 The User Study

For the experiment on reading, we used the commercial low-cost gaze tracker ERICA that is commonly used in usability research and as an input device for the disabled. The ERICA system does not allow free head movement, hence we used a chin rest for the experiment to stabilize the head position.

A group of nine people, six male, three female in the age from 23 to 47, took part in the user study. Every subject got three tasks. The first task presented a dialog with a poem of Edgar Allen Poe (23 lines, 150 words). The dialog presented feedback for the text already read and disappeared when totally read. The task was to read the text to make the dialog disappear. The second task was another dialog with a poem in the native language of the user (13 lines, 69 words), this time without providing feedback. The third task was a repetition of the second task, but this time with the demand to read the poem loudly.

5.3 Results

For the first task, all test users were able to let the dialog disappear (100%). Some of them complained that the feedback is faster than their reading and they felt being chased. In the second task, the dialog detected correctly complete readings in six cases (67%) and failed in the other three cases (33%). In the third task, the dialog correctly detected complete readings in five cases and failed in the other four cases.

The results of the second task were much better than expected, while the third task was worse than expected. Without visual feedback, the expectation was that users do not read carefully and the algorithm will not complete. Actually, the task given was to read the text, so the users did this carefully. Perhaps this would not be the case if another task had been given for which it is necessary to read something. The third task, reading loudly, had the intention to force the users to read the text slowly and carefully. However, the chin rest for head fixation obstructed speaking and the users moved their heads, which had a negative effect because the eye tracker calibration assumes a fixed head position.

A detection rate of 67% is sub-optimal and consequently compulsory reading should provide feedback, where the success rate is 100%. To detect whether a text was read carefully without feedback for the user, the values as introduced in 4.2 are more suitable.

When looking at the results, one should also consider the small font size. The font size of 20 pt used in our study was only slightly larger than the normal font of the system (16 pt), but much smaller than the font size of 48 pt used by Sibert, Gortuk and Lavine [5].

6 Discussion and Conclusions

We have outlined that novel technologies can provide new means for creating more effective user interfaces for E-learning systems. The scenarios show that having detailed knowledge of gaze and mouse movement will improve the experience for the learner and teacher.

Our user study shows that all components to build gaze-aware E-learning environments with fine-grained monitoring are already available. With falling prices for eye-trackers and standards for eye-tracker integration into conventional systems, E-learning could change significantly in the future.

Our pragmatic approach of using the gaze is easy to understand by teachers and learners and consequently well accepted as an improvement of the interface. Further research to extract more knowledge from the user's gaze as presented in [9] is necessary, but it should be applied with care to keep the E-learning systems understandable for teachers and learners.

Acknowledgments

The work has been conducted in the context of the research project Embedded Interaction ('Eingebettete Interaktion') and was partly funded by the DFG ('Deutsche Forschungsgemeinschaft').

References

1. Atterer, R., Wnuk, M., Schmidt, A.: Knowing the User's Every Move – User Activity Tracking for Website Usability Evaluation and Implicit Interaction. In: Proc. of the 15th International World Wide Web Conference (WWW2006), Edinburgh, Scotland (2006)
2. Reichle, E.D., Pollatsek, A., Fisher, D.L., Rayner, K.: Toward a Model of Eye Movement Control in Reading. Psychological Review 105(1), 125–127 (1998)

3. Campbell, C.S., Maglio, P.P.: A Robust Algorithm for Reading Detection. In: Proc. of the 2001 Workshop on Perceptive User interfaces. PUI '01., vol. 15, pp. 1–7. ACM Press, New York (2001)
4. Keat, F.T., Ranganath, S., Venkatesh, Y.V.: Eye Gaze Based Reading Detection. TENCON '03. Conference on Convergent Technologies for Asia-Pacific Region 2, 825–828 (2003)
5. Sibert, J.L., Gokturk, M., Lavine, R.A.: The Reading Assistant: Eye Gaze Triggered Auditory Prompting for Reading Remediation. In: Proc. of the 13th Annual ACM Symposium on User interface Software and Technology. UIST'00, pp. 101–107. ACM Press, New York (2000)
6. Nielsen, J.: Jakob Nielsen's Alertbox: F-Shaped Pattern For Reading Web Content April 17 (2006), http://www.useit.com/alertbox/reading_pattern.html.
7. Merten, C., Conati, C.: Eye-tracking to Model and Adapt to User Meta-cognition in Intelligent Learning Environments. In: Proc. of the 11th international Conference on Intelligent User Interfaces. IUI '06, 6th edn. pp. 39–46. ACM Press, New York (2006)
8. Duchowski, T.D.: Eye Tracking Methodology: Theory and Practice, pp. 31–42. Springer, Heidelberg (2003)
9. Iqbal, S.T., Bailey, B.P.: Using Eye Gaze Patterns to Identify User Tasks. The Grace Hopper Celebration of Women in Computing (2004)
10. Dickie, C., Vertegaal, R., Sohn, C., Cheng, D.: eyeLook: Using Attention to Facilitate Mobile Media Consumption. In: Proc. of the 18th Annual ACM Symposium on User interface Software and Technology UIST'05, pp. 103–106. ACM Press, New york (2005)
11. Jacob, R.J.: The Use of Eye Movements in Human-Computer Interaction Techniques: What You Look At is What You Get. ACM Trans. Inf. Syst. 9(2), 152–169 (1991)
12. Shaw, E., Johnson, L., Ganeshan, R.: Pedagogical Agents on the Web. In: Proc. of the Third Annual Conference on Autonomous Agents AGENTS '99, pp. 283–290. ACM Press, New York (1999)
13. Mueller, F., Lockerd, A.: Cheese: Tracking Mouse Movement Activity on Websites, a Tool for User Modeling. In: Proc. of the Conference on Human Factors in Computing Systems CHI 2001 Extended Abstracts, Seattle, Washington, USA (2001)
14. Ullrich, C., Melis, E.: The Poor Man's Eyetracker Tool of ActiveMath. In: Proc. of the World Conference on E-Learning in Corporate Government Healthcare and Higher Education eLearn-2002, 2313-2316, Montreal, Canada (2002)

Facial Expression Recognition Based on Color Lines Model and Region Based Processing

GeonAe Eom and Hyun-Seung Yang

Artificial Intelligence & Media Lab, Division of Computer Science,
EECS Department, KAIST, Korea
gaeom75@paradise.kaist.ac.kr, hsyang@kaist.ac.kr

Abstract. Facial expression involves various movements. We present various facial expressions as simple regions on facial area and get recognition rate. There are two steps for obtaining the expression regions. First step is to extract facial area from input image with color lines model and second step is to catch regions of expression on extracted facial area with active contour without edges method as a region based processing. We have tested this presentation method for facial expressions from the open facial expression database JAFFE(Japanese Female Facial Expressions). In this method, we can get a facial expression region without any manual works. In the future, we will compensate for lack of ambiguities among expressions with person specific method and this method will be extended to image sequence.

Keywords: facial expression, color lines model, active contour without edges.

1 Introduction

People have been interested in human and computer interaction and related techniques have been studied for a long time. There are many factors for interaction between human and computer, for example, voice, facial expression, gesture, and etc. Especially, facial expression may be one of the important roles in the interaction, because of the fact that facial expression makes up over 50% of a first impression [1].

Recently, researcher is applying a facial expression recognition technique in the field of not only human robot but also ubiquitous computing environment for giving a great service to people. But facial expression involves various movements. There is unique facial expression in each person. For example, a person who has an angry look in general is different with a person who has a smiley look. This makes facial expressions difficult [7]. In order to overcome this difficulty, we would like to extract simple and common regions from various facial expressions.

Research about a facial expression can be separated into the problem of representation and categorization of the facial expressions. Some approaches come from face recognition techniques in order to extract facial parameters and classify them. On the other hand some focus on movements of facial muscles or specific locations. Basically, there are template-based or feature-based approaches for facial data extraction, and rule-based methods or template-based methods for classification

C. Stephanidis (Ed.): Universal Access in HCI, Part II, HCII 2007, LNCS 4555, pp. 812–817, 2007.

according to extracting methods [1]. One of good template-based methods is the active appearance model which is introduced by cootes, et al[2][3]. This algorithm works well for representing and tracking of facial movements. But off-line training procedure is quite complicate for large face images with various facial expressions. Locations of facial features are labeled manually and iterative computation is accomplished for searching facial features from an input image. But usually, when we describe several facial expressions, we can express them such like Fig. 1. In this figure, it is simple, but we can recognize the expressions clearly. When we recognize a facial expression, we just consider around some area: eye, eye brow, or lip except a cheek, chin, or forehead. These differences are made by muscle's movement so that there are two kinds of features: permanent and transient facial features. Even though pucker on a face seems to be an importance part of facial expressions, they may prevent recognition. So we focus on a simple and common region representation from given face image. Whole procedure consists of three parts. First step is to detect face region and second is representation of feature regions. After that, NN classifier is applied for getting recognition rate. In this paper, we applied the color lines model [4] for detecting skin regions and the active contour without edges method (ACWE) [5] for representing a facial movement. The area of a various facial movement is indicated by the active contour method such like caricature. This method really captured features of various facial expressions, and these features are represented by a region.

In this paper, we will describe our proposed system in section 2 and experiment results will be in Section 3. Then we will discuss and conclude of our work in section 4.

Fig. 1. Description of Facial Expressions

2 Description of the Proposed Procedure

We propose a presentation of facial expressions as simple regions on facial area and get a recognition rate. There are two steps for obtaining the expression area. First step is to extract facial area from input image using color lines model and second step is to catch regions of expression on extracted facial area with active contour without edges method as a region based processing. After that, we get a recognition rate from NN classifier.

2.1 Detection of Facial Area with Color Lines Model

To use color is the most popular and simple method for detecting facial area. Color lines model suggested by Ido Omer and Michael Werman [4] gathers similar colors and separates different colors from given input image. Even though color histogram's distribution for real image does not follow the ideal linear assumption, neighborhood of points on each line is assumed by Gaussian distribution so that it can cover variations of image. In this model, RGB color space transforms into the space with polar coordinate. In order to find color lines, we separate polar coordinate space into several subintervals according to the bin size of angle and the distance. Each color line finds representative points from each subslice. These color lines make similar colors are intended to be gathered and different colors separated. Skin color is represented as a binary image as the following Fig. 1. Since each color area has unique color line, we can get a facial area affected from a specific skin color line as a white color and remaining areas are painted as a black. But if we paint a skin color area as a white directly, there are small holes inside face area that are made by illumination or facial components, eye brow, eye, nostril, and mouse, etc. So the points within the white area are covered after checking the pixel surrounding.

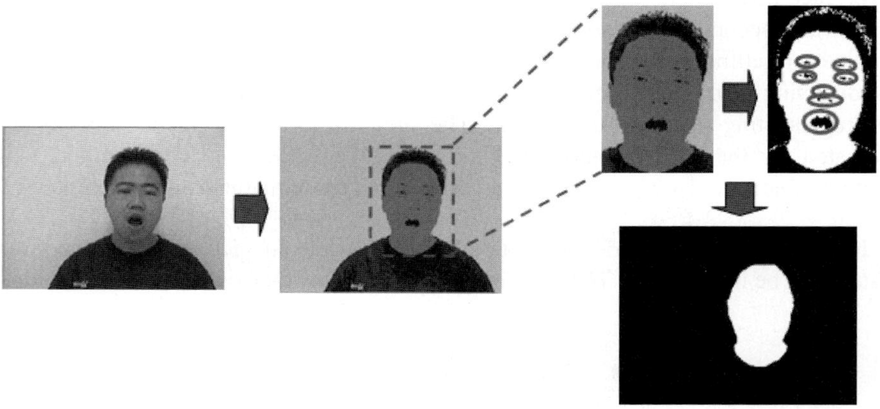

Fig. 2. First image is an input image and after using color lines model, we get the color clustered image. After painting skin color line as a white color, there remains some spots, eye, eye brow and lip, etc. Circles in the upper right image on third column show the spots. According to the condition around the spots, they are covered with the white color and finally, we can get the binary image which shows the facial area.

2.2 Region Based Processing with Active Contour Without Edges

When we describe several facial expressions, we can think them such like Fig. 1. In this picture, it is simple, but we can recognize the expressions clearly. This is the motivation of our approach.

We use the active contour without edges(ACWE) method [5] for describing facial expressions. Originally, ACWE method suggested by Tony chan and Luminita Vese based on Mumford-Shah functional and level set is one of curve evolving methods for detection of objects. We find this method can represents facial expressions like a caricature on a facial area. This method especially works well in image divided by two parts and when we focus on our facial area, clear-cut features can be extracted from this method. Before we apply this method, we accomplished a non-linear diffusion. Usually, input image has a noise. Non-linear diffusion is applied to each pixel points with gradient information from image so that it makes homogeneous area less smooth and area with noise much smooth along the boundary or corner. So we can get the clear facial expression regions after applying ACWE method on non-linear diffused image.

3 Experimental Results

We have two facial expression DB, one is K-DB which consists of color images of 5 KAIST students and the other is the open facial expression database JAFFE(Japanese Female Facial Expression) DB [6] which consists of grey images. So detection of face area is tested by using K-DB and region-based processing and recognition rate is tested by public database, JAFFE. Basically, facial expressions which is defined by Ekman are seven, neutrality, happiness, anger, surprise, sadness, disgust, and fear. Among these, we used just five facial expressions except disgust and fear, because these are related to person's mental state and emotion.

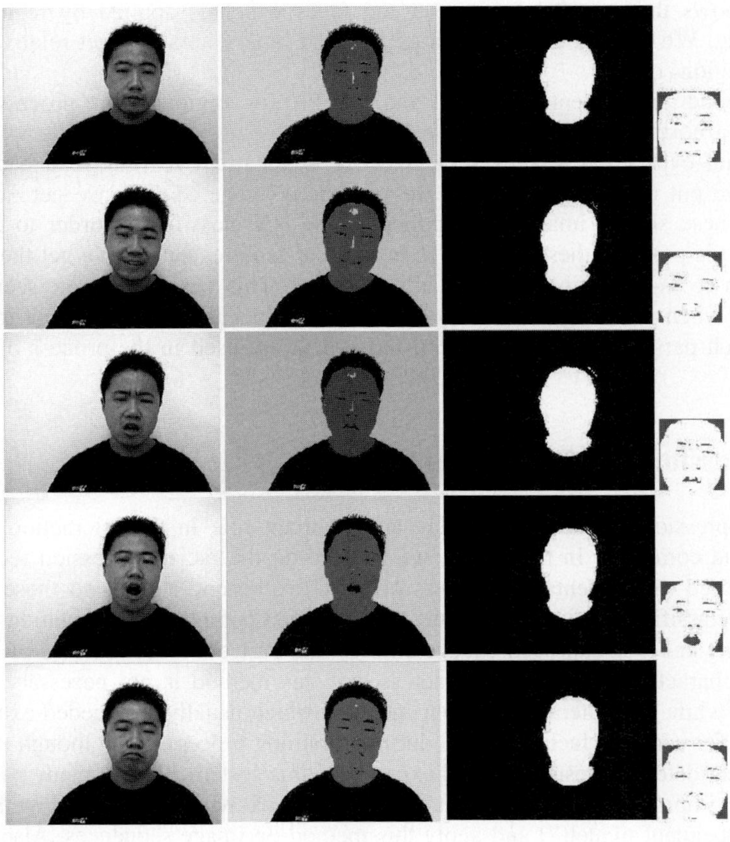

Fig. 3. First column is input images which consist of 5 facial expressions, Second column shows color clustered images from the first images

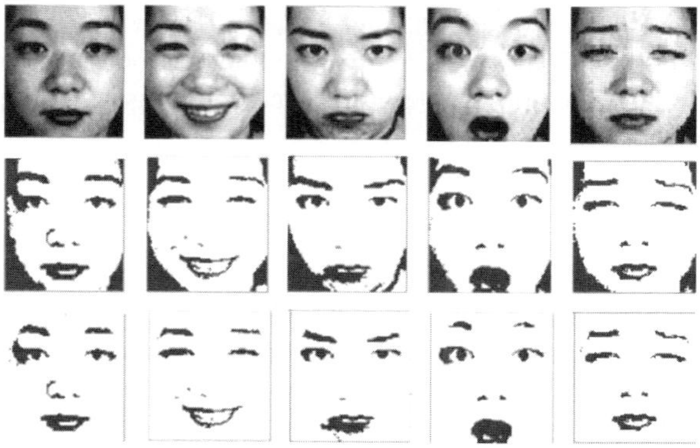

Fig. 4. Top : Input images for 5 different facial expressions, Middle : Region based processing images : Bottom : Masked images

First experiment focuses on the automatic presentation of facial feature region. Fig. 3 shows the detected face areas and faces which is applied by region based processing. We can get a facial area as a closed binary area and get relatively clear feature regions on that.

In second experiment, we used the JAFFE for region-based processing and assumed a normalized face image with two eyes as an input image. So we can get clear facial expression images such like Fig. 4. In order to remove a background region, we put the formal mask on the processed image. Finally we get expression region. These simple images are applied in the NN classifier in order to checking whether it is possible these features to be used as features so that we get the average 65% with cross-validation from the NN classifier. This recognition rate seems to be not good when we compared with other methods because mixed training images in which each person has different facial movement are used in the process of off-line training.

4 Discussion and Conclusion

Facial expression techniques are play an important role in the interaction between human and computer. In this paper, we focused on the facial expression recognition and proposed the presentation process of facial expression and tested those features with NN classifier. In our experiment, we simplified complex representation of facial expressions and our approach caught an essential part of it without loss of features. Another characteristic of our approach is that this method is not necessary to work manually while other iterative contour methods which usually are needed extra works manually for catching facial features during a training process. Even though this work shows clear detection result of facial expression, this system still has many parameters which can improve a detection result. In the future, we will combine this method with person dependent model[7] and apply this method on image sequences. Also we will integrate other complementary techniques in order to interact more efficiently between human and computer, for example, the voice analysis or gesture recognition, etc.

Acknowledgments. This research is supported by the ubiquitous computing and network(UCN) project, the ministry of information and communication (MIC) 21st century frontier R&D program in Korea.

References

1. Pantic, M., Leon J. M., Rothkrantz: Automatic Analysis of Facial Expressions: The state of the Art. IEEE Transactions on Pattern Analysis and Machine Intelligence, vol. 22(12) (2000)
2. Cootes, T.F., Edwards, G.J., Taylor, C.J.: Active Appearance Models. 5th European Conference on Computer Vision, vol. 2, pp. 484–498. Springer, Heidelberg (1998)
3. Crisinacce, D., Cootes, T.F.: Facial Feature Detection and Tracking with Automatic Template Selection
4. Omer, I., Werman, M.: Color Lines: Image Specific Color Representation. IEEE Computer Society Conference on Computer Vision and Pattern Recognition 2, 946–953 (2004)
5. Chan, T.F., Vese, L.A.: Active Contours Without Edges. IEEE Transactions on Image Processing, vol. 10(2) (2001)
6. accessed January 2007, http://www.kasrl.org/jaffe.html
7. Eom, G.A., Yang, H.S.: Person Dependent Facial Expression Recognition System, The 1st International Conference on Ubiquitous Robots and Ambient Intelligence, pp. 176–181 (2004)

A Real-Time Gesture Tracking and Recognition System Based on Particle Filtering and Ada-Boosting Techniques

Chin-Shyurng Fahn[1], Chih-Wei Huang[1], and Hung-Kuang Chen[2]

[1] Department of Computer Science and Information Engineering, National Taiwan University of Science and Technology, Taipei, Taiwan, R.O.C.
csfahn@csie.ntust.edu.tw
[2] Department of Electronic Engineering, National Chin-Yi University of Technology, Taichung, Taiwan, R.O.C.

Abstract. A real-time gesture tracking and recognition system based on particle filtering and Ada-Boosting techniques is presented in this paper. The particle filter, which is a flexible simulation-based method and suitable for non-linear tracking problems, is adopted to achieve hand tracking robustly. In order to avoid the influence of the other exposed skin parts of a human body and skin-colored objects in the background, our system further applies the motion information as a feature of the hand in addition to the skin color information. Compared with the conventional particle filters, our method leads to more efficient sampling and requires fewer particles. It results in lowering computational cost and saving much time for gesture recognition later. The gesture recognition uses the features derived from the wavelet transform, and employs an Ada-Boost algorithm which is excellent in facilitating the speed of convergence during the training. Hence, it is conducive to update new information and expand new gesture archives. The experimental results reveal our system is fast, accurate, and robust in hand tracking. Moreover, it has good performance in gesture recognition under complicated environments.

1 Introduction

With the fast development of computer technology in recent years, the interaction between humans and computers is becoming more and more important. Nowadays, both the keyboard and mouse are the standard pieces of equipments for people to interact with a computer. Nonetheless, this kind of interfaces restricts the communication between humans and computers to the manipulation of the devices. Alternatively, new Human Computer Interface (HCI) technology aiming at more rich, natural, and efficient ways of interactions between humans and computers appears in form of face tracking [1], hand tracking [2],[3], face recognition, gesture recognition [4], and so on, in these years. Of such new technology, gesture analysis has been established as one of the most important perceptual interfaces. As a key step of gesture analysis, the hand tracking, especially by monocular vision, is crucial to the success of the deployment of the vision-based user interface in new generation HCI systems.

C. Stephanidis (Ed.): Universal Access in HCI, Part II, HCII 2007, LNCS 4555, pp. 818–827, 2007.

A real-time gesture tracking and recognition system based on particle filtering and Ada-Boosting techniques is presented in this paper where a flow chart of this system is shown in Figure 1.

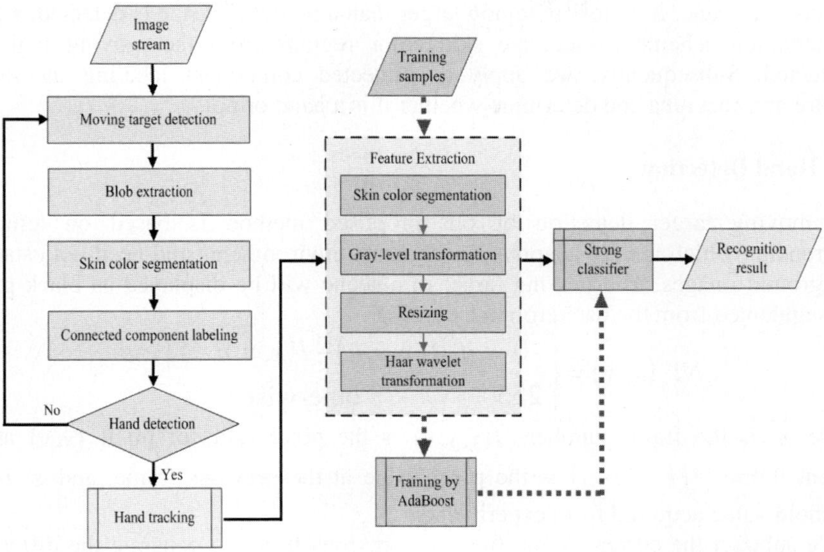

Fig. 1. The flow chart of our system

The particle filter, a flexible simulation-based method suitable for non-linear tracking problems, is adopted to achieve robust hand tracking [3], [5]. In order to avoid the influence of the other exposed skin parts of a human body as well as skin-colored objects in the background, our system makes use of the motion information as a feature of the hand in addition to the skin color information. Compared with the conventional particle filters, our method has a more efficient sampling scheme that requires fewer particles. It effectively reduces the computational cost of the tracking stage and implies more efficient gesture recognition.

The gesture recognition uses the features derived from the Harr wavelet transforms [6] and employs the Gentle Ada-Boost algorithm [7] which is excellent in facilitating the speed of convergence during the training. A great number of existing gesture recognition systems provides fine classification results. However, most of them need high-resolution image sequences and good segmentation of hand regions. Compared to these systems, our recognition system is able to achieve nice recognition results from more complex environments. Furthermore, the Ada-Boost algorithm for gesture recognition requires much less training time than the other machine learning methods such as the hidden Markov model and neural network to perform the same accuracy. Therefore, new gestures or training samples can be introduced or updated with much less efforts for various situations.

The discussion of hand tacking will be presented in Section 2 followed by the gesture recognition in Section 3. Some experimental results are shown in Section 4. Finally, the conclusions and remarks are given in Section 5.

2 Hand Tracking

In order to decrease the calculation time and improve the system performance, we can reduce the searching area while extracting hand regions by focusing on moving regions in a scene. If a moving region larger than a predefined size is detected, a color segmentation scheme to separate skin color regions from the moving region is conducted. Subsequently, we apply a connected component labeling method to acquire an exact area and determine whether it is a hand or not.

2.1 Hand Detection

The moving target detection of our proposed method is based on temporal differencing which is very adaptive for dynamic environments and need not establish background images. The moving target in a scene will be displayed as black pixels and segmented from the background by letting

$$NI_n(x,y) = \begin{cases} 0 & \text{if } |I(x,y,n) - I(x,y,n-1)| \geq \varepsilon \\ 255 & \text{otherwise} \end{cases}$$

where n is the frame number, $I(x,y,n)$ is the pixel value of point (x,y) at the current frame, $I(x,y,n-1)$ is the pixel value at the previous frame, and ε is the threshold value acquired from experiments.

We subtract the current frame from the previous frame to generate the difference image using the motion analysis method proposed in [8]. This method is to compute the absolute value of the differences in the neighborhood (we use a 9×9 mask) surrounding each pixel, then accumulates the difference value of each pixel in the mask. If the accumulated difference value exceeds a predetermined threshold, this pixel is assigned to a moving region.

With the motion analysis method, we can obtain the area of a moving target. To divide the hand region from the moving target, a skin color segmentation method is employed. First, we adopt the HSV color model to replace the RGB one. To aim at the extraction of skin color regions, we segment skin colors from others by H values which is ranged from 3 to 38. It is accomplished through the given upper and lower thresholds to discriminate skin color regions from non-skin ones. After segmenting the skin color region from an extracted moving target, we apply a connected component labeling method to obtain a more accurate area [9].

2.2 Tracking Scheme

The detection algorithm is used to find the complete hand region in the first frame; nonetheless, it is a time-consuming task. After detecting the hand region, we exploit the tracking process to surmount this problem. Our tracking method is activated after the initial location of a target is specified. On the other hand, the majority of the conventional methods employing detection together with tracking adopt a detect-then-track approach where the target is detected in the first frame and then turned to the tracker in the subsequent frames. A well-designed tracking scheme not only saves us a lot of calculation time but extracts the target from an image sequence precisely. To continuously understand the motion direction and trajectory of the target is the main purpose of tracking. Our system utilizes the particle filtering technique that is modified from [3] and [5] to implement the tracking algorithm.

The particle filter is one of flexible simulation-based methods for sampling from a sequence of probability distributions. The strength of these methods lies in their simplicity, flexibility, and systematic treatment of nonlinearity. Moreover, it can deal with extreme non-Gaussian and multimodal noise distributions. The particle filter approximates the sequence of probability distributions of interest using a large set of random samples, named particles. These particles are propagated over time using simple Importance Sampling and re-sampling mechanisms. The iterative process of the particle filter used in our system is summarized in Figure 2.

Given a sample set $S_{t-1} = \{(s_{t-1}^{(i)}, P_{t-1}^{(i)}) \mid j = 1,2,\cdots,n\}$ at time step $t-1$, perform the following steps:

1. **Propagating:** propagate each sample $s_{t-1}^{(i)}$ with probability $P_{t-1}^{(i)}$ by a dynamic model to obtain the sample set S_t.
2. **Weighting:** weigh the samples using both color and motion cues as:
   1) Calculate the distance between each sample and the target by
   $$Dis = \sqrt{1 - \frac{M}{M_t}}$$
   where M is a linear combination of the measurement of color and motion cues; M_t is the size of the sample.
   2) Weigh each sample with
   $$\pi^{(i)} = \frac{1}{\sqrt{2\pi}\sigma} e^{-\frac{Dis^2}{2\sigma^2}}$$
   where σ is the standard deviation of a Gaussian distribution.
3. **Selective re-sampling:** if $\pi^{(i)}$ exceeds or equals a threshold, select C_i even-weighted samples.
4. **Estimate:** obtain the state of the sample with the largest weight
   $$s_t^{(j)}, j = \arg\max_i \pi_t^{(i)}, i = 1,2,\cdots,n$$

Fig. 2. An iterative process of a particle filter

3 Gesture Recognition

We adopt the Ada-Boosting technique to train our samples whose sub-band information in the frequency domain is extracted from the Haar wavelet transform [6] as the features. The classification accuracy will be enhanced with the raise of the number of training samples, the iterations of boosting, and the suitability of features used for texture description. In order to improve the accuracy of classification, some preliminary processes are conducted before the wavelet transform.

During the tracking procedure, the human hand is represented by a rectangular window and the size of the window is changing with the size of the tracked hand. To reduce the influence of the background, the skin color segmentation method is again applied to extracting the real hand region. The Grey-level transformation is instantly performed after the skin color segmentation. Then we normalize the rectangular windows by resizing them to a fixed size. The smallest size of a hand region is about 60×60 pixels in our images; thus, we unify all the rectangular windows to this size. The Haar wavelet transform is performed on such a normalized rectangular window to obtain the second level sub-band LL2 as our hand features.

In this paper, we adopt the Gentle Ada-Boost algorithm [7] integrated with the Classification and Regression Trees (CARTs) as a weak classifier and utilize the GML Ada-Boost Matlab Toolbox provided by the Graphics and Media Laboratory [10] for training/constructing our strong classifier. A version of the Gentle Ada-Boost algorithm is given in Figure 3.

Given: training samples $S = \{(x_1, y_1), (x_2, y_2), \cdots, (x_m, y_m)\}$ for sample vector $x_i \in X$ and label $y_i \in \{-1,1\}$, weak classification space *H*, $H_1(x) = 0$, and integer *T* specifying the number of iterations

Initialize the distribution: $D_1(i) = 1/m$

For $t = 1, 2, \ldots, T$

(1) Fit the regression function $h_t(x)$ by weighted least squares of y_i to x_i with distribution $D_t(i)$

(2) Update $H_{t+1}(x) = H_t(x) + h_t(x)$

(3) Update $D_{t+1}(i) = D_t(i)\exp(-y_i h_i(x_i))$ and renormalize $D_{t+1}(i)$ such that $\sum_{i=1}^{m} D_{t+1}(i) = 1$

Output the final strong classifier: $H(x) = sign\left(\sum_{t=1}^{T} h_t(x)\right)$

Fig. 3. The Gentle Ada-Boost algorithm

We train and construct a unique strong classifier for each hand gesture through the Ada-Boost algorithm. By applying the features that are extracted from the rectangular window to the strong classifier, we can obtain a weight of the final prediction. In order to raise the accuracy of classification, we contemplate the weights of 10 consecutive rectangular windows and calculate the sum of these weights. Comparing the sum of weights for various strong classifiers, we can choose the largest one, and if this sum is greater than a predefined threshold, we think that the user is making a particular hand gesture.

4 Experimental Results and Discussion

In this section, we will implement our proposed method and analyze the experimental results. In order to demonstrate the effectiveness of the algorithms, some video sequences are tested. All the software of our real-time gesture tracking and recognition system is run on a personal computer using a Pentium 4 3.2 GHz CPU with 1 GB DDRAM. The developing environment includes the Borland C++ Builder 6, MATLAB 7.2, Windows XP Professional SP2 equipped with DirectX 9.0, and the image sequences with the resolution of 320 × 240 pixels. The throughput obtained is from 20 to 25 frames per second.

The accuracy measurements used for gesture tracking are based on the number of tracks in the reference data set as well as the number of tracks reported by the system. The notations and definitions of measuring our system performance are mc = A'/A, mf = R'/A, and mm = 1-R/A, which respectively symbolize the fraction of correct tracks, the fraction of reported tracks that are false alarms in which they do not correspond to true tracks, and the miss rate that should be zero for an ideal system.

In order to simplify tracking, we assume that there are no other exposed skin body parts of the same hand which is to be tracked. Moreover, we make the movement of the right hand is faster than other exposed skin body parts, especially than the head. Furthermore, we broadly classify the testing image sequences into three types: general, complicated, and speedy samples and label them as Types A, B, and C, respectively.

4.1 Type A: General Samples

We regard a video sample as a general one if the background of this sample is uncomplicated, the motion of a tracking target is evident, the environment is simple and under sufficient illuminant. For each testing video, we repeatedly execute it 10 times and record the experimental results. There are 11 video samples considered as a simple situation. Table 1 records the miss rates as well as the worst, average, and the best accurate rates of tracking for these 11 samples. The average accuracy of this type is better than 96% and even reaches 100%. Notice that all the experimental data are taken down by calculating the average values for each video sample.

Table 1. The Tracking Accuracy of General Samples

Measurement	Sample										
	A-1	A-2	A-3	A-4	A-5	A-6	A-7	A-8	A-9	A-10	A-11
Avg. m_f (%)	0.6	2.5	2.0	0.2	2.6	0.0	2.2	0.0	2.1	2.7	0.0
Avg. m_m (%)	0.2	1.1	0.1	0.2	1.4	0.0	0.1	0.0	0.0	0.1	0.0
Worst m_c (%)	98.0	88.8	91.5	99.0	90.0	100	94.9	99.6	95.8	95.8	100
Avg. m_c (%)	99.2	96.2	97.9	99.7	96.1	100	97.7	99.9	97.9	97.2	100
Best m_c (%)	100	99.1	100	100	99.2	100	99.5	100	99.6	99.1	100

4.2 Type B: Complicated Samples

We consider a testing video as a complicated sample if too many factors interfere with the tracking result; for instance, the hand is disturbed by human faces or skin-colored objects in the background, the hand region is too small, and the illuminant is not enough. We have 14 complicated samples and their experimental results are listed in Table 2.

Table 2. The Tracking Accuracy of Complicated Samples

Measurement	Sample													
	B-1	B-2	B-3	B-4	B-5	B-6	B-7	B-8	B-9	B-10	B-11	B-12	B-13	B-14
Avg. m_f (%)	3.1	5.6	3.9	1.8	5.4	6.9	4.0	2.4	5.2	2.8	5.6	1.5	5.2	2.5
Avg. m_m (%)	1.8	11.1	0.0	13.2	4.7	2.2	6.6	8.0	0.6	7.2	13.8	4.5	12.4	8.4
Worst m_c (%)	93.7	73.5	94.4	81.8	81.5	89.0	86.4	81.1	91.8	79.8	76.7	88.7	55.3	87.2
Avg. m_c (%)	95.0	83.4	96.1	84.9	90.0	90.9	89.5	89.6	94.2	90.0	80.6	94.0	82.4	89.1
Best m_c (%)	96.5	93.2	97.3	88.1	95.4	92.7	94.6	94.6	96.2	97.2	83.5	99.1	96.4	92.8

In this type of samples, the errors of tracking hands are usually caused by face disturbance. It is obvious that a human face is an integral skin color region and its size is often larger than that of a hand. Hence, when the hand moves near the face, the rectangular window tends to locate the target on the face region. But, if the hand continuously moves, the rectangular window constantly returns to the right position due to the effect of the motion information. Notice that the miss rate m_m becomes large in this type. It is because we set a threshold for the weight of the rectangular window, so our system will re-detect the hand region if the weight is less than the threshold. The re-detecting procedure could avoid unnecessary wrong tracks and diminish the false rate m_f, but frequently re-detecting actions would lead to the increase of m_m. Consequently, this threshold should be determined properly.

4.3 Type C: Speedy Samples

It will raise the tracking difficulty if the hand moves quickly. In our system, the average frame number per second is from 20 to 25, and if the hand movement range is over 100 pixels length (around one third width of a scene) in 10 consecutive frames, we identify this sample as a speedy one.

In general, the tracking accuracy of speedy samples is lower than those of the other two types. The experimental results are shown in Table 3. When the position of a hand changes too much in a short period, it usually exceeds the re-sampling scope of a particle filter. We can see that the differences between the worst and the best correct rates m_c in Samples C-2, C-3, and C-6 are very large. It is because the hand overlaps the human face or skin-colored objects and suddenly moves away at a high speed, while the particle candidates are slow in reacting and miss the hand region easily. Our system can keep tracking well if any one of the particle candidates just hits on the hand region. On the contrary, if the particle candidates do not catch the correct target, it will either abandon the tracking target then try to detect the hand region once more or keep tracking on the wrong target until the hand moves near the re-sampling scope of the particle filter. Attempting to enlarge the re-sampling range could slightly solve this problem. Nevertheless, the wider the re-sampling range is, the sparser the particle candidates are, and sometimes it would reduce the tracking precision.

Table 3. The Tracking Accuracy of Speedy Samples

Measurement	Sample						
	C-1	C-2	C-3	C-4	C-5	C-6	C-7
Avg. m_f (%)	1.0	10.0	4.0	10.8	11.0	8.8	2.0
Avg. m_m (%)	5.0	17.9	9.5	9.4	6.5	10.0	19.5
Worst m_c (%)	91.2	56.5	49.0	70.8	78.8	49.2	72.8
Avg. m_c (%)	94.0	72.2	86.6	79.9	82.5	81.3	78.6
Best m_c (%)	97.0	87.4	94.3	88.7	87.4	88.0	83.2

We compare the efficiency of the conventional [5], particle filter with mean shift [3], and our proposed methods. And the experimental results are recorded in Table 4.

Table 4. Comparison of the Three Hand Tracking Methods

Measurement	Method		
	Convention	Mean shift	Ours
Avg. execution time	47ms	25ms	17ms
Avg. frame number	21	39	58
Number of particles	100	20	20
Avg. accuracy (Type A)	91.7%	98.6%	98.3%
Avg. accuracy (Type B)	86.5%	91.0%	90.3%

Table 5 shows the average execution time of the mean shift method and our proposed method with different number of particles.

Table 5. Average Execution Time of the Mean Shift Method and Our Proposed Method

Number of particles	Avg. execution time (ms)	
	Mean shift	Ours
20	25	17
40	36	28
60	48	33

Our system can recognize three kinds of gestures: the palm, thumb, and victory gestures as Figure 4 illustrates. The positive and negative training samples are obtained manually from video sequences. Furthermore, in order to raise the variety of training samples, we also take the hand pictures as our samples directly. We totally have 2,100 training samples, and each kind of gestures includes approximately equal number of samples. The evaluation method of gesture recognition is to measure the accuracy of classifying the three particular kinds of gestures. We execute the gesture recognition procedure for each testing video 5 times to acquire more objective results and record the estimative effects for different kinds of gestures.

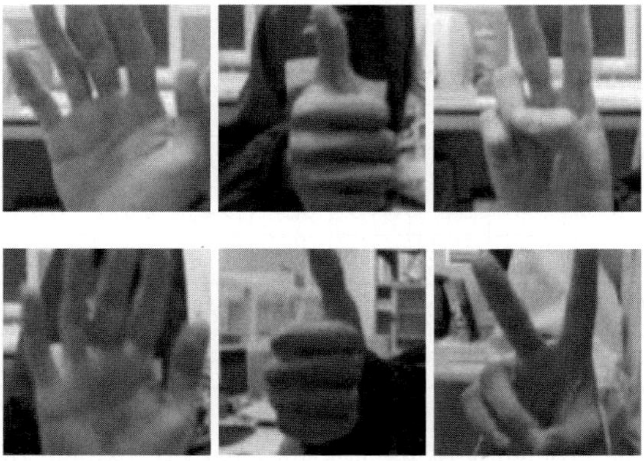

Fig. 4. Some samples of the palm, thumb, and victory gestures

Before we start training, a K-fold cross-validation procedure is applied. We adopt 5-fold cross-validation to estimate the accuracy of different system models in our experiments. From the model estimation, we find that the best performance is achieved while the Gentle Ada-Boost algorithm uses 24 CART splits and 500 iterations. In consideration of the tradeoff between accuracy and efficiency, we exploit the Gentle Ada-Boost algorithm with 24 CART splits and 500 iterations as our classification model.

The average recognition rates of the three kinds of gestures are shown in Table 6. As it can be seen from this table, the accuracy of the thumb gesture is much better than those of the other two. Comparing with the other two kinds of gestures, the shape of the thumb gesture is more stable and effortlessly to be recognized.

Table 6. Average Recognition Rates of the Three Kinds of Gestures

Accuracy	Gesture		
	Palm	Thumb	Victory
Average recognition rate (%)	80.9	96.9	81.4

5 Conclusions and Future Work

In this paper, we have presented a robust and efficient real-time gesture tracking and recognition system. The current system takes approximately 0.05-0.06 second a frame to complete all processes, including hand tracking and gesture recognition. During the tracking procedure, our method can use fewer particles to maintain exact hand tracking than the conventional particle filtering methods do, and results in low computational cost. Our tracking system is very robustly and precisely, which is not only suitable for tracking the hand behind a shelter or suffering from head disturbance, but also allows the slight oscillation of a scene. By employing a predefined threshold in the re-sampling step, our tracking system overcomes the degeneracy problem, saves much calculation time, and enhances the tracking accuracy.

The above computer vision based gesture tracking and recognition system is still far from achieving an ideal state of intelligence and flexibility. Although we have already proposed an acceptable system model, several parts require further improvement. At present, the observation phase of our tracking algorithm only uses color and motion cues. Some other cues, for example, texture features and the relative location of hands, can also be utilized, so that we can differentiate two hands from a head. Besides, the gesture recognition results are not good enough yet. Future work tends to improve the recognition rate of dynamic gestures by incorporating more features such as the contour, orientation, speed, and trajectory information as well as training with more and larger variety of gesture samples.

References

1. Bradski, G.R.: Computer vision face tracking for use in a perceptual user interface. Intel Technology Journal 2(2), 1–15 (1998)
2. Imagawa, K., Lu, S., Igi, S.: Color-based hands tracking system for sign language recognition. In: Proceedings of the Third IEEE International Conference on Automatic Face and Gesture Recognition, pp. 462–467 (1998)
3. Shan, C., Wei, Y., Tan, T., Ojardias, F.: Real time hand tracking by combining particle filtering and mean shift. In: Proceedings of the Sixth IEEE International Conference on Automatic Face and Gesture Recognition, pp. 669–674 (2004)
4. Liu, X., Fujimura, K.: Hand gesture recognition using depth data. In: Proceedings of the 6th IEEE Intern. Conf. on Automatic Face and Gesture Recognition, pp. 529–534 (2004)
5. Song, X.Q.: Real-time visual detection and tracking of multiple moving objects based on particle filtering techniques, Master Thesis, Department of Computer Science and Information Engineering, National Taiwan University of Science and Technology, Taipei, Taiwan, ROC (2005)
6. Kumar, S., Kumar, D.K., Sharma, A., McLachlan, N.: Classification of visual hand movements using multiresolution wavelet images. In: Proceedings of the International Conference on Intelligent Sensing and Information Processing, pp. 373–378 (2004)
7. Friedman, J., Hastie, T., Tibshirani, R.: Additive logistic regression: a statistical view of boosting. The Annals of Statistics 28(2), 337–407 (2000)
8. Graf, H.P., Cosatto, E., Gibbon, D., Kocheisen, M., Petajan, E.: Multi-modal system for locating heads and faces. In: Proceedings of the Second International Conference on Automatic Face and Gesture Recognition, pp. 88–93 (1996)
9. Suzuki, K., Horiba, I., Sugie, N.: Linear-time connected-component labeling based on sequential local operations. Computer Vision and Image Understanding Archive 89(1), 1–23 (2003)
10. Vezhnevets, A.: GML Ada-Boost Matlab Toolbox, Technique Manual, Graphics and Media Laboratory, Computer Science Department, Moscow State University, Moscow, Russian Federation (2006) http://research.graphicon.ru/

Enhancing Human-Computer Interaction with Embodied Conversational Agents

Mary Ellen Foster

Robotics and Embedded Systems Group
Department of Informatics, Technische Universität München
Boltzmannstraße 3, 85748 Garching bei München, Germany
foster@in.tum.de

Abstract. We survey recent research in which the impact of an embodied conversational agent on human-computer interaction has been assessed through a human evaluation. In some cases, the evaluation involved comparing different versions of the agent against itself in the context of a full interactive system; in others, it measured the effect on user perception of spoken output of specific aspects of the embodied agent's behaviour. In almost all of the studies, an embodied agent that displays appropriate non-verbal behaviour was found to enhance the interaction.

1 Introduction

An Embodied Conversational Agent (ECA) is a computer interface that is represented as a human body, and that uses its face and body in a human-like way in conversation with the user; see [1] for an overview of the field. The main benefit of ECAs as an interface metaphor is that they allow users to interact with a computer in the most natural possible setting: face-to-face conversation. Reeves and Nass [2] and others have demonstrated that, when computers produce social cues, users will respond socially, even if they are not conscious of this behaviour.

There is no longer any question that the production of language and its accompanying non-verbal behaviour are tightly linked [3–5]. The communicative functions of body language listed by Bickmore and Cassell [6] include conversation initiation and termination, turn-taking and interruption, content elaboration and emphasis, and feedback and error correction; non-verbal behaviours that can achieve these functions include gaze modification, facial expressions, hand gestures, and posture shifts, among others. Many of these behaviours have been implemented on embodied conversational agents to address many of these communicative functions.

In this paper, we investigate the impact of embodied agents on human-computer interaction by surveying a range of systems for which the impact of the agent has been directly evaluated. We first describe the two high-level techniques that have been used to evaluate embodied agents: system-level evaluation and evaluation of individual aspects. We then describe recent embodied-agent systems that have been evaluated using each of these techniques. At the end, we summarise the overall findings of these studies and draw conclusions regarding the ways in which an embodied agent can enhance the interaction with a computer system.

C. Stephanidis (Ed.): Universal Access in HCI, Part II, HCII 2007, LNCS 4555, pp. 828–837, 2007.

2 Evaluating Embodied Agents

Embodied agents are generally evaluated by measuring user responses to the output, in or out of context; automated evaluation has not been widely used in this area. Evaluation can take two forms [7]: the behaviour as a whole can be evaluated in the context of a system, or the individual modalities and behavioural aspects can be assessed separately.

System-level evaluation of an ECA has three aspects: the fluency and efficiency of the user-ECA interaction, the subjective user experience, and the effectiveness of the application in achieving its goals. These criteria are similar to the common evaluation criteria for multimodal dialogue systems described by Dybkjær et al. [8]; however, the addition of the ECA adds another modality whose settings can be varied, and that can potentially have an effect on any of the outcome variables.

Evaluation of individual aspects—e.g., non-verbal behaviour, audio-visual speech, or personality and emotion—is necessary to measure whether the way those behaviours are implemented in the ECA is understood by users as intended, and generally uses the following pattern. First, a model is implemented, based on a combination of documented behaviour from the literature and direct observation of human behaviours. The implemented model is then used to generate materials, and a judgement study is performed to measure whether participants are able to perceive the intended content in the output. Perception studies provide a different perspective on ECAs than system-level evaluation: passive observers may receive a different impression of an ECA than users who are directly engaged in interacting with the agent [e.g., 9].

In the following two sections, we describe a number of recent evaluations of each type. In Section 3, we describe a range of evaluations that have looked at the impact of the embodied agent on the overall system: in each case, we first describe the system and the role of the agent within it, and then describe the design and results of the evaluation study. In Section 4, we then summarise studies that have investigated the impact of specific embodied-agent behaviours directly.

3 System-Level Evaluations

In a system-level evaluation of an embodied agent, participants generally interact with a complete system under one of a range of conditions; various subjective and objective measures are then used to compare the different versions of the system. The conditions that are used can vary: in some cases, the system is run with and without the embodied agent; in others, different versions of the agent implement different behaviours; while in still others, the behaviours of participants interacting with an agent are compared to those of participants interacting with other humans.

3.1 REA: Social Dialogue and Embodiment

REA [10] is an embodied agent that acts as a real estate salesperson, answering user questions about properties in a database and showing users around a virtual house. REA is able to sense the user through cameras and a microphone and produces output including speech with intonation, facial expressions, and gestures of a fully-articulated body. In addition to supporting task-based dialogue in the real-estate domain, REA is also able to engage in social dialogue with the user: "small talk" in which social goals are primary and the task goals are left in the background. The primary function of small talk is to build rapport and trust and to allow the interlocutors to establish a style of interaction. Body language plays a critical role in human-human social dialogue: behaviours such as leaning forward, nodding, smiling, and direct gaze all contribute to feelings of warmth and trust in the interaction.

To measure the impact of REA's social dialogue, Bickmore and Cassell [6] performed an experiment in which participants interacted with one of two possible versions of REA: one version that employed only task-based dialogue, and one that used social dialogue as well. As an additional factor, half of the participants interacted with the fully embodied REA agent, while the other half talked with REA over a telephone. Participants answered a range of questions measuring their subjective impressions of REA, their degree of trust, and the amount that they were willing to spend on an apartment after having used the system. There was a complex interaction between the conditions: one main result was that participants that interacted with REA over the telephone preferred the social dialogue style, while participants that used the embodied version of REA preferred the task-based dialogue. Bickmore and Cassell hypothesise that this is due the body language used by REA inadvertently projecting an unfriendly personality.

3.2 MagiCster: Consistent Affective Facial Displays

The MagiCster project had two main goals: to develop believable embodied conversational agents making use of synchronised gaze, facial expression, gesture, body posture, and speech, and to evaluate agents in laboratory conditions to determine the aspects of the agents that are important for a range of human-computer interactions. As part of this project, the Greta embodied agent [11] was developed; this agent is able to display a range of performative facial displays such as surprise and feeling sorry for the user, and to combine them dynamically as needed to produce more complex expressions.

Berry et al. [12] describe an evaluation of the impact of Greta on users' responses to health-education materials. This study used two messages about healthy eating, one positively framed (emphasising the positive effects of eating well) and one negatively framed (emphasising the negative effects of not doing so). Participants were presented with one of the two messages and asked to rate the utterance on a number of scales, and were also asked several memory questions about the content of the utterance. In general, participants viewing messages presented by Greta performed worse on the memory task than those using a textual or speech-only presentation of the information; however, when Greta used facial displays that were consistent with the content of the speech, the performance impact was mitigated.

3.3 Gesturing Strategy and Agent Appearance

Buisine et al. [13] describe an experiment in which a range of multimodal gesturing strategies and agent appearances were compared in the context of a system that generated embodied technical explanations—for example, describing how to use a copy machine. The explanations contained many references to particular components of the machines, so there were several opportunities to make multimodal spatial references. Three different gesturing strategies were implemented for spatial references: redundancy (all relevant information is given in both speech and gesture), complementarity (half of the relevant information is given on each channel), and speech-only (all of the relevant information is given in speech, and the gestures have no semantic content). As another factor, agents with three different appearances were implemented: two male agents and one female.

In an evaluation, participants viewed explanations of each type produced by each of the agents; the dependent variables were users' subjective evaluations of the agents and their performance on a recall task. The presentations including speech only were judged to have lower quality than either of the other two types, particularly by the male participants; participants also reported more trust in the presentations that were judged to have higher quality. One of the male agents was perceived as significantly less likeable than the other two. The gender of the participant had a significant effect on their recall performance, but there was little effect of any of the experimental manipulations on this variable.

3.4 COMIC: Turn-Taking and Task Performance

The COMIC multimodal dialogue system adds a dialogue interface to a CAD-like application used in bathroom sales situations to help clients redesign their rooms. The input channels include speech recognition, along with handwriting and pen gestures provided either on a tablet display or with a mouse; the output combines synthesised speech, non-verbal behaviour of a talking head, deictic gestures using an on-screen pointer, and direct control of the underlying application. The nonverbal behaviour of the talking head performs several functions in COMIC. It gazes at objects on the screen as it describes them; it also uses facial expressions to convey the system state, for example using a "thinking" expression while processing input, looking confused if the user input was not understood, and looking happy when it was understood.

White et al. [14] describe an experiment designed to measure whether the non-verbal behaviours of the agent make a difference to users' interactions with the system. As a between-participants factor, the talking head was run in one of two modes: expressive, where all of the non-verbal behaviours of the head were enabled, and zombie, where all behaviours except lip movements were disabled. The results demonstrate that the expressive face mitigated the perception of slow system response and attracted the user's gaze more frequently. However, participants' performance on a recall measure was significantly lower with the expressive head than it was with the zombie head, especially for the male participants (whose overall recall performance was also lower).

3.5 Mel: Engagement in the Interaction

Mel [15] is a robot designed to resemble a penguin wearing glasses who acts as a host for visitors to a research lab. Its capabilities include participating in spoken dialogue, locating and tracking the position and gaze direction of the visitor, interpreting and responding to nodding behaviour during a conversation, and pointing and looking at objects in the environment. Mel leads the user through a demonstration of a research prototype, giving instructions on its use and describing how it works and how it can be useful. A specific goal for Mel was to maintain user engagement in the interaction. The level of engagement was monitored by tracking the verbal and non-verbal behaviour of the user, while a set of recipes based on observed human-human interactions were used to maintain engagement—for example, by looking at the user's face or repeating a prompt when the user attention wavers.

A study was conducted comparing the experience of two groups of users interacting with Mel. For one group, Mel employed its full range of non-verbal behaviour (mover mode); for the other group, the only motions were movements of the lips to accompany the speech (talker mode). These conditions are similar to the expressive and zombie conditions used in the evaluation of the COMIC system described above. The responses on a post-interaction questionnaire indicate that female participants reported more engagement in the interaction, regardless of condition; that participants in the talker condition found the robot more reliable; and that participants in the mover condition found the robot motions more appropriate. When the recordings of the interaction were analysed, it was found that participants in the mover condition had significantly longer interactions, coordinated their gaze with the robot more frequently, and looked back at the robot significantly more often.

3.6 GAMBLE: Deceptive Body Language

GAMBLE [9] is a scenario in which two human users play a dice game against an embodied agent. To win in this game, it is essential both to lie to your fellow players and to detect when they are lying to you. For the evaluation described by Rehm and André [9], two different versions of the agent were implemented: one that shows clues to deception in its facial expressions, and one that does not. In an initial study where the expressions were presented out of context, participants were able to detect these deceptive expressions; this study is summarised in Section 4. However, in the game context, there was no difference between participants' responses to the two versions of the agent: they caught the agent lying about 73% of the time for both versions, and incorrectly accused it of lying when it was telling the truth 54% of the time for both. Rehm and André propose that the lack of effect in this case is due to the fact that participants were concentrating on the task, rather than the details of the agent's expression.

In another analysis of the data from these interactions [16], it was found that participants looked at the agent approximately as often as they looked at the other human player when they were speaking to it. However, when addressed by the agent, participants looked at it much more often than they looked at the other human player when addressed by them.

3.7 MIT FitTrack: Relational Agents

The MIT FitTrack system [17] was designed to investigate the role of relational agents—embodied agents that are intended to build and maintain long-term social-emotional relationships with users. The system used an embodied agent to play the role of an exercise advisor who discussed physical activity with the user and encouraged them to become more physically active. The system output combined synthesised speech and synchronised non-verbal behaviour, using many of the same components as the REA system described in Section 3.1. It employed a range of behaviours in an effort to build and maintain a relationship with the user, including small talk, addressing the user as a friend, and displaying empathy and humour.

The effectiveness of the system was evaluated via a longitudinal study in which participants used the system daily for a month. Participants used the system in one of two modes: relational, in which the system employed its full range of relational behaviours in an effort to build a working relationship with the participant, and non-relational, in which the relational behaviours were all disabled. The outcomes were measured through a set of subjective questionnaires, and also by measuring the participants' exercise level before, during, and after the study. The participants in the relational condition displayed higher levels of trust and liking for the agent than did those using the non-relational version. Both groups of participants that used the FitTrack increased their physical activity more than a control group who did not use the system, but there was no significant difference between the two FitTrack groups on this measure.

3.8 iCat Home Companion: Social Intelligence

De Ruyter et al. [18] studied a home dialogue system that used the iCat user-interface robot to program a DVD recorder and participate in an online auction. The iCat is a platform for studying social human-robot interfaces: it is equipped with servos that can control many parts of the face to produce expressions, and is also able to produce lip-synchronised synthesised speech. A range of socially intelligent behaviours were implemented for the iCat: displaying attentive listening behaviour, responding to non-verbal cues of the user, and using expressive facial displays where appropriate. In the evaluation, the socially intelligent system was compared against a socially neutral version that used no facial displays apart for lip-synchronisation and that did not respond to or exhibit social cues. The results of the study indicated that participants rated the socially intelligent version as more social than the neutral version, and also expressed more satisfaction with the DVD player when they used the social iCat.

3.9 Evaluation Via Physiological Measures

Prendinger and colleagues have performed several studies in which the impact of embodied agents on an interaction is measured through physiological measures of the participants. In [19], they used a web-based system that displayed pictures of a Tokyo apartment and described them to a user. The system had three different presentation modes: an embodied agent that used synthesised speech and simple left/right deictic gestures, combined speech and incrementally-displayed text (with the same content in both), and speech only; the same synthetic voice was used for all presentation modes. They used eye-tracking to compare participants' responses to descriptions presented in the three modes. When the agent was present, participants followed its verbal and non-verbal navigation directions and mostly looked at the agent's face rather than other parts; with written text, participants looked at the box nearly twice as often as they did at the agent. On a questionnaire, participants rated the voice-only presentation to be significantly more useful for the task than either of the other presentation types.

In another study, Prendinger et al. [20] implemented a mathematical quiz game that included an embodied agent acting as quizmaster. The game included delays designed to frustrate the user (who was told that the game was in a development stage and could have bugs). The agent was able to produce a range of affective feedback, including apologising for delays in the system (with apologetic body language), looking happy when an answer was correct and sad when it was wrong, and using more polite language. In an experiment, participants used the system in one of two modes: with all of the affective feedback enabled, and with it all disabled. The results indicated that the affective agent reduced the stress of participants as measured by galvanic skin response, and also led participants to experience the quiz as less difficult.

4 Evaluation of Individual Aspects

In the previous section, we listed a number of studies where the impact of an expressive agent is evaluated in the context of an entire system. Other studies have looked at specific aspects of agents in isolation: for these studies, the general strategy is to test whether participants are able to perceive the intended prosodic or affective content of spoken output based on the body language of the agent that accompanies the utterance.

In a series of studies, Swerts and Krahmer [21] have investigated the influence of facial displays on users' perception of the prosody of an utterance. They found that congruent speech prosody and visual cues (nodding and eyebrow raises) are preferred to conflicting cues on these two channels; that correct facial displays enhance participants' ability to perceive stress in speech; and that the upper part of the face and the left side are the most relevant for perceiving the intended prosody.

Foster [22] has investigated the influence on facial displays of the intended user-model evaluation in the context of the COMIC multimodal dialogue system; this system is described in detail in Section 3.4. The studies used the RUTH talking head [23] to compare different methods of using data from a single-speaker corpus to select facial displays based on the intended user-model evaluation and other contextual factors. The results of these experiments demonstrate that participants are able to identify the intended user-model evaluation based on the motions of the talking head, and that they prefer outputs where the user model expressed in speech matches the facial displays.

Rehm and André [9] investigated the impact of facial cues to deception on users' responses to an agent, using the Greta talking head developed in the MagiCster project (Section 3.2). First, a set of deceptive facial expressions were created by "masking" negative emotions (anger, fear, disgust, sadness) with a smile. For the experiment, two versions of a number of videos were created in which Greta presented movie reviews: in one version, true smiles were used to accompany positive sentences such as I liked the happy ending, while the other version used expressions in which a smile was used to mask disgust; the same synthesised speech was used for both versions. Participants were shown a series of videos, half presented by each version of the agent. The version using deceptive facial displays was judged to be less reliable, less trustworthy, less convincing, less credible, and less certain about what it was saying. Note that, as described in Section 3.6, these facial displays did not make any difference in a task-based context.

Marsi and van Rooden [24] implemented selected facial signals of uncertainty on the RUTH talking head in the context of a multimodal question-answering system, and created videos including just the eyebrow motions, just the rigid head motions, or both. In an experimental study, participants were asked to use a five-point scale to rate the uncertainty level for a series of videos. Participants generally rated the videos intended to express certainty as being more certain than those intended to express uncertainty; however, when the eyebrow movements are investigated specifically, the brow movements designed to be uncertain were actually judged to be displaying certainty.

5 Summary

In general, the results of the studies described here indicate that an embodied agent can improve user satisfaction and engagement with a computer system, and in some cases (e.g., with the iCat companion) can even improve users' opinion of the objects being described by the system. Agent body language can also influence users' perception both of the prosody of synthesised speech and of various affective aspects of the speech.

However, not all of results were entirely positive: some agent implementations did not make any difference (e.g., the deceptive body language in the dice game), while others actually had an effect counter to what was intended (e.g., the inadvertently unfriendly body language of REA, the penalty on task performance for male participants with the expressive COMIC head, and the eyebrow motions that were judged to indicate certainty rather than uncertainty). In many cases, there was a differential effect of gender on participants' responses to the agent: female users generally seem to respond more positively to expressive embodied agents than do male users.

In summary, then, these studies demonstrate adding an expressive embodied interface agent to a computer system can often have a positive effect on users' interactions with that system. However, they also show that it is vital to test any particular agent implementation to ensure that it is having the intended effect on the target user group.

Acknowledgements. This work was supported by the EU FP6 IST Cognitive Systems Integrated Project "JAST" (FP6-003747-IP), http://www.euprojects-jast.net/.

References

1. Cassell, J., Sullivan, J., Prevost, S., Churchill, E. (eds.): Embodied Conversational Agents. MIT Press, Cambridge (2000)
2. Reeves, B., Nass, C.: The Media Equation: How people treat computers, television, and new media like real people and places. Cambridge University Press, Cambridge (1996)

3. Bavelas, J.B., Chovil, N.: Visible acts of meaning: An integrated message model of language in face-to-face dialogue. Journal of Language and Social Psychology 19(2), 163–194 (2000)
4. Kendon, A.: Gesture: Visible Action as Utterance. Cambridge University Press, Cambridge (2004)
5. McNeill, D. (ed.): Language and Gesture: Window into Thought and Action. Cambridge University Press, Cambridge (2000)
6. Bickmore, T., Cassell, J.: Social dialogue with embodied conversational agents. In: van Kuppevelt, J., Dybkjær, L., Bernsen, N.O. (eds.) Advances in Natural, Multimodal Dialogue Systems, Kluwer, New York (2005)
7. Ruttkay, Z., André, E., Johnson, W.L., Pelachaud, C. (eds.): Evaluating Embodied Conversational Agents. Dagstuhl Seminar Proceedings, 04121 (2006)
8. Dybkjær, L., Bernsen, N.O., Minker, W.: Evaluation and usability of multimodal spoken language dialogue systems. Speech Communication 43(1–2), 33–54 (2004)
9. Rehm, M., André, E.: Catch me if you can – exploring lying agents in social settings. In: Proceedings of the International Conference on Autonomous Agents and Multiagent Systems, pp. 937–944 (2005)
10. Cassell, J., Bickmore, T., Campbell, L., Vilhjálmsson, H., Yan, H.: Human conversation as a system framework: Designing embodied conversational agents. In: [1], pp. 29–63
11. Poggi, I., Pelachaud, C.: Performative facial expressions in animated faces. In: [1], pp. 154–188
12. Berry, D.C., Butler, L., de Rosis, F., Laaksolathi, J., Pelachaud, C., Steedman, M.: Final evaluation report. Deliverable 4.6, MagiCster project (2004)
13. Buisine, S., Abrilian, S., Martin, J.-C.: Evaluation of individual multimodal behaviour of 2D embodied agents in presentation tasks. In [25], pp. 217–238.
14. White, M., Foster, M.E., Oberlander, J., Brown, A.: Using facial feedback to enhance turn-taking in a multimodal dialogue system. In: Proceedings of HCI International 2005 Thematic Session on Universal Access in Human-Computer Interaction (2005)
15. Sidner, C.L., Lee, C., Kidd, C.D., Lesh, N., Rich, C.: Explorations in engagement for humans and robots. Artificial Intelligence 166(1–2), 140–164 (2005)
16. Rehm, M., André, E.: Where do they look? Gaze behaviors of multiple users interacting with an embodied conversational agent. In: Panayiotopoulos, T., Gratch, J., Aylett, R., Ballin, D., Olivier, P., Rist, T. (eds.) IVA 2005. LNCS (LNAI), vol. 3661, pp. 241–252. Springer, Heidelberg (2005)
17. Bickmore, T.W., Picard, R.W.: Establishing and maintaining long-term human-computer relationships. ACM Transactions on Computer-Human Interaction 12(2), 293–327 (2005)
18. de Ruyter, B., Saini, P., Markopoulos, P., van Breemen, A.: Assessing the effects of building social intelligence in a robotic interface for the home. Interacting with Computers 17(5), 522–541 (2005)
19. Prendinger, H., Ma, C., Yingzi, J., Nakasone, A., Ishizuka, M.: Understanding the effect of life-like interface agents through users' eye movements. In: Proceedings of the 7th international conference on Multimodal interfaces (ICMI 2005), pp. 108–115 (2005)
20. Prendinger, H., Mori, J., Ishizuka, M.: Using human physiology to evaluate subtle expressivity of a virtual quizmaster in a mathematical game. International Journal of Human-Computer Studies 62(2), 231–245 (2005)
21. Swerts, M., Krahmer, E.: On the perception of audiovisual cues to prominence (In Press)
22. Foster, M.E.: Evaluating the impact of variation in the generation of multimodal object descriptions. Ph.D. thesis, School of Informatics, University of Edinburgh (In submission) (2007)

23. DeCarlo, D., Stone, M., Revilla, C., Venditti, J.J.: Specifying and animating facial signals for discourse in embodied conversational agents. Computer Animation and Virtual Worlds 15(1), 27–38 (2004)
24. Marsi, E., van Rooden, F.: Expressing uncertainty with a talking head. In: Proceedings of the Workshop on Multimodal Generation (MOG 2007) (2007)
25. Pelachaud, C., Ruttkay, Z. (eds.): From Brows to Trust: Evaluating Embodied Conversational Agents. Springer, Heidelberg (2004)

Comparison Between Event Related Potentials Obtained by Syllable Recall Tasks and by Associative Recall Tasks

Mariko F. Funada[1], Miki Shibukawa[2], Tadashi Funada[3], Satoki P. Ninomija, and Yoshihide Igarashi[1]

[1] Department of Business Administration, Hakuoh Univ., Daigyoji, Oyama, Tochigi, Japan
[2] Department of Human Development, Hakuoh Univ., Daigyoji, Oyama, Tochigi, Japan
[3] Department of Mathematics, Rikkyo Univ. Nishiikebukuro, Toshimaku, Tokyo, Japan
{Mariko Funada,Miki Shibukawa, Tadashi Funada, Satoki P. Ninomija, Yoshihide Igarashi, funada}@hakuoh.ac.jp

Abstract. The final goal of this research is to establish some useful verbal communication systems between computers and persons, or between handicapped persons and normal persons. For a substantial progress toward the research goal, we investigate Event Related Potentials (ERP's for short) caused by Electroencephalograms (EEG's for short). By observing ERP's, we estimate recalled words, phrases, or sentences that may contain some homonyms or related words. In particular, we pay attention to the difference between ERP's caused by recalling a single syllable individually without other syllables and ERP's caused by recalling a syllable together with a word containing the syllable. From our observation of this difference, we believe that it may be useful to discuss the possibility of estimating a recalled word by combining ERPs caused by syllables.

Keywords: EEG, ERP, syllable recall, association.

1 Introduction

It would be nice if the progress of computer technology and brain science makes possible or easier for disabled or paralyzed individuals to communicate with their external surroundings. The research problem discussed in this paper has been motivated by this kind of desires and needs. Cognition events of a human being are controlled by electric signals sent from his/her brains. From this fact we intend to design a brain-computer interface using electroencephalograms (EEGs). As meaningful signals from the brain, event related potentials (ERPs) are measured from EEGs[1].

We show that ERPs are clearly related to cognitive events such as visual stimulation, auditory stimulation, and others. ERPs have been much studied in various areas, e.g., medical science, ergonomics, psychology, and others. The purpose of this paper is to confirm that the following assumption is acceptable or to give evidence for

C. Stephanidis (Ed.): Universal Access in HCI, Part II, HCII 2007, LNCS 4555, pp. 838–847, 2007.

the assumption. "We can guess correctly a word from ERP's obtained by recalling the syllables that are components of the word."

2 Methodology

2.1 Experiments

We repeat the following experiment four times:

1) The subjects: Two persons whose ages are 21 years old. We use "sub 1" and "sub 2" to identify them.
2) The place of the experiments: The laboratory of the first author at Hakuoh University.
3) Recalled words: We use five words. These are an apple, an orange, a strawberry, a banana, and a melon. Each of these words consists of three syllables in Japanese as follows: apple: ri-n-go, orange: mi-ka-n, strawberry: i-chi-go, banana: ba-na-na, melon: me-ro-n
4) Recalled Syllables: The fifty syllables used in Japanese are divided into ten groups as follows:
a-group {a, i, u, e, o}, ka-group {ka, ki, ku, ke,ko }, sa-group { sa, si, su, se, so}, ta-group { ta, ti, tu, te, to}, na-group {na,ni,nu ne,no}, ha-group {ha, hi, hu, he, ho}, ma-group { ma, mi, mu, me, mo}, ya-group {ya, yi, yu, ye, yo}, ra-group {ra, ri, ru, re, ro}, wa-group { wa, wi, wu, we, wo}
5) Stimuli: We use five sets of combinations of producing districts and products (fruit). Each of the combinations starts from two Chinese characters. One is a producing district followed by the other, a fruit name. When we use each combination as a stimulus to a subject, one syllable among the last three syllables is replaced by a pause. The experiments are to measure how the subject properly recalls the paused syllable from the producing district and other two syllables of the fruit name. These patterns are depicted in Fig.1, where the squares indicate positions of displayed syllables, and dark squares indicate positions of paused ones (i.e., not displayed ones).

Fig. 1. The formats of stimuli

We call five sequences of producing districts followed by fruit names containing pauses "a *term*". A term is repeated twice for each instance. Such a set of two terms are called "a *set*" or "a *set*" of experiments. Five sets are repeated. After another kind of experiments, the subjects take again five sets. The interval between two consecutive sets of the experiments is 1 minute for the rest of the subjects.
6) Syllable stimuli: We use similar formats for syllable stimuli to the formats explained in 5) above. The formats for syllable stimuli are shown in Fig.2, where

two problems are given. The first one consists of five syllables and the second one is a pause followed by 4 syllables. Other types of problems are also possible but we omit them here.

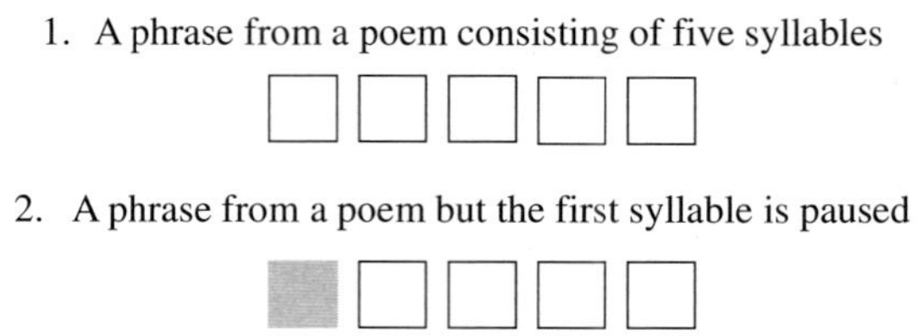

Fig. 2. Examples of formats for syllable stimuli

7) Display of stimuli: a sequence of stimuli is displayed on a 19 inches-CRT (cathode-ray tube) in front of the subjects. The size of the stimuli on the CRT is small enough for the subjects to see them without moving their eyes.
8) Tasks for each subject: A subject recalls five fruit names given in 3) above. When the first pattern in Fig.1 is displayed, the subject tries to determine which fruit he/she recalls. When the second pattern is displayed, the subject recalls the first syllables, when the third one is displayed, the subject recalls the second syllable, and so on. In this experiment, "recall" means to pronounce words in their mind without sound and moving their tongues.
9) A period for displaying a stimulus: Each stimulus in Fig.1 is displayed for 1 second. An interval between two consecutive stimuli is at random within the range from 800ms to1200ms.
10) Duration of an experiment: About 1.3 minutes are spent for a set of experiments, and 1 minutes are used for a short rest in the interval between two consecutive sets of experiments. Consequently the total experimental time for 5 sets of experiments is 6.5 minutes excluding intervals between sets.
11) EEGs: Single polar eight channels of "International 10-20 methods" are used for measuring EEG's. The measurement positions are Fp_1, Fp_2, C_3, C_4, O_3, O_4, C_z, and P_z. The base is A_1 connected to A_2.
12) The sampling frequency for A/D: 1 kHz.

2.2 Analysis

1) Recorded EEGs ($eeg_i(t)$, $i=1,2,\ldots 20$, $t=1,2,\ldots 1000$))are divided into five groups and four parts. Each EEG corresponds to a syllable or a problem .
2) The EEG's in each group are filtered by an adaptive filter made by the first author.
3) We normalize the filtered data ($EEG_i(t)$, $i=1,2,\ldots n$, $t=1,2,\ldots 1000$) by the average of them, $m(EEG_i)$ and the standard deviation $sd(EEGi)$.

$$NEEG_i(t) = \frac{EEG_i(t) - m(EEG_i)}{sd(EEG_i)} \tag{1}$$

4) We average the normalized twenty EEG's to obtain an ERP evoked by recalling a character and use a symbol $ERP_{kj}(t)$ to indicate the obtained ERP. "*k*" indicates a fruit name, and "*j*" indicates a pattern (format) of stimuli in Fig.1. (k=1,2,3,4,5, j=1,2,3,4, t=1,2,…1000)

$$EEG_{kj}(t) = \frac{1}{20}\sum_{i=1}^{20} NEEG_{kji}(t) \tag{2}$$

5) Since we repeated the experiments four times, we take the average of the four sampling data for $ERP_{kj}(t)$ to obtain a typical value of ERP for each syllable. We use $SERP_{kj}(t)$ as the average.

$$SERP_{kj}(t) = \frac{1}{80}\sum_{i=1}^{80} NEEG_{kji}(t) = \frac{1}{4}\sum_{i=1}^{4} ERP_{kji}(t) \tag{3}$$

3 Result

3.1 Recorded Data and Filtered Data

An example of measured data $eeg_i(t)$ is shown in Fig.3. The subject in Fig. 3 is "sub 1", and she recalls "a" in a syllable recalling task during the first set. The horizontal axis and the vertical axis of the graph are time in millisecond (ms) after a stimulus is displayed, and the amplitude of EEG's, respectively. The waves in the graph show the EEG's measured at C_4, C_3, Fp_2, and Fp_1. Various types of noises such as 50Hz alternating current, eye blinking, and electromyogram are also included in the EEG's.

The data after being filtered and normalized are shown in Fig.4. Noises such as alternating current, whose frequencies are higher than the fundamental frequency of EEGs, are attenuated.

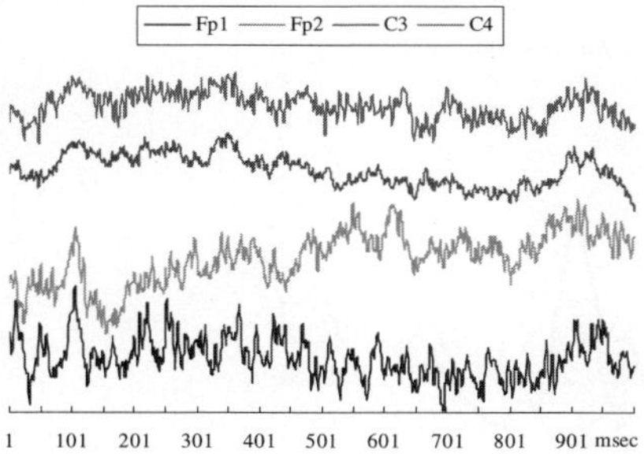

Fig. 3. An example of recorded data $eeg_i(t)$

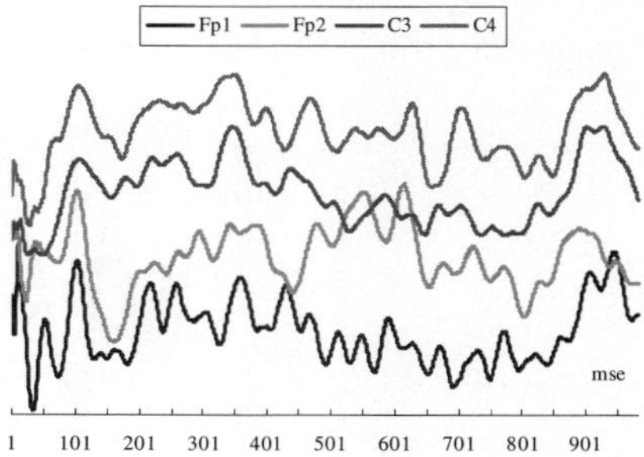

Fig. 4. The filtered and normalized data $NEEG_i(t)$

(sub-1, C3, The first "a" in the 1st set at the first experiment)

3.2 An ERP Obtained by an Associative Recall Task

The waves shown in Fig.5 are examples of $SERP_{kj}(t)$ (k=1, j=1,2,3,4, t=1,2,…,1000) obtained by averaging eighty measured data and by using the standard deviations of the EEG's, when "sub 1" recalling "ri-n-go" during her watch of the problem. The average EEG can be considered as a typical ERP. The arrows directing downwards or upwards indicate the potentials of ERP's. P_{100} and N_{200} are a kind of visual evoked potentials, P_{300} is the potentials concerned with the recognition of the problem, and N_{400} is considered as a potential related with the judgment from the context. Fig.6 is another example of $SERP_{kj}(t)$ (k=2, j=1,2,3,4, t=1,2,…,1000) obtained from "sub 2". The potentials of P_{100}, N_{200}, P_{300} and N_{400} also appear. The $SERP_{kj}(t)$ from "sub 1" and "sub 2" are a little different from each other, because the problems causing them are different from each other and the individual variation influences the potentials. Anyway, the $SERP_{kj}(t)$ (j=1) obtained by watching the problem is a bit different from the other for each subject: they have clearly positive and negative peaks after N_{400}. We call them P_{450} and N_{500} for "sub 1", and P_{500} and N_{550} for "sub 2".

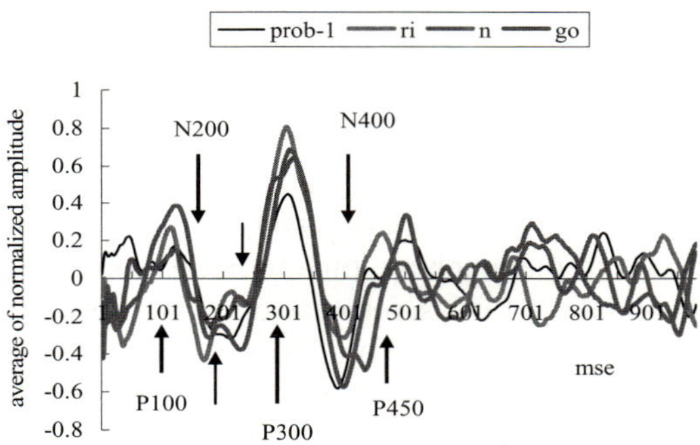

Fig. 5. An example of $SERP_{kj}(t)$ obtained by an Associative Recall Task (sub1, C3, recalling "ri-n-go")

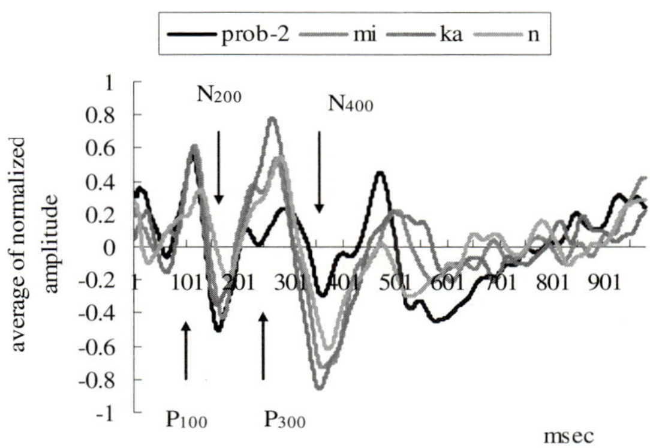

Fig. 6. An example of $SERP_{kj}(t)$ obtained by an Associative Recall Task(sub2, C3, recalling "mi-ka-n")

3.3 An ERP Obtained by a Syllable Recall Task

An example of an ERP obtained by a syllable recall task is shown in Fig.7. The potentials named P_{100}, N_{200}, P_{300} and N_{400} appear. It is estimated that the potentials exist about 450msec before the start. The ERP's contain various types of noise comparing with the ERP's in Fig.5 or in Fig.6. The reason why the noise remains is considered that the recalling syllable does not much depend on subjects but considerably depends on the the associative recalling task, the fruit name. Noise is also contained in the ERP's obtained from sub2.

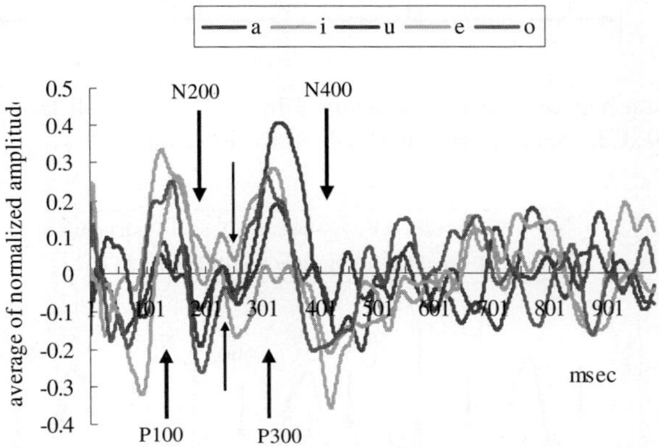

Fig. 7. An example of $SERP_{kj}(t)$ obtained by Syllable Recall Task (sub1, C3, recalling "a", "I", "u", "e", "o")

3.4 Comparison Between the ERP's of Both the Types

In Fig. 8, two waves of "ERP(t)'s" obtained by the two types of the syllable recalling tasks are shown in the order of the syllables of a fruit name ("ri-n-go"), and these waves are compared. We use ERP's obtained by recalling "ko" instead of "go" in the the syllable recalling tasks, since we did not record pronounced consonants in the syllable recalling tasks. Each ERP(t) wave of the associative recalling tasks is the result of plotting the values during the time interval, [100-500msec]-section, and standardizing them in the section. Moreover, the latencies are adjusted beforehand so that the latencies of P300 obtained the syllable task overlapped with the correspondence of P300 obtained by the associative task, because the noise does not sufficiently attenuate in the ERP's obtained by the syllable tasks. After some arrangement, the ERPs of the one type resemble the other type very much, and our result shows the possibility of estimating recalling a fruit name through the ERP's.

The ERP's in Fig.9 do not resemble each other. The results show that the difficulty to estimate the recalled fruit name through the ERP's.

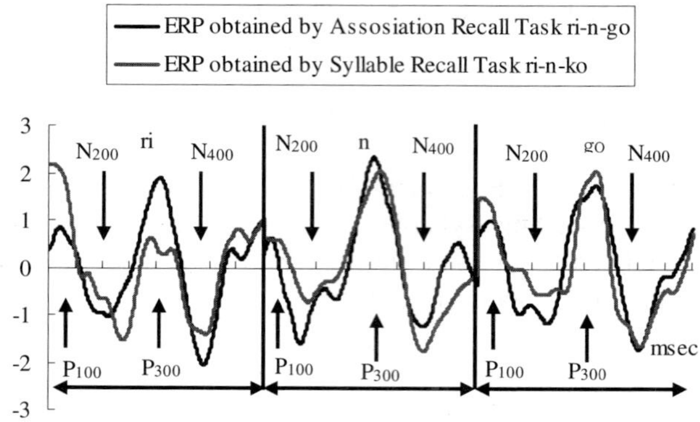

Fig. 8. Comparison between the ERP's obtained by a syllable recall task and an associative Recall Task (sub1, C3, recalling "ri", "n", "ko", and "ri-n-go")

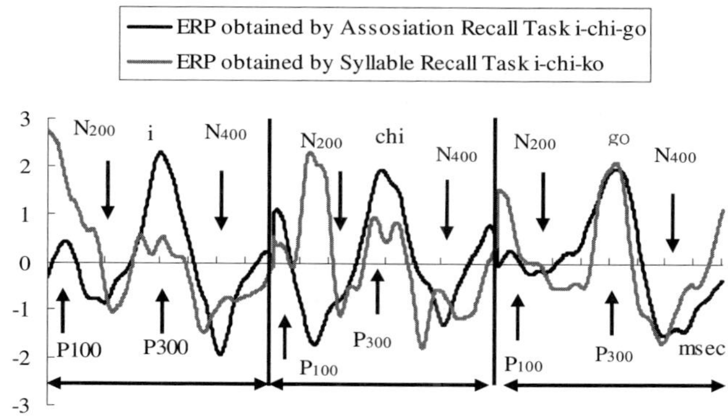

Fig. 9. Comparison between the ERP's obtained by a syllable recall task and an associative recall task (sub1, C3, recalling "i", "chi", "ko", and "i-chi-go")

3.5 Estimation of a Fruit Name Through ERP's

In order to estimate the recalled names of fruits, we use the following algorithm A. It uses the correlation between the ERPs in Fig.8 and Fig.9. The values of the correlation are 0.81 and 0.39 each in each type of the ERPs.

Table 1 shows the result of the detection ratio. If we use the average of the ERP's obtained by an associative recalling task, the correct detection ration is about 91.3%. But in the case where ERPs by a syllable recalling task are used, the average of correct detection ratio is about 65%. The difference between these two cases is about 25%.

[Algorithm A]

Step 1: we take out the part of $ERP_{kj}(t)$ (t=t1, t1+1, …, t2) from all $ERP_{kj}(t)$, and normalize them. (k=1,2,…,50, j=2,3,4)

Step 2: we selet parts of $ERP_{kj}(t)$ caused by the syllables of fruits and concatenate them. We represent the concatenated data as $mihon_i(t)(i=1,2,\ldots,5,\ t=1,2,\ \ldots,\ 3(t2-t1+1))$

Step 3: we take out the part of $ERP_{kj}(t)$ (t=t1, t1+1, …, t2) from all $ERP_{kj}(t)$, and normalize them. (k=1,2,…,5, j=2,3,4)

Step 4: we concatenate the normalized parts of $ERP_{kj}(t)$ for j=2,3, and 4 for each k. We represent the concatenated data as $LERP_i(t)(i=1,2,\ldots,5,\ t=1,2,\ \ldots,\ 3(t2-t1+1))$

Step 5: we calculate the correlation $r(i,j)$between $mihon_i(t)$ and $LERP_j(t)$ (t=1,2, …, $3(t2\text{-}t1+1)$) for all combinations i and j.

Step 6: if $r(i,j)$ has the maximum value among $r(i,k_2)$ k_2=1,2,…,5 or if $r(i,j)$ has the maximum value among $r(k_1,j)$ k_1=1,2,…,5, we estimate the subject visualized the jth words.

Table 1. Detection Ratio by the Algorithm A*

subjects	mihon	item	1st experiment	2nd experiment	3rd experiment	4th experiment
sub1	Averaged ERP by Assosiation Recall Task	ratio of correct answer	100%	100%	100%	100%
		number of addition	20	10	20	40
	Averaged ERP by Syllable Recall Task	ratio of correct answer	80%	40%	80%	100%
		number of addition	20	20	20	40
sub2	Averaged ERP by Assosiation Recall Task	ratio of correct answer	100%	40%	100%	80%
		number of addition	20	20	20	20
	Averaged ERP by Syllable Recall Task	ratio of correct answer	80%	40%	60%	40%
		number of addition	20	20	20	20

* Since we were not able to do the final experiment about sub1, the ERPs of the 4th experiment are the average of ERPs obtained at the 1st and the 3rd experiment.

4 Discussion

We discuss the features of ERP's and the effectiveness of the algorithm A.

The correlations given in Fig.10 shows how much the ERP's obtained by recalling "na" resemble the ERPs recalling the syllable of a fruit. The ERPs obtained by recalling "na" in a fruit name has high correlation with the ERPs of a task of the other type. This shows the possibility to estimate a recalling word through ERP's. However, the ERP's of recalling "n" have higher correlation with the ERP's recalling "na". This result explains the difficulties of the estimation. By the way, the algorithm A dose not use ERP's to estimate a fruit name, but it uses the linked ERPs. This means the algorithm is suitable for unstable data as shown in Fig.10.

Let us consider the arrangement of latencies. The ERPs in Fig.11 (a) shows the ERPs before the arrangement of latencies, and the ERPs in Fig.11 (b) are the ERPs after the arrangement. The comparison between the ERPs shows that some arrangement of latencies is required to estimate a fruit name. The latencies of ERPs by a syllable recalling task are observed about 10msec - 30msec later than the those by an associative recalling tasik. One of the reasons why this delay occurs is the length of problems. The phrases of the poem is 4 times longer than the problem of the associative recall task. A longer phrase requires more time to recognize them than a shorter one.

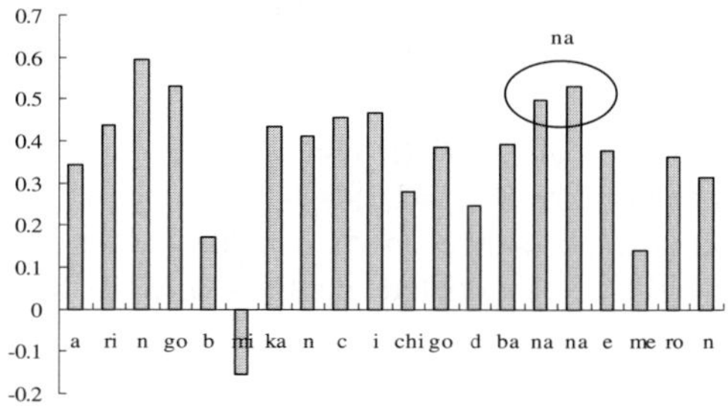

Fig. 10. Correlation between ERP obtained by recalling "na" and recalling fruit name

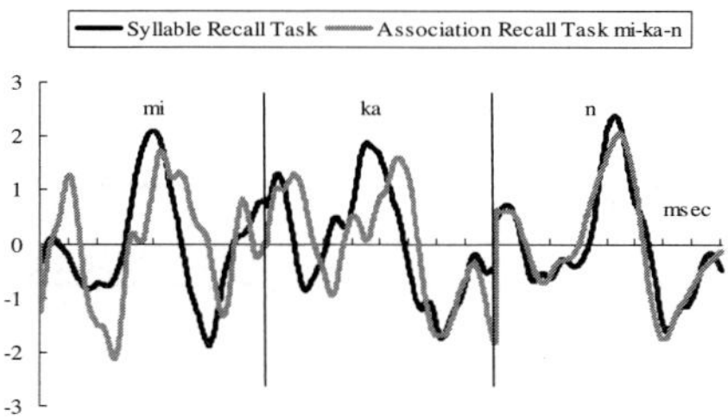

(a) ERPs without arrangement of latencies

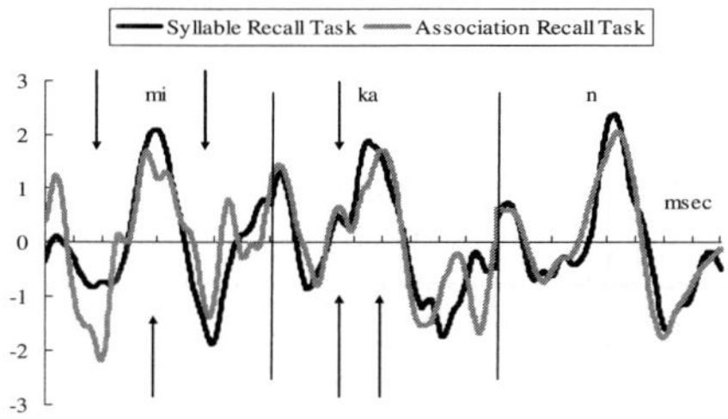

(b) ERPs after arrangement of latencies

Fig. 11. ERPs obtained by recalling "mi-kan-n" and "mi", "ka", and "n"

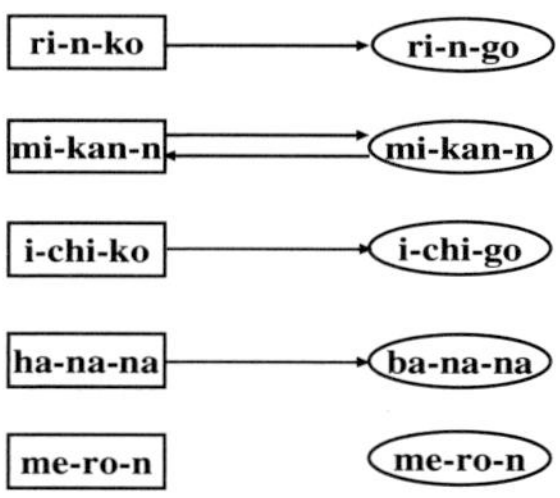

(i)The first experiment

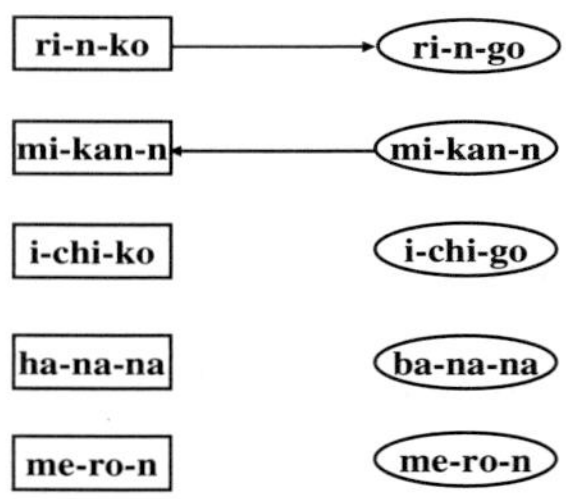

(ii) The second experiment

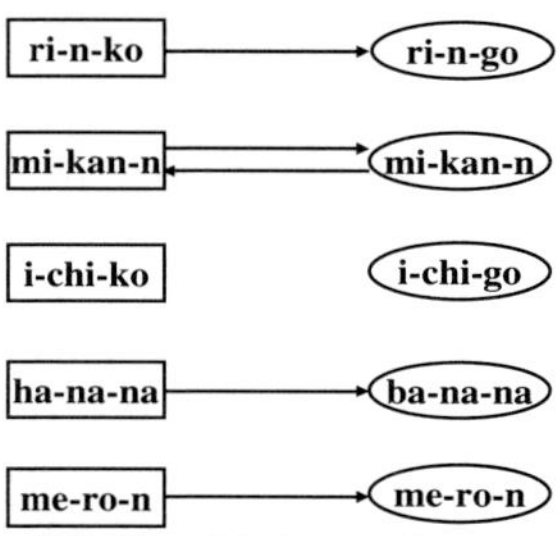

(iii) The third experiment

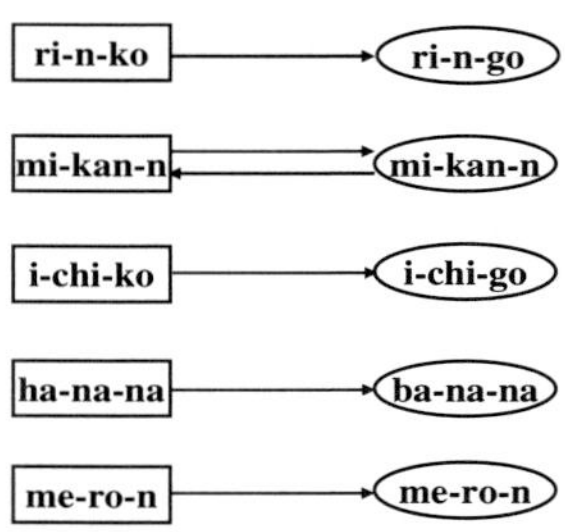

(iv) The forth experiment

Fig. 12. The rule used in Algorithm A to estimate a fruit name (sub1, C_3)

Fig.12 shows the rules used in the algorithm A to detect a correct fruit name. The rectangle means the ERP's obtained by the syllable task, and the oval means the ERP's obtained by the associative task. The allow shows the direction of the capability of the detection. In the forth case, all fruit names are detected correctly. The result shows the possibility of estimation of words or statements by using ERPs

5 Conclusion

The analysis of the experimental data and our claims are summarized as follows:

(1) We define "recall" as silent "pronunciation" without "tongue" moving. ERPs are caused by recalling the words. The words used in the experiments are five kinds of fruit in Japanese. ERPs caused by all Japanese syllable are measured.
(2) Most meaningfuly potential of ERPs for the estimation appears in the period [100msec, 550msec].
(3) Potential N_{400}-P_{450}-N_{500} (or N_{400}-P_{500}-N_{550}) appears when the subjects determine the recalling words.
(4) The words of fruits are almost completely estimated by the average of ERPs recalling them.
(5) It is difficult to estimate the recalled fruits by the linked ERPs caused by a syllable recall task, however it is not impossible.

The number of subjects in our experiments is too small. We must increase it to evaluate fairly our methods. We need further investigation to devise more effective methods to estimate the recalling words or statements.

References

1. Picton, T.W., et al.: Guideline for using human event-related potentials to study cognition: recording standards and publication criteria. Psychophysiology 37, 128–152 (2000)
2. Funada, M.F., Ninomija, S.P., et al.: Usability of EEG Signals for FES Control, -through Event Related Potentials Caused by Obscure Pictures. Proc. IFES, Austria, pp. 126–129 (2002)
3. Funada, M.F., Ito, Y., Ninomija, S.P.: On the relationship between Event Related Potentials and Stimuli of Characters, - Is it possible to realize a keyboard-less computer through ERP? proc. WC2003. Australia (2003)
4. Funada, M.F., Ito, Y., Ninomija, S.P.: Estimation Characters through Event Related Potentials. In: Proc. IEEE/EMBS, Mexico (2003)
5. Funada, M.F., Ninomija, S.P.: A Discrimination Algorithm of Event Related Potentials Evoked by Characters, BioMED2004, Austria, CD, pp. 1–6 (2004)
6. Funada, M.F., et al.: An Estimation of Homonyms Using Event Related Potentials Caused By Recalling Them in Mind, IASTED, Hawaii (2005)

Gaze as a Supplementary Modality for Interacting with Ambient Intelligence Environments

Daniel Gepner, Jérôme Simonin, and Noëlle Carbonell

LORIA, CNRS, INRIA & Nancy Université,
Campus Scientifique, BP 239, F54506, Vandoeuvre-lès-Nancy Cedex, France
{Daniel.Gepner,Jerome.Simonin,Noelle.Carbonell}@loria.fr

Abstract. We present our current research on the implementation of gaze as an efficient and usable pointing modality supplementary to speech, for interacting with augmented objects in our daily environment or large displays, especially immersive virtual reality environments, such as reality centres and caves. We are also addressing issues relating to the use of gaze as the main interaction input modality. We have designed and developed two operational user interfaces: one for providing motor-disabled users with easy gaze-based access to map applications and graphical software; the other for iteratively testing and improving the usability of gaze-contingent displays.

Keywords: gaze tracking, gaze pointing, gaze-contingent displays, gaze and speech human-computer interaction, multimodal human-computer interaction, ambient intelligence.

1 Context and Motivation

Thanks to recent advances in gaze tracking techniques, it is now possible to consider the integration of gaze as an input modality into user interfaces. Eye trackers have become much less intrusive while maintaining satisfactory accuracy (0.5° visual angle). Users have not any more to keep their head and body perfectly still like in the nineties; they can move them with sufficient amplitude to feel comfortable while sitting at desktop PCs. In addition, remote eye trackers can be embedded in screen frames and coupled with standard video cameras; instant vision-based detection of the user's actual gaze direction, head position and orientation is used to correct raw point of gaze measurements and to adjust the angle of the eye tracking infrared camera(s). As for head-mounted eye trackers, which place no constraint on people's movements and mobility, they have become much less intrusive: their size and weight have decreased so much that they can be attached to spectacles. Finally, calibration has become much simpler and quicker. So, it is reasonable to expect that, in a few years, user gaze direction will be reliably detected and followed through "invisible" wearable devices. Vision-based gaze detection and tracking, a truly non intrusive approach, appears as an appealing solution in the long term. However, considerable research efforts and scientific advances are still needed to achieve appropriate accuracy despite steady significant advances [3], [10].

C. Stephanidis (Ed.): Universal Access in HCI, Part II, HCII 2007, LNCS 4555, pp. 848–857, 2007.

While technical feasibility is in the process of being achieved, usability issues are yet to be further investigated. Gaze is obviously a useful human-computer interaction (HCI) modality for computer users with severe motor impairments [2], or for users who are engaged in demanding manual activities, such as pilots in cockpits; see the early study of gaze used to designate objects referred to in speech commands [8].

Contrastingly, the utility and usability of gaze as a supplementary input modality for able-bodied users has motivated much fewer studies and remains to be demonstrated. Gaze cannot of course supersede the mouse for pointing at, and selecting, graphical objects displayed on the screen of standard desktop PCs. As a pointing modality it can neither outmatch finger designation on a touch screen in efficiency and usability. However, its superiority to hand/arm gestures for remote pointing at large displays (e.g., "walls", reality centres or caves) is beyond doubt. Gaze pointing is faster, more precise and less tiring than gestures; hands are free and can be used to carry out other tasks, which may prove to be an invaluable advantage in some interaction contexts; in addition, it is more natural to use. Gaze, coupled with speech for expressing depth, can designate positions in a 3D virtual space more precisely and easily than 3D gestures; in particular, users have to mentally apply a homothetic transformation to their hand gestures and body moves to anticipate the actual span of these movements in a 3D virtual world, while planning them. Gaze pointing complemented with spoken phrases including action verbs is nevertheless inappropriate for manipulating virtual objects (e.g., on a Workbench screen), especially for shaping and deforming them. Therefore, gaze coupled with speech seems well suited to immersive virtual world exploration, but ill suited to virtual 3D object manipulation, as this form of input multimodality can be used for moving virtual objects but not for transforming them.

Research on the implementation of such concepts as 'Ambient Intelligence' and 'Ubiquitous/Pervasive Computing' is fast developing in the HCI scientific community. This evolution is likely to stimulate research on the integration of gaze into user interfaces as a remote pointing input modality. Ambient Intelligence (AmI), which subsumes Ubiquitous and Pervasive Computing, is a vision where humans are surrounded by computing and networking technology unobtrusively embedded in their surroundings. AmI lays emphasis on user friendliness, efficient and distributed services support, user empowerment, and advanced support to human interactions. This vision assumes a shift away from PCs to a variety of interactive "intelligent" agents which are unobtrusively embedded in our environment; see [5] for information on recent research advances on the implementation of AmI principles. Definitions of Ubiquitous and Pervasive Computing, [19], and [18], also put emphasis on "the integration of computation into our daily work practice to support our activities without being noticed" or even "visible"; which implies distributing interaction facilities in the environment and embedding them in everyday objects. So, future users of AmI and Ubiquitous/Pervasive Computing environments will be naturally induced to perform computer tasks while engaged in other non computing activities, at home or on the move. These parallel activities will sensibly reduce the perceptual and motor resources they will be able to invest in computing tasks. So, they will be confronted with similar computer access and interaction difficulties to those encountered by people with disabilities. Therefore, advances in research on Ambient Intelligence and progress in implementing this concept in software agents meant to support the general public in their daily activities are likely to significantly contribute to advancing the inclusion of people with disabilities in the fast developing Information Society, mainly by increasing computer access flexibility. They will also contribute to simplifying and unifying user-centred interface design, in-as-much as user interfaces meant to satisfy the needs and expectations of able-bodied users in a wide range of contexts of use will be easy to tailor to suit the specific needs of various communities of users with physical disabilities. The development of AmI in society will stimulate the progress of Universal Access.

These observations explain our interest for speech and gaze as a substitute multimodal command "language" for direct manipulation in some contexts of use, such as interaction with AmI artefacts or immersive virtual reality environments.

Our work on speech and gaze as a promising multimodal command "language" for interacting with augmented objects and large displays is presented in the following sections. We first specify our objectives. Then, the software tools that make up our experimental platform are described. Present research progress and outcomes are presented next. Future research directions are sketched in the conclusion.

2 Scientific Objectives

Our main objective is to design and implement an appropriate speech- and gaze-based command language for interacting with large displays. Design requirements include the following major constraints. This multimodal language should be:

- robust, that is, tolerant to ambient noise and atypical or faulty utterances,
- flexible to changes of context of use and inter-individual expression differences;
- effective and efficient, and capable of outmatching existing interaction facilities;
- usable: in particular, easy to use and to learn (i.e., transparent).

To be usable, gaze pointing, as an input modality supplementary to speech, should be implemented in compliance with the following specific requirements:

- The role of gaze should be limited to solving deictic and underspecified reference phrases included in speech commands. For instance, the pronouns "that" and "there" in Bolt's famous example "Put that there." are deictics which refer to objects or positions on the user's screen [4].
- Interpretation of deictic phrases should be mainly inferred from the analysis of gaze fixation positions on the display. Minimum constraints should be placed on users' eye movements. Of course, inference of referents matching deictics from spontaneous eye movements would be an ideal solution; it represents our ultimate goal. But present knowledge and modelling of gaze activity during human-computer tasks is insufficient for interpreting spontaneous gaze movements accurately and reliably. Therefore, at least for the time being, controlled gaze pointing is mandatory; see section 4 for a presentation of our current work on this issue. Nevertheless, implementation of this constraint should interfere as little as possible with users' spontaneous visual exploration strategies. So, users might be asked to "look once at the objects and/or locations on the display referred to ambiguously in the current command"; yet, they should be free to choose when to look at referents (i.e., before, during and/or

after the current verbal command), and for how long. In particular, dwells which have to last between 600 ms and 1 sec. to be reliably recognized in typing tasks on virtual keyboards [11] ought not to be required from users.

Research on speech- and gaze-based interaction is still in its early stages. Few studies have been published yet on the implementation and evaluation of gaze as a pointing modality: see, for instance, [17] and [6] for an assessment of pointing by gaze compared to standard pointing techniques, [13] for the use of this modality in pervasive computing environments, and [16] for its use in games. Multimodal interaction involving gaze has motivated fewer published studies; see, for instance, [20] on mutual disambiguation in gaze- and speech-based interaction.

One of the main difficulties is the well known "Midas touch" effect [9] which stems from the double origin of eye movement control: depending on the context and activity, gaze direction is either controlled by low-level perception mechanisms activated by the visual properties of objects in the environment (bottom-up control) or by intentional top-down processes. Fixations resulting from the latter processes are those which have the potential to yield information on the user's current intention. A way to avoid the Midas touch effect in gaze-based interaction is to avoid providing users with a visual feedback to their eye movements.

Our work on gaze as a supplementary input modality to speech is grounded on a main working hypothesis which is essential to obtain reliable and robust gaze and speech controlled user interfaces. We expect that users will behave as follows when using speech for controlling graphical software applications. There is some chance that they will glance at the graphical object on which the current oral command is designed to operate while planning the action they intend to perform on this object, and/or during the utterance of the command itself, and there is every chance that they will look at it once they have finished speaking, to check whether its execution by the system meets their expectations. If this assumption proves to be valid, it will be possible to distinguish between fixations driven by visual stimuli and those controlled by intents. Analysis of fixations occurring just before, somewhat after, and during the utterance of speech commands, is then likely to provide useful information on the object or action specified in the command.

3 Software Tools

Numerous advanced software tools are necessary for studying the potential of gaze as a pointing modality. We have developed a software platform comprising a set of components with the following functionalities:

- Robust real time computation of gaze fixations using a dispersion-based algorithm. This component is necessary for implementing gaze as an input modality. See [14] for descriptions of the main fixation computation algorithms and comparisons of their performances. We use a head mounted eye tracker (ASL-501) at two sampling rates, 60 Hz or 240 Hz. Results of real time fixation computation are identical to those of the ASL Eyenal batch processing software.
- Recording of rich traces of user interactions with any Windows application software. Time stamped traces include:

  - system and user generated events;
  - screen displays (from 4 to 8 screen copies per second) and mouse phantom (or cursor) positions on the screen;
  - coordinates of the user's gaze points on the screen, and speech from both user and system; plug-ins can be added to process other modalities.
- Synchronised play back of multimodal interactions from files of recorded traces. Eye fixations appear superimposed on the displays; optional visual markers display qualitative information on pupil diameter, fixation duration and size (i.e., spatial dispersion of samples included in each fixation).
- Assistance to manual annotation of displayed traces so as to facilitate their qualitative and quantitative analysis. Main annotation facilities include:
  - Manual or semi-automatic segmentation and labelling of visual and audio traces so as to define meaningful sequences of interactions. For instance, replacing all occurrences of a phrase in a text by another phrase represents a meaningful sequence of interactions with a word processor.
  - Manual or automatic definition of interest zones on the displays so as to determine what graphical objects are most frequently looked at by users during the execution of a given task.
- Implementation of the Wizard of Oz paradigm, an efficient rapid prototyping technique for simulating functionalities of innovative user interfaces which aim at reproducing human expertises too costly or difficult to implement appropriately, such as natural language understanding. Traces of users' interactions are simultaneously recorded on the user PC and sent to the wizard PC via local network. It is possible to filter the data sent to the wizard to avoid overcrowding his/her screen. Wizard-to-user information is also conveyed through the local network. An application dependent plug-in meant to assist the wizard in simulation of the user interface can be added to the software component running on the wizard's PC.

A version of this distributed platform has been developed under Linux with the aim of obtaining appropriate observation tools for studying gaze- and speech-based interaction with 3D virtual environments. The overall functionalities of this platform are identical to those of the Windows tools described above. Main specific features originate from the chosen 3D development environment, a multi-agent system (oRis, ENIB, France) which represents each 3D object in the animated scene as an agent. This feature impacts on the platform functionalities as follows:

- Implementation of the Wizard of Oz technique: 3D animations generated by oRis run on both workstations; this strategy makes it possible to limit wizard-to-user data exchanges to the oRis commands necessary for simulating the execution of the user's multimodal requests, and thus, to easily obtain smooth evolution of the animation on the user's screen.
- The play back includes the names of the objects gazed at by the user during fixations, since agents can be labelled.

In addition, the play back displays pupil diameter evolution, phonetic and orthographic transcripts of the user's oral commands together with a graphical representation of the speech signal. Transcripts are either done by human experts or generated by acoustic-phonetic decoders and speech recognition systems.

Eye tracking contribution to HCI research is twofold. First, data on eye movements are most useful and are increasingly used for assessing the ergonomic quality of advanced graphical user interfaces and interactive visualisations of very large data sets. We have used the software platform presented here for eliciting the possible influence of display spatial layout on the efficiency and comfort of visual search [15].

Secondly, eye tracking data analysis is quite obviously an essential source of knowledge for implementing gaze as a pointing modality. The next section presents our scientific contribution to this emerging research area, and demonstrates the usefulness of the software tools presented above.

4 Gaze, a Promising Pointing Modality

Our work on the implementation of gaze as an appropriate substitute modality for mouse pointing and selection in contexts where users interact with large displays, such as image walls or immersive virtual reality environments, is currently developing in three directions which are detailed next:

- prototyping of gaze controlled map-based applications,
- development of flexible gaze-contingent displays,
- design and development of "natural", gaze and speech command languages.

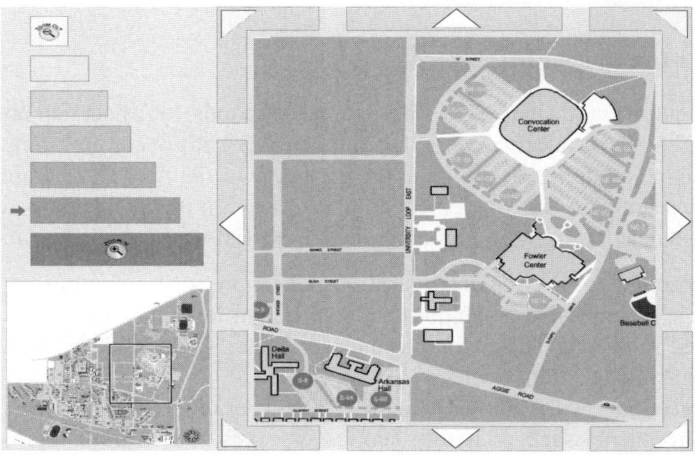

Fig. 1. Gaze-controlled user interface of the map-based application. Control buttons are in grey.

4.1 Gaze Control of Map-Based Applications

We have developed a prototype gaze controlled user interface for interacting with standard map applications. All the interaction facilities provided by applications on the Web, such as Mappy, can be activated using gaze sampled at a 60 Hz rate. This interface is presented in Figure 1. Looking at one of the four buttons surrounding the zoom-in window (on the right of the screen) moves the focus of the zoom to the right (left, top or bottom) by a fixed step the length of which can be adjusted by the user.

The zoom-in factor can be specified using the seven buttons on the top left of the screen. We are currently considering implementation of continuous zoom-in.

Looking at a point on the overall map (at the bottom of the screen on the left) causes the current content of the zoom-in window to be replaced by a portion of the map the contours of which are represented on the overall map by a black rectangular line; the centre of this rectangle coincides with the averaged positions of the samples included in the fixation; its size varies according to the zoom-in factor. To avoid the Midas touch effect without constraining the user's eye movements, we have proceeded like this: (i) when a fixation on the overall map is detected, the system waits for about 170 ms from the start of the fixation; then, (ii) it displays a blue circle around the averaged x, y coordinates of the 10 first samples in the fixation to warn the user that it will change the content of the zoom-in window about 200 ms later; (iii) if the user goes on fixating the same position on the overall map for about 200 ms (i.e., 12 samples), the system replaces the content of the zoom-in window with the portion of the overall map surrounding the averaged coordinates of the 22 first samples in the fixation. These thresholds have been determined from the data collected in [15].

This prototype which has been developed to test the usability of gaze pointing as an input modality has been evaluated by a few users who have judged it intuitive and comfortable to use. Potential applications include accessible graphical software for motor disabled people, and interaction with large graphical displays, for instance, digital wall maps in lecture rooms.

4.2 Gaze-Contingent Displays

A gaze-contingent display is a display that responds to where an observer looks within it. The most informative details are generated at the current point of gaze, and the display resolution is degraded at the periphery of the foveal or parafoveal field of vision. Research on the implementation of gaze-contingent displays, an emerging area, is fast developing; see [7] for a review. Potential application areas include:

- Interaction with complex distant visualisations or animations in cases when image compression techniques are insufficient for achieving satisfactory display speed and reactivity; for instance, remote surgery through Internet is a promising application area.
- Interaction with virtual reality applications, especially in immersive environments such as reality centres or caves, where gaze represents a more efficient and usable pointing modality than hand or finger gestures.

We have developed a robust gaze-contingent prototype which functions as a gaze-controlled lens: the display is blurred outside a circle the centre of which coincides with the averaged coordinates of the 4 first gaze samples (i.e., 70 ms or so) included in the current fixation. See Figure 2. The display resolution is highest inside this circle the diameter of which corresponds to the standard size of the foveal field of vision, that is, 5° visual angle. This prototype is operational, and its accuracy has been successfully tested by 5 participants who used it for exploring complex realistic displays. However, participants complained that the "lens" followed their eye movements too slowly, which obliged them to sensibly reduce their natural pace of visual exploration in an irritating way. A 70 ms lag between fixation start and "lens" move is indeed too long, but it is necessary for achieving reliable fixation detection. The decision of restricting the high resolution area on the display to the span of the foveal vision field was motivated by the will to test the actual accuracy of our prototype. Obviously, this area should be extended so as to also include the parafoveal vision field, which might reduce users' frustrations significantly. The same motive explains the absence of smooth resolution degradation. The study described in [1] differs from ours in that the gaze-contingent lens creates a fisheye deformation, and the task amounts to target search and selection in a grid of 9x9 boxes.

We are currently investigating two research directions in parallel so as to overcome the main usability weakness of contingent displays, that is, their insufficient reactivity by: (i) increasing the sampling frequency rate, from 60 Hz to 240 Hz, with a view to shortening fixation detection time; (ii) achieving a satisfactory trade-off between accuracy and time delay by analysing saccade velocity variations to predict next fixation approximate landing. An approach combining both strategies will also be tested. Finally, to further improve the usability of gaze-contingent displays, we shall test whether smooth degradation of resolution is actually more comfortable visually than stepwise reduction.

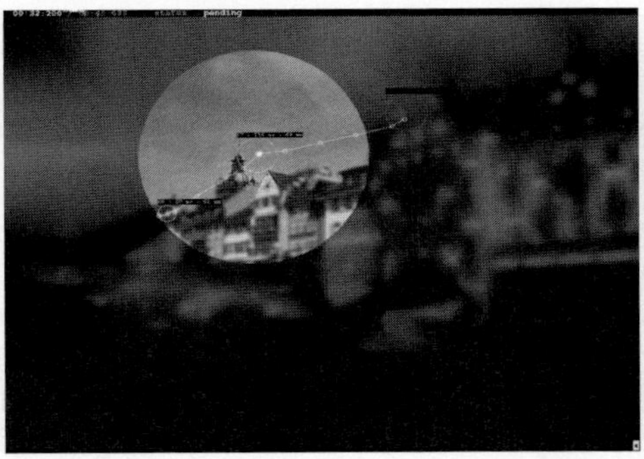

Fig. 2. Play back: gaze-controlled lens. Three of fixations are visible; the one on the right is starting

Fig. 3. Play back: Wizard of Oz simulation gaze- and speech-based interaction

4.3 Gaze, a Supplementary Modality to Speech

We have collected a corpus of realistic speech and gaze interactions with various 3D environments to acquire the necessary knowledge for implementing a "natural" style of input multimodality, using the Wizard of Oz technique for interpreting users' eye movements and oral commands. See Figure 3. 5 participants performed 5 scenarios lasting 4 min. each. They carried out two types of interactive tasks, manipulation of virtual objects and interaction with a reactive game. They had to comply with a few expression constraints only:

- the vocabulary they could use was restricted to a predefined list of words;
- during the last scenario only, they had to designate each object they had to move using a deictic and "looking at" the object they wanted to move, then at the new position it should occupy; during the previous 4 scenarios they could move their eyes freely.

Participants' speech commands have been segmented into words and phones by an expert phonetician; time-stamped orthographic and phonetic transcripts of the speech corpus are now available. Gaze fixations are currently analysed to determine which ones correspond to moments when the user's visual attention is focused on the 3D object that the current[1] command aims to act upon. Then, various algorithms will be designed to filter controlled and spontaneous eye movements with a view to identifying fixations on task objects alluded to in the current command, especially by underspecified reference phrases, thus contributing to reduce the ambiguity and imprecision of speech commands. These algorithms will be trained, tested and evaluated on the corpus of multimodal interactions presented in this section.

5 Conclusion

We have presented our work on the implementation of gaze as an appropriate input modality for pointing at virtual interactive objects in various contexts of use: user interfaces with graphical applications for people with motor disabilities, gaze-contingent displays, especially on large screens and multimodal, speech- and gazed-based interaction with immersive virtual environments and augmented reality interfaces.

In the short term, our research on the possible contribution of gaze to enriching HCI will be focused on the following goals:

- Improve gaze tracking accuracy by taking account of pursuit movements the occurrence of which is very frequent during interaction with animated scenes.
- Increase the reactivity of gaze-contingent displays by experimenting with various approaches.
- Assess the effective contribution of spontaneous or loosely controlled gaze to disambiguating imprecise references in speech commands, interpreting deictic phrases, and improving speech recognition accuracy (see [12]).

References

1. Ashmore, M., Duchowski, A.T., Shoemaker, G.: Efficient Eye Pointing with a Fisheye Lens. In: Proceedings of the 2005 CHCCS/ACM Conference on Graphics Interface (GI'05), University of Waterloo, Victoria, BC, May 9-11, 2005, pp. 203–210. School of Computer Science, Waterloo, Ontario (2005)
2. Bates, R., Istance, H.O.: Towards eye based virtual environment interaction for users with high-level motor disabilities. In: Proceedings of 5th International Conference Series on Disability, Virtual Reality and Associated Technologies (ICDVRAT'04), Oxford, UK, September 20-22, 2004, pp. 276–282 (2004)
3. Beymer, D., Flickner, M.: Eye Gaze Tracking Using an Active Stereo Head. In: Proceedings of IEEE Computer Society Conference on Computer Vision and Pattern Recognition (CVPR '03), Madison, Wisconsin, June 16-22, 2003, vol. 2, pp. 451–458 (2003)

[1] The oral command may be in progress or forthcoming or just completed.

4. Bolt, R.A.: Put-that-there: Voice and gesture at the graphics interface. In: Proceedings of the 7th International Conference on Computer Graphics and Interactive Techniques, Seattle, WA, July 14-18, 1980, pp. 262–270. ACM Press, New York (1980)
5. Carbonell: Ambient Multimodality: towards Advancing Computer Accessibility and Assisted Living. International Journal on Universal Access in the Information Society 5(1), 96–104 (2006)
6. Cournia, N., Smith, J.D., Duchowski, A.T.: Gaze vs. Hand-Based Pointing in Virtual Environments. In: Proceedings of International ACM Conference on Human Factors in Computing Systems (CHI 2003), Ft. Lauderdale (FL), April 5-10, 2003, pp. 772–773. ACM Press, New York (2003) Short Talks and Interactive Posters
7. Duchowski, A.T., Cournia, N., Murphy, H.: Gaze-Contingent Displays: a Review. Cyber Psychology and Behavior 7(6), 621–634 (2004)
8. Hatfield, F., Jenkins, E.A., Calhoun, G.: Principles and guidelines for the design of eye/voice interaction dialogs. In: Proceedings of 3rd Symposium on Human Interaction with Complex Systems (HICS'96), Dayton, Ohio, August 25-28, 1996, pp. 10–19 (1996)
9. Jacob, R.J.K.: Eye tracking in advanced interface design. In: Barfield, W., Furness, T.A. (eds.) Virtual Environments and Advanced Interface Design, pp. 258–288. Oxford University Press, Oxford, UK (1995)
10. Park, K.R.: Vision-based Facial and Eye Gaze Tracking. In: Biundo, S., Frühwirth, T., Palm, G. (eds.) KI 2004. LNCS (LNAI), vol. 3238, pp. 453–465. Springer, Heidelberg (2004)
11. Marajanta, P., Räihä, K.-J.: Twenty years of eye typing: systems and design issues. In: Proceedings of the 2002 Symposium on Eye Tracking Research and Applications, New Orleans, Louisiana, March 25-27, 2002, pp. 15–22 (2002)
12. Oviatt, S.L: Mutual disambiguation of recognition errors in a multimodal architecture. In: Proceedings of ACM SIGCHI Conference on Human Factors in Computing Systems (CHI '99), Pittsburgh, May 15-20, 1999, pp. 576–583. ACM Press, New York (1999)
13. Oyekoya, O.K., Stentiford, F.W.M.: Eye Tracking as a New Interface for Image Retrieval. Behavior and Technology Journal 22(3), 161–169 (2004)
14. Salvucci, D.D., Goldberg, J.H.: Identifying fixations and saccades in Eye-tracking protocols. In: Proceedings of the 2000 Symposium on Eye Tracking Ressearch and Applications (ETRA 2000), Palm Beach Gardens, Florida, November 6-8, 2000, pp. 71–78. ACM Press, New York (2000)
15. Simonin, J., Kieffer, S., Carbonell, N.: Effects of display layout on gaze activity during visual search. In: Costabile, M.F., Paternó, F. (eds.) INTERACT 2005. LNCS, vol. 3585, pp. 1054–1058. Springer, Heidelberg (2005)
16. Smith, J.D., Graham, N.T.C.: Use of Eye Movements for Video Game Control. In: Proceedings of International ACM Conference on Advances in Computer Entertainment Technology (ACE'2006), Hollywood, CA, June 14-16, 2006, p. 8. ACM Press, New York (2006) (The ACM Digital Library)
17. Tanriverdi, V., Jacob, R.J.K: Interacting with Eye Movements in Virtual Environments. In: Proceedings of International ACM Conference on Human Factors in Computing Systems (CHI 2000), The Hague, the Netherlands, April 1-6, 2003, pp. 265–272. ACM Press, New York (2000)
18. Want, R., Farkas, K.I., Narayanaswami, C.: Guest Editors' Introduction: Energy Harvesting and Conservation. IEEE Pervasive Computing 4(1), 14–17 (2005)
19. Weiser, M.: (1996) http://www.ubiq.com/hypertext/weiser/UbiHome.html
20. Zhang, Q., Imamiya, A.G.K., Mao, X.: A Gaze and Speech Multimodal Interface. In: Proceedings 24th International Conference on Distributed Computing Systems Workshops, Tokyo, Japan, March 23-26, 2004, pp. 208–213 (2004)

Integrating Multimodal Cues Using Grammar Based Models

Manuel Giuliani and Alois Knoll

Robotics and Embedded Systems Group
Department of Informatics, Technische Universität München
Boltzmannstraße 3, D-85748 Garching bei München, Germany
giuliani@in.tum.de, knoll@in.tum.de

Abstract. Multimodal systems must process several input streams efficiently and represent the input in a way that allows the establishment of connections between modalities. This paper describes a multimodal system that uses Combinatory Categorial Grammars to parse several input streams and translate them into logical formulas. These logical formulas are expressed in Hybrid Logic, which is very suitable for multimodal integration because it can represent temporal relationships between modes in an abstract way. This level of abstraction makes it possible to define rules for multimodal processing in a straightforward way.

1 Introduction

Multimodal systems are programs that are able to process several input streams and produce multimodal output. They record the utterances of a human user, combine them to build a conjoined interpretation, and derive their output from that interpretation. Therefore multimodal systems are more flexible and error-tolerant than systems that have only one input modality. In the best case, multimodal systems can be very natural to interact with, because the users do not have to learn how to operate the system: They can simply interact with it as they would with another human. To realise their full potential, multimodal systems must not only be able to recognise multiple modes, they also have to process the input information fast and in a way that allows a computer to reason over the input and determine the action it should execute.

This paper describes an approach for a multimodal system that involves an input processing based on a grammar formalism that is mainly used for language processing: Combinatory Categorial Grammar (CCG). By using OpenCCG, a Java-based implementation of the CCG, the input of speech recognition and other modes can be translated into Hybrid Logic formulas. These formulas can then be used to compute reactions by the system on a user input.

The structure of this paper is as follows. In Section 2 we review related work to our approach. Sections 3 and 4 introduce CCG and OpenCCG. Hybrid Logic is explained in Section 5 before our approach for a multimodal system is depicted in Section 6. Section 7 shows an example input processing, while Section 8 concludes this paper.

C. Stephanidis (Ed.): Universal Access in HCI, Part II, HCII 2007, LNCS 4555, pp. 858–867, 2007.

2 Related Work

Using grammars for the processing of multimodal cues has been proposed in different variations. The first who reported a grammatical framework for a multimodal interface were Shimazu, Arita, and Takashima [1]. They developed a Multimodal Definite Clause Grammar (MM-DCG) that was able to handle an arbitrary number of modes and stored temporal information inside the grammar. The DCG formalism that they used is suitable for a straightforward transformation of the grammar rules into Prolog code. However, MM-DCG assumes that the several modes are known from the beginning and ties them strictly together in the grammar. This leads to very domain-specific grammars that are hard to extend.

Johnston and Bangalore [2] use a multimodal context-free grammar to represent the input streams of speech recognition and pen input. The word entries of their grammar are composed of $n + 1$ components for the n input modes and one component for their joint meaning. Therefore, the grammar is also a semantic module which adds meaning to the input stream while parsing it. This approach is very useful for small domains. Johnston and Bangalore describe a grammar that was created for an application that manages contact details with speech and pen input in a PDA. The possible speech-gesture combinations for this example are limited and known in advance. That makes it possible to store them together in a single grammar. Also, the application does not change very much, hence they do not need a grammar that is easy to extend.

Nevatia, Zhao and Hongeng [3] introduce an event ontology that aims to display complex spatio-temporal events in a simple way. For that, they propose an Event Recognition Language (ERL) to specify possible events for a system that recognises certain events like human movements in a video stream. The events are divided into three classes: primitive events build the basis of the hierarchy, single-thread events are composed of primitive events, and multi-thread events are a number of single-thread events with a temporal/spatial/logical relationship. An approach like the ERL makes it possible for every user to specify complex events without worrying about the low-level processing of the underlying system.

Ryoo and Aggarwal [4] propose a general methodology for automated recognition of complex human activities. They use a representation scheme based on a context-free grammar (CFG). Similar to the ERL, this scheme can represent basic actions and complex actions. In this case the CFG allows the human actions that should be recognised by their system to be defined. In the program, they involve the CFG-based representation to recognise human activities in video streams automatically. The achieved recognition results are very high, but only for movements that correspond to the actions specified in the grammar. The probabilistic nature of human activity is not yet captured in their system.

3 Combinatory Categorial Grammar

Combinatory Categorial Grammar (CCG) was introduced by Ades [5] and Steedman [6]. It is an extension to the Categorial Grammar (CG) of Ajdukiewicz [7] and

Bar-Hillel [8]. Traditional context-free grammar formalisms use a top-down approach for parsing sentences. The structure of a language that should be parsed is stored in a set of rules, while the lexicon contains words with their assigned word categories. Categorial Grammars (CG) have a bottom-up approach in which the structure of a language is reflected in the lexicon of the grammar. Each word in the lexicon of a CG is assigned to a category that can be either atomic or complex. Example (1) shows the lexicon for a small grammar[1]:

(1) a. *loves* := (s\np)/np : $\lambda x.\ \lambda y.\mathbf{love}(x,y)$
b. *Peter* := np : **Peter**
c. *Mary* := np : **Mary**

This publication follows Mark Steedman by using the "result leftmost" notation. This notation utilises the slash operators / and \. The rightward-combining functor over domain β into range α is written α / β, while the leftward-combining functor is written $\alpha \backslash \beta$. For example, ditransitive verbs like *loves* use the category (s \ np) / np presented in (1a). They can be combined with a nominal phrase (np) that stands to the right of the verb. After that, they are combined with a np to the left of the verb to yield a sentence (s).

The combination of words to sentence constituents is done by a small set of rules. The simplest rules used in a CG are the rules of *Functional Application*, as displayed in (2):

(2) *Functional Application Rules*
a. $X/Y:f \quad Y:a \quad \Rightarrow \quad X:fa$ (>)
b. $Y:a \quad X\backslash Y:f \quad \Rightarrow \quad X:fa$ (<)

With the rules of Functional Application and the categories from the small grammar example in (1), the sentence "Peter loves Mary" can be parsed as shown in (3):

(3)
```
Peter    loves     Mary
-----  ----------  ----
 np    (s\np)/np    np
       ----------------->
             s\np
------------------------<
          np
```

In addition to the rules of Functional Application, CCG adds a couple of extra rules to the basic set of rules. The first of these extra rules are the rules of *Harmonic Functional Composition* that are introduced in (4). They allow the combination of contiguous words that do not build a sentence constituent together. The rules of forward and backward composition are depicted by "**>B**" and "**<B**" respectively.

(4) *Harmonic Functional Composition Rules*
a. $X/Y:f \quad Y/Z:g \quad \Rightarrow \quad X/Z:\lambda x.f(gx)$ (>**B**)
b. $Y\backslash Z:g \quad X\backslash Y:f \quad \Rightarrow \quad X\backslash Z:\lambda x.f(gx)$ (<**B**)

[1] The CCG rules and the grammar example in (1) use the λ-calculus for the display of semantics. The λ-calculus will not be explained in this paper, because OpenCCG - that will be illustrated in Section 4 - uses Hybrid Logic.

The second type of rules that are introduced by CCG are the *Type-Raising* rules. These rules turn atomic categories into functions over functions over this category. The Type-Raising rules are displayed in (5); the variable T is a variable that stands for all categories.

(5) *Type-Raising Rules*

a. $X : a \Rightarrow T/(T\backslash X) : \lambda f.fa$ (>**T**)

b. $X : a \Rightarrow T\backslash(T/X) : \lambda f.fa$ (<**T**)

4 OpenCCG

OpenCCG [9] is a Java-based implementation of the CCG formalism. It is capable of parsing and realising sentences. That means it can translate utterances into a logical form as well as take a given logical form and convert it back to a sentence. OpenCCG emerged from the Grok system and was extended by Michael White. In OpenCCG rules, categories, and lexicon entries are stored in a set of mandatory and optional XML files. Traditionally CCG uses the λ-calculus to represent parsed sentences, but OpenCCG uses the more flexible *Hybrid Logic* as proposed by Baldridge and Kruijff [10] to implement a dependency-based perspective on meaning. Hybrid Logic will be explained in the next section.

5 Hybrid Logic

Hybrid logic goes back to the hybrid tense logic by Prior [11], which is a hybridised version of ordinary tense logic. Although classical logic and modal logic are quite powerful in expressing relations between entities and their properties, they lack the ability to directly reference specific states at which a proposition holds. In standard modal logic, truth is relative to a set of points. These points are usually taken to represent worlds, times, space or states in a computer. Therefore only expressions that are for example relative to a set of times, like the sentence

(6) The sun is shining.

can be formalised in modal logic. This statement has different truth values at different times. The problem is that some statements in natural language are true exactly at one time only. For example the statement

(7) It is 7 o'clock 11 October 2006.

is only true at exactly 7 o'clock on the 11th of October 2006 and false at all other times. Example (6) can be formalised in modal logic, but this is not possible with example (7).

Therefore, a logic is needed with the ability to name states (or points, worlds, times) and reference them later. Hybrid logic extends modal logic to reach that goal. By introducing a new class of formulas, called *nominals*. Nominals are used to name states; they are true at exactly one state and are used instead of ordinary propositional symbols. Formulas can be formed by using standard boolean operators and a new *satisfaction operator*, which is depicted by @. The satisfaction operator makes it possible to formalise that a statement is true at a particular state. The formula $@_i p$ is defined as follows:

Definition 1. *$@_i p$ is true if and only if the proposition p is true in the unique state named by the nominal i*

Nominals and the satisfaction operator make it possible to formalise many relations that cannot be represented with standard modal temporal logic. The following sentence[2]

(8) Ed finished the book.

cannot be expressed by the modalities ⟨F⟩ and ⟨P⟩ (staying for future and past) alone, because these modalities do not state the exact point in time at which Ed finished the book. Through the addition of a nominal i it is possible to refer to that point in time:

(9) $\langle \mathrm{P} \rangle (i \wedge \textbf{Ed-finish-book})$

Hybrid logic is also suitable to represent linguistic meaning of sentences. This is done by a conjunction of modalised terms, which are tied by a nominal that names the head proposition of that conjunction. In Example (10), the hybrid logic representation of the sentence *Ed wrote a long book in London* is shown:

(10)
$$
\begin{aligned}
@_{h_1}(\textbf{write} \wedge \\
&\langle \mathrm{ACT} \rangle\ (\ d_0 \wedge \textbf{Ed}\ ) \wedge \\
&\langle \mathrm{PAT} \rangle\ (\ d_5 \wedge \textbf{book} \wedge \\
&\qquad\qquad \langle \mathrm{GR} \rangle\ (\ d_7 \wedge \textbf{long}\ )) \wedge \\
&\langle \mathrm{LOC} \rangle\ (\ d_9 \wedge \textbf{London}))
\end{aligned}
$$

The whole expression is dominated by the head proposition **write**, which is denoted by the nominal h_1. The modalities ⟨ACT⟩, ⟨PAT⟩, ⟨GR⟩ and ⟨LOC⟩ stand for the dependency relations *Actor*, *Patient*, *Locative* and *General Relationship* respectively. These relations are dependent on the head proposition. The hybrid logic term in Example (11) shows the general definition for the dependency relations:

(11) $@_h(\textbf{proposition} \wedge \langle \delta_i \rangle (d_i \wedge \textbf{dep}_i)$

The dependency relation $\langle \delta_i \rangle$ is associated with a nominal d_i. Each nominal d_i names a state where a dependent expressed as a proposition $\textbf{dep}_i$, should be evaluated. δ_i is a successor of h, the nominal identifying the head of the hybrid logic term.

6 Multimodal System

This section describes the multimodal system we propose for the grammar-based integration of several modes. As discussed in the previous sections, the system has to meet the following design criteria:

- The system must be independent from specific input modes. This ensures that the system can always be extended by additional modes.

[2] Examples (8), (9), and (10) are taken from [10].

- The data of the input modes must be accessible at a high level. For this the input processing and the complexity of the modes has to be transparent and the input streams must be represented on an abstract level.
- The time at which events like speech or gesture input occur must be captured and represented in the system. This happens both on a low level where timestamps of events are stored and also on a high level where the points in time are represented in an abstract representation.

Section 6.1 gives an overview, while several aspects of the proposed system are highlighted in Sections 6.2 to 6.4.

6.1 System Overview

Figure 1 shows an overview for our multimodal integration system. The input streams of the different modes are parsed by CCGs and represented on an abstract level by Hybrid Logic formulas. As mentioned in section 5, in Hybrid Logic formulas time points can be represented by nominals. These nominals are stored in the nominal-timestamp mapping module together with two timestamps that refer to the start and end time of an input stream. The Hybrid Logic formulas can be processed in two ways; on the one hand they are used to generate rules for the rule set of the system, while on the other hand the formulas can be processed directly in the online mode. For this, the set of rules must be already filled. The rules can be entered manually or learnt automatically from stored input data.

6.2 Input Modules

The several input modules have to register with the system before their input can be processed. The system has to make sure that an appropriate grammar is present for all registered input modules or that a new module can send well-formed Hybrid Logic formulas in any form. It is also imaginable that data sources from other multimodal systems may serve as input to our system. Since Hybrid Logic formulas can be represented in XML, any data that is in XML and involves information about input streams and timestamps can be transformed to Hybrid Logic formulas via XSLT stylesheets. The output of multimodal annotation tools like ELAN [12] or EXMARaLDA [13] can also be a source of data to the system.

The input modes that are used in our system are speech recognition, object recognition, face tracking, and gesture recognition. The use of grammars for parsing speech input is straightforward and common. For the other input modes we are planning to use a similar approach like in [3] and [4] that involves a hierarchy of actions/gestures. In this way, complex actions can be composed by primitive actions.

6.3 Nominal-Timestamp Mapping

The nominal-timestamp mapping module has two purposes. First, it stores every nominal with two timestamps for the start time and end time of the event that is denominated by the nominal. The method of determining timestamps for each event

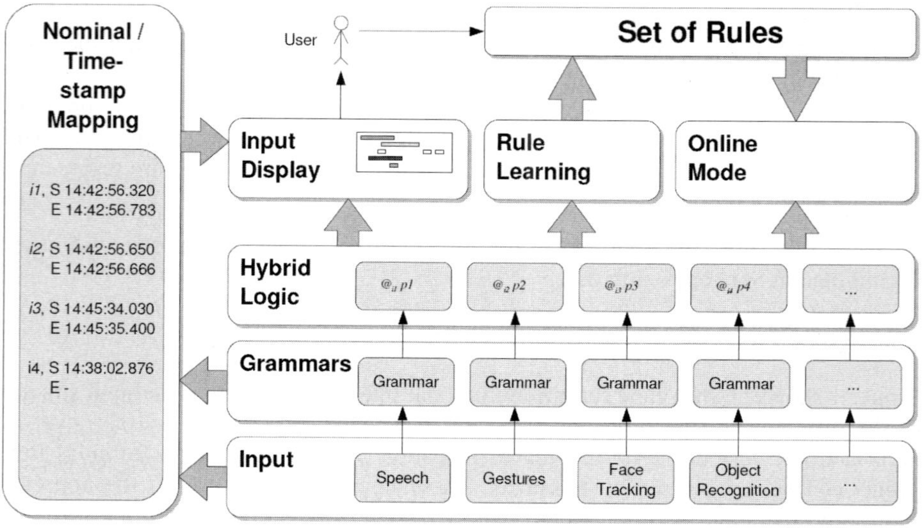

Fig. 1. Overview for the multimodal system

must be designed carefully. Especially as they differ for every input mode. For example, timestamps for speech recognition can be saved at the level of sentences or individual words, while the input from the face tracking component cannot be saved on a video frame level because the amount of data would be too large.

The second purpose of the nominal-timestamp mapping module is to allow other modules to compare the temporal relation between nominals. The four temporal relations that should be available are defined in the following list, these are similar to the interval relations reported by Allen in [14]:

precedes(x,y) Returns true if the end time of nominal x is earlier than the start time of nominal y.

succeeds(x,y) Returns true if the start time of nominal x is later than the end time of nominal y.

includes(x,y) Returns true if the start time of nominal x is earlier than the start time of nominal y and the end time of nominal x is later than the end time of nominal y.

includedBy(x,y) Returns true if the start time of nominal x is later than the start time of nominal y and the end time of nominal x is earlier than the end time of nominal y.

6.4 Grammars, Hybrid Logic Formulas

A grammar for speech processing has already been developed for German and English. It is written with OpenCCG and is designed for a specific task where a user instructs a robot to pick up and lay down objects like cubes, bolts and slats. See [15] for a complete description of the task and the robot assembly. The grammar can parse the following sentence types:

Statements	*"The bolt is yellow."*
Imperative Sentences	*"Take a slat!"*
Questions	*"Where is the red cube?"*
Confirmations	*"Yes." "No." "OK."*

The Hybrid Logic formulas representing the parsed sentences display their syntactic structure, as shown in Section 7.

The grammars for the other input modules like face tracking and gesture recognition are based on a hierarchy of actions. Thus, primitive actions build the basis of the hierarchy, while complex actions can be composed by combining those primary actions. For example, for the face tracking it is not suitable to generate logic formulas for every video frame that is captured by the video camera that is filming the user. It is rather desirable to join several frames to one action.

7 Processing Example

This section shows a full example how the processing of three input modes looks like. The three input modes are speech recognition, gesture recognition, and object recognition. The scenario of the example involves a robot, a user, and parts of a toy construction set. The user instructs the robot to pick up a certain object by pointing at a cube and saying *"Take this cube."*'. The sentence is passed by the speech recognition to the grammar, which yields the logical form presented in (12):

$$(12)\quad @_{x_1}(\langle\textsc{verb}\rangle\,\mathrm{take} \wedge \langle\textsc{noun}\rangle\,\mathrm{cube} \wedge \langle\textsc{deictic}\rangle\,\mathrm{this})$$

(13) displays the logical form that is generated by the gesture recognition:

$$(13)\quad @_{x_2}(\langle\textsc{gesture}\rangle\,\mathrm{pointAt})$$

The input by the object recognition is also parsed by a grammar. The corresponding logical form can be seen in (14):

$$(14)\quad @_{x_3}(\langle\textsc{object}\rangle\,\mathrm{cube})$$

The processing of the Hybrid Logic formulas involves the following steps: First, the collected Hybrid Logic formulas are displayed for the user in an abstract way. Figure 2 shows one possible way to present the input modes.

From this presentation, and with the help of the time relation functions of the nominal-timestamp mapping module, the developer can generate rules in a pseudo code that are then translated back into Hybrid Logic formulas. These rule formulas are stored in the set of rules afterwards and can be applied for input processing in the online mode afterwards. Example (15) shows a rule in pseudo code for the example given here:

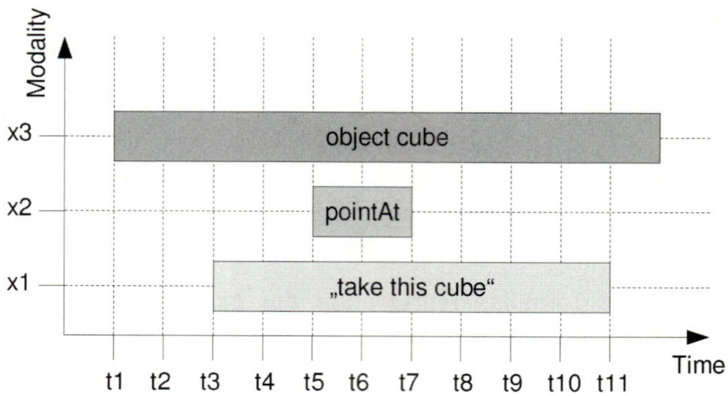

Fig. 2. Display of three input modes: Speech recognition x_1, gesture recognition x_2, and object recognition x_3

$$
\begin{array}{lll}
(15) & \text{if} & @_{x_1}(\langle\text{VERB}\rangle\ \text{take} \wedge \\
 & & \quad \langle\text{NOUN}\rangle\ O_1 \wedge \\
 & & \quad \langle\text{DEICTIC}\rangle\ \text{this}\ ) \\
 & \text{and} & @_{x_2}(\langle\text{GESTURE}\rangle\ \text{pointAt}\ ) \\
 & \text{and} & @_{x_3}(\langle\text{OBJECT}\rangle\ O_2\ ) \\
 & \text{and} & O_1 \equiv O_2 \\
 & \text{and} & \mathit{includes}(x_1, x_2) \\
 & \text{then} & \mathit{take}(\mathit{robot}, O_1)
\end{array}
$$

8 Conclusion

We described an approach for a multimodal system that uses Combinatory Categorial Grammars to parse input modes. The parsing process yields a representation of the modalities in Hybrid Logic, which is very useful for this task because it models temporal relationships. The proposed system displays the temporal connections between input modes on an abstract level, which allows the developer of the system to manually generate processing rules that enable the system to respond to user input appropriately.

Acknowledgements. This work was supported by the EU FP6 IST Cognitive Systems Integrated Project "JAST" (FP6-003747-IP), http://www.euprojects-jast.net/.

References

1. Shimazu, H., Arita, S., Takashima, Y.: Multi-modal definite clause grammar. In: Proceedings of the 15th Conference on Computational linguistics, pp. 832–836. Association for Computational Linguistics, Morristown, NJ, USA (1994)
2. Johnston, M., Bangalore, S.: Finite-state multimodal parsing and understanding. In: Proceedings of COLING-2000, Saarbruecken, Germany (2000)

3. Nevatia, R., Zhao, T., Hongeng, S.: Hierarchical language-based representation of events in video streams. In: IEEE Workshop on Event Mining (2003)
4. Ryoo, M.S., Aggarwal, J.K.: Recognition of composite human activities through context-free grammar based representation. In: CVPR '06: Proceedings of the 2006 IEEE Computer Society Conference on Computer Vision and Pattern Recognition, Washington, DC, pp. 1709–1718. IEEE Computer Society Press, Los Alamitos (2006)
5. Ades, A.E., Steedman, M.J.: On the order of words. Linguistics and philosophy 4, 517–558 (1982)
6. Steedman, M.: The syntactic process. MIT Press, Cambridge, MA (2000)
7. Ajdukiewicz, K.: Die syntaktische konnexität. Studia Philosophica 1, 1–27 (1935)
8. Bar-Hillel, Y.: A quasi-arithmetic notation for syntactic description. Language 29, 47–58 (1953)
9. White, M.: Efficient realization of coordinate structures in combinatory categorial grammar. Research on Language & Computation 4(1), 39–75 (2006)
10. Baldridge, J., Kruijff, G.J.: Coupling ccg and hybrid logic dependency semantics. In: Proceedings of the 40th Annual Meeting of the Association for Computational Linguistics (ACL 02), University of Pennsylania, Philadelphia, PA (2002)
11. Prior, A.: Past, Present and Future. Oxford University Press, Oxford (1967)
12. Brugman, H., Russel, A.: Annotating multi-media/multi-modal resources with elan. In: 4th International Conference on Language Resources and Evaluation (LREC2004), Lisbon (26.05.2004-28.05.2004 2004), pp. 2065–2068 (2004)
13. Schmidt, T., Wörner, K.: Erstellen und analysieren von gesprächskorpora mit exmaralda. Gesprächsforschung - Online-Zeitschrift zur verbalen Interaktion Ausgabe 6, 171–195 (2005)
14. Allen, J.F.: Maintaining knowledge about temporal intervals. Commun. ACM 26(11), 832–843 (1983)
15. Foster, M.E., By, T., Rickert, M., Knoll, A.: Human-robot dialogue for joint construction tasks. In: Proceedings, Eighth International Conference on Multimodal Interfaces (ICMI 2006), Banff (November 2006)

New Type of Auditory Progress Bar: Exploration, Design and Evaluation

Shuo Hsiu Hsu[1], Cécile Le Prado[1], Stéphane Natkin[1], and Claude Liard[2]

[1] CEDRIC Laboratory, Conservatoire National des Arts et Métiers, 292 rue St Martin, 75141 Paris Cedex 03, France
shuo-hsiu.hsu@orange.fr, cecile.leprado@free.fr, natkin@cnam.fr
[2] Brigitte Frybourg Laboratory, Conservatoire National des Arts et Métiers, 2 rue Conté case 211, 75003 Paris, France
liard@cnam.fr

Abstract. In this paper, we focus on the method to explore a different type of auditory progress bar by analyzing the characteristics of the visual progress bar and contexts of auditory application. A scenario of bearing in the forward/reverse modes of digital compass is selected to implement the auditory progress bar. The auditory cues play an interactive role in the bearing that they are altered according to the user's operating behavior. Composed of sound signal and silent pause, the auditory cues are generated from a formula based on the warm/cold metaphor. A method incorporating the foreground/background sounds is also designed to provide different ranges of progress information/progress update expressed through auditory cues. In this report four versions of auditory cues are presented as the solution to the interactive auditory progress bar and a pilot study is evaluated.

Keywords: Auditory progress bar, sound design.

1 Introduction

Progress bars are typical widgets in graphical user interfaces; the objective of the progress bar is to provide the user with information concerning the achievement of a task; primarily the information is about the task time. The study of Conn[2] indicated eight task properties to provide good time affordance for the progress bar in the graphical user interface. Progress bars vary between different applications; for example, a vending machine for hot drinks. The progress bar presents a simple process of making coffee. Other customary examples in computer user interface are shown in Fig.1, where the progress bar expresses more detailed information during the process of downloads. Previous studies [1][3][7] have proved that the auditory cues could be an alternative option to support visual feedback. Concerning the effectiveness of adding sounds to the progress bar, Crease and Brewster [3] developed an auditory progress bar composed of four musical tones referring to the different status' of a file transmission. Another study [9] is the application of the auditory progress bar in the telephone system, whereby the auditory progress bar indicates the waiting time on telephone lines.

C. Stephanidis (Ed.): Universal Access in HCI, Part II, HCII 2007, LNCS 4555, pp. 868–877, 2007.

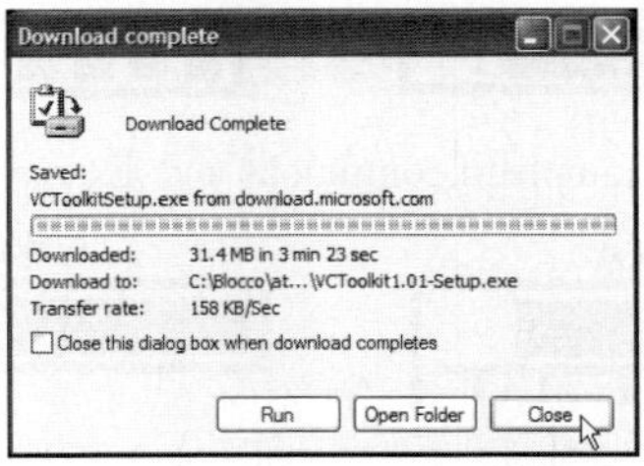

Fig. 1. The progress bar from the interface of downloads

2 Method

Progress bars are applied in various ways for different uses; they differ either from their forms or from the contents of messages. To discover other types of auditory progress bars, a systematic method is executed to explore possible applications. Firstly, two factors are used to analyze the visual progress bars: the external characteristics in visual presentation and the internal contents in transmitted information. Secondly, a cross table is adopted to generate all possible results composed by the two former factors. Finally, in order to choose the prospective application for the auditory progress bar, the interactivity, the contexts of auditory feedback and user scenarios are also considered.

2.1 Investigation of the Visual Progress Bar

The first step of investigating progress bars focuses on the external characteristics. By looking at the mode of usage of the visual progress bar, the evolution of visual presentation can be categorized as follows:

(1) The monotone and non-monotone bars: From the viewpoint of interactivity, the visual presentation of progress bars relates to the nature of the task. In the non-interactive tasks, the monotone progress bar indicates the progress of the task which can't manipulated by the user's operation; therefore, the progress bar performs regularly in a route from a starting point to an end point, as the example in Fig.1 shows. In the case of interactive tasks, its progress is represented by a non-monotone progress bar which acts in a repeated back and forth motion due to interaction between users and the interface.

(2) The continuous and discreet bars: Without additional measurement of the progress, visual presentation is one of the possibilities available for users to perceive the progress that the progress bar has made, either in the continuous or discreet form. In contrast to the transforming form of the continuous bar, the discreet bar is accumulated by certain sections equal to each other in size. Both examples are shown in Fig.2.

(3) The gradual and non-gradual bars: another way to display the progress of the task is how the progress bar works with a graduated scale to produce measured indications. The gradual progress bar in Fig.3 is defined by the measure to indicate the progress while a non-gradual progress bar has no scale.

Fig. 2. The example of continuous and discreet progress bar

Fig. 3. The example of gradual and non gradual progress bar

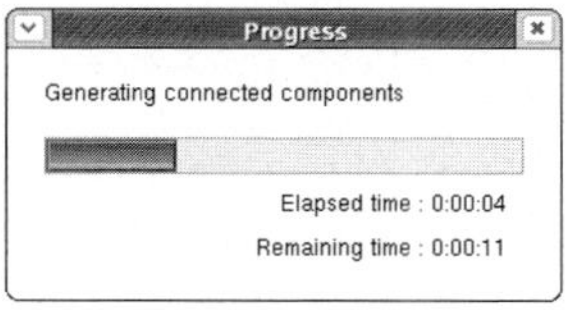

Fig. 4. The progress bar presents the value of ongoing time

The second step of the analysis is to find out what kind of information is conveyed by progress bars. Four types of information are presented: (1) the process: the progress bar represents the process of achievement for an ongoing task. (2) The value of the transmitted task: the progress bar can be used to present the value of the progress in the ongoing task as the example in Fig.4 demonstrates. (3) The change of status: The process of executing a task can be divided into different sections to indicate the progress status as shown in example Fig.5. (4) The variation of the evolution: in the non-monotone progress bar, users are aware of fluctuation of the progress in real time from the progress bar as shown in Fig.6.

Fig. 5. The progress bar presents the change of status in the video game Athens 2004

2.2 Generating Possible Progress Bar

The following stage is to explore the possible types of progress bar based on the analysis of the progress bar. Like the external characteristics, the modes of usage are defined in eight categories as listed in the rows on the left hand side of Table.1. Four kinds of internal information featured in a progress bar are shown at the top of the four columns in Table.1. A column with a star means that certain sort of usage possesses the attributes of one particular piece of information (Process, value, status, variation). In Table.1, two types of progress bar don’t match either column from the transmitted information. These two progress bars don't exist due to their incompatible elements (non-gradual and discreet). The results from Table.1 can be listed as six types of progress bar.

Fig. 6. The progress bar presents the variation of the motion from the player in the video game of Torino 2006

Table 1. Table composed of two types of characteristics. (M: Monotone, NM: Non monotone, G: Gradual, NG: Non gradual, C: Continuous, D: Discreet)

Information / Mode of usage			Process	Value	Status	Variation
M	G	C	*	*	*	
		D	*	*	*	
	NG	C	*			
		D				
NM	G	C	*	*	*	*
		D	*	*	*	*
	NG	C	*			*
		D				

2.3 Parameters Concerning the Auditory Progress Bar

To explore the possible application of an auditory progress bar from the generated results, six criterions based on the study of Edworthy [5] will be considered: (1) The concentration of vision and multi-tasking: when the working environment isn’t visually simple, the auditory feedback would be a possible solution to visual overloads from tasks. (2) The characteristics of tasks**:** the use of feedbacks from different modalities depends on the task's characteristics. Three conditions are discussed by three circles from the same center; the first inner circle proposes that the user performs tasks in a fixed place where feedbacks are easy to access. Factors which can possibly stir the annoyance of users due to being highly exposed to auditory messages are also taken into consideration. The extended middle circle shows that the operation in a mobile condition will intensify the priority to adopt the auditory feedback because of the visual feedback's inefficiency during the process. The outer circle shows a condition where visual feedbacks from the ongoing tasks are totally inaccessible for users; auditory feedback is transmitted from one end to the other in an operation carried out over a certain distance. (3) The duration of a task: the indication of the progress via auditory feedback can easily become annoying with the long duration of the task. (4) Various sources of sound from the surrounding environment could affect the use of auditory feedback. (5) Audio-only or audio-visual feedbacks: the auditory feedback could be an alternative option to replace the visual feedback, or it could play a role to enhance the effect of the visual feedback in the case that the visual and auditory feedbacks exist simultaneously. (6) Different conditions in vision: the use of auditory feedback will benefit various levels of sensory difficulties of vision. People with normal sensory abilities may experience different levels of sensory difficulties. For example, the modality of vision may not function well when overloaded or when there is low visibility underwater.

2.4 The Prospective Application for Auditory Progress Bar

In contrast to the study of Crease and Brewster[3] concerning the effectiveness of adding sounds to the visual progress bar, we aim to implement an auditory progress bar without any visual feedback. From analysis on the visual progress bar, we found that the parameter of variation in non-monotone progress bar showed an interactive condition between users and interface; such a parameter was considered to be an important factor in implementing a new type of auditory progress bar, which is most commonly found in video games. Beyond the domain of entertainment, a prospective non-gaming application was found in the electronic compass where it provided the modes of forward/reverse bearing; that is, according to the bearing relative to the target, whereby the user can trace the correct direction of the target without knowing the current bearing. This process of finding the target in this type of scenario can be regarded as a non-monotone progress bar because the status of the progress is manipulated by users according to the search conditions. In such a scenario of bearing, the auditory cue benefited bearing tasks where users could fully concentrate on the upcoming events, instead of being distracted by the visual feedback from the electronic compass.

3 Design of Auditory Progress Bar in Electronic Compass

There were several examples of using sound to indicate the bearing. Verbal sound such as speech was used to indicate the exact degrees of bearing in the auditory compass Tacktick[12]. In Smith-Kettlewell's project [6], the dynamic auditory cues of “beep-beep” and “ding-ding” were created to express the bearing of veering from a travel path. Another design aimed at finding the target via auditory cues can be found in AudioGPS[8]; different repeated tones were used for panning the direction, and the warm/cold metaphor was used in composing auditory cues to indicate the relative distance to the target. The manner in which to perceive the verbal sound was different from that to non-verbal sound. The verbal sounds conveyed more emotional and complex messages than non-verbal messages do. We decided to choose non-verbal sound to simplify and to eliminate cognitive factors about verbal language. Moreover, the non-verbal sounds are also more appropriate than the verbal sounds when aiming to express the relative progress of bearing without giving information concerning the four cardinal points or exact degree measurements.

3.1 Indication of the Progress in Finding Target

In the scenario of panning the target toward a 2-dimension space using an electronic compass, the process of bearing in a circular path can be transformed into a linear progress bar where auditory cues convey relative bearing. To design the auditory cues, we have two principles as followed: firstly, a "warm/cold" metaphor is used to express the progress of the ongoing task. Secondly, to feature the non-monotone progress bar, the content of the auditory cues has to express the message of variation during the task of searching for the target. Moreover, three sound parameters are adopted to generate the auditory cues: (1) the continuous and discrete sounds are used to indicate the process of reaching a target. (2) The stereo sound of the auditory cues indicates the relative position to the target (whether the user had passed the target or is approaching it). (3) Different duration from the sound signal and the silent pause: auditory cues composed by different durations of sound signal and silent pause would be created to express the progress.

3.2 Generation of the Auditory Cues

A mathematical equation based on the warm/cold metaphor is generated when we calculate the relative distance between the target (Xref) and the current heading(X) which is considered as two points on the circle of 360°. The relative distance (D) between Xref and X is calculated every 10 degrees from 0° to 360°. The result for each D is distributed as a hyperbolic curve as one example demonstrates in Fig.7. The output data of the equation from 0° to 360° is used to determine the duration for sound signal and silent pause in order to generate the auditory cues.

$$D = \frac{\left|1 + Sin\left(90 + \left|X - Xref\right|\right)\right|}{10\left|Sin\left(\left|X - Xref\right|\right)\right|} \qquad (1)$$

We designed four versions of the auditory cues by using the polarity (increasing and decreasing) of the duration for sound signal and silent pause; four versions are shown in Table.2. A beep sound (350Hz) was used as the basic unit for the sound signal.

3.3 Progress Sounds from the Different Grounds

Like the visual design of units on a ruler, different sizes of actual measurement markings are used to distinguish different levels of measuring. Therefore, we decided to apply two layers of auditory cues, foreground and background sounds, to express

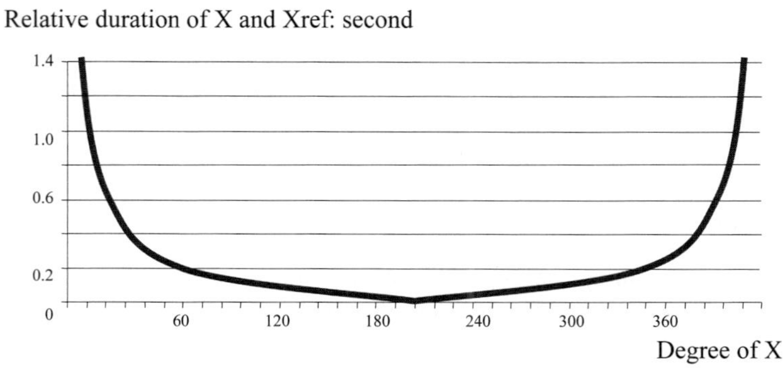

Fig. 7. The distribution of the curve D when Xref =0

Table 2. The 4 versions of auditory cues with different durations in the sound signal and the silent pause

Version	Duration of the sound	Duration of the silent pause
1		
2		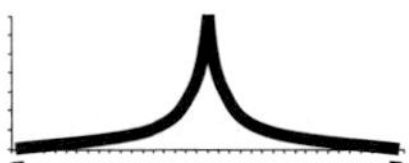
3		
4		

the progress in a different sense. The foreground progress sound generated by the equation presents the progress in details. The background process sound expresses the progress using a wide range of sounds, comprising a mixture of four pitches in total (D_2-9 73Hz, $A^{\#}_1$+32 59Hz, $C^{\#}_2$-7 69Hz, D_2+12 73Hz). Both layers of progress sound are dealt with increasing volume.

3.4 Sounds Concerning the Target

When the target is found, a continuous beep sound (2100Hz) is launched. If the user misses the target and passes it by, the auditory cues in stereo sound will help the user to distinguish the relative position of the target.

4 Experimental Design

A prototype of the electronic compass' interface was simulated in Macromedia Flash 8. Target finding tasks were executed via the laptop computer's headset. Subjects used the right and left keys on the external keyboard to simulate turning the compass without any visual feedback from the screen. The aim of this experiment was to determine if the designed auditory progress bars were able to enhance the awareness of the progress of the target orientation tasks. Four versions of auditory progress bar were implemented in four stages and each stage contained four tasks of finding targets in cardinal points without description in advance. A five-minute warm-up was provided for each subject at the beginning of each stage before starting the formal tasks; there were also five-minute breaks between each task. Moreover, the method of counterbalancing was used to even out carryout effects. An interview took place at the end of the tasks to collect subjects' opinions. A pilot study was carried out involving fourteen subjects, consisting of seven female and seven male students.

4.1 Results

From Fig.8, we found that the average time taken by subjects in version1 and version4 was less than that in version2 and version3. The average task time for male subjects was less than that for female subjects. We can refer to Table.2 when discussing this result, where the auditory progress bars were designed with decreasing duration of sound signal in version1 and version4, whilst the increasing duration of sound signal was used in version2 and version3. That is, subjects are used to the warm/cold metaphor in version1 and version4 when perceiving progress made from the auditory cues. Moreover, subjects expressed their preferences towards the four versions; four subjects preferred version1, version2 was preferred by two subjects, one subject preferred version3 and four subjects preferred version4. Three subjects made no comment.

With regard to the two-layer auditory progress bar's performance, ten subjects expressed that they couldn't identify its function while two subjects found the background sound was not evident. Furthermore, two other subjects even considered the auditory cues from the two layers progress to be incompatible and annoying. Ten of the fourteen subjects perceived the progress by using the foreground sound (different durations of sound signals and silent pauses) and the other four subjects followed the same method by using the background sound (different pitch of sound). One reason why we failed to receive positive response for the two-layer progress sound was due to the fact that the subjects had already established their personal preferences when faced with the priority of detecting and ignoring auditory stimuli. Thus, this caused the subjects to choose one dominating factor to perceive the progress and to screen the therefore redundant auditory messages. This situation could possibly be what the theory of gestalt in psychology describes.

In the process of finding targets, eight out of fourteen subjects considered the volume as the dominant factor in conveying much clearer messages of progress, while the duration pof the sound signal was regarded as the crucial factor by four subjects; another two subjects considered both the volume and the duration to be equally important. The auditory cues were composed by different duration of sound signal and silent pause to convey the progress information. Nevertheless, it is only natural that subjects needed to spend more time to distinguish the differences between the duration and the volume, especially when they encountered several auditory cues simultaneously.

Certain interesting findings were also discovered about the subjects' behavior when perceiving the progress made. There were two principal types of navigation methods adopted by the subjects: monotone navigation and non-monotone navigation. In adopting the first method, subjects moved the compass in one single direction (either clockwise or counterclockwise) to perceive the difference between the auditory cues. Using the other method, subjects took advantage of the different indications provided by the auditory cues when they changed their direction. Moreover, certain subjects carefully listened to each section of the auditory cues so that they could be sure of the differences between the auditory feedbacks, whereas some subjects preferred to speed up the bearing progress by skimming through some sections of the auditory cues. However, this finding could be accounted for, when taking into account the simulated control of the keyboard; subjects might not have had the same control behavior when holding a real compass.

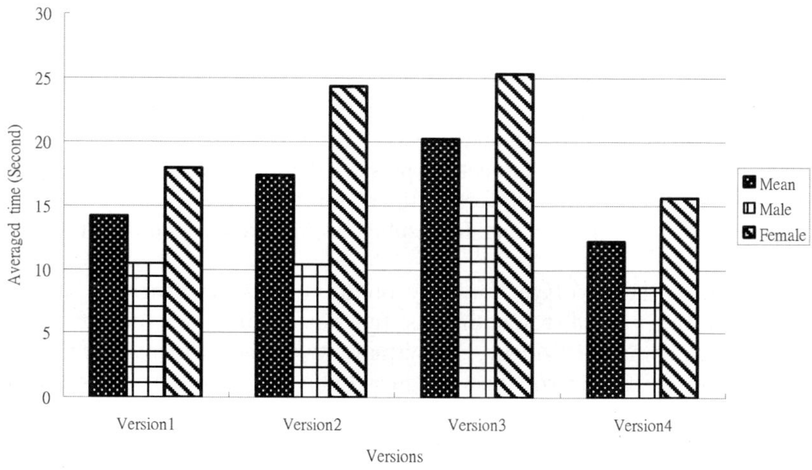

Fig. 8. Average time taken by subjects (male and female) for each version

5 Conclusions

The study aims at exploring the new type of auditory progress bar by using a systematic method. The coding of non-verbal sounds in the auditory progress bar can be regarded as one kind of earcon which conveys different messages to express the status of progress. Future work will continue to explore different applications in the audiovisual context where the auditory interface plays an essential role in enhancing usability and providing parallel feedback to support the visual interface.

Acknowledgments. We would like to thank our participants at CNAM for their participation in the experiment and thanks also goes to Chia-ching Chou for the technical support in Flash programming.

References

1. Blattner, M., Sumikawa, D., Greenberg, R.: Earcons and Icons: Their Structure And Common Design Principles. Human Computer Interaction 4, 11–44 (1989)
2. Conn, A.P.: Time affordances: the time factor in diagnostic usability heuristics. In: Proceedings of the SIGCHI conference on Human factors in computing systems (1995)
3. Crease, M.G., Brewster, S.A.: Making Progress with Sounds - The Design and Evaluation of An Audio Progress Bar. In: Proceedings of ICAD, British Computer Society (1998)
4. Deneen, B.J.: Electronic Compass for the Blind. <http://nsf-pad.bme.uconn.edu/1991/chapter_7.pdf>
5. Edworthy, J.: Does sound help us to work better with machines? Interacting with Computers 10, 401–409 (1998)
6. Flux-gate auditory compass <http://www.ski.org/rerc/5yrReport/General/IV.html#anchor151824>
7. Gaver, W.W.: Auditory Icons: Using Sound In Computer Interfaces. Human-Computer Interaction 2, 167–177 (1986)
8. Holland, S., Morse, D.R., Gedenryd, H.: Audio GPS: Spatial Audio in a minimal attention interface. In: 3rd International Workshop on HCI with Mobile Devices (2001)
9. Kortum, P., Peres, S.C., Knott, B., Bushey, B.: The Effects of Auditory Progress Bars on Consumer's Estimation of Telephone Wait Time. In: Proceedings of the 49th Annual Human Factors and Ergonomics Society. Orlando, FL (2005)
10. Leplâtre, G., Brewster, S.A.: Designing non-speech sounds to support navigation in mobile menus. In: Proceedings of ICAD (2000)
11. Norman, D.A.: Affordance, conventions, and design. interactions, Vol. 6(3) (1999)
12. The Tacktick <http://www.blindsailing.org>
13. Wogalter, M.S. (ed.): Handbook of Warnings. Lawrence erlbaum associates, Mahwah, New Jersey, London (2006)

Factors Influencing the Usability of Icons in the LCD Touch Screens

Hsinfu Huang[1], Wang-Chin Tsai[2], and Hsin-His Lai[1]

[1] Department of Industrial Design, National Cheng Kung University, No.1, University Road, Tainan City, Taiwan, R.O.C
p3893110@mail.ncku.edu.tw

[2] Graduate School of Design, National Yunlin University of Science and Technology 123 University Road, Section 3, Douliou, Yunlin, Taiwan, R.O.C.
g9031707@yuntech.edu.tw

Abstract. The purpose of this study was to investigate factors influencing the usability of icons in the LCD touch screens. In this study, subjects had to fill in the questionnaire and rated questions on 7-point Likert scales. 20 evaluation items were collected from relevant interface design guidelines. A total of 30 subjects, 10 none- experience users, 10 click-experience users (PDA user), 10 touch-experience users (LCD touch screens user), participated in the investigation. As main statistical test, a principal component analysis (PCA) was performed with SPSS/ PC. The results from the principal components analysis showed that the usability of touch icon was affected by seven factors: touch field, semantics quality, dynamics, hit quality, tactility, color quality and shape quality. Among these, touch field was the most important. Finally, the results of correlation analyses indicated that experience related to importance ratings for usability. Especially, subjects show significant difference in the size element ($p<0.05$). Further, user who has pen-click experience, such as PDA user, still show better performance for touch screen even if they use smaller icon.

Keywords: LCD touch screens, touch icons, usability, factors analysis.

1 Introduction

Computer graphic user interface (GUI) brings the visual operation to the user, and icons were often used on this interface [Näsänen & Ojanpää, 2003]. In the general situation, we execute tasks that control cursors to the goal by normal display-control relation in the working environment of VDT. With the development of touch panel technology, LCD touch screens have different interactive type. Compared to the type of gray screen in the past, current colored screen (16.7 million) seems more complicated. Besides, LCD touch screen was often used in the specialized working field, such as POS, kiosk, medical environment and industrial control using. [Sears, Plasisant and, Shneiderman, 1992]. Thus, a good touch-icon design will improve the user's performance, and reduce its fault.

C. Stephanidis (Ed.): Universal Access in HCI, Part II, HCII 2007, LNCS 4555, pp. 878–887, 2007.

Some of relevant studies determined anthropometry for workstation of touch-screen and make workstation more efficient [Beringer & Peterson, 1985 ; Sears ,1991 ; Schultz et al., 1998]. Schultz et al. [1998] indicated that Optimal viewing angle for touch-screen is between 19 and 54.5 degree off the horizontal. However, Touch-screen system was a complicated Human-Computer interface. Except workstation analysis for HCI, this study wish to focus attention on touch – screen usability. On the other hand, regardless of interface type, icons play an important role in the computer graphic user interface. We can already obtain some important icon design elements, including styling quality, message quality, meaningfulness, locatability, and metaphor [Huang et al., 2002]. According to this principle, interface designer can design useful icons. But it will be useful to design icons on the normal screens. Thus, there was a principle not confirmed in the design of touch-screen icon.

Obviously, operation of a touch screen was different from the normal screen. Apart from visual search, there was also a "touch" action involved in using a touch screen. However, there were few discussions on issues related to touching the target and icons using fingers. From the interface designer's perspective, in order to create a high-user friendly interface, he/she must understand the usability requirements, which must first be obtained from the users [Shneiderman & Plasisant, 2004]. Thus, the purpose of this study was to investigate factors affecting the usability of icons in the LCD touch screens. The findings could serve as a guide to design computer icons that were appropriate for touch screen interface, and make interface more user-friendly.

2 Methods

2.1 Subjects

A total of 30 subjects participated in this experiment. These subjects included 10 none-experience users, 10 click-experience users (PDA user) and 10 touch-experience users (LCD touch screen user). Their mean age was 29.18 (SD=2.67).

2.2 Materials and Stimuli

The materials were presented on 3M touch screen system (LCD/ MD17-5MS) with the max pixel resolution used was 1600 X 1200 and the frame rate was 80 Hz. The pixel size was 0.264mm X 0.264mm.Other specifications as follows: LCD Display (337.92mm X 270.34mm), Contrast Ratio (450:1), Brightness (260 cd/m2) and Response Time (16ms)。 The study designs a touch-screen interface of experiment by oneself, and executed by this screen. The pixel resolution used was 1024 X 768 and the frame rate was 70 Hz. In the experimental interface, there were various design icons with different feedback level and they were classified along the axis, as in Fig. 1. Subjects can experience the difference between operating the various touched icons.

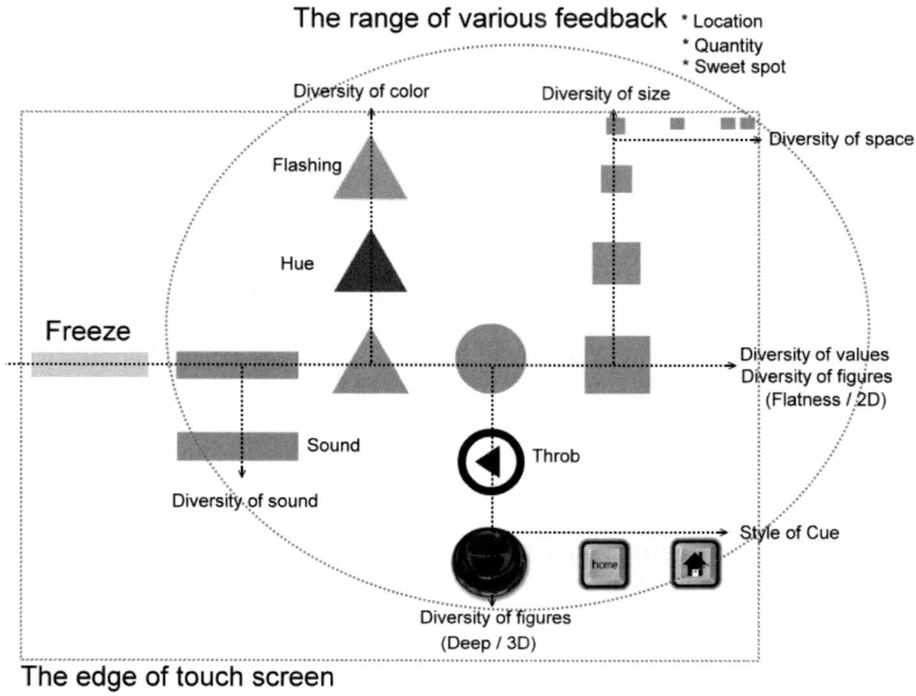

Fig. 1. Touch-screen icons in the experiment

2.3 Subjective Evaluation

According to method of Likert scale, the study makes usability of elements for touch-icons from relational journals. (Displays; Applied ergonomics; International journal of industrial ergonomics; Advances in human-computer interaction) or design guidelines of human-computer interface (Dix et al., 1998; Paiva, 2000; Shneiderman & Plasisant, 2004; Stone et al., 2005). Table 1 lists 20 items.

2.4 Procedures

Before the experiment, subjects were briefed on the rules and purpose of the experiment and were asked to fill in their personal details. Before the start of every test, the accuracy of touch screen was adjusted by the adjustment software. Subjects began with touching icon from the one's left side (Freeze/ None feedback of style). The touch icons adopted progressive interaction in the experimental interface. Subjects must touch every icon on the touch screen, as in Fig.2.

Subjects experienced all different interaction style, and perceived the different usability between operating the various touched icons. After the touch task finished, subjects were asked to rate the usability elements based on the importance of touch icon. Finally, subjects had to fill in the questionnaire and rated questions on 5-point Likert scales (1=not important at all; 5=most important).

2.5 Data Analysis

There were effective cases into the data analysis process. The following statistical methods were applied to data analysis: Descriptive statistical analysis, principal component analysis, and ANOVA.

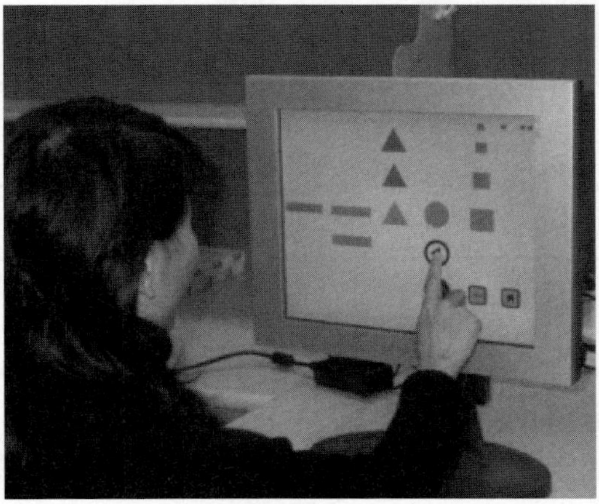

Fig. 2. The situation of experiment

Table 1. 20 elements of usability

Elements	Description
Location	The location of icon on the touch-screen
Quantity	The quantity of icon on the touch-screen
Density	The state of icons are intensive or loose
Values	The color of icon is light or deep
Chroma	The color of icon is light or deep
Hue	The type of color with icon
Size	Area of an icon on the touch-screen
Space	Distance between icon and icon
Sweet spot	Sensitive point that the icon is touched
Shape	Form of the static icon
Edginess	Resolution of the icon edge
Speed	The response time of icon is fast or slow
Depth	Degree of three-dimension of the icon
Flash	Flashing effect on the icon surface
Sound	Appear sound after icon is touched
Haptics	The user has simulated touch-sense psychologically
Displacement	The position of the icon will change after icon is touched, ex. Throb
Ideogram	The surface of the icon has guide of words
Symbol	The surface of the icon has guide of figure
Operation	The strategy of icon that user touch (Land-on/ Lift-off)

Table 2. Loadings of elements on the 7 main factors

Factor	1		2		3		4	
Elements	Size	0.80	Values	0.83	Operation	0.89	Displacement	0.78
	Location	0.75	Hue	0.82	Deep	0.61	Quantity	0.67
	Density	0.64	Chroma	0.65	Haptics	0.59	Speed	0.60
	Space	0.54					Sound	0.53
Cumulative %	21.58		36.20		48.22		56.38	
Eigenvalues	4.31		2.92		2.41		1.63	
Factor	5				6		7	
Elements	Sweet spot		0.76		Shape	0.85	Ideogram	0.89
	Flash		0.73		Edginess	0.58	Symbol	0.69
Cumulative %	63.77				70.29		75.67	
Eigenvalues	1.48				1.31		1.07	

3 Results

3.1 Factors of Usability

This study used the method of Principal Components Analysis to extract the factors of influencing the usability of icons in the LCD touch screens. The factor-loading matrix was created with the method of Varimax Orthogonal Rotation. Number of factors was determined based on the rule of Kaiser [1974] with eigenvalue greater than 1 for factor loading. The explained variation of seven factors was 75.67%. The results of relational analysis were displayed in Table 2.

About these seven factors influencing the usability of icons, factor 1 was named ''Touch field''. The Factor included size, location, space and Density. Lindberg & Näsänen [2003] indicated that icon spacing and size were influenced factors to human visual search when user watch graphic interface. Thus, even on the touch screens, they were still important factors with influence usability of touch icon, especially finger touch, which lead to inaccurate movements. Due to the reason that using touch screen with finger was less accurate than mouse, the space between the icons influence usability directly. Besides, it was less usability to users if icons were put at the corner of touch-screen.

Factor 2 was named ''Color quality''. The Factor included hue, values and chroma. On the touch-screens, icons with apposite color were attractive to users and can display status changes. According to connotations of different colors [Gotz, 1998], we can add positive and negative connotations on touched icons. For example, red color lets users feel attractive (positive connotations) and alarming (negative connotations). On the other hand, blue color gives refreshing (positive connotations) and aloof (negative connotations) impression. In summary, color attraction was an important principle of usability when users operate touch-screens.

Factor 3 was named ''Tactility''. The Factor included depth, haptics and operation. Different from the interface controlled by mouse, users touch icon with finger on the screen directly. It produces faster and more accurate performance on the human-computer interface when haptic (touch and force feedback) feedback was added [Brooks, 1988; Noma et al., 1996]. At this point, in order to improve usability of touch-icon, touch-icon can use three-dimension form to simulate psychological haptics. In the procedures of experiment, subjects consider three- dimension (not flat style) icon was better.

Factor 4 was named ''Dynamics''. The Factor included displacement, quantity, speed and sound. Marcus [1992] indicated that dynamics is a guide of icon design among them. Icons might also have associated sounds. Thus, dynamic interaction has direct influence on the usability of icons.

Factor 5 was named ''Hit quality''. The Factor included sweet spot and flash. In the situation of using touch-screen, users must touch icon with finger. If hit point (sweet spot) of icons were instable or insensitive, users will have setbacks. Thus, hit quality becomes a serious problem in the touch-screen.

Factor 6 was named ''Shape quality". The Factor included form of the static icon and resolution of the icon edge. Touch-screen often were used in the digital learning environment, various shapes can draw attention to touch for children. For touch-screen, user has a partiality for the uncomplicated and simple icon.

Finally, factor 7 was named ''Semantics quality". The Factor included ideogram and symbol. Icons plus words were effective in computing situations [Norman, 1991]. Obviously, this was suitable for touch-icons too. On the other hand, it was popular that using symbol figure on the icon. Thus, Semantics quality was a decisive factor whether information can transmit correctly for users.

The results of ANOVA on the mean ratings indicated significant differences ($F(6,527)=6.67$, $p<0.01$) among the seven factors. The results of Duncan t test were shown in table 3.

3.2 Importance of the Usability of Elements

This was clear form the results of descriptive Statistics. For users, sweet spot was regarded as major important guidance, and then space, location, size and sounds were the second. Users consider less important elements including operation, values, shape, and hue. And flash was ranked the least important. The results of ANOVA on the mean ratings indicated significant differences between 20 elements ($p<0.01$).

Table 3. The result of Duncan t test

Factor	Mean	Duncan grouping		
Touch field	5.76	A		
Semantics quality	5.32	A	B	
Dynamics	5.13		B	C
Hit quality	5.03		B	C
Tactility	4.97		B	C
Color quality	4.68			C
Shape quality	4.63			C

3.3 The Difference in Subjects' Experience

This study classifies two types of subject as touch experience and non- touch experience. And, the touch experience subjects include LCD touch-screen users and PDA users (click-experience on small screen). The results of usability evaluation to different experience were shown in fig. 3. Significant difference of icon size was seen between the different experiences using one-way ANOVA ($p<0.05$), and Duncan test showed {Exp (6.30), PDA (6.00)}> {PDA (6.00), Non-exp (5.10)}. Other elements have no significant effect. Special attention should be paid to compare different experience in the each factor. In the factor 2, non-touch experience users emphasize color quality than others. In the factor 3, LCD touch-screen users emphasize haptic feedback when they touch these icons. Besides, the result of lower mean showed that non-experience users have no idea about operation strategy of icon (Land-on/ Lift-off).

In the factor 5, all subjects think that sweet spot was a key to influencing the usability of icons.

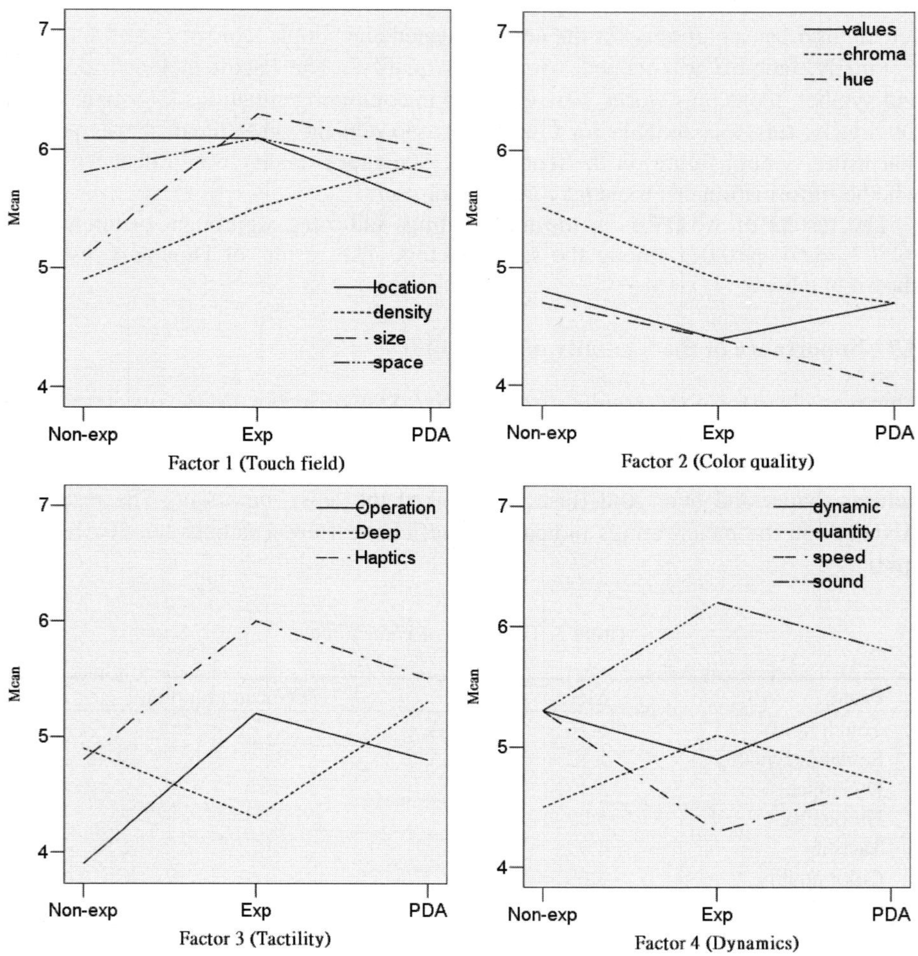

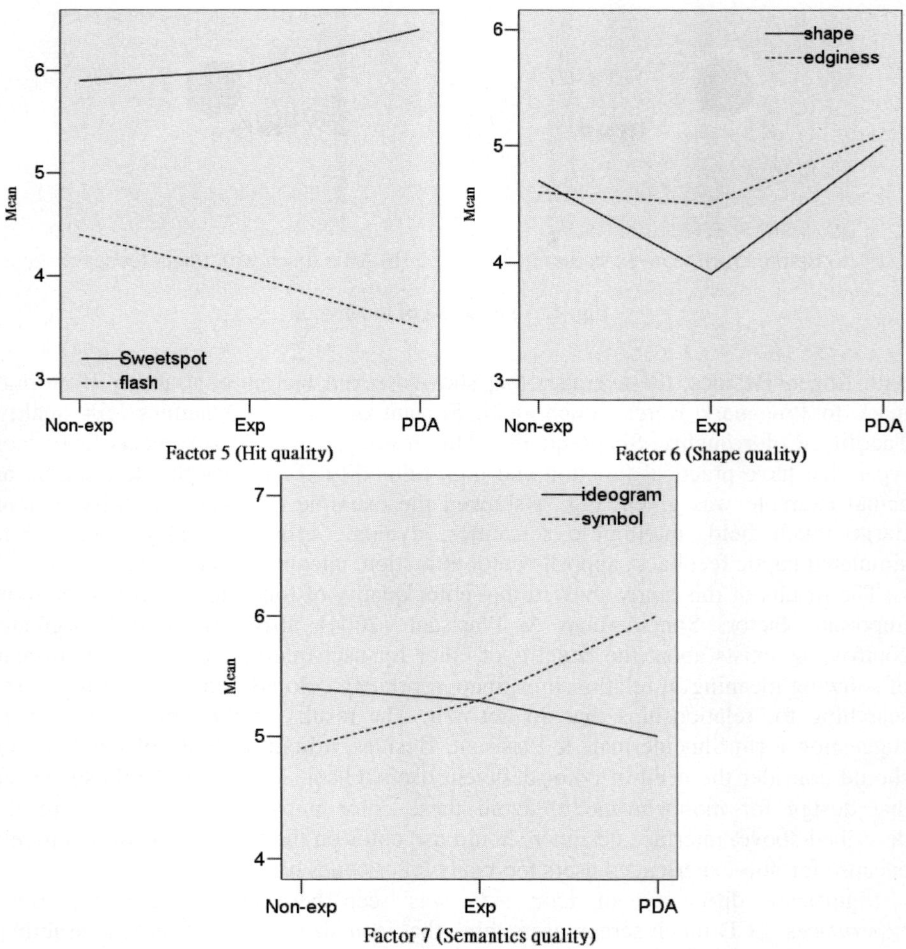

Fig. 3. The difference of 7 factors in subjects' experience

4 Discussion and Conclusions

In the computer world, icons were usually small (less than 1-inch-square or 64 by 64 piexel). Smaller icons were often used to save space or to be integrated within other objects [Plasisant and, Shneiderman, 1992]. However, small icon was not suitable for the touch screens because it will reduce usability. Subjects projected their usability of touch-icons upon subjective evaluation using Likert scale.

For Subjects, the elements that directly interact with finger are main factors influencing the usability of icons, such as sweet spot, size, location and displacement. On the other hand, subjects were not favor visual elements on the touch-icons, such as shape and color, especially flash effect. Thus, Touch-screens differ from traditional screen in that in addition to operation style, touch-screen users focus on interaction

(a) Before touch (convex status) (b) After touch with finger (concave status)

Fig. 4. An example of touch-icon

with finger. Besides, the averages that showed seven factors of usability from high mark to low mark were: Touch field, Semantics quality, Dynamics, Hit quality, Tactility, Color quality, Shape quality. This result indicated that subjects favor icon types that have practical function and high reliability. To clarify the description, an actual example was given. Fig. 4 showed the example of higher usability of icon (large touch field, intelligible semantics, dynamic effects, accurate sweet spot, simulated haptic feedback, apposite color attraction, uncomplicated shape).

The results of this study showed that color quality of touch-icon was not the most important factor. Shneiderman & Plasisant [2004] also indicated that greater controversy exists about the benefits of color for user-interface components. Instead of showing meaningful relationships, inappropriately colored fieds mislead users into searching for relationships that do not exit. The results of this study agreed with suggestion form Shneiderman & Plasisant. Besides, a high usability of touch-screen should consider the need of color-deficient users. Olson & Brewer [1997] suggested that design for monochrome to avoid these color impairment. From the results described above, interface designer should use color on the touch-icon conservatively because for non-experienced users too many color codes can cause confusion.

Significant difference of icon size was seen between the different users' experiences. LCD touch-screen users think that icon size strongly affect the usability. On the other hand, PDA users are used to using small screen, and using input device with higher accuracy, such as stylus. Thus, PDA users paid less attention to icon size than LCD touch-screen users. For novice, i.e. non-experienced users, they think that icon size weakly affect the usability. The possible reason is that, non-experienced users still at the stage of exploring for touch-screens. They have no accumulative experience of the setback about using touch-screen interface, and so unable to express the strong attention. However, all subjects still indicated that size is an important factor for usability of icons in the touch screens (Mean=5.10).

In this paper, the usability principles of touch-icon are constructed from experimental results. The relational results could serve as a guide to design touch-icons. A further study was done on the effect of fingertip pressure on touch performance.

Acknowledgements. The authors would like to acknowledge the contributions of Prof. Chang-Franw Lee in providing guidelines for material of this paper.

References

1. Beringer, D.B., Peterson, J.G.: Underlying behavioral parameters of the operation of touch-input devices: Biases, models, and feedback. Human Factors 27(4), 445–458 (1985)
2. Brooks, F.: Grasping reality though illusion: Interactive graphics serving science. In: Human factors in computing systems, pp. 1–11. ACM, New York (1988)
3. Götz, V.: Color and type for the screen. RotoVision, Berlin (1998)
4. Huang, S.-M., Shieh, K.-K., Chi, C.-F.: Factors affecting the design of computer icons. International Journal of Industrial Ergonomics 29, 211–218 (2002)
5. Kaiser, H.F.: An index of factorial simplicity. Psychometrika 30, 1–14 (1974)
6. Lindberg, T., Näsänen, R.: The effect of icon spacing and size on the speed of icon processing in the human visual system. Displays 24, 111–120 (2003)
7. Marcus, A. (ed.): Graphic design for electronic documents and user interface. ACM, New York (1992)
8. Näsänena, R., Ojanpää, H.: Effect of image contrast and sharpness on visual search for computer icons. Displays 24, 137–144 (2003)
9. Noma, H., Miyasato, T., Kishino, F.: A palmtop display for dexterous manipulation with haptic sensation. Proc CHI'96 conference: Human factors in computing systems, pp. 126–133. ACM, New York (1996)
10. Norman, K.: The psychology of menu selection: Designing cognitive control at the human/computer interface, Ablex, Norwood, NJ (1991)
11. Olson, J., Brewer, C.A.: An evaluation of color selections to accommodate map users with color vision impairments. Annals of the Association of American Geographics 87, 103–134 (1997)
12. Povlotsky, B., Dubrovsky, V.: Recommended versus preferred in design and use of computer workstations. In: Proceedings of the Human Factors Society, 32nd Annual Meeting, pp. 501–505 (1988)
13. Sear, A., Plaisant, C., Shneiferman, B.: A new era for touchscreen applications: High-precision, dragging, and direct manipulateion metaphors. Advances in human-computer interaction 3, 1–33 (1992)
14. Sears, A.: Improving touchscreen keyboards: Design issues and a comparison with other devices. Interacting with Computers 3(3), 251–269 (1991)
15. Shneiderman, B., Plasisant, C.: Designing the user interface. Addison-Wesley, Reading, MA (2004)
16. Stone, D., Jarrett, C., Woodroffe, M., Minocha, S.: Morgan Kaufmann Publishers, San Francisco (2005)

Natural Demonstration of Manipulation Skills for Multimodal Interactive Robots

Markus Hüser, Tim Baier-Löwenstein, Marina Svagusa, and Jianwei Zhang

University of Hamburg
Faculty of Mathematics, Informatics and Natural Sciences
Department Informatics, Group TAMS
{hueser,baier-loewenstein,9svagusa,zhang}@informatik.uni-hamburg.de

Abstract. This paper presents a novel approach to natural demonstration of manipulation skills for multimodal interactive robots. The main focus is on the natural demonstration of manipulation skills, especially grasping skills. In order to teach grasping skills to a multimodal interactive robot, a human instructor makes use of natural spoken language and grasping actions demonstrated to the robot. The proposed approach emphasizes on four different aspects of learning by demonstration: First, the dialog system for processing natural speech is considered. Second, an object detection and classification scheme for the robot is shown. Third, the correspondence problem is addressed by an algorithm for visual tracking of the demonstrator's hands in real time and the transformation of the tracking results into an approach trajectory for a robotic arm. The fourth aspect addresses the fine-tuning of the robot's hand configuration for each grasp. It introduces a criterion to evaluate a grasp for stability and possible reuse of a grasped object. The approach produces stable grasps and is applied and evaluated on a multimodal service robot.

1 Introduction

The field of human-robot interaction has seen a lot of advances in recent years. Especially, the way how robots can be programmed by simple teaching-by-showing via teach pendants, explicit robot programming languages, or task-level programming languages. The latter language enables the user to give sub-goals to the robot, rather then defining each single action the robot has to perform to solve a given problem. Although robot programming has been simplified by these developments, only a few and skilled experts are able to handle them. Robot programming still lacks the benefits of human teaching and learning such as a natural and versatile learning scheme of demonstration and imitation. In this paper we propose a framework for natural demonstration of manipulation skills, especially grasping skills. These skills are basic for a service robot and crucial to manipulation tasks and interaction with the environment. Service robots operate in scenarios which demand very flexible and robust behaviors like e.g. office environments. This robustness to non-static environments cannot be achieved by the classic robot programming techniques. Therefore, it is important to further simplify interaction between robots and humans.

C. Stephanidis (Ed.): Universal Access in HCI, Part II, HCII 2007, LNCS 4555, pp. 888–897, 2007.

The proposed framework meets these challenges through the integration of multi-modal techniques for human-robot-interaction and enables a user to program a service robot by the scheme of learning by imitation. The natural interaction between the user and the robot is emphasized by only using spoken dialog and gestures performed by the user. Neither additional sensors like data gloves, which have to be worn by the user, nor complicated sensor setups installed in the environment are needed.

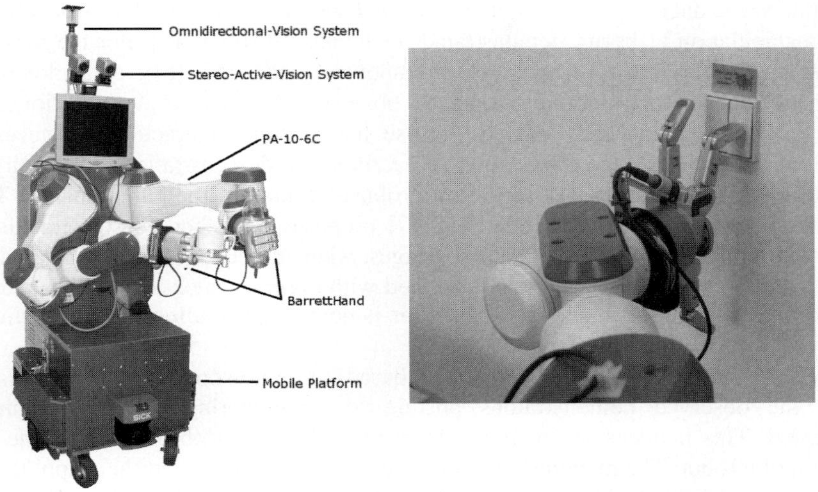

Fig. 1. TASER – TAMS Service robot (left), TASER operating a light switch (right)

The proposed approach is applied to the service robot of the TAMS Institute at the University of Hamburg, the **TA**MS-**Se**rvice-**R**obot (TASER). Figure 1 shows the robot TASER and how it is manipulating a light switch. The robot operates during normal workdays in an office environment. It is used as an experimental platform to point out the usability of the proposed approach.

The remainder of the paper is organized as follows: In section 2 an overview of related research is given. Section 3 covers natural demonstration of manipulation skills, whereas in section 3.1 the service robot TASER and the scenario is introduced. Section 3.2 describes the dialog system. Section 3.3 focuses on learning by demonstration and section 3.4 examines grasp analysis. Conclusions and future work are presented in Section 4.

2 Related Research

A good overview of learning by demonstration is given in [1]. A multimodal approach using language, vision and motor based on a hierarchical architecture is presented in [2]. It enables a student robot to learn three different behaviors ('go', 'pick', 'lift') from a teacher robot. A model for robot imitation also using language, vision and motor input based on the concepts of the modularity in the brain and mirror neuron system is given in [3].

To determine the best imitation strategy, a method for extracting goals and constraints of a demonstrated task is presented in [4]. Simple reaching tasks are considered and captured via magnetic field sensors and stereo-cameras and encoded into Hidden Markov Models (HMMs). Trajectories are reproduced according to a metric based on invariants of time, which measures the quality of reproduction.

The work of [5] is built on the closed-world assumption, which emphasizes the exact observation of the human operator. The whole work cell is modeled using accurate scene data acquired by data gloves and stereo cameras. In the work cell dual-arm manipulation tasks are demonstrated for humanoid robots [6]. For the reason of robust and accurate data acquisition (as shown in [4], [5], [6]), data gloves and magnetic sensors are common tools to observe the demonstrator's actions. But techniques for contact-free and easy-to-use human-robot-interaction interfaces are important to simplify the application of learning by demonstration. Especially the imitation of manipulation tasks requires a robust tracking of the human hands. There are many approaches to this topic, e.g. [7] proposes a method for the tracking of articulated finger motion in monocular images, where a geometric model of a hand is used to generate contours which are matched with observed monocular edge and skin color images. A hierarchical Bayesian filter is developed to allow the integration of temporal information.

In [8] a method for imitation learning based on visuo-somatic mapping, ranging from the observed demonstrator's posture to remembering the self-posture, is presented. This happens via mapping from the self-motion observation to the self-posture of a robot. The mapping from postures to posture space and the mapping from trajectories in posture space onto a motion-segment space is both done by SOMs. Optical flow from the demonstrator's motion is mapped onto a flow-segment space where flow data is connected with the corresponding motion segments in motion-segment space. The connection with self-motion is done via Hebbian Learning.

A brief overview of the special field of robot grasping is given in [9]. Canny et. al. [10] presents a grasp quality measure based on the approximation of the grasp wrench space (GWS). Due to the computational complexity of the problem Borst et. al. [11] presents a method to reduce the complexity by using a specialized task wrench space for object grasping. In [12] the author presents a method to generate grasps from prototypes using an object wrench space taking the object geometry into account. An efficient way to check form closure properties of a grasp is given in [13] where the authors present an approach to find form-closure grasps for n-hard fingers of 3-D objects, which are represented by a model of discrete points. In contrast Han et al. [14] suggest a method transforming the problem into linear matrix inequalities (LMIs), which solves grasp evaluation and grasp force optimization.

Most of the presented approaches above use the force or form-closure of a grasp wrench space as criterion for a grasp. This criterion guarantees resistance of the grasp against any external force, which might be applied to the grasped object. This often leads to large forces and torques at the grasping points. [15] considers this problem and proposes a method where a task wrench is generated and mapped to the grasp matrix in the form of a virtual contact acting with a certain magnitude. By the use of a LMI method it is possible to find the force necessary to resist the internal force.

3 Natural Demonstration of Manipulation Skills

In the following the approach to natural demonstration of manipulation skills and its implementation on the service robot TASER (section 3.1) is presented. The main focus is on the natural demonstration of grasping skills, which has to produce stable grasps and consider the reuse of the grasped object. For an easy and naturally-to-use application of this technique it is important to embed the learning process into a versatile interface for human-robot-interaction, which is capable of a dialog-driven communication between the robot and its user. The developed dialog system is intended to make the interaction between the robot and humans simpler and more intuitive and therefore uses speech-recognition alongside with speech-generation to drive the dialog (see section 3.2).

However natural demonstration also requires the robot to capture the data by itself without restricting the environment by the demands of special hardware, like data gloves, magnetic field sensors, head-mounted eye trackers or special sensor installations, which are cumbersome to set-up, calibrate and use. Therefore, only the onboard sensors (video, audio, laser) of the service robot TASER are used to gather data, when a human teacher demonstrates a grasping task. In doing so, it is important that the robot first detects an action and learns how to reproduce this action and then decides which type of grasp is suitable for further handling of the grasped object considering different constraints, e.g. like the fill level of a cup of tea. In the case of grasping a specific object, the robot has to detect the object (section 3.3), learn an approach trajectory and the tag point (section 3.4) as well as an adequate force for a stable grasp and the type of grasp with respect to the further handling of the grasped object (section 3.5).

3.1 The Service Robot TASER in Its Office Environment

A lot of service robots described in literature are built from special hardware which is designed for certain robot systems only. Furthermore, their manipulation and grasping skills seem to be rather limited because many robots only have a two-finger parallel jaw gripper. One of the particular objectives in building the robot TASER [16] was to assemble it mainly from off-the-shelf hardware.

TASER's mobile platform is equipped with a differential drive with integrated wheel encoders, two laser-range finders and a gyroscope for navigation. The localization reaches an accuracy of ±1cm in position and ±1° in orientation. The manipulator system of TASER currently consists of two Mitsubishi PA10-6C robot arms. A BH-262 BarrettHand and a micro-head camera are attached as a tool to each arm. With this design the system attains a humanlike workspace and silhouette. The PA10-6C has six degrees of freedom (DoF) and a kinematic length, which is similar to the length of a human arm. The BarretHand is a three-finger robot hand with 8 DoF, force sensors and a TorqueSwitch mechanism similar to a human hand [17].

TASER's interface for human-robot-interaction is intended to provide a simple and intuitive interaction between the robot and humans. The main sensors for the interaction are several camera systems mounted on the robot. In addition to the micro-head cameras on the hands, the system has a stereo-camera system mounted on a pan-tilt unit and an omnidirectional vision system (see Fig. 1). In order to teach TASER a grasping skill, a human instructor uses natural speech and demonstrates the grasping action to the robot. This involves a human instructor standing opposite the service robot (see Fig. 2) and demonstrating a grasping skill by saying 'start', performing the grasp and then saying 'stop'. This process is repeated several times until the robot has collected sufficient data to analyse according to forces and reusability.

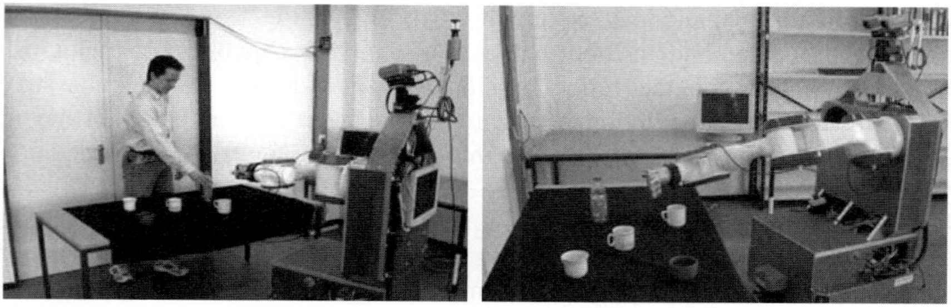

Fig. 2. Instructor demonstrates a grasping skill (left) and TASER reproduces the skill (right)

3.2 Dialog System

A finite-state based dialog system was developed for the robot. The robot can be queried for information or given a task through the dialog-system. It is a model of a finite-state automate, which contains a sequence of predetermined states [18] and is used to guide the user through a dialog. A rough overview of the dialog system is given in Fig. 3. Every time a dialog step is completed, which means that all the required information has been given by the user, the system state changes and reaches its end state. The advantage of a finite-state based system compared to a frame-based system, which has no predetermined dialog, or compared to an agent-based system, which includes intelligent behavior, is its simplicity. The semantics of the system is clear and intuitive. Moreover, as the user's responses are restricted, fewer technological demands are put on the system components, particularly the speech recognizer. Additionally, there is a smaller likelihood of errors in the more constrained system. An example of a dialog in which the system verifies the user's input [19] is given in table 1.

The instruction for grasping an object is received by speech recognition. The recognized sentence is passed to the verifier, which parses the instruction. The instruction is transferred to the speech output, which repeats it. If the user confirms the speech output to the dialog system, this confirmation is brought to the analyzer, which consists of the dialog manager, the context manager and the controller. If the user does not confirm the speech output of the robot, the dialog-system returns to the subsequent state of the last confirmed state. The user can then repeat his speech input. Thus, only instructions confirmed, are processed by the analyzer. Each command is assigned to a context and administrated by the context manager. The command ['Grab', 'Cup'] consists of a list, which defines current and further possible functions and objects in this context. In the example above, the possibility of two

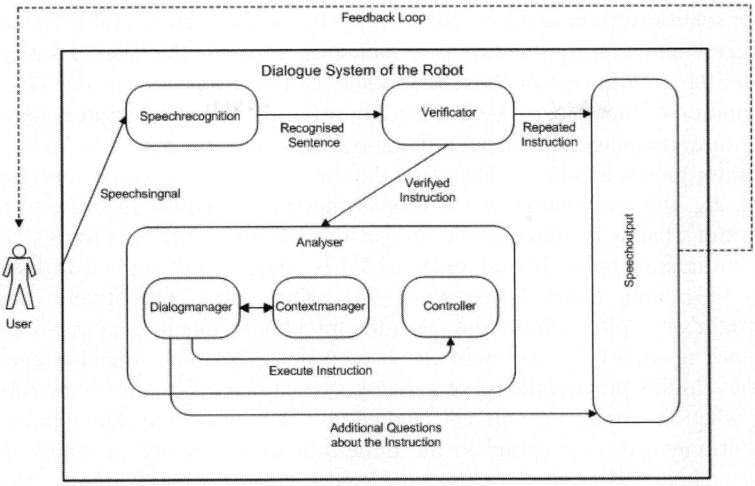

Fig. 3. Dialog system

identical cups, which can both be grasped is given. This constitutes a mnemonic ambiguity [20], which takes place when an input reference is ambiguous to the robot's context. The dialog manager gets the list from the context manager and initiates a speech output, which dissolves the ambiguous user instruction. After all these steps are accomplished, an order is sent by the dialog manager to the controller to execute the instruction.

Table 1. Resolved ambiguity in a dialog between user and robot

User	Robot
Get the cup.	
	May I bring you the cup?
Yes	
	There are two cups, would you like the green cup or the red cup?
The green cup	
	Do you want the red cup?
No	
	There are two cups, would you like the green cup or the red cup?
The green cup	
	Do you want the green cup?
Yes	
--- Robot is grasping the green cup ---	
	Done. Can I do something else for you?

3.3 Learning by Demonstration

Learning by demonstration is used to determine the trajectory of the instructor's hand while performing the grasping action and to estimate the tag point, where the hand touches the object. But before the robot can do so, it has to detect the object, its position and its orientation with the help of its stereovision system. This is done by the use of scale-invariant features (SIFT) [20]. To each object several SIFT key points are assigned and correspondence is established between the stereoscopic images. Therefore, the coordinates of those key points can be measured in 3D. The position and orientation of the object is determined by solving a linear equation system.

To learn a grasping skill through demonstration, it is necessary to know how the demonstrator grasps an object. Therefore the trajectory as well as the configuration of the hand, e.g. the articulation of the fingers, has to be known. In order to track the demonstrator's hands in stereoscopic images in real-time, active contours [21] and an expectation-maximization-like algorithm [22] is adapted and applied to local binary patterns [23] and color histograms [24]. The robot repetitively tracks the demonstrator's grasping actions and feeds the tracking results into a three-dimensional self-organizing map [24], to minimize discrepancies between intended and tracked trajectories. In this process the robot's dialog system is used to inform the robot about the time when the instructor will start and end his demonstration. The topology of the SOM is arranged to correspond to the three-dimensional space in which the user's hand is tracked. After convergence, the SOM gives a spatial description of the collected data and serves as the input data structure for an RL algorithm. The RL algorithm finds trajectories and hand configurations optimized for use by the robot arm and hand (Fig. 4) and serves as starting point for the following grasp analysis.

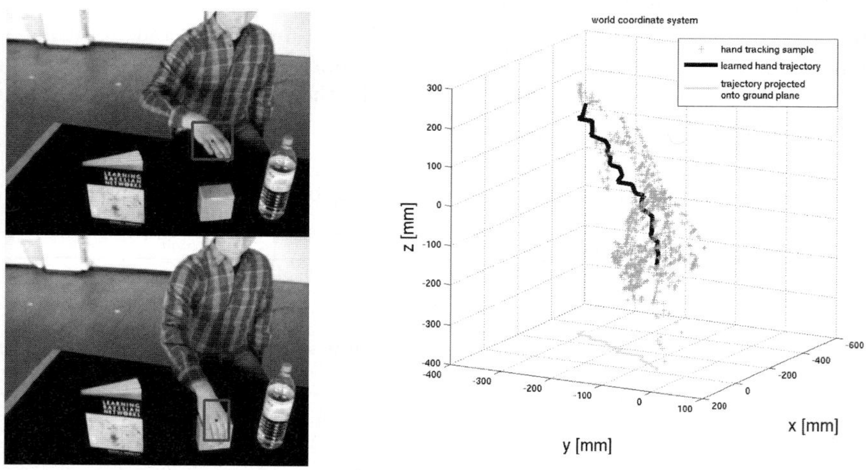

Fig. 4. Hand tracking results and generated trajectory of box grasping skill

3.4 Grasp Analysis

Most of the grasp evaluation criteria presented in section 2 are related to forces and torques. This is very useful if stability is the main criterion in grasping objects with an artificial hand. Our approach goes beyond this and defines a criterion which is related to the reusability of an object grasped with a certain grasp. The criterion has been introduced in [25] and [26]. For example the grasp shown in Fig. 5 might be very stable according to forces and torques, but it is unusable if somebody wants to fill something into the cup. For this reason we defined four sub-criteria related to

Fig. 5. Grasping a mug with a BarrettHand

operations being performed with a grasped object that is evaluated automatically during grasp analysis. A rating for the grasp is generated from the evaluation result. For each criterion, a list of constraints is defined which must be satisfied.

One of the four criteria is the operation *Pour-In*. It is defined as a gain in weight and a free area around the feed opening of the object. The free space around the ``feed opening" of e.g. the cup is defined as “keep-out-area” with the shape of a flat cylinder around the top of the object. The weight gain could be formulated in the form of a task wrench space, like in [12] or [15].

Similar to the Pour-In operation the operation *Pour-Out* can be defined as a loss in weight and a free area around the “feed-opening”. The keep-out-area makes sure that the opening is nod occluded by parts of the manipulator. Additionally, the grasp has to resist the forces which occur during the rotation movement.

The main criterion for a service robot is the *Handover* operation. It is defined by the free spaces on the object, which are needed to pass the object from one hand to the

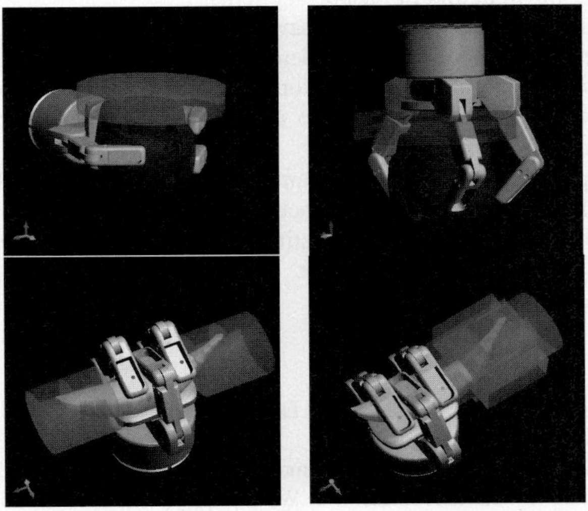

Fig. 6. Simulation of grasping a mug and evaluation of the Pour-In criterion (top row), evaluation of the Handover criterion for grasping a banana (bottom row)

other. The space is firstly defined by the shape of the object and secondly by the position which the opponent wants to grasp. Examples for handover grasp evaluation are shown in Fig. 6 (green volume marks spaces for possible Handover operations).

For some objects it is useful to define the operation *Movement* as a criterion for a grasp. For the evaluation of the criterion, the forces occurring during execution of a user-defined motion are considered. The motion can be defined via a transform or as a combination of basic movements like up, down, left, right, rotate etc. After the constrains for the selected criteria have been checked, a score for the object is built from a weighted sum of the four computed grasp criteria where s is the resulting score a_j is the factor of each constraint and C_j is the value for the constraint.

$$s = \sum_{j=1}^{n} a_j\ C_j \qquad (1)$$

If the user restricted the object's purpose to some of the criteria the weighted sum can yield different results in different contexts. E.g. it is useless to compute if Pour-Out and Pour-In operations are possible for a hammer.

4 Conclusions

The realization of a framework for natural demonstration of grasping skills on a multimodal interactive service robot has been presented. It enables the user to perform a natural human-like learning process with the service robot TASER. A dialog system based on natural spoken language makes the interaction between the robot and humans simpler and more intuitive. Furthermore, it is used to solve problems of ambiguity and keeps the users hands free while demonstrating a grasping action. Additionally the dialog system can be used to command the robot e.g. to carry out tasks like turning the light on or transporting items.

The criteria used for grasp evaluation have the great advantage that they are easy to understand, even if somebody has no idea about robotics or physics. They further simplify the interaction and communication process between the robot and a human instructor. They also enable the robot to choose task-specific grasps from a grasp database according to the current context.

The next step will be to extend the framework to increase TASER's usability. In this step the variety of the high-level functions like object grasping and multimodal interaction will be increased by more distinct manipulation of objects, like taking a printer's output and transport it to the user.

References

1. Billard, A., Siegwart, R.: Robot Learning from Demonstration. Robotics and Autonomous Systems, vol. 47(2 & 3) (June 30, 2004)
2. Weber, C., Elshaw, M., Zochios, A., Wermter, S.: A Multimodal Hierarchical Approach to Robot Learning by Imitation. In: Int. Workshop on Epigenetic Robotics: Modeling Cognitive Development in Robotic Systems, pp. 131–134. Genoa, Italy (2004)
3. Elshaw, M., Weber, C., Zochios, A., Wermter, S.: An Associator Network Approach to Robot Learning by Imitation through Vision, Motor Control and Language. In: Proc. of the Int. Joint Conference on Neural Networks, pp. 591–596. Budapest, Hungary (2004)

4. Calinon, S., Guenter, F., Billard, A.: Goal-Directed Imitation in a Humanoid Robot. ICRA, Barcelona (2005)
5. Ehrenmann, M., Zöllner, R., Rogalla, O., Vacek, S., Dillmann, R.: Observation in Programming by Demonstration: Training and Execution Environment. In: Third IEEE International Conference on Humanoid Robots, Karlsruhe, Germany (2003)
6. Zöllner, R., Asfour, T., Dillmann, R.: Programming by Demonstration: Dual-Arm Manipulation Tasks for Humanoid Robots. In: IEEE Int. Conf. IROS, pp. 479–488, Japan (2004)
7. Stenger, B.: DPhil Thesis: Model-Based Hand Tracking Using A Hierarchical Bayesian Filter. Department of Engineering, University of Cambridge, (March 2004)
8. Asada, M., Ogino, M., Matsuyama, S., Ooga, J.: Imitation Learning Based on Visuo-Somatic Mapping. In: Proceedings 9th Int. Symposium on Experimental Robotics (2004)
9. Bicchi, A., Kumar, V.: Robotic grasping and contact: a review. In: Proceedings of the IEEE International Conference on Robotics and Automation, pp. 348–353 (2000)
10. Ferrari, C., Canny, J.: Planning Optimal Grasps. In: Proceedings of the IEEE International conference on Robotics and Automation, pp. 2290–2295. Nice, France (1992)
11. Borst, C., Fischer, M., Hirzinger, G.: Grasp Planning: How to Choose a Suitable Task Wrench Space. In: Proceedings International Conference on Robotics and Automation, pp. 319–325. New Orleans, LA, USA (2004)
12. Pollard, N.S.: Parallel Algorithms for Synthesis of Whole-Hand Grasps. In: Proceedings of the IEEE International Conference on Robotics and Automation, Albuquerque, NM (1997)
13. Lui, Y., Lam, M.: Searching 3-D Form Closure Grasps in Discrete Domain. In: Proceedings IEEE Int. Conference on Intelligent Robots and System, Las Vegas, Nevada (2003)
14. Han, L., Trinkle, J., Li, Z.X.: Grasp Analysis as Linear matrix Inequality Problems. IEEE Transactions on Robotics and Automation 16(6), 663–674 (2000)
15. Haschke, R., Steil, J., Steuwer, I., Ritter, H.: Task-Oriented Quality Measures for Dextrous Grasping. In: IEEE Conf. on Computational Intelligence in Robotics and Automation (2005)
16. Westhoff, D., Baier, T., Hüser, M., Zhang, J.: A flexible software architecture for multi-modal service robots, Multiconf. on Comput. Engineering in Systems Applications (2006)
17. Kraiss, K.F.: Advanced Man Machine Interaction, Fundamentals and Implementation, pp. 153–162 (2006)
18. McTear, M.F.: Spoken Dialogue Technology, Enabling the Conversational User Interface, ACM Computing Surveys, vol. 34(1), pp. 90–169 (March 2002)
19. Kulyukin, V.: Human Robot Interaction through Gesture Free Spoken Dialogue in Autonomous Robots, vol. 16, pp. 239–257
20. Lowe, D.G.: Distinctive Image Features from Scale-Invariant Keypoints. International Journal of Computer Vision 60(2), 91–110 (2004)
21. Hüser, M., Baier, T., Zhang, J.: Imitation Learning of grasping skills through a multimodal service robot, 2005 IEEE ICRA Workshop on The Social Mechanisms of Robot Programming by Demonstration. Barcelona, Spain (2005)
22. Zivkovic, Z., Kröse, B.: An EM-like algorithm for color-histogram-based object tracking. In: IEEE Conference on Computer Vision and Pattern Recognition (2004)
23. Mäenpää, T., Pietikäinen, M.: Texture analysis with local binary patterns. In: Chen, C.H., Wang, P.S.P.: Handbook of Pattern Recognition & Computer Vision, 3rd
24. Hüser, M., Baier, T., Zhang, J.: Learning of demonstrated Grasping Skills by stereoscoopic tracking of human hand configuration, 2006 IEEE ICRA, Orlando, USA (May 15-19, 2006)
25. Hüser, M., Baier, T., Westhoff, D., Zhang, J.: Multimodal learning of demonstrated grasping skills for flexibly handling grasped objects, ISR/Robotik (2006)
26. Baier, T., Zhang, J.: Reusability-based Semantics for Grasp Evaluation in Context of Service Robotics. In: IEEE ROBIO 2006, Kunming, China (2006)

Smart SoftPhone Device for the Network Quality Parameters Discovery and Measurement

Jinsul Kim[1], Minsoo Hahn[1], and Hyun-Woo Lee[2]

[1] Digital Media Laboratory, Information and Communications University, Seoul, Korea

[2] BcN Interworking Technology Team, BcN Service Research Group, BcN Research Division, 161 Gajeong-dong, Yuseong-gu, Daejeon, 305-350, Korea

{jskim72,mshahn}@icu.ac.kr, hwlee@etri.re.kr

Abstract. Due to the shared nature of current network structures, guaranteeing the quality of service (QoS) of Internet applications from an end-to-end is sometimes difficult and then it has been requested to develop smart devices which have multi-modal functionality for ubiquitous network and computing environment. In this paper, we design smart SoftPhone device for guaranteeing QoS which can discover and measure various network parameters during realtime phone-call service through IP network. The smart SoftPhone for discovering and measuring of QoS-factors in realtime consists of four main blocks that is in order to control and measure various parameters independently based on UDP/SIP/RTP protocol during the end-to-end voice service. Also, we provide critical message report procedures and management schemes to guarantee QoS based on using smart SoftPhone device. For the reporting quality parameters optimally during establishing call sessions of VoIP service, we design critical management module blocks for call session and for quality reporting. To sum up, for the performance evaluation of the smart SoftPhone with scientific exactitude of quality factors, we examine the proposed technique based on the realtime phone-call service through heterogeneous network. The experimental results confirm that the developed smart SoftPhone is very useful to quality-measuring for the quality guaranteed realtime VoIP service and then it could also be applied to improve speech quality as a packet compensation device.

Keywords: VoIP, SoftPhone, QoS, IP Network, Measurement, Management.

1 Introduction

Today VoIP (Voice over IP) service is provided through the various access networks to Internet, allowing users to get call service anytime and anywhere. However, because voice transmission on the Internet is unreliable, the current best-effort technology cannot guarantee the QoS (Quality of Service) or reliability of VoIP services. Various studies on VoIP technology have tried to establish reliable services and evaluate QoS properties. To control many resources for future converged networks, developing smart devices which have multi-modal functionality for

C. Stephanidis (Ed.): Universal Access in HCI, Part II, HCII 2007, LNCS 4555, pp. 898–907, 2007.

applying pervasive network and computing are one of the hot research issues today. Also, with the increasing demand for internet telephony services by the VoIP technology, techniques for improving speech quality over IP networks are researched continually these days. Adaptive speech over VoIP systems requires mutual adaptation process with the guaranteed high quality during conversation on the phone. Overall, in this paper, according to the necessity of discovering of QoS and developing of smart device for VoIP services, we implement smart SoftPhone (UA) which is designed by modeling of 11 processing modules in 4 main blocks, to measure various network parameters and to provide high speech quality with the message procedures methodology of reporting and managing during sending and receiving voice packets on the smart SoftPhone.

The organization of this paper is as follows. Section 2 describes previous approaches on the identification and characterization of VoIP services by using related works. In section 3, we present our proposed functionality of smart SoftPhone for quality resource transmission and measurement. The message procedures for normal and abnormal calls are designed during establishing and releasing. In section 4, we describe how our smart SoftPhone works with GUI to measure quality level and to improve voice quality based on the proposed method. Finally, section 5 concludes the paper with possible future work.

2 Related Work

There have been many related research and development efforts in the field of QoS management and measurement for the past decade. Also, today multimedia quality management of IP networks has become an important issue with the development of realtime applications such as IP-phones, TV-conferencing and video streaming. Specifically, when voice data is mixed with various application data, there are worries that there will be a critical degradation in voice quality. For the measurement of network parameters, many useful management schemes proposed in this research areas [1]. Managing and Controlling of QoS-factor in realtime is required importantly for stable VoIP service. An important factor for VoIP-quality control technique involves the rate control, which is based largely on network impairments such as jitter, delay, packet loss rate, etc due to the network congestions [2] [3]. In order to support application services based on the NGN (Next Generation Network), an end-to-end QoS monitoring tool is developed with qualified performance analysis [4].

The second important factor is based on the factor that different parts of speech have different perceptual importance and each part of speech does not contribute equally to the overall voice quality [5]. Voice packets that are perceptually more important are marked, i.e. acquire priority in our approach. If there is any congestion, the packets are less likely to be dropped than the packets that are of less perceptual importance. The QoS schemes which are based on the priority marking are open loop ones and do not make use of changes in the network [6]. The third significant factor is that the standard RTCP packet type is defined for speech quality control in realtime without conversational speech quality reporting and managing procedures in detail through VoIP networks. The Realtime Transport Protocol (RTP) and RTP Control Protocol (RTCP) communications use the RTCP-Receiver Report to get back the information of the IP network conditions from RTP receivers to RTP senders. However, the original RTCP provides overall feedback on the quality of end-to-end networks [7]. The RTP Control Protocol Extended Reports (RTCP-XR) are a new VoIP management protocol which defines a set of metrics that contains information for assessing the VoIP call quality by the IETF [8]. The RTCP-XR reports the packet loss rate, the packet discard rate (because of jitter) and the distribution of lost/discarded packets. The loss/discard distribution describes calls in terms of bursts (periods during which the loss/discard rate is high enough to cause noticeable quality degradation) and gaps (periods during which lost or discarded packets occur infrequently and hence quality is generally acceptable). To guarantee call quality, the RTCP-XR can report the call quality directly in terms of the estimated R factor or the mean opinion score (MOS). The R factor is a conversational-quality metric in the range of 0 to 100. And the MOS-LQ is a perceptual listening-quality metric while the MOS-CQ is a conversational-quality metric, both in the range of 1 to 5. The RTCP-XR can be implemented as software is integrated into IP phones and gateways inexpensively. Then the messages containing key call-quality-related metrics are exchanged periodically between IP phones and gateways. However, the RTCP-XR is adequate to monitor the QoS-factor on end-to-end VoIP networks because it doesn't have speech quality monitoring functionality. To solve this problem, we propose upgrading some components in the RTCP-XR scheme. Because current IP networks are not designed to support the QoS, quality measurement becomes more important and urgent for more reliable higher quality multimedia services over IP networks. We explore impact of individual packet loss, delay, and jitter on the perceptual speech quality on the smart SoftPhone as one of VoIP systems. The evaluation of VoIP service quality is carried out by firstly encoding the input speech pre-modified with given network parameter values, and then decoded to generate degraded output speech signals.

In this paper, we implement smart SoftPhone device for guaranteeing QoS which can discover and measure various network parameters such as jitter, delay, and packet loss rate, etc., and then propose an end-to-end quality management scheme with the realtime message report procedures to manage the QoS-factors. The newly presented QoS-factor transmission mechanism for QoS managing over IP networks is assessed with the performance analysis in the realtime transmission of QoS parameters through VoIP network.

3 Smart SoftPhone with Discovering and Measuring Method

In this section, we clarify each functionality blocks and modules carried on smart SoftPhone for discovering and measuring realtime call-quality over IP network.

3.1 Modeling of Smart SoftPhone Functionality

In order to implement smart SoftPhone for high quality guaranteed, we design 11 critical modules for UA (User Agents) as illustrated in Fig.1. It comprises in four main blocks and each module is defined as follows:

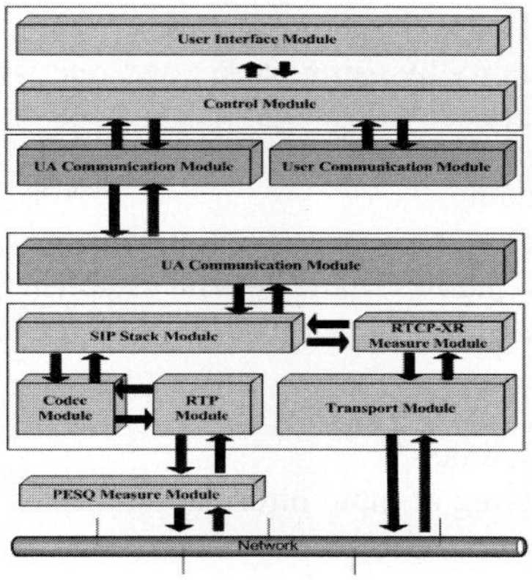

Fig. 1. Main processing blocks for UA (Smart SoftPhone) functionality

- SIP Stack Module -

- Analysis of every sending/receiving messages and creation response messages
- Sending to transport module after adding suitable parameter and header for sending message
- Analysis of parameter and header in receiving message from transport module
- Management and application of SoftPhone information, channel information, codec information, etc.
- Notify codec module of sender's codec information from SDP of receiving message and negotiate with receiver's codec
- Save up session and codec information

- Codec Module –

- Providing the encoding and decoding function about two different voice codecs (G.711/G.729)
- Processing of codec (encoding/decoding) and rate value based on SDP information of sender/receiver from SIP stack module

- RTP Module –

- Sending created data from codec module to other SoftPhone through RTP protocol

- RTCP-XR Measure Module –

- Formation of quality parameters for monitoring and sending/receiving information of quality parameters to SIP stack/transport modules

- Transport Module -

- Address messages from SIP stack module to network
- Address receiving message from network to SIP stack module

- PESQ Measure Module –
  - Measure voice quality by using packet and rate which is received from RTP module and network

- UA Communication Module -
  - In case of requesting call connection, interchange of information to SIP stack module through Windows Mail-Slot and establish SIP session connection
  - Address information to Control module in order to show information of SIP message to user

- User Communication Module -
  - Sending and receiving of input information through UDP protocol

- User Interface Module -
  - User give any command by using GUI and sending information to Control module

- Control Module -
  - Management of UA communication, user communication, and user information modules
  - Management of various optional information module

3.2 Message Report and QoS-Factor Management

In this paper, we propose realtime message report procedures and management scheme between VoIP-QM server and smart SoftPhones. The proposed method for the realtime message reporting and management consists of four main processing blocks, as illustrated in Fig.2. These four different processing modules implement call session module, UDP communication module, quality report message management module and quality measurement/computation/processing module. In order to control

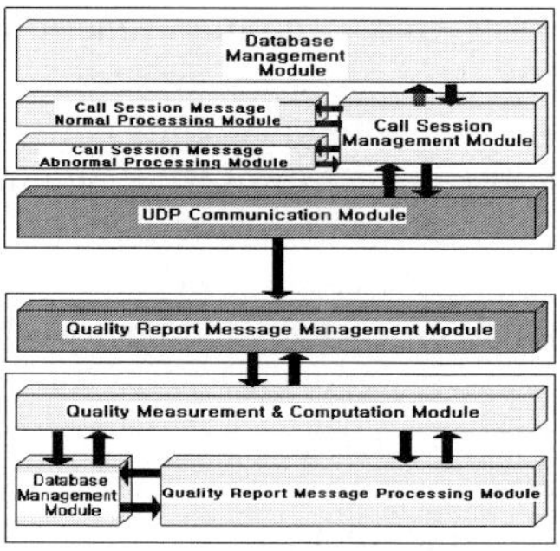

Fig. 2. Main processing blocks for call session & quality management /measurement

call session, we consider two cases, normal and abnormal processing (in Fig. 4 and 5) which are managing by call session management module and then it is automatically recorded in database management module according to session establish and release status. All of the call session messages are addressed to quality report message management module by UDP communication. After call-setup is completed, QoS-factor is measuring followed by computation of each quality parameters base on the message processing. Followed by each session establish and release, quality report messages are also recorded in database management module immediately.

3.3 Procedures of an End-to-End Call Session Based on SIP Protocol

An endpoint of SIP based Softswitch is known as smart SoftPhone (UA). That is, SIP client loosely denotes SIP end points where UAs run, such as SIP-phones and SoftPhones. Softswitch is intermediate network elements between the end points and engage in the routing of SIP messages from one UA to another UA based on a logical SIP address. Softswitch also performs functions of authentication, authorization, and signaling compression. A logical SIP URI address consists of a domain and identifies a UA ID number. The UAs belonging to a particular domain register their locations with the SIP Registrar of that domain by means of a REGISTER message. Fig. 3 shows SIP based Softswitch connection between UA#1-SoftPhone and UA#2-SoftPhone.

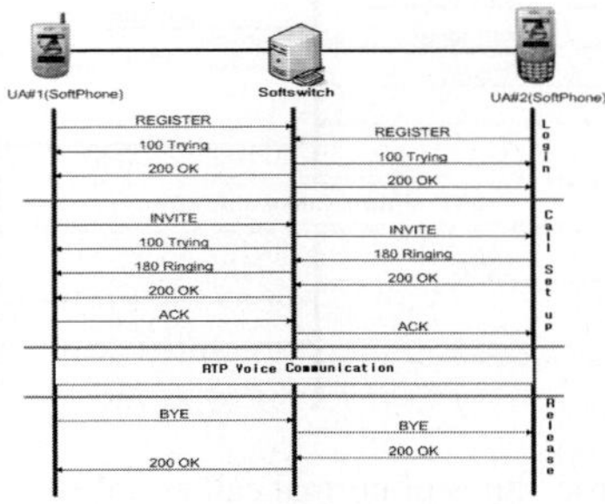

Fig. 3. Main Procedures of call establish/release between Softswitch and smart SoftPhoneï

3.4 Procedures of Normal Call Session Establish and Release

As illustrated in Fig.4, we present an efficient message flows and procedures between VoIP-QM server and smart SoftPhone (UA) in order to manage session information while normal call establishes and releases between Softswitch and UA. Following the message procedures, quality parameters are measuring as soon as the information of each session registered in VoIP-QM server.

First of all, after a caller UA which received a call-request sends INVITE message to Softswitch, the UA sends Msg.1 to VoIP-QM server and then VoIP-QM server sends response Msg.3 to the UA. Second, as soon as Softswitch receives 200OK message from 1-port Gateway after call established by SIP protocol, 1-port Gateway sends Msg.2 to VoIP-QM server and then VoIP-QM server sends response Msg.3 to the 1-port Gateway. Third, when Softswitch receives 200OK message from UA#1-SoftPhone after confirming above two procedures completed perfectly, the UA sends Msg.4 to VoIP-QM server and then VoIP-QM server sends response Msg.6 to the UA. Fourth, in order to release, as soon as UA#1-SoftPhone receives 200OK message from Softswitch, the UA sends Msg.5 to VoIP-QM server and then VoIP-QM server sends response Msg.6 to the UA. In detail, Msg.1 and Msg.2 are sending to VoIP-QM server. Sending point of Msg.1 in time is before call session established and after sending request message. Sending point of Msg.2 in time is after call session established and right before RTP communication is opened. Msg.3 is sent by the response message of Msg.1 and Msg.2. When RTP communication starts after call session established between Softswitch and UA, Msg.4 is sending to VoIP-QM server in order to receive each UA's SSRC information. As VoIP-QM server receives Msg.5 from UA, conversation time by SoftPhone is measuring and computing average of voice quality parameters over IP network. All of values which are measured in the realtime recorded in database management system. Finally, VoIP-QM server acknowledge to UA as response of Msg.5. As UA receive Msg.6, UA can know that the sending message normally up.

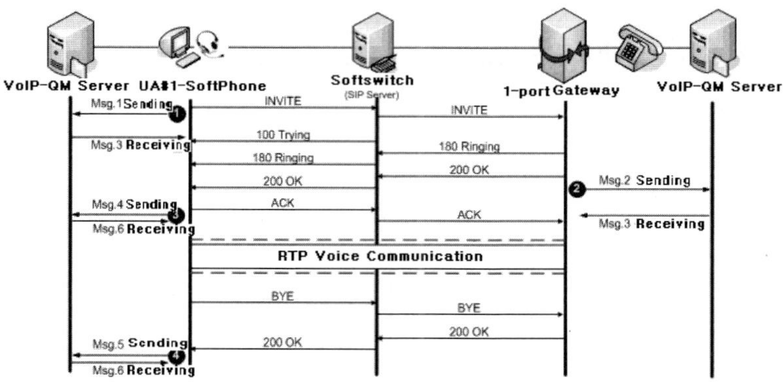

Fig. 4. Procedures of normal call establish/release case

3.5 Procedures of Abnormal Call Session Establish and Release

We present an efficient message flows and procedures in order to manage session information when abnormal situations are caused during call session is established and released. Following the message procedures, quality parameters are measuring after the information of each session registered in VoIP-QM server. When UA requests call-setup to Softswitch, it also notify to VoIP-QM server about the information of requesting call-setup. However, abnormal statuses are happen with several errors when system breaks out with some significant trouble. As illustrated in Fig.5 (a), when Softswitch doesn't response with 200OK messages, also abnormal status is occurred even though UA try to release of current call by sending BYE message. Third, when Softswitch doesn't response as soon as Softswitch receives INVITE message for call-setup from UA, the UA notify the status to VoIP-QM server by sending Msg.8 and then the VoIP-QM server sends Msg.6 for responding of the message as illustrated in Fig.5 (b).

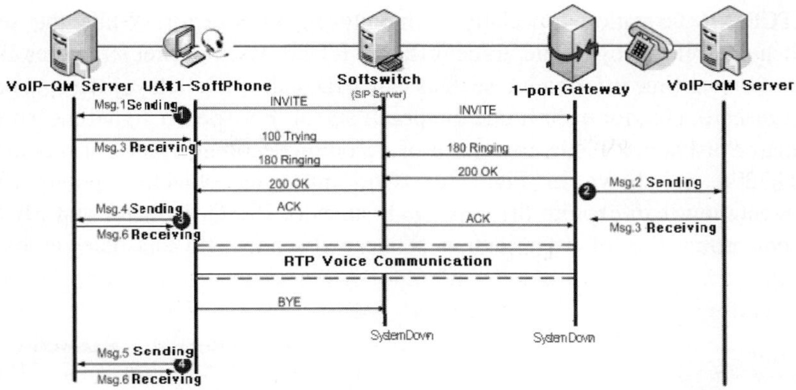

(a) Abnormal release case

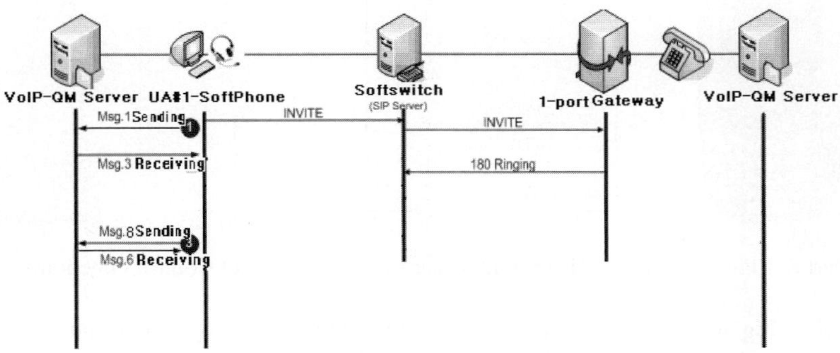

(b) No response case in Softswitch

Fig. 5. Procedures of abnormal call establish/release cases

4 Implementation of Smart SoftPhone

The main part of the Smart SoftPhone is implemented in MFC and C# in .Net environment for delivering and measuring of QoS-factor with various parameters transmission control in realtime. As illustrated in Fig.6 (a), the realtime VoIP packets delivering and measuring function on the smart SoftPhone is designed as various GUI function to manage an end-to-end speech quality over IP network. Smart SoftPhone has functionality for voice communication with other devices through SIP stack. The SIP stack implement to connect between network and any user's GUI of smart SoftPhone. We use Vocal 1.5.0 server in order for role of Softswitch, which is registration, establish, and release from smart SoftPhone. The user can call session establish and release by using GUI on smart SoftPhone which display the SIP message for sending and receiving to user. By the SIP message, the user checks current situation in realtime between caller and callee as shown in Fig.6 (b). Also, it measures voice quality by using objective measurement method which is called PESQ as standard from ITU-T and has reporting function network parameters which follows by RTCP-XR formation especially to monitoring QoS-factor. While the sessions establish and release by phone, three different RTCP-based packet structures BTs are modeled by realtime information such as caller ID, callee ID, delay, jitter, packet loss, packet discard, etc., for each frame of speech signal. For speech signal measurement, our smart SoftPhone designs to control of encoding/decoding voice packets in G.711 and G.729A as shown in Fig.6 (c). One important objective point with the implementation is to explore the measured values of PESQ, R-factor and MOS with time synchronization of each session at the end-sender and end-receiver by using NTP.

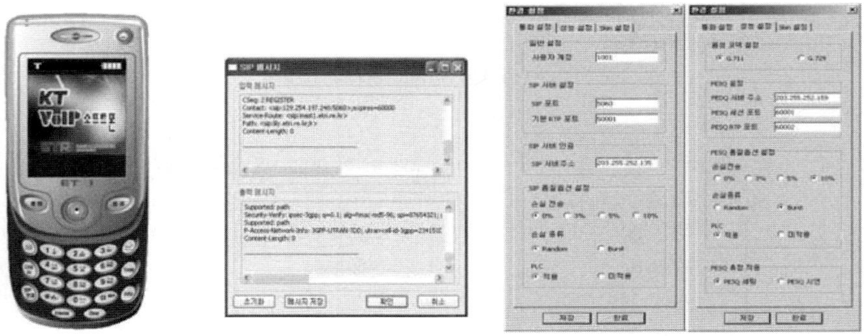

(a) Smart SoftPhone (UA) (b) SIP message (c) Control Function

Fig. 6. Implementation of smart SoftPhone for controlling functionality

5 Conclusion

In this paper, we implement smart SoftPhone for discovering and measuring of QoS-factors in realtime with various network parameters during phone-call service through IP network. Also, we provide critical message procedures applying RTCP-based packet structures BTs to manage call session with quality factors such as jitter, delay, loss, etc. For the reporting various quality parameters, we design management module for call session and for quality reporting. The presented QoS-factor transmission control mechanism is assessed in realtime environment and it is proved completely by the performance results which are obtained from the experiment. Finally, the performance evaluation of speech quality confirms that the smart SoftPhone device with proposed transmission procedure and management scheme is very useful to manage speech quality through IP network for the realtime Internet telephone service.

Acknowledgments. This research was partly supported by the ETRI (Electronics and Telecommunications Research Institute). The authors would like to thank Ph.D. Won Ryu as one of the project manager at ETRI, Korea for carefully reading and commenting.

References

1. Imai, S.: Voice Quality Management for IP Networks based on Automatic Change Detection of Monitoring Data. In: Kim, Y.-T., Takano, M. (eds.) APNOMS 2006. LNCS, vol. 4238, pp. 27–29. Springer, Heidelberg (2006)
2. Eejaie, R., Handley, M., Estrin, D.: RAP: End-to-end Rate-based Congestion Control Mechanism for Realtime Streams in the Internet. In: Proc. of IEEE INFOCOM, USA, (March 21-25, 1999)
3. Beritelli, F., Ruggeri, G., Schembra, G.: TCP-Friendly Transmission of Voice over IP. In: Proc. of IEEE International Conference on Communications, New York, USA, (April 2006)
4. Kim, C., et. al.: End-to-End QoS Monitoring Tool Development and Performance Analysis for NGN. In: Kim, Y.-T., Takano, M. (eds.) APNOMS 2006. LNCS, vol. 4238, pp. 27–29. Springer, Heidelberg (2006)
5. De Martin, J.C.: Source-driven Packet Marking for Speech Transmission over Differentiated-Services Networks. In: Proc. of IEEE ICASSP 2001, Salt Lake City, USA, (May 2001)
6. Cole, R.G., Rosenbluth, J.H.: VoIP over IP Performance Monitoring, Journal on Computer Communications Review, vol. 31(2) (April 2001)
7. Schulzrinne, H., Casner, S., Frederick, R., Jacobson, V.: RTP: A Transport Protocol for Real-Time Application, IETF RFC 3550 (July 2005)
8. Friedman, T., Caceres, R., Clark, A.: RTP Control Protocol Extended Reports, IETF RFC 3611 (November 2003)

BloNo: A New Mobile Text-Entry Interface for the Visually Impaired

Paulo Lagoá, Pedro Santana, Tiago Guerreiro, Daniel Gonçalves, and Joaquim Jorge

INESC-ID/Technical Superior Institute, Lisbon Technical University
Av. Rovisco Pais, 1049-001 Lisboa
{plagoa,psantana,tjvg,djvg,jaj}@immi.inesc.pt

Abstract. We present a new mobile text-entry method that relies on alphabet navigation and dismisses memorizing, offering visually impaired individuals an easy writing mechanism. Current mobile text-entry interfaces are not suitable for blind users and special braille devices are too heavy, large and cumbersome to be used in a mobile context. With the enormous growth of mobile communications and applications it was urgent to offer visually impaired individuals the ability to operate this kind of devices. Evaluation studies were carried and validated the navigation method as a new mobile text-entry interface for the target population.

Keywords: Mobile, Visually Impaired, Text-Entry, Accessibility, SMS.

1 Introduction

Nowadays, the mobile phone is an essential tool for most people. Tasks like making calls, using the Short Message Service (SMS), managing contacts and using the agenda are executed on a daily basis. SMS, in particular, have had an enormous growth in the past years: in 2000, 17 billion SMS messages were sent; in 2001, the number was up to 250 billion and 500 billion SMS messages in 2004. More than one trillion text messages were sent in 2005 [1]. This growth is related with the low costs to the user and social factors – it doesn't disturb the receiver, it provides diffusion and it doesn't demand an immediate answer. The number of services accessible by SMS has also been growing in the past years, including alerts, quizzes and advertising. However, for visually impaired individuals this service is very difficult or impossible to use. This is also true for the majority of applications available on a cell phone. Nowadays, mobile device potentialities are diverse and cell phones are commonly used as clocks, notebooks, and agendas, among others. As for SMS, the visually impaired are also deprived from using these services. Traditional mobile devices are not equipped with keyboards adapted to those users' needs nor do they provide any kind of feedback for their actions. Special hardware devices, although making possible for blind users to use mobile services, are too heavy and cumbersome to be carriable and especially, be used on a mobile context. Currently, visually impaired individuals have limited access to mobile devices, particularly, text-entry-based applications.

C. Stephanidis (Ed.): Universal Access in HCI, Part II, HCII 2007, LNCS 4555, pp. 908–917, 2007.

Fig. 1. Regular Mobile Phone Keypad

We present an interface that relies on alphabet navigation and dismisses memorizing, offering visually impaired individuals an easy writing mechanism. Moreover, menu navigation was also implemented and several practical tasks were evaluated with the target population.

2 Background

In the last few years, we have witnessed an enormous growth on mobile communications. Furthermore, with the increase of mobile device's memory and processing capabilities, cell phones became real mobile computers, gathering functionalities from digital cameras, games to management and organization applications. Although these devices are very similar to personal desktop computers their input and output capabilities are much more limited. Researchers leaned over this problem over the past few years trying to overcome mobile devices limitations and increase user's performance as well as easing mobile usage.

2.1 Mobile Devices Text-Entry Methods

Text introduction in mobile phones is done through a 12 key keypad (Fig. 1). Most keypads follow the ITU E.161 standard, featuring number keys 0-9 and two additional keys (* and #). The letters are spread through keys 2-9 alphabetically ordered, forming groups of three or four letters. The space character is usually assigned to the 0 key, but it depends on the mobile phone model. Several methods have been developed to introduce text in these devices and can be divided in two main categories: multi-press systems and predictive systems.

Multi-Press systems

Multi-press systems categorize all systems that require one or more key presses to enter a character. These systems don't use word or phrase prediction to help the user. The most known and used multi-press system is multi-tap which requires one or more button presses to obtain a certain character. A disambiguation problem arises when

Fig. 2. MessageEase: English keyboard configuration

the user wants to enter two or more consecutive characters present in the same key with two possible solutions: key press timeout, an acceptance button.

MessagEase [2] allows text introduction with two key presses. The system is based on the letter frequencies of certain language. According to these frequencies, the letters are induced into the keyboard. For the English language, the distribution is as on Figure. 2. To introduce such letters, the user presses the corresponding key twice (for example, to enter 'a', key 1 is pressed twice). To enter less frequent letters, the usage is as follows: to enter 'u', for example, the user presses the 5 key and then the 2 key (the 5 key works as a directional key). Less-Tap technique uses language knowledge to rearrange the letters within each button. This rearrangement is obtained from the letter frequencies for certain language. This way, the most frequent letter (from each group associated with the key) requires only one key press [3]. Two-key Input requires exactly two key presses for each letter. The first press selects the group of letters (for example, '4' selects GHI). The second press selects the letter from the group (for example, '2' selects 'h'). This approach solves the disambiguation problem present in other methods.

For blind individuals, multi-press systems are rather difficult to use as the user must memorize the letters associated with every key and must always be very careful with the amount of presses to achieve a given letter. As feedback is inexistent, the user can't have a notion on the message evolution. Multi-press frequency-based approaches are even worst that multi-tap as the alphabet sequence is lost and therefore memorizing needs increase.

Predictive Systems

Predictive input technologies use language knowledge to predict what text the user is going to enter. Letter anticipators predict the next letter based on the prefix entered by the user. Word completers predict the suffix of the introduced word or the remainder or even the entire phrase, featuring suggestions to the user. Hybrid systems combine the letter anticipators and the word completers [4].

T9 (Text on 9 keys) [5] is the most widely used predictive system on mobile phones. The system compares the sequence of keystrokes to words in a dictionary, in order to determine the intended word. If the user ends the word introduction and the displayed word isn't the desired, a "Next" button should be pressed, and all the words sharing the same key sequence are shown. If the word doesn't appear, the user should switch to multi-tap mode to entry the desired word. Using LetterWise, a text introduction method created by MacKenzie et al. [6], the user presses the key that features the desired letter. If the letter doesn't appear on the display screen, the user presses a "Next" key until the letter shows up. The prediction is done letter by letter, according to letter prefixes probabilities. The WordWise[7] method is similar to the T9, although in WordWise, when certain word isn't in the dictionary, LetterWise is the method in use to introduce the word (instead of Multi-tap). iTap, developed by Motorola, is very similar to T9: as the user writes, it compares the sequence of keystrokes to words in a dictionary, in order to determine the intended word. However, iTap also completes the words, featuring a list of possible suffixes of the word entered, and this is the main difference between the systems. eZiTap system, from Zi Corporation, combines multi-tap text introduction with word prediction, allowing an expert multi-tap user to improve performance without requiring any learning effort. As the user enters the desired word, a list of words sharing the same entered suffix is displayed. A "Next" key is used to navigate among the list.

Predictive systems with no visual feedback are prohibitive for blind people as the user isn't aware of the actual evolution of the system and the current message state. For example, using the T9 system, there isn't a relation between the key press and the letter appearing at the screen (it is affected by the predictive system frequencies) and it is not certain that, even when the correct keys are pressed, the word appears.

2.2 Visually Impaired Focused Approaches

Alternative devices were developed to overcome the difficulties arising from visual impairments. Typically, these products' goal is to serve as a Personal Digital Assistant (PDA) providing functionalities like Contact Management, Calculator, Notes, Clock or SMS (sending and receiving).

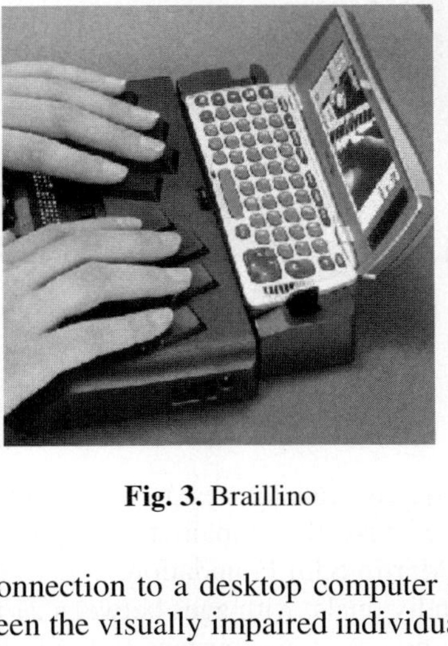

Fig. 3. Braillino

They normally allow connection to a desktop computer or a cell phone, acting as an interaction bridge between the visually impaired individual and the device.

Braillino, from Handy Tech Elektronik GmbH, is an electronic notebook adapted to the visually impaired that allows the connection to regular mobile devices through a docking station or bluetooth. It is also possible to connect it to a personal computer (Fig.3). It is based on a braille keyboard for input. It uses a software package called Taks&Braille that permits access to mobile phone funcionalities, offering braille output support and voice feedback (synthetic speech).

Alva Mobile Phone Organizer combines the funcionalities of a PDA and tri-band GSM cell phone allowing the users to make and receive calls, send and receive messages, take notes and manage contacts. Considering user interaction, it contains a twenty cells braille screen as well as speech synthesis and eight input braille keys.

There are several devices similar to Braillino or Alva Mobile Phone Organizer and they all share the same flaws: the large size and weight and the prohibitive costs when compared with regular mobile devices. Although it is true that blind users can use braille-Based devices to accomplish their goals, it is also true that these devices are too heavy and large to be carriable and used while on-the-move. Also, considering a usual scenario where a blind user handles a cane with one hand, it is impossible to operate this kind of devices (Fig. 4).

In a totally different scope are the screen readers, solutions that can be used in a regular mobile device, giving the users feedback on screen evolution and replacing visual feedback. Nuance Talks is an example of this type of assistive technology for the visually impaired. Although screen readers make possible for a blind user to use a mobile device, they still require for the user to memorize letter's placement. Considering performance issues, predictive systems are still very difficult to use.

Fig. 4. Alva Mobile Phone Organizer

3 Task Analysis

To identify the users' needs and capabilities as well as their common use of mobile phones we interviewed 8 visually impaired individuals. The interviews were conducted at Raquel and Martin Sain Foundation, a learning center for blind people, to six male and 2 female individuals, with ages between 21 and 64 years.

Considering mobile phone use, it was curious to verify that all users possess a cell phone and use it once or more a day to make calls. Only two of the users reported having problems to dial a number due to the lack of feedback and small keypad size. Normally, dialing isn't problematic and therefore this task is not the main concern of our work.

Half of the users (4) use the phone's contact list and they all share the same technique: memorize the contact's position in the list. Those who don't use the contact list justify it with lack of feedback from their phones. Although this result is somewhat surprising (we expected the contact list not to be used at all), the method is rather limited and lacks scalability as the users will only remember some important contact list positions.

Half of the users stated to send text messages (SMS) from which half stated to do it on a daily basis. All users that send SMS use Talks Screen Reader to get voice feedback but only one uses a predictive system (T9). The users generally agree that menu navegation is difficult and cumbersome and that the feedback is limited taking them to recurrently make mistakes.

4 Our Approach

Regular mobile device text-entry methods are suitable for visually capable individuals and seek to improve user's performance. Hence, it is possible for someone, with no experience, who doesn't remember the location of a letter, to easily look and recognize the key where that letter is. Those methods imply that the fingers *dance* through the keyboard, choosing letters and special characters, among ten or more keys. Once again, we easily overcome this issue appealing to vision. A blind user can't do that. The mark present at key '5' gives blind users the notion of the keypad layout but not feedback on the selected letter and, although users can make an effort to memorize a letter's placement, feedback is essential. Even SMS experts need to occasionally look at the words being written to ensure message correction. Moreover, expertise is acquired by using the method and receiving the feedback. Only after an extensive and successful use of the writing mechanisms the users can get used to them and, in some cases, no longer need constant visual feedback. Screen readers (such as Talks) overcome some of the issues as they offer the user feedback on the screen progress. However, keypad feedback is still inexistent which often leads to mistakes and sometimes giving up. Although users make sense on the message progress, they still have to know where to press to get the desired letter/action.

We can only offer visually impaired individuals mobile device accessibility if those devices can be easily available and usable. Therefore, based on user needs, capabilities, and available devices we decided that our method should be compatible with regular mobile phones and, therefore, with the regular 12 key keyboard layout requiring no-extra hardware (i.e. expensive and heavy braille keyboards).

When looking at the available solutions it is also clear that text-entry methods are not suitable for visually impaired individuals, even when using a screen reader, as memorization is still required. Therefore we designed our system not to require memorization or difficult adaptation stages. It is based on a new navigation-based text-entry method and speech synthesis feedback. Besides text-Entry based applications, BloNo provides the necessary feedback to navigate through menus and access applications.

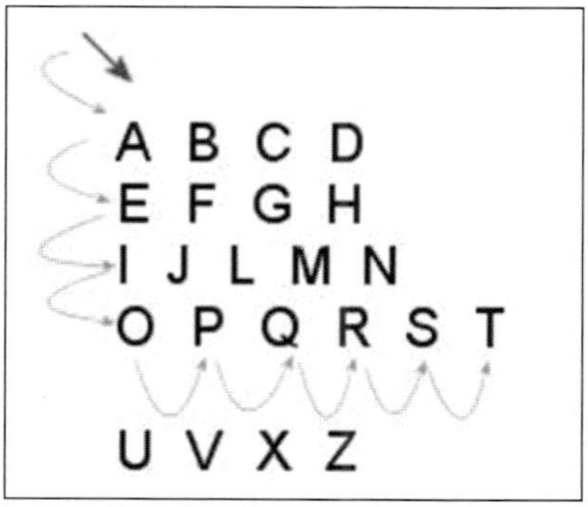

Fig. 5. Navigation method using two directions

4.1 Vowel Navigation Method

To accomplish our goals, a new text-entry system was developed. The alphabet was divided into five parts, each starting with a different vowel, as these are easy to remember unlike other arbitrarily chosen letters. Those parts were then used to create a character matrix (Fig. 5). We use the keyboard keys as a joystick to navigate that matrix. Keys '2' and '8' allow the user to navigate vertically through the vowels, while keys '4' and '6' will allow navigation through the rest of the alphabet horizontally (Fig. 5). Both the horizontal and the vertical navigations are cyclical, which means that the user can go, for instance, from the letter 'z' to the letter 'a', and from the vowel 'u' to 'a' (Fig. 6).

Using all directions will allow the user to reduce the number of key presses needed to reach to a certain letter. Comparing the approaches followed in Fig.5 and Fig. 6 we can state that, by using all the directions, the user needs only two strokes to reach the letter 't', instead of nine strokes (using only two directions). Also, the user receives voice feedback before accepting any letter (automatically after a configurable timeout), therefore reducing entry mistakes. The method requires little memorizing and even with low alphabet mental mapping the users can still, in a worst case scenario, navigate forward until they get to the desired letter (there are no wrong buttons, just shorter paths). This is a major issue for the visually impaired as they can totally rely on audio feedback before accepting any letter, increasing the text-entry task success and the motivation to improve the writing skills.

4.2 Automatic Word Finishing – AWF

To optimize user performance while introducing text, we developed a system that suggests (on user demand, by pressing the '9' key) a list of possible words that start with the prefix the user has entered. The user accepts the word by pressing the '5' key once. Punctuation characters can be selected by continuously pressing the '5' key.

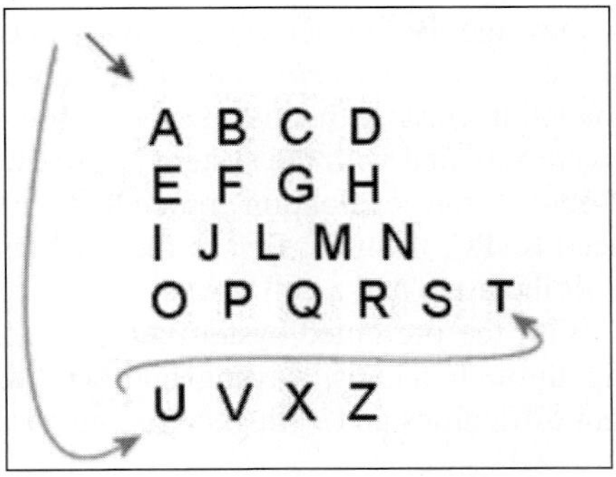

Fig. 6. Navigation method using four directions

4.3 Task-Aware Dictionaries

To enhance AWF performance we developed task-aware dictionaries. These are focused on the specific task being performed by the user and their goal is to reduce the spectrum of words suggested by the AWF. As an example, when entering a name on the contact list, the only words the user will need are names and surnames. In the same way, when entering an address, the user will only need street names.

5 Evaluation

Tests were made with five totally blind users assessing the new text entry interface as well as the techniques used to improve it, in a set of tasks including message writing and contact manipulation (Fig. 7). The tests were carried at Raquel and Martin Sain Foundation in a quiet room with no disturbances, with each student individually. All the five users presented 100% visual deficiency.

The test session start with a brief system presentation, followed by an ambientation phase. To support the evaluation method presentation, we printed a set of instructions and the description of the tasks in a braille manual. The evaluation consisted in six different tasks.

The first task consisted in writing, with no acceleration methods (i.e., AWK), the portuguese sentence – *Perdi o autocarro e não vou chegar a horas*. The text entry interface was well understood by all users with a mean of 2 words/minute ratio and a 1.4 error rate, after a brief 5 minutes training session. In the second task the users were asked to write the same sentence, but this time being able to use the AWF predicting system. The AWF mechanism reduced the number of keystrokes per character (KSPC) in 13.9%, the time to accomplish the tasks in 9.9% and the error rate to 1.

Adding a contact was tested in 3 different conditions: without AWF, with AWF and with AWF and task-aware dictionaries (names only). AWF mechanism improved the total time in 32.4% and task-aware dictionaries improved it by 14.5%, with a total time reduction of 42.2%.

Finally, the users were asked to send an SMS to a defined name in the contact list. This task gathered several steps: navigating menus, writing the text, choosing the contact and sending the message. Both the message and the contact in the contact list were pre-defined by us: the message was *sim* and the name was *Paulo Lagoá*. All the users successfully completed the task with a mean time of 104 seconds.

In general, all users were satisfied with the system and showed great improvements in their performance across the evaluation process (increased the number of words/minute and reduced KSPC, from the first to the final task). It is also important to notice that, although all the users had a cell phone, only one was capable of writing and sending messages. With the presented system all the users completed the tasks with success navigating through menus, writing and sending SMS and managing contacts without apparent difficulties and with good learning rates.

Fig. 7. Blind user testing the system

6 Conclusions and Future Work

While today mobile phones are a common tool used in everyday life, they strongly rely on visual feedback for their correct operation. As such, visually impaired users have trouble using them, contributing to frustration and social exclusion. Existing alternatives are not practical or depend on memorization, often leading to mistakes. We developed a new text-entry interface that requires no memorizing and no extra hardware making possible for any visually impaired individual to use a regular mobile device, accomplishing even the most difficult tasks like writing a message or managing contacts. We evaluated the interface with the target users and validated the approach, showing that users input words with an acceptable rate improving their performance quickly with almost no previous experience. As future work, we will study other text-entry interfaces as well as shortcut mechanisms that ease menu navigation, like accelerometers, RFID tags or voice recognition.

Acknowledgments. The authors would like to thank all users that participated in the studies described in this paper. This work was funded by Project BloNo, POSC: 248/4.2/C/REG.

References

1. GSMA's Hubbing Programme to Streamline Global Delivery of SMS Messages, GSM Association Press Release (2006)
2. Nesbat, S.B.: A System for Fast, Full-Text Entry for Small Electronic Devices. In: Proceeding of the Fifth International Conference on Multimodal Interfaces, ICMI 2003, Vancouver (November 5-7, 2003)
3. Pavlovych, A., Stuerzlinger, W.: Less-Tap: A Fast and Easy-to-learn Text Input Technique for Phones. Graphics Interface (2003)
4. Smith, J.: Thumbscript: Designing a general solution to the problem of text input in small devices - WHITE PAPER, Thumbscript Development (2000) www.thumbscript.com
5. Darragh, J.J., Witten, I.H., James, M.L.: The Reactive Keyboard: A Predictive Typing Aid, IEEE Computer, pp. 41–49 (1990)
6. Grover, D.L., King, M.T., Kuschler, C.A. Patent No. US5818437, Reduced keyboard disambiguating computer, Tegic Communications, Inc., Seattle, WA (1998) http://www.t9.com/
7. MacKenzie, I.S., Kober, H., Smith, D., Jones, T., Skepner, E.: LetterWise: Prefix-based disambiguation for mobile text input. In: Proc. UIST 2001, pp. 111–120. ACM, New York (2001)
8. MacKenzie, I.S., Kober, H., Gutowitz, H., Jones, T., Skepner, E.: Linguistically Optimised Text Entry on a Mobile Phone (2001)

Low-Cost Portable Text Recognition and Speech Synthesis with Generic Laptop Computer, Digital Camera and Software

Lauri Lahti[1] and Jaakko Kurhila[2]

[1] Department of Computer Science and Engineering, P.O. Box 5400, FIN-02015 Helsinki University of Technology, Finland
Lauri.Lahti@oi.fi
[2] Department of Computer Science, P.O. Box 68, FIN-00014 University of Helsinki, Finland
kurhila@cs.helsinki.fi

Abstract. Blind persons or people with reduced eyesight could benefit from a portable system that can interpret textual information in the surrounding environment and speak directly to the user. The need for such a system was surveyed with a questionnaire, and a prototype system was built using generic, inexpensive components readily available. The system architecture is component-based so that every module can be replaced with another generic module. Even though the system makes partly incorrect recognition of text in a versatile environment, the evaluation of the system with five actual users suggested that the system can provide genuine additional value in coping with everyday issues outdoors.

Keywords: Text recognition, speech synthesis, independent initiative.

1 Introduction

Coping with everyday life is an important issue for everyone [14]. As the use of technology has increased in everyday life, visually challenged or blind people have encountered new challenges and a need for adaptation in their routines. On the other hand, emergence of technical solutions has offered new possibilities to be an active and independent member of the society despite of the loss of sight. Research on various aspects of augmenting the eye sight with technical innovations is ongoing (see e.g. a face recognition system for social interactions [6], Braille interpretation for persons unable to read Braille [11], and way-finding with Braille output [15]).

It is evident that transforming visual textual information to speech can be of value since especially in urban areas direct and indirect textual information about the surrounding environment is largely available. Purpose-built systems for transferring text to speech in outdoor environment are being developed (see e.g. [4, 1]).

Since we live in an era of technology, many individuals have already a relatively lightweight laptop computer and a digital camera. These generic components can be combined into a low-cost portable text recognition and speech synthesis for outdoor use, if the components are bound together with appropriate software.

C. Stephanidis (Ed.): Universal Access in HCI, Part II, HCII 2007, LNCS 4555, pp. 918–927, 2007.

In this paper, we briefly describe the results of a survey that motivated the need for such a generic portable combination, describe the system and report the results of its use and performance in outdoor situations. The design principle behind the system is that the construction of the application should be component-based *and* use software that is easily available. The discussion in the end sketches the direction of porting the system into a digital mobile phone.

2 Survey of the Needs

In order to survey the demand for low-cost assistive technology for coping in everyday life, an email questionnaire was sent out to 450 members of the Finnish Federation of the Visually Impaired. A total of 29 persons replied to the questionnaire. Half of them had a complete loss of sight, and rest of them had a faint ability to perceive light or shapes. They represented fairly evenly age groups from twenties to sixties. Even though the questionnaire examined various aspects of assistive technology with 94 separate questions [8], the results reported in this article concentrate only on two specific issues: independent initiative and portable assistive technology for visually impaired users. The first issue of independent initiative was examined with two questions: “Do you try to cope with everyday problems by asking help from others or reading independently by yourself?” and “Would you like to manage your everyday activities more independently and how it could be the most beneficial for you?”

Several respondents state that they try to cope with the problems independently, but if they fail (after reasonable efforts), help from other people is sought. The justifications for this vary from “not wanting to be of trouble” to “lack of courage to seek help” and “not wanting outside people to know my personal affairs”.

A respondent concludes that "[...] of course I would like to cope with my everyday life as independently as possible. It is fairly tedious to work out schedules in order to get a guide to run errands. In my opinion, I would be more equal with others if I could run my errands on my time, and not when a family member or an aid has time.”

The second issue of portable assistive technology was examined with a question: “Special needs are being met with pocket-sized computers to alleviate the problems of everyday life wherever the user goes. What kind of features would be beneficial for you in this kind of assistive device?”

Out of 26 replies, 13 respondents brought up the wish of speech usage. An excerpt of a reply describes the possibilities of assistive technology in this area: “The computer should have a small Braille display and possibly speech synthesis. One could use it, for example, with an ATM machine, in order to know what the screen says. Similarly, it could be used with other screens, e.g. at bus, subway and railway stations. The computer could help when coping with new routes and it could substitute as a map, if it told street names and directions to aim at with a guide dog after entering the final destination to the system.”

Another respondent summarizes general needs: “When moving around, it would be undoubtedly good. But at the same time, it should have all the other things as well, such as phone, notebooks, address books, the Internet [...] but it should be an existing device, so that every assistive feature is just an add-on. This way, the accessibility and the price could be manageable. Nowadays the pricing of purpose-built assistive technology is out of reach. In addition, there are too many devices that provide only one or two services. Everything should be packaged into one portable device!"

After these results, it was clear that there is a need for a portable, low-cost solution to help in independent initiative that can serve multiple purposes. The idea of portable device for supplementing low vision or loss of sight is not particularly new; there already are various solutions [6, 7], and ongoing projects are under way [10]. Independent initiative in other contexts has also been researched [14].

The novel idea behind our system is that the construction of the assistive application should be based on devices and software that are already easily available — preferably freely downloadable — on the consumer market. The approach seemed to be cost-effective and provided an opportunity to tailor the assistive application with a large variety of modules. Without a doubt, existing software components combined in a novel way provides a considerable potential for a variety of computational tasks.

3 System Description

As machine vision is still limited in object recognition in everyday life [12, 2], the system was built to support only textual information, even though there are plenty of issues in textual recognition as well (see e.g. [3, 20, 19]).

3.1 Operation from the User's Viewpoint

After certain preparations the operation of the system is simple. The user points the camera to a view that needs to be interpreted and presses the left mouse button. The view is then captured by the camera and saved on the computer's hard drive. After that the image file is analyzed by a character recognition program. The text that can be found is transmitted to a speech synthesis program and the result can be heard from headphones. This procedure can be achieved with only one click with the mouse and the auditory interpretation of the texts in the scenery is acquired in 30 seconds.

The system searches one type of the characters at time: dark characters on light background or light characters on dark background. By rolling the wheel of the mouse forward the user can repeat the hearing of the current interpretation. If the user rolls the wheel of the mouse backwards the system offers interpretation made from the same picture but with inverted colors. By pressing the wheel of the mouse user can interrupt the hearing of the interpretation if it is necessary.

3.2 System Architecture

The final prototype of the portable system that provides text-to-speech synthesis in outdoor environment consists of mostly generic components: a laptop computer connected to a digital camera, easy-to-acquire software, a wheel-mouse and headphones. The laptop computer used was Toshiba Satellite Pro 4600 with a Pentium III processor (391 MHz). The camera was Canon PowerShot A95 with a CCD of 5 megapixels. The weight of the combination was less than 4 kilograms.

The operation of the system is based on the cooperation between software components running under Windows XP. The components used for the prototype were: Remote Capture software by Canon, TopOCR character recognition software by Topsoft [17], Mikropuhe speech synthesis by Timehouse [16], and Winamp media player by Nullsoft [13]. Remote Capture makes it possible to capture images directly from a Canon digital camera to the computer. TopOCR offers means to perform character recognition on any JPG image file. Mikropuhe is one of the leading software for producing synthesized speech in Finnish.

The cooperation is conducted in Autohotkey [9] macro environment. Autohotkey offers a scripting language for describing the desired flow of actions and their conditions within the operating system. On the top of the Autohotkey environment, a script is needed to allow the user to control the flow of data between the camera, OCR and speech synthesizer software. The script needed for the purpose was designed and written by the first author. All the other software components are generic in a sense that they are not custom-built for assistive technology. Therefore, it should be noted that even though the components were not all open source or freely distributable software, comparable components can be acquired free of charge. The decision to use relatively expensive speech synthesizer software was a language-related issue. The component-based architecture allows using any useful or easy-to-acquire components.

4 Text Recognition with the System

The quality of interpretation of the texts in the surrounding environment varies significantly. Due to challenges in the character recognition process, the system can normally offer only a suggestive interpretation. Normally, the system captures excerpts of text and thus conveys only a selection of the original text to the user. In addition, it is typical that optical character recognition software interprets random visual elements as characters, so that the end result can be difficult to comprehend. Thus the visually impaired users should not rely solely on this information but instead use it as a supplement for other observations concerning environment. Despite the distortion, it is often possible to recognize familiar words even from very short excerpts. Awareness of the context and common sense reasoning still leads to understanding of the text-to-speech interpretation.

Example in Figure 1 shows the quality of the system output in interpreting textual input in a typical condition. Of course, interpretations transcribed on paper do not match the user experience when perceived with speech synthesis.

Figure 1 has been taken towards a fence at a construction site. On the fence there is a sign that says: "*Työmaa-alue. Asiattomilta pääsy kielletty.*" (Construction site. Unauthorized access forbidden).

When this picture is analyzed by the system the text in this picture produces an interpretation: "*.-.,X.3=Tyomaa-alueAsiattomiltapääsykiellettyåö.*"

To eliminate confusing splitting of words the system concatenates all characters on purpose when producing the speech output. Especially in Finnish language, this should help in preserving the proper pronunciation and make the end result more understandable. Despite of the concatenation and some additional characters in the result, the original message is in practice quite recognizable. Even the loss of diacritic dots is tolerable to understand Finnish language. The design principle of using existing components forces to accept a certain level of robustness in the system.

Fig. 1. View at a construction site

5 User Tests

Two male and three female volunteers (aged 32 to 66) with varying visual disabilities tested the system in real life conditions. Two of the volunteers were not capable to read visual text at all. Three of the volunteers were able to read enlarged text with strong contrast. They all were relatively active users of computers.

During the testing the users were assisted by the first author. The assistance was for coordinating the activity and making a detailed recording of the opinions expressed. Some of the test locations were familiar to the volunteers.

5.1 Results

The evaluation consisted of a total of 35 different locations. In some locations, few additional trials were needed to optimize, for example, the framing of the textual information visible. In twenty locations the system could offer interpreted keywords that can be classified as "useful" or "rather useful". In four other locations the interpretations can be classified as "slightly useful". In the rest eleven locations, the system was not able to produce useful interpretations. When the experience of the system and its use grows, it is reasonable to believe that the ratio becomes better.

As it is often the case with speech synthesis, understanding the synthesized speech from the machine-made interpretation of the text was sometimes challenging. One source of inconvenience in this case is the intentional merging of the text into a long word, as motivated in Section 4. Another source for the difficulties appeared to be the special fonts used in many logos and advertisements. Moreover, random visual elements are often interpreted as characters. The defects in the interpreted texts were considered annoying but, on the other hand, they are much the same in results obtained in all traditional scanning and optical recognition of visual text.

Biased interpretations of the text received varied reactions from the users of the system. Additional characters give sometimes a misleading impression of looking at a timetable or a price list. Numeral information gets easily an uncertain sequencing and the existence of dots and commas is unclear. The system produces classical confusions with recognizing letter "O" and number zero or small letter "L" and number one. The volunteers mention similar difficulties with letter "B" and number eight or Roman numbering. However, the volunteers were already used to cope with these uncertainties with common sense and contextual information. For example, familiar prefixes in telephone numbers and Web addresses help to recognize the correct type of information.

5.2 Examples of Test Cases

Figure 2 presents a view to an exit from a subway station. There is an exit sign that says: "*Raitiovaunut Spårvagnar*" (Trams, in Finnish and in Swedish).

The system produced the following interpretation of the text: "*teRaitiovaunutSparvagnar*". The volunteer had no trouble in interpreting the output: "*Hey, that is the exit to go to tram tracks!*" The key issue is that the user can augment the output with existing knowledge to form a sense of the current context.

An opposing case to a successful interpretation in Figure 2 is presented in Figure 3. In Figure 3, there is a view towards a shop entrance: "*LAHJATALO PASTEL*" (GIFT HOUSE PASTEL, in Finnish).

The system produced the following interpretation of the text: "*LAHJATALOPASTEL*". The volunteer's response for the speech output is: "*Can I have it again? [2nd listening] Lahjatalopastel? Maybe a missing letter? Lahjatalo...*"

It is apparent that the volunteer did not know the presence of this particular gift shop, and could not connect the name "Pastel" to previous knowledge from the environment to the context. In this case, the addition of a clear space between the "gift shop" and "Pastel" could have helped understanding.

Other user test scenarios and results are presented in [8], containing details about the test users' characteristics and the process of interpretation in varying outdoor environment.

5.3 General Comments of the Use and Development Ideas

The volunteers gave versatile feedback about the usability of the system. One of the main concerns was how to point the camera to the essential textual objects so that a meaningful interpretation is possible. As one of the volunteers stated, without earlier experience, it is hard to know what kind of texts could be available in the environment. One volunteer proposed an idea that the system should offer instantly some text excerpts from the current view that would help in the framing of the view with the camera. It was evident that if the framing is difficult, the users often try to perceive the space by touching, or just by taking repeated shots towards different directions.

Fig. 2. Exit from a subway station to a tram stop

Fig. 3. Entrance to a shop with the shop name clearly visible

The volunteers proposed several novel ways to use the system. One of them is a situation where a user arrives to a new environment and wants to know what kind of shops, products and discounts are available. Textual signs and information boards are considered useful especially since they are typically written in a clear manner. The volunteers found that suitable purposes for the use of the system are shopping and traveling. In shops one can locate products, examine their properties and thus compare them. In public transportation one can check timetables and traffic routes.

The volunteers had divergent opinions about the usability of the system in everyday life. One user postulated that it is much faster to ask help from a passer-by than use the system. On the other hand, as seen in Section 2, some users note that they would not like to depend too much on the help from other people. One of the volunteers made an explicit point that he does not want to bother passers-by constantly. In addition, when alone at e.g. a bus stop, she might need to check the timetable independently. Another user feels that asking the names of the shops is tolerable but asking about advertisements or price comparisons is too intruding. This reason could encourage him to begin using the system although the speed of operation of the system might prove to be too slow after the initial excitement wears off.

The users point out that the usefulness of the system depends strongly on the easy portability and the capability to frame the view to be interpreted correctly. The users would appreciate the possibility to carry the system in a backpack and to use their hands only to take pictures. In addition, the framing of the views could be assisted by connecting it somehow to head movement. Also the procedures necessary to perform before the system is in operation raise some concern from the volunteers. To be truly usable, the procedure of setting up the system and starting it should be simple to do non-visually, as well as maintenance such as charging the batteries.

The results obtained by interpreting texts in a real-life surrounding environment with the system reflected the expectations of the volunteers. The accuracy of the interpretations was not high but yet often sufficient to give an overview of the textual content. Despite the limitations of the system, the volunteers considered the system to be generally useful since it adds to the independent initiative. One volunteer stated that he could begin to use even the rough prototype version right away in his everyday life.

6 Conclusions

The development of the system has positively shown that even with a quite modest level of technical expertise it is possible to create a useful computational solution for alleviating the problems of coping in everyday life. Existing devices and software can be harnessed to serve together in a novel way. From the perspective of software engineering, a truly open component-based architecture using existing modules enables to replace any component with a better component at any time. As long as copyright issues are taken sufficiently into account, this kind of product development can fruitfully support competition between manufacturers of different components. Due to the rapid rise of computing power and evolution in interoperability between components, today typical portable personal computers have the processing ability to carry on relatively demanding computational tasks.

To be useful, a device described in this article should be as portable as possible. In current research, the emphasis has been on mobile devices (see e.g. The Sypole Project [4]). The vOICe [10] project tries to convey visual imagery to aural information, and it has been implemented into a specific mobile phone (as The vOICe BEB), and is currently freely downloadable.

The vOICe BEB is a standalone application, so a natural direction for further development of portable text-to-speech is simply to use easy-to-acquire OCR and speech synthesis components, and integrate them into a mobile phone with a camera. In fact, some mobile phones will come already with an integrated speech synthesizer.

Simple OCR software could be used, and as the processing power in current mobile phones grows, better functionality can be achieved.

Components to build a working prototype into a mobile phone are already available. QuickTextScan from JSS Computing captures any text in the environment using the mobile phone's own camera and opens it for editing and passing to other applications [5]. Generic lightweight speech synthesis for mobile phones is also being developed (see e.g. VSpeak that provides a speech synthesizer working within the restrictions of contemporary mobile phones [18]).

Acknowledgments. The authors wish to thank the Finnish Federation of the Visually Impaired, people who replied to the survey, and especially those five persons that took part in the field trial. Moreover, the providers of software and hardware used in the prototype are gratefully acknowledged.

References

1. Technologies, C.A.: Inc. P2RD: Portable Print Reading Device (2004) http://www.catechnology.net/
2. Doermann, D., Liang, J., Li, H.: Progress in Camera-Based Document Image Analysis. In: ICDAR '03. Proc. seventh international conference on Document analysis and recognition, p. 606. IEEE Computer Society Press, Washington, DC, USA (2003)
3. Ezaki, N., Bulacu, M., Schomaker, L.: Text Detection from Natural Scene Images: Towards a System for Visually Impaired Persons. In: ICPR '04. Proc. Pattern Recognition, 17th international conference on (ICPR'04), vol. 2, pp. 683–686. IEEE Computer Society Press, Washington, DC, USA (2004)
4. Gaudissart, V., Ferreira, S., Mancas-Thillou, C., Gosselin, B.: Sypole: A Mobile Assistant for the Blind. In Proc. European Signal Processing Conference (EUSIPCO 2005), Antalya, Turkey (2005) http://tcts.fpms.ac.be/publications/papers/2005/eusipco05_vgsfcmbg.pdf
5. JSS Computing, Inc. QuickTextScan (2006) http://jsscomputing.com/quicktextscan/
6. Krishna, S., Little, G., Black, J., Panchanathan, S.: iCARE Interaction Assistant: A Wearable Face Recognition System for Individuals with Visual Impairments. In: Assets '05: Proc. 7th international ACM SIGACCESS conference on Computers and accessibility, pp. 216–217. ACM Press, New York, NY, USA (2005)
7. Krishna, S., Little, G., Black, J., Panchanathan, S.: A Wearable Face Recognition System for Individuals with Visual Impairments. In: Assets '05: Proc. 7th international ACM SIGACCESS conference on Computers and accessibility, pp. 106–113. ACM Press, New York, NY, USA (2005)
8. Lahti, L.: Computer-assisted acquisition of information for visually impaired (in Finnish). Master's thesis, University of Helsinki, Faculty of Science, Department of Computer Science, Report C-2006-32. (2006) http://ethesis.helsinki.fi/julkaisut/mat/tieto/pg/lahti/
9. Mallett, C.: AutoHotkey: Open Source Mouse and Keyboard Macro Program (2006) http://www.autohotkey.com/
10. Meijer, P.: The vOICe: A Synthetic Vision for the Blind (2006) http://www.seeingwithsound.com/
11. Mihara, Y., Sugimoto, A., Shibayama, E., Takahashi, S.: An Interactive Braille-Recognition System for the Visually Impaired Based on a Portable Camera. In: Proc. CHI'05: CHI '05 extended abstracts on Human factors in computing systems, pp. 1653–1656. ACM Press, New York, NY, USA (2005)

12. Nagel, H.-H.: Steps toward a Cognitive Vision System. AI Magazine 25(2), 31–50 (2004)
13. Nullsoft Ltd. Winamp: Media Player for Windows (2006) http://www.winamp.com/
14. Paradise, J., Mynatt, E.D., Williams, C., Goldthwaite, J.: Designing a Cognitive Aid for the Home: A Case-Study Approach. In: Assets '04: Proc. 6th international ACM SIGACCESS conference on Computers and accessibility, pp. 140–146. ACM Press, New York, NY, USA (2004)
15. Ross, D.A., Lightman, A.: Talking Braille: A Wireless Ubiquitous Computing Network for Orientation and Wayfinding. In: Assets '05: Proc. 7th international ACM SIGACCESS conference on Computers and accessibility, pp. 98–105. ACM Press, New York, NY, USA (2005)
16. Timehouse Oy. Mikropuhe: Finnish Speech Synthesis Software (2003) http://www.mikropuhe.com/mikropuhe.asp
17. TopSoft Ltd. TopOCR: Optical Character Recognition Software (2005) http://www.topocr.com/
18. VoiceSignal Technologies, Inc. VSpeak: Speech Synthesis for Mobile Phones (2006) http://www.voicesignal.com/solutions/applications.php3
19. Yang, J., Gao, J., Zhang, Y., Waibel, A.: Towards Automatic Sign Translation. In: HLT '01: Proc. 1st international conference on Human language technology research, pp. 1–6. Association for Computational Linguistics, Morristown, NJ, USA (2001)
20. Zandifar, A., Chahine, A.: A Video Based Interface to Textual Information for the Visually Impaired. In: ICMI '02: Proc. 4th IEEE international conference on Multimodal interfaces, p. 325. IEEE Computer Society, Washington, DC, USA (2002)

Human Interface for the Robot Control in Networked and Multi-sensored Environment

Hyun-Gu Lee[1], Yong-Guk Kim[2], Ho-Dong Lee[1], Joo-Hyung Kim[1], and Gwi-Tae Park[1,*]

[1] School of Electrical Engineering, Korea University, Seoul, Korea
{hglee99,juragic,proteus99,gtpark}@korea.ac.kr
[2] School of Computer Engineering, Sejong University, Seoul, Korea
ykim@sejong.ac.kr

Abstract. In this paper, we propose a human-robot interface in networked and multi-sensored environments. The human robot interface is an essential part of intelligent robotic system. Through the human robot interface, human being can interact with the robot. Especially, in multi-sensored environment, the human robot interface can be developed with remarkably extended functionality. Generally, handheld device such as PDA is a suitable for human robot interface because of its mobility and network ability. In this paper, we select PDA as device of human robot interface. In the implemented framework, the robot user can monitor what happens in multi-sensored environment and control the mobile robot easily and intuitively.

1 Introduction

Many researchers have been tried to make the robot more intelligent and serviceable. Consequently, the robotic system is widely used in various fields and become more important in our daily life. But, up to now, most robotic system has not fully intelligence and this leads to needs of human robot interface. Various and diverse researches on human robot interface are conducted. And now, human robot interface forms an essential part of successful robotic system.

Since the advent of computer network or internet, it changes extensively the whole industry as well as human being's life style. The robotic system is no exception to this fact. Many robot developers are carrying out research on fusion of computer network and robot with their own methodology and have been paid attention to human robot interface especially.

In this paper, in networked and multi-sensored environment, the range of human robot interface is extended to not only human and robot but also their surrounding environments. We are sure that such interface will be more easy, comfortable and powerful and leads to more intelligent robotic system.

In this paper, we propose human robot interface system in networked and multi-sensored environment.

The rest of this paper consists of several following sections.

[*] The corresponding author.

C. Stephanidis (Ed.): Universal Access in HCI, Part II, HCII 2007, LNCS 4555, pp. 928–935, 2007.

2 Robot in Networked and Multi-sensored Environments

2.1 System Architecture

Figure 1 shows interaction between human and robot in networked and multi-sensored environments. In this system, all resource such as sensors, robot and processing unit are connected via network. There are many sensors by which different sensory data will be collected from the surrounding environment. Those data are processed by using diverse algorithms, and the output from the process should be used for the robot actions or decision making. To make the mobile robot intelligent, it requires tremendous amount of computing power, in particular, when the action has to be made in the real time basis. But, in networked and multi-sensored environment, the robot can perform its tasks more easily and intelligent by sharing resources around it. The key point of this system is to relieve the burden of the processor within the robot, and so any intensive computation should be carried out in other processing units such as PC, which is distributed on the network.

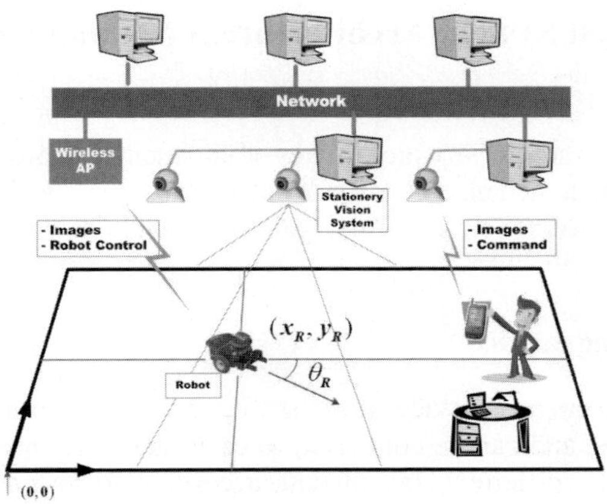

Fig. 1. Interaction between human and robot

In this system, the mobile robot is equipped with low performance PC, which functionality is restricted to only sensory data collection and robot control. The stationary vision system, mounted on wall or ceiling of room, observe the activity space of robot and human. The stationary vision system consists of image grabber and multiple cameras to cover wide area.

Handheld device such as PDA is convenient to use as interface with robot because of its mobility and small but acceptable computing power. Many researchers have been studies the possibility of handheld device as human robot interface. In Fig. 1, by using all resource through PDA, user can interact with robot more easily and intelligently. In networked and multi-sensored environment, user can see what robot see or what is happening in environment and give a command to robot through display screen and touchpad interface of PDA. In the present work, simple but intuitive interface of PDA has designed.

2.2 Middleware for Networked and Multi-sensored Environment

Generally, developing robot software is known as complex, tedious and error-prone task. Moreover, if the robot software is distributed over a network, its development imposes several additional problems such as concurrency issue, time delay and potential network failure. Hence, various methods for processing sensory data, controlling the robot and interfacing with the human must be integrated well-engineered piece of software. To resolve afore-mentioned problems and increase efficiency of the proposed framework, developing service by using middleware layers is needed.

CORBA is a widely recognized middleware standard for heterogeneous and distributed systems. By using CORBA's object model and its representation in the IDL(Interface Description Language), developers can implement network-based systems easily and transparently. In our system, we used the public domain implementation of CORBA, called ACE/TAO, as a middleware for the proposed system.

3 Services Based System Architecture for Human-Robot Interaction

We implement some services, which is key components of proposed system. Each service, which is implemented as CORBA object, has own specialized and cognitive task such as robot localization, robot navigation, obstacle detection, display for PDA and so on.

3.1 Data Streaming Service

In Fig. 1, many sensors and services are distributed in surrounding environment such as the activity space, and can be connected to each other via various network media. Each service needs a different kind of data according to its property and purpose. Especially, image acquired from stationary vision system can be used in diverse algorithm, obstacle detection, object recognition, robot localization and so on. These tasks need the image data acquired from the mobile robot or the stationary vision system. To support these tasks efficiently, the image streaming service, that is basic service of all services, is implemented. In our work, designing a flexible and efficient image streaming service is very important because bottleneck or time delay in image streaming service will make the entire system unstable.

Fig.2 shows streaming service interfaces implemented in this paper.

The image streaming service has two simple but important methods, Put and Get, as illustrated in Fig. 2. In the case of Get method, processing unit is able to retrieve image from robot on its demand. In otherwise case, if processing unit needs every image on time, it can be done by using Put. In this system, we adopt image compression such as MPEG and JPEG to the image streaming service because the size of image data is very larger than other sensory data and network bandwidth id limited.

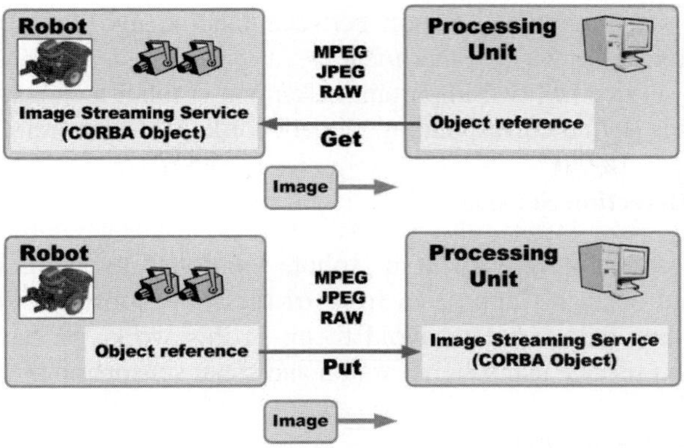

Fig. 2. Streaming service interfaces for different data type

3.2 Localization Service

The problem of robot localization is to find its location relative to the environment. Robot's location means the x and y coordinates and heading direction of a robot in a global coordinate system. Localization of the robot is a key component in many successful autonomous robot systems. If a robot does not know where it is relative to the environment, it is difficult to decide where to go and what to do.

In this work, a simple and robust localization strategy of the robots is introduced. The mobile robots don't need positioning sensors to localize themselves. By processing images from stationary vision systems, position of the robot can be determined. In this case, the robots only require patterns, which represent its identity, such as known color code or shape. According to a kind of pattern, various object recognition techniques can be used to determine the pose of the robots. The merit of this localization strategy is the resource sharing because many robots can use one localization system at the same time. Fig. 3 describes four steps of robot localization strategy used in this system.

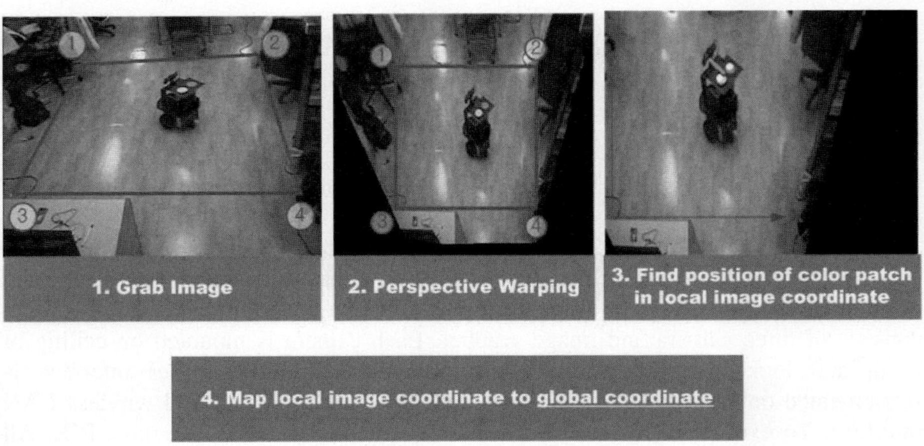

Fig. 3. Robot localization algorithm

At the final step, mapping relation between local image coordinate and global coordinate is already known by experiment.

Localization service has two important tasks: one is robot localization as shown in Fig. 3, the other is to find corresponding global coordinate to arbitrary image point.

3.3 Obstacle Detection Service

For safe and successful movement of robot, robot has to avoid obstacles while running. If some obstacles appear in front of the robot, obstacle detection service finds obstacles and help robot to avoid them. In this work, we have implemented obstacle detection service using stereo vision and sonar sensors on the robot.

3.4 Display Service for PDA

Display service, that is used to give variety of information to user, is designed for user interface mainly. Generally, PDA has low computing power and small resolution display than other processing unit such as PCs. Also, image data is compressed by the image streaming service. So, it is impossible for PDA to process all image data. To overcome these restrictions, display service creates the display contents for PDA and sends those data to PDA via wireless network. Figure 4 shows example of display service.

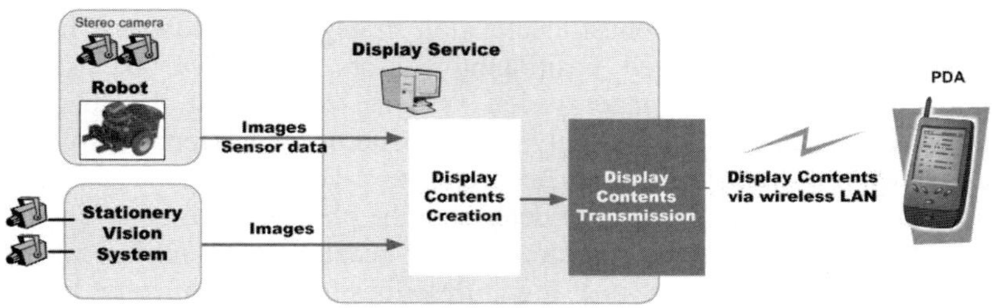

Fig. 4. Display service

4 Implementation

4.1 Hardware System

Figure 5 shows test space and hardware system of our implementation of the proposed system.

The robot system, Pioneer 2 DX, is equipped with stereo camera, MPEG hardware encoder and industrial PC. It can carry out basic behaviors such as navigation and obstacle avoidance as well as capturing stereo image. Stationary vision system consists of three camera and image grabber. Each camera is mounted on ceiling of room and look at some place, as illustrated in Fig. 5-(c). User interface is implemented on HP HX4700. This PDA has 624 Mhz processor and wireless LAN interface. To execute many services mentioned in this work, we use three PCs. All hardware systems are connected with each other via wired or wireless LAN interface.

(a) Robot(Pioneer 2 DX)

(b) Camera (Cannon VC-3)

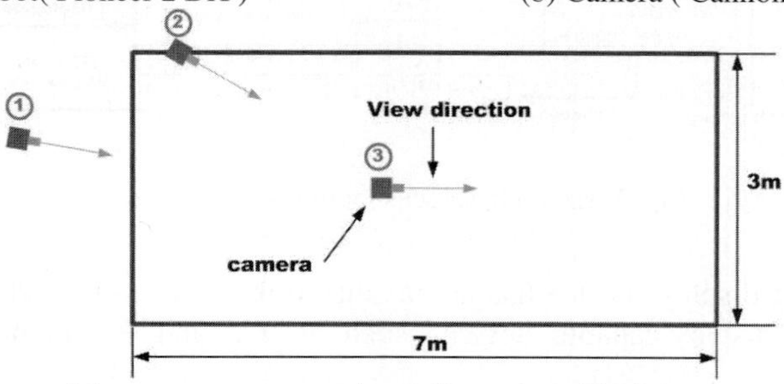

(c) camera arrangement and dimension of test space

Fig. 5. Test space and hardware system

4.2 User Interface Using PDA

Figure 6 shows display the process of service to support a user interface. Display service creates a new visual scene composing six images: Three images among these six images are acquired from cameras of stationary vision system, two images come from stereo camera of the mobile robot and one image is depth map resulted from stereo vision algorithm. Subsequently, display service automatically updates PDA screen with the newly created image. The update speed is about 5~7 frame per second because PDA has low network bandwidth of 11Mbps. The example screenshot of PDA is shown in Fig. 7.

Fig. 6. Display service for a PDA

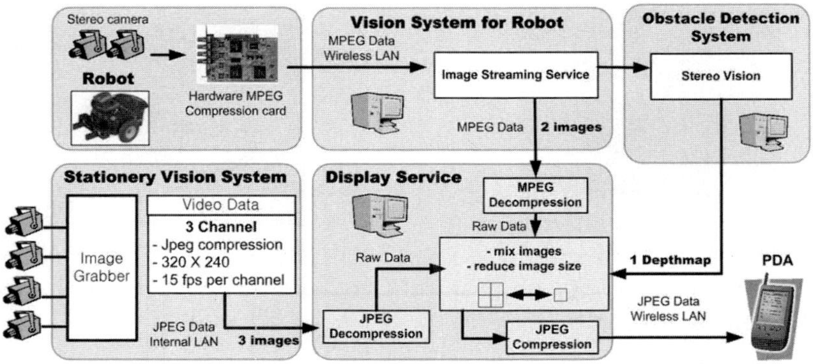

Fig. 7. Example screenshot of display service

The proposed display service has an advantage that it can be used not only PDA but also other display-capable devices such as TV and PC monitor with little modification.

4.3 Test Scenario of Interaction Between PDA and Robot

Through the user interface, user can monitor all images from robot and stationary vision system in real time basis. When user selects one image from the composed image, the selected image is only displayed on screen of PDA as shown in Fig. 8. This scheme enables user to control the robot in more detailed view. On PDA, if user

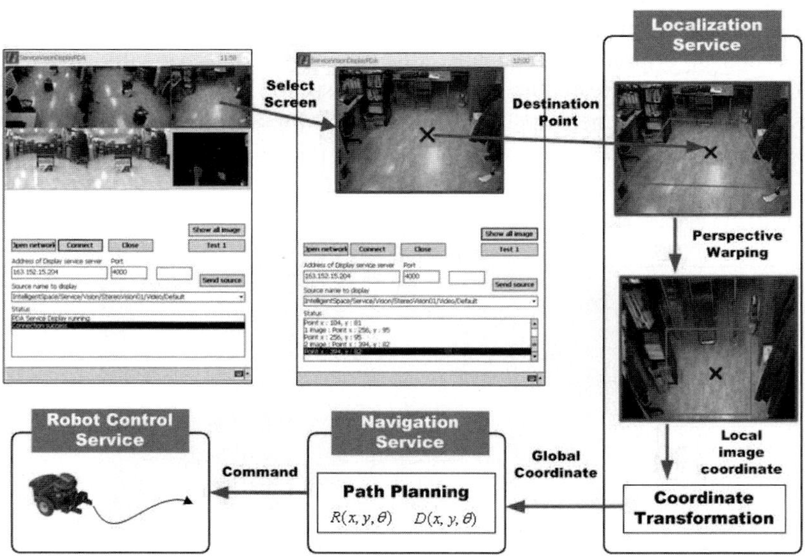

Fig. 8. Scenario for robot control using PDA

selects arbitrary point of image, user can know the global coordinate of selected point using localization service as well as current robot position. And then user can issue command of navigation to that point.

5 Conclusions

In this paper, we have designed and implemented human robot interface in networked and multi-sensored environments. From test scenario using implemented human robot interface, we verify that human robot interaction is done easily and intuitively through display service and PDA interface. The human robot interface is important because it compensate with lack of robot intelligence. Consequently, designing a good human robot interface is the key to the successful robot system.

References

1. Hori, T., Hirukawa, H., Suehiro, T., Hirai, S.: Networked Robots as Distributed Objects. In: IEEE/ASME Int. Conf, Advanced Intelligent Mechatronics, pp. 61–66 (1999)
2. Stevens, W.R.: UNIX Networking programming, 2nd edn. Prentice-Hall, Englewood Cliffs (1998)
3. Stallings, W.: Wireless Communications and networks. Prentice Hall, Englewood Cliffs (2002)
4. Richardson, I.E.G.: H.264 and MPEG-4 Video Compression: Video Coding for Next Generation Multimedia, Wiley (2003)
5. http://www.ijg.org
6. http://www.ffmpeg.org/

Gesture-Based Interactions on Multiple Large Displays with a Tabletop Interface

Jangho Lee[1], Jun Lee[1], HyungSeok Kim[2], and Jee-In Kim[2,*]

[1] Department of Computer Science & Engineering, Konkuk University, Seoul, Korea
[2] Department of Internet & Multimedia Engineering, Konkuk University, Seoul, Korea
{jangho,junlee,hyuskim,jnkm}@konkuk.ac.kr

Abstract. We like large displays. Also, we love to equip with multiple displays for exercising multiple tasks in parallel. It is not unusual to have multiple large displays in our offices. Therefore, we can see many widgets on multiple large displays and would like to select and manipulate them in more convenient and faster ways. Because the widgets are physically spread in multiple large displays, it is not easy for users to reach them easily. It follows that new interaction techniques must be provided.[1] New interaction techniques for accessing distant widgets on multiple large displays using a tabletop interface called 'u-Table' [2] are proposed in this paper. Hand gestures are mainly used on tabletop interfaces because of their intuitive, non-invasive and easy operations. We incorporate advantages of existing techniques such as intuitiveness of tabletop interfaces, fastness and simultaneity of existing interaction techniques such as Drag-and-pick [10] and Vacuum [11]. The proposed interaction techniques include fetching, sending, and manipulating distant widgets on multiple large displays. We expect our techniques can be applied various interfaces using hand gestures and heterogeneous displays.

Keywords: Multiple Large Displays, Hand Gestures, Tabletop Interfaces.

1 Introduction

A tabletop interface consists of a table-shaped display where displayed objects can be manipulated by touching the display. We extended the concept of the tabletop interface as a ubiquitous multimodal interaction platform, called 'u-Table' [2]. It provides touching interaction by utilizing computer-vision technology with camera under the table combined with the projected visual information from the projector under the table. In u-Table, the tabletop is used as a large touch-able screen. Output images are projected on the tabletop by rear-projection. u-Table also recognizes different devices using specially designed visual tags. The overall system is presented in Figure 1.

Hand gestures are commonly used to interact intuitively on tabletop interfaces [3]. In Augmented Surfaces [4], Hyperdragging can be used to move an object in a

[*] Corresponding author.

C. Stephanidis (Ed.): Universal Access in HCI, Part II, HCII 2007, LNCS 4555, pp. 936–942, 2007.

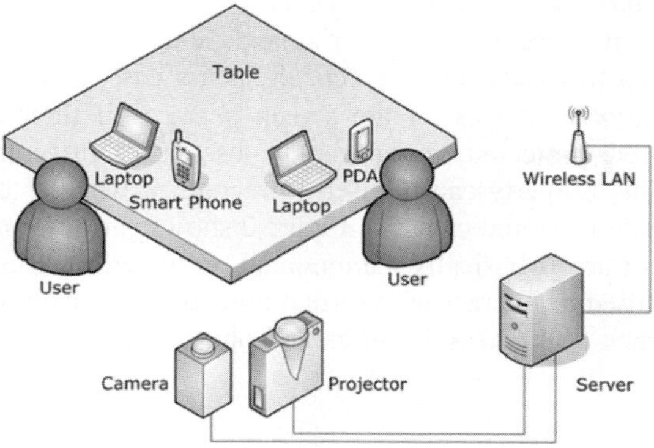

Fig. 1. System overview

notebook to a tabletop or a wall display. Interface Current [5] is a fluid interaction technique to support face-to-face collaboration. To access objects on the tabletop, it provides a controllable flow interface. In this paper, we propose intuitive hand gestures to access distant object.

The displays of tabletop interfaces are getting larger as the tabletop interfaces are considered as cooperative workspace [5][6]. In large display spaces, a user-accessible area is limited. Especially, a user cannot easily interact because of physical boundary problems [1]. On the large tabletop, objects may be placed far from a user when it is needed. When there is another user near the interest objects, the user can request that person to replace the objects to the user using techniques like the Throwing [7][8].

There are many techniques for accessing distant object in large displays. Multiple displays are generally used to make large display. There is a boundary problem with physically separated displays by bezels of each one, for example. Pick-and-drop [9] was used to move an object from a display to another display. Pick-and-drop enables a user to pick up an object on a display and drop it on another display. Throwing [7] can be used to move objects across larger distances. A first short stroke is used to move an object to the opposite direction and a longer stroke is used to correct direction. Drag-and-pop [10] can be used to get distant object with minimal movement. When a user begins to drag an icon to the target icon, icons of the candidate targets are arranged in front of the dragging icon. The user can rapidly drop the dragging icon to the target icon. Vacuum [11] improved Drag-and-pop at accessing multiple objects. A circular widget to make an arc of influence was used to select a target object. The performance of Vacuum was better than Drag-and-pop for selecting multiple targets.

In this paper, we introduce interaction techniques for multiple large displays using hand gestures on u-Table.

u-Table

u-Table is a tabletop user interface for sharing multimedia data in a ubiquitous computing environment [2]. A rear-projected screen is used to display images on u-Table. The rear-projected screen was chosen because this type of projection does not disturb images on the screen with user's hands and fingers. Most digitalized desk systems have used a front-projected screen. In such a case, hands and fingers of the users could contaminate images on the screen because of their shadows. Another point is that the rear-projected screen can be used as a diffuser which blurs the opposite image. This property can be used to recognize whether user's hands touch the screen or not without stereo cameras. Figure 2 shows various images of u-Table.

The u-Table interface is basically manipulated by fingertips. Multiple fingertips of multiple users are used to interact with virtual objects simultaneously. It can robustly and rapidly recognize users' hand gestures and physical objects using visual tags on the tabletop.

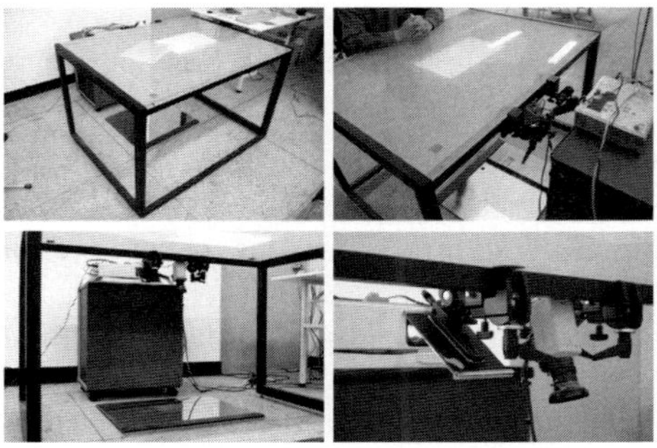

Fig. 2. Implementation of u-Table

3 Interactions

Our interaction techniques presented in this paper, 'Fetching' and 'Sending', are similar to Drag-and-Pop [10] and Vacuum [11]. Different from the conventional Drag-and-Pop or Vacuum techniques, we use hand gestures to reach objects on the

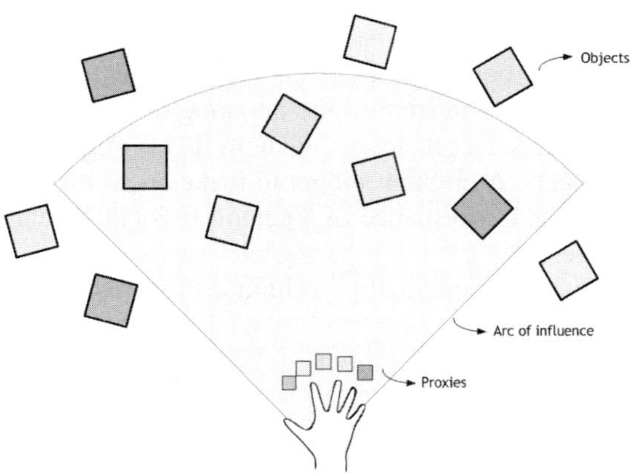

Fig. 3. Basic concept

displays instead of a pen or a mouse. Also, our method uses 'Proxies' and 'Drag Cursors' for fast interactions of fetching and sending widgets on multiple large screens.

The fetching and sending techniques are invoked by hand-gestures of drag-in and drag-out. After the drag-in hand gestures, an arc of its influence is created from the hand. The arc of the influence indicates range of accessible objects. The range can be tuned by adjusting fingers within the same gesture context.

The direction of the arc is decided by fingers of direction. Users can use all of their fingers and the direction is determined by fingers as shown in Figure 4.

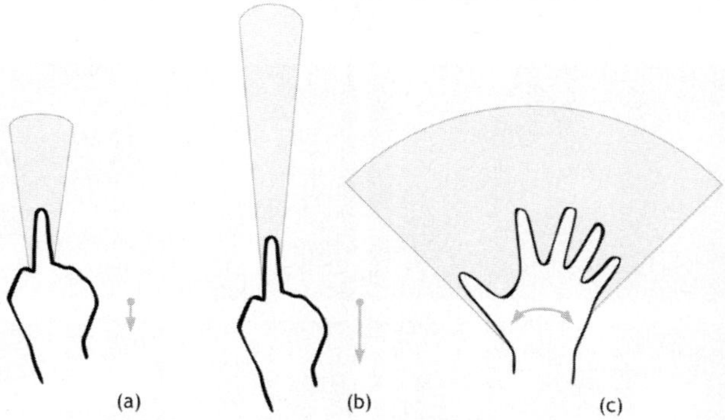

Fig. 4. Ranges set by finger gestures: (a) one finger for default (b) longer distance set by more drag-in actions by the finger (c) wider angle set by more (five in this example) fingers

The distance of the arc can be adjusted by amount of drag-in gestures. Figure 4-(b) shows that a user can set a longer range by more drag-in finger actions than 4-(a). The range can be multiplied to movement of the hand. The angle of the arc can be adjusted by angle of the hand. The angle of the arc can be changed as the number of fingers and the angle between the fingers are changed.

Proxy is a kind of hyperlink to a distant object. After a hand gesture to set an arc, objects in the arc are copied and appeared as proxies in front of the hand. The layout is similar to Drag-and-Pop and Vacuum but more convenient to hands. The proxies are laid as a shape of an arc as shown in Figure 5.

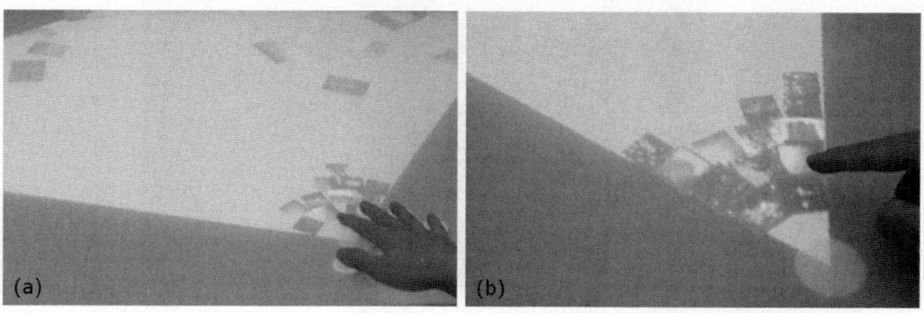

Fig. 5. Proxies: (a) Layout of proxies (b) selection of proxies by the fetching operation

The sending operation is a reverse operation of the fetching operation. It is used to move objects to a specific position on a display. The target position could be either other users or other devices on the table. The sending operation is invoked by drag-out. To indicate the position, a cursor of the target position is required. We implement the cursor using Hyperdragging [4]. The cursor is manipulated by hand gestures.

Figure 6 shows a cursor which represents a target position. Figure 6-(a) and Figure 6-(b) show process of adjusting distance by using drag-out gestures. The distance is illustrated by the cursor, the green dot at the end of the line. Figure 6-(c) and Figure 6-(d) illustrate an example of selecting range of the proxies.

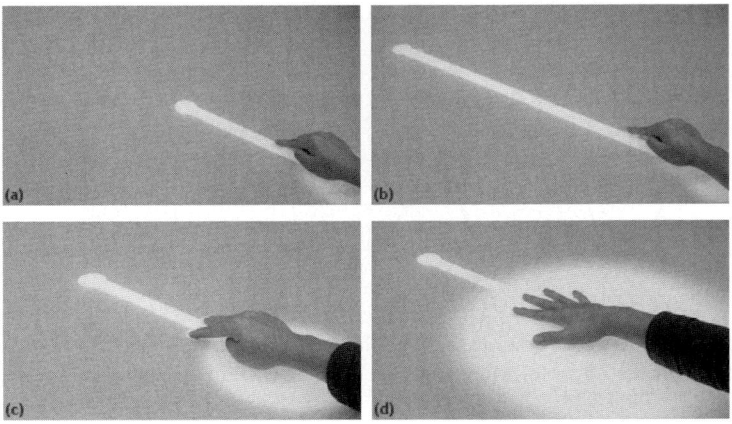

Fig. 6. Sending a widget with hand gestures

Proxies of the sending technique are selected by angle of the hand as shown in Figure 7. The user can easily adjust the position of the cursor and range of the proxies. After selection of the proxies, all of selected objects are transferred to the cursor position at once.

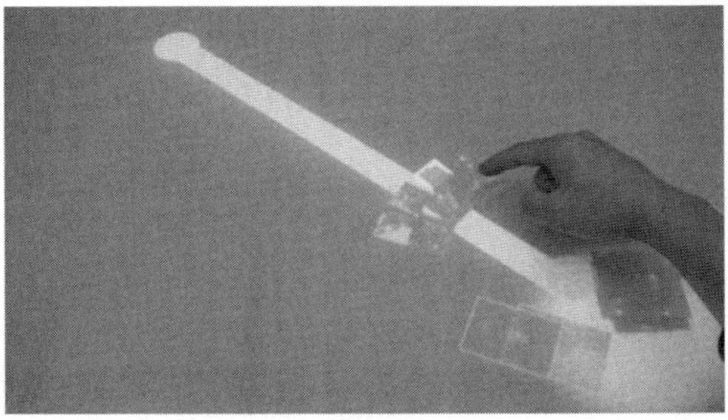

Fig. 7. Selection of proxies on sending

4 Applications

The fetching and sending techniques can be applied to various environments. In physically separated large displays, using the proposed techniques, users can easily move any object on various sized and located display even those displays are not controllable. Figure 8 shows an example of this case. A large wall display is located in front of the tabletop interface. Each display is physically separated but logically connected using these techniques. Users can fetch any object on the front display and send objects near the users to the front display as shown in Figure 8.

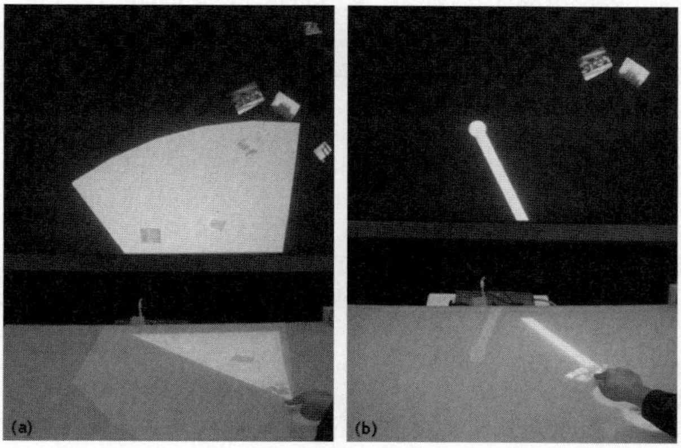

Fig. 8. Fetching and sending with multiple displays: (a) fetching objects from the front display (b) sending objects to the front display

When users want to manipulate a distant object, users can apply these techniques of fetching and sending. It is faster than physical movements, but still involves additional actions compared to the direct manipulation.

5 Conclusions

We introduce enhanced fast access techniques for distant objects. Users can easily send an object on the tabletop to another position using inertial widget. When a user wants to move entire objects, the user can use transformable tabletop. As an improvement to the inertial widget and transformable tabletop, we propose proxy-based enhancement for fetching and sending. The user can also manipulate the distant object directly using the direct manipulation technique on the proxy.

As future works, we are trying to apply the techniques to complex work processes, for example, classifying multimedia data along certain types and collaboration about data processing. We expect that our techniques can improve the performance of tabletop interfaces included large information displays environments. In addition to the proposed mechanism, we are investigating aspects of multi-user environment. In the multi-user environment where interaction counterpart can react intelligently, the interaction metaphor could be further simplified but with more interactivity on the task.

Acknowledgments. This work was supported by the Seoul City R&D Program, 'Building an Innovation Cluster of Digital Contents Industries for u-Life'.

References

1. Czerwinski, M., Robertson, G., Meyers, B., Smith, G., Robbins, D., Tan, D.: Large display research overview. CHI extended abstracts, pp. 69–74 (2006)
2. Lee, J., Kim, J.-I.: u-Table: A Tabletop Interface for Multiple Users. ICCSA, pp. 983–992 (2006)
3. Wu, M., Balakrishnan, R.: Multi-finger and whole hand gestural interaction techniques for multi-user tabletop displays. UIST, pp. 193–202 (2003)
4. Rekimoto, J., Saitoh, M.: Augmented Surfaces: A Spatially Continuous Work Space for Hybrid Computing Environments. CHI, pp. 378–385 (1999)
5. Hinrichs, U., Sheelagh, M., Carpendale, T., Scott, S.D., Pattison, E.: Interface Currents: Supporting Fluent Collaboration on Tabletop Displays. Smart Graphics, pp. 185–197 (2005)
6. Underkoffler, J., Ishii, H.: Urp: a luminous-tangible workbench for urban planning and design. CHI, pp. 386–393 (1999)
7. Geibler, J.: Shuffle, throw or take it! working efficiently with an interactive wall. CHI, pp. 265–266 (1998)
8. Reetz, A., Gutwin, C., Stach, T., Nacenta, M., Subramanian, S.: Superflick: a natural and efficient technique for long-distance object placement on digital tables. GI, pp. 163–170 (2006)
9. Rekimoto, J.: Pick-and-drop: a direct manipulation technique for multiple computer environments. UIST, pp. 31–39 (1997)
10. Baudisch, P., Cutrell, E., Robbins, D., Czerwinski, M., Tandler, P., Bederson, B., Zierlinger, Z.: Drag-and-Pop and Drag-and-Pick: Techniques for Accessing Remote Screen Content on Touch- and Pen-operated Systems. Interact, pp. 57–64 (2003)
11. Bezerianos, A., Balakrishnan, R.: The vacuum: facilitating the manipulation of distant objects. CHI, pp. 361–370 (2005)

3D Model Based Face Recognition by Face Representation Using PVM and Pose Approximation

Yang-Bok Lee[1], Taehwa Hong[2], Hyeon-Joon Moon[1], and Yong-Guk Kim[1]

[1] School of Computer Engineering, Sejong University, Seoul, Korea
yangbok@empal.com{hmoon,ykim}@sejong.ac.kr
[2] Samsung Electronics, Suwon, Korea

Abstract. Since a generative 3D face model consists of a large number of vertex points and polygons, a 3D model based face recognition system is generally inefficient in computation time. In this paper, we present a novel 3D face representation method to reduce the number of vertices and optimize its computation time and generate the 3D Korean face model based on the representation method. Also, a pose approximation method is described for initial fitting parameter. Finally, we evaluate the performance of proposed method with the face databases collected using a stereo-camera based 3D face capturing device and a web camera.

1 Introduction

Recently, a large number of researches on 3D based face recognition have been presented with various algorithms. It has several advantages over traditional 2D face recognition: First, 3D data provides absolute geometrical shape and size information of a face. Additionally, face recognition using 3D data is more robust to pose and posture changes since the model can be rotated to any arbitrary position. Also, 3D face recognition can be less sensitive to illumination since it does not solely depend on pixel intensity for calculating facial similarity. Finally, it provides automatic face segmentation information since the background is typically not synthesized in the reconstruction process [1].

V. Blanz, T. Vetter and S. Romdhani [2][3][4] proposed a method using 3D morphable model for face recognition robust to pose and illumination. They constructed a 3D morphable model with 3D faces acquired from a 3D laser-scanner, which are positioned in well calibrated cylindrical coordinates. Especially, texture information of 3D face is well defined in the reference frame where one pixel corresponds to one 3D vertex perfectly. Thereafter, they found appropriate shape and texture coefficient vectors of the model by fitting it to an input face using Stochastic Newton Optimization (SNO)[3] or Inverse Compositional Image Alignment (ICIA)[4][5] as a fitting. However, this approach has complexity and inefficiency problems caused by very large vertex number (about 80,000 ~ 110,000) despite of excellent performance.

C. Stephanidis (Ed.): Universal Access in HCI, Part II, HCII 2007, LNCS 4555, pp. 943–951, 2007.

In this paper we propose a novel 3D face representation method based on pixel-to-vertex map (PVM) and pose approximation method. Especially, through the representation method, it is possible to reduce the vertex number of each 3D face remarkably and all the 3D faces can be aligned with correspondence information based on the vertex number of a reference face simultaneously.

This paper is organized as follows. The PVM for 3D face representation and model generation are described in next section. Section 3 and Section 4 introduce the pose approximation process and the procedure of fitting the 3D model to an input image, respectively. Experimental results are presented in Section 5 based on a Korean database. Finally, conclusions and future work are discussed in Section 6.

2 3D Face Representation and Modeling

One of the most required parts in model-based face recognition system is clearly to generate a reliable face model. The reliability of the generated model has an important effect on the performance of the whole system. Then, model generation mainly depends on how well the face data are represented.

In most cases, a 3D face scan consists of texture intensity in 2D frame and geometrical shape in 3D. Especially, the shape information is represented by close connections of many vertices and polygons. Since the number of vertex points composing each of 3D face scans is different from each other, it is necessary to manipulate them to have the same number of vertices for consistent mathematical expression.

2.1 Shape Correspondence Using the Pixel-to-Vertex Map (PVM)

To achieve shape correspondence using the PVM, in the first place, we have manually registered three key features, which are left eye, right eye and mouth (from the 2D texture information of each 3D face scan). Thereafter, a fixed point for each of the features in texture coordinate is set and the features of each 3D face data are located in the fixed positions by rotating, translating and scaling. Then, the face region of a face data is separated from its background by adopting an elliptical mask.

PVM is a sort of binary image, which classifies pixels in the masked face region into ones mapped to a vertex and the opposite. We call the former active pixel (AP) and the latter inactive pixel (IP).

The procedures for the vertex correspondence using PVM are as follows:

- Construct each PVM matrix of M+1 3D face scans and build the vertex position matrix by stacking the position vector of the vertex mapping to each AP in a PVM. If the resolution of the texture frame is C by R, the PVM matrix of the ith scan, denoted by $\mathbf{M}_i$ and the vertex position matrix of the ith scan, denoted by $\mathbf{P}_i$ are obtained as

$$\mathbf{M}_i = \begin{bmatrix} m_{11}^i & m_{12}^i & \cdots & m_{1C}^i \\ m_{21}^i & & & \\ \vdots & & \ddots & \vdots \\ m_{R1}^i & & \cdots & m_{RC}^i \end{bmatrix}, \qquad m_{rc} = \begin{cases} 0, & \text{if } p_{rc} \text{ is IP} \\ 1, & \text{if } p_{rc} \text{ is AP} \end{cases}. \tag{1}$$

$$\mathbf{P}_i = [\mathbf{v}_1^i \quad \mathbf{v}_2^i \quad \cdots \quad \mathbf{v}_{s(\mathbf{M}_i)}^i]. \tag{2}$$

where p_{rc} is the pixel positioned at (r, c) in the texture frame and $s(\mathbf{M}_j)$ is size of the PVM, the number of the APs in the PVM. Also, $\mathbf{v}_j^i = [x_j \; y_j \; z_j]^T$ is the 3D position vector of the vertex mapping to the jth AP in the ith scan.

- Select a reference pixel-to-vertex map(RPVM), denoted by $\mathbf{M}^R$, by maximizing this criterion.

$$\mathbf{M}^R = \arg \max_{\mathbf{M}_j} s(\mathbf{M}_j). \tag{3}$$

The size of the RPVM, $s(\mathbf{M}^R)$ means the vertex number of a reduced subset. Then, all scans will be in correspondence with the vertex number. Likewise, the vertex position matrix of RPVM are denoted by $\mathbf{P}^R$.

- Compute each modified vertex position matrix of all scans except one selected for the RPVM.

$$\hat{\mathbf{v}}_k^i = \begin{cases} \mathbf{v}_{p(k)}^i, & \text{if } \mathrm{m}_{\mathrm{p(k)}}^{\mathrm{i}} \text{ is AP} \\ \mathbf{v}^N, & \text{if } \mathrm{m}_{\mathrm{p(k)}}^{\mathrm{i}} \text{ is IP} \end{cases}. \tag{4}$$

$$\mathbf{v}^N = \sum_{q=1}^{8} w_q \mathbf{v}_q. \tag{5}$$

$$w_j = \frac{\frac{1}{d_j}}{\sum_{j=1}^{8} \frac{1}{d_j}} \tag{6}$$

where $\hat{\mathbf{v}}_k^i$ is a modified vertex position vector, which is the same to the position of the original vertex if mapped to AP, otherwise should be acquired by an interpolation method. And, the subscripted $p(k)$ means the position of the pixel mapped to the vertex related to kth column in the $\mathbf{P}^R$. We have to seek an appropriate 3D position $\mathbf{v}^N$ for a vertex mapped to IP using linear combinations of the positions of vertices mapped to 8 nearest neighbor APs in the PVM of the target scan as defined in eq. (5) and (6).

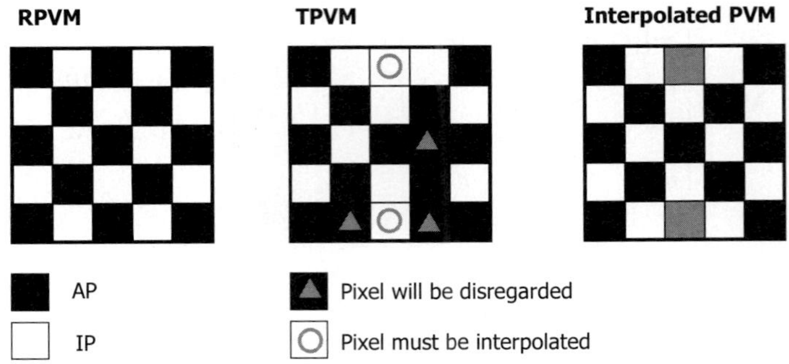

Fig. 1. Vertex correspondence by PVM

2.2 Face Model Generation

Through the PVM, it is possible that all 3D face data in our database are expressed with the same number of vertex points. Assume that there are N 3D face data in the database and they are expressed with V vertex points, shape and texture information can be written as eq.(7).

$$\mathbf{S} = \begin{bmatrix} x_1^1 & x_1^2 & \cdots & x_1^N \\ y_1^1 & y_1^2 & \cdots & y_1^N \\ z_1^1 & z_1^2 & \cdots & z_1^N \\ \vdots & \vdots & \vdots & \vdots \\ \\ x_V^1 & x_V^2 & \cdots & x_V^N \\ y_V^1 & y_V^2 & \cdots & y_V^N \\ z_V^1 & z_V^2 & \cdots & z_V^N \end{bmatrix}, \quad \mathbf{T} = \begin{bmatrix} t_1^1 & t_1^2 & \cdots & t_1^N \\ t_2^1 & t_2^2 & \cdots & t_2^N \\ \vdots & \vdots & \ddots & \vdots \\ t_V^1 & t_V^2 & \cdots & t_V^N \end{bmatrix} \tag{7}$$

We constructed separate models from shapes and textures of 100 Korean people by applying PCA [9][10] independently. The separate models are generated by linear combination of the shapes and textures as given by eq. (8).

$$\mathbf{S} = \mathbf{S}_0 + \sum_{j=1}^{N_S} \alpha_j \mathbf{S}_j, \qquad \mathbf{T} = \mathbf{T}_0 + \sum_{j=1}^{N_T} \beta_j \mathbf{T}_j. \tag{8}$$

where $\boldsymbol{\alpha} = [\alpha_1\ \alpha_2 \cdots \alpha_{N_S}]$ and $\boldsymbol{\beta} = [\beta_1\ \beta_2 \cdots \beta_{N_T}]$ are the shape and texture coefficient vectors (should be estimated by a fitting procedure). Also, $\mathbf{S}_0$ and $\mathbf{S}_j$ are the shape average model and the eigenvector associated with the jth largest eigenvalue of the shape covariance matrix, $\mathbf{T}_0$ and $\mathbf{T}_j$ in textures likewise.

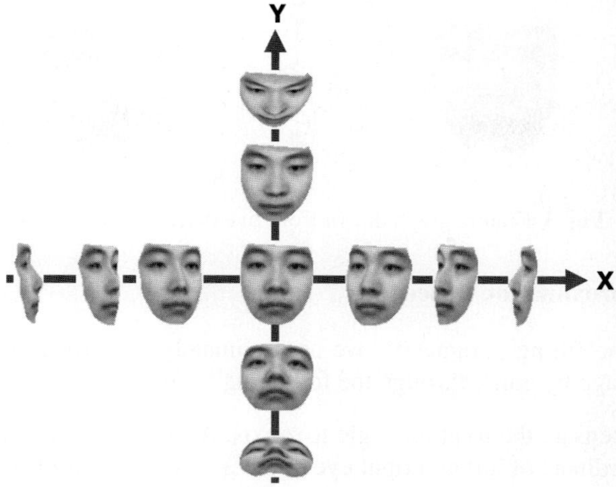

Fig. 2. A generative 3D average face model

3 Head Pose Analysis

Pose estimation is inevitably essential for implementing the face recognition system in pose varying environment. However, it is well known that it is not easy to determine accurately the pose of a face in 2D space, due to the absence of depth information to the camera axis (usually z-axis).

Our system also needs a pose estimation method for the robustness to pose variation certainly. Needless to say, the goal of our pose estimation is to compute not the accurate pose of the given face by an explicit mathematical expression but only the approximately estimated pose.

The proposed method is based on a topology of facial key features extracted from a detection algorithm or a manual registration, and a fixed marginal pose established by statistical analysis of the 3D data. Some assumptions must be preceded for the pose approximation as follows:

Assumption1. There is no variation to the z axis.

Assumption2. The pose variation to the y axis is considered in a selected marginal pose.

3.1 Marginal Pose

From the registered feature points, we can draw a graph named by feature graph as shown in Fig. 3.

Based on the feature graph, we define a marginal pose as a pose that allows the nose point N to be on the $\overline{LM}$ or $\overline{RM}$, which is the connected line of eye and mouth in right and left direction. We set up the statistical mean of 100 sample faces used for the generative model as the marginal pose.

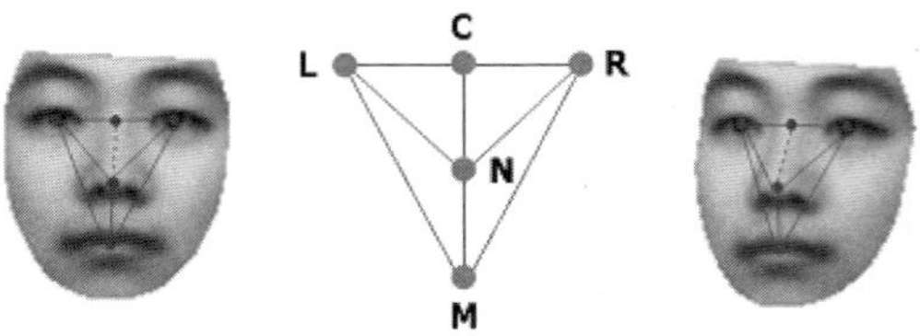

Fig. 3. Feature graph drawn from five detected feature points

3.2 Pose Approximation Procedure

To initialize the fitting parameters, we approximately perform pose estimation to a given input image by going through the following steps.

- Compensate the rotation angle to z-axis. An idea for achieving it is that each y coordinate of left and right eye in the image frame must be corresponded.
- Normalize the range of face region. Since each the face region of people is positioned at different range with each other, it is necessary for it to be ranged in same scope. We solve this problem by being identical the distance between C and M in y direction to the generative model' s.
- Decide if the given input face is frontal view or not. Inequality (9) shows the criterion we use.

$$\left|(\left|L_x - R_x\right|/2) - M_x\right| \le T_f \tag{9}$$

where T_f is a threshold value.

- Decide if the given input face is in range of the marginal pose or not. We can make a criterion for deciding it as the following:

$$f(x,y) = y - \left(\frac{L_y - M_y}{L_x - M_x}\right)x - \left(\frac{L_x M_y - L_y M_x}{L_x - M_x}\right) \tag{10}$$

- Decide if the given input image is right view or left view. The decision criterion of view is obtained from the fact that $\angle LCN$ may be an obtuse angle or an acute angle with respect to direction of view. By applying the second law of cosine in a triangle, $\angle LCN$ can easily be expressed.
- Estimate the pose of the given input image approximately. Assume that the input image is left view and its pose angle is smaller than the marginal pose. Then, our idea to estimate the pose of the input image is originated from the fact that the area of ΔLNM is also linearly changed when the pose is varied from frontal to the marginal pose. If the area of ΔLNM in the generative model with frontal pose is denoted by A_m and the marginal pose of the generative model is denoted by ϕ_m, the pose ϕ of an input image satisfying with the above conditions can be approximately estimated as defined in the following:

$$\phi = \frac{(A_m - A)}{A_m}\phi_m \tag{11}$$

where A is equal to the area of ΔLNM in the input image.

4 Fitting the 3D Model to a 2D Image

Shape and texture parameters of the generative 3D model are estimated by fitting it to a given input face. This is performed iteratively as close as possible to the input face. Fitting algorithms, called stochastic Newton optimization (SNO) and inverse compositional image alignment (ICIA) [5] were utilized in [3] and [4], respectively. It is generally addressed that SNO is more accurate but computationally expensive and ICIA is less accurate but more efficient in computation time [4].

We also explore the ICIA algorithm as a fitting method to guarantee the computational efficiency. When an input image is selected, the initial coefficients of shape and texture are set to zero and the projection parameters are appropriately decided by the pose approximation method introduced in previous section. Then, fitting steps are iterated until convergence to a given threshold value, minimizing the texture difference between the projected model image and the input image. During the fitting process, texture coefficients are updated without an additive algorithm at each iteration. But in case of shape coefficients, their updated values are not acquired with ease because of the nonlinear problem of structure from motion (SFM) [11]. To solve it, we recover the shape coefficients using SVD based global approach [12] after the convergence.

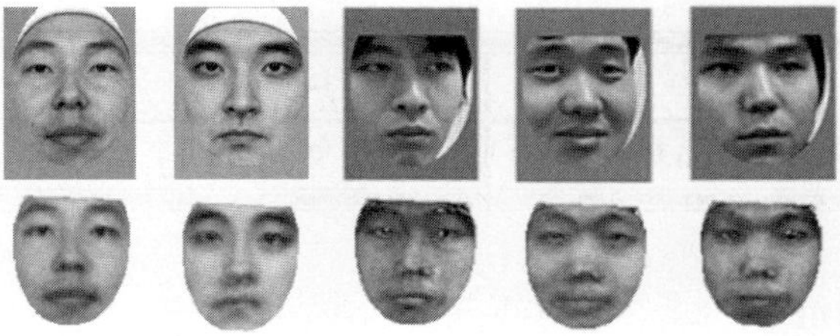

Fig. 4. Fitting results

5 Experimental Results

We evaluate our face recognition system based on a 3D model generated using proposed representation algorithm and pose approximation method in identification scenario [13]. For this, we constructed two databases from the Korean. One is composed of 3D face scans collected by a Geometrix Facevision 200, which is a stereo-camera based capturing device offering a 3D face scan including approximately 30,000 ~ 40,000 vertices and corresponding 2D texture image, the other is composed of 2D face images acquired from a general web camera. The data in the former have only frontal pose, therefore, are used for model generation and a few experiments with respect to the frontal poses. On the contrary, the latter was collected from 21 subjects during 3 sessions and contains 63 images with frontal pose and 51 images with profile pose ranged from 15°to 45°.

The experimental results to frontal and profile faces are depicted in Table 1 and 2. They report average recognition rate with rank 1 and fitting time. In both experiments, we utilized the L2 norm as a distance metric [13] and applied 50% as basis selection rate in texture and shape space.

The aim of the first experiment is to verify the influences of shape and texture parameters used as an identity parameter with respect to the system performance. Total 20 trials were done by randomly selecting 21 out of 62 subjects in 3D face database a trial. From the report of Table 1, we could find that shape parameter does not have great effects on system performance and model fitting time to only texture parameter is more efficient than to both shape and texture parameters on 1.73GHz Pentium-M and 1GB RAM. Also, we conducted the tests on 2D database containing the frontal and profile face images captured by a web camera. In this test, we selected 21 images and 51 images as probe set for frontal and profile pose, respectively.

Table 1. Recognition accuracy with rank 1 to frontal faces in 3D face database

	Only Texture	Texture & Shape
Average Recognition Rate (%)	92.1	93.3
Average Fitting Time (s)	0.9	5.6

Table 2. Recognition accuracy with rank 1 to frontal and profile faces in 2D face database

	Frontal	Profile
Average Recognition Rate (%)	89.9	83.2

6 Conclusion

A 3D model-based face recognition system was presented in this paper. A Korean 3D face model was generated from 100 3D face data. We introduced a method reducing and being identical with the number of vertex points and polygons constituting 3D shape for face representation. Practically, our 3D face model was represented with 4014 vertex points and 7980 polygons.

In the mean time, ICIA algorithm was adopted to fit the model to an input image. Especially, to initialize the fitting parameter, we proposed pose approximation method based on a marginal pose and the topology of some key features.

We found some facts from the experiments on the 3D and 2D databases. First, the shape parameters as identity parameter did not meaningfully improve the system performance in spite of increased computation time. Second, the experimental results showed that 3D model based face recognition system using the proposed representation method was further more efficient in computation time than the works in [4] even if it is somewhat less accurate. Lastly, we confirmed that in some measure

In future, we will plan to research solutions on the illumination problem, which is one of the most important issues in face recognition.

Acknowledgement. This research was performed for the Promotion and Support Program of Strategic Industry Innovation Cluster, one of the Collaboration Programs for Industry, Academy and Research Institute funded by City of Seoul, Korea.

References

1. Papatheodorou, T., Rueckert, D.: Evaluation of 3D Face Recognition Using Registration and PCA. In: Kanade, T., Jain, A., Ratha, N.K. (eds.) AVBPA 2005. LNCS, vol. 3546, pp. 997–1009. Springer, Heidelberg (2005)
2. Blanz, V., Vetter, T.: A Morphable Model for the Synthesis of 3D Faces. In: Computer Graphics, Annual Conference Series(SIGGRAPH), pp. 187–194 (1999)
3. Blanz, V., Vetter, T.: Face Recognition Based on Fitting a 3D Morphable Model. IEEE Transactions on Pattern Analysis and Machine Intelligence 25(9), 1063–1074 (2003)
4. Romdhani, S., Vetter, T.: Efficient, Robust and Accurate Fitting of a 3D Morphable Model. In: IEEE International Conference on Computer Vision (2003)
5. Baker, S., Matthews, I.: Equivalence and Efficiency of Image Alignment Algorithms. In: CVPR (2001)
6. Horn, B.K.P., Hilden, H.M., Negahdaripour, S.: Closed-Form Solution of Absolute Orientation Using Orthonormal Matrices. Journal of the Optical Society of America A 5, 1127–1135 (1988)
7. Besl, P.J., Mckay, N.D.: A Method for Registration of 3D Shapes. IEEE Transactions on Pattern Analysis and Machine Intelligence 14(2), 239–256 (1992)
8. Lu, X., Jain, A., Colbry, D.: Matching 2.5D Face Scans to 3D Models. IEEE Transactions on Pattern Analysis and Machine Intelligence 28(1), 31–43 (2006)
9. Turk, M., Pentland, A.: Eigenfaces for recognition. J. Cognitive Neuroscience 3, 71–86 (1991)
10. Vetter, T., Poggio, T.: Linear Object Classes and Image Synthesis from a Single Example Image. IEEE Transactions on Pattern Analysis and machine Intelligence 19(7), 733–742 (1997)
11. Bascle, B., Blake, A.: Separability of pose and expression in facial tracking and animation. In: Sixth International Conference on Computer Vision, pp. 323–328 (1998)
12. Romdhani, S., Canterakis, N., Vetter, T.: Selective vs. Global Recovery of Rigid and Non-rigid Motion. Technical report, CS Dept., Univ. of Basel (2003)
13. Moon, H., Phillips, P.: Computational and Performance Aspects of PCA-Based Face-Recognition Algorithms. Perception. 30, 303–321 (2001)

The Use of Interactive Visual Metaphors to Enhance Group Discussions Using Mobile Devices

John McGinn[1], Rich Picking[1], Liz Picking[2], and Vic Grout[1]

[1] School of Computing and Communications Technology, NEWI, University of Wales, Wrexham LL11 2AW, Wales, UK
[2] School of Health, Social Care and Sport & Exercise Sciences, NEWI, University of Wales, Wrexham LL11 2AW, Wales, UK
{j.mcginn,r.picking,l.picking,v.grout}@newi.ac.uk

Abstract. In this paper, we consider the problems of group discussions and collaborative decision-making, where one or more of the participants are using restrictive interfaces such as mobile phones or PDAs. We suggest possible solutions to some of these problems and present MAVis (Mobile Argumentation Visualizer), a web-based interface built upon upon a balance-beam visual metaphor. We report on user experiences of interacting with the visual metaphor, and on the challenges of transferring this to a multi-user environment supporting mobile devices.

Keywords: m-learning, collaborative working, decision-making, wicked problems, visual metaphors.

1 Introduction

In collaborative decision-making scenarios, where decisions are based on shared understanding through discussion, most, if not all problems encountered can be defined as *wicked problems* [1].

According to Conklin [2], wicked problems are intrinsically situated in socially complex settings. He summarizes their characteristics as follows:

- You don't understand the problem until you have developed a solution;
- Wicked problems have no stopping rule;
- Solutions to wicked problems are not right or wrong;
- Every wicked problem is essentially unique and novel;
- Every solution to a wicked problem is a "one-shot operation";
- Wicked problems have no given alternative solutions.

In this paper, we present an approach to the consideration of wicked problems in specific scenarios with m-learning characteristics. Example application areas in these scenarios include:

- Students on e-learning courses who need to communicate with fellow course members in remote or field locations;
- Students on traditional courses engaged in group activities;

C. Stephanidis (Ed.): Universal Access in HCI, Part II, HCII 2007, LNCS 4555, pp. 952–960, 2007.

- Students in work placements (e.g. medical, nursing and social work) who will be required to engage in multidisciplinary groups but may not be co-located;
- Collaboration between students in different countries and from different cultures.

It is self-evident that effective group and team working are essential transferable skills for students to acquire to enhance their employability and prepare them for post-University life. Current trends in the increasing internationalization and demographic diversity of Higher Education students however, present challenges for educators to preserve high-level critical thinking and reflective practice skills – both of which are enhanced by discussion, consultation and expert advice.

We have developed a suite of collaborative discussion tools, which use a simple visual metaphor to enhance group discussions [3, 4]. In this paper, we present the mobile version of this suite of tools, which we have called MAVis (Mobile Argumentation Visualizer).

We describe the background and history of MAVis, and the rationale for the visual metaphor we use. We then report our experiences of MAVis in an m-learning setting, and conclude with a reflection on this experience and a proposal for further work.

2 Background

By far the most common of all mobile devices is the telephone. The two most common communication channels utilized by mobile phone users are voice and SMS text messaging. In m-learning scenarios, we argue that there are inherent problems with relying on these channels alone, namely:

Voice –

- Requires temporal concurrency;
- Only one participant can contribute at a time;
- Remembering accurately what is said and by whom;
- Difficulty with accents;
- There is usually no auditable record;
- Problems for the hard of hearing.

Text -

- Requires manual dexterity;
- Multiple threads are difficult to track;
- Restricted real estate limits the text that can be viewed without scrolling;
- It is difficult to group related concepts;
- Like voice, it relies upon a common understanding of what language actually means.

We argue that in addition to these issues, neither channel lends itself very well to remote collaboration, because there is usually a lack of structure to the discussion without the physical presence of a chairperson to maintain order and to remind everyone of the objectives.

The increasing use of sophisticated mobile telephones and PDAs (Personal Digital Assistants) and the advance of the network infrastructure that supports them, present developers with opportunities to use more sophisticated visual channels in m-learning

[5, 6]. However, with these opportunities come the challenge of providing users with a valuable experience, given the constraints of mobile device size [7].

Our solution is to use a simple visual metaphor, known linguistically as the *argument-as-balance* metaphor [8], which we argue is easy to use, intuitive and efficient on screen real-estate. We now describe the rationale and history of our experience with this metaphorical approach in the context of collaborative discussion.

2.1 Rationale

The concept of linguistic metaphor is well-known in the fields of prose and poetry. For example, Lakoff and Johnson [8] describe the conceptual metaphor of *argument-as-war* with the following expressions:

Your claims are *indefensible*.
He *attacked every weak point* in my argument.
His criticisms were *right on target*.
I *demolished* his argument.
I never *won* an argument with him.
You disagree? Okay, *shoot*!
If you use that *strategy*, he'll *wipe you out*.
He *shot down* all of my arguments.

Lakoff and Johnson also describe the *argument-as-building* metaphor (if you don't *support* your argument with *solid* facts, the whole thing will *collapse*), the *argument-as-container* metaphor (that argument *has holes in it*), and the *argument-as-journey* metaphor (you're *going around in circles).*

Another common *argument-as* linguistic metaphor is the *argument-as-balance* metaphor, where rational argument is understood as a twin-pan balance of weights, the weight on each side representing the strength of counter arguments, for example: the debater *built up a weighty* argument; the jury *weighed* the merits of both sides; more facts might *tip the scale* [9].

In CSCW (computer-supported collaborative work), the visual metaphor has been identified by Eppler [10] as useful to organize content meaningfully and to present an overall message. Eppler also identifies visual metaphors in this context as being easy to use, easy to remember, and easy to understand. Eppler compares visual metaphors with concept maps, mind maps and conceptual diagrams. He concludes that for collaborative working, a combination of these techniques can be used for the greatest effect. However, for mobile devices, we argue that the physical limitations of the hardware do not support this approach. Certainly, the other techniques use much more screen space, and there are dangers of users being confused if they cannot easily view potentially complex diagrams and maps. The visual metaphor provides a better overview, as Eppler states (p.207):

"In order to summarize the discussion on a topic in a memorable and insightful way, a rich visual metaphor is used that positions all discussed items within an appealing and self-explanatory metaphoric structure."

Consequently, for collaborative m-learning applications, we have progressed with the visual metaphor, which we originally proposed for more generalized environments [3, 4].

2.2 History

On analysis of the alternative metaphorical interpretations of argumentation, we developed a tool which uses the argument-as-balance metaphor [3]. The tool is called DAVE (Decision and Argumentation Visualization Explorer). Developed in Macromedia Flash, it runs in a web browser or as a standalone application. It was originally developed to provide visual and intuitive support for presenting an argument, for communicating advice, and for assessing risk. Figure 1 shows an illustration of a patient's risk of contracting coronary heart disease, based on a number of medical factors.

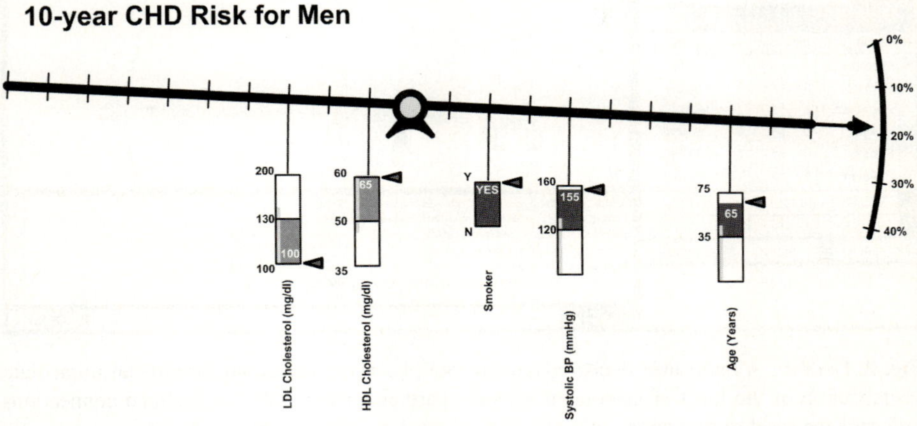

Fig. 1. DAVE A decision-support tool [3]. The contribution of *n* factors *(cf)* is the product of its magnitude and its importance *(I)* and *m* ameliorating factors *(af)* produce a contraindication in the same way. Thus: total indication = $\sum_{i=1}^{n} cf_i I_i - \sum_{i=1}^{m} af_i I_i$.

DAVIE (Decision and Argumentation Visualization International Explorer) was developed as an extension to DAVE [4]. It uses multiple instantiations of the central balance component of DAVE, which can be manipulated independently by participants. Our aim was to discover if it was possible to help a group develop a composite mental model of a problem area by using interactive graphical representations that show how each member of the group arrived at their stated opinions.

Conceived as a tool to support decision-making in multi-disciplinary teams across international and cultural boundaries, it has been useful as an analytical tool in conflict resolution situations and in training exercises where groups need to develop common conceptual maps. Each user selects and manipulates the factors in a given decision-making or problem scenario. The balance components are then collated in a stack formation into a single view which can be shared over the Internet. Correlation between factors on each balance is represented by connections from each balance component (Figure 2). DAVIE shows, for each member of a team, the relative importance that they attach to the various factors involved in reaching their own considered positions. Group members can then compare their own positions with those of other individual members or an average of the entire group. The intention is that team members can easily see how other people reach the opinions that they hold (or more precisely, how they justify them) in order that discussion can be focused towards resolving areas of fundamental difference.

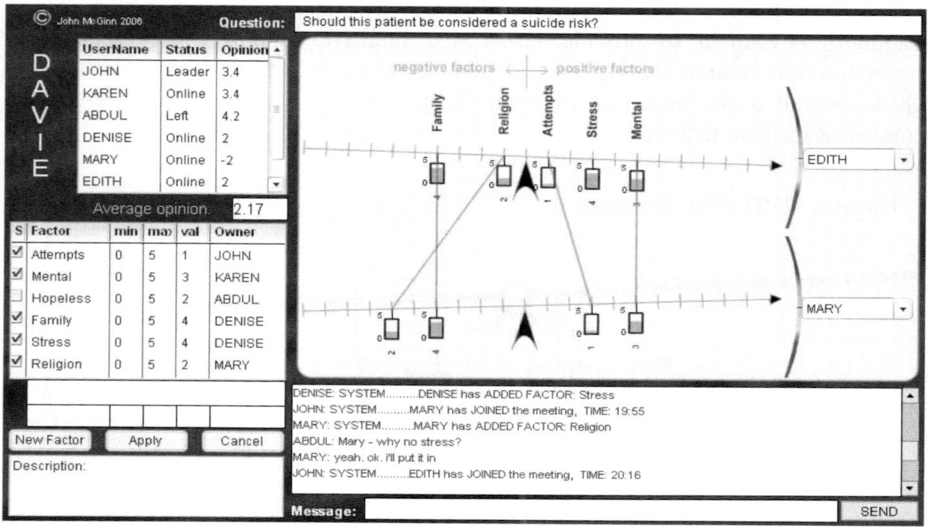

Fig. 2. DAVIE. A multi-user decision-support tool [4]. The connections provide an immediate visualization of the level of agreement between partners. The number of inclined connections indicates the level of disagreement between partners. It is also possible to identify partners who agree on the overall decision but for completely different reasons.

DAVIE can be used in a collaborative situation, where partners are given the opportunity to moderate and mediate the decision-making factors. Once a collective view has been reached, which may or may not result in total agreement, DAVIE can be used to complement discussion and act as an aide-memoire in conflict-resolution scenarios.

In the example in figure 2, students take on the roles of a multidisciplinary team assessing the suicide risk of a client. Students suggest factors for or against the proposition and these factors are then "owned" by appropriate members of the team. For example, Denise is playing the role of a social worker, so she is responsible for using her professional judgement to attach a value to the factors of *Family Support* and *Stress*. Once all of the factors are set out, each team member chooses which factors they consider to be significant and places them on the beam in positions that correspond to their perceived importance. Students are thus able to explore and determine areas of commonality and difference in order that they can better understand their own opinions and the cognitive models of the other participants.

There are two versions of DAVIE. The first version, DAVIEw, is used in a group or classroom situation. The application is presented with a data projector or an interactive whiteboard. It has been tested with groups of pre-registered Nursing students considering questions of medical intervention. Feedback from the students indicated that most of them found the visualization to be helpful or very helpful, although a minority commented that reducing life or death decisions to numbers or graphics was an inappropriate trivialization. This was not a view shared by professional practitioners to whom the application has since been presented.

We have also developed a remote version of the software, DAVIEr, which has been used by Computer Science students in the study of computer ethics. In this scenario, the students worked independently at their own machines but collaborated through a chat server. Again feedback was positive and students found the software useful after they were trained to use it. As in most exercises involving unstructured communication, the chat element of the application resulted in a large amount of trivial and irrelevant posting. However, the existence of a graphic that represents previously considered views allows a moderator to quickly refocus the discussion in a way that is difficult with a text-only interface.

3 MAVis

To support m-learning, we have developed a version of DAVIEr called MAVis (Mobile Argumentation Visualizer). It is web-based, written in Macromedia Flash and

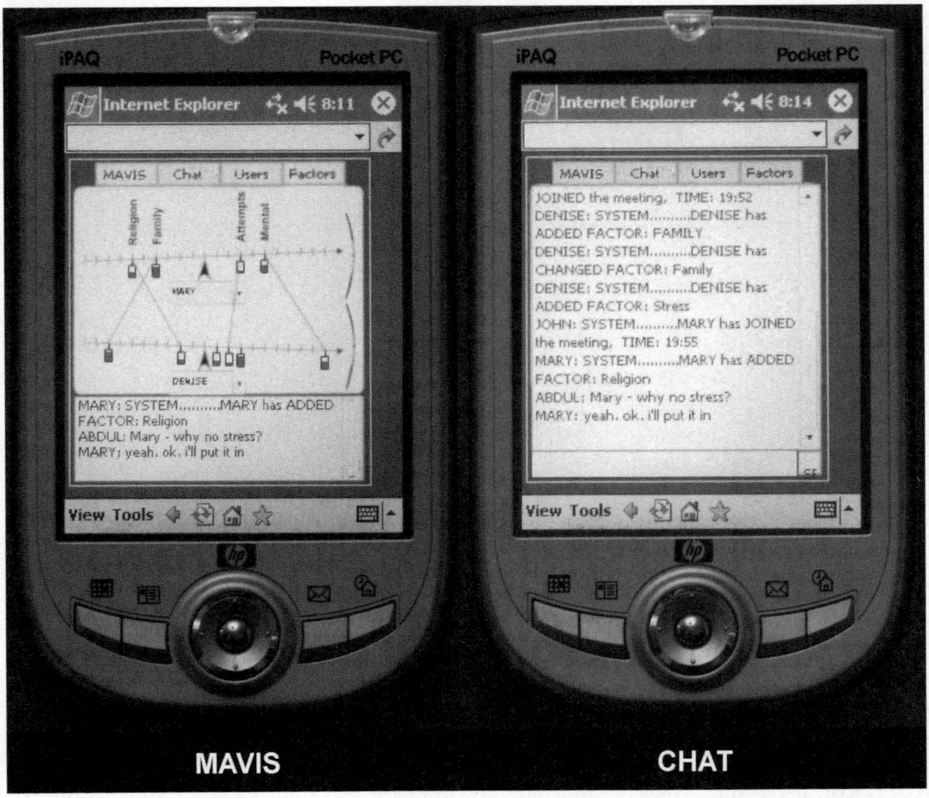

Fig. 3a. left) the main MAVis screen shows the interactive visual representations of the users' opinions and compares them to any other user. This screen also has a reduced text output panel so that the user can track incoming messages from other participants. **right)** the CHAT screen is a basic messaging client. This has an enlarged text output panel and a text input field.

operates through an XML socket server. MAVis and DAVIEr share the same messaging system and are therefore completely compatible. Almost all of the code is common. Messaging was facilitated in the development of the application through the XML socket server. MAVis incorporates the balance-beam visual metaphor, a chat client, a user status list, and a factors editor. Each feature is accessed via a series of tabs at the top of the user screen (figures 3a and 3b).

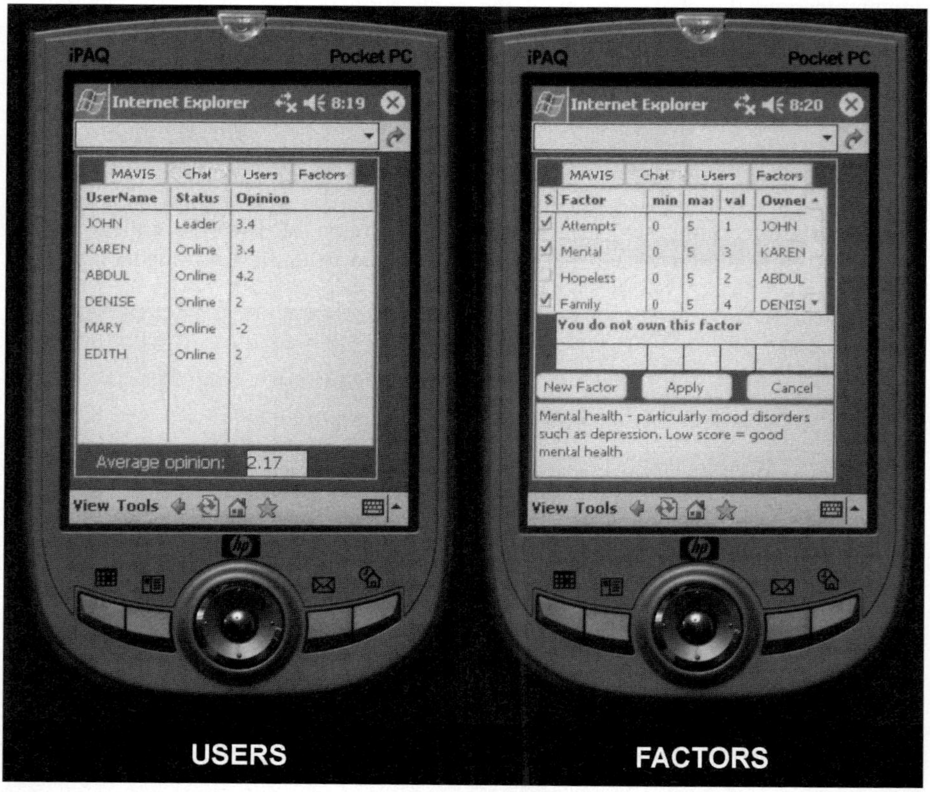

Fig. 3b. left) the USERS screen lists all of the participants, notes their status and displays a numerical representation of their opinions. **right)** the FACTORS screen lists all the factors that are being considered by everyone, together with their range and values. The screen also permits a user to add a new factor or edit one that they own. They can see descriptions of factors owned by other users but not edit them.

4 Discussion

We have used the MAVis interface as a client in Internet Explorer using the Macromedia FlashPlayer 7 plug-in in devices running Microsoft Pocket PC operating system. It is not yet possible for the MAVis device to be used by the moderator of a session because it lacks some of the necessary functionality, particularly the ability to save and restore sessions. However, users of MAVis have been able to engage fully with discussions being carried out between workstation devices. The main problem is one of speed. The application runs very slowly on a mobile device. It is slow to load over a wireless connection (around 120kB) and slow to operate because of the limited processing power and memory of the mobile device. The interface itself, however, works well.

Flash has proved to be very capable for the rapid development of MAVis and we believe that the use of visual metaphors to enhance text-based discussions has been sufficiently demonstrated to warrant further development of the application. The use of tabbed screens to switch between functional areas is simple and effective. The application needs to work much faster though to match the ease of use observed on the workstation client. We need to determine whether an alternative presentation such as popups for supplementary information would generate a better user experience.

5 Conclusion and Further Work

We have shown that visual metaphors can enhance discussions of wicked problems between remote parties. We have also demonstrated that this is possible on the restricted interfaces of current mobile devices.

More work needs to be done to determine whether response rates can be improved using Flash, or whether the application needs to be rewritten in a different language. We also need to test the application with other platforms and consider security issues.

Another avenue is to use the visual metaphors to enhance voice communication. This would certainly make the interface simpler but would severely limit the number of concurrent users.

Acknowledgments. Many thanks to Colin Moock (http://www.moock.org/unity) for his kind permission to use the UNITY 2 XML socket server for this project.

References

1. Rittel, H., Webber, M.: Dilemmas in a General Theory of Planning. In: Policy Sciences, vol. 4, pp. 155–169. Elsevier Scientific Publishing Company, Amsterdam (1973)
2. Conklin, J.: Dialogue Mapping: Building Shared Understanding of Wicked Problems. John Wiley, Chichester (2006)
3. McGinn, J., Picking, R.: The Argumentation-as Metaphor in Decision-making Visualization. In: 7th International Information Visualization Conference, London (2003)
4. McGinn, J., Picking, R., Mansour, F., Urena, R.: Computer-Aided International Decision-Making Using an As-Balance Metaphor. In: Proceedings of CSSI International Conference System Integration in Integrated Europe (ISIE), Liberec (2004)
5. E-marketer: Worldwide Mobile Connections to Reach Three Billion This Year. (February 1, 2007). Accessed (February 12th, 2007) http://www.emarketer.com
6. Datamonitor: Education Technology - Expanding Accessibility to Technology in Higher Education. (October 4, 2006) Accessed (February 12th, 2007) http://www.datamonitor.com

7. Bielawski, L., Matcalf, D.: Blended eLearning: Integrating Knowledge, Performance Support and Online Learning. HRD Press (2003)
8. Lakoff, G., Johnson, M.: Metaphors We Live By. University of Chicago Press, Chicago (1980)
9. Johnson, M.: The Body in the Mind. University of Chicago Press, Chicago (1987)
10. Eppler, M.J.: A Comparison Between Concept Maps, Mind Maps, Conceptual Diagrams, and Visual Metaphors as Complementary Tools for Knowledge Construction and Sharing. In: Information Visualization, vol. 5, pp. 202–210. Palgrave Macmillan, Oxford (2006)

An Accessible and Usable Soft Keyboard

Alexandros Mourouzis[1], Evangelos Boutsakis[1], Stavroula Ntoa[1], Margherita Antona[1], and Constantine Stephanidis[1,2]

[1] Foundation for Research and Technology – Hellas (FORTH), Institute of Computer Science, Heraklion, GR-70013, Greece
{mourouzi,boutsak,stant,antona,cs}@ics.forth.gr
[2] University of Crete, Department of Computer Science

Abstract. *AUK* is a 3x3 multi-tier onscreen keyboard. It supports various entry modes, including 1 to 10-key and joystick modes, allowing text entry with a remarkable range of devices. This paper presents the menu structure of *AUK*, the alternative entry modes, and several layouts for novice, moderate and expert users. The potential of *AUK*, as a text entry solution both for disabled and able-bodied users, is discussed. Overall, the work presented here is considered as a contribution to Universal Access and towards *ambient text entry*.

Keywords: Text entry, soft keyboard, Universal Access, Ambient Intelligence.

1 Introduction

Manual text entry, as the human process of communicating text to computer-based systems, is, in essence, an alternative way of *writing*. The main difference is that, in text entry, the storage medium is a computer memory rather than paper. Naturally, the medium itself poses certain limitations. Computers require users to select among a set of encoded characters[1], whereas paper, as a flat surface, implies the use of 2D symbols. However, the new medium brought along new options that changed writing forever. For instance, it enabled authors to act on transcribed texts without imposing restrictions for modifications, and to copy-and-paste text sections easily.

In these terms, text entry is merely a selection procedure [1], and can be defined as follows (adapted from [2]): *T(i, C, M)* is the human process of selecting from *a set of encoded characters C*[2] and *modifying options M* (backspace, delete, etc.), by means of a total number *i* of discrete and detectable *user actions* (e.g., tap a key).

According to [3], there have been two major waves of research on text entry, focussing on mainstream desktop computers and on mobile devices respectively. However, today a number of reasons call for practical solutions for further widening the potential user base and context of use of text entry systems. Such reasons include the need for inclusion into the information society [4] and the emergence of ambient intelligence environments [5]. This paper presents *AUK*, a multi-device soft keyboard for accessible, usable and efficient text entry across multiple contexts of use.

[1] Graphemes, symbols, etc., or a set of encoded strings of characters, i.e., words or sentences.
[2] E.g., the 95 printable ASCII characters based on English, numbered 32-126.

C. Stephanidis (Ed.): Universal Access in HCI, Part II, HCII 2007, LNCS 4555, pp. 961–970, 2007.

2 Background

Typing, originally introduced by mechanical typewriters, has been a diachronic entry method since the early emergence of computers and command line interfaces. In this method, there is a correspondence between characters and a set of keys spread across a device. Keyboards with different numbers of keys exist, but the 101-keys keyboard is predominant. In these terms, typing can be considered a *T(i, C, M)*, where *i* equals 101+, *C* includes 95+ characters[2], and *M* includes numerous options for modifying text. Such options are mainly of two types: navigation / selection (back, forward, home, select all, etc.) and modifying / processing functions (delete, backspace, copy-paste, etc.). Clearly, with a 101+ keys keyboard, *C* and *M* together exceed the number of input controls (i.e., of keys), thus *synchronous and asynchronous key combinations* (e.g., though the SHIFT and CAPS LOCK key) are employed to allow associating more than one character (or modifying option) to a single key.

With the emergence of graphical interfaces, menu-based text entry was introduced as a supplement of typing, allowing users to enter additional characters[3] not found on the keyboard through menus. In this *T(i, C, M)* case, if navigation across a characters set is made through the keys back, forward, down, up, and enter, *i* equals 5, *C* includes, for example, 256 characters[4], and *M* is an empty set. Such menus can be perceived as a primitive form of *soft* or *onscreen keyboards*. These are features of a program or operating system that generate a graphical keyboard operated through mouse, stylus, etc. Soft keyboards are particularly useful in two cases: (a) for making text entry accessible to people with manual dexterities - e.g., it can be combined with scanning techniques [6] and allow operation through few special switches; (b) for removing keypads from mobile devices and reducing their physical size – e.g., characters can be selected through tapping on a touch display. In both cases, soft keyboards are usually a representation of a full-size QWERTY keyboard.

With the emergence of mobile devices, typing and menu-based methods were combined to allow text entry through few-keys [3]. The success of SMS messaging on mobile phones raised the attention on 12-key keypads, with letters A-Z traditionally encoded on eight keys[5]. A number of 12-key entry methods exist so that more than one letters can be assigned to each key [7], but the most common are *multi-tap* and *dictionary-based disambiguation*[6] (for descriptions see [8, 9]).

Finally, other widely explored entry techniques include *speech*, *handwriting* or *sign language recognition* [1, 3, 9] and *virtual keyboards*[7] [10]. These techniques, up today, have failed to enter mainstream technologies, mainly because they do not reach acceptable levels of *speed* and *accuracy*, two primary *performance metrics* for text entry [3]. For details on text entry issues and methods, see [1, 3, 8, 9, and 11].

---

[3] Over the years, the volume of encoded characters increased dramatically and, ultimately, included characters from numerous writing systems around the world.

[4] From ISO 8859-1 (the most popular encoding in the Western world with 256 characters).

[5] See ITU E.161 international recommendation for telephone keypads at http://www.itu.int.

[6] The most common application is *T9* by Tegic Communications (http://www.t9.com).

[7] Although the term virtual keyboards (VKs) is often used interchangeably with soft keyboards, VKs are defined as touch-typing keyboards that do not have physical manifestation of the sensing areas [10], and thus should be perceived as different from onscreen keyboards.

3 The *AUK* Concept

The work presented here was originally motivated from previous experiences with scanning techniques for users with limited motor functionality of upper limbs. The evaluation of an accessible Web browser [12], which included a QWERTY-like soft keyboard operated via three special switches, indicated frustrating rates of *words per minute* (wpm)[8]. To overcome this barrier, the idea was put forward to use the layouts and current practices in mobile phones and implement a 12-key soft keyboard for offering movement minimisation and high learnability thanks to familiarity. Such a keyboard was anticipated to allow entry with various devices for typing (i.e., keypads), 2D indication and selection (e.g., a mouse), or simple selection (e.g., a single switch) if a scanning technique is built in. Then, having in mind that the letters A-Z on a 12-key keypad are typically encoded on eight keys, an 8-direction method[9] was explored for text entry also by means of a joystick: In that case, if one takes into account the joystick's default state (centre), there are 9 possible positions that can be mapped to a 3x3 grid, which leads us to the basic concept of *AUK*. That is, a multi-tier 3x3 menu system, consisting of a primary menu, where eight cells are used for entering letters and one cell is reserved for entering into additional, again 3x3, menus that accommodate extra characters and options.

Initially, letters were placed alphabetically, similarly to phone keypads (see Fig.1), and the *multi-tap* technique was considered for character disambiguation, employing *system timeout* to segment consecutive letters on the same key. The main benefit of such an approach is clear: familiarity. However, there are also some disadvantages recorded: (a) timeouts slow down users; (b) with an alphabetic layout, some frequent letters require more keystrokes than some less frequently needed letters [1]. Thus, as for people with reduced manual dexterity movement minimisation is a primary requirement, less *keystrokes per character* (KSPC [8]) were further pursued.

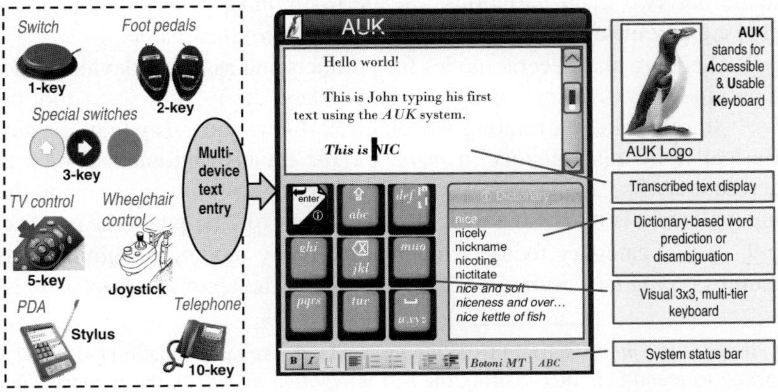

Fig. 1. Overview of *AUK*[10] soft keyboard for multi-device text entry (*stand-alone version*)

[8] The main reason is that the QWERTY layout has been designed for ten-fingers typing and not for linear or tree-based navigation as in scanning techniques.

[9] With one direction N, E, S, W, NE, ES, SW, WN used for each of the eight keys.

[10] About the *AUK* logo: According to wikipedia.com, auks are birds that look like, but aren't penguins; they are considered as a product of "*moderate convergent evolution*".

In summary, *AUK* supports (a) several different entry modes (1 to10-key, and joystick), rendering it appropriate for the widest possible range of input devices; (b) various layout configurations for different performance levels; and (c) the potential to integrate additional techniques, such as *text prediction* and *dictionary-based* or *prefix-based disambiguation*, as these ensure even lower KSPC values [3, 8, 10].

4 A Multi-tier 3x3 Menu Structure

AUK is similar to a multi-tier 3x3 menu system. Each 3x3 grid has eight virtual *character keys* and a *menu key* for entering or exiting alternative menus. Five *basic menus* can be interchanged sequentially[11] (Fig. 2). In the *primary menu* (1), the letters A-Z, the apostrophe, SPACE (SP), BACK (BK), and SHIFT (SH)[12] are placed on the character keys, and the menu key is used for *timeout kill*, swapping to menu (2), or entering a *linear menu* (D) for navigations, e.g., within a *word prediction list*[13]. Additionally, there are five *secondary menus*: *numerals* (6), *special characters* (7), *brackets* (8), *formatting options* (9), and *numeric operators* (10). Finally, menu (5) has a cell for selecting extra characters through menu (D), and an empty cell to allow space for adding new menus as necessary, thus rendering the structure extensible.

5 Entry Modes and Menu Layouts

The presented menu structure can be employed with various input methods. In particular, given *T(i, C, M)*, *AUK* supports text entry for:

- *i=9*. This is the basic mode of *AUK*, in which there is a correspondence between the nine *AUK* menu options (see Fig. 2) and nine keys (e.g., phone keypads). This mode has two main variations: (a) the *0-key mode* for *command without click* [15] e.g., by means of eye-tracking; and (b) the *joystick mode*.
- i<9. There are also several modes for products and assistive devices that have less than nine 'keys': *1-key*[14] (single switch or key, etc.); *2-key* (e.g., foot pedals); *3-key*[15] (three switches, rotating wheel, etc.); *4-key*; and *5-key* (e.g., pager keypad). Basically, in this category, a *menu cursor* travels, automatically or manually, across each 3x3 menu, always starting from a *home position*. Once the desired input element is reached, a *select button* is used for "tapping" the onscreen key.
- i>9. In this category focus is mainly on 10-key modes for number pads or 10-thumbs typing (see section 8). In the first case, the tenth key (*zero key*) is used for

---

[11] E.g., in the *9-key mode,* starting from the menu (1), the key combination 1-1-1-1-1 will result returning to menu (1), after visiting the *text navigation menu* (2), the *punctuation menu* (3), the *mode menu* (4), and the *extend menu* (5). If the user selects any *character key* in one of these menus, then the menu key changes to the *exit key* for returning directly to (1).

[12] SP, BK, and SH are very common [14]; in *AUK*, SP, being the most common key, is always the most easy to reach; the apostrophe, indicates missing letters, and thus is included here.

[13] If *dictionary-based* disambiguation is activated, then a list of alternative words is displayed.

[14] An automatic scanning technique is employed in this case.

[15] Two methods are used for the *3-key mode*: the *date stamp method* [see 985], and one proposed for *AUK*, through the buttons DOWN, RIGHT and SELECT, as this provides less KSPC.

timeout kill (single tap) and for the SH modifier (hold down). A second approach, mainly for 10-thumbs-typing, is to place the SP key alone, and use the tenth key for timeout kill (first tap) and BK (additional taps). Furthermore, in this second case, the space key may also be used for the CTRL modifier (hold down) and the tenth key for SH, whereas SH+SP is for entering menu (2) - see Fig. 4.

Indicatively, the arrangement of keys for the 3-, 9-, 10-key and joystick modes are presented in Fig. 3, along with the indicative entry scenarios presented in Table 1.

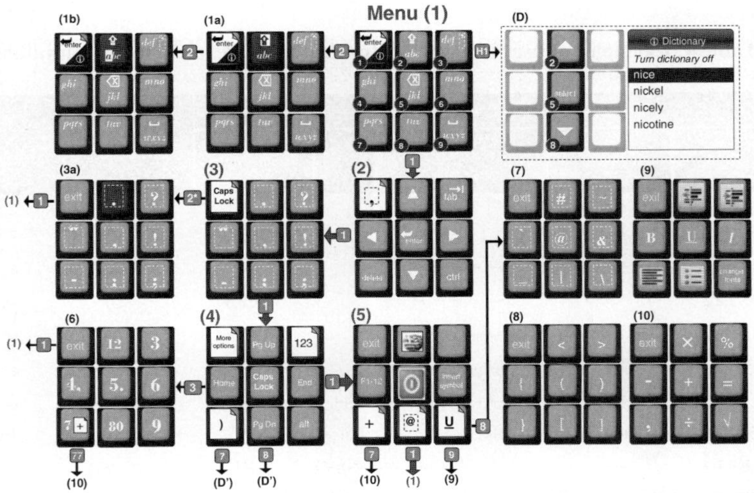

Fig. 2. The basic menu structure of *AUK* (for *i*=9)

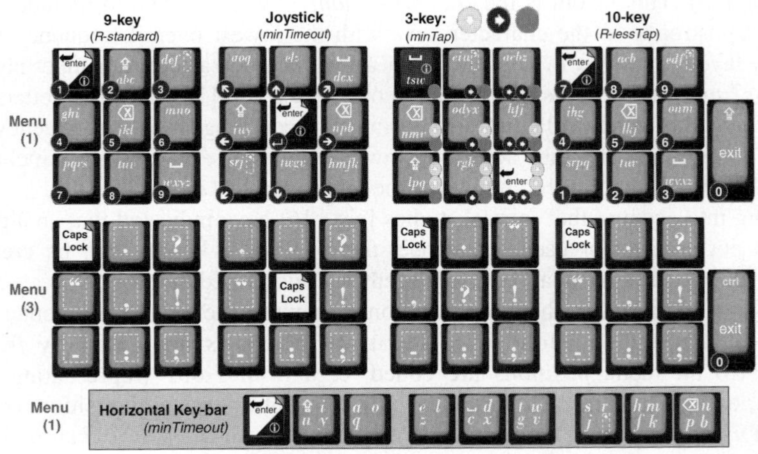

Fig. 3. Keys arrangement for modes 3-, 9-, 10-key and joystick. The bottom part shows the AUK menu as a horizontal bar for PDAs (see section 6).

6 Layouts for Novice, Moderate and Expert Performance

A significant amount of research has been conducted on 12-key text entry methods for mobile phones. Most efforts aim at achieving the upper limits of typing speed with a particular design, often at the expenses of an acceptable experience for novice users [3]. Yet, the ease of use for first-time users is critical for the success of any method. For this purpose, in addition to the entry mode described above, different A-Z letters layouts have been designed for novice, moderate and expert users. The following are layouts for multi-tap and involve the use of system timeout.

Table 1. Examples of user input, resulting transcribed text and menu transitions

User Input (with layouts in Fig. 3)				**Menus onscreen**‡	**Text** (transcribed)
9-key (*R-stan*)	Joystick (*minTout*)	3-key (*minTap*)	10-key (R-Lesstap)		
1	↗	↵	3	(1)	␣_
2,3	↵←,↑	↓,↓,↵,→,↵	0+9	(1)	E_
3,3,4,4,4	↑,←	→,↵,→,↵,↵	9,4	(1)	ei_
2,2,1,2,2,2	↖,↗,↗,↗	→,→,↵,→,→,↵,↵	8,0,8,8	(1)	ac_
3,3,8	↑,↓	→,↵,T, ↵,↵	9,2	(1)	et
3,3,9	↑,↗	→,↵,T, ↵	9,3	(1)	e␣_
3,3,1,1,1,2	↑,↵,↵,↵	→,↵,↓,↓,→,→,↵,↵,→,↵	9,7,7,2	(1>2>3>1)	e._
1+5	H↵,↵	H↵,→	1+5	(1>D>1)	*1st word*␣_
1,1,9,7,7,7,7	↵,↵,↘,↙	↓,↓,→,→,↵,→,↵,↵,↵,↵,↵	7,0+1	(1>2>1)	(ctrl+s)

T: system timeout _: text cursor's position ␣: SPACE H↵: Hold down key until system timeout

R-standard. This layout is the *standard phone layout*[5] adapted to include SP, BK, SH and apostrophe to the character keys with the lowest overall frequency (see the example layout for *9-key* in Fig. 3). This is a familiar and easy to remember layout.

R-lessTap. This layout is an adaptation of the *LessTap* [13], in which letters within each key of the standard layout are rearranged according to their frequency in the English Language[16] and thus achieving lower KSPC. *R-LessTap* simply includes the four extra options mentioned above (see the layout for *10-key* in Fig. 3).

Taking into account that several studies [e.g., 16] have indicated that an alphabetic order is not critical for user experience, more effective layouts can be created by disregarding the alphabetical order all together, as described below.

minTap. In this layout, the more common an input is, the easier it is to enter it. This is achieved through the following algorithm: (a) *inputs* are sorted by *frequency* order[17]; (b) all menu *positions* are coded, e.g., from *1-001* (representing the 1st position, on key 1, in menu *1*) up to *n-900* (representing the third position, on key 9, in menu *n*), and sorted by their *reachability* order (e.g., the *number of keystrokes* (KS) required to select each position); (c) the most frequent input (i.e., SP) is assigned to the position with the best reachability, and so on; (d) if an option can be assigned to

[16] E.g., see http://en.wikipedia.org/wiki/Letter_frequencies (used here for KSPC calculations).

[17] Frequency order used here: SP BS eta SH oinshrdlcumwfgypbv apostrophe kjxqz.

more than one positions that share equal reachability values, then it is placed on the key that currently has the lowest overall frequency[18]. An example appears in Fig. 3.

minTimout. In this layout, (a) letters on each key have the lowest possible *digraph frequencies* [11] in an *English text corpus* in order to have consecutive letters on the same key (and thus timeouts) less frequently[19], and (b) the letters on each key are arranged in decreasing *letter frequency* order – thus ensuring less 'taps' for frequent letters (see the layout used for the *joystick mode* in Fig. 3).

R-qwerty. In this layout, characters are grouped and arranged in a way that is related to the QWERTY layout. Such relation can be vision-based (e.g., having the letters "qwer" grouped together on the same key) or motor-based (i.e., with keys that are assigned to a specific finger[20] being grouped together (see Fig. 4).

In modes with i<9, there are three potential versions to be explored: (a) *persistent*, in which the virtual cursor snaps to home position after each character entry; (b) *static*, in which the cursor does not change position after each character entry, and (c) *dynamic*, in which the goal is to minimise the cursor-key distance to the next character (e.g., by moving the cursor on the most probable key, or by automatically rearranging entirely the characters layout). The latter, can also be applied in modes i>=9 for automatically rearranging the letters within each key, so that the first letter is always the most probable. In addition, *AUK* may have the following general modes: (a) multi-tap; (b) dictionary based disambiguation; (c) prefix based disambiguation [18]; (d) with or without *text prediction* [19] displayed though the *menu* (D); (e) synthetic speech output enabled for blind users. Finally, the following display options have been considered: (a) 3x3 keypad; (b) vertical or horizontal bar (e.g., for PDAs – see Fig. 3); and (c) cursor view (e.g., see Fig. 4).

7 Discussion: *Universal Access* to Text Entry

The proposed 3x3 structure shows a number of benefits. First of all, it complies with the fact that visual search involves "*combination of gestalting the area surrounding the current center of interest –3x3 matrix of letters– and using linear search ... as a back up strategy*" [17]. Yet, this structure offers access to a large and extensible input set, and thus *AUK* can operate as a stand-alone word processor or even as a plug-in for other applications. Furthermore, it is potentially easy to learn and use for users with different expertise, since: (a) functions can be placed as close to the user expectations, e.g., for improving novice experience [9], or according to their (individual or related) probabilities for expert performance; (b) onscreen visual[21] and aural feedback is provided for character entry and menu transitions; and (c) the backspace key is always the second most reachable option, thus allowing fast *error recovery* [20]. In addition, since *i* <=10, the input device operation can be easily blind, thus rendering *AUK* a *two-FOA* or even a *single-FOA* method[22] [3].

[18] So that frequent options are grouped with the less need ones without dispensing reachability.
[19] According to [1], the most frequent digrams account for over 80% of text in a language.
[20] In expert QWERTY typing each finger is assigned to specific keys.
[21] E.g., selected keys are highlighted (e.g., see (1a) and (1b)).
[22] The *focus of attention* (FOA) can single if AUK is visualised as cursor (see Fig. 4).

Table 2. Indicative performance rates of *AUK*, in comparison to other text entry methods, using a specific sentence that includes very common words in English Language[23]

Transcribed sententece: "As you have all said to her, she was not the one for him." (57 Chars; 14 words (from the 50 most frequent words in English); average word length 3; correlation with English: 0.8921)									
		T(i, C, M)		User actions		System actions		ARPI	
System (Char. layout)	**Method**	i	#C	Total	Mean	Total	Mean	Total	Mean
Desktop (QWERTY)	1- tap	101+	95+	57	1,000	0	0,000	57	1,000
Mobile keypad (standard)	T9	10	72+	60	1,053	0	0,000	60	1,053
AUK, joystick (minTap)	**directional**	**10**	**95+**	**79**	**1,386**	**2**	**0,035**	**81**	**1,421**
AUK, 10-key (R-lessTap)	**multi-tap**	**10**	**95+**	**79**	**1,386**	**4**	**0,070**	**83**	**1,456**
Mobile keypad (standard)	multi-tap	10	72+	116	2,035	4	0,070	120	2,105
AUK, 9-key (R-standard)	**multi-tap**	**9**	**95+**	**125**	**2,193**	**4**	**0,070**	**129**	**2,263**
FORTH Editor, 3-key [12]	manual scanning	3	95+	792	13,895	0	0,000	792	13,895
AUK, 3-key (minTap)	**manual scanning**	**3**	**95+**	**168**	**2,947**	**2**	**0,035**	**170**	**2,982**
Click-N-type	auto-scanning	1	95+	174	3,053	478	8,386	652	11,439
Microsoft On-screen keyboard	auto-scanning	1	95+	232	4,070	564	9,895	796	13,965
FORTH Editor, 1-key [12]	auto-scanning	1	95+	135	2,368	760	13,333	895	15,702
AUK, 1-key (minTap)	**auto-scanning**	**1**	**95+**	**174**	**3,053**	**118**	**2,070**	**292**	**5,123**
#C: length of Character set									

Regarding the potential user performance with various entry modes of the *AUK* system, the total number of *actions required per input* (ARPI[24] - i.e., *user actions*, such as taps, keystrokes or joystick movements, and *system actions*, such as timeouts or scanning intervals) was calculated in typing several sentences and compared to that of other techniques. These early results were very encouraging. In order to allow quick comparisons of *AUK* with other techniques, the average ARPI for typing a simple sentence that contains very frequent English words are presented in Table 2.

On the other hand, the fact that *AUK* supports numerous entry methods for *i* that ranges from 1 to 10+ renders the proposed text entry technique accessible from almost any device, including mainstream mobile devices and assistive technologies for people with disability (e.g., special switches and screen readers for blind users).

Under the light of the above, *AUK* is considered as a method that can potentially provide **Universal Access [4] to text entry** for anyone, regardless of the device used, the expertise of the user, or any other contextual parameter.

Currently, an interactive prototype of *AUK* has been implemented simulating the joystick and the 1-, 3-, 5-, 9- and 10-key modes through a desktop keyboard, and early tests are currently in progress for fine-trimming the *interface* of *AUK* and all layouts. Regarding near future plans: (a) the ARPI for each *AUK* entry mode and proposed character layout will be calculated using public corpora, and detailed comparison results with other techniques will be presented; (b) user performance will be estimated and predicted using theory-based methods such as Hick and Human's method and Fitt's Law; (c) user trials will be conducted with the interactive prototype of *AUK*, e.g., using the public phrase sets of MacKenzie and Sourkoreff[25]; (d) a version for Greek language will be implemented; (e) a mechanism for recording and employing personalised user corpora[26] will be developed and integrated; (f) plug-in versions of *AUK* will be developed for various platforms and applications; and (g) research will

---

[23] The correlation to English language was alculated with *AnalysePhrases* tool available at: http://www.yorku.ca/mack/PhraseSets.zip (Author: I. S. MacKenzie, 2001).

[24] This term is used in analogy to the term *keystrokes per character* (KSPC) introduced in [8].

[25] Available at http://www.yorku.ca/mack/PhraseSets.zip.

[26] Performance rates with *minTap* and *minTimeout* may be further improved by using individual user corpora for automatically rearranging the menu layouts accordingly.

be conducted to identify the frequency of all input options and the *dioption* frequencies (term used in analogy to digraph frequency) in desktop text entry in order to optimise the tree structure of the *AUK* menus, especially for 9-, and 10-key modes.

8 Towards Ambient Text Entry

Since the *AUK* approach is consistent and applicable across various (small) devices, it is anticipated to find application, and provide Universal Access, in the context of Ambient Intelligence environments [5]. In such an environment, the need will arise to provide ubiquitous and efficient text entry to displays of various sizes and characteristics, and in many cases without a traditional keyboard.

Additionally, *AUK* offers the possibility to achieve *ambient text entry*. If, for example, optical tracking through a portable camera is employed to track the movement of finger of a user, then *AUK* can support the development of a ubiquitous *virtual keyboard,* not necessarily visible, for 10-finger text entry. Such a technique could be based on the mapping of each finger to one of the virtual keys of AUK in the 10-key mode. For instance, assuming the mapping presented in Fig. 4 (right), if the user makes a discrete move of the small finger of the left hand, then the character ‘a’ will be entered. Alternatively, for visual feedback purposes, the 3x3 *AUK* menus can be presented in a cursor-like form within the text (see Fig. 4, left).

Overall, this approach has the potential to introduce significant advantages**. Text entry becomes *target-less* and *eyes-free* for all**, i.e., the user does not have to search for, and achieve physical contact with, a specific area (e.g., a key), thus **eliminating performance delays** due to time used (a) to visual scan in target identification (Hick and Human's method), and (b) to target selection (Fitt's Law). Furthermore, **finger and hand movement is minimised**, since there is no need to travel across a keyboard to reach different keys. On the other hand, using the cursor-like version of *AUK*, extra time is saved as the user does not have to focus from the text to the keyboard and back. Taking this a step further, a virtual mouse can be integrated. For instance, discrete finger moves can be reserved for typing and continuous ones for moving the mouse cursor, and inferring minimal hand travelling from the “keyboard” to the “mouse”. Finally and overall, **this approach is flexible and potentially adaptable to any user ability**, since it also works consistently and effectively for cases where i<10.

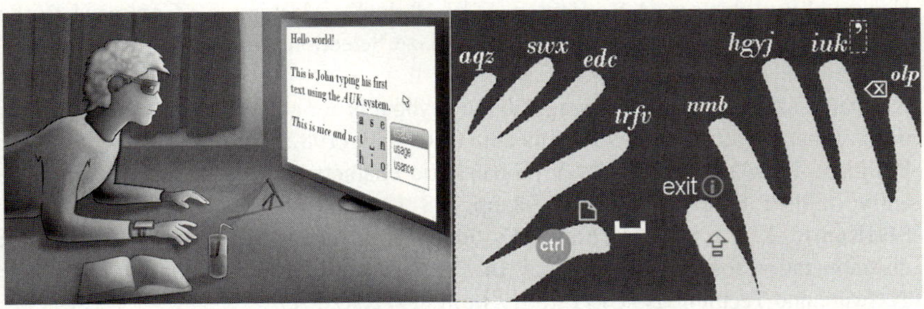

Fig. 4. Towards *ambient text entry for all* (sketch courtesy of Anthony Katzourakis)

Acknowledgments. Part of the work reported here has been carried out in the framework of the integrated project *ASK-IT* (Contract no 511298) funded by the European Commission.

References

1. Isokoski, P.: Manual Text Input: Experiments, Models, and Systems (PhD Thesis). University of Tampere, Tampere Finland (2004)
2. Sandnes, F.E., Thorkildssen, H.W., Arvei, A., Buverud, J.O.: Techniques for fast and easy mobile text-entry with three-keys. In: Proc. of the 37th Annual Hawaii International Conference on System Sciences (HICSS'04), pp. 1–10 (January 05-08, 2004)
3. MacKenzie, I.S., Soukoreff, R.W.: Text Entry for Mobile Computing: Models and Methods, Theory and Practice. Human-Computer interaction 17, 147–198 (2002)
4. Stephanidis, C., et al.: Toward an Information Society for All:HCI challenges and R&D recommendations. International Journal of Human-Computer Interaction 11(1), 1–28 (1998)
5. Emiliani, P.L., Stephanidis, C.: Universal access to ambient intelligence environments: Opportunities and challenges for people with disabilities. IBM Systems Journal 44(3), 605–619 (2005)
6. Edwards, A.D.N.: Extra-Ordinary Human-Computer Interaction: Interfaces for Users with Disabilities. Cambridge University Press, Cambridge (1995) ISBN 0-521-43413-0
7. Oniszczak, A., MacKenzie, I.S.: A comparison of Two Input Methods for Keypads on Mobile Devices. In: Proc. of NordiCHI'04, Tampere Finland, pp. 101–104 (October 23-27, 2004)
8. MacKenzie, I.S.: KSPC (Keystrokes per Character) as a Characteristic of Text Entry Techniques. In: Proceedings of the Fourth International Symposium on Human Computer Interaction with Mobile Devices, pp. 195–210. Springer, Heidelberg (2002)
9. Johansen, A.S., Hansen, J.P.: Augmentative and alternative communication: the future of text on the move. International Journal of UAIS 5, 125–149 (2006)
10. Kölsch, M., Turk, M.: Keyboards without Keyboards: A Survey of Virtual Keyboards. In: Sensing and Input for Media-centric Systems, SIMS 02 (2002)
11. Zhai, S., Hunter, M., Smith, B.A.: Performance Optimization of Virtual Keyboards. Human-Computer Interaction 17, 89–129 (2002)
12. Mourouzis, A., Ntoa, S., Boutsakis, E., Kartakis, G., Stephanidis, C.: Expert-based assessment of the ARGO Web browser for people with disability. In: Proc. of 8th European Conference for the Advancement of Assistive Technology in Europe (AAATE 2005), September 6-9, pp. 767–771. Lille, France (2005)
13. Pavlovych, A., Stuerzlinger, W.: Less-Tap: A Fast and Easy-to-learn Text Input Technique for Phones. In: Proc. of Graphics Interfaces, pp. 319–326 (2003)
14. Soukoreff, R.W., MacKenzie, I.S.: Input-based language modelling in the design of high performance text input techniques. In: Proc.of Graphifcs Interface, pp. 89–96 (2003)
15. Hansen, J.P., Johansen, A.S., Hansen, D.W., Itoh, K., Mashino, S.: Command Without a Click: Dwell Time Typing by Mouse and Gaze Selections. In: Proc. of INTERACT'03, pp. 121–128 (2003)
16. Norman, D.A., Fisher, D.: Why alphabetic keyboards are not easy to use: Keyboard layout doesn't much matter. Human Factors 24(5), 509–519 (1982)
17. Bellman, T., MacKenzie, I.S.: A probabilistic character layout strategy for mobile text entry. In: Proc. Graphics Interface '98, pp. 168–176 (1998)
18. MacKenzie, I.S., Kober, H., Smith, D., Jones, T., Skepner, E.: LetterWise: Prefix-based disambiguation for mobile text input. In: Proc.of the ACM Symposium on User Interface Software and Technology (UIST 2001), pp. 111–120 (2001)
19. Garay-Vitoria, N., Abascal, J.: Text Prediction Systems: A survey. International Journal on Universal Access in the Information Society (UAIS) 4(3), 188–203 (2006)
20. Soukoreff, R.W., MacKenzie, I.S.: Metrics for text entry research: An evaluation of MSD and KSPC, and a new unified error metric. In: Proc.of CHI 2003, pp. 113–120 (2003)

Ambient Documents: Intelligent Prediction for Ubiquitous Content Access

Gregory M.P. O'Hare[1], Michael J. O'Grady[1], Conor Muldoon[1], and Caroline A. Byrne[2]

[1] Adaptive Information Cluster (AIC), University College Dublin (UCD), Belfield, Dublin 4, Ireland

[2] Carlow Institute of T Carlow, Kilkenny Road, Carlow, Ireland

{Gregory.OHare,M.J.OGrady,Conor.Muldoon}@ucd.ie, Caroline.Byrne@itcarlow.ie

Abstract. Ubiquitous service delivery expects that content will be available where, when and how the user needs it. Consumers are becoming ever demanding and the consumers of ubiquitous services are no different in this regard. Their expectations escalate in terms of relevance, ease of access, recency, accuracy and latency of content supply. In addition they expect that the content be supplied proactively in anticipation of their needs together with delivery when they require it. This presupposes that content can be delivered relative to both the consumers location and their technological context. Within this paper we explore how traditional document access can be transformed and introduce *Ambient Documents* a new metaphor for document content access.

Keywords: Ubiquitous computing, Ambient Intelligence, ambient documents, intelligent agents.

1 Introduction

Ubiquitous computing seeks to attain a world of embedded computational infrastructures and artefacts where people can access services in an almost anytime-anywhere basis. This is an attractive vision and has motivated researchers for almost twenty years. Much of this research has focused on the enabling technologies – sensors, wireless networking technologies and on on. Significant progress has been made, and though it cannot be said that all problems have been resolved, it can be assumed that sufficient progress has been made such that practical issues such as data access, usability and so forth can now be explored. One initiative that aims to take accessibility and usability to the next stage is Ambient Intelligence (AmI) [1].

AmI was conceived in response to the realisation that ubiquitous computing systems could easily become unusable. A networked environment of artefacts competing for the user's attention could quickly result in the user being overwhelmed, and as such, being tempted to *switch-off*, both mentally, and, in the case of the ubiquitous computing system, by physically shutting the system down. Thus, AmI seeks to introduce intelligent techniques as a means of mediating between the user

C. Stephanidis (Ed.): Universal Access in HCI, Part II, HCII 2007, LNCS 4555, pp. 971–979, 2007.

and the services supported by the ubiquitous environment, some of which will involve access to a variety of electronic content. In this paper, the concept of an Ambient document as a means of document content access is introduced.

This paper is structured as follows. In the Section II, a description of the ambient document concept is provided. Two practical illustrations of ambient document construction and provision is provided in Section III. In Section IV, the use of intelligent techniques for anticipatory document provision and construction is outlined. Some related research is presented in Section IV, after which the paper is concluded.

2 Ambient Documents

Traditional document structure and access is predicated upon certain assumptions:

- Document retrieval is based on user requests (pull technology);
- Documents are generic;
- Documents are static;
- Documents are primarily comprised of text and images;
- Document content is always regulated;

Ambient documents radically challenge each of these assumptions. Such documents envisage a world where ambient documents exist almost as overlays upon the physical world. These overlays enable documents to be accessed in an ambient nature with content acquired and delivered in an intuitive manner.

Ambient Document Retrieval

The traditional pull model may still be used with Ambient Documents. However, it also incorporates the push/subscribe model to a far greater degree. In particular, the triggering parameters for pushing a document are intrinsically linked with various aspects of the user's context, and may be highly domain dependant. Ambient documents may be also anticipatory in that they can be dynamically constructed in anticipation of a future requirement, which may or may not arise.

Ambient Document Audience

Traditional documents are generic in the sense that they are written for a certain audience. In contrast, Ambient Documents are personalised for their audience, either as a group or individually. Their content is filtered and adapted such that it is of relevance to its readers and, in particular, to the pertinent aspects of the readers' profile that are dominant at the time of invocation.

Ambient Document Content

Ambient Documents are inherently dynamic entities. Their content is highly dependent of the prevailing situation or context of the user. What aspects of the user's context are of most significance depend on the application domain and the task being performed. Location is one obvious element but there are others. For example, if the document should include a forecast of the weather, then this must be gleaned from an appropriate source such that it is relevant to the current time and place.

Ambient Document Media

Traditionally, documents consisted of text and images. The WWW has challenged this assumption, and views documents as comprising various multimedia elements. Ambient Documents also subscribes to this view, though the selection of media elements is highly dependent on the user's context.

Ambient Document Ethos

Traditional documents are inherently regulated in their content and their structure. Ambient documents are unregulated in that their content and structure is highly dynamic. A typical example of this is a blog where the number of people contributing is unpredictable, and the contributed content varies in diverse ways.

Ambient Document Repositories

Ambient documents are inherently distributed and do not use a central repository or digital library. Such documents are frequently deployed at the very edge of networks and on devices of limited computational capabilities such as sensors.

Ambient Document Presentation

Ambient Documents do not presuppose the availability of a standard desktop workstation with a standard WIMP interface. Rather such documents can be accessed and viewed in a multimodal fashion. This may involve voice and gesture recognition for the input modality. For the display modality, audio and video may be used in cooperation with animated or virtual characters, via a range of physical media ranging from a smartphone interface to an Augmented Reality (AR) system.

3 Ambient Document Construction and Delivery

Constructing and delivering ambient documents to individuals and groups raises a number of challenges for designers, software engineers and service providers. The complexity of the process results from a combination of diverse target user groups, including experience and expectations, as well individual attributes such as language, age group and so on; diverse supporting infrastructure, including the capabilities of any embedded or mobile devices and prevailing networks; and other contextual elements, including location, time and so on. As an illustration of how such documents may be constructed and delivered, two examples are provided: one that conforms to a regulated ethos, and a second that is inherently unregulated.

3.1 Tourist Information Systems

Tourists are an example of an end-user group that is heterogeneous and mobile. As tourists explore their surrounding, an opportunity exists to deliver information to them in a timely basis. A number of systems have been described in the literature that aims to this, for example CRUMPET [2]. For the purposes of this discussion, the method adopted for Gulliver's Genie [3] [4] is presented and discussed in light of the ambient document concept.

When a tourist encounters a popular attraction, the Genie makes a presentation on this attraction available to them on their host device. The presentation itself utilises a combination of multimedia elements, namely, audio, images video and text. However, it is the nature and construction of the presentation that is of most interest. First of all, the context of the presentation is always relevant to the location and orientation of the tourist, that is, their spatial context. Secondly, the content is personalised for the tourist in question in two distinct ways. Initially, content is selected based on the tourist's personal profile. For example, an adult may be presented with material that would be pitched at level that would not be suitable for a child. After this initial pruning of content, the content is further filtered such that it is consistent with the tourist domain-specific model, in this case their cultural interests. Thirdly, and finally, all content is prioritised such that it coincides with the level of interest expressed by the tourist in previous interactions. The practical implication of this is that a dynamic model must be maintained at all times. Thus the presentation incorporates a number of diverse elements including a location-aware element, a content personalisation and customisation element, and a broad context-aware element.

If the ambient document attributes as listed in Section II are considered, it can be seen that the approach adopted by the Genie concurs with these. Gulliver's Genie adopts a data-push approach, although explicitly with the permission of the end-user. In a business model where the end-user pays, this is of critical importance. The Genie is designed to address the needs of a specific audience, namely tourists. However, the content is inherently dynamic, and adapted according to the location and profile of the tourist in question. Furthermore, this profile has a specific domain component, in this case a cultural interest sub-model. From a structural perspective, a range of multimedia elements are supported. Media browsing is nominally via standard navigation-pad manipulation, though activating the availability of the presentation itself can only be achieved by physically going the attraction in question. Hence, the interaction modality is multimodal, and incorporates both an implicit and explicit element. Technically, the content can be hosted on a centralised server, though a distributed approach is preferred. All content must be approved a priori, thus the presentation is regulated. Indeed, the adequate tagging of the content so that it can be matched with interested tourists is of fundamental importance.

However, the tourists themselves are oblivious to the ongoing suite of ongoing processes necessary to realize the service, as indeed they should be. From their perspective, a series of multimedia documents are presented to them for their perusal, at a time and in a location where they are of most interest. In this way, documents assume an ambient nature, and in the tourists' eyes, become perceived as a specific information overlay superimposed on the physical environment which can only be accessed at certain locations, which in this case, coincides with the location of tourist attractions.

3.2 GeoBlogging

Tourist activities are frequently solitary, and in an effort to address this, a blogging application was designed [5]. Blogging is a well known internet activity, but in this case, a geospatial element was added, hence the term geoblogging. The core idea is quite simple. As tourists explore their environment, they can access individual blog entries that have been made in their vicinity, or they can construct a blog entry themselves.

A blog entry may contain a combination of media elements, and it is at the discretion of the tourist as to which elements to use. Geospatial data and tourist profile are the two key parameters used for tagging the blog entry. Both will be used in the retrieval process: the geospatial data for matching the tourist's current geospatial context, and the tourist profile for filtering and prioritizing blog entries that are likely to be of most interest to the tourist.

Much of what was discussed previously about the Genie and ambient documents applies to the geoblogging applications. However, there is one critical difference. Blogging is an inherently unregulated activity. Where a blog entry is created, and accessed, cannot be predicted. The media elements used cannot be predicted. And the capability of the tourists' devices to render individual blogs must be factored into the retrieval process.

3.3 Intelligent Prediction

Ambient documents are almost invariable constructed on the fly, for example, the Genie presentations, and blog listings just described. This is a time consuming exercise, and one that could easily contribute to a poor end-user experience. One method of mitigating this difficulty concerns the predicting of content requirements in advance, and the subsequent preparation of content in anticipation of short term future access. Fundamental to this is a sophisticated model of the tourist's physical environment as well as an awareness of their spatial context. Based on this, their future route can be estimated and their future information needs anticipated. However, a degree of intelligence is necessary to do this. Gulliver's Genie adopts an approach termed intelligent precaching [6] as a mechanism for anticipating content requirements and the pre-caching of this content in the expectation that it can be pushed to the tourist. In the next section, a brief overview of approaches that can be adopted for using intelligent techniques for the production and dissemination of ambient documents is discussed.

4 Intelligent Techniques for Ambient Documents

There is a potentially serious conundrum at the heart of AmI. Ubiquitous computing is characterised by small lightweight distributed sensors and devices that are inherently limited from a computational perspective. However, intelligent techniques usually demand sophisticated software that will only operate satisfactorily on workstation-type environments. Reconciling these two issues requires significant effort and ingenuity from software engineers. Furthermore, even to make maximum use of the limited computational resources available calls for the facilitation of intelligent decision making. It is essential that these systems operate effectively and use efficient algorithms to minimise computational overhead. There are two broad approaches to achieving this, namely centralised and distributed.

- Centralised Intelligence can be centralised on a fixed network node. In this case, computational resources are not a serious problem. Thus the software designer has the luxury of choosing the AI techniques that are most appropriate. A key difficulty concerns system responsiveness. If, as may frequently be the case, there is a wireless networking component, this may become a bottleneck in the system, particularly if a significant amount of data must be transferred between a central network node and the host device to generate the predictive behaviour. This may have a detrimental effect on the usability of the system as a whole – something that should be avoided at all costs. Should the application seek to push data to the user, a small window of opportunity may exist to do this which must be taken advantage of. If not, the user may have moved on and an opportunity will be lost.

– Distributed Intelligence represents a second strategy for realizing the necessary intelligence for ubiquitous content access. In this case, the intelligence may be distributed throughout the network. One can easily envisage the sophisticated algorithms being run on fixed network nodes while some of the less computationally expensive algorithms may be deployed on the user's mobile device, or even on an embedded sensor. A practical implementation of the distributed AI approach is that of Multi-agent Systems (MAS). A MAS takes a decentralised approach to the problem of deploying intelligence in a distributed network. Though traditional MASs primarily targeted desktop environments, there have been a number of agent platforms reported in the literature that target mobile devices, and one of these, AFME, is described briefly in the following section. From an economic perspective, the number of cellular digital mobile phones is already greater than the number of desktop and notebook computers [7] and continues to grow at a considerably faster rate, particularly in developing countries. Thus the potential for the deployment of MASs in resource constrained computational environments is greater than that of networked desktop computers and laptops.

4.1 Agent Factory Micro Edition

Agent Factory Micro Edition (AFME) [8] is a minimised footprint agent platform specifically designed for resource constrained mobile devices. It is loosely based on Agent Factory [9], a pre-existing agent platform for personal computers. It uses a

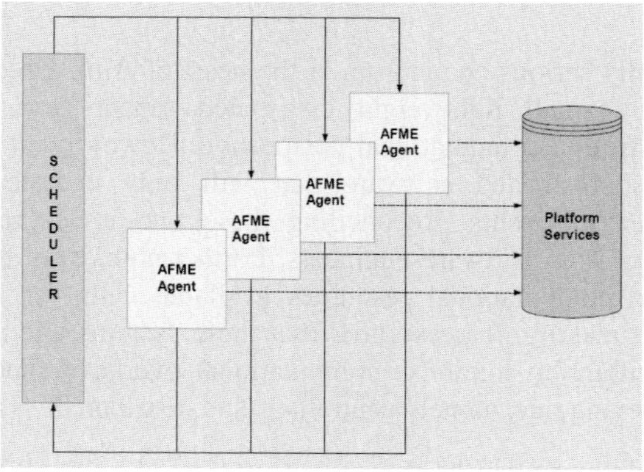

Fig. 1. A rchitecture of AFME

subset of the Agent Factory Agent Programming Language (AFAPL) and augments it with a number of features specific to AFME. AFAPL is founded on a logical formalism of belief and commitment. Rules that define the conditions under which agents should adopt commitments are used to govern and encode agent behaviour.

An AFME platform (Fig. 1) comprises a scheduler, several platform services, and a group of agents. The scheduler is responsible for the scheduling of agents to execute at periodic intervals. Rather than each agent creating a new thread when they begin operating, agents share a thread pool.

AFME delivers support for the creation of Belief, Desire, and Intention (BDI) [10] agents that follow a *sense-deliberate-act* cycle. Beliefs are, perhaps inaccurate, information that an agent has about the world. Desires are states in the world that agents wish to bring about. Intentions are desires that agents have committed resources to achieving. The control algorithm performs four functions. Preceptors are fired and beliefs are resolved within the belief resolution function. The beliefs are used within the deliberation process to identify the agent's desired states. Agents are resource bounded and will be unable to achieve all of their desires even if their desires are consistent. A subset is chosen, in the *intention selection process*, that maximises their self-interest with respect to their finite resources. The final function of the control algorithm concerns commitment management. Depending on the nature of the commitments adopted various actuators are fired.

In AFME agents are rational; sometimes they collaborate other times they compete depending on the context. In certain circumstances the developer will want to ensure that agents always behave in a particular manner. This type of behaviour is modelled, within AFME, through the use of fixed utility values that ensure that under such circumstances it is always in an agent's interest to behave in a certain fashion.

5 Related Research

Ambient documents are closely related to ubiquitous user interfaces, a number of which have been described in the literature. Most of these interfaces are concerned with the nature of the device, while ambient documents adopt a more holistic view, emphasising the construction process, though not at the expense of the rendering and visualisation element.

The Pervasive Adaptive Visualization and Interaction Service (PAVIS) is an approach to performing adaptive visualisation and user-interface generation based on device-specific information, such as resolution, screen size, and networking capability [11]. It aids the user in visualising data and interpreting information. The form visualisation takes has a considerable impact on how effectively the information is interpreted. The goal of PAVIS is to automatically generate user-interfaces that are best suited for the display device.

The User Interface Mark-up Language (UIML) [12] is an approach to simplifying the construction of multi-platform user interfaces. The goal of UIML is to reduce the development time of user interfaces for multiple device families through the construction of a generic interface vocabulary.

The Personal Universal Controller (PUC) [13] system automatically generates an intermediary interface for an appliance, such as stereos, copiers, elevators, and the non-driving functions of a car. PUC allows users to control appliances in their environment through a remote user interface. The remote control may be a graphical user interface on a PDA or mobile phone or speech recognition system that uses microphones in the room. The system provides a two-way communication channel between the appliance and the controller. This facilitates the transmission of the user's commands and enables the controller to receive feedback.

ICrafter [14] is a framework for the construction of *services* and ubiquitous user interfaces. The term services when used in this context is referring a devices, such as a light or a projector, or an application, such as Microsoft PowerPoint operating on a large screen, that provides useful functionality to users. The framework is concerned with the development of what are known as interactive workspaces. An interactive workspace is a technology rich space of interconnected computers, utility devices, and IO devices, where people come together to collaborate on a particular task, such as brainstorming.

6 Conclusion

As ubiquitous computing systems proliferate, the practical issues of data preparation, dissemination and access in such systems becomes increasingly important. The traditional view of documents as inherently static entities limits the potential and possibilities envisaged by the ubiquitous computing and AmI visions. In this paper, the concept of ambient documents has been introduced. Such documents offer a dynamic and radical view of document access, production and dissemination. Essential to the ambient document construct is the availability of a suite of intelligent techniques for content identification and filtering, as well as the prediction of future document usage. Having illustrated the potential of ambient documents in a mobile tourist information and blogging system, it is the authors' intention to investigate further the use of alternative interaction modalities as means of accessing and retrieving and navigating such documents.

Acknowledgments. This material is based upon works supported by the Science Foundation Ireland (SFI) under Grant No. 03/IN.3/1361.

References

1. Vasilakos, A., Pedrycz, W.: Ambient Intelligence, Wireless Networking, Ubiquitous Computing, Artec House (2006)
2. Poslad, S., Laamanen, H., Malaka, R., Nick, A., Zipf, A.: Crumpet: Creation of user-friendly mobile services personalised for tourism, Proceeding of the Second IEE International Conference on 3G Mobile Communication Technologies, London, UK (2001)
3. O'Hare, G.M.P., O'Grady, M.J., Gulliver's Genie, A.: Multi-Agent System for Ubiquitous and Intelligent Content Delivery, Computer Communications, vol. 26 (11) pp. 1177–1187 (2003)

4. O'Grady, M.J., O'Hare, G.M.P., Sas, C.: Mobile Agents for Mobile Tourists: A User Evaluation of Gulliver's Genie, Interacting with Computers Journal, vol. 17 (4), pp. 343–366 (2005)
5. Chen, J., O'Grady, M.J., O'Hare, G.M.P.: Autonomy and Intelligence - Opportunistic Service Delivery in Mobile Computing. In: Gabrys, B., Howlett, R.J., Jain, L.C. (eds.) KES 2006. LNCS (LNAI), vol. 4253, pp. 1201–1207. Springer, Heidelberg (2006)
6. O'Grady, M.J., O'Hare, G.M.P.: Just-In-Time Multimedia Distribution in a Mobile Computing Environment. IEEE Multimedia 11(4), 62–74 (2004)
7. Bratt, S.: Mobile Web Initiative, World Wide Web Consortium (W3C), MIT Research and Development Conference, Innovation for Industry (2005)
8. Muldoon, C., O'Hare, G.M.P., Collier, R., O'Grady, M.J.: Agent Factory Micro Edition: A Framework for Ambient Applications. In: Conti, R., Ruberti, A. (eds.) Proceedings of Intelligent Agents in Computing Systems (IACS 2) Workshop held in Conjunction with International Conference on Computational Science (ICCS) 2006. LNCS, vol. 3, pp. 727–734. Springer, Heidelberg (1973)
9. Collier, R.W., O'Hare, G.M.P., Lowen, T., Rooney, C.F.B.: Beyond prototyping in the factory of agents. In: Mařík, V., Müller, J.P., Pěchouček, M. (eds.) CEEMAS 2003. LNCS (LNAI), vol. 2691, pp. 383–393. Springer, Heidelberg (2003)
10. Rao, A.S., Georgeff, M.P.B.: Agents: From Theory To Practice. In: Proceedings of the First International Conference on Multi-Agent Systems (ICMAS'95), San Francisco, CA, pp. 312–319 (1995)
11. Alimohideen, J., PAVIS,: – Pervasive Adaptive Visualization and Interaction Service, CHI Workshop on Information Visualization and Interaction Techniques for Collaboration Across Multiple Displays, Montreal, Canada (2006)
12. Ali, M.-F., Marc Abrams, M.: Simplyfying Construction of Multi-Platform User Interfaces Using UIML, UIML Europe 2001 Conference (2001)
13. Nichols, J.: Automatically Generating User Interfaces, Pervasive Computing, Vienna, Austria (2004)
14. Ponnekanti, S.R., Lee, B., Fox, A., Hanrahan, P., Winograd, T.I.: A Service Framework for Ubiquitous Computing Environments. In: Abowd, G.D., Brumitt, B., Shafer, S. (eds.) Ubicomp 2001: Ubiquitous Computing. LNCS, vol. 2201, pp. 56–75. Springer, Heidelberg (2001)

Combining Pointing Gestures with Video Avatars for Remote Collaboration

Seon-Min Rhee[1] and Myoung-Hee Kim[1,2,*]

[1] Department of Computer Science and Engineering, Ewha Womans University, 11-1 daehyun-dong Seodaemun-gu, Seoul, 120-750, Korea
blue@ewhain.net

[2] Center for Computer Graphics and Engineering(CCGVR), Ewha Womans University, 11-1 daehyun-dong Seodaemun-gu, Seoul, 120-750, Korea
mhkim@ewha.ac.kr

Abstract. We present a simple and intuitive method of user interaction, based on pointing gestures, which can be used with video avatars in a remote collaboration. By connecting the head and fingertip of a user in 3D space we can identify the direction in which they are pointing. Stereo infrared cameras in front of the user, together with an overhead camera, are used to find the user's head and fingertip in a CAVE™-like system. The position of the head is taken to be the top of the user's silhouette, while the location of the user's fingertip is found directly in 3D space by searching the images from the stereo cameras for a match with its location in the overhead camera image in real time. The user can interact with the first object which collides with the pointing ray. In an experimental result, the result of the interaction is shown together with the video avatar which is visible to a remote collaborator.

Keywords: gesture interaction, immersive display, human-computer interaction.

1 Introduction

A spatially immersive display can be used to promote efficient remote collaboration by making a remote collaborator apparently visible in a local environment, and permitting them to manipulate shared virtual objects. In previous work [1] we proposed a stereo image based video avatar of a collaborator which can be merged into a virtual world. This allows users in remote VR environments to see each other. In addition to this feature, to create an efficient collaborative virtual workspace a simple and intuitive way of supporting interactions between the collaborator's and virtual objects needs to be provided. And the results of interactions need to be made visible to both collaborators. We achieve this with a tracking interface that can interpret pointing gestures.

To support vision-based user interaction in a virtual world, two categories have been studied. The first approach uses multiple images for pose estimation, in which an

* Corresponding author.

C. Stephanidis (Ed.): Universal Access in HCI, Part II, HCII 2007, LNCS 4555, pp. 980–986, 2007.

articulated body model is fitted to 3D data [2, 3, 4]. However, this approach does not permit real-time tracking of articulated structures. Second approach is gestural interaction using feature points. Kahn and Swain [5] were responsible for an early method of detecting pointing gestures, and Nickel and Stiefelhagen [6] have presented a method of pointing detection for human-machine interactions, using hidden Markov models. Kolesnik and Kulessa [7] used an overhead camera and segmented the silhouettes of users into two parts, corresponding to the body and an arm. But these three techniques have only been applied to interaction in a local environment.

We have implemented our method within a CAVE™-like system to support remote collaboration. Interpreting a user's gesture in such an environment is made more complicated because the background to the user is a changing image on the VR display, and not a static background. We therefore rely on infrared imaging to detect the user's movements robustly. We employ the concept of a pointing ray, which connects the head and the fingertip of a user in 3D. Images from two frontal and one overhead camera are used to detect the end-points of this ray. This gestural interaction is implemented in the context of our video avatars [1], so that a user can see their collaborator and their actions with respect to a virtual object.

This paper is organized as follows. In Section 2 we provide an overview of our approach to gestural interaction. In Section 3 we explain how we detect the position of the user's head and fingertip, which define a pointing gesture. We describe our implementation and present the results in Section 4, and conclusions follow in Section 5.

2 Overview

In a spatially immersive display environment such as a CAVE™-like system, uniform illumination can not be guaranteed because a changing virtual world is always being displayed. In our previous work [1] we used infrared images, which ignore the visible light from the screen, so as to achieve the static background which is essential for robust feature extraction, and we use the same environment in this current work. Fig. 1 shows our hardware setup and software organization. Two cameras and infrared light sources are installed on the upper front part of the screen and an overhead camera is attached to the ceiling.

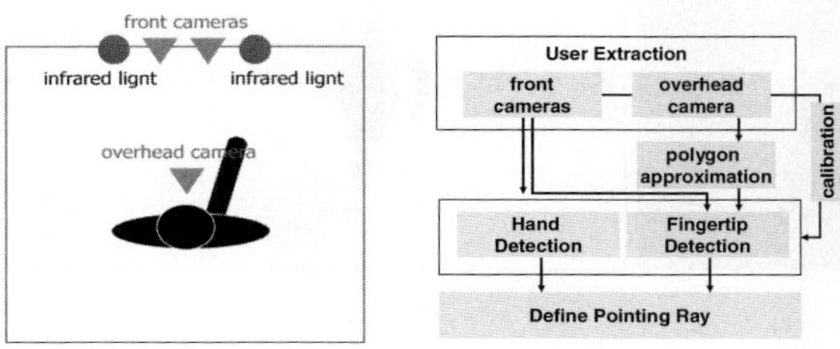

(a) (b)

Fig. 1. (a) Our hardware setup in a CAVE™-like system and (b) the software components that support gestural interaction

Gestures are analyzed using a pointing ray. While making simple pointing gestures, humans tend to look at the target object. The pointing ray is this line of sight, and it can be constructed by connecting the head and fingertip of a user. The use of an overhead camera makes it easier to find the fingertip, which is usually the body part that is farthest from the center of the body in the overhead camera image. We can construct the equation of a pointing ray P in terms of the 3D position of the head H, and the fingertip position F, as follows:

$$P = H + \alpha \frac{H - F}{|H - F|} \tag{1}$$

where α determines the length of the ray.

3 Analyzing Pointing Gestures

Prior to attempting detection of the user's head and fingertip the cameras must be calibrated. We use Tsai's method [8] to obtain internal and external camera parameters.

3.1 Head Detection

We use an efficient heuristic for head detection. If the silhouette of a user can be extracted robustly from an image, then the position of their head can simply be taken as the highest point on the silhouette. We can eliminate small irrelevant areas which are not related to the user's silhouette by region growing, as shown in Fig. 2(b). The seed point for region growing is the centroid of the region, which is defined as follows:

$$C = (\bar{x}, \bar{y}), \quad \bar{x} = \frac{\sum_{i=1}^{n} x_i}{n}, \quad \bar{y} = \frac{\sum_{i=1}^{n} y_i}{n} \tag{2}$$

where n is the number of points inside the silhouette, and their coordinates are (x_i, y_i).

(a) (b) (c)

Fig. 2. Head detection: (a) an original infrared image, (b) the initial attempt at silhouette extraction and (c) the result of improved extraction result by region growing. In (b) and (c) the detected head position is located in the red box.

Using the two head points in the images from the frontal cameras, the 3D position of the head can be calculated by triangulation [9].

3.2 Fingertip Detection

We locate a fingertip in 3D in two steps. First, the fingertip is found in the overhead camera image. We then search for its 3D position with the help of the two frontal camera images.

The process of fingertip detection using the overhead camera is summarized in Fig. 3. We assume that the fingertip will be the farthest point from the centroid of the silhouette of the user, as shown in Fig. 4(a). The centroid can be calculated using Equation (2), which was given in the previous section.

To find the farthest point from the centroid, we could check every point on the boundary of silhouette. However, to reduce the search time, we approximate the boundary by a polygon.

A distance function D_j is defined as $Dj = \sqrt{(x_j - \bar{x})^2 + (y_j - \bar{y})^2}$, $Vj = (x_j, y_j)$, where V_j is a vertex of the approximated boundary. Fig. 4(b) shows the value of this function for each vertex of an example polygon. If there is more than one most distant point, the brightest in the overhead camera image is chosen to represent the fingertip.

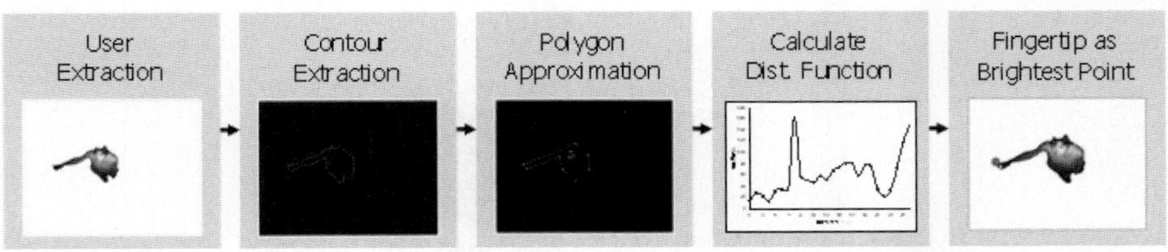

Fig. 3. Fingertip detection from the overhead camera image

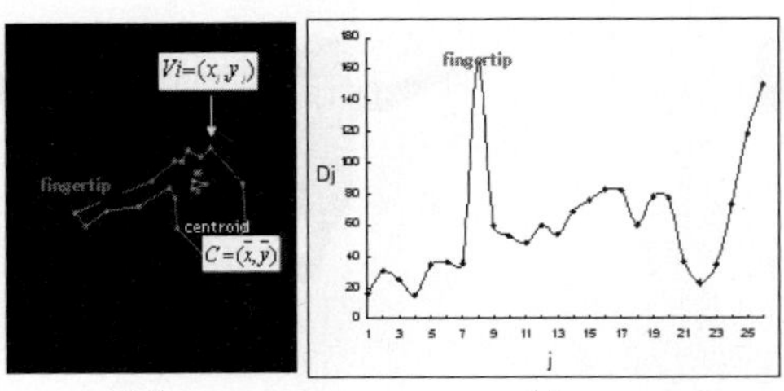

Fig. 4. (a) A polygon approximating the user's silhouette and (b) a plot of the distance function from the centroid of the silhouette to each vertex of the polygon

In the second step, we search for the 3D position of the fingertip with the help of the two frontal camera images (Π_1 and Π_2), as shown in Fig. 5(a). Because the infrared images only have a single channel of color information we cannot use a traditional stereo matching algorithm to find the 3D position of the point. We have therefore formulated a method of finding its 3D position directly, without using stereo matching.

The fingertip f3 on the image plane of the overhead camera image Π_3 can be reprojected into a 3D space along with the vector $\vec{P}$. The actual fingertip will be a point on this vector. Each point on $\vec{P}$ can be projected on to the image planes Π_1 and Π_2. If this point is the actual fingertip then the two projected points are also fingertips in their respective images and therefore both points will be within the silhouette of the user. Fig. 5(b) shows the result of fingertip detection in the overhead camera image and Fig. 5(c) and 5(d) shows projected fingertip candidates, which form an epipolar line.

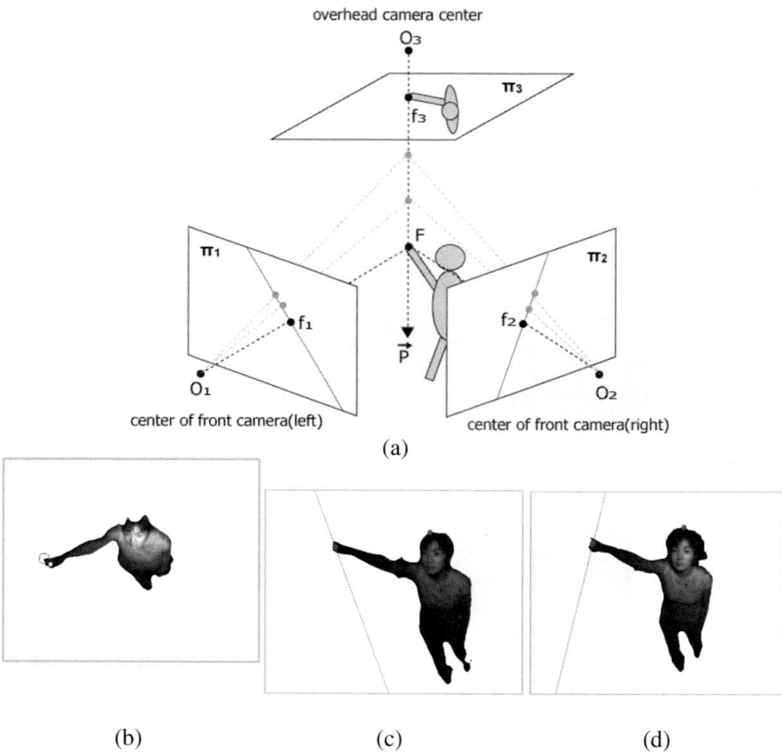

Fig. 5. (a) Conceptual view of fingertip detection: (b) shows the fingertip found in the overhead camera image, and (c) and (d) show the epipolar line of fingertip candidates. The final fingertip, which is within the user's silhouette in both images, is circled in red.

4 Implementation and Results

We used separate computers for detecting the pointing ray and for rendering the virtual world. To detect the head and fingertip we used an Intel Pentium 4 Dual CPU3.0GHz with 2GB RAM. The Flycapture [11] and OpenCV [12] libraries were used for image acquisition and processing. As a rendering server we used an Intel Pentium Xeon 2.4GHz with 2GB RAM, supporting the Blue-c API [10].

The 3D positions of the head and fingertip are transmitted to the rendering server. At this juncture their positions are expressed in a world coordinate system which is defined during camera calibration. Both head and fingertip points must be transformed into scene coordinates to support interaction with virtual objects in the scene.

The user is able to interact with the first object which collides with the pointing ray. An example of this form of interaction is shown in Fig. 6, in which the user selects a virtual object by pointing, and that object is then shown as a highlighted wireframe.

(a) (b) (c)

Fig. 6. Object selection using a pointing gesture. A user in the virtual environment points at the chess pieces in the order (a), (b) and (c). In each case the selected object is rendered as a highlighted wireframe.

5 Conclusion

We have proposed a simple but efficient method of interaction based on pointing gestures, which can be used with video avatars for collaboration in a spatially immersive virtual environment. We detect gestures from the 3D positions of the head and fingertip of the users, using two cameras installed in front of the screen and a third overhead camera. A pointing gesture can be used to select a virtual object to be manipulated. This results in a more powerful collaborative VR workspace in which our video avatars can operate. Users can see each other and collaborate within the same virtual world.

Acknowledgments. This work was supported by the Korean Ministry of Information and Communication (MIC) under the Information Technology Research Center (ITRC) Program. We would like to thank to Remo Ziegler (ETH Zurich, Switzerland) for the fruitful comments for this work.

References

1. Rhee, S.-M., Ziegler, R., Park, J., Naef, M., Gross, M., Kim, M.-H.: Low-Cost Telepresence in Collaborative Virtual Environment. IEEE Transaction on Visualization and Computer Graphics 13(1), 156–166 (2007)
2. Cheung, G.K.M., Baker, S., Kanade, T.: Shape-From-Silhouette of Articulated Objects and Its Use for Human Body Kinematics Estimation and Motion Capture. In: Proceedings of the IEEE Conference on Computer Vision and Pattern Recognition, pp. 77–84 (2003)

3. Mikic, I., Trivedi, M., Hunter, E., Cosman, P.: Human Body Model Acquisition and Tracking Using Voxel Data, International Journal of Computer Vision, vol. 53(3), 199–223 (2003)
4. Tollmar, K., Demirdijan, D., Darrell, T.: Gesture and Play - Exploring Full-Body Navigation for Virtual Environments. In: Proceedings of the Conference on Computer Vision and Pattern Recognition Workshop, vol. 5(47) (2003)
5. Kahn, R.E., Swain, M.J.: Understanding People Pointing: The Perseus System, International Symposium on Computer Vision. A Motion III, 11 (1995)
6. Nickel, K., Stiefelhagen, R.: Real-time Recognition of 3D-Pointing Gestures for Human-Machine-Interaction. In: Michaelis, B., Krell, G. (eds.) Pattern Recognition. LNCS, vol. 2781, pp. 557–565. Springer, Heidelberg (2003)
7. Kolesnik, M., Kulessa, T.: Detecting, Tracking and Interpretation of a Pointing Gesture by an Overhead View Camera. In: Proceedings of the Annual Symposium of the German Association for Pattern Recognition, pp. 429–436 (2001)
8. Tsai, R.Y.: An Efficient and Accurate Camera Calibration Technique for 3D Machine Vision. In: Proceedings of the IEEE Conference on Computer Vision and Pattern Recognition, pp. 364–374 (1986)
9. Taubin, G.: Camera Model and Triangulation, Note for EE-148: 3D Photography, CalTech (2001)
10. Naef, M., Staadt, O., Gross, M.: Blue-C API: A Multimedia and 3D Video Enhanced Toolkit for Collaborative VR and Telepresence. In: Proceedings of ACM SIGGRAPH International Conference on Virtual Reality Continuum and Its Applications in Industry, pp. 11–18 (2004)
11. FlyCapture® Software Development Kit, http://sourceforge.net/projects/opencvlibrary/
12. Open Computer Vision Library, http://sourceforge.net/projects/opencvlibrary/

Integrating Language, Vision and Action for Human Robot Dialog Systems

Markus Rickert, Mary Ellen Foster, Manuel Giuliani, Tomas By, Giorgio Panin, and Alois Knoll

Robotics and Embedded Systems Group
Department of Informatics, Technische Universität München
Boltzmannstraße 3, D-85748 Garching bei München, Germany
{rickert,foster,giuliani,by,panin,knoll}@in.tum.de

Abstract. Developing a robot system that can interact directly with a human instructor in a natural way requires not only highly-skilled sensorimotor coordination and action planning on the part of the robot, but also the ability to understand and communicate with a human being in many modalities. A typical application of such a system is interactive assembly for construction tasks. A human communicator sharing a common view of the work area with the robot system instructs the latter by speaking to it in the same way that he would communicate with a human partner.

1 Introduction

Joint action between humans and robots of various bodily structures (i.e., *N* robots with *M* humans) can be effectively supported by carrying on dialogs in natural language, by interpreting/generating facial expressions and gestures and by direct physical cooperation. It is not difficult to predict that the development of techniques for effective and efficient joint action based on multimodal communication flow between humans and artifacts is one of the most important requirements for the advancement of humanoid and service robotics in the wide sense. Once this development gains enough momentum, the requirements for ever-increasing responsiveness of the robots, for wider applicability to new scenarios, situations and object domains, and for an easy integration of the robots into scenarios with many cooperating robots and many cooperating humans will grow quickly.

There have been various attempts to design robots that directly interact with humans—for the purpose of "programming by demonstration" [1], for controlling their behavior within certain limits, or for "force amplification". These approaches, while working under controlled laboratory conditions, have not met with much success. We identify two main reasons for this failure: (i) Human instructions are perceived by the robot in just one modality, mostly through a fixed camera. This prevents the system from constructing cross-modal associations by evaluating clues from other modalities (sound, touch, etc.). It also prevents humans from giving additional explanations in *natural* modalities, e.g. combining hand movements with speech to give instructions. (ii) Partly due to mono-modality, the communication flow

C. Stephanidis (Ed.): Universal Access in HCI, Part II, HCII 2007, LNCS 4555, pp. 987–995, 2007.

for enabling joint action is not in the form of a dialog between human and robot. Such dialog becomes indispensable in the case of error conditions. Furthermore, the aspect of physical cooperation between the human and the robot system for the purpose of *instructing* the robot has rarely been addressed.

From a cognitive perspective, it is highly desirable that the robot systems autonomously realize cognitively adequate modes of interaction with humans— for dialog control, for synchronizing utterances with motor control and for lifelong learning and plasticity. To show how humans may communicate with robot systems naturally and multimodally, in a large-scale research effort, we are developing a system for joint action between robots and humans integrating vision, language, and

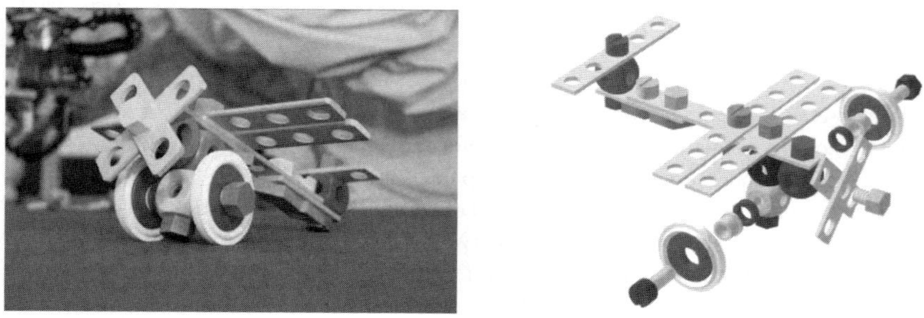

(a) (b)

Fig. 1. The Baufix aircraft toy scenario

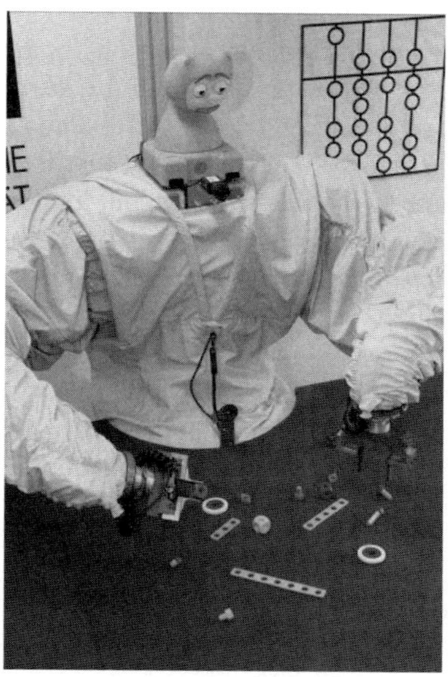

Fig. 2. Setup with two industrial robot manipulators and an animatronic head

cooperative action. To the best of our knowledge it is the only system that realizes joint action between humans and robots as well as between robots and that is controlled through multimodal dialog (primarily complex language utterances accompanied by gestures).

The scenario chosen for our system is the joint construction process of wooden toy—model of an aircraft or similar objects (Fig. 1). A human instructor with robot partner cooperates to build aggregates from elements of the toy construction set [2].

The setup (Fig. 2) consists of two industrial robot manipulators mounted to resemble human arms and an animatronic head [3] so that the user can interact with the system across a table. Various cameras are installed for the recognition of objects on the table and for tracking the user. Force/torque sensors and grippers (with position sensors) on each arm complete the installation.

2 Related Work

This system is partly based on previous work carried out at the University of Bielefeld [4,5,6]. These robots were controlled by a negotiating multi-agent system [7] that autonomously combined a large set of parametrized action primitives into action sequences based on the instruction and the environmental conditions. This system performed quite well given the state of the technology ten years ago. However, it did not have overly powerful recognition abilities, computer vision was slow, and so was the overall operation speed.

Several more recent systems have also considered the task of human-robot collaboration. Leonardo [8], for example, is a fully-embodied humanoid robot with social skills that allow it to learn and collaborate effectively in human settings. Mel the robotic penguin [9] acts as a host for a research lab, guiding visitors through the demonstration of a research prototype. The NASA peer-to-peer human-robot interaction system [10] is designed to allow humans and robots to collaborate on joint tasks: cooperation in this system mainly takes place when one agent asks another for help in dealing with a situation. The Karlsruhe humanoid robot [11] supports dialog-based human-robot collaboration in a kitchen environment.

3 Architecture

The system's architecture (Fig. 3) is divided into five high-level components, each with several functional modules. The data sent between the different modules is given timestamp to enable multimodal integration. Several computers are used to balance the processing load: for example, separate machines are used for object recognition and robot control. Inter-module communication is implemented using the Internet Communications Engine (Ice) [12], an object-oriented middleware which supports distributed heterogeneous systems. In this section we will give an overview of the different components and explain the connections between them.

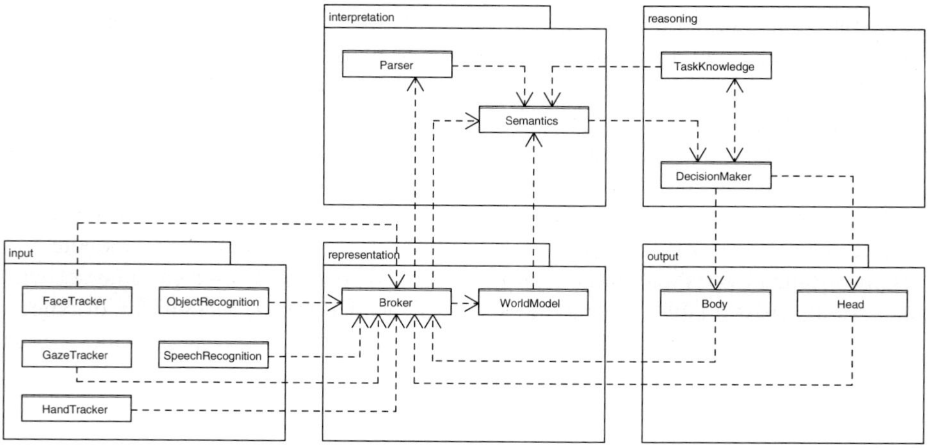

Fig. 3. Overview of the system's architecture

3.1 Input

In order to enable human-robot interaction with an emphasis on joint-action we require several input modalities. Apart from a focus on speech and verbal communication, we also support several non-verbal input channels.

The *SpeechRecognition* module is based on the Dragon NaturallySpeaking software [13], and provides speaker-independent limited-vocabulary speech recognition. The speech recognition hypotheses are passed on to the *Parser* module for further processing, as described in Section 3.2.

An implementation of template-matching based object recognition in combination with tracking is the core of the *ObjectRecognition* module, which is responsible for identifying the toy parts on the table. The position and orientation in world coordinates, as well as the type and color of the objects are determined using calibrated camera mounted on top of the table (Fig. 4(a)). The module is also able to detect overlapping objects to some degree. The use of template-matching will later provide the opportunity to introduce new templates into the system at run-time: if the system is unable to recognize an object, it can ask the user to identify it. The learned template is then stored for further use. The current implementation of this module also provides an early realization of the *HandTracking* module's functionality (Fig. 4(b)), which enables the user to refer to objects by pointing at them.

The *FaceTracker* system currently in use estimates the head position in space by tracking the external contour (Fig. 5(a)). It uses the Contracting Curve Density (CCD) algorithm, which has been improved for real time applications in [14]. The animatronic head uses this information in order to address the user during conversation.

The next version currently under development will provide a full 6 DOF estimation of the head position and orientation (Fig. 5(b)), together with an estimation of the user's gaze direction (Fig. 5(b)) for the *GazeTracker* module. For this purpose, we

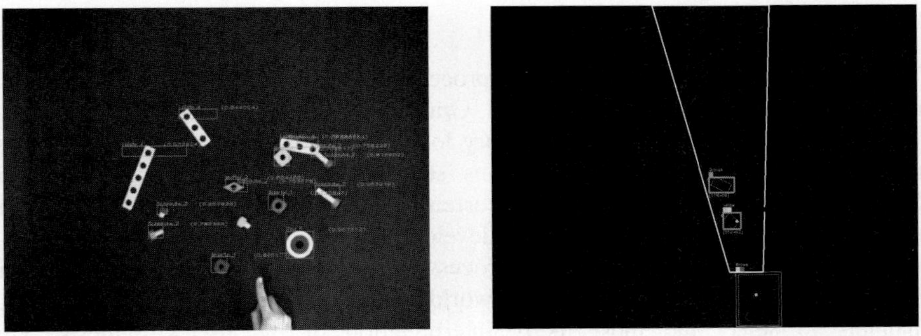

(a) (b)

Fig. 4. Object and hand recognition

adapt generic head model (Fig. 5(c)) [15] by fitting it to specific person's face using two photos, one from the front and one from the side view. After the initial head contour pose estimation, the 3D face template is matched to the underlying image by using fast Mutual Information optimization [16]. This provides more robust approach to deal with variations between expected and observed appearance due to changing lighting conditions, occlusions and other nonlinear effects. Two cameras, one mounted at the robot's base (gaze) and one just below the head (face) provide the input for these modules.

3.2 Representation

This part of the system is responsible for the symbolic representation of the different input channels. A core part in the communication of the system is provided by the *Broker* module. All information processed by the input and output modules is directed to this module, and other modules can register for the event types they are interested in. The data is then passed on to the relevant modules using Ice's publish/subscribe mechanism. This module also provides facilities for centralized logging of system activity for use in debugging and system evaluation.

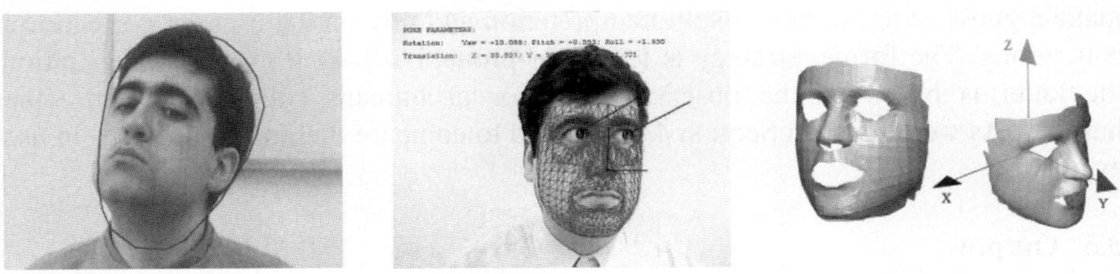

(a) (b) (c)

Fig. 5. Face tracking with external contour position and 6 DOF estimation

The *WorldModel* module provides a constantly-updated abstract representation of the current set of Baufix components in the world and their physical configuration.

3.3 Interpretation

The *Parser* module uses grammar to process utterances in natural language. It is based on the Combinatory Categorial Grammer (CCG), combination of regular categorial grammars and the combinatory logic [17]. This grammar is able to parse imperative sentences as well as questions, statements and confirmations. It uses the OpenCCG implementation [18] and currently supports sentences in the German language; an English grammar is under development.

The *Semantics* module responds to processed input from the speech recognizer and parser, and uses information from the world model and the other multimodal input channels to select the most likely interpretation of the user's requests. This interpretation is then passed to the *DecisionMaker* component described in the next section. If the user input cannot be fully interpreted—for example, because particular words in the speech were not understood correctly, if the multimodal input is unclear, or if reference cannot be unambiguously resolved—the interpreter does as much processing as it can and passes the result along.

3.4 Reasoning

The *TaskKnowledge* module creates plans for assembling the aircraft, but only abstractly, without considering the physical geometry of the pieces, arms, grippers etc. A "plan" in this sense is data structure in this module, and there can be any number of plans held in memory simultaneously, for example alternative suggestions for building particular aircraft. In addition, the system has notion of the "current plan" (for building the aircraft) which has been agreed on by the system and the user. At any given time, part of this plan has already been acted on, and the rest is to be done in the future. As part of the normal input processing, the system matches the perceived actions and utterances of the user against the current plan, so that the plan may advance without any action on the part of the robot.

The *DecisionMaker* module responds to interpreted messages from the input processing system and selects the appropriate system response. This decision is based on both the user input and the current state of the construction task. In the case of partially resolved input, the dialog manager can respond in one of two ways. It can either ask the user to clarify or repeat the request until it is fully understood, or it can make a guess as to the most likely interpretation and rely on the user for correction if it is wrong. The former strategy is less error-prone, but may lead to user frustration; the latter is based on the observed behavior of humans cooperating with other humans. As we discuss in Section 4, we intend to compare these two strategies in user evaluation.

3.5 Output

There are two main output channels in the system: actions of the robot manipulators, and embodied speech of the robot head. All output on both channels is sent to the Broker module for logging and so that it can be used to interpret utterances from the user.

The possible actions of the robot body are abstracted through set of action behaviors [19,20,21,22]. Parameterized sensorimotor actions can be chained together to customize new behaviors. These are executed on the robot using online real-time control instead of generating offline trajectories. Because of the live interaction with the human instructor, the system needs to be able to abort any action instantly and safely to provide "barge-in".

With given attractor position/force, the corresponding trajectory for the controller needs to be calculated online and the robot's velocity/acceleration constraints have to be considered. Different exit conditions, optionally combined with boolean operators, can be used to determine the next operation in this finite state machine. The screw action requires such complex combination to implement spiral search pattern for compensation, re-grasping due to cable limitations and the determination of the final force/torque limits. Fig. 6 shows such joint-action operation where the user is helping the robot with the assembly by holding slat.

(a) (b) (c) (d)

Fig. 6. Human and robot cooperating in an assembly

With online trajectory generation, a signal from the *DecisionMaker* module can activate the calculation of stop trajectory or the seamless switch to the next action at any time. The information from the robot's joint positions as well as from the gripper's position sensor are sent to the Broker module for further use. The *ObjectRecognition* can for example utilize this data to remove the manipulators from the top view image. Based on feedback from the gripper, the *DecisionMaker* can also determine errors during various actions in addition to information from the object recognition. If the goal was to pick up cube and the closed span does not match or indicates full close, then wrong object or no object has been picked up.

The linguistic content of the synthesized speech is created by OpenCCG, using the same OpenCCG-based grammar as the Parser module. The speech is synthesized using AT&T NaturalVoices [23] and is accompanied by lip-synchronization and other non-verbal behaviors of the animatronic head. Other non-verbal behaviors include gazing at the user while talking to them (using the position information from the face tracker), looking at objects on the table while manipulating them, and using nodding and other facial expressions to support the content of the speech.

4 Future Work

Future work for the JAST human-robot dialog system falls into two main categories: evaluating the current version of the system and continuing development of the next version. For the evaluation, we intend to investigate two aspects of the system: the non-verbal behavior of the talking head, and the dialog strategies used to respond to imperfectly understood output.

Previous studies with embodied agents [24] have shown that gaze feedback can increase engagement between human and an embodied robot agent; however, other studies with embodied agents have indicated that an expressive talking head may actually harm task performance in some cases [25]. We will employ widely-used paradigm to evaluate the impact of the non-verbal agent behavior on the interaction quality. Users will interact with the system in one of two modes: one in which the head uses its full repertoire of non-verbal gaze and expressive behavior, and one in which all behaviors except for lip-synchronization are disabled. The evaluation will also compare the impact on the dialog of the two strategies for responding to ambiguous output: waiting for complete clarification, or choosing an option arbitrarily and relying on the user for correction if necessary.

For the next version of the system, we aim to expand its technical capabilities in all areas. For input processing, we will continue development on the objectrecognition, gaze-tracking and hand-tracking modules; for the interpretation and reasoning modules, we aim to integrate more sophisticated assembly-planning knowledge and more full-featured dialog manager based on the Information State Update approach [26]; while on the output side, we will extend the robot's repertoire of actions and enhance the non-verbal displays of the talking head.

We will also expand the linguistic processing modules so that the system is able to work in English in addition to German.

Acknowledgments. This work was supported by the EU FP6 IST Cognitive Systems Integrated Project "JAST" (FP6-003747-IP), http://www.euprojects-jast.net/.

References

1. Erlhagen, W., Mukovskiy, A., Bicho, E., Panin, G., Kiss, C., Knoll, A., van Schie, H., Bekkering, H.: Goal-directed imitation for robots: a bio-inspired approach to action understanding and skill learning. Robotics and Autonomous Systems 54(5), 353–360 (2006)
2. Foster, M.E., By, T., Rickert, M., Knoll, A.: Human-robot dialogue for joint construction tasks. In: Proceedings of the International Conference on Multimodal Interfaces, pp. 68–71. ACM Press, New York (2006)
3. van Breemen, A.J.N., Yan, X., Meerbeek, B.: iCat: An animated user-interface robot with personality. In: Proceedings of the International Joint Conference on Autonomous Agents and Multiagent Systems, pp. 143–144. ACM Press, New York (2005)
4. Knoll, A., Hildebrandt, B., Zhang, J.: Instructing cooperating assembly robots through situated dialogues in natural language. In: Proceedings of the IEEE International Conference on Robotics and Automation (April 1997)
5. Zhang, J., Knoll, A.: A two-arm situated artificial communicator for human-robot cooperative assembly. In: Proceedings of the IEEE International Workshop on Human Robot Communication, pp. 292–299 (2001)
6. Knoll, A.: basic system for multimodal robot instruction. In: Kühnlein, P., Rieser, H., Zeevat, H. (eds.) Perspectives on Dialogue in the New Millennium. Pragmatics and Beyond New Series, vol. 114, John Benjamins, Amsterdam (2003)
7. Knoll, A.: Distributed contract networks of sensor agents with adaptive reconfiguration: Modelling, simulation, implementation. Journal of the Franklin Institute 338(6), 669–705 (September 2001)

8. Breazeal, C., Brooks, A., Gray, J., Hoffman, G., Kidd, C., Lee, H., Lieberman, J., Lockerd, A., Chilongo, D.: Tutelage and collaboration for humanoid robots. International Journal of Humanoid Robotics 1(2), 315–348 (2004)
9. Sidner, C.L., Dzikovska, M.: first experiment in engagement for human-robot interaction in hosting activities. In: Bernsen, N., Dybkjær, L., van Kuppevelt, J. (eds.) Advances in Natural Multimodal Dialogue Systems, Springer, Heidelberg (2005)
10. Fong, T.W., Kunz, C., Hiatt, L., Bugajska, M.: The human-robot interaction operating system. In: Proceedings of the International Conference on Human-Robot Interaction, ACM (2006)
11. Burghart, C., Mikut, R., Stiefelhagen, R., Asfour, T., Holzapfel, H., Steinhaus, P., Dillmann, R.: cognitive architecture for humanoid robot: first approach. In: Proceedings of the IEEE-RAS International Conference on Humanoid Robots, pp. 357–362 (2005)
12. Henning, M.: new approach to object-oriented middleware. IEEE Internet Computing 8(1), 66–75 (2004)
13. Nuance Communications, Inc.: Dragon NaturallySpeaking http://www.nuance. com/ naturallyspeaking/
14. Panin, G., Ladikos, A., Knoll, A.: An efficient and robust real-time contour tracking system. In: Proceedings of IEEE International Conference on Computer Vision Systems, IEEE Computer Society, 44 (2006)
15. Pighin, F., Hecker, J., Lischinski, D., Szeliski, R., Salesin, D.H.: Synthesizing realistic facial expressions from photographs. In: Proceedings of the International Conference on Computer Graphics and Interactive Techniques, pp. 75–84. ACM Press, New York (1998)
16. Moddemeijer, R.: On estimation of entropy and mutual information of continuous distributions. Signal Processing 16(3), 233–246 (1989)
17. Steedman, M.: The Syntactic Process. MIT Press, Cambridge, MA (2000)
18. White, M.: Efficient realization of coordinate structures in combinatory categorial grammar. Research on Language and Computation 4(1), 39–75 (2006)
19. Morrow, J.D., Khosla, P.K.: Manipulation task primitives for composing robot skills. In: Proceedings of the IEEE International Conference on Robotics and Automation, pp. 3354–3359 (1997)
20. Zhang, J., von Collani, Y., Knoll, A.: Interactive assembly by a two-arm robot agent. Journal of Robotics and Autonomous Systems 29(1), 91–100 (1999)
21. Thomas, U., Finkemeyer, B., Kröger, T., Wahl, F.: Error-tolerant execution of complex robot tasks based on skill primitives. In: Proceedings of the IEEE International Conference on Robotics and Automation, pp. 3069–3075 (2003)
22. Milighetti, G., Kuntze, H.-B.: Multi-sensor controlled skills for humanoid robots. In: Proceedings of the IFAC International Symposium on Robot Control (2006)
23. Jilka, M., Syrdal, A.K.: The AT&T German text-to-speech system: Realistic linguistic description. In: Proceedings of the International Conference on Spoken Language Processing, pp. 113–116 (2002)
24. Sidner, C.L., Lee, C., Kidd, C.D., Lesh, N., Rich, C.: Explorations in engagement for humans and robots. Artificial Intelligence 166(1–2), 140–164 (2005)
25. White, M., Foster, M.E., Oberlander, J., Brown, A.: Using facial feedback to enhance turn-taking in multimodal dialogue system. In: Proceedings of the International Conference on Human-Computer Interaction (2005)
26. Traum, D., Larsson, S.: The information state approach to dialogue management. In: Smith, R.W., van Kuppevelt, J. (eds.) Current and New Directions in Discourse and Dialogue, Kluwer Academic Publishers, Dordrecht (2003)

A New Gaze-Based Interface for Environmental Control

Fangmin Shi, Alastair Gale, and Kevin Purdy

Applied Vision Research Centre, Loughborough University
Loughborough LE11 3TU, United Kingdom
{f.shi, a.g.gale, k.j.purdy}@lboro.ac.uk

Abstract. This paper describes a new control system interface which utilises the user's eye gaze to enable severely disabled individuals control electronic devices easily. The system is based upon a novel human computer interface, which facilitates simple control of electronic devices by predicting and responding to the user's possible intentions, based intuitively upon their point of gaze. The interface responds by automatically pre-selecting and offering only those controls appropriate to the specific device that the user looks at, in a simple and accessible manner. It therefore affords the user conscious choice of the appropriate range of control actions required, which may be executed by simple means and without the need to navigate manually through potentially complex control menus to reach them. Two systems using the head-mounted and the remote eye tracker respectively are introduced, compared and evaluated in this paper.

1 Introduction

A number of diseases can progressively degenerate people's motor cells in the brain and spinal cord, greatly reducing their mobility. Statistics in 2006 [1, 2] showed that in Europe there were over three million patients suffering from ALS (Amyotrophic Lateral Sclerosis)/MND (Motor Neuron Disease), MS (Multiple Sclerosis), CP (Cerebral Palsy), SCI (Spinal Cord Injury), SMA (Spinal Muscular Atrophy), Rett Syndrome, Stroke, and TBI (Traumatic Brain Injury). All of these can gradually weaken patients' muscles and make them paralyzed, as well as impairing the ability to speak and breathe. In recent years there is evidence to suggest the incidence of these diseases is increasing. This is partly because these are more prevalent in an ageing population [3]. Due to the increasing personal and government cost on caregivers, the need for variable healthcare options attracts lots of interest from policy makers to encourage assistive technologies to be developed. As the intellect, memory or senses of such patients are unlikely to be affected by such diseases [3], a significant interest has also been generated from academics and industry in conducting research and development on assistive technologies to help them cope with their daily lives through the utilisation of their existing body functions, such as eye sight.

One of the useful assistive technologies for disabled and elderly people is the environmental control system. With it people are able to control their house lighting, open/close curtains and respond to the doorbell, for example. An environmental control system is normally designed to operate via a remote control comprising

C. Stephanidis (Ed.): Universal Access in HCI, Part II, HCII 2007, LNCS 4555, pp. 996–1005, 2007.

numerous buttons or menus. Consequently, this is a serious challenge for people with severe mobility impairment to manipulate such devices due to lack of fine finger movement skills. In fact, any development without an appropriate interface to meet the capabilities that a disabled individual has would be of little or no use to them.

Because mobility-restricted people often retain their sight and the ability to control their eye movements, many eye tracking systems have been developed to aid users by means of eye control technologies. These typically utilise a person's eye gaze to form a new human computer control interface so that a user is then able to use their eyes to create documents, browse the internet and even play games for fun. Many applications can be seen on the COGAIN website [1], which is a research network concerned with developing technologies on Communication by Gaze Interaction.

The means of making environmental controls accessible to people with such specialist needs is a large research issue. Within COGAIN, a couple of applications have shown a way to operate environmental controls via selecting on-screen computer icons representing each controllable device. The user, sitting in front of the screen, uses their eye gaze to navigate around the menu. By looking at either the "on" or "off" key (for instance) of the desired menu for a sufficient 'eye dwell' time, the appropriate device control is activated. Such system copes well with those disabled people who can make accurate eye selection. However, the difficulty of such selection methods would rise with increasing numbers of devices and control options, which directly result in increasing the complexity of the screen menu layout. In addition, such a system has a generic disadvantage in that the user randomly gazing at the screen could falsely trigger an action. Such a system also intrinsically requires the user to be positioned before a computer screen; in some cases this may not be desirable or practicable, in others it may compete with other activities the user is performing with the same screen.

In this paper a user-centric control design is presented, which allows an individual user to sit comfortably in, for instance, a wheelchair with an eye tracker monitoring his/her eye movement in real time. The user's direct eye gaze at a controllable device in their three dimensional environment would result in the system responding by offering simple control options specifically tailored to only the device in question. Currently the work employs a screen to present the options to the user but this could easily be of another type, such as an audible menu, as appropriate to the situation. Similarly, control input is currently achieved by eye-gaze, but other methods such as blow/suck tubes could be employed as necessary. Although the control interface is actuated in response to direct eye gaze, the control input is therefore a separate stage, making the complete process an indirect procedure. This method reduces accidental operation of devices and allows for more detailed control options, therefore increasing conscious control and autonomy for the user in controlling their environment. It is not simply a change of state, and the responsive interface can offer much more than a simple confirmation of the control action.

This research is currently being carried out under a research project named ART – Attention Responsive Technology. In the ART project, two types of eye trackers have been employed to track users' saccadic eye movements –a head mounted and a remote system. Their respective system developments have been described in previous papers [4, 5, 6]. The following sections of this paper will briefly introduce the ART architecture and the two types of ART system designs with the focus on a comparison of the two systems.

2 Attention Responsive Interface for Environmental Control

In order to achieve environmental control by means of eye gaze, the ART system is designed to have the following components:

- An eye tracker, which records the user' eye movements in real time and analyses the eye fixations when available.
- A scene object monitor, which is a compact computer vision unit, used to observe the user's environment in terms of his/her field of view. Any pre-known object in their field of view will be automatically identified and located by matching it with a pre-recorded image database of available controllable objects.
- A display to present the control options specific to the identified device. For instance, a simple ON or OFF choice may be popped up for an identified electric fan or a more complex range of options may be presented for controlling a TV. This display may comprise a compact screen, a touch sensitive screen or other technologies such as verbal menus, as most appropriate to the situation.
- A user-configurable means of allowing the user to make one or more control actions. For making a selection relative to a normal display screen menu, this can be again by eye control, by a switch or any other assistive input that is within the disabled individual's capabilities. For a touch sensitive screen, the user must be able to reach and touch the choice with suitable accuracy by some part of his/her body or a control stick or wand attached to them, for example on a head-band if they have suitable neck movement. Alternatively, a user could choose to use his/her eye blinks for indicating a selection.
- A wireless controller, which executes actual device control upon user initiation.

To illustrate how the ART system works, Fig. 1 shows the work flow. The ART system constantly monitors the user's eye movements. Any gaze fixation will trigger a scene image to be analysed, i.e. to identify and locate any controllable object. It will then be determined whether the eye fixation occupies the same location as a controllable object. If it does, then the control options specifically applicable to the identified device will be displayed and appropriate control action will be implemented. For example, when a user wants to open a curtain, what s/he needs to do is to simply look at the curtain. After an analysis to match his/her stable point of gaze at the curtain, two choices of OPEN and CLOSE are offered. By making one of the selections, the user's visual attention to the curtain will become an action as s/he wishes.

3 System Development - Common Units

The ART system has been designed with two different types of eye trackers, a head mounted and a remote system. The former affords a user with sufficient head rotation capabilities a wider field of view over which the system can accurately work. The latter remote system has the advantage of causing less physical intrusion and no long term discomfort, as it is not worn. It would also be much easier to set up with the user for each period of use, and so is considered a more acceptable solution for those who do not need or have a great deal of head movement. These different ways of tracking the eye gaze not only bring differences in system calibration procedures but also cause variations in setting up the scene camera. However, other functions are common in both systems.

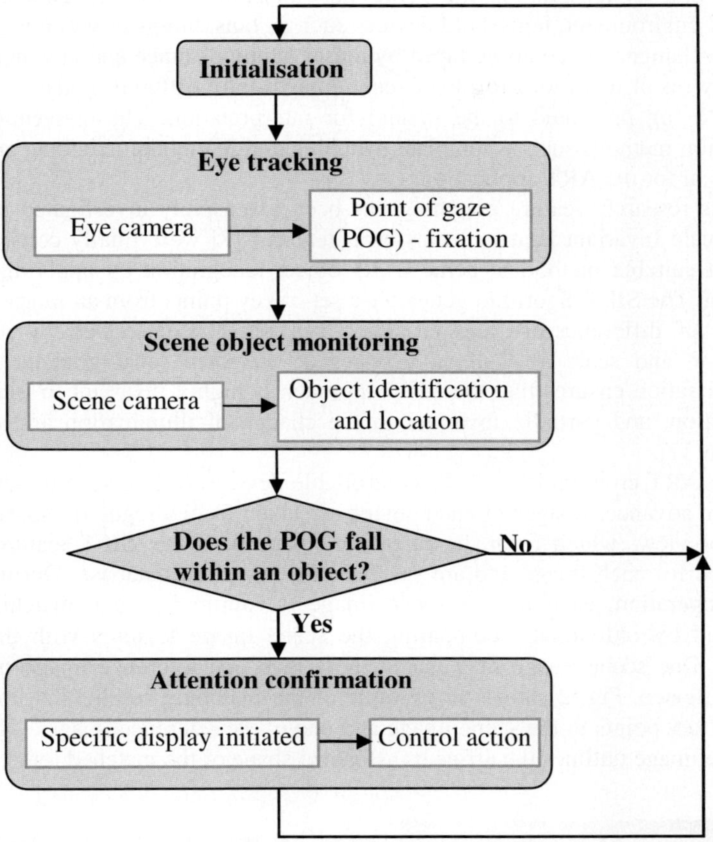

Fig. 1. ART system work illustration

3.1 Object Recognition

The main challenges for implementing the ART system design lie in:

1. How to recognise an object in three dimensional space
2. For a given gaze, how to know its position in the scene image coordinate system
3. Addressing issues of setup and maintenance, such as compatibility with typical environments and developing in-built procedures to add/ delete a new device
4. Building in sufficient capacity for user customisation in order to cater for their individual capabilities and requirements
5. Catering for the wider issues of its general use, over and above its basic operation. For example, considering how the system is set up with a user on a daily basis,

designing for none or less computer-literate carers to run it, maximising its robustness in a real-world situation and considering the consequence of system failure in situations where potentially vulnerable users may rely heavily upon it.

Items 2-4 will be addressed in the later sections of the paper. The first challenge exists in both systems and is one of the most difficult of them all. This is because in the ART environment, household devices such as fans, lamps or curtains, either solid or shape-changeable, could be faced by a user at any distance and any angle of view. This may result in various forms of scene images with different scales, rotations and lighting being presented to the system for interpretation. The conventional object recognition methods such as template matching and 3D model matching are therefore impractical for the ART application.

In this research, feature matching has been extensively investigated and Lowe's SIFT (Scale Invariant Feature Transform) features [7] were finally considered to be the most suitable method to achieve 3D object recognition by applying 2D image matching. The SIFT algorithm generates a set of key points from an image based on a pyramid of difference-of-Gaussian. Each key point is described by its location, orientation and scale as well as a series of weighted local gradient data. Such characterisation ensures that the SIFT approach is highly invariant to image scaling and rotation, and partially invariant to the change of illumination and the camera viewpoint [7].

In the ART environment all the controllable devices will need to be known to the system in advance. Images of each device are taken from a regularly spaced range of angles of view, which form the reference image database. SIFT features are then calculated for each image and are saved in the key point database. During real time system operation, each time a scene image is captured, image matching will be performed by individually comparing the scene image features with the database features. One scene image may match more than one reference image of the same indexed device. Fig. 2 shows an example of the matching result. The lines join the matched key points in the scene image and one of the reference images. The frame in the scene image outlines the affine transformed shape of the matched reference image.

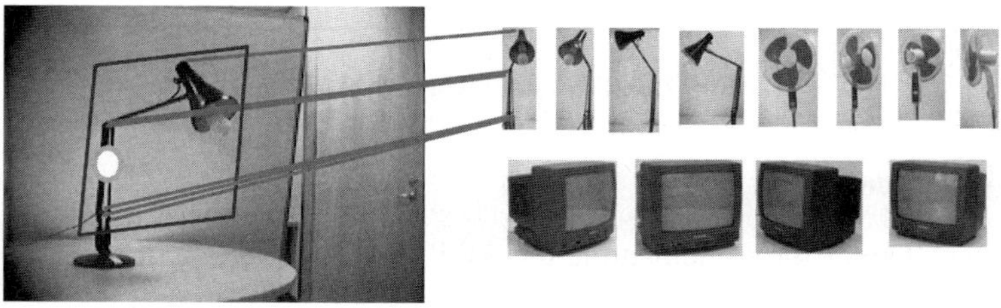

Fig. 2. SIFT feature matching identifies and locates the controllable device

3.2 User Interface

When a user's gaze at a device is detected, then an interface solely for that device is offered and the user can elect to operate the device or not. The physical user interface comprises two parts: an information display conveying the current state of the device and range of possible control actions, and a control input allowing the user to make the necessary control actions in a way that is appropriate to their abilities. Currently the display provides the necessary information visually and comprises a flat-panel interactive display. The user-configurable control input, currently provides three methods of control input to be utilised: simple switches, a touch sensitive screen and an eye blink to the screen, however many more options are possible ranging from a second stage of eye-control to more discrete transducers such as suck/blow tubes.

3.3 Device Control

Actual operation of the selected electronic device is accomplished through using the X10 control system which provides wireless environmental control from the user's interface [8]. The X10 communication protocol has been widely used in the area of home automation. It builds on the existing electrical wiring in the typical household. Each electrical device is plugged into an X10 modular device before it in turn is connected to the mains. Each modular device interprets control signals from a central transmitter.

As a home automation technology X10 has several advantages. It uses the existing wiring infrastructure in the building and so additional wiring is not necessary. X10 modules are cheap, easy to use, can be retro-fitted and are readily available. There are currently no other competing protocols that work as efficiently as X10 as a starting point in simple home automation applications. However, there are well known disadvantages for X10 in terms of its speed and reliability over long wiring runs and different circuits. A neighbouring X10 action may well change another system's X10 device status. As a consequence of its generically applicable nature the system is also relatively limited in the complexity of control operations it can interface with when dealing with more complicated devices having numerous possible states or levels to control. To overcome these, it is easy to upgrade to other home automation control technologies such as Insteon and Z-Wave, although both of these increase the cost of some usage complexities and higher market price.

4 ART System with Two Eye Trackers

4.1 ASL Head-Mounted Eye Tracker

The ART system is firstly designed with the ASL 501, a light weight head-mounted eye tracker. A laboratory-based prototype system and its software control interface have been developed and described in detail [4, 5].

Basically, a user needs to wear a head band, on which is mounted a compact eye camera, monitoring the eye illuminated by near infra-red light, as well as a compact scene camera, facing the user's field of view. The user's pupil size and the eye's line of gaze are computed by extracting the eye's pupil outline, which is highlighted by IR light reflecting back from the retina, and the light reflection from the cornea.

In this configuration, the relative position of the head, the eye camera and the scene camera is constant. A user simply needs to complete a subject calibration to establish this relationship once, unless any of these subsequently moves. In practice this is typically each time the system is positioned afresh on the user's head, as it is difficult to do so with exact duplication of previous positions. The nature of the ASL eye tracker has made the subject calibration very easy to follow. The procedure needs the user to sit in a comfortable position while wearing the head band and to look at nine calibration points consecutively on a target chart positioned in front of them. The system is nominally accurate to less than 1 degree of visual angle, which equates to an accuracy of approximately 35mm at a distance of 2m. In Fig. 3, using the calibrated parameters to verify the image points in the chart, there are statistically less than 10 pixels of error with an image size of 760x576 and at a distance of about 2m.

Fig. 3. ASL calibration with verified image points

Wearing both the eye and scene cameras on the head gives an easy way to set up the ART system with good accuracy, however, there are two main drawbacks with using this system. The first is that ambient lighting can significantly affect the pupil size and bright lights can also impede detection of the necessary infra-red reflections, thus leading to unstable line of gaze calculations. The second is concern about the user's comfort for prolonged periods of wearing the eye tracker on the head. The application of the ART system is expected to be one in which it is used for such extended periods of time by users, as it will facilitate autonomy throughout their daily life, so therefore comfort for the user is of vital importance.

4.2 Smarteye Remote Eye Tracker

To truly integrate the system into other assistive technologies, a less physically invasive system would be a distinct advantage. For this purpose, a new ART system using the Smarteye remote eye tracker has been developed [6]. There is a remote version of the ASL eye tracker available, but it was felt that in the ART project's particular application the Smarteye system would offer some advantages. Key amongst these was that it allows for greater head rotation and so an effectively wider total field of view, which could be important to users where head movement is possible and potentially also one of the few physical motor capabilities they may have available for them to utilise.

As the name suggests, the eye tracking with the Smarteye system is carried out remotely while a user sits comfortably in front of one to five small video cameras (eye cameras). There is no attachment at all to the user in this new configuration.

A three-camera Smarteye system is currently employed. The cameras are positioned completely independently from each other but are aimed to cover a range of likely user movements and head positions. The relative camera positions can then be calibrated by an automatic process through holding a calibration chart and making it visible to all three cameras. The Smarteye unit adopts a very different method from ASL to obtain the users' head position and eye line of gaze. Prior to any usage, it needs to generate a user's profile, which is a virtual 3D model of the user's head containing some prominent facial features. The features are marked in a series of snapshots to form the head and eye model and also used as a template in real time tracking of the head and the eyes. The Smarteye output is in three dimensions with reference to a World Coordinate System (WCS), which can be defined during the three-camera calibration process. This feature allows a great deal of user movement. The output can also be projected to a two dimensional plane in the World Coordinate System.

To develop the ART system, a scene camera is additionally integrated. We use a high resolution USB camera. This is positioned alongside the user's head and covers the scene which the user can reasonably view, or that part of the user's scene over which eye position can successfully be tracked, whichever is the smaller.

Fig. 4. Smart Eye calibration with verified image points

Like the ASL unit, the relationship among the user, the eye camera and the scene camera needs to be identified in order to relate the eye gaze position or direction to the scene. A similar calibration process to the ASL method is used to achieve this and Fig. 4 shows the calibration image with verified points. It can be seen that the Smarteye results have more error than those obtained from the ASL system. The average gaze accuracy is nearly 2 degrees with a larger error along the vertical axis than that along the horizontal axis. The errors are mainly due to noise in the head model generation; possibly resulting from the limited number of pixels in the eye images.

The absolute gaze error in comparison with the ground truth data with the Smarteye system is larger than with the ASL, however, it has the potential to still meets the ART system requirements well. Further investigation is currently being carried out to improve the Smarteye accuracy results in the ART system implementation.

4.3 System Integration and Comparison

Combining the different components described in Section 3 and either of the eye trackers above will form two complete ART systems. The systems work in different ways; however, as a result of the development carried out they will both successfully allow the detection of a purposeful gaze upon a controllable object if applicable. The circled star point imposed in Fig. 2 is an example of such a detected gaze falling within the identified object area. Both advantages and disadvantages of the two ART system approaches are evident as already discussed in the above context. Table 1 gives a comparison of the two ART systems in terms of their performance.

Table 1. System performance comparison with two ART systems

	ASL – based system	Smart Eye – based system
Measurement of eye line of gaze	By identifying pupil and corneal reflection and computing their separation	By computing the direction from the eye centre to the eye pupil known from the real time tracking of the head pose and the eye, based on the user's head/eye model
Calibration frequency	Once per session	Once per user
Calibration time	<30s	3 stages: 1. 3 eye camera calibration and definition of WCS: ≈10s 2. creation of subject's profile: ≈10 minutes 3. system calibration with scene camera: <30s
Requirement for the user during calibration	remaining perfectly still	No special restriction
Average gaze accuracy	<1°	2° or more
Sensitivity to ambient light	Sensitive to bright lights or daylight	Little
Allowable eye movement (horizontally/vertically)	50°/35° with no head movement. With head movement it is only limited by the physical ability to rotate head/body.	170°/60° also with no head movement
Attachment to user	Yes	No

5 Discussion and Conclusion

ART is especially designed to help individuals whose movements are severely restricted, or potentially for cases where other forms of control and movement are otherwise undesirable or impractical. ART system users also comprise patient's carers, system installers, maintainers etc. This paper has presented two different eye tracking units for direct detection of a user's attention to real household devices with a view to providing a more usable environmental control system.

The head mounted ASL system is easier to set up and gives more accurate gaze output, however, ambient light would affect it more and the requirement for a head band attachment to the user's head seems not practical for a long term usage. The remote Smarteye system completely releases the user from donning any attachment, but it needs more time to set up a user *initially* and its generic way of computing the eye gaze currently results in a larger error in our particular application (although this may be reduced by further investigation). Both systems also have a number of other components in common, i.e. the object identification and location, the control action and the initiation interface. The system evaluation with both able-bodied people and the disabled ART system potential users is currently being undertaken. To make an assistive device fully usable, apart from technical success, issues such as cost, reliability and human factors are all important, which will comprise further work on the project.

Acknowledgements. This research is funded by the ESRC/EPSRC PACCIT Programme. The work is also part of the COGAIN network.

References

1. COGAIN, Communication by Gaze Interaction (2006) http://www.cogain.org/, accessed
2. Bates, R., Donegan, M., Istance, H.O., Hansen, J.P., Rih, K.-J.: Introducing COGAIN – Communication by Gaze Interaction. In: Clarkson, J., Langdon, P., Robinson, P. (eds.) Designing Accessible Technology, pp. 77–84. Springer, Heidelberg (2006)
3. ASL/MND Alliance International. (Accessed 2007) http://www.alsmndalliance.org/
4. Shi, F., Gale, A.G., Purdy, K.J.: Eye-centric ICT control. In: Bust, P.D., McCabe, P.T. (eds.): Contemporary Ergonomics, Cambridge, pp. 215–223 (2006)
5. Shi, F., Gale, A.G., Purdy, K.J.: Helping People with ICT Device Control by Eye Gaze. In: Miesenberger, K., Klaus, J., Zagler, W., Karshmer, A. (eds.): Lecture Notes in Computer Science, Springer-Verlag, Berlin, pp. 480–487 (2006)
6. Shi, F., Gale, A.G., Purdy, K.J.: Exploring Eye Responsive Control – from a head mounted to a remote system. In: Bust, P.D., McCabe, P.T. (eds.): Contemporary Ergonomics, Nottingham (To appear 2007)
7. Lowe, D.G.: Distinctive Image Features from Scale-Invariant Keypoints. International Journal of Computer Vision 60(2), 91–110 (2004)
8. Gale, A.G., Shi, F., Purdy, K.J.: X10 - are you looking at me. In: de Waard, D. (ed.): Development in Human Factors in Transportation, Design, and Evaluation: Human Factors in Industrial and Consumer Products and Services conference, HFES Europe Chapter, Turin, Italy, pp. 285–294 (2006)

Geometry Issues of a Gaze Tracking System

Arantxa Villanueva, Juan J. Cerrolaza, and Rafael Cabeza

Public University of Navarre,
Campus Arrosadia sn., 31006 Pamplona, Spain
{avilla, rcabeza}@unavarra.es

Abstract. One of the most confusing aspects that one meets as he introduces himself into gaze tracking is the variety, in terms of hardware equipment, of available systems providing solutions to the same matter, i.e. determining subject's gaze. Calibration permits adjusting trackers based on different hardware and image features to the subject. The negative aspect of calibration is that it permits the system to work properly but at the expense of a lack of control over the intrinsic behavior of the tracker. The objective of this work is to overcome this obstacle to explore more deeply the elements of a tracker from a purely geometrical point of view. Alternative models based on image features are evaluated. As result of this study a model has been constructed based on minimal calibration using one camera and multiple lighting with acceptable accuracy level.

Keywords: gaze-tracking, video-oculography, calibration, PoR, LoS.

1 Introduction

Among existing tracking technologies, systems incorporating video-oculography (VOG) use a camera or a number of cameras and try to determine the movement of the eye using the information obtained after studying the captured images. Normally they include infrared lighting in order to produce specific effects in the obtained images. The non intrusive nature of the trackers employing videooculography renders it an attractive technique. Video-oculographic eye tracking techniques can be divided into two main groups. Methods that measure the eye movements inside its orbit and methods that calculate the gaze direction, i.e. Line of Sight (LoS). For the methods of the second type if the position of the gazed area, such as a screen, is known the Point of Regard (PoR) is determined as the gazed point. The number of commercial systems and experimental trackers devoted to calculating PoR that incorporate VOG is really large and they admit multiple variations in terms of hardware, i.e. number of cameras and number of lighting sources. However, their basis seems to be the same; the image of the eye captured by the camera will change when the eye rotates or translates in 3D space. In fact most of them work in an acceptable way and can be used in real applications. However, from another point of view it seems essential to explore more deeply into the geometry and behavior of these systems. This will help to explain and

C. Stephanidis (Ed.): Universal Access in HCI, Part II, HCII 2007, LNCS 4555, pp. 1006–1015, 2007.

correct most of the problems arisen during tracking sessions as the subject moves his head or the tracking is lost. The arisen matter is evident: "what is the connection between the image in the camera and the observed point?" This study tries to analyze the mathematical connection between the image and the observed point in depth. Interesting works have been presented devoted to mathematical modelling of gaze tracking systems. The most relevant are the ones presented by Beymer&Flickner [1], Ohno&Mukawa [2] and Shih&Liu [3] and more recently the results by Guestrin&Eizenman [4] and Hennessey et al. [5]. All of them deal with single camera or stereo trackers that use some kind of infrared lighting. The work by Shih&Liu [3], from our point of view, presents high mathematical rigor.

We would like to emphasize the theoretical essence of the present paper. Although experimental results are included we consider that our main contribution is the construction of a geometrical basis and models as result of our work. The link between the image and the observed point is found deducing the minimal requirements of a system in terms of number of cameras or illuminators. Narrowly related with the hardware necessities, the most interesting features of the image for gaze determination can be identified. As a consequence of this finding a model for a gaze tracking system fully based on identifiable and recognizable variables is constructed. In the next section a more proper introduction to the studied matter is carried out. Sections 3 and 4 are devoted to the analysis of alternative models and to the construction of the final model for a gaze tracking system. Section 5 presents the experimental results and finally the conclusions obtained are exposed in section 6.

2 Eye Tracking System Models

Regardless of the hardware used the goal of any tracker is to establish a connection between the features provided by the technology, i.e. image analysis results, and gaze. Quadratic or cubic expressions based on unknown coefficients that are deduced by means of the well-known calibration procedure are used to this end. Calibration consists in asking the subject to gaze at a 3x3/4x4 grid of known markers on the screen. This permits systems with fully different hardware and image features to work acceptably, but prevents researchers from determining the minimal system requirements and geometrical properties. The objective of this work is to overcome this obstacle and to build a geometrical model based on physical parameters for the gaze tracking system. The procedure selected in order to accomplish the work is to analyze separately the alternative features that can be extracted from the image. We define a model as a connection between the fixated point and alternative features extracted from the image, expressed as a function of hardware and subject parameters describing the gaze tracking system setup. The models proposed are based on single point features such as the center of the pupil and the glint, based on shapes such as the pupil ellipse or based on combinations of points and shapes. First a geometrical analysis is conducted for the models in which projective relations among the elements of the system are studied from a purely geometrical point of view. In this step corneal refraction is obviated and the determination of the gaze direction in a free head movement scenario is pursued for the models. Secondly corneal refraction is considered for those models that satisfied the previous step introducing additional limitations to the model. Figure 1 sketches the analysis for each model.

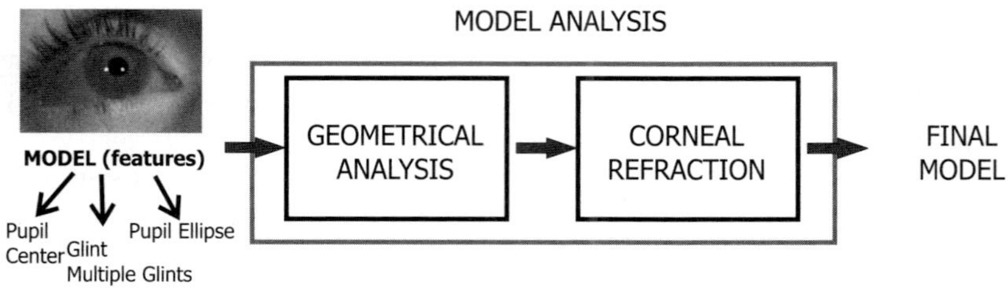

Fig. 1. Each model based on alternative image features is analyzed geometrically and from the point of view of corneal refraction

3 Geometrical Analysis

From a geometrical point of view the objective should be to find a model that can determine the 3D position of the gaze in a free head movement environment. The gaze line can be easily approximated by the visual axis. On the other hand the optical axis of the eyeball can be approximated as its symmetry axis. Optical and visual axes of the eye present an angular offset nasally whose value is about 5±1°. Once the 3D position of the optical axis is calculated with respect to a reference system, the visual axis can be calculated supposing that the horizontal angular offset between both axes is known and applying the corresponding torsion described in [6] in order to achieve an agreement with the eyeball orientation described by Listing's and Donder's laws. The optical axis of the eye contains three principal points of the eyeball since it is approximated as its symmetry axis, i.e. *A*, eyeball center, *C*, corneal center and *E*, pupil center. Therefore the geometrical matter is reduced to determine two points of the optical axis. Figure 2 represents a simplified description of the problem. Then the visual axis can be easily derived from it as it has been explained before. To follow the alternative models are introduced. Much effort has been made in order to simplify the most cumbersome mathematical aspects and to pay more attention in the obtained conclusions. More details can be found in [7].

Center of the Pupil and Corneal Reflection. First the models resulting from each feature separately are studied. Regarding to the center of the pupil if affine projection is assumed, the center of the pupil in the image can be approximated to the projection of point *E*. Regardless of the exact mathematical expressions relating the involved variables, the selected image feature gives just information about one principal point of the optical axis, i.e. *E*.

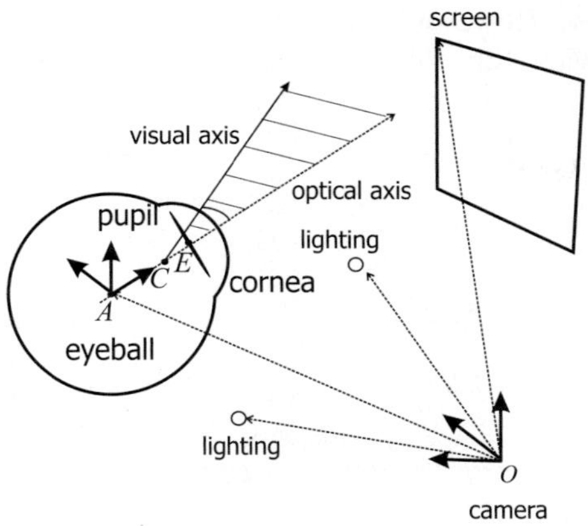

Fig. 2. Principal points of the system. The optical axis contains the center of the eyeball *A*, corneal center *C* and pupil center *E*.

On the other hand the corneal reflection or glint in the image is a consequence of the reflection caused by the illumination source on the corneal surface and in the best case can provide information about the corneal center position *C*. These two features separately provide information about one principal point of the optical axis, i.e. *E* or *C* respectively. Therefore the optical axis can hardly be solved. An acceptable behavior of the model could be expected in a fixed head situation (fixed *A*). However, free head movement is pursued and consequently these models are rejected.

It is commonly assumed that the distance between these two features in the image compensates for possible head movements during a tracking session but from the point of view of this work this approximation is not valid and there exists a dependence between this vector value and the head position. In order to simplify the analysis let us propose a rough approximation of both features. Assuming affine projection one could back-project the center of the pupil from the image generating the line r_m. Considering a coaxial location of the led with respect to the camera we define r_r as the back-projection of the glint into 3D space. Close approximations of points *E* and *C* are contained in r_m and r_r respectively. Knowing the distance between *E* and *C* does not solve the indetermination, since more than one combination of points in r_m and r_r can be found at the desired distance and therefore there is no unique solution. Therefore once again the 3D optical axis position is not determined (see figure 3).

Multiple Glints. Following the law of reflection each illuminator will result in a plane containing the incident ray, the reflected ray and the normal at the point of incidence. Consequently the corneal center *C* as well as the projection center of the camera *O* will be contained in the plane. It is deduced that if more than one illuminator are used, *C* contained in the normal, and *O* contained in the reflected ray, will be contained in the resulting intersection line of the planes [3]. Once the corneal 3D line is deduced knowing the corneal radius by means of a calibration process one could deduce the corneal center 3D position. Consequently it is stated that two illumination sources, i.e. two glints, are enough in order to determine the 3D position of the corneal center. However it does not add anything new, from a purely geometrical point of view, since A and E remain unknown and the optical axis is not determined.

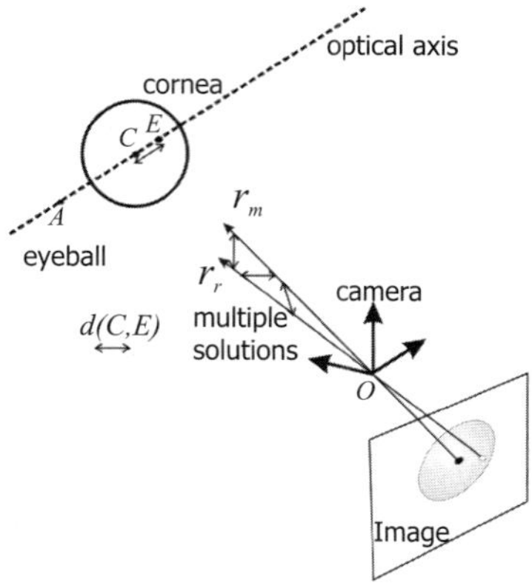

Fig. 3. The combination of pupil center and glint position does not allow determining the optical axis of the eye since multiple combinations can be found in r_r and r_m having the same distance

Pupil Center + Multiple Glints. From preceding sections we know that employing two glints leads to the 3D determination of the corneal center C. This breaks the indetermination arisen for the model based on the center of the pupil and one glint. In other words once C is found, the center of the pupil can be easily found knowing r_m and the distance between both points. The advantage with respect to the single glint model is that the introduction of a second illuminator resolves the position of the corneal center. No approximation has been considered for the estimation of C whereas affine projection is assumed for the center of the pupil.

The Projected Pupil Ellipse. It is already known that the projection of the pupil results in a shape that can be approximated by an ellipse [1] [2]. The back-projection of the pupil from the image into 3D space would be a cone, i.e. back projection cone, and it could be assured that there is at least one plane that intersects the cone in a circular section containing the pupil. The theory about conics claims that parallel intersections of a quadric result in equivalent conic sections. Considering the back projection cone as a quadric, it is clear that if we find a plane with a circular section for the specific quadric, i.e. back projection cone, infinite pupils of different sizes could be defined employing intersecting parallel planes. The direction of the planes that result in circular sections is not a trivial task and is derived from [8]. The absolute conic that using homogenous coordinates (x^0, x^1, x^2, x^3) is defined as $x^0 = 0$;

$$\sum_{i=1}^{3} (x^i)^2 = 0 \tag{1}$$

lying on the plane at infinity is the place of all the cyclic sections. The intersection of a quadric with the absolute conic is a circumference. The mathematical solution of this intersection finds out the direction of the parallel planes or sets of parallel planes that intersect the quadric with a circular shape. For the case under analysis two possible solutions resulting in circular sections of the cone are found. Two groups of an infinite number of planes can be calculated, each of them intersecting the back-projection cone in a circular shape of different sizes and containing a suitable solution for the gaze tracking matter. Consequently no solution can be provided for the optical axis since the size of the 3D pupil is supposed to be unknown and variable during a tracking session and consequently not valid to select one of the intersections.

The Pupil Ellipse + Glint. To simplify the analysis once again we deduce a 3D line by means of the back-projection of the glint in the image which is supposed to contain an approximation of *C*, i.e. r_r. Each possible plane intersecting the back-projection cone in a circumference determines a pupil center *E* and an optical axis that is calculated as the 3D line perpendicular to the pupil plane that crosses *E* (see figure 4). The solution is easily deduced if the distance between the center of the pupil *E* and the corneal center *C* is known. The pupil plane for which the optical axis meets the r_r line at the known distance from *E* will be selected as solution to the tracking problem. In addition the intersection between the optical axis and the r_r line will be the corneal center *C*. Therefore the introduction of the glint permits the selection of one of the planes for each one of the two possible orientations (see The Projected Pupil Ellipse). However a more rigorous mathematical analysis leads to conclude that just one solution is possible as the second one requires the assumption that the center of the cornea, *C*, remains closer to the camera than the center of the pupil *E* and this situation is not feasible.

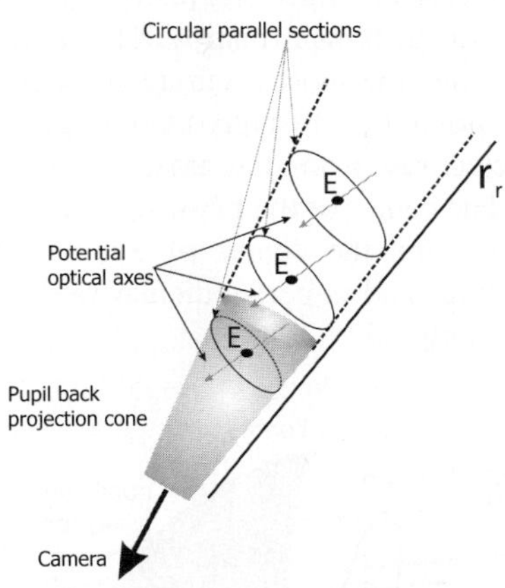

Fig. 4. Each plane intersects the cone in a circle resulting in an optical axis crossing its center *E* perpendicularly. The correct optical axis is the one that intersects r_r at the right distance, i.e. *d(C, E)*.

The Pupil Ellipse + Multiple Glints. It is already known that the combination of two glints and the center of the pupil provides a solution to the tracking problem. Therefore at least the same result is expected if the pupil ellipse is considered since it contains the value of the center. The most outstanding difference amongst models based on the pupil ellipse with one or multiple glints is the fact that employing the information provided exclusively by the glints, the corneal center can be accurately determined. Consequently the data about the distance between both centers, i.e. pupil and corneal centers can be ignored. The known point *C* must be located in one of the optical axes calculated from the circular sections and crossing perpendicularly the corresponding center *E*. The optical axis among the possible ones that contains the previously calculated *C* will be selected as solution for the tracking problem.

4 Refraction Analysis

Since any ray of light coming from the back part of the eye suffers refraction and consequently a deviation in its direction when it crosses the corneal surface the obtained pupil image must be considered as the projection of a virtual pupil. The opposite path could be studied and any point of the pupil contour in the image can be back-projected from the image and refracted in the cornea. Starting from the pupil image in the camera the cornea, i.e. its center and radius, must be known to apply refraction. Consequently the model based on the pupil ellipse and the glint fails this analysis since it does not accomplish a previous determination of the corneal center. Contrary to this model the one based on the pupil center and two glints makes a prior computation of the corneal center, however, it can no longer be assumed it is the center of the real pupil the one contained in r_m but the center of the virtual pupil. One could expect that *E* will be contained in a 3D line obtained as a consequence of the refraction of r_m when crossing the cornea. Although this approximation can be considered as valid in some cases it is geometrically not true, since refraction through a spherical surface is not a linear transformation. The model based on two glints and the shape of the pupil provides the most accurate solution to the matter. The model deduces the value of *C* employing exclusively the two glints of the image. Then each pupil contour back-projected ray from the image is calculated and its refraction estimated into the cornea. The center of the pupil should be a point located at a known distance from *C* that represents the center of a circle whose perimeter is fully contained in the refracted lines and is perpendicular to the line connecting pupil and corneal centers as shown in figure 5.

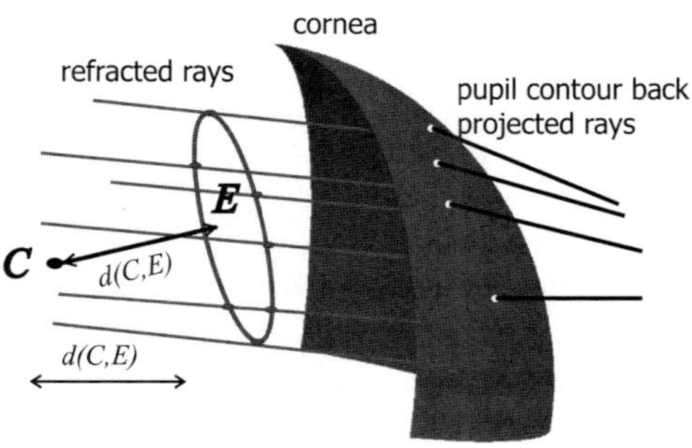

Fig. 5. The pupil center *E* is deduced from the refracted rays of the pupil contour from the image. It represents the center of a circumference that contains all the refracted rays and is connected to *C* perpendicularly at the correct distance *d(C, E)*.

5 Experimental Results

From the prior analysis, the model based on two glints and the shape of the pupil appears as the only potential model for the gaze tracking system. When a real eye tracking system is considered, real hardware must be considered. That means that certain intrinsic tolerances and noise of the elements composing the eye tracker need to be introduced. The reduced size of the glint in the image at certain user camera distances introduces certain indetermination in the position of the corneal reflection and consequently in the corneal center computation. Based on the experimental indetermination value of this feature a formal study was carried out that showed the sensitivity of the corneal center estimation with respect to glint position indetermination. In order to reduce the sensitivity the solution adopted by this study, is to increase the number of illumination sources in order to obtain an average value for the point *C*. If more than two illuminators are employed, alternative pairs can be used to estimate the pursued point. An average of the obtained values by means of the possible combinations reduces the sensitivity of the model to glint indetermination. Consequently a model based on the pupil ellipse and multiple lighting is proposed. Ten users were selected for the test. The working distance was selected in the range 400-500 mm from the camera. Figure 6a shows the selected fixation marks uniformly distributed in the gazing area whose position is known with respect to the camera. The position in mm for each point is shown. Ten consecutive images were acquired and grabbed for each fixation. The images have been captured with a calibrated Hamamatsu C5999 camera and digitalized by a Matrox Meteor card with a resolution of 640x480 (RS-170). The LEDs used for lighting have a spectrum centered at 850 nm. Four LEDs were selected to produce the needed multiple glints. They were located in the lower part of the camera and its positions with respect to the camera were measured. The images present a dark pupil and four bright glints (see figure 6b). The next step was to process each image separately to extract the glints coordinates and the ellipse of the pupil. As said in the introduction, this paper deals with geometrical modelling of gaze tracking systems. From this point of view aspects such as image processing algorithms used and additional experimental details are obviated to focus the reader in the results obtained for the proposed geometrical model.

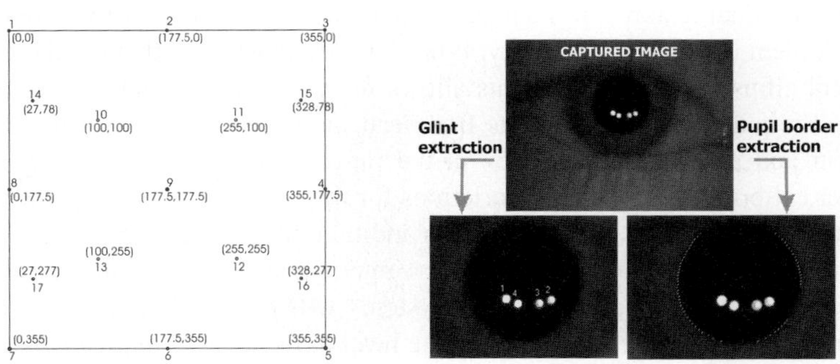

Fig. 6. a) Test points. b) From each image the glints positions and the pupil contour are extracted.

Once the hardware is defined and in order to apply the constructed model based on the ellipse and glints positions, some individual subject characteristics need to be calculated such as corneal radius, angular offset between optical and visual axes and the distance between corneal and pupil centers. The constructed model based on multiple glints and pupil shape permits, theoretically, determining this data by means of a single calibration mark. In the practice and in order to increase the confidence on the obtained values, three fixations were selected for each subject to estimate a mean value for these parameters. The aim of table 1 is to show a quantitative evaluation of the model competence for two, three and four LEDs. For each subject the average error for the 17 fixation marks was calculated in visual degrees since this is the most significative measurement of the model performance. It is clear that the model with four LEDs presents the lowest errors. In average the model with two LEDs presents an error of 1.08° the model with three LEDs 0.89° and the model with four 0.75°. Therefore it can be said that, in average, the models with three and four LEDs render acceptable accuracy values (<1°). As expected an increase in the number of illumination sources results in an improvement of the system tracking capacity.

Table 1. Error quantification (degree) of the final model using 2, 3 and 4 LEDs for ten users

Subject	1	2	3	4	5	6	7	8	9	10
2LED	1.47	0.85	1.46	0.90	0.92	0.97	1.24	0.78	1.19	1.06
3LED	1.06	0.80	1.35	0.58	0.75	0.78	1.20	0.79	0.74	0.86
4LED	1.04	0.76	1.01	0.62	0.72	0.71	0.62	0.65	0.59	0.80

6 Conclusions

The intrinsic connection between the captured image from the eye and gaze has been explored. A model for a video-oculographic eye tracking system has been constructed. A model is understood as a geometrical connection between subject's gaze and the variables describing the elements of the system together with the data extracted from the image. The objective was not to find the most robust system but to find out the minimal features of the image that are necessary in order to solve the gaze tracking problem in an acceptable way. It has been demonstrated that the model based on the pupil ellipse and multiple glints allows for a competent tracking and matches the pursued requirements, i.e. permits free head movement, has minimal calibration requirement and presents an accuracy in the range of the already existing systems with longer calibrations and more restrictions for the head. Theoretically one point of calibration is enough to adjust the model. In addition the minimal hardware needed by the system is also determined, i.e. one camera and multiple infrared lighting. Geometrical modelling of gaze tracking systems will provide a theoretical basis to find out image-gaze connections that tolerate head movement, explain and correct the loss of accuracy during a tracking session and allow for simpler and shorter calibration procedures.

Acknowledgments

COGAIN (511598): Communication by Gaze Interaction. Network of Excellence FP6-2003-IST-2.

References

1. Beymer, D., Flickner, M.: Eye gaze tracking using an active stereo head. In: Proceedings of the IEEE Conference on Computer Vision and Pattern Recognition. vol. 2, Wisconsin, pp. 451–458 (2003)
2. Ohno, T., Mukawa, N.: A free head, simple calibration, gaze tracking system that enables gaze-based interaction. In: Proceedings of the Eye Tracking Research and Applications Symposium, San Antonio (TX), pp. 115–122 (2004)
3. Shih, S.W., Liu, J.: A novel approach to 3-D gaze tracking using stereo cameras. IEEE Transactions Systems Man. and Cybernetics Part -B 34(1), 234–245 (2004)
4. Guestrin, E., Eizenman, M.: General theory of remote gaze estimation using pupil center and corneal reflections. IEEE Transactions on Biomedical Engineering 53(6), 1124–1133 (2006)
5. Hennessey, C., Noureddin, B., Lawrence, P.: A single camera eye-gaze tracking system with free head motion. In: ETRA '06: Proceedings of the 2006 symposium on Eye tracking research and applications, pp. 87–94. ACM Press, New York (2006)
6. Fry, G., Treleaven, C., Walsh, R., Higgins, E., Radde, C.: Definition and measurement of torsion. In: American Journal of Optometry and Archives of American Academy of Optometry. vol. 24., Philadelphia, pp. 329–334 (1947)
7. Villanueva, A.: Mathematical Models for Video Oculography. Thesis, Public University of Navarra, Pamplona, SPAIN (2005)
8. Hartley, R.I., Zisserman, A.: Multiple View Geometry in Computer Vision, 2nd edn. Cambridge University Press, Cambridge (2004) ISBN: 0521540518

Adaptive Context Aware Attentive Interaction in Large Tiled Display

Chee-Onn Wong, Dongwuk Kyoung, and Keechul Jung

Human-Centered Interface (HCI) Laboratory, Department of Media, Soongsil University, Seoul, South Korea
{cheeonn, kiki227, kcjung}@ssu.ac.kr

Abstract. We propose a conceptual model towards a context-based attentive interaction. Our focus is to improve the interaction between the user and the application of large tiled display by introducing user context and user attention. Interaction in our proposed system adapts user's visual attention region with the user's changing context based on head movement to achieve an immersive interaction with the tile display. Our experiment uses computer vision to track the user's presence and projects the most attentive regions in a tiled display in high resolution. User will be able to see other regions in higher resolution according to the head movement. At the same time, user attention is captured and modeled to learn the attentive regions to be displayed for other users. This paper will show the experimental result of the effectiveness of the perceptual interaction in a large tiled display environment.

Keywords: Tiled display, attentive user interface, context aware, perceptual interaction.

1 Introduction

The development of information and digital media makes it possible to explore into an immersive interaction experience. Perceptual interaction incorporates the perception based on the context environment that the system is situated, and enabling a desired interaction to take place accordingly. According to [1], once a computer has the perceptual ability to know who, what, when, where, and why, then probabilistic rules derived by statistical learning methods are normally sufficient for the computer to determine a good course of action.

Knowing the user's context and attention will ease the interaction. Allowing user to navigate freely in the system with pre-identified preferences and cue will help the user to get the selected information and guide the user to the user's preferred tasks. For reality and naturalness of a visual interface, it is necessary to provide immersion feeling and natural, efficient interaction with displayed objects [2].

An optimal system is a system that is smart to know what the user's current context and at the same time, prioritize the information according to the user's task. This improves the user's interaction and thus gradually making the interface invisible and focuses on user's task and solves the problem of information overload.

C. Stephanidis (Ed.): Universal Access in HCI, Part II, HCII 2007, LNCS 4555, pp. 1016–1025, 2007.

Tiled display offers greater number of pixels and has the potential to allow more applications with higher resolution display to operate. Image visualization on large screen increases the perceptual load of the user [3]. Our motivation for this paper is to provide attentive regions to be displayed in high resolution that will direct the user's focus to the specific object in a large tiled display. Our goal is also to provide a focused attentive display region for users by a bi-resolution to be projected for users.

The rest of this paper is organized as follow. Section 2 provides some related research and the achievement. Section 3 presents our proposed system overview, the framework involved and the technology used. Section 4 describes detailed implementation followed by Section 5 outlines the experimental result and finally in section 6 we present our conclusion and future work.

2 Related Research

Research on tiled display and its interaction has shown an inclination towards two directions. One main direction is on large display in virtual environment and another direction is interaction in a larger working space environment. Large display has an advantage of projecting high resolution display and interaction within the environment creates an immersive feel for the user.

2.1 System with Large Display in Virtual Environment

Research work had been carried out extensively on large display in virtual environment. Goo et al. in [4] developed an interactive virtual learning environment to evaluate the effects of guided or unguided style virtual reality (VR) learning on user attention. Large display with learning content of underwater world displayed to user while eye tracking system and various physiological sensors are used to detect user's attention state.

Li et al. presented a low cost off-the-shelf display using two projectors and render real-time 3D geometric alignment with hardware acceleration for each graphics pipeline [5]. Tao et al. in [6] demonstrated an isolation of display size and resolution as independent variables by using three different display technologies. They further show how users working with large display become less reliant on wayfinding aids to acquire spatial knowledge and construct cognitive map of virtual environments.

2.2 Tiled Display and Interaction

Human Computer Interaction (HCI) is becoming one of the most important research issues in the field of computing. It has received much attention as new paradigms of interaction evolve in different kinds of applications. Tiled display interaction as proposed by [10] utilizes avatar and gesture in a large projected display and user appears on screen to interact with icons and other items. User behavior in tiled display is observed with nine monitors to form a tiled display in [11]. User's interaction is observed for different given tasks in the regions of the tiled display. Other interaction within the large display using real time computer vision algorithm that track all ten fingers of user's hand for direct manipulation experience using finger manipulations and gestures [12].

2.3 Perceptual Interface and Attentive Interaction

Perceptual User Interfaces (PUIs) use alternate sensing modalities to replace or complement traditional mouse, keyboard, trackball and joystick input: specialized devices are exploited to provide the user with alternate interaction channels, such as speech, hand gesture, etc. [13]. With advances in computer vision, a lot of research effort has been focused on designing vision-based PUI, which are the systems that use a video camera to detect the visual cues of the user, such as motion of the face, to control a program [14, 15].

Lee et.al in [16] develop the attentive interaction design toolkit, a vision-based input toolkit that gives users an analysis of faces found in a given image stream, including facial expression, body motion and attentive activities. The attention meter will measure the level of attention by users towards the system.

3 System Overview

Our proposed system intended to provide an immersive perceptual interaction that augments user's interest based on the intention and attention that the user is currently situated, the related content of interest and hassle-free perceptual interaction. The system is based on the conceptual model of context aware attentive interaction as shown in Fig. 1.

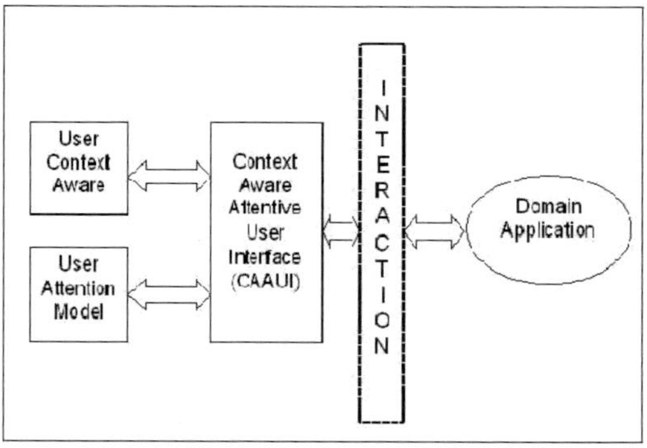

Fig. 1. Conceptual model of context aware attentive interaction

The user context aware recognizes input that is available to the context application. The information will be diverted to the application directly through the Context Aware Attentive User Interface (CAAUI). The attention model deals with user adaptation, learning, reasoning and planning for selected data to be displayed based on user's past, present and expected preference. An intermediate context aware attentive user interface (CAAUI) will act as an intelligent perceptual interface between the user and the application and optimally distribute tasks between user and system.

3.1 Interaction in Tiled Display

Tiled display system has an advantage of larger display with high resolution. Our proposed model is simulated in a large tiled display application prototype developed in our laboratory. We use two projectors to display a large display and render a low resolution data for maximizing the computational efficiency and minimizing user's perceptual load. User context aware detects the presence of users and head motion tracking of the user using a AR marker. Upon detection of the user's presence, image in the tiled display will be displaying the essential attentive regions in high resolution based on the outcome of the learning model from user's viewing behavior in the past (user attentive model). Other regions remain in low resolution.

Tiled display provides an environment for perceptual interaction. The system configuration for the tiled display uses two projectors whereby each capable to project high and low resolution. This is to minimize the computational power by only showing the attentive areas with high resolution to users. The display is divided into eight equal sections.

User will interact with the display directly with the head orientation detection with a marker. User wears a cap with AR marker and a camera detects the user's head movement to display the image cluster on high resolution. The remaining clusters will be projected in low resolution. The rationale of our implementation is we want to direct the user's attention to the focused area while minimizing the user's perceptual load. At the same time, computational power will be minimized in terms of displaying low resolution in unattended areas.

Our system in geometric calibration solves non-linear distortion using the method of dividing a small rectangular area. It changes non-linear distortion into linear distortion. It computes warping functions for each small rectangular. Warping function is determined using keystone correction method and four corner points. Fig. 2 shows the relationship between the frames of reference that are relevant to the problem of automatic keystone correction. The relationship between the three frames of reference corresponding to the source image frame, camera image frame and projected image frame is shown in Fig. 2(a). Fig. 2(b) shows the application image can be appropriately pre-warped, using the mapping W so that it appears rectilinear after projection through a misaligned projector.

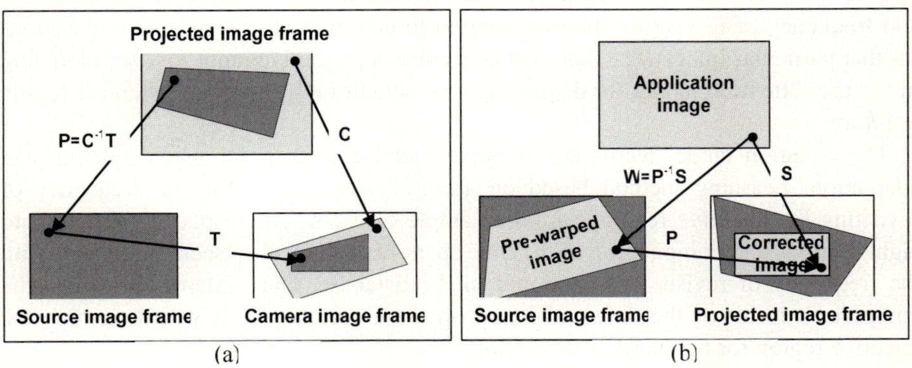

Fig. 2. Relationship between the frames

3.2 Head Direction Orientation Using AR Marker

Our prototype deploys using AR ToolKit for head direction orientation during perceptual selection by the user. User wears a normal cap with AR Marker following the user's head direction when user views the large image in the display.

AR ToolKit [17] identifies the position of the marker in the camera coordinate system. The marker following the user's head position is computed and tracked. Fig. 3 shows the coordinate system used in AR ToolKit [17]. We use this concept to determine the head orientation and position using this coordinate system [18,19,20].

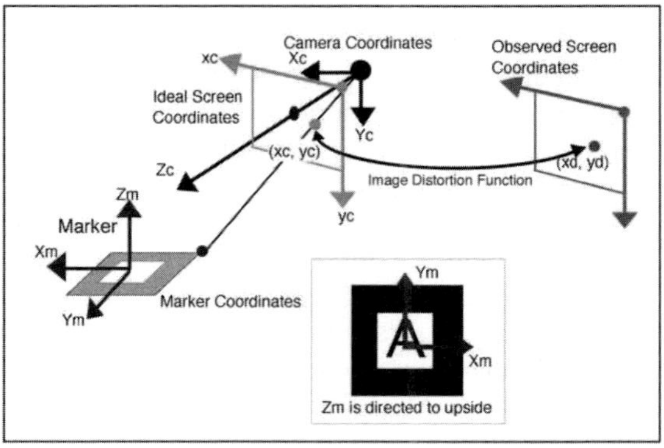

Fig. 3. Coordinate system used in AR ToolKit

4 System Description

The first component of the prototype consists of detecting the user's presence. We use a web camera as an initial set up to detect the user's present and projects the attentive regions with high resolution to capture user's attention. This is based on the second component; the attentive model that is built with an unsupervised learning method. The user's preference of the attentive region in the display will be projected as high resolution so that user's perceptual load is minimized. The attentive model uses time and frequency of re-visiting the same region to determine the most attentive regions for that particular image. The data will be used as a predictive input for user modeling in the user attention model for displaying as a default high resolution attentive region in future.

The attention model learns the attentive viewing regions for user modeling and adaptation. Learning method based on accumulative time spent and frequency of revisiting the attentive regions across a sample of users. The display is divided into eight sections and computation of the time spent in each focused section together with the frequency of revisit will be stored in the database. Our system will obtain the comparison result of the data and based on these parameters, it will determine the attentive region for that particular display.

Rendering of images onto the tiled display uses two computers with two different projectors which projects both high and low resolution areas that are depending on the region of focus. User's selections of region to be displayed as a focused region (high resolution) rely on the marker detection of the user's head direction orientation. The description is depicted in Fig. 4.

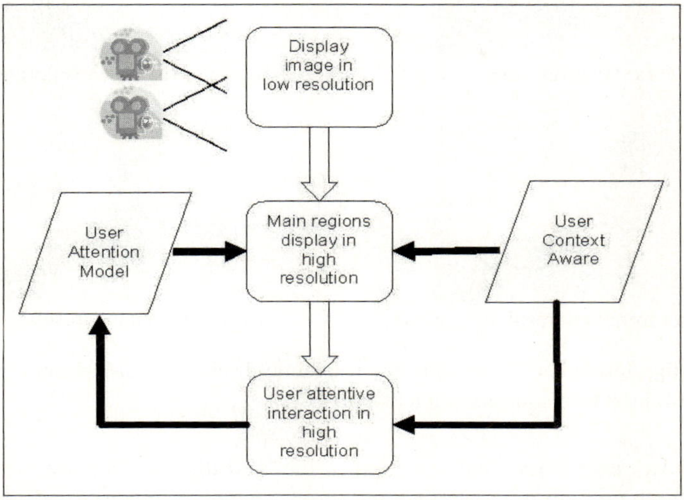

Fig. 4. Overview of the interaction in tiled display

System configuration for the prototype utilizes simple off the shelf equipments. The screen size is 3m X 2m (width X height in meter). Two projectors and one web camera are used to set up the environment. AR marker is used to track the orientation direction of the user's head. The tracking is built with AR Toolkit.

5 Experimental Result

Our experiment shows the tiled display operated by the user's presence detection and by default showing the attentive region when the user is near to the display. User will be detected by a camera and display of high and low resolution takes place. Fig. 5 shows a comparison of an image projected by (a) high resolution, (b) low resolution, (c) inset from high resolution (zoom) and (d) inset from low resolution (zoom). The prototype will display a high resolution as in 5(a) when the region is selected. Otherwise, it will display a low resolution as in 5(b). The high and low resolution display has a clear distinct difference with the quality of projection in the overall display of an image and thus contributes to the minimizing of the computation power as a whole. Our tiled display projects a total of 8 sections (4 sections for each projector) and display accordingly when user's selection is detected via the AR marker. Low resolution is four times lower pixel than the high resolution.

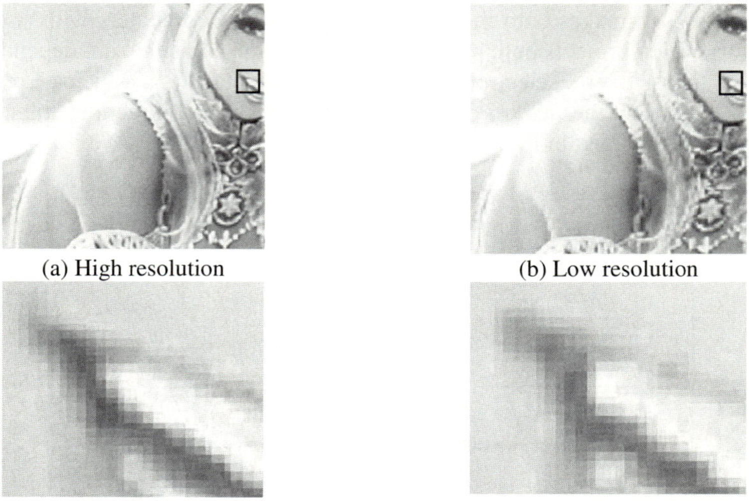

(a) High resolution (b) Low resolution

(c) Inset from high resolution (zoom) (d) Inset from low resolution (zoom)

Fig. 5. (a) High resolution display, (b) low resolution display, (c) inset from high resolution (zoom) and (d) inset from low resolution (zoom)

Fig. 6 shows user perceptual selection in the tiled display. We use two projectors projecting high and low resolution and user's head orientation will be captured according to the direction that the user prefers. This is also to minimize the perceptual load of the user when the user is focusing on a small part of a large display. This concept is based on the attentive display [17] that refers to the demand for rendering power and display resolution, but it is different from parallel display approach. Instead of requiring additional hardware, attentive display make more out of available hardware by directing display and computation resources to where they count most. AR marker is used to trace the head orientation.

(a) Upper left direction (b) Lower right direction (c) AR marker

Fig. 6. (a) and (b) User direction orientation with high resolution display on selected area and (c) AR marker on user's head for direction orientation

An attentive model based on calculation of time and revisit of each user will determine the most attentive region in that particular display. The attentive model acts as an intelligent component to pre-define the attentive area for each display based on the accumulative user's data. It is modeled with a learning capability that learns the attentive region based on viewing parameters.

The overall system configuration of our prototype is shown in Fig. 7. Our experimental result shows a reduction of processing time and minimizes the computational power by projecting images to large display with combination of high and low resolution. We use the method of focusing only the essential based on the attention from the user and thus reduce the overall computational power. We averaged out the iterations of testing and the computation time is summarized in Table 1.

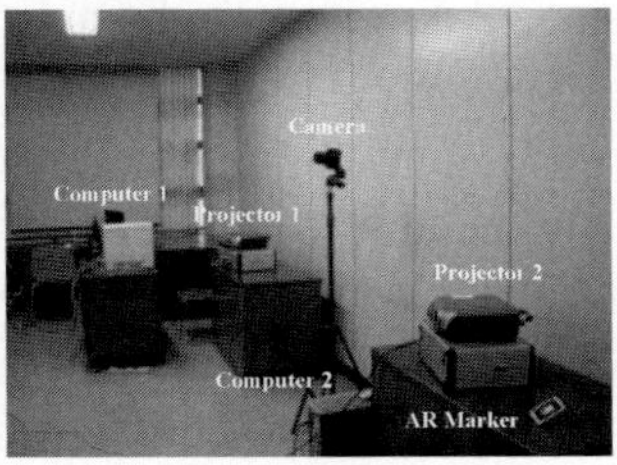

(a) Hardware setup

(b) User interaction

Fig. 7. Overall system configuration

Table 1. Comparison of computational power and accuracy of head orientation

Number of regions displayed (per projector)	Computational time (seconds)
0	0.2105
1	0.2890
2	0.3435
3	0.4220
4	0.4925

6 Conclusion and Future Work

We proposed a perceptual interaction in a tiled display setting. Our prototype follows the conceptual model of context aware attentive interaction. User interacts with the tiled display based on their head orientation with the direction of user's view. This will lighten the user's perceptual load and minimize the computational power. At the same time, user's interaction data will be constantly feed as an input to the attention model in order to display the most attentive region in a particular display to the new users.

There are several advantages in our proposed model. By redirecting the user's attention to their focus of interest, users' experiencing an immersive perceptual interaction with lighter perceptual burden in a large tiled display. Context aware that reasons the user's cues together with attention model that prioritize and learn user's behavior will decrease user's perceptual load thus interacting directly with the desired attentive information. Minimal computational resources needed to render high resolutions only on selected attentive regions.

Future work will be the possibility to include other context aware input and improving calibration of visual attention based on both head tracking and eye tracking without using a marker. Real time tracking of the human head movement with direction orientation detection will enhance the perceptual and immersive feel when interacting in a tiled display.

Acknowledgments. This work was supported by grant No.(R01-2006-000-11214-0) from the Basic Research Program of the Korea Science & Engineering Foundation.

References

1. Pentland, A.: Perceptual Intelligence. Communications of the ACM, vol. 43(3) (2000)
2. Ahn, S.C., Kim, I.J., Kim, H.G.: Interactive Immersive Display. The 14th International Conference on Artificial Reality and Telexistence (ICAT, TSI workshop (2004) pp. 63–68 (2004)
3. Baudisch, P., DeCarlo, D., Duchowski, A.T., Geisler, W.S.: Focusing on the essential: Considering attention in dislay design, Comunications of the ACM, vol. 46(3) (2003)
4. Goo, J.J., Park, K.S., Lee, M.H., Park, J., Hahn, M.S., Ahn, H.G., Picard, R.W.: Effects of Guided and Unguided Style Learning on User Attention in a Virtual Environment. International Conference on E-Learning and Games (Edutainment 2006) pp. 1208–1222 (2006)
5. Li, Z.Y., Varshney, A.: A Real-Time Seamless Tiled Display System for 3D Graphics. In: Proceedings of Seventh Annual Symposium on Immersive Projection Technology (IPT (2002)
6. Tao, Ni., Bowman, D.A., Jian, Chen.: Displays : Increased display size and resolution improve task performance in information-rich virtual environment. In: Proceedings of the conference on graphics interface (GI'06) (2006)
7. Jo, D., Kang, H., Lee, G.A., Son, W.: Xphere: A PC Cluster based Hemispherical Display System. IEEE Virtual Reality Conference VR, 312 (2006)
8. Vertegaal, R., Shell, J.S., Chen, D., Mamuji, A.: Designing for Augmented Attention: Towards a Framework for Attentive User Interfaces. Computers in Human Behavior 22, 771–789 (2006)
9. Tahboub, K.A.: Intelligent Human-Machine Interaction Based on Dynamic Bayesian Networks Probabilistic Intention Recognition. Journal of Intelligent and Robotic Systems 45, 31–52 (2006)
10. Ahn, S.C., Lee, T.S., Kim, I.J., Kwon, Y.M., Kim, H.G.: Large display interaction using video avatar and hand gesture recognition. In: Campilho, A., Kamel, M. (eds.) ICIAR 2004. LNCS, vol. 3211, pp. 261–268. Springer, Heidelberg (2004)
11. Ball, R., North, C.: Analysis of user behavior on high-resolution tiled displays. In: Costabile, M.F., Paternó, F. (eds.) INTERACT 2005. LNCS, vol. 3585, pp. 350–363. Springer, Heidelberg (2005)
12. Malik, S., Ranjan, A., Balakrishnan, R.: Interacting with large displays from a distance with vision-tracked multi-finger gestural input. The 7th Annual ACM Symposium on User Interface Software and Technology (UIST05) (2005)

13. Iannizzotto, G., Rosa, F.L., Costanzo, C., Lanzafame, P.: A multimodal perceptual user interface for collaborative environment. In: Roli, F., Vitulano, S. (eds.) ICIAP 2005. LNCS, vol. 3617, pp. 115–122. Springer, Heidelberg (2005)
14. Gorodnichy, D.O., Roth, G.: Nouse 'Use your nose as a mouse' perceptual vision technology for hands-free games and interfaces. Image and Video Computing NRC 47140 12(12), 931–942 (2004)
15. Gorodnichy, D.O.: Perceptual cursor – a solution to the broken loop problem in vision-based hands-free computer control devices. NRC/ERB 1133, NRC48472 (2006)
16. Lee, C.H.J., Wetzel, J., Selker, T.: Enhancing interface design using attentive interaction design toolkit. International conference on computer graphics and interactive techniques (ACM SIGGRAPH, Educators program (2006), http://www.hitl.washington.edu/artoolkit/
17. Kato, H., Billinghurst, M.: Marker tracking and HMD calibration for a video-based augmented reality conferencing system. In: Proceedings of the 2nd International workshop on Augmented Reality (IWAR99) (1999)
18. Billinghurst, M., Kato, H., POupyrev, I.: The MagicBook: A transitional AR Interface. Computers and Graphics, pp. 745–753 (2001)
19. Billinghurst, M., Kato, H.: Collaborative augmented reality. Communications of the ACM 45(7), 64–70 (2002)

Improvements of Chord Input Devices for Mobile Computer Users

Fong-Gong Wu, Chun-Yu Chen, and Chien-Hsu Chen

Department of Industrial Design, National Cheng Kung University, 1, Ta-Hsueh Road, Tainan, TW 70101, Taiwan
fonggong@mail.ncku.edu.tw,
Jimmy.Chen@quantatw.com, chenhsu@mail.ncku.edu.tw

Abstract. This study will be using a tablet computer as an example to study mobile products and make a comparison with keyboard and mouse by providing an input device consisting of a new form of touch pen in combination with chord input. The goal is to find the best combination of input device, minimizing harm caused by the input device and provide a reference for further input device designs. Therefore the NEW chord keyboard and touch pen conforms to the needs of a new mobile product and it becomes the best combination of this experiment which can be considered for future product design references.

Keywords: mobile device, input device, touch pen, chord input.

1 Introduction

Every input device has its unique characteristics which are not necessarily suitable for all products. An unsuitable input tool would slow down search of the database and cause inefficiency [1]. Furthermore, this might also cause frustration in the learning process; influence the result of the study and efficiency of the computer equipment. Therefore, in this mobile era, aiming at input needs of a mobile product, it is necessary to provide a suitable new mobile input device and study it [2] [3] [4].

This study will be using a tablet computer as an example to study mobile products and make a comparison with keyboard and mouse by providing an input device consisting of a new form of touch pen in combination with chord input. The goal is to find the best combination of input device, minimizing harm caused by the input device and provide a reference for further input device designs. The focus of this research is as follows:

a. Providing different combinations of chord grouping with touch pens and finding data for the most efficient and accurate input.
b. Study of gestures of different combinations of chord grouping with touch pens to minimize harm caused by the input device.
c. Make a comparison to find the advantages and disadvantages of keyboards and computer mouse.
d. Investigate the relationship between underlying elements and grouping methods; and their influence on efficiency.

C. Stephanidis (Ed.): Universal Access in HCI, Part II, HCII 2007, LNCS 4555, pp. 1026–1035, 2007.

2 Method

Input devices are being classified into two categories, pointing and text input. Most studies in the past focused only on the efficiency or design of keyboard input; there are hardly any complete evaluations on the integration of input device research. This study will include pointing device and keyboard input research and undergo different combinations of chord grouping with touch pens in various experiments. These experiment results are being compared with the available keyboards and mouse to obtain the best input device design.

2.1 Research of Existing Keyboard and Mouse Input

Keyboard and mouse are the most common input devices used nowadays; most computer users have accepted and became accustomed to this combination. But this combination is not the best selection for input gesture and efficiency. Due to the development of icons on computer user interface, a mouse is used much more often than a keyboard. The development of the internet has also resulted in the frequent use of a mouse. This experiment makes use of a mouse and keyboard for the purpose of comparison; based on its common usage and the problem that arises from its usage. The experiment will start by testing a mouse and keyboard, it will act as a procedure to adjust to the experiment and furthermore to act as a standard of comparison for the new input combination.

2.2 Formulating Combination of Touch Pen and Chord Keyboard

In the vast amount of input devices, this research focuses on the future of mobile products. It puts into consideration various new types of input combination based on gestures and input efficiency, with the goal of providing the best combination for input devices. The pointing device we have chosen is a touch pen; this is based on the fact that human's reliability on the usage of pens has not decreased due to technological development [5]. This experiment uses a touch pen merely as a simple pointing device. It hopes to reach the input efficiency of a mouse and avoid the physical harm caused by the usage of a mouse. In terms of text inputs, a chord keyboard is considered due to its size and input efficiency. Due to the lack of usage in academic studies, learning curve of the input device will be an element of this study. This study hopes that the chord keyboard which has been seen as a special input device will be recognized for common usage; promoting common usage of the device.

2.3 Selection of Chord Keyboard Grouping

This experiment requires the collocation of chord keyboard and touch pen; based on their individual characteristics and arrangement, "Single-hand control" and "text-number input" is chosen. Product reliability, popularity and developmental stage are also placed under consideration. The following three sets of keyboard are used as experiment variables:

The first set of keyboard uses "BAT" chord input (see the Fig.1. source: BAT quick reference guide [6]), the arrangement is based on how one memorize the order of the alphabet to form words with meanings. For the subjects, it is a brand new concept of input learning process. This cascade theory grouping might hasten input method of the subject due to its difference from existing keyboards.

The second set of keyboard uses "HALF" chord input (see the Fig.2). HALF chord keyboard is the most popular and reliable chord keyboard. The arrangement uses QWERT keyboard reflection theory grouping which is directly related to existing keyboards [6]. This type of guided chord might decrease learning curve of the user and efficiently reach the speed at which normal input devices has.

The third set of keyboard uses "NEW" chord input (see the Fig.3). NEW chord arrangement uses the principles of English text input of a mobile phone and develops a new form of grouping. This arrangement is based on text orders. A mobile phone is the most commonly used mobile product, which should help with the learning curve of the user groups; decreasing learning period and reaching sustainable efficiency.

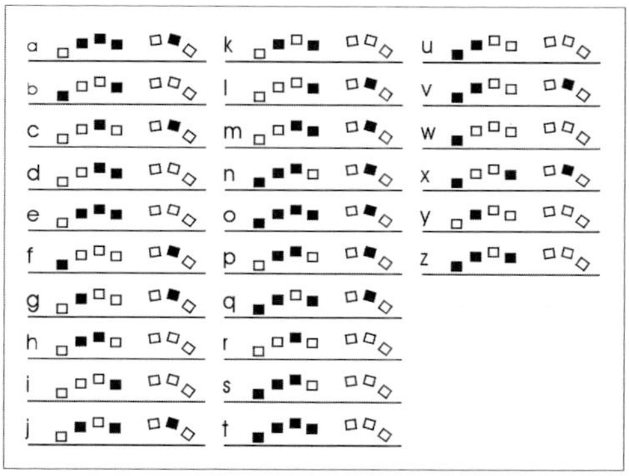

Fig. 1. "BAT" chord input [6]

Fig. 2. "HALF" chord input

Fig. 3. "NEW" chord input

2.4 Experiment Design and Planning

2.4.1 Experiment Variables

a. Independent variable: This is based on the popularity and grouping characteristics of three different sets of chord keyboards. The first one, BAT chord keyboard has a characteristic of creating order from memory. The second one is HALF with the characteristics of the reflection characteristic. The last type, the NEW chord keyboard has a ordering similar to existing mobile phones. These three keyboards are all paired with touch pen. A QWERTY keyboard is paired with a mouse that acts as a pointing device for the task.

b. Dependant variable:

(a) Input rate: CPM, characters per minute.
(b) Error rate: the number of errors typed per hundred words.
(c) Operating gesture: the elbow, wrist and upper body gesture.
(d) The record of wrist deflection angle.
(e) Objectivity chart: comfort of the shoulder and wrist and the learning curve.

2.4.2 Subjects

15 voluntary subjects (7 females and 8 males), the subjects have over three years of keyboard, mouse input and mobile text message input experience. Their ability of typing words per minute is between 20 to 30 words per minute. All the subjects are right-handed.

2.4.3 Experiment Equipment

Three sets of chord keyboard including BAT chord keyboard, Half chord keyboard, NEW chord keyboard, QWERTY keyboard; a touch pen, tablet computer, mouse and digital camera; 0.5mm black tape and transparent tapes for wrist deflection adjustment.

2.4.4 Experiment Task

The experiment task consists mainly of pointing and text input. The pointing task includes clicking and dragging; clicking refers to the clicking of buttons. "Begin task" and "complete task" buttons are clicked accordingly. Dragging is designed to dragging computer icons on a user interface. Text input tasks require the subjects to enter the assigned alphabet; when an error is made, the subject is asked to delete the mistake and enter the correct text.

The experiment enters the instruction page, after reading the instructions the task of pointing and text inputting is proceeded. The experiment begins by clicking on the start button and enters the dragging task screen where the subject has to drag the image into a block. Next page can be accessed by clicking on the link where the task of English text input begins. One hundred texts are entered according to the screen display, the font size is 14, and the text contents are simple extracts from the children's fable "The Little Prince". The alphabet contents are distributed normally to avoid rare texts and display common input texts. The two tasks are criss-crossed and the pointing and text inputting tasks are being executed five times.

2.4.5 Experiment Procedure

a. Phase one: In order to understand the learning curve and operating gesture, phase one is preceded in five days, each procedure undergoes 30-40 minutes. A practice session of 10 minutes is proceeded before entering the actual program. 15 subjects are divided equally between BAT chord keyboard, Half chord keyboard and NEW chord keyboard. All three groups are collocated with a touch pen. The experiment instructions and settings are introduced on the first day where existing keyboard and mouse are used. This is done to familiarize experiment procedure and record it as a criterion for comparison, the comparison is made with a chord keyboard paired with a touch pen. Subjects are asked to fill in objectivity satisfactory chart based on the effect that a chord keyboard does on their shoulder and wrist. From the second to the fifth day, the subject undergoes a practice session of ten minutes where they directly proceed to experiment task with a chord keyboard and touch pen. Objectivity satisfactory chart is filled in at the end of the tasks. The time needed for the training and experiment of the first phase is around four hours.

b. Phase two: After the end of phase one; to understand the effect of recall on the chord keyboard, the second phase of the experiment is conducted one week after the initial practice. The duration of the experiment is two days and the procedure and content is the same as phase one.

c. Phase three: Based on the result of the first two experiments, the best combination is selected through reviewing the input rate, learning curve and input gesture. Phase three is then proceeded; the same subjects are used and the duration is five days. The experiment content is the same as phase one and after observations of eight hours of training, the best input combination is gained.

2.5 Statistics and Analytical Method

The data of this experiment is used mainly for the purpose of gaining input rate and detecting deflection during wrist operation. Statistical methods are then used to analyze relations between different combinations of chord grouping; using the software SPSS version 10.0 to process raw data.

3 Results

3.1 Research of Existing Keyboard and Mouse Input

3.1.1 Text Input Rate Analysis

At the end of phase one, the input rate of the three sets of chord keyboard and touch pen are processed into Paired Samples T Test. In the 95% (α=0.05) reliability region [-18.9276,-13.4631] which does not include the T value (-12.915). After five days of training, the input rate has remarkable improvement showing that the subjects have learned efficiently during phase one of the experiment.

In order to investigate the input rate of each group, the result of input rate and grouping from phase one of the experiment undergoes One-Way ANOVA. The test of homogeneity of variance can be seen from Table1, a noticeable standard is set at 0.05 and there was not any noticeable difference from the groups with the exception of the results from day three. Each separate group undergoes ANOVA; the input rate from day three also undergoes ANOVA after it undergoes inverse transformation also conforms to the test of homogeneity. From the result of ANOVA through day one to day five, one can see that the salience is smaller than the level of significance of 0.05. This implies that the text input of this phase can differentiate from the difference of the chord keyboard.

3.1.2 Phase One Input Rate and ANOVA

In order to understand the differentiation of the input rate from the various groups after phase one of the experiment, Scheffe's test is applied to investigate the relation of various group input rates on day five. According to Table2, the salience of BAT and Half is 0.002, and the salience of BAT and NEW is 0.015, using Scheffe's method. Both results are smaller than the level of significance of 0.05. The salience of Half and NEW is 0.467, higher than the level of significance of 0.05. This indicates that there is a significant difference between the input rate of Half and BAT, and NEW and BAT. There is no significant differences with the combination of Half and NEW. Furthermore, according to Table3, Scheffe's method groups together Half and NEW and isolates BAT.

Table 1. The test of homogeneity of variance

	Levene	significance
DAY 1	0.559	0.586
DAY 2	2.474	0.126
DAY 3	5.962	0.016∗
DAY3(reciproca)	1.263	0.318
DAY 4	1.732	0.220
DAY 5	0.994	0.416

Table 2. The multiple comparison of input rates from day 5 of phase one

Rate input according to the fifth day variance			Salience	95% confidence interval	
	Group	Group		Lower bound	Upper bound
Scheffe	BAT	Half	0.002∗	-14.43	-3.79
		NEW	0.015∗	-12.00	-1.39
	Half	BAT	0.002∗	1. 79	14.43
		NEW	0.467	-2.88	7.74
	NEW	BAT	0.015∗	1. 36	12.00
		Half	0.467	-7.74	2.88

Table 3. Scheffe's rate grouping correlation table from day 5 of phase one

	Group	Sample number	Alpha=0.05	
			1	2
Scheffe	BAT	5	36.046	
	Half	5		45.160
	NEW	5		42.730
	Salience		1.000	0.467

Through the numbers of Table4, one can find text input rates of different groups. On day one, Half keyboard of the second group had the highest input rate(32.75cpm), and the BAT keyboard of the first group had the lowest input rate(16.27cpm). There is obvious differences on the input rates, showing that the Half keyboard has the best input rates is the most adaptive keyboard. The subjects have trouble adapting to the BAT keyboard due to the memorizing of the orders; the input rate is remarkably lower than the other two. After five days of training, there is remarkable progress with the input rate from all three groups. The input rate of BAT is 37.64cpm, the input rate of Half is 45.12cpm and the input rate of NEW is 42.73cpm. Although Half keyboard is still slightly higher than the other two, NEW keyboard has reached a 62.88% input rate within five days, which is remarkably higher than the other two groups. The growing rate of Half keyboard had a higher rate but its rate increased minimally compared with the other two groups after two days; there is even a further decrease in the input rate on the fourth day. The input rate of BAT and NEW increased steadily and its difference with Half is reduced remarkably on the fifth day.

3.1.3 Pointing Device Input Rate Analysis

The touch pen performed just as well as a mouse, both device can be clicked and dragged at the designated spot in a short period. Therefore, using a touch pen as a pointing device requires no learning for the subject to use it just as efficient as a mouse.

Table 4. Text input rate of phase one compared with normal text input

		Day 1	Day 2	Day 3	Day 4	Day 5	Progress rate	Comparison with normal keyboard (%)
Group 1 (BAT)	Input rate (cpm)	16.27	22.56	28.72	31.62	37.64	21.37	37.64/77.2 =48.75%
	Standard deviation	2.19	3.47	3.59	3.67	3.37		
Group2 (Half)	Input rate (cpm)	32.75	39.6	44.13	42.93	45.16	12.41	45.16/91.27 =49.47%
	Standard deviation	3.73	4.53	5.97	3.96	2.75		
Group 3 (NEW)	Input rate (cpm)	24.98	32.15	36.89	40.21	42.73	17.75	42.73/67.95 =62.88%
	Standard deviation	3.11	2.08	2.32	2.53	2.78		

3.1.4 Error Rate Analysis

Based on the error rate of day one, BAT keyboard had a remarkable error rate (8.7%) than Half keyboard (2.9%) and NEW keyboard (2.95%). This shows that BAT is more difficult to use initially, the other two keyboards uses existing keyboard grouping which lowered the input error rate.

In order to investigate the error rates of each group, the error rate and the various groups of phase one undergoes One-Way ANOVA. The test of homogeneity of variance salience is higher than the level of significance which is 0.05. This shows that the variance of various groups are the same, and the error rate variance of each group can be analyzed. After five days of training, according to Table5, error rates of all three sets of chord keyboard decreased accordingly and they are not far from the error rate of normal keyboard (1.0%-1.4%). This shows that after a short period of practice, the input error rate can be adjusted to the levels of a normal keyboard. Overall, NEW keyboard have kept the error rate minimal and at a steady decease. This shows that a grouping that is similar to the groupings of a mobile phone will lower the error rate of the subject.

3.2 Phase Two Experiment Result and Analysis

After a week of experiment training is stopped, phase two of the training experiment is continued which consists of duration of two days. A Paired Samples T Test is done on the three new sets of chord keyboards and touch pen. After stopping a week from the training, the salience is 0.01 which reaches salience from day five of phase one and day one of phase two. This indicates that there is a remarkable degeneracy in the input rate. But compared with the second day which had a salience of 0.262 showing no noticeable change. This indicates that the subject could recall the new form of input and there are no significant differences to the learning of chord keyboard during phase one.

In order to investigate the relation of the input rate of various groups, the input rate and groups undergoes One-Way ANOVA. After the test of homogeneity, the level of significance is set at 0.05. The input rate of day one undergoes square transformation to conform to the test of homogeneity, so they can undergo variance analysis. After the training stops for a week, on day one of phase two, BAT keyboard's input rate is 24.98cpm, Half keyboard's input rate is 41.33cpm and NEW keyboard's input rate is 42.55cpm. There is a decline in the input rate of the three set of keyboards. BAT keyboard showed that after a period of learning, the memorization for the grouping decreases and therefore slows down the input rate. The other two groups makes an alteration to existing input method which helps with the memorization of the keyboard formation. Therefore, the input rate will not decline after a week of not using the keyboard.

The second day of phase two, the input rates of all three sets increased. BAT and Half is close to the input rate of day five from phase one. NEW has even improved by 7.48cpm, indicating that after a short period of practice, the grouping of chord keyboard can be memorized and recovered to the previous standard. NEW keyboard did not have a decline and furthermore rapidly grow, surpassing Half keyboard to become the most fast input rate of the three groups. Memorization of this phase had the best evaluation. Therefore this keyboard is chosen as the candidate for the next phase to seek combination with the most efficient input rate.

3.3 Phase Three Experiment Result and Analysis

After the analysis of the two previous phases, the input rate, error rate and input gesture are placed under consideration. NEW keyboard and a touch pen is the best input combination. Duration of five days in carried out for phase three of the experiment, the experiment aims to understand the best input rate of this keyboard under a long period of learning.

A ten minute practice time is given before the beginning of phase three to recover the familiarity of the user to the keyboard. The subjects should have inputted around 6000 to 7000 texts at the end of phase three. The duration of the experiment is around eight hours. The final experiment result shows that the five subjects averaged a 60.06cpm, the slowest being 55.18cmp and the fastest being 66.67cpm. In comparison with a normal QWERTY keyboard that averaged 67.95cpm, NEW keyboard has 88.38% of existing keyboard input rate. This indicates that NEW keyboard can replace original text input function after training and it is very likely to surpass input rate of normal keyboards in the future.

4 Discussion

After the input training of phase one (around 4 hours), input rates from all three keyboards showed remarkable progress. All three sets of keyboard showed around 50% of input rate of normal keyboards. The NEW keyboard even succeeded to 60% of the original input rate. This indicates that after learning, the chord keyboard showed a remarkable input rate in a short period of time.

In comparison to the new concept of the BAT keyboard, NEW and half showed a higher input rate and a lower error rate. This indicates that using existing grouping will help the user with the familiarization of the chord keyboard and requires a shorter period of learning. A suggestion is using existing grouping and make changes to develop a new keyboard.

On day one of the experiment, the error rate of BAT is 8.7%, NEW and Half's error rates are both under 3%. After the training of phase one (around four hours), the error rate of all three set of keyboards are kept under 2%. This is not far from the error rates of normal keyboards which is 1-1.5%. This indicates that experience with existing mobile and keyboard grouping will help lowering the error rate of the user. After learning, error rates of all threes sets are lowered effectively.

After a week of not using the keyboard, the memorization experiment from phase two showed that users using all three set of keyboards showed slight decline in its input rate. The BAT keyboard declined from the original 37.64cpm to 24.98cpm, showing the biggest decline of all three. But on the second day, the subjects could recover the input rate they gained from phase one, NEW even surpassed the input rate of phase one and increased the rate by 7.48cpm.

After the evaluation of the previous two phases, the input rate gained through the combination of a NEW keyboard and a touch pen showed the most potential. This combination can reach the input rate standard of normal keyboard and mouse after eight hours of training. The chord keyboard is small in size which can be carried around, the touch pen has an intuitional operating gesture and requires less wrist bending and pressurizing. Therefore the NEW chord keyboard and touch pen conforms to the needs of a new mobile product and it becomes the best combination of this experiment which can be considered for future product design references.

Acknowledgments. The authors would like to thank the National Science Council of the Republic of China for financially supporting this research under Contract No. NSC 93-2213-E-006-078

References

1. Nishinaka, Y., Tsujino, Y., Tokura, N.: A pointing method for graphics. Systems and Computer in Japan 21, 13–22 (1990)
2. Wu, F.G., Luo, S.: Design and Evaluation Approach for Increasing Stability and Performance of Touch Pens in Screen Handwriting Tasks. Applied Ergonomics 37(3), 319–327 (2006)
3. Wu, F.G., Luo, S.: Performance of the Five-Point Grip Pen in Three Screen-based Tasks. Applied Ergonomics 37(5), 629–639 (2006)
4. Wu, F.G., Huang, H.Y., Chen, C.H.: Chord Input Arrangement for the Mobile Computer. 11th International Conference on Human-Computer Interaction. Las Vegas, USA, file 87 (2005)
5. Parush, S., Lavanon-Erez, N., Weintraub, N.: Ergonomic factors influencing handwriting performance. Work. 11, 295–305 (1998)
6. Matias, E., MacKenzie, I.S., Buxton, W.: One-Handed Touch-Typing on a QWERTY keyboard. Human-Computer Interaction 11, 1–27 (1996)

A Study of Control Performance in Low Frequency Motion Workstation

Yi-Jan Yau[1], Chin-Jung Chao[2], Sheue-Ling Hwang[1], and Jhih-Tsong Lin[1]

[1] Institute of Industrial Engineering and Engineering Management, National Tsing Hua University, Hsinchu, Taiwan 30013, Republic of China
[2] Office of Industrial Safety and Environment Protection, Chung-Shan Institute of Science and Technology, Tao-Yuan, Taiwan 32500, Republic of China
d927814@oz.nthu.edu.tw, c356028@yahoo.com.tw,
slhwang@ie.nthu.edu.tw, d947808@oz.nthu.edu.tw

Abstract. Many studies have found the performance of using non-keyboard input devices (NKID) was affected by motion environment, but few of them have considered the interaction between motion direction and the approach angle on manipulating NKID. In this study, an experiment was conducted to investigate the effect of different approach angles (0o, 45o, 90o, 135o, 180o, 225o, 270o, 315o, 360o) and motion directions (roll and pitch) on the performance (movement time and error rate) of using trackball. The results showed that the main effect of approach angle on movement time was significant, whereas there was neither significant interaction nor the main effect of motion direction. The effects of approach angle and motion direction on the error rate were not significant. Some suggestions on the control console and interface design were proposed based on the results of the experiment.

Keywords: Motion; Trackball; Roll; Pitch.

1 Introduction

There were 97% of organizations used mouse as an information input device [1], but some work situations such as in a moving vehicle (e.g. car, air or maritime vessel), or in a small work station where there is no place for mouse placement and manipulation, are not suitable for using mouse as an input device. As a result, mouse was replaced by trackball, joystick or touch screen in these special work environments. Grant et al. [2] indicated that trackball was a conventional input device used on battleship and the users generally faced with targets located at different angles from a start position; hence, manipulating trackball to execute the point-and-click task is one of the major input tasks on ship and most of this type tasks are carried out on two dimensions visual display interface. It means that the users need to manipulate trackball to select icons, menus, or targets on different angles of the presented interface as quickly and accurately as possible. Many researches have investigated the effects of approach angle of mouse on the performance of executing the point-and-click task. Boritz, et al. [3] indicated that the selection time was affected

C. Stephanidis (Ed.): Universal Access in HCI, Part II, HCII 2007, LNCS 4555, pp. 1036–1044, 2007.

by the angle of approach with mouse. Mackenize and Buxton [4] found that in comparison with 0o and 90o, the mouse movement time was longer at the 45o of approach angle. Whisenand and Emurian [5] pointed out that the approach angle of mouse was a reliable factor affecting the movement time of target selection. Hancock and Booth [6] indicated that the movement time would depend on the approach angle by using Tablet PC and Smart-Board. From literature review, it seems that very few studies have explored the effects of approach angle on manipulating trackball.

Some researches have pointed out that the performance of using joystick, control level was degraded due to the severe ship motion, car motion or helicopter vibration [7-11]. However, few studies have investigated the effects of motion direction of vehicle as well as the approach angle of cursor on manipulating trackball. On the other hand, for most mouse and trackball users, the requirements of manipulative ways and musclulo-skeletal groups were different. However, in comparison with the researches on interface design for mouse users, fewer studies have considered the trackball users.

In order to improve the performance of input task under motion environment with trackball, the interface designers need to consider the effects of targets (icon, menu) layout and the motion direction at the same time. The purpose of this study was to investigate the effects of motion direction and approach angle on executing point-and-click task by using an off-the-shelf trackball (Logitech TrackMan Wheel).

2 Methods

2.1 Subjects

Twelve male subjects from Chung-Shan Institute of Science and Technology (CSIST) attended to this experiment. They were all right-handed and familiar with using mouse but had no experience on using trackball. Their ages were from 22 to 30 years and the mean was 26.5. They all had 0.8 corrected visual acuity or better as well as normal color vision.

2.2 Apparatus

The experiment was carried out in a cabin loaded on Stewart motion platform with capacity displacements of heave, sway and surge being ±200mm, ±250mm and ±250mm respectively, and the angles of roll, pitch, and yaw ±15o, ±15o and ±17o. The whole-body motions of present experiment were roll (0.3 Hz, ± 8°) and pitch (0.3Hz, ± 8°) produced by the motion platform. The point-and-click tasks were performed with a Pentium-class desktop PC running Window XP with ADVANTECH FPM-3175TVR-T 17"Color TFT LCD with1024 x 768 resolutions. The input device was Logitech TrackMan Wheel (LTW) thumb trackball and experimental software was developed by Visual C++. Since the approach angle of cursor was highly dependent on the orientation of trackball, the position of LTW trackball was directly headed to the north (90o) to keep the same approach angles of the cursor and trackball in this experiment. The Topcon ACP-8 and Standard Pseudo Isochromatic charts were used to measure visual acuity and the color vision of the subjects.

2.3 Procedure

Participants were interviewed to gather their basic information prior to the experiment and were requested to evaluate their health condition and motion sickness by filling out questionnaires in the beginning, middle, and at the end of experiment. The motion sickness was assessed with the Misery Scale (MISC) which was developed and validated at the TNO Human Factors Research Institute [12] and widely used by NATO [13]. Participants were instructed to adjust the seat height and distance to screen to fit their comfort, and use their preferred hand to move the cursor to capture the targets as quickly and accurately as possible. A 60-minute practice was offered to subjects to practice multi-directional point-and-click tasks by using Logitech TrackMan Wheel thumb trackball under roll and pitch motion directions before experiment. At the beginning of experiment, participants positioned the cursor toward the center circle of operating interface and clicked it to commence a trial. A pair of circle targets (diameter = 23 pixels) of which one was filled green with a black crosshair pointer (+) and another was filled red with a black minus sign (-) appeared. Participant moved the cursor to and clicked the green circle, and then, moved to and clicked the red circle. The black crosshair or minus sign turned into white while the subject successfully clicked inside the boundary of the green or red circle. An error was defined as the click outside the red circle and a beep was sounded while click outside the green or red circles. Time was recorded between two successful clicks. Once successfully selected, another new pair of circles randomly appeared. This process continued until all trials in a set were completed. A set consisted of twenty-four times of point-and-click trials (1 motion situation; 3 different distances; 8 different angles). The distances between the pairs of circles were 230, 460 and 690 pixels, and the approach angles were 0°, 45°, $90^{o,}$ 135°, 180°, 225°, 270°, 315°, $360\,^o$. Fig. 1 shows the experimental interface layout and a sample condition. Each participant completed ten repeat sets (a block) of point-and-click tasks under roll and pitch respectively. In order to prevent order effect, ordering of motion direction was counterbalanced. A fully within-subjects repeated measures design was applied. The independent variables, motion directions (2 levels, roll and pitch) and approach angles (8 levels, 0o~360o) were all within-subject factors. Dependent variables were the mean movement time (MMT) (millisecond) and error rate (ER). The movement time was the time between two successive clicks, and MMT was the arithmetic mean of the movement time on each approach angle. The error was the targets selected outside the circle target and the ER was the percentage of error occurred on each approach angle in each block. A two-way repeated measure ANOVA was used to examine the effects of motion type and approach angle on the movement time and error rate. The subjective evaluations for the difficulty of motion direction of platform and approach angle of cursor on point-and-click task were performed after each block. The participants selected the correspondent number on seven points scale, ranging from 1 (very difficult) to 7 (very easy). For further analysis of the difficulty of each approach angle, the participants chose the three most difficult approach angles under each motion direction. The subjective questionnaire was analyzed by nonparametric tests. The Friedman's analysis of variance by ranks was used to analyze the effect of difficult degree of manipulating trackball under different motion directions and approach angles.

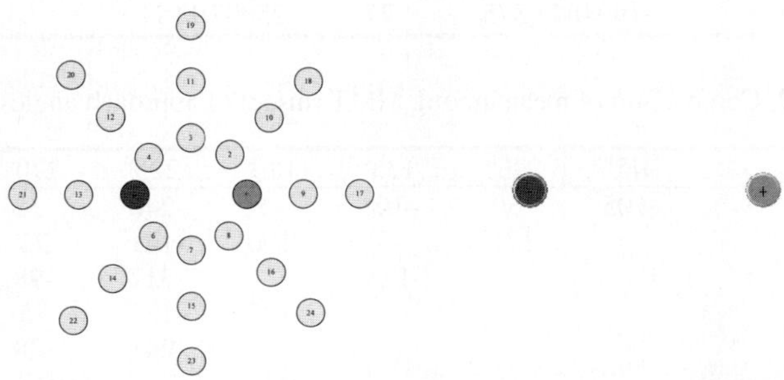

(a) Interface design layou (b) A sample experimental condition

Fig. 1. Experimental interface layout and a sample condition

3 Results

No subject suffered from motion sickness since their motion sickness index scores were all very low (= 0 or 1); hence, the performance on point-and-click task were directly affected by the motion and approach angle.

3.1 Mean Movement Time

The results of ANOVA indicated that main effect of approach angle on the mean movement time was significant ($F_{7,77} = 5.736$, $P < 0.001$) whereas the motion direction and the interaction were not significant (Table 1). Table 2 lists the pairwase comparison of the means. The pairwase comparison demonstrated that the shortest movement time was reached at the approach angle of 90° and the longest movement time was occurred at the angle of 225°. Furthermore, the comparison between different approach angles revealed that the movements along the vertical and horizontal axes seemed faster than that of movements along the diagonals. The relationship between mean movement time and approach angle is showed in Fig. 2. Fig. 3 presents the average mean movement time of cursor movement in various approach angles and motion directions. Although the effect of motion direction on movement time was not significant, there was a tendency that the movement speed on pitch was slower than that of on roll direction at all approach angles except at the angle 135°.

Table 1. ANOVA results of movement time

Source	Sum of Squares	df	Mean Square	F	Sig.
Motion Direction (M)	95586.750	1	95586.750	.601	.455
Error (M)	1750144.125	11	159104.011		
Approach Angle (A)	1649398.313	7	235628.330	5.736	.000
Error(A)	3163007.062	77	41078.014		
M *A	168964.250	7	24137.750	.932	.487
Error (M*A)	1994847.875	77	25907.115		

Table 2. Comparison of mean among MMT (msec) of approach angles

	Mean	0°	45°	90°	135°	180°	225°	270°	315°
0°	1787	-	-105*	66	-108	-5	-246*	-32	-149*
45°	1892		-	171*	-3	100	-141*	73	-44
90°	1721			-	-173*	-71	-312*	-98	-215*
135°	1894				-	103	-138*	75	-41
180°	1791					-	-241*	-28	-144*
225°	2032						-	213*	97
270°	1819							-	-116
315°	1935								-

Comparison of means between movement time (msec) of approach angles
(* : p<0.05)

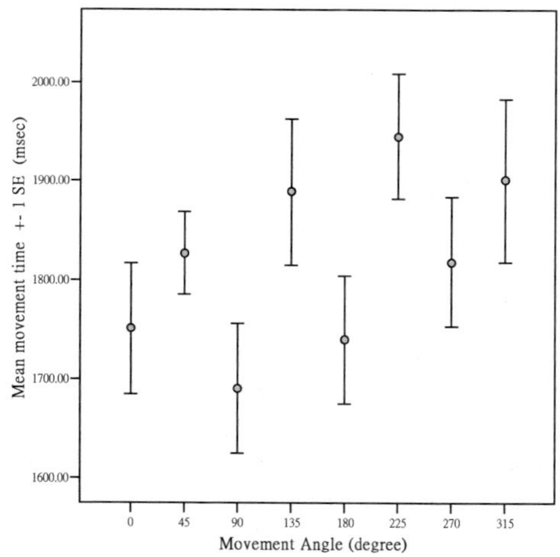

Fig. 2. Average MMT (± 1 SE) for the approach angle

3.2 Accuracy

Table 3 lists the error rate in various approach angles and motion directions. The results of ANOVA indicated that neither the motion direction nor the approach angle was significant on accuracy. The interaction effect between motion direction and approach angle was not significant.

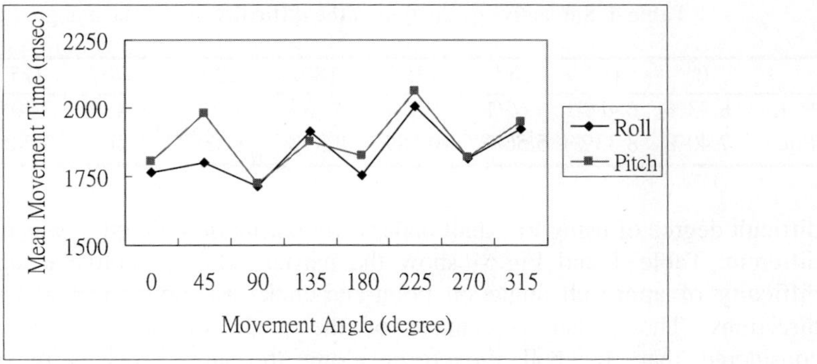

Fig. 3. Average MMT in various approach angles and motion directions

Table 3. Error rate in various approach angles and motion directions

	0°	45°	90°	135°	180°	225°	270°	315°	Average
Roll	8.33%	6.48%	4.63%	9.26%	4.63%	10.18%	6.48%	3.70%	6.71%
Pitch	7.40%	8.33%	5.56%	10.18%	8.33%	8.33%	5.56%	3.70%	7.17%

3.3 Subjective Measurement

The results of a Friedman's test indicated that the difficult degree of manipulating trackball along different angles was significantly different ($p<0.01$), whereas the

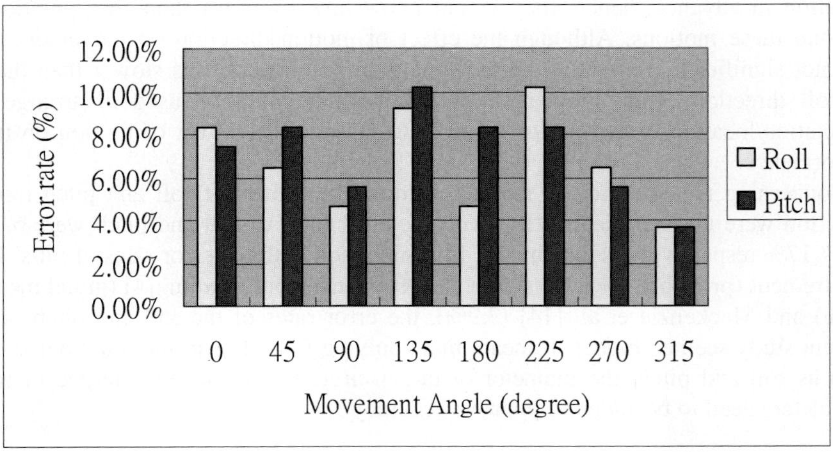

Fig. 4. Subjective evaluation of the difficulty of approach angle

Table 4. Subjective evaluation of the difficulty of approach angle (%)

	0°	45°	90°	135°	180°	225°	270°	315°	Average
Roll	8.33%	6.48%	4.63%	9.26%	4.63%	10.18%	6.48%	3.70%	6.71%
Pitch	7.40%	8.33%	5.56%	10.18%	8.33%	8.33%	5.56%	3.70%	7.17%

difficult degree of using trackball under different motion direction was not significant different. Table 4 and Fig. 4 show the participants' subjective evaluation of the difficulty of approach angle on point-and-click task under roll and pitch motion directions. The higher percentage of the angle meant that more participants considered that trackball movement along the angle was more difficult than movement along the other angles. In general, as observed in Figure 3, movements along the angles of 45o, 135o, 225o and 315o were more difficult than movements along the angles of 0o, 90o, 180 and 270o under roll and pitch motion directions.

4 Discussions

4.1 Motion Direction

The results of experiment demonstrated that the effects of motion directions, i.e. roll and pitch, on the speed of cursor movement and accuracy of target selection by using Logitech TrackMan Wheel (LTW) thumb trackball on point-and-click task were not significant. This finding is consistent with the results of subjective evaluations of the present study. The participants felt that the difficulty of manipulating LTW to execute the point–and-click task under roll and pitch was not different. The possible explanations for this could be (1) the effects of the motion direction were alleviated by various approach angles and (2) the participants could predicate the motion direction in advance, hence, they would know how to adjust their manipulation to respond these motions. Although the effect of motion direction on movement time was not significant, generally, the movement speed on pitch was slower than that of on roll direction. This implication of this finding could be used to arrange the orientation/location of the control console to alleviate the effect of motion on input performance.

Concerning the accuracy of target selection, the effects of roll and pitch motion direction were not significant. However, the error rates of roll and pitch were 6.71% and 7.17% respectively (see Table 3). In comparison with the error rates of Fitts' Law requirement (probably 4%), the studies of MacKenzie and Buxton, [4] (grand mean is 4.6%) and Mackenzie et al. [14] (3.9%), the error rates of the roll and pitch of the present study seemed higher. It meant that applying Fitts' law to motion environment such as roll and pitch, the diameter of target circle needed to be enlarged or more parameters need to be added to improve accuracy.

4.2 Approach Angle

The approach angle of cursor (or approach angle of trackball) significantly affected the movement time but not the accuracy. The experimental results revealed that the cursor movements along the vertical and horizontal directions seemed faster than that of movements along the four diagonal directions and the fastest movement direction occurred at approach angle 90° whereas the slowest reached at the angle of 225°. This finding is also consistent with the results of subjective evaluations of the present study that movements along the angles of 135°, 225°, 315° and 45°, were more difficult than along the other angles. The results not only confirmed the findings of MacKenzie and Buxton [4] that the speed of movements along 90° and 0° was faster than that of movement along 45o with mouse but also extended their findings to 270 °, 180° and other diagonal directions with trackball. This result also confirmed the findings of Whisenand and Emurian [5] who suggested that arranging target-type objects with the approach angles of 0°, 180 ° and 270 ° on interface would improve the target selection performance with a mouse. The more likely explanations of these results could be attributed to the nature of human physical structures that movement is more rapidly in certain directions than in other directions [15] and differences in the musclulo-skeletal groups required to manipulate cursor movements in different directions [16].

5 Conclusion

This study indicated that the approach angle significantly affected the movement time of manipulating trackball to execute the point-and-click task; however, the effect of motion direction is little. Movement were generally faster along the vertical and horizontal lines in comparison with movement along the diagonals; furthermore, movement along the angle of 225o seems slower than movement along other directions. The performance differences founded in this study have definite implications for arrangement of control console and user interface design, especially for time and safety critical systems. The important and critical controls such as buttons or icons should be placed on the vertical or horizontal direction of the interface to achieve a better movement performance. For completely understanding the effects of motion direction and approach angle on non-keyboard input device (NKID), more NKID such as touch screen, joystick and other type of trackball as well as more motion directions should be included.

References

1. Woods, V., Hastings, S., Buckle, P., Haslam, R.: Ergonomics of using a mouse or other non-keyboard input device, Health and Safety Executive (2002)
2. Grandt, M., Pfendler, C., Mooshage, O.: Empirical Comparison of Five Input Devices for Anti-Air Warfare Operators. In: 8th International Command and Control Research and Technology Symposium (ICCRTS) on Information Age Transformation Washington, DC (2003)
3. Boritz, J., Booth, K., Cowan, W.: Fitts' law studies of directional mouse movement, in Graphics Interface,Canadian Human Machine Communications Society. Canada (1991)
4. MacKenzie, I.S., Buxton, W.: Extending Fitts' law to two dimensional tasks. In: Proceedings of the CHI '92 Conference on Human Factors in Computing Systems (1992)

5. Whisenand, T.G., Emurian, H.H.: Effects of Angle of approach on Cursor Movement with a Mouse: Consideration of Fitts' Law. Computer in Human Behavior 12(3), 481–495 (1996)
6. Hancock, S.M., Booth, K.S.: Improving Menu Placement Strategies for Pen Input, in Graphics Interface. Ontario, London (2004)
7. Lewis, C.H., Griffin, M.J.: A review of the effects of vibration on visual acuity and continuous manual control., part. II-Continuous manual control. Journal of Sound and Vibration. 56(3), 415–457 (1978)
8. McLedo, P., Poulton, C., Ross, H.D., Lewis, W.: The influence of ship motion on manual control skills. Ergonomics 23, 623–634 (1980)
9. McLeod, R., Griffin, M.: A review of the effects of whole-body translational vibration on continuous manual control performance. Journal of Sound and Vibration 133(1), 55–115 (1989)
10. Hill, S.G., Tauson, R.A.: Soldier Performance Issues in C2 On the Move. In: 10th International Command and Control Technology Symposium (ICCRTS) (2005)
11. Griffin, M.J.: Handbook of Human Vibration. Academic Press, London (1990)
12. Wertheim, A.H., Ooms, J., De Regt, G.P., Wientjes, C.J.E.: Incidence and severeness of sea sickness: validation of rating scale. TNO Human Factors Research Institute (1992)
13. Colwell, J.L.: NATO: Questionnaire: Correlation between ship motion, fatigue, sea sickness and naval task performance, in Human Factor in Ship Design and Operation. London (2000)
14. Mackenzie, I.S., Seller, A., Buxton, W.: A comparison of input devices in elemental pointing and dragging tasks. In: Proceedings of the CHI '91 Conference on Human Factors in Computing Systems (1991)
15. McCormick, E.J., Sanders, M.S.: Human Factors in Engineering and Design. McGraw-Hill Book Company, New York (1992)
16. Grossman, T., Balakrishnan, R.: A Probabilistic Approach to Modeling Two-Dimensional Pointing. ACM Transactions on Computer-Human Interaction 12(3), 435–459 (2005)

An Ambient Display for the Elderly*

Yeo-Jin Yoon[1], Han-Sol Ryu[1], Ji-Man Lee[1], Soo-Jun Park[2], Seong-Joon Yoo[1], and Soo-Mi Choi[1,**]

[1] Department of Computer Engineering, Sejong University, Seoul, Korea
[2] Electronics and Telecommunications Research Institute, Korea
smchoi@sejong.ac.kr

Abstract. The demand for systems to assist in the care of the elderly is continually increasing. We propose an ambient display that allows casual and implicit interaction with an elderly user. The display system recognizes the user and measures the distance between the user and the display using information from an RFID reader and an ultrasonic sensor. It uses this information to adjust the level of detail of the displayed information. If the user is far from the display, a black-and-white image is displayed that does not attract attention. But when the user's approach is recognized, the display provides three-dimensional spatial navigation through the image space. When the user is very close to the display, they can interact directly using the touch screen. In the event of an emergency, LEDs attached around the display call the user's attention by flashing the light.

Keywords: ambient display, implicit interaction, ubiquitous computing.

1 Introduction

As ubiquitous computing becomes increasingly available, new computing environments that take into account the physical capabilities of the elderly are the subject of current research. In particular, demand for health care systems that relate to the everyday life of the elderly is increasing. Such systems need to provide an interface suitable for elderly people who are not accustomed to the computing environment. In this paper, we present an ambient display system that reacts to the behavior of elderly people, without requiring excessive attention from the user.

Together with an analysis of elderly people's behavior, systems using a digital frame-type display have been studied in projects relating to ubiquitous health care, such as at Georgia Institute of Technology and Intel Research Center in Seattle. In the AwareHome project at Georgia Tech, indirect interactions with remote family members are facilitated using the Digital Family Portraits display [1]. This display looks like a picture, but can provide family members who live at a distance with information about their elderly relative's everyday life, including their health,

* This work was supported by the Korean Ministry of Information and Communication under the Leading Technology Development Program.

** Corresponding author.

C. Stephanidis (Ed.): Universal Access in HCI, Part II, HCII 2007, LNCS 4555, pp. 1045–1051, 2007.

environment, relationships and activities. Such information is summarized every week and gives the user a feeling that they are talking to the distant family members through the frame. The CareNet display [2] developed by Intel enables the user to access information directly by operating the menus of a touch screen, and it also allows images to be edited.

These existing picture-like displays do not necessarily capture the interest of the elderly, because they only show pictures and permit only explicit interactions, for instance through the menus of a touch screen. Additionally, visually small and complicated interfaces, like that of the CareNet display make it difficult for elderly people to find the information they require.

We are proposing a display system enhances the user's memory of the people shown in pictures, and adequately captures the interest of elderly people. This system can be operated by explicit interaction methods, such as a menu or by implicit interaction, which is derived by the behavior of the elderly person. The user is identified by means of an RFID reader, and based on this it will show pictures of a particular individual (see Section 3). In addition, the system can adjust the level of detail of the display interface depending on the user's proximity by measuring the distance between the user and the display using the ultrasonic sensor.

The rest of this paper is made up as follows: Section 2 briefly explains the proposed system; in Section 3, the equipment and methods used for implicit interaction by the elderly are explained; in Section 4, methods of generating a three-dimensional space from a two-dimensional picture, as an aid to memory, are presented, together with results, and lastly we draw some conclusions and future work.

2 An Ambient Display System

Main components of the proposed system are a radio-frequency identification tag and reader for user recognition, an ultrasonic sensor for detecting proximity, a touch screen monitor for displaying pictures, and an illuminated frame for indicating urgent situations. The RFID reader identifies the user who is approaching the display and shows them an appropriate image. The ultrasonic sensor measures the distance between the display and the user, and provides images with an appropriate resolution.

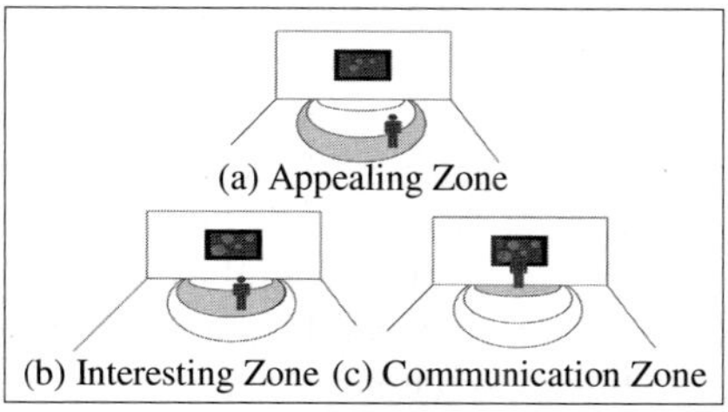

Fig. 1. Display zones corresponding to user proximity

Measurements of user proximity are divided into three ranges, which correspond to different scenarios as follows:

In the Appealing Zone, the ultrasonic sensor reacts to the presence of a user, and the display changes from black-and-white to color. Nevertheless, the picture-like display does not demand excessive attention, although explicit interaction using an air mouse can be provided if necessary.

In the Interesting Zone, both the ultrasonic sensor and the RFID recognize the user, and the image on the display becomes three-dimensional. Display of the image includes a navigation function that zooms in and out depending on the closeness of the user and his/her direction of movement.

In the Communication Zone, the user is very close to the display, and explicit interaction becomes possible. The user can operate menus directly using the touch screen, and access detailed information.

When the user is outside all three zones, the system looks like a framed picture, and shows black-and-white images, but it can also delivers urgent information regardless of the user's location. If a situation critical to the user or environment occurs, the lamps light up and a warning message is displayed on the screen.

If an elderly person is hurt in a fall, or exhibits unusual behavior such as failing to get up in the morning, the display system can inform a relative at a remote location. The relative can properly react using a phone call and let other visit the elderly person.

3 Implicit Interaction

The ubiquitous computing environment is being developed through studies of implicit interaction techniques, such as user recognition, and on non-standard explicit interactions. This work is built on sensor techniques, including computer vision, RFID, ultrasonic, infrared, and gyro sensors. Non-standard explicit interactions are more suitable for the elderly, who do not find a keyboard and mouse easy to use. We provide navigation uses implicit interaction when a user is too distant for explicit interaction.

Our system uses a 900MHz RFID reader (Infinity 210 UHF: SIRIT) to recognize a user. When the user enters the sensor reaction zone, the RFID reader recognizes the tag (Class 1 Generation 2) and confirms their identity using the ID on the tag. The tag can be a bracelet or a small sticker which can be worn without inconvenience. The reaction zone of our RFID extends about 2.4 meters from the display, if an external antenna is deployed.

When more than one user is recognized, the RFID sensor can differentiate between them. The user wearing the tag that reacts most strongly to the RFID reader receives the highest priority (see Fig. 2).

The distance between the display and the user is in measured by the RFID and an active ultrasonic sensor, which reads a pulse in the direction of the priority user. The distance is calculated from the round-trip time of the ultrasonic wave, and the direction in which the user is moving can also be determined from a sequence of measurements. The images on the display are modified as the user moves closer or farther away. The maximum detection range of the ultrasonic sensor is about 5 meters, which includes all three display zones.

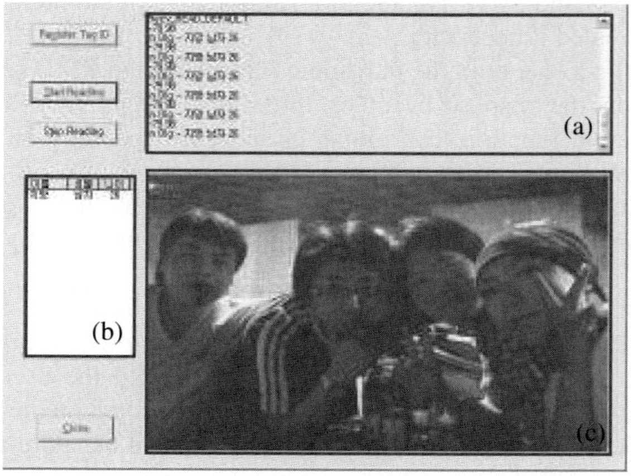

(a) RFID reader (b) Priority of recognized IDs (c) Picture related to the highest-priority ID

Fig. 2. User recognition and picture selection by the RFID reader

(a) (b)

Fig. 3. RFID reader (a) and ultrasonic sensor (b)

4 Picture-Based Three-Dimensional Spatial Navigation

When a user enters the Interest Zone, the display begins three-dimensional navigation within the scene being displayed. We use the "Tour into the Picture (TIP)" method first proposed by Horry [5], and subsequently developed to apply to many document types of images and videos.

TIP is based on three kinds of images as shown in Fig. 4: an original image, a mask image and a background image. In our system, a three-dimensional model is derived from the mask image in order to separate the foreground and background. The vanishing point or vanishing lines in the two-dimensional image, and the coordinates of the four corners, are used to find the coordinates locating the foreground model within the background model.

(a) Original image (b) Mask image (c) Background image

Fig. 4. Processing an image using vanishing-line information

The three-dimensional space that is created in this way provides navigation inside the Interest Zone based on the changing the distance between the user and the display. As the user approaches the display, the foreground image within the three-dimensional space comes to meet them.

Fig. 5. Three-dimensional spatial navigation

Fig. 5 shows what happens as a user approaches the display. The user gets the feeling that they are actually moving within images that are displayed by this method of navigation. Such a system is likely to induce the curiosity of an elderly person and help their memory of the situation.

We also use the hybrid images technique [9] to achieve a variety of interaction effects based on the position of the user. Two images, referred to as hybrid images, are combined into a single image by applying low-frequency to one image and high-frequency filtering to the other. We use this technique alternate between different images, depending on the location of the user.

Fig. 6 shows the application of the hybrid images technique to a foreground image from the three-dimensional spatial navigation system. The two facial images show the same face with different expressions. One image is converted to a high-frequency image using the Fast Fourier Transform and the other to a low-frequency image using a Gaussian filter. The facial expression of the person can then be changed by image morphing as the user moves nearer to, or farther from, the display. This technique can also be applied to other images and to text, allowing different information to be provided as the distance between the user and the display changes.

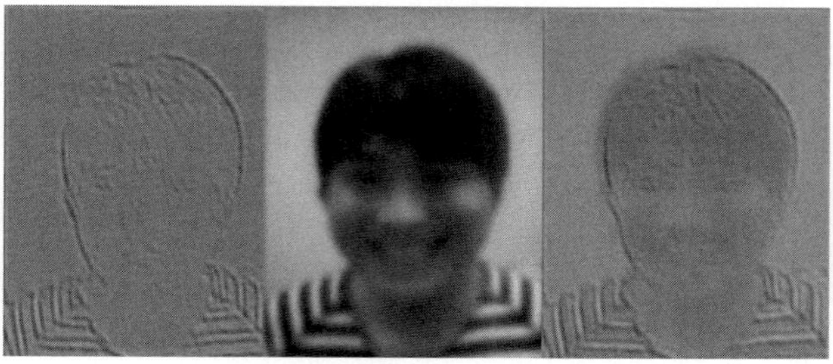

(a) Fast-Fourier Transformed image (b)Gaussian filtered image (c) Hybrid image (a)+(b)

Fig. 6. Utilization of hybrid image

5 Conclusion

We have presented an ambient display to help the memory of the elderly. It operated on the basis of implicit interactions such as user recognition and closeness of approach. We have used the TIP method that enables a flat picture to be perceived as a three-dimensional space, through the interaction of many kinds of sensors.

In the near future, we plan to test the usability of this system using the elderly persons, with both pictures and information delivery. For information that has no connection with the display zones, we will explore methods of structured delivery that are suitable for different kinds of information.

As the number of elderly people living alone increases, this sort of display will become increasingly useful. By allowing information about the wellbeing of an elderly person, and the medicines they are taking, to be acquired by the display, further application areas are opened up, including the ubiquitous health care which is likely to develop in years to come.

References

1. Mynatt, B.E., Rowan, J., Craighill, S.: Digital Family Portraits: supporting peace of mind for extended family members. In: Proc.CHI'01, pp. 333–340. ACM Press, New York (2001)
2. Consolvo, S., Roessler, P., Shelton, B.E.: The CareNet Display: lessons learned from an in home evaluation of an ambient display. In: Davies, N., Mynatt, E.D., Siio, I. (eds.) UbiComp 2004. LNCS, vol. 3205, pp. 1–17. Springer, Heidelberg (2004)
3. Wisneski, C., Ishii, H., Dahley, A., Gorbet, M., Brave, S., Ullmer, B., Yarin, P.: Ambient displays: turning architectural space into an interface between people and digital information. In: Proc.Couild (1998)
4. Yoon, Y.S., Sohn, T.W.: UI for Supporting old age's prospective memory, journal of the HCI Society of Korea, pp. 94–100 (2006)
5. Horry, Y., Anjyo, K., Arai, K.: Tour Into the Picture: using a spidery mesh interface to make animation from a single image. In: Proc. ACM SIGGRAPH, pp. 225–232 (1997)

6. Pyo, S.H.: Tour Into the Picture (TIP) Using a vanishing line, Master's thesis, CS Dept, KAIST (1999)
7. Kang, H.W., Pyo, S.H., Anjyo, K., Shin, S.Y.: Tour Into the Picture using a vanishing line and it's extension to panoramic images. In: Proc. Of EUROGRAPHICS, pp. 132–141 (2001)
8. Chu, S.H., Tai, C.L.: Animating Chinese landscape paintings and panorama using multi-Perspective modeling. In: Proc. of Computer Graphics International (2001)
9. Oliva, A., Torralba, A., Schyns, P.G.: Hybrid images, ACM SIGGRAPH, pp. 520–530 (2006)

Personal Companion: Personalized User Interface for U-Service Discovery, Selection and Interaction*

Hyoseok Yoon, Hyejin Kim, and Woontack Woo

GIST U-VR Lab.,
Gwangju 500-712, South Korea
{hyoon,hjinkim,wwoo}@gist.ac.kr

Abstract. In this paper, we propose a mobile user interface named personal companion which enables selection and interaction of u-services based on context of user. Personal companion selects u-services from a list of discovered services, supports camera-based selection with embedded marker and personalizes UI of the selected service in ubiquitous computing environment. In order to verify its usefulness, we implemented personal companion on PDA and UMPC platform and deployed into smart home testbed for selecting and interacting with u-services. The proposed personal companion is expected to play a vital role in ubiquitous computing environment by bridging users and u-services.

Keywords: mobile user interface, camera-based interaction, personalization, embedded marker.

1 Introduction

Recent interest and increased awareness for future computing paradigms such as ubiquitous computing and context-aware computing are getting more attention from both researchers and end-users alike. In these future computing environments, users are served by pervasive and ubiquitous intelligent services for highly personalized and easy-to-use services. Ultimately, the goal is to realize the vision of Mark Wesier who envisioned technologies which disappear into everyday life of users [1].

However, the traditional desktop-based interface and interaction methods have limitations in getting and using the services in the ubiquitous computing environment (u-service, hereafter). This limitation arises, because u-service is characterized by properties such as *ubiquity* and *context-awareness*. Especially *ubiquity* of u-service builds upon the assumption of *mobility* of users, and *context-awareness* requires acquiring and analyzing information of users and the environment. Moreover, all these functionality should be available anywhere and anytime in a form of compact-sized computing resource. A viable approach is introduced with recent advancement

* This research is supported by the UCN Project, the MIC 21st Century Frontier R&D Program in Korea.

C. Stephanidis (Ed.): Universal Access in HCI, Part II, HCII 2007, LNCS 4555, pp. 1052–1061, 2007.

in mobile device such as PDA, cell-phone and hand-held PC, and many researchers are pursuing to include both intelligence and functionalities into the mobile device [2][3]. Moreover, a mobile user interface plays an important role of a bridge and a *transitional interface* [4] to support different interactive spaces for users in ubiquitous computing environment. To realize this, we need fundamental technologies such as service discovery for getting available service list and functions, selection method for effectively selecting relevant items among a myriad of services, and interaction methods for user and service interaction.

In this paper, we propose a user interface for ubiquitous computing environment named *personal companion* based on the three aforementioned fundamental technologies. The proposed interface enables interaction with u-service by supporting service discovery and filtering, camera-based interaction method, and personalization of user interface. The remainder of the paper is structured as follows. Related works on mobile device as an interface are described in section 2. The design considerations for personal companion are explained in section 3. In section 4, we describe features of personal companion in detail. Prototype implementations are discussed in section 5, and we conclude with a remark for future work in section 6.

2 Related Work

Currently, several projects use mobile device as an intermediary for user and environment. In this section, we review on-going or recent related works in aspect of service discovery, service selection and interaction.

In TRON project [5], they developed Ubiquitous Communicator (UC) for recognizing and acquiring detailed information on RFID-tagged objects. For sensing purpose, small-sized RFID (Radio Frequency IDentification) and barcode are attached to everyday objects and digitized information is embedded. When RFID reader in UC reads digitized information, it is decoded into URL where detailed information can be retrieved. They have developed this idea into applications such as food traceability system and drug traceability system to identify product and trace back product information, i.e., where it is produced and who produced it. ubiController [6] is a mobile user interface for ubiquitous computing implemented on PDA platform. It provides controllability to users for discovering services and controlling it universally. Here middlewares such as UPnP[1] and ubi-UCAM [7] are utilized to detect changes in services and environment. Context of user such as current location, orientation and speed are used to provide situation-awareness in GUI. Moreover, multi-user is supported through mediation in conflict situations by recommendation and sharing personal media contents with other users. In an effort to interact with distributed services in the environment, Voyager framework [8] which is developed as a part of 2Wear project[2], proposed a dynamically distributed interface, *ambient dialogue* to realize disappearing computing and to maximize mobility of users.

There are other recent works using a mobile device with camera and tags such as a camera-based framework [9], EMI^{2}lets [10], u-Photo [11] and Vidgets [12]. In the

---

[1] UPnP, http://www.upnp.org
[2] 2Wear project, http://2wear.ics.forth.gr

camera-based framework, visual codes are used for interaction where a relative distance and angle between camera and visual tags are used for generating input commands like direction, i.e., up, down, right, left and rotation. In EMI^{2}lets framework, a mobile device is used as a universal remote controller for controlling smart objects. The framework includes EMI^{2}Proxy which is a representtative agent for a user, EMI^{2}Object which stands for smart object agent and EMI^{2}BehaviourRepository to support logical operation. For service and smart object discovery, a Jini-like service discovery method[3] which uses Bluetooth and TRIP tag is used. In u-Photo project, they have created a metadata structure for including appliance control and sensor information into digital still image. Through this metadata structure called u-Photo, user can interact using a metaphor of *"take a picture of service/device and control"* to connect physical, virtual and networked devices. Also in Vidgets, camera on mobile device is used to recognize visual markers and to control multiple services universally. Table 1 shows a summary of related work considering service discovery, selection and interaction.

Table 1. Summary of related work

Project	Service Discovery	Service Selection	Service Interaction
UC	RFID/Barcode	RFID Reader	Product traceability
ubiController	UPnP	Image-based	Control and contents sharing
Voyager	Bluetooth	Proximity-based	Interface composition
CamPhoneFrame	Visual Code	Camera-based	Direction and rotation input
EMI^{2}lets	Jini-like	Proximity/Camera	Service control
u-Photo	LED/Eyemark	Camera-based	Service control
Vidgets	Visual Marker	Camera-based	Service control

As we can observe from Table 1, many researchers are using visual tags or markers with built-in camera. This follows recent trend in market, since most cellular phones sold now have built-in camera. However, distinguishable markers and tags do not assimilate well into the environment, which result in visually awkward and divided attention for user to notice two separate things, an object and a marker. Also in projects where Bluetooth is used suffered from low network performance and limited by ranges. Therefore we avoid using Bluetooth method alone for service discovery. Most researches covered service control and some form of information augmentation. A few works used mobile device as an input device which displayed possibilities of a versatile user interface as performance of mobile device advances. This also opens a door for new interaction methods and extended application areas.

3 Design of Personal Companion

Personal companion focuses on mobility and support for ubiquitous computing environment. Therefore we defined and followed a set of guidelines for personal companion. Moreover, we also introduce a novel *embedded marker* to reduce visual interference of markers in camera-based interaction.

[3] JINI, http://www.jini.org

3.1 Design Guidelines for User Interface

In order to provide users with more effective user-centered mobile UI, we have considered user's efficiency in performing tasks and flexibility of meeting user's various demands. For an increased efficiency, functions and contents that a user prefers are provided at initial stage. Additional functions and contents are accessible through short cut menus. Moreover, to provide a consistent UI for users, frequently used function keys such as back and exit are placed in the static area of mobile user interface, so no matter what menu page user is on, the static area is associated with consistent functions. Default menu interface is based on icons and we give it a textual description as well to reduce misunderstanding. In case of flexibility in mobile user interface, we allow users to configure own interface by choosing preferred fonts, colors and menu styles.

3.2 Embedded Marker

Personal companion supports interaction with services through camera and embedded marker. Figure 1 shows the concept of embedded marker where an embedded marker is created using an object as a part of a marker or making a marker out of a part of an object.

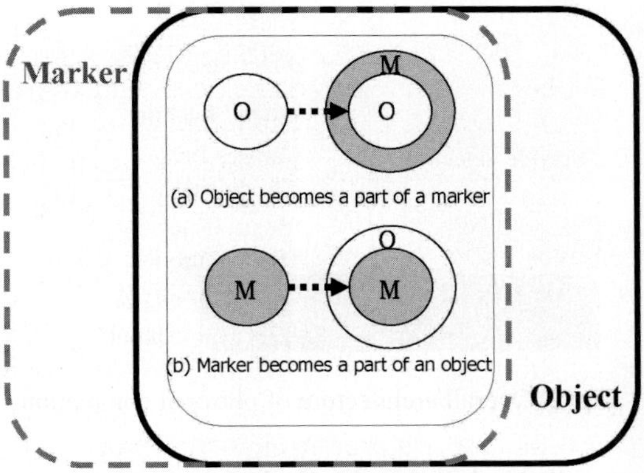

Fig. 1. Concept diagram of embedded marker

We refrain from using the conventional visual markers, because it is visually awkward to eyes of users. Especially, the marker stands out when used in colorful background, grabs attention of users in multiple marker cases, separates user's attention to an actual object and a marker, and does not give semantics in arbitrarily shaped patterns. In our approach, the embedded marker can bring a user's attention into a focused match and does not need to make an arbitrary pattern. Therefore users can get a hint for what information will be delivered from the actual object and marker. Such idea is realized in prototypes in screen saver like marker, a marker based on physical features of an object, and a marker embedded in contents.

4 Functions of Personal Companion

Personal companion is consisted of logical modules for service discovery, service selection and service interaction. For service discovery, UPnP-based method is used. In service selection, there are camera-based selection module (which is comprised of image acquisition and pattern matching module) and direct list-based selection module. For service interaction modules, user interface personalization, reconfiguration and camera-based interaction are included. Figure 2 shows the overall architecture of personal companion.

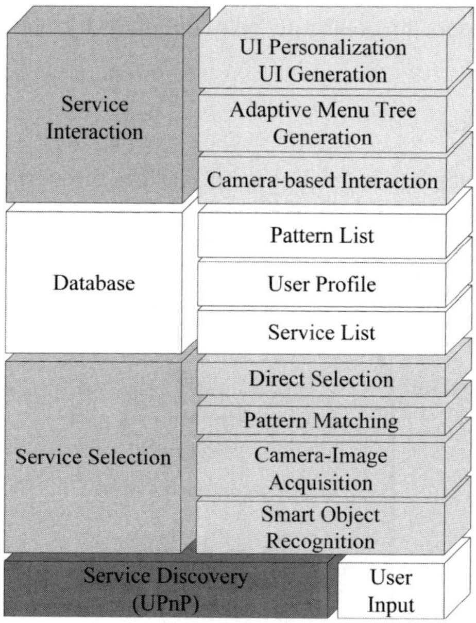

Fig. 2. Overall architecture of personal companion

Table 2. Roles of individual components

Module	Roles
Service Discovery	Discover services in the environment
Smart Object Recognition	Recognize smart objects
Camera-image Acquisition	Acquire image through camera input
Pattern Matching	Compare acquired image with patterns
Direct Selection	Select a service from service list
Service List	A database to save service list
User Profile	A database for user profile
Pattern List	A database for patterns
Camera-based Interaction	Input mode for navigation
Adaptive Menu Tree Generation	Generate personalized menu tree
UI Generation	Generate personalized UI
UI Personalization	Personalize control menu

Table 2 shows a brief summary of each component's roles in personal companion architecture.

4.1 Service Discovery

A distinguished characteristic of ubiquitous computing environment is ubiquity of services. Since users are able to move in and out of environments, there is a need for certain mechanism to tell users what kind of services are available and what can they do with it. In ubiquitous computing environment, service discovery is a process of making ubiquitous and invisible services into visible and personal services. There are several service discovery protocols available [13]. For personal companion, we utilize service discovery protocol known as UPnP where user's mobile device acts as an UPnP control point and services in the environment are implemented as UPnP services. However, UPnP itself does not support use of context; therefore we concurrently used it with our context-aware application framework, ubi-UCAM [7] to utilize context information in both UPnP service and UPnP control point. Once personal companion is run, it searches for new devices and services in the environment. When a new device or service is discovered, its information is saved onto the service database which is accessed for service control.

4.2 Service Selection

There are two possible selection methods, list-based and camera-based. In list-based selection method, service information stored in service database is provided to the user in a list. In this step, icons or tab controls of menu which visually symbolize each service are used as shown in figure 3. Through this association, users can easily select services and intuitively know physical devices, multiple devices as well as logical but invisible services.

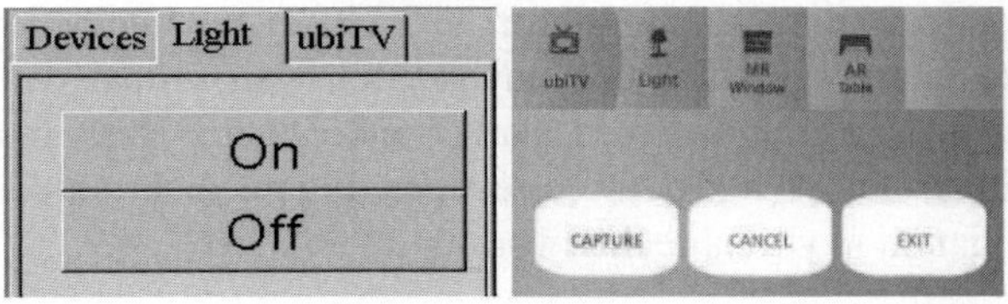

Fig. 3. Visualization of services as tab menu in UMPC and PDA

Second method is camera-based selection method. Due to inefficiency of the first method in a scenario with a large number of services, we provide alternative selection method. It is inefficient and difficult to list several items in one screen, therefore we introduce camera-based method which uses user's explicit command or aid. Typically, taking a picture with a camera reflects a user's direct intention of owning and keeping particular moment or information. We extend this notion further to include service control as well. A similar concept is popularized and used in many other works [9][10][11][12][14]. When the user takes a picture with personal companion, acquired image is compared with patterns in pattern database to identify the object in the picture.

4.3 Service Personalization

After a service is selected through discovery and selection steps, a user interface to control and access functions and contents of the service is generated. Here, *personalization* takes place as a filtering mechanism to tailor services to users. We do not provide all functions and contents to user at one moment, since the screen size of a mobile device is limited. Therefore we utilize preference of users to assign preferred contents and functions higher priority values. As a result, most preferred items are listed first and placed in top menu for easy accessibility. This way, personal companion recommends and guides user's next action. Personalization is classified into two categories. First category is personalization in functions and contents of a service, so different users have different levels of control and access. Second category is personalization in appearance of user interface. In this category, user's preference is used to construct appearance of user interface. Personal companion supports both categories of personalization. For personalizing functions and contents, it filters based on media service genres and for appearance personalization, it customizes colors, fonts, and menu styles according to user's profile [15].

4.4 Service Interaction

When a personalized user interface is generated, the user can interact with services through camera-based interaction. Personal companion provides various interaction possibilities using a camera on the mobile device. First example is controlling smart object after recognition, so it acts as a universal remote controller to discover multiple services and control them. Another example includes an interaction with marker-embedded contents where a user can navigate through virtual reality by tracking relative distance and position between marker and camera. Here, mobile device can be used as an input device for giving directions. Figure 4 shows controlling a light service and navigation in virtual reality world.

Fig. 4. Interaction with services, controlling a light service and VR navigation

5 Implementation and Experiment

The proposed user interface is implemented on PDA and UMPC platform and tested in ubiHome [16] smart home testbed as shown in figure 5.

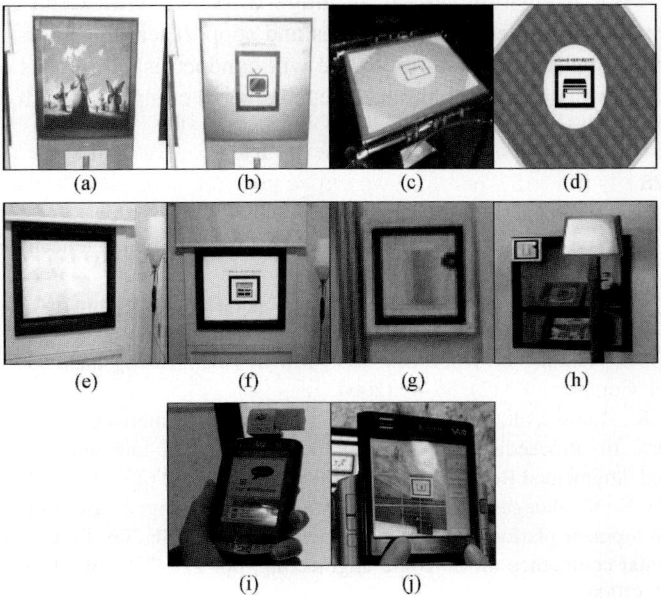

Fig. 5. Smart Objects and embedded marker prototypes, (a)(b) ubiTV embedded marker, (c)(d) ARTable embedded marker, (e)(f) MRWindow embedded marker, (g)(h) ubiLight switch embedded marker and ubiLight, (i)(j) PDA and UMPC version of personal companion

Earlier prototype is developed for PDA using Pocket PC 2003, and then it is also tested on PDA running Windows Mobile 5.0. In UMPC platform running Windows XP operating system, it was easier to develop applications and performance was much better than PDA platform. Figure 5 (i) and (j) shows the implemented PDA and UMPC version of personal companions. By using these two mobile platforms, we discovered, selected and interacted with u-services. Also prototypes of embedded markers are designed as shown in Figure 5 (a) to (h). Figure 5 (a) to (f) shows each smart object and corresponding embedded marker prototype, in a form of screen saver which turned into a marker when a user comes into the effective service area. Figure 5 (g) and (h) show an embedded marker using physical feature of a light switch.

6 Conclusion

In this paper, we introduced personal companion for discovering, selecting, and interacting with u-services. Personal companion comes with service discovery capability so it can discover u-services and visualize it for easier selection. For selection methods, we introduced a list-based selection method which is useful for a smaller set of services while camera-based selection method is presented for a larger number of services. When a u-service is selected, the preference of the user is reflected to personalize the interface and its functions. For service interaction, personal companion is used as a universal remote controller and as a directional input device for the VR navigation system. In future work, we will extend the interaction scope to support augmented reality services and support learning in usage of mobile UI to better personalize it. Furthermore, we will conduct usability tests on mobile UI designs and implemented prototypes to update personal companion with the feedback.

References

1. Weiser, M.: The computer for the 21st century. Scientific American 265(3), 94–104 (1991)
2. Ballagas, R., Borchers, J., Rohs, M., Sheridan, J.G.: The smart phone: A ubiquitous input device. IEEE Pervasive Computing 5(1), 70–77 (2006)
3. Myers, B.A., Nichols, J., Wobbrock, J.O., Miller, R.C.: Taking handheld devices to the next level. Computer 37(12), 36–43 (2004)
4. Grasset, R., Looser, J., Billinghurst, M.: Transitional interface: concept, issues and framework. In: Proceedings of the Fifth IEEE and ACM International Symposium on Mixed and Augmented Reality (ISMAR 2006), pp. 231–232 (2006)
5. Sakamura, K.: Challenges in the age of ubiquitous computing: a case study of t-engine, an open development platform for embedded systems. In: ICSE '06: Proceeding of the 28th international conference on Software engineering, pp. 713–720. ACM Press, New York, NY, USA (2006)
6. Yoon, H., Woo, W.: ubicontroller: Situation-aware mobile user interface for ubiquitous computing environment. In: Ubicomp (2006)
7. Oh, Y., Shin, C., Jang, S., Woo, W.: ubi-ucam 2.0: A unified context-aware application model for ubiquitous computing environments. In: Proc. The first Korea/Japan Joint Workshop on Ubiquitous Computing & Networking Systems 2005 (UbiCNS 2005). Jeju, Korea (2005)
8. Savidis, A., Stephanidis, C.: Distributed interface bits: dynamic dialogue composition from ambient computing resources. Personal Ubiquitous Comput. vol. 9(3) (2005)
9. Rohs, M., Zweifel, P.: A conceptual framework for camera phone-based interaction techniques. In: Gellersen, H.-W., Want, R., Schmidt, A. (eds.) PERVASIVE 2005. LNCS, vol. 3468, Springer, Heidelberg (2005)
10. de Ipia, D.L., Vzquez, J., Garca, D., Fernndez, J., Garca, I., Sainz, D., Almeida, A.: Emilets: A reflective framework for enabling ami. Journal of Universal Computer Science 12(3), 297–314 (2006)
11. Suzuki, G., Aoki, S., Iwamoto, T., Maruyama, D., Koda, T., Kohtake, N., Takashio, K., Tokuda, H.: u-photo: Interacting with pervasive services using digital still images. In: Pervasive, pp. 190–207 (2005)
12. Tokunaga, E., Kimura, H., Kobayashi, N., Nakajima, T.: Virtual tangible widgets: seamless universal interaction with personal sensing devices. In: ICMI '05: Proceedings of the 7th international conference on Multimodal interfaces, pp. 325–332. ACM Press, New York, NY, USA (2005)

13. Edwards, W.K.: Discovery systems in ubiquitous computing. Pervasive Computing, IEEE 5(2), 70–77 (2006)
14. Kohtake, N., Iwamoto, T., Suzuki, G., Aoki, S., Maruyama, D., Kouda, T., Takashio, K., Tokuda, H.: u-photo: A snapshot-based interaction technique for ubiquitous embedded information. In: Proceedings of The Second International Conference on Pervasive Computing (Pervasive 2004) Advances in Pervasive Computing, pp. 389–392 (2004)
15. Suh, Y., Kang, D., Woo, W.: Context-based user profile management for personalized services. In: Proceedings of The First International Workshop on Personalized Context Modeling and Management for UbiComp Applications (ubiPCMM'05), pp. 64–73 (2005)
16. Jang, S., Shin, C., Oh, Y., Woo, W.: Introduction of ubihome testbed. In: Proc. The first Korea/Japan Joint Workshop on Ubiquitous Computing & Networking Systems 2005 (UbiCNS 2005) (2005)

Author Index

Printing: Mercedes-Druck, Berlin
Binding: Stein+Lehmann, Berlin